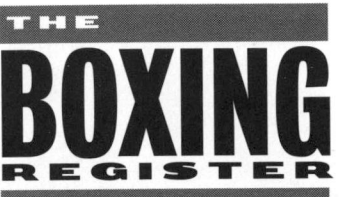

THE BOXING REGISTER

INTERNATIONAL BOXING HALL OF FAME
Official Record Book

3RD EDITION

By James B. Roberts and Alexander G. Skutt

McBooks Press
Ithaca, New York

Book and cover design by Rider Design

Library of Congress Cataloging-in-Publication Data

Roberts, James B., 1962–
    The boxing register: International Boxing Hall of Fame official record book,
3rd ed. / by James B. Roberts and Alexander G. Skutt.
      p. cm.
    Includes bibliographical references and index.
    ISBN 1-59013-020-0
    1. Boxing—Records. 2. Boxers (Sports)—Biography. 3. Boxing—History.
4. International Boxing Hall of Fame. I. Skutt, Alexander G., 1948– .
II. International Boxing Hall of Fame. III. Title.

796.8'3—dc20   2002106053

Additional copies of this book may be ordered from any bookstore or directly from McBooks Press, Inc., ID Booth Building, 520 North Meadow Street, Ithaca, NY 14850. Please include $4.00 postage and handling with mail orders. New York State residents must add sales tax. All McBooks Press publications can also be ordered by calling toll-free 1-888-BOOKS11 (1-888-266-5711).

The Boxing Register and other boxing books and memorabilia are available from the International Boxing Hall of Fame, One Hall of Fame Drive, Canastota, NY 13032, 1-315-697-7095.

Visit the McBooks Press website at
www.mcbooks.com

Printed in the United States of America

9 8 7 6 5 4 3 2 1

CONTENTS

FOREWORD

I GREW UP WITH BOXING. I must have been seven or eight years old when I had a kind of vision—boxing gloves flashed through my mind—that let me know that the sport was going to play a big part in my life. Of course, living in Canastota, New York may have had something to do with that. I was born and raised in this village of 5,000 people. It has produced two world champions as well as a number of trainers, managers, boxing writers, and other participants of the sport. Canastota loves boxing and has supported it for a long time.

I was born in 1956, the year Canastota's Carmen Basilio lost the world welter-weight to title to Johnny Saxton and then won it back again. As I grew up, I heard stories about Carmen from my father and other townspeople. By the time I was ten or eleven, I was mowing lawns and doing odd jobs to earn enough money for my subscription to *The Ring* and the boxing books I wanted, like Nat Fleischer's series on how to box, how to train, or how to manage a fighter.

You can imagine my excitement when up-and-coming Canastota boxer, Billy Backus, moved in next door. Billy was fighting top ten opponents in the welter-weight division. I often went to Syracuse to watch his bouts, and at the age of 14, I sat in his corner for his victorious championship fight against Jose Napoles. After that, I accompanied Billy to subsequent fights. I spent time in the dressing room, I watched him train in the gym, and I paid attention to everything that went on around me. I even got in the ring a few times myself, mostly for the experience. I knew trying out the boxer's role would give me more insight into the sport.

By the time I was in my late teens, I had started training some amateurs, and I learned as much as I could about what it was like to run a gym. I was interested in the concept of inspiring troubled youth to direct their energies into learning to box. I was able to follow my interest in promotion in my early twenties, when I rented the Syracuse War Memorial several times and put on boxing shows. I dealt with the matchmakers, and I saw firsthand what happens when a match falls apart 48 hours before the show and how you put it back together again.

If you add to this background my interest as a fan, historian and collector, I've been very fortunate in seeing and experiencing just about every aspect of the sport. As executive director of the International Boxing Hall of Fame, I now help to preserve the history of boxing.

IN 1984, THE HALL OF FAME WAS JUST AN IDEA, operating out of a borrowed office with a desk, a phone, a pencil and a pad of paper. From finding out what a "feasibility study" was, to having one done, to the first Induction Weekend, and now plans for expansion, the Hall has fulfilled many purposes. It's a place where the rich history of boxing can be maintained and where visitors can develop a deeper understanding of the world's oldest sport. It's also a place where attitudes like Willie Pep's "keep on punchin'" or Muhammad Ali's "dare to be great" continue to be inspirations.

The Hall of Fame is also a way for Canastota to say thank you to the sport and to those who have kept it alive. The village has become a second hometown to many in the boxing world. Canastota has an appreciation of the sport, and the Hall is a way of getting boxers to come here and be thanked for everything they have given us. Friendships among townspeople and international boxers have developed, and as Canastota continues to extend its hospitality, more and more boxers feel comfortable coming here.

The International Boxing Hall of Fame is proud to now have its own official record book, *The Boxing Register*, which gives boxing fans, as well as newcomers to the sport, something to study and enjoy long after their visit to the Hall of Fame. Those who have boxing in their blood will appreciate it as a way to keep memories alive. Those who are just learning about boxing will be exposed to the excitement of the sport's unparalleled competition. The book also touches on the cultural and social significance of boxing, and through the life stories of many of the boxers in this book, it will be obvious that boxing has—as it continues to do—provided many young people with a way to turn their lives around.

Boxing is an international, equal-opportunity sport that transcends borders and ethnic differences. Controlled boxing, with judges and referees and gloves, is a healthy outgrowth of humankind's natural instinct to fight. It is both an art and a science, and it is very much about personal achievement. *The Boxing Register* offers a look into the lives and careers of the best in this unique sport.

EDWARD BROPHY
Canastota, New York

ACKNOWLEDGMENTS

THE AUTHORS RECEIVED A GREAT DEAL OF HELP FROM THE BOXING COMMUNITY in creating this updated third edition of *The Boxing Register*. First, we want to thank Executive Director Edward Brophy, Historian Jeff Brophy, the Board of Directors, and the rest of the IBHOF staff for their help. They warmly welcomed us to their exciting museum and gave us access to their excellent library. Jeff Brophy is a knowledgeable and meticulous researcher who demonstrated an endless willingness to review our work, answer our questions, and locate invaluable news clippings and magazine articles in the Hall of Fame's extensive files.

We are extremely grateful for the generosity of Anibal Miramontes of Fight Fax, Inc., and his predecessor Phill Marder, who gave us fight-by-fight records of all the Modern Era boxers. The information we present on fighter's weigh-in weights is largely based on the data they provided. Fight Fax publishes the mammoth annual, *The Boxing Record Book,* which contains the complete records of all contemporary boxers. Fight Fax also provides the boxing community with an excellent service by providing up-to-the-minute records of fighters via fax transmission. They can be reached by phone at 856-638-0505.

The Ring magazine has been a vitally important part of boxing since 1922. It is now published by London Publishing Co., 7002 West Butler Pike, Ambler, PA 19002, which also publishes several other boxing magazines. We want to thank publisher Stuart Saks for giving us access to *The Ring*'s amazing archive of boxing photographs. Editor-in-chief Nigel Collins and the rest of London's sports staff were very hospitable and informative.

Any boxing record book owes a huge debt to the long series of boxing annuals that were published from 1941 to 1987: *The Ring Record Book and Boxing Encyclopedia*. These volumes were edited for many years by *The Ring* founder Nat Fleischer and, for the last few years of their existence, by the distinguished boxing historian, Herbert G. Goldman. Recently, Mr. Goldman has been researching and writing an eagerly-awaited new boxing reference book. He kindly took time to review and correct much of our new material.

One of the finest boxing sites on the Internet is the Cyber Boxing Zone. Mike DeLisa and his associates publish a lively and insightful monthly on-line magazine. They are also building a very valuable encyclopedia of the fight-by-fight records of past champions. Mike was generous in sharing some of the fruits of their research by checking this manuscript prior to publication. Visit them at www.cyberboxingzone.com.

Tracy Callis, a prominent boxing historian associated with both Cyber Boxing Zone and the International Boxing Research Organization, also reviewed our new material and shed light on several perplexing matters. Laurence Fielding of the IBRO provided much useful additional information.

Ed Maloney, publisher of the Hall of Fame's website at www.ibhof.com, was very helpful in vetting parts of the manuscript before publication—a service that he also provided for earlier editions.

Wendy Skinner of McBooks Press, original editor of *The Boxing Register*, is a fine writer who truly appreciates the terrible allure of boxing. The authors thank her for her Herculean efforts in bringing the first edition of this book into existence. We also want to acknowledge the outstanding editorial work of Ellen Potter, Devon Stout, Patricia Zafiriadis, S.K. List, Romana Mancini, and Corinne Wright.

Michael Rider of Rider Design created the striking design for *The Boxing Register*. Mary Bolles provided patient, thoughtful, and meticulous production work. Judith Kip compiled the excellent index.

ABBREVIATIONS

Opponents' Designation

♛ World Champion
⑩ Top Ten Contender
★ Member, International Boxing Hall of Fame

Ring Records

TB	Total Bouts
KO	Knockouts
W	Wins by Decision
WF	Wins by Foul or Disqualification
KO'd	Knocked Out ("KO by")
L	Losses by Decision
LF	Losses by Foul or Disqualification
ND	No-Decision Bouts

Results

KO	Knock-out Win
TKO	Technical Knock-out Win
W	Win by Decision
WF	Win by Foul or Disqualification
TW	Technical Win
D	Draw
KO'd	Knock-out Loss ("KO by")
TKO'd	Technical Knock-out Loss
L	Loss by Decision
LF	Loss by Foul or Disqualification
TL	Technical Loss
ND	No-Decision Bout
ND-W	No-Decision Bout with "Newspaper-Win"
ND-L	No-Decision Bout with "Newspaper-Loss"
ND-D	No-Decision Bout with "Newspaper-Draw"
NC	No Contest
Exh	Exhibition

NO-DECISION BOUTS

The authors have provided, where possible, the "newspaper result" of no-decision bouts—early 20th century fights where by state law or other rule judges did not render official decisions when the bout went the distance. However, because of their unofficial nature, these newspaper results have not been included in the totals of wins, losses, and draws listed at the top of each boxer's record.

Title Bouts

For	Fought for a title and lost
Lost	Lost a title
Reg	Regained a title formerly held
Ret	Retained a title by winning or drawing
Won	Won a title for the first time
Vac	Fought for a vacant title (no current titleholder)

Weight Divisions

symbol	division	modern weight limits	contested since
H	Heavyweight*	Over 190 lbs.	1719
C	Cruiserweight	176-190	1979
LH	Light Heavyweight*	169-175	1903
SM	Super Middleweight	161-168	1984
M	Middleweight*	155-160	1853
JM	Junior Middleweight	148-154	1962
W	Welterweight*	141-147	1888
JW	Junior Welterweight~	136-140	1922 (except 1935–1946)
L	Lightweight*	131-135	1896
JL	Junior Lightweight+	127-130	1921 (except 1934–1949)
FE	Featherweight*	123-126	1890
JFE	Junior Featherweight#	119-122	1922 (except 1924–1976)
B	Bantamweight*	116-118	1887
JB	Junior Bantamweight	113-115	1980
FL	Flyweight*	109-112	1913
JFL	Junior Flyweight	106-108	1975
S	Strawweight	105 and under	1988

* Long-contested titles, historically the most widely recognized and prestigious
~ Called Super Lightweight by the WBC
+ Called Super Featherweight by the WBC
# Called Super Bantamweight by the WBC

Sanctioning Bodies

EBU	European Boxing Union
IBF	International Boxing Federation
NABF	North American Boxing Federation
NBA	National Boxing Association
NYSAC	New York State Athletic Commission
USBA	United States Boxing Association
WBA	World Boxing Association
WBC	World Boxing Council
WBO	World Boxing Organization

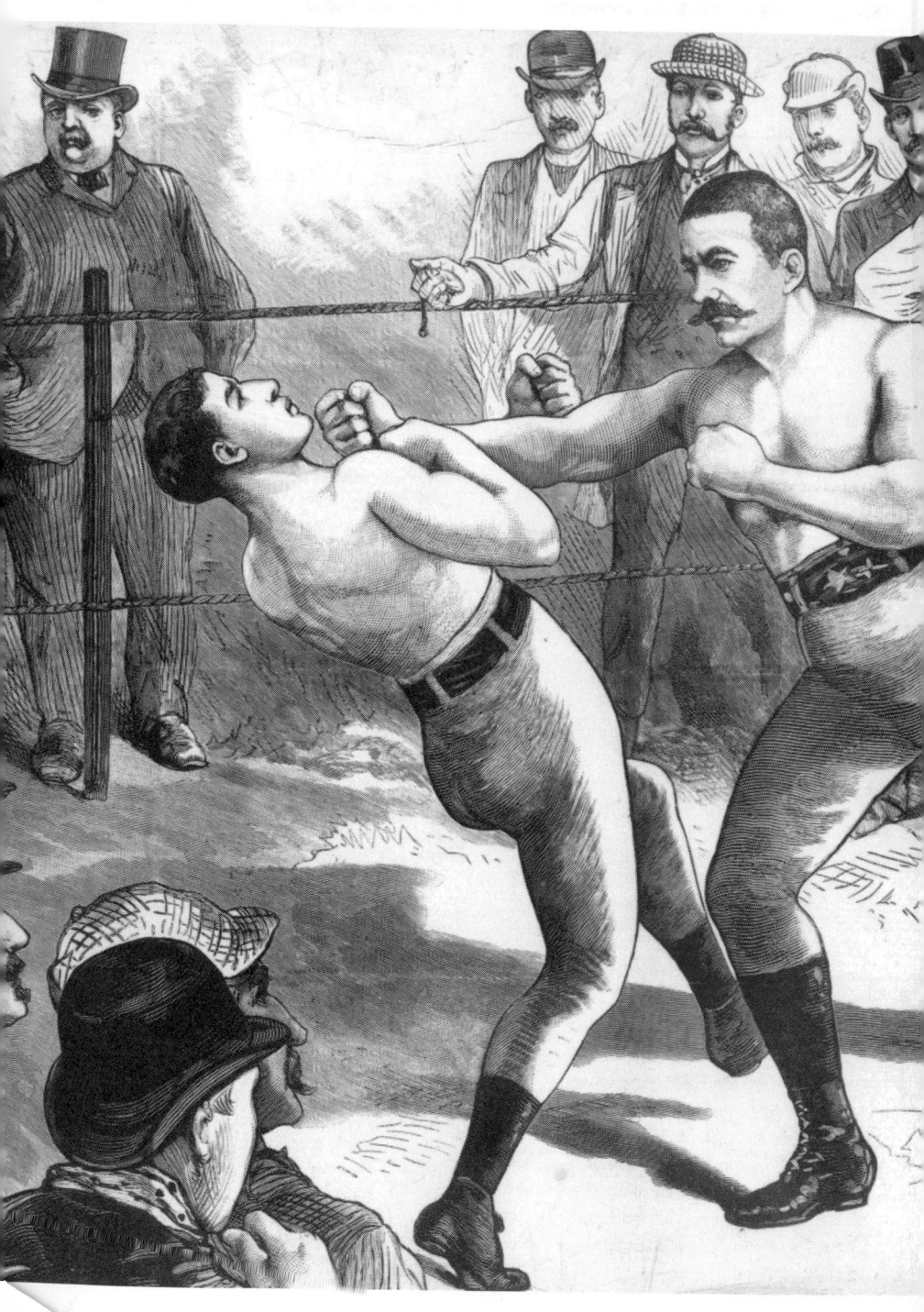

THE
PIONEERS

From Bare Knuckle Brawlers to The Boston Strong Boy

WHILE THE ANCIENT CIVILIZATIONS of Egypt, and later Greece and Rome, provide the first recorded history of hand-to-hand combat as an organized public spectacle, the origins of modern boxing are to be found in eighteenth-century England, where the first bare knuckle champions were recognized. The Pioneers inducted into the International Boxing Hall of Fame all fought in the bare knuckle era. Now largely forgotten by all but boxing historians, these early fighters laid the foundations of boxing as we know it today.

The typical early contest was an unregulated, no-holds-barred battle. The "ring" was defined by the circle of spectators. There was no referee, nor any rounds or time limits. Gloves had yet to be introduced and, beyond the fighters' personal sense of sportsmanship, there were no rules. The object was to fight until one man could no longer go on. Bouts routinely lasted for hours and while fists were considered the primary weapon, no tactic—including strangling, gouging, throwing, kicking, sometimes even using a small cudgel—was forbidden. For many decades, no consideration was given to the relative weight of the opponents, and no organization existed to give

Daniel Mendoza's three bouts with Richard Humphries captured England's imagination.

James Figg taught the use of the sword, cudgel, and fist.

claimed and wore the crown from 1719 until his death in 1740. He operated Figg's Amphitheatre in London and did much to establish boxing as a popular sport. In 1743, a subsequent champion, Jack Broughton, wrote a set of rudimentary rules for governing behavior in the ring. Broughton's Rules stood until 1838, when the more detailed London Prize Ring Rules were introduced.

Until the appearance of Daniel Mendoza, English champion from 1791 to 1795, fisticuffs was largely a contest of brawn. Stamina and sheer brute strength often determined the winner of a marathon bout. Mendoza, a middleweight by modern standards, introduced a wider range of ring skills and strategies for overcoming an opponent, and the anything-goes crudity of the early fights began to give way to the science of boxing.

Americans invaded the English boxing scene when black freemen Bill Richmond and Tom Molineaux arrived in the early 1800s to challenge English fighters. Molineaux became the first African-American to fight in a title bout when he met Tom Cribb in 1810. The first organized bout in the United States took place in 1816 in New York when Americans Jacob Hyer and Tom Beasley fought under English rules. In 1836, English champion James ("Deaf") Burke followed Irish titleholder Sam O'Rourke to New Orleans for a rowdy set-to that ended when spectators rushed the ring. Five years later, Hyer's son Tom and a fighter called Yankee Sullivan met in the first recognized American championship

official recognition to champions or challengers. To set up a title bout, a fighter would issue, often in writing, a challenge or response to the champion's open invitation to take on worthy contenders.

Fisticuffs as a sport first arose in the working class, sometimes as the result of a grudge or dispute, but as bare knuckle fights gained popularity, the upper classes—even royalty—took notice. Wealthy patrons sponsored fighters, arenas, and schools where "the noble art of self-defense" was taught. The ring soon became a square, permanently enclosed with wooden rails or heavy rope.

Boxing's first recognized champion was Hall of Famer James Figg, who

A CHRONOLOGY OF PIONEER HALL OF FAMERS

Name	Birth	Death	Nationality	Weight	Approx. Reign	Page
James Figg	1695	1734	British	Heavyweight	1719–1734	25
Jack Broughton	1704	1789	British	Heavyweight	1738–1750	17
Tom Johnson	1750	1797	British	Heavyweight	1784–1791	28
Benjamin Brain	1753	1794	British	Heavyweight	1791–1794	16
Daniel Mendoza	1764	1836	British	Heavyweight	1794–1795	32
John Jackson	1769	1845	British	Heavyweight	1795	27
Dutch Sam	1775	1816	British	Lightweight	—	23
Jem Belcher	1781	1811	British	Heavyweight	1800–1803	15
Bill Richmond	1763	1829	American	Heavyweight	—	36
Hen Pearce	1777	1809	British	Heavyweight	1803–1806	35
Tom Cribb	1781	1848	British	Heavyweight	1808–1822	20
Tom Molineaux	1784	1818	American	Heavyweight	—	33
Barney Aaron	1800	1850	British	Lightweight	—	14
Tom Spring	1795	1851	British	Heavyweight	1823–1824	38
Jem Ward	1800	1884	British	Heavyweight	1825–1827	42
Young Dutch Sam	1808	1843	British	Lightweight	—	24
James Burke	1809	1845	British	Heavyweight	1833–1839	18
William Thompson	1811	1880	British	Heavyweight	1839–40, 1845–50	41
Nat Langham	1820	1871	British	Middleweight	—	30
Tom Sayers	1826	1865	British	Middle/Heavy	1858–1860	37
John C. Heenan	1835	1873	American	Heavyweight	—	26
Tom King	1835	1888	British	Heavyweight	1863	29
Jem Mace	1831	1910	British	Heavyweight	1866–1871	31
John Morrissey	1831	1878	American	Heavyweight	—	34
Arthur Chambers	1847	1925	American	Lightweight	—	19
Mike Donovan	1847	1918	American	Middleweight	—	21
Paddy Duffy	1864	1890	American	Welterweight	—	22
John L. Sullivan	1858	1918	American	Heavyweight	1882–1892	39–40

fight. In 1860, American John Heenan ("The Benecia Boy") travelled to England to face English champion Tom Sayers in the first transatlantic title fight to be well-publicized on both sides of the ocean.

Boxing began to resemble its modern-day form more closely when Englishman John Graham Chambers, under the sponsorship of the Marquess of Queensberry, devised a new set of rules in 1867. The Queensberry Rules, as they came to be known, established three-minute rounds with a minute's rest in between, and called for the use of protective gloves. The new rules were universally adopted, and John L. Sullivan ("The Boston Strong Boy"), who was American champion from 1882 to 1892, was both the last bare knuckle titleholder and the first heavyweight to be crowned under the Queensberry Rules.

While boxing in England had become an acceptable pastime, with many boxers touring in circuses or performing at fairs, it was illegal in much of the United States, and most early fights were held in out-of-the-way places to avoid police intervention. By the time the enormously popular Sullivan came along, police often looked the other way. Boxing exhibitions were often staged in vaudeville theatres, and audiences expanded to include ladies and top-hatted gentlemen.

BARNEY AARON
The Star of the East

Right-handed; 138 lbs.

Hall of Fame Induction: 2001

Born: 11/21/1800, Aldgate, England

Died: 1850

One of the top lighter-weight fighters of early nineteenth-century England, Barney Aaron enjoyed boxing even as a young boy. Aaron's first recorded fight was in 1819 when he was challenged by William Connelly, known as the Rosemary Lane Champion. Aaron beat the more experienced Connolly in sixteen rounds over 33 minutes. In his next fight Aaron suffered defeat at the fists of the heavier Manny Lyons. Worn out after 75 minutes of battle, Aaron was unable to continue. He avenged this loss in a 50-minute rematch victory.

With a few more wins, Aaron established a solid reputation as one of the best lightweights of that era. On March 19, 1823, he attended the fights at Mousley Hurst. A third bout was added to the bill when a purse was offered, and Tom Collins and Aaron rose to the challenge. Aaron dominated the fight until an injury to his left hand forced him to quit. His performance attracted notice, however, and he now began to fight on a more regular basis. Aaron's 1823 and 1824 victories over Ned Stockman, Lenney (twice), Frank Redmond, and Pete Warren, earned him a reputation as one of the best lightweights in England. Called The Star of the East, Aaron was considered the greatest Jewish fighter since Hall of Famer Dutch Sam.

Aaron next challenged Arthur Matthewson, who was undefeated and known as one of the top small fighters of his day. The two battled through 57 rounds until Matthewson caught Aaron with a shot to the throat, knocking him out. A blow to the throat also spelled defeat for Aaron in a match against Dick Curtis on February 27, 1827, though the match was considered a great exhibition of fighting skill on the part of both combatants.

Aaron continued to fight until April 1, 1834, when he lost to Tom Smith, the East End Sailor Boy, seven years his junior. While he met with defeat in some of his toughest battles, Aaron left behind a sterling reputation in the prize ring. In retirement, he served as an attendant at ringside for important fights, while making his living as a fishmonger. His namesake son immigrated to America in 1855 and soon began to box as Young Aaron. Young Aaron twice held the American lightweight championship, in 1857–58 and in 1867.

SELECTED BOUTS

Date	Year	Opponent	Location	Result / Duration	Title
—	1819	William Connelly	—	W 16 rounds	—
Mar 19	1823	Tom Collins	Moulsey Hurst, Surrey, Eng.	L stopped by injury 30 min.	—
May 6	1823	Ned Stockton	Blindlow Heath, Sussex, Eng.	W 40 rounds	—
Aug 5	1823	Lenney	Harpenden Common, Eng.	W 11 rounds	—
Nov 11	1823	Lenney	Moulsey Hurst	W 21 rounds	—
Dec 30	1823	Frank Redmond	Moulsey Hurst	W 29 rounds	—
Apr 6	1824	Peter Warren	Colbrook, England	W 29 rounds	—
June 21	1824	Arthur Matthewson	—	L 57 rounds	—
Feb 27	1827	Dick Curtis	Andover, England	L 50 min.	—
Oct 23	1827	Frank Redmond	near St. Albans, England	W 42 rounds	—
Apr 1	1834	Tom Smith	Greenstreet Green, Kent, Eng.	L 20 rounds	—

JEM BELCHER

A very agile, quick-hitting fighter, Jem Belcher held the English prize ring title for five years at the beginning of the nineteenth century. Born in Bristol, the home of many of boxing's early champions, Belcher first fought professionally in his hometown in 1798 when he defeated Jack Britton. A year later, Belcher fought Jack Bartholomew to a 51-round draw. At the time, Bartholomew was considered the champion in many quarters because he had beaten title-claimant Tom Owen. When Belcher triumphed over Bartholomew in a seventeen-round rematch in 1800, he was hailed as the new champion.

In 1803, Belcher lost sight in one eye when he was struck by the ball in a game of racquets. Half-blind, Belcher avoided defending his title for two years, fighting exhibition bouts only. In 1805, Belcher's former protégé, Henry Pearce, made a claim to the championship because of Belcher's inactivity. The weakened Belcher agreed to fight but, hurt by the loss of the eye and his intemperate lifestyle, he could not stand up to the aggressive, slugging Pearce. Belcher submitted after eighteen rounds.

Perhaps Belcher should have retired to his pub, The Jolly Brewer, after the Pearce defeat. Instead, he agreed in 1807 to fight Hall of Famer Tom Cribb, a champion in the making. The fight attracted a large crowd. For the first twenty rounds, Belcher dominated. Then Cribb hit Belcher over his good eye, nearly closing it. Belcher's hands were seriously injured and his punches were weak. Finally, after 41 rounds, the incapacitated Belcher could not go on. In a rematch two years later, Cribb outclassed Belcher again and won in 31 rounds. The defeat was particularly painful for Belcher because he had wagered his entire fortune on his own victory. He served four weeks in prison for starting a fracas after the fight, and while there, became seriously ill. A ruined man, Belcher died in 1811 and was honored at a well-attended funeral.

Right-handed; 5'11½"; 166–182 lbs.

English Champion 1800–1805

Hall of Fame Induction: 1992

Born: 4/15/1781, Bristol, England

Died: 7/30/1811

SELECTED BOUTS

Date	Year	Opponent	Location	Result / Duration		Title
Mar 16	1798	Jack Britton	Bristol, England	W	33 min.	—
Apr 15	1799	Paddington Jones	Wormwood Scrubbs, England	W	33 min.	—
Aug 15	1799	♛ Jack Bartholomew	Uxbridge, England	D	51 rounds	For-England-H
May 15	1800	♛ Jack Bartholomew	Finchley, England	W	17 rounds	Won-England-H
Dec 22	1800	Andrew Gamble	Wimbledon, England	W	5 rounds	Ret-England-H
Mar 16	1801	Joe Berks	Camberwell, England	W	14 rounds	Ret-England-H
Nov 25	1801	Joe Berks	Hurley, England	W	16 rounds	Ret-England-H
Aug 20	1802	Joe Berks	London	W	14 rounds	Ret-England-H
Apr 12	1803	Jack Firley	Linton, England	W	11 rounds	Ret-England-H
Dec 6	1805	Henry Pearce★	Near Doncaster, England	L	18 rounds	Lost-England-H
Apr 8	1807	Tom Cribb★	Moulsey Hurst, England	L	41 rounds	—
Feb 1	1809	Tom Cribb★	Epsom Downs, England	L	31 rounds	—

BENJAMIN BRAIN
Big Ben

Right-handed; 5'10"; 196 lbs.
English Champion 1791–94
Hall of Fame Induction: 1994
Born: 1753, Bristol, England
Died: 4/8/1794

Benjamin ("Big Ben") Brain outweighed most men and even most professional fighters in the England of the 1780s. A coal miner by trade, Brain was a valiant fighter whose career spanned twenty years. Brain was born in the port city of Bristol, in southwestern England. His first recorded fight took place in 1774, when he defeated Jack Clayton, the champion of Kingswood.

In 1786, when Brain battled John Boone ("The Fighting Grenadier"), toughs broke into the ring and ganged up on Brain. In the resulting melee, Brain suffered a beating that almost closed his eyes. When order was restored and a surgeon had lanced the swelling around Brain's eyes, Big Ben resumed fighting. Within ten minutes, he forced Boone to quit in defeat.

In 1789, Brain was scheduled to fight the English champion, Hall of Famer Tom Johnson. When Brain fell ill and cancelled the bout, he forfeited the large sum of money he had put up for the fight. Two years later, Brain got his chance to fight Johnson for the title at Wrotham-in-Kent. Brain battered Johnson's nose effectively, and Johnson broke a finger in the course of the eighteen-round battle. Brain, then 37, prevailed, to take the title from the 40-year-old Johnson.

Brain's toppling of Johnson is sometimes seen to mark the end of the first era of boxing, when men stood toe-to-toe and punched and grappled until one of them could no longer go on. There is no question that the early brawlers were courageous, but the boxers who came after Brain began to rely on more than just strength and stamina.

Soon after winning the championship in 1791, and with no challengers coming forward, Brain retired from boxing. The title was then declared vacant. Three years later, there was still no champion, although a suitable challenger had come forward. Brain agreed to return to the ring as the acknowledged titleholder and was scheduled to fight Will Wood in February of 1794 in a comeback bout. However, Brain was stricken with an illness and was unable to fight. He died in April 1794, still considered the champion.

SELECTED BOUTS

Date	Year	Opponent	Location	Result / Duration		Title
—	1774	Jack Clayton	England	W	—	—
Oct 31	1786	John Boone	Bloomsbury, England	W	app. 40 min.	—
Oct 31	1788	W. Corbally	Navestock, England	W	20 min.	—
Oct 23	1789	Jack Jacombs	Banbury, England	W	2 hrs. 5 min.	—
—	1789	Tom Tring	Dartford, England	W	12 rounds	—
Aug 30	1790	William Hooper	Chapel Row Level, Eng.	D	180 rounds	—
Jan 17	1791	♛ Tom Johnson★	Wrotham, England	W	18 rounds	Won-England-H

JACK BROUGHTON
The Father of Boxing

Jack Broughton is remembered both for his skill as a fighter and for the innovations he brought to the free-for-all fisticuffs that preceded modern boxing. In Broughton's time, there were few standards of fair play. Bare-handed combat between two men was seen as a civilized advance over dueling with swords or guns, but "the manly art of boxing" was an anything-goes sport with no written code. Broughton came to realize, however, that a well-placed punch could often do more damage than some of the less refined gambits. More than any other fighter before him, Broughton saw the advantage of sizing up a rival and adjusting his methods to overcome a perceived weakness. In 1738, Broughton defeated George Taylor, a student of England's first champion, James Figg, to win the title.

Right-handed; 5'11"; 196–200 lbs.
English Champion 1738–1750
Hall of Fame Induction: 1990
Born: 1704, Cirencester, England
Died: 1/8/1789

Broughton devised "Broughton's Rules" in 1743, two years after he unintentionally killed ring opponent George Stevenson. While still allowing many avenues of attack, Broughton's Rules introduced the now-familiar prohibition against hitting an "adversary when he is down," banned all but the fighters and their seconds from the ring, and gave a downed man half a minute to get up. Broughton also invented "mufflers," forerunners of modern boxing gloves, for use in training and exhibition matches.

Boxing was a popular diversion of the aristocratic class in the early eighteenth century, and like many early fighters, Broughton had a patron, the Duke of Cumberland. Cumberland abruptly withdrew his support, however, when Broughton lost the title to Jack Slack, Figg's grandson and a butcher by trade, in 1750. The bout with Slack lasted only fourteen minutes because Broughton could not recover from a blinding punch. Boxing historian Pierce Egan reported that Cumberland had thousands of pounds riding on the match and pushed Broughton to fight on even after his eyes had swollen shut. He shouted accusatorially at his fighter, "What are you about, Broughton? You can't fight! You're beat!" According to Egan, the courageous Broughton replied, "I can't see my man, your Highness; I am blind, but not beat; only let me be placed before my antagonist, and he shall not gain the day yet." After this defeat, Broughton never fought again, and he turned his academy, a popular boxing arena, into a profitable antique shop.

Broughton, who lived to be 85 years old, was buried in Westminster Abbey in remembrance of his contribution to English boxing. He earned lasting recognition as "The Father of the English School of Boxing" and as the "Father of the Science of the Art of Self-Defense." His Rules survived for almost 100 years, to be superceded by the London Prize Ring Rules in 1838.

SELECTED BOUTS

Date	Year	Opponent	Location	Result / Duration		Title
Circa	1733	Tom Pipes	England	W	—	—
Circa	1733	Bill Gretting	England	W	—	—
—	1738	George Taylor	England	W	—	Won-England-H
Feb 17	1741	♛ George Stevenson	London	W	40 min.	—
Apr 10	1750	Jack Slack	England	L	14 min.	Lost-England-H

JAMES BURKE
The Deaf 'Un

Right-handed; 5'8½"; 175–178 lbs.

English Champion 1833–1839

Hall of Fame Induction: 1992

Born: 12/8/1809, St. Giles, London, England

Died: 1/8/1845

James ("Deaf") Burke was the first British champion to fight on American soil. He was also the most active champion of his day, fighting twenty bouts, some of gruelling duration. Burke learned to box while working as a waterman on the Thames River. An older boxer gave Burke instruction and put him in the ring against Ned Murphy in 1828. The two battled for 50 rounds, until the match was called a draw because of darkness. Burke fought more marathon bouts in the next few years, including a three-hour victory over Bill Fitzmaurice and a two-hour-and-fifty-minute loss to Bill Cousens.

Burke was unsuccessful in attempts to be matched against champion Jem Ward, but when Ward retired, Burke fought Harry Macone for the title. In a brutal match, Burke triumphed in 59 rounds. The next year, Burke battled challenger Simon Byrne. By the nineteenth round, Burke was on the ground and his ear had been bitten through. The two men fought doggedly for more than three hours, however. Burke finally tapped an exhausted Byrne to the ground in the 99th round. Byrne died three days after the fight. Burke was not blamed, but he avoided competitions and fought only exhibitions for a time.

The Irish champion Sam O'Rourke challenged Burke for the title, but Burke declined when O'Rourke insisted that the fight be held in Ireland. O'Rourke then travelled to America, where he constantly denigrated Burke's abilities and courage. On hearing of the insults, Burke decided to meet his challenger in New Orleans in 1836. In the first round, Burke threw O'Rourke to the ground with a cross-buttock hold. In the next round, one of O'Rourke's seconds threw Burke into O'Rourke's grasp. By the third round, the fight had degenerated into a violent free-for-all. The crowd surged into the ring, and Burke was forced to flee the scene on horseback in fear for his life.

On his return to England, Burke faced Bendigo Thompson in the first championship match conducted under the more stringent London Prize Ring Rules, adopted in 1838. Thompson won on a foul in the tenth round. Burke fought twice more before retiring in 1843. Penniless, he died of tuberculosis less than two years later.

SELECTED BOUTS

Date	Year	Opponent	Location	Result / Rounds		Title
Feb 4	1828	Ned Murphey	England	D	50	—
Aug 6	1828	Thomas ("Bull") Hands	England	W	12	—
Jun 9	1829	Bill Fitzmaurice	Herpenden Cmn., Eng.	W	166	—
—	1832	Harry Macone	Lockington Bottom, Eng.	W	59	Won-Vac England-H
May 30	1833	Simon Byrne	near London	W	99	Ret-England-H
May 6	1836	Samuel O'Rourke	New Orleans	NC	3	—
Aug 21	1837	Tom O'Connell	Harts Island, NY	W	10	—
Feb 12	1839	Bendigo Thompson★	Heather, England	LF	10	Lost-England-H
Jun 13	1843	Bob Castles	Rainham Ferry, England	W	37	—

ARTHUR CHAMBERS

Arthur Chambers began fighting at the age of sixteen after a brief stint in the Royal Navy. His first fight on October 1, 1864, was a triumph, a twenty-round victory over his hometown opponent, Arthur Webber. Over the next eight years, Chambers won eight recorded bouts and drew four times. His lone defeat was at the hands of Jem Brady in a fight that lasted one hour and twenty minutes, until it was interrupted by police, then continued the next day for another three and one quarter hours before Brady's eventual victory.

Chambers next travelled to New York. In the manner of the day, he issued public challenges to fighters under one hundred twenty pounds, but found no takers. Finally, he was paired with a fellow Englishman, the American lightweight champion, Billy Edwards. Each side put up two thousand dollars, the money and championship to go to the victor. The fight, held on Squirrel Island, Canada, north of Detroit, on September 4, 1872, proved more difficult than Chambers anticipated. He absorbed a solid beating for 25 rounds. After coming to scratch for the 26th, Chambers clinched with Edwards and immediately claimed that Edwards had bitten him. The referee examined Chambers, found tooth marks, and awarded Chambers the victory on a foul. Rumors circulated that Chambers's second—not Edwards—had bitten him prior to the start of the 26th round to dupe the referee.

Right-handed; 5'4½"; 115–125 lbs.

American Lightweight Champion 1872–73, 1879

Hall of Fame Induction: 2000

Born: 12/3/1847, Salford, Lancashire, England

Died: 5/25/1925

The next year, Chambers defeated the highly regarded George Seddons. In 1877, he was forced to retire after the middle finger of his left hand was amputated, but two years later he returned to answer the challenge of Professor Johnny Clark, who claimed the lightweight title. Chambers proved his fighting mettle in a marathon 136 round, two-hour and twenty-minute victory over Clark, and then retired for good.

In retirement, Chambers remained active in the boxing world, serving as advisor and backer of John L. Sullivan, and also opened a bar in Philadelphia.

SELECTED BOUTS

Date	Year	Opponent	Location	Result / Rounds		Title
Oct 1	1864	Arthur Webber	Mode Wheel, near Manchester, England	W	20	—
Nov 15	1864	Fred Finch	London	W	64	—
Nov 8	1865	Ned Evans	Hazlehead Bridge, England	W	44	—
Aug 7	1866	Jem Brady	Southport Place, England	NC	28	—
Aug 8	1866	Jem Brady	Barton Moss, England	L	63	—
Feb 19	1867	Dick Goodwin	Acton, Cheshire, England	D	105	—
Sep 29	1868	Tom Scattergood	Manchester	W	40	—
Oct 6	1870	George Fletcher	Manchester	W	56	—
Sep 4	1872	Billy Edwards	Squirrel Island, Canada	WF	26	Won-Amer-L
Aug 3	1873	George Seddons	Long Island, NY	W	39	Ret-Amer-L
Mar 27	1879	Johnny Clark	Chippewa Falls, Canada	W	136	Won-Amer-L

TOM CRIBB

Right-handed; 5'10"; 196–199 lbs.

English Champion 1809–1822

Hall of Fame Induction: 1991

Born: 7/8/1781, Hanaham, Gloucestershire, England

Died: 5/11/1848

One of the first fighters to actually train for bouts, Tom Cribb is remembered as the master of milling on the retreat, or attacking and then stepping away. He held the championship for thirteen years and defeated the first fighters to arrive from America. Cribb worked for a time on the wharves of London, where he survived a couple of near-fatal accidents. Once he was crushed between two coal barges. Another time a five hundred-pound load of oranges fell on his chest.

Cribb's first recorded fight was a victory over George Maddox. He then defeated the black American fighter, Bill Richmond, in a 90-minute bout before facing former champion Jem Belcher in 1807. Belcher came close to winning at one point, but Cribb's second initiated a discussion concerning bets which lasted long enough to allow Cribb to get back on his feet. Cribb was able to close Belcher's one good eye to gain the victory. In a rematch in 1809, Cribb won easily and was generally considered to be the champion

In 1810, Cribb fought Tom Molineaux, a former American slave and the first black to fight for a championship. On an extremely cold day in December, the fighters battered each other mercilessly. In the nineteenth round, Molineaux held Cribb so that Cribb could not either hit him or fall down. A crowd of spectators rushed the ring, and Molineaux suffered a broken finger in the unruly scene. When the fight resumed, Molineaux seized control for the next several rounds, but eventually Cribb managed to close both of the challenger's eyes. Molineaux also began shivering from the weather and, after 33 rounds, could not continue.

Before a rematch with Molineaux, Cribb went to Scotland to train. Using runs and long walks, Cribb reduced his weight and improved his stamina. He also stayed away from alcohol, reportedly no small sacrifice. The fight was short for those days, and brutal. Molineaux dominated the early rounds until Cribb—with nose and mouth bleeding and both eyes swollen—turned to body punching. In the ninth round, Cribb knocked his opponent down with a left to the jaw. Molineaux did not get up in time, but Cribb, wanting to prove his worth, allowed the fight to continue. In the eleventh, he knocked Molineaux unconscious.

Cribb then retired except for one comeback bout, a victory over Jack Carter in 1820. Careers as the owner of a public house and as a coal merchant did not bring lasting success to Cribb, who died at age 68.

SELECTED BOUTS

Date	Year	Opponent	Location	Result / Rounds		Title
Oct 8	1805	Bill Richmond★	Hailsham, Sussex, Eng.	W	90 min.	For-England-H
Jan 7	1805	George Maddox	Wood Green, England	W	76	—
Apr 8	1807	Jem Belcher★	Moulsey Hurst, England	W	41	—
Feb 1	1809	Jem Belcher★	Epsom Downs, England	W	31	Won-England-H
Dec 18	1810	Tom Molineaux★	Copthall Common, England	W	33	Ret-England-H
Sep 28	1811	Tom Molineaux★	Thistleton, England	W	11	Ret-England-H

MIKE DONOVAN
Professor

Mike Donovan, who came to be known as "Professor" in honor of his long career as boxing instructor at the New York Athletic Club, was born in Chicago on September 27, 1847. While still a teenager, he enlisted with the Union Army and served in the Civil War.

After the war, Donovan went to New Orleans where he trained under veteran boxer Frank Kendrick. He then traveled up the Mississippi to St. Louis. In July 1866, in a 92-round fight, Donovan lost on a foul to Billy Crowley.

By 1872 Donovan had moved his base of operations to New York City. He became a popular attraction at Harry Hill's, the legendary fight club and tavern. The next year he fought the toughest bout of his career, against Jim Murray. The pair battled for 44 bloody rounds until police intervened.

Right-handed; 148 lbs.
Hall of Fame Induction: 1998
Born: 9/27/1847, Chicago
Died: 3/24/1918

In April 1878, Donovan faced William McClellan for the American middleweight crown, but lost on a foul in fourteen rounds. In 1881, Donovan gained some recognition as the American middleweight champion when he battered title claimant George Rooke for two rounds before police stopped the fight.

In 1880 and 1881, Donovan fought two exhibitions with the up-and-coming John L. Sullivan. Though Donovan's great defensive skills enabled him to survive both these fights with draws, Sullivan's punching power convinced Donovan that the heavyweight crown was beyond his reach.

Donovan retired after defeating 180-pound Walter Watson in October 1884. In addition to a purse, he was awarded the position of boxing instructor at the New York Athletic Club. Donovan worked at the club for over thirty years. One of his pupils was Theodore Roosevelt, who later invited Donovan to the White House to spar.

In 1888, Donovan came out of his ring retirement to fight middleweight champion Jack Dempsey ("The Nonpareil"). Though Donovan had not fought in four years and was 41 years old, he forced the action from the start. Dempsey had to flee along the ropes to escape Donovan's attack. After six rounds the referee called the fight a draw.

When World War I started, Donovan served as a boxing instructor for recruits in the New York area. He died of pneumonia on March 24, 1918. Donovan's son, referee Arthur Donovan, is also a member of the International Boxing Hall of Fame, and his grandson, Art, is a member of the Pro Football Hall of Fame.

SELECTED BOUTS

Date	Year	Opponent	Location	Result / Duration		Title
Jul	1866	Billy Crowley	St. Louis	LF	92 rounds	—
Jun	1873	Jim Murray	Philadelphia	D	44 rounds	—
Apr 5	1878	William McClellan	San Francisco	LF	14 rounds	For-Amer-M
May 18	1878	William McClellan	—	W	7 rounds	—
Feb	1880	John L. Sullivan★	Boston	Exh	4 rounds	—
Apr 25	1881	George Rooke	New York	W	2 rounds	—
Mar 21	1881	John L. Sullivan★	Boston	Exh	4 rounds	—
Oct 17	1884	Walter Watson	New York	W	7 rounds	—
Nov 15	1888	Jack Dempsey (Nonpareil)★	Brooklyn	D	6 rounds	—
May	1891	William McClellan	New York	W	48 seconds	—

PADDY DUFFY

Right-handed; 5'7"; 135–142 lbs.
Welterweight Champion 1888–89
Hall of Fame Induction: 1994
Born: 11/12/1864, Boston, MA
Died: 7/10/1890

Considered the first welterweight champion, Paddy Duffy, like John L. Sullivan, was an Irish-American from Boston. His first fight, at age nineteen, was a knockout victory over Skin Doherty in 1884.

Duffy won his first four bouts before fighting three draws with Paddy Sullivan. After one loss in a bout with Jack C. McGee, Duffy never lost again. He fought in Baltimore, Washington, and Philadelphia in 1886 and 1887 before returning to Boston, where he entered a four-fight series with Jack McGinty. Their first two fights ended in draws. Duffy won a six-round decision in the third fight and solidified his reputation by knocking out McGinty in the ninth round of the fourth fight.

At this point, Duffy sported a record of 21-1-11, which earned him the right to face William McMillan, the English welterweight champ. Fighting at Fort Foote in Vancouver, Canada, Duffy knocked McMillan out in seventeen rounds to claim the world title.

In Duffy's next fight, he faced Tom Meadows, the Australian champion, in San Francisco. At the time, the welterweight division had an upper weight limit of 142 pounds. Duffy tipped the scales for this bout at 140 while Meadows came in at 143. The two battled for 45 rounds before Duffy won on a foul. Duffy never fought again and died in 1890 at the age of 25.

SELECTED BOUTS

Date	Year	Opponent	Location	Result / Rounds		Title
Feb	1884	Skin Doherty	Boston	KO	3	—
May	1884	Paddy Sullivan	Gloucester, MA	D	6	—
Jun	1884	Paddy Sullivan	Lowell, MA	D	6	—
Jun	1884	Paddy Sullivan	Boston	D	6	—
Dec 19	1884	Jack C. McGee	Boston	KO'd	2	—
Jan 28	1886	Bill Young	Baltimore	D	6	—
Mar	1886	Bill Young	Baltimore	KO	2	—
Apr 22	1886	Bill Nally	Washington	KO	4	—
May	1886	Danny Shea	Baltimore	KO	7	—
June	1886	Charles Gleason	Philadelphia	W	4	—
June	1886	Butler's Unknown	Philadelphia	W	4	—
Oct	1886	Charles Gleason	Philadelphia	D	4	—
May	1887	Jack McGinty	Boston	D	6	—
Jun	1887	Jack McGinty	Boston	D	6	—
Oct	1887	Jack McGinty	Boston	W	6	—
Feb 9	1888	Jack McGinty	Boston	KO	9	—
Oct 30	1888	William McMillan	Vancouver, B.C.	KO	17	Won-Vac World-W
Mar 29	1889	Tom Meadows	San Francisco	WF	45	Ret-World-W

DUTCH SAM
The Terrible Jew

Dutch Sam (born Samuel Elias) never fought at more than 134 pounds, but he often defeated men more than thirty pounds heavier. Sam came from the Whitechapel area of London that would later produce Jackie ("Kid") Berg and Ted ("Kid") Lewis.

As legend has it, Sam first began to box formally after Harry Lee, a man active in the fight game, noticed Sam in a fight and taught him the basics of boxing. Fighting Lee himself, Sam recorded his first victory on October 12, 1801. Sam impressed ring observers with his extremely well-muscled physique although he stood only 5'6½". Despite his lack of size, Sam was known as the hardest hitter of his era and earned the nickname, "The Man with the Iron Hand."

In 1804 Sam fought his first major battle, facing the "Pride of Westminster," Caleb Baldwin, a bigger and more experienced pugilist. For twenty rounds Baldwin dominated, attempting to fight inside to utilize his superior size. Sam held Baldwin at bay by firing uppercuts to his face, then began to gain strength and hammered away at Baldwin until he knocked him out in the 37th round.

Right-handed; 5'6½"; 133 lbs.
Hall of Fame Induction: 1997
Born: 4/4/1775 London
Named: Samuel Elias
Died: 7/3/1816

Sam's most important fights were with Tom Belcher. When they first met in 1806, Belcher, the brother of Hall of Famer Jem Belcher, was considered England's top boxer at the 140-pound level. The two engaged in a hard-fought battle that lasted 57 rounds before Belcher succumbed. In the rematch Sam had the edge. The fight ended in controversy when a wild swing by Sam hit Belcher in the face while Belcher was on his way to the ground. Belcher's supporters argued that Sam had committed a foul. Ring officials could not agree on the proper ruling, so the fight ended without a winner. In their final meeting, Sam defeated Belcher in 36 rounds. Daniel Mendoza seconded Sam in this battle.

After defeating Ben Medley in 1810, Sam announced his retirement. A man who had always boasted that he could train on gin, Sam drank heavily. He fought once more in 1814 against William Nosworthy, with whom he had gotten into a dispute while drunk. The years of drinking and lack of training had rendered Sam a much less physically impressive version of his former self. Nosworthy easily defeated him in nine rounds.

This defeat did not tarnish Sam's overall reputation as a scientific fighter with incredibly strong hands and a hard punch. Sam and Mendoza rank as the two greatest Jewish fighters of the Pioneer era, and historians believe Sam was the first boxer to use the uppercut. Sam died in 1816. His son, Young Dutch Sam, followed in his father's footsteps and had a very successful ring career.

SELECTED BOUTS

Date	Year	Opponent	Location	Result / Duration		Title
Oct 12	1801	Harry Lee	—	W	—	—
Aug 7	1804	Caleb Baldwin	Woodford Green, England	W	37 rounds	—
Apr 27	1805	Bill Britton	Shepperton, England	W	30 rounds	—
Feb 8	1806	Tom Belcher	Virginia Water, England	W	57 rounds	—
Jul 28	1807	Tom Belcher	Moulsey Hurst, England	ND	34 rounds	—
Aug 21	1807	Tom Belcher	Crawley Common, England	W	36 rounds	—
May 10	1808	Bill Cropley	—	W	25 min.	—
May 10	1810	Ben Medley	Moulsey Hurst	W	49 rounds	—
Dec 8	1814	Bill Nosworthy	Moulsey Hurst	L	9 rounds	—

YOUNG DUTCH SAM

Right-handed; 5'9"; 137 lbs.

Hall of Fame Induction: 2002

Born 1/30/1808, London

Named: Samuel Evans

Died: 11/4/1843

With Young Dutch Sam's 2002 induction, he and his father, Dutch Sam, join referee Arthur Donovan and Professor Mike Donovan as the only father-son combinations in the International Boxing Hall of Fame. His father was still an active fighter when Young Dutch Sam (Samuel Evans) was born in London on January 30, 1808. Like his father, Young Dutch Sam was not a heavyweight. He stood about 5'9" and never weighed more than 145 pounds.

As a youngster, Young Dutch Sam gained employment with Pierce Egan—Hall of Famer, early boxing journalist, and publisher. Evans worked as a "runner" for Egan's weekly newspaper, *Pierce Egan's Life in London*. The runner's job was to distribute the paper to pubs frequented by "the Fancy" (as sports fans were then termed). Through Egan, Sam met Hall of Famer Gentleman Jackson, who—years before—had defeated Mendoza for the heavyweight championship. Soon after meeting Jackson, Sam abandoned the newspaper business for the prize ring.

In his first recorded fight, when he was only fifteen, he defeated Bill Dean. Young Dutch displayed a mixture of power and speed in the ring. His movements were very graceful and yet he had the ability to inflict great punishment with his left hand as he did when he cut Gypsy Cooper to ribbons with his left jab in 1826 at Gravesend. Hughes Ball, a wealthy and socially prominent member of the Fancy, became Sam's patron. In one of Sam's best-remembered bouts, it took 30 rounds and a total of 3 hours and 35 minutes for Sam to finally vanquish Dick Davis on June 19, 1827 at Havensham.

Surviving records of Young Dutch's career show only victories in his sixteen battles between 1823 and 1834. He may also have had a few losses, however. A quote by one of his contemporaries Charles Knight in his autobiography recounts a match in which he "saw Young Dutch Sam fall across the ropes with a broken arm."

Tragedy struck on March 13, 1838, while Sam was acting as a second to Owen Swift in his bout with Brighton Bikl. Bikl died in the ring and Swift, Sam, and all the other participants were arrested and tried. Some of the defendants were sentenced to prison, but all were soon released. Sam retired from the ring and opened a public house or "pub." Young Dutch Sam died at the age of 35.

SELECTED BOUTS

Date	Year	Opponent	Location	Result / Duration	Title
—	1823	Bill Dean	England	W 45 min.	—
Oct 18	1825	Harry Jones	Shere Mere, England	W 18 rounds	—
Apr 25	1826	Gypsy Cooper	Gravesend, England	W 18 rounds	—
Jun 8	1826	Bill Carroll	Ascot, England	W 16 rounds	—
Apr 27	1827	Jack Cooper	Andover, England	W 9 rounds	—
Jun 19	1827	Dick Davis	Havensham, England	W 30 rounds	—
Apr 7	1829	Ned Neale	Ludlow, England	W 78 rounds	—
Jun 24	1834	Tom Gaynor	Andover, England	W 17 rounds	—

JAMES FIGG

Although fisticuffs as a sport started in England about 40 years before his rise to prominence, James Figg is considered to have been the first heavyweight boxing champion. He was also the first to teach and promote boxing both as a skill and a competitive sport.

Six feet tall and a multi-talented athlete, Figg was an expert fencer and was a popular performer in fairs. He gained fame for his skill in exhibitions with the sword and the cudgel before adding bare knuckle fighting to his repertoire. By 1719, Figg's claim to the bare knuckle championship was secure. He fended off several challengers, including three-time opponent Ned Sutton. Figg defeated Sutton with his fists, sword, and cudgel.

With the backing of a patron, the Earl of Peterborough, Figg opened a fighting academy in London on what is now known as Tottenham Court Road. His advertising card, designed for him by the artist William Hogarth, proclaimed him "master of the noble science of defence" and offered to teach gentlemen in the use of "the small backsword and quarterstaff at home and abroad." Hogarth was a great friend of Figg's and also painted a portrait showing the fighter in a lace shirt and wig, holding his clenched fists before him.

Right-handed; 6'; 185 lbs.
First English Champion 1719–1734
Hall of Fame Induction: 1992
Born: 1695, Thame, Oxfordshire, England
Died: 12/8/1734

Figg later established Figg's Amphitheatre in Oxford Road, one of several London arenas devoted to staging matches in the growing sport of prizefighting. In these permanent venues, the "ring" that had originally been formed by spectators, sometimes holding a rope in their hands, became an elevated square platform, enclosed with wooden rails. Figg popularized sparring as a public entertainment, and his school was frequented by the upper classes, with noblemen often arriving in groups to try their hand at boxing or fencing.

Since bare knuckle exhibitions were also tremendously popular with the working classes, Figg continued to make appearances in public, often at London's Southwark Fair, in a boxing booth where he would take on all comers. Fighting infrequently in formal matches, Figg retained the championship until his retirement in 1734 when his premier student, George Taylor, declared himself successor to the title.

Figg, who socialized with the Prince of Wales and other members of the royal family, died in 1740, leaving a wife and several children. Although some considered him a better swordsman than boxer, Figg is called "The Father of Boxing" for his role in popularizing and teaching the sport.

SELECTED BOUTS

Date	Year	Opponent	Location	Result / Duration		Title
Circa	1720	Timothy Buck	England	W	—	—
Circa	1720	Tom Stokes	England	W	—	—
Circa	1720	Bill Flanders	England	W	—	—
—	1723	Chris Clarkson	England	W	30 min.	—
—	—	Ned Sutton (3 bouts)	England	W	—	—

JOHN C. HEENAN
The Benicia Boy

Right-handed; 6'2"; 182–195 lbs.

Hall of Fame Induction: 2002

Born: 5/2/1835, Troy, NY

Named: John Carmel Heenan

Died: 10/28/1873

The son of Irish immigrant parents, Heenan worked as an unskilled laborer before moving to California in 1852, where he swung a hammer in the workshops of the Pacific Mail Steamship Company in Benicia. The 6'2", 200-pound Heenan was very muscular and earned a reputation for toughness.

Heenan returned to the East and obtained a position in the New York Customs House. Soon after, he began to issue challenges to American heavyweight champion John Morrissey through the *New York Sun*. On July 3, 1858, Heenan published a card issuing a formal challenge, and Morrissey agreed to fight.

In order to avoid police interference, the fight took place in Canada. Held on October 20, 1858, with stakes of $5,000 a side, the match drew bets from around the country. Heenan entered the ring suffering from an abscess in his leg, and though he got off to a strong start, the veteran Morrissey began to dominate as the bout continued. By the eleventh round, Heenan, weakened by the abscess, collapsed. The victorious Morrissey refused Heenan a rematch, and never fought again.

Unable to fight Morrissey, Heenan set his sights on Tom Sayers, who, as the British champion, was the de facto champion of the world. Enthusiasm in the U.S. about that meeting surpassed even the excitement over the Morrissey fight, and many believe that no sporting event between the years 1825 and 1875 attracted as much attention.

On April 17, 1860, Heenan met Sayers in a field at Farnborough, England. Heenan was eight years younger, five inches taller, and much heavier, but Sayers was favored. The pair battled for more than two hours, neither gaining a decisive upper hand. In the 37th round, constables attempted to push through the crowd to the ring to stop the fight. According to some accounts, Heenan thrust Sayer's throat against the ropes, which were then cut. The referee called the fight a draw, but the timekeeper called the fighters back for another five rounds before the confusion in and around the ring forced the end of the match. Again, the match was ruled a draw.

Heenan had only one more major fight, facing champion Tom King at Wadhurst, England, on December 10, 1863. Relying on superior strength and wrestling tactics, Heenan ignored defense and was soundly defeated in 24 rounds, although controversy surrounded the bout.

Plagued by consumption and pneumonia, Heenan never fought again. His health had long been in decline, and at Green Run Station, Wyoming, he was forced by illness to leave the train in which he was travelling. Heenan died shortly thereafter.

SELECTED BOUTS

Date	Year		Opponent	Location	Result / Duration		Title
Oct 20	1858		John Morrissey★	Long Pt. Island, Canada	L	11	For-Vac America-H
Apr 17	1860	♛	Tom Sayers	Farnborough, England	D	42	For-England-H
Dec 10	1863	♛	Tom King	Wadhurst, Kent, England	L	24	For-England-H

JOHN JACKSON
Gentleman Jackson

Winning England's prize ring championship in the third and final fight of his sparse career, John Jackson exemplified the "gentleman boxer." The son of a builder, Jackson was of a higher socioeconomic status than his predecessors and he hobnobbed successfully with the nobility. He dressed well and behaved in a polite manner, and so brought an often-missing gentility to the sport.

A great athlete, Jackson was also an accomplished sprinter and long jumper. He first fought professionally in 1788 when he defeated the more experienced and previously unbeaten William Fewterel. Jackson proved himself to be a fine two-handed puncher, using his left more than most fighters of his time. Jackson next fought George Ingelston. Jackson won the first two rounds, but in the third, as he was attempting to finish Ingelston, Jackson skidded on the slippery ring surface. Historians disagree as to whether Jackson turned his ankle or broke his leg, but in any case, he was down, and Ingelston was declared the winner.

The loss stung Jackson badly and he retired from the ring, having only fought twice. Not until six years later, in 1795, did the chance to fight the highly skilled Daniel Mendoza for the title finally motivate Jackson to return. Jackson scored an easy victory in nine rounds totaling eleven minutes, although he prevailed through the use of a questionable tactic. Jackson grabbed Mendoza's long hair with one hand. With Mendoza held before him, Jackson slugged him mercilessly with his free hand. This maneuver was not against the rules of the time, and Jackson won the fight without penalty.

Right-handed; 5'11"; 202 lbs.

English Champion 1795

Hall of Fame Induction: 1992

Born: 9/25/1769, London, England

Died: 10/7/1845

Content in the knowledge that he had at last won the title, Jackson retired again. He turned his attention to operating his London boxing academy, where he instructed many members of the nobility, including Lord Byron. Jackson encouraged fighters at his academy to use "mufflers," the hand covering that Hall of Famer Jack Broughton invented for training and sparring.

During King George IV's coronation, Jackson was recruited to assemble guards to keep order. He assembled a complement of eighteen prizefighters. A popular sports celebrity of his day, Jackson was a favorite of the more common people as well as the aristocrats. He died at the age of 76, and at his grave, a statue of a crouching lion was erected to symbolize his great skill and strength.

SELECTED BOUTS

Date	Year	Opponent	Location	Result / Duration		Title
Jun 9	1788	William Fewterel	Smitham Bottom, Eng.	W	1 hr. 7 min.	—
Mar 12	1789	George Ingelston	England	L	20 min.	—
Apr 15	1795	♛ Daniel Mendoza★	Hornchurch, England	W	9 rounds	Won-England-H

TOM JOHNSON

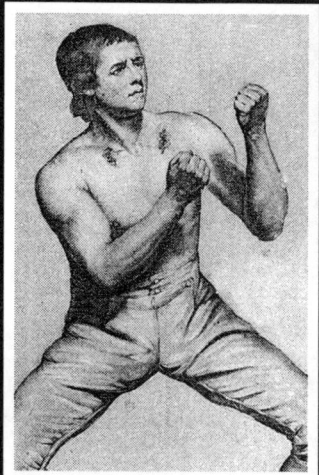

Right-handed; 5'10"; 202 lbs.

English Champion 1784–91

Hall of Fame Induction: 1995

Born: 1750, Derby, England

Named: Thomas Jackling

Died: 1/21/1797

Tom Johnson restored to boxing a modicum of credibility and public respect—lost since the days of Hall of Famer Jack Broughton. After Broughton's demise in 1750, the title was held for ten years by Jack Slack, inventor of the paralyzing rabbit punch and accused fixer of fights. By the time Slack was defeated, crooked fights were common. The championship bounced from one fighter to another, and by the 1780s, no one had a firm hold on it.

Born in Derby, Johnson worked for many years as a stevedore on London's wharves. In 1783, he became champion almost by chance when he offended a fighter named Jack Jarvis. This led to a challenge and a boxing match in which Johnson convincingly defeated Jarvis in just fifteen minutes. After this victory, some acclaimed Johnson as the champion. No one had held the title since Irishman Duggan Fearns defeated Harry Sellers in a 90-second fight, reputed to have been fixed. When Fearns abruptly disappeared from the scene, the title became vacant.

Johnson defeated the Croydon Drover in 1784, and later that year, triumphed over Stephen ("Death") Oliver. At this point, Johnson declared himself champion. In 1786, Johnson whipped four more opponents easily, then faced the Irish champion Michael Ryan the next year. The two champions fought ferociously. When Ryan landed a hard punch to Johnson's temple, sending him reeling against the ropes, Johnson's second entered the ring and grabbed Ryan. Ryan could have claimed victory on the foul but did not. Given time to recover, Johnson came back to defeat Ryan ten minutes later. He also won a rematch.

Johnson's next fight was a grueling 62-round battle with Isaac Perrins. Though he suffered several knockdowns, Johnson hung on to win. In 1791, the aging Johnson lost his title to Ben Brain in eighteen rounds.

By the time he retired, Johnson had amassed a small fortune, but within a year, he had spent and gambled it all away. He then taught boxing in Ireland until his death in 1797. Johnson's refusal to engage in "crosses," as fixed fights were called, rekindled the public's interest in boxing and restored much-needed integrity to the sport.

SELECTED BOUTS

Date	Year	Opponent	Location	Result	/ Duration	Title
Jun	1783	Jack Jarvis	Walworth, England	W	15 min.	—
Mar	1784	Croydon Drover	England	W	27 min.	—
Jun	1784	Stephen ("Death") Oliver	England	W	35 min.	Won-Vac England-H
Jan 18	1787	Bill Warr	Okingham, England	W	1 hr. 40 min.	Ret-England-H
Dec 19	1787	Michael Ryan	England	W	30 min.	Ret-England-H
Feb 11	1789	Michael Ryan	Rickmansworth	W	33 min.	Ret-England-H
Nov 22	1789	Isaac Perrins	Banbury, England	W	62 rounds	Ret-England-H
Jan 17	1791	Benjamin Brain★	England	L	18 rounds	Lost-England-H

TOM KING
The Fighting Sailor

Born on England's seacoast, Tom King became a sailor at an early age and travelled to Africa, among other ports. He learned to box in the British Royal Navy where he fought both bare fisted and with gloves. King later worked as a foreman on the London docks. After King defeated a bully known as Brighton Bill, Hall of Famer Jem Ward took an interest in King and began to train him. King scored a one-round victory over a top dockyard fighter, Bill Clamp, in his first professional bout.

King defeated Tom Truckle and Young Broome before taking a shot at the championship, held by Hall of Famer Jem Mace, in 1862. For the first half of the 43-round match, King dominated Mace, nearly closing both of his eyes. Mace recovered, however, and took control from the 30th round until the end of the fight. A knockdown blow to the throat put King out of commission.

In a rematch less than a year later, Mace again appeared to be getting the better of King, whose face was badly battered. In the nineteenth round, Mace went in for the kill, but left himself open for a right cross to the face from King.

Right-handed; 6'2"; 175 lbs.

English Champion 1863

Hall of Fame Induction: 1992

Born: 8/14/1835, Stepney, London, England

Died: 10/3/1888

Mace was knocked down, and only frantic efforts by his seconds enabled him to start the next round. Mace struggled into the 21st round when King simply pushed him down. Mace's seconds then threw in the sponge, and King was the champion.

Although King refused to fight Mace again, he did agree to a match with John Heenan, the American known as the Benicia Boy, who had earlier fought Tom Sayers to a draw. Heenan relied on his superior strength and wrestling tactics, foolishly ignoring defensive fighting. The more accomplished King easily took the measure of Heenan and won a 24-round fight, absorbing very little punishment himself.

After successfully defending the English boxing crown against Heenan, King retired. Unlike many professional fighters of his time—and many since—King did not live out his remaining days in poverty. He became an accomplished oarsman and a very successful bookmaker. He married the daughter of a ship owner and amassed considerable wealth before his death.

SELECTED BOUTS

Date	Year	Opponent	Location	Result / Rounds		Title
—	1859	Bill Clamp	—	W	1	—
Nov 27	1860	Tom Truckle	Kentish Marshes, England	W	49	—
Oct 21	1861	Young Broome	Farnborough, England	W	43	—
Jan 28	1862	♛ Jem Mace★	Godstone, England	L	43	For-England-H
Nov 26	1862	♛ Jem Mace★	Medway, England	W	21	Won-England-H
Dec 10	1863	John C. Heenan★	Wadhurst, England	W	24	Ret-England-H

NAT LANGHAM

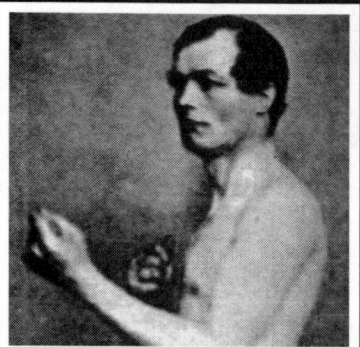

Right-handed; 5'10"; 152–156 lbs.

Middleweight Champion 1843–57

Hall of Fame Induction: 1992

Born: May 1820, Hinckley, Leicestershire, England

Died: 9/1/1871

Considered the best middleweight of his day, Nat Langham compiled a fine record which included a victory over Hall of Famer Tom Sayers. Born in Hinckley, England, Langham worked as a farm laborer before moving to London to work briefly as a delivery man. Langham's earliest recorded bouts took place in Hinckley, but he honed his skills in London where he came under the direction of former heavyweight champion Ben Caunt. Using sharp, well-timed blows—especially with his left, which Tom Sayers called the "Pickaxe"—Langham carved out several impressive victories. A win over William Ellis in 1843 gave Langham the middleweight title.

In 1851, Langham suffered the only defeat of his career, at the hands of Harry Orme. The battle raged for 117 rounds. Langham cut Orme's mouth and nose in the first round. Langham's shots raised a mouse under each eye but an Orme hip-toss dazed Langham in the eleventh. The fighting continued for two hours and forty-six minutes. Finally, Langham gave up the struggle after Orme threw him again, and Orme had the victory.

When Langham faced the highly respected George Guttridge, the two fought for an hour and twenty-five minutes. In the first ten rounds, Langham had the advantage. For the next 40, Guttridge appeared to improve. From the 51st until the 93rd, Langham took control until Guttridge finally conceded.

Langham also fought the up-and-coming Tom Sayers. In the 61st round, Langham closed both of Sayers's eyes and knocked him to the ground, ending the fight. After this grueling fight, Sayers attempted to secure a rematch but none was forthcoming. Langham then retired to open the Cambrian Stores, a tavern. He also owned a boxing booth and founded the Rum-rum-Pas Club for aristocratic ring patrons. He remained active in boxing and as a tavern owner for many years. He did come out of retirement once, in part to settle a family dispute with his former mentor, Caunt, who was also his wife's uncle. The two fought to a 60-round draw in 1857.

SELECTED BOUTS

Date	Year	Opponent	Location	Result / Rounds		Title
—	1842	Tom Lowe	England	W	43	—
—	1842	Bill Croazier	England	W	8	—
—	1842	Ned Ellis	England	W	8	—
Feb 9	1843	William Ellis	—	W	8	Won-England-M
Jun 12	1845	Doc Campbell	—	W	27	—
May 4	1847	William Sparks	—	W	67	—
May	1851	Harry Orme	—	L	117	—
Oct 18	1853	Tom Sayers★	Lakenheath, England	W	61	Ret-England-M
—	1854	George Guttridge	—	W	93	Ret-England-M
Sep 9	1857	Ben Caunt	—	D	60	—

JEM MACE
The Gypsy

Jem Mace brought a more scientific style of fighting to the ring than did most of his predecessors. Before making fighting his career, Mace worked as an apprentice cabinetmaker and as a fiddler. He defeated Slasher Slack in his first professional fight in 1855.

Mace's success brought him the attention of Nat Langham, who hired him to man his touring boxing booth, taking on all comers. In 1861, Mace agreed to fight Sam Hurst, considered the champion by virtue of his victory over title-claimant Tom Paddock. Hurst, a noted wrestler, outweighed Mace by about one hundred pounds. Mace eluded Hurst's rushes and in the eighth round, knocked him unconscious.

As champion, Mace toured the country in a circus before facing Tom King in 1862. Mace had taken notes on King's style, an unusual practice in those days. On a cold, rainy January day, Mace struggled for 22 rounds with the larger King, who outweighed him by about 25 pounds. King's punches closed Mace's left eye and almost closed his right. In the 30th round, Mace backheeled King, who fell on his head. In the 43rd, a left to the throat and a throw to the ground ended it for King.

In the rematch, King upset Mace to win the championship. When King refused to fight Mace again, Mace picked a fight with him on the street. When King retired, Mace was again considered the champion. With boxing in a decline in England, Mace travelled to the United States. In 1870 and 1871, he fought the American champion Joe Coburn. Police stopped the first bout, held in Port Ryeson, Canada, before a winner was determined. In the second fight, in Bay St. Louis, Mississippi, the two fought to a draw. Mace continued to fight sporadically until he was in his sixties.

Right-handed; 5'9½"; 144–168 lbs.

English Champion 1866–71

Hall of Fame Induction: 1990

Born: 4/8/1831, Beeston, Norwich, England

Died: 3/3/1910

Mace also helped foster the growth of boxing in Australia when he toured there. He taught Australia's top trainer, Larry Foley, many fine points of the sport which Foley later imparted to such notables as Bob Fitzsimmons, Peter Jackson, and Young Griffo. Mace spent the last years of his life back in England, where he died at the age of 79.

SELECTED BOUTS

Date	Year	Opponent	Location	Result / Rounds		Title
Oct 2	1855	Slasher Slack	Mildenhall, England	W	9	—
Sep 21	1858	Bob Brettle	Near Thames Haven, England	L	2	For-England-W
Sep 20	1860	Bob Brettle	Near Foolness Island, England	W	5	Won-England-W
Jun 18	1861	♔ Sam Hurst	Medway Island, England	W	8	Won-England-H
Jan 28	1862	Tom King★	Godstone, England	W	43	Ret-England-H
Nov 26	1862	Tom King★	Near Thames Haven	L	21	Lost-England-H
Sep 1	1863	Joe Goss	London	W	19	Won-England-M
Aug 6	1866	Joe Goss	London	W	21	Ret-England-H
May 10	1870	Tom Allen	Kennerville, LA	W	10	Won-World-H
Nov 30	1871	Joe Coburn	Bay St. Louis, MS	D	12	Ret-World-H
Feb 7	1890	Charlie Mitchell★	Glasgow	L	4	—

DANIEL MENDOZA

Right-handed; 5'7"; 160–168 lbs.

English Champion 1794–95

Hall of Fame Induction: 1990

Born: 7/5/1764, London, England

Died: 9/3/1836

Daniel Mendoza was the first to truly put the "science" in the Sweet Science. More than any previous fighter, Mendoza relied on footwork, jabs, and defense rather than pure brute force. Although relatively small at 5'7" and 160 pounds, Mendoza's speed and agility allowed him to triumph over larger, slower opponents. Lauded by early boxing historian Pierce Egan as "a complete artist" and "a star of the first brilliancy," Mendoza was a very popular fighter who enjoyed a short reign as England's champion.

Of Spanish heritage, Mendoza was the first Jewish fighter to gain prominence. He grew up in London's East End in poor surroundings and worked as a glass cutter, laborer, assistant to a green grocer, and an actor before making a career of fighting. His first recorded fight was a victory over Harry the Coalheaver. After he defeated Sam Martin ("The Bath Butcher") in 1787, Mendoza established a reputation as a fighter of the first rank.

In 1788, Mendoza embarked on a bitter three-fight series with Richard Humphries. Mendoza lost the first fight when he suffered a leg injury and threw in the towel after 29 minutes. In the rematch the following year, Mendoza thoroughly dominated Humphries to win in 52 minutes. Mendoza also won the third encounter in fifteen minutes.

With the retirement of Ben Brain, Mendoza claimed the championship. His grip on the title was solidified with a victory over Bill Warr in 1794. As champion, Mendoza toured England, Scotland, and Ireland demonstrating his skills as part of the Aston Circus. While in Ireland, Mendoza thrashed Squire Fitzgerald, who had made derogatory remarks about Mendoza's skills and ethnicity.

Mendoza held the title until 1795 when John Jackson rather easily knocked him out in nine rounds. Mendoza retired only to return, for financial reasons, at the age of 41 with a victory over Harry Lee in 1806. He even fought one losing effort in 1820. He ran boxing schools and owned a tavern in retirement. Mendoza's contributions to boxing had a lasting impact. His impressive ring displays further popularized boxing, and by teaching and example, he advanced the use of more sophisticated tactics in the ring.

SELECTED BOUTS

Date	Year	Opponent	Location	Result / Duration		Title
—	—	Harry the Coalheaver	England	W	40 min.	—
—	1787	BIll Warr	England	W	23 rounds	—
Jan 9	1788	Richard Humphries	Odiham, England	L	29 min.	—
May 6	1789	Richard Humphries	Stilton, England	W	52 min.	—
Sep 29	1790	Richard Humphries	Doncaster, England	W	15 min.	—
May 14	1792	Bill Warr	Croyden, England	W	23 rounds	—
Nov 12	1794	Bill Warr	Bexley Common, Eng.	W	15 min.	Won-England-H
Apr 15	1795	John Jackson★	Hornchurch, England	L	9 rounds	Lost-England-H
Jul 4	1820	Tom Owen	Banstead Downs, Eng.	L	12 rounds	—

TOM MOLINEAUX
The Virginia Slave

Tom Molineaux was the first American to fight in England for the heavyweight title. Born a slave, he was raised on a plantation in Virginia owned by Algernon Molineaux. He participated in fights with slaves from neighboring plantations as arranged by the plantation owners. Before one of these bouts, Algernon Molineaux promised his fighter freedom should he win. Molineaux won the fight and was granted his freedom. He traveled to New York, where he worked as a porter and a laborer on the docks.

Hearing of better opportunities for fighters in England, Molineaux joined a ship as a deckhand and set sail for England. In London, he declared himself to be the American champion even though no such title existed. Molineaux further boasted that he could beat anyone, including the retired champion, Hall of Famer Tom Cribb. Eager to prove the superiority of British fighters, Cribb arranged for his protégé, Bill Burrows ("The British Unknown") to fight Molineaux. Seconded and trained by Bill Richmond, another African-American fighter, Molineaux overpowered the "Unknown" with short arm jolts and

Right-handed; 5'8½"; 185–198 lbs.

Hall of Fame Induction: 1997

Born: 3/23/1784, Georgetown, MD

Died: 8/4/1818

blows to the head. Richmond, a free New Yorker, had fought Cribb several years earlier.

Cribb came out of retirement to face Molineaux on December 18, 1810 on a cold, rainy day. Molineaux drew first blood in the second round. In the 28th, Molineaux floored Cribb, who failed to come to scratch within thirty seconds. Under the rules, Molineaux should have been declared the winner. However, Cribb's second accused Molineaux of hiding bullets in his hands to give his punches more power. The referee searched Molineaux, found no foreign objects, and then let the revived Cribb continue. By the 33rd round, Molineaux was exhausted, shivering from the cold, and dazed from hitting his head on a ring post. He fell to the ground, unable to continue.

Molineaux immediately challenged Cribb for a rematch. While Cribb trained arduously, Molineaux, now estranged from Richmond, preferred carousing. Molineaux dominated for five rounds. A Cribb right knocked the wind out of him in the sixth. Molineaux never recovered and was knocked out in the eleventh when a Cribb right broke his jaw.

Molineaux never again fought for the title. Beset by problems with alcohol, Molineaux toured rural areas of England, Ireland, and Scotland in a traveling boxing and wrestling show. While in Ireland, he fell ill, possibly with tuberculosis, and died at the age of 34.

SELECTED BOUTS

Date	Year	Opponent	Location	Result / Duration		Title
Jul 14	1810	Bill Burrows	England	W	1 hr.	—
Aug 21	1810	Tom Blake	England	W	8 rounds	—
Dec 18	1810	Tom Cribb★	Copthall Common, England	L	33 rounds	—
May 21	1811	Jim Rimmer	England	W	21 rounds	—
Sep 28	1811	Tom Cribb★	Thistleton Gap, England	L	11 rounds	—
Apr 2	1813	Jack Carter	England	WF	25 rounds	—
—	1813	George Cooper	Scotland	D	10 rounds	—
May 31	1814	Bill Fuller	Auchineaux, Scotland	WF	2 rounds	—
Mar 10	1815	George Cooper	Edinburgh, Scotland	L	14 rounds	—

JOHN MORRISSEY
Old Smoke

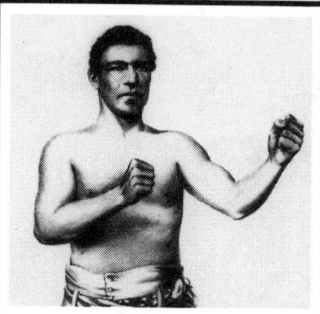

Right-handed; 5'11"; 175 lbs.
American Heavywt. Champ 1858
Hall of Fame Induction: 1996
Born: 2/12/1831, Templemore, Ireland
Died: 5/1/1878

A poor Irish immigrant, John Morrissey grew up in Troy, New York. He was allowed one year of school before becoming a manual laborer. Head of a gang of young toughs, Morrissey had frequent run-ins with the police—an inauspicious start for a man who later became a U.S. congressman.

After Morrissey took a bartending job in Troy, his boss tried to arrange a boxing match between Morrissey and "Dutch" Charlie Duane. When the young fighter went to New York City to challenge Duane at a Tammany Hall hangout, he was badly beaten by the unfriendly crowd. Morrissey stayed in the city, however, as a hired bully, enforcing the political loyalty of recent immigrants. Morrissey was dubbed "Old Smoke," when he and another "immigrant runner" knocked over a coal stove in a saloon fight and Morrissey was pinned to the burning embers before going on to win.

In 1851, Morrissey made his way to California as a stowaway in search of gold. His first organized prize fight took place in 1852 when he challenged Englishman George Thompson, then the California champion. Thompson had the upper hand, but when Morrissey's supporters brandished weapons, he fouled Morrissey in the twelfth round to forfeit the match.

Morrissey then returned to New York to challenge veteran fighter Yankee Sullivan. The fight was held at Boston Corners where New York, Connecticut, and Massachusetts meet, to stymie state authorities who might try to halt the match. Sullivan was 41, and Morrissey just 22, but for 37 rounds, the quicker and more scientific Sullivan thrashed Morrissey, who displayed his great ability to absorb a beating. Then onlookers stormed the ring. When the fighters were called to come to scratch for the 38th round, Sullivan was fending off Morrissey's second, Orville ("Awful") Gardner. The referee gave Morrissey the fight, in violation of a rule of that day which stated a fight must be stopped until the ring was clear. Morrissey parlayed his "win" into starting a bar and a gambling house. He used his connections to avoid convictions for shooting two waiters, three separate charges of assault with intent to kill, and possible involvement in the murder of a political foe.

In 1858, Morrissey faced another Troy native son, John C. ("Benicia Boy") Heenan, for what was considered the American heavyweight championship. Heenan fought well but was suffering from an earlier leg injury, and also broke his hand on a corner post during the fight. He collapsed in the eleventh round.

Morrissey then retired from the ring. He opened a gambling house and then a racetrack in Saratoga Springs, New York, helping to establish the town as a popular resort and horse racing center. He later testified against Tammany Hall political leader, Boss Tweed, which helped speed the breakup of his organization. Morrissey was elected to two terms in Congress and two in the New York State Senate before his death in 1878.

SELECTED BOUTS

Date	Year	Opponent	Location	Result / Rounds		Title
Aug 31	1852	George Thompson	California	WF	12	—
Oct 12	1853	Yankee Sullivan	Boston Corners, NY	W	38	—
Oct 20	1858	♛ John C. Heenan★	Long Pt. Island, Canada	W	11	Won-Amer-H

HENRY ("HEN") PEARCE
The Game Chicken

Although he did not possess the boxing skill of his immediate predecessor, Jem Belcher, Henry Pearce used his great strength and slugging ability to take the championship. Like Belcher, Pearce hailed from Bristol, England. Pearce started fighting in and around Bristol, although his first recorded bout is listed as having taken place in London in 1803 when he beat Jack Firley.

In 1805, he fought a memorable battle with his friend John Gully, an inmate of debtors' prison. The two staged a bout on the prison grounds with Gully getting the best of Pearce by a small margin. Impressed with his opponent's showing, Pearce arranged for a sponsor to pay Gully's debts so that he could be released from prison. The two then met in Hailsham for a public battle. Pearce dominated Gully early in the fight, knocking him down in each of the first seven rounds. In the eighteenth round, Gully came back to bloody Pearce badly. Two rounds later, one of Pearce's eyes was almost swollen shut. The two fighters battled on, both bruised and bleeding. From the 33rd round until the end of the fight, Pearce controlled the action. After an hour and ten minutes, Pearce's persistent attack sufficiently weakened Gully so that he could not continue.

Pearce laid full claim to the title in his next fight, when he battled Jem Belcher. Although blind in one eye from an accident, Belcher agreed to the challenge. The slugging Pearce outfought Belcher for eighteen rounds to win the undisputed championship. Pearce never fought again. He toured the

Right-handed; 5'9"; 175 lbs.
English Champion 1803–06
Hall of Fame Induction: 1993
Born: 1777, Bristol, England
Died: 4/30/1809

country after the Belcher victory, celebrating in high fashion. According to contemporary accounts, Pearce was drunk more often than sober. He contracted tuberculosis and other ailments and died in 1809, only four years after winning the championship.

SELECTED BOUTS

Date	Year	Opponent	Location	Result / Rounds		Title
Jun 3	1803	Jack Firley	London	W	10	—
Aug 12	1803	Joe Berks	London	W	15	—
Jan 23	1804	Joe Berks	Wimbledon, England	W	24	—
Mar 11	1805	Elias Spray	Hampton, England	W	29	—
Apr 27	1805	Stephen Carte	Shepperton, England	W	25	—
Oct 8	1805	John Gully	Hailsham, England	W	64	—
Dec 6	1805	♔ Jem Belcher★	near Doncaster, England	W	18	Won-England-H

BOXING GLOVES While it may seem to the uninitiated that boxing gloves were introduced to lessen injury to an opponent's face and body, in fact, they were invented to protect the attacker's hands. Many an early bare-fisted fight was lost because of hand injuries. Over the years, gloves evolved from the early "mufflers" used in training to the padded mittens now in use. To inflict injury to the opponent and not to one's hands is still the object, although modern gloves are a far cry from those used in Greek and Roman times. In the fights to the death of ancient times, gloves were often studded or covered with spikes.

RINGFACT

BILL RICHMOND
The Black Terror

Right-handed; 5'9"; 152–175 lbs.

Hall of Fame Induction: 1999

Born: 8/5/1763, Cuckold's Town, Richmond (Staten Island), NY

Died: 12/29/1829

Bill Richmond, the first African-American fighter to gain prominence in British boxing, was born to slaves belonging to Dr. George C. Charlton, a minister. Not much is known about Richmond's youth, but at the start of the Revolutionary War Dr. Charlton left New York for England, leaving his slaves behind. Richmond, the story goes, occupied his time sparring with British soldiers under the command of General Earl Percy, later the Duke of Northumberland, and because of his fistic prowess and his good character was made Percy's valet and accompanied him to England in 1777. Percy paid for Richmond to serve as an apprentice cabinetmaker, and Richmond learned the trade well, working as a journeyman in both York and London.

Richmond's first recorded fight was on August 25, 1791. Richmond was part of a large crowd at the racetrack in York, when George Moore insulted him and challenged him to a fight. Onlookers formed a ring on the spot and offered a purse to the winner. Though Moore outweighed him by approximately 50 pounds, Richmond easily dispensed with him.

Despite this success, Richmond declined offers to become a prizefighter and continued as a cabinetmaker for the next seven years, fighting only in response to insults and personal affronts. After thrashing Frank ("The York Bully") Meyers in an impromptu match, reportedly over a woman, Richmond decided to turn to fighting on a full-time basis.

His early career saw a loss to George Maddox and wins over Youssop ("The Jew") and Jack Holmes, also known as Tom Tough. But Richmond faced a sterner test of his abilities when he fought future champion and Hall of Famer Tom Cribb on October 8, 1805. Giving away almost 30 pounds, Richmond displayed a knack for avoiding Cribb's heavy blows, and landed some of his own. He struggled gamely, but clearly took the worst of the fighting before succumbing in the 25th round of a 90-minute fight.

Though he never again contended for the championship, Richmond continued to box for the next five years. He then opened a public house and taught boxing, holding lessons at the Royal Tennis Court in London. In his sixth decade, he fought twice more, scoring victories, and then continued to fight exhibitions and impromptu battles for another six years. Richmond frequently served as a second and trainer, as he did for Tom Molineaux, another African-American, in his unsuccessful title fight against Tom Cribb.

SELECTED BOUTS

Date	Year	Opponent	Location	Result / Rounds		Title
Aug 25	1791	George ("Dockey") Moore	York, England	W	25 min.	—
—	—	Frank Meyers	York	W	—	—
—	—	Whipmaker Green	London	W	10 min.	—
Jan 23	1804	George Maddox	Wimbledon Commons, Eng.	L	3 rounds	—
May 21	1805	Youssop ("The Jew")	Blackheath, England	W	6 rounds	—
Jul 8	1805	Jack Holmes	Cricklewood Green, Eng.	W	26 rounds	—
Oct 8	1805	Tom Cribb★	Hailsham, Sussex, Eng.	L	90 min.	For-England-H
Aug 9	1809	George Maddox	Near Margate, Kent, Eng.	W	52 rounds	—
Nov 12	1818	Jack Carter	—	W	3 rounds	—

TOM SAYERS
The Napoleon of the Prize Ring

Although a middleweight or lighter by modern standards, Tom Sayers fought in the first great international heavyweight championship match against American John C. Heenan. Sayers, who never topped 152 pounds, routinely took on opponents of all sizes.

In 1849, Sayers defeated Abe Couch in his first professional fight. His next fight was broken up by the police after nine rounds, then later reconvened to end in a 39-round draw when darkness fell. In 1853, Sayers met the acknowledged middleweight champion, Nat Langham. By the 61st round, Sayers's eyes had swollen shut and his seconds threw in the towel.

After an impressive victory over Harry Poulson, Sayers fought a tough draw with Aaron Jones and whipped him soundly in the rematch. Sayers then met Bill Perry, who at that time called himself the heavyweight champion. Perry outweighed Sayers by 50 pounds and won the early rounds of the match, but in the tenth, Sayers split Perry's lip and his seconds called an end to the fight. Although his evasive tactics led some to accuse Sayers of cowardice, he had fought a very smart fight that won him the heavyweight championship.

Right-handed; 5'8½"; 152 lbs.

English Champion 1858–60

Hall of Fame Induction: 1990

Born: 5/25/1826, Brighton, Sussex, England

Died: 11/8/1865

Sayers mounted four successful defenses before facing Heenan, a claimant to the American heavyweight title. For the first time, a match in England aroused interest on both sides of the Atlantic, and was well-reported in the newspapers. Heenan outweighed Sayers by 46 pounds and towered six inches above him. The fight was bloody from the beginning, and in the sixth round, Sayers broke his right arm blocking a punch. In the eighth, Heenan broke his left hand. Sayers then targeted Heenan's eyes, and although the American dominated the fight, he was rapidly becoming blinded. In the 37th, Heenan held Sayers helpless against the ropes, which someone suddenly cut. The crowd surged inside the ring and the referee deserted, but the two bloody battlers continued for five rounds until the match ended in a draw. The courage of both competitors was much admired, and boxing interest in the U.S. soared. Sayers retired after the fight and died of tuberculosis and diabetes six years later.

SELECTED BOUTS

Date	Year	Opponent	Location	Result / Rounds		Title
Mar 19	1849	Abe Couch	Greenhithe, England	W	6	—
Oct 18	1853	♛ Nat Langham★	Lakenheath, England	L	61	For-England-M
Jan 29	1856	Harry Poulson	Appledore, England	W	109	—
Jun 16	1857	♛ Bill Perry	Down R. Thames, Eng.	W	10	Won-England-H
Sep 21	1857	Bob Brett	Leashford, England	W	7	—
Jan 5	1858	Bill Benjamin	Isle of Grain, England	W	3	—
Jun 15	1858	Tom Paddock	Kent, England	W	21	Ret-England-H
Apr 5	1859	Bill Benjamin	near Ashford, England	W	11	—
Apr 17	1860	John C. Heenan★	Farnborough, England	D	42	Ret-England-H

TOM SPRING

Right-handed; 5'11½"; 186 lbs.

English Champion 1821–24

Hall of Fame Induction: 1992

Born: 2/22/1795, Townhope, Herefordshire, England

Named: Thomas Winter

Died: 8/20/1851

One of the most scientific of the early fighters, Tom Spring possessed a style that distinguished him from most of his contemporaries. Not known for his punching power and troubled by bad hands, Spring had good defense, fine footwork and a solid left. Spring first fought at the age of seventeen while working as a butcher in Hereford. His first recorded professional bout was a win over the towering John Hollands.

In 1818, Spring twice faced Ned Painter, a more experienced fighter, for a win and a loss. As the first bout began, Spring hit Painter on the side of the throat, sending him down. When Painter toppled to the ground, his head and shoulder struck a stake holding the ring together. Badly injured, Painter nevertheless fought through the 31st round before succumbing. In the rematch, Painter opened a gash over Spring's right eye with a hard right. Spring continued to bleed but hung on for 42 rounds before quitting.

After defeating Jack Carter in 1819, Spring went on an exhibition tour of England, sparring with the champion Tom Cribb. When Cribb retired in 1821, he handed the title to Spring. Challengers were slow to take Spring up on his offer to fight anyone in England until Spring signed to fight Bill Neat in 1823. Though denigrated as a "lady's maid fighter" for his lack of punching power, Spring scored a knockdown in the first round and cut Neat in the next. The fight ended in 37 minutes with Spring the winner.

Spring next fought two tough battles with the Irish fighter Jack Langan. The fights presented a great contrast in styles—Spring was quick and athletic and Langan was big, slow and ponderous. Spring won both marathon battles against Langan. He was forced to retire largely because of his ruined hands, a common hazard for bare knuckle fighters. Except for one fight with Painter, Spring's ability to avoid punishment and hit often, though without much power, enabled him to triumph over his opponents. His "Spring's Harlequin Step," in which he feinted briefly into his opponent's range, evaded the reactive punch and then scored a hit himself, was an especially effective move.

Well-respected for his kindness and gentlemanly demeanor outside of the ring, Spring became a prosperous innkeeper upon his retirement.

SELECTED BOUTS

Date	Year	Opponent	Location	Result / Rounds		Title
—	c.1814	John Hollands	England	W	—	—
Sep 9	1817	Jack Stringer	Moulsey, England	W	29	—
Apr 1	1818	Ned Painter	Mickleham Downs, England	W	31	—
Aug 7	1818	Ned Painter	Russia Farm, England	L	42	—
May 4	1819	Jack Carter	Crawley Downs, England	W	71	—
Dec 20	1819	Ben Burn	England	W	11	—
Feb 20	1821	Tom Oliver	Arlington Corners, England	W	25	—
May 17	1823	Bill Neat	Hinckley Downs, England	W	8	Won-Vac England-H
Jan 7	1824	Jack Langan	Worcester, England	W	77	Ret-England-H
Jun 8	1824	Jack Langan	Warwick, England	W	76	Ret-England-H

John L. Sullivan
The Boston Strong Boy

John L. Sullivan was an extraordinarily popular figure in the late ninteenth century, a living hero whose prowess in the ring brought him lasting fame. Sullivan remains well known even today, over one hundred years after his last fight. Born to Irish immigrant parents in the town of Roxbury, neighboring Boston, Sullivan apparently inherited his solid physique—he was 5'10" tall and weighed 190 pounds—from his mother, who equalled her grown son's stature. Sullivan's father, although an aggressive scrapper himself, was barely 5'3".

Sullivan briefly attended Boston College in an effort to satisfy his mother's desire to have him become a priest. He worked for a short time as a hod carrier, his father's profession, before becoming an assistant plumber, and then attempting to learn the tinsmith trade. His stint as a plumber reportedly ended when he broke his employer's jaw in a dispute about the proper pipe to use on a job. A versatile athlete, Sullivan played semi-pro baseball in the Boston area. The Cincinnati Red Stockings offered him a contract, which he declined.

From an early age, Sullivan showed great proficiency with his fists. As a teenager, he would fight in Boston barrooms, issuing a challenge that he "could lick any man in the house." He also engaged in weightlifting exhibitions, hefting and sometimes throwing kegs of beer. Sullivan turned to fighting more seriously at the age of eighteen when he engaged in three- and four-

Right-handed; 5'10½"; 190 lbs.

Heavyweight Bare Knuckle Champion 1882–89, Heavyweight (Queensberry Rules) Champion 1885–92

Hall of Fame Induction: 1990

Born: 10/15/1858, Roxbury, MA

Named: John Lawrence Sullivan

Died: 2/2/1918

round amateur bouts. Sullivan's big break came when he went to the Dudley Street Opera House in Boston in 1877. One of the acts featured heavyweight boxer Tom Scannel, who skipped rope, shadowboxed, and sparred with partners chosen from the audience. Often, the sparring partner was in on the act and would box two furious rounds before succumbing in the third. This night, Sullivan, urged on by the crowd, climbed the stage to face Scannel. Scannel, offering to shake hands, suddenly slugged Sullivan instead. In return, Sullivan blasted Scannel with a half-dozen rapid blows and knocked him into the orchestra pit.

The scene at the opera house launched young Sullivan on his professional career. In 1878, he knocked out Cockey Woods in Boston. In 1880, he boxed exhibitions with noted scientific boxer Professor Mike Donovan and former champion Joe Goss. Sullivan outclassed them both. The next year he scored an eight-round knockout over John Flood, known as the Bull's Head Terror. Fighting on a barge in the Hudson River to evade the authorities, Sullivan made short work of Flood, knocking him down eight times. Both fighters wore tight, unpadded gloves.

The next year Sullivan met Paddy Ryan, the heavyweight champion—at least in American eyes—in Mississippi City, Mississippi. It was a bare knuckle contest, and basically one-sided. Sullivan dominated the fight and knocked Ryan out in the eighth round with a right to the jaw. Sullivan was now considered the world champion although there was some disagreement among British and Australian followers of the sport. In addition to his regular bouts, Sullivan went on an American tour, challenging anyone to stay in the ring with him for four rounds for a $1,000 prize. He took on all comers. Only Tug Wilson, an English fighter, went the distance.

In 1883, Sullivan faced British Empire champion, Charlie Mitchell, in a gloved bout. Although Sullivan was winning the fight when the police stepped in to prevent the battered Mitchell from absorbing more punishment, Mitchell had shocked Sullivan and his fans by knocking him down in the first round. Five years later, the two met at the estate of Baron Rothschild in France. They battled in a rain-soaked ring for 39 rounds to a draw.

In 1889, Sullivan fought one of his most famous bouts with Jake Kilrain in the last significant bare knuckle bout in boxing. Kilrain was hailed by Richard Fox, the publisher of the *Police Gazette*, as the new champion. Fox disliked Sullivan for a perceived slight in a bar and had long searched for an opponent to topple him. Sullivan's weight had ballooned to 240 flabby pounds, and he went into extensive training with champion wrestler William Muldoon to trim down to 205. In the fight, Sullivan got off to a good start by tripping and hip-tossing Kilrain to win the first two rounds. Sullivan was thrown in the third. From then on, Kilrain fought on gamely but Sullivan had the better of it. Beaten and battered, Kilrain could not come to scratch for the 76th round.

Sullivan did not fight for three years after the Kilrain match and instead toured as the hero in a mawkish play called *Honest Hearts and Willing Hands*. He continued to box in exhibitions, and to carouse. In one exhibition, against Gentleman Jim Corbett, both fighters sparred in full evening attire.

In 1892, Sullivan faced Corbett in earnest in New Orleans as part of the Carnival of Champions, fought under the Queensberry Rules. The fighters wore five-ounce gloves. The contrast in styles was obvious. The powerful, steadfast Sullivan had little use for ring trickery or defense, while Corbett was known for his peerless boxing ability. Young and agile, Corbett outboxed Sullivan, who was out of condition as a result of his indulgent lifestyle. Corbett stayed clear of the champion for twelve rounds. By the seventeenth, Corbett's forays were wearing Sullivan down and he had a clear advantage. Corbett knocked out Sullivan in the 21st round.

Sullivan never fought again. He did some acting and, surprisingly, swore off alcohol. Previously known for his prodigious drinking, Sullivan became a temperance lecturer. He retired to a Massachusetts farm, having depleted most of the $1 million he had earned in his public career. Sullivan's vast renown and charismatic style did much to advance the sport of boxing in America.

SELECTED BOUTS

Date	Year	Opponent	Location	Result / Rounds		Title
—	1878	Cockey Woods	Boston	TKO	5	—
Feb 7	1882	♛ Paddy Ryan	Mississippi City, MS	KO	9	Won-BK World-H
Oct 17	1883	James McCoy	McKeesport, PA	TKO	1	—
May 14	1883	Charlie Mitchell★	New York	W	3	—
Jan 19	1885	Paddy Ryan	New York	TKO	1	—
Aug 29	1885	Dominick McCaffrey	Cincinnati	W	6	Won-Vac M of Q World-H
Nov 13	1886	Paddy Ryan	San Francisco	KO	3	—
Mar 10	1888	Charlie Mitchell★	Chantilly, France	D	39	Ret-BK World-H
Jul 8	1889	Jake Kilrain	Richburg, MS	TKO	75	Ret-BK World-H
Sep 7	1892	James J. Corbett★	New Orleans	KO'd	21	Lost-M of Q World-H

WILLIAM THOMPSON
Bendigo

The name of William ("Bendigo") Thompson is inextricably linked with that of Ben Caunt by their three epic battles. Thompson, one of a set of triplets, was called Abednego, later shortened to Bendigo. As a boxer, he was often known by his nickname alone.

Thompson started fighting professionally in 1832 with a victory over Joe Hanley, and in 1835, he faced Caunt for the first time. According to contemporary reports, Caunt was incensed by Thompson's tactic of falling to the ground when in difficulty. In the 22nd round, Caunt hit the kneeling Thompson and lost the fight on a foul.

Thompson won his next three fights before facing Caunt again. Caunt came into the ring in less than the best fighting condition. A great athlete, Thompson easily eluded Caunt's clumsy attacks. However, in the fifth round Caunt caught Bendigo against the ropes and nearly strangled him. Thompson continuously peppered Caunt with shots to the body. In the thirteenth, Caunt again nearly strangled Thompson. In the 50th round, Caunt alleged that Thompson had illegally kicked him, but the claim was disallowed. In the 75th round, Thompson lost on a foul when he slipped to the ground without having been hit. Some observers believed that Thompson

Left-handed; 5'9½"; 165 lbs.

English Champion: 1839–40, 1845–50

Hall of Fame Induction: 1991

Born: 10/11/1811, Nottingham, England

Died: 8/23/1880

intentionally fell to avoid further punishment, while others believed that Thompson had the fight well in hand and would have won.

In his next battle, Thompson faced the champion James ("Deaf") Burke. Fighting under the new London Prize Ring Rules, Thompson dominated the fight. In the tenth, a badly beaten Burke head-butted Thompson and was disqualified. In 1840, the new champion, after watching some steeplechase races, exuberantly tried to turn a somersault and fell, seriously injuring his leg. He did not fight for six years until he faced Caunt for the third time. Thompson entered this bout crouching to make himself less of a target and eluded many of Caunt's thrusts. Thompson dominated the fight and earned the victory when Caunt sat down in the 93rd round without getting hit.

Thompson then retired only to return for one fight in 1850, a victory over Tom Paddock. A hard drinker and an innkeeper, Thompson turned to preaching in his later years, especially concerning himself with temperance issues. Although some questioned his sincerity, he continued his ministry for many years.

SELECTED BOUTS

Date	Year	Opponent	Location	Result / Rounds		Title
Oct	1832	Joe Hanley	England	W	16	—
Jul 21	1835	Ben Caunt	Nottingham, England	WF	22	—
Jun 13	1837	Bill Looney	Chapel-en-le-Frith, Eng.	W	99	—
Apr 3	1838	Ben Caunt	Shelby, England	LF	75	—
Feb 12	1839	♛ James ("Deaf") Burke ★	Heather, England	WF	10	Won-England-H
Sep 9	1845	♛ Ben Caunt	Stoney Stratford, England	WF	93	Reg-England-H
Jun 5	1850	Tom Paddock	Mildenhall, England	WF	49	Ret-England-H

JEM WARD
The Black Diamond

Right-handed; 5'10"; 175 lbs.

English Champion: 1825–31

Hall of Fame Induction: 1995

Born: 12/26/1800

Died: 4/3/1884

Although an excellent fighter, Jem Ward—English champion for most of the period from 1825 to 1831—was the first boxer to be disciplined by a governing body for throwing a fight. Ward turned professional at the age of fifteen with a victory over George Robinson. He remained unbeaten until 1822 when he lost to Bill Abbott, a fighter most observers considered to be far inferior to Ward. After many rounds, Ward shouted to Abbott loud enough that those at ringside could hear, "Now, Bill, look sharp, hit me and I'll go down." When Abbott then hit Ward, he collapsed. The Pugilistic Society conducted an inquiry into the match. Ward confessed that he had been paid one hundred pounds to lose. The Pugilistic Society expelled Ward and barred him from fighting in any ring under its control.

The next year Ward was attending a bout and, when the main event ended quickly, he was called upon to enter the ring against Ned Baldwin, whom he easily defeated. Still unable to clear his name, Ward toured England with other boxers. He defeated Joe Rickens while pretending to be an unschooled farm boy named Sawney Wilson, so as to get better betting odds.

In 1823, the Pugilistic Society reinstated Ward. He lost his next bout to Josh Hudson. In 1825, he challenged the champion Tom Cannon, who was seconded by Hall of Famers Tom Spring and Tom Cribb. On an intensely hot day, Ward won easily. Ward very briefly lost the title when Peter Crawley defeated him in 1827. Crawley retired within days, and Ward reclaimed the championship. He held it until 1831 when he retired.

A fine fighter and powerfully built man, Ward received criticism for refusing to face the younger challenger, James Burke. Ward had some success as an artist, and his paintings were displayed in London and Liverpool. He also enjoyed playing the violin and flute. Among his retirement ventures, he sang in concerts and operated a tavern.

SELECTED BOUTS

Date	Year	Opponent	Location	Result / Duration		Title
May 6	1816	George Robinson	Stepney, England	W	45 min.	—
Jun 18	1816	Bill Wall	Limehouse Fields, England	W	2 hrs.	—
Jul 27	1817	George Webb	Limehouse Fields	W	3 min.	—
Jul 4	1819	Nick Murphy	Barking, England	W	35 min.	—
Sep 29	1820	Mike Hayes	Isle of Dogs, England	W	40 min.	—
Nov 11	1823	Josh Hudson	Moulsey Hurst, England	L	15 rounds	—
Jun 21	1824	Phil Sampson	Colnbrook, England	W	26 rounds	—
Dec 28	1824	Phil Sampson	Stony Stratford, England	W	27 rounds	—
Jul 19	1825	♛ Tom Cannon	Warwick, England	W	10 rounds	Won-England-H
Jan 2	1827	Peter Crawley	Royston, England	L	11 rounds	Lost-England-H
May 27	1828	Jack Carter	Shepperton, England	W	17 rounds	Ret-England-H
Jul 12	1831	Simon Byrne	Willeycutt, England	W	33 rounds	Ret-England-H

The bare-knuckle boxing era effectively ended with a seventy-five round war on July 8, 1889, in Richburg, Mississippi. Two rival claimants for the bare-knuckle heavyweight title battled for two hours and sixteen minutes in blistering heat until a bested Jake Kilrain threw in the sponge and John L. Sullivan again was universally acclaimed as champion.

WHO RULES?

Boxing's Governing Bodies

WHEN BOXING WAS A GROWING SPORT in England, it produced one champion at a time. A man achieved acclaim by defeating the current champion or, if no champion existed, through other accomplishments in the ring. There were no organizations to supervise the conduct of boxing and boxers, but fans and historians could follow a fairly cohesive lineage of champions. By the early twentieth century, when eight weight classes were established, each division had its own champion.

Today, the potential exists for 68 champions to hold titles offered by four dominant boxing organizations. The World Boxing Association (WBA), the World Boxing Council (WBC), the International Boxing Federation (IBF), and the World Boxing Organization (WBO) each has its own version of seventeen weight-division titles. Several other organizations also offer titles, with the result that one can no longer get a simple answer to the question: Who's the heavyweight (or any weight) champ?

The history of boxing's governing bodies reaches back to England where the sport was largely unregulated until 1891 when Hall of Famer Lord Lonsdale helped establish the National Sporting Club. This club regulated English boxing for 38 years, during which time it formally defined and standardized the eight recognized weight classes and presented Lonsdale Belts to British champions. The British Boxing Board of Control was established around 1930 and continues to regulate boxing in the United Kingdom. The British board is affiliated with the European Boxing Union (EBU), which in 1946 replaced the International Boxing Union (IBU), first formed in 1911 in Paris. The EBU continues to administer boxing through its affiliate members in European countries.

Meanwhile, the United States was slower to organize any type of regulation for the sport. Richard K. Fox, publisher of the popular *Police Gazette,* instituted the practice of distributing championship belts in the U.S. in the late 1880s, when he presented a belt to Jake Kilrain, who was perhaps less deserving of the honor than John L. Sullivan, the more widely accepted champion. Fox continued to present belts to fighters he deemed worthy, but the *Police Gazette* had no function as an official sanctioning body.

With passage of the Walker Law in 1920, boxing became legal in the state of New York under the purview of the New York State Athletic Commission (NYSAC). New York quickly became the center of boxing, and served as a model for other states interested in legalizing the sport. In February 1921, representatives of fifteen state ath-letic commissions met in Manhattan's Flatiron Building to form the National Boxing Association (NBA). The group's stated objective was to standardize rules and regulations in the sport. Of equal concern, particularly to Abe J. Greene, the New Jersey state boxing commissioner, was finding a way to keep boxing's growing profits from concentrating solely in New York.

However, even though it was founded in New York City, the NBA failed to capture NYSAC as a member. The state commission refused to join, citing a prohibition in state law. In reality, New York did not wish to share its power or potential revenue. The state's refusal to join the fledgling NBA created, in effect, two sanctioning bodies and, often, the NBA and NYSAC crowned different champions in the same weight class. New York maintained its considerable power in boxing through the 1960s, when the sport's crime-riddled promotional structure was exposed, and other venues for headline fights began to dominate.

Lennox Lewis has held four major heavyweight championships (WBC, WBA, IBF, and IBO) although never more than three simultaneously.

In the ongoing conflict between the NBA and NYSAC, disputes over the real champion in a given weight class were often settled by Nat Fleischer, editor of *The Ring* magazine. Under Fleischer's authority, the magazine issued monthly rankings of contenders and awarded championship belts.

Following World War II, boxing gained considerable ground in Mexico, South America, Australia, Asia, and Africa. In response to this expansion, the NBA changed its name to the World Boxing Association (WBA) in 1962. Nevertheless, the WBA remained primarily a U.S. organization because of its voting scheme: Each state commission was granted one vote, while each foreign country also had only a single vote, regardless of its level of boxing activity. This imbalance gave a boxing-poor state like New Hampshire, for instance, an equal vote with countries like Argentina or Mexico, which were home to hundreds of bouts each year.

Disputes were often settled by Nat Fleischer, editor of The Ring.

American domination of the WBA led promoter and matchmaker George Parnassus and others to form the World Boxing Council (WBC) in 1963. Parnassus, who often showcased lighter-weight Latin American contenders, believed these fighters were not accurately or fairly represented in the WBA's rankings. As originally established, the World Boxing Council (WBC) consisted of eleven countries organized into continental federations with two votes granted to each federation.

Predictably, the WBA and WBC often had different champions in the same weight classes. In the 1970s and '80s, both sanctioning bodies doubled the number of weight classes, adding to the panoply of champions.

In 1976, fight manager Jose ("Pepe") Cordero of Puerto Rico engineered changes in the WBA which ended its control by United States interests. Under the rules of the organization, Cordero realized that if each state had a vote then, by rights, so should the provincial boxing commissions in other nations. That year, representatives of provincial commissions appeared at the WBA convention, seized control of the organization from the Americans and have retained it ever since.

In 1983, a third major sanctioning body formed when Bob Lee, head of the United States Boxing Association (USBA), attempted to gain the presidency of the

WBA. When his attempt failed, he took the USBA from under the WBA umbrella and formed the International Boxing Federation (IBF), a body that now offers its own array of seventeen titles.

The World Boxing Organization (WBO), yet another outgrowth of the WBA, was formed when a disgruntled Latin American contingent and some Americans bolted from the WBA. The WBO, of course, supports its own titles and champions. Other sanctioning bodies have been formed in recent years, including the International Boxing Association (IBA), the International Boxing Organization (IBO), the World Boxing Union (WBU), the World Boxing Federation (WBF), and the International Boxing Council (IBC), but the four described here—the WBA, WBC, IBF, and WBO—are generally considered to have the most clout by the boxing media.

The multiplication of sanctioning bodies has drawn some criticism from the public and the boxing media. Fans must puzzle out which "world champion" is really the best, or why the boxer who is apparently the best in a particular weight class may not hold a championship belt. A second and more serious charge leveled at the sanctioning bodies is that the rating systems are at best inaccurate and at worst corrupt. Rankings have reportedly been purchased, and often, one organization's rankings bear little resemblance to those of another, or to the independent rankings of *The Ring*.

Despite these problems, some proponents of boxing's growth and renewed popularity support the proliferation of titles. More boxers can compete for titles, adding excitement to the sport and possibly enhancing the quality of the fights. Since title fights tend to carry higher purses, more boxers are allowed opportunities to gain financial reward. Television producers and advertisers tend to be more attracted to bouts they can bill as title fights, and the economic benefit for arenas, casinos, and tourism must be considered as well.

Fans would undoubtedly appreciate more guidance in interpreting the tangle of titles. The governing bodies themselves need to recognize the public's distaste for anything less than fairness in rankings, as well as the great value of having tournaments that would produce "super-champions" in each of the weight classes. The interest generated in seeing champions fight each other would do much to justify the existence of many titles.

THE OLD-TIMERS

The Sweet Science Becomes an American Passion

BOXING WAS BORN IN ENGLAND, but it grew up in America. The sport was embraced by the growing nation, and by the time the last of the bare knuckle fighters had faded into history, the United States was the principal proving ground for ring hopefuls. In the early twentieth century, boxing as a crowd-pleasing, money-making endeavor flourished first in the American West, then moved east to capture the attention of the entire country. While Britain, Australia, and the West Indies produced occasional champions, with Europe, Asia, South America, and Africa joining in later, nowhere was the sport as popular as in the United States.

Until the 1920s, public prizefighting was illegal in most states, and matches often had to be conducted in secret locations, or as so-called "sparring sessions" in private clubs. Police intervention was still a hazard, and it was not uncommon for boxers to find themselves confined to a local jail for several days following a raided fight. Fixed bouts were not uncommon, and it could be as dangerous to be a spectator as it was to be a boxer because of the police raids or eruptions of violence among spectators.

Legal attempts to clean up the sport sometimes backfired. The Frawley Law, passed in 1911, ended a ten-year period when authorities tried to ban boxing completely. It was decided that fixes would be less likely to occur if only a knockout could be recognized as a win. If both men were still on their feet at the end of a match, it was called a no-decision bout, with no official winner. The no-decision regulation was

intended to foil crooked gamblers by making it harder to influence the boxers, referees, or judges. However, the newspaper reporters—who often identified the supposed winners of no-decision bouts—were still vulnerable to payoffs. The arrival of the Walker Law in New York State in 1920 put an end to the no-decision era when it set up more stringent regulations as well as an athletic commission to oversee the sport. The Walker Law was quickly emulated by other states.

Because the West had fewer restrictions, it dominated boxing in the early part of the century. Operating in California, James Coffroth became the nation's first great boxing promoter and, in 1910, Tex Rickard arranged what was probably the most anticipated clash up to that time—the Jack Johnson–James J. Jeffries heavyweight championship match in Reno, Nevada.

Boxing began to shed its unsavory reputation when influential people like former President Theodore Roosevelt recommended controlled fisticuffs to promote health and fitness. This view, as well as a growing public acceptance of the sport as conducted on a professional level, led to its legalization in many states.

With the passage of the Walker Law, the center of boxing activity shifted to New York City and environs. Boxing came to be seen as a legitimate, major athletic pursuit, and when the first million-dollar gate was realized, promoters set up other high-profit matches. Boxing produced larger-than-life heroes like Jack Dempsey and Gene Tunney, acknowledged pillars of "The Golden Age of Sport," along with such stars as baseball's Babe Ruth and tennis player Bill Tilden. Boxer celebrities like Max Baer mixed show business into their careers, and several boxers retired to become film or stage actors.

This period of growth also saw formal establishment of the traditional eight weight classes: heavyweight, light heavyweight, middleweight, welterweight, lightweight, featherweight, bantamweight, and flyweight. Reports of fights were brought to a much wider audience through films, radio broadcasts, increased newspaper coverage, and the establishment of the seminal boxing publication, *The Ring.*

Although the era grappled with racism as increasing numbers of African-American boxers entered the ring, many fighters—including blacks—built substantial careers, fighting frequently and over long periods of time. Unlike the earliest pugilists, who may have fought only a dozen recorded bouts, or later boxers, for whom 40 fights could make an entire career, it was not unusual for fighters in the Old-Timers era to record two hundred or more encounters.

LOU AMBERS
The Herkimer Hurricane

LIGHTWEIGHT

Right-handed; 5'6"; 131–140 lbs.

104 bouts, 6/16/1932 to 2/28/1941

Managers: Nicanor Rafael 1932–33, Dave Steinberg 1933–34, Al Weill 1934–41

Lightweight Champion 1936–38, 1939–40

Hall of Fame Induction: 1992

Born: 11/8/1913, Herkimer, NY

Named: Luigi Guiseppe D'Ambrosio

Died: 4/24/1995

One of the top lightweights of the 1930s, Lou Ambers built a reputation as a clever, aggressive boxer. Ambers first picked up the rudiments of boxing in a church basement gym in his native Herkimer, New York. When the Great Depression forced his family's restaurant to close and Ambers ended up working in a furniture factory, he decided to try boxing as a career. After fighting in amateur "bootleg" bouts for a few dollars a fight, Ambers entered the professional ranks with a second-round knockout of Frankie Curry in 1932. Ambers continued his winning ways as a pro, going undefeated in his first 32 fights. He earned the attention of *The Ring* and was named its ninth-best lightweight contender in the 1933 annual rankings.

In 1935, Ambers fought his idol, Tony Canzoneri, for the world lightweight title vacated by Barney Ross. Ambers had previously been Canzoneri's sparring partner. Canzoneri quite easily dispatched Ambers, winning a fifteen-round decision. The next year Ambers faced Canzoneri for the title again. Fighting in Madison Square Garden before a crowd of 18,026, Ambers avenged the earlier defeat to claim the title. He scored with straight lefts—cutting Canzoneri under the eye—and with right uppercuts. Ambers maintained a healthy respect for Canzoneri's slugging ability and avoided serious damage while earning a unanimous decision.

Ambers faced the sternest

Ambers (L) engages in some relaxed sparring with boyish Marty Servo who later beat Freddie Cochrane for the welterweight crown.

IN THE RING	WON 90	LOST 8	DRAWS 6	TB 104	KO 30	W 60	WF 0	D 6	KO'd 2	L 6	LF 0	ND 0

Date	Year		Opponent	Site	Result / Rounds		Title
SELECTED BOUTS							
Jun 16	1932		Frankie Curry	—	KO	2	—
Sep 26	1932		Ray Meyers	New York	W	5	—
Jan 11	1935	⑩	Harry Dublinsky	New York	W	10	—
Mar 1	1935	⑩	Sammy Fuller	New York	W	15	—
Apr 24	1935		Harold Hughes	Providence, RI	KO	5	—
May 10	1935	⑩	Tony Canzoneri★	New York	L	15	For-Vac World-L
Jul 1	1935		Fritzie Zivic★	Pittsburgh	W	10	—
Jan 3	1936	⑩	Frankie Klick	New York	W	10	—
Feb 7	1936	⑩	Baby Arizmendi	New York	W	10	—
Sep 3	1936	♛	Tony Canzoneri★	New York	W	15	Won-World-L
Oct 28	1936	⑩	Eddie Cool	Philadelphia	L	10	—
Nov 20	1936	⑩	Jimmy McLarnin★	New York	L	10	—
Dec 29	1936		Stumpy Jacobs	Rochester, NY	TKO	7	—
Feb 10	1937	⑩	Davey Day	New York	W	10	—
Apr 5	1937	⑩	Pedro Montanez	New York	L	10	—
Apr 18	1937		Phil Baker	New Haven, CT	W	10	—
May 7	1937	⑩	Tony Canzoneri★	New York	W	15	Ret-World-L
Sep 23	1937	⑩	Pedro Montanez	New York	W	15	Ret-World-L
Jun 7	1938	⑩	Baby Arizmendi	Los Angeles	W	10	—
Jul 17	1938		Henry Armstrong★	New York	L	15	Lost-World-L
Feb 24	1939	⑩	Baby Arizmendi	New York	TKO	11	—
May 26	1939		Paul Junior	Boston	TKO	8	—
Aug 22	1939	♛	Henry Armstrong★	New York	W	15	Reg-World-L
Apr 25	1940		Norment Quarles	Charleston, SC	W	10	—
May 10	1940	⑩	Lew Jenkins★	New York	TKO'd	3	Lost-NY World-L
Feb 14	1941		Norment Quarles	Hartford, CT	W	10	—
Feb 28	1941	♛	Lew Jenkins★	New York	TKO'd	7	—

challenge to his title when he met the feather- and welterweight champion, Henry Armstrong, in Madison Square Garden in 1938. Armstrong knocked Ambers down in the fifth and sixth rounds. Although Ambers recovered sufficiently to gash Armstrong's left eye and mouth, Armstrong continued to fight, swallowing blood so that the damage to his mouth would not be apparent enough to force the referee to stop the fight. Armstrong won a split decision to take the lightweight title. Ambers won the title back in a rematch in Yankee Stadium the next year. It was a vicious fight in which Armstrong lost five rounds because of his low blows. Ambers delivered several telling punches to Armstrong's face and closed one of his eyes to win a split decision. A proposed third fight between these two well-matched fighters never took place.

In 1940, Ambers lost the title when Lew Jenkins stopped him in three rounds. After losing the rematch to Jenkins in seven rounds, Ambers retired. He operated a restaurant and was involved in public relations after leaving the ring.

ABE ATTELL

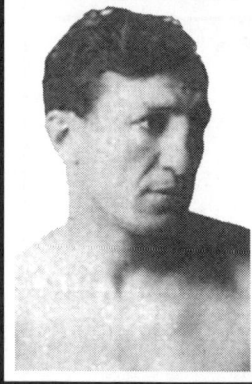

FEATHERWEIGHT

Right-handed; 5'4"; 118–130 lbs.

171 bouts, 8/19/1900 to 1/8/1917

Managers: Al Lippe, Jack McKenna, Tim McGrath, Zeke Abrams, Ike Bloom, Lob Kohn, Billy Nolan, George Weedon, Jack Kearns, Dan Morgan, John Reisler

Featherweight Champion 1901–12

Hall of Fame Induction: 1990

Born: 2/22/1884, San Francisco, CA

Named: Abraham Washington Attell

Died: 2/7/1970

Long-reigning featherweight champion Abe Attell defended the title fourteen times over nine years, although at times his claim to the championship was disputed. A small, quick, and clever boxer, Attell learned to fight in the streets of San Francisco as a Jewish boy growing up in an Irish neighborhood. He quickly found boxing success at the amateur level, then turned professional in 1900 at age sixteen, knocking Kid Lennett out in two rounds. Later, Attell confided that Lennett had been one of the neighborhood toughs who had given him a thrashing in the street.

Although eventually known more for his skillful boxing than his punching ability, Attell scored knockouts in fifteen of his first sixteen fights, and 21 of his first 25. Attell credited Hall of Famer George Dixon, whom he fought three times in 1901, with inspiring him to develop an easier, more graceful style. Between Attell's first and second fights—both draws—with the aging Dixon, he worked to emulate Dixon's apparently effortless movements. He beat Dixon in the third match, a fifteen-round bout advertised by Attell's manager, Jack McKenna, as a fight for the vacant featherweight championship.

Although Attell claimed the title, which then had a 122 lb limit, others asserted that Young Corbett's victory over Terry McGovern later that year made Corbett the featherweight champ. Attell's hold on the title was strengthened in 1903, when he beat Johnny Reagan in 20 rounds. He was generally accepted as the champion until he faced Tommy Sullivan in St. Louis the next year. Sullivan scored a knock-

Abe Attell (R) and Harlem Tommy Murphy fought to a 20-round draw in a long, bloody war in Daly City, CA on August 3, 1912.

IN THE RING	WON 91	LOST 9	DRAWS 18	TB 171	KO 53	W 36	WF 2	D 18	KO'd 4	L 5	LF 0	ND 51	NC 2

Date	Year	Opponent	Site	Result / Rounds		Title
SELECTED BOUTS						
Aug 19	1900	Kid Lennett	San Francisco	KO	2	—
Aug 24	1901	George Dixon★	Denver	D	10	—
Oct 20	1901	George Dixon★	Cripple Creek, CO	D	20	—
Oct 28	1901	George Dixon★	St. Louis	W	15	—
Sep 3	1903	Johnny Reagan	St. Louis	W	20	Won-Vac-World-FE
Feb 1	1904	Harry Forbes	St. Louis	KO	5	Ret-World-FE
Feb 22	1906	♛ Jimmy Walsh	Chelsea, MA	W	15	Ret-World-FE
Jul 4	1906	Frankie Neil	Los Angeles	W	20	Ret-World-FE
Oct 30	1906	Harry Baker	Los Angeles	W	20	Ret-World-FE
Dec 7	1906	Jimmy Walsh	Los Angeles	KO	8	Ret-World-FE
May 24	1907	Kid Solomon	Los Angeles	W	20	Ret-World-FE
Feb 28	1908	Eddie Kelly	San Francisco	KO	7	Ret-World-FE
Jan 1	1908	♛ Owen Moran★	San Francisco	D	25	Ret-World-FE
Mar 31	1908	♛ Battling Nelson★	San Francisco	D	15	—
Apr 30	1908	Tommy Sullivan	San Francisco	KO	4	Ret-World-FE
Nov 25	1908	Freddie Welsh★	Vernon, CA	L	15	—
Dec 11	1908	Ad Wolgast★	Los Angeles	ND-W	10	—
Jan 14	1909	Freddie Weeks	Goldfield, NV	KO	10	Ret-World-FE
Feb 19	1909	Jim Driscoll★	New York	ND-L	10	—
Oct 24	1910	Johnny Kilbane★	Kansas City	W	10	Ret-World-FE
Nov 13	1910	Frankie Conley	New Orleans	D	15	Ret-World-FE
Feb 22	1912	Johnny Kilbane★	Vernon, CA	L	20	Lost-USA-World-FE
Jan 8	1917	Phil Virgets	New Orleans	KO'd	4	—

out over Attell in five rounds, but Attell discounted the win, alleging that Sullivan had been over the weight limit. Most boxing experts agreed. When Attell knocked Sullivan out in four rounds in 1908, this dispute was settled. Attell tried to move up to the lightweight class in 1908. He fought Hall of Famer and future champion, Battling Nelson, to a draw in a fight Attell claimed to have won.

Attell lost his title in 1912 to Johnny Kilbane in Vernon, California in a twenty-round decision. The two fighters had split two previous meetings. Kilbane earned the lasting enmity of Attell by claiming that Attell had coated his back with chloroform. Attell insisted the substance was a cooling slather of cocoa butter.

Attell continued to fight for another year before retiring. His one-fight comeback was a knock-out loss to Phil Virgets. In retirement, Attell operated a succession of bars. He was involved in baseball's 1919 Black Sox Scandal—when gamblers bribed eight players on the Chicago team to throw the World Series—although he was not actually convicted of any crime.

By his own admission, Attell did not always perform at his best. Sometimes his goal was to get a lucrative return match with the same opponent. Nevertheless, he only lost nine times in his 171-fight career.

MAX BAER
The Livermore Larruper

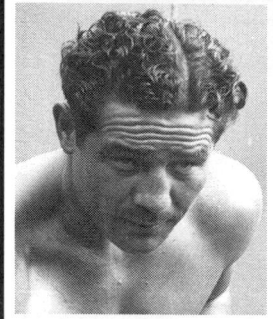

HEAVYWEIGHT

Right-handed; 6'2½"; 205–215 lbs.
84 bouts, 5/16/1929 to 4/4/1941
Manager: Ancil Hoffman
Heavyweight Champion 1934–35
Hall of Fame Induction: 1995
Born: 2/11/1909, Omaha, NE
Named: Maximillian Adalbert Baer
Died: 11/21/1959

Possessing perhaps the most powerful right hand in heavyweight history, Max Baer was a flashy performer who wisecracked and clowned his way through his career. Although he never fully realized his tremendous potential, Baer won the heavyweight title, and his showmanship entertained an America rocked by the Great Depression. Born in Omaha, Baer moved with his family to Colorado and then to California. He dropped out of school after eighth grade to work with his father on a cattle ranch, where he built his great physical strength doing range work.

Early in his career, Baer trained with a zeal he did not demonstrate later. He turned pro in 1929 and won 22 of his first 24 fights, nine with first-round knockouts. Baer was in supreme condition and dangerous in the ring. In 1930, he was charged with manslaughter when Frankie Campbell, brother of baseball player Dolph Camilli, died as a result of a Baer knockout. Ultimately cleared of criminal charges, Baer was suspended from fighting in California for a year.

Baer quit boxing for several months after Campbell's death, then lost four of his next six fights, partly because of his reluctance to go on the attack. One victor, Hall of Famer Tommy Loughran, told Baer that he was looping and telegraphing his punches. Jack Dempsey helped Baer shorten his punches and took an interest in him for the rest of his career. In 1932, Baer knocked Ernie Schaaf unconscious in the tenth round of what had been a fairly even fight. Not long after, Schaaf died following a bout with Primo Carnera. The death was attributed in part to the beating administered by Baer.

In 1933, in the best fight of his career, Baer beat Max Schmeling at Yankee Stadium before 60,000 fans. Baer hammered Schmeling so thoroughly, referee Arthur Donovan stopped the fight in the tenth round. Now in line

Tony ("Two Ton") Galento hugs Baer in an effort to postpone his fate—an 8th-round KO in Jersey City in July 1940.

IN THE RING	WON **72**	LOST **12**	DRAWS **0**	TB 84	KO 53	W 19	WF 0	D 0	KO'd 3	L 7	LF 2	ND 0

Date	Year	Opponent	Site	Result / Rounds		Title

SELECTED BOUTS

Date	Year	Opponent	Site	Result / Rounds		Title
May 16	1929	Chief Caribou	Stockton, CA	KO	2	—
Apr 22	1930	Ernie Owens	Los Angeles	W	10	—
Jun 25	1930	Ernie Owens	Oakland	KO	5	—
Jul 15	1930	Les Kennedy	Los Angeles	L	10	—
Dec 19	1930	⑩ Ernie Schaaf	New York	L	10	—
Jan 16	1931	Tom Heeney	New York	KO	3	—
Feb 6	1931	⑩ Tommy Loughran★	New York	L	10	—
Apr 7	1931	Ernie Owens	Portland, OR	KO	2	—
May 5	1931	⑩ Johnny Risko	Cleveland	L	10	—
Jul 4	1931	Paolino Uzcudun	Reno	L	20	—
Nov 9	1931	⑩ Johnny Risko	San Francisco	W	10	—
Nov 23	1931	Les Kennedy	Oakland	KO	3	—
Jan 29	1932	⑩ King Levinsky	New York	W	10	—
Feb 22	1932	Tom Heeney	San Francisco	W	10	—
Jul 4	1932	⑩ King Levinsky	Reno	W	20	—
Aug 31	1932	⑩ Ernie Schaaf	Chicago	W	10	—
Sep 26	1932	⑩ Tuffy Griffiths	Chicago	KO	10	—
Jun 8	1933	⑩ Max Schmeling★	New York	KO	10	—
Jun 14	1934	♛ Primo Carnera	Long Island City, NY	TKO	11	Won-World-H
Jun 13	1935	⑩ Jim Braddock★	Long Island City	L	15	Lost-World-H
Sep 24	1935	⑩ Joe Louis★	New York	KO'd	4	—
Apr 15	1937	⑩ Tommy Farr	London	L	12	—
Mar 11	1938	⑩ Tommy Farr	New York	W	15	—
Jun 1	1939	⑩ Lou Nova	New York	TKO'd	11	—
Jul 2	1940	⑩ Tony Galento	Jersey City, NJ	KO	8	—
Apr 4	1941	⑩ Lou Nova	New York	TKO'd	8	—

for the world heavyweight title, Baer fought Primo Carnera in 1934. At the Madison Square Garden Bowl, before a throng of 50,000, Baer knocked the giant Carnera down eleven times in eleven rounds.

Baer was now at the height of his fame. He starred in a movie, *The Prizefighter and the Lady* (banned in Germany because Baer's grandfather was Jewish), and lived the high life. He was romantically linked to innumerable starlets, socialites, chorus girls, and Broadway actresses before marrying in 1935.

Baer frittered away the title to James J. Braddock in his first defense. He fought with an injured right hand, and his half-hearted, joking effort lost him the fifteen-round decision. He had been champion for a year. Three months later, Joe Louis demolished Baer in four rounds.

Baer continued to fight for another six years, compiling a record of 30-4 in that time. In retirement, Baer acted, had a successful nightclub act both individually and with Slapsie Maxie Rosenbloom, and refereed boxing and wrestling matches. Baer's son, Max Jr., became famous in his own right for playing the role of Jethro Bodine in the long-running television comedy series, *The Beverly Hillbillies*.

JIMMY BARRY
The Little Tiger

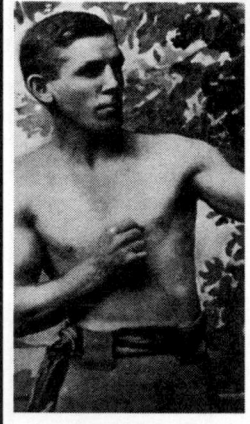

FLYWEIGHT

Right-handed; 5'2"; 95–115 lbs.

70 bouts, 1891 to 9/1/1899

Managers: Dominick O'Malley, Charles E. ("Parson") Davies

World 100 lbs Champ 1893

USA World 102 lbs Champ 1894

USA World 105 lbs Champ 1894–95

USA World 110 lbs Champ 1895–99

World 108 lbs Champ 1897–99

Hall of Fame Induction: 2000

Born: 3/7/1870, Chicago, IL

Died: 4/5/1943

A flyweight fighter in the early days of gloved boxing, before the division was established, Jimmy Barry is one of a select few Hall of Famers who never lost a match. The diminutive Barry came under the tutelage of former lightweight boxer Harry Gilmore, impressing him with his two-handed power. Barry's first match was against Jack Larson at McGurn's Handball Court in Chicago, and though Larson was more experienced and outweighed the newcomer by ten pounds, Barry knocked him out in the third.

Barry became a regular at McGurn's, then ventured out of Illinois to the Columbian Athletic Club in Roby, Indiana to face the well-regarded "Portland Cyclone" Jimmy Shea on July 10, 1893. Though he once again gave away a considerable amount of weight—fourteen pounds—Shea's handlers threw in the towel after only three rounds. Later that year in Roby, Barry knocked out touring Londoner Jack Levy in seventeen rounds to win what was billed as the "World 100-lb Championship," and on June 2, 1894, he defeated Jim Gorman in eleven rounds at the famed Olympic Club in New Orleans to claim the world 102-lb title.

Next, "The Little Tiger" faced his greatest rival, Casper Leon, for the American paperweight title, contested at 105 pounds. Barry, a clever boxer and two-handed puncher, was considered the premier small man in the Midwest, while Leon was top in the East. The fight went twenty rounds before a Barry right turned the tide, leading to a knockout victory in the 28th. In a rematch on March 30, 1895, in Chicago, the police intervened and stopped the bout in the fourteenth round.

A Sicilian by birth, but fighting out of New York, Casper Leon was Barry's most frequent opponent.

IN THE RING	WON 59	LOST 0	DRAWS 9	TB 70	KO 39	W 20	WF 0	D 9	KO'd 0	L 0	LF 0	ND 0	NC 2

Date	Year	Opponent	Site	Result / Rounds		Title
SELECTED BOUTS						
—	1891	Jack Larson	Chicago	KO	1	—
—	1891	Barney McCall	Chicago	W	4	—
Sep 3	1892	Frank Murphy	Springfield, IL	KO	7	—
Feb 12	1893	Billy Murphy	Chicago	KO	1	—
Jul 10	1893	Jimmy Shea	Roby, IN	TKO	4	—
Dec 5	1893	Jack Levy	Roby	KO	17	Won-World-100 lbs
Jun 2	1894	♔ Jimmy Gorman	New Orleans	W	11	Won-USA World-102 lbs
Sep 15	1894	Casper Leon	Lamont, IL	KO	28	Won-USA World-105 lbs
Mar 30	1895	Casper Leon	Chicago	D	14	Ret-USA World-110 lbs
Oct 21	1895	Jack Madden	Maspeth, NY	KO	4	Ret-USA World-105 lbs
Feb 18	1896	Young Spitz	Chicago	KO	8	—
Jul 24	1896	Casper Leon	Elmira, NY	NC	6	—
Jan 10	1897	Harry Dally	Chicago	KO	2	—
Jan 30	1897	Sammy Kelly	New York	D	20	—
Mar 1	1897	Jack Ward	New York	W	20	—
Apr 23	1897	Jimmy Anthony	San Francisco	W	20	—
Dec 6	1897	Walter Croot	London	KO	20	Won-World-108 lbs
May 30	1898	Casper Leon	New York	D	20	Ret-USA World-110 lbs
Jun 3	1898	Steve Flanagan	Philadelphia	D	6	—
Nov 21	1898	Casper Leon	Chicago	D	6	—
Dec 29	1898	Casper Leon	Davenport, IA	D	20	Ret-USA World-110 lbs
Sep 1	1899	Harry Harris ★	Chicago	D	6	—

Though called a draw, Barry was generally considered the winner. Leon fought him four more times, all either draws or no decisions.

Barry next faced Walter Croot at the National Sporting Club in London, seeking acknowledgment as the world paperweight champion. For the first sixteen rounds, the fight was fairly even, but in the seventeenth, Barry's attack began to wear on Croot. In the twentieth, an exhausted Croot attempted to launch one last barrage in hopes of a victory, but Barry landed a right which dazed Croot and then knocked him out with a left to the head and a right to the jaw. Croot never regained consciousness and died the next morning. Charged with manslaughter, Barry was exonerated when it was determined that Croot died of a skull fracture sustained when his head hit the unpadded wooden floor.

Though cleared of wrongdoing in Croot's death, Barry was deeply affected by the incident and immediately announced his retirement. After his return to the United States, he came out of retirement and fought nine more times, with two wins, seven draws, and no knockouts. Before the fatality, Barry generally won by knockout, and he admitted that Croot's death affected his fighting style. In his last fight against future bantam champ and Hall of Famer Harry Harris, on September 1, 1899, most observers believed that Harris won but that the referee called the match a draw to enable Barry to again retire undefeated.

BENNY BASS
The Little Fish

FEATHERWEIGHT

Right-handed; 5'1½"; 120–135 lbs.

239 bouts, 1/29/1921 to 5/7/1940

Manager: Phil Glassman

Featherweight Champion 1927–28

Junior Lightweight Champion 1929–31

Hall of Fame Induction: 2002

Born: 12/4/1904, Kiev, Ukraine, Russia

Died: 6/25/1975

Another of the many great fighters who earned their stripes in Philadelphia, Benny Bass arrived at the City of Brotherly Love by a circuitous route.

Bass was born in Kiev, at a time when Russian Jews were the victims of frequent pogroms. His father immigrated to the U.S. in 1907, and three years later, he sent for his wife and five sons. They survived a shipwreck near Ireland and reached America.

As a boy, Bass developed a keen interest in boxing, fighting his first amateur match when he was twelve. A scheduled fighter, Young Smithy, fell ill before his bout at the Gayety Theater and allowed Bass to fight in his place. Bass knocked out his opponent in the first round.

For the next few years, Bass boxed regularly as an amateur while holding a day job. It was during this time that he came to the attention of Harry McGrath, the head of the AAU boxing program in Philadelphia. Under McGrath's guidance, the sixteen-year-old Bass turned professional on January 29, 1921, in a no-decision bout against Matty Dechter. He fought frequently over the next few years in the Philadelphia area, then took Phil Glassman as his manager in 1923. By 1924, Bass was a main event fighter in small clubs along the East Coast.

In 1926, Kid Kaplan vacated the featherweight title and Bass, as the next ranked contender, signed to face Red Chapman for the NBA championship in Philadelphia on September 12, 1927. The match was a ten-round slugfest, highlighted by a double knockdown. At its conclusion, Bass was awarded the decision and the title.

He did not hold the title for long. His first defense came on February 10, 1928, in Madison Square Garden, against Hall of Famer Tony Canzoneri. Bass suffered a broken collarbone in the third, but battled back courageously. While he lasted the full fifteen rounds, he lost a unanimous decision

Benny Bass won a unanimous, bloody ten-round decision from Red Chapman at Municipal Stadium in Philadelphia on September 12, 1927, to claim the NBA version of the Featherweight Championship. The fighters rose from a double knockdown in the ninth to finish the legendary battle. Frank McCracken refereed.

IN THE RING	WON 152	LOST 28	DRAWS 5	TB 239	KO 69	W 80	WF 3	D 5	KO'd 3	L 14	LF 11	ND 52	NC 2

Date	Year	Opponent	Site	Result / Rounds	Title
SELECTED BOUTS					
Jan 29	1921	Matty Dechter	Philadelphia	ND-W 6	—
Apr 29	1924	ⓞ Johnny Brown	Philadelphia	KO 3	—
Sep 24	1925	ⓞ Eddie Anderson	Philadelphia	W 10	—
Nov 2	1925	ⓞ Lew Mayrs	Philadelphia	KO 2	—
Jan 11	1926	ⓞ Leo ("Kid") Roy	Philadelphia	W 10	—
Jun 8	1926	ⓞ Andy Martin	Providence	L 12	
Jul 29	1926	ⓞ Johnny Farr	New York	W 10	—
Oct 1	1926	ⓞ Babe Herman	Philadelphia	W 10	—
May 2	1927	ⓞ Chick Suggs	Philadelphia	W 10	—
Aug 10	1927	ⓞ Johnny Farr	Cleveland	W 10	—
Sep 12	1927	ⓞ Red Chapman	Philadelphia	W 10	Won-Vac NBA-FE
Jan 2	1928	ⓞ Pete Nebo	Philadelphia	W 10	—
Feb 10	1928	♛ Tony Canzoneri★	New York	L 15	For-World-FE, Lost-NBA-FE
Jun 18	1928	♛ Pete Nebo	Philadelphia	L 10	—
Sep 10	1928	ⓞ Harry Blitman	Philadelphia	KO 6	—
Jan 14	1929	ⓞ Davey Abad	Philadelphia	W 10	—
Jan 28	1929	Red Chapman	Philadelphia	KO 1	—
Dec 20	1929	♛ Tod Morgan	New York	KO 2	Won-World-JL
Jul 21	1930	ⓞ Tony Canzoneri★	Philadelphia	L 10	—
Jan 5	1931	ⓞ Lew Massey	Philadelphia	W 10	Ret-NBA-JL
Jul 15	1931	ⓞ Kid Chocolate★	Philadelphia	TKO'd 7	Lost-NBA-JL
Mar 8	1933	ⓞ Joe Ghnouly	St. Louis	W 10	—
Dec 27	1933	ⓞ Eddie Cool	Philadelphia	W 10	—
Apr 30	1934	ⓞ Anacleto ("Cleto") Locatelli	Philadelphia	L 10	—
Jul 31	1934	ⓞ Johnny Jadick	Philadelphia	W 10	—
Jul 27	1937	ⓞ Henry Armstrong★	Philadelphia	KO'd 4	—
May 7	1940	ⓞ Tommy Spiegel	Philadelphia	L 10	—

and his crown. Over the next year and a half, Bass fought frequently, recording wins over Harry Blitman, Chapman, and others.

On December 20, 1929, Bass fought for a new title—this time the junior lightweight belt held by Tod Morgan. Though he was not known as a knockout artist, Bass stopped Morgan in just two rounds at Madison Square Garden.

Bass fought Canzoneri again in a non-title bout on July 21, 1930, but lost the ten-round decision. The champ successfully defended his title on January 5, 1931, with a decision over Lew Massey, and on July 15 of that same year, Bass put his belt on the line against Hall of Famer Kid Chocolate. "The Cuban Bon Bon" proved to be too much for Bass, who was stopped short in the seventh round.

While Bass never had a chance to claim another championship, he was nowhere near retiring from the ring. He moved up to lightweight as a ranked contender in 1932 and 1933, and continued to fight in and around Philadelphia until Tommy Spiegel gained a ten-round decision over him on May 7, 1940.

In retirement, Bass was very active in the Veteran Boxers Association, and he enjoyed attending fights and other boxing functions.

PAUL BERLENBACH
The Astoria Assassin

LIGHT HEAVYWEIGHT

Right-handed; 5'10½"; 165–180 lbs.
52 bouts, 10/4/1923 to 9/28/1933
Manager: Dan Hickey
Light Heavyweight Champ 1925–26
Hall of Fame Induction: 2001
Born: 2/18/1901, New York
Died: 9/30/1985

Paul Berlenbach was the only man to ever win both an AAU national wrestling championship and a world boxing title. Left deaf and mute by scarlet fever at age two, the accidental touch of a downed electrical wire when he was fifteen miraculously restored Berlenbach's hearing and speech.

Berlenbach first became interested in wrestling at a local gymnastics club, where he came to the attention of Nat Pendleton, himself a national wrestling champion. Pendleton got Berlenbach a membership at the New York Athletic Club, and the latter went on to great success, as an amateur free-style wrestler.

While campaigning as a wrestler, Berlenbach began boxing lessons with Dan Hickey at the New York Athletic Club. Though an ungainly fighter, Berlenbach's left hand packed tremendous punching power. Hickey changed him to a right-hander to bring his powerful left closer to his opponent, taught him the rudiments of boxing, and became his manager. Meanwhile, Berlenbach continued to star as a wrestler winning the 1922 and 1923 AAU national championships.

On October 4, 1923, Berlenbach launched his pro-boxing career with a first-round knockout of Jimmy Roberts, and went on to win his next eight fights with KOs, four in the first round. On March 14, 1924, he faced future champion and Hall of Famer Jack Delaney. The more experienced Delaney knocked Berlenbach down three times in the fourth, and the referee stopped the fight.

Berlenbach shrugged off the loss and won fourteen of his next seventeen bouts with no losses, including a knockout of former light heavyweight champ Battling Siki. Then, on May 30, 1925, in front of 45,000 fans at Yankee Stadium, Berlenbach abandoned his puncher style and boxed light heavyweight champion Mike McTigue to a fifteen-round decision to win the light heavyweight ti-

Referee Patsy Haley sends Berlenbach (L) to a neutral corner while Jimmy Slattery takes the count in their September 11, 1925, title bout in Yankee Stadium.

IN THE RING	WON 39	LOST 8	DRAWS 3	TB 52	KO 33	W 6	WF 0	D 3	KO'd 3	L 4	LF 1	ND 1	NC 1

Date	Year	Opponent	Site	Result / Rounds		Title
SELECTED BOUTS						
Oct 4	1923	Jimmy Roberts	New York	KO	1	—
Mar 14	1924	Jack Delaney★	New York	KO'd	4	—
Aug 15	1924	Joe ("Hambone") Kelly	Boston	KO	5	—
Aug 27	1924	⑩ Young Stribling★	New York	D	6	—
Oct 1	1924	Johnny Gill	Jersey City, NJ	ND-W	10	—
Jan 30	1925	Young Tony Marullo	New York	W	12	—
Mar 13	1925	Battling Siki	New York	TKO	10	—
May 30	1925	♛ Mike McTigue	New York	W	15	Won-World-LH
Sep 11	1925	⑩ Jimmy Slattery	New York	TKO	11	Ret-World-LH
Dec 11	1925	⑩ Jack Delaney★	New York	W	15	Ret-World-LH
Mar 19	1926	⑩ Johnny Risko	New York	L	10	—
Jun 10	1926	⑩ Young Stribling★	New York	W	15	Ret-World-LH
Jul 16	1926	⑩ Jack Delaney★	Brooklyn	L	15	Lost-World-LH
Jan 28	1927	⑩ Mike McTigue	New York	TKO'd	4	—
Nov 25	1927	♛ Mickey Walker★	Chicago	L	10	—
Dec 9	1927	⑩ Jack Delaney★	Chicago	KO'd	6	—
May 22	1928	Larry Estridge	New York	TKO	8	—
Mar 31	1931	Eddie Clark	Brooklyn	KO	3	—
Sep 28	1933	Carl Knowles	Atlanta, GA	L	10	—

tle, which he then successfully defended against Jimmy Slattery before facing Delaney again. Tex Rickard paired the two for the opening bout of the new Madison Square Garden on December 11, 1925: Berlenbach won a fifteen-round decision.

Like most light heavyweights, Berlenbach wanted the fatter purses and greater attention of the top heavyweights, but his attempt to move up in 1926 ended in a loss to Johnny Risko. After winning a decision over Hall of Famer Young Stribling, Berlenbach again faced Delaney, this time in front of a crowd of 49,000 at Ebbets Field. Delaney outboxed Berlenbach and took the championship.

After the loss of his title, Berlenbach's fortune seemed to change. He broke with Hickey, and on January 28, 1927, he was KO'd in four rounds by McTigue. After that fight, he briefly retired, disillusioned with boxing and its fans. He returned to the ring later that year, but lost to Hall of Famer Mickey Walker and again to Delaney, who knocked him out in the sixth round. After winning two fights in 1928, he retired again, returned to wrestling in 1929, and came back briefly for five boxing matches in '31 and one in '33. By this time, however, the Astoria Assassin's skills had faded.

Berlenbach's real estate investments soured during the Great Depression, and he was forced to turn to a succession of odd jobs, such as bartending, refereeing, and selling newspapers. Later, he was hired by Jacob Ruppert, owner of the New York Yankees and Ruppert Breweries, as a goodwill ambassador.

JAMES J. BRADDOCK
The Cinderella Man

HEAVYWEIGHT

Right-handed; 6'2½"; 162–199½ lbs.

86 bouts, 4/14/1926 to 1/21/1938

Manager: Joe Gould

World Heavyweight Champion 1935–37

Hall of Fame Induction: 2001

Born: 6/7/1905, New York, NY

Named: James Walter Braddock

Died: 11/29/1974

James J. Braddock's "rags to riches" story captured the nation's attention during his brief reign as heavyweight champion of the world.

Braddock grew up in Northern New Jersey, and had a notable amateur career, winning New Jersey's state light heavyweight and heavyweight amateur titles. Braddock turned professional on April 14, 1926, with a four-round, no-decision bout against Al Settle. Campaigning as a light heavyweight, Braddock knocked out his next eleven opponents, eight of them in the first round, and on January 28, 1927 made his Madison Square Garden debut with a one-round knockout of George LaRocco.

A decision against Pete Latzo and knockout victories over Tuffy Griffith and Jimmy Slattery earned Braddock a shot at the light heavyweight title held by Hall of Famer Tommy Loughran on July 18, 1929. Though a solid boxer-puncher, Braddock was outfought by the gifted Loughran in a fifteen round decision.

The loss, coupled with a broken knuckle that required medical care Braddock could not afford, derailed the fighter's promising career. Over the next five years, Braddock fought 33 times but won just eleven bouts.

In 1934, Braddock's manager, Joe Gould, got Braddock a fight on the undercard of the Max Baer–Primo Carnera heavyweight championship fight against Corn Griffin. Braddock, now a heavyweight, was viewed as a mere "opponent" for the up-and-coming Griffin, yet he surprised everyone with a third-round knockout. Propelled by a victory over Hall of Famer John Henry Lewis, Braddock next fought top contender Art Lasky, and decisioned him at Madison Square Garden to earn a shot against Max Baer for the heavyweight title.

Braddock was given no chance against the hard-hitting, though light-training, Baer. But if Baer did not take the fight seri-

Champion Max Baer's (R) hands are low as Braddock hones in on his target during their June 13, 1935, heavyweight championship bout in Long Island City, NY.

IN THE RING	WON 46	LOST 23	DRAWS 4	TB 86	KO 27	W 19	WF 0	D 4	KO'd 2	L 20	LF 1	ND 11	NC 2

Date	Year	Opponent	Site	Result / Rounds		Title
SELECTED BOUTS						
Apr 14	1926	Al Settle	West Hoboken, NJ	ND-D	4	—
Jan 28	1927	George LaRocco	New York	KO	1	—
Feb 1	1927	Johnny Alberts	Wilkes Barre, PA	KO	4	—
Oct 17	1928	⑩ Pete Latzo	Newark, NJ	W	10	—
Nov 30	1928	⑩ Gerald ("Tuffy") Griffith	New York	KO	2	—
Jan 18	1929	⑩ Leo Lomski	New York	L	10	—
Mar 11	1929	⑩ Jimmy Slattery	New York	TKO	9	—
Jul 18	1929	♛ Tommy Loughran★	New York	L	15	For-World-LH
Nov 15	1929	⑩ Maxie Rosenbloom★	New York	L	10	—
Jan 17	1930	⑩ Leo Lomski	Chicago	L	10	—
Jan 23	1931	⑩ Ernie Schaaf	New York	L	10	—
Nov 10	1931	⑩ Maxie Rosenbloom★	Minneapolis	NC	2	—
Dec 4	1931	⑩ Al Gainer	New Haven	L	10	—
May 13	1932	Charley Retzlaff	Boston	L	10	—
Sep 21	1932	⑩ John Henry Lewis★	San Francisco	L	10	—
Nov 9	1932	⑩ Lou Scozza	San Francisco	TKO'd	6	—
Jun 14	1934	John ("Corn") Griffin	New York	TKO	3	—
Nov 16	1934	⑩ John Henry Lewis★	New York	W	10	—
Mar 22	1935	⑩ Art Lasky	New York	W	15	—
Jun 13	1935	♛ Max Baer★	Long Island City, NY	W	15	Won-World-H
Jun 22	1937	⑩ Joe Louis★	Chicago	KO'd	8	Lost-World-H
Jan 21	1938	⑩ Tommy Farr	New York	W	10	—

ously, Braddock did. He scored effectively with both hands to take command of the battle by the eighth round, and continued to pepper Baer with jabs to win the championship on a fifteen-round decision. Journalist Damon Runyon christened the upset winner "The Cinderella Man."

Braddock signed on to defend his title against Max Schmeling in the summer of 1936, but arthritis in his right hand forced the fight's postponement. Braddock's manager, Gould, then broke his contract with Madison Square Garden, ostensibly because of opposition to the German Schmeling by the Non-Sectarian Anti-Nazi League. It is likely, however, that the real reason Braddock bypassed the Schmeling fight was an amazing offer from promoter Mike Jacobs of $500,000 or half the gate and radio revenues (whichever was greater), plus ten percent of Jacobs's profits from all his heavyweight title promotions for the next ten years, should Braddock fight and lose to a different opponent: Joe Louis. On June 22, 1937, in Comiskey Park, Chicago, in front of 45,000 fans, Braddock came out strong in the first round, knocking down Louis with a right uppercut, but the more talented Louis quickly asserted his dominance and knocked Braddock out in the eighth. Braddock would fight just one more time.

In retirement, Braddock was in the military surplus business, and operated electrical generators and welding equipment.

WELTERWEIGHT

Right-handed; 5'8"; 118–150 lbs.

342 bouts, 10/7/1905 to Aug. 1930

Managers: G.F. Thiel 1906, Marcus Williams 1906–10, Charlie Redman 1910–11, Jack Costello 1911–12, Dan Morgan 1912–25

Welterweight Champion 1915, 1916–17, 1919–22

Hall of Fame Induction: 1990

Born: 10/14/1885, Clinton, NY

Named: William J. Breslin

Died: 3/27/1962

Jack Britton was a masterful boxer whose career spanned 25 years. He was 37 when Mickey Walker took the welterweight title from him, and he continued to fight top contenders until his retirement at age 44. An Irish street scrapper from Clinton, New York, Britton's earliest professional bouts took place in 1904 and 1905 at small boxing clubs in Milwaukee and Chicago. Although he was a talented fighter, Britton languished in the lower ranks until he teamed up with manager Dan Morgan, who insisted his boxers live clean and train hard. Under Morgan's guidance, Britton's career took off.

Britton fought three times against Hall of Famer Packey McFarland. Their first match was a draw and the next two were no-decisions, but all were memorable for the ring artistry displayed by the two fighters. In 1915, Britton won a twelve-round decision over Mike Glover to stake a claim as the welterweight champion. After Ted ("Kid") Lewis also defeated Glover, the stage was set for Lewis and Britton to meet, with the winner to be acclaimed as champion. The bout became the first in a twenty-fight rivalry between Britton and the closely matched Lewis. Enemies from the onset, Britton and Lewis exchanged threats and then refused to speak to each other. In the ring, both spurned the customary handshake. In a wild bout, the hard-hitting Lewis won the decision and the championship.

Most of the Britton–Lewis matches were officially no-decision bouts, but in 1916, Britton won a decision over Lewis to take the welterweight title. For the next six years, the two fighters monopolized the championship. Lewis regained it in a twenty-round decision in 1917. In 1919, Britton knocked out Lewis in the ninth round to

Welterweight champ Jack Britton fought many top contenders in his 25-year career. He was 44 before he finally quit the ring.

IN THE RING	WON 104	LOST 27	DRAWS 21	TB 344	KO 28	W 72	WF 4	D 21	KO'd 1	L 24	LF 2	ND 190	NC 2

Date	Year		Opponent	Site	Result / Rounds		Title
SELECTED BOUTS							
Nov 11	1904		Jack Nelson	Milwaukee	W	6	—
Oct 7	1905		Tommy Shea	Chicago	L	6	—
Jan 30	1911		Packey McFarland ★	Memphis, TN	D	8	—
Mar 7	1913		Packey McFarland ★	New York	ND-L	10	—
Dec 8	1913		Packey McFarland ★	Milwaukee	ND-L	10	—
Mar 26	1915		Ted ("Kid") Lewis ★	New York	ND-L	10	—
Jun 22	1915	♛	Mike Glover	Boston	W	12	Won-World-W
Aug 31	1915		Kid Lewis ★	Boston	L	12	Lost-World-W
Sep 27	1915	♛	Ted ("Kid") Lewis ★	Boston	L	12	For-World-W
Jan 20	1916	♛	Ted ("Kid") Lewis ★	Buffalo	ND-W	10	—
Feb 15	1916	♛	Ted ("Kid") Lewis ★	Brooklyn	ND-W	10	—
Apr 24	1916	♛	Ted ("Kid") Lewis ★	New Orleans	W	20	Reg-World-W
Oct 17	1916		Ted ("Kid") Lewis ★	Boston	W	12	—
Nov 14	1916		Ted ("Kid") Lewis ★	Boston	D	12	—
Mar 26	1917		Ted ("Kid") Lewis ★	Cleveland	ND-L	10	—
May 19	1917		Ted ("Kid") Lewis ★	Toronto	ND-L	10	—
Jun 6	1917		Ted ("Kid") Lewis ★	St. Louis	ND-D	12	—
Jun 14	1917		Ted ("Kid") Lewis ★	New York	ND-D	10	—
Jun 25	1917		Ted ("Kid") Lewis ★	Dayton, OH	L	20	Lost-World-W
Mar 6	1918	♛	Ted ("Kid") Lewis ★	Atlanta	ND-D	10	—
May 2	1918	♛	Ted ("Kid") Lewis ★	Scranton, PA	ND-D	10	—
May 24	1918	♛	Ted ("Kid") Lewis ★	New York	ND-W	6	—
Jun 20	1918	♛	Ted ("Kid") Lewis ★	New York	ND-W	6	—
Mar 17	1919	♛	Ted ("Kid") Lewis ★	Canton, OH	KO	9	Reg-World-W
Jul 28	1919		Ted ("Kid") Lewis ★	Jersey City, NJ	ND-W	8	—
Aug 23	1920		Lou Bogash	Bridgeport, CT	D	12	Ret-World-W
Feb 7	1921		Ted ("Kid") Lewis ★	New York	W	15	Ret-World-W
Feb 17	1922		Dave Shade	New York	D	15	Ret-World-W
Jun 13	1922		Benny Leonard ★	New York	WF	13	Ret-World-W
Nov 1	1922		Mickey Walker ★	New York	L	15	Lost-World-W
Aug	1930		Rudy Marshall	Stamford, CT	L	10	—

take it back. Britton remained the champion until 1922. In his last successful title defense, Britton fought lightweight champion Benny Leonard at the New York Velodrome before approximately 18,000 fans. Leonard knocked Britton down in the thirteenth round, then hit him again before he got up, giving Britton the victory on the foul. Some ringside observers believed that Leonard deliberately went for the foul because he didn't want to hold two titles.

Britton lost the welterweight belt in Madison Square Garden later that year to the much younger Mickey Walker, who floored Britton three times. Though he never again contended for the title, Britton continued to fight for seven more years, pushed beyond his prime when he lost his ring earnings in failed Florida land investments. He left the ring to become a boxing instructor and mentor to young athletes in New York City, where he and Morgan continued the close association that had built one of boxing's strongest careers.

The Elongated Panamanian

BANTAMWEIGHT

Right-handed; 5'11"; 112–126 lbs.

155 bouts, 1922 to 12/4/1942

Manager: Dave Lumiansky

Bantamweight Champion 1929–35

Hall of Fame Induction: 1992

Born: 7/5/1902, Colon, Panama

Named: Alfonso Teofilo Brown

Died: 4/11/1951

Tall, thin, and all muscle, Panama Al Brown held the world bantamweight title for six years. He was born in Panama's Canal Zone and as a young man was employed as a clerk with the United States Shipping Board. He became interested in boxing while watching bouts between U.S. military personnel and, when encouraged by his boss, gave the ring a try.

Brown had surprising punching power and an incredible 76" reach. He turned professional at age 20 and won the Isthmus flyweight title in his third fight, with a decision over Sailor Patchett. Brown's performance caught the attention of fight manager Dave Lumiansky, who took him to New York. Brown was unbeaten in his first seventeen bouts in the U.S. and was ranked as the third-best flyweight in the 1924 annual rankings of *The Ring*. By 1926, Brown had moved up to the bantamweight level and was ranked sixth by *The Ring*. He then spent a year in Paris, where he was a great favorite of French fight fans, compiling a 6-2-1 record in nine bouts.

In 1929, Brown challenged Vidal Gregorio for the vacant world bantamweight title. The fight took place in Queensboro Stadium in Long Island City, with 15,000 looking on. Brown dominated the fight and

Brown (L) uses his long reach to dig into Baltazar Sangchili's ribs on his way to a 15-round win in this 1938 bout in Paris.

IN THE RING	WON 123	LOST 18	DRAWS 10	TB 155	KO 55	W 64	WF 4	D 10	KO'd 0	L 16	LF 2	ND 4

Date	Year	Opponent	Site	Result / Rounds		Title
SELECTED BOUTS						
—	1922	Jose Moreno	Colon, Panama	W	6	—
Aug 22	1923	Johnny Breslin	New York	D	4	—
Oct 16	1925	⑩ Johnny Breslin	New York	W	10	—
Nov 10	1926	Antoine Merlo	Paris	KO	2	—
Apr 2	1927	Eugene Criqui	Paris	W	10	—
Sep 13	1928	⑩ Kid Francis	New York	W	12	—
Oct 23	1928	⑩ Alf ("Kid") Pattenden	Paris	D	15	—
Apr 9	1929	Joe Cadman	Paris	TKO	3	—
Jun 18	1929	⑩ Vidal Gregorio	Long Island City, NY	W	15	Won-Vac World-B
Jul 26	1929	⑩ Battling Battalino	Hartford, CT	L	10	—
Feb 8	1930	Johnny Erickson	New York	WF	4	Ret-World-B
Jul 23	1930	⑩ Domenico Bernasconti	Brooklyn	W	10	—
Oct 4	1930	Eugene Huat	Paris	W	15	Ret-World-B
Aug 15	1931	⑩ Pete Sanstol	Montreal	W	15	Ret-World-B
Oct 27	1931	⑩ Eugene Huat	Montreal	W	15	Ret-World-B
Dec 15	1931	⑩ Newsboy Brown	Los Angeles	L	10	—
Jan 18	1932	⑩ Eugene Huat	Paris	W	10	—
Jul 10	1932	Kid Francis	Marseilles, France	W	15	Ret-World-B
Sep 19	1932	⑩ Emile Pladner	Toronto	KO	1	Ret-World-B
Mar 19	1933	Domenico Bernasconi	Milan	W	12	Ret-World-B
Jul 3	1933	⑩ Johnny King	London	W	15	Ret-World-B
Oct 1	1933	Georges LePerson	Algiers, Algeria	W	10	—
Nov 12	1933	Alfredo Magnolfi	Casablanca, Morocco	W	10	—
Dec 9	1933	Luigi Quadrini	Oran, Algeria	W	10	—
Feb 19	1934	Young Perez	Paris	W	15	Ret-World-B
Nov 1	1934	Young Perez	Tunis, Tunisia	KO	10	Ret-World-B
Dec 24	1934	♛ Freddie Miller★	Paris	L	10	—
Mar 18	1935	⑩ Baltazar Sangchili	Valencia, Spain	L	10	—
Jun 1	1935	⑩ Baltazar Sangchili	Valencia	L	15	Lost-World-B
Sep 11	1935	Pete Sanstol	Oslo, Norway	L	10	—

easily won the decision. Over the next six years, Brown, a true world champion, defended his title in New York, Paris, Montreal, Marseilles, Toronto, Milan, London, and Tunis, and fought non-title bouts in many other cities around the world.

The merry-go-round stopped in Valencia, Spain, in 1935, when Baltazar Sangchilli beat Brown in a fifteen-round decision and walked off with the title. Brown kept fighting, mostly in Paris and New York, and finally back home in Panama. He twice retired and twice came back, until he at last quit the ring in 1942. Although the money had poured in during his globe-trotting days, Brown died penniless in New York in 1951, after a bout with tuberculosis.

TOMMY BURNS

HEAVYWEIGHT

Right-handed; 5'7"; 158–184 lbs.
60 bouts, 1900 to 7/16/1920
Heavyweight Champion 1906–1908
Hall of Fame Induction: 1996
Born: 6/17/1881, Chesley, Ontario
Named: Noah Brusso
Died: 5/10/1955

A largely forgotten and sometimes belittled champion, Tommy Burns held the heavyweight title for nearly three years and set a record for the most consecutive defenses by knockout. Burns, who acted as his own manager, also made a lot of money, an accomplishment that distinguishes him from many top fighters. When, badly overmatched, he finally fell to Jack Johnson, there was no question that he displayed great courage.

Burns was a French-Canadian who excelled as a lacrosse and hockey player in his youth. He polished his boxing skills in mining camps and turned professional in 1900, first fighting as a lightweight. Two years later he won the Michigan state middleweight title, which he successfully defended three times. Burns was small and fast, holding his hands low and darting in and out to score punches. It was a technique that often worked against larger, slower men. He had a fairly long reach for his height—he was only 5'7"—and preferred to score on the inside, especially with left hooks.

In a light heavyweight match in 1904, Hall of Famer Philadelphia Jack O'Brien proved too much for him, but Burns continued to beef up, heading for the heavyweight division. In 1905, when he knocked out Dave Barry in San Francisco, promoter Tom McCarey proposed matching him with heavyweight champ Marvin Hart. Although Johnson and some other black fighters may have been better qualified, the color bar was still very strong, and McCarey was looking for white contenders. The fight with Hart took place in Los Angeles in 1906, with retired heavyweight champ James J. Jeffries refereeing. Burns outboxed Hart in twenty rounds and took the championship and a purse of $15,000.

Burns then launched his series of defenses. He KO'd Fireman Jim Flynn, then fought O'Brien to a draw before winning a twenty-round decision in the rematch. He scored a one-round knockout of Australian contender Bill Squires, then added Squires to his camp as a sparring partner. With Johnson on his heels, Burns took his title on a world tour, recording knockout

Burns (R) was the first true world champion, defending his title in England, Ireland, France, Australia, and the U.S. He knocked out sometime sparring partner Bill Squires in all three of their meetings.

IN THE RING	WON 46	LOST 5	DRAWS 8	TB 60	KO 37	W 9	WF 0	D 8	KO'd 2	L 3	LF 0	ND 1

Date	Year	Opponent	Site	Result / Rounds		Title

SELECTED BOUTS

Date	Year	Opponent	Site	Result	Rounds	Title
—	1900	Fred Thornton	Detroit	KO	5	—
Dec 26	1902	Tom McCune	Detroit	KO	7	Won-Mich. State-M
Sep 25	1903	Jimmy Duggan	Houghton, MI	KO	9	Ret-Mich. State-M
Oct 12	1903	Jack Hammond	Sioux Ste. Marie, MI	KO	3	Ret-Mich. State-M
Dec 31	1903	Tom McCune	Detroit	W	10	Ret-Mich. State-M
Oct 7	1904	Phila. Jack O'Brien★	Milwaukee	L	6	—
Aug 31	1905	Dave Barry	San Francisco	KO	20	—
Oct 17	1905	Jack (Twin) Sullivan	Los Angeles	L	20	—
Feb 23	1906 ♛	Marvin Hart	Los Angeles	W	20	Won-World-H
Oct 2	1906	Fireman Jim Flynn	Los Angeles	KO	15	Ret-World-H
Nov 28	1906	Phila. Jack O'Brien★	Los Angeles	D	20	Ret-World-H
May 8	1907	Phila. Jack O'Brien★	Los Angeles	W	20	Ret-World-H
Jul 4	1907	Bill Squires	Colma, CA	KO	1	Ret-World-H
Dec 2	1907	James ("Gunner") Moir	London	TKO	10	Ret-World-H
Feb 10	1908	Jack Palmer	London	KO	4	Ret-World-H
Mar 17	1908	Jem Roche	Dublin	KO	1	Ret-World-H
Apr 18	1908	Jewey Smith	Paris	KO	5	Ret-World-H
Jun 13	1908	Bill Squires	Paris	TKO	8	Ret-World-H
Aug 24	1908	Bill Squires	Sydney	KO	13	Ret-World-H
Sep 2	1908	Bill Lang	Melbourne	KO	6	Ret-World-H
Dec 26	1908	Jack Johnson★	Sydney	TKO'd	14	Lost-World-H
Apr 7	1910	Bill Lang	Sydney	W	20	Won-Vac Brit Emp-H
Jan 26	1914	Battling Brant	Taft, CA	KO	4	—
Jul 16	1920	Joe Beckett	London	TKO'd	7	For-Brit Emp-H

victories in London, Dublin, Paris, Sydney, and Melbourne. Three times, he put Squires in the ring as his opponent.

Johnson, who had followed Burns to London and Paris, finally secured a title bout in Sydney the day after Christmas, 1908. Promoted by canny Australian entrepreneur Hugh D. ("Huge Deal") McIntosh, the fight was timed to coincide with the arrival in Sydney of the American fleet. Johnson was to receive $5,000 and Burns $30,000, the largest amount ever earned by a boxer for a single fight up to that time. Burns was the three-to-one favorite, but Johnson was unquestionably the superior fighter. He was bigger, faster, stronger, and more skilled as a boxer. He took revenge for the racist insults he had endured, battering and taunting Burns, who though bloodied and bruised, hung on for fourteen rounds. When police finally entered the ring, McIntosh, who was refereeing, conceded that Johnson had won.

Burns took a year off, then beat Bill Lang for the vacant British Empire heavyweight title, which he relinquished the next year. He fought only five more times, ending his career with a failed comeback effort against Joe Beckett in London in 1920. In retirement, Burns owned a tavern in Bremerton, Washington before becoming an evengelist. He died of a heart attack in 1955.

L I G H T W E I G H T

Right-handed; 5'5"; 118–140 lbs.

175 bouts, 7/24/1925 to 11/1/1939

Manager: Sammy Goldman

Featherwt. Champ 1927–28,
Lightwt. Champ 1930–33, 1935–36,
Jr. Welterwt. Champ 1931–32, 1933

Hall of Fame Induction: 1990

Born: 11/6/1908, Slidell, LA

Died: 12/9/1959

One of the best in an era of excellent fighters, Tony Canzoneri was an aggressive combatant who lit into his opponents with zeal and power. He was knocked out only once, in the final fight of his career. Canzoneri bounced in and out of titleholder status in three weight classes, and he fought in 22 championship bouts in the ten years he stayed at his peak.

Louisiana-born Canzoneri started boxing as an amateur in New Orleans and continued the pursuit after moving to New York City with his family. He won New York State's amateur bantamweight title in 1924 and turned professional the next year at age sixteen. Within two years, Canzoneri was ready to challenge Bud Taylor for the vacant NBA bantamweight title. The results of the heated battles with Taylor were a draw and a loss for Canzoneri. Soon afterward, Canzoneri abandoned the bantamweight class and moved to featherweight, going for the vacant world featherweight title against Hall of Famer Johnny Dundee. Canzoneri outboxed the aging Dundee to win the belt, then went after NBA featherweight champ Benny Bass to unify the title. Canzoneri won a decision over Bass, but lost the title to French boxer Andre Routis seven months later.

In 1929, Canzoneri moved up to lightweight but failed to snare the title from champion Sammy Mandell in a ten-round decision. The years 1930 and '31 saw three furious battles between Canzoneri and Jackie ("Kid") Berg, a gutsy, aggressive fighter well-prepared to meet Canzoneri's attacks. Canzoneri lost to Berg on points in a non-title bout, but stunned the boxing world later in 1930 by knocking out lightweight champ Al Singer in 66 seconds at New York's Polo Grounds to gain the world lightweight crown. The next year Canzoneri avenged

Canzoneri floors Joe Glick in this 1930 bout in Brooklyn. Glick got up, but Canzoneri won the decision.

IN THE RING	WON **137**	LOST **24**	DRAWS **10**	TB 175	KO 44	W 93	WF 0	D 10	KO'd 1	L 22	LF 1	ND 4

Date	Year	Opponent	Site	Result / Rounds		Title

SELECTED BOUTS

Date	Year	Opponent	Site	Result / Rounds		Title
Jul 24	1925	Jack Gardner	Rockaway, NY	KO	1	—
Mar 26	1927	ⓦ Bud Taylor	Chicago	D	10	For-Vac NBA-B
Jun 24	1927	ⓦ Bud Taylor	Chicago	L	10	For-Vac NBA-B
Oct 24	1927	Johnny Dundee★	New York	W	15	Won-Vac World-FE
Feb 10	1928	♛ Benny Bass★	New York	W	15	Ret-World-FE
Sep 28	1928	ⓦ Andre Routis	New York	L	15	Lost-World-FE
Aug 2	1929	♛ Sammy Mandell★	Chicago	L	10	For-World-L
Sept 11	1930	ⓦ Billie Petrolle★	Chicago	L	10	—
Jan 17	1930	ⓦ Jackie ("Kid") Berg★	New York	L	10	—
Nov 14	1930	♛ Al Singer	New York	KO	1	Won-World-L
Apr 24	1931	♛ Jackie ("Kid") Berg★	Chicago	KO	3	Ret-World-L & Won-World-JW
Jul 13	1931	Cecil Payne	Los Angeles	W	10	Ret-World-JW
Sep 10	1931	ⓦ Jackie ("Kid") Berg★	New York	W	15	Ret-World-L & JW
Oct 29	1931	Phillie Griffin	Newark	W	10	Ret-World-JW
Nov 20	1931	ⓦ Kid Chocolate★	New York	W	15	Ret-World-L & JW
Jan 18	1932	ⓦ Jackie Jadick	Philadelphia	L	10	Lost-World-JW
Jul 18	1932	♛ Jackie Jadick	Philadelphia	L	10	For-World-JW
Nov 4	1932	ⓦ Billy Petrolle★	New York	W	15	Ret-World-L
May 21	1933	♛ Battling Shaw	New Orleans	W	10	Reg-World-JW
Jun 23	1933	ⓦ Barney Ross★	Chicago	L	10	Lost-World-L & JW
Sep 12	1933	♛ Barney Ross★	New York	L	15	For-World-L & JW
May 10	1935	ⓦ Lou Ambers★	New York	W	15	Won-Vac World-L
Oct 4	1935	ⓦ Al Roth	New York	W	15	Ret-World-L
May 8	1936	ⓦ Jimmy McLarnin★	New York	W	10	—
Sep 3	1936	ⓦ Lou Ambers★	New York	L	15	Lost-World-L
Oct 5	1936	ⓦ Jimmy McLarnin★	New York	L	10	—
May 7	1937	♛ Lou Ambers★	New York	L	15	For-World-L
Nov 1	1939	Al ("Bummy") Davis	New York	TKO'd	3	—

his earlier loss to Berg, knocking him out in the third round and taking the junior welterweight title in the process. Canzoneri won the fifteen-round rematch, then added to his winning streak with a decision over the great boxer Kid Chocolate.

Canzoneri lost the junior welterweight title in 1932 and won it back in 1933. He lost both his lightweight and junior welterweight titles to Barney Ross in Chicago Stadium on a decision and also lost a rematch with Ross several months later.

In 1935, Canzoneri won his last championship when he decisioned Hall of Famer Lou Ambers for the lightweight title vacated by Ross. In two subsequent rematches, Ambers defeated Canzoneri to take and retain the title. Canzoneri fought until 1939 when Al ("Bummy") Davis knocked him out in the third round—the first time Canzoneri had been on the short end of a fight that did not go the distance. He quit the ring and in retirement backed Broadway shows, had a nightclub act, and operated a restaurant.

GEORGES CARPENTIER
The Orchid Man

LIGHT HEAVYWEIGHT

Right-handed; 5'11½"; 126–175 lbs.
109 bouts, 11/1/1908 to 9/15/1926
Manager: Francois Descamps
Light Heavyweight Champ 1920–22
Hall of Fame Induction: 1991
Born: 1/12/1894, Lens, France
Died: 10/28/1975

Perhaps the greatest European fighter of all time, Georges Carpentier competed in virtually every weight class. He started fighting in the *savatte* style—in which the use of the feet was allowed—but his manager, Francois Descamps, quickly switched him to conventional boxing. Carpentier's formidable skills allowed him to become a professional in 1908 at just fourteen years old, fighting as either a flyweight or a bantamweight.

In 1911, Carpentier knocked out Robert Eustache to win the French welterweight title. He also triumphed over Young Joseph in a knock-out win for the European welterweight title. The next year he added the European middleweight title. Carpentier's collection of titles grew in 1913 when he claimed the European light heavyweight title with a second-round knockout of Bandsman Rice and the European heavyweight title with a fourth-round knockout of Bombardier Billy Wells.

Carpentier had great success against bigger men. He won a victory on a foul over Gunboat Smith in 1914 to claim the white heavyweight championship. The advent of World War I interrupted Carpentier's boxing career. He served in the French military as an observation pilot and was decorated twice. Already popular, Carpentier was hailed as a true hero in France.

In 1920, Carpentier came to the United States and became a favorite of

An enormous throng of over 80,000 fans saw Carpentier fall to champ Jack Dempsey in a 4th-round knockout in this July 2, 1921 heavyweight title fight at Boyle's Thirty Acres in Jersey City, NJ.

IN THE RING	WON **88**	LOST **14**	DRAWS **6**	TB 109	KO 56	W 28	WF 4	D 6	KO'd 8	L 4	LF 2	ND 1

Date	Year	Opponent	Site	Result / Rounds		Title

SELECTED BOUTS

Date	Year	Opponent	Site	Result / Rounds		Title
Nov 1	1908	Ed Salmon	Mais-Laffitte, France	WF	13	—
Feb 19	1909	George Gloria	Paris	KO'd	6	—
Jun 15	1911	Robert Eustache	Paris	TKO	16	Won-France-W
Aug 29	1911	Dixie Kid★	Trouville, France	TKO'd	5	—
Oct 23	1911	Young Joseph	London	KO	10	Won-Europe-W
Feb 29	1912	Jim Sullivan	Monte Carlo	KO	2	Won-Vac Eur-M
Apr 4	1912	George Gunther	Paris	W	20	Ret-Europe-M
May 23	1912	Willie Lewis	Paris	W	20	Ret-Europe-M
Oct 23	1912	Billy Papke★	Paris	LF	17	—
Feb 12	1913	Bandsman Rice	Paris	KO	2	Won-Vac Eur-LH
Jun 1	1913	Bomb. Billy Wells	Ghent, Belgium	KO	4	Won-Vac Eur-H
Dec 8	1913	Bomb. Billy Wells	London	KO	1	Ret-Europe-H
Mar 21	1914	Joe Jeannette★	Paris	L	15	—
Jul 16	1914	Ed ("Gunboat") Smith	London	WF	6	Won-White-H
Jul 19	1919	Dick Smith	Paris	KO	8	Ret-Europe-H
Dec 4	1919	Joe Beckett	London	KO	1	Ret-Europe-H
Oct 12	1920	♛ Battling Levinsky★	Jersey City, NJ	KO	4	Won-World-LH
Jul 2	1921	♛ Jack Dempsey★	Jersey City	KO'd	4	For-World-H
May 11	1922	Ted ("Kid") Lewis★	London	KO	1	Ret-World-LH
Sep 24	1922	Battling Siki	Paris	KO'd	6	Lost-World-LH
May 6	1923	Marcel Nilles	Paris	KO	1	Won-France-H
May 31	1924	⑩ Tommy Gibbons★	Michigan City, IN	ND	10	—
Jul 24	1924	⑩ Gene Tunney★	New York	TKO'd	15	—
Jun 17	1926	⑩ Tommy Loughran★	Philadelphia	L	10	—
Sep 15	1926	Rocco Stramaglia	Coeur d'Alene, ID	KO	3	—

American fans as well. He knocked out Battling Levinsky in four rounds in Jersey City to claim the world light heavyweight title. The next year, master promoter Tex Rickard paired Carpentier with Jack Dempsey for the heavyweight championship of the world. Over 80,000 people paid $1,789,238 to attend the match at Boyle's Thirty Acres in Jersey City. Blessed with extremely quick hands and feet and a strong right, Carpentier believed that he had a good chance to defeat Dempsey, even though the champion outweighed him by twenty pounds. In the second round, Carpentier broke his thumb with a punch that sent Dempsey reeling into the ropes. In the fourth, Dempsey knocked Carpentier down. Carpentier rose at the count of nine, but a left to the face and a right to the heart sent him down again, this time for the knockout.

In 1922, Carpentier defended his light heavyweight title with a one-round knockout of Hall of Famer Ted ("Kid") Lewis but then lost it to Battling Siki, who knocked him out in six. Carpentier lost to the future heavyweight champion Gene Tunney in the fifteenth when his corner threw in the towel to protect him from further punishment. Carpentier remained active through 1926. In retirement, he acted in French movies and music hall shows and operated a restaurant.

JOE CHOYNSKI
Chrysanthemum, The California Terror

LIGHT HEAVYWEIGHT

Right-handed; 5'10"; 168–172 lbs.

79 bouts, 11/14/1888 to 11/24/1904

Hall of Fame Induction: 1998

Born: 11/8/1868, San Francisco, CA

Named: Joseph Bartlett Choynski (coy-EN-ski)

Died: 1/24/1943

Although never a titleholder, San Francisco's "Chrysanthemum" Joe Choynski fought many of the most famous boxers of the late nineteenth and early twentieth centuries.

Despite his father's intellectual life—Yale graduate Isadore Choynski was a writer who eventually published a San Francisco newspaper focused on exposing municipal corruption and anti-Semitism—the younger Choynski followed a decidedly different career path. Choynski dropped out of high school and worked in a succession of jobs, among them blacksmith and candy puller before becoming a professional boxer in 1888.

Although not an overly large man at 170 pounds, Choynski made a name for himself fighting top heavyweights. Early in his pro career, Choynski fought three wars with his neighbor, fellow San Franciscan and future heavyweight champion, Jim Corbett. Among fight fans, their rivalry was intensified because Choynski was a Jewish laborer while Corbett was a Gentile who worked in a bank. The first bout between the two was held in rural Fairfax, California and was stopped by the local sheriff in the fourth round. The next week Corbett and Choynski met again on a barge off Benicia in San Francisco Bay. Boxing historian Frank Menke described this fight as "one of the epics of pugilism, for [its] duration of savagery."

Choynski donned a spectator's driving gloves when Corbett refused to fight bare-knuckled. The seams of the riding gloves created welts on Corbett's face and body, while Corbett's punches left Choynski's face badly bruised and bloody. In the third round, Corbett broke two knuckles on his left hand; then he broke his right thumb in the fourteenth. Finally, in the 27th round, Corbett knocked out

Choynski (R) poses in a face-off with the much larger Jim Jeffries before their November 30, 1897 meeting in San Francisco. The 20-round fight ended in a draw. Jeffries, less than two years later, would take the heavyweight championship from Bob Fitzsimmons.

IN THE RING	WON 50	LOST 14	DRAWS 6	TB 79	KO 25	W 22	WF 3	D 6	KO'd 10	L 4	LF 0	ND 8	NC 1

Date	Year	Opponent	Site	Result / Rounds	Title
SELECTED BOUTS					
Nov 14	1888	George Bush	San Francisco	KO 2	—
May 30	1889	Jim Corbett★	San Francisco	NC 4	—
Jun 5	1889	Jim Corbett★	Benecia, CA	KO'd 27	—
Jul 15	1889	Jim Corbett★	San Francisco	L 4	—
Feb 10	1891	Joe Goddard	Sydney	KO'd 4	—
Jul 20	1891	Joe Goddard	Melbourne	KO'd 4	—
Dec 17	1891	Billy Woods	San Francisco	KO 34	—
Dec 20	1891	♛ John L. Sullivan★	San Francisco	Exh 3	—
Jun 17	1894	♛ Bob Fitzsimmons★	Boston	D 5	—
Mar 21	1896	Kid McCoy★	New York	ND 4	—
Apr 16	1896	Tom Sharkey	San Francisco	L 8	—
Nov 30	1897	Jim Jeffries★	San Francisco	D 20	—
Mar 11	1898	Tom Sharkey	San Francisco	D 8	—
Mar 24	1899	♛ Kid McCoy★	San Francisco	L 20	—
Oct 6	1899	♛ Kid McCoy★	Chicago	D 8	—
Jan 12	1900	♛ Kid McCoy★	New York	KO'd 4	—
Feb 23	1900	Joe Walcott★	New York	KO'd 7	—
May 8	1900	Tom Sharkey	Chicago	KO'd 2	—
Feb 25	1901	Jack Johnson★	Galveston, TX	KO 3	—
Sep 29	1902	Jack O'Brien★	Chicago	L 6	—
Mar 30	1903	Jack O'Brien★	Philadelphia	ND-L 6	—
Nov 24	1904	Jack Williams	Philadelphia	ND 6	—

the barely conscious Choynsky. Six weeks later the pair fought for a third time with Corbett winning a four-round decision.

In 1890, Choynski traveled to Australia where he twice lost to the Australian champion, Joe Goddard. On June 18, 1894, Choynski fought a five-round draw with future heavyweight champion Bob Fitzsimmons in a bout which was stopped by police. On November 30, 1897, Choynski fought to a draw with another future champion, young Jim Jeffries, who outweighed him by approximately fifty pounds.

In 1901, Choynski faced a third future heavyweight champion, Jack Johnson. Choynski knocked Johnson out in the third round. Johnson would not suffer another knockout for fourteen years. After the fight, Choynski and Johnson were arrested for participating in a mixed-race match. In jail for four weeks, the two were allowed to box to entertain their fellow inmates, providing excellent training for Johnson. In a 1940 interview, Johnson called Choynski "the hardest puncher in the last fifty years."

Choynski remained in fine physical condition after his 1904 retirement. For ten years, he was the boxing and athletic instructor for the Pittsburgh Athletic Club. He later became a chiropractor, worked in the insurance business, and served as a consultant for the movie "Gentleman Jim." He died on January 24, 1943 in Cincinnati.

JAMES J. CORBETT
Gentleman Jim

HEAVYWEIGHT

Right-handed; 6"1"; 178–190 lbs.
19 bouts, 1884 to 8/14/1903
Manager: William A. Brady
Heavyweight Champion 1892–97
Hall of Fame Induction: 1990
Born: 9/1/1866, San Francisco, CA
Named: James John Corbett
Died: 2/18/1933

James J. Corbett gained lasting fame when he knocked out the hugely popular John L. Sullivan to take the heavyweight title in 1892. The first heavyweight to win a championship under the Marquess of Queensberry Rules, Gentleman Jim was a masterful boxer who also prided himself on his social respectability. Although grieving fans of Sullivan were slow to accept Corbett, the new champ's decent lifestyle attracted a better sort of audience for the fights.

Corbett grew up in a large Irish family in San Francisco, where his father owned a livery stable. A street fighter as a boy, Corbett completed high school and took a job as a bank clerk. He led another life outside the bank, however, sharpening his pugilistic skills by taking on all comers on saloon stages. Corbett's formal training began when—with the blessing of the bank's president—he was taken under the wing of English boxing instructor Walter Watson at San Francisco's Olympic Club. He fought his first professional bout, a knockout, at age eighteen.

Corbett's career took off when he faced Joe Choynski for a three-fight series in 1889. Choynski, who went on to defeat Jack Johnson, was an extremely hard puncher. The first fight was stopped by police after just four rounds, but six days later the two met again on the blistering hot deck of a barge in San Francisco Bay. It was a bloody fight. The seams on Choynski's gloves cut Corbett, and in the third round, Corbett broke his left hand with a punch to Choynski's head. Finally, in the 27th round, a battered Corbett knocked out Choynski with a left hook.

Corbett won a rematch with Choynski and the next year decisioned Jake Kilrain who had earlier fought an epic, though losing, battle with Sullivan. Cor-

Relentlessly banging at the champion, Corbett (R) dropped John L. Sullivan in the 21st round of their 1892 title bout in New Orleans.

IN THE RING	WON 11	LOST 4	DRAWS 3	TB 19	KO 7	W 4	WF 0	D 3	KO'd 3	L 0	LF 1	ND 0	NC 1

Date	Year	Opponent	Site	Result / Rounds		Title
SELECTED BOUTS						
—	1884	Frank Smith	Salt Lake City	KO	2	—
—	—	Duncan McDonald	Evanston, WY	D	8	—
May 30	1889	Joe Choynski★	Fairfax, CA	NC	4	—
Jun 5	1889	Joe Choynski★	Benecia, CA	KO	27	—
Jul 15	1889	Joe Choynski★	San Francisco	W	4	—
Jul 29	1889	Dave Campbell	Portland, OR	D	10	—
Feb 18	1890	Jake Kilrain	New Orleans	W	6	—
Apr 14	1890	Dominick McCaffrey	Brooklyn	W	4	—
May 21	1891	Peter Jackson★	San Francisco	D	61	—
Jun 26	1891	♛ John L. Sullivan★	San Francisco	Exh	4	—
Oct 8	1891	Ed Kinney	Milwaukee	W	4	—
Feb 16	1892	Bill Spilling	—	KO	1	—
—	1892	Bob Caffrey	—	KO	1	—
Sep 7	1892	♛ John L. Sullivan★	New Orleans	KO	21	Won-World-H
Jan 25	1894	Charlie Mitchell★	Jacksonville, FL	KO	3	Ret-World-H
Mar 17	1897	Bob Fitzsimmons★	Carson City, NV	KO'd	14	Lost-World-H
Nov 22	1898	Tom Sharkey	New York	LF	9	—
May 11	1900	♛ James J. Jeffries★	Coney Island	KO'd	23	For-World-H
Aug 30	1900	Charles ("Kid") McCoy★	New York	KO	5	—
Aug 14	1903	♛ James J. Jeffries★	San Francisco	KO'd	10	For-World-H

bett then faced Hall of Famer Peter Jackson, a black fighter with whom Sullivan had refused to tangle. The two great boxers battled for 61 rounds until the fight was stopped and declared a draw.

Corbett was slowly gaining on Sullivan, first meeting him in a high society exhibition where both men wore evening clothes. The theatrical Corbett, who would later have a lengthy career in movies, plays, and vaudeville, did not strike many blows but he did not allow Sullivan to hit him either.

In 1892 in New Orleans, Corbett and Sullivan met in earnest, with the heavyweight title at stake. Under the Queensberry Rules, the fighters wore light gloves. Throughout the fight Corbett made Sullivan chase him to land a punch. Sullivan finally knocked Corbett down with a hard right in the seventeenth, but in round 21, Corbett shot a left hook to Sullivan's jaw, followed it up with a flurry of punches, and finished Sullivan with a right.

Corbett lost the title in 1897 when the lighter Bob Fitzsimmons knocked him out in fourteen rounds. Corbett tried to regain his title from his former sparring partner, James J. Jeffries, in 1900. Although he still displayed great boxing skills, Corbett was knocked out in the 23rd round. Three years later Jeffries knocked him out again, and Corbett quit. In retirement, he continued his stage career.

The Chicago Spider, The Cherry Picker from Logan Square

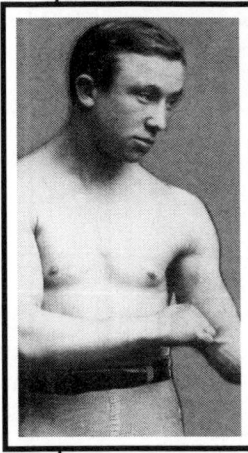

BANTAMWEIGHT

Right-handed; 5'0"; 102–117 lbs.

93 bouts, 1/18/1905 to 3/16/1920

Manager: E.E.("Pop") Coulon 1905–11, Emil Thierry 1911–14

USA World 105 lbs Champ 1907–09

USA World 108 lbs Champ 1909

USA World 112 lbs Champ 1910

USA World Bantamweight Champ 1910–14

Hall of Fame Induction: 1999

Born: 2/12/1889, Toronto

Died: 10/29/1973

Coulon's father, a piano manufacturer and fight manager, instructed him in the fine points of boxing from a very young age. When he was fifteen, he was sent to New York to study boxing with his cousin, George ("Elbows") McFadden, who had previously knocked out Hall of Famer Joe Gans.

Coulon turned pro when he KO'd Young Bennie in Chicago on January 18, 1905. He won his first 26 fights, twelve of them by knockout, before facing Kid Murphy in Milwaukee on March 1, 1907. Murphy won the ten-round decision and claimed the American version of the world paperweight title. Coulon avenged his defeat in a rematch on January 8, 1908, with a decision in ten, and claimed the world title. This was an era of conflicting title claims and championship fights made at two, or three, pound intervals; most British observers considered ten-round fights inadequate to decide championships.

On February 19, 1910, Coulon decisioned English contender Jim Kendrick, and two weeks later he faced Kendrick again in a widely recognized bantamweight championship fight. Coulon outlasted Kendrick and knocked him out in the nineteenth round. Coulon successfully defended his title numerous times at a weight limit of either 115 or 116 lbs. However, in a rematch with Kid Williams in Vernon, California, the challenger quickly fractured two of Coulon's ribs, knocked him out in the third, and took his title.

Coulon stayed out of the ring for two years after this loss, and never received another title shot. He served in the army during World War I as a physical instructor, and after the war fought twice in Paris. After European standout Charles Ledoux knocked him out in six rounds, Coulon retired.

After his fighting days, Johnny Coulon (L) still had a few tricks up his sleeve. A finger placed on Joe Louis's neck makes the 120-pound Coulon unliftable!

IN THE RING	WON 52	LOST 6	DRAWS 4	TB 93	KO 30	W 22	WF 0	D 4	KO'd 3	L 3	LF 0	ND 30	NC 1

Date	Year	Opponent	Site	Result / Rounds		Title

SELECTED BOUTS

Date	Year	Opponent	Site	Result	Rounds	Title
Jan 18	1905	Young Bennie	Chicago	KO	6	—
Mar 1	1907	Kid Murphy	Milwaukee	L	10	For-USA World-105 lbs
Jan 8	1908	Kid Murphy	Peoria, IL	W	10	Won-USA World-105 lbs
Jan 29	1908	Kid Murphy	Peoria	W	10	Ret-USA World-105 lbs
Feb 20	1908	Cooney Kelley	Peoria	KO	9	Ret-USA World-105 lbs
Mar 13	1908	Young Terry McGovern	Los Angeles	W	10	Ret-USA World-105 lbs
Feb 11	1909	Kid Murphy	New York	TKO	5	Ret-USA World-105 lbs
May 28	1909	Tibby Watson	Dayton, OH	KO	10	Won-USA World-108 lbs
Jan 29	1910	Earl Denning	New Orleans	KO	9	Won-USA World-112 lbs
Feb 19	1910	Jim Kendrick	New Orleans	W	10	Ret-USA World-112 lbs
Mar 6	1910	Jim Kendrick	New Orleans	KO	19	Won-USA World-B (115 lbs)
Apr 11	1910	Young O'Leary	New York	ND-D	10	Ret-USA World-B (115 lbs)
Apr 25	1910	Frankie Burns	Brooklyn	ND-L	10	Ret-USA World-B (115 lbs)
May 12	1910	Phil McGovern	New York	ND-W	10	Ret-USA World-B (115 lbs)
Jun 8	1910	Frankie Burns	New York	ND	10	Ret-USA World-B (115 lbs)
Dec 3	1910	Charlie Harvey	New Orleans	W	10	Ret-USA World-B (115 lbs)
Jan 19	1911	Terry Moran	Memphis, TN	KO	2	Ret-USA World-B (115 lbs)
Feb 26	1911	Frankie Conley	New Orleans	W	20	Ret-USA World-B (116 lbs)
Mar 22	1911	George Kitson	Akron, OH	TKO	5	Ret-USA World-B (116 lbs)
Mar 28	1911	Harry Forbes	Kenosha, WI	ND-W	10	Ret-USA World-B (116 lbs)
Apr 20	1911	Phil McGovern	Kenosha	ND-W	10	Ret-USA World-B (116 lbs)
Jan 11	1912	George Kitson	South Bend, IN	KO	3	Ret-USA World-B (116 lbs)
Feb 3	1912	Frankie Conley	Vernon, CA	W	20	Ret-USA World-B (116 lbs)
Feb 18	1912	Frankie Burns	New Orleans	W	20	Ret-USA World-B (116 lbs)
Oct 18	1912	Kid Williams ★	New York	ND-L	10	—
Nov 20	1912	Charley Goldman ★	Brooklyn	ND-W	10	—
Jun 9	1914	♛ Kid Williams ★	Vernon, CA	KO'd	3	Lost-USA World-B (116 lbs)
May 14	1917	♛ Pete Herman ★	Racine, WI	TKO'd	3	—
Mar 16	1920	Charles Ledoux	Paris	KO'd	6	—

The end of his fighting career did not lead to the end of his productive life. Coulon toured with vaudeville groups and made many friends in his travels, including European heads of state, actors, and even Ernest Hemingway. During his travels he devised a popular trick: he would ask someone to lift him and usually—since he weighed only 120 pounds—they were successful. Coulon would then place a finger on the lifter's neck and ask them to try again, where-upon they would inevitably fail. Such luminaries as Jack Dempsey, Primo Carnera, and Joe Louis fell victim to this stunt.

Returning to Chicago, Coulon and his wife, Marie, opened a gym in 1923. Heavyweight champs, from Dempsey to Ali, trained there when in the Chicago area, and countless amateur boxers learned to fight under Coulon's direction. Coulon always had an interest in the underprivileged in his neighborhood and helped many poor youngsters, once saving a community youth center that was on the brink of closing its doors. He briefly appeared in the 1969 movie *Medium Cool*, which contains scenes filmed in his gym.

LES DARCY

MIDDLEWEIGHT

Right-handed; 5'6"; 147–165 lbs.

49 bouts, 1910 to 9/30/1916

Manager: Tim O'Sullivan

Australian World Middleweight Champion 1915–16

Hall of Fame Induction: 1993

Born: 10/31/1895, East Maitland, NSW, Australia

Named: James Leslie Darcy

Died: 5/24/1917

Les Darcy had a short but brilliant fighting career that came to an unglamorous end when the young boxer died far from home. Considered one of the greatest middleweights of all time, Darcy proved his mettle in his native Australia. Born in New South Wales, he started boxing as an amateur at age fifteen and quickly turned professional. He won his first sixteen fights before challenging the veteran Bob Whitelaw for the Australian welterweight title. Darcy lost the twenty-round decision but, in a rematch, knocked Whitelaw out in five.

Darcy graduated from regional bouts to fighting in Sydney Stadium, and promoters began to import talent to challenge him. He lost his first two fights in Sydney, one by decision and one by foul, to American Fritz Holland. The next year Darcy faced another American, Jeff Smith, in what was considered a contest for the Australian world middleweight title. When Darcy complained of a low blow at the end of the fifth round, the referee believed that Darcy did not want to continue and awarded the decision to Smith. In a rematch, Darcy was awarded the victory when Smith punched him in the groin.

As Australian world middleweight champ, Darcy defeated such top-flight visiting Americans as Eddie McGoorty, Billy Murray, Jimmy Clabby, George Chip, George ("K.O.") Brown, and Buck Crouse, as well as knocking out Smith and Holland in rematches.

American Jimmy Clabby bends to avoid punishment from Darcy (R) in one of their two meetings in Sydney. Darcy took 20-round decisions both times.

IN THE RING	WON 45	LOST 4	DRAWS 0	TB 49	KO 29	W 15	WF 1	D 0	KO'd 0	L 2	LF 2	ND 0

Date	Year	Opponent	Site	Result / Rounds		Title
SELECTED BOUTS						
—	1910	Sid Pasco	Maitland, Australia	KO	2	—
Nov 3	1913	Bob Whitelaw	Newcastle, Australia	L	20	For-Australia-W
Mar 21	1914	Bob Whitelaw	Maitland	KO	5	—
Jul 18	1914	Fritz Holland	Sydney	L	20	—
Sep 12	1914	Fritz Holland	Sydney	LF	18	—
Jan 23	1915 ♛	Jeff Smith	Sydney	LD	5	For-Australia World-M
Mar 13	1915	Fritz Holland	Sydney	W	20	—
May 1	1915	Fritz Holland	Melbourne	KO	13	—
May 22	1915 ♛	Jeff Smith	Sydney	WF	2	Won-Australia World-M
Jun 12	1915	Mick King	Sydney	TKO	10	Won-Australia-M & Ret-Australia World-M
Jul 31	1915	Eddie McGoorty	Sydney	TKO	15	Ret-Australia World-M
Sep 4	1915	Billy Murray	Sydney	W	20	Ret-Australia World-M
Oct 9	1915	Fred Dyer	Sydney	TKO	6	Ret-Australia World-M
Oct 23	1915	Jimmy Clabby	Sydney	W	20	Ret-Australia World-M
Nov 1	1915	Billy Murray	Melbourne	KO	6	—
Dec 27	1915	Eddie McGoorty	Sydney	KO	8	—
Jan 15	1916	George ("K.O.") Brown	Sydney	W	20	—
Feb 19	1916	Harold Hardwick	Sydney	KO	7	Won-Australia-H
Mar 25	1916	Les O'Donnell	Sydney	KO	7	Ret-Australia-H
Apr 8	1916	George ("K.O.") Brown	Sydney	W	20	—
May 13	1916	Alex Costica	Sydney	TKO	5	Ret-Australia World-M
Jun 3	1916	Buck Crouse	Sydney	KO	2	—
Jun 24	1916	Dave Smith	Sydney	KO	12	Ret-Australia-H
Aug 16	1916	Dave Smith	Brisbane, Australia	KO	11	Ret-Australia-H
Sep 9	1916	Jimmy Clabby	Sydney	W	20	Ret-Australia World-M
Sep 30	1916	George Chip	Sydney	KO	9	Ret-Australia World-M

Darcy's opponents are said to have admired his courage, stamina, and punching power. In 1916, Darcy KO'd Harold Hardwick to capture the Australian heavyweight title.

Darcy was Australia's best known sportsman at the time his country mobilized to join the Allied cause in World War I. Because Darcy failed to enlist in the military, public opinion turned against him. He escaped the mounting controversy by stowing away on an oil tanker, the S.S. Cushing, bound for New York. In America he was vilified by the press and labeled a "slacker." New York's governor refused to issue a license for a fight involving Darcy. Other states' governors followed suit and a six-month tour, promoted by Tex Rickard, failed to materialize. To regain favor, Darcy signed an oath of allegiance to the U.S. and joined the armed services (with the understanding that he would be given furloughs to fight). However, he collapsed a few days later and died in Memphis of blood poisoning from an infected tooth. His body was shipped home, where he was mourned as a hero.

JACK DELANEY
Bright Eyes

LIGHT HEAVYWEIGHT

Right-handed; 5'11½"; 158–178 lbs.

93 bouts, 10/1919 to 4/21/1932

Managers: Al Jennings 1919–1922, Pete Reilly 1923–1928, Billy Prince 1932

Light Heavyweight Champion 1926–1927

Hall of Fame Induction: 1996

Born: 3/18/1900, St. Francis du Lac, Quebec

Named: Ovila Chapdelaine

Died: 11/27/1948

Jack Delaney was one of the most popular fighters of the 1920s. A French-Canadian born in Quebec, Delaney moved with his parents to Holyoke, Massachusetts and then Bridgeport, Connecticut. He started to fight professionally in 1919. In his first three years, he compiled a record that included a regional title win and only three losses in nearly 30 fights.

In 1924, under the direction of Pete Reilly, Delaney decisioned future light heavyweight champion Tommy Loughran. Less than a month later, in Madison Square Garden, Delaney had his first clash with former AAU wrestling champion Paul Berlenbach. The fight, billed as "The Wrestler versus The Boxer," pulled in $50,000, a new record for the Garden. In the first round, Delaney, who had a smooth, graceful style, eluded Berlenbach's crude rushes and peppered him with punishing left jabs. Berlenbach knocked Delaney down in the second round. When Delaney saw Berlenbach before him, he dropped back to the canvas to get a new count, a move that would disqualify him today. The two fighters traded knockdowns in the third, but then Delaney took control so completely that Berlenbach had difficulty finding his corner. Delaney knocked the wrestler down twice in the fourth round before the referee ended the fight. Berlenbach went on to become light heavyweight champion when he defeated Mike McTigue in 1925.

Delaney scored two knockouts over Tiger Flowers before facing Berlenbach again. He lost to the champ in a fifteen-round decision, but then embarked on an eleven-fight winning streak that led to a rematch. The fight was held in Brooklyn's Ebbets Field and drew a crowd of 41,000 and a gate of $450,000. Delaney was the popular favorite and was loudly cheered by female fans known as "Delaney's screaming mamies." Delaney

Delaney (seated) won this heavyweight fight against Paolino Uzcudun by foul in the seventh round on August 11, 1927. Trainer Pete Reilly is reaching through the ropes displaying Delaney's dented protective cup.

IN THE RING	WON 77	LOST 10	DRAWS 2	TB 93	KO 44	W 31	WF 2	D 2	KO'd 3	L 7	LF 0	ND 2	NC 2

Date	Year	Opponent	Site	Result / Rounds		Title
SELECTED BOUTS						
Oct	1919	Steve August	Bridgeport, CT	W	4	—
Feb 13	1922	Lou Bogash	Bridgeport	W	15	—
Aug 31	1923	Jimmy Darcy	New York	W	10	—
Feb 19	1924	⑩ Tommy Loughran★	Boston	W	10	—
Mar 14	1924	⑩ Paul Berlenbach★	New York	KO	4	—
Oct 3	1924	⑩ Jimmy Slattery	New York	L	6	—
Jan 16	1925	⑩ Tiger Flowers★	New York	KO	2	—
Feb 13	1925	⑩ Jimmy Slattery	New York	L	6	—
Feb 26	1925	⑩ Tiger Flowers★	New York	KO	4	—
Jul 16	1925	⑩ Tommy Loughran★	Philadelphia	D	10	—
Dec 11	1925	♛ Paul Berlenbach★	New York	L	15	For-World-LH
Feb 5	1926	Johnny Risko	New York	W	10	—
Mar 15	1926	⑩ Mike McTigue	New York	KO	4	—
Mar 22	1926	⑩ Maxie Rosenbloom★	Philadelphia	W	10	—
Jun 3	1926	Tommy Burns★	Brooklyn	TKO	2	—
Jul 16	1926	♛ Paul Berlenbach★	Brooklyn	W	15	Won-World-LH
Dec 10	1926	Jamaica Kid	Waterbury, CT	KO	3	—
Feb 18	1927	Jimmy Maloney	New York	L	10	—
Aug 11	1927	Paolino Uzcudun	New York	WF	7	—
Sep 14	1927	Johnny Risko	Cleveland	L	10	—
Dec 9	1927	⑩ Paul Berlenbach★	Chicago	KO	6	—
Mar 1	1928	Tom Heeney	New York	L	15	—
Apr 30	1928	Jack Sharkey★	New York	KO'd	1	—
Mar 3	1932	Phil Johnson	Bridgeport	KO	2	—
Mar 29	1932	Frank Willis	Stamford, CT	KO	3	—
Apr 21	1932	Leo Williams	Hartford, CT	KO	1	—

fought as Reilly had directed, looking to pile up points rather than try for a knockout. He staggered Berlenbach in the first round with a right cross to the jaw. In the fifth, a left hook dropped Berlenbach to one knee. Delaney controlled the remaining rounds and won the light heavyweight title.

Early in 1927, Delaney relinquished his championship in order to pursue the heavyweight crown. He was matched against Jimmy Maloney, as a step to a challenge of then-heavyweight champion Gene Tunney. Delaney lost to Maloney, in part because of an injured hand—reportedly the result of a misplaced punch intended for a porter on a train. The loss sidetracked Delaney's quest. He defeated Paolino Uzcudun on a questionable foul before ending the year with a knockout of Berlenbach in their last meeting.

In his last important fight, Delaney suffered a one-round knockout by future heavyweight champion Jack Sharkey. Delaney never threw a punch and it was speculated that he may have been intoxicated. After one more fight, Delaney retired, although he made a brief three-fight comeback in 1932. Delaney returned to Bridgeport where he operated a number of businesses. He also ran a tavern in New York and refereed. He died of cancer in 1948.

JACK DEMPSEY
The Nonpareil

MIDDLEWEIGHT

Right-handed; 5'8"; 140–148 lbs.
64 bouts, 4/7/1883 to 1/18/1895
Middleweight Champion 1884–91
Hall of Fame Induction: 1992
Born: 12/15/1862, County Kildare, Ireland
Named: John Kelly
Died: 11/2/1895

Now largely overshadowed by his namesake, the heavyweight champion Jack Dempsey, the original Jack Dempsey was a boxer of enormous talent. At the peak of his career, he was the best around, which earned him the nickname "The Nonpareil" (without equal). Born in Ireland, Dempsey came to New York as a child and worked in a Brooklyn barrel factory before venturing into wrestling and then boxing. He turned professional as a lightweight in 1883, at the age of twenty.

Dempsey was unbeaten in his first fourteen fights. In 1884, he earned a chance to battle George Fulljames, who had recently claimed the middleweight championship. Dempsey knocked Fulljames out in the 22nd round to become the American — some said world — middleweight champion.

Fighting on both coasts, Dempsey remained undefeated until 1889 when he fought George LaBlanche in San Francisco. In their first encounter, three years before, Dempsey had knocked LaBlanche out in thirteen rounds. This time the two battled for 32 rounds. Dempsey was getting the better of LaBlanche when

Police intervened in the 11th round to end the 1883 Coney Island, NY bout between Jack Dempsey and Harry Force held in the shadow of the elevated train tracks. This was Dempsey's third recorded fight.

IN THE RING	WON 50	LOST 3	DRAWS 8	TB 64	KO 26	W 24	WF 0	D 8	KO'd 3	L 0	LF 0	ND 0	NC 3

Date	Year	Opponent	Site	Result / Rounds		Title
SELECTED BOUTS						
Apr 7	1883	Ed McDonald	Maspeth, NY	KO	21	—
Aug 14	1883	Jack Boylan	Flushing, NY	KO	23	—
Sep 17	1883	Soap McAlpine	New York	D	4	—
Feb 28	1884	Jim Barry	New York	KO	3	—
Mar 2	1884	Joe Hennessey	New York	KO	4	—
Mar 4	1884	Tom Sullivan	New York	KO	2	—
Mar 6	1884	Bill Dacey	Coney Island	KO	9	—
May 1	1884	Jack Bowles	New York	W	6	—
Jul 9	1884	Tom Henry	Rockaway, NY	NC	3	—
Jul 30	1884	George Fulljames	Great Kills, NY	KO	22	Won-Vac Amer-M
Sep 4	1884	Mike Dempsey	Rockaway	KO	7	—
Nov 30	1884	Mike Malone	Philadelphia	KO	2	—
Mar 19	1885	Charles Bixamos	New Orleans	KO	5	—
May 4	1885	Tom Barry	San Francisco	KO	5	—
Feb 3	1886	Jack Fogarty	New York	KO	27	Ret-Amer-M
Mar 14	1886	George LaBlanche	Larchmont, NY	KO	13	Ret-Amer-M
Dec 13	1887	Johnny Reagan	Manhasset, NY	TKO	45	Ret-Amer-M
Nov 15	1888	Mike Donovan★	Brooklyn	D	6	—
Aug 22	1889	Mike Dempsey	San Francisco	KO	7	—
Aug 27	1889	George LaBlanche	San Francisco	KO'd	32	—
Feb 18	1890	Aus. Billy McCarthy	San Francisco	TKO	28	Won-World-M
Jan 14	1891	Bob Fitzsimmons★	New Orleans	TKO'd	13	Lost-World-M
Mar 2	1893	Mike Keogh	Portland, OR	W	4	—
Sep 6	1894	Aus. Billy McCarthy	New Orleans	D	20	—
Jan 18	1895	♛ Tommy Ryan★	Coney Island	TKO'd	3	For-World-W

the challenger executed a pivot punch which dropped Dempsey in his tracks. The pivot punch was thrown using a backhand motion so that the puncher's elbow, forearm or fist would connect with the victim's head. This move was declared illegal, and though Dempsey lost the fight, he was permitted to retain the title.

Dempsey became undisputed middleweight champion with his victory over Australian Billy McCarthy. In 1891, he faced Hall of Famer Bob Fitzsimmons in New Orleans. Fitzsimmons, who would later go on to take the heavyweight championship, dominated the fight. He knocked Dempsey down thirteen times in thirteen rounds and pleaded with him to give up. Dempsey refused, reportedly saying, "A champion never quits." Finally, Dempsey went down in the thirteenth for the knockout defeat. A punch to the throat in this fight affected Dempsey's speech for the remainder of his life.

Though only 28 at the time of the Fitzsimmons fight, Dempsey fought only three more times. Hall of Famer Tommy Ryan stopped him in the third round in his final fight in 1895. By this time, Dempsey was already weakened by the tuberculosis which would claim his life later that year.

JACK DEMPSEY
The Manassa Mauler

HEAVYWEIGHT

Right-handed; 6'¾"; 170–195 lbs.
81 bouts, 8/17/1914 to 9/22/1927
Managers: Jack Kearns 1917–23,
Leo P. Flynn 1927
Heavyweight Champion 1919–26
Hall of Fame Induction: 1990
Born: 6/24/1895, Manassa, CO
Named: William Harrison Dempsey
Died: 5/31/1983

A ferocious fighter and one of the Roaring Twenties' most famous personalities, Jack Dempsey embodied the spirit of a brash America that still had frontiers and believed anything was possible. From beginnings as an itinerant miner and fruit picker, Dempsey became a roughneck Adonis who ruled the ring as heavyweight champ. He married a Hollywood actress, cared enough about his appearance to have his flattened nose rebuilt, and always gave fight fans a show to remember.

Born in Manassa, Colorado, Dempsey came from a large, poor family. He managed to get through eighth grade before setting out on his own, following rumors of work from town to town. Like his two older brothers—professional boxers who both called themselves "Jack" Dempsey in honor of Jack Dempsey, The Nonpareil—Dempsey frequently tested his mettle in bars and saloons, challenging

Snarling with a terrible ferocity, Dempsey (R) follows a series of crushing uppercuts with left hooks to the face to take the heavyweight championship title from Jess Willard on Independence Day 1919.

IN THE RING	WON 61	LOST 6	DRAWS 8	TB 81	KO 50	W 10	WF 1	D 8	KO'd 1	L 5	LF 0	ND 6

Date	Year	Opponent	Site	Result / Rounds		Title
SELECTED BOUTS						
Aug 17	1914	Young Herman	Ramona, CO	D	6	—
Nov 2	1914	Young Hancock	Salt Lake City	KO	1	—
Jun 24	1916	Andre Anderson	New York	ND-W	10	—
Jul 8	1916	Wild Burt Kenny	New York	ND-W	10	—
Jul 14	1916	John Lester Johnson	New York	ND-D	10	—
Feb 13	1917	Jim Flynn	Murray, UT	KO'd	1	—
Mar 28	1917	Willie Meehan	Oakland	L	4	—
Aug 10	1917	Willie Meehan	San Francisco	D	4	—
Sep 7	1917	Willie Meehan	San Francisco	D	4	—
Oct 2	1917	Ed ("Gunboat") Smith	San Francisco	W	4	—
Feb 14	1918	Jim Flynn	Ft. Sheridan, IL	KO	1	—
May 3	1918	Billy Miske	St. Paul, MN	ND-W	10	—
Jul 27	1918	Fred Fulton	Harrison, NJ	KO	1	—
Sep 13	1918	Willie Meehan	San Francisco	L	4	—
Nov 6	1918	♛ Battling Levinsky	Philadelphia	KO	3	—
Nov 28	1918	Billy Miske	Philadelphia	ND-W	6	—
Dec 30	1918	Ed ("Gunboat") Smith	Buffalo	KO	2	—
Jul 4	1919	♛ Jess Willard	Toledo, OH	TKO	3	Won-World-H
Sep 6	1920	Billy Miske	Benton Harbor, MI	KO	3	Ret-World-H
Dec 14	1920	Bill Brennan	New York	KO	12	Ret-World-H
Jul 2	1921	Georges Carpentier★	Jersey City, NJ	KO	4	Ret-World-H
Jul 4	1923	Tommy Gibbons★	Shelby, MT	W	15	Ret-World-H
Sep 14	1923	Luis Angel Firpo	New York	KO	2	Ret-World-H
Sep 23	1926	⑩ Gene Tunney★	Philadelphia	L	10	Lost-World-H
Jul 21	1927	⑩ Jack Sharkey★	New York	KO	7	—
Sep 22	1927	♛ Gene Tunney★	Chicago	L	10	For-World-H

any man to beat him. He first fought professionally in 1914 and adopted the name Jack when his brothers retired.

At the start of his career, Dempsey fought mostly in the West. In 1917, he suffered his only knock-out loss when Fireman Jim Flynn leveled him in one round. Shortly afterward, Dempsey linked up with manager Jack Kearns, who guided him to the heavyweight title. Dempsey's record for the rest of 1917 and 1918 included fourteen one-round knockouts. Beautiful to watch in the ring, the great Western brawler's bobbing, weaving style inspired more than one writer to compare him to a coiled cobra.

In 1919, Dempsey took the heavyweight crown from Jess Willard, who out-weighed him by 58 pounds but fell victim to Dempsey's crouching, weaving attacks. Dempsey knocked Willard down seven times in the first round, then worried the exhausted champ through two more rounds for a TKO. Dempsey defended the title twice in 1920. The next year, promotional genius Tex Rickard set up a bout between Dempsey, an alleged draft-dodger, and French war hero Georges Carpentier. The title fight at Boyle's Thirty Acres in Jersey City broke all

Dempsey might have regained the championship in this 1927 fight in Chicago but was slow to go to a neutral corner after downing Gene Tunney. Tunney benefited from the "long count" and won in ten.

previous records for gate earnings. A throng of 80,000 paid nearly $1.8 million to see Dempsey knock out Carpentier in the fourth round.

Dempsey defended his title twice more in the next five years, earning a decision over Tommy Gibbons and knocking out Argentinian Luis Firpo in a topsy-turvy contest at New York's Polo Grounds. In the first round, Dempsey knocked Firpo down seven times, and Firpo knocked Dempsey down twice, once sending him through the ropes onto the press tables. The knockout came in the second round.

Dempsey never fought Hall of Famer Harry Wills, a top contender, because Rickard refused to arrange a mixed-race title bout. When the New York State Athletic Commission reacted by cancelling Dempsey's license, Rickard signed his star to fight Gene Tunney in Philadelphia in 1926. Tunney triumphed in a ten-round decision.

A crowd of 102,000 filed into Soldier Field in Chicago to watch the rematch a year later. The match became famous as "The Battle of the Long Count." Dempsey knocked down Tunney in the seventh, but the start of the count was delayed because Dempsey was unaware of Illinois boxing rules and was slow in going to a neutral corner. Tunney rose at the count of nine—although he had really been down for about fourteen seconds—and recovered to win a decision. Dempsey supporters believed that the fight turned on the referee's action, while Tunney partisans maintained that Tunney would have gotten up and won the fight anyway.

A few months later, Dempsey retired. He boxed exhibitions, managed and promoted fighters, and officiated at boxing and wrestling matches. Dempsey also served as a Commander in the Coast Guard in World War II and owned a popular New York City restaurant.

Luis Angel Firpo knocks Dempsey through the ropes and onto the press tables in New York's Polo Grounds in 1923. The champ scrambled back into the ring and knocked out Firpo in the second round.

JACK DILLON
The Hoosier Bearcat

LIGHT HEAVYWEIGHT

Right-handed; 5'7½"; 140–175 lbs.

245 bouts, 4/18/1908 to 1/12/1923

Managers: Sam Marburger 1912–20, Al Harter 1920–23

Light Heavyweight Champ 1914–16

Hall of Fame Induction: 1995

Born: 2/2/1891, Frankfort, IN

Named: Ernest Cutler Price

Died: 8/7/1942

Some called light heavyweight Jack Dillon "Jack the Giant Killer" for his ability to handle the most unstoppable heavyweights of the day. A prolific fighter who travelled the U.S. and Canada setting up fights as often as he could, Dillon had stamina, strength, and intelligence. He turned welterweight pro in his native Indiana at the age of seventeen, but soon moved up to the middleweight division and fought for two years before being handed his first loss, a ten-rounder with Eddie McGoorty.

In 1912, Dillon scored a third-round knockout against Hugo Kelly, and promptly claimed the world light heavyweight title, uncontested since Philadelphia Jack O'Brien had won it some years earlier. By 1914, Dillon was officially recognized as champion, when he won a decision over Battling Levinsky. Later that year, a referee cut short a Dillon–K.O. Brown meeting after three rounds, saying the fighters were just going through the motions.

Dillon, who did sometimes carry weaker fighters, was apparently affected by the criticism that followed that bout and began to fight heavyweights who were invariably larger. He defeated such big men as Al Weinert, Tom Cowler, and Fireman Jim

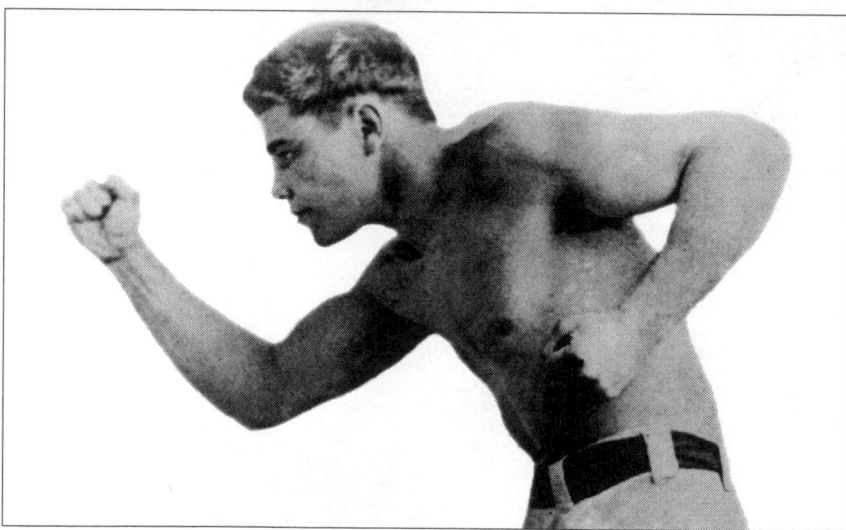

Dillon, here demonstrating his dangerous right uppercut, felled many a larger fighter. He first claimed the light heavyweight crown with his victories over Hugo Kelly in 1912 and Al Norton in 1914.

IN THE RING	WON **94**	LOST **7**	DRAWS **14**	TB 245	KO 64	W 30	WF 0	D 14	KO'd 2	L 5	LF 0	ND 129	NC 1

Date	Year	Opponent	Site	Result / Rounds		Title

SELECTED BOUTS

Date	Year	Opponent	Site	Result / Rounds		Title
Apr 18	1908	Kid Brown	Indianapolis	D	6	—
Oct 21	1910	George Chip	Pittsburgh	ND-W	6	—
Jan 24	1911	George Chip	Dayton, OH	W	15	—
Apr 28	1911	George Chip	Terre Haute, IN	ND	10	—
Oct 23	1911	Battling Levinsky★	Philadelphia	ND-W	6	—
Feb 10	1912	George Chip	Pittsburgh	ND-W	6	—
Mar 23	1912	Frank Klaus	San Francisco	L	20	—
May 3	1912	Frank Klaus	New York	ND-L	10	—
May 28	1912	Hugo Kelly	Indianapolis	KO	3	—
Jul 25	1912	George Chip	Indianapolis	ND	10	—
Oct 19	1912	George Chip	Pittsburgh	ND-D	6	—
Apr 14	1913	George Chip	Youngstown	ND-W	12	—
Apr 17	1913	Battling Levinsky★	Rochester, NY	ND-D	10	—
Apr 14	1914	Battling Levinsky★	Butte, MT	W	12	Won-Vac World-LH
May 29	1914	Battling Levinsky★	Indianapolis	ND-W	10	—
Jun 15	1914	Bob Moha	Butte	W	12	Ret-World-LH
Mar 16	1915	Ed ("Gunboat") Smith	Milwaukee	ND-W	10	—
Jul 5	1915	George Chip	Kansas City	D	10	—
Jul 16	1915	Zulu Kid	Far Rockaway, NY	ND-W	10	—
Feb 8	1916	Battling Levinsky★	Brooklyn	ND-D	10	—
Mar 14	1916	Ed ("Gunboat") Smith	Brooklyn	ND-W	10	—
Apr 25	1916	Battling Levinsky★	Kansas City	W	15	Ret-World-LH
Jul 13	1916	Battling Levinsky★	Baltimore	ND-L	10	—
Sep 12	1916	Battling Levinsky★	Memphis, TN	D	8	—
Oct 24	1916	Battling Levinsky★	Boston	L	12	Lost-World-LH
Nov 19	1916	Mike Gibbons★	St. Paul, MN	ND-L	10	—
Feb 16	1917	Ed ("Gunboat") Smith	New Orleans	W	20	—
Jul 30	1917	Harry Greb★	Pittsburgh	ND-L	10	—
Sep 3	1917	Mike Gibbons★	Terre Haute	ND-L	10	—
Oct 17	1917	Zulu Kid	Montreal	ND-W	10	—
Mar 4	1918	Harry Greb★	Toledo, OH	ND-L	12	—
Jan 12	1923	Joe Walters	Bicknell, IN	ND	10	—

Flynn. Dillon defeated Flynn twice, knocking him out in 1916 only a year after Flynn had defeated Jack Dempsey.

Dillon lost the world light heavyweight title to Battling Levinsky in 1916 in their ninth meeting. Levinsky employed ring science to avoid Dillon's still powerful punches and won on points. Dillon continued to fight for seven years after losing the title. A workmanlike fighter who did not vigorously seek the spotlight, Dillon's aggressive attacking style against bigger men won him a place in ring history. Dillon left boxing in 1923, not much richer than when he started. He retired to Florida where he lived next door to a small restaurant he owned and ran. He died in 1942.

WELTERWEIGHT

Right-handed; 5'8"; 138–155 lbs.

154 bouts, 3/2/1900 to 3/14/1920

Managers: Bill Jacobs and Charlie Gavin

Welterweight Championship Claims 1904–1912

Hall of Fame Induction: 2002

Born: 12/23/1883, Fulton, MO

Named: Aaron Lister Brown

Died: 4/6/1934

The Dixie Kid was born in Fulton, Missouri, and fought locally as an amateur with four bouts at age fifteen. By 1900, he had moved to California where he fought seventeen pro bouts in 1900 and 1901, compiling a record of 10–5–2. With age came more skill and power, and 1902 and 1903 saw the Kid win thirteen fights, twelve of them by knockout.

After recording knockouts over Al Neil and John Solomon in 1904, the Kid earned the chance to face Joe Walcott, the welterweight champion of the world. This meeting, on April 29, 1904 in San Francisco, was a rare championship bout in which both fighters were blacks. The more experienced Walcott—who had won the title from Jim ("Rube") Ferns two and one-half years earlier—held the advantage in the first nineteen rounds. In the twentieth, referee James ("Duck") Sullivan stopped the fight and awarded the title to the Kid on a foul. Walcott's manager, Hall of Famer Tom O'Rourke, stormed into the ring and punched Sullivan in the mouth; the promoter and fans who'd bet on Walcott stormed the ring. Sullivan escaped, but he never officiated another title bout. Later it was discovered that the referee had bet on the Kid.

No matter the controversy, the Kid claimed the championship. He fought non-title bouts in 1904 and 1905, including a six round no decision bout with Hall of Famer Philadelphia Jack O'Brien.

There are no recorded Dixie Kid fights from 1907 to 1908, while the Kid served a prison sentence for assault. Returning to the ring, the Kid's championship status was in doubt, and most boxing groups thought his title forfeit. He fought frequently in the next two years—primarily in no decision bouts in Philly—but also in New York and Memphis. In a foray into Boston, he was knocked out by Hall of Famer Sam Langford and again the next time the pair met, in Memphis on January 10, 1910.

In 1911, the Kid left the U.S. to fight the rest of his career in Eng-

The Dixie Kid (C) is nicely turned out to watch the 1914 Jockeys and Variety Artists Football Match.

IN THE RING	WON 80	LOST 29	DRAWS 12	TB 154	KO 58	W 19	WF 3	D 12	KO'd 6	L 20	LF 3	ND 30	NC 3

Date	Year	Opponent	Site	Result / Rounds		Title

SELECTED BOUTS

Date	Year	Opponent	Site	Result	Rounds	Title
Mar 2	1900	Cuter Kid	Los Angeles	D	3	—
Feb 14	1901	Henry Lewis	Stockton	KO'd	4	—
Feb 9	1904	Al Neil	Oakland	KO	1	—
Feb 26	1904	John Solomon	Fresno	KO	11	—
Apr 29	1904	♛ Joe Walcott★	San Francisco	WF	20	Won-World-W*
Nov 12	1904	Philadelphia Jack O'Brien★	Philadelphia	ND-L	6	—
Dec 26	1904	Young Peter Jackson	Baltimore	D	15	—
Sep 28	1909	Sam Langford★	Boston	TKO'd	5	—
Jan 10	1910	Sam Langford★	Memphis	KO'd	3	—
Nov 24	1910	Frank Mantell	Waterbury, CT	NC	4	—
Jan 17	1911	Mike ("Twin") Sullivan	Buffalo	ND-D	10	—
Aug 29	1911	Georges Carpentier★	Trouville, France	TKO	5	—
Nov 9	1911	Johnny Summers	Liverpool, England	KO	2	Won-Vac GB World-W
Jan 18	1912	♛ Harry Lewis	Liverpool	TKO'd	8	—
Apr 24	1912	George Bernard	Paris	KO	10	Ret-GB & France Word-W
Oct 4	1912	Marcel Thomas	Paris	L	15	Lost-IBU World-W
Mar 14	1920	Paul Buisson	Marseille, France	L	12	—

*Result was suspect.

land, France, and Ireland. He knocked out Hall of Famer Georges Carpentier in Trouville, France, on August 29, 1911. When Harry Lewis, who had claimed the welterweight title in 1908, stopped the Kid in eight rounds on January 18, 1912, all doubt ended about the Kid's title contention.

In Paris on April 24, 1912, the Kid regained another welterweight title in a most unusual way when he met George Bernard of France in a twenty-rounder recognized by Britain and France as a championship bout. Late in the tenth, Bernard dropped to the canvas writhing from a claimed low blow. Referee Willie Lewis waited until after the start of the eleventh round to award the match to Bernard as a win by foul, but three doctors who examined him later were unconvinced. The decision was reversed and the Dixie Kid was declared the winner.

The Kid continued to be a very active fighter for some four years after the Bernard fight, but his long career had taken its toll and his record was just 23-17-6. On March 14, 1920, he returned for one last fight, and lost a twelve round decision to Paul Buisson in Marseille, France.

The Kid is often remembered for his unique fighting style—his hands at his sides, and his chin jutting towards his opponent, daring him to strike. Very fast and a master counterpuncher, his favorite move was a right uppercut, followed by a left hook to the head.

Extremely inventive outside the ring, the Kid was granted a number of patents in the 1920s, but as time passed he sank into a world of drug abuse and squandered his ring earnings. On April 6, 1934, the penniless Kid fell from a tenement window in Los Angeles, by accident or by design, and died.

GEORGE DIXON
Little Chocolate

FEATHERWEIGHT

Right-handed; 5'3½"; 101–126 lbs.

130 bouts, 11/1/1886 to 12/10/1906

Manager: Tom O'Rourke

Bantamwt. Champ 1890,
Featherwt. Champ 1891–97, 1898–1900

Hall of Fame Induction: 1990

Born: 7/29/1870, Halifax, Nova Scotia, Canada

Died: 1/6/1909

George Dixon became the first black man to win a world boxing title when he captured the bantamweight crown in England and then successfully defended it in America. He later added the world featherweight title, which he held for a total of eight years. Considered to be one of the finest small boxers ever, Dixon was well-respected for both his grace and power. He became interested in fighting while assisting a photographer who took posed boxing pictures. Dixon entered the pro ring in his native Halifax, Nova Scotia in 1886 at the age of sixteen.

Under the guidance of manager Tom O'Rourke, Dixon fought Cal McCarthy at the Union Athletic Club in Boston in 1890 for the American version of the featherweight title. Wearing two-ounce gloves, Dixon and McCarthy battled for 70 rounds, only to have the exhausting fight called a draw. That same year Dixon travelled to England to face Nunc Wallace, the holder of the British version of the world bantamweight title. Dixon easily vanquished Wallace, scoring a knockout in the eighteenth round.

Dixon returned to America to lay further claim to the title by knocking out bantamweight challenger Johnny Murphy. Dixon also knocked out McCarthy in a rematch in 1891. By 1892, he had outgrown the bantamweight division and began competing solely as a featherweight. With a fourteenth-round knockout of Fred Johnson in Coney Island in 1892, Dixon asserted his claim to the featherweight title.

Dixon participated in the three-day Carnival of Champions at the Olympia Club in New Orleans, where most of boxing's top contenders met. Dixon was matched against the amateur champion Jack Skelly, who was

Including the hundreds of unrecorded exhibitions in vaudeville halls, Dixon may have fought as many as 800 times.

IN THE RING	WON 50	LOST 26	DRAWS 44	TB 130	KO 27	W 22	WF 1	D 44	KO'd 5	L 20	LF 1	ND 7	NC 3

Date	Year		Opponent	Site	Result / Rounds		Title
SELECTED BOUTS							
Nov 1	1886		Young Johnson	Halifax, N.S.	KO	3	—
Feb 7	1890		Cal McCarthy	Boston	D	70	For-Amer-115 lbs
Jun 27	1890	♛	Nunc Wallace	London	KO	18	Won-Vac World-114 lbs
Oct 23	1890		Johnny Murphy	Providence, RI	KO	40	Ret-World-114 lbs
Mar 31	1891		Cal McCarthy	Troy, NY	KO	22	Ret-World-115 lbs
Jul 28	1891		Abe Willis	San Francisco	KO	5	Ret-World-115 lbs
Jun 27	1892		Fred Johnson	Coney Island	KO	14	Won-World-118 lbs
Sep 6	1892		Jack Skelly	New Orleans	KO	8	Ret-World-118 lbs
Aug 7	1893		Eddie Pierce	Coney Island	KO	3	Ret-World-120 lbs
Sep 25	1893		Solly Smith	Coney Island	KO	7	Ret-World-120 lbs
Jun 29	1894		Young Griffo★	Boston	D	20	—
Jan 19	1895		Young Griffo★	Coney Island	D	25	—
Aug 27	1895		Johnny Griffin	Boston	W	25	Ret-World-FE
Oct 28	1895		Young Griffo★	New York	D	10	—
Nov 27	1896		Frank Erne	New York	L	20	Lost-World-122 lbs
Mar 24	1897		Frank Erne	New York	W	25	Reg-World-122 lbs
Oct 4	1897		Solly Smith	San Francisco	L	20	Lost-World-120 lbs
Jun 6	1898		Eddie Santry	New York	W	20	Reg-World-FE
Jul 1	1898		Ben Jordan	New York	L	25	Lost-World-FE
Nov 11	1898	♛	Dave Sullivan	New York	WD	10	Reg-World-FE
Nov 29	1898		Oscar Gardner	New York	W	25	Ret-World-FE
Jan 17	1899		Young Pluto	New York	KO	10	Ret-World-FE
May 15	1899		Kid Broad	Buffalo	W	20	Ret-World-FE
Jun 2	1899		Joe Bernstein	New York	W	25	Ret-World-FE
Jul 11	1899		Tommy White	Denver	W	20	Ret-World-FE
Aug 11	1899		Eddie Santry	New York	D	20	Ret-World-FE
Nov 2	1899		Will Curley	New York	W	25	Ret-World-FE
Nov 21	1899		Eddie Lenny	New York	W	25	Ret-World-FE
Jan 9	1900		Terry McGovern★	New York	TKO'd	8	Lost-World-FE
Jun 23	1900	♛	Terry McGovern★	Chicago	L	6	—
Aug 24	1901		Abe Attell★	Denver	D	10	—
Oct 20	1901		Abe Attell★	Cripple Creek, CO	D	20	—
Oct 28	1901		Abe Attell★	St. Louis	L	15	—
Jan 24	1903		Jim Driscoll★	London	D	6	—
Dec 10	1906		Monk the Newsboy	Providence	L	15	—

white. Dixon controlled the action from the start, broke Skelly's nose, and knocked him out in the eighth. White fans at the match reacted with shock and disgust, and to keep peace, the Olympia Club decided not to conduct any more mixed-race matches. The racist reaction to this fight led to limited black access to other matches, including heavyweight championships.

A long string of title defenses was interrupted by only a few quickly-avenged defeats. Terry McGovern finally bested Dixon in 1900 to take the crown away. Dixon lost a non-title rematch with McGovern and never again contended for the title, though he continued to fight until 1906. Dixon died, penniless, three years after retiring.

Peerless Jim

FEATHERWEIGHT

Right-handed; 5'6"; 122–126 lbs.
69 bouts, 1901 to 10/20/1919
Manager: Charles Harvey
British World Featherweight
Champion 1912–13
Hall of Fame Induction: 1990
Born: 12/15/1880, Cardiff, Wales
Died: 1/31/1925

Like Jimmy Wilde before him, Welshman Jim Driscoll (also known as Jem Driscoll) got his start fighting in the boxing booths of the British Isles. There a fighter offered all comers a chance to beat him. After fighting hundreds of bouts in the booths, Driscoll turned professional in 1901 at the age of eighteen and promptly won his first ten fights by knockout. In his next fight, he decisioned Joe Ross to win the Welsh featherweight title. Driscoll was quick and elusive in the ring. He had great hand speed, which he combined with enough power to rack up 35 knockouts in 69 fights.

In 1907, Driscoll won the vacant British featherweight title with a seventeenth-round knockout of Joe Bowker. After adding the British Empire featherweight title in 1908, Driscoll avenged one of the few defeats of his career by beating Harry Mansfield in a rematch. He next travelled to the United States, where he won a newspaper decision over the tough Leach Cross. Driscoll fought a no-decision match with world featherweight champ Abe Attell at the National Athletic Club

Charles Ledoux (L) handed Driscoll his only knock-out loss, in the last fight of Driscoll's career, at the National Sporting Club of London, in 1919. Here Driscoll holds Ledoux at bay with his jab.

IN THE RING	WON 52	LOST 3	DRAWS 6	TB 69	KO 35	W 15	WF 2	D 6	KO'd 1	L 1	LF 1	ND 8

Date	Year	Opponent	Site	Result / Rounds		Title

SELECTED BOUTS

Date	Year	Opponent	Site	Result / Rounds		Title
—	1901	Bill Radford	Cardiff, Wales	KO	2	—
Dec 24	1901	Joe Ross	Cardiff	W	10	Won-Wales-FE
Sep 29	1902	Harry Mansfield	Cardiff	D	10	—
Jan 24	1903	George Dixon★	London	W	6	—
—	1903	Harry Mansfield	Cardiff	W	10	—
—	1903	Harry Mansfield	Cardiff	W	6	—
Aug 29	1904	Harry Mansfield	Cardiff	L	10	—
Dec 26	1905	Harry Mansfield	Wednesbury, Eng.	TKO	15	—
May 28	1906	Joe Bowker	London	W	15	—
Jun 3	1907	Joe Bowker	London	KO	17	Won-Vac Britain-FE
Feb 24	1908	Charlie Griffin	London	WF	15	Won-Vac Brit Emp-FE
Aug 17	1908	Harry Mansfield	Cardiff	W	6	—
Nov 13	1908	Matty Baldwin	New York	ND-W	6	—
Dec 29	1908	Matty Baldwin	Boston	W	12	—
Feb 10	1909	Leach Cross	New York	ND-W	10	—
Feb 19	1909 ♛	Abe Attell★	New York	ND-W	10	—
Feb 14	1910	Seaman Arthur Hayes	London	TKO	6	Ret-Britain-FE
Apr 18	1910	Spike Robson	London	KO	15	Ret-Britain-FE
May 25	1910	Pal Moore	Philadelphia	ND-D	6	—
Dec 20	1910	Freddie Welsh★	Cardiff	LF	10	—
Jan 30	1911	Spike Robson	London	TKO	11	Ret-Britain-FE
Jun 3	1912	Jean Poesy	London	KO	12	Won-Vac Eur & Vac Brit World-FE
Jan 27	1913	Owen Moran★	London	D	20	Ret-Brit, Eur & Brit World-FE
Mar 10	1919	Pedlar Palmer	London	TKO	4	—
Oct 20	1919	Charles Ledoux	London	TKO'd	16	—

in New York. Though Driscoll failed to knock Attell out, he completely dominated the fight. Driscoll left the ring unmarked, but Attell had one eye closed and a badly swollen nose. Driscoll later claimed that he and Attell had agreed that the title would change hands based on the newspaper decision, the unofficial vote by ringside reporters. Attell, who had clearly been outboxed, did not acknowledge that such an agreement had been made.

After the Attell fight, Driscoll went back to Britain, returning to the United States only once more, to fight Pal Moore in Philadelphia. In 1912, Driscoll knocked out Jean Poesy in twelve rounds to win the vacant British and European world featherweight titles. The next year, Driscoll retired undefeated. He served in the British military during World War I, then attempted a comeback in 1919. He fought twice before losing to Charles Ledoux by a technical knockout. Driscoll was ahead in the Ledoux fight but became exhausted by the sixteenth round. After this defeat, Driscoll quit the ring for good. He was suffering from tuberculosis, and six years later died of pneumonia after a long stretch of ill health.

JOHNNY DUNDEE
The Scotch Wop

FEATHERWEIGHT

Right-handed; 5'4½"; 120–130 lbs.

335 bouts, 8/10/1910 to 12/5/1932

Managers: Scotty Monteith 1910–20, Jimmy Johnston 1920–29

Jr. Lightwt. Champ 1921–23, 1923–24, NY World Featherwt. Champ 1922–23, Featherwt. Champ 1923–24

Hall of Fame Induction: 1991

Born: 11/22/1893, Sciacca, Sicily, Italy

Named: Giuseppe Carrora

Died: 4/22/1965

Johnny Dundee fought an amazing 335 times from 1910 until 1932. In 1911 alone, he entered the ring 47 times, enough to equal an entire career for many fighters. A master of ring trickery and dazzling footwork, Dundee presented a variety of styles which opponents found very difficult to decipher. He was especially adept at launching punches while bouncing off the ropes. Not much of a knockout artist, Dundee nevertheless outboxed the best fighters of his era.

Born in Italy as Giuseppe Carrora, Dundee was brought to New York as an infant and grew up in "Hell's Kitchen," where his family ran a fish market. Dundee was a street brawler who caught the attention of manager Scotty Monteith. Monteith gave his young charge a new name and shaped his early career. Dundee never fought as an amateur, but went right into professional boxing at age sixteen. Almost half of his bouts were no-decisions, although newspaper reporters at ringside declared him the winner of a majority of these matches.

In 1913, Dundee travelled to California to face world featherweight champion Johnny Kilbane, another boxer with an inscrutable style. The referee stopped the match in the twentieth round and declared it a draw, but most observers thought Dundee appeared to be winning. Dundee fought eight no-decision bouts against Hall of Famer Benny Leonard between 1915 and 1920. Though

Dundee might have enjoyed a better record if he had always fought as a featherweight. He was less successful as a lightweight.

IN THE RING	WON 90	LOST 31	DRAWS 19	TB 335	KO 22	W 67	WF 1	D 19	KO'd 2	L 29	LF 0	ND 194	NC 1

Date	Year		Opponent	Site	Result / Rounds		Title
SELECTED BOUTS							
Aug 10	1910		Skinny Bob	New York	ND-L	4	—
Sep 4	1912	♛	Johnny Kilbane★	New York	ND-L	10	—
Apr 29	1913	♛	Johnny Kilbane★	Vernon	D	20	For-World-FE
Jan 1	1914		Freddie Welsh★	New Orleans	ND-L	10	—
Mar 2	1915		Benny Leonard★	New York	ND-W	10	—
Mar 8	1916		Benny Leonard★	New York	ND-L	10	—
Jun 12	1916		Benny Leonard★	New York	ND-W	10	—
Nov 15	1916		Benny Leonard★	Philadelphia	ND-W	6	—
Mar 26	1917		Lew Tendler★	Philadelphia	ND	6	—
Oct 1	1917		Lew Tendler★	Philadelphia	ND	6	—
Jan 20	1919	♛	Benny Leonard★	Newark	ND-L	8	—
Jun 16	1919	♛	Benny Leonard★	Philadelphia	ND-L	6	—
Sep 17	1919	♛	Benny Leonard★	Newark	ND-L	8	—
Jan 9	1920	♛	Benny Leonard★	Jersey City, NJ	ND-L	8	—
Nov 18	1921		George ("K.O.") Chaney	New York	WF	5	Won-Vac World-JL
May 5	1922		Lew Tendler★	Philadelphia	L	15	
Jul 6	1922		Jack Sharkey★	New York	W	15	Ret-World-JL
Aug 15	1922		Danny Frush	Brooklyn	KO	9	Won-Vac NY World-FE
Aug 28	1922		Pepper Martin	New York	W	15	Ret-World-JL
Feb 2	1923		Elino Flores	New York	W	15	Ret-World-JL
May 30	1923		Jack Bernstein	New York	L	15	Lost-World-JL
Jul 26	1923	♛	Eugene Criqui	New York	W	15	Won-World-FE
Dec 17	1923	♛	Jack Bernstein	New York	W	15	Reg-World-JL
Jun 20	1924	⑩	Kid Sullivan	Brooklyn	L	10	Lost-World-JL
Oct 24	1927	⑩	Tony Canzoneri★	New York	L	15	For-Vac World-FE
Dec 5	1932		Mickey Greb	Orange, NJ	W	6	—

Leonard generally had the edge, newspaper accounts gave Dundee three of these battles. In 1921, Dundee faced George ("K.O.") Chaney for the vacant world junior lightweight title and won on a foul in the fifth round. While still holding that title, Dundee faced Danny Frush for what was, in some circles, considered to be the world featherweight title. Dundee knocked Frush out in the ninth round, for the last knockout of his career.

In 1923, Dundee lost the junior lightweight title to Jack Bernstein, but regained it in their rematch. Then Dundee conquered Eugene Criqui, the generally accepted featherweight champion, in a bout at New York's Polo Grounds. With 40,000 fans watching, Dundee dominated the fight and won the championship. In 1924, he lost the junior lightweight title and gave up the featherweight title because he could no longer make the weight. Dundee continued to fight until 1932 but his best days were clearly behind him. He lost most of his ring earnings investing in a mediocre stable of race horses.

BANTAMWEIGHT

Right-handed; 5'4", 115–121 lbs.

72 bouts, 9/1/1930 to 12/2/1940

Manager: Arturo Gigante 1930–34, Lou Brix 1934–40

NBA Bantamweight Champion 1934–1935, 1935–1936

Bantamweight Champion 1936–1937, 1938–1939

Hall of Fame Induction 2002

Born: 3/23/1913, Barceloneta, Puerto Rico

Died: 11/17/1979

Sixto Escobar was the first world champion to come from Puerto Rico. He was the sixth child of a labor boss in the sugar cane fields in Barceloneta, a small town west of San Juan. Though his father was massively built, Sixto never grew taller than 5'4".

Escobar fought twenty-three times as an amateur, winning all but three. He turned professional at seventeen in a six-round decision over Luis Perez in September 1930. Though the earliest fights were in San Juan, he soon moved to Venezuela, where he lost a bid for that country's lightweight title on March 19, 1932.

In 1934, Escobar exploded onto the world boxing stage in Holyoke, Massachusetts, where he knocked out bantamweight contender Bobby Leitham in the seventh round. Two weeks later he defeated future featherweight champion Joey Archibald in a ten round decision. After knocking out Leitham yet again, Escobar faced Baby Casanova in Montreal on June 26, 1934 for the vacant NBA bantamweight title. Escobar knocked Casanova out in nine rounds to win NBA recognition as the bantamweight titleholder.

On August 7, 1935 he fought Pete Sanstol in a bout at the Montreal Forum in front of 10,000 fans. Escobar started out strong, and by the end of the ninth, Sanstol's face was so swollen that his left eye was completely closed. Escobar won the twelve round decision.

In his next fight on August 26, Escobar put his title on the line against Lou Salica in Madison Square Garden. Salica won the fifteen round decision, but in the rematch, less than three months later, Escobar regained the NBA crown, again by decision. On August

Escobar only required two hard punches and one minute and forty-nine seconds to retain his bantamweight title versus Carlos ("Indian") Quintana on October 13, 1936 in Madison Square Garden. The ref is Hall of Famer Arthur Donovan.

IN THE RING	WON 46	LOST 23	DRAWS 3	TB 72	KO 22	W 24	WF 0	D 3	KO'd 0	L 23	LF 0

Date	Year	Opponent	Site	Result / Rounds		Title
SELECTED BOUTS						
Sep 1	1930	Luis Perez	San Juan, PR	W	6	—
Nov 15	1931	Enrique Chafferdet	Caracas	L	10	—
Mar 19	1932	Jose T. Rosales	Caracas	L	12	For-Venezuela-FE
Jan 9	1933	Enrique Chafferdet	Caracas	D	10	—
Feb 11	1933	Enrique Chafferdet	Caracas	L	10	—
May 7	1934	⓪ Bobby Leitham	Holyoke, MA	KO	7	—
Jun 5	1934	⓪ Bobby Leitham	Montreal	TKO	5	—
Jun 26	1934	⓪ Baby Casanova	Montreal	KO	9	Won-Vac NBA-B
Aug 8	1934	Eugene Huat	Montreal	W	15	Ret-NBA-B
May 28	1935	⓪ Joey Archibald	New York	KO	6	—
Aug 7	1935	Pete Sanstol	Montreal	W	12	—
Aug 26	1935	⓪ Lou Salica	New York	L	15	Lost-NBA-B
Nov 15	1935	♛ Lou Salica	New York	W	15	Reg-NBA-B
Aug 31	1936	♛ Tony Marino	New York	TKO	13	Won-World-B
Oct 5	1936	⓪ Harry Jeffra	Baltimore	L	10	—
Oct 13	1936	Carlos ("Indian") Quintana	New York	TKO	1	Ret-World-B
Dec 9	1936	⓪ Harry Jeffra	New York	L	10	—
Feb 21	1937	⓪ Lou Salica	San Juan	W	15	Ret-World-B
Sep 23	1937	⓪ Harry Jeffra	New York	L	15	Lost-World-B
Feb 20	1938	♛ Harry Jeffra	San Juan	W	15	Reg-World-B
Apr 19	1938	⓪ K.O. Morgan	Detroit	L	10	—
Nov 1	1938	⓪ Henry Hook	Toronto	L	10	—
Apr 2	1939	⓪ K.O. Morgan	San Juan	W	15	Ret-World-B
Aug 14	1939	Jimmy Perrin	New Orleans	L	10	—
Oct 4	1939	⓪ Tony Olivera	Oakland	L	10	—
Dec 2	1940	Harry Jeffra	Baltimore	L	10	—

31, 1936, Escobar met Tony Marino, the acknowledged world title-holder. Escobar knocked Marino out in thirteen rounds to become the undisputed bantamweight champion of the world.

Later that year, Escobar lost two non-title fights to Harry Jeffra. After another successful defense in San Juan against Salica, Escobar put up his belt against Jeffra on September 23, 1937, at the Polo Grounds in a fight night dubbed "The Carnival of Champions." Escobar lost his crown in a fifteen-round decision.

In the rematch on February 20, 1938, at Escambron Beach Park in San Juan stadium named in his honor, Escobar delighted his fans when he decisioned Jeffra to retake the title, but after this fight his career quickly deteriorated. When Jeffra defeated him on December 2, 1940, Escobar retired, though he was only 27.

In the ring, Escobar became best known for a lethal right cross and for his great stamina. He was never knocked out. Escobar moved forward throwing left jabs and hooks to create an opening for his magnificent right. In retirement, he served in the U.S. Army in World War II, owned real estate in Puerto Rico, and worked in public relations.

BOB FITZSIMMONS
Ruby Robert

HEAVYWEIGHT

Right-handed; 5'11¾"; 150–175 lbs.
115 bouts, 1883 to 2/20/1914
Manager: Martin Julian
Middleweight Champion 1891–97,
Heavyweight Champion 1897–99,
Light Heavywt. Champion 1903–05
Hall of Fame Induction: 1990
Born: 5/26/1863, Helston, Cornwall,
England
Named: Robert James Fitzsimmons
Died: 10/22/1917

The first triple titleholder in history, Bob Fitzsimmons won the world middleweight, heavyweight, and light heavyweight championships in a career that spanned 27 years. As a young man, Fitzsimmons worked as a blacksmith, and his punches held the power of an iron hammer hitting an anvil. He defied age, consistently fought larger men, and was crafty and resilient in the ring.

Born in England, Fitzsimmons moved to New Zealand with his family as a small boy. School was a luxury and, before long, Fitzsimmons went to work as a carriage painter and in a foundry. His interest in boxing heated up when he entered an amateur boxing tournament supervised by visiting Hall of Famer Jem Mace. Weighing just 140 pounds, Fitzsimmons knocked out four larger opponents and won the heavyweight division of the contest.

In 1885, Fitzsimmons moved to Australia, where most of his early professional bouts took place. Over the next seven years, he posted a record of 21-2, with 24 no-decisions. In 1890, he travelled to America where three knockout bouts earned him a chance to fight world middleweight champion Jack Dempsey (The Nonpareil). Fitzsimmons proved to be more than Dempsey's equal and, after a vicious battle, he knocked the champion out in the thirteenth round.

Fitzsimmons defended his middleweight crown just once before aiming at the heavyweight title. He knocked out fellow contender Peter Maher in one round in 1896 and, later that year, delivered an eighth-round wallop that floored heavyweight Tom Sharkey. Referee Wyatt Earp, the former lawman, called the punch a low blow and disqualified Fitzsimmons, to the dismay of most observers, who thought the punch was fair.

In 1897, Fitzsimmons faced heavyweight champion James J. Corbett in Carson City, Nevada for the title. The balding,

Fitzsimmons (L) parries a blow from the scantily-clad James J. Corbett, as he heads toward a 14th-round knockout and the title.

						IN THE RING							

IN THE RING — **WON 74** **LOST 8** **DRAWS 3** | **TB** 115 | **KO** 67 | **W** 7 | **WF** 0 | **D** 3 | **KO'd** 7 | **L** 0 | **LF** 1 | **ND** 30

Date	Year	Opponent	Site	Result / Rounds		Title

SELECTED BOUTS

Date	Year	Opponent	Site	Result / Rounds		Title
—	1883	Arthur Cooper	Timaru, NZ	KO	3	—
Feb 11	1888	Billy McCarthy	Sydney	ND	4	—
Nov 10	1888	Jim Hall	Sydney	ND	4	—
Nov 24	1888	Jim Hall	Sydney	ND	4	—
Nov 30	1889	Professor West	Sydney	KO	1	—
Feb 10	1890	Jim Hall	Sydney	KO'd	4	For-Australia-M
May 17	1890	Frank Allen	San Francisco	TKO	1	—
May 29	1890	Aus. Billy McCarthy	San Francisco	KO	5	—
Jan 14	1891	♛ Jack Dempsey (Nonpareil)★	New Orleans	TKO	13	Won-World-M
Mar 2	1892	Peter Maher	New Orleans	KO	12	—
Mar 8	1893	Jim Hall	New Orleans	KO	4	—
Jun 17	1894	Joe Choynski★	Boston	D	5	—
Sep 26	1894	Dan Creedon	New Orleans	KO	2	Ret-World-M
Feb 21	1896	Peter Maher	Langtry, TX	KO	1	—
Dec 2	1896	Tom Sharkey	San Francisco	LF	8	—
Mar 17	1897	♛ James J. Corbett★	Carson City, NV	KO	14	Won-World-H
Jun 9	1899	James J. Jeffries★	Coney Island	KO'd	11	Lost-World-H
Apr 30	1900	Ed Dunkhorst	Brooklyn	KO	2	—
Aug 10	1900	Gus Ruhlin	New York	KO	6	—
Aug 24	1900	Tom Sharkey	Coney Island	KO	2	—
Jul 25	1902	♛ James J. Jeffries★	San Francisco	KO'd	8	For-World-H
Nov 25	1903	♛ George Gardner	San Francisco	W	20	Won-World-LH
Jul 23	1904	Phila. Jack O'Brien★	Philadelphia	ND-L	6	—
Dec 20	1905	Phila. Jack O'Brien★	San Francisco	TKO'd	13	Lost-World-LH
Jul 17	1907	Jack Johnson★	Philadelphia	KO'd	2	—
Dec 27	1909	Bill Lang	Sydney	KO'd	12	For-Australia-H
Feb 20	1914	Jersey Bellew	Bethlehem, PA	ND-W	6	—

spindly-legged Fitzsimmons (John L. Sullivan called him "a fighting machine on stilts") did not look like a potential heavyweight champion. He was 34 years old, to Corbett's 30, and weighed sixteen pounds less. Corbett landed seriously damaging blows for most of the fight. Fitzsimmons was bleeding badly, but his blacksmith's arm won him the fight in the fourteenth round when he slammed a paralyzing blow into Corbett's solar plexis, the nerve center just below the breastbone. Corbett went down with a horrified gasp, and Fitzsimmons took the title. He wore the crown for two uncontested years before losing it to James J. Jeffries, who knocked him out in the eleventh round.

Fitzsimmons continued boxing and in 1903, at 40 years old, he knocked George Gardner down four times in twenty rounds to win the light heavyweight title. He lost the title to Philadelphia Jack O'Brien in 1905, but continued to fight on and off for the next nine years. He lost a two-round knockout to Jack Johnson in one of his last fights. In retirement, Fitzsimmons toured the vaudeville circuit before becoming an evangelist.

TIGER FLOWERS
The Georgia Deacon

MIDDLEWEIGHT

Left-handed; 5'10"; 157–169 lbs.
157 bouts, 1918 to 11/12/1927
Manager: Walk Miller
Middleweight Champion 1926
Hall of Fame Induction: 1993
Born: 8/5/1895, Camille, GA
Named: Theodore Flowers
Died: 11/16/1927

Tiger Flowers was the first African-American to become a world middleweight champion. Born in Georgia, Flowers began fighting in 1918, when he was working in a Philadelphia shipbuilding plant. He started his professional boxing career at the age of 23, much later than most who plan to reach the top. A southpaw, Flowers was sometimes called a "left-handed Harry Greb," because of the way he hit opponents with the side of his fist. Flowers was a deeply religious man who recited a passage from Psalm 144 before every bout.

Flowers won his first 25 fights before experiencing a knockout at the hands of Panama Joe Gans. In 1922 and 1923, Flowers racked up several wins, interrupted by knockout losses to Kid Norfolk, Sam Langford, and the Jamaica Kid. In 1924, *The Ring* magazine rated Flowers the top contender for champion Harry Greb's middleweight title. Flowers earned a title shot after losing a controversial decision to light heavyweight Mike McTigue. The judges for this special holiday-time bout, held December 23 in New York, were Bernard Gimbel, the department store magnate, and Peter J. Brady, a banker. These unqualified judges gave the decision to McTigue, although nearly all expert observers thought the fight belonged to Flowers.

The high point of Flowers's (R) career was this fifteen-round decision over Harry Greb to take the middle-weight title on February 26, 1926 in New York. Flowers died within two years of this triumph.

IN THE RING	WON 115	LOST 14	DRAWS 6	TB 157	KO 53	W 56	WF 6	D 6	KO'd 9	L 3	LF 2	ND 21	NC 1

Date	Year	Opponent	Site	Result / Rounds		Title
SELECTED BOUTS						
—	1918	Bill Hooper	Brunswick, GA	KO	11	—
—	1922	Kid Norfolk	—	KO'd	3	—
Feb 21	1922	Gorilla Jones	Juarez, Mexico	KO	4	—
Jun 5	1922	Sam Langford★	Atlanta	KO'd	2	—
Jul 26	1922	Jamaica Kid	Covington, KY	TKO'd	2	—
Apr 20	1923	Jamaica Kid	Toledo, OH	ND-W	12	—
May 8	1923	Kid Norfolk	Springfield, OH	KO'd	1	—
May 15	1923	Tom King	Juarez	W	15	—
Sep 3	1923	Jamaica Kid	Atlanta	W	10	—
Mar 3	1924	Jamaica Kid	Fremont, OH	ND-W	12	—
Mar 29	1924	Lee Anderson	New York	W	12	—
Jun 27	1924	Jamaica Kid	Grand Rapids, MI	ND-W	10	—
Jul 21	1924	Jamaica Kid	Covington	WF	3	—
Aug 21	1924	♛ Harry Greb★	Fremont	ND-L	10	—
Sep 15	1924	Jamaica Kid	Columbus, OH	ND-W	12	—
Oct 11	1924	Jamaica Kid	New York	TKO	9	—
Feb 5	1925	Jamaica Kid	Dayton, OH	KO	10	—
Mar 20	1925	Lou Bogash	Boston	W	10	—
Dec 23	1925	⑩ Mike McTigue	New York	L	10	—
Feb 26	1926	♛ Harry Greb★	New York	W	15	Won-World-M
Aug 19	1926	⑩ Harry Greb★	New York	W	15	Ret-World-M
Oct 15	1926	⑩ Maxie Rosenbloom★	Boston	LF	9	—
Dec 3	1926	⑩ Mickey Walker★	Chicago	L	10	Lost-World-M
Feb 18	1927	Lou Bogash	Boston	W	10	—
Jul 4	1927	⑩ Maxie Rosenbloom★	Chicago	D	10	—
Nov 9	1927	⑩ Maxie Rosenbloom★	Detroit	D	10	—
Nov 12	1927	Leo Gates	New York	TKO	4	—

In February of 1926, Flowers met Greb for the title in Madison Square Garden in front of a crowd of 16,311. Flowers got off to a good start and staggered Greb in the first round. Greb cut Flowers in the second and the fourth. As the fight went on, the battle degenerated into a wrestling match with considerable holding, gouging, and low blows. Flowers won a unanimous decision to capture the title. He also won an August rematch with Greb. Just four months later, Flowers lost his title to Mickey Walker in Chicago, even though Flowers had dominated the fight. The judges' questionable decision was investigated by the Illinois State Athletic Commission, but Walker still held the title.

Flowers tried for most of the next year to obtain a rematch with Walker. Still a top contender, he twice fought to a draw with Hall of Famer Maxie Rosenbloom. In November of 1927, Flowers was hospitalized for an operation to remove scar tissue from around his eyes. He died as a result of the procedure, which was similar to the surgery that had claimed the life of Harry Greb the previous year.

JOE GANS
The Old Master

LIGHTWEIGHT

Right-handed; 5'6¼"; 131–137 lbs.
155 bouts, 1891 to 3/12/1909
Manager: Al Herford
Lightwt. Champ 1902–04, 1906–08
Hall of Fame Induction: 1990
Born: 11/25/1874, Baltimore, MD
Named: Joseph Gaines
Died: 8/10/1910

The first native-born black American to win a world title, Joe Gans impressed the boxing community with his scientific approach to the sport. Gans never moved more than a few inches to avoid a punch, studied his opponents' strengths and weaknesses much more intently than other fighters of the time, and directed his punches with pinpoint accuracy to key points of weakness.

Gans's first-known boxing experience took place at the Monumental Theater in Baltimore when he won a "battle royal," a wild contest in which several black fighters entered the ring at once to fight until one remained. Gans's superiority in this brutal exhibition attracted the interest of boxing manager Al Herford, who directed Gans to a professional career. Gans started boxing professionally in 1891 in Baltimore. Over the rest of the decade, he compiled an enviable record of 58-3-6 with two no-decisions.

In 1900, Gans, then 26 years old, faced Frank Erne for the world lightweight title. Erne peppered Gans with a blistering left jab throughout the fight, seriously cutting Gans' left eyelid. Realizing that to continue would risk blindness, Gans asked that the fight be stopped in the twelfth round. Gans spent hours analyzing Erne's style until he developed a strategy to counteract that murderous left.

In their rematch two years later, Gans executed his plan perfectly and knocked Erne out in one round to recapture the lightweight title.

Also in 1900, Gans met Hall of Famer Terry McGovern, who knocked him out in the second round after four earlier knockdowns. This match raised eyebrows as few believed Gans would fall to the wildly swinging McGovern. Later, Gans regretfully admitted to taking a dive in this fight.

Never weighing more than 137 pounds, Gans often

Gans (R) shakes hands with champ Battling Nelson before the start of their marathon 1906 title fight in Goldfield, NV.

IN THE RING	WON 120	LOST 8	DRAWS 9	TB 155	KO 85	W 30	WF 5	D 9	KO'd 5	L 3	LF 0	ND 18

Date	Year	Opponent	Site	Result / Rounds		Title

SELECTED BOUTS

Date	Year	Opponent	Site	Result / Rounds		Title
—	1891	Dave Armstrong	Baltimore	KO	12	—
Nov 18	1895	Young Griffo★	Baltimore	D	10	—
Sep 21	1897	Young Griffo★	Philadelphia	D	15	—
Mar 23	1900	♛ Frank Erne	New York	TKO'd	12	For-World-L
Dec 13	1900	Terry McGovern★	Chicago	KO'd	2	—
May 12	1902	♛ Frank Erne	Fort Erie, Ont.	KO	1	Won-World-L
Jun 27	1902	George McFadden	San Francisco	KO	3	Ret-World-L
Jul 24	1902	Rufe Turner	Oakland	KO	15	Ret-World-L
Sep 17	1902	Gus Gardner	Baltimore	KO	5	Ret-World-L
Oct 13	1902	Kld McPartland	Fort Erie	KO	5	Ret-World-L
Jan 1	1903	Gus Gardner	New Britain, CT	WF	11	Ret-World-L
Mar 11	1903	Steve Crosby	Hot Springs, AR	KO	11	Ret-World-L
May 29	1903	Willie Fitzgerald	San Francisco	KO	10	Ret-World-L
Jul 4	1903	Buddy King	Butte, MT	KO	4	Ret-World-L
Nov 2	1903	Jack Blackburn★	Philadelphia	ND-D	6	—
Dec 8	1903	Sam Langford★	Boston	L	15	—
Mar 25	1904	Jack Blackburn★	Baltimore	W	15	—
Sep 30	1904	♛ Joe Walcott(Barbados)★	San Francisco	D	20	For-World-W
Oct 31	1904	Jimmy Britt	San Francisco	WF	5	Ret-World-L
Jun 29	1906	Jack Blackburn★	Philadelphia	ND-D	6	—
Sep 3	1906	♛ Battling Nelson★	Goldfield, NV	WF	42	Ret-World-L
Jan 1	1907	Kid Herman	Tonopah, NV	KO	8	Ret-World-L
Sep 9	1907	Jimmy Britt	San Francisco	TKO	6	Ret-World-L
Sep 27	1907	George Memsic	Los Angeles	W	20	Ret-World-L
May 14	1908	Rudy Unholz	San Francisco	KO	11	Ret-World-L
Jul 4	1908	Battling Nelson★	Colma, CA	KO'd	17	Lost-World-L
Sep 9	1908	♛ Battling Nelson★	Colma	KO'd	21	For-World-L
Mar 12	1909	Jabez White	New York	ND-W	10	—

fought heavier men. He lost a fifteen-round decision to Hall of Famer Sam Langford in 1903 and fought to a draw with Joe Walcott in an attempt to take the welterweight title in 1904. Gans relinquished the lightweight title to fight Walcott, though in some quarters he still was considered the titleholder.

In 1906, Gans met Battling Nelson in Goldfield, Nevada, in a fight arranged by Tex Rickard. Neither Nelson nor Rickard had much regard for black fighters. Gans, although he was the defending champion, was offered only one-third of the purse, and Nelson insisted that Gans make the 133-pound weight limit, rigidly enforced with three weigh-ins on the day of the fight. Gans knocked Nelson down a couple of times and each time helped him up. In the 42nd round, Nelson felled Gans with a low blow. The referee called the punch a foul and declared Gans the winner. Nelson knocked Gans out in the rematch to take the title, and then knocked Gans out again in their third meeting. At the time of his last two fights with Nelson, Gans already had begun to feel the effects of tuberculosis. He died from the disease in 1910.

FRANKIE GENARO

FLYWEIGHT

Right-handed; 5'2½"; 110–116 lbs.

130 bouts, 10/15/1920 to 3/3/1934

Managers: Harry Garsh, Phil Bernstein, Joe Jacobs, Billy McCarney

American Flyweight Champion 1923–25

NBA Flyweight Champion 1928–29

NBA-IBU Champion 1929–31

Hall of Fame Induction: 1998

Born: 08/26/1901, New York, NY

Named: Frank DiGennaro

Died: 12/27/1966

Frankie Genaro was one of the top flyweights in an era that included Hall of Famers Pancho Villa, Fidel LaBarba, Jimmy Wilde, and Benny Lynch. A popular fighter, Genaro used speed and science in the ring as he took on fly-, bantam-, and featherweights.

Born Frank DiGennaro in New York City, Genaro started boxing as a teenager under the name of a cousin, Al DeVito. In 1919, Genaro won the New York State, Metropolitan Association, and National AAU flyweight titles and capped his stunning amateur career by winning a gold medal in the 1920 Olympic Games in Antwerp. Genaro turned professional later that year.

Fighting primarily in New York, Genaro twice defeated Charley Phil Rosenberg and suffered his first loss at the hands of Harry Leonard in a twelve-round decision. He took on future flyweight champ Pancho Villa twice, for a no-decision and a win.

On March 1, 1923, Genaro met Villa, then owner of the American flyweight title, for the third time. Throughout most of the fight, Villa was the aggressor. However, Genaro scored often enough to earn the judges' approval and with it, the title. The booing crowd thought neither fighter had worked hard enough, but gave the edge to Villa.

Genaro then set his sights on the world flyweight title held by Jimmy Wilde. Wilde had virtually retired but agreed to come to the United States for one last title bout. However, when Genaro's manager could not reach an agreement with Wilde, the champ fought Villa. Villa knocked out Wilde in the seventh round to take the world title. When Villa died on July 14, 1925, Genaro became the "uncrowned" champion.

Genaro defended his American title on August 22, 1925 against 1924 Olympic gold medalist Fidel LaBarba, who took the title with a decision. In 1927 Genaro unsuccessfully challenged for the vacant NBA world flyweight title against Frenchy Belanger in Tor-

The diminutive Genaro clowns with Charly Kranchi, middleweight champ of Switzerland.

IN THE RING	WON 82	LOST 21	DRAWS 8	TB 130	KO 19	W 58	WF 5	D 8	KO'd 5	L 13	LF 3	ND 19	NC 0

Date	Year	Opponent	Site	Result / Rounds		Title
SELECTED BOUTS						
Oct 15	1920	Joe Colletti	New York	WF	3	—
Feb 16	1921	Joe Colletti	Poughkeespie, NY	D	12	—
Apr 9	1921	Joe Colletti	Brooklyn	W	10	—
Aug 12	1921	Joe Colletti	Saratoga, NY	W	12	—
May 24	1922	Charley Phil Rosenberg	New York	W	12	—
Jul 6	1922	Pancho Villa ★	Jersey City, NJ	ND-W	12	—
Aug 18	1922	Harry Leonard	New York	L	12	—
Aug 22	1922	Pancho Villa ★	Brooklyn	W	10	—
Mar 1	1923	⑩ Pancho Villa ★	New York	W	15	Won-American-FL
Jun 26	1925	Kid Williams ★	Baltimore	W	12	—
Aug 22	1925	⑩ Fidel La Barba ★	Los Angeles	L	10	Lost-American-FL
Nov 28	1927	⑩ Albert Belanger	Toronto	L	10	For-Vac-NBA-FL
Feb 6	1928	⑩ Albert Belanger	Toronto	W	10	Won-NBA-FL
Mar 2	1929	⑩ Emile Pladner	Paris	KO'd	1	Lost-NBA-FL
Apr 18	1929	⑩ Emile Pladner	Paris	WF	5	Reg-NBA-IBU-FL
Oct 17	1929	Ernie Jarvis	London	W	15	Ret-NBA-IBU-FL
Jun 10	1930	Albert Belanger	Toronto	W	10	Ret-NBA-IBU-FL
Dec 26	1930	⑩ Midget Wolgast★	New York	D	15	For-Vac-World-FL
Mar 25	1931	Victor Ferrand	Madrid	D	15	Ret-NBA-IBU-FL
Jul 30	1931	Jackie Harmon	Waterbury, CT	KO	6	Ret-NBA-IBU-FL
Oct 3	1931	⑩ Valentin Angelmann	Paris	W	15	Ret-NBA-IBU-FL
Oct 27	1931	Victor Perez	Paris	KO'd	2	Lost-NBA-IBU-FL
Apr 5	1933	Joey Archibald	Fall River, MA	W	10	—
Mar 3	1934	Little Pancho	Oakland, CA	KO'd	9	—

onto. In the rematch less than two months later, Genaro outpunched and out-boxed Belanger. In contrast to the Villa title fight, Genaro fought furiously and clearly won the decision.

In 1929, Genaro took his title to Europe to face highly regarded Emile ("Spider") Pladner in Paris. Pladner knocked Genaro out in the first round. In the rematch six weeks later, Genaro regained the title on a foul. Genaro fought in England, France, Germany, and Italy before returning to New York to face the New York world flyweight champ Midget Wolgast on December 26, 1930 in Madison Square Garden. After fifteen rounds the fight was called a draw with each fighter retaining his title.

The next year Genaro lost his title when Young Perez knocked him out in the second round. At thirty, Genaro did not have much left. He compiled a record of 6-5, including a victory over future featherweight champ Joey Archibald. Age and an aggressive career had taken its toll on this fine fighter. He retired after Little Pancho knocked him out in 1934. In retirement Genaro was involved in sales and real estate. He owned lakefront property in Cochecton, New York where he planned to open a resort. He also worked for the Department of Marine Aviation in New York for fifteen years. Genaro died on December 27, 1966.

MIKE GIBBONS
St. Paul Phantom

MIDDLEWEIGHT

Right-handed; 5'9"; 148 lbs.

127 bouts, 1/11/1908 to 5/16/1922

Manager: George Barton

Hall of Fame Induction: 1992

Born: 7/20/1887, St. Paul, MN

Named: Mike J. Gibbons

Died: 8/31/1956

Although he never became a champion, Mike Gibbons is considered by many boxing historians to be one of the top ten middleweights of all time. Gibbons learned to box at the YMCA in his native St. Paul. He turned professional at the age of nineteen with a third-round knockout of Roy Moore and was unbeaten in his first fourteen fights before losing a decision to Jimmy Clabby. A footwork wizard who could wear an opponent out with his defensive maneuvers, Gibbons could punch hard, too. As a young fighter, he built a reputation that put him in line for the middleweight championship.

In 1912, the middleweight division had no recognized champion. More than half a dozen fighters, including Gibbons and Eddie McGoorty, claimed a right to the title. Gibbons signed to fight McGoorty with the winner to be declared champion. The heavier McGoorty was the favorite by far, and Gibbons employed

Mike Gibbons (R) spars with his brother, Hall of Famer Tommy Gibbons atop the American Building in New York City on March 12, 1917. Tommy, who fought both Dempsey and Tunney, outweighed Mike by 24 lbs.

IN THE RING	WON 62	LOST 3	DRAWS 4	TB 127	KO 38	W 23	WF 1	D 4	KO'd 0	L 3	LF 0	ND 58

Date	Year	Opponent	Site	Result / Rounds		Title
SELECTED BOUTS						
Jan 11	1908	Roy Moore	St. Paul, MN	KO	3	—
Mar 12	1910	Jimmy Clabby	St. Paul	L	10	—
Apr 17	1911	Gus Christie	Milwaukee	ND	8	—
May 5	1911	Gus Christie	Milwaukee	ND	10	—
Sep 1	1911	Jimmy Clabby	Milwaukee	ND	10	—
Nov 10	1911	Young Sherman	New York	KO	4	—
Dec 4	1912	Eddie McGoorty	New York	ND	10	—
May 13	1913	Gus Christie	Boston	W	12	—
Jan 21	1915	Jimmy Clabby	Milwaukee	ND	10	—
Mar 2	1915	Eddie McGoorty	Hudson, WI	ND	10	—
May 31	1915	Soldier Bartfield	Brooklyn	ND	10	—
Sep 11	1915	Packey McFarland ★	Brooklyn	ND	10	—
May 18	1916	Ted ("Kid") Lewis ★	New York	ND	10	—
Nov 10	1916	Jack Dillon ★	St. Paul	ND	10	—
Feb 10	1917	Harry Greb ★	Philadelphia	ND	6	—
Jul 4	1917	George Chip	Youngstown, OH	ND	12	—
Sep 3	1917	Jack Dillon ★	Terre Haute, IN	ND	10	—
Apr 26	1918	Packey McFarland ★	Camp Dodge, IA	Exh	6	—
Jan 31	1919	George Chip	Duluth, MN	ND	10	—
Mar 4	1919	Soldier Bartfield	St. Paul	ND	10	—
Apr 22	1919	Soldier Bartfield	San Francisco	W	4	—
May 19	1919	George ("K.O.") Brown	Memphis, TN	ND	8	—
Jun 12	1919	George Chip	Terre Haute	ND	10	—
Jun 23	1919	Harry Greb ★	Pittsburgh	ND	10	—
May 16	1922	Danny Fagan	Winnipeg, Man.	KO	2	—

his ring choreography not to beat McGoorty but to keep him from winning. Gibbons constantly backpedaled and put on a great display of footwork but he did not really fight. The newspapers awarded McGoorty the decision, but the fight's lack of action kept him from gaining general acclaim as the titleholder. Asked by a reporter why he had not fought more vigorously, Gibbons replied, "Because you and every other writer said that McGoorty would beat me, simply because he was ten pounds heavier than me. I decided to prove you were wrong, and that he couldn't lay a glove on me. And he didn't. That's all I cared about."

Gibbons continued to fight successfully after the McGoorty fight, and proved his mettle in a 1916 match with Hall of Famer Jack Dillon. At the time, Dillon was reputed to have the best punch in all of boxing. For ten rounds, Gibbons eluded Dillon's attack and countered beautifully when Dillon missed him. Gibbons won every round of the fight, according to those at ringside.

Gibbons fought for another six years, taking on Harry Greb, among others. Even the blurringly fast Greb was confused by Gibbons, by then known as the "Phantom of St. Paul." Greb shouted to his manager, "From now on, match me with one guy at a time."

HEAVYWEIGHT

Right-handed; 5'9½"; 172 lbs.

106 bouts, 9/5/1911 to 6/5/1925

Manager: Eddie Kane

Hall of Fame Induction: 1993

Born: 3/22/1891, St. Paul, MN

Died: 11/19/1960

Like his older brother Mike, Tommy Gibbons is best remembered for a fight in which he kept a champion at bay. Widely acknowledged as a stellar fighter in several weight classes, Gibbons held his own with heavyweight king Jack Dempsey and was knocked out only once in his career.

Gibbons learned to box at the YMCA in his hometown of St. Paul. He turned professional at the age of twenty and recorded knockouts in his first three fights. At the start of his career, Gibbons fought as a welterweight. As he added weight, he moved up in class until he eventually contended for the heavyweight title. Gibbons battled Hall of Famer Harry Greb four times from 1915 to 1922, losing the only one of the four bouts in which a decision was rendered. He also fought multiple bouts with George ("K.O.") Brown, Joe Herrick, George Chip, Gus Christie, Silent Martin, Billy Miske, Clay Turner, Burt Kenny, and Chuck Wiggins. Only Miske beat Gibbons, and he won on a foul.

Initially, Gibbons was famed for his speed and boxing ability. However, as he gained weight, he developed a more powerful punch. In 1921, Gibbons won 21 fights by knockouts, with ten of them coming in the first round. Although not all of the victories were against top competition, Gibbons succeeded in making enough of a name for himself to earn a shot at Dempsey's heavyweight title.

The title fight took place in Shelby, Montana. The city fathers wanted to put the town on the map by hosting a heavyweight championship bout. Jack Kearns, Dempsey's manager, agreed to have his fighter perform there if Dempsey were paid $310,000. Kearns also insisted on using his own referee, James Dougherty. Gibbons, hungry for the championship, agreed to

Gibbons floors Georges Carpentier in the seventh round of a ten-round no-decision bout before a huge throng in Michigan City, IN on May 31, 1924.

IN THE RING	WON 57	LOST 4	DRAWS 1	TB 106	KO 47	W 10	WF 0	D 1	KO'd 1	L 2	LF 1	ND 43	NC 1

Date	Year	Opponent	Site	Result / Rounds		Title

SELECTED BOUTS

Date	Year	Opponent	Site	Result / Rounds		Title
Sep 5	1911	Oscar Kelly	Minneapolis	KO	5	—
Jul 12	1912	Tommy Nelson	New York	KO	1	—
Feb 9	1914	George ("K.O.") Brown	Hudson, WI	ND	10	—
Mar 24	1914	Billy Miske	Hudson	ND	3	—
Apr 20	1914	George ("K.O.") Brown	Superior, WI	ND	10	—
Jul 12	1915	Billy Miske	St. Paul, MN	ND	10	—
Nov 16	1915	Harry Greb★	St. Paul	ND	10	—
Mar 23	1917	♛ Battling Levinsky★	St. Paul	ND	10	—
Aug 22	1917	George Chip	St. Paul	ND	10	—
Sep 3	1917	Gus Christie	Dayton, OH	W	15	—
Apr 26	1918	Gus Christie	Terre Haute, IN	W	10	—
May 3	1918	George Chip	Des Moines, IA	W	12	—
Apr 11	1919	George Chip	Denver	W	10	—
Jun 19	1919	Billy Miske	Minneapolis	ND	10	—
Jul 4	1919	George ("K.O.") Brown	Denver	ND	12	—
Feb 3	1920	George ("K.O.") Brown	Peoria, IL	ND	10	—
May 15	1920	Harry Greb★	Pittsburgh	ND	10	—
Jul 31	1920	Harry Greb★	Pittsburgh	ND	10	—
Mar 13	1922	Harry Greb★	New York	L	15	—
Oct 13	1922	Billy Miske	New York	LF	10	—
Nov 13	1922	George Ashe	Detroit	KO	1	—
Dec 15	1922	Billy Miske	St. Paul	W	10	—
Apr 30	1923	Chuck Wiggins	New Orleans	KO	10	—
Jul 4	1923	♛ Jack Dempsey★	Shelby, MT	L	15	For-World-H
May 31	1924	Georges Carpentier★	Michigan City, IN	ND	10	—
Jun 5	1925	ⓦ Gene Tunney★	New York	KO'd	12	—

be paid beyond expenses only if there were money left over after Dempsey's cut. Dempsey got paid, but because the fight drew only about 7,000 spectators, Gibbons received nothing. In fact, the fight was a financial disaster for Shelby and three banks failed as a result of backing the fiasco.

Still, it was a good fight. Dempsey hit Gibbons with some solid shots, notably in the eleventh and fifteenth rounds, but Gibbons parried and slipped away from punches that would have scored against a less-accomplished fighter. It was later rumored that Kearns told Dempsey to be sure to go a full fifteen rounds so that his agent could get out of town with Dempsey's purse before the local promoters reconsidered. The stories surrounding the fight do little to diminish Gibbons's achievement; most observers believed that he could not have been knocked out under any circumstances.

It took Dempsey's nemesis, Gene Tunney, to finally stop Gibbons. In a fight in 1925, Tunney dropped Gibbons in the twelfth round. It was the first and only time he was knocked out. Gibbons then retired, never having won a championship. In retirement, he sold insurance and served four terms as sheriff of St. Paul.

HARRY GREB
The Pittsburgh Windmill

MIDDLEWEIGHT

Right-handed; 5'8"; 142–170 lbs.

299 bouts, 5/29/1913 to 8/19/1926

Managers: James M. ("Red") Mason 1913–20, 1923–26, George Engel 1921–22

Middleweight Champion 1923–26

Hall of Fame Induction: 1990

Born: 6/6/1894, Pittsburgh, PA

Named: Edward Henry Greb

Died: 10/22/1926

Possibly the most fearless fighter ever to enter the ring, Harry Greb is remembered both for the frequency with which he fought and for the great ferocity he displayed. He came up against the best fighters of his day, demolishing many of them with bloodthirsty enthusiasm. He often challenged Jack Dempsey, but the two never fought. In a career which spanned thirteen years, Greb fought 299 times, and won 264, including so-called newspaper decisions. He was only knocked out twice, once in his first year of fighting, and once when he broke his arm throwing a punch.

Greb began his pro career at the age of eighteen in his native Pittsburgh, fighting mostly in and around his hometown for the first few years. Rising through the ranks, he triumphed over the likes of George ("K.O.") Brown, Jack Dillon, Eddie McGoorty, Gunboat Smith, and Tommy Gibbons. In 1922, Greb faced the unbeaten Gene Tunney in Madison Square Garden for the American light heavyweight title. Greb immediately swarmed all over Tunney, relentlessly attacking him from every angle. In a gory battle, Tunney's nose splashed

Harry Greb (R) poses with Johnny Wilson, referee Jack O'Sullivan, and announcer Joe Humphrys before contesting the title on August 31, 1923 in New York.

IN THE RING	WON 105	LOST 8	DRAWS 3	TB 299	KO 48	W 55	WF 2	D 3	KO'd 2	L 5	LF 1	ND 183

Date	Year	Opponent	Site	Result / Rounds	Title
SELECTED BOUTS					
May 29	1913	Frank Kirkwood	Pittsburgh	ND-W 6	—
Nov 16	1915	Tommy Gibbons★	St. Paul, MN	ND-L 10	—
Feb 10	1917	Mike Gibbons★	Philadelphia	ND-L 6	—
Sept 6	1917	Battling Levinsky★	Pittsburgh	ND-W 10	—
Mar 4	1918	Jack Dillon★	Toledo, OH	ND-W 12	—
Apr 28	1919	Battling Levinsky★	Conton. OH	ND-W 12	—
Jun 23	1919	Mike Gibbons★	Pittsburgh	ND-W 10	—
Jul 31	1920	Tommy Gibbons★	Pittsburgh	ND-W 10	—
May 23	1922	Gene Tunney★	New York	W 15	Won-USA-LH
Jan 30	1923	Tommy Loughran★	New York	W 15	Ret-USA-LH
Feb 23	1923	Gene Tunney★	New York	L 15	Lost-USA-LH
Aug 31	1923	♛ Johnny Wilson	New York	W 15	Won-World-M
Dec 3	1923	Bryan Downey	Pittsburgh	W 10	Ret-World-M
Dec 10	1923	Gene Tunney★	New York	L 15	For-USA-LH
Dec 25	1923	Tommy Loughran★	Pittsburgh	W 10	—
Jan 18	1924	⑩ Johnny Wilson	New York	W 15	Ret-World-M
Mar 24	1924	Fay Keiser	Baltimore	TKO 12	Ret-World-M
Jun 26	1924	⑩ Ted Moore	New York	W 15	Ret-World-M
Aug 21	1924	⑩ Tiger Flowers★	Fremont, OH	ND-W 10	—
Sep 17	1924	⑩ Gene Tunney★	Cleveland	ND-D 10	—
Mar 27	1925	⑩ Gene Tunney★	St. Paul	ND-L 10	—
Jul 2	1925	Mickey Walker★	New York	W 15	Ret-World-M
Jul 16	1925	⑩ Maxie Rosenbloom★	Cleveland	ND-W 10	—
Nov 13	1925	⑩ Tony Marullo	New Orleans	W 15	Ret-World M
Feb 26	1926	⑩ Tiger Flowers★	New York	L 15	Lost-World-M
Aug 19	1926	♛ Tiger Flowers★	New York	L 15	For-World-M

blood from 40 seconds into the first round; Greb soon reopened scars on Tunney's forehead. The lighter, faster, more experienced Greb overwhelmed the "Fighting Marine" and took the fifteen-round decision. Although he was denied a chance to face the world titleholder, Georges Carpentier, Greb successfully defended his American title against Hall of Famer Tommy Loughran before facing Tunney in a rematch. This time Tunney won a controversial decision. Referee Patsy Haley apparently penalized Greb for holding and hitting and other roughhouse tactics in awarding Tunney the fight. The two would battle three more times with Tunney winning one and with two no-decisions.

In his first bout after the second Tunney fight, Greb dropped to middleweight and captured the world title with a fifteen-round decision over Johnny Wilson. Greb held the title until 1926 when Tiger Flowers dethroned him. Greb failed to reclaim the title in a return bout.

A remarkably tough competitor, Greb had suffered a detached retina in a fight in 1921 against Kid Norfolk. A month later, Greb was back in the ring, and he continued to fight for five years, half-blind. Greb's life came to an untimely end in 1926 when he died while undergoing surgery to repair facial injuries caused by boxing and an auto accident.

Y:UNG GRIFF:

FEATHERWEIGHT

Right-handed; 5'4"; 122–135 lbs.
219 bouts, 1886 to 9/25/1911
Featherweight Champ 1890–93
Hall of Fame Induction: 1991
Born: 4/15/1869, Sofala, NSW, Australia
Named: Albert Griffiths
Died: 12/7/1927

One of the greatest defensive fighters of all time, Young Griffo compiled an outstanding record while eschewing traditional training methods. Born in Australia, the illiterate Griffo got his first experience fighting while selling newspapers on the docks of Sydney. When noted Australian boxer Larry Foley saw him in a street fight, Foley added Griffo to his stable of fighters. Griffo first started boxing under the old London Prize Ring Rules in 1886.

In 1889, Griffo won an eight-round decision over Nipper Peakes to take the Australian featherweight title. The next year, he scored a fifteenth-round knockout of Torpedo Billy Murphy in Sydney to win a version of the world featherweight title. Though Griffo successfully defended this title once, he did not gain widespread acclaim as the title holder.

In 1893, Griffo journeyed to the United States and dazzled fans with his incredible ability to avoid getting hit. He used to boast that he could stand on a

Griffo ducks out of danger in the last stanza of his twelve-round decision victory over Horace Leeds at the Seaside Athletic Club of Coney Island, NY on March 4, 1895. Insets 1 and 2 show other bouts that day.

IN THE RING	WON 63	LOST 9	DRAWS 37	TB 219	KO 32	W 28	WF 3	D 37	KO'd 4	L 4	LF 1	ND 110

Date	Year	Opponent	Site	Result / Rounds		Title
SELECTED BOUTS						
—	1886	Joe Francis	Sydney	KO	3	—
May 1	1888	Joe Pluto	Melbourne	D	8	—
Sep 1	1888	Joe Pluto	Melbourne	D	4	—
Dec 12	1889	Joe Pluto	Melbourne	D	70	—
Dec 27	1889	Nipper Peakes	Melbourne	W	8	Won-Australia-FE
Mar 29	1890	Chiddy Ryan	Sydney	W	4	—
Sep 2	1890	♛ Billy Murphy	Sydney	TKO	15	Won-World-126 lbs
Mar 12	1891	George Powell	Sydney	WD	20	Ret-World-126 lbs
Jul 25	1892	Jim Barron	Darlinghurst, Australia	D	22	For-Australia-L
—	1892	Chiddy Ryan	Sydney	D	45	
Nov 13	1893	Young Scotty	Chicago	W	6	—
Feb 10	1894	Kid Lavigne★	New York	D	8	—
May 5	1894	Billy Murphy	Boston	W	8	—
Jun 29	1894	♛ George Dixon★	Boston	D	20	—
Aug 27	1894	Jack McAuliffe★	New York	L	10	—
Jan 19	1895	♛ George Dixon★	Coney Island	D	25	—
Oct 12	1895	Kid Lavigne★	Maspeth, NY	D	20	—
Oct 28	1895	♛ George Dixon★	New York	D	10	—
Nov 18	1895	Joe Gans★	Baltimore	D	10	—
Feb 3	1896	Hugh Behan	New York	KO'd	1	—
Sep 21	1897	Joe Gans★	Philadelphia	D	15	—
Jul 10	1900	Joe Gans★	New York	KO'd	8	—
Feb 10	1904	Tommy White	Chicago	KO'd	1	—
Sep 25	1911	Honey Mellody	Philadelphia	ND	6	—

handkerchief and dodge punches without taking a step in any direction. Griffo fought a host of notables, usually competing as a lightweight, although he did not earn a title shot. He fought three draws with George Dixon, which could have gone Griffo's way had the rules allowed the rendering of a decision. He also lost a controversial decision to Hall of Famer Jack McAuliffe, who barely touched Griffo in ten rounds.

Griffo did not treat his boxing career seriously. Usually, he did not train at all for his fights. If legend is to believed, he often arrived in the ring drunk or hung over. Even so, he was able to win more than his share of fights while absorbing only a minimal amount of punishment. By 1900, the years of hard living had slowed Griffo, and he suffered a knockout by Joe Gans. Griffo continued to fight until 1904 and made an abortive comeback in 1911. In retirement, the hard-drinking, wise-cracking Griffo used up his fame and money until he was reduced to panhandling in Times Square. He became a familiar figure, spending his days perched on the steps of the Rialto Theater. When Griffo died in 1927, promoter Tex Rickard reportedly paid for the funeral.

HARRY HARRIS
Human Scissors, Human Hairpin

BANTAMWEIGHT

Right-handed; 5'7¾"; 115 lbs.

52 bouts, 4/5/1896 to 6/3/1907

British World Bantamweight (115 lbs.) Champion 1901

Hall of Fame Induction: 2002

Born: 11/18/1880; Chicago, IL

Died: 6/5/1959

Unlike many boxing greats, Harry Harris's productive career did not end with his last ring battle.

As a 90-pound teenager, Harris, along with his twin brother Sam, began taking boxing lessons at the Bill O'Connell gym in Chicago. It was O'Connell who recommended the Harris boys to Chicago newspaper artist Ed Carey—also a local amateur bantamweight—as sparring partners. Gaining experience with Carey, Harry Harris decided to try his hand as a professional, and debuted at fifteen in a five-round decision over Dennis Mahoney on April 5, 1896.

After turning pro, Harris formed a friendship with Hall of Famer Kid McCoy. The two sparred together in Chicago and toured in a traveling show, taking on all comers. McCoy was a mentor to Harris, and taught him many tricks of the trade, including his famed "Corkscrew Punch." Lean and lanky, Harris cut an unlikely figure as a boxer. But with his extraordinarily long reach, long, thin legs, and surprising power, he handled both boxers and sluggers with equal panache.

In 1898, Harris first became known to the New York fight crowd when he fought and won a five-bout series there, three by knockout. He suffered his first loss the next year, a six-round decision to Steve Flanagan. Also in 1899, Harris fought one of the defining matches of his career when he faced undefeated Hall of Famer and bantamweight champion Jimmy Barry. Though Harris dominated the six-round battle, the referee called the fight a draw out of respect for Barry's record.

When Terry McGovern vacated the bantamweight title in 1900, Harris was viewed as the successor to the title. He defeated future welterweight champ Buddy Ryan and Caspar Leon in

Hall of Fame middleweight Charles ("Kid") McCoy (L) was a friend and mentor to the younger (and lighter) Harris (R).

IN THE RING	WON 38	LOST 2	DRAWS 7	TB 52	KO 14	W 23	WF 1	D 7	KO'd 0	L 2	LF 0	ND 5

Date	Year	Opponent	Site	Result / Rounds		Title
SELECTED BOUTS						
Apr 5	1896	Dennis Mahoney	Chicago	W	5	—
Sep 9	1898	George Ross	New York	W	10	—
Feb 7	1899	Steve Flanagan	Chicago	L	6	—
May 19	1899	Torpedo Billy Murphy	Chicago	KO	4	—
Sep 1	1899	Jimmy Barry★	Chicago	D	6	—
Sep 22	1899	Steve Flanagan	Chicago	D	6	—
Oct 14	1899	Steve Flanagan	Chicago	D	6	—
Jan 20	1900	Barney ("Kid") Abel	Chicago	KO	3	—
Oct 16	1900	Casper Leon	Chicago	W	6	—
Oct 26	1900	Johnny Reagan	Chicago	W	6	—
Oct 30	1900	Kid McFadden	Chicago	W	6	—
Nov 27	1900	Clarence Forbes	Chicago	L	6	—
Mar 18	1901	Thomas ("Pedlar") Palmer	London	W	15	Won-British World-B (115 lbs)
Apr 15	1901	Harry Ware	London	W	15	—
Feb 27	1902	Austin Rice	Chicago	D	6	—
Mar 26	1902	Danny Dougherty	Philadelphia	ND	6	—
Mar 31	1906	Jack Goodman	New York	ND	3	—
Jun 3	1907	Harlem Tommy Murphy	New York	WF	8	—

that same year, then sailed to England in hopes of meeting Harry Ware— Britian's top bantam. The fight never materialized.

Instead, Harris signed to meet Pedlar Palmer on March 18, 1901, at London's National Sporting Club. In contrast to Harris's unusually long,thin physique, Palmer was a sinewy 5'3". He started out strong, moving inside and working the body while avoiding Harris's left. Harris was too skilled to be baffled by Palmer for long. In the fifth round, instead of jabbing with a straight left, he turned his throw into a part hook, part uppercut that connected with Palmer's jaw, knocking him down. Harris won an easy decision and claimed the 115 lbs. title.

When he returned to the U.S., the top bantamweights avoided him. Around this time, he met A. L. Erlanger, of Klaw and Erlanger, a New York theatrical firm. Harris impressed Erlanger, who employed him as treasurer and theater manager until 1916.

Harris did not retire entirely from the ring. He tried unsuccessfully to land a fight with featherweight champion Abe Attell. After fighting a no-decision match with Barney ("Kid") Abel in 1905, and three no-decision bouts with Jack Goodman in 1906 and 1907, Harris, now fighting as a lightweight, defeated Harlem Tommy Murphy on a foul on June 3, 1907, and then retired.

Harris continued to box for fun at the City Athletic Club, where he gave instruction to future heavyweight champion Gene Tunney. He also sparred with financier J. Robinson Duff, who persuaded him to leave Broadway for Wall Street. Harris became a member of the New York Curb Exchange, later known as the American Stock Exchange. He continued there until his retirement.

PETE HERMAN

BANTAMWEIGHT

Right-handed; 5'2"; 105–125 lbs.
144 bouts, 9/30/1912 to 4/24/1922
Managers: Jerome Gargano, Doc Cutch, Sammy Goldman, Red Walsh
Bantamweight Champ 1917–20, 1921
Hall of Fame Induction: 1997
Born: 2/12/1896, New Orleans, LA
Named: Peter Gulotta
Died: 4/13/1973

One of the toughest competitors ever to hold the bantamweight title, Pete Herman was a fast, durable fighter with two-fisted punching power that was especially effective at close range.

Born Peter Gulotta, Herman went to work as a shoeshine boy in New Orleans at the age of twelve. He and his friend, Eddie Coulon, went to a gym to box during their lunch hours. When Coulon began fighting professionally, Herman decided to turn pro as well. In his first bout, at age sixteen, he fought to a draw with Coulon. He quickly became a formidable opponent for any bantamweight.

In 1914, Herman fought well in a no-decision, non-title bout with bantam champ Kid Williams. Less than two years later, he again faced Williams, this time with the title on the line. Under the terms of the contract, the champion had his choice of referee. Williams named his friend Billy Rocap. The fight went twenty rounds, a heated contest all the way, with much of the fighting conducted in close. According to most ringside observers, Herman had won, but Rocap gave the fight to Williams.

Herman fought Williams again on January 9, 1917. This time, Herman chose Rocap to officiate, convinced the referee would not risk his reputation by making another questionable decision. The battle raged for the full twenty rounds. Herman knocked Williams down twice. Rocap awarded the fight and the championship to Herman, who was just twenty years old. On April 27, 1917, Herman fought the other bantamweight who campaigned with the same last name. He engaged in a ten-round no-decision bout with "Pekin" Kid Herman.

For close to four years, Herman met a wide range of opponents, including Williams in a no-decision fourth match, but only defended the title once. In this period, Herman suffered an injury that would dramatically change his life. In a charity benefit match, his right eye was permanently damaged.

On December 22, 1920, Herman fought Joe Lynch in a title match in New York. His declining vision made worse by the thick tobacco smoke in the hall, Herman lost to Lynch. He

Herman (L) sends bantam champ Jimmy Wilde through the ropes in their London, January 13, 1921 non-title battle. The stunned Wilde failed to hear the bell to begin the 14th round. The referee finally called a halt to the bout after 17 rounds.

IN THE RING	WON 67	LOST 12	DRAWS 8	TB 144	KO 21	W 46	WF 0	D 8	KO'd 1	L 10	LF 1	ND 57

Date	Year	Opponent	Site	Result / Rounds		Title
SELECTED BOUTS						
Sep 30	1912	Eddie Coulon	New Orleans	D	6	—
Jun 30	1914	♛ Kid Williams★	New Orleans	ND-D	10	—
May 1	1915	Young Zulu Kid	New Orleans	D	10	—
Nov 6	1915	Young Zulu Kid	New Orleans	W	15	—
Nov 15	1915	Memphis Pal Moore	Memphis	L	8	—
Feb 7	1916	♛ Kid Williams★	New Orleans	D	20	For-World-B
Feb 28	1916	Lou Tendler★	Philadelphia	ND-L	6	—
Jan 9	1917	♛ Kid Williams★	New Orleans	W	20	Won-World-B
Feb 16	1917	Johnny Ertle	Milwaukee	ND-W	10	—
Apr 27	1917	Pekin Kid Herman	Peoria, IL	ND	10	—
May 14	1917	Johnny Coulon★	Racine, WI	TKO	3	—
Jun 13	1917	Kid Williams★	Philadelphia	ND-L	6	—
Nov 5	1917	Frankie Burns	New Orleans	W	20	Ret-World-B
May 4	1918	Jack Sharkey	Philadelphia	ND	6	—
Sep 6	1918	Young Zulu Kid	Jersey City, NJ	ND-W	8	—
Mar 24	1919	Memphis Pal Moore	Memphis	ND-L	8	—
May 23	1919	Johnny Ertle	Minneapolis	KO	5	—
Sep 1	1919	Joe Lynch	Waterbury, CT	ND-L	10	—
Sep 15	1919	Jack Sharkey	Detroit	ND-D	10	—
Nov 12	1919	Joe Lynch	Philadelphia	ND-W	6	—
Jan 7	1920	Johnny Ritchie	New Orleans	KO	8	—
Dec 22	1920	Joe Lynch	New York	L	15	Lost-World-B
Jan 13	1921	♛ Jimmy Wilde★	London	TKO	17	—
Jul 25	1921	♛ Joe Lynch	Brooklyn	W	15	Reg-World-B
Sep 23	1921	Johnny Buff	New York	L	15	Lost-World-B
Dec 9	1921	Packy O'Gatty	Brooklyn	KO	1	—
Apr 24	1922	Roy Moore	Boston	W	10	—

then went to England to face Hall of Famer Jimmy Wilde. Wilde balked at going into the ring because of a dispute over Herman's weight. The Prince of Wales, who was in attendance, went to Wilde's dressing room and persuaded him to compete. When the fight finally took place, Herman scored a TKO over the lighter Wilde in seventeen rounds. The Prince, later King Edward VII, became friendly with Herman and remained in contact with him over the years.

At Brooklyn's Ebbets Field, on July 25, 1921, with poor vision in both eyes, Herman used an effective body attack to decision Lynch and regain the title. He was able to hold it just two months before losing to Johnny Buff. In his last fight, against Roy Moore, Herman could not see his opponent and could only hit him when they clinched. Despite this handicap, Herman won the decision.

Herman retired at age 26. Shortly thereafter, he became totally blind. He opened a cafe, Pete Herman's, in the French Quarter in New Orleans and received a lifetime appointment to the Louisiana State Athletic Commission. Nat Fleischer, the founder of The Ring, ranked Herman as the second-greatest bantamweight of all time.

PETER JACKSON

HEAVYWEIGHT

Right-handed; 6'1½"; 192 lbs.

85 bouts, 1882 to 12/2/1899

Hall of Fame Induction: 1990

Born: 7/3/1861, St. Croix, West Indies

Died: 7/13/1901

Racial prejudice was the only thing that kept Peter Jackson from his chance to win the world heavyweight crown. A world-class fighter, Jackson was not always granted the kind of competition he deserved. Born in the Virgin Islands, Jackson moved with his family to Australia when he was six years old. When his parents returned to the Caribbean, Jackson stayed in his new homeland. He became an excellent swimmer and diver and found work on ships at the age of fourteen. As a young man, Jackson used his fists to help quell a mutiny, and the incident received attention in the Australian press. Larry Foley, who had also handled Young Griffo, sought Jackson out and started him on his professional career.

Jackson won the Australian heavyweight title in 1886 with a knockout of Tom Leeds in the 30th round. Having difficulty securing bouts in Australia and eager to prove his worth, Jackson travelled to the United States in 1888. However, most top fighters shunned him for racial or competitive reasons. John L. Sullivan, the heavyweight champion and the most famous American boxer, stated, "I will not fight a Negro. I never have, and I never shall." Although Sullivan had actually faced a black opponent previously, he would not change his stance regarding Jackson.

Jackson knocked out George Godfrey, another black fighter, and several white opponents who agreed to fight him as he travelled across the country. He then journeyed to England where he beat Jem Smith in

Jackson (L) outboxed Gus Lambert in Troy, NY on March 5, 1890. After four rounds, police called a halt to the bout, which is officially recorded as a "no-contest." Starting in 1892, Jackson virtually abandoned the ring for nearly six years, touring as an actor in Uncle Tom's Cabin and other plays.

IN THE RING	WON 45	LOST 4	DRAWS 5	TB 85	KO 30	W 12	WF 3	D 5	KO'd 3	L 1	LF 0	ND 31

Date	Year	Opponent	Site	Result / Rounds		Title
SELECTED BOUTS						
—	1882	Jack Hayes	Sydney	D	5	—
Jul 26	1884	Bill Farnan	Melbourne	KO'd	3	For-Australia-H
Oct 4	1884	Bill Farnan	Melbourne	D	6	—
Sep 25	1886	Tom Leeds	Sydney	KO	30	Won-Australia-H
Aug 24	1888	George Godfrey	San Francisco	KO	10	—
Dec 27	1888	Joe McAuliffe	San Francisco	KO	24	—
Apr 26	1889	Patsy Cardiff	San Francisco	W	10	—
May 1	1889	Shorty Kincaid	Virginia City, NV	W	2	—
Jul 11	1889	Sailor Brown	Chicago	KO	4	—
Jul 30	1889	Mile Lynch	Buffalo	KO	2	—
Aug 5	1889	Paddy Brennan	Buffalo	KO	1	—
Nov 11	1889	Jem Smith	London	WF	3	—
Dec 25	1889	Peter Maher	Dublin	KO	2	—
Mar 5	1890	Gus Lambert	Troy, NY	NC	4	—
Apr	1890	Dick Keating	Louisville, KY	KO	1	—
May 19	1890	Ed Smith	Chicago	W	5	—
Jul 23	1890	Tom Johnson	Maryville, CA	W	4	—
Oct 21	1890	Joe Goddard	Melbourne	D	3	—
May 21	1891	James J. Corbett★	San Francisco	D	61	—
Jan 12	1892	Al Fish	Chicago	W	2	—
Jan 12	1892	Jack Dalton	Chicago	KO	3	—
—	1892	Jem Smith	London	KO	2	Won-Brit Emp-H
May 30	1892	Frank Slavin	London	KO	10	Ret-Brit Emp-H
Mar 22	1898	James J. Jeffries★	San Francisco	KO'd	3	—
Aug 24	1899	Jim Jeffords	Vancouver, B.C.	KO'd	4	—
Dec 2	1899	Billy Warren	Melbourne	D	25	—

two rounds to claim the championship of the British Empire. Jackson dominated the fight and forced Smith to resort to wrestling to avoid a knockout.

Back in the U.S., Jackson found an adequate foe in future heavyweight champion James J. Corbett. In 1891, at the California Athletic Club in San Francisco, the two battled to a 61-round draw. Jackson displayed great boxing ability, although some observers believed that the 30-year-old fighter's punches were not the incredibly powerful weapons they had once been. Corbett later stated in his autobiography that Jackson could have beaten any heavyweight Corbett ever saw.

Over the next several years, Jackson fought when he could obtain a match, acted, and ran a boxing school in London. In 1898, an over-the-hill Jackson lost to future champion James J. Jeffries on a third-round knockout. Shortly thereafter, Jackson returned to Australia to fight the tuberculosis which ultimately killed him.

JOE JEANNETTE

H E A V Y W E I G H T

Right-handed; 5'10"; 185–205 lbs.

157 bouts, 11/11/1904 to
11/11/1919

Manager: Dan McKetrick

Hall of Fame Induction: 1997

Born: 8/26/1879, North Bergen, NJ

Named: Joseph Jennette

Died: 7/2/1958

Like Sam Langford, the fighter he most admired, Joe Jeannette was barred from fighting for the heavyweight championship not for lack of skill but because of the color of his skin. Racism, promoters' fear of riots, and economic considerastions made it nearly impossible for Black boxers to get bouts against top whites.

Born in New Jersey, Jeannette learned to fight in street brawls as a youth. On a dare, he became a professional fighter at the age of 25. Jeannette quickly moved into the first rank of black heavyweights. Within two years of turning pro, Jeannette had fought Jack Johnson seven times, with one win, one loss, one draw, and four no-decisions.

Because most of the white heavyweights of the day refused to face black fighters, black heavyweights were repeatedly matched against each other. Jeannette fought Langford fifteen times, resulting in a record of 3–6–2 with four no-decisions. He fought Sam McVey five times, with a record of 1–1–2 with one no-decision. Jeannette also fought multiple battles with Morris Harris (4), Black Bill (10), Battling Jim Johnson (9), and Hall of Famer Harry Wills (three no-decisions). Because the records for early black fighters are often incomplete or contradictory, it is quite possible that Jeannette actually faced these opponents many more times.

Jeannette's most famous fight occurred on April 17, 1909, when he met McVey in Paris. The pair had fought a lackluster bout there two months before. The dissatisfied crowd had showered the ring with programs and other debris, and rumors began to circulate that the two had treated the fight as a mere exhibition. Eager to dispel that notion, Jeannette and McVey agreed to fight to the finish with no round limit. The resulting battle was one of the greatest marathons in boxing history. McVey scored the first of his 27 knockdowns in the first round. In the sixteenth McVey countered a Jeannette uppercut with a right to the jaw that most likely would have finished Jeannette—had he not been saved by the bell. Jeannette went down in the next round, the 21st time in seventeen rounds that he had hit the canvas. Looking beaten after nineteen rounds, Jean-

Jeannette rests against the ropes as Englishman Ben Taylor receives the ten count in the 3rd round of their January 23, 1909 Paris bout.

IN THE RING	WON 79	LOST 9	DRAWS 6	TB 157	KO 66	W 8	WF 5	D 6	KO'd 2	L 7	LF 0	ND 62	NC 1

Date	Year	Opponent	Site	Result / Rounds		Title
SELECTED BOUTS						
Nov 11	1904	Morris Harris	Philadelphia	ND-L	6	—
May 9	1905	Jack Johnson★	Philadelphia	ND-L	6	—
Nov 25	1905	Jack Johnson★	Philadelphia	WF	2	—
Dec 2	1905	Jack Johnson★	Philadelphia	ND-L	6	—
Dec 25	1905	Sam Langford★	Lawrence, MA	TKO	8	—
Jan 16	1906	Jack Johnson★	New York	ND-L	3	—
Mar 14	1906	Jack Johnson★	Baltimore	L	15	—
Apr 5	1906	Sam Langford★	Chelsea, MA	L	15	—
Sep 20	1906	Jack Johnson★	Philadelphia	ND-D	6	—
Nov 26	1906	Jack Johnson★	Portland, ME	D	10	—
Jan 11	1907	Sam Langford★	Lawrence	D	12	—
Apr 15	1907	Sam McVey★	New York	ND-W	10	—
Mar 3	1908	Sam Langford★	Boston	D	12	—
Sep 1	1908	Sam Langford★	New York	ND-L	6	—
Feb 20	1909	Sam McVey★	Paris	L	20	—
Apr 17	1909	Sam McVey★	Paris	TKO	50	—
Sep 6	1910	Sam Langford★	Boston	L	15	—
Sep 5	1911	Sam Langford★	New York	ND-D	10	—
Jul 1	1913	Harry Wills★	New Orleans	ND	10	—
Dec 20	1913	Sam Langford★	Paris	L	20	—
Mar 21	1914	Georges Carpentier★	Paris	W	15	—
Jun 9	1914	Harry Wills★	New Orleans	ND-D	10	—
Apr 13	1915	Sam Langford★	Boston	W	12	—
May 12	1916	Sam Langford★	Syracuse, NY	KO'd	7	—
Sep 14	1917	Sam Langford★	Toledo, OH	ND-W	12	—
Oct 30	1919	Harry Wills★	Jersey City, NJ	ND-L	8	—
Nov 11	1919	Barley Madden	Bayonne, NJ	WF	4	—

nette miraculously revived and seized control of the fight. As the bout moved past the 40-round mark, Jeannette began to floor McVey with regularity, but still could not put him away. In the 42nd, Jeannette dropped McVey seven times. Finally, after 49 rounds, McVey could not continue. Despite having been knocked down 27 times, Jeannette had triumphed in this unbelievable test of endurance, courage, and boxing ability. This fight underscores Jeannette's indomitable will.

In one of his few bouts against a top-quality white opponent, Jeannette decisioned Hall of Famer Georges Carpentier in 1914 when the young European champ was only twenty. In later years, Jeannette lamented the fact that champion Jack Johnson refused to give him a title bout, saying, "Jack forgot about his old friends after he became champion and drew the color line against his own people."

Jeannette continued to fight until his retirement in 1919 at the age of 40. While existing records credit him with slightly over 150 fights, Jeannette believed that he had actually fought about 400 times. After leaving the ring, he worked as a referee, operated a gym, and ran a limousine rental company.

JAMES J. JEFFRIES
The Boilermaker

HEAVYWEIGHT

Right-handed; 6'2½"; 206–227 lbs.

21 bouts, 1896 to 7/4/1910

Manager: William A. Brady

Heavyweight Champ 1899–1905

Hall of Fame Induction: 1990

Born: 4/15/1875, Carroll, Ohio

Named: James Jackson Jeffries

Died: 3/3/1953

One of the finest heavyweights in history, James J. Jeffries retired undefeated but, six years later, was coaxed into an ill-fated comeback fight with Jack Johnson.

Jeffries moved with his family from Ohio to a Los Angeles-area farm at the age of seven. As a youth, he was a great athlete who distinguished himself in boxing, wrestling, and track. While working as a boilermaker and for a meat packing company, among other jobs, Jeffries boxed at the East Side Athletic Club. In his first professional fight, he knocked out Hank Griffin in the fourteenth round. Nineteen at the time, Jeffries waited until he was 21 to box professionally fulltime, honoring a promise to his parents.

Jeffries fought draws with Gus Ruhlin and Joe Choynski in 1897. The next year, he won five fights, including a knockout victory over Peter Jackson and a decision over Tom Sharkey, whom Jeffries would later call his toughest opponent. He also went to New York, where he agreed to fight twice in one night. He won a decision over Bob Armstrong, but broke his thumb and had to cancel the second bout. Jeffries was shaken by the crowd's boos and returned to California.

Jeffries then came under the direction of a new manager, William A. Brady, who was able to sign his man for a match with the world heavyweight champion, Bob Fitzsimmons, at the Coney Island Athletic Club. Jeffries embarked on an arduous training regimen for this bout. With the help of middleweight Tommy Ryan he devised a new fighting style which he intended to try out against the lanky Fitzsimmons. Jeffries fought in a crouch with his left arm extended and his face protected by his right forearm. He developed a terrific left hook, as well as a straight left he could throw out of the crouch, often at short range and with great effect.

In the championship

Author Jack London led the chorus that urged Jeffries (L) out of retirement to face Jack Johnson in Reno, NV on July 4, 1910.

	WON	LOST	DRAWS	TB	KO	W	WF	D	KO'd	L	LF	ND
IN THE RING	**18**	**1**	**2**	21	15	3	0	2	1	0	0	0

Date	Year	Opponent	Site	Result / Rounds		Title
SELECTED BOUTS						
—	1896	Hank Griffin	Los Angeles	KO	14	—
—	1896	Jim Barber	Los Angeles	KO	2	—
Jul 2	1896	Dan Long	San Francisco	KO	2	—
Apr 9	1897	T. Van Buskirk	San Francisco	KO	2	—
May 19	1897	Henry Baker	San Francisco	KO	9	—
Jul 17	1897	Gus Ruhlin	San Francisco	D	20	—
Nov 30	1897	Joe Choynski★	San Francisco	D	20	—
Feb 28	1898	Joe Goddard	Los Angeles	KO	4	—
Mar 22	1898	Peter Jackson★	San Francisco	KO	3	—
Apr 22	1898	Pete Everett	San Francisco	KO	3	—
May 6	1898	Tom Sharkey	San Francisco	W	20	—
Aug 5	1898	Bob Armstrong	New York	W	10	—
Jun 9	1899	♛ Bob Fitzsimmons★	Coney Island	KO	11	Won-World-H
Nov 3	1899	Tom Sharkey	Coney Island	W	25	Ret-World-H
Apr 6	1900	Jack Finnegan	Detroit	KO	1	Ret-World-H
May 11	1900	James J. Corbett★	Coney Island	KO	23	Ret-World-H
Nov 15	1901	Gus Ruhlin	San Francisco	TKO	5	Ret-World-H
Jul 25	1902	Bob Fitzsimmons★	San Francisco	KO	8	Ret-World-H
Aug 14	1903	James J. Corbett★	San Francisco	KO	10	Ret-World-H
Aug 26	1904	Jack Munroe	San Francisco	TKO	2	Ret-World-H
Jul 4	1910	♛ Jack Johnson★	Reno	KO'd	15	For-World-H

bout, Jeffries knocked Fitzsimmons down in the second round. Early in the fight, Fitzsimmons landed some hard punches, but Jeffries's blows were more effective. In the tenth, Jeffries knocked the champion down twice with powerful lefts. In the eleventh, Jeffries finished off Fitzsimmons with a left hook and a right uppercut.

The new champion then won a very tough 25-round decision over Sharkey before facing the former champion James J. Corbett. Jeffries had previously served as Corbett's sparring partner and welcomed the chance to best him in the ring. Corbett had the advantage in the first ten rounds and, after twenty rounds, still had a clear lead. But in the 23rd, Jeffries knocked Corbett out with a straight left and then a left hook to the jaw.

Jeffries defended his title four more times with four knockout victories before retiring. Included among his victims were Fitzsimmons, Corbett, and Ruhlin. After six years of retirement, at age 35, Jeffries returned to the ring in an attempt to wrest the championship from Jack Johnson. Though out of shape at the time he signed for the match, Jeffries brought himself into condition. Touted as a "Great White Hope," Jeffries was nevertheless no match for Johnson, who knocked him out in the fifteenth round.

In retirement, Jeffries owned a bar and a farm where he bred prize cattle, although a series of poor investments forced him to declare bankruptcy in the 1920s. He also performed in boxing exhibitions in vaudeville and acted in movies.

JACK JOHNSON
The Galveston Giant, Li'l Arthur

HEAVYWEIGHT

Right-handed; 6'¼"; 185–221 lbs.

123 bouts, 1897 to 5/15/1928

Managers: Morris Hart, Johnny Connors, Alec McLean, Sam Fitzpatrick, Abe Arends, George Little, Tom Flanagan, Sig Hart

Heavyweight Champion 1908–15

Hall of Fame Induction: 1990

Born: 3/31/1878, Galveston, TX

Named: John Arthur Johnson

Died: 6/10/1946

The first African-American heavyweight champion, Jack Johnson dared to crash through the color bar that had created two classes of boxers since the sport's beginnings. A gaudy, bold character who lived just as he wanted, Johnson enraged the defenders of white supremacy with his refusal to accept anything less than equality. He was beloved by blacks and some whites, but thoroughly hated and eventually conquered by those who saw him as a threat to America's divided society.

The son of a former slave, Johnson grew up poor in Galveston, Texas where at that time, blacks were forbidden to use the same sidewalks as whites. He got a little schooling, then went to work on the docks and elsewhere. Johnson honed his fighting skills in "battle royals," racist spectacles in which several black men

Johnson (R) and champion Tommy Burns met for the title in Rushcutter's Bay Arena, Sydney on December 26, 1908. After Burns was thoroughly battered, police stepped in and the referee declared Johnson the victor.

IN THE RING	WON **77**	LOST **13**	DRAWS **14**	TB 123	KO 48	W 26	WF 3	D 14	KO'd 7	L 5	LF 1	ND 19

Date	Year	Opponent	Site	Result / Rounds		Title

SELECTED BOUTS

Date	Year	Opponent	Site	Result / Rounds		Title
—	1897	Jim Rocks	Galveston, TX	KO	4	—
Feb 25	1901	Joe Choynski★	Galveston	KO'd	3	—
Nov 4	1901	Hank Griffin	Bakersfield, CA	L	20	—
Dec 27	1901	Hank Griffin	Oakland	D	15	—
Oct 31	1902	George Gardner	San Francisco	W	20	—
Feb 3	1903	Denver Ed Martin	Los Angeles	W	20	Won-Black-H
Feb 27	1903	Sam McVey★	Los Angeles	W	20	Ret-Black-H
Oct 27	1903	Sam McVey★	Los Angeles	W	20	Ret-Black-H
Apr 22	1904	Sam McVey★	San Francisco	KO	20	Ret-Black-H
Oct 18	1904	Denver Ed Martin	Los Angeles	KO	2	Ret-Black-H
Mar 28	1905	Marvin Hart	San Francisco	L	20	—
May 9	1905	Joe Jeannette★	Philadelphia	ND-W	6	—
Mar 14	1906	Joe Jeannette★	Baltimore	W	15	—
Apr 26	1906	Sam Langford★	Chelsea, MA	W	15	—
Jul 17	1907	Bob Fitzsimmons★	Philadelphia	KO	2	—
Nov 2	1907	Jim Flynn	San Francisco	KO	11	—
Dec 26	1908 ♛	Tommy Burns★	Sydney	TKO	14	Won-World-H
May 19	1909	Phila. Jack O'Brien★	Philadelphia	ND-D	6	—
Sep 9	1909	Al Kaufman	San Francisco	ND-W	10	Ret-World-H
Oct 16	1909	Stanley Ketchel★	Colma, CA	KO	12	Ret-World-H
Jul 4	1910	James J. Jeffries★	Reno	KO	15	Ret-World-H
Jul 4	1912	Jim Flynn	Las Vegas, NM	WD	9	Ret-World-H
Dec 19	1913	Jim Johnson	Paris	D	10	Ret-World-H
Jun 27	1914	Frank Moran	Paris	W	20	Ret-World-H
Apr 5	1915	Jess Willard	Havana	KO'd	26	Lost-World-H
Apr 23	1916	Arthur Craven	Barcelona, Spain	KO	1	—
Apr 3	1918	Blink McCloskey	Madrid	W	4	—
May 17	1920	George Roberts	Tijuana, Mexico	KO	3	—
Feb 22	1923	Homer Smith	Montreal	W	10	—
May 2	1926	Pat Lester	Nogales, Mexico	W	15	—
May 15	1928	Bill Hartwell	Kansas City, KS	KO'd	7	—

fought at once until the last man standing was declared the winner. White audiences then tossed coins to the victor. These crude free-for-alls were often the only venues available to black fighters, and only the very best emerged.

Johnson turned professional in 1897 with a knockout victory over Jim Rocks. West Coast champion Joe Choynski took Johnson down in 1901, then taught him ring tactics when both were jailed after police raided the fight. In 1903, Johnson won a twenty-round decision over Denver Ed Martin for the black heavyweight title, which he defended four times in the next two years. In 1905, he lost a decision to future heavyweight champion Marvin Hart. Two years later, Johnson scored a second-round knockout of former heavyweight champion Bob Fitzsimmons.

Even though he was an obvious contender for the crown, Johnson was repeat-

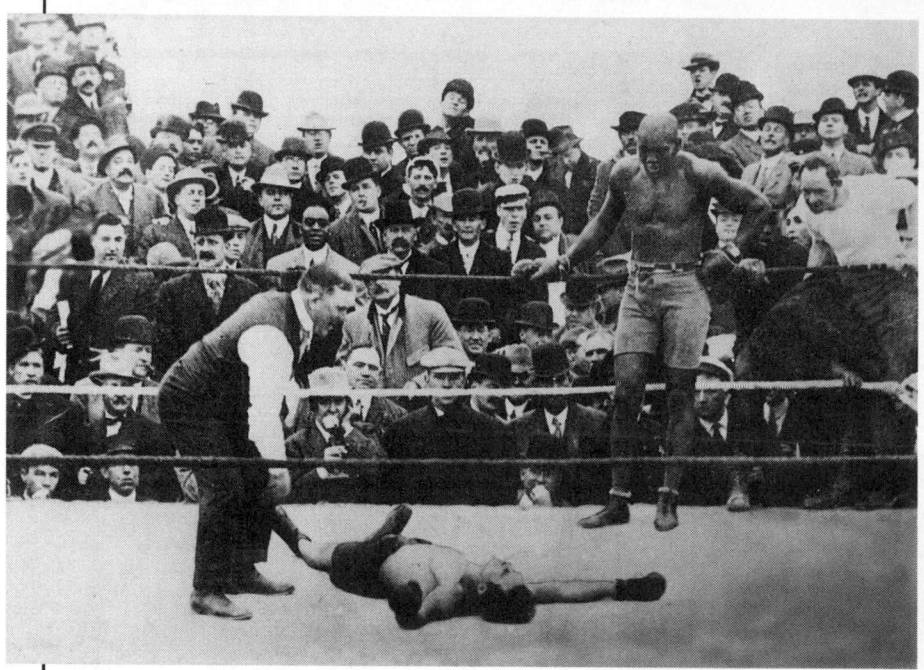

Outweighed by 35 pounds, Stanley Ketchel survived twelve rounds before succumbing to Johnson's knockout punch on October 16, 1909 in Colma, CA. Ketchel floored Johnson earlier in that same twelfth round.

edly refused a shot at the heavyweight title because of his race. He was finally given his chance in 1908 when he faced champion Tommy Burns in Australia in a stadium erected especially for the fight, in Rushcutter's Bay near Sydney. Johnson won on a technical knockout in the fourteenth round to become the first black heavyweight champion of the world.

White society was outraged, and Johnson rubbed salt in the wound by flaunting his fame and wealth. The search was already on for a "Great White Hope" to reclaim the crown. In 1909, middleweight champion Stanley Ketchel tried to topple Johnson. When Ketchell floored Johnson in the twelfth, the champion rose and knocked Ketchel out with one vicious punch. After the match, Johnson claimed that he had agreed to carry Ketchel and had become outraged when Ketchel knocked him down.

Finally, white hopes were pinned to former champion James J. Jeffries, who was persuaded to come out of retirement to face Johnson on July 4, 1910 in Reno, Nevada. Jeffries, who hadn't been in the ring for six years, trained hard for the fight. Movie cameras recorded the battle, which Johnson clearly dominated. Jeffries was totally defenseless by the fifteenth, when Johnson went for the easy knockout. Blacks in cities across the country burst into an extended celebration, starting race riots in which several people died. The films of Jeffries's demolition by the black champ were never shown.

Meanwhile, Johnson's bi-racial love life sent his enemies scurrying for revenge, and eventually he was convicted of transporting a minor across state lines for immoral purposes, even though the teenaged white woman was Johnson's wife. To avoid prison, Johnson fled to Canada and then Europe, where he twice defended his title in Paris.

In 1915, Johnson was persuaded to fight the huge 6'6" Jess Willard in a title bout in Havana. By then 37 years old, Johnson tired as the fight passed the twenty-round mark. In the 26th, Willard knocked Johnson out with a left to the body and a jab to the head. A promise from the fight's promoter to get Johnson safely back into the U.S. failed to materialize, and the fighter continued to live in exile. In 1920, Johnson surrendered to federal authorities and served eight months in Kansas's Leavenworth prison. After his release, he fought sporadically until 1928 when he retired at the age of 50. Johnson also acted in Hollywood movies, owned a Chicago nightclub, and fought bulls in Spain during his long career. He was working as an amusement arcade entertainer when he died in a car accident in 1946. Sports historian Arthur Ashe later called Johnson the most significant black athlete in history.

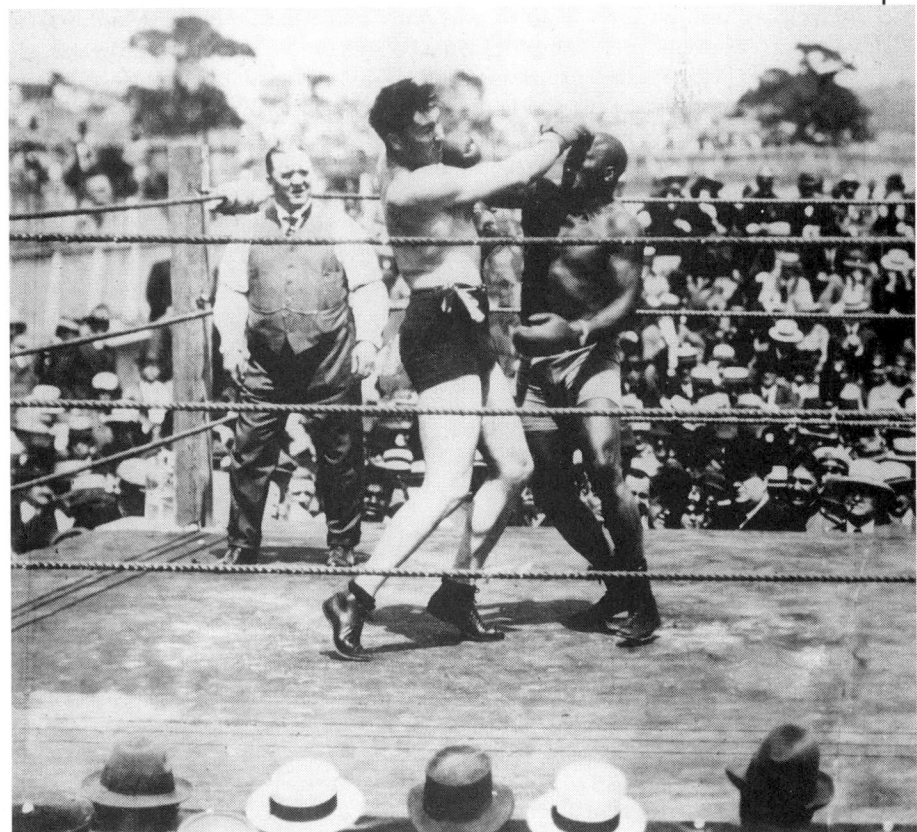

Jess Willard and Johnson exchange blows in the April 5, 1915 fight in Havana that resulted in the loss of Johnson's crown. Referee Jack Welch counted the supine, glassy-eyed Johnson out in the 26th round.

The Michigan Assassin

MIDDLEWEIGHT

Right-handed; 5'9"; 142–170 lbs.
64 bouts, 5/2/1904 to 6/10/1910
Managers: Joe O'Connor 1904–09,
Willus Britt 1909–10
Middleweight Champion 1908–10
Hall of Fame Induction: 1990
Born: 9/14/1886, Grand Rapids, MI
Named: Stanislaus Kiecal
Died: 10/15/1910

Stanley Ketchel is considered by some to be the greatest middleweight of all time. A natural fighter who was never formally trained, Ketchel propelled himself to fame and the middleweight championship in just six years. Sadly, his career ended when he was murdered at age 24. Ketchel's life often resembled a torrid movie script. Orphaned at fourteen, he ran away from his adoptive home and lived as a hobo, travelling through the Canadian and American West. In Butte, Montana, he worked as a bouncer and also took on all comers in fights at a local theatre. He fought his first recorded professional bout—a one-round knockout—in 1903.

Ketchel lost only twice in his first 42 matches, all fought in Montana. In 1907, he went to California, where he won matches with several well-respected fighters, and by 1908, he had achieved national prominence. His twentieth-round knockout of Jack (Twin) Sullivan earned him the vacant world middleweight title. In his first three months as champion, Ketchel decisioned Billy Papke, and knocked out Hugo Kelly and Joe Thomas. In the rematch with Papke, the challenger punched Ketchel in the head as the fighters were meeting in the center of the ring to shake hands. The referee merely chided Papke, and the fight commenced. Still dazed by the illegal punch, Ketchel never seized control of the fight and was knocked out in the twelfth round. Six weeks later, Ketchel fought Papke with a savage fury and knocked him out in the eleventh, becoming the first middleweight champion to regain a lost title.

In 1909, Ketchel fought some of the most memorable battles of his career. In a no-decision bout against light heavyweight champion Philadelphia Jack O'Brien, Ketchel absorbed a solid beating for six rounds, but came back to knock O'Brien down four times in the ninth and tenth rounds. The fight would have been a knockout if O'Brien hadn't been saved by the bell. In their rematch, Ketchel demolished O'Brien in three rounds.

World champion boxers visit Ketchel's grave—Jimmy Clabby (#2 from left), Johnny Kilbane (3), Johnny Coulon (4), and Luther McCarthy (5).

IN THE RING	WON 52	LOST 4	DRAWS 4	TB 64	KO 49	W 3	WF 0	D 4	KO'd 2	L 2	LF 0	ND 4

Date	Year	Opponent	Site	Result / Rounds		Title

SELECTED BOUTS

Date	Year	Opponent	Site	Result	Rounds	Title
May 2	1904	Kid Tracy	Butte, MT	KO	1	—
May 11	1904	Maurice Thompson	Butte	L	6	—
Oct 21	1904	Maurice Thompson	Butte	L	10	—
Mar 23	1907	Mike McClure	Redding, CA	KO	7	—
May 3	1907	Benny Hart	Marysville, CA	KO	8	—
May 23	1907	George Brown	Sacramento	KO	3	—
Sep 2	1907	Joe Thomas	Colma, CA	KO	32	—
Dec 12	1907	Joe Thomas	San Francisco	W	20	—
Feb 22	1908	♛ Mike (Twin) Sullivan	Colma	KO	1	—
May 9	1908	Jack (Twin) Sullivan	Colma	KO	20	Won-Vac World-M
Jun 4	1908	Billy Papke★	Milwaukee	W	10	Ret-World-M
Jul 31	1908	Hugo Kelly	San Francisco	KO	3	Ret-World-M
Aug 18	1908	Joe Thomas	San Francisco	KO	2	Ret-World-M
Sep 7	1908	Billy Papke★	Vernon, CA	TKO'd	12	Lost-World-M
Nov 26	1908	♛ Billy Papke★	Colma	KO	11	Reg-World-M
Mar 26	1909	♛ Phila. Jack O'Brien★	New York	ND-W	10	—
Jun 2	1909	Tony Caponi	Schenectady, NY	KO	4	—
Jun 9	1909	♛ Phila. Jack O'Brien★	Philadelphia	KO	3	—
Jul 5	1909	Billy Papke★	Colma	W	20	Ret-World-M
Oct 16	1909	♛ Jack Johnson★	Colma	KO'd	12	For-World-H
Apr 27	1910	Sam Langford★	Philadelphia	ND-W	6	—
Jun 10	1910	Jim Smith	New York	KO	5	—

Feeling bold after his strong performances, Ketchel agreed to challenge Jack Johnson for the heavyweight championship. The champ far outweighed Ketchel and was at the peak of his career. For the first six rounds, Ketchel stayed out of Johnson's way. In the seventh, Ketchel caught Johnson with a stinging left to the jaw. Ketchel went on the attack in the eighth and on into the tenth round. Meanwhile, Johnson landed enough punches to bloody Ketchel's face. The moment of truth came in the twelfth round, when Ketchel pounded a right into Johnson's jaw that threw the champ off balance. To the roaring of the crowd, Johnson briefly sat down on the canvas but rose up enraged and blasted Ketchel with a right to the jaw. Ketchel, his mouth a ruin, fell and stayed down for the count.

After the loss to Johnson, Ketchel continued to rack up victories. In 1910, determined to get another shot at the championship, he went to a ranch in Conway, Missouri to train. In this remote locale, the melodrama of Ketchel's life caught up with him. He died with a bullet in his lung, shot by a jealous hired hand who claimed the handsome prizefighter tried to steal his ladyfriend. The killer, Walter Dipley, was convicted of first-degree murder and served 23 years in prison.

Had he not died, Ketchel might have accomplished much more, perhaps even winning the heavyweight championship. At it was, he built a great record as middleweight champion and recorded 49 knockouts in 64 fights.

K CH C LA E
The Cuban Bon Bon

FEATHERWEIGHT

Right-handed; 5'6"; 120–132 lbs.
146 bouts, 2/10/1928 to 12/18/1938
Manager: Luis Gutierrez
Jr. Lightweight Champ 1931–33,
NY World Featherwt. Champ 1932–34
Hall of Fame Induction: 1991
Born: 1/6/1910, Cerro, Cuba
Named: Eligio Sardinias-Montalbo
Died: 8/8/1988

One of the most popular fighters in New York from the late 1920s to the late 1930s, Kid Chocolate dazzled fans with his speed and two-handed punching ability. Chocolate, a Cuban whose birth name was Eligio Sardinias-Montalbo, first started fighting as a newspaper boy in Havana, defending his sales turf. After he won an amateur boxing tournament sponsored by the newspaper *La Noche*, Chocolate came under the guidance of the newspaper's sports editor, Luis Gutierrez. Neither Gutierrez nor Chocolate knew a lot about boxing at that point and part of Chocolate's training was to watch films of famous fights.

Chocolate never lost a fight as an amateur and racked up 21 knockouts in 21 bouts as a pro before taking on New York in 1928 at the age of eighteen. Chocolate quickly made a name for himself, and his fights moved from small clubs to Madison Square Garden. By 1929, he was ranked the top featherweight contender in the annual ratings by *The Ring*. In 1930, Chocolate faced his stiffest challenge when he met Hall of Famer Jackie ("Kid") Berg at the Polo Grounds with 40,000 fans watching. Berg outweighed Chocolate by almost ten pounds. Chocolate's best round of the fight was the third, when he pounded Berg with jarring uppercuts to the head. As the fight went on, however, Berg's relentless attack tired Chocolate. Berg won a fairly close decision, handing Chocolate the first defeat of his career.

Later that same year, Chocolate lost decisions to Fidel LaBarba and featherweight champion Battling Battalino. Ringside observers said Chocolate appeared

Kid Chocolate, here posing in bag gloves, first saw pro boxing in films shown in Havana theatres.

IN THE RING	**WON** **131**	**LOST** **9**	**DRAWS** **6**		*TB* 146	*KO* 50	*W* 80	*WF* 1	*D* 6	*KO'd* 2	*L* 7	*LF* 0	*ND* 0

Date	Year		Opponent	Site	Result / Rounds		Title
SELECTED BOUTS							
Feb 10	1928		Kid Sotolongo	Havana	KO	5	—
Aug 25	1928		Nick Mercer	Brooklyn	KO	3	—
Sep 17	1928		Sammy Tisch	New York	W	10	—
May 22	1929	⑩	Fidel LaBarba★	New York	W	10	
Aug 29	1929		Al Singer	New York	W	12	—
Aug 7	1930	♔	Jackie ("Kid") Berg★	New York	L	10	—
Nov 3	1930	⑩	Fidel LaBarba★	New York	L	10	—
Dec 12	1930	♔	Battling Battalino	New York	L	15	For-World-FE
Jul 15	1931	♔	Benny Bass★	Philadelphia	TKO	7	Won-World-JL
Nov 20	1931	♔	Tony Canzoneri★	New York	L	15	For-World-L
Apr 10	1932		Davey Abad	Havana	W	15	Ret-World-JL
Jun 22	1932		Johnny Farr	Pittsburgh	W	10	—
Jul 18	1932	⑩	Jackie ("Kid") Berg★	Long Island City, NY	L	15	—
Aug 4	1932	⑩	Eddie Shea	Chicago	W	10	Ret-World-JL
Aug 10	1932		Johnny Farr	Cincinnati	W	10	—
Oct 4	1932		Johnny Farr	Detroit	W	10	—
Oct 13	1932	⑩	Lew Feldman	New York	TKO	12	Won-Vac NY World-FE
Dec 9	1932	⑩	Fidel LaBarba★	New York	W	15	Ret-NY World-FE
May 1	1933		Johnny Farr	Philadelphia	W	10	Ret-World-JL
May 19	1933	⑩	Seaman Watson	New York	W	15	Ret-NY World-FE
Jul 15	1933		Nic Bensa	Madrid	W	10	—
Nov 24	1933	⑩	Tony Canzoneri★	New York	KO'd	2	—
Dec 4	1933	⑩	Frankie Wallace	Cleveland	W	10	—
Dec 25	1933	⑩	Frankie Klick	Philadelphia	TKO'd	7	Lost-World-JL
Apr 16	1934	⑩	Frankie Wallace	San Francisco	W	10	—
Dec 18	1938		Nicky Jerome	Havana	D	10	—

slightly listless. Chocolate was back in top form by July of 1931, when he won his first title with a technical knockout over junior lightweight champion Benny Bass. The same year, Chocolate attempted to add the lightweight title to his holdings, but fell victim to the blistering attack of champion Tony Canzoneri, who won by decision.

In 1932, Chocolate lost a rematch with Berg, but claimed New York's world featherweight title when he TKO'd Lew Feldman at Madison Square Garden. Chocolate defended this particular title twice before relinquishing it, allegedly for failing to make the weight.

By 1933, Chocolate clearly was on the downside of his career. Canzoneri knocked him out in two rounds, and he lost his junior lightweight championship when Frankie Klick scored a technical knockout over him in seven. He continued to fight until 1938 against second-rate competition.

Although he was sometimes criticized for not training seriously enough for important bouts, Chocolate was recognized as a consummate ring artist: skillful, quick, and powerful. His ring earnings spent on New York night life and grand good times, Chocolate retired to Cuba, where he operated a gym.

FEATHERWEIGHT

Right-handed; 5'5"; 122–126 lbs.

142 bouts, 12/2/1907 to 6/2/1923

Manager: Jimmy Dunn

Featherweight Champion 1912–23

Hall of Fame Induction: 1995

Born: 4/18/1889, Cleveland, OH

Named: John Patrick Kilbane

Died: 5/31/1957

The man who ended the featherweight championship reign of Abe Attell, Johnny Kilbane spent much of his life in the public eye. Kilbane defended the featherweight title for eleven years and, in retirement, became a senator in the Ohio state legislature. A Cleveland native, Kilbane started fighting professionally in the Ohio area in 1907 with three victories, according to the somewhat spotty records of his early career.

Kilbane was a good scientific boxer who could also punch. He fought Attell three times, twice in championship bouts. In 1910, he lost a decision to Attell. Two years later, on a extremely hot night in Vernon, California, Kilbane took the crown from Attell with a twenty-round decision. Kilbane scored frequently with his left jab, while Attell resorted to heeling, butting, and elbowing. After the fight, Kilbane claimed that Attell had coated his back with chloroform in an attempt to daze his opponent. Attell said it was cooling cocoa butter and, for many years, bore ill will towards Kilbane for this charge, which Kilbane often repeated. Through five title bouts, including one in 1913, in which he fought Hall of Famer Johnny Dundee to a draw, Kilbane defended his crown until 1923.

In 1917, Kilbane attempted to move up in class and faced the lightweight champion Benny Leonard in a

On February 22, 1912 in Vernon, CA, Kilbane triumphs over Abe Attell, ending Attell's eleven-year grip on the featherweight crown.

	WON 51	LOST 4	DRAWS 7	TB 142	KO 25	W 25	WF 1	D 7	KO'd 2	L 2	LF 0	ND 78	NC 2
IN THE RING													

Date	Year	Opponent	Site	Result / Rounds		Title

SELECTED BOUTS

Date	Year	Opponent	Site	Result / Rounds		Title
Dec 2	1907	Tom Mangan	Cleveland	W	3	—
Jan 1	1908	Tommy Kilbane	Lorain, OH	W	3	—
Feb 10	1908	Tommy Kilbane	Cleveland	D	4	—
Nov 25	1908	Tommy Kilbane	Cleveland	W	25	—
Dec 31	1909	Tommy Kilbane	Canton, OH	W	15	—
Oct 24	1910	♛ Abe Attell ★	Kansas City	L	10	For-World-FE
Jan 31	1911	♛ Abe Attell ★	Cleveland	NC	4	—
May 6	1911	Joe Rivers	Vernon, CA	L	20	—
May 30	1911	Jimmy Walsh	Canton	ND-W	12	—
Sep 16	1911	Joe Rivers	Vernon, CA	KO	16	—
Dec 23	1911	Charley White	Cleveland	ND-W	12	—
Feb 22	1912	♛ Abe Attell ★	Vernon, CA	W	20	Won-World-FE
May 21	1912	Jimmy Walsh	Boston	D	12	Ret-World-FE
Sep 4	1912	Johnny Dundee ★	New York	ND-D	10	
Apr 29	1913	Johnny Dundee ★	Vernon, CA	D	20	Ret-World-FE
Jun 10	1913	Jimmy Fox	Oakland	TKO	6	Ret-World-FE
Sep 16	1913	Jimmy Walsh	Boston	W	12	Ret-World-FE
Mar 17	1915	Kid Williams ★	Philadelphia	ND-W	6	—
Apr 29	1915	Benny Leonard ★	New York	ND-W	10	
Sep 4	1916	George ("K.O.") Chaney	Cedar Point, OH	KO	3	Ret-World-FE
Mar 26	1917	Eddie Wallace	Bridgeport, CT	D	12	Ret-World-FE
May 1	1917	Freddie Welsh ★	New York	ND-W	10	—
Jul 25	1917	♛ Benny Leonard ★	Philadelphia	KO'd	3	—
Apr 21	1920	Alvie Miller	Lorain, OH	KO	7	Ret-World-FE
May 25	1921	Freddy Jacks	Cleveland	ND-W	10	—
Sep 17	1921	Danny Frush	Cleveland	KO	7	Ret-World-FE
Jun 2	1923	Eugene Criqui	New York	KO'd	6	Lost-World-FE

non-title fight. Kilbane could not handle the heavier Leonard and was knocked out in three rounds. World War I put Kilbane's professional boxing career on hold while he served as a boxing instructor at Camp Sherman.

In 1921, Kilbane again defended his title in Cleveland with a knockout of Danny Frush. In 1923, at age 34, he returned to the ring after almost two years of inactivity to face Eugene Criqui at New York's Polo Grounds. Reportedly, Kilbane received $75,000 to come back. At the time, Criqui was the European champion. Past his prime, Kilbane could not handle the punching power of Criqui, who had the champ sagging on the ropes and knocked him out in the sixth.

Never known for his knock-out power, Kilbane knew how to put forth just enough effort to win. If necessary, he could throw a mean punch, but for the most part, he was content to outbox an opponent and avoid getting hit.

In retirement, Kilbane refereed and operated a gym as well as serving in the state senate. He was clerk of the Cleveland Municipal Court when he died in 1957.

F L Y W E I G H T

Right-handed; 5'3"; 112–124 lbs.
95 bouts, 9/18/1924 to 2/13/33
Manager: George Blake
1924 Olympic Flyweight Gold
Medalist
Flyweight Champion 1927
Hall of Fame Induction: 1996
Born: 9/29/1905, New York, NY
Died: 10/3/1981

A championship boxer who gave up his title to attend Stanford University, Fidel LaBarba was one of the first fighters to parlay an Olympic gold medal into a professional career. A converted lefty, LaBarba was a great defensive fighter whose weaving style often kept him from getting hit. He was never knocked out.

LaBarba was the son of Italian immigrants. He grew up in Los Angeles where he became a paperboy, often using his fists to claim a busy street corner. At age fourteen, he came under the direction of manager George Blake. He fought successfully as an amateur, and in 1924, won top flyweight honors at the national Amateur Athletic Union tournament in Boston, then went on to Paris to win a gold medal at the Olympics. He turned pro later that year while still attending high school.

LaBarba's third professional fight was against Hall of Famer Jimmy McLarnin, a far more experienced fighter. When the referee gave McLarnin the decision in the four-round bout, Blake and LaBarba grabbed the judges' slips from the referee's hand. Two of the three judges had awarded LaBarba the fight, but the referee's decision stood. In two rematches, LaBarba held McLarnin to a four-round draw, but lost on points in his first ten-rounder.

In 1925, LaBarba challenged Frankie Genaro for the American flyweight title. LaBarba won a convincing ten-round decision. That year, *The Ring* placed LaBarba at the top of its flyweight rankings. In 1927, LaBarba faced Elky Clark for the world flyweight title, vacant since the death of Pancho Villa. LaBarba outboxed Clark in every round and knocked him down—but not out—five times to win the championship.

In 1928, never having defended his title, LaBarba announced he was leaving boxing to attend Stanford. A year later, he was back in the ring, this time campaigning as a bantamweight. LaBarba won all five of his fights that year. Over the next two years, LaBarba compiled a strong record. He split two decisions with Kid Choco-

LaBarba was undefeated when he retired as flyweight champion in 1927 to enter Stanford and study journalism. One year later he returned to the ring as a bantamweight.

Date	Year	Opponent	Site	Result / Rounds		Title

SELECTED BOUTS

Date	Year	Opponent	Site	Result	Rounds	Title
Sep 18	1924	Pat Pringle	Los Angeles	KO	1	—
Oct 28	1924	Jimmy McLarnin ★	Vernon, CA	L	4	—
Nov 11	1924	Jimmy McLarnin ★	Vernon	D	4	—
Jan 13	1925	Jimmy McLarnin ★	Vernon	L	10	—
Aug 22	1925	♛ Frankie Genaro ★	Los Angeles	W	10	Won-Amer-FL
Jul 8	1926	Georgie Rivers	Los Angeles	W	10	Ret-Amer -FL
Oct 5	1926	⑩ Newsboy Brown	Vernon	D	10	—
Jan 21	1927	⑩ Elky Clark	New York	W	12	Won-Vac World-FL
Feb 14	1927	⑩ Johnny Vacca	Boston	L	10	—
Mar 22	1927	⑩ Johnny Vacca	Boston	L	10	—
Jul 12	1927	Memphis Pal Moore	Chicago	W	10	—
Aug 23	1927	⑩ Johnny Vacca	Los Angeles	W	10	—
Nov 23	1928	Ray Ravini	San Francisco	KO	8	—
Jan 26	1929	Billy McAllister	Sydney	KO	9	—
Mar 16	1929	Willie Smith	Sydney	TKO	12	—
May 22	1929	⑩ Kid Chocolate ★	New York	L	10	—
Aug 30	1929	Jackie Mandell	Hollywood	TKO	8	—
Oct 12	1929	Kid Francis	Paris	L	12	—
Mar 4	1930	Santiago Zorilla	Los Angeles	W	10	—
Nov 3	1930	⑩ Kid Chocolate ★	New York	W	10	—
May 22	1931	♛ Battling Battalino	New York	L	15	For-World-FE
Jul 20	1931	Jackie Mandell	Stockton, CA	KO	1	—
Nov 27	1931	Santiago Zorilla	Hollywood	KO	6	—
Jan 1	1932	⑩ Baby Arizmendi	Mexico City	L	10	—
Mar 11	1932	⑩ Varias Milling	Hollywood	W	10	—
Apr 22	1932	⑩ Petey Sarron	Detroit	W	10	—
Jun 28	1932	Bobby Gray	San Jose, CA	KO	8	—
Dec 9	1932	♛ Kid Chocolate ★	New York	L	15	For-NY World-FE
Dec 29	1932	♛ Tommy Paul	Chicago	L	10	—
Jan 27	1933	⑩ Seaman Watson	New York	L	12	—
Feb 13	1933	Mose Butch	Pittsburgh	W	10	—

late, then in 1931, moved up to featherweight to challenge Battling Battalino for the world featherweight title. Battalino took the decision in fifteen hard-fought rounds.

In 1932, while training for a challenge to Kid Chocolate for the New York featherweight title, LaBarba seriously injured his eye. He fought Chocolate anyway, but, hampered by obscured vision, narrowly lost the decision. LaBarba fought three more times, losing twice, before retiring from the ring. Later, his injured eye was removed.

LaBarba returned to Stanford, where he earned a degree in journalism. He worked as a sportswriter before entering the army in World War II. He later worked in public relations, and was a screenwriter and technical advisor for boxing movies, until a series of heart attacks forced his retirement. La Barba died in 1981 in Los Angeles.

SAM LANGFORD
The Boston Tar Baby

HEAVYWEIGHT

Right-handed; 5'8"; 139–204 lbs.
291 bouts, 4/11/1902 to 8/2/1926
Managers: Joe Woodman
Hall of Fame Induction: 1990
Born: 3/4/1883, Weymouth, Nova Scotia, Canada
Named: Samuel E. Langford
Died: 1/12/1956

One of many top black boxers denied a chance to fight for a championship largely because of racial discrimination, Sam Langford took on every fighter he could, from lightweight to heavyweight, in his 24-year career. He combined great punching power and agility with intelligence and courage. Those who agreed to face Langford often considered him so dangerous they would request assurances that he be merciful in the ring. Because the pool of his potential opponents was so limited, Langford at times held back in hopes of a rematch.

Born in Canada, Langford began his professional boxing career in 1902 at the age of nineteen with a knockout victory over Jack McVicker in Boston. Quickly rising to prominence, Langford defeated Joe Gans in 1903. The next year, he fought to a draw with Joe Walcott. In 1906, though he was outweighed by at least twenty pounds, Langford faced the future heavyweight champion of the world, Jack Johnson. Langford lost the fifteen-round decision and never really had Johnson in trouble although, years later, exaggerated accounts circulated that Langford had nearly beaten Johnson. Once he was champion, Johnson refused to give Langford a title shot.

In 1910, Langford fought a very tough, six-round no-decision bout against the aggressive middleweight champion, Stanley Ketchel. Langford scored well in the early rounds, but Ketchel took control towards the end of the fight. Newspaper accounts generally awarded the decision to Ketchel, although the verdict could have gone either way. Langford was never given

Langford finishes Ian Hague in four rounds on May 24, 1909 in London. Some of the best boxers spurned Langford's challenges.

IN THE RING	WON 167	LOST 38	DRAWS 37	TB 293	KO 117	W 48	WF 2	D 37	KO'd 9	L 29	LF 0	ND 48	NC 3

Date	Year	Opponent	Site	Result / Rounds		Title
SELECTED BOUTS						
Apr 11	1902	Jack McVicker	Boston	KO	6	—
Dec 8	1903	♛ Joe Gans★	Boston	W	15	—
Sep 5	1904	Joe Walcott (Barbados)★	Manchester, NH	D	15	—
Apr 5	1906	Joe Jeannette★	Chelsea, MA	W	15	—
Apr 26	1906	Jack Johnson★	Chelsea	L	15	—
Jan 11	1907	Joe Jeannette★	Lawrence, MA	D	12	—
Dec 21	1908	Jim Flynn	San Francisco	KO	1	—
Apr 27	1910	♛ Stanley Ketchel★	Philadelphia	ND-L	6	—
Sep 6	1910	Joe Jeannette★	Boston	W	15	—
Aug 15	1911	♛ Phila. Jack O'Brien★	New York	KO	5	—
Apr 8	1912	Sam McVey★	Sydney	W	20	—
Dec 20	1913	Joe Jeannette★	Paris	W	20	—
May 1	1914	Harry Wills★	New Orleans	L	10	—
Oct 1	1914	Joe Jeannette★	New York	ND-W	10	—
Nov 26	1914	Harry Wills★	Los Angeles	KO	14	—
Apr 13	1915	Joe Jeannette★	Boston	L	12	—
Jan 3	1916	Harry Wills★	New Orleans	L	20	—
Feb 11	1916	Harry Wills★	New Orleans	KO	19	—
Apr 7	1916	Sam McVey★	Syracuse, NY	ND-W	10	—
Apr 25	1916	Harry Wills★	St. Louis	L	8	—
May 12	1916	Joe Jeannette★	Syracuse, NY	KO	7	—
Apr 14	1918	Harry Wills★	Panama City	KO'd	6	—
Jul 4	1919	Harry Wills★	St. Louis	L	8	—
Sep 30	1919	Harry Wills★	Syracuse, NY	ND-L	10	—
Apr 19	1920	Harry Wills★	Denver	L	15	—
Aug 14	1920	Sam McVey★	East Chicago, IN	ND-D	10	—
Jan 17	1922	Harry Wills★	Portland	L	10	—
Jun 5	1922	Tiger Flowers★	Atlanta	KO	2	—
Aug 2	1926	Brad Simmons	Drumright, OK	TKO'd	1	—

an opportunity to fight for Ketchel's title. In 1911, Langford made short work of former light heavyweight champion Philadelphia Jack O'Brien with a fifth-round knockout.

Because of his difficulty in finding matches, Langford often fought the same opponents—especially other black fighters in a similar predicament—over and over. Langford and Harry Wills tangled eighteen times. Wills knocked Langford out twice and generally had the better of the series, although it must be noted that the first meeting occurred when Langford was 31 years old. Langford had more than ten fights each against Sam McVey, Joe Jeannette, Jim Barry, Jeff Clarke, and Bill Tate.

After almost three hundred recorded bouts, Langford retired at the age of 43. In his last years in the ring, he was troubled by eye problems which eventually resulted in blindness. When he retired at last, he struggled to live comfortably until a sportswriters' fund for his care was established.

GEORGE ("KID") LAVIGNE
The Saginaw Kid

LIGHTWEIGHT

Right-handed; 5'3½"; 128–140 lbs.
56 bouts, 9/7/1886 to 12/25/1909
Manager: Sam Fitzpatrick
Lightweight Champion 1896–99
Hall of Fame Induction: 1998
Born: 12/6/1869, Bay City, Michigan
Named: George Henry Lavigne
(luh VEEN)
Died: 3/9/1928

John L. Sullivan said of George ("Kid") Lavigne, "Of all the fighters of the present day, Kid Lavigne is the one I most admire. He is the grandest little man of our time." At his peak the slim, fair-haired Lavigne displayed tremendous stamina, heart, and punching power.

Lavigne was born in Bay City, Michigan to French-Canadian parents. He turned professional in Saginaw in 1886 with a one-round knockout at age seventeen. In 1887, Lavigne took on the far more experienced George Siddons. The pair battled for 77 rounds in Saginaw before the fight was called a draw. They fought to a 55-round draw in the rematch.

After continued success in Michigan, Lavigne traveled to California. In 1894, he fought to a draw with master stylist Young Griffo. Later that year Lavigne administered such a beating to Andy Bowen, a fighter of some renown, that Bowen died after the fight.

Another draw with Griffo set the stage for Lavigne's greatest fight ever, against Joe Walcott on December 2, 1895 in Maspeth, New York. Under the terms of a special advance agreement, Walcott had to knock Lavigne out in fifteen rounds or less in order to win. In one of the most grueling fights in boxing history, Walcott attacked Lavigne relentlessly. Lavigne, an ear torn, one eye closed, and his mouth bloody, but showing an incredible will to win, took control in the fourteenth. By the close of the fifteenth, the great Walcott refused to quit but clearly had nothing left. Lavigne was awarded the victory, although many believed the brutal battle should have ended in a draw.

Lavigne then journeyed to England to challenge Dick Burge in a twenty-round bout for the vacant world lightweight title. British boxing fans were amazed that the angelic-looking, boyish man who stood only 5'3" was the ferocious Kid Lavigne. Although Burge was the larger fighter, at the end of the sixteenth he had

Lavigne (C) trained in London prior to his June 1, 1896 fight with Dick Burge. A victory gave Lavigne the vacant world lightweight championship. Here, he is flanked by Sam Fitzpatrick (L), his manager and Michael ("Dad") Butler (R), his trainer.

IN THE RING	WON 35	LOST 6	DRAWS 10	TB 56	KO 19	W 16	WF 0	D 10	KO'd 4	L 2	LF 0	ND 5	NC 0

Date	Year	Opponent	Site	Result / Rounds		Title
SELECTED BOUTS						
Sep 7	1886	Morris McNally	Saginaw, MI	KO	1	—
Mar 1	1887	George Siddons	Saginaw	D	77	—
Apr 26	1887	George Siddons	Grand Rapids, MI	D	55	—
Nov 20	1891	Joe Soto	San Francisco	W	30	—
Aug 10	1892	Jim Burge	San Francisco	D	50	—
Feb 10	1894	Young Griffo★	New York	D	8	—
Oct 12	1895	Young Griffo★	Maspeth, NY	D	20	—
Dec 2	1895	Joe Walcott★	Maspeth	W	15	—
Jun 1	1896	Dick Burge	London	KO	17	Won-Vac-World-L
Oct 27	1896	Jack Everhardt	New York	TKO	24	Ret-World-L
Feb 8	1897	Kid McPartland	New York	W	25	Ret-World-L
Apr 30	1897	Eddie Connolly	New York	TKO	11	Ret-World-L
Oct 29	1897	Joe Walcott★	San Francisco	TKO	12	Ret-World-L
Mar 17	1898	Jack Daly	Cleveland	D	20	Ret-World-L
Apr 11	1898	Jack Daly	Philadelphia	ND	6	—
Sep 28	1898	Frank Erne	Coney Island	D	20	Ret-World-L
Nov 25	1898	Tom Tracy	San Francisco	W	20	—
Mar 10	1899	♛ Mysterious Billy Smith	San Francisco	TKO'd	14	For-World-W
Apr 25	1899	Andy Davy	Berlin, NH	D	10	—
Jul 3	1899	Frank Erne	Buffalo	L	20	Lost-World-L
May 25	1902	Jimmy Britt	San Francisco	KO'd	8	—
Dec 25	1909	Dick Nelson	Detroit	L	6	—

to be helped to his corner after Lavigne landed a savage right hook. In the seventeenth, Lavigne fired a right to the jaw which knocked Burge out and gave Lavigne the championship.

Returning home, Lavigne won his first six title defenses, but many speculated that his disdain for training and excessive consumption of alcohol were taking their toll. His trainer, Biddy Bishop, once said, "Keeping Lavigne sober between fights was a tremendous achievement, and it is with great pride that I look back at the masterpiece of my career in training, keeping the Kid away from the bottle for eleven whole days." On March 10, 1899, Lavigne attempted to add the welterweight title to his list of honors when he faced Mysterious Billy Smith in San Francisco. Lavigne had trained diligently for this fight, and the press marveled at his physical condition. However, Smith's rights to Lavigne's left side fractured a rib, and in the fourteenth another right staggered Lavigne, who fell against the ropes. Five more rights to the jaw rendered him helpless. Lavigne's brother rushed into the ring claiming foul, but referee Jim McDonald stopped the fight and declared Smith the winner.

Lavigne lost the lightweight title to Frank Erne in 1899. In his next fight, Lavigne was knocked out by George McFadden. Lavigne fought very little over the next ten years before officially retiring in 1909. Outside the ring he held a variety of odd jobs until becoming a night watchman at the Ford Motor Company plant in Detroit in the 1920s. He died March 9, 1928.

BENNY LEONARD
The Ghetto Wizard

LIGHTWEIGHT

Right-handed; 5'5"; 123–153 lbs.

212 bouts, 1911 to 10/7/1932

Managers: Buck Areton 1911–14, Louis Wallach 1914, Billy Gibson 1914–25, Jack Kearns and Joey Leonard 1931–32

Lightweight Champion 1917–23

Hall of Fame Induction: 1990

Born: 4/7/1896, New York, NY

Named: Benjamin Leiner

Died: 4/18/1947

Perhaps the greatest lightweight of all time, Benny Leonard possessed superb boxing skills as well as potent punching power. He fought over two hundred times and suffered only four knockouts: three early in his career and the fourth in his final fight. Born on the East Side of New York, Leonard learned to fight in neighborhood battles and turned pro in 1911 at just fifteen years of age. In his inaugural bout he was knocked out in the third round.

By 1915, Leonard was working his way to the top of the lightweight ranks. A scientific boxer whose poise in the ring led observers to say fighting scarcely even mussed his hair, Leonard fought a series of no-decision bouts with Hall of Famer Johnny Dundee. He also performed well in no-decision matches with Hall of Famer Johnny Kilbane and lightweight champion Freddie Welsh. In 1917, Leonard challenged Welsh for the title. He skillfully hammered away at Welsh, knocking him out in the ninth round.

Leonard held the lightweight title for six years. In his first defense, he knocked out Kilbane, then featherweight champ, in three rounds. Leonard also successfully held several other challengers at bay. In 1922, Leonard set his sights on the welterweight crown and challenged champion Jack Britton. In a well-attended fight at

Leonard, sporting monogrammed trunks, squares off with Richie Mitchell. After trading knockdowns, a shaken Leonard ended it with a sixth-round TKO.

IN THE RING	WON 85	LOST 5	DRAWS 1	TB 212	KO 69	W 15	WF 1	D 1	KO'd 4	L 0	LF 1	ND 121

Date	Year	Opponent	Site	Result / Rounds	Title

SELECTED BOUTS

Date	Year	Opponent	Site	Result / Rounds		Title
—	1911	Mickey Finnegan	New York	TKO'd	3	—
Nov 2	1912	Special Delivery Hirsch	New York	ND-L	10	—
Feb 18	1914	Irish Patsy Cline	New York	ND-W	10	—
Mar 2	1915	Johnny Dundee★	New York	ND-L	10	—
Apr 29	1915	♛ Johnny Kilbane★	New York	ND-L	10	—
Mar 8	1916	Johnny Dundee★	New York	ND-W	15	—
Mar 31	1916	♛ Freddie Welsh★	New York	ND-W	10	—
Jun 12	1916	Johnny Dundee★	New York	ND-L	10	—
Jul 28	1916	♛ Freddie Welsh★	Brooklyn	ND-L	10	—
May 28	1917	♛ Freddie Welsh★	New York	TKO	9	Won-World-L
Jul 25	1917	Johnny Kilbane★	Philadelphia	TKO	3	Ret-World-L
Oct 19	1917	Jack Britton★	New York	ND-W	10	—
Jun 25	1918	Jack Britton★	Philadelphia	ND-W	6	—
Sep 23	1918	♛ Ted ("Kid") Lewis★	Newark	ND-L	8	—
Jan 20	1919	Johnny Dundee★	Newark	ND-W	8	—
Jun 16	1919	Johnny Dundee★	Philadelphia	ND-W	6	—
Sep 4	1919	Soldier Bartfield	Philadelphia	ND-W	6	—
Feb 9	1920	Johnny Dundee★	Jersey City	ND-W	8	—
Jul 5	1920	Charlie White	Benton Harbor, MI	KO	9	Ret-World-L
Nov 26	1920	Joe Welling	New York	TKO	14	Ret-World-L
Jan 14	1921	Richie Mitchell	New York	TKO	6	Ret-World-L
Feb 10	1922	Rocky Kansas	New York	W	15	Ret-World-L
Jun 26	1922	♛ Jack Britton★	New York	LF	13	For-World-W
Jul 27	1922	Lew Tendler★	Jersey City	ND-W	12	—
Jul 23	1923	Lew Tendler★	New York	W	15	Ret-World-L
Aug 1	1924	Pal Moran	Cleveland	ND-W	10	—
Oct 6	1931	Pat Silvers	Long Island City, NY	KO	2	—
Nov 23	1931	Buster Brown	Baltimore	W	10	—
Apr 11	1932	Buster Brown	New York	W	10	—
May 16	1932	Marty Goldman	Newark	KO	2	—
Oct 7	1932	⑩ Jimmy McLarnin★	New York	TKO'd	6	—

New York's Velodrome, Leonard knocked Britton down in the thirteenth round, then in an uncharacteristic move, hit Britton again during the referee's count. Britton was given the win because of Leonard's foul. Leonard fought left-hander Lew Tendler twice. A no-decision twelve-rounder in Jersey City was very close and earned Tendler the right to try for the title. The two met in 1923 in Yankee Stadium with nearly 60,000 fans looking on. Leonard outboxed his closely matched rival to win in fifteen rounds.

Leonard retired in 1925, but hard times brought him back to the ring in 1931. He won the first nineteen fights of his comeback before Jimmy McLarnin knocked him out in six rounds. Leonard then retired for good. In 1947, he died of a heart attack in the ring at St. Nicholas Arena in New York while refereeing a match.

LIGHT HEAVYWEIGHT

Right-handed; 5'11"; 162–199½ lbs.

289 bouts, 1909 to 1/15/1929

Managers: Fred Douglas 1910–13, Dan Morgan 1913–22, Al Lippe 1926–29

World Light Heavyweight Champ 1916–20

Hall of Fame Induction: 2000

Born: 6/10/1891, Philadelphia, PA

Named: Barney Lebrowitz

Also Fought as: Barney Williams

Died: 2/12/1949

Battling Levinsky—never reluctant to enter the ring—fought at least 289 times. While the exact total is unknown and some fights remain unrecorded, his bouts probably exceed 300.

Levinsky began fighting as Barney Williams at the age of seventeen or eighteen. His career took off under the managerial aegis of Hall of Famer Dumb Dan Morgan. According to Morgan, Levinsky appeared at Morgan's New York office and said, "I think I'm a fighter. I want a chance." He got it as a substitute heavyweight on that night's card at St. Nicholas Arena, pitted against the 40-pound heavier Porky Flynn in a no-decision bout. At the close of the fight, Morgan had ring announcer Joe Humphreys proclaim, "Morgan's new find is now named 'Battling Levinksy,' and he defies any Irishman in the country to lick him."

Levinsky was a supreme defensive fighter, who scored enough points to win "newspaper decisions" in the no-decision bouts that comprised more than half his career totals. No knockout artist, he stopped his opponent short of the distance in less than twelve percent of his fights.

Dan Morgan touted Levinsky's durability with a tale of New Year's Day 1915. Levinsky supposedly fought a ten-round, no-decision bout with Bartley Madden in the morning in Brooklyn, followed by another ten-round, no-decision in the afternoon with Soldier Kearns in Manhattan, and then by a train ride to Waterbury, Connecticut, where Levinsky faced Gunboat Smith in a twelve-round, no-decision contest to close the day. Only the last fight actually happened!

Though he often fought heavyweights, Levinsky was not one of them,

Gentleman Jim Corbett (L) won his world title 24 years before Battling Levinsky (R) took the light-heavyweight crown.

IN THE RING	WON 77	LOST 19	DRAWS 15	TB 289	KO 34	W 42	WF 1	D 15	KO'd 3	L 13	LF 3	ND NC 178 0

Date	Year		Opponent	Site	Result / Rounds		Title
SELECTED BOUTS							
	1909		Paddy Burns	Pottsville, PA	ND	6	—
Oct 23	1911		Jack Dillon★	Philadelphia	ND-L	6	—
Apr 17	1913		Jack Dillon★	Rochester, NY	ND-D	10	—
Jul 20	1913		Dan ("Porky") Flynn	New York	ND-D	10	—
Jan 27	1914		Alfred ("Soldier") Kearns	New York	ND-D	10	—
Apr 14	1914		Jack Dillon★	Butte, MT	L	12	For-Vac World-LH
May 29	1914	♛	Jack Dillon★	Indianapolis, IN	ND-L	10	—
Feb 8	1916	♛	Jack Dillon★	Brooklyn	ND-D	10	—
Apr 25	1916	♛	Jack Dillon★	Kansas City, MO	L	15	For-World-LH
Jul 13	1916	♛	Jack Dillon★	Baltimore	W	10	—
Sep 12	1916	♛	Jack Dillon★	Memphis, TN	D	8	—
Oct 24	1916	♛	Jack Dillon★	Boston	W	12	Won-World-LH
Mar 23	1917		Tommy Gibbons★	St. Paul	ND-L	10	—
Sep 6	1917		Harry Greb★	Pittsburgh	ND-L	10	—
Nov 6	1918		Jack Dempsey★	Philadelphia	KO'd	3	—
Feb 17	1919		Harry Greb★	Buffalo	ND-L	10	—
Jul 14	1919		Harry Greb★	Philadelphia	ND-L	6	—
Oct 12	1920		Georges Carpentier★	Jersey City, NJ	KO'd	4	Lost-World-LH
Jan 13	1922		Gene Tunney★	New York	L	12	For-USA-LH
Nov 11	1926		Young Stribling★	Des Moines, IA	ND-L	10	—
Jan 15	1929		Herman Weiner	Hagerstown, MD	KO'd	1	—
Oct 21	1930		Joe Sims	Brooklyn	KO	3	—

and he and Morgan set their sights on the light heavyweight title held by Hall of Famer Jack Dillon. On April 25, 1916, in Kansas City, Dillon won the fifteen-round decision. When Dillon put the title on the line again on October 24 in Boston, the pair's ninth meeting, most ring pundits did not give Levinsky much of a chance, nor did Dillon. Yet Levinsky handled Dillon's pressing attack and scored enough with a left jab and left hook to win the twelve-round match.

Levinsky was in no hurry to defend his title and spent the next four years fighting non-title bouts, including six no-decisions against Harry Greb and a three-round knockout loss to a young Jack Dempsey. On October 12, 1920, he finally put the title up for grabs against Georges Carpentier in Jersey City, and was knocked out in four rounds. In 1922, Levinsky faced Gene Tunney for the American light heavyweight title, and lost a twelve-round decision in a rather lackluster fight. Actually, few of Levinsky's fights were ever exciting. Sportswriter Damon Runyon noted, "If you have seen one of Levinsky's fights, you have seen them all. They are of a piece. There is rarely any prospect of the unexpected occurring in his battles. He will be there at the finish, but so will the other fellow."

After the loss to Tunney, Levinsky retired, but was lured back to the ring four years later. Following a first-round knockout loss to Herman Weiner on January 15, 1929, Levinsky again retired. Nearly two years later, he fought one more bout.

JO N HENRY LEWI

LIGHT HEAVYWEIGHT

Right-handed; 5'11"; 140–181 lbs.

117 bouts, 1928 to 1/25/1939

Managers: Ernie Lira, Larry White, Frank Schuler, Gus Greenlee

Light Heavyweight Champ 1935–39

Hall of Fame Induction: 1994

Born: 5/1/1914, Los Angeles, CA

Died: 4/18/1974

John Henry Lewis was the first black American to win the light heavyweight championship, a title he held for four years. And as with many light heavyweights, Lewis often fought larger heavyweights to gain more attention and bigger purses. Lewis was not the first fighter in his family. His great-great uncle was Tom Molineaux, an early bare knuckle heavyweight who travelled to England to challenge for the title.

Born in California, Lewis moved to Arizona when his father got a job as trainer for the University of Arizona athletic teams. Lewis's father also opened a gym in Phoenix. At a very early age, Lewis and his brother Christy were put to work at the gym, fighting "midget boxing" exhibitions. Later, the Lewises toured the Southwest in such exhibitions.

Given this early training, Lewis was well-prepared to turn professional at the age of fourteen as a welterweight. Three years later Lewis won a decision over Lloyd Phelps to take what was considered to be the Arizona middleweight championship. In 1932, Lewis

Lewis (L) traps Len Harvey in the corner during a successful title defense in Wembley Stadium on November 9, 1936.

IN THE RING	WON 103	LOST 8	DRAWS 6	TB 117	KO 60	W 43	WF 0	D 6	KO'd 1	L 7	LF 0	ND 0

Date	Year		Opponent	Site	Result / Rounds		Title
SELECTED BOUTS							
—	1928		Buster Grant	Phoenix	W	4	—
Sep 21	1932		Jim Braddock★	San Francisco	W	10	—
Oct 26	1932		Lou Scozza	San Francisco	W	10	—
Nov 16	1932	♛	Maxie Rosenbloom★	San Francisco	L	10	—
Jul 10	1933	♛	Maxie Rosenbloom★	San Francisco	W	10	—
Jul 31	1933	♛	Maxie Rosenbloom★	San Francisco	W	10	—
Nov 16	1934		Jim Braddock★	New York	L	10	—
Mar 13	1935		Emilio Martinez	Denver	W	10	—
Apr 12	1935	♛	Bob Olin	San Francisco	W	10	—
Jul 17	1935	⑩	Maxie Rosenbloom★	Oakland	L	10	—
Jul 24	1935		Abe Feldman	New York	L	10	—
Oct 31	1935	♛	Bob Olin	St. Louis	W	15	Won-World-LH
Nov 29	1935	⑩	Maxie Rosenbloom★	San Francisco	L	10	—
Jan 29	1936		Emilio Martinez	Denver	L	10	—
Mar 13	1936	⑩	Jock McAvoy	New York	W	15	Ret-World-LH
Nov 9	1936		Len Harvey	London	W	15	Ret-World-LH
May 4	1937		Emilio Martinez	St. Louis	W	10	—
Jun 3	1937		Bob Olin	St. Louis	TKO	8	Ret-World-LH
Apr 25	1938		Emilio Martinez	Minneapolis	KO	4	Ret-World-LH
Oct 28	1938		Al Gainer	New Haven, CT	W	15	Ret-World-LH
Jan 25	1939	♛	Joe Louis★	New York	KO'd	1	For-World-H

received wide attention when he decisioned future heavyweight champion James J. Braddock in San Francisco and lost a close decision in a non-title bout with light heavyweight champion Maxie Rosenbloom.

The next year, Lewis scored two victories over Rosenbloom, a closely matched rival who came back to defeat Lewis twice. Lewis lost a rematch with Braddock in his first New York appearance in 1934. Managed by the owner of the Pittsburgh Crawfords Negro League baseball team, Gus Greenlee, Lewis fought as often as possible in an attempt to secure a shot at the title. In 1935, he got his chance, fighting for the light heavyweight belt against Bob Olin in St. Louis. But being champ apparently didn't mean being paid. Under the terms of his contract, Lewis forfeited his purse when the sparse crowd failed to provide the minimum expected gate.

Lewis possessed all of the attributes of a great boxer. He had the speed of a welterweight, was aggressive, skilled at defense, and a master puncher. The lack of financial reward was a problem, however. In 1939, Lewis signed for a heavyweight title fight against his friend, Joe Louis. Although it was not widely known, Lewis was almost blind in one eye and had been for some years. Joe Louis gave his friend a chance for a big payday before the eye problem forced him to retire. Louis made short work of the challenger, knocking him out in one round. This fight was the only knockout Lewis suffered in 117 fights. Lewis retired after this defeat.

WELTERWEIGHT

Right-handed; 5'8½"; 116–166 lbs.

282 bouts, 9/13/1909 to 12/13/1929

Managers: Charles Rose, Freeman Bernstein, Jimmy Johnston, Charles Harvey

Welterweight Champion 1915–16, 1917–19

Hall of Fame Induction: 1992

Born: 10/24/1894, London England

Named: Gershon Mendeloff

Died: 10/20/1970

Perhaps the best pound-for-pound boxer England has ever produced, Ted ("Kid") Lewis began fighting as a fly-weight and battled in every division, including heavy-weight, during his lengthy career. He won numerous British and European titles and was twice welterweight champion of the world.

Born in London's East End, Lewis was attracted as a boy to boxing matches in a neighborhood theatre. He first fought professionally at the age of fourteen, when he earned sixpence for defeating another youngster. Fighting frequently and for little reward, Lewis became an excellent boxer. In 1913, he won the British feath-erweight title with a knock-out victory over Alec Lambert, and he added the European featherweight title the next year.

In 1914, Lewis travelled to the United States with his sights set on the world welterweight title. In 1915, he faced Hall of Famer Jack Britton in the first of many battles between the two well-matched boxers. The fight was a no-decision bout in which Lewis was generally acknowledged to be the winner. A few months later, Lewis took the welterweight crown from Britton with a twelve-round decision in Boston. For the next six years, Lewis and Britton fought bitterly in rematch after

Tom Gummer is on the receiving end of a left on the way to a first-round knockout by Lewis (R) in Brighton, England on February 16, 1922.

IN THE RING	WON 173	LOST 30	DRAWS 14	TB 282	KO 71	W 99	WF 3	D 14	KO'd 7	L 18	LF 5	ND 65

Date	Year		Opponent	Site	Result / Rounds		Title
SELECTED BOUTS							
Sep 13	1909		Johnny Sharpe	London	L	6	—
Apr 9	1911		Nat Brooks	London	W	10	—
Oct 6	1913		Alec Lambert	London	TKO	17	Won-Britain-FE
Feb 2	1914		Paul Til	London	WF	12	Won-Vac Eur-FE
Mar 26	1915		Jack Britton★	New York	ND-W	10	—
Aug 31	1915	♛	Jack Britton★	Boston	W	12	Won-World-W
Apr 24	1916		Jack Britton★	New Orleans	L	20	Lost-World-W
May 18	1916		Mike Gibbons★	New York	ND-L	10	—
Jun 25	1917	♛	Jack Britton★	Dayton, OH	W	20	Reg-World-W
May 17	1918		Johnny Tillman	Denver	W	20	Ret-World-W
Mar 17	1919		Jack Britton★	Canton, OH	KO'd	9	Lost-World-W
Mar 11	1920		Johnny Bee	London	KO	4	Won-Britain-W
Jun 9	1920		Johnny Basham	London	KO	9	Ret-Brit-W & Won-Eur-W
Nov 19	1920		Johnny Basham	London	KO	19	Ret-Brit & Eur-W
Feb 7	1921		Jack Britton★	New York	L	15	For-World-W
Jun 27	1921		Jack Bloomfield	London	W	20	Won-Britain-M
Oct 14	1921		Johnny Basham	London	KO	12	Ret-Brit-M & Won-Eur-M
May 11	1922	♛	Georges Carpentier★	London	KO'd	1	For-World-LH
Jun 19	1922		Frankie Burns	London	KO	11	Won-Brit Emp-M
Nov 20	1922		Roland Todd	London	W	20	Ret-Brit, Brit Emp & Eur-M
Feb 15	1923		Roland Todd	London	L	20	Lost-Brit, Brit Emp & Eur-M
Jul 3	1923		Johnny Brown	London	W	20	Ret-Brit-W & Won-Brit Emp-W
Nov 26	1923		Tommy Milligan	Edinburgh	L	20	Lost-Brit & Brit Emp-W
Dec 13	1929		Johnny Basham	London	TKO	3	—

rematch. In 1916, Britton reclaimed the welterweight title with a twenty-round decision. Lewis took back the crown in 1917 and held it until Britton knocked Lewis out in the ninth round in 1919. Altogether, Britton and Lewis met at least twenty times, although Lewis later claimed that the two had battled even more frequently.

Lewis returned to England in 1919 and over the next three years won British welterweight, middleweight, and light heavyweight titles, and the European middleweight and British Empire middleweight titles. He KO'd the skillful Johnny Basham three times, and overwhelmed middleweight Jack Bloomfield in a fierce twenty-round bout.

In 1922, Lewis challenged Hall of Famer Georges Carpentier for the world light heavyweight title but was knocked out in one round. The knock-out punch took Lewis by surprise, when he turned his head to catch a comment from the referee.

Lewis continued to fight for the next seven years in Europe, the United States, and South Africa. He fought 282 bouts officially, though he estimated that he actually fought many more. Known as one of the first combination punchers, Lewis attacked relentlessly and with great stamina. Lewis fought until he was 35. In retirement, he was involved in several businesses, including a nightclub.

LIGHT HEAVYWEIGHT

Right-handed; 5'11"; 140–192 lbs.

172 bouts, 12/9/1919 to 1/18/1937

Manager: Joe Smith

Light Heavyweight Champ 1927–29

Hall of Fame Induction: 1991

Born: 11/29/1902, Philadelphia, PA

Named: Thomas Patrick Loughran

Died: 7/7/1982

A gifted boxer with one of the greatest left hands in history, Tommy Loughran started his career as a middleweight, then went on to dominate the light heavyweight ranks in the late 1920s. Later, he jumped to the heavyweight division where he also compiled a solid record.

Manager Joe Smith handled Loughran from the start of his career. Fighting in the Philadelphia area, Loughran was undefeated in his first 43 bouts. In 1922, he faced ferocious Harry Greb in the first of six meetings. In this no-decision bout, Greb was generally credited with the victory. In the same year, Loughran took on the then-unbeatable Gene Tunney. Tunney knocked Loughran down in the first round, but Loughran held his own in the fairly even match. In 1923, Loughran fought Greb again, for one win, two losses, and a no-decision. Their final meeting in 1924 was a draw.

Loughran broke his right hand early in his career and as time went on, relied almost exclusively on his powerful left. His finely-honed boxing skills caught the public's attention when he served as a sparring partner for Jack Dempsey before the first Dempsey–Tunney fight. Loughran's ability to handle the powerful Dempsey won him many admirers.

In 1927, Loughran faced

Known as one of the cleverest boxers in history, Loughran was a sugar broker after his fight career. He also refereed several important bouts.

IN THE RING	WON 94	LOST 23	DRAWS 9	TB 172	KO 17	W 76	WF 1	D 9	KO'd 2	L 21	LF 0	ND 45	NC 1

Date	Year	Opponent	Site	Result / Rounds		Title
SELECTED BOUTS						
Dec 9	1919	Eddie Carter	Philadelphia	KO	2	—
Jul 10	1922	Harry Greb★	Philadelphia	ND-L	8	—
Aug 24	1922	Gene Tunney★	Philadelphia	ND-L	8	—
Jan 15	1923	Harry Greb★	Pittsburgh	ND-L	10	—
Jan 30	1923	Harry Greb★	New York	L	15	For-USA-LH
Oct 11	1923	♕ Harry Greb★	Boston	W	10	—
Dec 25	1923	♕ Harry Greb★	Pittsburgh	L	10	—
Oct 13	1924	♕ Harry Greb★	Philadelphia	D	10	—
Jun 17	1926	Georges Carpentier★	Philadelphia	W	10	—
Oct 7	1927	⑩ Mike McTigue	New York	W	15	Won-Vac NY World-LH
Dec 12	1927	Jimmy Slattery	New York	W	15	Won-World-LH
Jan 6	1928	⑩ Leo Lomski	New York	W	15	Ret-World-LH
Jun 1	1928	⑩ Pete Latzo	Brooklyn	W	15	Ret-World-LH
Jul 16	1928	⑩ Pete Latzo	Wilkes-Barre, PA	W	10	Ret-World-LH
Mar 28	1929	♕ Mickey Walker★	Chicago	W	10	Ret-World-LH
Jul 18	1929	Jim Braddock★	New York	W	15	Ret-World-LH
Sep 26	1929	⑩ Jack Sharkey★	New York	KO'd	3	—
Feb 6	1931	⑩ Max Baer★	New York	W	10	—
Dec 18	1931	King Levinsky	New York	L	10	—
Jan 10	1933	⑩ King Levinsky	Philadelphia	W	10	—
Sep 27	1933	Jack Sharkey★	Philadelphia	W	15	—
Mar 1	1934	♕ Primo Carnera	Miami	L	15	For-World-H
Jan 18	1937	⑩ Sonny Boy Walker	Philadelphia	W	10	—

Mike McTigue for the vacant world light heavyweight title. For fourteen rounds, Loughran dominated the fight. McTigue rallied in the fifteenth, but Loughran hung on to win a convincing victory. He defended the title five times before he gave it up to seek the heavyweight crown. In 1929, he faced Jack Sharkey as part of a series of bouts which would determine the successor to retired heavyweight champion Tunney. Fighting in Yankee Stadium before approximately 45,000 fans, Loughran scored with hard jabs in the first round, but in the third, Sharkey landed a right to the temple which sent Loughran to the canvas. Though he got up, Loughran was out on his feet, and referee Louie Magnolia stopped the fight.

Loughran continued to fight over the next four years and beat many top heavyweights such as Max Baer and Sharkey (in a rematch). In 1934, he got another shot at the title, then held by the lumbering Primo Carnera. Carnera outweighed Loughran by 86 pounds, the biggest weight differential for any title fight in history. En route to a decision in fifteen rounds, Carnera stepped on Loughran's foot, breaking a toe. Loughran never again challenged for the title. He continued to fight for three years before retiring, still acclaimed as a master of footwork and boxing skill.

BENNY LYNCH
The Kid from the Gorbals

F L Y W E I G H T

Right-handed; 5'5"; 109–119 lbs.
111 bouts, 4/24/1931 to 10/3/1938
NBA-IBU Flyweight Champion 1935–38
World Flyweight Champion 1937–38
Hall of Fame Induction: 1998
Born: 4/2/1913, Clydesdale, Scotland
Named: Samuel Benjamin John Lynch
Died: 8/6/1946

Scottish champion Benny Lynch earned a reputation as one of the greatest and most popular flyweights of all time. Although he rarely fought outside the Glasgow area and never traveled beyond the British Isles, Lynch gained national and international recognition.

Born in Clydesdale, Scotland, Lynch fought as a boy in amateur competitions. He also toured Scotland with boxing booths, taking on all comers, before turning professional at age eighteen.

On May 16, 1934 he won a close fifteen-round decision over Jim Campbell to capture the Scottish flyweight title. In the rematch six weeks later, Lynch won again. Also that year he defeated Italian champion Carlo Cavagnoli, French champion Valentin Angelmann, and Spanish champion Pedrito Ruiz.

Lynch then persuaded Jackie Brown, NBA, British, and International Boxing Union (IBU) flyweight champion, to come to Scotland for a non-title match. Lynch outboxed Brown but came away with only a draw. On September 9, 1935, Lynch met Brown again. This time the fight, at Manchester's Belle Vue Stadium, was for Brown's titles. Using superior foot speed and an awe-inspiring left hook, Lynch knocked down Brown ten times in less than two rounds before the champion surrendered. The first Scots world champion, Lynch was literally the toast of the country, feted in many taverns and pubs.

On January 19, 1937, Lynch met Small Montana, who held the New York State version of the world flyweight title, to unify the crown in London's Wembley Arena. Although Montana started fast, Lynch weathered his attacks and won a fifteen-round decision to become the undisputed world champion at the age of 23. Few observers would have guessed that Lynch would retire from boxing in less than two years and that he would be dead in nine.

In his first title defense, against nineteen-year-old former blacksmith Peter Kane, Lynch dominated. He knocked Kane down several times, but at one point when the challenger slipped and fell, Lynch offered him a hand to help

Hands still wrapped, Lynch (L) accepts the flyweight belt from Hall of Famer Lord Lonsdale.

IN THE RING	WON 83	LOST 13	DRAWS 15	TB 111	KO 34	W 48	WF 1	D 15	KO'd 1	L 11	LF 1	ND 0

Date	Year	Opponent	Site	Result / Rounds		Title
SELECTED BOUTS						
Apr 24	1931	Young Bryce	Glasgow, Scotland	KO	2	—
May 23	1931	Packy Boyle	Glasgow	L	6	—
Mar 25	1933	Jim Brady	Glasgow	W	12	—
May 2	1933	Jim Brady	Dundee, Scotland	D	12	—
Oct 10	1933	Willie Vogan	Edinburgh	KO	2	—
Nov 9	1933	Bob Fielding	Liverpool, England	D	10	—
Feb 1	1934	Jim Brady	Edinburgh	W	12	—
Mar 21	1934	Carlo Cavagnoli	Glasgow	W	12	—
May 16	1934	Jim Campbell	Glasgow	W	15	Won-Scottish-FL
Jun 27	1934	Jim Campbell	Glasgow	W	15	Ret-Scottish-FL
Sep 26	1934	⑩ Valentin Angelmann	Glasgow	W	12	—
Nov 7	1934	Pedrito Ruiz	Glasgow	W	12	—
Mar 4	1935	♛ Jackie Brown	Glasgow	D	12	—
Sep 9	1935	♛ Jackie Brown	Manchester, England	TKO	2	Won-NBA-IBU-FL
Mar 2	1936	⑩ Jimmy Warnock	Belfast	L	12	—
Sep 16	1936	⑩ Pat Palmer	Glasgow	KO	8	Ret-NBA-IBU-FL
Jan 19	1937	♛ Small Montana	London	W	15	Won-Vac-World-FL
Mar 1	1937	Len Hampston	Manchester	LW	5	—
Mar 22	1937	Len Hampston	Leeds, England	TKO	10	—
Jun 2	1937	⑩ Jimmy Warnock	Glasgow	L	10	—
Oct 13	1937	♛ Peter Kane	Glasgow	KO	13	Ret-NBA-IBU-FL
Mar 24	1938	♛ Peter Kane	Liverpool	D	15	Ret-NBA-IBU-FL
Jun 29	1938	⑩ Jackie Jurich	Paisley, Scotland	KO	12	—
Sep 28	1938	Kayo Morgan	Glasgow	L	12	—
Oct 3	1938	Aurel Toma	London	KO'd	3	—

him up. In the thirteenth, however, Lynch dropped Kane twice more to end the fight. Their rematch was a draw.

Lynch was next scheduled to defend his title against American Jackie Jurich. The fight, postponed twice because Lynch was injured, finally took place on June 29, 1938. Lynch weighed in 6½ pounds over the flyweight limit so the fight had to be held as a non-title event. Lynch knocked Jurich down six times before scoring a twelfth-round knockout. After the fight, Lynch received a stiff fine for not making weight and was stripped of the title.

Lynch moved up to bantamweight and, after suffering the first knockout of his career at the hands of Aurel Toma on October 3, 1938, he retired. Lynch returned to the boxing booths and held a variety of jobs. Although he continued to be very popular in Scotland, he drank excessively.

On the morning of August 6, 1946, a policeman found him lying ill. He was taken to a hospital where it was determined that he was suffering from pneumonia brought on by malnutrition and alcoholism. He died later that day. Knowledgeable fight fans remember Lynch for his brief dominance of the flyweight division, surprising power for his size, fine footwork, boxing ability, and sportsmanship.

SAMMY MANDELL
The Rockford Sheik, The Boxing Beau Brummel

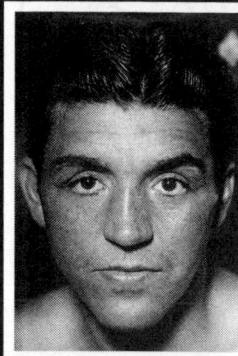

L I G H T W E I G H T

Right-handed; 5'8"; 110–146 lbs.

187 bouts, 1/14/1920 to 6/27/1934

Managers: Eddie Long 1920–1924, Eddie Kane 1920–1931, Hugh Shannon 1933

Lightweight Champion 1926–1930

Hall of Fame Induction: 1998

Born: 2/2/1904, Piana dei Greci, Sicily

Named: Salvador Mandala

Died: 11/7/1967

A Midwest favorite, Sammy Mandell outboxed two great Hall of Famers, Jimmy McLarnin and Tony Canzoneri. He held the world lightweight title for four years.

Of Italian-Albanian descent, Mandell came to the United States with his father at the age of three and settled in Rockford, Illinois. Mandell's two older brothers boxed, and he followed them into the sport, turning professional in 1920 at the age of fifteen. Most of his early fights were no-decision bouts. His modified ring name was designed to boost his appeal to Jewish boxing fans.

In 1924, Mandell fought tough junior lightweight Jack Bernstein three times, scoring one win, one draw, and one no-decision. Dubbed "The Rockford Sheik" by a Chicago sportswriter because of his good looks, Mandel also scored a newspaper victory in a no-decision bout with Hall of Famer Johnny Dundee. In its inaugural annual rankings, *The Ring* rated Mandell as the third-best lightweight.

With champion Benny Leonard's retirement in January 1925, the division title became vacant. Mandell won a twelve-round decision over the highly-rated Sid Terris on February 6, which Mandell thought should have earned him recognition as the titleholder. When the recognition was not forthcoming, Mandell entered the New York State Athletic Commission's eight-man elimination tournament to determine a new champion. But Mandell lost on a foul to Jimmy Goodrich in the first round of the tournament, and Rocky Kansas became champion after defeating tournament-winner Goodrich.

On July 3, 1926, Mandell met Kansas for the title in Chicago's Comiskey Park. Rain fell throughout the fight and soaked the ring. Kansas, 35, had the edge in strength and experience, but the light-hitting Mandell was a quicker and bet-

Lightweight champion Rocky Kansas lost a 1926 10-round decision and the title in Chicago's Comiskey Park to 22-year-old Mandell (R), who was 13 years his junior.

IN THE RING	WON 82	LOST 21	DRAWS 9	TB 187	KO 32	W 49	WF 1	D 9	KO'd 6	L 14	LF 1	ND 73	NC 2

Date	Year	Opponent	Site	Result / Rounds		Title
SELECTED BOUTS						
Jan 14	1920	Stub Lowery	Camp Grant, IL	ND-W	4	—
Jul 31	1923	Sailor Larson	Peoria, IL	ND-W	8	—
Dec 17	1923	⑩ Sid Terris	New York	D	10	—
Jan 11	1924	⑩ Jack Bernstein	New York	D	15	—
May 15	1924	⑩ Jack Bernstein	Louisville	ND-W	12	—
Jun 9	1924	⑩ Johnny Dundee★	East Chicago	ND-W	10	—
Sep 12	1924	Dick Hoppe	Los Angeles	W	4	—
Nov 7	1924	⑩ Jack Bernstein	New York	W	12	—
Feb 6	1925	⑩ Sid Terris	New York	W	12	—
May 8	1925	⑩ Jimmy Goodrich	Long Island City, NY	LF	6	—
Jul 3	1926	♛ Rocky Kansas	Chicago	W	10	Won-World-L
Apr 4	1927	⑩ Jackie Fields	Los Angeles	ND-D	12	—
Nov 15	1927	⑩ Spug Meyers	Chicago	W	10	—
Jan 13	1928	⑩ Billy Petrolle★	Minneapolis	ND-W	10	—
Feb 23	1928	Jackie Fields	Chicago	W	10	—
May 21	1928	⑩ Jimmy McLarnin★	New York	W	15	Ret-World-L
Jun 26	1928	Jack Zivic	Los Angeles	TKO	7	—
Aug 2	1929	⑩ Tony Canzoneri★	Chicago	W	10	Ret-World-L
Aug 28	1929	Frankie Frisco	Petoskey, MI	TKO	3	—
Nov 4	1929	⑩ Jimmy McLarnin★	Chicago	L	10	—
Mar 1	1930	⑩ Jimmy McLarnin★	Chicago	L	10	—
Jul 17	1930	⑩ Al Singer	New York	KO'd	1	Lost-World-L
Oct 2	1930	Spug Meyers	Cedar Rapids, IA	ND-W	10	—
Jun 27	1934	Joe Bernal	Oakland, CA	KO'd	6	—

ter boxer. He fought a methodical, systematic fight and took the ten-round decision.

Mandell fought 23 non-title fights before meeting top contender and future Hall of Famer Jimmy McLarnin on May 21, 1928. Fighting for his title in the Polo Grounds before a paid crowd of 20,290, Mandell put on, in the words of New York Times writer James P. Dawson, "an exhibition of ring wizardry which stamps him as a worthy successor to the great boxers of the ring who have held the lightweight title." Although the hard-hitting McLarnin took several rounds, the fight was Mandell's. Later, in two non-title rematches, McLarnin beat Mandell by decision.

The next year Mandell successfully defended his title against Tony Canzoneri in Chicago Stadium with a split decision. Mandell held the title until July 17, 1930 when Al Singer surprised the boxing world with a stunning first-round knockout of the champ. Never before had Mandell received the count of ten. Mandell continued to box for four more years but never again contended for the title.

In retirement, Mandell kept his hand in boxing as a promoter and manager for a time. He then worked as a security guard in a Chicago bank before a stroke in 1957 left him incapacitated until his death ten years later.

The Napoleon of the Prize Ring

LIGHTWEIGHT

Right-handed; 5'6"; 128–141 lbs.
36 bouts, 10/19/1884 to 9/30/1897
Manager: Billy Madden
Lightweight Champion 1886–94
Hall of Fame Induction: 1995
Born: 3/24/1866, Cork, Ireland
Died: 11/5/1937

Jack McAuliffe, lightweight champion for eight years, is one of only a handful of fighters to have retired undefeated. Born in Ireland, McAuliffe moved with his family to Bangor, Maine as a child. Like many top boxers of the period, he learned to fight in the streets. At sixteen, he became convinced that he could become a boxer when he defeated an English sailor in a bare knuckle bout in the basement of a Bangor storehouse.

According to legend, McAuliffe later worked in a Williamsburg, New York cooperage where fellow employee Jack Dempsey (The Nonpareil) gave the younger fighter boxing lessons and advice. McAuliffe turned professional in 1884 with a knockout victory over Jake Karcher and, two years later, knocked out Jack Hopper to win the American lightweight title.

McAuliffe further asserted his claim to the title when Jimmy Mitchen, a top contender, refused to face him. When he knocked out Billy Frazier, McAuliffe's grip on the world lightweight title was solidified, although McAuliffe reportedly was five pounds over the weight limit, and Frazier complained of a fast count in the 21st and final round.

In 1887 in Revere, Massachusetts, McAuliffe met British titleholder Jem

McAuliffe (L) defended his world lightweight title in an eleven-round victory over Billy Dacey on October 10, 1888 at Dover, NJ.

IN THE RING	WON 30	LOST 0	DRAWS 5*	TB 36	KO 22	W 8	WF 0	D 5*	KO'd 0	L 0	LF 0	ND 1

*includes 1 TD

Date	Year	Opponent	Site	Result / Rounds		Title

SELECTED BOUTS

Date	Year	Opponent	Site	Result	Rounds	Title
Oct 19	1884	Jake Karcher	Brooklyn	KO	17	—
Jan 13	1886	Jack Hopper	New York	W	6	—
Feb 27	1886	Jack Hopper	Cedarhurst, NY	KO	17	Won-Amer-L
Apr 21	1886	Joe Heiser	New York	W	4	—
Jul 24	1886	Ed Carroll	Philadelphia	TKO	1	—
Jul 31	1886	Charles McCarthy	Philadelphia	KO	3	—
Oct 29	1886	Billy Frazier	Boston	KO	21	Won-Vac World-L
Jan 14	1887	Harry Gilmore	Lawrence	KO	28	Ret-World-L
Nov 16	1887	Jem Carney	Revere, MA	D	74	Ret-World-L
Oct 10	1888	Billy Dacey	Dover, NJ	KO	11	Ret-World-L
Dec 17	1888	Sam Collyer	Brooklyn	KO	2	—
Dec 26	1888	Jake Hyams	Brooklyn	KO	9	—
Feb 23	1889	Billy Myer	Judson, IN	D	64	Ret-World-L
Feb 28	1889	Billy Boltz	Elgin, IL	KO	1	—
Mar 21	1890	Jimmy Carroll	San Francisco	KO	47	Ret-World-L
Sep 11	1891	Austin Gibbons	Hoboken, NJ	TKO	6	—
Jun 22	1892	Billy Frazier	New York	KO	3	—
Sep 5	1892	Billy Myer	New Orleans	KO	15	Ret-World-L
Dec 16	1892	Billy Myer	Chicago	W	6	—
Jan 16	1894	Jem Ryan	San Francisco	W	6	—
Aug 27	1894	Young Griffo★	Coney Island	W	10	—
Nov 20	1896	Jimmy Carroll	San Francisco	W	10	—
Sep 30	1897	Phila. Tommy Ryan	Scranton, PA	W	10	—

Carney in a long, bloody, and disorderly match held after dark at a secret location, in an attempt to forestall police interference. Spectators were advised to arrive in small groups at a nearby hotel where they were carefully screened for several hours before the fight. Later, they were escorted by lantern light to the site, a barn where, as the story goes, a Salvation Army band was practicing. Finally, all was ready and the long fight started. McAuliffe was knocked down in the seventh round but got up without a problem. The two then went round after round. By the 60th, McAuliffe was visibly tiring, and his backers were getting nervous. In the 70th round, Carney knocked McAuliffe down again and probably would have won, had McAuliffe's friends not rushed into the ring to help their man. Four rounds later, Carney again knocked McAuliffe down, and McAuliffe's supporters again interfered. The referee declared the match a draw to stop the unruly behavior before the police arrived. Twenty-seven years later in London, Carney and McAuliffe re-enacted their epic fight.

In 1892, McAuliffe won a rematch with Frazier and knocked out Billy Myer in the famous Carnival of Champions in New Orleans. Two years later, McAuliffe was awarded a questionable decision over Hall of Famer Young Griffo. McAuliffe retired in 1894 but came back to fight four more times in 1896 and 1897.

CHARLES ("KID") M⊃ ⊃ : ⊽
The Corkscrew Kid

MIDDLEWEIGHT

Right-handed; 5'11"; 142–173 lbs.

107 bouts, 6/2/1891 to 8/4/1916

Manager: Ben Benton

Middleweight Champion 1897

Hall of Fame Induction: 1991

Born: 10/13/1872, Rush County, IN

Named: Norman Selby

Died: 4/18/1940

One of the most controversial figures in boxing history, Charles ("Kid") McCoy was also one of the best and most popular fighters of the 1890s. Inventor of the damaging "corkscrew" punch, which added a twist at the moment of impact, McCoy slashed and mauled opponents, sometimes to excess. He delighted in such ring tactics as pointing excitedly into the crowd and then slugging the unwary opponent who was gullible enough to look away.

McCoy's difficult life was marked by violence outside the ring and ended tragically. Born in rural Indiana as Norman Selby, McCoy reportedly adopted his ring name when he ran away from home as a youth. He began fighting professionally in 1891 at the age of seventeen and scored knockouts in twelve of his first eighteen fights.

In 1896, McCoy faced welterweight champion Tommy Ryan in a non-title event. A one-time sparring partner for Ryan, McCoy pretended to be weak and ill-trained for the fight. He asked Ryan to take it easy on him because he was only fighting for the loser's purse. Ryan was taken by surprise when McCoy turned tiger and battered him badly before knocking him out in the fifteenth round.

In 1897, McCoy knocked out Dan Creedon to win the world middleweight title. McCoy never defended this title but sought instead to move up to the heavyweight division. He earned a decision over tough Gus Ruhlin in 1898, suffered a loss to Tom Sharkey, and decisioned Joe Choynski in San Francisco in 1899. McCoy's performance overshadowed a lesser boxer named Peter McCoy, who had fought in San Francisco days earlier, and inspired the newspaper headline,

Kid McCoy's trademarked weapon was the "corkscrew" punch—delivered with a final punishing twist that could tear an opponent's skin.

IN THE RING	WON 86	LOST 6	DRAWS 6	TB 107	KO 64	W 20	WF 2	D 6	KO'd 4	L 2	LF 0	ND 6	NC 3

Date	Year	Opponent	Site	Result / Rounds		Title
SELECTED BOUTS						
Jun 2	1891	Pete Jenkins	St. Paul, MN	W	4	—
Nov 25	1895	Ted White	London	L	10	—
Mar 2	1896	♛ Tommy Ryan★	Maspeth, NY	KO	15	—
Mar 21	1896	Joe Choynski★	New York	ND	4	—
May 18	1896	Mysterious Billy Smith	Boston	WF	6	—
Sep 8	1897	♛ Tommy Ryan★	Syracuse, NY	NC	5	—
Nov 12	1897	George LaBlanche	Dayton, OH	KO	1	—
Nov 12	1897	Beach Ruble	Dayton	KO	1	—
Dec 17	1897	Dan Creedon	Long Island City, NY	TKO	15	Won-Vac World-M
May 20	1898	Gus Ruhlin	Syracuse	W	20	—
Jan 10	1899	Tom Sharkey	New York	KO'd	10	—
Mar 24	1899	Joe Choynski★	San Francisco	W	20	—
Oct 6	1899	Joe Choynski★	Chicago	D	8	—
Jan 1	1900	Peter Maher	Coney Island	KO	5	—
Jan 12	1900	Joe Choynski★	New York	KO	4	—
May 29	1900	♛ Tommy Ryan★	Chicago	W	6	—
Aug 30	1900	James J. Corbett★	New York	KO'd	5	—
Apr 22	1903	Jack Root	Detroit	L	10	For-Vac World-LH
May 14	1904	Phila. Jack O'Brien★	Philadelphia	ND-D	6	—
Jul 25	1908	Peter Maher	New York	KO	2	—
Aug 4	1916	Artie Sheridan	Mission, TX	W	4	—

"Choynski is Beaten by the Real McCoy," which coined a lasting phrase.

McCoy continued his quest for the heavyweight title in 1900 with knock-out victories over Peter Maher, Choynski, and Jack Bonner, and decisions over Ryan and Creedon. He then faced James J. Corbett. McCoy did not perform well, and when Corbett knocked him out in the fifth round, rumors flew that the fight was fixed. Corbett left for Europe immediately afterward, adding fuel to the mystery. When Vice President Theodore Roosevelt, a proponent of boxing, declared that both fighters were honest, the story died. McCoy lost a decision to Jack Root in 1903 for the newly created light heavyweight title. He continued to fight off and on until 1916, when he retired at the age of 43.

McCoy led a stormy life outside the ring. He was married eight times to six different women. He owned a tavern, a gym, appeared in early movies, and worked as a salesman and a detective. In 1924, he was convicted of manslaughter for shooting and killing Theresa Moers, a woman with whom he was living. He also wounded three other people in the course of the incident. McCoy's melodramatic courtroom re-enactment of what he claimed was Moer's suicide probably saved him from the death penalty. Sentenced to 24 years in prison, he served seven before he was released on parole. He married again and worked for the Ford Motor Company for several years following his parole. McCoy committed suicide in 1940.

The Pride of the Stockyards; The Chicago Flash

L I G H T W E I G H T

Right-handed; 5′8″; 130–140 lbs.

104 bouts, 1904 to 9/11/1915

Manager: Emil Theiry

Hall of Fame Induction: 1992

Born: 11/1/1888, Chicago, IL

Named: Patrick McFarland

Died: 9/23/1936

One of several excellent World War I-era fighters who never won titles, Packey McFarland held his own with the very best. Not a brawler by nature, McFarland gained experience fighting in the Chicago stockyards. When he knocked out a fellow employee in a lunch-hour match, McFarland decided to adopt boxing as his vocation. Turning pro at the age of sixteen, McFarland initially fought on handball courts in the Irish neighborhoods of Chicago.

Because the crowds demanded it, McFarland employed a fine knock-out punch in his early encounters. Later, as his career developed, McFarland became better known for his boxing skill. In fact, he expressed a distinct lack of interest in knocking out opponents, preferring to win by decision. Going east for the first time, McFarland decisioned highly touted Bert Keyes in Boston in 1908. He then

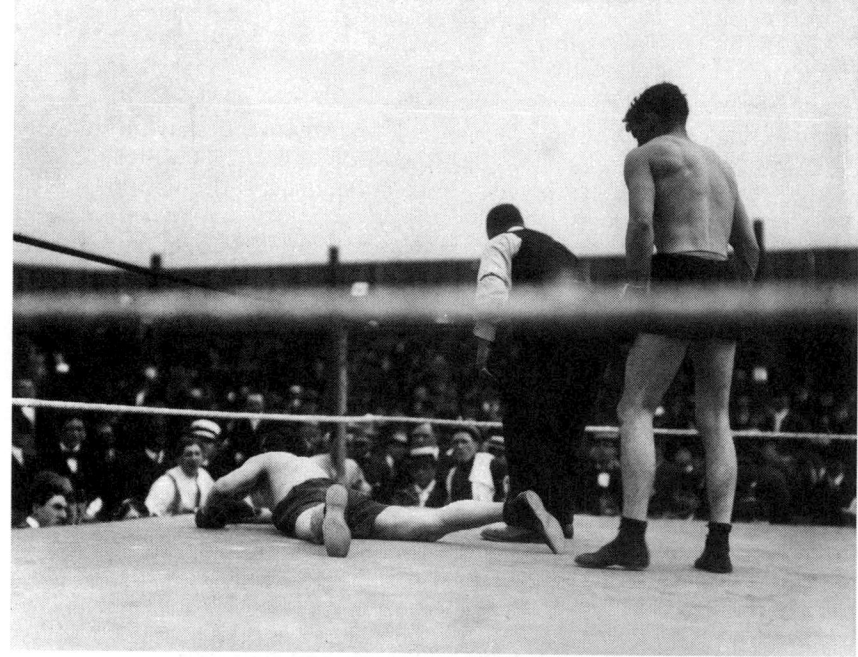

Jimmy Britt was a skillful fighter, but on April 11, 1908 in Colma, CA, he couldn't withstand Packey McFarland's greater punching power. He was knocked out in the sixth round.

IN THE RING	WON 64	LOST 1	DRAWS 5	TB 104	KO 47	W 17	WF 0	D 5	KO'd 1	L 0	LF 0	ND 34

Date	Year	Opponent	Site	Result / Rounds		Title
SELECTED BOUTS						
—	1904	Dusty Miller	—	KO'd	5	—
Jan 24	1905	Jack Walker	Chicago	KO	4	—
Feb 10	1905	Jack Meyers	South Bend, IN	KO	3	—
Nov 21	1907	Kid Herman	Davenport, IA	ND	15	—
Jan 14	1908	Bert Keyes	Boston	W	12	—
Jan 28	1908	Young Loughrey	Philadelphia	ND	6	—
Feb 21	1908	Freddie Welsh★	Milwaukee	W	10	—
Apr 11	1908	Jimmy Britt	Colma, CA	KO	6	—
Jul 4	1908	Freddie Welsh★	Los Angeles	D	25	—
Aug 7	1908	Phil Brock	Los Angeles	KO	7	—
Nov 18	1908	Tommy Murphy	Philadelphia	ND	6	—
Sep 19	1909	Ray Bronson	New Orleans	D	20	—
Apr 1	1910	Dick Lee	Plymouth, England	KO	9	—
May 30	1910	Freddie Welsh★	London	D	20	—
Jun 18	1910	Jack Goldswain	London	KO	3	—
Jan 9	1911	Johnny McCarthy	Kansas City	W	10	—
Jan 30	1911	Jack Britton★	Memphis, TN	D	8	—
Mar 20	1911	Billy Ryan	Oswego, NY	KO	4	—
May 12	1911	Tommy Kilbane	Buffalo	ND	10	—
Jul 3	1911	Young Ahearn	Albany, NY	KO	8	—
Nov 30	1911	Tommy Murphy	San Francisco	W	20	—
Apr 26	1912	Matt Wells	New York	ND	10	—
Oct 11	1912	Tommy Kilbane	Winnipeg, Alb.	KO	10	—
Mar 7	1913	Jack Britton★	New York	ND	10	—
Oct 17	1913	Tommy Murphy	New York	ND	10	—
Nov 20	1913	Kid Alberts	Waterbury, CT	ND	10	—
Dec 8	1913	Jack Britton★	Milwaukee	ND	10	—
Sep 11	1915	Mike Gibbons★	Brooklyn	ND	10	—

won a decision over Freddie Welsh before fighting him to a 25-round draw in a rematch in Los Angeles. A third bout with Welsh in London also resulted in a draw.

Though McFarland was highly regarded, he was never given a shot at the lightweight title held by Battling Nelson. In 1908, the two nearly came to blows outside the Hotel Astoria in New York. In fairness to Nelson, McFarland usually fought above the lightweight limit, which was then 133 pounds.

McFarland fought Jack Britton three times. The first bout, held in Memphis, was called a draw, although Chicago newspapers declared Britton the winner. In two no-decision rematches, Britton and McFarland fought very evenly. McFarland closed his career by fighting in a much ballyhooed contest with the clever Hall of Famer Mike Gibbons, but the ten-round fight was a flop with neither fighter landing any significant punches.

In retirement, McFarland managed his sizable investments, was director of two banks, and also served on the Illinois State Athletic Commission.

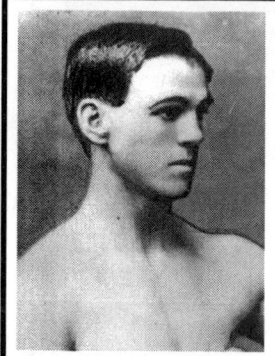

FEATHERWEIGHT

Right-handed; 5'4"; 112–127 lbs.

78 bouts, 4/3/1897 to 5/27/1908

Managers: Sam Harris and Joe Humphreys

Bantamwt. Champ 1899–1900, Featherweight Champ 1900–01

Hall of Fame Induction: 1990

Born: 3/9/1880, Johnstown, PA

Named: John Terrence McGovern

Died: 2/26/1918

One of the hardest hitters in the history of the featherweight division, Terry McGovern captured both the bantamweight and featherweight titles. In his prime, McGovern was a fearless, powerful puncher who recorded 38 knockouts in his first 62 fights. Not much for fancy maneuvers, McGovern simply went after his opponents with a ferocious will to win.

McGovern, who grew up in Brooklyn, never went to school. He was a newsboy and later worked at a variety of jobs. As a laborer in a lumber yard, McGovern handled himself well in the occasional fights there, and his boss encouraged him to become a fighter. He turned pro in 1897 at the age of seventeen.

Within two years, McGovern was a contender for the vacant world bantamweight title. He faced British bantamweight champ Tom ("Pedlar") Palmer for the crown in 1899. Though previously unbeaten, Palmer could not last one round with the solid-punching McGovern, who knocked him out in less than two minutes. The next year McGovern took the world featherweight title from a declining George Dixon with an eighth-round knockout in Madison Square Garden.

McGovern (L) shakes hands with Young Corbett before one of their battles. Corbett was the only opponent to ever knock out McGovern. He KO'd him twice.

IN THE RING	WON 60	LOST 4	DRAWS 4	TB 78	KO 42	W 17	WF 1	D 4	KO'd 2	L 1	LF 1	ND 10

Date	Year	Opponent	Site	Result / Rounds		Title

SELECTED BOUTS

Date	Year	Opponent	Site	Result / Rounds		Title
Apr 3	1897	Jack Shea	Brooklyn	KO	1	—
May 5	1898	George Munroe	Yonkers, NY	D	20	—
Jun 11	1898	George Munroe	Coney Island	KO	24	
Aug 4	1898	George Munroe	Brooklyn	WF	7	—
Apr 28	1899	Joe Bernstein	New York	W	25	—
Jul 1	1899	Johnny Ritchie	Tuckahoe, NY	KO	3	—
Sep 12	1899	♛ Tom ("Pedlar") Palmer	Tuckahoe, NY	KO	1	Won-World-B
Jan 9	1900	♛ George Dixon★	New York	TKO	8	Won-World-FE
Feb 1	1900	♛ Eddie Santry	Chicago	KO	5	Ret-World-FE
Mar 9	1900	Oscar Gardner	New York	KO	3	Ret-World-FE
Jun 12	1900	Tommy White	Coney Island	KO	3	Ret-World-FE
Jun 23	1900	George Dixon★	Chicago	W	6	—
Jul 16	1900	♛ Frank Erne	New York	KO	3	—
Nov 2	1900	Joe Bernstein	Louisville	KO	7	Ret-World-FE
Dec 13	1900	Joe Gans★	Chicago	KO	2	—
Apr 30	1901	Oscar Gardner	San Francisco	KO	4	Ret-World-FE
May 29	1901	Aurelio Herrera	San Francisco	KO	5	Ret-World-FE
Nov 28	1901	Young Corbett	Hartford, CT	KO'd	2	Lost-World-FE
Mar 31	1903	♛ Young Corbett	San Francisco	KO'd	11	For-World-FE
Mar 14	1906	Battling Nelson★	Philadelphia	ND-L	6	—
Oct 17	1906	♛ Young Corbett	Philadelphia	ND-W	6	—
May 27	1908	Spike Robson	New York	ND-L	6	—

McGovern successfully defended his featherweight title several times in 1900 and 1901. He also scored a third-round knockout over the world lightweight champion Frank Erne in a non-title bout. He beat Hall of Famer Joe Gans in two rounds in 1900, although Gans later admitted to throwing the fight.

McGovern's toughest opponent was Young Corbett, a fighter from Denver whose fierce attitude rivaled the ruthlessness that McGovern exhibited. A fight between the two, who were only seven months apart in age, was set up in 1901 in Hartford, with McGovern's title at stake. Observors have said that Corbett unnerved the champion by not showing any fear or deference toward him. Passing by McGovern's dressing room on his way to the ring, Corbett shouted, "Come on out, you Irish rat, and take the licking of your life." Corbett and McGovern each scored a knockdown in the first round, but in the second, Corbett handed McGovern the first knockout of his career. McGovern tried to win back the title from Corbett in 1903 but was knocked out again.

McGovern fought infrequently for the next five years, never regaining his earlier skill. In the latter stages of his career, McGovern's behavior became erratic, and he spent time in various sanitariums. He collapsed while serving as a referee at an Army camp during World War I and died soon after.

JIMMY McLARNIN
Baby Face

WELTERWEIGHT

Right-handed; 5'6"; 112–147 lbs.

77 bouts, 1923 to 11/20/1936

Manager: Pop Foster

Welterwt. Champ 1933–34, 1934–35

Hall of Fame Induction: 1991

Born: 12/19/1906, Inchacore, Ireland

Named: James Archibald McLarnin

Jimmy McLarnin was a hard hitter who could target a punch with devastating accuracy. His bouts with Hall of Famer Barney Ross are remembered as some of the very best contests in any weight class or era. Born in Ireland, McLarnin grew up in Vancouver, Canada. Fight manager Pop Foster took McLarnin under his wing at an early age and trained him for the professional ranks. Foster debuted McLarnin in Canada at age sixteen as a flyweight, then took his young star to California, pitting him against increasingly tough opponents. In 1925, McLarnin decisioned Hall of Famer Pancho Villa in the Filipino's last fight.

In 1928, McLarnin challenged Sammy Mandell for the world lightweight championship. Mandell won a convincing decision over the young McLarnin, who nevertheless was lauded for his courage and willingness to fight. Later, in two non-title bouts, McLarnin won decisions over Mandell. McLarnin defeated

McLarnin (R) won his last fight, decisioning Lou Ambers in ten on November 20, 1936 in New York. Ambers had won the lightweight crown just two months earlier, but this meeting was a non-title bout.

IN THE RING	WON 62	LOST 11	DRAWS 3	TB 77	KO 20	W 41	WF 1	D 3	KO'd 1	L 10	LF 0	ND 1

Date	Year	Opponent	Site	Result / Rounds		Title
SELECTED BOUTS						
—	1923	George Ainsworth	—	W	4	—
Feb 22	1924	Eddie Collins	Oakland	KO	3	—
Oct 28	1924	Fidel LaBarba★	Vernon, CA	W	4	—
Nov 11	1924	Fidel LaBarba★	Vernon	D	4	—
Jan 13	1925	⑩ Fidel LaBarba★	Vernon	W	10	—
Jul 4	1925	♛ Pancho Villa★	Oakland	W	10	—
Feb 24	1928	Sid Terris	New York	KO	1	—
May 21	1928	♛ Sammy Mandell★	New York	L	15	For-World-L
Nov 4	1929	♛ Sammy Mandell★	Chicago	W	10	—
Dec 13	1929	⑩ Ruby Goldstein★	New York	KO	2	—
Mar 1	1930	♛ Sammy Mandell★	Chicago	W	10	—
Sep 11	1930	♛ Al Singer	New York	KO	3	—
Nov 21	1930	⑩ Billy Petrolle★	New York	L	10	—
May 27	1931	⑩ Billy Petrolle★	New York	W	10	—
Aug 20	1931	⑩ Billy Petrolle★	New York	W	10	—
Aug 4	1932	⑩ Lou Brouillard	New York	L	10	—
Oct 7	1932	Benny Leonard★	New York	TKO	6	—
Dec 16	1932	⑩ Sammy Fuller	New York	KO	8	—
May 29	1933	♛ Young Corbett III	Los Angeles	KO	1	Won-World-W
May 28	1934	⑩ Barney Ross★	Long Island City, NY	L	15	Lost-World-W
Sep 17	1934	♛ Barney Ross★	Long Island City	W	15	Reg-World-W
May 28	1935	⑩ Barney Ross★	New York	L	15	Lost-World-W
May 8	1936	♛ Tony Canzoneri★	New York	L	10	—
Oct 5	1936	⑩ Tony Canzoneri★	New York	W	10	—
Nov 20	1936	♛ Lou Ambers★	New York	W	10	—

Billy Petrolle, Benny Leonard, and others to earn a shot at the welterweight title held by Young Corbett III. The fight was held in Los Angeles in 1933. McLarnin was on fire. Within seconds, he floored the champ with a right to the chin, then knocked him down again with three lefts. Two more blows sent Corbett sprawling and it was all over before the bell sounded to end the first round.

The next year, McLarnin defended his title against Ross, the lightweight and junior welterweight champ, in the Madison Square Garden Bowl before a crowd of 65,000. In a split decision, Ross won the championship. In the rematch four months later, Ross fought in furious flurries and McLarnin boxed magnificently, even with one eye completely closed from the twelfth round on. This time, McLarnin won and reclaimed his title. McLarnin faced Ross for a third time at the Polo Grounds in 1935 with 40,000 fans looking on. Jack Dempsey refereed. The two champions went at each other relentlessly for fifteen rounds, and Ross was declared the winner on a unanimous decision. McLarnin then split two fights with Tony Canzoneri and defeated Lou Ambers before leaving the ring. In retirement, McLarnin pursued a business career and also acted, golfed, and lectured.

HEAVYWEIGHT

Right handed; 5'10½"; 200–215 lbs.

97 bouts, 4/12/1902 to 8/2/1921

Manager: Billy Roche 1902–03, Spider Kelly 1904, Frank Carillo 1906–07, Frank Bernard 1907, and Cal McClain 1912

Unofficial Black Heavyweight Champ 1909, 1915

Hall of Fame Induction: 1999

Born: 5/17/1884 Waelder, TX

Named: Samuel E. MacVea

Died: 12/23/1921

Like fellow black Hall of Famers Sam Langford and Joe Jeannette, Sam McVey never fought for the heavyweight title. McVey grew up in California. As a youth McVey worked in an Oxnard livery stable, where he joined in occasional informal boxing matches. His success in these bouts drew the attention of the stable's owner, Billy Roche, who quickly arranged to manage McVey. His first recorded fight was a six-round knockout victory over George Sullivan on April 12, 1902, in Oxnard.

McVey won his first seven fights by knockout before he was paired with Hall of Famer and future heavyweight champion Jack Johnson in a bout advertised as for "The Negro Heavyweight Title." The inexperienced McVey was no match for Johnson, and he lost. When the rematch ended in another twenty-round decision for Johnson, Roche severed his connection with McVey. In the third McVey–Johnson fight, McVey was KO'd in the twentieth round.

In 1907, McVey left California for the first time, fighting Joe Jeannette in a no-decision battle in New York. Then McVey set sail for Europe, fighting once in England before moving on to France, where black heavyweights were generally well accepted. On February 20, 1909, McVey won a twenty-round decision over Jeannette in a particularly lackluster bout. Rumors circulated that the two combatants had treated the fight merely as an exhibition. A rematch on April 17, 1909, turned out to be one of the greatest displays of endurance in ring history. The powerful McVey, who often charged opponents with his left arm extended, knocked Jeannette down 27 times and nearly finished him with a right to the jaw in the sixteenth round. Jeannette was

McVey (L) met "Chicago Jim" Barry in Sydney, Australia on March 16, 1912. Barry (not to be confused with Hall of Famer Jimmy Barry, also from Chicago) lasted a full twenty rounds and lost on points.

IN THE RING	WON 63	LOST 12	DRAWS 7	TB 97	KO 48	W 14	WF 1	D 7	KO'd 5	L 7	LF 0	ND 13	NC 2

Date	Year	Opponent	Site	Result / Rounds		Title
SELECTED BOUTS						
Apr 12	1902	George Sullivan	Oxnard, CA	KO	6	—
Feb 26	1903	Jack Johnson★	Los Angeles	L	20	For-Black-H
Oct 27	1903	Jack Johnson★	Los Angeles	L	20	For-Black-H
Apr 22	1904	Jack Johnson★	San Francisco	KO'd	20	For-Black-H
Feb 20	1909	Joe Jeannette★	Paris	W	20	Won-Vac Black-H
Apr 9	1909	Cyclone Billy Warren	Paris	KO	2	Ret-Black-H
Apr 17	1909	Joe Jeannette★	Paris	TKO'd	50	Lost-Black-H
Jul 20	1911	George ("The Boer") Rodel	Liverpool, England	KO	1	—
Apr 11	1912	Sam Langford★	Sydney	L	20	For Black-H
Aug 3	1912	Sam Langford★	Sydney	L	20	For-Black-H
Oct 10	1912	Sam Langford★	Perth, Australia	TKO'd	11	For-Black-H
Dec 26	1912	Sam Langford★	Sydney	KO'd	13	For-Black-H
Dec 20	1914	Harry Wills★	New Orleans	W	20	—
Jun 29	1915	Sam Langford★	Boston	W	12	Won-Black-H
Sep 7	1915	Harry Wills★	Boston	L	12	Lost-Black-H
Apr 7	1916	Sam Langford★	Syracuse, NY	ND-W	10	For-Black-H
Aug 12	1916	Sam Langford★	Buenos Aires	D	20	For-Black-H
Feb 17	1918	Harry Wills★	Panama City	KO'd	5	—
Sep 8	1920	Harry Wills★	Philadelphia	NC	6	For-Black-H
Aug 2	1921	Jeff Clark	Lancaster, PA	ND-D	10	—

saved by the bell, and in the later rounds began to take control of the fight, knocking McVey down seven times in the 42nd. After 49 rounds, McVey could not continue. Though he suffered defeat, his tremendous performance showcased his slugging power and fighting spirit.

On April 1, 1911, McVey met Sam Langford for the first time in a fight that ended in a twenty-round draw. In the course of his career, McVey would fight Langford fifteen times, Jeannette five, another black heavyweight, Battling Jim Johnson, seven times, and Hall of Famer Harry Wills five. Unable to secure bouts with top white opponents—or with Jack Johnson when he was champion—the top black fighters were forced to face each other repeatedly. In Liverpool, England, on July 20, 1911, McVey scored a first-round knockout over George ("The Boer") Rodel, a rare white adversary.

Later that year, the globe-trotting McVey next moved his operations to Australia, campaigning there for three years. He faced Langford six times Down Under. McVey returned to the United States from 1914 to 1916, then embarked on a Latin American tour, which ended when Wills knocked him out in Panama City. By this time, McVey's career was winding down. He did not fight for over two and a half years before making a brief eight-fight comeback before retiring.

Unfortunately, McVey's retirement did not last long. In 1921, he contracted pneumonia and died. Jack Johnson paid for the funeral and for the debts of his one-time rival.

FEATHERWEIGHT

Left-handed; 5'5"; 122–132 lbs.

248 bouts, 4/4/1927 to 4/1/1940

Managers: Danny Davis 1927–31, Pete Reilly 1931–37, Dom and Tony Vairo 1938

NBA Featherweight Champ 1933–34, World Featherweight Champ 1934–36

Hall of Fame Induction: 1997

Born: 4/3/1911, Cincinnati, OH

Died: 5/8/1962

Although Freddie Miller rarely strayed far from his hometown of Cincinnati for his first 95 fights, by the end of his career few fighters could claim to have fought in as many places as the diminutive southpaw. Miller donned the gloves in virtually every major city in the United States. Abroad, he campaigned in England, Scotland, Spain, France, Ireland, Mexico, Cuba, Belgium, South Africa, Wales, and Venezuela. Through all his travels, Miller impressed observers as one of the greatest left-handers in boxing history.

Miller turned professional at the age of sixteen with a third-round knockout of Billy Barnes in Cincinnati. A knockout victory would prove to be somewhat unusual for Miller, who recorded knockouts in fewer than twenty percent of his fights. Miller won 71 of his first 75 fights which led *The Ring* to recognize him as the third-best featherweight contender in its annual rankings for 1929. It is astonishing that Miller was a veteran of 75 pro bouts at the age of eighteen.

In 1930 and 1931, Miller was ranked by *The Ring* as a junior lightweight even though he managed to make weight as a featherweight in a bout with Battling Battalino for his world title. Battalino decisioned Miller in ten rounds. In their rematch six months later, Miller and Battalino engaged in a shameful performance. At the time both fighters were managed by Pete Reilly. Beforehand, the fighters agreed that Miller could win the title. However, Miller and Battalino performed this charade so artlessly that the referee declared the fight no contest. In 1932, Miller was dropped from The *Ring*'s annual rankings.

Miller rebounded on January 13, 1933 in Chicago, when he faced NBA world featherweight champion Tommy Paul. In this battle, their fourth meeting, Miller took the decision in ten rounds. The next year, Miller gained recognition as the undisputed featherweight champion when he decisioned Nel Tarleton in Liverpool, England. Also in 1934, Miller earned decisions over Hall of Famers Chalky Wright and Panama Al

Miller sends IBU featherweight champion Nel Tarleton to his knees. In their September 20, 1934 Liverpool meeting, Miller gained a unified world title.

	WON	LOST	DRAWS	TB	KO	W	WF	D	KO'd	L	LF	ND	NC
IN THE RING	**208**	**28**	**7**	248	42	163	3	7	1	25	2	1	4

Date	Year	Opponent	Site	Result / Rounds		Title
SELECTED BOUTS						
Apr 4	1927	Billy Barnes	Ft. Thomas, KY	KO	3	—
Jan 1	1929	⑩ Cecil Payne	Cincinnati	W	10	—
Jan 29	1930	⑩ Bushy Graham	Cincinnati	D	10	—
Oct 2	1930	⑩ Johnny Farr	Cincinnati	W	10	—
Nov 13	1930	⑩ Johnny Farr	Cincinnati	L	10	—
Jun 11	1931	⑩ Eddie Shea	Cincinnati	W	10	—
Jul 23	1931	♛ Battling Battalino	Cincinnati	L	10	For-World-FE
Jan 27	1932	♛ Battling Battalino	Cincinnati	NC	3	For-World-FE
Jan 13	1933	⑩ Tommy Paul	Chicago	W	10	Won-NBA-FE
Feb 28	1933	⑩ Baby Arizmendi	Los Angeles	W	10	Ret-NBA-FE
Mar 21	1933	⑩ Speedy Dado	Los Angeles	W	10	Ret-NBA-FE
Jun 12	1933	⑩ Baby Arizmendi	San Francisco	L	10	—
Jan 1	1934	Jackie Sharkey	Cincinnati	W	10	Ret-NBA-FE
Feb 7	1934	⑩ Petey Sarron	Cincinnati	W	10	—
Jun 8	1934	Albert ("Chalky") Wright★	El Centro, CA	W	10	—
Sep 20	1934	⑩ Nel Tarleton	Liverpool, England	W	15	Won-Vac World-FE
Dec 24	1934	♛ Panama Al Brown★	Paris	W	10	—
Feb 17	1935	Jose Girones	Barcelona	KO	1	Ret-World-FE
Jun 12	1935	⑩ Nel Tarleton	Liverpool	W	15	Ret-World-FE
Oct 22	1935	⑩ Vernon Cormier	Boston	W	15	Ret-World-FE
Feb 18	1936	Johnny Pena	Seattle	W	12	Ret-World-FE
Mar 2	1936	⑩ Petey Sarron	Coral Gables, FL	W	15	Ret-World-FE
May 11	1936	⑩ Petey Sarron	Washington, DC	L	15	Lost-World-FE
Feb 9	1937	⑩ Jackie Wilson	Pittsburgh	L	10	—
Apr 26	1937	⑩ Jackie Wilson	Cincinnati	L	10	—
Jul 31	1937	⑩ Petey Sarron	Johannesburg, South Africa	W	10	—
Sep 4	1937	⑩ Petey Sarron	Johannesburg	L	12	For-World-FE
Oct 24	1938	⑩ Leo Rodak	Washington, DC	L	15	For-NBA-FE
Dec 5	1938	⑩ Sammy Angott ★	Louisville, KY	L	10	—
Apr 1	1940	Herschel Joiner	Cincinnati	TKO'd	8	—

Brown. As champion, Miller took on all comers in a wide range of venues. He defended the world featherweight title successfully five times in three years and fought 48 non-title fights, winning 41.

On May 11, 1936, Miller put his title on the line against Petey Sarron. Miller had previously defeated Sarron three times, with the most recent victory coming only two months before. However, Sarron decisioned Miller to take the title. Miller defeated Sarron in a non-title bout in the rematch, but when they fought for the title in Johannesburg, South Africa, Sarron retained the crown. This was the first time that two Americans ever fought for a world title on foreign soil.

Miller did not get another chance at Sarron but did unsuccessfully battle Leo Rodak for the Maryland version of the world featherweight title in 1938. After suffering the only knockout defeat of his career, at the hands of Herschel Joiner, Miller retired. Though only 28, Miller had fought 248 times in thirteen years.

C AR E EL

HEAVYWEIGHT

Right-handed; 5'9"; 130–175 lbs.

47 bouts, 1877 to 1/23/1894

Managers: George ("Pony") Moore and Billy Thompson

Hall of Fame Induction: 2002

Born: 11/24/1861, Birmingham, England

Named: Charles Watson Mitchell

Died: 4/3/1918

Though no bigger than a modern-day middleweight, Charlie Mitchell took on the top heavyweights of his day and floored the great champion he most yearned to beat—John L. Sullivan.

A game, scientific fighter, who was skillful with both gloves and bare knuckles, Mitchell started fighting as a bare knuckle lightweight at sixteen. The next year, he fought English lightweight champ Billy Kennedy to a draw in a gloved match. Mitchell held court at a series of taverns in England from 1878 through 1880, where he took on all comers.

In 1881, Mitchell's pugilistic career began to take off. He fought a draw with Jack Burke for the welterweight championship of England. In April, 1882, Mitchell beat Ned Harnatty in a middleweight competition, and later that year he defeated six opponents—some much bigger than he—to win the heavyweight championship of England in a tournament staged to find a challenger for John Sullivan. As the winner, Mitchell came to the United States in 1883.

Sullivan agreed to fight Mitchell on May 14, 1883, in Madison Square Garden. The fight received a great deal of attention, and *Police Gazette* publisher Richard K. Fox touted the chances of the smaller Mitchell. At the start of the match, Sullivan charged Mitchell, firing lefts and rights, but the challenger used his superior speed to avoid many wild blows. Sullivan, who outweighed Mitchell by 40 pounds, landed enough punches to knock Mitchell down several times and dominate the action. Police stopped the fight after three rounds, but in the first, a quick left by Mitchell had knocked Sullivan down for the first time in his career.

Mitchell fought exhibitions for the next year or so, both in the U.S. and in England. On March 26, 1884, a fight with Jake Kilrain in Boston was called a draw after the police intervened. Next up was a Sullivan rematch. On the day of the fight, June 30, 1884, there were rumors that Mitchell had malaria and that Sullivan was on a binge, and indeed the latter arrived at Madison Square Garden so drunk that he announced he was sick and unable to fight.

ROUND 9.—MITCHELL LANDED WELL

Mitchell (R) connects to the mouth in a solid ninth round in his uphill bare-knuckle battle to defeat heavyweight champion of the world, John L. Sullivan. Several times both fighters tumbled to the grass in an exhausted heap.

IN THE RING	WON 31	LOST 3	DRAWS 12	TB 47	KO 7	W 24	WF 0	D 12	KO'd 1	L 2	LF 0	ND 0	NC 1

Date	Year	Opponent	Site	Result / Rounds		Title
SELECTED BOUTS						
Jan 11	1878	Bob Cunningham	Birmingham, England	W	50 min.	—
—	1879	Billy Kennedy	London	D	4	For-England-L
Jun 16	1881	Jack Burke	Winkfield, England	D	25	For-England-W
Apr 4	1882	Ned Harnatty	Chelsea Baths	W	3	—
Feb 17	1883	Jack Clarke	Newcastle, England	TKO	1	Won-North England-H
May 14	1883	John L. Sullivan★	New York	L	3	—
Jun	1883	Garrett	Syracuse, NY	W	1	—
Oct 2	1883	William Sheriff	Flushing, NY	D	7	—
Mar 20	1884	Joe Denning	New York	W	4	—
Mar 26	1884	Jake Kilrain	Boston	D	4	—
May 12	1884	Billy Edwards	New York	KO	3	—
Oct 13	1884	Dominick McCaffrey	New York	L	4	—
Oct 21	1884	Jack Burke	New York	D	4	—
Nov 24	1884	Jack Burke	New York	D	3	—
Feb 23	1885	John F. Scholes	Toronto	W	4	—
May 22	1885	Mike Cleary	San Francisco	D	4	—
Jun 29	1885	Jack Burke	Chicago	D	6	—
May 16	1886	Jack Burke	Chicago	D	10	—
Jun 11	1886	Patsy Cardiff	Minneapolis	W	6	—
Mar 10	1888 ♛	John L. Sullivan★	Chantilly, France	D	39	For-World-H
Feb 7	1890	Jem Mace★	Glasgow, Scotland	W	4	Won-England-H
Mar 2	1892	Arthur Upham	New Orleans	TKO	3	—
Jan 25	1894 ♛	Jim Corbett★	Jacksonville, FL	KO'd	3	For-World-H

Mitchell continued his ambitious fight schedule. When Sullivan toured England, his manager arranged another fight with Mitchell at the estate of Baron Alphonse Rothschild in Chantilly, France, the parties agreeing to fight for $2,500 a side. Sullivan knocked Mitchell down in the first, second, and third rounds, but Mitchell kept moving, trying to wear down his big opponent. In the seventh, Mitchell threw Sullivan to the turf for the first time. The ninth round was also a good one for Mitchell; he connected with Sullivan's jaw. For a total of 39 rounds, the fighting continued, Sullivan attacking and Mitchell dodging. Finally, with both fighters moving as though in slow motion, they agreed to a draw.

Though he was unsuccessful in his title bid, Mitchell remained active in boxing both as a fighter and as a second for Jake Kilrain in his famous battle with Sullivan. On February 7, 1890, Mitchell met 58-year-old Hall of Famer Jem Mace in a fight billed as the heavyweight championship of England. Police broke up the match with Mitchell leading.

On January 25, 1894, Mitchell once again fought for the world heavyweight title, now held by Jim Corbett. The younger Corbett proved to be too much for Mitchell, knocking him out in three rounds. Though Mitchell continued to fight exhibitions, he would never again fight for the championship.

OWEN MORAN
"The Fearless"

BANTAMWEIGHT

Right-handed; 5'4", 102–130 lbs.
107 bouts, 1900 to 8/21/1916
Manager: Charley Harvey
Brit World Bantam Champ 1907
Hall of Fame Induction: 2002
Born: 11/4/1884, Birmingham, England
Died: 3/17/1949

Though he was never widely acclaimed as a champion, Owen Moran is considered one of the greatest British fighters of all time.

Moran started boxing in carnival booths around 1900, adeptly taking on all comers. He was spotted by Captain Cleveland, a former amateur boxer and "man of means," who was impressed by Moran's skill. In his first major bout, Moran lost a tough, twenty-round decision to ring veteran Digger Stanley on June 17, 1901. Shortly after the Stanley fight, Cleveland arranged for Charley Harvey to manage Moran.

Harvey quickly signed Moran to fight Harry Slough at Leicester's Mafeking Gymnasium. At first, Slough pushed the less experienced Moran around the ring, but the challenger went the full fifteen rounds to be declared the winner. In 1904, he earned a six-round decision over Hall of Famer George Dixon.

Moran then went to the United States, where he debuted in a six-round, no-decision bout with Danny Dougherty. The 5'4" Moran impressed observers with his speed and double-fisted attack. A Philadelphia sportswriter reported, "I can't believe this Moran is an Englishman. He fights like an American." Back in England, Moran faced another fine fighter in Abe Attell's brother, Monte, beating him in an easy twenty-round bout.

In 1907, Harvey brought Moran to the U.S. for an extended stay. In Philadelphia, on October 19, 1907, Moran battered Tommy O'Toole in a six-round, no-decision bout. Harvey then took Moran to the West Coast, where he arranged a fight for Moran with Frankie Neil, considered the lightweight champion of California. He pounded Neil to the verge of collapse, eased up to let him recover, then hammered him again, knocking him out in the sixteenth round.

Outraged California fight fans persuaded featherweight champion Abe Attell to put his

In San Francisco, on November 26, 1910, Battling Nelson "The Durable Dane" suffers the second knock-out of his distinguished career at the hands of Owen Moran. Referee Ben Selig administers the ten-count.

IN THE RING	WON 67	LOST 16	DRAWS 5	TB 107	KO 34	W 33	WF 0	D 5	KO'd 2	L 9	LF 5	ND 19

Date	Year	Opponent	Site	Result / Rounds		Title
SELECTED BOUTS						
—	1900	Bill Lovesey	Birmingham, Eng.	KO	2	—
Jun 17	1901	Digger Stanley	Birmingham	L	20	—
Oct 9	1901	Harry Slough	Leicester, Eng.	W	15	—
May 30	1904	Joe Bowker	London	L	20	For-English-B (116 lbs)
Oct 17	1904	George Dixon★	London	W	6	—
Oct 29	1904	Harry Ware	Newcastle, Eng.	TKO	3	Won-English-B (116 lbs)
Jan 23	1905	Digger Stanley	London	W	20	—
Mar 12	1905	Danny Dougherty	Philadelphia	ND-W	6	—
May 15	1905	Monte Attell	London	W	15	—
Apr 22	1907	Al Delmont	London	W	20	Won-Brit World-B (116 lbs)
Jul 22	1907	Young Pierce	Liverpool	KO	18	—
Nov 22	1907	Frankie Neil	San Francisco	TKO	17	—
Jan 1	1908	♛ Abe Attell★	San Francisco	D	25	For-World-FE
Apr 7	1908	Ad Wolgast★	New York	ND-W	6	—
Sep 7	1908	♛ Abe Attell★	Colma, CA	D	23	For-World-FE
Apr 1	1910	♛ Abe Attell★	New York	ND-D	10	—
Jun 24	1910	Abe Attell★	Los Angeles	ND-L	10	—
Nov 9	1910	♛ Abe Attell★	Philadelphia	ND-D	6	—
Nov 26	1910	Battling Nelson★	San Francisco	KO	11	—
Mar 14	1911	Packey McFarland★	New York	ND-L	10	—
Jul 4	1911	Ad Wolgast★	San Francisco	KO'd	13	For-World-L
Jan 27	1913	♛ Jem Driscoll★	London	D	20	For-British World-FE
May 31	1915	Llew Edwards	London	LF	11	For-Vac British-FE
Aug 21	1916	Billy Marchant	Liverpool	LF	2	—

title on the line against Moran on New Year's Day, 1908, in San Francisco. Moran had to slim down to 120 pounds. The fight was called a draw and a return battle was scheduled for 23 rounds in Colma, California, on September 7, 1908. Once again, the two Hall of Famers battled to a draw.

On November 26, 1910, Moran faced Battling Nelson. Early in the fight, Nelson winked at friends at ringside to show that Moran would be an easy opponent, but by the eleventh round, Nelson was visibly weakened. Although Moran was bleeding profusely from his nose and eyes, a right to the side of the neck knocked the Durable Dane unconscious.

On July 4, 1911, Moran returned to San Francisco to challenge for the lightweight title held by Wolgast. Throughout the fight, Moran complained of Wolgast's butts and low blows. A punch to Moran's midsection doubled him over in the thirteenth, and Wolgast then fired a right behind Moran's ear to knock him out. To his death, Moran claimed the body blow was low.

Moran continued to fight for another five years, winning only three of his last fifteen bouts. A twenty-round draw with Jim Driscoll for the British featherweight title was the final highlight of Moran's distinguished career.

BATTLING NELSON
The Durable Dane

LIGHTWEIGHT

Right-handed; 5'7½"; 120–140 lbs.

131 bouts, 9/3/1896 to 4/17/1917

Managers: John Robinson, Ted Murphy, Billy Nolan

Lightweight Champion 1908–10

Hall of Fame Induction: 1992

Born: 6/5/1882, Copenhagen, Denmark

Named: Oscar Matthew Nielson

Died: 2/7/1954

One of the toughest boxers in ring history, Battling Nelson twice held the world lightweight title. Slight of build but relentless in both delivering and enduring beatings, Nelson spooked more than one opponent with his unblinking resistance. His trademark punch was a short left hook aimed at the liver, with thumb and forefinger extended to provide greater penetration. A Dane by birth, Nelson grew up in a suburb of Chicago. He fought professionally for the first time against a fighter in a travelling circus. Challenged to last three rounds, the fourteen-year-old Nelson knocked Wallace's Kid out in one.

Nelson's career blossomed in 1904. He knocked out Martin Canole, Eddie Hanlon, and Young Corbett and won a decision against the hard-hitting Aurelio Herrera, who once flipped Nelson into an involuntary somersault with a powerful punch. In December 1904, Nelson lost to Jimmy Britt in a fight for the vacant white lightweight title. The next year Britt and Nelson again squared off. In the eighteenth round, Nelson caught Britt with a flurry of punches and knocked him out. In 1906, Nelson met black champion Joe Gans in Nevada, in a Tex Rickard promotion. Gans had won the lightweight title in 1904 but relinquished it to fight for (and win) the welterweight title. Gans knocked Nelson down

In Washington, DC, Nelson poses with Captain J.W. Thompson, Company M of the 14th Infantry, and a special patriotic punching bag.

IN THE RING	WON 59	LOST 19	DRAWS 19	TB 131	KO 38	W 20	WF 1	D 19	KO'd 3	L 14	LF 2	ND 33	NC 1

Date	Year	Opponent	Site	Result / Rounds		Title
SELECTED BOUTS						
Sep 3	1896	Wallace's Kid	Hammond, IN	KO	1	—
Apr 6	1899	Eddie Penny	Chicago	KO	1	—
Apr 6	1904	Spider Welsh	Salt Lake City	KO	16	—
Nov 29	1904	Young Corbett	San Francisco	KO	10	—
Dec 20	1904	Jimmy Britt	San Francisco	L	20	For-Vac White-L
Feb 28	1905	Young Corbett	San Francisco	TKO	9	—
May 22	1905	♛ Abe Attell★	Philadelphia	ND-L	6	—
Jun 6	1905	Jack O'Neil	Philadelphia	ND-W	6	—
Sep 9	1905	♛ Jimmy Britt	Colma, CA	KO	18	Won-White-L
Mar 14	1906	Terry McGovern★	Philadelphia	ND-W	6	—
Sep 3	1906	Joe Gans★	Goldfield, NV	LF	42	For-World-L
Jul 31	1907	Jimmy Britt	San Francisco	L	20	—
Mar 31	1908	♛ Abe Attell★	San Francisco	D	15	—
Jul 4	1908	♛ Joe Gans★	Colma	KO	17	Won-World-L
Sep 9	1908	Joe Gans★	Colma	KO	21	Ret-World-L
May 29	1909	Dick Hyland	Colma	KO	23	Ret-World-L
Jun 22	1909	Jack Clifford	Oklahoma City	TKO	5	Ret-World-L
Jul 13	1909	Ad Wolgast★	Los Angeles	ND-L	10	—
Jan 21	1910	Eddie Lang	Memphis, TN	KO	8	Ret-World-L
Feb 22	1910	Ad Wolgast★	Richmond, CA	TKO'd	40	Lost-World-L
Nov 26	1910	Owen Moran★	San Francisco	KO	11	—
Nov 28	1912	Leach Cross	New York	ND-L	10	—
Oct 13	1913	Ad Wolgast★	Milwaukee	ND-L	10	—
Apr 17	1917	♛ Freddie Welsh★	St. Louis	ND-L	12	—

several times but could not knock him out. In the 33rd round, Gans broke his hand but continued to fight. Finally, in the 42nd round, Nelson hit Gans with a low blow and lost on the foul. Two years later, Nelson reclaimed the title with a seventeenth-round knockout of Gans. In their third meeting, Nelson again recorded a knock-out victory.

In 1909, Nelson met his fiercest opponent, Ad Wolgast, in a bloody no-decision fight that newspaper reporters gave to Wolgast. The next year the two fought in a brutally wild brawl for the title. In the 22nd round, Nelson knocked Wolgast down hard, but Wolgast surprised the crowd by getting up before the ten count. Both of Nelson's eyes swelled shut, and by the start of the 40th round, he was so nearly blind that he took his fighting stance opposite one of the ring posts. At that point, the referee stopped the fight, and Wolgast was the champion.

Nelson continued to fight for seven more years but never again contended for the championship. He lost the newspaper decision in a return match with Wolgast in 1913 when both men were past their primes. Nelson lost his career earnings and died in poverty.

BILLY PAPKE
The Illinois Thunderbolt

MIDDLEWEIGHT

Right handed; 5'8¾"; 150–162 lbs.
62 bouts, 3/24/1906 to 4/8/1919
Managers: Tom Jones and Al Lippe
Middleweight Champion 1908
Hall of Fame Induction: 2001
Born: 9/17/1886, Spring Valley, IL
Named: William Herman Papke
Died: 11/26/1936

Billy Papke's violent life led to the middleweight championship of the world, but also to a tragic and untimely demise. Papke became known for his fistic prowess at age six. His youth was spent fighting, working, and playing baseball, and he soon followed his father to the local mines, where workers staged impromptu boxing matches.

Papke turned pro on March 24, 1906, outpointing the "Mexican Wonder" over four rounds in LaSalle, IL. In the next eighteen months, fighting mostly in Illinois, he accrued a record of seventeen wins and three draws before his first big fight—at age 21—a newspaper decision over former British champion Pat O'Keefe in Philadelphia.

After beating Hugo Kelly on March 6, 1908, Papke earned a title shot against one of the greatest fighters ever, Hall of Famer Stanley Ketchel. Ketchel opened the June 4, 1908, match in Milwaukee with a quick left hook, downing Papke. Though Papke shook it off and fought for another ten rounds, he complained that Ketchel had hit him when he was reaching out to shake hands. Ketchel won the decision and retained his title, but Papke served notice that he would not be duped again.

The rematch was held on Labor Day, September 7, 1908, at the James J. Jeffries Athletic Club in Vernon, California, with Jeffries himself serving as referee. At the start of the fight, Papke stunned Ketchel with a right to the face when Ketchel extended *his* arm to shake hands, and proceeded to knock him down five times in the first round. By the ninth, Papke had closed

Referee Jim Jeffries restarts the action in the brutal September 7, 1908, bout in which Papke (L) took the title from the battered Stanley Ketchel.

IN THE RING	WON **37**	LOST **11**	DRAWS **6**	TB 62	KO 30	W 6	WF 1	D 6	KO'd 1	L 8	LF 2	ND 8	NC 0

Date	Year	Opponent	Site	Result / Rounds		Title
SELECTED BOUTS						
Mar 24	1906	Mexican Wonder	LaSalle, IL	W	4	—
Mar 6	1908	Hugo Kelly	Milwaukee	W	10	—
Jun 4	1908	♛ Stanley Ketchel ★	Milwaukee	L	10	For-World-M
Aug 13	1908	Frank Mantell	Boston	KO	1	—
Sep 7	1908	♛ Stanley Ketchel ★	Vernon, CA	TKO	12	Won-World-M
Nov 26	1908	Stanley Ketchel ★	Colma, CA	KO'd	11	Lost-World-M
Mar 19	1909	Fireman Jim Flynn	Los Angeles	L	10	—
Jul 5	1909	♛ Stanley Ketchel ★	Colma	L	20	For-World-M
Jun 21	1910	Jack ("Twin") Sullivan	Boston	W	12	—
Feb 11	1911	Cyclone Johnny Thompson	Sydney	L	20	—
Jun 8	1911	Jim Sullivan	London	KO	9	—
Oct 31	1911	Bob Moha	Boston	L	12	—
Jun 29	1912	Marcel Moreau	Paris	KO	16	Won-French-M
Oct 23	1912	Georges Carpentier ★	Paris	WF	17	—
Mar 5	1913	Frank Klaus	Paris	LF	15	For-Vac-World-M
Apr 8	1919	Soldier Jacob Bartfield	San Francisco	L	4	—

both of Ketchel's eyes. In the eleventh round, he knocked Ketchel through the ropes. Finally, in the twelfth, Papke, covered with the other man's gore from wrist to shoulder, knocked Ketchel down twice. Jeffries stopped the fight, one of the bloodiest matches in history. Papke won the middleweight championship, believing that his own sneak attack repaid Ketchel for his previous early blow.

Papke soon faced Ketchel for a third time on Thanksgiving Day, 1908, in Colma, California. Hoping to lull Papke, now called the "Illinois Thunderbolt," into a false sense of security, Ketchel's camp spread rumors that he was drinking heavily, while he actually trained vigorously for the match. He knocked Papke out in the eleventh round. Ketchel won their fourth battle, July 5, 1909, with a twenty-round decision.

Ketchel was murdered in October of 1910, and Papke claimed his title, yet losses hurt his reputation. He travelled to London and knocked out the British champ, Jim Sullivan, for what some considered the middleweight title. After an extremely lackluster fight against Bob Moha in 1911, Papke briefly retired.

Soon he was back, and on June 29, 1912, Papke knocked out Marcel Moreau in Paris to win the French crown. Finally he faced Frank Klaus in Paris on March 5, 1913, in a fight universally recognized as for the middleweight championship. Papke was knocked down twice and then was disqualified for butting in the fifteenth round. He fought twice more before leaving the sport.

In retirement, Papke owned real estate and trained his son, Billy Jr., who tried his hand at boxing. Papke's later life was marred by conflict with his estranged wife, Edna. On Thanksgiving Day, 1936, he left his job as a greeter at ex-boxer Fireman Jim Flynn's tavern in Los Angeles and went to Edna's apartment with his .38 revolver. Papke killed her and then turned the gun on himself.

BILLY PETROLLE
The Fargo Express

LIGHTWEIGHT

Right-handed; 5'7"; 130–144 lbs.

160 bouts, 10/27/1922 to 1/24/1934

Manager: Jack Hurley

Hall of Fame Induction: 2000

Born: 1/10/1905, Berwick, PA

Named: William Michael Petrolle

Died: 5/14/1983

A tough crowd-pleaser, Billy Petrolle defeated three Hall of Famers, yet was never a champion himself. Petrolle's family moved to Fargo, North Dakota, when he was a small boy. His father was a laborer for the Northern Pacific Railroad, and Petrolle left school in seventh grade to join him in the shops. Lured by the $60 offered for bouts at the Elks Club of Fargo, Petrolle entered a match. He later explained, "I would have fought Jack Dempsey for sixty bucks. It was more than I made for two weeks in the shops. I knocked the kid out in the second round, and when they counted ten over him, I knew I was never going back." After two more bouts at the Elks Club, promoter/manager Jack Hurley began training Petrolle, teaching him to both jab and hook with his left.

Petrolle is credited with 160 fights during his career, though his total may have exceeded 250. Dubbed "The Fargo Express" after a cartoonist pictured him as a runaway locomotive, Petrolle was always ready to fight, entering the ring for at least 76 bouts in his first four years as a boxer. Petrolle went the distance against champion and Hall of Famer Sammy Mandell on January 13, 1928, in a non-title, no-decision bout, but later that year he knocked out Hall of Famer Kid Berg. Then a beating at the hands of King Tut in a no-decision fight in October, 1928 kept him out of the ring for four months. Though 1929 brought a "newspaper" victory over former lightweight champ Jimmy Goodrich, a loss to Tut in Detroit sent Petrolle into retirement.

Patsy Haley counts out Eddie Ran in Madison Square Garden on January 22, 1932. Petrolle scores a sixth-round knockout.

IN THE RING	WON 83	LOST 21	DRAWS 10	TB 160	KO 62	W 17	WF 4	D 10	KO'd 3	L 17	LF 1	ND 45	NC 1

Date	Year	Opponent	Site	Result / Rounds		Title
SELECTED BOUTS						
Oct 27	1922	Kid Fogarty	Fargo, ND	KO	2	—
Mar 1	1926	⑩ Louis ("Kid") Kaplan	Hartford, CT	L	10	—
Jun 15	1927	⑩ Billy Wallace	New York	L	10	—
Jan 13	1928	♛ Sammy Mandell★	Minneapolis	ND-L	10	—
Jun 21	1928	⑩ Bruce Flowers	Detroit	W	10	—
Jul 26	1928	⑩ Jackie ("Kid") Berg★	Chicago	D	10	—
Aug 24	1928	⑩ Jackie ("Kid") Berg★	Chicago	TKO	5	—
Oct 16	1928	⑩ King Tut	Minneapolis	ND-L	10	—
Sep 12	1929	⑩ King Tut	Detroit	L	10	—
Sep 11	1930	⑩ Tony Canzoneri★	Chicago	W	10	—
Oct 10	1930	♛ Jackie ("Kid") Berg★	New York	L	10	—
Nov 21	1930	⑩ Jimmy McLarnin★	New York	W	10	—
Feb 27	1931	⑩ King Tut	New York	KO	4	—
May 27	1931	⑩ Jimmy McLarnin★	New York	L	10	—
Aug 20	1931	⑩ Jimmy McLarnin★	New York	L	10	—
Dec 30	1931	⑩ Billy Townsend	New York	KO	7	—
Jan 22	1932	Eddie Ran	New York	KO	6	—
Nov 4	1932	♛ Tony Canzoneri★	New York	L	15	For-World-L
Mar 22	1933	⑩ Barney Ross★	Chicago	L	10	—
Jul 12	1933	⑩ Bep Van Klaveren	New York	TKO	4	—
Sep 8	1933	⑩ Sammy Fuller	Boston	D	10	—
Oct 21	1933	⑩ Sammy Fuller	Brooklyn	W	10	—
Jan 24	1934	♛ Barney Ross★	New York	L	10	—

Petrolle launched a comeback four months later, scoring a decision against Hall of Famer Tony Canzoneri on September, 1930. On November 21, he faced Hall of Famer Jimmy McLarnin, and though McLarnin was heavily favored, Petrolle emerged victorious.

Petrolle's star dimmed the next year as he faced two defeats at the hands of McLarnin. He rebounded with a knockout victory over former champion Battling Battalino in a ferocious twelve-round battle on March 24, 1932, winning with a left jab followed by a right under the heart. Unfortunately, Petrolle injured his left arm, which had become his biggest weapon in the ring. Nevertheless, he won the rematch and earned a title shot against Canzoneri. Petrolle had trouble making weight for the fight, and though only 27, he was past his prime. He lost a fifteen-round decision to Canzoneri, and after two losses to Hall of Famer Barney Ross in 1933 and '34, Petrolle again retired.

Petrolle was an aggressive fighter who favored a crouched stance, his head bobbing from side to side. He attacked the body more than most boxers, and his left hook was a devastating weapon. As a good-luck charm, Petrolle always entered the ring wrapped in a red and green Navajo blanket. He fought ten current or former champions and defeated five of them, yet he lost his one title shot. In retirement, Petrolle operated a foundry, then a religious goods shop.

LIGHT HEAVYWEIGHT

Right-handed; 5'10½"; 155–165 lbs.
179 bouts, 12/12/1896 to 6/17/1912
Light Heavyweight Champ 1905–12
Hall of Fame Induction: 1994
Born: 1/17/1878, Philadelphia, PA
Named: James Francis Hagen
Died: 11/12/1942

Philadelphia Jack O'Brien was one of the most colorful fighters of the early twentieth century. A showman and a shrewd self-publicist, O'Brien was a great boxer as well. His strong left jab and solid right were complemented by his skill at blocking punches and countering attacks. Debuting as a lightweight, O'Brien turned professional at age eighteen in 1896 in his native Philadelphia. As he matured, O'Brien moved into the welterweight and then middleweight classes. Ultimately he fought light heavyweights and heavyweights, even though he never weighed more than 165 pounds.

In 1901 O'Brien sailed for England, where he hoped to build up his record. O'Brien won all nineteen of his fights there, fifteen by knockout. Not all of his opponents were of the first rank, but O'Brien nevertheless sent reports of his victories to the Associated Press, which alerted American fans to his success. Returning to the United States in glory (and reportedly with eighteen trunks of new clothes), O'Brien was greeted at the dock by the mayor of Philadelphia and a crowd of 10,000 fans. O'Brien hit the lecture circuit with Major Anthony J. Drexel Biddle, a prominent Philadelphian and avid boxing fan who encouraged young men to emulate O'Brien's "muscular Christianity."

O'Brien prepares for a violin performance. After he retired from the ring, O'Brien stayed close to the world of boxing and often attended important bouts.

IN THE RING	WON 100	LOST 6	DRAWS 16	TB 179	KO 51	W 41	WF 8	D 16	KO'd 3	L 3	LF 0	ND 57

Date	Year	Opponent	Site	Result / Rounds		Title
SELECTED BOUTS						
Dec 12	1896	Isadore Strauss	Philadelphia	D	6	—
Feb 14	1900	Young Peter Jackson	San Francisco	TKO'd	13	—
Feb 25	1901	Harry Smith	Newcastle, England	TKO	4	—
Mar 3	1902	Andy Walsh	Philadelphia	TKO	3	—
Apr 11	1902	♛ Joe Walcott (Barbados)★	Philadelphia	ND-W	6	—
Sep 29	1902	Joe Choynski★	Chicago	W	6	—
Nov 19	1902	Marvin Hart	Philadelphia	ND-D	6	—
Mar 30	1903	Joe Choynski★	Philadelphia	ND-W	6	—
Apr 20	1903	♛ Joe Walcott (Barbados)★	Boston	D	10	—
May 5	1903	Marvin Hart	Philadelphia	ND-L	6	—
Jan 27	1904	♛ Tommy Ryan★	Philadelphia	ND-W	6	—
May 14	1904	Charles ("Kid") McCoy★	Philadelphia	ND-D	6	—
Jul 23	1904	♛ Bob Fitzsimmons★	Philadelphia	ND-W	6	—
Nov 12	1904	Dixie Kid★	Philadelphia	ND-W	6	—
Mar 24	1905	Young Peter Jackson	Baltimore	WF	2	—
Apr 7	1905	Young Peter Jackson	Baltimore	W	10	—
Dec 20	1905	♛ Bob Fitzsimmons★	San Francisco	TKO	13	Won-World-LH
Nov 28	1906	♛ Tommy Burns★	Los Angeles	D	20	For-World-H
May 8	1907	♛ Tommy Burns★	Los Angeles	L	20	For-World-H
Jun 10	1908	Jack Blackburn★	Philadelphia	ND-W	6	—
Mar 26	1909	♛ Stanley Ketchel★	New York	ND-L	10	—
May 19	1909	♛ Jack Johnson★	Philadelphia	ND-D	6	—
Jun 9	1909	♛ Stanley Ketchel★	Philadelphia	TKO'd	3	—
Aug 15	1911	Sam Langford★	New York	TKO'd	5	—
Jun 17	1912	Ben Koch	Philadelphia	ND-L	6	—

Over the next few years, O'Brien fought such notables as Joe Choynski, Joe Walcott (Barbados), and Young Peter Jackson. By 1905, his string of successes allowed him to challenge Bob Fitzsimmons, the recognized world light heavyweight titleholder. Fitzsimmons, then 44, also claimed the heavyweight title, vacant since the retirement of James J. Jeffries. Fitzsimmons collapsed after thirteen rounds with O'Brien. Now acknowledged as the light heavyweight champ and, in some quarters, as the heavyweight champ, O'Brien embarked on a vaudeville tour to capitalize on his fame.

In 1906, O'Brien fought to a draw with the more widely recognized heavyweight titleholder, Tommy Burns, in Los Angeles. In a rematch, Burns won the twenty-round decision. In 1909, Stanley Ketchel made his eastern debut against O'Brien at the National Athletic Club in New York. O'Brien dominated the first six rounds, but in the ninth, Ketchel knocked him down. In the tenth, O'Brien was decked twice and only the bell saved him from a knockout. O'Brien retired in 1912, never having defended his light heavyweight title.

After a financial reversal resulting in bankruptcy, O'Brien operated a successful gym in New York.

MAXIE ROSENBLOOM
Slapsie Maxie

LIGHT HEAVYWEIGHT

Right-handed; 5'11"; 160–188 lbs.

299 bouts, 9/24/1923 to 6/26/1939

Manager: Frank Bachman

Light Heavyweight Champ 1930–34

Hall of Fame Induction: 1993

Born: 9/6/1904, Leonard's Bridge, CT

Died: 3/6/1976

Few fighters stepped into the ring more often than Maxie Rosenbloom, who fought 299 times in sixteen years. Raised on the Lower East Side of New York, Rosenbloom left school after third grade and later served time in reform school. Reportedly, actor George Raft spotted the young Rosenbloom in a street brawl and advised him to become a boxer. Rosenbloom had an unusual style. He was a weak puncher and often slapped at his opponents with an open hand—earning him the nickname "Slapsie"—but he was a consummate defensive fighter and did whatever was necessary to avoid getting hit. He won the vast majority of his fights, although he only recorded nineteen knockouts in his entire professional career.

Rosenbloom turned pro at the age of nineteen and quickly became ranked as a contender, placing tenth in the 1925 annual rankings by *The Ring*. In 1927, Rosenbloom faced Jimmy Slattery—who had already beaten him twice—for the vacant NBA light heavyweight title. Slattery again won the decision. Over the next couple of years, Rosenbloom kept up a rigorous schedule, battling 46 times in 1928 and 1929.

In 1930, Rosenbloom again faced Slattery in a title fight. Rosenbloom took the decision in fifteen rounds and won the world light heavyweight championship, as recognized by the New York State Athletic Commission. Most ring experts considered Rosenbloom the best light heavyweight in the game, and he was acclaimed as the undisputed champion when he defeated Lou Scozza in July of 1932.

Rosenbloom held the title un-

Toward the end of his career, Rosenbloom fought mostly on the West Coast, where the popular fighter operated two restaurants.

Date	Year	Opponent	Site	Result / Rounds		Title
SELECTED BOUTS						
Sep 24	1923	Nick Scanlon	New York	W	6	—
Mar 3	1925	Hambone Kelly	New York	W	6	—
Jul 16	1925	♛ Harry Greb★	Cleveland	ND-L	10	—
Aug 22	1925	⑩ Jimmy Slattery	Brooklyn	L	6	—
Jan 1	1926	⑩ Jimmy Slattery	Buffalo	L	10	—
Jan 11	1926	⑩ Art Wiegand	Buffalo	L	6	—
Oct 15	1926	♛ Tiger Flowers★	Boston	WF	9	—
Mar 17	1927	⑩ Young Stribling★	Boston	L	10	—
Jun 21	1927	⑩ Leo Lomski	New York	L	12	—
Jul 4	1927	⑩ Tiger Flowers★	Chicago	D	10	—
Aug 30	1927	⑩ Jimmy Slattery	Hartford, CT	L	10	For-Vac NBA-LH
Nov 9	1927	⑩ Tiger Flowers★	Detroit	D	10	—
Mar 5	1928	⑩ Cuban Bobby Brown	Pittsburgh	W	10	—
Jul 31	1928	Ted ("Kid") Lewis★	New York	WF	6	—
Aug 24	1928	⑩ Leo Lomski	Long Branch, NJ	D	10	—
Nov 22	1928	⑩ Cuban Bobby Brown	Jersey City, NJ	W	10	—
Nov 15	1929	⑩ Jim Braddock★	New York	W	10	—
Jun 25	1930	♛ Jimmy Slattery	Buffalo	W	15	Won-World-LH
Oct 22	1930	Abie Bain	New York	TKO	11	Ret-World-LH
Aug 5	1931	⑩ Jimmy Slattery	Brooklyn	W	15	Ret-World-LH
Nov 10	1931	Jim Braddock★	Minneapolis	NC	2	—
Jul 14	1932	⑩ Lou Scozza	Buffalo	W	15	Ret-World-LH
Nov 16	1932	⑩ John Henry Lewis★	San Francisco	W	10	—
Mar 10	1933	⑩ Adolf Heuser	New York	W	15	Ret-World-LH
Mar 24	1933	⑩ Bob Godwin	New York	TKO	4	Ret-World-LH
Jul 10	1933	⑩ John Henry Lewis★	San Francisco	L	10	—
Jul 31	1933	⑩ John Henry Lewis★	San Francisco	L	10	—
Nov 3	1933	⑩ Mickey Walker★	New York	W	15	Ret-World-LH
Feb 5	1934	⑩ Joe Knight	Miami	D	15	Ret-World-LH
May 8	1934	⑩ Mickey Walker★	Los Angeles	L	10	—
Nov 16	1934	⑩ Bob Olin	New York	L	15	Lost-World-LH
Jul 17	1935	⑩ John Henry Lewis★	Oakland	W	10	—
Nov 29	1935	♛ John Henry Lewis★	Chicago	W	10	—
Jun 26	1939	Al Ettore	Hollywood	KO	3	—

til 1934, when he lost a decision to Bob Olin, although many sports writers at ringside believed Rosenbloom had won. Along the way, Rosenbloom fought John Henry Lewis, winning three of their five matches. Rosenbloom had a reputation of fighting just about anyone who would get in the ring with him. He once asked for a match with Joe Louis. As the story goes, Louis was confident of winning but declined because he feared Rosenbloom would make him look bad.

A lively character, Rosenbloom didn't devote much time to training. Although he stayed away from alcohol, he enjoyed gambling, the company of women, and late night celebrations. Rosenbloom parlayed his colorful reputation into a successful acting and night club career, often portraying a punch-drunk fighter.

BARNEY ROSS
The Pride of the Ghetto

WELTERWEIGHT

Right-handed; 5'7"; 130–145 lbs.

81 bouts, 8/31/1929 to 5/31/1938

Managers: Willis ("Gig") Rooney 1929–30, Sam Pian and Art Winch 1930–38

Lightweight Champ 1933–35, Jr. Welterweight Champ 1933–35, Welterwt. Champ 1934, 1935–38

Hall of Fame Induction: 1990

Born: 12/23/1909, New York, NY

Named: Beryl David Rosofsky

Died: 1/17/1967

Barney Ross was a tough fighter whose excellent physical fitness and stamina made him a champion three times over. He held world titles in the lightweight, junior welterweight, and welterweight classes. Ross grew up in Chicago, where he was raised by Orthodox Jewish parents who wanted him to become a Hebrew teacher. His family was opposed to fighting of any kind, but after his father was killed in a holdup and Ross became the breadwinner, he convinced his mother he could make money in the ring. A fast, clever, and hard-hitting boxer, Ross won the 1929 Inter-City Golden Gloves Championship and turned pro later that year.

Fighting mostly in the Chicago area as a lightweight, Ross compiled a record of 40-2-2 and in 1932 was ranked as the third-best lightweight contender by *The Ring*. In 1933, Ross won a ten-round decision over Tony Canzoneri at Chicago Stadium for both the lightweight and the junior welterweight championships. Canzoneri and his manager, Sammy Goldman, disputed the decision. To silence

Ross (L) is about to connect with a left cross in one of his series of bouts with welterweight contender Filipino Ceferino Garcia, who, in 1939, took the world middleweight title from Fred Apostoli.

IN THE RING	WON 72	LOST 4	DRAWS 3	TB 81	KO 22	W 50	WF 0	D 3	KO'd 0	L 4	LF 0	ND 2

Date	Year	Opponent	Site	Result / Rounds		Title

SELECTED BOUTS

Date	Year		Opponent	Site	Result	Rounds	Title
Aug 31	1929		Ramon Lugo	Los Angeles	W	6	—
Oct 21	1929		Virgil Tobin	San Francisco	KO	2	—
Nov 19	1929		Joey Barth	Chicago	W	5	—
Oct 21	1932	⑩	Battling Battalino	Chicago	W	10	—
Mar 22	1933	⑩	Billy Petrolle★	Chicago	W	10	—
May 4	1933	⑩	Joe Ghnouly	St. Louis	W	10	—
Jun 23	1933	♛	Tony Canzoneri★	Chicago	W	10	Won-World-L & JW
Jul 26	1933		Johnny Farr	Kansas City	KO	6	Ret-World-JW
Sep 12	1933	⑩	Tony Canzoneri★	New York	W	15	Ret-World-L & JW
Nov 17	1933	♛	Sammy Fuller	Chicago	W	10	Ret-World-JW
Jan 24	1934	⑩	Billy Petrolle★	New York	W	10	—
Feb 7	1934		Pete Nebo	Kansas City	W	12	Ret-World-JW
Mar 5	1934	⑩	Frankie Klick	San Francisco	D	10	Ret-World-JW
Mar 27	1934	⑩	Bobby Pacho	Los Angeles	W	10	Ret-World-JW
May 28	1934	♛	Jimmy McLarnin★	Long Island City, NY	W	15	Won-World-W
Sep 17	1934	⑩	Jimmy McLarnin★	Long Island City	L	15	Lost-World-W
Dec 10	1934	⑩	Bobby Pacho	Cleveland	W	12	Ret-World-JW
Jan 28	1935	⑩	Frankie Klick	Miami	W	10	Ret-World-JW
Apr 9	1935		Henry Woods	Seattle	W	12	Ret-World-JW
May 28	1935	♛	Jimmy McLarnin★	New York	W	15	Reg-World-W
Sep 13	1935	⑩	Ceferino Garcia	San Francisco	W	10	—
Nov 29	1935	⑩	Ceferino Garcia	Chicago	W	10	—
Nov 27	1936	⑩	Izzy Jannazzo	New York	W	15	Ret-World-W
Sep 23	1937	⑩	Ceferino Garcia	New York	W	15	Ret-World-W
May 31	1938		Henry Armstrong★	Long Island City	L	15	Lost-World-W

any thought that he had been the beneficiary of a hometown bias, Ross made sure a rematch was promptly scheduled on Canzoneri's home turf at the Polo Grounds in New York. In the bloody fifteen-rounder, Ross was again the victor by decision.

In 1934 and '35 Ross engaged in three title fights with welterweight champion Jimmy McLarnin. Ross and McLarnin traded knockdowns in the first fight, which Ross won by decision, becoming the new champion. In a rematch held at the Madison Square Garden Bowl, McLarnin decisioned Ross to reclaim the title. In the third fight, however, Ross outlasted McLarnin to win by a unanimous decision. Again welterweight champ, Ross had by this time relinquished his lightweight and junior welterweight titles. Ross lost the welterweight title in 1938. He was so thoroughly battered by Henry Armstrong that fans shouted for the referee to stop the action, but Ross refused to go down in what was to be his last fight.

Ross enlisted in the Marines in World War II and was decorated for his bravery at Guadalcanal, but he became addicted to the morphine used to ease the pain from his war injuries. Eventually he overcame his addiction and wrote an autobiography, *Monkey on My Back*, later made into a motion picture starring Cameron Mitchell.

TOMMY RYAN

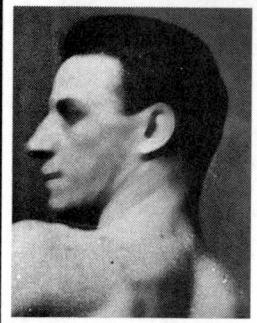

MIDDLEWEIGHT

Right-handed; 5′7¾″; 142–158 lbs.

105 bouts, 1887 to 3/4/1907

Welterweight Champ 1894–98,
Middleweight Champ 1898–1907

Hall of Fame Induction: 1991

Born: 3/31/1870, Redwood, NY

Named: Joseph Youngs

Died: 8/3/1948

An intelligent, adaptable fighter, Tommy Ryan held world titles in both the welterweight and middleweight divisions. He also schooled several of his contemporaries, including champions James J. Jeffries and Gentleman Jim Corbett, in some of the finer points of boxing. Ryan helped Jeffries develop the crouch he used when he wrested the heavyweight title from Bob Fitzsimmons, and later, he showed Corbett how to counteract the same maneuver.

Born Joseph Youngs, Ryan changed his name after he ran away from home. He honed his boxing skills in lumber camps, then turned professional in 1887 as a lightweight. He scored knockouts in seventeen of his first eighteen bouts, the exception being a 57-rounder with Jimmy Murphy that ended without a decision.

In 1893, Ryan began a five-battle series (not counting an exhibition) with the brawling Mysterious Billy Smith. The first two contests were draws. The third, held

1) Ryan floors Jack Dempsey (The Nonpareil) in the third at Coney Island on January 18, 1895.
2) Referee Hurst calls the fight a TKO. 3) Dempsey pleads in vain for Police Captain Clayton to intercede.

IN THE RING	WON 86	LOST 3	DRAWS 6	TB 105	KO 68	W 17	WF 1	D 6	KO'd 1	L 1	LF 1	ND 4	NC 6

Date	Year	Opponent	Site	Result / Rounds		Title
SELECTED BOUTS						
—	1887	John Case	—	KO	5	—
Apr 30	1889	M. Shaughnessy	Detroit	KO	23	—
Jun 18	1889	M. Shaughnessy	Detroit	KO	46	—
Aug 10	1889	Jimmy Murphy	Grand Rapids, MI	NC	57	—
Aug 29	1893	Mysterious Billy Smith	Coney Island	D	6	—
Jan 9	1894	Mysterious Billy Smith	Boston	D	6	—
Jun 1	1894	Jack Pitts	Minneapolis	KO	3	—
Jul 26	1894 ♛	Mysterious Billy Smith	Minneapolis	W	20	Won-World-W
Jan 18	1895	Jack Dempsey★	Coney Island	TKO	3	Ret-World-W
May 27	1895	Mysterious Billy Smith	Coney Island	NC	18	Ret-World-W
Mar 2	1896	Charles ("Kid") McCoy★	Maspeth, NY	KO'd	15	—
Nov 25	1896	Mysterious Billy Smith	Maspeth	WF	9	Ret-World-W
Dec 23	1896	Bill Payne	Syracuse, NY	KO	4	Ret-World-W
Feb 24	1897	Tom Tracy	Syracuse	TKO	9	Ret-World-W
Sep 8	1897	Charles ("Kid") McCoy★	Syracuse	NC	5	—
Jun 13	1898	Tommy West	New York	TKO	14	Ret-World-W
Oct 24	1898	Jack Bonner	Coney Island	W	20	Won-Vac World-M
Sep 18	1899	Frank Craig	Coney Island	TKO	10	Ret-World-M
May 29	1900	Charles ("Kid") McCoy★	Chicago	L	6	—
Mar 4	1901	Tommy West	Louisville, KY	TKO	17	Ret-World-M
Mar 14	1902	Mysterious Billy Smith	Kansas City	KO	4	—
Jun 24	1902	Johnny Gorman	London	KO	3	Ret-World-M
Sep 15	1902	Kid Carter	Fort Erie, Ont.	KO	6	Ret-World-M
Jan 27	1904	Phila. Jack O'Brien★	Philadelphia	ND-L	6	—
Mar 4	1907	Hugo Kelly	Rochester, NY	D	6	—

in Minneapolis, was a challenge for Smith's welterweight title. After twenty rounds, the Minneapolis police interrupted the fight. Ryan, judged to be in the lead at that point, was awarded the championship.

Ryan easily resisted an attempt by Jack Dempsey (The Nonpareil) to take the title in 1895, stopping the older boxer in the third round. The next year, Ryan faced his former sparring partner Kid McCoy in a non-title match. Ryan trained lightly for this bout and lost by knockout in the fifteenth round. Supposedly, McCoy tricked Ryan by telling him that he was not in shape.

In 1898, after triumphing in a brutal brawl with Tommy West, Ryan turned his attention to the middleweight ranks. He captured the championship with a twenty-round decision over Jack Bonner. Ryan never relinquished this title, holding it until his retirement in 1907. This ten-year hold on the middleweight crown is unrivaled.

Following his retirement, Ryan travelled the vaudeville circuit and performed in boxing exhibitions with Fitzsimmons. He also managed boxers, ran a gym in Syracuse, New York, and invested in several businesses in California, where he eventually settled.

JACK SHARKEY
The Boston Gob

HEAVYWEIGHT

Right-handed; 6'; 188–205 lbs.

55 bouts, 1/29/1924 to 8/18/1936

Manager: Johnny Buckley

Heavyweight Champion 1932–33

Hall of Fame Induction: 1994

Born: 10/26/1902, Binghamton, NY

Named: Joseph Paul Cukoschay

Died: 8/17/1994

Although he held the heavyweight championship for barely a year, Jack Sharkey was a well-respected boxer with great ring skills and an arsenal of punches. Over the years, he faced eleven opponents who either were or had been world champions, and he was the only man to fight both Joe Louis and Jack Dempsey. Sharkey learned to box in the Navy, where he became champion of the Atlantic Fleet. He turned pro in 1924, adopting his ring name in imitation of Jack Dempsey and Sailor Tom Sharkey. At the beginning of his career, Sharkey was a hard hitter, knocking out four of his first five opponents. Later, several hand injuries required him to evolve into more of a boxer, although he could still command a variety of punches, including a devastating left hook.

By 1925, *The Ring* ranked Sharkey as the seventh top contender for Jack Dempsey's heavyweight title. By the next year, he had risen to the number two spot in the same listing. Sharkey helped pave the way to a title challenge by defeating the formidable Harry Wills in 1926 at Brooklyn's Ebbets Field with 42,000 fans looking on. Wills gave away the win with a foul in the thirteenth, but the fight had been Sharkey's all the way.

In 1927, Sharkey faced Dempsey, who had lost the championship to Gene

Sharkey (L) takes a ten-round decision from the tough Young Stribling on February 27, 1929 at Flamingo Park in Miami. Official attendance was 30,102 and Sharkey's share of the receipts was $100,000.

IN THE RING	WON 38	LOST 13	DRAWS 3	TB 55	KO 14	W 21	WF 3	D 3	KO'd 4	L 8	LF 1	ND 1

Date	Year	Opponent	Site	Result / Rounds		Title
SELECTED BOUTS						
Jan 29	1924	Billy Muldoon	Boston	KO	1	—
Mar 18	1924	Eddie Record	Boston	L	10	—
Apr 25	1924	Eddie Record	Boston	KO	7	—
Sep 17	1925	⑩ Johnny Risko	Boston	W	10	—
Oct 12	1926	⑩ Harry Wills★	Brooklyn	WF	13	—
Mar 3	1927	⑩ Mike McTigue	New York	TKO	12	—
Jul 21	1927	⑩ Jack Dempsey★	New York	KO'd	7	—
Jan 13	1928	⑩ Tom Heeney	New York	D	12	—
Mar 12	1928	⑩ Johnny Risko	New York	L	15	—
Apr 30	1928	⑩ Jack Delaney★	New York	KO	1	—
Jun 21	1928	Leo Gates	St. Louis	KO	3	—
Dec 10	1928	⑩ Arthur DeKuh	Boston	W	10	—
Jan 25	1929	K.O. Christner	New York	W	10	—
Feb 27	1929	Young Stribling★	Miami	W	10	—
Sep 26	1929	⑩ Tommy Loughran★	New York	KO	3	—
Feb 27	1930	⑩ Phil Scott	Miami	KO	3	—
Jun 12	1930	⑩ Max Schmeling★	New York	LF	4	For-Vac World-H
Jul 22	1931	⑩ Mickey Walker★	Brooklyn	D	15	—
Oct 12	1931	⑩ Primo Carnera	Brooklyn	W	15	—
Jun 21	1932	♛ Max Schmeling★	Long Island City, NY	W	15	Won-World-H
Jun 29	1933	⑩ Primo Carnera	Long Island City	KO'd	6	Lost-World-H
Sep 18	1933	King Levinsky	Chicago	L	10	—
Sep 27	1933	⑩ Tommy Loughran★	Philadelphia	L	15	—
Aug 18	1936	⑩ Joe Louis★	New York	KO'd	3	—

Tunney just the year before, in Yankee Stadium. More than 72,000 fans paid $1.8 million to be there, a record gate for a non-title fight. Sharkey dominated the early going and came close to knocking Dempsey out. In the seventh, Dempsey peppered Sharkey with low blows. When Sharkey, grimacing in pain, turned to the referee to protest, Dempsey caught him with a left hook and knocked him out.

In 1930, Sharkey fought Max Schmeling for the vacant heavyweight title in Yankee Stadium before another huge crowd. Sharkey won the first three rounds, but was disqualified in the fourth when Schmeling fell to the canvas claiming a foul. In the rematch two years later, Sharkey won the decision and the world championship. He lost the title in his first defense to the ungainly giant, Primo Carnera. Sharkey dominated for the first five rounds. In the sixth, Carnera caught Sharkey with a wild right uppercut which knocked him out. Carnera was rumored to be under the control of mobsters, and noted writers such as Dan Parker and Paul Gallico believed underworld money had convinced Sharkey to take a fall. Sharkey vehemently denied the charge.

Sharkey lost his final fight on a third-round knockout to Joe Louis. In retirement, he operated a bar, refereed, made personal appearances at sportsmen's shows, and fished.

MIDDLEWEIGHT

Right handed; 5'10"; 127–162 lbs.

134 bouts, 1/12/1928 to 5/23/1941

Manager: Dave Miller

NY/NBA Middleweight Champion
1936–38

Hall of Fame Induction: 1999

Born: 12/18/1912, Tacoma, WA

Named: Frederick Earle Steele

Died: 8/23/1984

Perhaps the finest American middleweight of the 1930s, Freddie Steele—who grew up far from America's major boxing centers—decided to become a boxer at age six, when he watched pro Tod Morgan train. Morgan, another product of Washington State, went on to become world junior lightweight champion.

Steele began training at a local gym when he was twelve. The owner, Dave Miller, was so impressed with Steele's dedication and slugging ability that he soon had the young fighter sparring with pros and ultimately became his manager. Steele himself turned pro at age fifteen when he decisioned Hermosa Villa in four rounds in Tacoma, Washington, and by age eighteen he had fought professionally at least 39 times, winning 32; the remaining bouts were draws.

In 1932, Steele knocked out future champion Ceferino Garcia twice, and the next year beat Leonard Bennett, despite suffering a broken jaw. In 1935, he defeated such impressive opponents as Baby Joe Gans, future champion Fred Apostoli, and former champions Gorilla Jones and Vince Dundee, breaking Dundee's jaw in three places in a fight punctuated with at least eleven knockdowns.

On July 11, 1936, Steele defeated Babe Risko in Seattle in a fifteen-round decision to win recognition from both the NBA and New York Athletic Commission as the world middleweight champion. Steele was an active champion, defending his title four times during the next fifteen months, with points wins over Risko and Jones and knockout victories over Frankie Battaglia and Ken Overlin. He also won eight non-title bouts in the same period.

Boxing fans were now

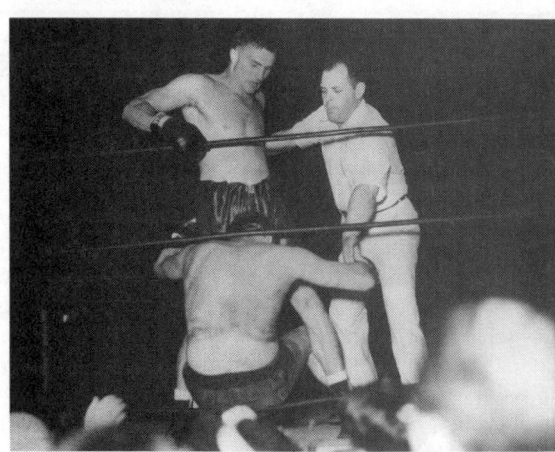

Vince Dundee, former middleweight champ from Baltimore, suffered a savage body attack, eleven knockdowns, a broken jaw, and a possible concussion at the hands of Freddie Steele before their July 30, 1935, fight was stopped in the third round.

IN THE RING	WON 120	LOST 4	DRAWS 9	TB 134	KO 60	W 60	WF 0	D 9	KO'd 3	L 1	LF 0	ND 0	NC 1

Date	Year	Opponent	Site	Result / Rounds		Title
SELECTED BOUTS						
Jan 12	1928	Hermosa Villa	Tacoma, WA	W	4	—
May 18	1932	Ceferino Garcia	Seattle	KO	2	—
Sep 20	1932	Ceferino Garcia	Los Angeles	KO	2	—
Jan 17	1933	Leonard Bennett	Seattle	W	6	—
May 22	1934	⑩ William ("Gorilla") Jones	Seattle	D	10	—
Jan 24	1935	⑩ Baby Joe Gans	Tacoma	KO	3	—
Apr 1	1935	⑩ Fred Apostoli	San Francisco	KO	10	—
Jul 30	1935	⑩ Vince Dundee	Seattle	TKO	3	—
Sep 17	1935	William ("Gorilla") Jones	Seattle	W	10	—
Mar 24	1936	⑩ Eddie ("Babe") Risko	Seattle	W	10	—
Jul 11	1936	⑩ Eddie ("Babe") Risko	Seattle	W	15	Won-NY/NBA World-M
Nov 17	1936	⑩ Gus Lesnevich	Los Angeles	KO	2	—
Jan 1	1937	William ("Gorilla") Jones	Milwaukee	W	10	Ret-NY/NBA World-M
Feb 10	1937	⑩ Eddie ("Babe") Risko	New York	W	15	Ret-NY/NBA World-M
May 11	1937	⑩ Frank Battaglia	Seattle	KO	3	NY/NBA World-M
Sep 11	1937	Ken Overlin	Seattle	KO	4	NY/NBA World-M
Jan 7	1938	♛ Fred Apostoli	New York	KO'd	9	—
Feb 19	1938	Carmen Barth	Cleveland	TKO	7	Ret-NY/NBA World-M
Jul 28	1938	⑩ Al Hostak	Seattle	KO'd	1	Lost-NBA World-M
May 23	1941	Jimmy Casino	Hollywood	TKO'd	5	—

clamoring for a unification bout between Steele and IBU World champion Fred Apostoli. Negotiations broke down due to a disagreement over money, but Steele agreed to meet Apostoli in a non-title bout. In a prior fight, Steele had knocked out a then-inexperienced Apostoli, but this time Apostoli battered Steele in a brutal bout until the referee stopped the contest in the ninth round. Steele defended his championship once more with a seventh-round knockout of Carmen Barth, but was stripped of the New York crown for not agreeing to a title match with Apostoli.

Steele still reigned as the NBA world middleweight champion, but he put that belt on the line on July 28, 1938, against Al Hostak at Civic Stadium in Seattle. For the first time, Steele entered the ring without the support of manager Dave Miller, who had died suddenly at age 36. Hostak launched an impressive first-round flurry and knocked Steele out at one minute and forty-three seconds of the first round. After this defeat, Steele, only twenty-five, retired from the ring. A brief comeback attempt three years later ended with a knockout by Jimmy Casino.

After his boxing career, Steele made a living as a Hollywood actor, capitalizing on a golfing friendship with Bing Crosby. He appeared in such films as *Gentleman Jim, G.I. Joe, Hail the Conquering Hero,* and *Deep Purple,* but his acting career didn't last long. Steele later became a longshoreman, then operated a restaurant in Westport, Washington.

YOUNG STRIBLING
King of the Canebrakes

H E A V Y W E I G H T

Right-handed; 5'11½"; 172 lbs.

285 bouts, 1/17/1921 to 9/22/1933

Manager: W. L. Stribling

Hall of Fame Induction: 1996

Born: 12/26/1904, Bainbridge, GA

Named: William Lawrence Stribling. Jr.

Died: 10/2/1933

Young Stribling knocked out 125 opponents, setting a record that only Archie Moore topped. Stribling failed to win a championship, but his career was still going strong when he died in a motorcycle accident at the age of 28.

Stribling's mother, a vaudeville acrobat, claimed she wanted him to be a boxer from the time he was a baby. "When he was six weeks old, I started rolling him around the bed just as you would a lump of dough. When he was two years old, I started him on leg and arm exercises," she later told an interviewer. Stribling's parents put him and his kid brother in their vaudeville act as juvenile boxers. When the family retired from the stage, they settled in Macon, where Stribling got formal boxing instruction at the YMCA. His first professional bout was a four-round decision in 1921 over a tough Atlanta newsboy named Kid Domb.

A bantamweight at age sixteen, Stribling added bulk steadily. He fought successfully as a middleweight in the Atlanta area and then, in 1923, gained national attention when he was matched in a non-title bout with light heavyweight champion Mike McTigue. Their first fight ended in a hotly contested draw. When the two met again six months later, Stribling knocked McTigue down in the tenth round, but New Jersey boxing regulations stipulated that only a knockout could be counted as a victory. Stribling had to be content with a "newspaper win," granted by ringside reporters.

Stribling (C) poses with his parents. W.L. Stribling was his son's manager; "Ma" Stribling, a powerful athlete herself, served as Young Stribling's trainer.

For all but a brief period, Stribling was managed by his father; his mother, "Ma" Stribling, handled much of her son's training. Stribling beat Hall of Famer Tommy Loughran twice in 1924, and was second in *The Ring*'s rankings of light heavyweight contenders that year. He would remain in *The Ring*'s top ten rankings, as either a light heavy- or a heavyweight, through 1931. The magazine ranked him as the top heavyweight in 1928.

A 1926 title bout with light heavy-

IN THE RING	WON 221	LOST 12	DRAWS 14	TB 285	KO 125	W 93	WF 3	D 14	KO'd 1	L 9	LF 2	ND 36	NC 2

Date	Year		Opponent	Site	Result / Rounds		Title
SELECTED BOUTS							
Jan 17	1921		Kid Domb	Atlanta	W	4	—
Oct 4	1923	♛	Mike McTigue	Columbus, GA	D	10	—
Mar 31	1924	♛	Mike McTigue	Newark, NJ	ND-W	12	—
May 2	1924		Tommy Burns★	Toronto	W	10	—
Jun 26	1924	⑩	Tommy Loughran★	New York	W	6	—
Aug 27	1924	⑩	Paul Berlenbach★	New York	D	6	—
Mar 28	1925	⑩	Tommy Loughran★	San Francisco	W	10	—
Mar 25	1926	⑩	Jimmy Slattery	New York	W	10	—
Jun 10	1926	♛	Paul Berlenbach★	New York	L	15	For-World-LH
Nov 11	1926		Battling Levinski★	Des Moines, IA	ND-W	10	—
Jan 23	1928	⑩	Martin Burke	Miami	KO	1	—
Aug 13	1928	⑩	Martin Burke	Mobile, AL	KO	1	—
Jan 21	1929		Sully Montgomery	Memphis	KO	2	—
Feb 27	1929	⑩	Jack Sharkey★	Miami	L	10	—
Nov 4	1929		Maurice Grizelle	Paris	W	10	—
Nov 18	1929	⑩	Primo Carnera	London	LF	4	—
Dec 7	1929	⑩	Primo Carnera	Paris	WF	7	—
May 8	1930		Hans Schoenrath	London	KO	3	—
Dec 12	1930	⑩	Tuffy Griffiths	Chicago	W	10	—
Jul 3	1931	♛	Max Schmeling★	Cleveland	KO'd	15	For-World-H
Feb 26	1932	⑩	Ernie Schaaf	Chicago	L	10	—
Nov 5	1932		Tony Gora	Adelaide, Australia	KO	6	—
Dec 17	1932		Don McCorkindale	Johannesburg	W	12	—
Mar 6	1933		Pierre Charles	Paris	L	5	—
Aug 2	1933		Benny O'Dell	Rome	KO	2	—
Sep 22	1933	♛	Maxie Rosenbloom★	Houston	W	10	—

weight champion Paul Berlenbach was a disappointment for Stribling, who had overtrained and tired badly in the later rounds. He scored a string of knockouts in 1928, however, and the next year faced heavyweight Jack Sharkey. Sharkey was staggered by a right to the heart, but when Stribling failed to follow up with more punches, Sharkey recovered. Later Sharkey said, "Had our positions been reversed, I could—in fact, I would—have murdered him." Jim Corbett considered Stribling the best feinter he ever saw but lamented Stribling's unwillingness to follow up with a solid punch. However, Stribling, recorded over one hundred knockouts using his "buckshot" punch, a right to the jaw following a right-left feint.

Stribling got another chance at a title when he fought heavyweight champion Max Schmeling in 1931. Stribling was reeling by the tenth round and was knocked down in the fifteenth. Referee George Blake stopped the fight with just fourteen seconds left in the final round. Again, it was speculated that Stribling had overtrained.

Stribling's last fight was a win over Maxie Rosenbloom in 1933. In October of that year, Stribling was struck by a car while riding his motorcycle home from a round of golf. He died in a hospital two days later.

LEW TENDLER

LIGHTWEIGHT

Left-handed; 5'6"; 118–147 lbs.

169 bouts, 1913 to 6/18/1928

Manager: Phil Glassman

Hall of Fame Induction: 1999

Born: 9/28/1898, Philadelphia, PA

Died: 11/5/1970

Though never a champion, Lew Tendler is considered one of the greatest left-handed fighters of all time. Tendler learned to fight on the streets as a boy, and after his father's death in 1908, he used his fists to gain and keep the most lucrative newspaper-selling corner in Philadelphia.

Encouraged to become a prizefighter, Tendler sought the advice of Phil Glassman, head of the Philadelphia Newsboys' Association and manager of several local boxers. Glassman managed Tendler for his whole career, starting with a fight at the Broadway Athletic Club, where Tendler fought a six-round, no-decision bout with Mickey Brown, the champion of the newsboys. Tendler earned $17.50 for the fight, based on his own ticket sales, and when his mother learned what he could get paid for boxing, she recanted her disapproval.

Tendler's early career consisted mainly of local no-decision bouts, fighting 96 no-decisions overall. At sixteen, he received a chance to fight Johnny Kilbane for the featherweight title, but Glassman turned it down because he felt Tendler was not yet ready. In 1916, Tendler performed well in a no-decision bout with Hall of Famer Pete Herman—who had fought to a draw for the bantamweight title three weeks earlier—and the next year fought two no-decision bouts against Hall of Famer Johnny Dundee. Tendler suffered his first defeat at the hands of Rocky Kansas, but in 1919, he knocked out George ("K.O.") Chaney in one round.

A victory over Johnny Dundee on May 5, 1922, established Tendler as the top contender for Hall of Famer Benny Leonard's lightweight title. Tex Rickard paired the two at Boyle's Thirty Acres near Jersey City—where, the pre-

Lew Tendler works out on the speed bag.

IN THE RING	WON 59	LOST 11	DRAWS 2	TB 169	KO 38	W 21	WF 0	D 2	KO'd 1	L 7	LF 3	ND 96	NC 1

Date	Year	Opponent	Site	Result / Rounds		Title
SELECTED BOUTS						
Nov 6	1913	Mickey Brown	Philadelphia	ND	6	—
Feb 28	1916	Pete Herman★	Philadelphia	ND-W	6	—
Mar 26	1917	Johnny Dundee★	Philadelphia	ND-L	6	—
Oct 1	1917	Johnny Dundee★	Philadelphia	ND-W	6	—
Oct 29	1917	Rocky Kansas	Philadelphia	ND-W	6	—
Sep 18	1918	George ("K.O.") Chaney	Philadelphia	ND	6	—
Jan 1	1919	Rocky Kansas	Buffalo	ND-W	10	—
Jun 4	1919	George ("K.O.") Chaney	Philadelphia	KO	1	—
Jun 13	1919	Packey Hommey	Newark, NJ	ND-W	8	—
Nov 8	1919	George Erne	Philadelphia	KO	2	—
May 19	1920	Pinky Mitchell	Milwaukee	ND-W	10	—
Oct 21	1921	Rocky Kansas	New York	L	15	—
May 5	1922	♛ Johnny Dundee★	New York	W	15	—
Jul 27	1922	♛ Benny Leonard★	Jersey City, NJ	ND-L	12	For-World-L
Jul 24	1923	♛ Benny Leonard★	New York	L	15	For-World-L
Jan 1	1924	Nate Goldman	Philadelphia	L	10	—
Jun 2	1924	♛ Mickey Walker★	Philadelphia	L	10	For-NBA World-W
Jan 19	1925	Jack Zivic	Pittsburgh	KO'd	5	—
Mar 16	1925	Nate Goldman	Philadelphia	W	10	—
Jun 8	1925	Jack Zivic	Philadelphia	W	10	—
Mar 15	1927	Young Harry Wills	Los Angeles	KO	8	—
Jan 2	1928	Jack McFarland	Philadelphia	KO	8	—
Jun 18	1928	Nate Goldman	Philadelphia	KO	5	—

vious year, Jack Dempsey had fought Georges Carpentier in boxing's first million-dollar gate. Fifty-five thousand fans paid a total of $367,862 to see the July 27, 1922, fight. Tendler cut Leonard's eye in the first, nearly knocked him down in the fourth, and in the eighth hit him with a right and a left to the face and another left to the chin. Leonard looked as though he might fall, but he pulled through and the fight went to its twelve-round conclusion. Officially a no-decision contest, the bout did not lead to the title changing hands. Despite his troubles in the fourth and eighth, Leonard won the newspaper decision.

The Cromwell Athletic Club and matchmaker Jimmy Johnston staged a rematch at Yankee Stadium on July 24, 1923. A crowd of 58,519 paid $452,648 to see the fight, a tremendous figure for the lightweight class. Leonard outboxed Tendler and won the fifteen-round decision. Tendler then moved up to welterweight and fought champion and Hall of Famer Mickey Walker on June 2, 1924, but he lost the ten-round decision. Tendler retired in 1928 after knocking out Nate Goldman.

Tendler was a somewhat unorthodox fighter. He was one of the few lefties who could jab and hook effectively with his right hand, though his most effective punch was a straight left to the body. In retirement, he operated successful restaurants in Philadelphia and Atlantic City.

GENE TUNNEY
The Fighting Marine

HEAVYWEIGHT

Right-handed; 6'½"; 155–192 lbs.

83 bouts, 7/3/1915 to 7/26/1928

Managers: Bill Jacob 1915–18, Billy Roche and Sammy Kelly 1919–20, Frank ("Doc") Bagley 1920–22, Billy Gibson 1923–28

Heavyweight Champion 1926–28

Hall of Fame Induction: 1990

Born: 5/25/1897, New York, NY

Named: James Joseph Tunney

Died: 11/7/1978

Gene Tunney—bright, good-looking, and an acknowledged pillar of the 1920s' "Golden Age of Sports"— was never as popular among boxing fans as the man he defeated to become heavyweight champion of the world. Tunney outfought Jack Dempsey in 1926, and he retained the title in the famous "long count" rematch a year later. Tunney's relative intellectualism, reticence in public, and scientific boxing style distanced him from fight fans and the press. Despite this lack of contemporary acclaim, Tunney is remembered as a great fighter who lost only once in his career and was the first heavyweight champion to retire—and stay retired—as the titleholder.

Although he later found his way into high society, Tunney's origins were strictly working class. He grew up in New York, where his father was a longshoreman. He learned to fight in the streets, and the gift of a pair of boxing gloves when he was ten is often cited as significant to his development. Still, Tunney did not pursue boxing in earnest until his teens, when he frequented the Greenwich Village Athletic Club at night after working all day as a typist for a steamship company.

Twenty-nine-year-old Gene Tunney signs a contract to meet Jack Dempsey for the heavyweight championship on September 23, 1926. Tunney is flanked by his manager Billy Gibson (R) and promoter Tex Rickard.

IN THE RING	WON 61	LOST 1	DRAWS 1	TB 83	KO 45	W 16	WF 0	D 1	KO'd 0	L 1	LF 0	ND 19	NC 1

Date	Year	Opponent	Site	Result / Rounds		Title
SELECTED BOUTS						
Jul 3	1915	Bobby Dawson	New York	TKO	9	—
Aug	1915	Battling Genrimo	New York	KO	3	—
Dec 5	1918	Victor Marchand	Paris	KO	2	—
Dec	1918	Howard Morrow	Romorantin, France	KO	6	—
Dec	1918	Tommy Gavigan	Romorantin	D	12	—
Apr 26	1919	Ted Jamieson	Paris	W	10	—
Nov 14	1919	Dan O'Dowd	Bayonne, NJ	ND-W	8	—
Jun 28	1920	Ole Anderson	Jersey City, NJ	TKO	3	—
Jul 2	1921	Soldier Jones	Jersey City	TKO	7	—
Oct 14	1921	Jack Burke	New York	TKO	3	—
Jan 13	1922	Battling Levinsky★	New York	W	12	Won-Vac Amer-LH
Apr 10	1922	Jack Burke	Pittsburgh	TKO	9	—
May 23	1922	Harry Greb★	New York	L	15	Lost-Amer-LH
Aug 24	1922	Tommy Loughran★	Philadelphia	ND-W	8	—
Feb 23	1923	Harry Greb★	New York	W	15	Reg-Amer-LH
Jul 31	1923	Dan O'Dowd	Long Island City, NY	W	12	—
Dec 10	1923	♛ Harry Greb★	New York	W	15	Ret-Amer-LH
Jul 24	1924	Georges Carpentier★	New York	TKO	15	—
Sep 17	1924	Harry Greb★	Cleveland	ND-D	10	—
Mar 27	1925	Harry Greb★	St. Paul, MN	ND-W	10	—
Jun 5	1925	⑩ Tommy Gibbons★	New York	KO	12	—
Nov 18	1925	⑩ Johnny Risko	Cleveland	ND-W	12	—
Dec 29	1925	⑩ Dan O'Dowd	St. Petersburg, FL	KO	2	—
Sep 23	1926	♛ Jack Dempsey★	Philadelphia	W	10	Won-World-H
Sep 22	1927	⑩ Jack Dempsey★	Chicago	W	10	Ret-World-H
Jul 26	1928	⑩ Tom Heeney	New York	TKO	11	Ret-World-H

He turned pro in 1915 with a TKO over Bobby Dawson, a far more experienced boxer.

When World War I erupted, Tunney joined the Marines. While stationed in France, he won the American Expeditionary Force light heavyweight championship. Back in the United States, Tunney continued his ring success. In 1921, he stopped Soldier Jones on the undercard of the Dempsey–Carpentier fight in Jersey City. The next year, Tunney decisioned Battling Levinsky to win the American light heavyweight title. Tunney's first defense came just months later against Hall of Famer Harry Greb, a fighter whose tornado-like attacks were feared by many fighters. In a brutal match, Greb used a variety of tactics—some of questionable legality. It was Tunney's only loss. His nose was broken by a headbutt, his eyes were nearly swollen shut and his face was covered in blood, but Greb couldn't knock him out. The fight went the full fifteen and Greb won the decision. In a rematch the next year, Tunney avenged the loss. He won a fifteen-round decision over Greb by slamming him with a series of body punches on the advice of master ring technician, Benny Leonard.

Tunney fought in eleven professional bouts before he joined the Marines in 1917, when the U.S. entered World War I.

Tunney's (R) only loss came at the hands of Harry Greb on May 23, 1922. Tunney avenged the defeat that same year.

Tunney then turned his attention to his longtime goal, the heavyweight title held by Jack Dempsey. In 1926, Tunney signed to face Dempsey in Philadelphia at the Sesquicentennial Stadium. The match could not be held in New York because that state's athletic commission banned Dempsey for refusing to defend his title against African-American contender, Harry Wills. Tunney trained purposefully. He studied films of Dempsey, and he brought many former Dempsey opponents or sparring partners to his camp to learn as much about the champ's style as possible. In interviews, he exuded confidence (although he was belittled by the press for reading a book while in training). Thanks to the promotional genius of Tex Rickard, the fight attracted 120,757 fans who paid almost $2 million in hopes of seeing Tunney get his comeuppance. In the first round, Tunney countered a left hook with a chopping right to the cheek which staggered Dempsey. Tunney then out-boxed the Manassa Mauler for the remaining nine rounds of the fight to win the decision and the championship.

Dempsey demanded a rematch and the two met in 1927 at Soldier Field in Chicago. Over one hundred thousand fans showed up, and the $2.6 million gate set a record. Through the first six rounds, Tunney was leading the fight, although neither fighter had seriously damaged the other. In the seventh, Dempsey stunned Tunney with a right cross to the temple, then followed it up with

A barrage from Jack Dempsey felled Tunney in the seventh round of their September 22, 1927 rematch in Chicago. When Dempsey delayed in retreating to a neutral corner, Tunney had time to recover.

six more strong blows, knocking Tunney down. Under Illinois boxing rules, Dempsey had to go to a neutral corner before the count could begin. Instead, Dempsey went to Tunney's corner, an action that would have been legal in New York. By the time referee Dave Barry got Dempsey to the neutral corner, Tunney had been down for at least four seconds. Tunney rose at the delayed ten count and continued the battle. Tunney won the decision, although the "long count" tainted the fight in the minds of many fans.

Tunney fought one more time, scoring an eleventh-round TKO over title challenger Tom Heeney, before retiring. He married a steel heiress and, interrupted by a stint in the Navy in World War II, had a very successful business career. An object of interest to literary sportsmen, Tunney counted Ernest Hemingway and George Bernard Shaw among his friends. One of his four children, John, became a United States Senator.

PANCHO VILLA

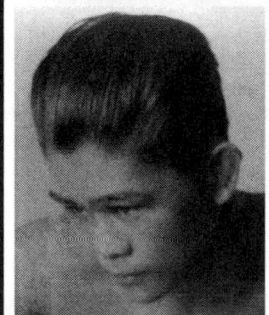

FLYWEIGHT

Right-handed; 5'1"; 109–115 lbs.

105 bouts, 1919 to 7/4/1925

Manager: Frank A. Churchill

Flyweight Champion 1923–25

Hall of Fame Induction: 1994

Born: 8/1/1901, Iloilo, Philippines

Named: Francisco Guilledo

Died: 7/14/1925

Pancho Villa is considered by many to be the greatest Asian fighter in boxing history. Just over five feet tall, Villa was explosive and unrelenting in the ring. He had fought 105 times, sometimes with as little as a week between bouts, by the time of his death at age 24. Born Francisco Guilledo on the island of Panay in the Philippines, Villa often fought with other boys in his village. His reputation with his fists brought him to the attention of promoter Frank Churchill in Manila. Impressed with the then-80-pound fighter, Churchill began handling Villa and, reportedly, named him after the famous Mexican bandit.

Villa fought exclusively in the Philippines from 1919 through April 1922, often facing much larger men. In that time, he lost only three fights and captured two Filipino titles. In 1922, Churchill took Villa to the United States. The young Filipino fought two no-decision bouts in New Jersey, losing—according to the newspapers—to Abe Goldstein and Frankie Genaro. The America press and public were at first slow to take notice of Villa. Churchill had difficulty arranging fights in major venues until, for almost no money, he got Villa and another Filipino, Elino Flores, on a card at Ebbets Field, home of the Brooklyn Dodgers. Each fighter won his bout, and the crowd gave Villa a standing ovation.

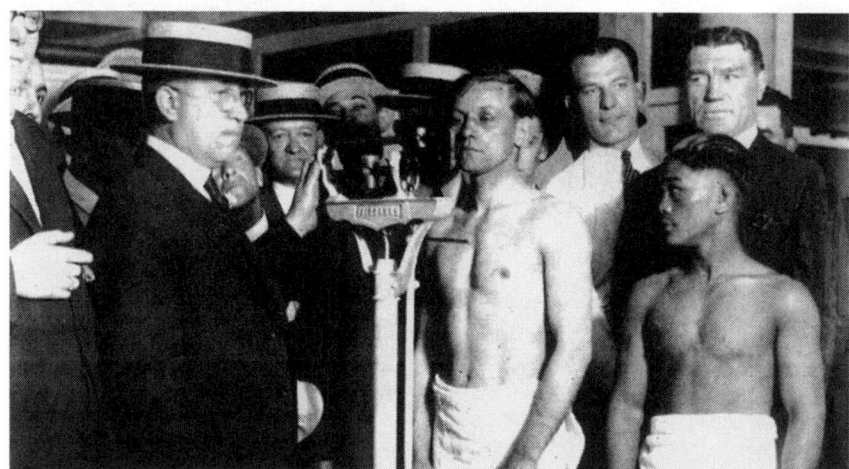

Philadelphia Jack O'Brien stands directly behind Villa as towel-wrapped Jimmy Wilde is weighed in for the defense of his flyweight title. Villa triumphed with a seven-round knockout of the aging star.

IN THE RING	WON 73	LOST 5	DRAWS 4	TB 105	KO 22	W 51	WF 0	D 4	KO'd 0	L 4	LF 1	ND 23

Date	Year	Opponent	Site	Result / Rounds		Title
SELECTED BOUTS						
—	1919	Kid Castro	Manila, Philippines	W	4	—
Jun 7	1922	Abe Goldstein	Jersey City, NJ	ND-L	12	—
Jul 6	1922	Frankie Genaro ★	Jersey City	ND-L	12	—
Jul 19	1922	Battling Murray	Averne, NY	W	6	—
Jul 29	1922	Terry Miller	Asbury Park, NJ	ND-W	12	—
Aug 2	1922	Johnny Hepburn	New York	W	6	—
Aug 22	1922	Frankie Genaro ★	New York	L	10	—
Sep 14	1922	Johnny Buff	New York	KO	11	Won-Amer-FL
Nov 17	1922	Abe Goldstein	New York	W	15	Ret-Amer-FL
Dec 29	1922	Terry Martin	New York	W	15	Ret-Amer-FL
Jan 1	1923	Battling Murray	Philadelphia	ND-W	8	—
Mar 1	1923	Frankie Genaro ★	New York	L	15	Lost-Amer-FL
May 11	1923	Battling Murray	Chicago	ND-W	10	—
May 24	1923	Bobby Wolgast	Philadelphia	ND-L	8	—
Jun 18	1923	♛ Jimmy Wilde ★	New York	KO	7	Won-World-FL
Jul 31	1923	Kid Williams ★	Philadelphia	ND-L	8	—
Oct 13	1923	Benny Schwartz	Baltimore	W	15	Ret-World-FL
Dec 10	1923	Patsy Wallace	Philadelphia	ND-W	8	—
Feb 8	1924	Georgie Marks	New York	W	15	Ret-World-FL
May 30	1924	Frankie Ash	Brooklyn	W	15	Ret-World-FL
Jul 28	1924	Battling Murray	Atlantic City	ND-W	6	—
Mar 9	1925	Francisco Pilapel	Manila	KO	8	—
May 1	1925	Clever Sencio	Manila	W	15	Ret-World-FL
Jul 4	1925	Jimmy McLarnin ★	Oakland	L	10	—

Three months after his arrival in the U.S., Villa knocked out Johnny Buff in eleven rounds to win the American flyweight title. Genaro took the title back in 1923 in a 15-round decision that most observers believed belonged to Villa. Meanwhile, British flyweight champion Jimmy Wilde had come to New York seeking the world title. Although Genaro was a likely opponent, the now wildly popular Villa was considered a better draw. In the match at New York's Polo Grounds, Villa displayed his relentless, attacking style, peppering Wilde with punches from both hands. In the seventh round, Villa battered Wilde to a state of helplessness, ending the fight and Wilde's career.

Although a proposed rematch with Genaro never took place, Villa defended his title several times in the U.S. and the Philippines. Villa fought in a non-title bout with Jimmy McLarnin on July 4, 1925 in Oakland. Weak from the recent extraction of a wisdom tooth, Villa lost the decision. It was to be his last fight. Another visit to the dentist resulted in the discovery of an infection and the extraction of three more teeth. Villa ignored the dentist's instructions to rest and return for a follow-up visit, and instead indulged in a week-long party. The infection worsened, and by the time Villa's trainer, Whitey Ekwert, discovered the fighter's distress and rushed him to the hospital, it was too late. Villa died in the hospital of Ludwig's Angina, an infection of the throat cavity.

JOE WALCOTT
The Barbados Demon

WELTERWEIGHT

Right-handed; 5'1½"; 133–148 lbs.
135 bouts, 2/28/1890 to 11/13/1911
Manager: Tom O'Rourke
Welterweight Champion 1901–04
Hall of Fame Induction: 1991
Born: 3/13/1873, Barbados, British West Indies
Died: 10/4/1935

In 1950, when Nat Fleischer published his listings of the all-time best fighters in each weight class, he ranked Joe Walcott as the greatest of the welterweights. Walcott was a tough, skillful fighter willing to take on all comers from welterweight to heavyweight. Not quite 5'2", Walcott was nevertheless powerfully built and had a long reach that allowed him to compete with much larger men. He had great stamina and withstood beatings that would have finished most fighters.

Born in Barbados, Walcott grew up in his family's adopted home of Massachusetts. Although not a street brawler, Walcott excelled in both boxing and wrestling. While working as an elevator operator in a Boston hotel, Walcott began his professional career under the direction of promoter Tom O'Rourke. He won his first fight with a second-round knockout of Tom Powers.

After tallying a 46-4-8 record, including 30 wins by knockout, Walcott faced Kid Lavigne in San Francisco in 1897 for the world lightweight title. A natural welterweight, Walcott was weakened by the necessity of making the lower weight limit. Lavigne retained the title with a twelve-round decision. Walcott scrapped with Mysterious Billy Smith for the welterweight title in 1898. Smith and Walcott always put on a good show and they fought for 20 anything-goes rounds with the win going to Smith. In 1900, Walcott knocked out Joe Choynski, the heavyweight who went on to vanquish Jack Johnson the next year.

A few times in his long career, Walcott was forced to throw a fight. In a bout with Tommy West, Walcott, who was boxing well, simply quit at the end of the eleventh round. O'Rourke later told Fleischer, "Walcott didn't dare to win that night. I got the tip... he must lose.

George ("Kid") Lavigne gets the worst of it from Walcott, but was credited with the December 2, 1895 victory in Maspeth, NY. The combatants had agreed beforehand that Walcott could only win by knockout.

IN THE RING	WON	LOST	DRAWS	TB	KO	W	WF	D	KO'd	L	LF	ND	NC
	92	**25**	**24**	134	58	34	0	24	9	12	4	21	2

Date	Year	Opponent	Site	Result / Rounds		Title
SELECTED BOUTS						
Feb 28	1890	Tom Powers	Boston	KO	2	—
Jun 5	1893	Paddy McGuigan	Newark	W	10	—
Mar 1	1895	Mysterious Billy Smith	Boston	D	15	—
Dec 2	1895	George ("Kid") Lavigne★	Maspeth, NY	L	15	—
Oct 29	1897	♛ George ("Kid") Lavigne★	San Francisco	TKO'd	12	For-World-L
Apr 4	1898	Mysterious Billy Smith	Bridgeport, CT	D	25	—
Dec 6	1898	♛ Mysterious Billy Smith	New York	L	20	For-World-W
Apr 25	1899	Dan Creedon	New York	KO	1	—
Nov 25	1899	Dan Creedon	Chicago	W	6	—
Nov 29	1899	Dan Creedon	Utica, NY	W	20	—
Feb 23	1900	Joe Choynski★	New York	TKO	7	—
May 4	1900	Mysterious Billy Smith	New York	W	25	—
Sep 24	1900	Mysterious Billy Smith	Hartford, CT	TKO	10	—
Sep 27	1901	George Gardner	San Francisco	W	20	—
Dec 15	1901	♛ Jim ("Rube") Ferns	Fort Erie, Ont.	TKO	5	Won-World-W
Apr 11	1902	Phila. Jack O'Brien★	Philadelphia	ND-L	6	—
Apr 25	1902	George Gardner	San Francisco	L	20	—
Jun 23	1902	Tommy West	London	W	15	Ret-World-W
Apr 1	1903	Billy Woods	Los Angeles	D	20	Ret-World-W
Apr 20	1903	Phila. Jack O'Brien★	Boston	D	10	—
Apr 29	1904	Dixie Kid★	San Francisco	LF	20	Lost-World-W
Sep 5	1904	Sam Langford★	Manchester, NH	D	15	—
Sep 30	1904	♛ Joe Gans★	San Francisco	D	20	—
Oct 16	1906	Billy ("Honey") Mellody	Chelsea, MA	L	15	For-Vac World-W
Nov 29	1906	♛ Billy ("Honey") Mellody	Chelsea	TKO'd	12	For-World-W
Nov 13	1911	Henry Hall	Eastport, ME	ND	6	—

. . . If West had been stopped in that twelfth round . . . I'd probably have been laying nice, peaceful and natural on the next slab."

Walcott was given another shot at the welterweight title in 1901 when the fought Jim ("Rube") Ferns. Walcott won easily with a fifth-round knockout. He retained his title until 1904, when he lost on a foul in the twentieth round to the Dixie Kid in the first world title match between two blacks. When the Dixie Kid outgrew the welterweight class later that year, Walcott was unofficially considered to have reclaimed the title. In 1906, Honey Mellody won a fifteen-round decision over Walcott to become the new welterweight champ.

Walcott held his own against much larger fighters, such as Sam Langford and Philadelphia Jack O'Brien. In addition to his recorded bouts, Walcott is reputed to have fought many other times. He retired in 1911 at the age of 38. In retirement, he worked as a fireman, a porter on a freighter, and as a handyman at Madison Square Garden. Jimmy Walker, then Mayor of New York, is said to have interceded with Garden officials to obtain this job for the down-and-out fighter who had once been a star. Walcott died in 1935 when struck by a car in Massillon, Ohio.

MICKEY WALKER
The Toy Bulldog

MIDDLEWEIGHT

Right-handed; 5'7"; 140–170 lbs.

163 bouts, 2/10/1919 to 12/1/1935

Managers: Johnny Anthes 1919–20, Jack Bulger 1920–23, Joe Diegnan 1923–25, Jack Kearns 1925–34, Bill Duffy 1934–35

Welterweight Champion 1922–26, Middleweight Champion 1926–31

Hall of Fame Induction: 1990

Born: 7/13/1901, Elizabeth, NJ

Named: Edward Patrick Walker

Died: 4/28/1981

Hard hitting, hard drinking Mickey Walker was a classic brawler who loved fighting for its own sake. He ran through millions of dollars during his lucrative career, living the life of a playboy whose off-hours carousing did little to affect his prowess in the ring. Compact and heavily-muscled, Walker had a repertoire of punches to mince the opposition, no matter what their weight class. He was a champion for nine years, holding the welterweight and middleweight titles successively.

Walker began his ring career at age seventeen in his native Elizabeth, New Jersey. He built a good record in the New Jersey area from 1919 to 1921, then in 1922, battered an aging Jack Britton in Madison Square Garden to take the world welterweight crown. At the top of the heap, Walker attracted Jack Dempsey's estranged manager Jack Kearns, and in 1925 the two formed a longtime partnership that included indulging in the flashy lifestyle Walker enjoyed.

Walker defended his welterweight title several times before challenging Harry Greb for the middleweight championship in 1925. A crowd of 65,000 filled New York's Polo Grounds to see these two aggressive fighters meet. Walker opened up early to try to wear down the champ, but Greb's speed was too much for him. Greb hung on to his title, winning the fifteen-round decision.

In 1926, Walker lost the welterweight title to Pete Latzo in a ten-round decision in Scranton, Pennsylvania, Latzo's home turf. Still title-hungry, Walker went after Tiger

Walker (L) held the welterweight title on July 2, 1925 when he moved up to middleweight to challenge Harry Greb.

IN THE RING	WON 93	LOST 19	DRAWS 4	TB 163	KO 60	W 33	WF 0	D 4	KO'd 5	L 11	LF 3	ND 46	NC 1

Date	Year	Opponent	Site	Result / Rounds		Title
SELECTED BOUTS						
Feb 10	1919	Dominic Orsini	Elizabeth, NJ	ND	4	—
Sep 14	1922	Artie Bird	New York	KO	8	—
Nov 1	1922	♛ Jack Britton★	New York	W	15	Won-World-W
Mar 22	1923	Pete Latzo	Newark	ND-W	12	Ret-World-W
Oct 8	1923	Jimmy Jones	Newark	NC	9	Ret-World-W
Jun 2	1924	⑩ Lew Tendler★	Philadelphia	W	10	Ret-World-W
Oct 1	1924	Bobby Barrett	Philadelphia	KO	6	Ret-World-W
Jul 2	1925	♛ Harry Greb★	New York	L	15	For-World-M
Sep 21	1925	⑩ Dave Shade	New York	W	15	Ret-World-W
May 20	1926	⑩ Pete Latzo	Scranton, PA	L	10	Lost-World-W
Dec 3	1926	♛ Tiger Flowers★	Chicago	W	10	Won-World-M
Jun 30	1927	⑩ Tommy Milligan	London	KO	10	Ret-World-M
Jun 21	1927	Ace Hudkins	Chicago	W	10	Ret-World-M
Nov 25	1927	⑩ Paul Berlenbach★	Chicago	W	10	—
Mar 28	1929	♛ Tommy Loughran★	Chicago	L	10	For-World-LH
Oct 29	1929	⑩ Ace Hudkins	Los Angeles	W	10	Ret-World-M
Feb 25	1931	Johnny Risko	Miami	W	10	—
Apr 10	1931	Bearcat Wright	Omaha, NE	W	10	—
Jul 22	1931	⑩ Jack Sharkey★	Brooklyn	D	15	—
Apr 29	1932	⑩ King Levinsky	Chicago	W	10	—
Jun 24	1932	⑩ Johnny Risko	Cleveland	L	12	—
Sep 26	1932	⑩ Max Schmeling★	Long Island City, NY	TKO'd	8	—
Nov 3	1933	♛ Maxie Rosenbloom★	New York	L	15	For-World-LH
May 8	1934	♛ Maxie Rosenbloom★	Los Angeles	W	10	—
Dec 1	1935	Eric Seelig	New York	TKO'd	7	—

Flowers's middleweight crown, which he took in a controversial decision. In 1929, Walker attempted to add the light heavyweight title to his list of laurels but lost a ten-round decision to Hall of Famer Tommy Loughran.

After defeating Ace Hudkins in October of 1929, Walker did not again defend the middleweight title, formally relinquishing it in 1931. That year, with his sights on the heavyweight belt, Walker battled future heavyweight champion Jack Sharkey to a draw (though a majority of the reporters at ringside believed that Walker won the fight). He also took on and conquered Bearcat Wright, a fighter who outweighed him by one hundred pounds and stood almost a foot taller. After suffering a beating at the hands of Max Schmeling, Walker returned to the light heavyweight ranks. He lost a fifteen-round decision in a title fight with Maxie Rosenbloom, although he beat Rosenbloom in a non-title rematch.

After losing to Eric Seelig on a seventh-round TKO in 1935, Walker retired. His ring earnings largely spent, Walker did some acting, operated a tavern, and worked as a salesman for a distillery. He later became an artist whose primitive-style paintings earned critical acclaim and also worked as sports editor of the *Police Gazette*.

FREDDIE WELSH
The Welsh Wizard

LIGHTWEIGHT

Right-handed; 5'7"; 130–140 lbs.

168 bouts, 12/21/1905 to 4/15/1922

Managers: Jack Clancy 1905–13, Harry Pollock 1913–22

British Lightweight Champ 1909–11, 1912–14, World Lightweight Champ 1914–17

Hall of Fame Induction: 1997

Born: 3/5/1886, Pontypridd, Wales

Named: Frederick Hall Thomas

Died: 7/29/1927

Considered one of the greatest defensive fighters in boxing history, Freddy Welsh parlayed excellent boxing skills, fantastic footwork, and expert use of his left jab into the lightweight championship of the world. Born in Wales, in the same region that produced Hall of Famer Jimmy Wilde, Welsh learned the basics of boxing in his homeland. He competed in amateur tournaments in Scotland under the name Freddy Welsh so that his mother would not know that her son, Frederick Hall Thomas, was a fighter.

When he was sixteen, Welsh ran away to the United States with three other boys. After a year he came back to Wales, but soon returned to America. Looking for work, Welsh rode the rails to the Dakotas to labor in the farm fields. He eventually got a job in a New York gymnasium where he honed his boxing skills.

Welsh turned professional at the age of eighteen with a knockout victory over Young Williams in Philadelphia. He fought 25 times in 1906 with all but three of those fights no-decision bouts. He then returned to the British Isles where he won thirteen fights in a row, including ten by knockout. Not known as a slugger, Welsh would only record twenty more knockouts during the remainder of his career.

Back in the United States, in 1908, Welsh lost a close decision and then fought to a draw with Packey McFarland. Then, frustrated at his inability to land a title shot against lightweight champion Battling Nelson, Welsh returned to England to contend for the first Lonsdale Belt offered by the National Sporting Club. He won a fairly easy twenty-round decision over Johnny Summers to take the belt. Welsh beat Hall of Famer Jim Driscoll on a foul to retain the belt before losing to Matt Wells, but he defeated Wells in the rematch. Still, Welsh could not get a shot at the world title. Nelson's van-

In Cardiff, Wales, two Welshmen, both Hall of Famers, vie for the Lonsdale belt, symbolic of British lightweight supremacy. Welsh (L) beat Jim Driscoll by disqualification on December 20, 1910.

IN THE RING	WON 76	LOST 4	DRAWS 6	TB 168	KO 32	W 40	WF 4	D 6	KO'd 1	L 3	LF 0	ND 82

Date	Year	Opponent	Site	Result / Rounds		Title
SELECTED BOUTS						
–	1905	Young Williams	Philadelphia	KO	3	—
Feb 18	1907	Seaman Hayes	London	W	6	—
Feb 21	1908	Packey McFarland★	Milwaukee	L	10	—
Jul 4	1908	Packey McFarland★	Los Angeles	D	25	—
Nov 25	1908	Abe Attell★	Vernon, CA	W	15	—
Nov 8	1909	Johnny Summers	London	W	20	Won-Britain-L
May 30	1910	Packey McFarland★	London	D	20	—
Dec 20	1910	Jim Driscoll★	Cardiff, Wales	WF	10	Ret-Britain-L
Feb 27	1911	Matt Wells	London	L	20	Lost-Britain-L
Nov 11	1912	Matt Wells	London	W	20	Reg-Britain-L
Dec 16	1912	Hugh Mehegan	London	W	20	Ret-Britain-L
Jan 1	1914	Johnny Dundee★	New Orleans	ND-W	10	—
Apr 28	1914	Leach Cross	Los Angeles	W	20	—
Jul 7	1914	♛ Willie Ritchie	London	W	20	Won-World-L
Nov 2	1914	Ad Wolgast★	New York	TKO	8	—
Mar 6	1916	Ad Wolgast★	Milwaukee	ND-W	10	—
Mar 31	1916	Benny Leonard★	New York	ND-L	10	—
Jul 4	1916	Ad Wolgast★	Denver	WF	11	Ret-World-L
Jul 28	1916	Benny Leonard★	Brooklyn	ND-W	10	—
Sep 4	1916	Charley White	Colorado Springs, CO	W	20	Ret-World-L
Apr 17	1917	Battling Nelson★	St. Louis	ND-W	12	—
Apr 20	1917	Rocky Kansas	Buffalo	ND-L	10	—
May 1	1917	Johnny Kilbane★	New York	ND-L	10	—
May 28	1917	Benny Leonard★	New York	TKO'd	9	Lost-World-L
Apr 15	1922	Archie Walker	Brooklyn	L	10	—

quisher, the new champ Ad Wolgast, signed for a fight with Welsh that was canceled when Wolgast was stricken with appendicitis.

Finally, Welsh met world lightweight champion Willie Ritchie in London for the title. In a very close fight, Welsh adopted a defensive posture which allowed Ritchie few clear shots at him. From time to time Welsh scored in close. Ritchie recorded the only knockdown of the fight in the twelfth round. The referee, the sole judge in the fight, scored the first nineteen rounds even and gave the twentieth and final round to Welsh.

Welsh defended his title twice and fought a host of no-decision bouts before facing Benny Leonard in a title contest on May 28, 1917. The great Leonard broke through Welsh's usually impenetrable defenses to knock him down three times in the ninth round before the referee stopped the fight. This bout was the only time in Welsh's career that he was stopped before the final bell.

Welsh served as a captain in the U.S. Army during World War I. After the war he fought five times before retiring, after a loss to Archie Walker. For some years Welsh operated a health farm in New Jersey before he lost it to foreclosure. He died in a New York hotel room in 1927 at the age of 41, unemployed and nearly penniless.

JIMMY WILDE
Ghost with a Hammer in His Hand; Mighty Atom

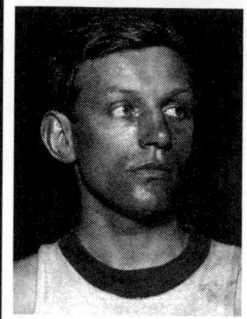

FLYWEIGHT

Right-handed; 5'2½"; 94–109 lbs.

149 bouts, 12/26/1910 to 6/18/1923

Manager: Teddy Lewis

Flyweight Champion 1916–23

Hall of Fame Induction: 1990

Born: 5/15/1892, Tylorstown, Glamorganshire, Wales

Died: 3/10/1969

Heavyweight champion Gene Tunney lauded Jimmy Wilde as "the greatest fighter I ever saw." The frail-looking Wilde, whose skinny limbs and protruding ribs belied the power of his punches, became the first flyweight champion to be recognized in the United States as well as in Britain. The flyweight class was established in England in 1909 by the National Sporting Club, but American recognition of the division did not come until 1916, the year Wilde took the world title.

Wilde was born in Wales in the same area that produced Freddie Welsh and Jim Driscoll. The son of a poor coal miner, Wilde worked as a pit boy as a child, hacking coal from channels too narrow for a grown man. When he began boxing in 1908 at the age of sixteen, he weighed just 74 pounds. He competed in boxing booth tournaments in his home of Tylorstown, taking on all comers. His first recorded professional match was a knockout of Ted Roberts in 1911.

Wilde won the British 98-pound title in 1913 when he recorded an eighteen-round technical knockout over Billy Padden. In 1915, he failed in his bid to win the British and European flyweight championships in the first loss of his career when Tancy Lee stopped him in seventeen. The next year, however, Wilde won wide acclaim as flyweight champion when he defeated Joe Symonds in London with a TKO in twelve. He also trounced Lee in a rematch in 1916 to unify the British and European flyweight titles. Later the same year, Wilde

Wilde's (R) June 18, 1923 meeting with Pancho Villa was his last bout. After his knockout loss, Wilde turned to sports writing.

IN THE RING	WON 131	LOST 3	DRAWS 2	TB 149	KO 99	W 31	WF 1	D 2	KO'd 3	L 0	LF 0	ND 13

Date	Year	Opponent	Site	Result / Rounds		Title

SELECTED BOUTS

Date	Year	Opponent	Site	Result / Rounds		Title
Dec 26	1910	Les Williams	Pontypridd, Wales	ND	3	—
Jan 20	1912	Matt Wells' Nipper	London	KO	1	—
Jan 1	1913	Billy Padden	Glasgow, Scotland	TKO	18	Won-Britain-98 lbs.
Jul 19	1913	Young Dando	Tonypandy, Wales	W	15	—
Sep 23	1913	Young Dando	Cardiff, Wales	W	20	—
Dec 6	1913	Young Dando	Merthyr, Wales	WF	10	—
Apr 27	1914	Alf Mansfield	Leeds, England	W	20	—
Sep 28	1914	Alf Mansfield	London	TKO	10	—
Jan 25	1915	Tancy Lee	London	TKO'd	17	For-Britain & Europe-FL
Jan 24	1916	Tommy Noble	London	TKO	11	—
Jan 27	1916	Jimmy Morton	Liverpool	KO	2	—
Feb 14	1916	Joe Symonds	London	TKO	12	Won-Britain-FL
Apr 24	1916	Johnny Rosner	Liverpool	TKO	11	Ret-Britain-FL
May 29	1916	Tommy Harrison	London	TKO	8	—
Jun 26	1916	Tancy Lee	London	TKO	11	Won-Eur-FL & Ret-Britain-FL
Nov 9	1916	Tommy Noble	Liverpool	TKO	15	—
Dec 18	1916	Young Zulu Kid	London	KO	11	Won-World-FL
Mar 12	1917	George Clark	London	TKO	4	Ret-Brit, Eur & World-FL
May 16	1919	Alf Mansfield	London	TKO	13	—
Jul 17	1919	Memphis Pal Moore	London	W	20	—
Dec 6	1919	Jack Sharkey★	Milwaukee	ND-W	10	—
Apr 12	1920	Young Zulu Kid	Windsor, Ont.	ND-W	10	—
Jan 13	1921	Pete Herman★	London	TKO'd	17	—
Jun 18	1923	Pancho Villa★	New York	KO'd	7	Lost-World-FL

knocked out Young Zulu Kid of the U.S. to gain universal acceptance as the world champion.

Wilde kept fighting and winning until former bantamweight champ Pete Herman hammered him for seventeen rounds in 1921 in London and Wilde collapsed from exhaustion. Still considered the flyweight champion, Wilde did not fight for over two years until he put his title on the line against the very hot Pancho Villa at the Polo Grounds in New York in 1923. In the first two rounds, Wilde fought well, but a hard right from Villa at the end of the second dazed him. Villa then pounded the champ at will until the fight ended in the seventh.

Wilde retired after the fight with Villa, putting his amazing seven-year career to bed. Veteran ring observers marveled for years at Wilde's power. He punched harder and more accurately than many men who outweighed him by 30 or 40 pounds. His scrawny physical appearance remained a source of scrutiny throughout his career, and once he became champion, several doctors studied him, trying to determine the unique source of his strength. His unorthodox training methods, which included competing in the boxing booths even after he became champion and using his wife as a sparring partner, have all fueled the boxing world's interest in this unusual star.

BANTAMWEIGHT

Right-handed; 5'1"; 110–124 lbs.

202 bouts, 7/18/1910 to 9/3/1929

Managers: Sam H. Harris, Dave Warnick, Max Waxman

Bantamweight Champ 1914–1917

Hall of Fame Induction: 1996

Born: 12/5/1893, Copenhagen, Denmark

Named: John Gutenko

Died: 10/18/1963

Kid Williams, who fought for nineteen years, is considered one of the top bantamweights of all time. Born in Denmark, Williams came to the United States with his parents in 1904. The family settled in a poor section of Baltimore, where Williams found work as a newsboy, often fighting for the choicest spots to sell papers.

Williams's skill with his fists attracted the attention of Baltimore matchmaker John Barrett, who persuaded the sixteen-year-old to enter his first professional match. The fight was held at Baltimore's Gayety Theatre in 1910. Williams attacked his opponent, Shep Farren, in an all-out fury and knocked him out in the fifth round. After this victory Barrett gave Gutenko a more "American-sounding" name to use in the ring.

Flamboyant manager Sam Harris soon latched onto Williams and controlled him—and his earnings—until the end of the fighter's career. Williams churned through a succession of opponents until he was matched against the more experienced George ("K.O.") Chaney, who handed him his first loss in 1911.

In 1912, Williams fought bantamweight champion Johnny Coulon in a non-title bout. The no-decision fight was deemed Williams's win by the newspapers, and the fans agreed, loudly cheering as he dominated Coulon in eight of the ten rounds. In 1914, Williams KO'd European bantamweight champ Eddie Campi. Five months later, he met Coulon again—this time for the world title—in Vernon, California, then a hotbed of boxing. The match was slated to go 20 rounds if necessary, but Williams wasted little time in vanquishing Coulon. By the third round, bleeding and with two fractured ribs, Coulon fell to a right cross to the chin.

Williams, at 21, was bantamweight champion of the

Dave Wartnick (L) was one of Kid Williams' managers. In his long career, the short, solidly-built Williams fought over 200 battles.

IN THE RING	WON 104	LOST 17	DRAWS 9	TB 202	KO 55	W 43	WF 6	D 9	KO'd 3	L 9	LF 5	ND 71	NC 1

Date	Year	Opponent	Site	Result / Rounds		Title
SELECTED BOUTS						
Jul 18	1910	Shep Farren	Baltimore	KO	5	—
Jul 10	1911	George ("K.O.") Chaney	Baltimore	L	20	—
Jul 27	1911	Young McFarland	New York	KO	5	—
Sep 14	1912	Mickey Brown	New York	TKO	8	—
Oct 18	1912	♛ Johnny Coulon★	New York	ND-W	10	—
Dec 11	1912	♛ Charles Ledoux	Philadelphia	ND-W	6	—
Feb 12	1913	Eddie Campi	Los Angeles	W	20	—
Jul 15	1913	♛ Charles Ledoux	Los Angeles	TKO	15	—
Jan 31	1914	♛♛ Eddie Campi	Los Angeles	KO	12	Won-Brit World-B
Jun 9	1914	♛ Johnny Coulon★	Vernon, CA	KO	3	Won-World-B
Jun 30	1914	Pete Herman★	New Orleans	ND-D	10	—
Dec 19	1914	Joe O'Donnell	Philadelphia	TKO	3	—
Mar 17	1915	♛ Johnny Kilbane	Philadelphia	ND-L	6	—
Sep 10	1915	Johnny Ertle	St. Paul, MN	LF	5	—
Oct 28	1915	Memphis Pal Moore	Memphis	L	8	—
Dec 6	1915	Frankie Burns	New Orleans	D	20	Ret-World-B
Feb 7	1916	Pete Herman★	New Orleans	D	20	Ret-World-B
Sep 4	1916	Frankie Burns	Baltimore	ND-W	10	—
Jan 9	1917	Pete Herman★	New Orleans	L	20	Lost-World-B
Jan 29	1918	Joe Lynch	Philadelphia	TKO'd	4	—
Mar 2	1921	Tommy Ryan★	Pittsburgh	ND-W	10	—
Jul 31	1923	Pancho Villa★	Philadelphia	ND-W	8	—
Dec 22	1923	Danny Lee	New York	KO	1	—
Jun 26	1925	Frankie Genaro★	Baltimore	L	12	—
Dec 14	1928	Willie Parrish	Baltimore	TKO	5	—
Sep 3	1929	Bobby Burns	Baltimore	KO'd	2	—

world. He went on to face some top talent, fighting a tough ten-round draw with Pete Herman in New Orleans in his first fight after winning the championship. He lost a no-decision bout to featherweight champ Johnny Kilbane in 1915 and later that year, in St. Paul, lost on a controversial foul to Johnny Ertle.

Williams met Herman again in New Orleans 1916, this time for the title. Herman clearly had the best of the fight, which was nevertheless declared a draw by referee Billy Rocap, a friend of Williams's. A year later, the two were back in New Orleans for another title challenge by Herman, who won the twenty-round decision.

Williams continued to fight for another twelve years. A tiny powerhouse at 5'1", Williams had an aggressive, attacking style which made him a formidable opponent to the end of his career. A profligate spender, Williams was also often bilked out of a fair share of his purses. He left the ring almost as poor as he entered it. He held jobs as a taxi driver, salesman, and steel worker. In 1934, he was sentenced to a year in jail for failure to support his wife and children. He tried, at the age of 42, to make a comeback as a boxer, but the Maryland State Athletic Commission refused to issue him a license. In 1957, Williams was arrested for drunkenness. He died in Baltimore in 1963.

HARRY WILLS
The Black Panther

HEAVYWEIGHT

Right-handed; 6'4"; 220 lbs.

103 bouts, 1910 to 8/4/1932

Managers: Jim Buckley and Paddy Mullins

Hall of Fame Induction: 1992

Born: 5/15/1889, New Orleans, LA

Died: 12/21/1958

One of the greatest heavyweights to never fight for a championship, Harry Wills was hampered during his entire career by the color bar that limited opportunities for black fighters. An undeniable rival for Jack Dempsey's crown, Wills was nevertheless shut out of a chance at the title. The race barrier may also have provided a convenient way for white boxers, wary of Wills's extraordinary size and power, to avoid facing him in the ring.

Wills worked as a longshoreman before turning to pro boxing in 1910. Initially he relied almost entirely on his bulk to win fights, but with time, Wills developed fine boxing skills and speed in the ring. Wills found several worthy opponents among a growing class of black heavyweights. He fought Hall of Famer Sam Langford eighteen times and got the better of the series. He also battled Sam McVey, Joe Jeannette, Jeff Clarke, Kid Cotton and Roughhouse Ware. Wills travelled around the country and to Panama to participate in these fights, which were often held in less than ideal conditions.

Wills floors Luis Angel Firpo before a crowd of 80,000 people at Boyle's Thirty Acres on September 1, 1924. The twelve-round bout was officially a no-decision contest, but the result was clear.

IN THE RING	WON 65	LOST 8	DRAWS 2	TB 103	KO 47	W 18	WF 0	D 2	KO'd 4	L 1	LF 3	ND 25	NC 3

Date	Year	Opponent	Site	Result / Rounds		Title
SELECTED BOUTS						
—	1910	Kid Ravarro	—	KO	1	—
May 1	1914	Sam Langford★	New Orleans	ND	10	—
Nov 26	1914	Sam Langford★	Vernon, CA	KO'd	14	—
Dec 20	1914	Sam McVey★	New Orleans	L	20	—
Sep 7	1915	Sam McVey★	Boston	W	12	—
Jan 3	1916	Sam Langford★	New Orleans	W	20	—
Feb 11	1916	Sam Langford★	New Orleans	KO'd	19	—
Feb 7	1917	Jim Johnson	St. Louis	KO'd	2	—
Apr 14	1918	Sam Langford★	Panama	KO	6	—
May 19	1918	Sam Langford★	Panama	KO	7	—
Sep 30	1919	Sam Langford★	Syracuse, NY	ND	10	—
Nov 5	1919	Sam Langford★	Tulsa, OK	W	15	—
Apr 19	1920	Sam Langford★	Denver	W	15	—
Jul 26	1920	Fred Fulton	Newark	KO	3	—
Oct 10	1921	Ed ("Gunboat") Smith	Havana	KO	1	—
Nov 18	1921	Ed Martin	Portland, OR	KO	1	—
Jan 17	1922	Sam Langford★	Portland	W	10	—
Sep 1	1924	⑩ Luis Angel Firpo	Jersey City	ND-W	12	—
Oct 12	1926	⑩ Jack Sharkey★	Brooklyn	LF	13	—
Jul 13	1927	⑩ Paolino Uzcudun	Brooklyn	KO'd	4	—
Aug 4	1932	Vinko Jankassa	Brooklyn	KO	1	—

Wills demonstrated his prowess to white audiences in 1920 when he knocked out white contender Fred Fulton in the third round at the First Regiment Armory in Newark, New Jersey. Fulton fell victim to Wills's tremendous strength and body punching. Although this victory thrust Wills into the status of top contender for Jack Dempsey's heavyweight crown, promoter Tex Rickard balked at holding a mixed-race title bout. In 1924, James A. Farley, chairman of the New York State Athletic Commission, announced the commission would not sanction a title match for Dempsey unless Wills was the opponent. Dempsey gave up his license to fight in New York, and Rickard instead signed Gene Tunney to fight Dempsey in Philadelphia. Reportedly, rival promoter Floyd Fitzsimmons attempted to arrange a Dempsey–Wills bout and paid Wills $50,000 in advance, which Wills could keep if the fight did not take place. As a result of Rickard's interference, the fight never happened. Some charged that Dempsey was afraid to fight Wills, but Wills never publicly made that assertion.

Wills fought Luis Angel Firpo in 1924 and was generally acclaimed the winner in a no-decision bout. In 1926 and past his prime, Wills fought future champion Jack Sharkey and was behind on points when he fouled Sharkey and was disqualified. Wills continued to fight until 1932. Had history been different, he could well have been heavyweight champion of the world. After his retirement, Wills prospered managing his New York real estate interests.

AD WOLGAST
The Michigan Wildcat

LIGHTWEIGHT

Right-handed; 5'4¼"; 118–133 lbs.

134 bouts, 6/10/1906 to 9/6/1920

Managers: Frank Mulkern 1906–08, Tom Jones 1908–15, and Larney Lichtenstein 1915–17

World Lightweight Champ 1910–12

Hall of Fame Induction: 2000

Born: 2/8/1888, Cadillac, MI

Named: Adolph Wolgust

Died: 4/14/1955

Extremely aggressive, Ad Wolgast rose to the top of the lightweight ranks with little concern for defense and a great ability to take a punch. Tragically, he paid a terrible price for too many blows to the head. Wolgast first saw a pro fight in Petoskey, Michigan. When he didn't have enough money for a ticket, Wolgast told the promoter he was a promising young amateur and found himself being matched with Kid Moore. Wolgast won the fight in a six-round decision—though Moore outweighed him by 27 pounds.

Wolgast fought his first two years as a pro primarily in Grand Rapids and Milwaukee before moving on to fight in California. There, he knocked out two opponents, but largely fought no-decision bouts. On July 13, 1909, Wolgast, now dubbed the "Michigan Wildcat," met Hall of Famer and lightweight champion Battling Nelson in Los Angeles for a no-decision, non-title fight. The newspaper decision in the bloody brawl went to Wolgast.

On February 22, 1910, Wolgast and Nelson met again in a "distance" title fight scheduled for forty-five rounds. Nelson had the advantage in the early rounds, but by the 40th his vision was so impaired that he took his fighting stance opposite one of the ring posts, and the referee stopped the fight. Wolgast was the new world lightweight champion.

Wolgast made his fifth title defense against Mexican Joe Rivers. He managed to force Rivers into accepting as referee Jack Welch, who was known to encourage the wild brawling-style fight that favored Wolgast. Rivers began well, and a discouraged Wolgast nearly did not answer the bell for the thirteenth, coming out only when his cornerman threatened him with a bottle. Wolgast unleashed a hard left to River's groin, while Rivers smashed him with a right-left combination to the jaw. Both fighters fell, Wolgast on top of Rivers, and Welch started a count on Rivers while

Referee Ed W. Smith is about to step in and stop this brutal fight in the 40th round. Battling Nelson (L) is blinded by Ad Wolgast's attack in Richmond, CA, on February 22, 1910.

IN THE RING	WON 60	LOST 12	DRAWS 13	TB 134	KO 40	W 19	WF 1	D 13	KO'd 4	L 4	LF 4	ND 49	NC 0

Date	Year	Opponent	Site	Result / Rounds		Title
SELECTED BOUTS						
Jun 10	1906	Kid Moore	Petoskey, MI	W	6	—
Dec 11	1908	Abe Attell★	Los Angeles	ND-L	10	—
Jul 13	1909	Battling Nelson★	Los Angeles	ND-W	10	—
Feb 22	1910	♛ Battling Nelson★	Richmond, CA	TKO	40	Won-World-L
Jun 10	1910	Jack Redmond	Milwaukee	ND-L	10	—
Feb 8	1911	K.O. Brown	Philadelphia	ND-L	6	—
Mar 17	1911	George Memsic	Vernon, CA	TKO	9	Ret-World-L
Mar 31	1911	Anton LaGrave	San Francisco	TKO	5	Ret-World-L
May 27	1911	California Frankie Burns	San Francisco	TKO	17	Ret-World-L
Jul 4	1911	Owen Moran★	San Francisco	KO	13	Ret-World-L
May 11	1912	Willie Ritchie	San Francisco	ND-D	4	—
Jul 4	1912	Mexican Joe Rivers	Vernon	TKO	13	Ret-World-L
Nov 28	1912	Willie Ritchie	Daly City, CA	LF	16	Lost-World-L
Oct 13	1913	Battling Nelson★	Milwaukee	ND-W	10	—
Jan 23	1914	Mexican Joe Rivers	Milwaukee	ND-W	10	—
Nov 2	1914	♛ Freddie Welsh★	New York	TKO'd	8	—
Mar 6	1916	♛ Freddie Welsh★	Milwaukee	ND-L	10	—
Jul 4	1916	♛ Freddie Welsh★	Denver	LF	11	For-World-L
Sep 6	1920	Lee Morrissey	San Bernardino, CA	D	4	—

helping Wolgast back to his feet. When his count reached ten, Welch raised Wolgast's arm in victory, then hurriedly fled as a mob rushed the ring. Wolgast retained his title in this notorious "double knockout" fight.

His next title defense came against Willie Ritchie on November 28, 1912. Wolgast came out fighting, but in the sixteenth Ritchie landed a long wild right to the jaw, spinning Wolgast around and nearly sending him down. Braced with one fist on the canvas, Wolgast launched two low blows to Ritchie, and referee Jim Griffen stopped the fight, awarding the victory to Ritchie on a foul.

After losing two fights in a row in 1913, Wolgast spoke of retirement, yet later that year he scored a newspaper victory in a no-decision fight with Nelson in Milwaukee. His retirement put on hold, he next challenged Freddy Welsh in a bout billed as the lightweight championship, but the fight was stopped in the eighth round when Wolgast's arm was broken. (Technically, the 1914 match wasn't for the belt—both fighters weighed in over the 135 lbs limit.) Meetings two years later ended with a newspaper loss to Welsh and with a loss by foul.

Wolgast's all-attack fighting style resulted in numerous injuries, including broken arms, hands, and ribs, cauliflowered ears and extensive brain damage. In 1917, Wolgast fought just once and was knocked out in the second round. He fought only one more bout, in 1920. Jack Doyle, a boxing promoter in Vernon, California, was appointed as Wolgast's guardian, and allowed him to "train" for nonexistent fights. By 1927, Wolgast was institutionalized and remained so for the rest of his life.

F L Y W E I G H T

Right-handed; 5'3½"; 107–135 lbs.

212 bouts, 10/8/1925 to 3/14/1940

Managers: Jimmy Coster, Chris Dundee, Johnny Keyes, Al Ketchel, Al Lippe, Eddie Walker

New York World Flyweight Champion 1930–35

Hall of Fame Induction: 2001

Born: 7/18/1910, Philadelphia

Named: Joseph Robert Loscalzo

Died: 10/19/1955

Midget Wolgast made a meteoric rise to the top of the flyweight division, winning a world title at the age of nineteen. Wolgast enjoyed fighting as a boy, and engaged in many schoolyard brawls, often with bigger kids. Unfortunately, his fighting instinct also led to his expulsion from public school for striking a teacher, but he returned after six weeks of reform school.

After he left school, Wolgast got a job installing hardwood floors. To learn more about fighting he also became a janitor at a local boxing gym. The lure of the ring proved strong, and Wolgast began to train in secret. He caught the eye of trainer/manager Jimmy Coster, who coached him for six months before putting him in the ring for the first time. The fifteen-year-old Wolgast decisioned Al Ketchel in the October 8, 1925, match and earned $12 for his efforts. He adopted the name Wolgast in honor of popular Philadelphia boxer Bobby Wolgast, and Midget, obviously, because of his size. By 1928, he was ranked as the ninth best flyweight in *The Ring*'s annual ratings.

In 1929, Wolgast compiled a record of 16-0-1 (plus two NDs), including victories over ranked contenders Phil Tobias and Ruby Bradley, and his ranking rose to number two. In late 1929, the New York State Athletic Commission declared Willie La Morte's flyweight title vacant, and Wolgast, now jointly managed and trained by Hall of Famer Chris Dundee and Jimmy Coster, was paired with Black Bill on March 21, 1930, for the New York version of the world title. Wolgast scored consistently with left hooks in the second, third, and fourth rounds, but Bill battled back with body shots in the fifth and sixth. The fight again went Wolgast's way in the seventh, and though Bill fought back desperately, opening a cut over Wolgast's eye in the final round, the decision and the title went to Wolgast.

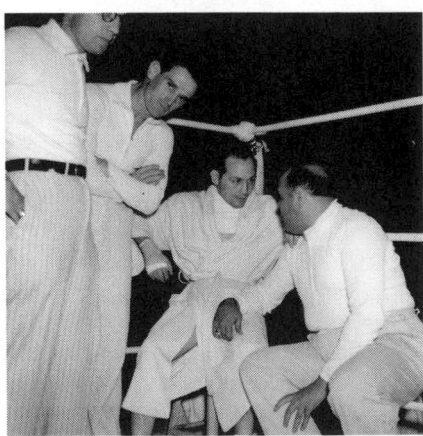

Midget Wolgast is surrounded by his nattily attired brain trust. Wolgast held the New York–version of the flyweight title during a period when there was no universally recognized champion.

IN THE RING	WON **149**	LOST **35**	DRAWS **16**	TB 212	KO 16	W 133	WF 0	D 16	KO'd 6	L 28	LF 1	ND 12	NC 0

Date	Year	Opponent	Site	Result / Rounds		Title

SELECTED BOUTS

Date	Year	Opponent	Site	Result	Rounds	Title
Oct 8	1925	Al Ketchel	Philadelphia	W	6	—
Nov 5	1926	Jimmy Britt	Philadelphia	W	6	—
Nov 3	1927	⑩ Willie Davies	New York	W	10	—
Jan 23	1928	⑩ Billy Kelly	Scranton, PA	L	10	—
Jan 26	1929	⑩ Phil Tobias	Philadelphia	W	10	—
Mar 21	1930	⑩ Black Bill	New York	W	15	Won-Vac NY World-F
May 16	1930	⑩ Willie La Morte	New York	TKO	6	Ret-NY World-F
Dec 19	1930	⑩ Willie Davies	Toronto	W	10	—
Dec 26	1930	♛ Frankie Genaro★	New York	D	15	For-World-F
Feb 23	1931	⑩ Ruby Bradley	Holyoke, MA	W	10	—
Jul 13	1931	⑩ Ruby Bradley	Brooklyn	W	15	Ret-NY World-F
Sep 8	1931	⑩ Happy Atherton	Indianapolis	W	10	—
Dec 2	1931	⑩ Speedy Dado	Oakland	W	10	—
Mar 18	1932	⑩ Little Pancho	Honolulu	W	10	—
Jul 13	1933	⑩ Lew Farber	Brooklyn	L	10	—
Sep 27	1933	⑩ Bobby Leitham	Montreal	L	10	—
Oct 30	1933	⑩ Jackie Brown	London	W	12	—
Nov 13	1933	⑩ Valentin Angelmann	Paris	D	10	—
Sep 4	1934	⑩ Henry Moreno	New Orleans	L	10	—
Nov 9	1934	⑩ Pablo Dano	Hollywood	L	10	—
Jan 25	1935	⑩ Young Tommy	Hollywood	W	10	—
Jul 3	1935	⑩ Small Montana	Sacramento	L	10	—
Sep 16	1935	⑩ Small Montana	Oakland	L	15	Lost-NY World-F
Nov 5	1935	♛ Small Montana	Los Angeles	W	10	—
Nov 27	1935	⑩ Henry Armstrong★	Oakland	L	10	—
Mar 14	1940	Bill Morris	Lancaster, PA	L	6	—

Only two months later, he successfully defended the title against Willie La Morte, winning with one of his infrequent knockouts in the sixth round. On December 26, 1930, Wolgast met NBA and International Boxing Union champion Frankie Genaro in Madison Square Garden for a unification bout, but the fight ended in a draw and both men retained their titles.

Though he fought frequently over the next four years, Wolgast made only one title defense, a victory over Ruby Bradley. His skills declined; his wondrous speed did not seem quite so fast; his difficult-to-defend-against style—which featured Wolgast switching from conventional to southpaw and back—no longer seemed so confusing. In his personal life, Wolgast's marriage collapsed. The diminutive Romeo was romantically linked to Mae West—amongst others. He spent considerably more time inside barrooms than in the practice ring. On September 16, 1935, he lost his title to Small Montana in a ten-round decision.

Though he was only 25 years old, Wolgast was finished as a serious title contender. He continued to box for another four and a half years with a record of 15-19-3, and was knocked out five times. In retirement, he trained young boxers. Wolgast died of a heart attack in a Philadelphia bar in 1955.

FIXES
AND FALLEN HEROES

The Seamy Side of Boxing

THROUGHOUT ITS COLORFUL HISTORY, boxing has had more than its share of scandal, both inside and outside the ring. Almost from its very beginnings, the sport has attracted a criminal element, and many fighters and non-combatants have risen from environments where obeying the law is less relevant than economic or physical survival. The violence that is prized in the ring has at times erupted in boxers' private lives, and stints in reform school or prison are woven into several champions' histories.

TAKING A DIVE

A continuing theme in boxing's checkered history is the fixing of fights. The sport is very susceptible to rigging. First, it involves only two active participants, and only one needs to be convinced to throw a fight. Fixing team sports, in which there are many players and where events can occur more haphazardly, is much less practical. Furthermore, boxing is essentially an entrepreneurial endeavor in which individual fighters must guard their own financial interests. Lacking the kind of central authority established in other professional sports, boxing does not have rigorous procedures for self-regulation. Certain boxers, with the control of their careers in the hands of trainers and managers and perhaps living from purse to purse, have been vulnerable to manipulation.

While no one can say for certain when the first fight was thrown, the first known fix by a Hall of Famer took place in 1822 when Englishman Jem Ward threw his fight with Bill Abbott. In more modern times, allegations of fixed fights have arisen many times, although the charges have rarely been proven. For instance, it was rumored that Stanley Ketchel was to allow the great black heavyweight, Jack Johnson, to beat him, and in return, Johnson would take it easy on the lighter Ketchel. When Ketchel knocked Johnson down, some say Johnson was outraged at the betrayal. In any case, he responded with a ferocious attack which ended the fight quickly.

Action in other heavyweight boxing matches has raised cries of "fix" as well. Many suspected Hall of Famer Jack Sharkey of giving less than his best effort when he lost the heavyweight championship to the ungainly giant, Primo Carnera. Sharkey vehemently denied the charges for the rest of his life, but Carnera had known underworld connections and won other fights in which his opponents took dives. Reportedly, Carnera's handlers arranged the fixes without his knowledge.

In the sixties, the two Muhammad Ali–Sonny Liston title fights raised some eyebrows. In the first, then-champion Liston quit between rounds, refusing to get up from his stool because of an injured shoulder. Although an examination after the fight did reveal an injury, the seeming invincibility of Liston and the shady figures with whom he associated cast doubt on the legitimacy of the fight's outcome. In the second fight, Ali floored Liston with a short right which Ali dubbed the "anchor punch." But some at ringside called it the "phantom punch" because they never saw it. Confusion over the count by referee Jersey Joe Walcott contributed to the perception that the fight was not on the level. As with most boxing fix stories, the charges were never substantiated. It was never implied that Ali himself was knowingly involved.

Shown here in happier times, Alicia Muñiz strolls along with her common-law husband middleweight Carlos Monzon. Muñiz's life came to an end in 1988 when Monzon threw her to her death from a balcony.

Publicly confirmed fixes include middleweight Jake LaMotta's admitted fall to Billy Fox in return for a promised title shot. Rocky Graziano was suspended by the New York State Athletic Commission for not reporting a bribe offer, and Harold Johnson had his license suspended for collapsing against Julio Mederos without being hit. Fans and boxing commissions alike have undoubtedly been duped at other times by unscrupulous figures whose influence on boxing has diminished the sport's integrity.

BEHIND BARS

With some notable exceptions, boxing has always tended to draw its participants from the lower socioeconomic strata. The streets of urban neighborhoods have been a wellspring of aspiring boxers. Historically, youngsters particularly adept with their fists have been urged to channel their aggressiveness through formal boxing instruction.

Unavoidably, the type of environment which fosters a career in boxing may also lead to tangles with the law. Several great boxers served time in youth detention centers or prison. In his autobiography, *Somebody Up There Likes Me*, Rocky Graziano details the many youthful misdeeds that landed him in reform school. Former heavyweight champion Sonny Liston learned to box in prison, and the young Mike Tyson was discovered by trainer Cus D'Amato while serving time in an Upstate New

York detention center. Even fighters who came to be highly respected for strength of character, such as Archie Moore and Floyd Patterson—both former chairmen of the New York State Athletic Commission—served time in reform schools.

Some boxers have been involved in criminal activities in their adult lives as well. Liston, who was strongly linked to St. Louis racketeer John Vitale, was arrested numerous times, although sometimes he may have been a victim of police harassment. Hall of Famer Kid McCoy, whose gradual decline ended with suicide, was convicted of killing a woman with whom he lived and shooting three other people. Carlos Monzon, former middleweight champion and a national hero to Argentinians, was convicted of killing the mother of his youngest child by throwing her off a second-story balcony, and Hall of Fame trainer Jack Blackburn killed his wife and shot two others. More recently, in a case which received national attention, Tyson was convicted of rape and served over three years in prison before his release in 1995.

Criminality is by no means the norm for successful boxers—many have had stable home lives or followed their boxing careers with public service or youth work—but for some, the violence that defines the sport is not confined to the squared circle.

CORRUPTION AND CONTROL

Boxing has been tainted with widespread corruption at various times in its history. During the period from the late 1940s to the early 1960s, the New York City-based International Boxing Club (IBC) dominated the promotion of boxing. Though owned primarily by James Norris (a member of the family which owned the Detroit Red Wings in the National Hockey League) and Arthur Wirtz (who had ties to the NHL Chicago Blackhawks), the IBC fell under the influence of mobster Frankie Carbo. Carbo and his associates also controlled the Boxing Managers Guild of New York and the International Boxing Managers Guild, which gave them strong influence over two aspects of the fight game: staging fights and controlling fighters.

Interestingly, a plan by declining champion Joe Louis to maintain an interest in heavyweight championship fights coincided with the IBC's early activities. Louis, who realized his reign as champ would soon come to an end, set up a corporation in hopes of getting exclusive contracts with top heavyweights. Promoters would have to go through Joe Louis Enterprises, Inc. to sign the fighters. Norris bought Louis out for $150,000 and a twenty percent share of IBC's stock in return for the contracts Louis had landed with Ezzard Charles, Jersey Joe Walcott, Lee Savold, and Gus Lesnevich. Although ostensibly employed by the IBC, Louis quickly faded from the scene.

Norris then arranged for Madison Square Garden to buy out its promoter, Mike Jacobs, and also to buy out the only major competitor, the Tournament of Champions. These purchases gave Norris and the IBC a virtual monopoly on boxing promotion in the U.S. Norris controlled the Garden and owned Chicago Stadium, the

Detroit Olympia, and the St. Louis Arena. The IBC promoted 36 of 44 championship fights held between May 1949 and May 1953.

Norris assured the IBC of obtaining quality fighters by making payments to the Boxing Managers Guild, and Carbo helped Norris line up fighters for IBC promotions. Although the very wealthy Norris had the arenas and promotional contracts, he needed Carbo to provide fighters through his links to managers such as Frank ("Blinky") Palermo.

Carbo's behind-the-scenes machinations dominated boxing for several years. Although Floyd Patterson, the heavyweight champion of the late 1950s and early '60s, resisted the IBC, the organization still wielded an incredible amount of influence over the sport. Lightweight champion Ike Williams fell under IBC control and later testified that, although he did not succumb, he had often been pressured by Palermo to throw fights. Williams also said he was sometimes cheated out of purses. The mob's influence on boxing also extended to deciding who got title shots based on which fighters were under their control. Patterson's manager, Cus D'Amato, refused to allow him to fight IBC fighters. While this stand helped somewhat in diminishing the importance of the corrupt IBC, the competitive aspect of the sport suffered as Patterson faced less than top contenders.

The mob's influence extended to deciding who got title shots.

Trainer Ray Arcel apparently ran afoul of the IBC when he began promoting fights for the ABC television network. Arcel's matches competed with those run by the IBC. Following threats to get out of television, Arcel was struck on the head with a lead pipe in 1953. Arcel recovered but, while the assault was never officially linked to the IBC, he nevertheless ended his association with the network and, in fact, stayed away from boxing for almost twenty years.

A significant factor in the demise of the IBC was the action of the Justice Department to prosecute for anti-trust violations. In 1959, the U.S. Supreme Court upheld a lower court decision which ordered Norris and Wirtz to sell their holdings in Madison Square Garden, dissolved the IBC in Illinois and New York, and set a limit on the number of championship fights which could be held in IBC venues.

In a New York State criminal prosecution, Carbo was sentenced to two years in prison for undercover matchmaking and managing. However, Carbo's conviction and the breakup of the IBC did not end the criminal influence on boxing. Carbo and Palermo were eventually convicted of trying to extort money from California promoter Jackie Leonard after the Don Jordan–Virgil Akins welterweight championship fight. Carbo was sentenced to 25 years in prison, and Palermo received a fifteen-year sentence. With the decline of Norris, Wirtz, Carbo, and Palermo, the influence of organized crime greatly diminished in boxing, although some assert that the criminal element still has a presence in the sport.

The reputation of premier fight promoter Don King, a hugely successful figure in today's boxing scene, makes many observers uneasy. King, convicted of manslaughter in 1967 in connection with the death of a rival in the Cleveland numbers racket, has since survived numerous scrapes with law enforcement authorities. An FBI sting operation, three grand jury probes, an income tax evasion case, and prosecution for insurance fraud all failed to prove King guilty of wrongdoing.

Many questions about King's complex dealings seem to arise from an apparent conflict of interest when he acts as both promoter and manager. According to a 1991 *Sports Illustrated* article by a former FBI agent who had investigated King's alleged mob connections, then-heavyweight champion Larry Holmes, managed by King, said in private that he feared for his safety if he cooperated with the government. Former heavyweight champion Buster Douglas reportedly paid $7 million in a lawsuit settlement to get out from under King's influence. WBC titleholder Julio Cesar Chavez has spoken against King. At King's 1995 insurance fraud trial, Chavez testified that he never saw $350,000 in training expenses that King attempted to recover from Lloyd's of London when a Chavez fight was canceled due to injury.

STAYING ALIVE

At its best, boxing is an unparalleled physical art. At its worst, it is a killer and maimer of good men. Blindness, hearing loss, mental impairment, respiratory or speech difficulties, paralysis, and death are among the possibilities that lurk just behind the glory of being a star in satin trunks. While serious injuries and deaths do occur in other sports—skiing and auto racing, for instance—boxing is perhaps the only sport where death and injuries are viewed as "part of the game." Financial or other pressures have led more than one hurt or sick boxer to fight at extreme risk to his health.

According to the 1982 *Ring Record Book*, between 1918 and 1981 over 400 amateur and professional fighters died as a result of injuries suffered in the ring.

The well-publicized case of Gerald McClellan, a 27-year-old boxer who received very severe injuries in his super middleweight title fight with Nigel Benn in 1995, renewed calls for mandatory headgear or the outright abolition of boxing. A six-inch blood clot was removed from McClellan's brain in emergency surgery following the title bout. The young fighter suffered almost total hearing and sight loss, cannot walk, and will need lifelong care.

One of the more distasteful aspects of boxing injuries is the long-range effect on the brain of numerous blows to the head. The once-comic image of the punch-drunk fighter is a tragic reality for some ring veterans. One-time heavyweight contender Jerry Quarry died at age 53 after suffering from the form of dementia pugilistica that resembles Alzheimer's disease. Sports fans are familiar with the transformation of Muhammad Ali from a quick-witted, swaggering champion to a soft-spoken, slow-moving figure because of Parkinson's syndrome, perhaps exacerbated by his ring career. Brain injuries have shortened the productive lives of many other boxers and former boxers.

A disturbing article by Dr. Ira Classon written for the National Parkinson's Foundation summarizes recent research about the brain damage that boxers often sustain during their ring careers.

Dr. Classon's own studies, as well as work by other researchers indicates that "15–40 percent of ex-boxers have been found to have symptoms of chronic brain injury. Recent work, employing detailed psychological testing and MRI scanning, has shown that most professional boxers (even those without symptoms) have some degree of brain damage." Fortunately, "today's boxers have fewer bouts and shorter careers, resulting in fewer blows to the head and less cumulative brain injury."

Being the best at something excruciatingly difficult is a timeless lure.

Examinations of hundreds of former boxers reveals that "symptoms usually begin near or shortly after the end of a boxer's career. On occasion they are first noticed after a particularly hard bout. Symptoms develop an average of 16 years after beginning the sport, although some cases have occurred as early as 6 years after becoming a boxer. [Brain disorders] can occur in all weight classes but [are] seen most often in the heavier divisions, and champion boxers run as much risk of sustaining chronic brain injury as less skilled journeymen."

Classon's findings are that "boxers with less than 20–30 professional bouts usually do not have any symptoms of brain injury those with 25–50 bouts often show MRI and psychological test abnormalities without obvious symptoms. Boxers with more than 50 professional bouts often have obvious symptoms of brain injury as well as MRI and psychological test abnormalities."

The dangerous nature of boxing has periodically led to calls for reforms, ranging from more thorough and frequent medical examinations to protective headgear. At various times, Congress has held hearings to discuss federal control of boxing and, from time to time, movements to ban the sport have arisen.

Boxing has been a part of human history for centuries, however, and it may never be "civilized" out of existence. The promise of prize money, as well as the possibility of being the very best at something excruciatingly difficult, is a timeless lure to talented young men. And for some who love the sport, the real-life metaphor of rise and decline, of glorious win and devastating loss, stands as an elemental human truth that must be acted out regardless of the risks involved.

THE MODERN ERA
Boxing Waxes and Wanes but the Great Stars Shine

BOXING'S MODERN PERIOD is perhaps best defined by the stars it produced. Names like Joe Louis, Archie Moore, Rocky Marciano, Sugar Ray Robinson, Joe Frazier and, of course, Muhammad Ali are indelibly etched into our collective memory of an era that saw boxing wax and wane. International champions arrived to challenge American dominance as boxing flourished in Japan, the Philippines, Thailand, Mexico, Puerto Rico, South America, and elsewhere. Champions such as Alexis Arguello of Nicaragua, Japan's Fighting Harada, and Filipino Gabriel ("Flash") Elorde built careers in their home countries, then went abroad to continue their winning ways. In order to be classified as modern-era boxers, Hall of Fame inductees must have ended their careers after 1942.

The modern era also saw the rise of the boxer as national hero. Audiences often identified with "their" fighters. African-American star Joe Louis, who was careful not to arouse a backlash of racism, was an unparalleled hero to American blacks in the 1930s and '40s. Louis was further lionized as a symbol of freedom in the Western world when he fought German champion Max Schmeling, manipulated as an icon of Aryan supremacy, on the eve of World War II.

Racism as a deterrent to non-whites was largely overcome in the modern era of boxing. The door Louis opened was flung wide with the emergence of a pantheon of great black fighters from the 1950s on. Headliners like Floyd

Patterson and Sonny Liston were still largely handled by whites, however. The next transition came when blacks took positions as trainers, managers, and promoters. With the appearance in the 1970s of powerful and controversial promoter Don King, African-American influence in boxing continued to strengthen. The broadening in-

ternational scope of boxing, with more fighters coming from countries beyond the United States, especially in the lower weight classes, has also populated the sport with many different ethnic groups.

Television coverage had a great effect on boxing. Evolving from novelty broadcasts in the 1940s to extensive network exposure in the 1950s, televised bouts brought boxing many new fans but also seriously damaged the gate for live fights. This likewise contributed to the decline of small boxing venues where neophyte boxers typically started their careers. But as other broadcast entertainment crowded out television coverage of boxing, the public shifted its attention away from the fights.

Public wariness was aroused when the 1950s and '60s saw the exposure of corruption and organized crime in boxing. Mobster Frankie Carbo was shown to exert considerable influence on the International Boxing Club, the dominant promoter for Madison Square Garden, and Blinky Palermo, manager for many fighters during this period, was closely associated with Carbo.

Meanwhile, interest in amateur boxing as an Olympic sport was keen. During this era, success in the Olympics became an important springboard to a successful professional career in the ring. Americans Floyd Patterson, Muhammad Ali, Joe Frazier, George Foreman, Sugar Ray Leonard, Leon Spinks, Michael Spinks, Italian Nino Benvenuti, and Pascual Perez of Argentina are all notable boxers whose Olympic laurels preceded world titles.

Among the many forces that have shaped boxing's modern era, perhaps none has been more influential than the career and personality of heavyweight Muhammad Ali. Olympic gold medal winner in 1960, Ali was brash, flamboyant, and extremely talented. His star-wattage persona sold out his 1963 Madison Square Garden bout with Doug Jones despite the fact that it took place during a New York City newspaper strike, and his fame never stopped growing. He outraged both the boxing organizations and the U.S. government by becoming a Black Muslim and protesting the Vietnam War. Stripped of his heavyweight championship title, Ali was nevertheless hailed as "The People's Champion," and recognized worldwide as the most famous athlete ever.

Another change in boxing in the modern era has been the rise of some important new boxing venues. Manhattan's Madison Square Garden is still regarded as the "Mecca of Boxing." However, most high-profile bouts now take place at gam-

bling casinos in Las Vegas, Atlantic City, Connecticut, Mississippi, and elsewhere throughout the U.S.

Don King has emerged as the most influential man in boxing. His promotional accomplishments are unprecedented. His mega-promotion of the 1974 "Rumble in the Jungle" between Muhammad Ali and George Foreman paid a then-unheard-of $10 million in purses and drew an estimated one billion television viewers worldwide. He produced the HBO elimination series that resulted in Mike Tyson being crowned the undisputed heavyweight champion. In 1994, King promoted a record 47 world title bouts. After Mike Tyson's release from prison, King carefully directed Tyson's comeback attempt until Tyson's career was again derailed—this time by his suspension for biting Evander Holyfield's ears.

Bob Arum, another very important promoter, is head of Top Rank. He has promoted the widely watched boxing series on ESPN as well as countless major bouts over the last twenty years. He promoted the November 5, 1994 fight in which George Foreman beat Michael Moorer to regain the world championship that he had lost in 1974 to Muhammad Ali.

The modern era of boxing has also seen fragmentation of the direct lineage of champions with a proliferation of weight classes and titles. The number of fully contested weight divisions has more than doubled, from eight to seventeen, and the number of sanctioning bodies has grown dramatically.

In the early years of the new century, some highly skilled and popular boxers are claiming their places in history. Roy Jones, Jr. dominates his light heavyweight division so thoroughly that he faces the inevitable pressure to bulk up and take on heavyweights.

Sugar Shane Mosley, Bernard Hopkins, and Felix Trinidad are three outstanding fighters in the mid-range weight divisions who show great heart and class as well as magnificent skills.

Lennox Lewis unified the heavyweight championship and secured all four significant championship bouts with his second win over Evander Holyfield, British-born Lewis was a likeable, intelligent and soft-spoken champion—and the first Brit to wear the heavyweight crown since Bob Fitzsimmons a century earlier.

And a hitherto untapped audience may be emerging as more women show an interest in boxing workouts for fitness and follow the careers of outstanding female boxers such as Christy Martin and Lucia Rijker.

MUHAMMAD ALI
The Louisville Lip; The Greatest

HEAVYWEIGHT

Right-handed; 6'3"; 186–236 lbs.

61 bouts, 10/29/1960 to 12/11/1981

1960 Olympic Light Heavyweight Gold Medalist

Heavyweight Champion 1964–67, 1974–78, 1978–79

Hall of Fame Induction: 1990

Born: 1/17/1942, Louisville, KY

Named: Cassius Marcellus Clay, Jr.

In all of boxing history, Muhammad Ali stands alone. In early boasts, he called himself "The Greatest," and by the time his storied career came to an end, most fight fans agreed. Ali had also become the best-known athlete in the world and, very possibly, the best-loved as well.

Cassius Clay—who used his birth name until he became a Black Muslim in 1964—grew up in a quiet black neighborhood of Louisville, Kentucky. He was a popular student in high school, where his stunning self-confidence made him noteworthy even then. He had been focussed on boxing since he was twelve and

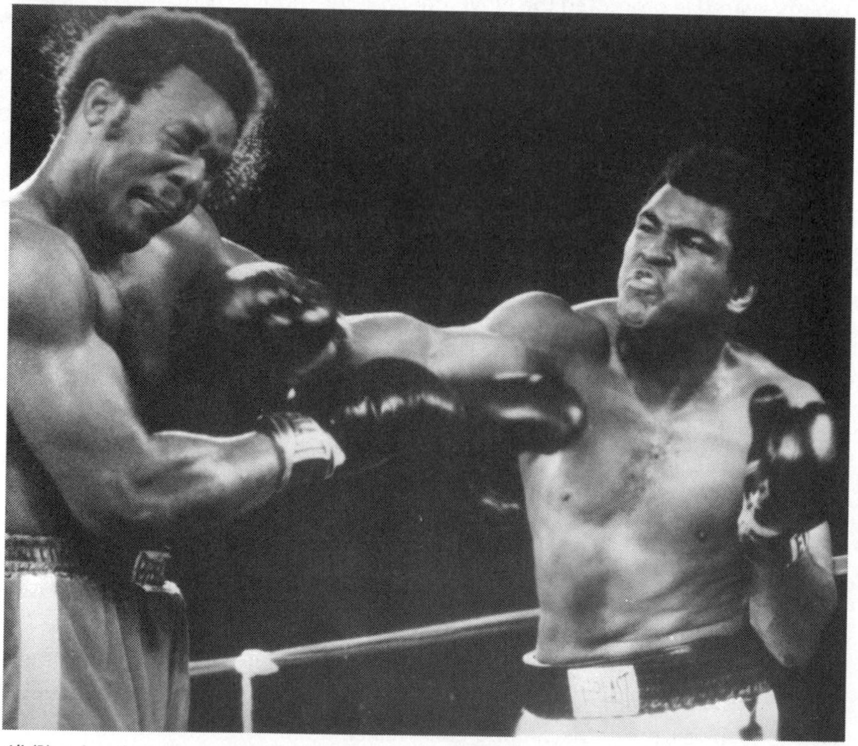

Ali (R) springs from the ropes to knock out George Foreman and regain the heavyweight championship in the eighth round of the 1974 "Rumble in the Jungle." Foreman recovered the crown twenty years later.

IN THE RING	WON 56	LOST 5	DRAWS 0	TB 61	KO 37	W 19	WF 0	D 0	KO'd 1	L 4	LF 0

Date	Opponent	Site	Result / Rounds		Title	Wt.
1960						
Oct 29	Tunney Hunsaker	Louisville, KY	W	6	—	186
Dec 27	Herbert Siler	Miami	KO	4	—	190
1961						
Jan 17	Anthony Sperti	Miami	TKO	3	—	195
Feb 7	Jimmy Robinson	Miami	TKO	1	—	193
Feb 21	Donnie Fleeman	Miami	TKO	7	—	190
Apr 19	Lamar Clark	Louisville	KO	2	—	192
Jun 26	Duke Sabwedong	Las Vegas	W	10	—	194
Jul 22	Alonzo Johnson	Louisville	W	10	—	192
Oct 7 ⑩	Alex Miteff	Louisville	TKO	6	—	188
Nov 29	Willi Besmanoff	Louisville	TKO	7	—	193
1962						
Feb 10	Lucian Banks	New York	TKO	4	—	194
Feb 28	Jack Wagner	Miami	TKO	4	—	195
Apr 23	George Logan	Miami	TKO	4	—	196
May 19 ⑩	Billy Daniels	New York	TKO	7	—	196
Jul 20 ⑩	Alejandro Lavorante	Los Angeles	KO	5	—	199
Nov 15 ⑩	Archie Moore★	Los Angeles	TKO	4	—	204
1963						
Jan 24	Charles Powell	Pittsburgh	KO	3	—	205
Mar 13 ⑩	Doug Jones	New York	W	10	—	202
Jun 18	Henry Cooper	London	TKO	5	—	207
1964						
Feb 25 ♛	Sonny Liston★	Miami	TKO	7	Won-World-H	210
1965						
May 25 ⑩	Sonny Liston★	Lewiston, ME	KO	1	Ret-World-H	206
Nov 22 ⑩	Floyd Patterson★	Las Vegas	TKO	12	Ret-World-H	210
1966						
Mar 29 ⑩	George Chuvalo	Toronto	W	15	Ret-World-H	214
May 21	Henry Cooper	London	TKO	6	Ret-World-H	201
Aug 6 ⑩	Brian London	London	TKO	3	Ret-World-H	209
Sep 10 ⑩	Karl Mildenberger	Frankfurt, Germany	TKO	12	Ret-World-H	203
Nov 14	Cleveland Williams	Houston	TKO	3	Ret-World-H	210
1967						
Feb 6 ♛	Ernie Terrell	New York	W	15	Ret-World-H	212
Mar 22 ⑩	Zora Folley	New York	TKO	7	Ret-World-H	211
1970						
Oct 26 ⑩	Jerry Quarry	Atlanta	TKO	3	—	213
Dec 7 ⑩	Oscar Bonavena	New York	TKO	15	—	212
1971						
Mar 8 ♛	Joe Frazier★	New York	L	15	For-World-H	215
Jul 26 ⑩	Jimmy Ellis	Houston	TKO	12	Won-Vac NABF-H	220
Nov 17	Buster Mathis	Houston	W	12	Ret-NABF-H	227
Dec 26	Jurgen Blin	Zurich, Switzerland	KO	7	—	226
1972						
Apr 1 ⑩	McArthur Foster	Tokyo	W	15	—	226
May 1	George Chuvalo	Vancouver, B.C.	W	12	Ret-NABF-H	217
Jun 27 ⑩	Jerry Quarry	Las Vegas	TKO	7	Ret-NABF-H	216

Date		Opponent	Location	Result	Round	Title	Wt
Jul 19		Alvin Lewis	Dublin	TKO	11	—	217
Sep 20	⑩	Floyd Patterson★	New York	TKO	7	—	218
Nov 21	♛	Bob Foster★	Stateline, NV	KO	8	Ret-NABF-H	221
1973							
Feb 14	⑩	Joe Bugner	Las Vegas	W	12	—	217
Mar 31	⑩	Ken Norton★	San Diego	L	12	Lost-NABF-H	221
Sep 10	⑩	Ken Norton★	Inglewood, CA	W	12	Reg-NABF-H	212
Oct 20		Rudy Lubbers	Jakarta, Indonesia	W	12	—	217
1974							
Jan 28	⑩	Joe Frazier★	New York	W	12	Ret-NABF-H	215
Oct 30	♛	George Foreman	Kinshasa, Zaire	KO	8	Reg-World-H	216
1975							
Mar 24	⑩	Chuck Wepner	Cleveland	TKO	15	Ret-World-H	223
May 16	⑩	Ron Lyle	Las Vegas	TKO	11	Ret-World-H	224
Jul 1	⑩	Joe Bugner	Kuala Lumpur, Malaysia	W	15	Ret-World-H	224
Oct 1	⑩	Joe Frazier★	Quezon, Philippines	TKO	14	Ret-World-H	224
1976							
Feb 20		Jean Coopman	San Juan, PR	KO	5	Ret-World-H	226
Apr 30	⑩	Jimmy Young	Landover, MD	W	15	Ret-World-H	230
May 24		Richard Dunn	Munich, Germany	TKO	5	Ret-World-H	220
Sep 28	⑩	Ken Norton★	New York	W	15	Ret-World-H	221
1977							
May 16	⑩	Alfredo Evangelista	Landover	W	15	Ret-World-H	221
Sep 29	⑩	Ernie Shavers	New York	W	15	Ret-World-H	225
1978							
Feb 15	⑩	Leon Spinks	Las Vegas	L	15	Lost-World-H	225
Sep 15	♛	Leon Spinks	New Orleans	W	15	Reg-World (WBA)-H	221
1980							
Oct 2	♛	Larry Holmes	Las Vegas	TKO'd	11	For-Vac World (WBC)-H	217
1981							
Dec 11	⑩	Trevor Berbick	Nassau, Bahamas	L	10	—	236

trained with the single-mindedness of a future champion. He started boxing at the amateur level in his hometown and captured the AAU and Golden Gloves titles in 1959 and 1960. He competed in the 1960 Olympics in Rome, where he won a gold medal in the light heavyweight division.

Ali first boxed professionally in 1960, at age eighteen, with a win over a boxer named Tunney Hunsaker. In subsequent early bouts, it was quickly apparent that Ali possessed unbelievable hand and foot speed for someone his size. As he developed, he displayed a stinging jab and a strong right hand. Ali liked to hold his hands low and evade punches to the head by simply bobbing out of harm's way.

The brash young fighter's knack for self-promotion nearly rivalled his ring skills. He mugged for the cameras, talked in rhymes, and boasted that he was not only the greatest, but also the prettiest of all time. He began to predict, with unnerving accuracy, the round in which he would stop opponents ("They all fall/In the round I call"). In a time when interest in boxing had waned, Ali dramatically revitalized the sport. He was a one-man show, full of swagger and contempt, and the press and public embraced him.

Ali proved over and over, with great talent and boxing intelligence, that he

A vital aspect of Ali's speed, besides his fancy footwork, was his remarkable ability to dodge punches by bending and twisting his torso. Here he eludes the mighty Sonny Liston en route to taking the title.

was much more than an entertaining huckster. In 1961, Ali knocked out Alex Miteff, who had been considered a top contender the previous year. In 1962 and 1963, he defeated such daunting adversaries as George Logan, Billy Daniels, Archie Moore, Doug Jones, and Henry Cooper.

Having emerged as the top heavyweight contender, Ali faced the formidable Sonny Liston for the world championship in 1964. Many observers gave Ali little chance against big, bad Liston. But Ali dominated the fight and, though nearly blinded for two rounds by a foreign substance used by Liston's corner (perhaps liniment or a coagulant applied to a cut and then transferred to Liston's gloves), won when Liston refused to answer the bell for the seventh round, claiming an injured shoulder. After the victory, Ali announced that he had become a member of the Nation of Islam, the Black Muslim religion, and had changed his name.

Ali's conversion upset some fans. The jokester had gotten serious about race and politics. It cost him some popularity and probably, though never acknowledged, influenced his future as a titleholder. When Ali agreed to give Liston a return match, the WBA took the title away—ostensibly because the rematch contract was a violation of WBA rules. Ali continued to be outspoken, particularly in statements against the Vietnam War.

In his second fight with Liston, Ali triumphed in one round, apparently using his famed "anchor punch." As with the first Liston fight, this rematch was shrouded in controversy. Some thought that Liston took a dive. After flooring Liston, Ali did not immediately move to a neutral corner. Liston eventually rose from the

canvas and the fight resumed. It was only when Nat Fleischer, editor of *The Ring*, shouted from ringside that Liston had been down for at least a count of ten, that referee Jersey Joe Walcott stopped the fight.

Ali's refusal, on religious grounds, to accept induction into the armed forces caused him to be stripped of his undisputed world title in 1967. Furthermore, Ali faced imprisonment for his action and was barred from

People around the world responded positively to Muhammad Ali's expressive face, charismatic personality, and shameless self-promotion.

boxing while his case was litigated. He called himself "The People's Champion" and continued to be recognized as the world heavyweight titleholder in Great Britain and Japan. Ultimately, in June 1971, the U.S. Supreme Court ruled in Ali's favor, after he returned to the ring in an October 1970 conquest over Jerry Quarry.

In his last fights before his banishment, Ali had combined stylish footwork with great punching power. Most experts concede that upon his return, the older, slightly heavier fighter was not quite the equal of the 1967 Ali. Ali met the new champion, Joe Frazier, in the "Fight of the Century" in Madison Square Garden in 1971. In an extremely hard-fought battle, Frazier won the decision, handing Ali his first defeat. In one of the greatest series in ring history, the two met twice more in battles of strength, skill, and courage, with Ali emerging as the victor both times. Ali scored a technical knockout over Frazier in their final bout, called the "Thrilla in Manila" and considered by many to be one of the greatest fights of all time.

Ali reclaimed the heavyweight championship in 1974 when he knocked out the previously unbeaten George Foreman. Dubbed the "Rumble in the Jungle," the match was held in Kinshasa, Zaire. Ali used his "rope-a-dope" strategy in which he leaned against the ropes and allowed Foreman to punch himself out. After Foreman tired, Ali knocked him out.

Ali lost his title to the unproven Leon Spinks in 1978, but reclaimed it in the rematch later that same year. He then announced his retirement only to make ill-fated comeback attempts against Larry Holmes and Trevor Berbick. Plagued by ill health in retirement, Ali remains a respected public figure.

Ali courageously fought for eleven rounds with a broken jaw on March 31, 1973 in San Diego, when Ken Norton handed him his second career loss. Ali won their rematch six months later.

SAMMY ANGOTT
The Clutch

LIGHTWEIGHT

Right-handed; 5'8"; 128–155 lbs.
133 bouts, 3/1/1935 to 8/8/1950
Manager: Charlie Jones
Lightweight Champion 1941–42
NBA Lightweight Champion 1940–41, 1943–44
Hall of Fame Induction: 1998
Born: 1/17/1915, Washington, PA
Named: Salvatore Engotti
Died: 10/22/1980

A tough, scrappy fighter who held his own with Hall of Famers Willie Pep, Henry Armstrong, and Beau Jack, Sammy Angott seldom scored knockouts but twice captured the lightweight title.

Reared in Washington, Pennsylvania as Salvatore Engotti, Angott won his first professional bout in 1935 at the age of twenty. By 1938 he was ready to challenge Leo Rodak, the top-ranked featherweight. In the first of three matches held in Pittsburgh, Rodak outfought Angott to take a ten-round decision. In the rematch, Angott dramatically avenged his defeat with a first-round knockout and, in the third match, Angott won a ten-round decision. As 1940 dawned, Angott's career was solidly established and *The Ring* rated him the second-best lightweight contender.

The next year, Angott met Davey Day for the vacant NBA lightweight title, previously held by Lou Ambers. The fight was in Angott's adopted home base of Louisville the night before the Kentucky Derby. Former heavyweight champ Jack Dempsey, the referee and sole judge of the fight, awarded the decision to Angott.

The new champion fought only non-title fights for the next year and a half. In his most notable battles, he defeated Bob Montgomery but lost to the heavier Fritzie Zivic and a young Sugar Ray Robinson. In late 1941, Angott successfully defended his title against Lew Jenkins in New York before 11,346 fans. Jenkins, who had defeated Ambers, held the New York version of the world title. Angott dominated with ease but never went for the knockout. The crowd, disappointed in both fighters, booed constantly from the sixth round on.

Angott started 1942 with a non-title decision over Montgomery in Madison Square Garden. Uncharacteristically, Angott abandoned his cautious approach and slugged it out with Montgomery, knocking him down in the ninth. Four months later the pair met again at Shibe Park in Philadelphia, before a crowd of 16,000. Angott started fast and held off a furious rally by Montgomery to win a narrow split decision.

Between the Montgomery bouts, Angott fended off Allie Stolz, winning a hotly contested split decision. After another loss to Robinson and a win over Aldo Spoldi, Angott surprised the boxing world by announcing his retirement, at the age of 27, to work in a steel mill to support the war effort. Angott also told reporters that his right hand was injured and had not responded to treatment.

Even so, Angott returned to the ring on March 19, 1943, with a non-title win over the previously undefeated featherweight champion Willie Pep. Later that

Date	Opponent	Site	Result / Rounds		Title	Wt.
1935						
Mar 1	Tony Marengo	New York	W	4	—	—
Apr 30	Charlie Vaughn	New York	W	6	—	—
May 14	Al Gillette	New York	W	6	—	—
Jun 26	Jimmy Ferry	Washington, PA	KO	1	—	—
Jul 22	Jackie Wilson	Pittsburgh	L	6	—	—
Nov 25	Al Farone	Pittsburgh	W	6	—	—
Dec 31	Dick Cabello	New York	W	6	—	—
1936						
Jan 14	Eddie Hannon	New York	W	6	—	—
Mar 11	Solly Ambrosso	New York	W	6	—	—
Mar 25	Leonard Del Genio	New York	L	8	—	—
May 5	Johnny Morro	New York	D	8		
Jun 2	Joe Boscarino	New York	W	10		
Jun 17	Lee Shepard	Pittsburgh	L	10		
Jun 22	Eddie Mc Geever	New York	L	8		
Jul 14	Victor Vallee	New York	W	6		
Jul 30	Billy Miller	Pittsburgh	W	6		
Aug 10	Harry Krause	Pittsburgh	W	10		
Aug 24	Tommy Spiegel	Millvale, PA	L	8		
Sep 10	Harry Krause	Pittsburgh	W	10		
Sep 29	Lee Sheppard	Pittsburgh	KO	4		
Oct 12	Lee Sheppard	Pittsburgh	L	10		
Nov 23	Harry Krause	Pittsburgh	L	8		
Dec 7	Lloyd Pine	Louisville, KY	W	10		
1937						
Feb 22	Johnny Hutchinson	Pittsburgh	L	8		
Mar 8	Lloyd Pine	Louisville	D	10		
Mar 22	Dave Barry	Louisville	W	10		
Apr 18	Jimmy Buckler	Louisville	W	10		
May 10	Louis Gallop	Chicago	KO	4		
May 17	George Feist	Chicago	W	6	—	—
Jun 3	Pete Lello	Chicago	KO	5	—	—
Jul 12	Jimmy Christy	Chicago	W	10	—	—
Aug 12	Everett Rightmire	Milwaukee	W	10	—	—
Aug 23	Jimmy Christy	Chicago	W	10	—	—
Sep 20	Billy Marquart	Chicago	L	8	—	—
Oct 18	Johnny Pena	Chicago	W	10	—	—
Oct 25	Jimmy Vaughn	Louisville	W	10	—	—
Nov 8	Wishy Jones	Louisville	W	10	—	—
Nov 16	Billy Marquart	Chicago	L	8	—	—
Dec 6	Lew Massey	Louisville	W	10	—	—
1938						
Feb 7	Harvey Woods	Chicago	W	8	—	—
Feb 15	Victor Vallee	New York	W	10	—	—
Feb 25	Everett Simmington	Chicago	W	8	—	—
Mar 7	Everett Rightmire	Louisville	W	10	—	—
Mar 22	Jackie Wilson	Milwaukee	W	10	—	—
May 6	⑩ Wesley Ramey	Louisville	W	10	—	—

Date		Opponent	Location	Result	Rounds	Notes	
May 23		Frankie Covelli	Chicago	W	10	—	—
Jun 1		Irving Eldridge	Pittsburgh	W	10	—	—
Jun 15		Roger Bernard	Milwaukee	W	10	—	—
Jun 28		Tommy Spiegel	Pittsburgh	W	10	—	—
Jul 4		Lee Sheppard	Pittsburgh	KO	7	—	—
Jul 25		Leo Rodak	Pittsburgh	L	10	—	—
Aug 8		Nick Camarata	Chicago	W	10	—	—
Aug 15		Leo Rodak	Pittsburgh	KO	1	—	—
Sep 2		Wishy Jones	Louisville	W	10	—	—
Sep 16	⑩	Wesley Ramey	Dallas	W	10	—	—
Sep 27		Leo Rodak	Pittsburgh	W	10	—	—
Oct 7		Lloyd Pine	Louisville	W	10	—	—
Nov 14		Norment Quarles	New Orleans	W	10	—	—
Dec 5		Freddie Miller	Louisville	W	10	—	—
1939							
Jan 23		Joey Ferrando	Pittsburgh	KO	10	—	—
Jan 30		Eddie Brink	Pittsburgh	KO	5	—	—
Apr 14	⑩	Aldo Spoldi	York, PA	W	10	—	—
May 3		Milton Aron	Chicago	W	10	—	—
Jun 27		Howard Scott	Louisville	W	10	—	—
Jul 17	⑩	Petey Sarron	Pittsburgh	W	10	—	—
Aug 28		Billy Marquart	Pittsburgh	W	10	—	—
Oct 6	⑩	Davey Day	Chicago	W	10	—	—
Nov 3	⑩	Alberto Arizmendi	Chicago	W	10	—	—
Dec 8	⑩	Davey Day	Chicago	L	12	—	—
1940							
Feb 2	⑩	Pete Lello	New York	D	10	—	—
Mar 1		Baby Boy Breese	Milwaukee	W	10	—	—
May 3	⑩	Davey Day	Louisville	W	15	Won-Vac NBA-L	134
Jun 25		Alberto Arizmendi	Los Angeles	D	10	—	—
Jul 24		Nick Castiglione	Chicago	W	10	—	—
Aug 28		Fritze Zivic	Pittsburgh	L	10	—	—
Nov 4		George Latka	San Francisco	D	10	—	—
Nov 25	⑩	Bob Montgomery★	Philadelphia	W	10	—	—
Dec 18		Don Eddy	Miami	W	10	—	—
1941							
May 2		Dave Castilloux	Louisville	W	12	—	—
May 19		Lenny Mancini	Cleveland	W	10	—	—
Jun 1		Lloyd Pine	Chicago	W	10	—	—
Jun 24		Henry Hurst	Toronto	W	10	—	—
Jul 21		Sugar Ray Robinson★	Philadelphia	L	10	—	—
Aug 12		Jimmy Tygh	Pittsburgh	KO	3	—	—
Sep 8		Pete Galiano	Washington, PA	KO	6	—	—
Sep 19		Lee Sheppard	Akron, OH	KO	1	—	—
Oct 31		Chino Lopez	Pittsburgh	KO	6	—	—
Dec 19	♔	Lew Jenkins★	New York	W	15	Won-World-L	133
1942							
Mar 6	⑩	Bob Montgomery★	New York	W	12	—	—
May 15		Allie Stolz	New York	W	15	Ret-World-L	134
Jul 7	⑩	Bob Montgomery★	Philadelphia	W	12	—	—
Jul 31	⑩	Sugar Ray Robinson★	New York	L	10	—	—
Sep 28		Aldo Spoldi	New Orleans	W	10	—	139
1943							
Mar 19	♔	Willie Pep★	New York	W	10	—	134
Jun 11	⑩	Henry Armstrong★	New York	L	10	—	138

Oct 1	Ⓦ	Joey Peralta	Detroit	W	10		—	—
Oct 27	Ⓦ	Luther White	Los Angeles	W	15	Won-Vac-NBA-L	134	
Dec 17		Bobby Ruffin	New York	W	10		—	—

1944

Jan 28	Ⓦ	Beau Jack★	New York	D	10		—	—
Mar 8	Ⓦ	Juan Zurita	Hollywood	L	15	Lost-NBA-L	135	
Apr 4		Aaron Perry	Washington, DC	W	10		—	141
Jun 7	Ⓦ	Ike Williams★	Philadelphia	L	10		—	140
Aug 1		Aaron Perry	Washington, DC	W	12		—	—
Sep 6	Ⓦ	Ike Williams★	Philadelphia	L	10		—	—
Nov 10		Jimmy McDaniels	New York	L	10		—	144

1945

Aug 20		Gene Burton	Pittsburgh	D	10		—	142
Sep 19	Ⓦ	Ike Williams★	Pittsburgh	KO	6		—	140
Oct 24		Danny Kapilow	Washington, DC	W	10		—	—
Dec 10		Danny Kapilow	Pittsburgh	W	10		—	142

1946

Mar 4	Ⓦ	Sugar Ray Robinson★	Pittsburgh	L	10		—	143
Jul 8	Ⓦ	Beau Jack★	Washington, DC	KO'd	7		—	—

1947

Feb 17		George Dixon	Wheeling, OH	TKO	1		—	—
Feb 24		John Bryant	Canton, OH	KO	5		—	—
Feb 27		Jackie McFarland	Mansfield, OH	KO	2		—	—
Mar 14		Nick Castiglione	Chicago	KO	4		—	—
Mar 24		Teddy Davis	Wheeling, OH	TKO	3		—	—
Apr 9		Cal Elphante	Zanesville, OH	KO	3		—	—
May 16	Ⓦ	Johnny Bratton	Chicago	W	10		—	—

1948

Feb 17		Eddie Pusey	Louisville	KO	2		—	—
Mar 15		Rudy Zadell	Cumberland, KY	W	10		—	—
Jun 11		Buster Miles	Huntington, WV	W	10		—	—

1949

Mar 3		Johnny Bryant	Clarksburg, VA	KO	2		—	—
Aug 5		Billy Suddeth	Topeka	W	10		—	—
Oct 19		Don Williams	Worcester, MA	L	10		—	143
Dec 12		Tony Riccio	Newark, NJ	L	10		—	146

1950

Jan 2	Ⓦ	Sonny West	Baltimore	D	10		—	—
Jan 23		Clem Custer	Baltimore	KO	8		—	—
Feb 20		Ralph Zanelli	Providence, RI	W	10		—	—
Mar 20	Ⓦ	Sonny West	Baltimore	L	10		—	—
May 10		John Davis	Oakland, CA	L	10		—	144
Jun 22		Tim Dalton	Davenport, IA	W	10		—	—
Jun 26		Kid Azteca	El Paso	W	10		—	—
Aug 8	Ⓦ	Sonny West	Detroit	L	10		—	—

year Angott reclaimed the vacant NBA lightweight title with a decision over Slugger White in the baseball stadium of the Pacific Coast League Hollywood Stars. The next year, Angott lost his title in a fifteen-round decision to Juan Zurita. This was Angott's last title bout.

Angott moved up to welterweight and was a ranked contender in that class in 1944 and 1945. He continued to fight through 1950. In retirement, Angott lent his fame to many charitable activities, and worked for a manufacturing plant in Canton, Ohio. He died in 1980 after suffering a blood clot on the brain.

A L E X S A R G U E L L O
Flaco de Explosivo

L I G H T W E I G H T

Right-handed; 5'10"; 122–143 lbs.

88 bouts, 8/1/1968 to 1/21/1995

WBA Featherwt. Champ 1974–77
WBC Super Featherwt. Champ 1978–80
WBC Lightwt. Champ 1981–83

Hall of Fame Induction: 1992

Born: 4/19/1952, Managua, Nicaragua

The first Nicaraguan to be inducted into the Hall of Fame, Alexis Arguello transcended poverty and political strife in his home country to hold titles in three different weight classes during his long career. Arguello was a master offensive boxer and tactician who could adapt his fighting to take advantage of his opponents' weaknesses. He would wait patiently for an opening and then strike with damaging accuracy. Of his 80 professional victories, 64 were knockouts.

A street fighter as a youth, Arguello learned ring basics from a brother-in-law in Managua, and quickly parlayed his skills into an escape from his hardscrabble life. When his family's poverty forced him to leave school at 14 to work on a dairy farm, Arguello dedicated himself to boxing. After a year of amateur fighting, he turned pro in 1968 at age 16. Fighting exclusively in Nicaragua in the early stages of his career, Arguello racked up 34 wins, many by knockout, and only two losses.

By 1974, Arguello's world was expanding. *The Ring* ranked him the second-best contender for the featherweight title, and in February, Arguello fought outside Nicaragua for the first time, travelling to Panama to challenge Ernesto Marcel for the WBA featherweight belt. Marcel squeaked by Arguello on a fifteen-round decision. Marcel retired in June, and in July, Ruben Olivares KO'd Japanese fighter Zensuke Utagawa to take the vacant title. Arguello then went after Olivares. The two met in November of 1974, at the Fabulous Forum in Inglewood, California before a crowd of 14,313. It was Arguello's first fight in the United States. Both boxers were in top condition, and the fight was close. Arguello narrowly won the first five rounds, then Olivares came back to take control. He hurt Arguello in the eighth, ninth, and tenth rounds. In the thirteenth, Arguello saw his opening and knocked Olivares down

Arguello (L) staggers Ray ("Boom Boom") Mancini with a left on the way to a 14-round KO in their October 1981 bout in Atlantic City.

IN THE RING	WON 80	LOST 8	DRAWS 0	TB 88	KO 64	W 16	WF 0	D 0	KO'd 4	L 4	LF 0

Date		Opponent	Site	Result / Rounds		Title	Wt.
1968							
Aug 1		Cachorro Amaya	Managua, Nicaragua	TKO'd	1	—	—
Dec 14		Alacran Espinoza	Managua	W	4	—	—
1969							
Jan 23		Burrito Martinez	Managua	KO	3	—	—
Apr 26		Alacran Espinoza	Managua	L	6	—	—
1970							
Jul 29		Carlos Huete	Managua	W	8	—	—
Aug 12		Ricardo Donoso	Managua	KO	2	—	—
Sep 7		Marcelino Beckles	Managua	TKO	8	—	—
Oct 17		Mario Bojorge	Managua	KO	3	—	—
Nov 14		Jose Urbina	Managua	KO	1	—	—
Dec 5		Julio Morales	Managua	KO	3	—	—
Dec 19		Armando Figueroa	Managua	TKO	1	—	—
1971							
Feb 12		Tony Quiroz	Managua	KO	6	—	—
Mar 13		Raton Hernandez	Managua	W	10	—	—
Apr 17		Raton Hernandez	Managua	W	10	—	—
May 1		Mauricio Buitrago	Managua	KO	7	—	—
Jun 5		Kid Chapula	Managua	KO	1	—	—
Jun 26		Marcial Loyola	Managua	TKO	2	—	—
Jul 17		Hurricane Clay	Managua	TKO	5	—	—
Aug 14		Catalino Alvarado	Managua	KO	1	—	—
Sep 4		Ray Mendoza	Managua	TKO	4	—	—
Oct 2		Hurricane Clay	Managua	W	10	—	—
Nov 18		Vicente Worrel	Managua	KO	2	—	—
1972							
Feb 8		Guillermo Barrera	Managua	KO	1	—	—
Apr 11		Tanquecito Gonzalez	Managua	KO	2	—	—
Jun 22		Jorge Reyes	Managua	TKO'd	6	—	—
Aug 16		Fernando Fernandez	Managua	KO	1	—	—
Sep 23		Jorge Benitez	Managua	KO	1	—	—
Nov 17		Guillermo Ortiz	Managua	KO	2	—	—
Dec 12		Rafael Gonzalez	Managua	TKO	7	—	—
1973							
Mar 30		Fernando Fernandez	Managua	TKO	2	—	—
Apr 22		Magalio Lozada	Managua	W	10	—	—
May 26		Kid Pascualito	Managua	KO	3	—	—
Jun 30		Octavio Gomez	Managua	KO	2	—	—
Aug 25		Ignacio Lomeli	Masaya, Nicaragua	KO	1	—	—
Oct 17		Sigfredo Rodriguez	Managua	TKO	9	—	—
Nov 27	⑩	Jose Legra	Masaya	KO	1	—	—
1974							
Jan 8		Raul Martinez	Managua	KO	1	—	—
Feb 16	♛	Ernesto Marcel	Panama City	L	15	For-WBA-FE	123
Apr 27		Enrique Garcia	Masaya	KO	3	—	—
May 20	⑩	Art Hafey	Masaya	KO	5	—	—
Aug 29		Oscar Aparicio	Masaya	W	12	Won-Cent Am-FE	—
Sep 21		Otoniel Martinez	Masaya	KO	1	—	—
Nov 23	♛	Ruben Olivares★	Inglewood, CA	KO	13	Won-WBA-FE	124
1975							
Feb 8		Oscar Aparicio	San Salvador, El Salvador	W	10	—	—

Date		Opponent	Location	Result	Round	Notes	
Mar 15	⑩	Leonel Hernandez	Caracas, Venezuela	TKO	8	Ret-WBA-FE	126
May 31		Rigoberto Riasco	Managua	TKO	2	Ret-WBA-FE	126
Jul 18		Rosalio Muro	San Francisco	TKO	2	—	128
Oct 12	⑩	Royal Kobayashi	Tokyo	KO	5	Ret-WBA-FE	125
Dec 20		Saul Montano	Managua	KO	3	—	—

1976

Feb 1		Jose Torres	Mexicali, Mexico	W	10	—	127
Apr 10		Modesto Concepcion	Managua	KO	2	—	—
Jun 19		Salvador Torres	Inglewood	KO	3	Ret-WBA-FE	125

1977

Feb 19		Godfrey Stevens	Managua	KO	2	—	—
May 14		Alberto Herrera	Managua	KO	1	—	—
Jun 22		Cocoa Sanchez	New York	TKO	4	—	—
Aug 3		Jose Fernandez	New York	TKO	1	—	131
Aug 27		Benjamin Ortiz	San Juan, PR	W	10	—	—
Sep 29		Jerome Artis	New York	TKO	2	—	134
Dec 18	⑩	Enrique Solis	Managua	KO	5	—	—

1978

Jan 28	♛	Alfredo Escalera	Bayamon, PR	TKO	13	Won-WBC-JL (SFE)	129
Mar 25		Mario Mendez	Las Vegas	TKO	3	—	—
Apr 29		Rey Tam	Inglewood	TKO	5	Ret-WBC-JL (SFE)	129
Jun 3		Diego Alcala	San Juan	KO	1	Ret-WBC-JL (SFE)	129
Jul 26	⑩	Vilomar Fernandez	New York	L	10	—	135
Nov 10	⑩	Arturo Leon	Las Vegas	W	15	Ret-WBC-JL (SFE)	130

1979

Feb 4	⑩	Alfredo Escalera	Rimini, Italy	KO	13	Ret-WBC-JL (SFE)	129
Jul 8	⑩	Rafael Limon	New York	TKO	11	Ret-WBC-JL (SFE)	130
Nov 16	⑩	Bobby Chacon	Inglewood	TKO	7	Ret-WBC-JL (SFE)	129

1980

Jan 20	⑩	Ruben Castillo	Tucson	TKO	11	Ret-WBC-JL (SFE)	130
Mar 31		Gerald Hayes	Las Vegas	W	10	—	131
Apr 27		Rolando Navarrete	San Juan	TKO	5	Ret-WBC-JL (SFE)	130
Aug 9		Cornelius Boza-Edwards	Atlantic City	TKO	8	—	135
Nov 14		Jose Ramirez	Miami	W	10	—	136

1981

Feb 7		Robert Vasquez	Miami	TKO	3	—	136
Jun 20	♛	Jim Watt	London	W	15	Won-WBC-L	134
Oct 3	⑩	Ray ("Boom Boom") Mancini	Atlantic City	TKO	14	Ret-WBC-L	135
Nov 21		Roberto Elizondo	Las Vegas	KO	7	Ret-WBC-L	135

1982

Feb 13		James Busceme	Beaumont, TX	KO	6	Ret-WBC-L	135
May 22	⑩	Andy Ganigan	Las Vegas	KO	5	Won-Vac World (WBC)-L	133
Jul 31		Kevin Rooney	Atlantic City	KO	2	—	140
Nov 12	♛	Aaron Pryor★	Miami	KO'd	14	For-WBA-JW	138

1983

Feb 26		Vilomar Fernandez	San Antonio, TX	W	10	—	140
Apr 24		Claude Noel	Atlantic City	TKO	3	—	140
Sep 9	♛	Aaron Pryor★	Las Vegas	KO'd	10	For-WBA-JW	139

1985

Oct 25		Pat Jefferson	Anchorage, AK	KO	5	—	142

1986

Feb 9		Billy Costello	Reno	TKO	4	—	143

1994

Aug 27		Jorge Palomares	Miami Beach	W	10	—	142

1995

Jan 21		Scott Walker	Las Vegas	L	10	—	142

with a short left hook. Olivares got up but fell later in the same round to a flurry of punches from which he could not recover.

Arguello kept his WBA featherweight title until 1977 when he relinquished it because he could no longer comfortably make the weight. In 1978 in Puerto Rico, Arguello faced Alfredo Escalera for the WBC super featherweight title. Arguello scored a thirteenth-round knockout. He defended this belt several times over the next two years before he gave it up and set his sights on the lightweight title.

In 1981, Arguello won his third title with a decision over WBC lightweight champ Jim Watt. Later that year, future WBA champ, Ray ("Boom Boom") Mancini put Arguello to the test in a hard-fought battle which Arguello won with a TKO in the

Sinewy Arguello knocked out future Tyson trainer Kevin Rooney (R) in two rounds on July 31, 1982 in Atlantic City.

fourteenth. The next year, his knockout victory over Andy Ganigan, titleholder in the short-lived WAA, led to Arguello's acclaim as world lightweight champion. Trying for a fourth belt, Arguello challenged Aaron Pryor for the WBA junior welterweight title. Pryor was 27 and in top condition. Arguello, at 31, was still fit, but fighting the younger man took all his strength. In the first five rounds, Arguello carefully probed the tireless Pryor. In the middle rounds, Arguello dominated, inflicting serious damage. But Pryor withstood Arguello's attacks and, in the fourteenth round, came back to pound Arguello so effectively that the referee stopped the fight. Rumors that Pryor's turnaround was boosted by an illegal substance in his water bottle or by less than the required padding in his gloves were never substantiated. In the rematch less than a year later, Arguello was knocked out in the tenth. He then retired for two years before making a two-fight comeback. After another stretch of retirement, during which he was elected to the Hall of Fame, Arguello again returned to the ring for one win in 1994 and one loss in 1995.

After a period of living abroad, Arguello returned to Nicaragua in 1990 when the Sandinistas left power. Although initially a Sandinista supporter, Arguello had switched his allegiance when the Sandinista government seized his property and bank account. He fought briefly as a Contra in the early 1980s after a brother was killed in the conflict. A national hero who still loves his country passionately, Arguello works with amateur boxers in Nicaragua.

HENRY ARMSTRONG
Homicide Hank

WELTERWEIGHT

Right-handed; 5'5½"; 120–147 lbs.

181 bouts, 7/27/1931 to 2/14/1945

Managers: Wirt Ross, 1932–36; Eddie Mead, 1936–41; George Moore, 1942–45

Featherweight Champion 1937–38, Lightweight Champion 1938–39, Welterweight Champion 1938–40

Hall of Fame Induction: 1990

Born: 12/12/1912, Columbus, MS

Named: Henry Jackson

Died: 10/24/1988

At a time when boxing had only eight weight classes, Henry Armstrong simultaneously held world titles in three of them. Armstrong collected everything but money in his impressive career. He was a knockout artist with a killer punch and a killer attitude in the ring. His incessant windmill style dazed his opponents, and he was extraordinarily resistant to battering. Poorly paid or cheated out of most of his ring earnings, Armstrong could rarely afford the high life of a champion, but prizefighting has never seen a more deserving bearer of its top honors.

Born in Mississippi as Henry Jackson, Armstrong moved to St. Louis with his family when he was four. As a boy, he joined in neighborhood street brawls, and soon decided he wanted to become a fighter. He finished high school (where he read an original poem at graduation) before briefly appearing in the amateur ranks as Melody Jackson. His first professional bouts, one win and one loss, took place in the Pittsburgh area, where Armstrong lived for a short time. He then moved to Los Angeles, where he resumed his amateur status, fighting as Henry Armstrong. He won his next 85 fights while making a living operating a shoeshine parlor. Armstrong officially turned pro after failing to make the 1932 Olympic boxing team.

Lou Ambers (R) got a beating and the win in his 1939 rematch with Armstrong. The referee took five rounds from Hank for low blows.

IN THE RING	WON 151	LOST 21	DRAWS 9	TB 181	KO 101	W 50	WF 0	D 9	KO'd 2	L 17	LF 2

Date	Opponent	Site	Result / Rounds		Title	Wt.
1931						
Jul 27	Al Iovino	North Braddock, PA	KO'd	3	—	120
Jul 31	Sammy Burns	Millville, PA	W	6	—	124
1932						
Aug 30	Eddie Trujillo	Los Angeles	L	4	—	—
Sep 27	Al Greenfield	Los Angeles	L	4	—	—
Oct	Max Tarley	—	W	4	—	—
Nov	Young Bud Taylor	—	KO	2	—	—
Dec	Vince Trujillo	—	KO	2	—	—
Dec 13	Gene Espinosa	Los Angeles	W	4	—	—
Dec 31	Young Corpus	Los Angeles	W	4	—	—
1933						
Jan	Steve Harkey	Los Angeles	W	4	—	—
Feb 3	Johnny Ryan	Ventura, CA	W	6	—	—
Feb 17	George Dundee	Ventura	W	6	—	—
Mar 21	Paul Wangley	Los Angeles	KO	4	—	—
Apr 28	Perfecto Lopez	Ventura	W	6	—	—
May 31	Max Tarley	Los Angeles	KO	3	—	—
Jun 7	Ricky Hall	Pismo Beach, CA	TKO	3	—	—
Jul 11	Baby Manuel	Los Angeles	L	6	—	—
Aug 8	Bobby Calmes	Los Angeles	KO	5	—	—
Aug 30	Hoyt Jones	Los Angeles	D	4	—	—
Sep 5	Perfecto Lopez	Los Angeles	D	4	—	—
Sep 7	Joe Sanchez	Ventura	KO	4	—	—
Sep 28	Perfecto Lopez	Ventura	W	8	—	—
Oct 11	Perfecto Lopez	Los Angeles	D	4	—	—
Oct 19	Johnny Granone	Sacramento, CA	TKO	6	—	—
Nov 3	Kid Moro	Pismo Beach	W	10	—	—
Nov 23	Kid Moro	Stockton, CA	D	10	—	—
Dec 14	Gene Espinosa	Sacramento	KO	7	—	—
1934						
Jan 26	Baby Manuel	Sacramento	W	10	—	—
Feb 13	Benny Pelz	Los Angeles	W	6	—	—
Mar 8	Perfecto Lopez	Bakersfield, CA	W	8	—	—
Mar 17	Young Danny	Los Angeles	KO	1	—	—
May 4	Kid Moro	Watsonville, CA	D	10	—	—
May 10	Mark Diaz	Ventura	W	8	—	—
May 22	Johhny DeFoe	Los Angeles	KO	5	—	—
Jun 5	Vicente Torres	Los Angeles	W	4	—	—
Jun 14	Davey Abad	Sacramento	W	10	—	—
Jul 17	Perfecto Lopez	Los Angeles	W	6	—	—
Aug 28	Perfecto Lopez	Los Angeles	KO	5	—	—
Sep 13	Max Tarley	Sacramento	KO	3	—	—
Nov 3	⑩ Baby Arizmendi	Mexico City	L	10	—	—
Dec 2	Joe Conde	Mexico City	KO	7	—	—
Dec 15	Ventura Arana	Mexico City	KO	5	—	—
1935						
Jan 2	⑩ Baby Arizmendi	Mexico City	L	12	For-Vac CA-Mex World-FE	126
Feb 15	⑩ Baby Casanova	Mexico City	LF	4	—	—

Date	Opponent	Location	Result	Rounds	Title	
Mar 19	Sal Hernandez	Los Angeles	KO	2	—	—
Mar 31	Davey Abad	Mexico City	L	10	—	—
Apr 6	Tully Corvo	Sacramento	KO	5	—	—
Apr 16	Frankie Covelli	Los Angeles	W	8	—	—
May 28	Davey Abad	Los Angeles	W	10	—	—
Jun 25	Varias Milling	Los Angeles	W	10	—	—
Sep 8	Perfecto Lopez	San Francisco	D	8	—	—
Oct 21	Lester Marston	Oakland	KO	7	—	—
Nov 12	Leo Lomelli	Oakland	KO	6	—	—
Nov 27	⑩ Midget Wolgast ★	Oakland	W	10	—	—
Dec 6	Alton Black	Reno	KO	8	—	—
1936						
Jan 1	Joe Conde	Mexico City	L	10	—	—
Feb 26	Ritchie Fontaine	Oakland	L	10	—	—
Mar 31	Ritchie Fontaine	Los Angeles	W	10	—	—
Apr 17	Alton Black	Reno	KO	8	—	—
May 19	⑩ Bobby Leyvas	Los Angeles	KO	4	—	—
Jun 22	Johnny DeFoe	Butte, MT	W	10	—	—
Aug 4	⑩ Baby Arizmendi	Los Angeles	W	10	Won-CA-Mex World-FE	125
Aug 28	Juan Zurita	Los Angeles	KO	4	—	—
Sep 3	Buzz Brown	Portland, OR	W	10	—	—
Sep 8	Dommy Ganzon	Sacramento	KO	1	—	—
Oct 27	⑩ Mike Belloise	Los Angeles	W	10	—	—
Nov 2	Gene Espinosa	Los Angeles	KO	1	—	—
Nov 17	Joey Alcanter	St. Louis	TKO	6	—	—
Dec 3	⑩ Tony Chavez	St. Louis	LF	8	—	—
1937						
Jan 1	Baby Casanova	Mexico City	KO	3	—	—
Jan 19	⑩ Tony Chavez	Los Angeles	KO	10	—	—
Feb 2	Moon Mullins	Los Angeles	TKO	2	—	—
Feb 19	Varias Milling	San Diego	KO	4	—	—
Mar 2	Joe Rivers	Los Angeles	KO	4	—	—
Mar 12	⑩ Mike Belloise	New York	KO	4	—	—
Mar 19	Aldo Spoldi	New York	W	10	—	—
Apr 6	⑩ Pete DeGrasse	Los Angeles	KO	10	—	—
May 4	Frankie Klick	Los Angeles	KO	4	—	—
May 28	Wally Hally	Los Angeles	KO	4	—	—
Jun 9	Mark Diaz	Pasadena, CA	KO	4	—	—
Jun 15	Jackie Carter	Los Angeles	KO	4	—	—
Jul 8	Alf Blatch	New York	TKO	3	—	—
Jul 19	Lew Massey	Brooklyn	TKO	4	—	—
Jul 27	Benny Bass ★	Philadelphia	KO	4	—	—
Aug 13	Eddie Brink	New York	KO	3	—	—
Aug 16	Johnny Cabello	Washington, DC	TKO	2	—	—
Aug 31	Orville Drouillard	Detroit	TKO	5	—	—
Sep 9	Charley Burns	Pittsburgh	KO	4	—	—
Sep 16	Johnny DeFoe	New York	TKO	4	—	—
Sep 21	Bobby Dean	Youngstown, PA	KO	1	—	—
Oct 18	Joe Marcienti	Philadelphia	KO	3	—	—
Oct 29	♛ Petey Sarron	New York	KO	6	Won-World-FE	124
Nov 19	⑩ Billy Beauhuld	New York	TKO	5	—	—
Nov 23	Joey Brown	Buffalo	KO	2	—	—
Dec 6	⑩ Tony Chavez	Cleveland	TKO	1	—	—
Dec 12	Johnny Jones	New Orleans	KO	2	—	—

Campaigning as a featherweight, Armstrong fought often—his bouts were sometimes only days apart—and with great success. In 1934, *The Ring* ranked him as the sixth-best featherweight contender in its annual rankings. In 1936, Armstrong won a ten-round decision over Baby Arizmendi for the California-Mexico version of the world featherweight title. By 1937, Armstrong was unstoppable. He fought 27 times and won 27 times, 26 by knockout. Among his victims was Petey Sarron, acclaimed as the world featherweight titleholder. Armstrong knocked Sarron out in six to lay undisputed claim to the championship.

But 1938 was the greatest year of Armstrong's career. In May, he challenged Barney Ross for the welterweight title. The fight was held in the open-air Madison Square Garden Bowl in front of 28,290 fans. Although Armstrong struggled to make the maximum weight, the end was near for Ross, who was unaware that his career had peaked. For fifteen rounds, Armstrong gave the champ a merciless shellacking that had the crowd calling for the fight to be stopped.

With the featherweight and welterweight titles firmly in hand, Armstrong then faced Lou Ambers for the lightweight championship. In a very fierce fight, Armstrong knocked Ambers down in the fifth and sixth rounds, but Ambers cut Armstrong's mouth and eyes so seriously that the referee considered stopping the fight. Fighting without a mouthpiece so that he could swallow the blood flow-

Armstrong (R) took the title from Lou Ambers on August 7, 1938. Armstrong scored knockdowns in the 5th and 6th. However Amber's late comeback made the split-decision victory controversial.

1938

Date		Opponent	Location	Result	Rds	Title	Wt
Jan 12		Enrico Venturi	New York	KO	6	—	—
Jan 21		Frankie Castillo	Phoenix	TKO	3	—	—
Jan 22		Tommy Brown	Tucson	KO	2	—	—
Feb 1	⑩	Albert ("Chalky") Wright★	Los Angeles	TKO	3	—	—
Feb 9		Al Citrino	San Francisco	TKO	4	—	—
Feb 25	⑩	Everett Rightmire	Chicago	TKO	3	—	—
Feb 28		Charley Burns	Minneapolis	TKO	2	—	—
Mar 15	⑩	Baby Arizmendi	Los Angeles	W	10	—	—
Mar 25		Eddie Zivic	Detroit	TKO	4	—	—
Mar 30		Lew Feldman	New York	KO	5	—	—
May 31	♛	Barney Ross★	Long Island City, NY	W	15	Won-World-W	147
Aug 17	♛	Lou Ambers★	New York	W	15	Won-World-L	134
Nov 25	⑩	Ceferino Garcia	New York	W	15	Ret-World-W	147
Dec 5		Al Manfredo	Cleveland	TKO	3	Ret-World-W	147

1939

Date		Opponent	Location	Result	Rds	Title	Wt
Jan 10	⑩	Baby Arizmendi	Los Angeles	W	10	Ret-World-W	147
Mar 4		Bobby Pacho	Havana	TKO	4	Ret-World-W	147
Mar 16		Lew Feldman	St. Louis	KO	1	Ret-World-W	147
Mar 31	⑩	Davey Day	New York	KO	12	Ret-World-W	147
May 25	⑩	Ernie Roderick	London	W	15	Ret-World-W	147
Aug 22	⑩	Lou Ambers★	New York	L	15	Lost-World-L	135
Oct 9		Al Manfredo	Des Moines, IA	TKO	4	Ret-World-W	141
Oct 13		Howard Scott	Minneapolis	KO	2	Ret-World-W	141
Oct 20		Ritchie Fontaine	Seattle	KO	3	Ret-World-W	147
Oct 24		Jimmy Garrison	Los Angeles	W	10	Ret-World-W	147
Oct 30		Bobby Pacho	Denver	TKO	4	Ret-World-W	147
Dec 11		Jimmy Garrison	Cleveland	KO	7	Ret-World-W	147

1940

Date		Opponent	Location	Result	Rds	Title	Wt
Jan 4		Joe Ghnouly	St. Louis	KO	5	Ret-World-W	147
Jan 24		Pedro Montanez	New York	TKO	9	Ret-World-W	147
Mar 1	♛	Ceferino Garcia	Los Angeles	D	10	For-World-M	142
Apr 26		Paul Junior	Boston	TKO	7	Ret-World-W	147
May 24		Ralph Zanelli	Boston	TKO	5	Ret-World-W	147
Jun 21		Paul Junior	Portland, ME	TKO	3	Ret-World-W	144
Jul 17		Lew Jenkins★	New York	TKO	6	—	—
Sep 23		Phil Furr	Washington, DC	KO	4	Ret-World-W	146
Oct 4	⑩	Fritzie Zivic★	New York	L	15	Lost-World-W	142

1941

Date		Opponent	Location	Result	Rds	Title	Wt
Jan 17	♛	Fritzie Zivic★	New York	TKO'd	12	For-World-W	141

1942

Date		Opponent	Location	Result	Rds	Title	Wt
Jun 1		Johnny Taylor	San Jose, CA	KO	4	—	—
Jun 24	⑩	Richard ("Sheik") Rangel	Oakland	W	10	—	—
Jul 3		Reuben Shank	Denver	L	10	—	—
Jul 20		Joe Ibarra	Sacramento	TKO	3	—	—
Aug 3		Aldo Spoldi	San Francisco	TKO	7	—	—
Aug 13		Jackie Burke	Ogden, UT	W	10	—	—
Aug 26		Rodolfo Ramirez	Oakland	KO	8	—	—
Sep 7		Johnny Taylor	Pittman, NV	KO	3	—	—
Sep 14		Leo Rodak	San Francisco	KO	4	—	—
Sep 30		Earl Turner	Oakland	KO	4	—	—
Oct 13	⑩	Juan Zurita	Los Angeles	KO	2	—	—
Oct 26	⑩	Fritzie Zivic★	San Francisco	W	10	—	—
Dec 4		Lew Jenkins★	Portland, OR	KO	8	—	—
Dec 14		Saverio Turiello	San Francisco	KO	4	—	—

Date		Opponent	Location	Result	Rounds		
Jan 5		Jimmy McDaniels	Los Angeles	W	10	—	—
Mar 2	⑩	Willie Joyce	Los Angeles	L	10	—	—
Mar 8	⑩	Tippy Larkin	San Francisco	KO	2	—	—
Mar 22		Al Tribuani	Philadelphia	W	10	—	—
Apr 2	♛	Beau Jack★	New York	L	10	—	138
Apr 30		Saverio Turiello	Washington, DC	TKO	5	—	—
May 7		Tommy Jessup	Boston	KO	1	—	—
May 24	⑩	Maxie Shapiro	Philadelphia	KO	7	—	—
Jun 11	⑩	Sammy Angott★	New York	W	10	—	140
Jul 24	⑩	Willie Joyce	Hollywood	W	10	—	140
Aug 6		Jimmy Garrison	Portland, OR	W	10	—	140
Aug 14		Joey Silva	Spokane, WA	W	10	—	—
Aug 27	⑩	Sugar Ray Robinson★	New York	L	10	—	140

1944

Jan 14		Aldo Spoldi	Portland, OR	KO	3	—	—
Jan 26		Saverio Turiello	Kansas City	KO	7	—	—
Feb 7		Lew Hanbury	Washington, DC	KO	3	—	—
Feb 23		Jimmy Garrison	Kansas City	TKO	5	—	—
Feb 29		Jackie Byrd	Des Moines	KO	4	—	—
Mar 14		Johnny Jones	Miami	KO	5	—	—
Mar 20	⑩	Frankie Wills	Washington, DC	W	10	—	142
Mar 24	⑩	Ralph Zanelli	Boston	W	10	—	—
Apr 25	⑩	John Thomas	Los Angeles	W	10	—	140
May 16	⑩	Ralph Zanelli	Boston	W	10	—	—
May 22		Aaron Perry	Washington, DC	TKO	6	—	140
Jun 2	⑩	Willie Joyce	Chicago	L	10	—	140
Jun 15	⑩	Al Davis	New York	KO	2	—	141
Jun 21		Nick Latsios	Washington, DC	W	10	—	142
Jul 4	⑩	John Thomas	Los Angeles	L	10	—	—
Jul 14	⑩	Luther ("Slugger") White	Hollywood	D	10	—	137
Aug 21	⑩	Willie Joyce	San Francisco	W	10	—	139
Sep 15		Aldo Spoldi	St. Louis	KO	2	—	141
Nov 4	⑩	Mike Belloise	Portland, OR	KO	4	—	—

1945

Jan 17		Chester Slider	Oakland	D	10	—	140
Feb 6		Genaro Rojo	Los Angeles	W	10	—	140
Feb 14		Chester Slider	Oakland	L	10	—	141

ing in his mouth, Armstrong went the distance and won a split decision to become boxing's first simultaneous triple titleholder.

Armstrong voluntarily relinquished the featherweight title in 1938. In 1939, Ambers took the lightweight title back in a rematch in which Armstrong was severely penalized for low blows. Armstrong failed to attain the middleweight title in 1940 when he fought hard-hitting Ceferino Garcia to a draw. That same year, he lost the welterweight belt, the last of his titles, to Fritzie Zivic. Zivic repeatedly worked Armstrong's eyes, which were scarred and vulnerable to cutting. Armstrong, who considered Zivic a dirty fighter, could not beat him in the rematch. When they met a third time, Armstrong won, but Zivic was no longer champion. Armstrong continued to box into 1945, though the days of his unbeatable rapid-fire attack were behind him. In retirement, Armstrong overcame alcoholism and became an ordained Baptist minister.

CARMEN BASILIO
The Upstate Onion Farmer

MIDDLEWEIGHT

Right-handed; 5'6½"; 143–155 lbs.

79 bouts, 11/24/1948 to 4/25/1961

Managers: Johnny DeJohn and Joe Netro

Welterwt. Champ 1955–56, 1956–57; Middlewt. Champ 1957–58

Hall of Fame Induction: 1990

Born: 4/2/1927, Canastota, NY

From the farm country around Canastota, New York sprang one of boxing's toughest heroes, Carmen Basilio. Twice welterweight champ, Basilio had the nerve to challenge—and beat—middleweight king Sugar Ray Robinson in one of the most brutal matches of ring history. An all-out fighter who took as many punches as he delivered, Basilio bore the badges of his profession on his angular face—flattened nose, scarred cheeks, and split eyebrow. Built low to the ground, Basilio was a game fighter who looked mean and who fought with great courage.

Basilio's father, Joseph, an onion farmer, was a boxing fan who inspired his son's early interest in the sport. Basilio fought some bouts in the Marine Corps before turning professional in 1948, at the age of 21. In 1953, he decisioned Hall of Famer Ike Williams and then defeated Billy Graham to win the New York State welterweight championship. After fighting Graham to a draw in a rematch the same year, Basilio faced Kid Gavilan for the welterweight championship of the world. Fighting in the War Memorial Auditorium in Syracuse, New York before 6,803 fans, Basilio came close to knocking Gavilan out in the second round. Gavilan, however, rose at the count of nine and prevailed in a fifteen-round decision.

Basilio got another chance to fight for the welterweight title when he faced the new champion, Tony DeMarco, in the Syracuse War Memorial in 1955. In a wild, bloody brawl, DeMarco

At Yankee Stadium in September 1957, Basilio (R) relentlessly battered away at Sugar Ray Robinson and took his crown.

led through eight rounds. In the tenth, Basilio floored DeMarco twice. DeMarco managed to avoid a knockout but succumbed in the twelfth when the referee stopped the fight. Basilio lost his title to Johnny Saxton in 1956. Basilio had Saxton seriously shaken up, but the challenger's corner reportedly fabricated a delay in replacing a damaged glove, giving Saxton time to recover sufficiently to win a decision. Basilio won the rematch six months later to reclaim the title.

In 1957, Basilio fought what many consider to be the finest battle of his career. He moved up to middleweight in a bid to topple the enduring Sugar Ray

IN THE RING	WON 56	LOST 16	DRAWS 7	TB 79	KO 27	W 29	WF 0	D 7	KO'd 2	L 14	LF 0

Date	Opponent	Site	Result / Rounds		Title	Wt.
1948						
Nov 24	Jimmy Evans	Binghamton, NY	KO	3	—	145
Nov 29	Bruce Walters	Syracuse, NY	KO	1	—	145
Dec 8	Eddie Thomas	Binghamton	KO	2	—	—
Dec 16	Rollie Johns	Syracuse	W	6	—	142
1949						
Jan 5	Johnny Cunningham	Binghamton	D	6	—	—
Jan 19	Jay Parlin	Binghamton	D	6	—	—
Jan 25	Ernie Hall	Syracuse	KO	2	—	—
Feb 19	Luke Jordan	Rochester, NY	W	6	—	—
Apr 20	Elliott Throop	Syracuse	KO	1	—	—
May 2	Connie Thies	Rochester	L	6	—	—
May 8	Jerry Drain	Syracuse	KO	3	—	143
May 18	Johnny Clemons	Syracuse	KO	3	—	145
Jun 7	Johnny Cunningham	Syracuse	KO	2	—	146
Jul 12	Jesse Bradshaw	Syracuse	TKO	2	—	—
Jul 21	Sammy Daniels	Utica, NY	W	8	—	—
Aug 2	Johnny Cunningham	Utica	L	8	—	—
Aug 17	Johnny Cunningham	Syracuse	W	8	—	145
Sep 7	Tony DiPelino	Rochester	W	8	—	—
Sep 30	Jackie Parker	Syracuse	TKO	3	—	—
1950						
Jan 10	Sonny Hampton	Buffalo	W	8	—	—
Jan 24	Cassill Tate	Buffalo	W	8	—	—
Feb 7	Adrien Mourguiart	Buffalo	KO	7	—	—
Mar 6	Lew Jenkins	Syracuse	W	10	—	—
Mar 27	Mike Koballa	Brooklyn	L	8	—	147
Apr 12	Gaby Ferland	New Orleans	D	10	—	—
May 5	Gaby Ferland	New Orleans	KO	1	—	—
Jun 21	Guillermo Giminez	New Orleans	TKO	8	—	140
Jul 31	Guillermo Giminez	New Orleans	TKO	9	—	141
Aug 28	Eddie Giosa	New Orleans	L	10	—	145
Dec 15	Vic Cardell	New York	L	10	—	—
1951						
Mar 9	Floro Hita	Syracuse	W	8	—	—
Apr 12	Eddie Giosa	Syracuse	W	10	—	—
May 29	Lester Felton	Syracuse	L	10	—	—
Jun 18	Johnny Cesario	Utica	L	10	—	—

Date		Opponent	Location	Result	Rds	Title	Weight
Sep 17		Shamus McCray	Syracuse	W	8	—	—
Sep 26		Ross Virgo	New Orleans	L	10	—	—
1952							
Feb 4		Emmett Norris	Wilkes-Barre, PA	W	10	—	—
Feb 28		Jimmy Cousins	Akron, OH	W	8	—	—
Mar 31		Jackie O'Brien	Wilkes-Barre	W	10	—	—
May 29	⑩	Chuck Davey	Syracuse	D	10	—	—
Jul 16	⑩	Chuck Davey	Chicago	L	10	—	—
Aug 20	⑩	Billy Graham★	Chicago	L	10	—	—
Sep 22		Baby Williams	Miami	W	10	—	—
Oct 20		Sammy Giuliani	Syracuse	KO	3	—	—
Nov 18		Chuck Foster	Buffalo	TKO	5	—	—
1953							
Jan 12		Ike Williams★	Syracuse	W	10	—	—
Feb 28		Vic Cardell	Toledo, OH	W	10	—	—
Apr 11		Carmine Fiore	Syracuse	TKO	9	—	—
Jun 6	⑩	Billy Graham★	Syracuse	W	12	Won-NY State-W	147
Jul 25	⑩	Billy Graham★	Syracuse	D	12	Ret-NY State-W	147
Sep 18	♛	Kid Gavilan★	Syracuse	L	15	For-World-W	147
Nov 28		Johnny Cunningham	Toledo	TKO	4	—	—
Dec 19	⑩	Pierre Langlois	Syracuse	D	10	—	—
1954							
Jim 16		Italo Scortichini	Miami	D	10	—	—
Apr 17	⑩	Pierre Langlois	Syracuse	W	10	—	—
May 15		Italo Scortichini	Syracuse	W	10	—	—
Jun 26		Al Andrews	Syracuse	W	10	—	—
Aug 17		Ronnie Harper	Fort Wayne, IN	TKO	2	—	—
Sep 10		Carmine Fiore	New York	W	10	—	—
Oct 15		Allie Gronik	Syracuse	W	10	—	—
Dec 16		Ronnie Harper	Akron	TKO	4	—	—
1955							
Jan 21		Peter Muller	Syracuse	W	10	—	—
Jun 10	♛	Tony DeMarco	Syracuse	TKO	12	Won-World-W	145
Aug 10		Italo Scortichini	New York	W	10	—	—
Sep 7		Gil Turner	Syracuse	W	10	—	—
Nov 30	⑩	Tony DeMarco	Boston	TKO	12	Ret-World-W	145
1956							
Mar 14	⑩	Johnny Saxton	Chicago	L	15	Lost-World-W	146
Sep 12	♛	Johnny Saxton	Syracuse	TKO	9	Reg-World-W	146
1957							
Feb 22	⑩	Johnny Saxton	Cleveland	KO	2	Ret-World-W	147
May 16		Harold Jones	Portland, OR	TKO	4	—	—
Sep 23	♛	Sugar Ray Robinson★	New York	W	15	Won-World-M	153
1958							
Mar 25	⑩	Sugar Ray Robinson★	Chicago	L	15	Lost-World-M	159
Sep 5		Art Aragon	Los Angeles	TKO	8	—	155
1959							
Apr 1		Arley Selfer	Augusta, GA	TKO	3	—	—
Aug 28	⑩	Gene Fullmer★	San Francisco	TKO'd	14	For-Vac NBA-M	156
1960							
Jun 29	♛	Gene Fullmer★	Salt Lake City	TKO'd	12	For-NBA-M	156
1961							
Jan 7	⑩	Gaspar Ortega	New York	W	10	—	—
Mar 11		Don Jordan	Syracuse	W	10	—	—
Apr 22	♛	Paul Pender	Boston	L	15	For-World-M	159

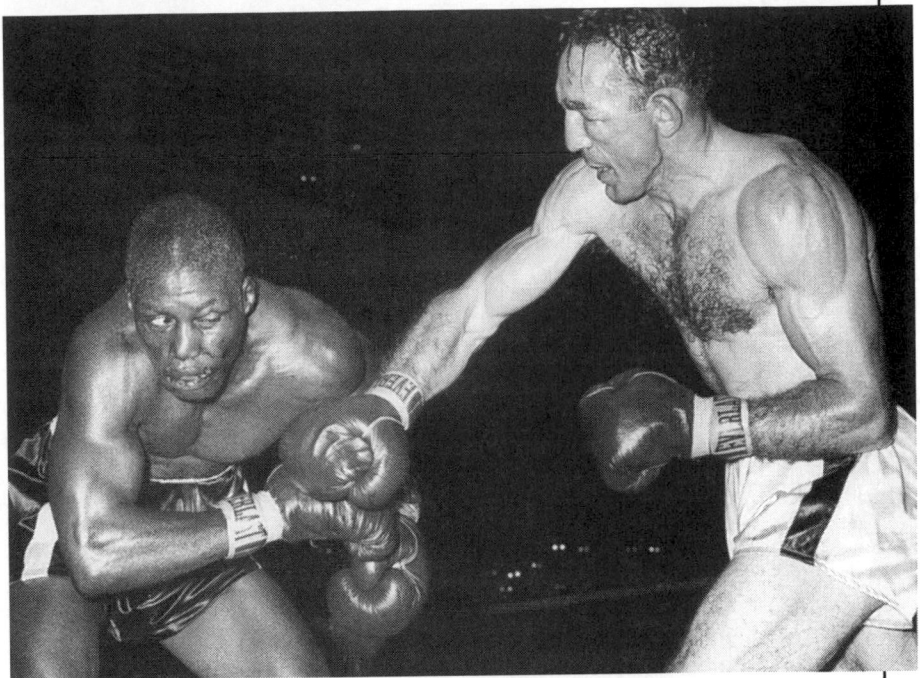

Basilio (R) is on the familiar home turf of Syracuse's War Memorial Auditorium when he takes out Johnny Saxton in the 9th with a booming right to regain the world welterweight title on September 12, 1956.

Robinson. Robinson had lost and regained the title four times, and had recently come out of a short retirement. He was 37; Basilio was 30. The contest, later ranked the twelfth greatest fight of all time by *The Ring*, took place in Yankee Stadium before a crowd of 38,000. At the start of the fight, Robinson jabbed Basilio persistently and effectively. He bloodied Basilio's nose in the third round and cut his left eye in the fourth. Basilio dominated in the fifth and continued to press Robinson in the following rounds. There was no holding back as each fighter felt the effect of many resounding, jarring punches. At times, each man appeared dazed and ready to drop. After fifteen rounds had finally gone by, the bloody and exhausted Basilio went down on one knee to pray. A few moments later, it was announced that he had won the split decision to take the middleweight title. The rematch six months later was just as gruesome, with Basilio fighting one-eyed from the sixth round on. This time, Robinson won the decision. In three later bids, Basilio failed to claim the middleweight title from subsequent champions Gene Fullmer and Paul Pender.

Basilio's aggressive, charging style and powerful left hook enabled him to win championships in two weight classes and to have a long and memorable career. In retirement, he worked as a physical education instructor at LeMoyne College in Syracuse and as a Genesee Brewery representative. Basilio's hometown of Canastota is also the site of the International Boxing Hall of Fame. Basilio is a frequent visitor to the shrine that honors him and other great boxers of the past.

WILFRED BENITEZ

JUNIOR MIDDLEWEIGHT

Right-handed; 5'10"; 140–160 lbs.

62 bouts, 11/22/1973 to 9/18/1990

Junior Welterwt. Champ 1976–1979,
Welterweight. Champ 1979,
WBC Junior Middleweight
(Super Welterweight) Champ 1981–82

Hall of Fame Induction: 1996

Born: 9/12/1958, Bronx, NY

A talented fighter who sometimes got away with perfunctory preparation for formidable opponents, Wilfred Benitez became a triple titleholder at the age of 22. Born in New York the youngest of eight children, Benitez was brought up on boxing. His father, Gregorio ("Goyo"), had boxed as a boy in Puerto Rico and often set up playground matches for his sons in the Bronx, charging passersby a quarter to watch.

At seven, Benitez moved with his family to Puerto Rico where he fought in the regional Golden Gloves tournament and turned professional at the age of fifteen. Winning his first eleven fights, he returned to New York to face Al Hughes in Madison Square Garden's Felt Forum. Barely sixteen, Benitez was legally too young to fight in New York, but carried a baptismal certificate showing he was older.

A year later in San Juan, he challenged Antonio ("Kid Pambele") Cervantes, the WBA junior welterweight champion. Training seriously for this fight, Benitez

Benitez's right shakes welterweight champion Carlos Palomino (L). Benitez took the title in a 15-round decision on January 14, 1979 in an outdoor arena in San Juan.

IN THE RING	WON 53	LOST 8	DRAWS 1	TB 62	KO 31	W 22	WF 0	D 1	KO'd 4	L 4	LF 0

Date	Opponent	Site	Result / Rounds		Title	Wt.
1973						
Nov 22	Hiram Santiago	San Juan, PR	KO	1	—	—
Nov 30	Jesse Torres	St. Martin, VI	KO	2	—	—
1974						
Jan 7	Hector Amadia	San Juan	KO	4	—	—
Jan 26	Joe ("Hawk") York	St. Martin	KO	2	—	—
Feb 18	Roberto Flanders	San Juan	TKO	4	—	142
Apr 1	Victor Mangual	San Juan	W	8	—	141
Apr 30	Juan Disla	San Juan	TKO	3	—	143
May 11	Sonny Lake	St. Martin	KO	1	—	—
Jun 21	Ives St. Jean	St. Martin	KO	1	—	—
Jun 26	Carlos Crispin	San Juan	TKO	3	—	—
Aug 31	Sonny Lake	St. Martin	TKO	5	—	—
Sep 16	Al Hughes	New York	TKO	5	—	138
Oct 25	Terry Summerhayes	New York	TKO	6	—	144
Dec 2	Lawrence Hafey	New York	W	8	—	145
1975						
Jan 4	Francisco Rodriguez	San Juan	TKO	7	—	142
Feb 8	Santiago Rosa	San Juan	KO	4	—	143
Mar 31	Wilbur Seales	San Juan	TKO	4	—	—
May 5	Santos Solis	San Juan	W	10	—	—
Jun 9	Angel R. Garcia	San Juan	W	10	—	145
Jun 28	Joe Henry	San Juan	TKO	8	—	—
Aug 1	Eyue Jeudy	St. Martin	KO	4	—	—
Aug 19	Young Woodall	St. Martin	KO	4	—	—
Sep 1	Marcelino Alicea	San Juan	TKO	2	—	140
Oct 20	Omar Piton	New York	TKO	6	—	143
Dec 13	Chris Fernandez	San Juan	W	10	—	—
1976						
Mar 6	♛ Antonio Cervantes★	San Juan	W	15	Won-World-JW	138
May 31	Emiliano Villa	San Juan	W	15	Ret-World-JW	140
Oct 16	⑩ Tony Petronelli	San Juan	TKO	3	Ret-World-JW	140
1977						
Feb 2	⑩ Harold Weston	New York	D	10	—	144
Mar 6	⑩ Mel Dennis	Marion, OH	W	8	—	146
Jun 2	Roberto Gonzalez	St. Thomas, VI	KO	1	—	—
Jul 1	Easy Boy Lake	St. Thomas	KO	1	—	—
Aug 3	Ray Guerrero	New York	TKO	15	Ret-World-JW	139
Nov 18	⑩ Bruce Curry	New York	W	10	—	—
1978						
Feb 4	⑩ Bruce Curry	New York	W	10	—	145
Aug 25	⑩ Randy Sheilds	New York	TKO	6	—	145
Dec 5	Vernon Lewis	New York	W	10	—	147
1979						
Jan 14	♛ Carlos Palomino	San Juan	W	15	Won-World-W	146
Mar 25	⑩ Harold Weston	San Juan	W	15	Ret-World-W	147

Date		Opponent	Location	Result	Rds	Title	Wt
Nov 30	⑩	Sugar Ray Leonard★	Las Vegas	TKO'd	15	Lost-World-W	144
1980							
Mar 9		Johnny Turner	Miami Beach	TKO	9	—	150
Aug 1	⑩	Tony Chiaverini	Las Vegas	TKO	8	—	154
Dec 12	⑩	Pete Ranzany	Sacramento, CA	W	10	—	150
1981							
May 23	♛	Maurice Hope	Las Vegas	TKO	12	Won-WBC-JM (SW)	153
Nov 13		Carlos Santos	Las Vegas	W	15	Ret-WBC-JM (SW)	153
1982							
Jan 30	⑩	Roberto Duran	Las Vegas	W	15	Ret-WBC-JM (SW)	152
Dec 3	⑩	Thomas Hearns	New Orleans	L	15	Lost-WBC-JM (SW)	152
1983							
May 18		Tony Cerda	Las Vegas	W	10	—	158
Jul 16	⑩	Mustafa Hamsho	Las Vegas	L	12	—	157
1984							
Feb 11		Stacy McSwain	Detroit	W	10	—	154
Jul 14	⑩	Davey Moore	Monte Carlo	TKO'd	2	—	154
1985							
Mar 30		Mauricio Bravo	Oranjestad, Aruba	KO	2	—	155
Jul 6		Danny Chapman	Washington, DC	TKO	7	—	153
Aug 21		Kevin Moley	New York	W	10	—	154
1986							
Feb 15	⑩	Matthew Hilton	Montreal	KO'd	9	—	152
Jul 2		Paul Whittaker	New Orleans	W	10	—	158
Sep 17		Harry Daniels	Baltimore, MD	W	10	—	164
Nov 28		Carlos Herrera	Salta, Argentina	TKO'd	7	—	155
1990							
Mar 8		Ariel Conde	Phoenix	KO	7	—	158
May 23		Pat Lawlor	Tucson	L	10	—	158
Aug 24		Sam Wilson	Denver	W	10	—	160
Sep 18		Scott Papsadora	Winnipeg, Man.	L	10	—	159

outboxed the champ and won a decision to become the youngest boxer ever to win a world title. He defended his belt three times, but a scheduled rematch with Cervantes was postponed after Benitez crashed his car. When he failed to reschedule quickly enough, the WBA stripped him of the title.

In the meantime, Benitez's chronic habit of lax preparation had begun to surface. After just twelve days of training to fight Harold Weston, he clowned around in the ring and only managed to score a draw. Fighting Bruce Curry with barely a week's training, he was knocked down three times and just squeaked out a split decision.

As he matured physically, Benitez moved up to welterweight and faced champion Carlos Palomino in San Juan. Although contracted to Hall of Famer Jimmy Jacobs, Benitez was still trained by his father and, at Jacobs's direction, by another Hall of Famer, Emile Griffith, as well. Nearing the Palomino fight, Griffith and Goyo Benitez clashed over the tactical approach Wilfred should use, but Griffith prevailed. Benitez scored a split decision and won his second world title.

In many of Benitez's best performances, he employed an unusual defensive tactic. He spread his legs wide while keeping his feet flat on the floor. From this position, he quickly moved his upper body, dodging his opponents' punches.

In 1981 Benitez moved up to junior middleweight and attempted to gain his third world crown. Here he crumples Maurice Hope against the ropes for a 12-round TKO victory and the WBC belt.

Later in 1979, Benitez took on Sugar Ray Leonard, his stiffest challenge to date, with minimal preparation estimated at something between two and nine days. Nevertheless, Benitez nearly went the distance, until the fight was stopped in the final seconds. Even though Leonard knocked Benitez down twice and won, Sugar Ray openly admired his opponent's ring skills.

In 1981, Benitez moved up to junior middleweight and faced WBC champion Maurice Hope. Jacobs had turned down a bigger paycheck for a potential match with Thomas Hearns to have Benitez fight Hope for a third world title. In the ring, Hope did some damage, but Benitez did much more, knocking out two of Hope's teeth and, in the twelfth round, the fighter himself.

This bout may have marked the high point of Benitez's career. A year later he defeated Roberto Duran but lost his very next fight by decision to Hearns. An attempt to move up to middleweight under the training of Victor Machado and Cus D'Amato failed with a loss by decision to Mustafa Hamsho. Back under the direction of his father, Benitez broke his ankle in a fight with Davey Moore. He continued to fight but never again contended for a title.

By the age of 37, Benitez had squandered his ring earnings and suffered from chronic traumatic encephalopathy. He was recently awarded a newly instituted boxer's pension by the Puerto Rican government. Benitez is remembered for his remarkable defensive skills in the ring and his facility for fighting both right- and left-handed. "At one time," observed promoter Teddy Brenner, "he was the best fighter in the world."

GIOVANNI ("NINO") BENVENUTI

MIDDLEWEIGHT

Right-handed; 5'11"; 153–164 lbs.

90 bouts, 1/20/1961 to 5/9/1971

Manager: Bruno Amaduzzi

1960 Olympic Welterweight Gold Medalist

Jr. Middlewt. Champion 1965–66, Middlewt. Champion 1967, 1968–70

Hall of Fame Induction: 1992

Born: 4/26/1938, Trieste, Italy

Name: Carmine Tilelli

A handsome idol of the Italian public as well as many fans around the world, Giovanni ("Nino") Benvenuti moved from Olympic stardom to the professional ring with great ease. He is best remembered for three bitter fights in 1967 and 1968 with Hall of Famer Emile Griffith, for the middleweight championship.

Born the son of a fisherman in Trieste, Benvenuti was one of four boys in the family who all aspired to boxing careers. He began boxing as an amateur in his native Italy, where he won 120 fights and lost none. An all-round athlete, he engaged in some unconventional training methods, such as swimming, to stay in top form. He had a wide repertoire of punches, as well as speed and good defensive moves. Benvenuti capped his amateur career by earning a gold medal in the welterweight division

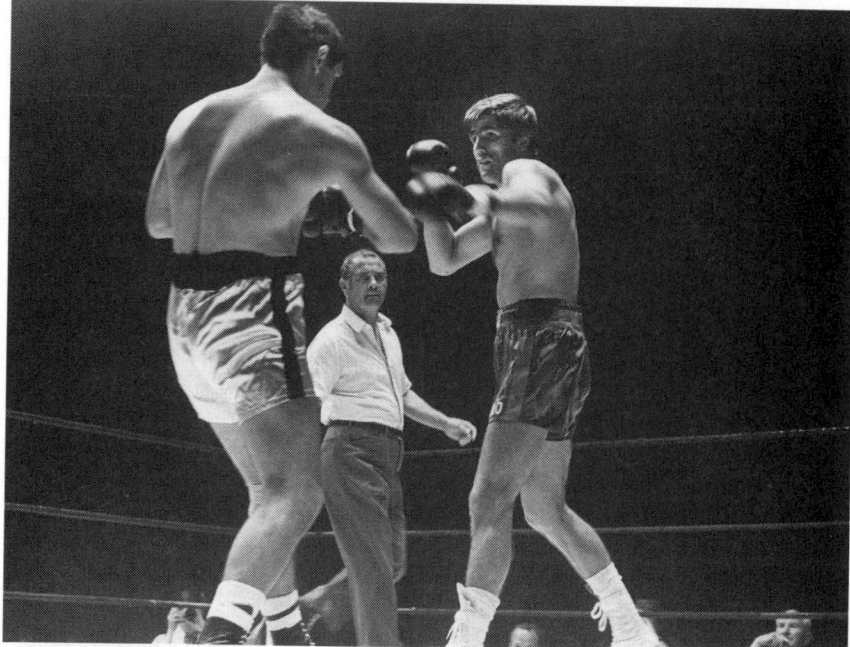

Benvenuti (R) measures Art Hernandez with a short jab. This September 17, 1968 non-title bout was a ten-round victory for Benvenuti. Earlier in 1968, he had regained the middleweight title.

IN THE RING	WON 82	LOST 7	DRAWS 1	TB 90	KO 35	W 42	WF 5	D 1	KO'd 3	L 4	LF 0

Date	Opponent	Site	Result / Rounds		Title	Wt.
1961						
Jan 20	Ali Allala	Trieste, Italy	W	6	—	—
Feb 10	Nicola Sanmartino	Rome	TKO	3	—	—
Feb 27	Ali Allala	Naples, Italy	KO	1	—	—
Mar 14	Sahib Mosri	Bologna, Italy	TKO	3	—	—
Apr 7	Nick Maric	Milan	W	6	—	—
Apr 21	Pierre Mondino	Florence	W	6	—	—
May 3	Daniel Brunet	Naples	WD	3	—	—
May 16	Michel Francois	Turin, Italy	KO	4	—	—
Jun 7	Henri Cabelduc	Bologna	W	6	—	—
Jun 17	Marc Desforneaux	Trieste	W	6	—	—
Oct 2	Retmia Mahrez	Bologna	TKO	3	—	—
Nov 1	Angelo Brisci	Trieste	KO	1	—	—
Nov 9	Jesse Jones	Rome	WD	6	—	—
Dec 20	Giuseppe Catalano	Rome	W	8	—	—
1962						
Jan 19	George Aldridge	Rome	KO	6	—	—
Feb 19	Jose Riquelme	Bologna	W	8	—	—
Mar 8	Manfred Haas	Turin	W	8	—	—
Mar 17	Gianni Lommi	Milan	TKO	5	—	—
Apr 1	Jim Hegerle	Rome	TKO	4	—	—
May 1	Hector Constance	Trieste	W	10	—	—
Jun 2	Jean Ruellet	Cagliari, Italy	W	8	—	—
Jun 22	Heini Freytag	Rome	W	8	—	—
Jul 12	Gino Rossi	Trieste	W	10	—	—
Aug 2	Mahmout Le Noir	Lignano, Italy	W	8	—	—
Aug 30	Giuseppe Gentiletti	Senigallia, Italy	TKO	2	—	—
Sep 28	Diego Infantes	Rome	W	8	—	—
Oct 18	Daniel Leullier	Padua, Italy	W	10	—	—
Nov 30	Isaac Logart	Rome	W	10	—	—
Dec 26	Giampaolo Melis	Bologna	TKO	2	—	—
1963						
Mar 1	Tomasso Truppi	Rome	KO	11	Won-Vac Italy-M	160
Apr 5	Georges Estatoff	Turin	KO	6	—	—
Apr 24	Jean Ruellet	Alejandria, Italy	W	10	—	—
May 23	Jimmy Beechman	Rome	W	10	—	—
Jun 7	Tony Montano	Rome	W	10	—	—
Aug 31	Francesco Fiori	Priverno, Italy	KO	3	Ret-Italy-M	160
Sep 16	Willy Niederau	Prato, Italy	TKO	6	—	—
Sep 27	Victor Zalazar	Rome	TKO	2	—	—
Oct 18	⑩ Gaspar Ortega	Rome	W	10	—	—
Nov 7	Jackie Cailleau	Prato	W	10	—	—
Nov 15	Lou Gutierrez	Rome	TKO	7	—	—
Dec 13	⑩ Teddy Wright	Rome	W	10	—	—
1964						
Feb 28	Memo Ayon	Rome	KO	5	—	—
Mar 18	Michel Diouf	Bologna	W	10	—	—
Apr 10	Sugar Boy Nando	Rome	W	10	—	—

Date		Opponent	Location	Result	Rounds	Title	Weight
May 28		Jimmy Beechman	Bologna	TKO	2	—	—
Jul 30		Fabio Bettini	San Remo, Italy	W	12	Ret-Italy-M	160
Sep 18		Denny Moyer	Rome	W	10	—	160
Oct 9		Abrao DeSouza	Rome	WD	7	—	—
Nov 27		Aristeo Chavarin	Rome	KO	4	—	—
Dec 19		Juan Duran	Milan	W	10	—	158
1965							
Jan 22		Art Hernandez	Rome	TKO	3	—	—
Feb 12		Tommaso Truppi	Bologna	TKO	5	Ret-Italy-M	160
Feb 26		Mick Lehaly	Milan	W	10	—	—
Mar 18		Dick Knight	Bologna	KO	6	—	—
Apr 2		Rip Randall	Rome	W	10	—	—
Apr 30		Milo Calhoun	Genoa, Italy	W	10	—	—
Jun 18	♛	Sandro Mazzinghi	Milan	KO	6	Won-World-JM	153
Aug 15		Daniel Leullier	Senigallia	TKO	7		
Oct 15	⑩	Luis Folledo	Rome	TKO	6	Won-Vac Europe-M	160
Nov 5		Johnny Torres	Turin	WD	7	—	—
Nov 15		James Shelton	Bologna	W	10	—	—
Dec 17	⑩	Sandro Mazzinghi	Rome	W	15	Ret-World-JM	153
1966							
Feb 4	⑩	Don Fullmer	Rome	W	12	—	—
Mar 11		Clarence James	Turin	W	10	—	—
May 14		Jupp Elze	Berlin	KO	14	Ret-Europe-M	159
Jun 25	⑩	Ki-Soo Kim	Seoul	L	15	Lost-World-JM	153
Sep 23		Harry Scott	Rome	W	10	—	—
Oct 21		Pascal Di Benedetto	Rome	TKO	11	Ret-Europe-M	160
Dec 2		Ferd Hernandez	Rome	W	10	—	—
Dec 23		Renato Moares	Rome	KO	9	—	—
1967							
Jan 19		Manfred Graus	Bologna	KO	2	—	—
Mar 3		Milo Calhoun	Rome	W	10	—	—
Apr 17	♛	Emile Griffith★	New York	W	15	Won-World-M	159
Sep 29	⑩	Emile Griffith★	New York	L	15	Lost-World-M	159
1968							
Jan 19		Charley Austin	Rome	W	10	—	—
Mar 4	♛	Emile Griffith★	New York	W	15	Reg-World-M	160
Jun 7		Yoshiaki Akasaka	Rome	KO	2	—	161
Jul 5		Jimmy Ramos	Turin	TKO	4	—	162
Sep 17		Art Hernandez	Toronto	W	10	—	163
Oct 14	⑩	Doyle Baird	Akron, OH	D	10	—	—
Dec 14	⑩	Don Fullmer	San Remo	W	15	Ret-World-M	160
1969							
May 26	⑩	Dick Tiger★	New York	L	10	—	164
Oct 4	⑩	Fraser Scott	Naples	WD	7	Ret-World-M	160
Nov 22	⑩	Luis Rodriguez★	Rome	KO	11	Ret-World-M	159
1970							
Mar 13		Tom Bethea	Melbourne	TKO'd	8	—	163
May 23		Tom Bethea	Umag, Yugoslavia	KO	8	Ret-World-M	160
Sep 12	⑩	Doyle Baird	Bari, Italy	KO	10	—	—
Nov 7	⑩	Carlos Monzon★	Rome	KO'd	12	Lost-World-M	159
1971							
Mar 17		Jose Chirino	Bologna	L	10	—	163
May 9	♛	Carlos Monzon★	Monte Carlo, Monaco	TKO'd	3	For-World-M	160

Frank Sinatra was one of Nino Benvenuti's biggest fans. The handsome boxer with the playboy image looked more like a tennis star than a prize-fighter. He was a hero to the adoring Italian public.

in the 1960 Olympics, the same year Muhammad Ali participated in the games. Looking back on his entire boxing career, Benvenuti commented, "Winning the Olympic medal was my biggest thrill."

The following year, Benvenuti turned professional and continued to win. He triumphed in his first 65 professional fights—along the way winning the Italian and European middleweight titles, as well as the world junior middleweight title. Although the junior middleweight division was not well established in 1965, when Benvenuti defeated countryman Sandro Mazzinghi in Milan, he was recognized as a world champion. But a year later, Benvenuti lost that title when he suffered his first loss, to Korean Ki-Soo Kim.

As early as 1963, Benvenuti had been placed among the top ten middleweights in the annual rankings by *The Ring*. In 1967, he had his first opportunity to fight for the world middleweight championship when he travelled to the United States to face Emile Griffith in Madison Square Garden. Over 18,000 fans had come to watch the former Olympian scrap with Griffith. Although Griffith knocked the Italian challenger down in the fourth round, Benvenuti used his superior size and reach to keep Griffith away with jabs and hooks. When Griffith did venture inside, Benvenuti traded punches with the champion on an equal basis. Benvenuti won the title in a fifteen-round decision.

In their rematch in New York's Shea Stadium, Griffith used an effective attack to Benvenuti's body to regain the championship. The two foes met a third time in a bout which helped open the new Madison Square Garden, with Benvenuti regaining the championship by decision. He held the belt until 1970 when Carlos Monzon knocked him out in the twelfth round. After losing to Monzon again, Benvenuti retired to the business world. His suave manner and good looks later led to appearances in Italian movies.

JAC KIE ("KID") BE G
The Whitechapel Whirlwind

JR. WELTERWEIGHT

Right-handed; 5'9"; 134–153 lbs.

192 bouts, 6/8/1924 to 5/19/1945

Managers: Harry Levene (England), Frank Jacobs, and Sol Gold

Jr. Welterweight Champion 1930–31

Hall of Fame Induction: 1994

Born: 6/28/1909, London, England

Named: Judah Bergman

Died: 4/22/1991

Trained by Hall of Famer Ray Arcel, Jackie ("Kid") Berg boxed professionally for over two decades, during which time he recorded 157 wins. Like many fighters of his time, he fought frequently, sometimes with as little as a week between bouts. Berg is the first modern-era Hall of Fame inductee from England, the cradle of prizefighting.

Berg, born Judah Bergman in Whitechapel in London's East End, was an early devotee of the boxing matches staged at a theatre in his district. In 1924, when he was just fourteen, he convinced the show promoters to let him compete. Berg's energetic, attacking style was an instant success with the fans. He fought exclusively in London until 1928 with a record of 53 wins, three losses, and three draws. Ready to challenge a broader field of opponents, Berg arrived in the United States early in 1928. He fought primarily in Chicago before moving on to New York the following year.

Berg performed well in New York and quickly became a favorite in Madison Square Garden. Berg's swarming, continuous attack earned him the nickname, "The Whitechapel Whirlwind." His handlers played up his Jewish ethnicity by having him enter the ring wearing a tallis (prayer shawl) and tefilin (small leather box containing sacred scripture). In 1928, Berg was ranked as the ninth-best lightweight by *The Ring*. In 1929, he advanced to second top contender in the magazine's annual rankings. In

When Berg won the junior welterweight title in 1930, that division had only been contested for five years.

Date	Opponent	Site	Result / Rounds		Title	Wt.
1924						
Jun 8	Young Johnny Gordon	London	TKO	8	—	—
Jul 7	Charley Harwood	London	TKO	7	—	—
Jul 20	Syd Lyons	London	TKO	3	—	—
Aug 3	Billy Clarke	London	D	10	—	—
Aug 21	Billy Clarke	London	W	10	—	—
Sep 21	Teddy Pullen	London	KO	1	—	—
Oct 2	Jimmy Wooder	London	D	10	—	—
Oct 16	Albert Hicks	London	W	10	—	—
Nov 3	Young Clancy	London	W	15	—	—
Nov 10	Jimmy Wooder	London	W	10	—	—
Nov 20	Harry Miller	London	TKO	6	—	—
Nov 27	Fred Patten	London	W	15	—	—
Dec 7	Teddy Sheperd	London	TKO	9	—	—
Dec 11	Fred Saunders	London	TKO	14	—	—
Dec 15	Arthur Lloyd	London	W	10	—	—
Dec 26	Billy Colebourne	London	TKO	6	—	—
1925						
Jan 8	Albert Colcombe	London	TKO	13	—	—
Jan 26	Billy Streets	London	W	15	—	—
Feb 9	Arthur Lloyd	London	W	15	—	—
Feb 26	Billy Streets	London	TKO	9	—	—
Mar 12	Johnny Cuthbert	London	L	15	—	—
Apr 6	Sid Carter	London	W	15	—	—
Apr 19	George Davis	London	WF	6	—	—
May 21	Ted ("Kid") Lewis★	London	TKO	10	—	—
Jun 7	Billy Shepherd	London	TKO	13	—	—
Jun 18	Johnny Cuthbert	London	L	15	—	—
Jun 28	Jack Slattery	London	TKO	9	—	—
Jul 16	Joe Samuels	London	TKO	15	—	—
Jul 26	George Green	London	TKO	11	—	—
Aug 6	Fred Green	London	W	15	—	—
Aug 20	Fred Green	London	W	15	—	—
Aug 30	Johnny Britton	London	W	15	—	—
Sep 10	Norman Radford	London	KO	14	—	—
Oct 15	Johnny Cuthbert	London	TKO	11	—	—
Oct 29	Johnny Curley	London	W	15	—	—
Nov 12	Ernie Swash	London	WF	2	—	—
Nov 26	Battling Van Dyke	London	W	15	—	—
1926						
Feb 11	Harry Corbett	London	L	15	—	—
Mar 18	Andre Routis	London	W	15	—	—
Apr 26	Harry Corbett	London	D	15	—	—
May 16	Mick Hill	London	W	15	—	—
Jun 21	Andre Routis	London	WF	3	—	—
Jul 8	Henry Hebrans	London	TKO	5	—	—
Jul 29	Paul Gay	London	TKO	6	—	—
Aug 29	Harry Corbett	London	W	15	—	—
Oct 10	Phil Bond	London	W	16	—	—

Date		Opponent	Location	Result		Notes	
Nov 21		Billy Gilmore	London	TKO	8	—	—
Dec 19		Omer Saerens	London	WF	9	—	—
1927							
Jan 13		Walter Wright	London	TKO	2	—	—
Jan 23		Joe Claes	London	W	15	—	—
Feb 27		Paul Fritsch	London	TKO	8	—	—
Apr 21		Alf Simmons	London	WF	8	—	—
May 29		Bob Miller	London	TKO	6	—	—
Sep 18		Robert Sirvain	London	TKO	6	—	—
Sep 29		Jack Kirk	London	KO	13	—	—
Oct 11		Raymond Jansin	London	WF	7	—	—
Nov 7		Vittorio Venturi	London	W	10	—	—
Dec 4		Lucien Vinez	London	W	15	—	—
1928							
Feb 27		Jack Donn	London	WF	10	—	—
May 31	⑩	Pedro Amador	Chicago	W	10	—	—
Jun 7		Johnny Mellow	Detroit	W	10	—	—
Jun 14	⑩	Freddie Mueller	Chicago	W	10	—	—
Jul 12		Mike Watters	Chicago	TKO	9	—	—
Jul 26	⑩	Billy Petrolle★	Chicago	D	10	—	—
Aug 24	⑩	Billy Petrolle★	Chicago	TKO'd	5	—	—
Oct 8		Spug Meyers	Chicago	WF	3	—	—
Dec 6		Alf Mancini	London	W	15	—	—
1929							
Jan 12		Lucien Vinez	London	W	15	—	—
May 10	⑩	Bruce Flowers	New York	W	10	—	—
May 23	⑩	Bruce Flowers	New York	W	10	—	—
Jun 11	⑩	Estanislao Loayza	New York	D	10	—	—
Jul 12		Herman Perlick	Chicago	W	10	—	—
Jul 24	♛	Mushy Callahan	Brooklyn	W	10	—	—
Aug 5		Joe Trabon	New York	TKO	5	—	—
Aug 19		Harry Wallace	New York	TKO	9	—	—
Aug 29		Spug Meyers	New York	W	10	—	—
Sep 16		Georgie Balduc	Brooklyn	WF	2	—	—
Sep 30		Phil McGraw	New York	W	10	—	—
Oct 21	⑩	Bruce Flowers	New York	W	10	—	—
Nov 2		Tommy Gerval	New York	KO	2	—	—
Nov 18		Eddie Elkins	New York	W	10	—	—
Nov 30		Artie DeLuca	New York	W	6	—	—
Dec 18		Tony Caragliano	New York	WF	2	—	—
1930							
Jan 16	⑩	Tony Canzoneri★	New York	W	10	—	—
Feb 18	♛	Mushy Callahan	London	TKO	10	Won-World-JW	137
Apr 4	⑩	Joe Glick	New York	W	10	—	—
Apr 7		Jackie Philips	Toronto	W	10	—	—
May 29		Al Delmont	Newark	TKO	4	—	—
Jun 11		Herman Perlick	Long Island City, NY	W	10	—	—
Jul 10		Henry Perlick	Newark	W	10	—	—
Aug 7	⑩	Kid Chocolate★	New York	W	10	—	—
Sep 3		Buster Brown	Newark	W	10	—	—
Sep 18	⑩	Joe Glick	Long Island City	W	10	—	—
Oct 10	⑩	Billy Petrolle	New York	W	10	—	—
1931							
Jan 23		Goldie Hess	Chicago	W	10	—	138
Jan 30		Herman Perlick	New York	W	10	—	—

Date		Opponent	Location	Result	Rounds	Notes	
Apr 10	⑩	Billy Wallace	Detroit	W	10	—	138
Apr 24	👑	Tony Canzoneri★	Chicago	KO'd	3	For-World-L & Lost-World-JW	—
May 8	⑩	Tony Herrera	New York	W	10	—	—
May 18		Ray Kiser	Pittsburgh	W	10	—	—
Jun 22		Tony Lambert	Newark	TKO	8	—	—
Jul 24		Teddy Watson	Jersey City, NJ	KO	7	—	—
Jul 27		Phillie Griffin	Newark	W	10	—	—
Aug 4		Jimmy McNamara	New York	W	10	—	—
Sep 10	👑	Tony Canzoneri★	New York	L	15	For-World-L & For-World-JW	—
Dec 14		Maurius Baudry	London	TKO	5	—	—

1932

Date		Opponent	Location	Result	Rounds	Notes	
Mar 21		Buster Brown	New York	W	10	—	—
Apr 1	⑩	Sammy Fuller	New York	D	10	—	—
May 20	👑	Sammy Fuller	New York	L	12	—	138
Jun 29		Mike Sarko	New York	W	6	—	—
Jul 18	👑	Kid Chocolate★	New York	W	15	—	—

1933

Date		Opponent	Location	Result	Rounds	Notes	
Apr 27		Cleto Locatelli	London	L	10	—	—
May 28		Louis Saerens	London	KO	4	—	—
Jul 8		George Rose	Cardiff, Wales	TKO	5	—	—
Jul 14		Eugene Drouhin	London	TKO	8	—	—
Sep 30		Harry Wallace	New York	TKO	4	—	—
Oct 19		Tony Falco	New York	L	10	—	—

1934

Date		Opponent	Location	Result	Rounds	Notes	
Jan 12		Cleto Locatelli	New York	L	10	—	—
Apr 14		Jackie Flynn	London	W	10	—	—
May 12		Len Wickwar	Leicester, England	WF	6	—	—
May 29		Jimmy Stewart	Liverpool, England	TKO'd	3	—	—
Jul 10		Joe Kerr	Liverpool	TKO	6	—	—
Aug 19		Nicholas Wilke	London	TKO	9	—	—
Oct 29		Harry Mizler	London	TKO	10	Won-Britain-L	135
Dec 2		Alfred Bastin	London	TKO	4	—	—

1935

Date		Opponent	Location	Result	Rounds	Notes	
Jan 21		Gustave Humery	London	TKO	8	—	—
Feb 25		Gustave Humery	Paris	L	10	—	—
Apr 1		Gustave Humery	London	L	10	—	—
May 19		Harry Brown	London	KO	3	—	—
Oct 21		Peter McKinley	London	W	10	—	—
Nov 14		Pat Butler	London	TKO	4	—	—

1936

Date		Opponent	Location	Result	Rounds	Notes	
Jan 11	⑩	Laurie Stevens	Johannesburg	L	12	For-Brit Emp-L	135
Apr 24	⑩	Jimmy Walsh	Liverpool	TKO'd	9	Lost-Britain-L	135
Jul 22	⑩	Aldo Spoldi	Brooklyn	TKO'd	2	—	—

1937

Date	Opponent	Location	Result	Rounds	Notes	
Jan 24	Ivor Pikens	London	W	10	—	—
Feb 7	Pat Haley	London	WF	10	—	—
Feb 11	George ("Panther") Purchase	West Ham, England	TKO	12	—	—
Feb 21	Harry Mason	London	TKO	5	—	—
Mar 22	Louis Saerens	Bristol, England	D	10	—	—
Apr 11	Pat Haley	Cricklewood, England	TKO	9	—	—
May 6	Alby Day	London	W	10	—	—
Aug 14	Jack Lewis	Poole, England	D	10	—	—
Oct 4	Jake Kilrain	London	TKO	6	—	—
Nov 1	George Odwell	London	TKO'd	10	—	—
Dec 6	Charlie Chetwynd	Manchester, England	TKO	5	—	—

Date		Opponent	Location	Result	Rounds		
Dec 13		Leo Phillips	Birmingham, England	W	10	—	—
1938							
Feb 10		Silvio Zangrillo	Brooklyn	KO	8	—	—
Mar 5		Larry Anzalone	Brooklyn	W	8	—	—
Mar 15		Vincent Pimpinella	Brooklyn	W	10	—	—
Mar 29	⑩	Frankie Wallace	Brooklyn	W	8	—	—
Apr 9		Johnny Horstman	Brooklyn	W	8	—	—
May 3		Ray Napolitano	Brooklyn	W	8	—	—
Jun 7		Johnny McHale	Brooklyn	W	8	—	—
Jun 15		Augie Arellano	Long Island City	D	8	—	—
Jun 30		Johnny Horstman	Brooklyn	W	8	—	—
Jul 12		Johnny McHale	Brooklyn	W	8	—	—
Jul 25		Freddie ("Red") Cochrane	Newark	L	10	—	—
Aug 5		Pete Cara	Brooklyn	W	8	—	—
Oct 11		Johnny McHale	Brooklyn	W	8	—	—
Oct 25		Joey Greb	New York	W	8	—	—
Nov 22		Frankie Cavanna	Brooklyn	W	8	—	—
1939							
Feb 3		Baby Breese	Hollywood, FL	L	10	—	—
Mar 10	⑩	Pedro Montanez	New York	KO'd	5	—	—
Apr 4		Pete Galiano	Brooklyn	W	8	—	—
Apr 11		Marine Bunker	Bermuda	KO	8	—	—
Jun 6		Tippy Larkin	Garfield, NJ	W	10	—	—
Jun 26	⑩	Milt Aron	Chicago	TKO'd	6	—	—
Jun 30		Mike Piskin	Long Branch, NJ	L	10	—	—
Jul 11		Johnny Rohrig	Garfield	W	10	—	—
Aug 1		Joey Greb	Garfield	W	8	—	—
Oct 12		Paddy Roche	Southampton, England	W	10	—	—
Nov 30		Paddy Roche	Nottingham, England	TKO	5	—	—
1940							
Jan 25		Harry Davis	Hackney, England	W	10	—	—
Feb 5		George Reynolds	Bristol, England	W	10	—	—
Feb 29		Eddie Ryan	London	WF	6	—	—
Mar 8		Paddy Roche	Dublin	TKO	4	—	—
Mar 10		Dick Bradshaw	Hackney	TKO	3	—	—
Apr 4		Harry Davis	Hackney	TKO	8	—	—
1941							
Jan 20		Harry Craster	London	W	10	—	—
Feb 20		Harry Charman	London	W	6	—	153
Feb 27		Harry Mizler	London	W	10	—	—
Apr 21		Eric Boon	London	WF	2	—	—
May 30		Ernie Roderick	London	L	10	—	—
Jul 24		Arthur Danahar	London	TKO'd	5	—	—
Nov 2		George Odwell	Stoke Newington, England	L	10	—	—
Nov 24		Joe Connolly	Leeds, England	TKO	8	—	—
1942							
Feb 5		Paddy Roche	Newcastle, England	TKO	4	—	—
Mar 12		Joe Connolly	Glasgow, Scotland	TKO	4	—	—
1943							
May 22		Gordon Woodhouse	Handcross, England	L	6	—	—
1945							
Mar 1		Eric Dolby	London	KO	4	—	—
Mar 8		Jimmy Brunt	London	W	8	—	—
May 19		Johnny McDonald	Coventry, England	KO	5	—	—

those years, Berg was 4-0-1 against lightweight and junior welterweight contenders.

In 1930, Berg faced Hall of Famer Tony Canzoneri, who would soon become lightweight champ. In the first two rounds, Berg attempted a stand-up boxing style, which wasn't successful. From the third round until the end of the fight, Berg went back to his typical style and won the decision. In his next fight, held in London, Berg knocked out American Mushy Callahan to win the world junior welterweight title. Later that year in a non-title fight, Berg won a split decision over the previously unbeaten Kid Chocolate—a natural featherweight. Berg forced the action and chased Chocolate all over the ring.

The next year he again faced Canzoneri, this time for the lightweight title. Berg could not handle Canzoneri and was knocked out in the third round. In the rematch, Berg performed well but lost the fifteen-round decision. Most of the boxing world believed that Canzoneri had taken the junior welterweight belt from Berg, while simultaneously successfully defending his own lightweight crown. But Berg still asserted the belt was his. Berg's disputed claim

Jackie ("Kid") Berg handed the brilliant Cuban, Kid Chocolate, his first defeat in 161 fights. Berg outweighed Chocolate by nearly ten pounds.

to the junior welterweight title ended when he lost to Sammy Fuller in 1932. That same year, he won another decision over Chocolate.

Though Berg continued to fight in the U.S., Britain, and elsewhere, he never again challenged for a world title. He held the British lightweight title for two years before losing it to Jimmy Walsh in 1936. Berg retired in 1945, after 21 years as a fighter, then worked as a movie stunt man in England.

JIMMY BIVINS

HEAVYWEIGHT

Right-handed; 5'10"; 157–187 lbs.

112 bouts, 1/15/1940 to 10/28/1955

Managers: Wilfred ("Whizzbang") Carter 1940–42, Claude Shane 1942–53

Hall of Fame Induction: 1999

Born: 12/6/1919, Dry Branch, GA

Named: James Louis Bivins

Not so long ago, when there were just eight weight classes and one champion in each, even fighters considered all-time greats in the sport were not guaranteed a chance at a championship belt. Jimmy Bivins is one such boxer. Few fighters have maintained as high a level of excellence as Bivins for such a long time, or fought so many quality opponents.

Bivins's family moved to Cleveland when he was two. He worked an assortment of jobs while in school, and he was a good student. After graduation, Bivins began visiting local gyms. In his first fight against a more experienced boxer, Bivins easily dominated his opponent. His performance attracted the attention of Wilfred ("Whizbang") Carter, an amateur trainer who entered Bivins in the Golden Gloves competition, where he won the 126-pound novice title. The next year Bivins won the 147-pound open division title, finished second in the nationals, then turned professional.

Carter continued as Bivins's trainer and Charles ("Claude") Shane Jr. became Bivins's manager. On January 15, 1940, Bivins made his pro debut as a welterweight with a one-round triumph against Emory ("KO") Morgan. Bivins soon moved to middleweight and quickly faced top competition. On April 8, 1940, Bivins won an eight-round decision over Nate Bolden, and in September decisioned Hall of Famer Charley Burley. Bivins closed 1940 splitting two decisions with Anton Christoforidis, who would win the NBA light heavyweight title in his next fight. In his incredible debut year, Bivins won nineteen of twenty fights against some excellent opponents.

While Bivins continued to face very high-quality opponents, his chances for a title shot in 1942 were hurt when titles were frozen for the duration of WWII. He started the year with a punishing ten-round decision over former middleweight champion Billy Soose, who retired after the fight. Bivins

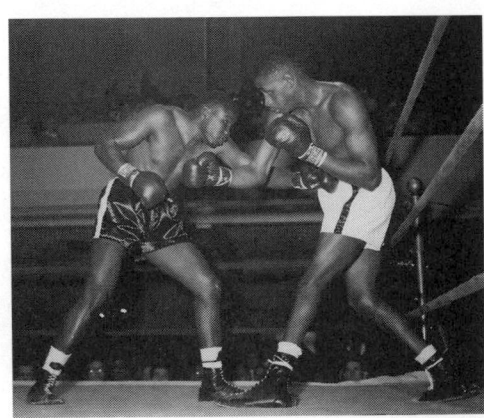

After suffering three losses in a row, Bivins (L) still had enough left for a ten-round decision over seventh-ranked light heavyweight contender Doc Williams on November 21, 1951 in New York. Here Bivins connects to the belt line.

IN THE RING	WON 86	LOST 25	DRAWS 1	TB 112	KO 31	W 55	WF 0	D 1	KO'd 5	L 20	LF 0

Date		Opponent	Site	Result / Rounds		Title	Wt.
1940							
Jan 15		Emory Morgan	Cleveland	TKO	1	—	147
Feb 12		Tito Taylor	Chicago	W	6	—	—
Feb 26		Joe Sutka	Chicago	W	8	—	—
Mar 18		Joe Sutka	Chicago	W	8	—	—
Mar 27		Young Flowers	Cleveland	KO	3	—	—
Apr 8		Nate Bolden	Chicago	W	8	—	—
Apr 15		Johnny Dean	Cleveland	KO	3	—	—
Apr 25		Enzo Ionozzi	Cleveland	KO	1	—	—
May 13		Paul Frazier	Chicago	KO	1	—	—
Jun 13		Homer Jackson	Pittsburgh	TKO	1	—	—
Jun 24		Frankie Hughes	Chicago	W	8	—	—
Jul 1		Mose Brown	Pittsburgh	W	6	—	—
Jul 15		Paul Frazier	Chicago	W	8	—	—
Aug 5		Johnny Barbara	Chicago	KO	2	—	—
Sep 3	⑩	Charley Burley★	Pittsburgh	W	10	—	—
Sep 9		Johnny Barbara	Chicago	TKO	7	—	—
Sep 23		Larry Kellum	Pittsburgh	KO	1	—	—
Oct 22		Vincent Pimpinella	Cleveland	W	10	—	—
Nov 15	⑩	Anton Christoforidis	Cleveland	W	10	—	—
Dec 2	⑩	Anton Christoforidis	Cleveland	L	10	—	—
1941							
Feb 9		Pete Tamalonis	Cleveland	TKO	1	—	—
Mar 5	⑩	Teddy Yarosz	Cleveland	W	10	—	—
Apr 2		Buddy Knox	Cleveland	W	10	—	172
Jul 2		Curtis Sheppard	Pittsburgh	W	10	—	—
Jul 14		Lem Franklin	Chicago	TKO'd	9	—	—
Sep 11		Tony Musto	Cleveland	L	10	—	—
Oct 20	⑩	Nate Bolden	Chicago	W	10	—	—
Nov 17	⑩	Melio Bettina	Cleveland	L	10	—	—
1942							
Jan 13	⑩	Billy Soose	Cleveland	W	10	—	—
Mar 11	♛	Gus Lesnevich	Cleveland	W	10	—	—
Apr 17	⑩	Bob Pastor	Cleveland	L	10	—	—
Jun 22	⑩	Joey Maxim★	Cleveland	W	10	—	—
Jul 23		Joe Muscato	Cleveland	KO	5	—	—
Sep 15		Tami Mauriello	Cleveland	W	10	—	177
Oct 20	⑩	Bob Pastor	Cleveland	W	10	—	—
Nov 27		Lee Savold	New York	W	10	—	175
1943							
Jan 7		Ezzard Charles★	Cleveland	W	10	—	174
Feb 26	⑩	Anton Christoforidis	Cleveland	W	15	—	175
Mar 12	⑩	Tami Mauriello	New York	W	10	—	—
Apr 6		Watson Jones	Los Angeles	W	10	—	179
Apr 26		Pat Valentino	San Francisco	W	10	—	176
Jul 8	⑩	Lloyd Marshall	Cleveland	KO	13	—	174
Aug 24		Herbert Marshall	Washington, DC	KO	6	—	—
Sep 15	⑩	Melio Bettina	Cleveland	W	10	—	—
Dec 1		Lee Q. Murray	Cleveland	W	10	—	—
1944							
Feb 29	⑩	Lee Q. Murray	Cleveland	W	10	—	—

Date		Opponent	Location	Result	Rounds		
Feb 5		George Parks	Washington	TKO	4	—	188
Feb 19		Buddy Walker	Baltimore	KO	2	—	—
Feb 27		Johnny Flynn	Cleveland	W	10	—	—
Mar 16	⑩	Melio Bettina	New York	D	10	—	—
Jun 12		Buddy Scott	Washington	KO	4	—	188
Jul 26	⑩	Curtis Sheppard	Pittsburgh	W	10	—	—
Aug 22	⑩	Archie Moore★	Cleveland	KO	6	—	186
Sep 26		Yancey Henry	Washington	W	10	—	185

1946

Date		Opponent	Location	Result	Rounds		
Jan 7		Watson Jones	San Francisco	TKO	6	—	187
Jan 22		Johnny Haynes	Los Angeles	KO	2	—	187
Jan 29	⑩	Billy Smith	Oakland	W	10	—	186
Feb 10		Yancey Henry	Baltimore	KO	10	—	—
Feb 25	⑩	Jersey Joe Walcott★	Cleveland	L	10	—	—
Jun 20	⑩	Lee Q. Murray	Cleveland	L	10	—	—
Nov 12	⑩	Ezzard Charles★	Pittsburgh	L	10	—	—
Dec 5		Colion Chaney	Akron, OH	KO	5	—	—

1947

Date		Opponent	Location	Result	Rounds		
Jan 16		Johnny Flynn	Washington	W	10	—	—
Feb 3		Booker Beckworth	Chicago	KO	4	—	—
Feb 17	⑩	Curtis Sheppard	Pittsburgh	W	10	—	—
Mar 10	⑩	Ezzard Charles★	Cleveland	KO'd	4	—	—
Apr 21	⑩	Curtis Sheppard	Baltimore	W	10	—	—
May 9	⑩	Lee Q. Murray	Detroit	L	10	—	—
Jun 2		Omelio Agramonte	Baltimore	KO	2	—	—
Jun 9	⑩	Lee Q. Murray	Baltimore	W	10	—	—
Jul 1		Bobby Zander	Los Angeles	W	10	—	181
Sep 8	⑩	Archie Moore★	Baltimore	TKO'd	9	—	—
Nov 12		Sid Peaks	Chicago	W	10	—	—

1948

Date		Opponent	Location	Result	Rounds		
Jan 13		Johnny Shkor	Buffalo	W	10	—	—
Mar 1		Johnny Haynes	Baltimore	KO	4	—	—
Mar 9	⑩	Turkey Thompson	Los Angeles	W	10	—	185
Apr 12	⑩	Billy Thompson	Philadelphia	TKO	7	—	—
Apr 20		Pat Valentino	Cleveland	W	10	—	—
Aug 28	⑩	Archie Moore★	Baltimore	L	10	—	187
Sep 13	⑩	Ezzard Charles★	Washington	L	10	—	178
Oct 11	⑩	Johnny Flynn	Philadelphia	W	10	—	—
Nov 17	⑩	Joe Louis★	Cleveland	Exh	6	—	—
Dec 7	⑩	Joey Maxim★	Cleveland	L	10	—	178

1949

Date		Opponent	Location	Result	Rounds		
Mar 21	⑩	Rusty Payne	Pittsburgh	W	10	—	—
Apr 11	⑩	Archie Moore★	Toledo, OH	KO'd	8	—	—
Jun 20		Willie Bean	Cleveland	W	10	—	—
Jul 5	⑩	Leonard Morrow	Los Angeles	L	10	—	—
Jul 15		Watson Jones	Las Vegas	KO	2	—	—
Sep 21	⑩	Leonard Morrow	Oakland	W	10	—	—
Sep 27		Clarence Henry	Los Angeles	TKO	8	—	—
Oct 26	⑩	Harold Johnson★	Philadelphia	L	10	—	—

1950

Date		Opponent	Location	Result	Rounds		
Feb 1		Willis Applegate	Miami	W	10	—	—
Feb 6		Sid Peaks	Newark, NJ	L	10	—	—

1951

Date		Opponent	Location	Result	Rounds		
Jan 22		Young Willis	Baltimore	KO	4	—	—
Feb 12		Ted Lowry	Baltimore	W	10	—	—

Feb 21	⑩	Archie Moore★	New York	TKO'd	9		—	—
May 4		Willie Bean	Hollywood	W	10		—	—
May 18		Bobby Mitchell	Phoenix	W	10		—	—
May 29		Willie Bean	Los Angeles	W	10		—	—
Jun 26	⑩	Clarence Henry	Los Angeles	L	10		—	—
Aug 15	⑩	Joe Louis★	Baltimore	L	10		—	180
Nov 5	⑩	Bob Baker	Pittsburgh	L	10		—	—
Nov 21	⑩	Charley ("Doc") Williams	New York	W	10		—	—
1952								
Mar 31		Aaron Wilson	Baltimore	TKO	3		—	—
Sep 19		Coley Wallace	New York	KO	9		—	—
Oct 22		Wesbury Bascom	St. Louis	W	10		—	—
Nov 3	⑩	Tommy Harrison	Providence, RI	L	10		—	—
Nov 26	⑩	Ezzard Charles★	Chicago	L	10		—	—
1953								
Apr 6		Tommy Harrison	Miami	L	10		—	—
Apr 24		Claude Rolfe	Tampa	W	10		—	—
Jun 9		Chubby Wright	Huntington, WV	W	10		—	—
1955								
Aug 31		Dan Moray	Cleveland	KO	3		—	—
Oct 28		Mike DeJohn	Cleveland	W	6		—	—

next defeated light heavyweight champion Gus Lesnevich in a non-title bout in Cleveland, but the win hurt his chances for a title match. After the fight, Lesnevich's manager said, "This guy is too good for us—now or ever." Bivins did lose to heavyweight Bob Pastor in his next fight, but he avenged that defeat later in the year. He also decisioned Hall-of-Famer Joey Maxim and top heavyweight contenders Tami Mauriello and Lee Savold.

The next year opened with a decision over Hall of Famer Ezzard Charles, whom he knocked down four times. The next month, Bivins decisioned Christoforidis for the "duration" light heavyweight title. On March 12, 1943, Bivins won eight of ten rounds for an easy decision against Mauriello for the "duration" heavyweight title. Bivins fought only once in 1944 before he was inducted into the army, but he returned from the service as strong as before with a sixth-round knockout of Hall of Famer Archie Moore. On February 25, 1946, Bivins lost a disputed split decision to Hall of Famer and future heavyweight champion, Jersey Joe Walcott. Had Bivins won, he might have received the title shot against Louis instead of Walcott.

Bivins bounced in and out of top-ten-contender status in the late '40s. Though he beat heavyweight contender Rusty Payne and light heavyweight contender Leonard Morrow, in 1949 he lost decisions to Morrow and to Hall of Famer Harold Johnson, and was knocked out by Archie Moore shortly after rejoining the fight gam. Bivins fought his last bout on October 28, 1955, when he decisioned up-and-coming Mike DeJohn.

In retirement, Bivins worked for a Cleveland bakery and as a trainer of amateurs, gym owner, and boxing commissioner. Sadly, in 1998 Bivins was found imprisoned by his son-in-law and daughter in a dirty attic. He was in terrible health when he was rescued, and after hospitalization he came under the care of a family and friends, while his son-in-law pleaded guilty to elder abuse.

JOE BROWN
Old Bones

LIGHTWEIGHT
Right-handed; 5'7½"; 130–142 lbs.
161 bouts, 1/13/1946 to 4/24/1970
Managers: Lester Majoue and
Louis Chattard 1946–1955,
Lou Viscusi 1955–1970
Lightweight Champion 1956–1962
Hall of Fame Induction: 1996
Born: 5/18/1926, New Orleans, LA
Died: 11/21/1997

Known for a strong right as well as his fine left jabs and hooks, Joe ("Old Bones") Brown was born in New Orleans and brought up in Baton Rouge. A carpenter like his father, he honed his boxing skills with the Navy in the Pacific, although he had a single pro bout in 1943.

After the war, Brown resumed his professional career with a series of fights in New Orleans. In spite of an out-of-the-gate loss to Leonard Ceasar, for the rest of 1946 he established a 5-1-1 record, with all his wins by decision. Over the next two years, Brown main-

In a close match between two veterans, Joe Brown (R) wrests the lightweight crown from Wallace ("Bud") Smith in New Orleans on August 24, 1956.

IN THE RING	WON 104	LOST 44	DRAWS 13	TB 162	KO 47	W 57	WF 0	D 13	KO'd 9	L 33	LF 2	NC 1

Date	Opponent	Site	Result / Rounds		Title	Wt.
1943						
Sep 3	Leonard Ceasar	New Orleans	W	4	—	—
1946						
Jan 13	Leonard Ceasar	New Orleans	L	5	—	—
Jan 20	Johnny Monroe	New Orleans	W	6	—	—
Mar 22	Leonard Ceasar	New Orleans	D	6	—	—
Mar 29	Leonard Ceasar	New Orleans	W	8	—	—
Apr 5	Frankie Adams	New Orleans	W	6	—	—
Jun 28	Herbert Jones	New Orleans	W	8	—	—
Jul 26	Buster Tyler	New Orleans	L	10	—	—
Oct 18	Bob Weatherley	New Orleans	W	8	—	—
1947						
Mar 7	Buster Tyler	New Orleans	D	10	—	—
Mar 28	Melvin Bartholomew	New Orleans	L	10	—	—
Apr 18	Jimmy Carter★	New Orleans	W	10	—	—
May 2	⑩ Sandy Saddler★	New Orleans	KO'd	3	—	—
Jul 4	Melvin Bartholomew	New Orleans	W	10	—	—
Jul 23	Freddie Latson	Norwalk, CT	W	6	—	—
Aug 6	Danny Webb	Montreal	W	10	—	—
Sep 24	Dan Robinson	Jersey City, NJ	W	8	—	—
Oct 6	Ernie Butler	Newark, NJ	KO	5	—	—
Oct 21	⑩ Arthur King	Toronto	W	8	—	—
Nov 10	⑩ Arthur King	Toronto	L	8	—	—
Dec 15	Joey Bagnato	Toronto	KO	1	—	—
1948						
Feb 28	Bobby McQuillar	New Orleans	D	10	—	—
May 7	Bobby McQuillar	New Orleans	L	10	—	—
Jul 25	Luther Burgess	New Orleans	D	10	—	—
Oct 1	⑩ Freddie Dawson	New Orleans	L	10	—	—
Oct 26	Frank Cockrell	San Antonio, TX	KO	5	—	—
Nov 18	Arthur Persley	New Orleans	W	10	—	—
Dec 3	⑩ Johnny Bratton	New Orleans	KO'd	4	—	—
1949						
Mar 22	Booker Ellis	St. Paul, MN	W	6	—	—
Mar 28	Luther Rawlings	Chicago	W	10	—	—
Apr 25	Joe Sgro	Chicago	W	8	—	—
May 10	Hugh Sublett	South Bend, IN	W	8	—	—
May 23	John LaBroi	Chicago	D	8	—	—
May 27	Leroy Willis	New Orleans	W	10	—	—
Jun 6	Willie Russell	Cincinnati	W	10	—	—
Dec 5	Ike Jenkins	Philadelphia	W	6	—	—
1950						
Jan 20	Milton Scott	Chicago	KO	2	—	—
Feb 6	Danny Womber	Chicago	W	8	—	—
Feb 22	Dave Marsh	Chicago	W	4	—	—
Jun 16	⑩ John L. Davis	Hollywood	L	10	—	—
Sep 22	Jack Hassen	Melbourne	KO	8	—	—
Oct 30	Charley Williams	Sydney	KO	1	—	—

Date		Opponent	Location	Result	Rds		
Nov 27		Howell Steen	Sydney	NC	10	—	—
Dec 14		Bernie Hall	Broken Hill, Australia	TKO	11	—	—
1951							
Feb 20	⑩	Tommy Campbell	Los Angeles	L	10	—	—
Mar 10		Baby Ortiz	Ocean Park, CA	KO	2	—	—
Apr 13		Teddy Davis	New Orleans	W	10	—	—
Apr 27		Lester Felton	New Orleans	W	10	—	—
May 11		Clarence Johnson	New Orleans	W	10	—	—
May 25	⑩	Virgil Akins	New Orleans	W	10	—	—
Jul 6	⑩	Virgil Akins	New Orleans	W	10	—	—
Aug 31	⑩	Tommy Campbell	New Orleans	KO	1	—	—
Sep 28		Stonewall Jackson	New Orleans	TKO	5	—	—
Dec 6	⑩	Virgil Akins	St. Louis	L	10	—	—
1952							
Feb 4		Walter Haines	Miami	D	6	—	—
Feb 15		Walter Haines	New Orleans	D	10	—	—
Mar 14		Walter Haines	New Orleans	W	10	—	—
Mar 28		Calvin Smith	New Orleans	TKO	7	—	—
Jun 10		Jerry Turner	Tampa	TKO	5	—	—
Jul 11		Melvin Bartholomew	New Orleans	W	10	—	—
Jul 18		Marshall Clayton	New Orleans	TKO	9	—	—
Aug 22		Jimmy Taylor	New Orleans	W	10	—	—
Oct 10	⑩	George Araujo	New York	KO'd	7	—	—
Dec 10		Don Bowman	Cleveland	KO	1	—	—
1953							
Jan 7		Joey Greenwood	Cleveland	W	8	—	—
Apr 22	⑩	Orlando Zulueta	Baltimore	D	10	—	—
Jun 9		Luther Rawlings	Miami Beach	D	10	—	—
Dec 29		Cliff Dyes	Miami Beach	TKO	9	—	—
1954							
Feb 8		Charlie Smith	Providence, RI	LD	6	—	—
Mar 24		Isaac Logart	Miami Beach	W	10	—	—
Jun 20		Federico Plummer	Colon, Panama	TKO	9	—	—
Jul 25		Wilfredo Brown	Colon	KO	4	—	—
Aug 31		Nat Jackson	New Orleans	KO	4	—	—
Sep 28		Carl Coates	New Orleans	L	10	—	—
Dec 29		Antonio Armenteros	Miami	L	6	—	—
1955							
Jan 18		Antonio Armenteros	New Orleans	TKO	7	—	—
Jan 30		Tito Despaigne	Colon	KO	4	—	—
Mar 6		Bobby Rosado	Colon	W	10	—	—
Mar 20		Antonio Armenteros	Colon	W	10	—	—
Jun 16		Junius West	Colon	KO	3	—	—
Aug 1	⑩	Arthur Persley	New Orleans	L	12	—	—
Oct 31		Jimmy Hackney	New Orleans	W	10	—	—
Nov 8		Ray Rojas	Houston	TKO	7	—	—
Dec 13		Ray Portilla	Houston	TKO	5	—	136
1956							
Feb 6		Arthur Persley	New Orleans	TKO	9	—	—
May 2	♛	Wallace ("Bud") Smith	Houston	W	10	—	—
Jun 5		Eddie Brant	Beaumont, TX	TKO	3	—	—
Aug 24	♛	Wallace ("Bud") Smith	New Orleans	W	15	Won-World-L	133

1957

Date		Opponent	Location	Result		Notes	Weight
Feb 13	⑩	Wallace ("Bud") Smith	Miami Beach	TKO	11	Ret-World-L	134
Mar 12		Armand Savoie	Houston	W	10	—	—
Jun 19	⑩	Orlando Zulueta	Denver	TKO	15	Ret-World-L	134
Jul 30		Gilberto Holguin	San Antonio	W	10	—	—
Aug 21	⑩	Joey Lopes	Chicago	D	10	—	—
Nov 12		Kid Centella	Houston	W	10	—	—
Dec 4	⑩	Joey Lopes	Chicago	TKO	11	Ret-World-L	133

1958

Date		Opponent	Location	Result		Notes	Weight
Jan 24		Ernie Williams	Washington, DC	TKO	5	—	—
Feb 26		Orlando Echevarria	Havana	KO	1	—	—
May 7	⑩	Ralph Dupas	Houston	TKO	8	Ret-World-L	134
Jul 23	⑩	Kenny Lane	Houston	W	15	Ret-World-L	134
Nov 5	⑩	Johnny Busso	Miami Beach	L	10	—	—

1959

Date		Opponent	Location	Result		Notes	Weight
Feb 11	⑩	Johnny Busso	Houston	W	15	Ret-World-L	134
Jun 3	⑩	Paolo Rosi	Washington, DC	TKO	9	Ret-World-L	132
Aug 27		Santiago Ramirez	Baton Rouge, LA	KO	8	—	—
Sep 9		Gale Kerwin	Columbus, OH	TKO	4	—	—
Sep 26		Joey Parks	Albuquerque, NM	D	10	—	—
Dec 2	⑩	Dave Charnley	Houston	TKO	6	Ret-World-L	134
Dec 14		Joey Parks	New Orleans	W	10	—	—

1960

Date		Opponent	Location	Result		Notes	Weight
Mar 21		Ray Portilla	San Antonio	TKO'd	6	—	—
Aug 25		Harlow Irwin	Minneapolis	TKO	5	—	—
Oct 4	⑩	Battling Torres	Houston	KO	4	—	—
Oct 28	⑩	Cisco Andrade	Los Angeles	W	15	Ret-World-L	135
Dec 7		Giordano Campari	Milan	L	10	—	—

1961

Date		Opponent	Location	Result		Notes	Weight
Mar 7		Joey Parks	Houston	W	10	—	138
Apr 18	⑩	Dave Charnley	London	W	15	Ret-World-L	134
Oct 28	⑩	Bert Somodio	Quezon, Philippines	W	15	Ret-World-L	135

1962

Date		Opponent	Location	Result		Notes	Weight
Apr 21	⑩	Carlos Ortiz★	Las Vegas	L	15	Lost-World-L	134
Aug 24	⑩	Luis Molina	San Jose, CA	L	10	—	—

1963

Date		Opponent	Location	Result		Notes	Weight
Jan 22		Tony Noriega	Houston	KO	6	—	—
Feb 25	⑩	Dave Charnley	Manchester, England	KO'd	6	—	—
Apr 20	⑩	Manuel Alvarez	Monterrey, Mexico	KO	8	—	—
May 21		Joey Lopes	Sacramento, CA	TKO	8	—	—
Jun 22	⑩	Alfredo Urbina	Monterrey	L	10	—	—
Aug 10	⑩	Nicolino Locche	Buenos Aires	L	10	—	—
Sep 14		Pedro Galasso	Rio de Janeiro	TKO	5	—	—
Nov 11	⑩	Carlos Hernandez	Maracaibo, Venezuela	KO'd	3	—	—

1964

Date		Opponent	Location	Result		Notes	Weight
Apr 2	⑩	Manuel Gonzalez	Odessa, TX	L	10	—	—
Apr 28	⑩	Paul Armstead	Sacramento	L	10	—	—
May 5		Tony Perez	San Jose	W	10	—	—
May 25	⑩	Paul Armstead	San Francisco	L	10	—	—
Jun 21		Esteban Santamaria	Colon	W	10	—	135
Aug 25		Ricardo Medrano	Austin, TX	LD	10	—	—
Sep 14		Hector (Chino) Diaz	Omaha, NE	KO	8	—	—

Date	Opponent	Location	Result	Rounds		
Oct 3	Percy Hayles	Kingston, Jamaica	L	10	—	—
Nov 21	Levi Madi	Johannesburg	W	10	—	—
Dec 19	Jonas Maoto	Johannesburg	KO	6	—	—
1965						
Feb 9	Levi Madi	Cape Town	W	10	—	—
Feb 27	Joe N'gidi	Johannesburg	L	10	—	—
Mar 9	Vic Andretti	London	TKO'd	5	—	138
May 18	Joey Olguin	Sacramento	L	10	—	138
Jun 29	Porfirio Zamora	Corpus Christi, TX	W	10	—	—
Aug 27	Antonio Herrera	Cali, Columbia	L	10	—	—
Oct 2	Mario Rossito	Barranquilla, Colombia	L	10	—	—
Nov 13	⑩ Frankie Narvaez	San Juan, PR	L	10	—	—
1966						
Mar 11	Bruno Arcari	Turin, Italy	L	10	—	—
Apr 15	Jarmo Bergloef	Helsinki, Finland	D	10	—	—
May 14	Josiah Nakedi	Bloemfontein, S. Africa	KO	9	—	—
Jun 4	Enoch Nhlapo	Johannesburg	W	10	—	—
Jun 25	Joe N'Gidi	Durban, South Africa	L	10	—	—
Jul 30	Joe N'Gidi	Johannesburg	L	10	—	—
Aug 30	Rodwell LeKay	Lourenco Marques, Mozambique	W	10	—	—
1967						
Jun 16	Porfirio Zamora	Baton Rouge	TKO	8	—	—
Jun 26	Joe Barrientes	New Orleans	W	10	—	—
Aug 1	⑩ Percy Pugh	New Orleans	L	10	—	—
Sep 11	Benito Juarez	New Orleans	W	10	—	—
Dec 23	Nathaniel Jackson	Pensacola, FL	KO	5	—	—
1968						
Apr 23	Vic Graffio	Beaumont, TX	TKO	8	—	—
Jun 9	⑩ Chango Carmona	Mexico City	TKO'd	4	—	133
Sep 11	Ricardo Medrano	Beaumont	L	10	—	—
Nov 6	Jose Garcia	Beaumont	KO'd	9	—	—
1969						
Aug 12	Steve Freeman	Houston	D	10	—	—
1970						
Apr 24	Ramon Flores	Tucson	W	10	—	—
Aug 24	Dave Oropeza	Phoenix	L	10	—	144

tained a modest record of 15-8-4, winning a decision over future lightweight champion Jimmy Carter, but losing by knockout to Hall of Fame featherweight Sandy Saddler and the formidable welterweight Johnny Bratton.

In the early 1950s, Brown's career ran hot and cold, as did his ranking. But by 1955, ready to improve on his erratic record and overcome general dismissal as a "fancy Dan" (a fine defensive fighter with little power), he began working with trainer Bill Gore. Almost immediately, he racked up knockouts in consecutive fights with Ray Rioja, Ray Portilla, and Arthur Persley.

A non-title decision over lightweight champion Wallace ("Bud") Smith set the stage for a title-making rematch. On August 24, 1956, a partisan crowd jammed New Orleans' Municipal Auditorium, hoping to see the hometown Brown beat Smith. Starting off quickly in the first, Brown led the scoring with both rights and

Brown (R) defended his lightweight title twelve times including two rough wins against Britisher Dave Charnley. In their second meeting in London on April 18, 1961, Charnley bulls in while sustaining damage.

lefts. Sustaining a broken hand in the second round, Brown nevertheless resourcefully outboxed his opponent for much of the fight. Hurt in the twelfth, he used both hands to knock Smith down in the fourteenth and, by the final round, had claimed a split decision and the title. In the rematch, Brown won by knockout.

Over the next six years, Brown defended his title successfully eleven times, twice knocking out Ralph Dupas and winning a close decision over tough southpaw Kenny Lane. On April 21, 1962, he faced Hall of Famer Carlos Ortiz in the Las Vegas Convention Center. Much younger and quicker, Ortiz used snapping left jabs to keep Brown from mounting an effective attack and won an easy decision. Brown's manager, Lou Viscusi, blamed his fighter's loss on tonsillitis, although he'd been cleared ahead of time by the state's physician.

Brown lost his next fight—and thus a shot at a rematch with Ortiz—and never again challenged for the title. He continued to box for another eight years until the age of 44, often in such far-flung venues as South America, South Africa, and Finland.

KEN BUCHANAN

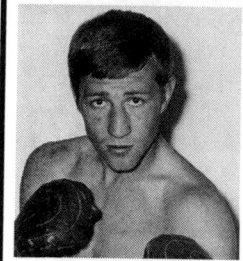

LIGHTWEIGHT

Right handed; 5'7½"; 126–138 lbs.
69 bouts, 9/20/1965 to 1/25/1982
Manager: Eddie Thomas
Lightweight Champion 1970–1972
Hall of Fame Induction: 2000
Born: 6/28/1945, Edinburgh, Scotland

One of the top Scots fighters of all time, Buchanan yearned to be a boxer from the time he was a small boy. He cajoled his father to let him join a boxing club when he was only eight, and although younger than the minimum age of nine, he won a medal in his first year.

An accomplished amateur fighter, Buchanan participated in the European championships in Moscow in 1963 and in Berlin in 1965. That year he also won the British Amateur Boxing Association featherweight title.

After his ABA title win, Buchanan turned professional and signed with manager Eddie Thomas. Thomas, who also managed Howard Winstone, a top featherweight, decided that Buchanan would be most successful as a lightweight. Buchanan's first professional fight was on September 20, 1965, when he knocked out Brian Tonks in the second round. Buchanan won his first sixteen bouts before winning the vacant Scottish lightweight title on January 23, 1967, with a ten-round decision over John McMillan. On February 19, 1968, Buchanan knocked out Maurice Cullen in eleven rounds to win the British lightweight title.

Buchanan started off 1969 with a decision over contender Frank Narvaez and won his next three fights before abruptly announcing his retirement at only 24. The impetus for this shocking announcement was an attempt to sever his contract in a dispute with Thomas, his manager. When the British Boxing Board of Control ruled in Thomas's favor, Buchanan did retire, only to return on November 11, 1969, with a second round knockout of Vincenzo Pitardi.

On January 29, 1970, Buchanan left Britain for the first time to fight Miguel Velazquez for the vacant European lightweight title in Madrid. Though much favored, Buchanan lost a fifteen-round decision. Later that year, he faced lightweight cham-

A tired Ken Buchanan wins a Lonsdale Belt, emblematic of the British championship, with his lightweight knockout victory over Maurice Cullen. Because Buchanan won a total of three British championships, he was given permanent possession of his belt.

IN THE RING	WON 61	LOST 8	DRAWS 0	TB 69	KO 27	W 34	WF 0	D 0	KO'd 1	L 7	LF 0

Date		Opponent	Site	Result / Rounds		Title	Wt.
1965							
Sep 20		Brian Tonks	London	TKO	2	—	126
Oct 18		Vic Woodhall	Manchester, England	TKO	2	—	—
Nov 1		Billy Williams	London	TKO	3	—	—
Nov 22		Joe Okezie	London	TKO	3	—	—
Dec 13		Junior Cassidy	London	W	8	—	—
1966							
Jan 24		Tommy Tiger	London	W	8	—	—
Mar 7		Manley Brown	London	TKO	4	—	—
Apr 4		Tommy Tiger	London	W	8	—	—
Apr 19		Chris Elliot	Manchester	W	8	—	—
May 11		Junior Cassidy	Manchester	W	8	—	—
Jul 12		Brian Smith	Aberavon, England	TKO	1	—	—
Aug 6		Ivan Whiter	London	W	8	—	—
Sep 6		Mick Laud	London	W	8	—	—
Oct 17		Antonio Paiva	London	W	10	—	—
Nov 29		Al Keen	Leeds, England	W	8	—	—
Dec 19		Phil Lundgren	London	W	10	—	—
1967							
Jan 23		John McMillan	Glasgow, Scotland	W	10	Won-Scots-L	135
Feb 14		Tommy Garrison	London	W	10	—	—
May 11		Franco Brondi	Paisley, Scotland	TKO	3	—	—
Jun 28		Winston Laud	London	W	8	—	—
Jul 26		Rene Roque	Aberavon	W	10	—	—
Sep 14		Al Rocca	London	TKO	7	—	—
Oct 30		Jim ("Spike") McCormack	London	W	12	—	134
1968							
Feb 19		Maurice Cullen	London	KO	11	Won-British-L	135
Apr 22		Leonard Tavarez	London	W	8	—	—
Jun 10		Ivan Whiter	London	W	8	—	—
Oct 23		Angel Robinson Garcia	Mayfair, England	W	10	—	131
Dec 11		Ameur Lamine	Hamilton, Scotland	TKO	3	—	—
1969							
Jan 2	⑩	Frank Narvaez	Piccadilly, England	W	10	—	—
Feb 17		Mike Cruz	Mayfair	TKO	5	—	132
Mar 5		Jose Luis Torcida	Solihull, England	W	10	—	—
Jul 14		Jerry Gracy	Nottingham, England	TKO	1	—	—
Nov 11		Vincenzo Pitardi	Mayfair	TKO	2	—	—
1970							
Jan 29	⑩	Miguel Velazquez	Madrid	L	15	For-Vac Eur-L	135
Feb 23		Leonard Tavarez	Piccadilly	W	10	—	134
Apr 6		Chris Fernandez	Nottingham	W	10	—	—
May 12		Brian Hudson	London	KO	5	Ret-Brit-L	135
Sep 26	♛	Ismael Laguna★	San Juan	W	15	Won-World-L	134
Dec 7		Donato Paduano	New York	W	10		136
1971							
Feb 12	⑩	Ruben Navarro	Los Angeles	W	15	Ret-World-L	134
May 10	⑩	Carlos Hernandez	London	TKO	8	—	—
Sep 13	⑩	Ismael Laguna★	New York	W	15	Ret-World-L	133

1972							
Mar 28	⑩	Al Ford	London	W	10	—	—
Apr 29		Andries Steyn	Johannesburg	TKO	3	—	136
Jun 26	⑩	Roberto Duran	New York	TKO'd	14	Lost-World-L	133
Sep 20		Carlos Ortiz★	New York	TKO	7	—	—
Dec 4		Chang-Kil Lee	New York	TKO	2	—	—
1973							
Jan 29		Jim Watt	Glasgow	W	15	Reg-Brit-L	133
Mar 27		Hector Matta	London	W	10	—	136
May 29		Frankie Otero	Miami Beach	W	10	—	132
Sep 1		Edwin ("Chuchu") Malave	New York	TKO	7	—	137
Oct 11	⑩	Frankie Otero	Toronto	TKO	6	—	134
Dec 6		Miguel Araujo	Copenhagen	KO	1	—	—
1974							
Feb 7		Jose Peterson	Copenhagen	W	10	—	—
Apr 4		Joe Tetteh	Copenhagen	KO	3	—	—
May 1		Antonio Puddu	Cagliari, Italy	KO	6	Won-Eur-L	135
Nov 21		Winston Noel	Copenhagen	TKO	2	—	—
Dec 16		Leonard Tavarez	Paris	TKO	14	Ret-Eur-L	135
1975							
Feb 27	♛	Ishimatsu Suzuki	Tokyo	L	15	For-WBC-L	133
Jul 25		Giancarlo Usai	Cagliari	TKO	12	Ret-Eur-L	135
1979							
Jun 28		Benny Benitez	Randers, Denmark	W	8	—	—
Sep 6		Eloi De Souza	Randers	W	8	—	—
Dec 6		Charlie Nash	Copenhagen	L	12	For-Eur-L	135
1980							
May 15		Najib Daho	London	KO	7	—	135
Oct 20		Des Gwilliam	Birmingham, England	W	8	—	136
1981							
Jan 26		Steve Early	Edgebaston, Scotland	L	12	—	137
Apr 4		Langton Tinago	Salisbury, England	L	10	—	—
Nov 24		Lawrence Williams	London	L	8	—	—
1982							
Jan 25		George Feeney	Piccadilly	L	8	—	138
1983							
*Mar 8		Johnny Claydon	London	KO	7	—	—

Unsanctioned bout, not included in totals

pion Ismael Laguna in San Juan, Puerto Rico. The fight was held on September 26, 1970, at Hiram Bithorn Stadium, and temperatures soared over 100 degrees. Buchanan started off well against the favored Laguna, but in the fourth and fifth, Laguna frequently connected with Buchanan's body and head. The challenger recovered in the sixth, and while the champ again took charge in the seventh, Laguna soon appeared to be faring worse than his opponent from the intense heat. Buchanan pinned Laguna against the ropes in the twelfth, then got the better of him over the next three rounds to earn a split decision, winning on two cards, 145-144 and 144-143, and losing on one, 143-144.

Buchanan had won, but the WBC refused to recognize him as champion—the California Athletic Commission had previously suspended Laguna for breaking a contract to defend his title. The Laguna fight marked the end of Buchanan's association with Thomas. For his efforts in 1970, the Boxing Writers Association of America awarded Buchanan the Edward J. Neil Trophy for Fighter of the Year.

In his first bout after winning the title, Buchanan fought in Madison Square Garden on the undercard of the Ali–Bonavena fight, easily defeating Donato Paduano and winning over the New York fans. He traveled to California for his next fight and decisioned Ruben Navarro, a late substitute for Mando Ramos, on February 12, 1971, before 10,360 spectators at the L.A. Sports Arena. It was after this bout that Buchanan finally received official WBC recognition of his championship.

He did not maintain the WBC title for long. After defeating Laguna in a rematch in Madison Square Garden on September 13, 1971, Buchanan was stripped of the title for fighting Laguna instead of the WBC's top contender, Pedro Carrasco.

On June 26, 1972, in Madison Square Garden, Buchanan's championship reign came to an end when he faced the brawling Roberto Duran. Duran attacked Buchanan from every angle, even used his head as a weapon. Though Buchanan fought well, Duran had the edge as the fight wore on. Duran received a warning for hitting below the belt in the thirteenth, and the fight ended with a blow (perhaps from Duran's knee) to Buchanan's groin that floored the champion. He could not continue, the punch was ruled legal, and Buchanan lost the title.

Buchanan knocked out fading Hall of Famer Carlos Ortiz in his next fight, and on January 29, 1973, he won a Lonsdale Belt when he decisioned Jim Watt in Glasgow for the British lightweight title. On May 1, 1974, he knocked out Antonio Puddu to win the European championship, and the next year he traveled to Tokyo to face WBC lightweight champion Ishimatsu Suzuki for a world title. Buchanan lost a close split decision. After one more fight, a defense of his European belt, Buchanan retired.

Four years later, financial reverses forced Buchanan back into the ring. While he won four of his first five fights, he dropped his last four against fighters who would once have presented no challenge to him. He officially retired after losing to George Feeney on January 25, 1982, though he did continue to fight in unlicensed bouts. After further financial setbacks, Buchanan was forced to work as a carpenter and, for a time, lived in a oneroom apartment in Glasgow, claiming unemployment benefits. Buchanan has written two autobiographies, *High Life and Hard Times* and *The Tartan Legend*.

Ken Buchanan batters Ruben Navarro against the ropes in Buchanan's first world lightweight title defense, before a large crowd in Los Angeles on February 12, 1971.

CHARLEY BURLEY

M I D D L E W E I G H T

Right-handed; 5'9½"; 142–162 lbs.

98 bouts, 9/29/1936 to 7/22/1950

Managers: Phil Goldstein 1936–42 and Tommy O'Loughlin 1942–1950

Hall of Fame Induction: 1992

Born: 9/6/1917, Bessemer, PA

Named: Charles Duane Burley

Died: 10/16/1992

Charley Burley had an excellent, if frustrating, career as a black fighter up against the color bar. Part of an outstanding crop of boxers to come out of the Pittsburgh area in the late 1930s and early '40s, Burley entered the pro ranks in his hometown in 1936. In his first eighteen months of fighting, Burley compiled an outstanding record of 16 wins and one loss, and he was given a chance to fight a prominent local fighter, Hall of Famer Fritzie Zivic. Burley lost a decision to the far more experienced Zivic, but he later beat Zivic twice.

Despite his success, or perhaps because of it , Burley had great difficulty getting matches with the top fighters. Normally a middleweight , Burley faced heavyweights who sometimes outweighed him by as much as 50 pounds. Not all prizefighting greats refused to face him. He lost two decisions to a much heavier Ezzard Charles and defeated the great Archie Moore. However, proposed fights against Billy Conn, Sugar Ray Robinson, a fourth fight against Zivic, and bouts with other champions never materialized.

Though unable to gain a title shot as a

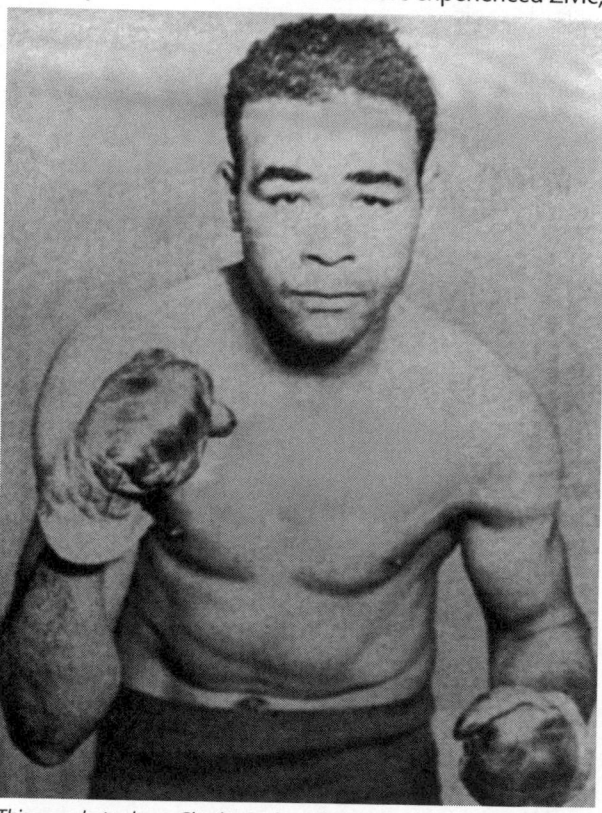

This rare photo shows Charley Burley as he appeared around the time he won the California middleweight title from Jack Chase in 1943.

IN THE RING	WON 84	LOST 11	DRAWS 2	TB 98	KO 50	W 34	WF 0	D 2	KO'd 0	L 11	LF 0	NC 1

Date	Opponent	Site	Result / Rounds		Title	Wt.
1936						
Sep 29	George Leggins	Pittsburgh	KO	4	—	—
Oct 22	Ralph Gizzy	Pittsburgh	W	6	—	—
Nov 9	Eddie Wirko	Pittsburgh	TKO	5	—	—
1937						
Jan 22	Ralph Gizzy	Oil City, PA	KO	2	—	—
Feb 8	Ray Collins	Oil City	TKO	5	—	—
Apr 15	Johnny Folio	McKeesport, PA	TKO	5	—	—
Apr 19	Ray Gray	Pittsburgh	W	6	—	—
May 3	Sammy Grippe	Pittsburgh	W	6	—	—
May 27	Keith Goodballet	Pittsburgh	TKO	2	—	—
Jun 24	Mickey O'Brien	Pittsburgh	W	10	—	—
Aug 9	Remo Fernandez	Pittsburgh	TKO	7	—	—
Aug 16	Sammy Grippe	Millvale, PA	TKO	6	—	—
Sep 9	Eddie Dolan	Pittsburgh	L	8	—	—
1938						
Jan 27	Tiger Jackson	Pittsburgh	KO	2	—	—
Feb 3	Johnny Folio	Pittsburgh	W	4	—	—
Feb 10	Carl Turner	Pittsburgh	W	4	—	—
Mar 3	Art Tate	Pittsburgh	KO	2	—	—
Mar 21	⑩ Fritzie Zivic★	Pittsburgh	L	10	—	—
Jun 1	Mike Barto	Millvale	KO	4	—	—
Jun 13	⑩ Fritzie Zivic★	Millvale	W	10	—	—
Aug 2	Leon Zorrita	Millvale	TKO	6	—	—
Aug 22	⑩ Cocoa Kid	Millvale	W	16	—	—
Nov 3	Werther Arcelli	Pittsburgh	KO	1	—	—
Nov 21	Billy Soose	Pittsburgh	W	10	—	—
1939						
Jan 10	Sonny Jones	Pittsburgh	TKO	7	—	—
Jun 20	⑩ Jimmy Leto	Millvale	L	10	—	—
Jul 17	⑩ Fritzie Zivic★	Pittsburgh	W	10	—	—
Aug 28	⑩ Jimmy Leto	Pittsburgh	W	10	—	—
Oct 23	Mickey Makar	Pittsburgh	KO	1	—	—
Dec 1	⑩ Holman Williams	New Orleans	L	15	—	—
1940						
Feb 12	⑩ Nate Bolden	Pittsburgh	W	10	—	—
Apr 12	Baby Kid Chocolate	New Orleans	KO	5	—	—
Apr 26	Sammy Edwards	New Orleans	KO	2	—	—
Jun 17	Carl Dell	Holyoke, MA	W	10	—	—
Jul 29	⑩ Georgie Abrams	Millvale	D	10	—	—
Aug 19	Kenny LaSalle	Millvale	W	10	—	—
Sep 3	⑩ Jimmy Bivins★	Millvale	L	10	—	—
Oct 18	Eddie Peirce	Pittsburgh	W	10	—	—
Nov 11	Vincent Pimpinella	Washington, DC	W	10	—	—
1941						
Mar 31	Babe Synnott	Pittsburgh	TKO	5	—	149

Date		Opponent	Location	Result	Rounds		
Apr 18		Eddie Ellis	Boston	TKO	5	—	—
Jun 2		Ossie Harris	Millvale	TKO	9	—	150
Jul 14		Gene Buffalo	Philadelphia	KO	5	—	—
Aug 25		Otto Blackwell	Millvale	W	8	—	—
Sep 25	⑩	Antonio Fernandez	Philadelphia	W	10	—	—
Dec 12		Ted Morrison	Minneapolis	KO	2	—	—
Dec 23		Jerry Hayes	Eau Claire, WI	KO	4	—	—
1942							
Jan 9		Shorty Hogue	Minneapolis	KO	10	—	—
Jan 23		Jackie Burke	Minneapolis	TKO	5	—	—
Feb 6		Milo Theodorescu	San Diego	TKO	4	—	—
Feb 13		Willard ("Big Boy") Hogue	San Diego	TKO	6	—	—
Feb 26	⑩	Holman Williams	Minneapolis	W	10	—	—
Mar 13		J.D.Turner	Minneapolis	TKO	6	—	—
Apr 10		Cleo McNeal	Minneapolis	KO	5	—	—
Apr 20		Phil McQuillan	New York	TKO	1	—	—
Apr 24		Joe Sutka	Chicago	TKO	4	—	—
Apr 30		Sonny Wilson	Minneapolis	TKO	2	—	—
May 25	⑩	Ezzard Charles★	Pittsburgh	L	10	—	—
Jun 23	⑩	Holman Williams	Cincinnati	W	10	—	—
Jun 29	⑩	Ezzard Charles★	Pittsburgh	L	10	—	—
Aug 14	⑩	Holman Williams	New Orleans	TKO	9	—	—
Oct 16	⑩	Holman Williams	New Orleans	L	15	—	157
Nov 13		Cecilio Lozada	San Diego	TKO	2	—	156
Dec 13	⑩	Lloyd Marshall	Los Angeles	L	10	—	152
1943							
Feb 3		Harvey Massey	Oakland	KO	9	—	—
Feb 19	⑩	Jack Chase	Hollywood	W	10	—	—
Mar 3		Aaron Wade	Oakland	W	10	—	—
Apr 19	⑩	Cocoa Kid	New Orleans	D	10	—	—
May 14	⑩	Holman Williams	Hollywood	NC	10	—	154
Jun 26		Bobby Birch	San Diego	W	10	—	—
1944							
Mar 3		Bobby Berger	San Diego	KO	5	—	—
Mar 20		Aaron Wade	San Diego	W	10	—	—
Apr 3	⑩	Jack Chase	Hollywood	KO	9	Won-CA-M	159
Apr 21	⑩	Archie Moore★	Hollywood	W	10	—	162
May 12		Al Gilbert	San Diego	TKO	4	—	158
Jun 23		Frankie Nelson	Hollywood	TKO	6	—	160
Aug 28		Gene Buffalo	San Francisco	TKO	5	—	—
Sep 11	⑩	Jack Chase	San Francisco	TKO	12	—	—
1945							
Mar 12	⑩	Joe Carter	San Francisco	W	10	—	—
Jul 11	⑩	Holman Williams	Buffalo	L	12	—	—
Jul 26		Oscar Boyd	Pittsburgh	KO	2	—	—
Aug 20	⑩	Aaron Wade	Pittsburgh	W	10	—	—
Sep 4		Dave Clark	Cincinnati	KO	1	—	—
Sep 28		Walter Duval	New Orleans	TKO	4	—	—
Oct 8	⑩	Billy Smith	San Francisco	W	10	—	—
1946							
Mar 14		Charley Dotson	Pittsburgh	TKO	3	—	—
Apr 8		Paul Peters	San Francisco	TKO	1	—	—

Date		Opponent	Location	Result	Rounds		
Apr 24	⑩	Billy Smith	Oakland	W	10	—	—
Jul 16		Charley Banks	Pittsburgh	W	10	—	—
Aug 5	⑩	Bert Lytell	Pittsburgh	W	10	—	—
1947							
Feb 17	⑩	Bert Lytell	Baltimore	L	10	—	—
Aug 8		Larry Cartwright	Huntington, WV	TKO	7	—	—
1948							
Mar 24		Battling Blackjack	Phoenix	KO	3	—	—
1949							
Apr 3	⑩	Charley Williams	New Orleans	W	10	—	—
Jul 25		Willie Wright	Pittsburgh	W	8	—	—
1950							
Feb 2		Chuck Higgins	Pittsburgh	KO	1	—	—
Mar 2		Buddy Hodnett	Pittsburgh	TKO	7	—	159
Jul 22		Pilar Bastidas	Lima, Peru	W	10	—	—

welterweight, middleweight, or light heavyweight, Burley did receive recognition in *The Ring*'s annual ratings of fighters. From 1939 through 1941, Burley was considered among the top five welterweight contenders. In 1942 and from 1944 through 1946, Burley was judged at least the third-best middleweight contender.

Racism was an undeniable force in preventing this talented fighter from receiving an opportunity to fight for a title. Ineffective management and Burley's unwillingness to take a dive probably also contributed. Burley asserted that he could have had a bout with Robinson, but he would have had to throw the first of a scheduled three-fight series deliberately. And, as with many strong African-American fighters, the question of whether white fighters were afraid to face him is unresolved. For a short time, Zivic became Burley's manager, perhaps so he would not have to fight him.

As with the Negro League diamond stars active before the integration of major league baseball, the descriptions of Burley's skills by his contemporaries are more indicative of his quality than is his record. Archie Moore called Burley the toughest man he fought in 234 fights. Trainer Eddie Futch said, "Charley Burley was the finest all-around fighter I ever saw." Futch added that Burley could do it all, box and punch.

Burley continued to fight until 1950. After retiring from the ring, he worked for the City of Pittsburgh.

STARE-DOWN

Sonny Liston intimidated his opponents, even before punches flew, with a steady menacing stare during the referee's instructions. Joe Frazier and Mike Tyson also were disconcerting starers. Shirley Povich, long-time sportswriter for the *Washington Post* credits Jack Sharkey with originating the tactic at the weigh-in for his July 1927 fight with Jack Dempsey. Dempsey seemed shaken by the stare, asking his seconds, "What's he doing?"

RINGFACT

MIGUEL ANGEL CANTO
El Maestro

FLYWEIGHT

Right-handed; 5'1": 108–113 lbs.

74 bouts, 2/5/1969–7/24/1982

WBC Flyweight Champion 1975–79

Hall of Fame Induction: 1998

Born: 1/30/49, Merida, Mexico

Named: Miguel Angel Canto Solis

Mexico's Miguel Canto was known for his superb speed, footwork, counterpunching ability, and stamina. Despite a lack of knock-out power, he was an active champion who held the WBC flyweight belt for over four years.

Born in Merida, in the Yucatan Peninsula, Canto learned to fight in the streets. He began formal training as a boxer at the age of thirteen. Four years later he won the Yucatan amateur flyweight title. Canto turned professional in 1969 after his father's death.

Canto quickly developed a rivalry with future-ranked flyweight Vicente Pool, whom he defeated three times in less than six months. Their final battle gave Canto the Yucatan State flyweight title. Canto's manager, Jesus Rivero, who would later handle Oscar de la Hoya, brought Tarcisio Gomez from Mexico City to Merida to face Canto. The undersized Canto, weighing less than the flyweight limit of 112 pounds, lost to the bigger and more experienced Gomez.

The fight with Gomez became a turning point for Canto, who trained hard

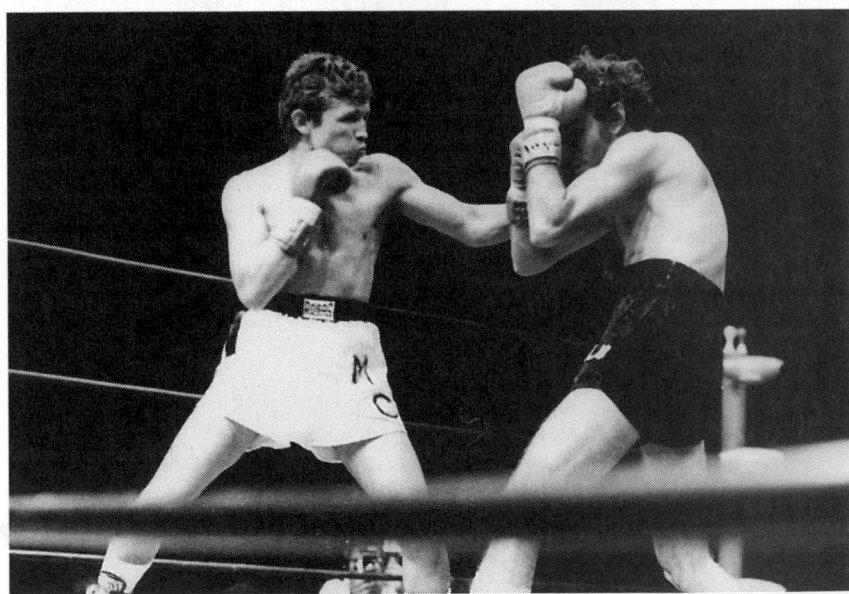

After taking the title belt, Canto (L) avenged his 1973 loss to Betulio Gonzalez with two successful title defenses in 1975 and 1976.

IN THE RING	WON 61	LOST 9	DRAWS 4	TB 74	KO 15	W 45	WF 1	D 4	KO'd 5	L 4	LF 0

Date	Opponent	Site	Result / Rounds		Title	Wt.
1969						
Feb 5	Raul Hernandez	Merida, Mexico	TKO'd	3	—	—
May 5	Pedro Martinez	Merida	W	4	—	—
Aug 13	Pedro Carrillo	Mexico City	TKO'd	4	—	—
Dec 6	Vicente Pool	Chetumal, Mexico	W	8	—	—
1970						
Jan 21	Rudy Granados	Merida	W	10	—	—
Feb 4	Joe Calvario	Merida	D	10	—	—
Mar 4	Vicente Pool	Merida	W	10	—	—
Mar 21	Baby Albornoz	Chetumal	TKO	9	—	—
Apr 8	Alex Basilio	Merida	TKO	6	—	—
Apr 29	Ranita Torres	Merida	D	8	—	—
May 27	Vicente Pool	Merida	W	12	Won-State-FL	112
Jun 24	Jose Cetina	Merida	W	12	Ret-State-FL	110
Oct 14	Tarcisio Gomez	Merida	L	10	—	109
Nov 11	Arturo Velazquez	Merida	W	10	—	109
Dec 9	Jose Medrano	Merida	W	10	—	109
1971						
Jan 21	Pedro Martinez	Cansahcab, Mexico	KO	2	—	—
Feb 14	Francisco Montalvo	Cansahcab	TKO	6	—	—
Mar 17	Marcus Gomez	Merida	TKO	6	—	110
Apr 4	Tigre Bracamontes	Merida	W	8	—	—
Apr 29	Jose Cetina	Merida	W	10	—	—
May 14	Gavilan Martinez	Tekax, Mexico	W	10	—	111
Jun 2	Mario Garcia	Merida	TKO	10	—	111
Jul 14	Pedro Lopez	Merida	KO	3	—	111
Jul 28	Domingo Ledesma	Merida	W	10	—	111
Sep 1	Roberto Alvarez	Merida	W	10	—	110
Oct 20	Alberto Morales	Merida	W	10	—	111
Dec 1	Luis Urrunaga	Merida	W	10	—	—
1972						
Jan 22	Constancio Garcia	Merida	W	12	Won-Mexican-FL	112
Mar 15	Jose Vargas	Merida	W	10	—	112
Apr 5	Armando Villa	Merida	TKO	4	—	113
May 20	Ricardo Delgado	Merida	W	12	Ret-Mexican-FL	110
Jul 26	Jose Valencia	Merida	W	10	—	110
Sep 27	Jose Corral	Merida	TKO	3	—	112
Nov 18	Alberto Morales	Merida	W	12	Ret-Mexican-FL	111
1973						
Jan 31	Ignacio Espinal	Merida	D	10	—	112
Mar 24	Tarcisio Gomez	Merida	TKO	2	Ret Mexican-FL	110
May 2	Rudy Billones	Merida	W	10	—	111
May 26	Luis Garcia	Tenosique, Mexico	TKO	7	—	111
Jun 29	Alfredo Rodriguez	Chetumal	KO	5	—	111
Aug 4 ⑩	Betulio Gonzalez	Caracas, Venezuela	L	15	For-Vac-WBC-FL	111
Nov 17	Lupe Hernandez	Merida	W	12	Ret-Mexican-FL	112
1974						
Feb 13 ⑩	Tony Moreno	Merida	TKO	5	—	—
Apr 27	Manuel Montiel	Merida	W	12	Ret-Mexican-FL	110
Jun 8	Pablito Jimenez	Merida	W	10	—	112

Date		Opponent	Location	Result	Rounds	Title	
Aug 17		Alberto Morales	Mexico City	W	10	—	111
Oct 25		Ricardo Delgado	Valladolid, Mexico	W	10	—	112
1975							
Jan 8	♛	Shoji Oguma	Sendai, Japan	W	15	Won-WBC-FL	111
Mar 8	⑩	Ignacio Espinal	Merida	W	10	—	113
May 24	⑩	Betulio Gonalez	Monterrey, Mexico	W	15	Ret-WBC-FL	111
Jul 18		Lupe Madera	Cozumel, Mexico	TKO	9	—	115
Aug 23		Jiro Takada	Merida	TKO	11	Ret-WBC-FL	111
Dec 13	⑩	Ignacio Espinal	Merida	W	15	Ret-WBC-FL	112
1976							
Mar 13		Francisco Marquex	Mexico City	W	10	—	—
May 15		Susumu Hanagata	Merida	W	15	Ret-WBC-FL	111
Oct 3	⑩	Betulio Gonzalez	Caracas	W	15	Ret-WBC-FL	111
Nov 20		Orlando Javierto	Los Angeles	W	15	Ret-WBC-FL	112
1977							
Apr 24		Reyes Arnal	Caracas	W	15	Ret-WBC-FL	111
Jun 15		Kimio Furesawa	Tokyo	W	15	Ret-WBC-FL	112
Sep 17		Martin Vargas	Merida	W	15	Ret-WBC-FL	112
Nov 30		Martin Vargas	Santiago, Chile	W	15	Ret-WBC-FL	112
1978							
Jan 4	⑩	Shoji Oguma	Tokyo	W	15	Ret-WBC-FL	111
Apr 18	⑩	Shoji Oguma	Tokyo	W	15	Ret-WBC-FL	112
Nov 20		Tacomron Vibonchai	Houston	W	15	Ret-WBC-FL	111
1979							
Feb 10		Antonio Avelar	Merida	W	15	Ret-WBC-FL	111
Mar 18		Chan-Hee Park	Pusan, Korea	L	15	Lost-WBC-FL	111
Sep 9	♛	Chan-Hee Park	Seoul	D	15	For-WBC-FL	112
1980							
Aug 16		Alfredo Hernandez	Merida	W	10	—	112
Oct 18		Orlando Maldonado	Guadalajara	WF	6	—	113
1981							
Feb 22	⑩	Sung-Jun Kim	Merida	W	10	—	113
Mar 29		Gabriel Bernal	Villahermosa, Mexico	L	10	—	112
Jun 6		Gabriel Bernal	Merida	W	10	—	113
Aug 29	⑩	Candido Tellez	Villahermosa	TKO'd	4	—	113
Oct 31		Alfredo Hernandez	Torreon, Mexico	TKO'd	7	—	113
1982							
Jul 24		Rodolfo Ortega	Merida	TKO'd	9	—	—

to gain needed strength. He went on to win his next fourteen bouts and, on January 22, 1972, he took the Mexican flyweight title from Constancio ("Rocky") Garcia. Fighting exclusively in Merida, Canto successfully defended the title twice in 1972.

In 1973, Canto traveled to Caracas, Venezuela to challenge Betulio Gonzalez for the vacant WBC flyweight title. Although he lost to Gonzalez, Canto moved up to third in *The Ring's* flyweight rankings for 1973. Five more victories in 1974 gave Canto the top spot on *The Ring* list.

On January 8, 1975 Canto again challenged for the WBC title, then held by Shoji Oguma of Japan. Canto was the aggressor in the bout and used his unusually long reach to fire rights and lefts to his opponent's body. Canto earned a majority decision to take the title.

After eleven successful title defenses, Canto met Oguma in a rematch in 1978 in Tokyo. Canto won a hotly contested split decision. He won on two scorecards—147-146 by the United States judge and 147-145 by the Mexican judge. Oguma came out ahead on the Japanese judge's card by a score of 148-145. When the decision was announced, the overwhelmingly Japanese crowd threw debris into the ring. In the rematch, again held in Tokyo, Canto retained his title with a fifteen-round decision.

After decisioning future champion Antonio Avelar on February 10, 1979, Canto held a flyweight record of fourteen successful title defenses. There would not be a fifteenth. On March 18, 1979, Canto met Chan-Hee Park in Pusan, South Korea. Chan-Hee built up a significant lead in the early rounds. Although Canto made a spirited comeback starting in the eleventh round, he could not overcome Chan-Hee's early lead. Canto's career weakness, the lack of real knock-out power, kept him from ending the fight. Although it was close on two of the three cards, the challenger earned a unanimous decision. In the rematch six months later, Canto was knocked down in the fifth round but seized control in the later rounds. Again the fight went the full fifteen rounds. This time, however, it was ruled a draw. The Mexican judge favored Canto; the Korean judge favored Chan-Hee; and the Italian referee called it even.

Canto briefly retired in 1979 following the draw in South Korea. He became involved in a wide variety of business ventures, including a restaurant and a hotel, but he returned to boxing in 1980. He won four of his first five comeback fights but was stopped in the next three in less than regulation. In a fight against Candido Tellez, he suffered his first knockout since 1969. After Rodolfo Ortega stopped him in the ninth round on July 24, 1982, Canto retired for good.

Like his idol and stylistic model, Willie Pep, Canto is remembered as a classy ring general with fourteen successful title defenses to his credit.

Demonstrating his signature speed and balance, Canto (L) avoids a blow by Ignacio Espinal. They met three times: Canto won twice; one fight was a draw.

JIMMY CARTER

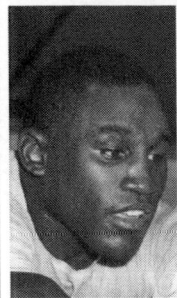

L I G H T W E I G H T

Right handed; 5'6"; 129–145 lbs.

119 bouts, 3/14/1946 to 4/1/1960

Manager: Willie Ketchum

Lightweight Champion 1951-52, 1952-54, 1954-55

Hall of Fame Induction: 2000

Born: 12/15/1923, Aiken, SC

Named: James Walter Carter

Died: 9/21/1994

The first three-time lightweight champion, Jimmy Carter received neither the publicity nor the accolades normally accorded to world title holders. Carter once remarked, "I know it sounds strange, but I don't care what they say about me. I win most of my fights."

Carter moved from South Carolina to Harlem when he was nine. As a member of the Army Corps of Engineers during WWII, Carter boxed while serving in France, England, and the Pacific.

After his discharge, Carter turned professional on March 14, 1946, with a four-round decision over Clifton Bordies in Newark. The following year, he faced two future Hall of Famers, dropping a ten-round decision to Joe Brown in New Orleans and battling Sandy Saddler to a ten-round draw. By 1949, Carter was discouraged by his lack of progress, but his manager, Willie Ketchum, persuaded him to keep at it. That year, he traveled extensively for the first time, scoring wins in New York, Detroit, and California, and two wins out of three fights in Australia.

In 1950, Carter began to attract national attention. He decisioned future champion Wallace ("Bud") Smith, defeated veteran Jesse Underwood, and closed the year with a draw against third-rated contender Tommy Campbell.

Carter earned his first shot at the lightweight title of Hall of Famer Ike Williams. Perhaps because the fight was televised, it attracted only 3,594 fans to Madison Square Garden on May 25, 1951.

Williams had great difficulty making weight. Carter dominated the fight, knocking Williams down three times before referee Petey Scalzo stopped the contest in the fourteenth round with Williams pinned against the ropes. Carter, the new title holder, got only about $4,000 for his efforts

On April 1, 1952, Carter successfully defended his title against Lauro Salas. In a rematch on May 14, Salas—ranked by some oddsmakers as the 15–1 underdog—shocked the boxing world when he cap-

Kid Gavilan's (L) reign as welterweight champion began exactly one week before Jimmy Carter's (R) first term as lightweight champ.

IN THE RING	WON 80	LOST 30	DRAWS 9	TB 119	KO 30	W 50	WF 0	D 9	KO'd 3	L 27	LF 0

Date	Opponent	Site	Result / Rounds		Title	Wt.
1946						
Mar 14	Clifton Bordies	Newark, NJ	W	4	—	130
Apr 5	Joe Krikis	New York	W	4	—	130
Apr 8	Ray Morris	Newark	KO	5	—	—
Apr 19	George Wright	New York	W	6	—	—
May 1	Johnny LaRusso	Long Island City, NY	W	6	—	—
May 7	Lou Daniels	New York	KO	3	—	—
May 28	Leo LeBron	New York	W	6	—	—
May 31	Johnny LaRusso	New York	L	4	—	—
Jun 12	Lou Langley	New York	KO	1	—	—
Jul 9	Joey Monterio	Norwalk, CT	W	6	—	—
Jul 29	Paul Midiri	New York	D	6	—	130
Aug 12	Ray Lewis	New York	L	6	—	—
Aug 26	Al Turner	Brooklyn	KO	5	—	—
Sep 5	Johnny Johnson	New York	KO	4	—	129
Sep 16	Danny Carabella	Brooklyn	L	8	—	—
Oct 2	Paul Midiri	Long Island City	W	8	—	—
Oct 19	Charley Noel	New York	W	8	—	—
Nov 5	Bill Williams	New York	KO	7	—	134
Dec 2	Eddie Smith	New York	W	8	—	—
Dec 17	Ruby Garcia	New York	KO	3	—	133
1947						
Jan 7	Walter Keene	New York	W	8	—	134
Feb 24	Walter Lewis	New York	W	8	—	—
Mar 18	Eddie White	New York	TKO	4	—	133
Mar 28	Walter Stevens	New York	W	6	—	—
Apr 18	Joe Brown★	New Orleans	L	10	—	—
May 12	Johnny Johnson	New York	W	8	—	—
May 27	Chico Morales	New York	KO	7	—	131
Jun 3 ⑩	Sandy Saddler★	Washington, DC	D	10	—	—
Jul 22	Thompson Harmon	New York	KO	5	—	—
Sep 8	Henry Polowitzer	New Haven, CT	W	8	—	—
Sep 16	Patsy Spataro	New York	KO	7	—	—
Sep 29	Dave Williams	New Haven	D	8	—	—
Oct 27	Dave Williams	New Haven	D	8	—	—
Nov 18 ⑩	Charles ("Cabey") Lewis	Hartford	KO'd	7	—	—
Dec 9	Al Pennino	New York	D	8	—	—
1948						
Jan 27	Thompson Harmon	New York	W	8	—	134
Mar 9	Charley ("Cabey") Lewis	New York	W	10	—	132
Mar 29	Cal Smith	Boston	W	8	—	135
Apr 18	Willie Russell	Cincinnati	W	10	—	—
May 21	Bobby McQuillar	New Orleans	L	10	—	—
Jun 29	Phil Burton	Springfield, IL	W	10	—	—
Jul 12	Wilfredo Miro	Springfield	W	10	—	—
Jul 20	Woody Winslow	New York	D	8	—	—
Jul 26	Julie Kogan	Springfield	KO	8	—	—
Aug 9	George Smith	Springfield	W	10	—	—
Aug 30	Joey Angelo	Springfield	W	10	—	—

Date		Opponent	Location	Result			
Sep 27		Isaac Jenkins	New Haven	W	8	—	—
Nov 1	⑩	Sonny Boy West	Baltimore	L	10	—	—
Dec 6		Louis Joyce	Holyoke, MA	W	10	—	—
1949							
Jan 17		Harold Jones	New York	W	10	—	—
Jan 31		Talmadge Bussey	Detroit	W	10	—	—
Apr 4		Nick Diaz	Ocean Park, CA	TKO	6	—	135
Apr 22		Archie Whitewater	San Francisco	KO	6	—	—
May 23		Mario Trigo	Ocean Park	TKO	8	—	134
Sep 16		Norman Gent	Melbourne	L	12	—	—
Oct 4		Charlie Ashenden	Sydney	KO	4	—	—
Oct 28		Bernie Hall	Melbourne	W	12	—	—
Nov 29	⑩	Rudy Cruz	Los Angeles	L	10	—	135
1950							
Mar 28	⑩	Wallace ("Bud") Smith	Cincinnati	W	10	—	—
Jul 25		Jesse Underwood	Cincinnati	W	10	—	133
Oct 6	⑩	Tommy Campbell	New Orleans	D	10	—	—
1951							
Jan 30		Calvin Smith	Philadelphia	L	10	—	—
Feb 7		Percy Bassett	New York	W	10	—	—
Mar 5		Percy Bassett	Philadelpia	L	10	—	—
May 25	♛	Ike Williams★	New York	TKO	14	Won-World-L	135
Jun 18		Chick Boucher	Fall River, MA	KO	4	—	—
Jul 2		Ronnie Harper	Flint, MI	KO	5	—	—
Jul 10		Enrique Bolanos	Los Angeles	TKO	7	—	—
Aug 2	⑩	Del Flanagan	Minneapolis	TKO	7	—	—
Aug 14		Mario Trigo	Los Angeles	W	10	—	—
Aug 28	⑩	Art Aragon	Los Angeles	L	10	—	—
Nov 14	⑩	Art Aragon	Los Angeles	W	15	Ret-World-L	134
1952							
Jan 21		Mario Trigo	Philadelphia	W	10	—	—
Feb 5		Alan McFater	Toronto	W	9	—	—
Mar 12		Luther Rawlings	Chicago	W	10	—	—
Apr 1	⑩	Lauro Salas	Los Angeles	W	15	Ret-World-L	134
May 14	⑩	Lauro Salas	Los Angeles	L	15	Lost-World-L	134
Sep 1		Basil Marie	Dartmouth, NS, Canada	W	10	—	—
Oct 15	♛	Lauro Salas	Chicago	W	15	Reg-World-L	135
Dec 9		Archie Whitewater	Oakland	W	10	—	—
Dec 16		Freddie ("Babe") Herman	Sacramento, CA	D	10	—	—
1953							
Jan 12	⑩	Eddie Chavez	San Francisco	L	10	—	—
Feb 16		Armand Savoie	Montreal	L	10	—	—
Apr 24		Tommy Collins	Boston	TKO	4	Ret-World-L	134
Jun 12	⑩	George Araujo	New York	TKO	13	Ret-World-L	135
Sep 12		Johnny Cunningham	Miami	L	10	—	—
Sep 28		Ben Miloud	Johnstown, PA	KO	8	—	—
Oct 15		Carlos Chavez	Los Angeles	KO	6	—	—
Nov 11		Armond Savoie	Montreal	KO	5	Ret-World-L	133
1954							
Feb 8		Billy Lauderdale	Nassau, Bahamas	W	10	—	—
Mar 5	⑩	Paddy DeMarco	New York	L	15	Lost-World-L	135
Jun 2		Charley Riley	St. Louis	KO	2	—	—
Aug 4		Glen Flanagan	Chicago	W	10	—	—
Sep 22		Freddie Herman	San Francisco	W	10	—	—
Nov 17	♛	Paddy DeMarco	San Francisco	KO	15	Reg-World-L	135

1955							
Jan 26		Bobby Woods	Spokane, WA	W	10	—	—
Feb 11	Ⓣ	Tony DeMarco	Boston	D	10	—	—
Apr 20		Orlando Zulueta	Washington, DC	L	10	—	—
Jun 29	Ⓣ	Wallace ("Bud") Smith	Boston	L	15	Lost-World-L	134
Oct 19	♛	Wallace ("Bud") Smith	Cincinnati	L	15	For-World-L	135
1956							
Feb 1	Ⓣ	Cisco Andrade	Chicago	L	10	—	—
Mar 5		Phil Burton	Quebec City, Quebec, Canada	W	10	—	—
Mar 29		Don Jordan	Los Angeles	W	10	—	138
May 3	Ⓣ	Art Aragon	Los Angeles	W	10	—	138
Jun 21		Lauro Salas	Los Angeles	W	10	—	
Sep 11	Ⓣ	Larry Boardman	Boston	KO'd 8		—	139
1957							
May 23		Buddy McDonald	Spokane	W	10	—	—
Sep 7		Mickey Northup	Hollywood, CA	W	10	—	—
Oct 8	Ⓣ	Willie Toweel	London	L	10	—	137
1958							
Jan 14	Ⓣ	Joey Lopes	Sacramento	L	10	—	—
Mar 11	Ⓣ	Joey Lopes	Sacramento	L	10	—	—
Jul 19		Jimmy Grow	Hollywood	KO 7		—	138
Sep 9	Ⓣ	Al Nevarez	Ciudad Juarez, Mexico	L	10	—	139
Sep 23		Rudy Jordan	Fresno, CA	KO'd 6		—	139
1959							
Aug 11		Kildo Nunez	San Jose, CA	W	10	—	—
Oct 13		Jimmy Smith	Richmond, CA	KO 3		—	—
Nov 10		Kildo Nunez	Richmond	KO 4		—	—
Nov 24		Art Ramponi	Oakland	L	10	—	—
1960							
Feb 25		Jimmy Grow	Boise, ID	L	10	—	—
Apr 1		Luis Garduno	Mesa, AZ	L	10	—	145

tured the lightweight title in a split decision. On October 15, a mere five months later, Carter decisioned Salas to regain the crown.

Carter's second stint as champion ended when he lost on points to Paddy DeMarco on March 5, 1954. Once again he regained his title in a rematch, stopping DeMarco in the fifteenth round. Carter thus became the first fighter to win the lightweight belt three times. A solid, if unspectacular and methodical fighter, Carter combined good boxing skills with a decent punch that brought him many victories.

Carter's third championship reign proved to be his shortest, as Wallace ("Bud") Smith decisioned him seven months later. Smith won their rematch as well.

Then-Vice President Richard Nixon (L) meets Jimmy Carter in Washington, DC.

In retirement, Carter worked for fifteen years in a Ford assembly plant, then as a teacher's aide.

MARCEL CERDAN
The Casablanca Clouter

MIDDLEWEIGHT

Right-handed; 5′8″; 143–163 lbs.

110 bouts, 11/4/1934 to 6/16/1949

Managers: Lucien Roupp and Jo Longman

Middleweight Champ 1948–49

Hall of Fame Induction: 1991

Born: 7/22/1916, Sidi Bel-Abbes, Algeria

Died: 10/27/1949

One of the most popular boxers in the era immediately after World War II, Marcel Cerdan died tragically in a plane crash as he was flying back to the United States from Paris to attempt to reclaim the world middleweight title.

Cerdan was born into a boxing family in Algeria, then a French possession. His father, a butcher by trade, promoted amateur bouts in Casablanca, and two of his brothers preceded him into the professional prize ring. Cerdan quit school at the age of eleven to work along the waterfront. At eighteen, he started fighting professionally under the guidance of manager Lucien Roupp. Cerdan won his first 34 fights before facing Omar Kouidri in Casablanca for the French welterweight title. Cerdan took the decision

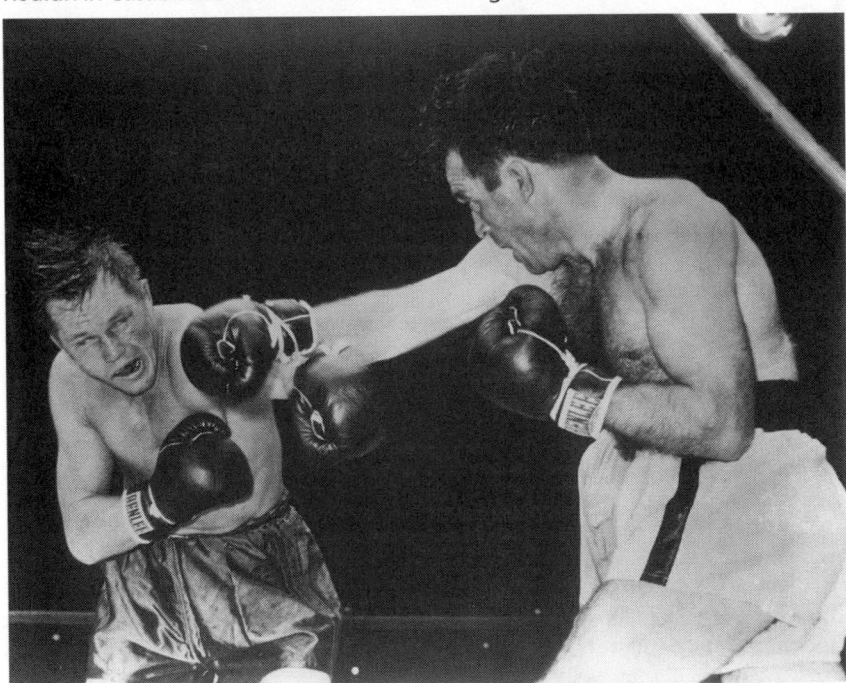

A right cross rocks the already-battered Tony Zale (L) as Cerdan inflicts more damage. Zale couldn't answer the bell for the 12th round and Cerdan took the middleweight belt on September 21, 1948.

IN THE RING	WON 106	LOST 4	DRAWS 0	TB 110	KO 61	W 45	WF 0	D 0	KO'd 1	L 1	LF 2

Date	Opponent	Site	Result / Rounds		Title	Wt.
1934						
Nov 4	Marcel Bucchianer	Meknes, Morocco	W	6	—	—
Nov 12	Benazra	Meknes	TKO	5	—	—
1935						
Feb 16	Perez Tercero	Casablanca, Morocco	W	10	—	—
Apr 13	Privat	Casablanca	TKO	5	—	—
Apr 13	Benazra	Casablanca	W	10	—	—
Jul 5	Mac Perez	Casablanca	TKO	2	—	—
Jul 19	Joseph Sarfati	Casablanca	W	10	—	—
Aug 8	Mestre	Casablanca	W	10	—	—
Nov 23	Mac Perez	Casablanca	W	10	—	—
Dec 14	Mac Perez	Casablanca	W	10	—	—
1936						
Mar 4	Antoine Abad	Casablanca	W	10	—	—
Apr 7	M. Hergane	Casablanca	W	10	—	—
Apr 11	Joseph Martinez	Taza, Morocco	TKO	9	—	—
May 23	M. Ricardo	Casablanca	KO	5	—	—
May 27	Kid Abadie	Casablanca	KO	3	—	—
Jun 6	M. Castillanos	Casablanca	W	10	—	—
Jul 19	Joseph Sarfati	Casablanca	W	10	—	—
Aug 2	Al Francis	Oran, Algeria	KO	6	—	—
Oct 17	Primo Rubio	Casablanca	W	10	—	—
Nov 2	Aisa Attaf	Casablanca	KO	1	—	—
Nov 21	Jean Debeaumont	Casablanca	W	10	—	—
1937						
Jan 16	Aisa Attaf	Algiers, Algeria	KO	8	—	—
Jan 30	Maurice Naudin	Algiers	KO	3	—	—
Mar 2	Omar Kouidri	Rabat, Morroco	W	10	—	—
Apr 3	Omar Kouidri	Algiers	W	10	—	—
Jul 3	Ali Omar	Algiers	KO	5	—	—
Aug 2	Kid Marcel	Oran	W	10	—	—
Sep 13	Eddy Rabak	Casablanca	KO	6	—	—
Oct 7	Louis Jampton	Paris	W	10	—	—
Oct 21	Jean Morin	Paris	W	10	—	—
Dec 18	Ifergane	Rabat	W	10	—	—
1938						
Jan 6	Charles Feodorowich	Paris	KO	2	—	—
Jan 13	Eddie Ran	Paris	KO	2	—	—
Jan 20	Jean Zides	Paris	KO	9	—	—
Feb 21	Omar Kouidri	Casablanca	W	12	Won-France-W	147
Mar 12	Charles Pernot	Algiers	W	10	—	—
Mar 25	Lucien Krawsyck	Paris	W	10	—	—
Apr 13	Eddy Rabak	Paris	W	10	—	—
May 5	Anacleto Locatelli	Paris	W	12	—	—
May 20	Gustave Humery	Paris	KO	6	—	—
Jun 4	Jean Morin	Algiers	W	10	—	—
Jul 3	Victor Deckmyn	Oran	W	10	—	—
Sep 15	Al Baker	Paris	W	10	—	—

Date	Opponent	Location	Result		Notes	Weight
Oct 27	Amadeo Deyana	Paris	W	10	—	—
Nov 10	Alfredo Katter	Paris	KO	4	—	—
Nov 24	Omar Kouidri	Paris	W	12	Ret-France-W	147

1939

Date	Opponent	Location	Result		Notes	Weight
Jan 9	Harry Craster	London	LD	5	—	—
Jan 21	Ercole Buratti	Algiers	W	10	—	—
Feb 4	Al Baker	Brussels	KO	7	—	—
Feb 20 ⑩	Saverio Turiello	Paris	W	12	—	—
Mar 22	Felix Wouters	Brussels	W	12	—	—
May 21	Roger Cadot	Marseilles, France	KO	6	—	—
Jun 3 ⑩	Saverio Turiello	Milan	W	15	Won-Europe-W	147
Jun 18	Anacleto Locatelli	Marseilles	W	10	—	—

1941

Date	Opponent	Location	Result		Notes	Weight
Jan 19	Young Raymond	Algiers	KO	1	—	—
Jan 26	Young Raymond	Casablanca	TKO	6	—	—
Feb 2	Victor Fortes	Casablanca	TKO	7	—	—
Mar 9	Victor Janas	Casablanca	W	10	—	—
Apr 13	Victor Fortes	Oran	TKO	2	—	—
May 4	Omar Kouidri	Oran	TKO	6	—	—
Jun 22	Francois Blanchard	Marseilles	KO	6	—	—
Jul 20	Joe Brun	Oran	TKO	2	—	—
Sep 13	Roland Coureau	Algiers	TKO	9	—	—
Dec 31	Robert Seidel	Vichy, France	KO	3	—	—

1942

Date	Opponent	Location	Result		Notes	Weight
Feb 21	Fred Flury	Nice, France	KO	7	—	—
Apr 26	Gustave Humery	Paris	KO	1	—	—
May 17	Fernand Viez	Paris	W	10	—	—
Jun 28	Gaspard de Ridder	Paris	KO	1	—	—
Jul 25	Victor Janas	Algiers	TKO	2	—	—
Aug 2	Ben Frely	Marseilles	KO	3	—	—
Aug 15	Victor Buttin	Algiers	LD	8	—	—
Sep 30	Jose Ferrer	Paris	TKO	1	Ret-Europe-W	147

1943

Date	Opponent	Location	Result		Notes	Weight
Aug 8	John McCoy	Oran	KO	2	—	—
Sep 12	Omar Kouidri	Algiers	W	10	—	—
Oct 13	Larry Cisneros	Oran	KO	6	—	—
Oct 31	Bulldog Milano	Casablanca	KO	2	—	—
Dec 26	James Toney	Oran	KO	2	—	—
Dec 29	Larry Cisneros	Algiers	KO	2	—	—

1944

Date	Opponent	Location	Result		Notes	Weight
Jan 30	Willie Sampson	Casablanca	KO	2	—	—
Oct 21	Bouaya	Casablanca	KO	1	—	—

1945

Date	Opponent	Location	Result		Notes	Weight
Mar 9	Joe Brun	Paris	TKO	7		
May 13	Jean Despeaux	Paris	KO	5	—	—
Jun 3	Oscar Menozzi	Marseilles	KO	3	—	—
Jun 24	Edouard Tenet	Croix de Berny, France	W	10	—	—
Oct 19	Tommy Davies	Paris	KO	1	—	—
Nov 30	Assane Diouf	Paris	KO	3	Won-France-M	160
Dec 8	Victor Buttin	St. Etienne, France	KO	3	—	—

1946

Date	Opponent	Location	Result		Notes	Weight
Jan 13	Agustin Guedes	Lisbon, Portugal	KO	1	—	—
Jan 18	Edouard Tenet	Paris	W	12	Ret-France-M	160
Feb 24	Jose Ferrer	Barcelona, Spain	KO	4	—	—
Apr 14	Joe Brun	Nice	KO	2	—	—

Date		Opponent	Location	Result	Rds	Title	Wt
May 25		Robert Charron	Paris	W	12	Ret-France-M	160
Jul 7	Ⓝ	Holman Williams	Paris	W	10	—	—
Oct 20		Jean Pankowiak	Paris	KO	5	—	—
Dec 6	Ⓝ	Georgie Abrams	New York	W	10	—	160
1947							
Feb 2		Leon Foquet	Paris	KO	1	Won-Vac Europe-M	160
Feb 11		Bert Gilroy	London	KO	4	—	161
Mar 28		Harold Green	New York	KO	2	—	—
Oct 7		Billy Walker	Montreal	TKO	1	—	—
Oct 31	Ⓝ	Anton Raadik	Chicago	W	10	—	—
1948							
Jan 26		Giovanni Manca	Paris	KO	2	Ret-Europe-M	160
Feb 9		Jean Walzack	Paris	KO	4	Ret-Europe-M	160
Mar 12		Lavern Roach	New York	TKO	8	—	156
Mar 25		Lucien Krawsyck	Paris	W	10	—	—
May 23	Ⓝ	Cyrille Delannoit	Brussels	L	15	Lost-Europe-M	160
Jul 10	Ⓝ	Cyrille Delannoit	Brussels	W	15	Reg-Europe-M	160
Sep 21	♛	Tony Zale ★	Jersey City, NJ	TKO	12	Won-World-M	158
1949							
Mar 29	Ⓝ	Dick Turpin	London	KO	7	—	—
May 8		Lucien Krawsyck	Casablanca	KO	4	—	—
Jun 16	Ⓝ	Jake LaMotta ★	Detroit	TKO'd	10	Lost-World-M	159

in twelve rounds. In 1939, he added the European welterweight crown with a victory over Saverio Turiello.

With the outbreak of World War II, Cerdan served in the French Navy before his artillery unit was disbanded by the Germans. He boxed several times in occupied Paris after France fell to the Nazi invasion. A meeting with Spanish middleweight champion Jose Ferrer, whom Cerdan knocked out in one round, irritated the Germans, and Cerdan wisely fled, using forged travel permits. He then joined the Free French Navy. Cerdan first became known to American audiences when he won two major Inter-Allied boxing tournaments in 1944 and 1945. American fans liked him, even when he beat American boxers.

After the war, Cerdan won the French and European middleweight titles. In 1946, he traveled to the United States to face the tough Georgie Abrams. Cerdan won a ten-round decision and, at the close of that year, was rated the fourth-top contender for the middleweight title by *The Ring* in its annual rankings. Cerdan finally fought Tony Zale for the world championship in 1948 at Roosevelt Stadium in Jersey City. Cerdan used his superior speed, quickness, and punching accuracy to pile up a lead over Zale before knocking him down with a left hook at the end of the eleventh round. Zale could not come out for the twelfth round, and Cerdan was the champion.

The next year Cerdan defended his title against Hall of Famer Jake LaMotta. In the first round, LaMotta wrestled Cerdan to the canvas, damaging the champ's shoulder. Cerdan, who once knocked an opponent out with a broken hand, fought one-armed until he could not continue. In the tenth round, he conceded defeat. The rematch was postponed when LaMotta claimed an injury.

Cerdan's plane crashed on its way to the United States for the LaMotta rematch. The entire boxing community mourned the French fighter's passing.

ANTONIO CERVANTES
Kid Pambele

JUNIOR WELTERWEIGHT

Right-handed; 5'10"; 121–143 lbs.

79 bouts, 1/31/1964 to 12/9/1983

Manager: Ramiro Machado

Junior Welterweight Champion 1972–76, 1977–80

Hall of Fame Induction: 1998

Born: 12/23/1945, San Basilio de Palenque, Colombia

The first Colombian to win a world championship, Antonio Cervantes is also the first native of Colombia to be inducted into the International Boxing Hall of Fame.

Cervantes arose from an unusual heritage and upbringing. While approximately 90 percent of Colombians are either white or Indian, Cervantes hails from the all-black San Basilio de Palenque, a town with a population of about 3,000. The founders of the town were slaves who rebelled against their Spanish masters in the late 1500s. Through the use of guerrilla warfare, the former slaves maintained their forest settlement and their freedom.

Ultimately, Palenque became part of Colombia, but certain vestiges of its origin remained. For instance, young boys and girls in Palenque were traditionally trained in the arts of war, including fist fighting. Today, the town's children still engage in organized fighting, seen as a noble pastime. Often, boys become members of a "cuadro," fighting each other and the members of other cuadros. In addition to Cervantes, tiny Palenque has since produced three other champions: middleweight Rodrigo Valdez, junior featherweight Ricardo Cardona, and flyweight Prudencio Cardona.

Hard-hitting Cervantes leaves Alfonso Frazer spread-eagled on the canvas and takes the junior welterweight title in Panama City on October 28, 1972.

IN THE RING	WON 66	LOST 12	DRAWS 1	TB 79	KO 36	W 30	WF 0	D 1	KO'd 2	L 10	LF 0

Date	Opponent	Site	Result / Rounds		Title	Wt.
1964						
Jan 32	Juan Martinez	Cerete, Colombia	W	6	—	—
Feb 28	Rodolfo Marquez	Valledupar, Colombia	W	4	—	—
Apr 21	Rodolfo Marquez	Maria La Baja, Colombia	KO	3	—	—
May 5	Oscar Gonzalez	Medellin, Colombia	W	8	—	—
Jun 20	Felix Salgado	Barranquilla, Colombia	W4	—		—
1965						
Oct 2	Antonio Yi	Barranquilla	W	6	—	—
1966						
Jan 19	Rafael Donado	Cartagena, Colombia	KO	2	—	—
Mar 19	Antonio Yi	Cartagena	W	6	—	—
Apr 29	Jose Godoy	Cartagena	W	6	—	121
May 10	Jesus Cardenas	Turbaco, Colombia	TKO	7	—	—
May 24	Jose Godoy	Calamar, Colombia	W	6	—	—
Jun 24	Jose Zuniga	Cartagena	W	6	—	—
Jul 29	Reynaldo Lopez	Cartagena	D	8	—	123
Sep 23	Cipriano Zuluaga	Monteria, Colombia	L	10	—	—
Nov 6	Cipriano Zuluaga	Monteria	L	10	—	—
1967						
Feb 3	Victor Cano	Bogota, Colombia	L	8	—	—
Apr 2	Eleodoro Pitalua	Cartagena	W	6	—	—
May 20	Eleodoro Pitalua	San Andres, Colombia	W	10	—	—
Jun 3	Reynaldo Lopez	San Andres	W	10	—	—
Jul 14	Nestor Rojas	Caracas, Venezuela	L	8	—	—
Aug 5	Rafael Rojas	Barranquilla	KO	5	—	—
1968						
Jan 21	Eleodoro Pitalua	Cartagena	W	10	—	—
Aug 31	Jose Godoy	Bogota	W	8	—	—
Nov 25	Orlando Ruiz	Caracas	KO	1	—	—
Dec 20	Cruz Marcano	Caracas	KO'd	4	—	—
1969						
Feb 9	Jesus Gonalez	Cartagena	TKO	2	—	—
Apr 15	Frank Leroy	Caracas	KO	2	—	—
May 15	Jose Torres	Cartagena	KO	2	—	—
Jun 4	Milton Mendez	Cartagena	W	10	—	—
Aug 15	Francisco Bolivar	Caracas	L	10	—	—
Nov 10	Antonio Gomez	Caracas	L	10	—	—
1970						
Feb 20	Pedro Chirinos	Caracas	W	10	—	—
Mar 12	Diego Tovar	Caracas	KO	1	—	—
Nov 6	Jorge Rodriguez	San Jose, CA	KO	8	—	—
Dec 10	Rodolfo Gonzalez	Los Angeles	TKO	8	—	135
1971						
Feb 18	❿ Enrique Jana	Los Angeles	TKO	8	—	—
May 28	Lupe Ramirez	Caracas	W	10	—	—
Jul 10	Gerardo Ferrat	Valencia, Venezuela	W	10	—	—

Oct 18	Julio Viera	Caracas	W	10	—	—
Dec 11	♛ Nicolino Locche	Buenos Aires	L	15	For-World-JW	138

1972

Mar 10	Jose Escudero	Barranquilla	KO	1	—	—
Apr 26	Frank Medina	Barranquilla	KO	8	—	141
Aug 19	Lupe Ramirez	Maracay, Venezuela	W	10	—	—
Oct 28	⑩ Alfonso Frazer	Panama City	TKO	10	Won-World-JW	139

1973

Feb 16	Josue Marquez	Hato Rey, PR	W	15	Ret-World-JW	140
Mar 17	Nicolino Locche	Maracay	TKO	10	Ret-World-JW	139
Apr 28	Benny Huertas	Cali, Colombia	KO	1	—	—
May 19	⑩ Alfonso Frazer	Panama City	TKO	5	Ret-World-JW	139
Jul 20	Rey Mercado	Barranquilla	TKO	5	—	—
Sep 8	⑩ Carlos Gimenez	Bogota	TKO	5	Ret-World-JW	139
Dec 5	Lion Furuyama	Panama City	W	15	Ret-World-JW	139

1974

Mar 20	Chang-Kil Lee	Cartagena	KO	6	Ret-World-JW	140
Jun 8	Pedro Adigue	Maracay	KO	5	—	—
Jul 28	⑩ Victor Ortiz	Cartagena	KO	2	Ret-World-JW	139
Oct 26	Shinichi Kadoto	Tokyo	KO	8	Ret-World-JW	140

1975

Mar 15	Ray Guerrero	Caracas	TKO	2	—	—
May 17	⑩ Esteban De Jesus	Panama City	W	15	Ret-World-JW	139
Sep 20	Kiyoshi Kazama	Caracas	TKO	6	—	—
Nov 15	⑩ Hector Thompson	Panama City	TKO	8	Ret-World-JW	139

1976

Mar 6	Wilfred Benitez★	San Juan, PR	L	15	Lost-World-JW	140
May 22	Javier Ayala	Maracay	KO	1	—	—
Jul 17	Beau Jaynes	Maracay	W	10	—	—
Oct 16	Ariel Maciel	Maracay	KO	2	—	—
Nov 13	⑩ Saoul Mamby	Maracay	W	10	—	—

1977

Mar 19	Adriano Marrero	Maracay	W	10	—	—
Jun 25	Carlos Gimenez	Maracaibo, Venezuela	TKO	6	Won-Vac-World-JW	139
Nov 5	Adriano Marrero	Maracay	W	15	Ret-World-JW	139

1978

Mar 10	Johnny Copeland	Caracas	TKO	3	—	—
Apr 28	Tongta Kiatvayupak	Udon Thani, Thailand	KO	6	Ret-World-JW	140
Aug 26	Norman Sekgapane	Mmabatho, South Africa	TKO	9	Ret-World-JW	139

1979

Jan 18	⑩ Miguel Montilla	New York	W	15	Ret-World-JW	140
Aug 25	⑩ Kwang-Min Kim	Seoul	W	15	Ret-World-JW	139

1980

Mar 29	⑩ Miguel Montilla	Cartagena	TKO	7	Ret-World-JW	139
Aug 2	⑩ Aaron Pryor★	Cincinnati	KO'd	4	Lost-World-JW	139

1981

Dec 4	⑩ Lennox Blackmoore	Bogota	KO	9	—	—

1982

Apr 2	Jerome Artis	Cartagena	W	10	—	—

1983

Mar 26	Amancio Castro	Cartagena	W	12	Won-Vac-CenAm-JW	140
Jul 30	Sergio Alvarez	Cartagena	TKO	11	Ret-CenAm-JW	140
Dec 9	Danny Sanchez	Miami	L	10	—	—

Cervantes had three formal amateur bouts before turning professional at the age of eighteen in 1964. Venezuelan Ramiro Machado, who believed that the raw Cervantes could develop into a fine fighter, purchased Cervantes' contract and moved him to Venezuela. Cervantes' uncle nicknamed his nephew "Kid Pambele" after a favorite Nicaraguan fighter.

In 1970, Cervantes outfought his first ranked opponent, Enrique Jana. The next year, Cervantes challenged for the world junior welterweight title held by Niccolino Loche. Fighting gamely on Loche's home turf, Luna Park in Buenos Aires, Cervantes lost a fifteen-round decision.

After Loche lost the title to Alfonso ("Peppermint") Frazer, Cervantes faced Frazer in the champion's native Panama on October 28, 1972. Cervantes knocked Frazer down three times before the fight was stopped in the tenth round. The first world champion in Colombian history, Cervantes became a national hero. He met with the president and other national political leaders and, through his influence, electricity was first brought to Palenque.

Cervantes defended his title successfully ten times. In these ten defenses, the power-punching Cervantes recorded seven knockouts. Cervantes' reign came to an end in 1976 when he lost a split decision to Hall of Famer Wilfred Benitez. Benitez, just seventeen, became the youngest-ever world champion. After the loss, Cervantes continued to pursue the title, scoring victories over future champion Saoul Mamby and

In Independence Stadium, Mmabatho, Bophuthatswana on August 26, 1978, Cervantes (R) successfully defends his WBA junior welterweight belt with a nine-round TKO of Norman ("Pangaman") Sekgapane.

ranked contender Adriano Marrero. On June 25, 1977 in Maracaibo, Venezuela, Cervantes fought Carlos Giminez to determine a new WBA junior welterweight champion. Cervantes stopped Giminez in the sixth round.

Cervantes defended his title six times over the next three years. It took another Hall of Famer to dethrone Cervantes. Aaron Pryor scored a TKO in the fourth round of their August 2, 1980 bout. (This fight was on the same card as Hearns–Cuevas, when Tommy Hearns took the WBA welterweight title.) Cervantes won the Central American and Caribbean Super Lightweight titles before retiring in 1983.

Shortly before the end of Cervantes' career, Colombia's national boxing commission suspended him for 90 days for drunken and improper behavior. Although Cervantes invested in apartments, a ranch, houses, and Colombian boxing promotions, he spent much of his earnings on drugs, drinking, and partying. Reportedly, he had several brushes with the law including an arrest for beating up drug dealers. Hospitalized for drug and alcohol addiction in Colombia, Cervantes was then sent to a Cuban psychiatric hospital. After his release, he worked as a trainer in Cartagena, Colombia, not far from Palenque.

JEFF CHANDLER
Joltin' Jeff

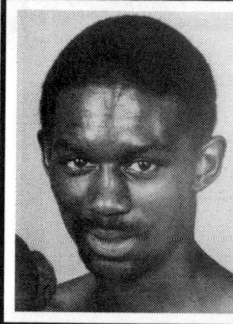

BANTAMWEIGHT

Right-handed; 5'7"; 113–121 lbs.

37 bouts, 2/25/1976 to 4/7/1984

Manager: "KO" Becky O'Neil

WBA Bantamweight Champion
1980–1984

Hall of Fame Induction: 2000

Born: 9/3/1956, Philadelphia

In 1980, Jeff Chandler became the first American in 30 years—since the championship reign of Manuel Ortiz—to hold the world bantamweight title.

Unlike many boxers, Chandler had not set his sights on boxing at an early age. Chandler did not box formally until he was nineteen, but he learned a good bit about fighting on the streets of South Philly. The son of a construction worker, he joined street gangs while attending Bartlett Junior High at the same time as fellow Hall of Famer Matthew Saad Muhammad.

After high school, Chandler worked in construction, but a trip to a local gym with one of his friends galvanized his interest in boxing. After only two months of training, Chandler won his first amateur fight. His next bout was less successful—a loss to the more experienced Johnny Carter—but shortly thereafter Chandler turned professional.

On February 25, 1976, Chandler fought a four-round draw with lefty Mike Dowling, and less than two months later he recorded his first victory in a four-round decision over Chico Vivas. At that point in his career, Chandler had not yet developed the punching power that would be central to his success, yet he went undefeated through his next seven fights of which six were decision victories.

In 1978, KO Becky O'Neil and her husband, Willie, took Chandler under their wings. The O'Neills were long-time Philadelphia fight fans who took a liking to Chandler after watching some of his early fights. A former vaudevillian and national jitterbug champion, the diminutive Mrs. O'Neill became Chandler's manager, while her husband trained him. The pair developed a close bond with Chandler, regarding him as one of their

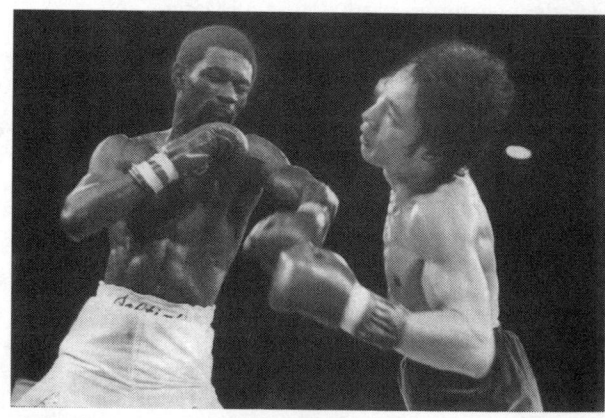

Chandler's (L) first meeting with tough Japanese bantamweight Eijiro Murata ended in a draw, but his next two title defenses were knockout victories. Chandler sends a stunned Murata to the canvas with a left hook.

IN THE RING	WON 33	LOST 2	DRAWS 2	TB 37	KO 18	W 15	WF 0	D 2	KO'd 1	L 1	LF 0

Date	Opponent	Site	Result / Rounds		Title	Wt.
1976						
Feb 25	Mike Dowling	Scranton, PA	D	4	—	117
Apr 13	Chico Vivas	Philadelphia	W	4	—	118
Jun 8	Mike Frazier	Philadelphia	W	4	—	116
Aug 6	John Glover	Philadelphia	W	4	—	116
Oct 14	Larry Huffin	Wilmington, DE	KO	3	—	116
Nov 30	Tony ("Pee Wee") Stokes	Philadelphia	W	4	—	115
1977						
Feb 21	Fernando Sanchez	Philadelphia	W	6		117
Jun 15	John Glover	Philadelphia	W	6	—	116
Oct 25	Tony Reed	Philadelphia	W	8	—	115
1978						
Mar 14	Tony Hernandez	Philadelphia	KO	2	—	117
May 24	Jose Luis Garcia	Philadelphia	KO	5	—	116
Jun 19	Roque Moreno	Philadelphia	KO	5	—	117
Aug 24	Sergio Reyes	Philadelphia	W	8	—	116
Oct 24	Andres Torres	Philadelphia	W	10	—	117
Dec 5	Rafael Gandarilla	Philadelphia	KO	9	—	116
1979—						
Apr 3	Davey Vasquez	Philadelphia	W	10	—	118
May 14	Justo Garcia	Philadelphia	W	10	—	118
Jul 31	Alberto Cruz	Atlantic City	KO	3	—	114
Sep 26	Baby Kid Chocolate	Upper Darby, CT	KO	9	Won-Vac-USBA-B	117
Dec 4	Francisco Alvarado	Upper Darby	KO	7	—	118
1980						
Feb 1	Javier Flores	Philadelphia	KO	10	Won-Vac-NABF-B	118
Mar 29	Andres Hernandez	Atlantic City	W	12	—	116
Jul 12	Gilberto Villacana	Atlantic City	KO	4	—	117
Jul 31	Gustavo Martinez	Atlantic City	KO	8	—	118
Nov 14 ♛	Julian Solis	Miami	KO	14	Won-World-B	118
1981						
Jan 31 ⑩	Jorge Lujan	Philadelphia	W	15	Ret-World-B	113
Apr 4 ⑩	Eijiro Murata	Tokyo	D	15	Ret-World-B	115
Jul 25 ⑩	Julian Solis	Atlantic City	KO	7	Ret-World-B	115
Dec 10 ⑩	Eijiro Murata	Atlantic City	KO	13	Ret-World-B	117
1982						
Mar 27 ⑩	Johnny Carter	Philadelphia	KO	6	Ret-World-B	117
Oct 27	Miguel Iriarte	Atlantic City	KO	9	Ret-World-B	117
1983						
Mar 13 ⑩	Gaby Canizales	Atlantic City	W	15	Ret-World-B	118
May 22	Hector Cortez	Atlantic City	W	10	—	121
Jul 23 ⑩	Oscar Muniz	Atlantic City	L	10	—	121
Sep 10	Eijiro Murata	Tokyo	KO	10	Ret-World-B	118
Dec 17 ⑩	Oscar Muniz	Atlantic City	KO	6	Ret-World-B	116
1984						
Apr 7 ⑩	Richard Sandoval	Atlantic City	KO'd	15	Lost-World-B	118

family. Meanwhile, promoter Russell Peltz also became a part of the growing Chandler team.

For his part, Chandler continued to rack up victories. On September 26, 1979, Chandler knocked out Baby Kid Chocolate in nine rounds to win the vacant USBA bantamweight title. Two fights later, Chandler added the vacant North American Boxing Federation bantamweight title, stopping Javier Flores in ten rounds. He was subsequently offered a title shot against WBC super bantamweight champ Wilfredo Gomez. Knowing that Chandler had difficulty bulking up to the 118-pound bantamweight limit, let alone the 122-pound super bantamweight level, O'Neill turned down the fight. She and Chandler also rejected an offer to fight WBC bantamweight champion Lupe Pintor in a non-title match, not wanting to have to defeat him twice to win the championship.

In 1980, it appeared that Chandler was in line for a fight against Pintor, but on July 31 of that year, he fought Pintor's sparring partner, Gustavo Martinez, in Atlantic City. He easily defeated Martinez with an eight-round knockout, and the proposed Pinter title fight never materialized. Martinez had reportedly warned Pintor away from "Joltin' Jeff."

Instead, Chandler signed on to face WBA bantamweight champion Julian Solis—as yet undefeated—on November 14, 1980. The fight was held at the Miami Jai-Alai Fronton before a crowd of over five thousand fans, many of whom taunted Chandler as he waited in his corner for the opening bell. They were forced to eat their words as Chandler took command from the start. He spun Solis

Chandler (R) is on his way to a six-round successful title defense when he lands this counterpunch to the left cheek of Oscar Muniz in Atlantic City on December 17, 1983

away from him after a clinch and followed with a left hook that knocked the champ to the canvas. When Solis made a move to get inside, Chandler warded him off with right uppercuts and cut Solis's right eye in the third. He continued to hold firm as Solis annoyed him with a lunging left hook, followed by clutching and grabbing. Chandler landed a left hook in the eighth that hurt the champ. Though Solis rallied towards the end of each of the next few rounds, he never hurt Chandler. Finally, Chandler drove Solis against the ropes with a succession of potent rights, continuing the barrage until the referee stopped the fight at 1:05 of the fourteenth round.

Chandler's first title defense came less than three months later on January 31, 1981, when he faced former champion Jorge Lujan in the ballroom of a Philadelphia hotel before a national television audience. Lujan's side-to-side movement allowed him to slip many of Chandler's shots. However the champion landed enough left hooks and hard, straight rights to win a unanimous decision.

In his next defense, Chandler managed a draw against Eijiro Murata in Tokyo. He followed this fight with three against old opponents, knocking out Solis and Murata, and then his old amateur foe, Carter. Yet outside the ring Chandler began to run into problems. He was charged with possession of cocaine and marijuana. Though he claimed he was set up, he received six months probation. Then, two months before his scheduled fight with Miguel Iriarte, Chandler was stabbed in the back with a broken bottle after an altercation with a motorist that quickly escalated into a large brawl. He did not postpone the upcoming fight, and Chandler managed to stop Iriarte in the ninth.

In a non-title fight on July 23, 1983, Chandler suffered his first defeat at the hands of Oscar Muniz. Chandler accepted the fight on short notice and didn't take his opponent seriously. In their rematch, this time with the title at stake, Chandler opened a cut over Muniz's left eye in the second round and continued to administer punishment into the seventh round, when the fight was stopped with Chandler the victor.

Chandler's title reign came to an abrupt end on April 7, 1984, when Richie Sandoval dominated him over fifteen rounds to win an easy decision. Though only 27, Chandler retired after undergoing cataract surgery later that year. He considered returning to the ring, but he never did. In his relatively short career, Chandler had become known as a stylish fighter, and a hard-hitting boxer. In retirement, he works as a trainer.

Chandler's (R) title proved unattainable for world-ranked fellow Philadelphian Johnny Carter. Carter succumbed in six on March 27, 1982.

EZZARD CHARLES
The Cincinnati Cobra

HEAVYWEIGHT

Right-handed; 6'; 160–190 lbs.

122 bouts, 3/15/1940 to 9/1/1959

Managers: Jake Mintz and Tom Tannas

NBA Heavywt. Champ 1949–50, World Heavywt. Champ 1950–51

Hall of Fame Induction: 1990

Born: 7/7/1921, Lawrenceville, GA

Named: Ezzard Mack Charles

Died: 5/27/1975

One of the most underrated of the former heavyweight champions, Ezzard Charles compiled an outstanding record in his nineteen-year professional career. He fought in thirteen championship bouts and triumphed over some of the best boxers of his day.

Charles was born in Georgia but grew up in Cincinnati. As an amateur, he was unbeatable, winning 42 consecutive fights, including Golden Gloves and other tournament championships. He turned professional in 1940 after winning the 1939 National Amateur Athletic Union middleweight title. Charles started fighting as a middleweight before moving up to light heavyweight and, ultimately, to the heavyweight division. He earned a reputation as both a clever boxer and a hard puncher. Among those vanquished early in his career are Hall of Famers Charley Burley, Joey Maxim, and Archie Moore.

The death of an opponent shocked Charles in 1948. He was fresh from his third victory over Moore, when he faced Sam Baroudi in Chicago. In the final round of this fight, Charles unleashed a devastating knockout attack. Baroudi never recovered and died a few days after the fight. Baroudi's death affected Charles deeply, and observers saw a change in his style from that point on. Although he was criticized for being too conservative, Charles no longer possessed the desire to finish his opponents off in the manner which had earned him the nickname, "The Cincinnati Cobra."

In 1949, Charles decisioned Jersey Joe Walcott in Chicago to win the National Boxing Association heavyweight title—vacant after Joe Louis's retirement. Charles defended this title three times, but it

An over-the-hill Joe Louis (R) grimaces from a blow to his side by Charles on September 27, 1950. Charles won the vacant heavyweight championship.

IN THE RING	WON 96	LOST 25	DRAWS 1	TB 122	KO 58	W 38	WF 0	D 1	KO'd 7	L 17	LF 1

Date	Opponent	Site	Result / Rounds		Title	Wt.
1940						
Mar 15	Medley Johnson	Middletown	KO	3	—	—
Mar 20	Jimmy Brown	Reading, PA	KO	2	—	—
Mar 27	John Reeves	Cincinnati	W	6	—	—
Apr 2	Charley Banks	Cincinnati	W	6	—	—
Apr 10	Kid Ash	Portsmouth, OH	KO	3	—	—
Apr 16	Charley Banks	Cincinnati	KO	2	—	—
Apr 24	Remo Fernandez	Cincinnati	KO	6	—	—
May 10	Eddie Fowler	Portsmouth	KO	3	—	—
May 17	Pat Wright	Middletown	KO	4	—	—
Jun 5	Frankie Williams	Cincinnati	KO	7	—	—
Jun 12	John Reeves	Columbus, OH	KO	4	—	—
Jun 24	Bradley Lewis	San Francisco	KO	3	—	—
Sep 23	Marty Simmons	Cincinnati	W	10	—	—
Oct 3	Billy Hood	Cincinnati	KO	2	—	—
Dec 2	Charley Jerome	Cincinnati	KO	2	—	—
1941						
Feb 10	Billy Bengal	Cincinnati	W	10	—	—
Feb 22	Slaka Cavrich	Cincinnati	KO	2	—	—
Mar 10	Floyd Howard	Cincinnati	KO	7	—	—
Mar 31	Joe Sutka	Cincinnati	W	10	—	—
May 12	Rudy Kozole	Cincinnati	W	10	—	—
Jun 9 ⑩	Ken Overlin	Cincinnati	L	10	—	—
Jul 21	Al Gilbert	Cincinnati	KO	6	—	—
Oct 13	Pat Mangini	Cincinnati	KO	1	—	—
Nov 17 ⑩	Teddy Yarosz	Cincinnati	W	10	—	—
1942						
Jan 12 ⑩	Anton Christoforidis	Cincinnati	KO	3	—	—
Mar 2 ⑩	Ken Overlin	Cincinnati	D	10	—	—
Apr 8	Billy Pryor	Cincinnati	W	10	—	—
May 13 ⑩	Kid Tunero	Cincinnati	L	10	—	—
May 25 ⑩	Charley Burley★	Pittsburgh	W	10	—	—
Jun 29 ⑩	Charley Burley★	Pittsburgh	W	10	—	—
Jul 14	Steve Mamakos	Cincinnati	KO	1	—	—
Jul 27 ⑩	Booker Beckwith	Pittsburgh	KO	9	—	—
Aug 17 ⑩	Jose Basora	Pittsburgh	KO	5	—	—
Sep 15 ⑩	Mose Brown	Pittsburgh	KO	6	—	—
Oct 27 ⑩	Joey Maxim★	Pittsburgh	W	10	—	—
Dec 1 ⑩	Joey Maxim★	Cleveland	W	10	—	—
1943						
Jan 7 ⑩	Jimmy Bivins★	Cleveland	L	10	—	—
Mar 31 ⑩	Lloyd Marshall	Cleveland	KO'd	8	—	—
1946						
Feb 18	Al Sheridan	Cincinnati	KO	2	—	—
Mar 25	Tee Hubert	Cincinnati	W	10	—	—
Apr 1	Billy Duncan	Pittsburgh	KO	4	—	—
Apr 15	Georgie Parks	Pittsburgh	KO	6	—	—
May 13	Tee Hubert	Cincinnati	KO	4	—	—
May 20 ⑩	Archie Moore★	Pittsburgh	W	10	—	—

Date		Opponent	Location	Result	Rounds	Title	
Jun 13		Sheldon Bell	Youngstown, OH	KO	5	—	—
Jul 29	⑩	Lloyd Marshall	Cincinnati	KO	6	—	—
Sep 23	⑩	Billy Smith	Cincinnati	W	10	—	—
Nov 12		Jimmy Bivins★	Pittsburgh	W	10	—	—
1947							
Feb 17	⑩	Billy Smith	Cleveland	KO	5	—	—
Mar 10		Jimmy Bivins★	Cleveland	KO	4	—	—
Apr 4		Erv Sarlin	Pittsburgh	W	10	—	—
May 5	⑩	Archie Moore★	Cincinnati	W	10	—	—
Jul 14	⑩	Fitzie Fitzpatrick	Cincinnati	KO	5	—	—
Jul 25	⑩	Elmer Ray	New York	L	10	—	—
Sep 16		Joe Matisi	Buffalo	W	10	—	—
Sep 29	⑩	Lloyd Marshall	Cincinnati	KO	2	—	—
Oct 16		Al Smith	Akron, OH	KO	4	—	—
Oct 27		Clarence Jones	Huntington	KO	1	—	—
Nov 3		Teddy Randolph	Buffalo	W	10	—	—
Dec 2	⑩	Fitzie Fitzpatrick	Cleveland	KO	4	—	—
1948							
Jan 13	⑩	Archie Moore★	Cleveland	KO	8	—	—
Feb 20		Sam Baroudi	Chicago	KO	10	—	—
May 7	⑩	Elmer Ray	Chicago	KO	9	—	—
May 20		Erv Sarlin	Buffalo	W	10	—	—
Sep 13	⑩	Jimmy Bivins★	Washington, DC	W	10	—	—
Nov 14		Walter Hafer	Cincinnati	KO	7	—	—
Dec 10	⑩	Joe Baksi	New York	KO	11	—	—
1949							
Feb 7		Johnny Haynes	Philadelphia	KO	8	—	—
Feb 28	⑩	Joey Maxim★	Cincinnati	W	15	—	—
Jun 22	⑩	Jersey Joe Walcott★	Chicago	W	15	Won-Vac-NBA-H	—
Aug 10	⑩	Gus Lesnevich	New York	TKO	7	Ret-NBA-H	—
Oct 14	⑩	Pat Valentino	San Francisco	KO	8	Ret-NBA-H	—
1950							
Aug 15		Freddie Beshore	Buffalo	TKO	14	Ret-NBA-H	—
Sep 27	⑩	Joe Louis★	New York	W	15	Won-Vac-World-H	—
Dec 5	⑩	Nick Barone	Cincinnati	KO	11	Ret-World-H	—
1951							
Jan 12	⑩	Lee Oma	New York	TKO	10	Ret-World-H	—
Mar 7	⑩	Jersey Joe Walcott★	Detroit	W	15	Ret-World-H	—
May 30	♛	Joey Maxim★	Chicago	W	15	Ret-World-H	—
Jul 18	⑩	Jersey Joe Walcott★	Pittsburgh	KO'd	7	Lost-World-H	—
Oct 10	⑩	Rex Layne	Pittsburgh	TKO	11	—	—
Dec 12	♛	Joey Maxim★	San Francisco	W	12	—	—
Dec 21		Joe Kahut	Portland, OR	KO	8	—	—
1952							
Jun 5	♛	Jersey Joe Walcott★	Philadelphia	L	15	For-World-H	—
Aug 8	⑩	Rex Layne	Ogden, UT	L	10	—	—
Oct 8		Bernie Reynolds	Cincinnati	KO	2	—	—
Oct 24	⑩	Cesar Brion	New York	W	10	—	—
Nov 26	⑩	Jimmy Bivins★	Chicago	W	10	—	—
Dec 15		Frank Buford	Boston	TKO	7	—	—
1953							
Jan 14		Wes Bascom	St. Louis	TKO	9	—	—
Feb 4	⑩	Tommy Harrison	Detroit	TKO	9	—	—
Apr 1		Rex Layne	San Francisco	W	10	—	—
May 12		Bill Gilliam	Toledo, OH	W	10	—	—
May 26		Larry Watson	Milwaukee	KO	5	—	—

Date		Opponent	Location	Result	Rounds		
Aug 11	⑩	Nino Valdes	Miami Beach	L	10	—	—
Sep 8	⑩	Harold Johnson★	Philadelphia	L	10	—	—
Dec 16	⑩	Coley Wallace	San Francisco	KO	10	—	—
1954							
Jan 13	⑩	Bob Satterfield	Chicago	KO	2	—	—
Jun 17	♛	Rocky Marciano★	New York	L	15	For-World-H	—
Sep 17	♛	Rocky Marciano★	New York	KO'd	8	For-World-H	—
1955							
Feb 18	⑩	Charley Norkus	New York	W	10	—	—
Apr 11		Vern Escoe	Edmonton, Alberta	KO	3	—	—
Apr 27	⑩	John Holman	Miami Beach	KO'd	9	—	—
Jun 8	⑩	John Holman	Cincinnati	W	10	—	—
Jul 13	⑩	Paul Andrews	Chicago	W	10	—	—
Aug 3	⑩	Tommy Jackson	Syracuse, NY	L	10	—	—
Aug 31	⑩	Tommy Jackson	Cleveland	L	10	—	—
Nov 14		Toxie Hall	Providence, RI	L	10	—	—
Dec 6		Toxie Hall	Rochester, NY	W	10	—	—
Dec 22		Bob Albright	San Francisco	W	10	—	—
Dec 29	⑩	Young Jack Johnson	Los Angeles	KO'd	6	—	—
1956							
Apr 21		Don Jasper	Windsor, Ont.	KO	9	—	—
May 21	⑩	Wayne Bethea	New York	L	10	—	—
Jun 19		Bob Albright	Phoenix	KO	7	—	—
Jul 13		Pat McMurtry	Tacoma, WA	L	10	—	—
Aug 13		Harry Matthews	Seattle	L	10	—	—
Oct 2		Dick Richardson	London	LD	2	—	—
1958							
Aug 28		Johnny Harper	Fairmont, WV	W	10	—	—
Sep 30		Alfredo Zuany	Juarez, Mexico	L	10	—	—
Oct 27		Donnie Fleeman	Dallas	KO'd	6	—	—
1959							
Jul 3		Dave Ashley	Cincinnati	KO	7	—	—
Jul 30		George Logan	Boise, ID	KO'd	8	—	—
Sep 1		Alvin Green	Oklahoma City, OK	L	10	—	—

took a victory over the deposed king to gain him universal recognition as the world champion. Charles and Louis, who came out of retirement in an effort to recapture his crown, met in Yankee Stadium in 1950. Overweight and past his prime, Louis was no match for Charles, who out-pointed the Brown Bomber with relative ease. Many thought Charles could have knocked out the ex-champ, but Charles appeared to ease off in the later rounds when he had the fight well in hand.

Walcott was Charles's most threatening nemesis, and although Charles held him off in a title challenge in March 1951, Jersey Joe came back to take the crown in July. The fight was held in Forbes Field in Pittsburgh, and Charles fell in the seventh round to a knockout left hook. Charles failed in an attempt to win the title again in 1952 when Walcott outboxed him, and two tries against Walcott's successor, Rocky Marciano, were also unsuccessful.

In retirement, Charles made bad investments in a number of business ventures. He also wrestled professionally. He died in 1975, virtually penniless and after having suffered for several years from lateral sclerosis of the spine, an ailment that eventually paralyzed him from the waist down.

BILLY CONN
The Pittsburgh Kid

LIGHT HEAVYWEIGHT

Right-handed; 6'; 135–187 lbs.
76 bouts, 6/28/1934 to 11/25/1948
Manager: Johnny Ray
Light Heavyweight Champ 1939–41
Hall of Fame Induction: 1990
Born: 10/8/1917, Pittsburgh, PA
Named: William David Conn, Jr.
Died: 5/29/1993

Best known as the contender who could have knocked off Joe Louis's heavyweight crown if he'd been less eager, Billy Conn was a light heavyweight champ with the talent to fight heavyweights on their own terms. Known as "The Pittsburgh Kid," Conn started fighting as a youth in the alleys of the East Liberty section of Pittsburgh. Idolizing another Pittsburgh fighter, Harry Greb, Conn started working in the gym at a young age under the guidance of Johnny Ray. He never fought as an amateur, but went straight into the professional ranks at age sixteen.

Conn began as a lightweight and, as he grew, advanced through the welterweight, middleweight, and light heavyweight ranks. He fought mostly in the Pittsburgh area, where he compiled an impressive record. Not a great puncher, Conn used clever boxing skills and an indomitable spirit to pile up his victories. By 1938, Conn was ranked as the ninth-best light heavyweight contender in *The Ring*'s annual rankings.

Hall of Famer Georges Carpentier looks on from the referee's spot as brothers Jackie and Billy Conn (R) prepare to spar. Carpentier preceded Billy Conn by nineteen years as light heavyweight champion.

IN THE RING	WON 63	LOST 12	DRAWS 1	TB 76	KO 14	W 49	WF 0	D 1	KO'd 3	L 9	LF 0

Date	Opponent	Site	Result / Rounds		Title	Wt.
1934						
Jun 28	Dick Woodward	Fairmont, WV	L	4	—	—
Jul 20	Johnny Lewis	Charleston, SC	KO	3	—	—
Aug 30	Bob Dronan	Parkersburg, WV	W	6	—	—
Sep 27	Paddy Gray	Pittsburg	W	4	—	—
Nov 12	Pete Leone	Wheeling, WV	TKO'd	3	—	—
1935						
Jan 29	Johnny Birek	Pittsburgh	W	6	—	—
Feb 25	Ray Eberle	Pittsburgh	L	6	—	—
Mar 13	Stanley Nagy	Wheeling	W	4	—	—
Apr 8	George Schlee	Pittsburgh	KO	1	—	—
Apr 25	Ralph Gizzy	Pittsburgh	L	4	—	—
Jun 3	Ray Eberle	Millvale, PA	W	6	—	—
Jun 10	Ralph Gizzy	Millvale	L	6	—	—
Jul 9	Teddy Movan	Millvale	L	4	—	—
Jul 29	Ray Eberle	Millvale	W	5	—	—
Aug 19	Teddy Movan	Millvale	L	4	—	—
Sep 9	George Leggins	Pittsburgh	W	4	—	—
Sep 10	Johnny Yurcini	Washington, PA	W	6	—	—
Oct 7	Johnny Yurcini	Johnstown, PA	W	6	—	—
Oct 14	Teddy Movan	Pittsburgh	D	6	—	—
Nov 18	Steve Walters	Pittsburgh	W	6	—	—
1936						
Jan 27	Johnny Yurcini	Pittsburgh	TKO	4	—	—
Feb 3	Kid Cook	Pittsburgh	W	6	—	—
Feb 17	Kid Cook	Pittsburgh	W	8	—	—
Mar 16	Steve Nickleash	Pittsburgh	W	6	—	—
Apr 13	Steve Nickleash	Pittsburgh	W	6	—	—
Apr 27	General Burrows	Pittsburgh	W	6	—	—
May 19	Dick Ambrose	Pittsburgh	W	6	—	—
May 27	Honeyboy Jones	Pittsburgh	W	8	—	—
Jun 3	Honeyboy Jones	Pittsburgh	W	10	—	—
Jun 15	General Burrows	Pittsburgh	W	8	—	—
Jul 30	Teddy Movan	Pittsburgh	W	8	—	—
Aug 10	Teddy Movan	Pittsburgh	W	8	—	—
Sep 8	Honeyboy Jones	Pittsburgh	W	10	—	—
Sep 21	Roscoe Manning	Pittsburgh	KO	5	—	—
Oct 19	Charlie Weise	Pittsburgh	W	10	—	—
Oct 22	Ralph Chong	Pittsburgh	W	10	—	—
Dec 2	Jimmy Brown	Pittsburgh	KO	9	—	—
Dec 28	⑩ Fritzie Zivic★	Pittsburgh	W	10	—	—
1937						
Mar 11	⑩ Babe Risko	Pittsburgh	W	10	—	—
May 3	Vince Dundee	Pittsburgh	W	10	—	—
May 27	⑩ Oscar Rankins	Pittsburgh	W	10	—	—
Jun 30	⑩ Teddy Yarosz	Pittsburgh	W	12	—	—

Aug 13	Ⓚ	Young Corbett III	San Francisco	L	10		—	—
Sep 30	Ⓚ	Teddy Yarosz	Pittsburgh	W	15		—	—
Nov 8	Ⓚ	Young Corbett III	Pittsburgh	W	10		—	—
Dec 16	Ⓚ	Solly Krieger	Pittsburgh	L	12		—	—
1938								
Jan 24		Honeyboy Jones	Pittsburgh	W	12		—	—
Apr 4		Domenic Ceccarelli	Pittsburgh	W	10		—	—
May 10		Eric Seelig	Pittsburgh	W	10		—	—
Jul 25	Ⓚ	Teddy Yarosz	Pittsburgh	L	12		—	—
Sep 14	Ⓚ	Ray Actis	San Francisco	KO	8		—	—
Oct 27		Honeyboy Jones	Pittsburgh	W	10		—	—
Nov 28		Solly Krieger	Pittsburgh	W	12		—	—
1939								
Jan 6		Fred Apostoli	New York	W	10		—	—
Feb 10		Fred Apostoli	New York	W	15		—	—
May 12		Solly Krieger	New York	W	12		—	—
Jul 13	♛	Melio Bettina	New York	W	15	Won-Vac World-LH	170	
Aug 14	Ⓚ	Gus Dorazio	Philadelphia	KO	8		—	—
Sep 25	Ⓚ	Melio Bettina	Pittsburgh	W	15	Ret-World-LH	172	
Nov 17	Ⓚ	Gus Lesnevich	New York	W	15	Ret-World-LH	171	
1940								
Jan 10		Henry Cooper	New York	W	12		—	—
Jun 5	Ⓚ	Gus Lesnevich	Detroit	W	15	Ret-World-LH	173	
Sep 6	Ⓚ	Bob Pastor	New York	KO	13		—	—
Oct 18		Al McCoy	Boston	W	10		—	—
Nov 29	Ⓚ	Lee Savold	New York	W	12		—	—
1941								
Feb 27		Ira Hughes	Clarksburg, WV	KO	4		—	—
Mar 6		Dan Hassett	Washington, DC	KO	5		—	—
Apr 4		Gunnar Barlund	Chicago	TKO	8		—	—
May 26		Buddy Knox	Pittsburgh	KO	8		—	—
Jun 18	♛	Joe Louis★	New York	KO'd	13	For-World-H	174	
1942								
Jan 12		Henry Cooper	Toledo, OH	W	12		—	176
Jan 28		J.D. Turner	St. Louis	W	10		—	—
Feb 13		Tony Zale★	New York	W	12		—	—
1946								
Jun 19	♛	Joe Louis★	New York	KO'd	8	For-World-H	187	
1948								
Nov 15		Mike O'Dowd	Macon, GA	KO	9		—	—
Nov 25		Jackie Lyons	Dallas	KO	9		—	—

In 1939, Conn faced Melio Bettina in New York for the world light heavyweight championship—vacant since the retirement of John Henry Lewis. Conn fell behind in the first six rounds and lost the thirteenth but otherwise dominated the fight. He won the decision to take the title. Conn also won the rematch later that year and twice defended his title against Gus Lesnevich.

In 1941, Conn relinquished the light heavyweight title in order to challenge Joe Louis for the world heavyweight championship. The fight was held in New York's Polo Grounds before 54,486 fans, including 6,000 Conn supporters from Pittsburgh. Louis had been on top for four years. He was 27; Conn was 24. Conn weighed in at 169 pounds, while Louis tipped the scales at 199. Conn looked good, dancing away from Louis's punches and landing a few speedy blows when Louis was off-guard. Although Louis won the first two rounds, Conn won the third and, by the twelfth, was ahead on two cards and even on the third. With a win by decision in the making, Conn made a tactical error in the unlucky thirteenth. Instead of continuing to fight in the same style with which he had built his lead, Conn attempted to take Louis out. He launched into Louis with abandon. Conn's more offensive posture enabled Louis to penetrate, and he knocked Conn out with a right to the jaw. Louis later conceded that the fight had been one of the closest of his career.

A scheduled rematch was postponed due to family problems that demanded Conn's attention. Next, Conn broke his hand, which delayed the rematch until after the end of World War II. Before the rematch finally took place in Yankee Stadium, Louis said of Conn, "He can run but he can't hide." Louis was right. Louis won easily, knocking Conn out in the eighth. Conn fought twice more and then retired.

Conn starred in a movie about himself, called *The Pittsburgh Kid*. Much later, he and his wife were the subjects of a lengthy article by Frank Deford in *Sports Illustrated* titled, "The Boxer and The Blonde."

Conn (L) connects solidly with a jab to Joe Louis's heart. Conn twice challenged the much-larger Louis for the heavyweight championship. In their first meeting, in 1941, he came remarkably close to victory.

Right-handed; 5'8"; 133–173 lbs.

50 bouts, 11/14/1971 to 9/25/1989

Manager: Lupe Sanchez

WBA Welterweight Champion 1976–1980

Hall of Fame Induction: 2002

Born: 12/27/1957, Santo Tomis, Mexico

Named: Isidro Pipino Cuevas Gonzalez

A very popular fighter both in his native Mexico and in the United States, Pipino Cuevas won the world welterweight title when he was just eighteen years old.

Cuevas was born in the Colonia Panamericana section of Mexico City. One of eleven children, Cuevas learned to fight in his tough neighborhood, where he spurned the local gangs, but fought his own individual battles. When he was thirteen, his father, a butcher, took Cuevas to a Mexico City gym to learn to fight properly and to channel his aggression more productively than in street combat. Before he finally became a full-time boxer, Cuevas worked for his father, shined shoes, and sold gum on the street.

Cuevas bypassed the apprenticeship of a lengthy amateur boxing career and turned pro at fourteen, with his first fight on November 14, 1971. He made an inauspicious debut, and was knocked out in the second round. Undeterred, he compiled a seven and five record in his first twelve fights as he gained experience.

By 1974, Cuevas began to exhibit his great ability by winning all four of his fights, three of them one-round knockouts. The next year, he won the Mexican welterweight title with a tenth-round knockout of Jose Palacios, who was later a ranked contender. Cuevas relinquished the belt just seven months later, setting his sights on a world championship. Toward that end, he made his first appearance in the United States on June 2, 1976, when he faced Andy ("Hawk") Price, who had fought 28 fights to Cuevas's twenty. Price won a split decision. WBA welter-

In the sixth round of his first WBA title defense, Cuevas fells Shoji Tsujimoto at Jissen Rinri Stadium in Kanazawa, Japan, on October 27, 1976.

IN THE RING	WON 35	LOST 15	DRAWS 0	TB 50	KO 31	W 4	WF 0	D 0	KO'd 6	L 9	LF 0

Date		Opponent	Site	Result / Rounds		Title	Wt.
1971							
Nov 14		Al Castro	Mexico City	KO'd	2	—	134
1972							
Jan 1		Jose Arias	Mexico City	TKO	4	—	—
Mar 4		Mario Roman	Mexico City	L	6	—	—
May 25		Rielero Rodriguez	Mexico City	TKO	2	—	—
Jun 22		Pancho Benitez/Paco Tapia	Mexico City	TKO	2	—	—
Aug 20		Juan Pablo Oropeza	Mexico City	L	8	—	—
Dec 7		Raul Martinez	Mexico City	KO	1	—	134
1973							
Mar 1		Sergio Alejo	Mexico City	TKO	4	—	133
May 13		Memo Cruz	Mexico City	L	10	—	—
Aug 4		Jose Figueroa	Mexico City	TKO	3	—	144
Oct 7		Octavio Amparan	Mexico City	TKO	7	—	133
Nov 24		Eleazar Delgado	Mexico City	L	10	—	—
1974							
May 11		Salvador Ruvalcaba	Mexico City	KO	1	—	145
Jun 12		Sugar Sanders	Mexico City	TKO	1	—	—
Aug 21		Jose Luis Pena	Mexico City	KO	1	—	—
Oct 26		Sammy Garcia	Mexico City	KO	3	—	143
1975							
Jan 25		Ruben Vasquez	Mexico City	W	10	—	145
Jul 12		Carlos Obregon	Mexico City	W	10	—	145
Sep 27		Jose Palacios	Mexico City	KO	10	Won-Mexico-W	147
1976							
Apr 3		Rafael Piamonte	Mexicali, Mexico	KO	1	—	—
Jun 2		Andy Price	Los Angeles	L	10	—	146
Jul 17	♛	Angel Espada	Mexicali	TKO	2	Won-WBA-W	146
Oct 27		Shoji Tsujimoto	Kanazawa, Japan	TKO	6	Ret-WBA-W	145
1977							
Mar 13	Ⓦ	Miguel Angel Campanino	Mexico City	KO	2	Ret-WBA-W	146
Aug 6	Ⓦ	Clyde Gray	Los Angeles	KO	2	Ret-WBA-W	145
Nov 19	Ⓦ	Angel Espada	San Juan	TKO	12	Ret-WBA-W	147
1978							
Mar 4	Ⓦ	Harold Weston	Los Angeles	TKO	10	Ret-WBA-W	146
May 20	Ⓦ	Billy Backus	Inglewood, CA	TKO	2	Ret-WBA-W	146
Sep 9	Ⓦ	Pete Ranzany	Sacramento, CA	TKO	2	Ret-WBA-W	146
1979							
Jan 29		Scott Clark	Los Angeles	TKO	2	Ret-WBA-W	146
Jul 30	Ⓦ	Randy Shields	Chicago	W	15	Ret-WBA-W	146
Dec 8	Ⓦ	Angel Espada	Los Angeles	TKO	10	Ret-WBA-W	146
1980							
Apr 6		Harold Volbrecht	Houston	KO	5	Ret-WBA-W	146
Aug 2	Ⓦ	Thomas Hearns	Detroit	KO'd	2	Lost-WBA-W	146
1981							
Feb 7		Bernardo Prada	Los Angeles	KO	2	—	147
Jun 25		Joergen Hansen	Houston	TKO	2	—	—
Nov 7	Ⓦ	Roger Stafford	Las Vegas	L	10	—	147

1983					
Jan 29 ⑩	Roberto Duran	Los Angeles	TKO'd	4	— 149
1984					
Mar 1	Mauricio Bravo	Los Angeles	TKO	1	— 150
Jul 12	Jun-Suk Hwang	Los Angeles	L	10	— 150
1985					
Mar 7	Herman Montes	Los Angeles	KO'd	3	— 152
1986					
Feb 25	Felipe Vaca	Inglewood	W	4	— 159
Mar 4	Steve Little	Sacramento	L	10	— 153
Jul 25	Louis Mateo	Chicago	TKO	3	— 155
Oct 4	Lorenzo Garcia	Salta, Argentina	L	10	— 152
Dec 19	Jorge Vaca	Guadalajara, Mexico	KO'd	2	— —
1987					
Jul 25	Daniel Valenzuela	Mexico City	KO	6	— 173
1989					
May 29	Francisco Carballo	Tijuana	KO	4	— —
Jul 31	Martin Martinez	Tijuana	KO	1	— —
Sep 25	Lupe Aquino	Tijuana	KO'd	2	— 160

weight champion Angel Espada was in attendance at the fight, and he picked Cuevas to be his next opponent, expecting that he would be a pushover.

On July 17, 1976, only six weeks after losing to Price, Cuevas entered the ring with Espada in Mexicali, Mexico, for the welterweight crown. The eighteen-year-old made short work of the champion and stopped him in just two rounds to win the world title. In the rematch a year later, one of Cuevas's toughest fights, he scored a technical knockout against Espada in twelve rounds, and broke Espada's jaw in the bargain.

Cuevas did not shy away from defending his title. He won ten defenses by knockout, against such opponents as Espada, contenders Clyde Gray, Harold

Cuevas hones his reflexes on the speed bag.

Weston, and Pete Ranzany, and former champion Billy Backus. In his only victorious title defense that actually went the distance, Cuevas emerged with a unanimous decision on July 30, 1979, over Randy Shields in front of nearly 4,500 fans at the International Amphitheater in Chicago. As usual, Cuevas was the aggressor in the fight. A head butt opened a cut above Shields's right eye in the fourth round, and though Shields jabbed to throw off Cuevas's rhythm and was never knocked down, the champ took the fight on all three cards: 73–71, 71–70 and 73–67.

The fight against Shields was an anomaly because Cuevas did not do any real damage to him with his vaunted left hook. Never fighting on the defensive, Cuevas liked to move forward, work the body, and then unleash his lethal left. He became extremely popular with Mexican fans, though he rarely smiled—even outside the ring.

After knocking out Harold Volbrecht, the confident Cuevas signed on to another defense, this time against Thomas ("Hit Man") Hearns, the Motor City Cobra, in the challenger's hometown of Detroit, on August 2, 1980. Hearns brought Cuevas's title reign to an end with a knockout in the second round.

Six months later, a capacity crowd packed the Olympic Auditorium in Los Angeles to see Cuevas fight for the first time since losing his title. Thousands more had to be turned away. Cuevas did not disappoint, knocking out Bernardo Prada in two rounds. After a decision loss to tenth-ranked contender Roger Stafford on November 7, 1981, Cuevas stayed away from the ring again, this time for over a year, before returning to face Roberto Duran on January 29, 1983. Duran proved too much for Cuevas, knocking him out in four rounds.

Cuevas fought only nine times in the next four years, and won only four of those fights. Finally, after an long hiatus of almost two years, Cuevas fought three times in Tijuana in 1989. When Lupe Aquino beat him with a second-round knockout on September 25, 1989, Cuevas retired for good. Though the last nine years of his career had been a disappointment, Cuevas is remembered for his four-year title reign and his willingness to take on all challengers to his crown.

After his retirement, Cuevas purchased land for each of his brothers and sisters and a new house with a five-horse stable for his parents. He has been active in a number of business ventures in Mexico, including a string of butcher's shops, a restaurant, and a security business. He has even worked in the Mexico City government.

Cuevas enjoys a stroll with boxing writer Rose Trentman and his manager, Lupe Sanchez. Trentman later became a New York State Boxing Commissioner.

GABRIEL ("FLASH") ELORDE

JR. LIGHTWEIGHT

Left-handed; 5'6"; 118–137 lbs.

117 bouts, 6/16/1951 to 5/20/1971

Manager: Lope Sarreal

Jr. Lightweight Champion 1960–67

Hall of Fame Induction: 1993

Born: 3/22/1935, Bogo, Cebu, Philippines

Died: 1/2/1985

Gabriel ("Flash") Elorde, of the Philippines, entered the international boxing scene of the 1950s to become the world junior lightweight champion. A frequent defender of his crown, Elorde had a seven-year reign as champ. Elorde began his career in his hometown of Cebu at the age of sixteen. The next year he won the Filipino bantamweight title, the first of his many Asian and Filipino honors. Within a year, Elorde added the Oriental bantamweight crown to his ring honors. Other regional championships he acquired during his career include the Oriental featherweight, Filipino lightweight, and Oriental lightweight titles.

Elorde first caught the attention of American boxing enthusiasts when he faced world featherweight champion Sandy Saddler in an over-the-weight (nontitle) match in Manila. Elorde won a ten-round decision over Saddler, earning the

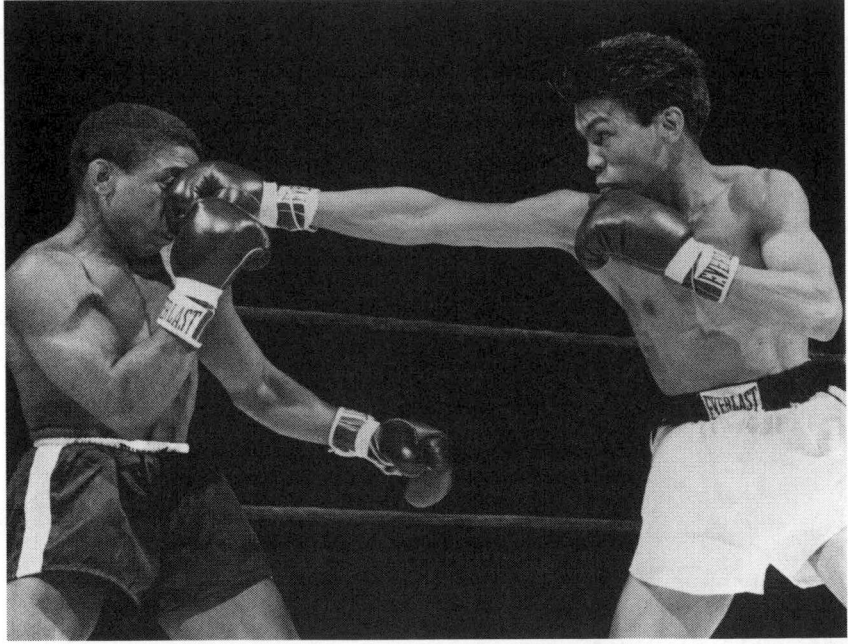

Quick-jabbing Elorde (R) connects to the face of Miguel Berrios in one of their two 1956 meetings. Berrios triumphed in both ten-round decisions. The year 1956 saw Elorde fighting entirely in the U.S.

IN THE RING	WON 88	LOST 27	DRAWS 2	TB 117	KO 33	W 54	WF 1	D 2	KO'd 4	L 23	LF 0

Date	Opponent	Site	Result / Rounds		Title	Wt.
1951						
Jun 16	Kid Gonzaga	Cebu, Philippines	KO	4	—	—
Jun 23	Young Basilian	Cebu	KO	3	—	—
Jun 30	Mike Sanchez	Cebu	W	5	—	—
Jul 14	Kid Santos	Cebu	KO	5	—	—
Jul 28	Star Mercado	Cebu	KO	1	—	—
Aug 11	Fighting Chavez	Cebu	KO	1	—	—
Aug 20	Fighting Chavez	Cebu	KO	7	—	—
Sep 8	Little Patilla	Cebu	KO	6	—	—
Sep 15	Star Flores	Cebu	W	10	—	—
Oct 16	Kid Independence	Cebu	KO'd	10	—	—
Dec 1	Lucky Strike	Cebu	KO	5	—	—
1952						
Jan 30	Tenejeros Boy	Davao, Philippines	W	8	—	—
Feb 24	Little Dundee	Davao	L	8	—	—
Mar 16	Tommy Romulo	Davao	D	10	—	—
May 3	Benny Escobar	Caloocan, Philippines	W	8	—	—
May 10	Paulito Escarlan	Caloocan	W	6	—	—
May 31	Tanny Campo	Caloocan	W	8	—	—
Jul 26	Tanny Campo	Manila	W	12	Won-Philippines-B	118
Aug 12	Little Dundee	Davao	KO	4	Ret-Philippines-B	118
Oct 18	Hiroshi Horiguchi	Tokyo	W	12	Won-Orient-B	118
Nov 18	Akiyoshi Akanuma	Tokyo	D	10	—	—
1953						
Feb 18	Willie Brown	Manila	KO	4	—	—
Mar 15	Al Cruz	Manila	W	10	—	—
May 20	Larry Bataan	Manila	L	12	For-Orient-FE	126
Jul 6	Akiyoshi Akanuma	Tokyo	W	12	Ret-Orient-B	118
Aug 8	Shigeji Kaneko	Nishinomiya, Japan	L	10	—	—
Oct 8	Noboru Tanaka	Tokyo	W	10	—	—
Nov 25	Masashi Akiyama	Tokyo	L	10	For-Japan-JL	127
1954						
Jan 21	Kiyoaki Nakanishi	Tokyo	W	10	—	127
Apr 21	Hiroshi Okawa	Tokyo	W	10	—	128
Jun 29	Shigeji Kaneko	Tokyo	L	12	For-Orient-FE	125
Aug 5	Roy Higa	Tokyo	W	10	—	—
Aug 18	Tommy Romulo	Manila	W	12	Won-Philippines-L	131
Nov 20	Katsumi Kosaka	Manila	KO	8	—	—
Nov 27	Masashi Akiyama	Manila	W	10	—	130
1955						
Jan 12	Masashi Akiyama	Tokyo	L	10	—	131
Apr 15	Severo Fuentes	Manila	W	10	—	—
Jun 15	Leo Alonzo	Manila	L	12	Lost-Philippines-L	135
Jul 20	♛ Sandy Saddler★	Manila	W	10	—	129
Oct 3	Shigeji Kaneko	Tokyo	L	10	—	—
1956						
Jan 18	♛ Sandy Saddler★	San Francisco	TKO'd	13	For-World-FE	125
Apr 23	Cleo Lane	San Francisco	KO	1	—	129

Date		Opponent	Location	Result	Rounds	Title	Weight
May 8		Chico Rosa	Stockton, CA	W	10	—	129
Jun 11		Gil Velarde	San Francisco	TKO	7	—	130
Jun 26		Cecil Schoonmaker	Stockton	KO	9	—	130
Jul 24		Dave Gallardo	San Jose, CA	W	10	—	—
Aug 22	⑩	Miguel Berrios	San Francisco	L	10	—	129
Oct 16		Luke Sandoval	San Jose	KO	2	—	130
Nov 9	⑩	Miguel Berrios	New York	L	10	—	—
1957							
Feb 5		Hidemi Wada	Osaka, Japan	KO	5	—	130
Mar 16		Tommy Romulo	Manila	W	12	Reg-Philippines-L	135
Apr 27		Hideto Kobayashi	Nagoya, Japan	W	12	Won-Vac Orient-L	135
Jun 23		Omsap Laempapha	Bangkok	L	12	Lost-Orient-L	135
Aug 4		Salika Yontrakit	Bangkok	KO	3	—	—
Sep 24		Shigeji Kaneko	Tokyo	L	10	—	130
Oct 23		Leo Alonzo	Manila	W	12	Reg-Philippines-L	135
1958							
Mar 2		Hiroshi Okawa	Tokyo	W	12	Reg-Orient-L	135
May 3		Javellana Kid	Manila	W	12	Ret-Orient-L	131
Jun 10	⑩	Ike Chestnut	Honolulu	W	10	—	128
Sep 2		Hisao Kobayashi	Tokyo	W	12	Ret-Orient-L	135
Nov 15		Keiichi Ishikawa	Manila	TKO	6	Ret-Orient-L	132
Dec 27		Kiyoaki Nakanishi	Davao	TKO	3	—	—
1959							
Feb 6		Takeo Sugimori	Tokyo	W	12	Ret-Orient-L	135
Feb 23	⑩	Paolo Rosi	San Francisco	L	10	—	—
Mar 31		Teddy Davis	Stockton	W	10	—	133
May 25	⑩	Sonny Leon	Caracas, Venezuela	W	10	—	130
Jun 15		Vicente Rivas	Caracas	L	10	—	—
Jul 29		Solomon Boysaw	Cleveland	L	10	—	—
Oct 7		Hisao Kobayashi	Tokyo	W	12	Ret-Orient-L	135
Nov 26		Isami Ikeyama	Tokyo	TKO	4	—	—
Dec 15		Nursery Kid	Manila	W	10	—	—
1960							
Mar 16	♛	Harold Gomes	Quezon, Philippines	KO	7	Won-World-JL	130
Jul 9		Hachiro Ito	Manila	TKO	5	—	135
Aug 17	⑩	Harold Gomes	San Francisco	KO	1	Ret-World-JL	130
Oct 17		Sakuzi Shinozawa	Manila	W	12	Ret-Orient-L	135
Dec 16		Vicente Rivas	Manila	W	10	—	—
1961							
Mar 19		Joey Lopes	Manila	W	15	Ret-World-JL	130
May 31		Giordano Campari	Manila	W	10	—	—
Sep 2		Teruo Kosaka	Manila	W	12	Ret-Orient-L	135
Dec 16	⑩	Sergio Caprari	Manila	TKO	1	Ret-World-JL	130
1962							
Mar 10		Somkiat Katmuangyon	Manila	KO	2	Ret-Orient-L	135
Apr 30		Teruo Kosaka	Tokyo	L	12	Lost-Orient-L	135
Jun 23	⑩	Auburn Copeland	Manila	W	15	Ret-World-JL	130
Aug 4		Teruo Kosaka	Cebu	W	12	Reg-Orient-L	135
Nov 17		Isarasak Puntainorasing	Manila	TKO	3	—	—
Dec 21		Solomon Boysaw	Manila	W	10	—	—
1963							
Feb 16	⑩	John Bizzarro	Manila	W	15	Ret-World-JL	130
Jun 1		Tsunstomi Miyamoto	Manila	TKO	9	Ret-Orient-L	135
Aug 3	⑩	Love Allotey	Manila	W	10	—	—
Nov 16	⑩	Love Allotey	Quezon	WD	11	Ret-World-JL	130

1964							
Feb 15	♔ Carlos Ortiz★	Manila	TKO'd	14	For-World-L	135
May 8	Tadashi Matsumoto	Manila	W	12	Ret-Orient-L	135
Jul 27	⑩ Teruo Kosaka	Tokyo	TKO	12	Ret-World-JL	130
Nov 21	⑩ Kang-II Suh	Manila	W	12	Ret-Orient-L	135
1965						
Feb 27	⑩ Rene Barrientos	Manila	W	12	Ret-Orient-L	135
Jun 5	⑩ Teruo Kosak	Quezon	KO	15	Ret-World-JL	130
Aug 5	Frankie Narvaez	New York	W	10	—	135
Dec 4	⑩ Kang-II Suh	Quezon	W	15	Ret-World-JL	130
1966						
Mar 19	⑩ Ismael Laguna★	Tokyo	W	10	—	135
Jun 9	Yoshiaki Numata	Tokyo	L	12	Lost-Orient-L	135
Aug 7	Percy Hayles	Quezon	W	10	—	
Oct 22	Vicente Derado	Quezon	W	15	Ret-World-JL	130
Nov 14	♔ Carlos Ortiz★	New York	KO'd	14	For-World-L	134
1967						
Feb 2	⑩ Kang-II Suh	Manila	W	10	—	—
Apr 25	Fujio Mikami	Honolulu	W	10	—	—
Jun 15	⑩ Yoshiaki Numata	Tokyo	L	15	Lost-World-JL	130
Oct 28	Akihisa Someya	Manila	L	10	—	—
1969						
Feb 15	Eugenio Espinoza	Quito, Ecuador	L	10	—	137
Apr 26	⑩ Jaguar Kakizama	Quezon	L	10	—	—
1970						
Apr 10	Mongai Munchai	Manila	KO	5	—	—
May 16	Isao Ichihara	Davao	KO	9	—	—
Jun 27	Kenji Iwata	Manila	W	10	—	136
Aug 28	Chico Andrade	Manila	TKO	5	—	134
Oct 31	Tatsunao Mitsuyama	Quezon	W	10	—	—
Dec 18	Isao Ichihara	Agana, Guam	L	10	—	—
1971						
Feb 14	Isao Ichihara	Quezon	KO	6	—	—
May 20	Hiroyuki Murakami	Tokyo	L	10	—	—

right to face the champ for his title. The bout, which took place at the Cow Palace in San Francisco in 1956, marked Elorde's first appearance in America. The win was awarded to Saddler, despite the fact that he trailed on points, when it was stopped in the thirteenth round to prevent further damage to a cut over Elorde's eye.

For the next few years, Elorde honed his skills with fights in American, Japanese, and Pacific Rim cities. Loaded down with Asian titles, Elorde again climbed into the ring in 1960, for a chance at a world title. He faced Harold Gomes, holder of the world junior lightweight title. This weight class had been reinstituted in 1959 after not having a champion for almost 25 years. Elorde knocked Gomes out in seven rounds. In a return match, Elorde laid Gomes out in less than two minutes. Elorde proved to be a lasting champion. Fighting mostly on home turf, he successfully defended the title ten times before losing it on a decision to Yoshiaki Numata in 1967. Elorde twice attempted to take Carlos Ortiz's world lightweight title, but both times he was stopped in the fourteenth round. After losing his title to Numata, Elorde fought once more and then did not box for over a year before returning to the ring for ten more fights.

JEFF FENECH
Marrickville Mauler

FEATHERWEIGHT

Right-handed; 5'7½"; 116–135

32 bouts, 10/12/1984 to 5/18/1996

IBF Bantamweight Champion 1985-1987

WBC Junior Featherweight Champion 1987-1988

WBC Featherweight Champion 1988-1989

Hall of Fame Induction: 2002

Born: 5/28/1964, Sydney

Named: Jeffrey Fenech

Jeff Fenech is one of a select group of fighters who have won world titles in three weight classes. Some long-time ring observers may grouse that this is easier today than in years past due to the expanded number of sanctioning bodies and weight divisions, but Fenech's masterful achievement is still worthy of great praise.

Born in Sydney, the son of Maltese immigrants, Fenech learned to fight in the streets, running with a rough crowd and spending time in a home for troubled boys. Eventually Fenech arrived at a gym run by Johnny Lewis, who became his trainer for the majority of his career. In 1984, Fenech represented his country in the Los Angeles Olympics, where he lost in the quarterfinals to Redzep Redzepovski of Yugoslavia. It was a questionable loss, as the judges 3–2 decision in Fenech's favor was overturned by the five-member jury. After the fight, Fenech said to the media, "I've worked so hard for the chance to win Australia's first boxing gold medal at the Olympics, only to have the chance taken away by a bunch of senile old men."

Shortly after returning home from the Olympic Games, Fenech began his professional career with a second-round knockout of Bobby Williams. After recording five more knockouts,

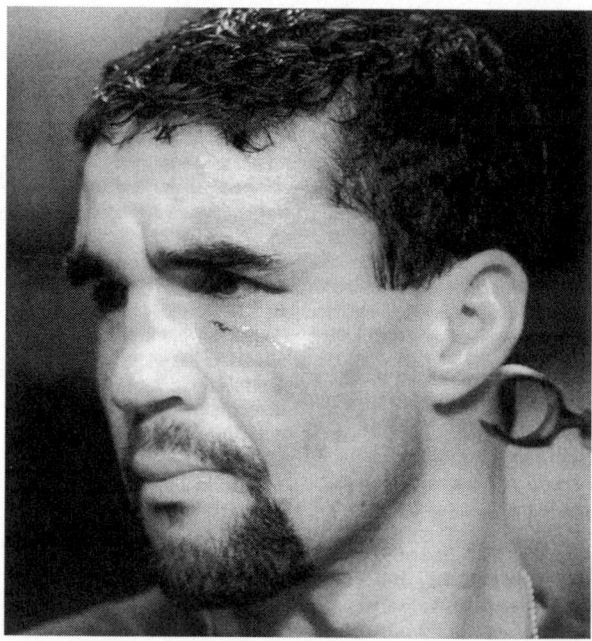

Always a tough customer, here Fenech sports some swelling and a cut under his left eye.

IN THE RING	WON 28	LOST 3	DRAWS 1	TB 32	KO 21	W 6	WF 1	D 1	KO'd 3	L 0	LF 0

Date	Opponent	Site	Result / Rounds		Title	Wt.
1984						
Oct 12	Bobby Williams	Marrickville, Australia	KO	2	—	116
Oct 26	Percy Israel	Marrickville	KO	7	—	118
Nov 30	Junior Thompson	Marrickville	KO	2	Won-Australia-JB	115
Dec 15	Iliesa Manila	Suva, Australia	KO	2	—	—
1985						
Feb 1	Wayne Mulholland	Dapto, Australia	TKO	5	—	117
Mar 4	Rolando Navarro	Sydney	TKO	4	—	—
Apr 26 ♛	Satoshi Shingaki	Sydney	TKO	9	Won-IBF-B	118
Jun 14	John Matienza	Sydney	TKO	6	—	121
Jul 26	John Farrell	Brisbane	TKO	9	—	120
Aug 23	Satoshi Shingaki	Sydney	TKO	4	Ret-IBF-B	118
Nov 4	Kenny Butts	Brisbane	TKO	2	—	—
Dec 2 ⑩	Jerome Coffee	Sydney	W	15	Ret-IBF-B	118
1986						
Apr 11 ⑩	Daniel Zaragoza	Perth	W	10	—	123
Jul 18	Steve McCrory	Sydney	TKO	14	Ret-IBF-B	118
1987						
Apr 3	Tony Miller	Melbourne	W	12	Won-Australia-FE	125
May 8	Samart Payakaroon	Sydney	KO	4	Won-WBC-JFE	122
Jul 10 ♛	Greg Richardson	Sydney	TKO	5	Ret-WBC-JFE	122
Oct 16	Carlos Zarate★	Sydney	TW	4	Ret-WBC-JFE	122
Dec 11	Osmar Avila	Sydney	KO	1	—	126
1988						
Mar 7 ⑩	Victor Callejas	Sydney	TKO	10	Won-WBC-FE	126
Aug 12	Tyrone Downes	Melbourne	KO	5	Ret-WBC-FE	126
Nov 30	George Navarro	Melbourne	KO	5	Ret-WBC-FE	126
1989						
Apr 8 ⑩	Marcos Villasana	Melbourne	W	12	Ret-WBC-FE	125
Nov 24 ⑩	Mario Martinez	Melbourne	W	12	—	132
1991						
Jan 19	John Kalbhenn	Adelaide, Australia	TKO	4	—	133
Jun 28 ♛	Azumah Nelson	Las Vegas	D	12	For-WBC-JL	128
Sep 13	Miguel Francia	Melbourne	W	10	—	132
1992						
Feb 28 ♛	Azumah Nelson	Melbourne	TKO'd	8	For-WBC-JL	130
1993						
Jun 7 ⑩	Calvin Grove	Melbourne	KO'd	7	—	131
1995						
Nov 18	Tito Tovar	Atlantic City	TKO	8	—	135
1996						
Mar 9	Mike Juarez	Melbourne	TKO	2	—	132
May 18 ♛	Philip Holiday	Melbourne	KO'd	2	For-IBF-L	134

Fenech challenged Satoshi Shingaki for the IBF bantamweight title on April 26, 1985. Though he had only six professional fights under his belt, Fenech thoroughly dominated the champion and knocked him out in the ninth round, seizing a world championship at the age of 21. He improved his record in the rematch, downing Shingaki in only three rounds.

Fenech defended his title against top contender Jerome Coffee in a fifteen-round decision, the first fight where Fenech was forced to go the whole distance. It was also one of the first times he used his boxing skills to win a fight; his reputation was that of a raw brawler rather than a skilled ring tactician. Fenech then achieved a sort of revenge against his perceived Olympic injustice when he knocked out American Steve McCrory in the fourteenth round of a title defense on July 18, 1986. McCrory was the gold medal winner in Los Angeles in Fenech's weight class.

Fenech was now having trouble meeting the bantam weight limit, and he vacated his title to move up to super bantamweight. On May 8, 1987, he faced WBC super bantamweight champ Samart Payakaroon. Fenech had an easy time of it, knocking out Payakarun at 2:42 of the fourth round. Two doctors had to rush into the ring to extract Payakarun's tongue from his throat. The former champ revived after six minutes and spent the night in the hospital.

Fenech also successfully defended his new title, starting with a knockout victory over Greg Richardson. He then defeated aging Hall of Famer Carlos Zarate with a technical decision: the fight was stopped in the fourth round because Fenech's eye was injured by an accidental head butt.

After less than a year as champion, Fenech again vacated his title to move up another weight class. On March 7, 1988, at the Sydney Entertainment Center, Fenech fought Victor Callejas for the vacant WBC featherweight title. His right crosses knocked Callejas down in the third and eight, and Callejas was staggered many times in the fight before it was stopped in the tenth. Fenech had now become a three-division champion. After the fight, he boasted that he had broken his right hand a month earlier and had won the championship match with only one hand.

After decisioning Marcos Villasana on April 8, 1989, Fenech announced his retirement. He had broken both his hands in the Villasana fight. He returned to the ring seven months later and won a decision over Mario Martinez, but his right hand was injured again, and he was forced to undergo corrective surgery. After another absence, this one of a little over a year, Fenech returned to knock out Johnny Kalbhenn, setting the stage for one of the most memorable fights of his career.

Fenech was now given a title shot against Azumah Nelson for the WBC super featherweight title. He was bidding to become a champion in four weight classes, and for the first time in his career he fought in the United States. Indeed, it was only his second fight outside of Australia. Held on June 28, 1991, in Las Vegas on the undercard of a Mike Tyson–Razor Ruddock main event, the fight opened with Fenech as the aggressor. Nelson fought back, meeting Fenech's advances with jabs and hooks that made Fenech miss. Nelson won the first two rounds before he spent the next three fighting against the ropes. Fenech unleashed a barrage, but failed to land many clean punches. Nelson bobbed and weaved, threw uppercuts and hooks, then tried moving and jabbing in the sixth. Despite these maneuvers, Fenech stayed with Nelson, and appeared to be weakening him. In the twelfth round, Fenech scored with a right and then fired a torrent of punches that had Nelson wobbly at the end of the fight. The verdict, however, was a disappointing draw, with one judge scoring the fight even, the others splitting. Most observers believed that Fenech should have been the victor.

Before the rematch, held at the Princes Park football grounds in Melbourne, Australia, Fenech boasted, "The only way they're going to take [Nelson] home to Ghana is in a body bag." Fortunately for Nelson, however, Fenech did not make good on his prediction. Nelson knocked Fenech down three times before the fight was called in the eighth round for Fenech's first defeat.

Fenech did not fight again for fifteen months. When he did get back into the ring, Calvin Grove knocked him out in the seventh round. He required 30 stitches to repair the damage Grove had caused to his face. Fenech announced his retirement the next day. He did fight twice more, but after Philip Holiday knocked him out in the second round of an IBF lightweight title fight on May 18, 1996, Fenech retired for good.

Fenech now trains and manages fighters, in addition to running his own gym. He is also active in broadcasting. Fenech's biography, *Jeff Fenech: I Love Youse All*, by Terry Smith was published in Australia in 1993.

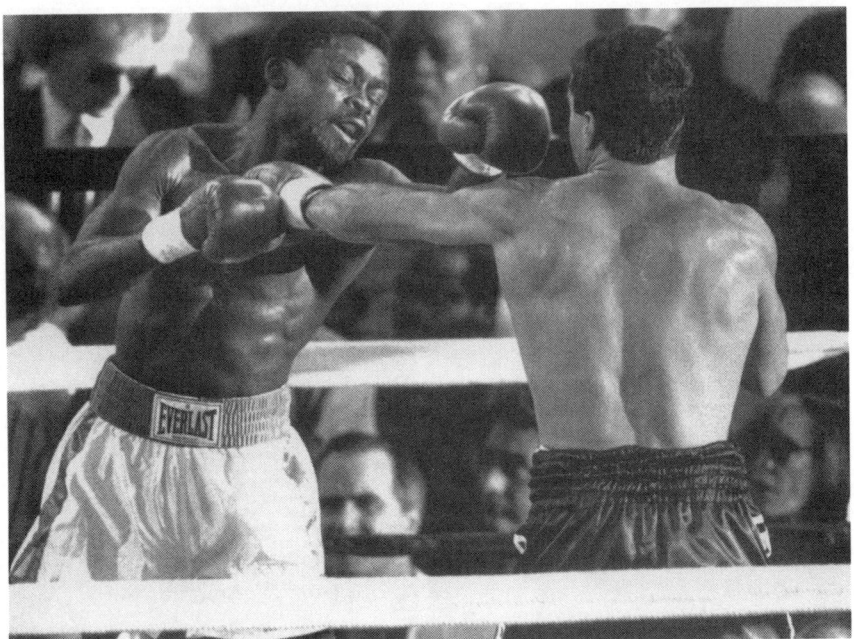

Fenech connects with a straight left to Azumah Nelson's throat in their hard-fought draw on June 28, 1991, in Las Vegas.

BOB FOSTER

LIGHT HEAVYWEIGHT

Right-handed; 6'3"; 170–188 lbs.

65 bouts, 3/27/1961 to 6/3/1978

Light Heavyweight Champ 1968–74

Hall of Fame Induction: 1990

Born: 12/15/1938, Albuquerque, NM

Named: Robert Lloyd Foster

One of the top fighters of the late 1960s and early '70s, light heavyweight champion Bob Foster did not always receive the acclaim due him because he labored in one of boxing's more anonymous divisions. At times overshadowed by the more glamorous heavyweight fighters of the era, Foster nevertheless was almost unbeatable in his weight class.

Foster first fought as an amateur in his native New Mexico, and also boxed while serving in the Air Force. He was undefeated in over one hundred amateur bouts and earned a place on the 1959 Pan American Games team. He abandoned his goal of fighting in the 1960 Olympics when the only slot offered him was as a middleweight. The light heavyweight spot on the team went to Muhammad Ali, then known as Cassius Clay.

Turning pro in 1961, Foster won his first nine fights before Doug Jones knocked him out in eight rounds in 1962. Jones was a top heavyweight contender

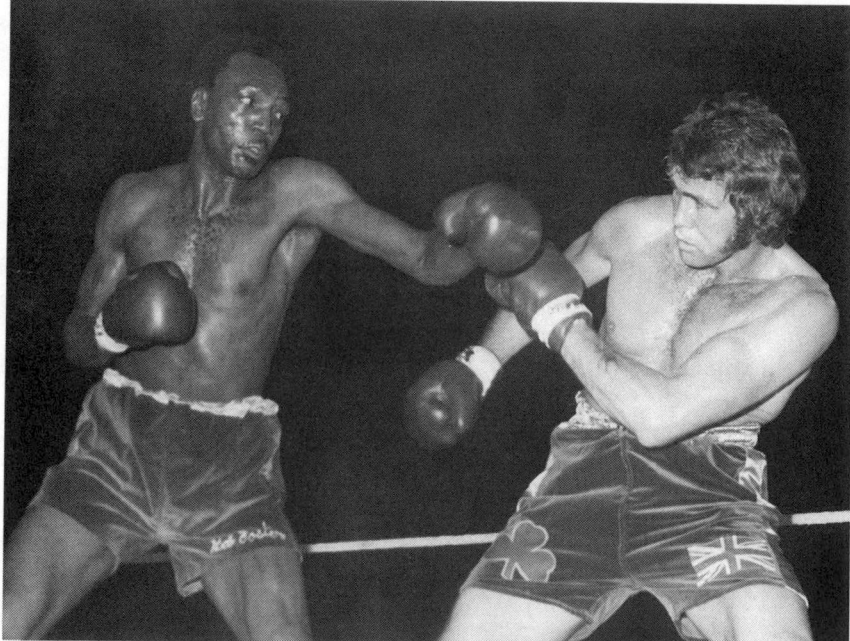

Foster's first overseas match was this 14-round knockout of Chris Finnegan (R) in London on September 26, 1972. Less than two months later, Foster met Ali for the NABF heavyweight title.

IN THE RING	WON 56	LOST 8	DRAWS 1	TB 65	KO 46	W 10	WF 0	D 1	KO'd 6	L 2	LF 0

Date	Opponent	Site	Result / Rounds		Title	Wt.
1961						
Mar 27	Duke Williams	Washington, DC	KO	2	—	—
Apr 3	Clarence Ryan	New York	W	4	—	—
May 8	Billy Johnson	New York	W	4	—	—
Jun 22	Ray Bryan	Montreal	KO	2	—	—
Aug 8	Floyd McCoy	Montreal	W	6	—	—
Nov 22	Ernie Knox	Norfolk, VA	KO	4	—	—
Dec 4	Clarence Floyd	Toronto	TKO	4	—	—
1962						
May 19	Billy Tisdale	New York	KO	2	—	—
Jun 27	Bert Whitehurst	New York	W	8	—	—
Oct 20	⑩ Doug Jones	New York	TKO'd	8	—	174
1963						
Feb 18	Richard Benjamin	Washington, DC	KO	1	—	—
Apr 29	Curtis Bruce	Washington, DC	KO	4	—	—
Nov 6	⑩ Mauro Mina	Lima, Peru	L	10	—	—
Dec 11	Willi Besmanoff	Norfolk	TKO	3	—	—
1964						
Feb 25	Dave Bailey	Miami	KO	1	—	—
May 8	Allen Thomas	Chicago	KO	1	—	—
Jul 10	⑩ Ernie Terrell	New York	KO'd	7	—	183
Nov 23	Norm Letcher	San Francisco	KO	1	—	—
Dec 11	Don Quinn	Norfolk	KO	1	—	—
Dec 11	⑩ Henry Hank	Norfolk	TKO	10	—	—
1965						
Jan 15	Roberto Rascon	Albuquerque, NM	KO	2	—	—
Mar 21	Dave Russell	Norfolk	TKO	6	—	—
May 24	Chuck Leslie	New Orleans	TKO	3	—	—
Jul 26	Henry Hank	New Orleans	W	12	—	—
Dec 6	⑩ Zora Folley	New Orleans	L	10	—	—
1966						
Dec 6	Leroy Green	Norfolk	KO	2	—	—
1967						
Jan 16	Jim Robinson	Washington, DC	TKO	1	—	—
Feb 27	⑩ Andres Selpa	Washington, DC	TKO	2	—	—
May 8	⑩ Eddie Cotton	Washington, DC	TKO	3	—	174
Jun 9	Henry Matthews	Roanoke, VA	TKO	2	—	—
Oct 25	Levan Roundtree	Washington, DC	KO	8	—	—
Nov 20	Eddie Vick	Providence, RI	W	10	—	—
Dec 5	Sonny Moore	Washington, DC	KO	5	—	—
1968						
May 24	♛ Dick Tiger★	New York	KO	4	Won-World-LH	173
Jul 29	Charley Polite	Springfield, MA	TKO	3	—	179
Aug 26	Eddie Vick	Albuquerque	TKO	9	—	—
Sep 9	⑩ Roger Rouse	Washington, DC	TKO	5	—	—
1969						
Jan 22	Frank DePaula	New York	TKO	1	Ret-World-LH	171
May 24	⑩ Andy Kendall	Springfield	TKO	4	Ret-World-LH	174
Jun 19	Levan Roundtree	Atlanta	TKO	4	—	—

Date		Opponent	Location	Result	Rds	Title	Wt
Nov 2		Chuck Leslie	New Orleans	TKO	5	—	—
1970							
Feb 24		Bill Hardney	Orlando	TKO	4	—	—
Mar 9		Cookie Wallace	Tampa	KO	6	—	177
Apr 4		Roger Rouse	Missoula, MT	TKO	4	Ret-World-LH	174
Jun 27	⑩	Mark Tessman	Baltimore	KO	10	Ret-World-LH	173
Nov 18	♛	Joe Frazier★	Detroit	KO'd	2	For-World-H	188
1971							
Mar 2		Hall Carroll	Scranton, PA	KO	4	Ret-World (WBC)-LH	174
Apr 24		Ray Anderson	Tampa	W	15	Ret-World (WBC)-LH	170
Aug 17		Vernon McIntosh	Miami	TKO	3	—	182
Oct 29		Tommy Hicks	Scranton	TKO	8	Ret-World (WBC)-LH	174
Dec 16	⑩	Brian Kelly	Oklahoma City, OK	TKO	3	Ret-World (WBC)-LH	174
1972							
Apr 7	♛	Vicente Rondon	Miami	KO	2	Ret-World-LH	175
Jun 27	⑩	Mike Quarry	Las Vegas	KO	4	Ret-World-LH	173
Sep 26	⑩	Chris Finnegan	London	KO	14	Ret-World-LH	174
Nov 21	⑩	Muhammad Ali★	Stateline, NV	KO'd	8	For-NABF-H	180
1973							
Aug 21	⑩	Pierre Fourie	Albuquerque	W	15	Ret-World-LH	173
Dec 1	⑩	Pierre Fourie	Johannesburg	W	15	Ret-World-LH	174
1974							
Jun 17	⑩	Jorge Ahumada	Albuquerque	D	15	Ret-World-LH	174
1975							
Jun 28		Bill Hardley	Santa Fe, NM	KO	3	—	179
1976							
May 8		Al Bolden	Missoula	KO	3	—	183
Aug 28		Harold Carter	Missoula	W	10	—	186
Sep 25		Al Bolden	Spokane, WA	TKO	6	—	181
1977							
Sep 2		Bob Hazelton	Willemstad, Curacao	KO	10	—	—
1978							
Feb 9		Mustapha Wasajja	Copenhagen	TKO'd	5	—	—
Jun 3		Bob Hazelton	Wichita, KS	TKO'd	2	—	—

at that time. Foster was KO'd by heavyweight contender Ernie Terrell in 1964 and lost to another tough heavyweight, Zora Folley the next year. By 1965, although Foster had achieved recognition as the third-rated light heavyweight in *The Ring's* annual rankings, he was having second thoughts about boxing as a career. He went to work in a munitions plant and fought only once in 1966. But by 1967, Foster was back in the ring and at the height of form. He racked up seven straight wins, six by knockout, and in 1968, got a shot at the light heavyweight title held by Nigerian dynamo Dick Tiger.

The fight with Tiger drew 11,547 fans to Madison Square Garden. Tiger hurt Foster in the first round, but Foster seized command in the third. In the next round, Foster nailed Tiger with a right uppercut followed by a left hook for a knockout, the first of Tiger's career. This sensational sequence was named the "round of the year" by *The Ring*. Foster had little trouble defending his title over the next six years, knocking out eleven of fourteen opponents. Fast, young British champion Chris Finnegan, who may have been Foster's toughest challenger, was felled in the fourteenth round of their match in 1972. After fighting to a draw with Jorge Ahumada in 1974, Foster announced his retirement, only to make a comeback attempt the next year. This effort ended with two consecutive knockout losses in 1978.

Foster's forays into the heavyweight ranks were often disappointing. In an article in the September 1968 issue of *The Ring*, Foster declared, "My goal is to be the first light heavyweight champion in history to win the heavyweight title." Foster failed to achieve this objective, suffering knockouts at the hands of Joe Frazier and Muhammad Ali, among others. He fought Frazier for the world heavyweight title in 1970 and challenged Ali for the NABF heavyweight title in 1972. That Foster reached for the heavyweight title does not detract from his solid domination of the light heavyweight division.

After retirement, Foster began a long career in law enforcement in his hometown of Albuquerque, New Mexico.

Muscles knotted with the effort, Foster digs into a heavy bag. Vulnerable against the best heavyweights of his day, Foster's record was nearly perfect when he fought against light heavyweights.

JOE FRAZIER
Smokin' Joe

H E A V Y W E I G H T

Right-handed; 5'11½"; 197–229 lbs.

37 bouts, 8/16/1965 to 12/3/1981

Manager: Yancy Durham

1964 Olympic Heavyweight Gold Medalist

Heavyweight Champion 1970–73

Hall of Fame Induction: 1990

Born: 1/12/1944, Beaufort, SC

Named: Joseph William Frazier

Joe Frazier was a great heavyweight champion who put up the toughest resistance Muhammad Ali ever faced. As one half of the 1971 "Fight of the Century," he was the first man to defeat Ali. And only Ali and George Foreman ever beat him.

Frazier was born on a farm in Beaufort, South Carolina. After marrying at the age of fifteen, Frazier moved north, eventually settling in Philadelphia and working in a slaughterhouse. He went to a gym in an effort to lose weight and there received his first formal boxing training. He fought well as an amateur, losing only once—to huge Buster Mathis in the 1964 Olympic trials. When Mathis dropped out because of an injury, Frazier took his place and won the gold medal in the heavyweight division.

Frazier turned professional the next year in Philadelphia and won his first

Frazier (R) bores in on Ali in the March 8, 1971 "Fight of the Century" in Madison Square Garden while shrugging off the painful effects of Ali's long jab. Frazier floored Ali in the 15th and won the unanimous decision.

IN THE RING	WON 32	LOST 4	DRAWS 1	TB 37	KO 27	W 5	WF 0	D 1	KO'd 3	L 1	LF 0

Date		Opponent	Site	Result / Rounds		Title	Wt.
1965							
Aug 16		Woody Goss	Philadelphia	TKO	1	—	203
Sep 20		Michael Bruce	Philadelphia	KO	3	—	—
Sep 28		Ray Staples	Philadelphia	KO	2	—	—
Nov 11		Abe Davis	Philadelphia	KO	1	—	—
1966							
Jan 17		Mel Turnbow	Philadelphia	KO	1	—	199
Mar 4		Dick Wipperman	New York	TKO	5	—	199
Apr 4		Charley Polite	Philadelphia	TKO	2	—	197
Apr 28		Don Smith	Pittsburgh	KO	3	—	—
May 19		Chuck Leslie	Los Angeles	KO	3	—	—
May 26		Memphis Jones	Los Angeles	KO	1	—	198
Jul 25		Billy Daniels	Philadelphia	TKO	6	—	202
Sep 21	⑩	Oscar Bonavena	New York	W	10	—	204
Nov 21		Eddie Machen	Los Angeles	TKO	10	—	—
1967							
Feb 21		Doug Jones	Philadelphia	KO	5	—	205
Apr 11		Jeff Davis	Miami Beach	KO	5	—	207
May 4		George Johnson	Los Angeles	W	10	—	203
Jul 19	⑩	George Chuvalo	New York	TKO	4	—	—
Oct 17		Tony Doyle	Philadelphia	TKO	2	—	—
Dec 18		Marion Connors	Boston	KO	3	—	—
1968							
Mar 4		Buster Mathis	New York	KO	11	Won-Vac NY World-H	204
Jun 24	⑩	Manuel Ramos	New York	TKO	2	Ret-NY World-H	203
Dec 10	⑩	Oscar Bonavena	Philadelphia	W	15	Ret-NY World-H	203
1969							
Apr 22		Dave Zyglewicz	Houston	KO	1	Ret-NY World-H	204
Jun 23	⑩	Jerry Quarry	New York	TKO	7	Ret-NY World-H	203
1970							
Feb 16	♛	Jimmy Ellis	New York	TKO	5	Won-Vac World-H	205
Nov 18		Bob Foster★	Detroit	KO	2	Ret-World-H	209
1971							
Mar 8	⑩	Muhammad Ali★	New York	W	15	Ret-World-H	205
1972							
Jan 15		Terry Daniels	New Orleans	TKO	4	Ret-World-H	215
May 25		Ron Stander	Omaha, NE	TKO	5	Ret-World-H	217
1973							
Jan 22	⑩	George Foreman	Kingston, Jamaica	TKO'd	2	Lost-World-H	214
Jul 2	⑩	Joe Bugner	London	W	12	—	208
1974							
Jan 28	⑩	Muhammad Ali★	New York	L	12	For-NABF-H	209
Jun 17	⑩	Jerry Quarry	New York	TKO	5	—	212
1975							
Mar 1		Jimmy Ellis	Melbourne	TKO	9	—	200
Sep 30	♛	Muhammad Ali★	Quezon, Philippines	TKO'd	14	For-World-H	203
1976							
Jun 15	⑩	George Foreman	New York	KO'd	5	—	224
1981							
Dec 3		Floyd Cummings	Chicago	D	10	—	229

eleven fights by knockout, four in the first round. In 1966, Frazier began to face opponents who were or had once been ranked contenders. He knocked out Billy Daniels and Eddie Machen and decisioned Oscar Bonavena. In its 1966 rankings of the top heavyweights, *The Ring* placed Frazier as the sixth-best contender. After victories over Doug Jones and Canada's "Man of Steel," George Chuvalo, in 1967, Frazier was considered the top contender for the heavyweight title. Just three years after launching his professional career, Frazier was ready to face champions on their own terms.

After Muhammad Ali was stripped of his title for refusing induction into the armed forces, the New York State Athletic Commission paired Frazier with his old amateur opponent, Buster Mathis, for its version of the world title. Madison Square Garden boxing officials Harry Markson and Teddy Brenner staged the bout as part of the opening festivities of the new Garden. Frazier and Mathis fought evenly for the first six rounds. But from the seventh round on, Frazier dominated the fight with his aggressive style and trademark left hook, then pounded Mathis to the canvas in the eleventh round for the knockout. He defended the New York title four times, conquering Bonavena, Dave Zyglewicz, Manuel Ramos, and Jerry Quarry. In 1970, Frazier unified the heavyweight championship with a fifth-round knockout of WBA champion Jimmy Ellis.

Later that year, Ali was cleared to begin fighting again. Eager to regain his championship, he challenged Frazier. Enmity brewed as the two fighters signed to fight on March 8, 1971 at Madison Square Garden. Ali bragged about his undiminished prowess and denigrated "stand-in" champion Frazier as a white man's pawn, a charge that infuriated Frazier. The bout was dubbed "The Fight of the Century," and few fights in recent times have attracted as much attention. An estimated 300 million fans watched it on closed-circuit television or via satellite, resulting in a gross of about $23 million for the promoters. The fight lived up to its billing. Ali dazzled the fans by battering Frazier with thundering combinations in the first rounds, but Frazier fought in close and worked at wearing Ali down. At times, each man appeared uncertain of how to stay on his feet and, in the eleventh, the two propped each other up in a staggering embrace. Frazier finally launched the magic punch and knocked Ali down in the fifteenth, only the third time that feat had ever been accomplished. He had plainly won the fight and proven with great spirit and courage that he was the world champion.

In 1973, Frazier lost the title to George Foreman, who knocked him down six times in two rounds. Foreman may have had the title, but the Ali-Frazier rematch was the hot ticket. The 1974 bout attracted a crowd of 20,748 to Madison Square Garden and set a non-title, indoor gate record of $1,053,688. Frazier landed more power punches, but Ali scored more frequently to win a unanimous decision. Frazier complained that Ali held him behind the head.

The two great champions met for a final clash in the Philippines, in 1975, with Ali's world title on the line. Called the "Thrilla in Manila," this fight is considered one of the greatest battles of all time. Ali scored often early in the fight, but Frazier seized control of the middle rounds and by the end of ten, the contest was even. In the twelfth, however, Ali unleashed a blistering two-handed attack which cut Frazier's mouth and swelled his left eye nearly shut. Ali continued the onslaught until Frazier's trainer, Eddie Futch, stopped the fight after fourteen rounds.

After another knockout loss to Foreman in 1976, Frazier retired, although he did make a brief one-fight comeback five years later. In retirement, the popular Frazier has trained fighters and sung with his band, the Knockouts.

Frazier trains on the speed bag at the Concord Hotel, a Catskill Mountain resort north of New York City. Frazier was reknowned for wearing down his opponents with a determined and relentless attack.

GENE FULLMER

MIDDLEWEIGHT

Right-handed; 5'8"; 157–162 lbs.

64 bouts, 6/9/1951 to 8/28/1963

Manager: Marv Jensen

Middleweight Champ 1957,
NBA Middlewt. Champ 1959–62

Hall of Fame Induction: 1991

Born: 7/21/1931, West Jordan, UT

The small town of West Jordan, Utah, produced boxer Gene Fullmer, whose aggressive, crowd-pleasing style twice earned him the middleweight crown. Not a particularly polished fighter, Fullmer was an all-out slugger who made up for his lack of science with raw punching power. He fought in thirteen title bouts and for the last four years of his career, Fullmer fought exclusively in championship matches. Although his face bore the evidence of many blows that hit their marks, only Sugar Ray Robinson and Dick Tiger were able to knock Fullmer out.

Fullmer, reportedly named Gene after heavyweight champion Gene Tunney, started boxing at age eleven. His amateur record, which included a string of knockouts, was an impressive 70 wins with only four losses. He won four Utah

Carmen Basilio's defense is down as Fullmer (R) jabs. Fullmer beat Basilio on late-round TKOs in San Francisco in 1959 and Salt Lake City in 1960. Both fights were for the NBA middleweight title.

IN THE RING	WON 55	LOST 6	DRAWS 3	TB 64	KO 24	W 31	WF 0	D 3	KO'd 2	L 4	LF 0

Date	Opponent	Site	Result / Rounds		Title	Wt.
1951						
Jun 9	Glen Peck	Logan, UT	KO	1	—	—
Jun 16	Andy Jackson	West Jordan, UT	KO	1	—	—
Jun 23	Gary Carr	Midvale, UT	KO	3	—	—
Jul 2	Eddie Duffy	Vernal, UT	KO	1	—	—
Jul 9	Eddie Duffy	Salt Lake City	KO	2	—	—
Jul 16	Lamar Peterson	West Jordan	KO	1	—	—
Aug 1	Carlos Martinez	San Francisco	KO	1	—	—
Aug 24	Sam Healy	Hurricane, UT	KO	1	—	—
Aug 25	Buddy Sloane	Hurricane	KO	2	—	—
Sep 7	Charley Cato	West Jordan	KO	4	—	—
Sep 14	Sam Healy	Vernal	KO	4	—	—
Sep 25	Garth Panter	Salt Lake City	W	10	—	—
Oct 3	Gary Hanley	West Jordan	KO	1	—	—
Oct 10	Rudy Zadell	Pittsburgh	W	6	—	—
Oct 17	Ray Jones	Vernal	KO	1	—	—
1952						
Aug 8	Mickey Rhodes	Ogden, UT	KO	6	—	—
Sep 20	Armando Cotero	Hollywood	W	6	—	—
1954						
Feb 6	Kid Leon	West Jordan	KO	1	—	—
Apr 26	Charley Cato	Salt Lake City	KO	1	—	—
May 17	Andy Anderson	Salt Lake City	TKO	7	—	—
Jun 5	Kid Rico	Salt Lake City	TKO	1	—	—
Jul 12	Govan Small	Salt Lake City	W	10	—	—
Jul 29	Reno Abellira	West Jordan	W	10	—	—
Aug 16	Dick Wolfe	West Jordan	KO	4	—	—
Nov 8	Jackie LaBua	Brooklyn	W	10	—	—
Nov 15	Peter Muller	Brooklyn	W	10	—	—
1955						
Jan 31	Marcel Assire	Brooklyn	W	10	—	—
Feb 14	Paul Pender	Brooklyn	W	10	—	—
Mar 21	Govan Small	Salt Lake City	W	10	—	—
Apr 4	Gil Turner	Brooklyn	L	10	—	—
Jun 20	Gil Turner	Salt Lake City	W	10	—	—
Jul 26	⑩ Del Flanagan	Butte, MT	W	10	—	—
Sep 12	Al Andrews	Ogden	W	10	—	—
Sep 28	⑩ Bobby Boyd	Chicago	L	10	—	—
Nov 25	⑩ Eduardo Lausse	New York	L	10	—	—
1956						
Jan 4	⑩ Rocky Castellani	Cleveland	W	10	—	—
Feb 17	Gil Turner	New York	W	10	—	157
Apr 20	⑩ Tiger Jones	Cleveland	W	10	—	—
May 25	⑩ Charley Humez	New York	W	10	—	158
Sep 22	Moses Ward	West Jordan	KO	3	—	—
1957						
Jan 2	♛ Sugar Ray Robinson★	New York	W	15	Won-World-M	157
Jan 28	Wilf Greaves	Salt Lake City	W	10	—	160

Date		Opponent	Location	Result	Rounds	Title	Weight
Feb 18		Ernie Durando	Denver	W	10	—	—
May 1	⑩	Sugar Ray Robinson★	Chicago	KO'd	5	Lost-World-M	159
Jun 7	⑩	Tiger Jones	Chicago	W	10	—	—
Sep 4		Chico Veja	West Jordan	W	10	—	—
Nov 15	⑩	Neal Rivers	New York	W	10	—	—
1958							
Mar 3		Milo Savage	Salt Lake City	W	10	—	—
Jul 7		Jimmy Hegerle	West Jordan	W	10	—	—
Sep 11	⑩	Spider Webb	Salt Lake City	W	10	—	—
Nov 10		Joe Miceli	Salt Lake City	KO	2	—	—
1959							
Jan 9		Milo Savage	San Antonio, TX	W	10	—	—
Feb 20		Wilf Greaves	New York	W	10	—	—
Aug 28	⑩	Carmen Basilio★	San Francisco	TKO	14	Won-Vac NBA-M	159
Dec 4	⑩	Spider Webb	Logan	W	15	Ret-NBA-M	159
1960							
Apr 20	⑩	Joey Giardello★	Bozeman, MT	D	15	Ret-NBA-M	160
Jun 29	⑩	Carmen Basilio★	Salt Lake City	TKO	12	Ret-NBA-M	159
Dec 3	⑩	Sugar Ray Robinson★	Los Angeles	D	15	Ret-NBA-M	159
1961							
Mar 4	⑩	Sugar Ray Robinson★	Las Vegas	W	15	Ret-NBA-M	159
Aug 5	⑩	Florentino Fernandez	Ogden	W	15	Ret-NBA-M	159
Dec 9	⑩	Benny Paret	Las Vegas	KO	10	Ret-NBA-M	159
1962							
Oct 23	⑩	Dick Tiger★	San Francisco	L	15	Lost-NBA-M	160
1963							
Feb 23	♛	Dick Tiger★	Las Vegas	D	15	For-WBA-M	160
Aug 28	⑩	Dick Tiger★	Ibadan, Nigeria	TKO'd	7	For-Vac World-M	160

Golden Glove titles and five Inter-Mountain Amateur Athletic Union championships, although he lost in the Western finals of the 1948 Olympic welterweight trials. Fullmer worked as a welder in the mining industry before turning pro in 1951 in his home state. His first eleven fights were knockouts, all accomplished in four rounds or fewer.

Fullmer's first fights outside his region came in 1954 when Teddy Brenner matched him against Jackie LaBua and Peter Muller in Brooklyn. Fullmer won both fights by decision. In 1955, Fullmer decisioned future champ Paul Pender and split two decisions with Gil Turner.

Fullmer continued to work his way through the ranks, methodically dispensing with opponents until nothing stood in the way of a middleweight title shot. He was viewed as a top contender when he faced champ Sugar Ray Robinson in January, 1957 in Madison Square Garden for the title. Robinson had been on top for a long time, and he was the definite favorite. Fullmer was relentless, mauling the older boxer and hanging in tight to deliver forceful body punches. With a left to the jaw and a right to the body, he knocked Robinson to the canvas in the seventh, and just three seconds were left in the count when the champ got up. The fight went the distance with neither fighter scoring another decisive punch, but Fullmer's persistent attack obviously tired Robinson, and the judges unanimously awarded Fullmer the win. Fullmer's reign as Robinson's vanquisher was short, however. In May, when Robinson took back the championship with a decisive five-round knockout in Chicago Stadium, many observers felt Fullmer's time had come and gone.

Fullmer was far from finished, however, and he took another crack at a championship in 1959 when he faced Carmen Basilio for the vacant NBA middleweight title in San Francisco's Cow Palace. Basilio and Fullmer were two of a kind: fast, hard-hitting boxers who could withstand immense punishment in the ring. Fullmer battered his opponent until the fourteenth round, when the referee called a halt after Fullmer bulled Basilio over. After the fight, Basilio exclaimed, "Fullmer kicked the hell out of me."

Fullmer successfully defended his title against both Basilio and Robinson, as well as top contenders Joey Giardello, Spider Webb, Florentino Fernandez, and Benny Paret. He met Robinson twice in title bouts, first fighting to a draw and then winning a fifteen-round decision. Dick Tiger finally ended Fullmer's winning streak in 1962 with a fifteen-round decision in Candlestick Park. Fullmer challenged Tiger twice more, in his final two professional appearances. He fought Tiger to a draw in Las Vegas in 1963 in an attempt to regain the NBA title and travelled to Nigeria that same year to battle for the vacant world middleweight crown. Tiger leveled Fullmer in seven.

Fullmer then retired to Utah, where he operated a successful mink ranch for many years. A Mormon, he reportedly donated ten percent of his considerable ring earnings to the church.

Fullmer (R) keeps the pressure on a reeling Gil Turner. Fullmer won 10-round decisions in Salt Lake City and New York avenging Turner's victory in their first meeting in Brooklyn in 1955.

KHAOSAI GALAXY
The Thai Tyson

JUNIOR BANTAMWEIGHT

Left-handed; 5'4"; 114–121 lbs.

51 bouts, 12/17/1980 to 12/12/1991

Manager: Niwat Laosunwanawat

WBA Jr. Bantamweight Champion 1984–91

Hall of Fame Induction: 1999

Born: 5/15/1959, Napa, Petchaboon, Thailand

Named: Sura Saenkham

Also fought as: Khaosai Vangchamphoo

Although he is virtually unknown in the United States, Khaosai Galaxy is regarded by many as the greatest junior bantamweight ever, and certainly the greatest boxer to emerge from Thailand. From his southpaw stance, Galaxy moved forward relentlessly, punishing his opponents with devastating left-handed body shots.

Galaxy grew up in a small rice-growing village in northeastern Thailand. When Khaosai and his twin brother Khaokor were five, their mother, an enthusiastic fight fan, gave them two pairs of boxing gloves. Sparring and training together as they grew, the young boxers both became world champions.

Galaxy started his career as a kick boxer, mastering Muay Thai, the ancient and extremely popular Thai combat sport. Galaxy made the switch to conventional boxing in 1980, and quickly found success using only his hands. He won his first several bouts before he faced Sakda Saksuree for the bantamweight championship of Thailand. Galaxy lost the fight in a ten-round decision, the only defeat of his entire career. He avenged himself upon Saksuree only six weeks later with a knockout victory in six rounds, though this time the fight was not for a belt. Finally, on January 25th of the next year, Galaxy knocked out Sakdisami Chorsirirat in seven rounds to win the Thai bantamweight title.

Galaxy won his next eleven fights by knockout, none of them lasting longer than the fifth round, and though he continued to fight exclusively in Thailand, he was becoming known as a leading junior bantamweight. Junior bantamweight was a new weight class with a 115-pound limit. The WBC crowned its first champion in 1980, with the WBA following suit in 1981. WBA junior bantamweight champion Jiro Watanabe

Song-Uhm Jae (L) managed to last ten rounds with Galaxy at Rajdamnern Stadium, in Bangkok, by covering up and easing his punishment. Galaxy was only eight months away from a title shot.

IN THE RING	WON 50	LOST 1	DRAWS 0	TB 51	KO 44	W 6	WF 0	D 0	KO'd 0	L 1	LF 0

Date	Opponent	Site	Result / Rounds		Title	Wt.
1980						
Dec 17	Pukk Sithrum	Bangkok	KO	5	—	119
Dec 31	Sansung Sithkempetch	Bangkok	KO	3	—	119
1981						
Jan 26	Prasong Sithkempetch	Bangkok	KO	1	—	118
May 13	Sakdi Porntavee	Bangkok	KO	3	—	121
Jun 10	Thaene Singchaowang	Bangkok	KO	1	—	118
Jun 24	Phichitsuk Korusayarm	Bangkok	W	10	—	117
Jul 29	Sakda Saksuree	Bangkok	L	10	For-Thai-B	117
Aug 29	Mornsakdi Muangsurin	Bangkok	TKO	3	—	—
Sep 10	Sakda Saksuree	Bangkok	KO	6	—	—
Oct 14	Tsuguyuki Toma	Bangkok	KO	4	—	118
1982						
Jan 25	Sakdisami Chorsirinat	Bangkok	KO	7	Won-Thai-B	117
Mar 10	Katsuyuki Ohashi	Bangkok	KO	3	—	119
Apr 14	Yuh-Ok Joo	Bangkok	KO	4	—	116
May 24	Ali Formentera	Bangkok	KO	5	—	117
Jul 10	Agus Suyanto	Bangkok	KO	4	—	116
Aug 26	Adan Uribe Perez	Bangkok	KO	4	—	115
Oct 13	Willie Jensen	Bangkok	KO	2	—	116
Nov 27	Mun-Kyun Joo	Korat, Thailand	KO	4	—	116
Dec 24	Marciano Sekiyama	Bangkok	KO	4	—	118
1983						
Feb 23	Jose Luis Soto	Bangkok	KO	2	—	117
May 10	Luis Ibanez	Bangkok	KO	3	—	117
Jun 30	Montsayarm Mahachai	Bangkok	KO	3	—	—
Aug 3	Chang-Young Park	Bangkok	W	10	—	117
Oct 12	Gil Ragas	Bangkok	TKO	7	—	116
Dec 14	Noritetsu Kato	Bangkok	TKO	5	—	117
1984						
Mar 14	Song-Uhm Jae	Bangkok	W	10	—	117
Jul 11	Val De Vera	Bangkok	TKO	7	—	116
Sep 2	Yun-Lee Moon	Bangkok	KO	2	—	117
Nov 21	Eusebio Espinal	Bangkok	KO	6	Won-Vac WBA-JB	114
1985						
Mar 6	Dong-Choon Lee	Bangkok	KO	7	Ret-WBA-JB	115
Jul 17	Rafael Orono	Bangkok	TKO	5	Ret-WBA-JB	115
Dec 23 ⑩	Edgar Montserrat	Bangkok	TKO	2	Ret-WBA-JB	115
1986						
Nov 1	Israel Contreras	Willemstad, Curaçao	KO	5	Ret-WBA-JB	114
1987						
Feb 28	Ellyas Pical	Djakarta	TKO	14	Ret-WBA-JB	114
Jun 25	Sap-Chun Chung	Bangkok	KO	3	—	118
Oct 12	Byung-Kwan Chung	Bangkok	KO	3	Ret-WBA-JB	115

1988						
Jan 26	Kongtorani Payakaroon	Bangkok	W	12	Ret-WBA-JB	115
May 9	Kap-Sup Song	Bangkok	TKO	7	—	118
Sep 12	Jun Llano	Bangkok	TKO	3	—	117
Oct 9	Chang-Ho Choi	Seoul	KO	8	Ret-WBA-JB	115
1989						
Jan 15	Tae-Il Chang	Samutprakarn, Thai.	KO	2	Ret-WBA-JB	115
Apr 8	Kenji Matsumura	Yokohama, Japan	W	12	Ret-WBA-JB	114
Jul 29	Alberto Castro	Surin, Thai.	TKO	10	Ret-WBA-JB	115
Oct 31	Kenji Matsumura	Kobe, Japan	TKO	12	Ret-WBA-JB	115
1990						
Mar 29	Ari Blanca	Bangkok	KO	5	Ret-WBA-JB	115
Jul 5	Shunichi Nakajima	Chiang Mai, Thai.	KO	7	Ret-WBA-JB	115
Sep 29	Yong-Kang Kim	Suphanburi, Thai.	KO	6	Ret-WBA-JB	115
Dec 9	Ernesto Ford	Petchaboon, Thai.	KO	6	Ret-WBA-JB	115
1991						
Apr 5	Jae-Suk Park	Samut Songkram	TKO	5	Ret-WBA-JB	115
Jul 20	⑩ David Griman	Samutprakarn	TKO	5	Ret-WBA-JB	115
Dec 12	⑩ Armando Castro	Bangkok	W	12	Ret-WBA-JB	115

defeated Payao Pooltarat on July 5, 1984, to unify the championship, but the WBA then stripped Watanabe of its title.

In order to fill the now-vacant WBA junior bantamweight championship, the WBA paired Galaxy with Eusebio Espinal in Bangkok on November 21, 1984. Before the fight, the previously unbeaten Espinal boasted that he would finish Galaxy with a knockout. In the fifth round, Galaxy unleashed a thundering body attack and knocked Espinal down for the eight count. He followed up in the sixth with right and left hooks to Espinal's midsection until Espinal fell to the canvas at two minutes and sixteen seconds of the round. Crowned champion, Galaxy held the WBA title until he retired.

Each of the combatants analyzed the bout in postfight interviews. Galaxy stated, "Espinal's left hooks were strong. But I found his weakness at his midsection in the third round. From the next round on, I opened up my body attacks. My fight plan worked well."

Espinal praised the victor: "Khaosai was a ferocious puncher, and he never stopped coming forward."

In 1985, Galaxy knocked out all three challengers to his title. In 1986, he fought only once, leaving Thailand for Willemstad, Curaçao, to face unbeaten Israel Contreras on November 1, 1986. Though Contreras was the aggressor in the first two rounds, Galaxy knocked him down in the third and fourth. A pair of Galaxy uppercuts and a right to the jaw in the fifth set up the finishing blow—a sharp left hook to Contreras's head. The challenger did not recover from that punch for several minutes.

Galaxy mounted another title defense on July 29, 1989, against top WBA junior bantamweight contender Alberto Castro. As his body matured, Galaxy had to work hard to make weight, and he faced Castro somewhat weakened by weight loss. In the second round, Castro, not cowed by the champ's power and reputation, countered a looping right hook with a sharp right. Galaxy went down, sprung up quickly, but was unsteady for the remainder of the round.

Behind solid lefts in the third, the experienced champion recovered some momentum. The bout was touch and go through the sixth, and Castro nearly floored Galaxy with a sixth-round right to the chin. Somehow, he managed to stay aloft on his rubbery legs. In the same round, the champ also suffered a cut over his eye. The seventh proved the turning point when Galaxy concentrated his legendary power on Castro's midsection. By the tenth, the game Colombian was beaten. At one point in that round, Castro turned his back on the champ to try to avoid the pounding to his body. After a final desperate flurry, Castro waived his arm to show the referee that he could endure no more and walked back to his corner. Khaosai Galaxy, "The Thai Tyson," was still the WBA junior bantamweight title-holder.

The Castro fight serves as a good example of Galaxy's style. An aggressive southpaw fighter with strength and the determination to come back after hitting the canvas, he overwhelmed opponents with both right and left hands and was especially effective in going to the body. Galaxy punched with incredible power, especially with his left.

After the Castro fight, Galaxy made seven more successful title defenses before retiring in the wake of an eighth defense—a twelve-round decision over Armando Castro on December 12, 1991. His last fight was attended by eleven thousand fans at Bangkok's Thepsapin Stadium. Galaxy accepted gifts for 35 minutes before the fight started.

In his nineteen title defenses, Galaxy knocked out sixteen of his opponents. He scored wins over future WBA flyweight champion David Griman, three-time IBF junior bantamweight champion Ellyas Pical, two-time WBC junior flyweight champion Rafael Orono, and flyweight champion Yong-Kang Kim. A national hero in Thailand, Galaxy has stayed active in boxing since his retirement. His twin brother, Khaokor, also won the WBA bantamweight title, making them the first set of twins to both be world champions.

An intense Galaxy connects with a hard right to the chin of Yong-Kang Kim on September 29, 1990. Galaxy won with a sixth-round KO.

VICTOR GALINDEZ

LIGHT HEAVYWEIGHT

Right-handed; 5'10", 160–190 lbs.

70 bouts, 5/10/1969 to 6/14/1980

WBA Light Heavyweight Champion 1974–1978

Hall of Fame Induction: 2002

Born: 11/2/1948, Vedia, Buenos Aires, Argentina

Named: Victor Emilio Galindez

Died: 10/26/1980

One of the greatest "large" South American fighters of all time, Victor Galindez twice won the light heavyweight world championship.

As a child, Galindez worked on his uncle's farm, in a butcher shop, as a bootblack, and as a newsboy. When he was sixteen, his friends urged the imposing Galindez to try his hand at boxing. A local promoter drafted the big Argentine for one of his shows in Lujan, near Buenos Aires, and his fight career had begun.

After boxing for pay in unregulated bouts, Galindez made a foray into amateur boxing. He represented Argentina in the 1967 Pan American Games and the 1968 Olympics, where he was defeated in the first round of the tournament. He officially turned pro with a fourth-round knockout of Ramon Ruiz on May 10, 1969, in Buenos Aires. In 1970, Galindez fought ten times and compiled a 5-3-1 record, with one no contest.

On November 28, 1970, Galindez challenged for the Argentine light heavyweight title. He lost a twelve-round decision to Avenamar Peralta, but won their first rematch. Two more meetings in 1971 would go to Peralta. Also that year, Galindez won two of three fights against future light heavyweight contender Jorge Ahumada.

His prospects improved in 1972. He faced Carlos Santagada on January 22. Galindez trailed after seven rounds of the ten-round battle. However, in the eighth he stopped Santagada short with a furious assault. On July 22, Galindez decisioned Juan Aguilar to win the Argentine light heavyweight title. Afterwards he declared, "I am a new fighter," and he certainly seemed to be, following up with two successful title defenses against Peralta and two wins and one draw with Aguilar.

Billy Douglas (L) faces off against Galindez on August 21, 1976, in Buenos Aires. Galindez won by decision. Douglas later managed the boxing career of his son, James ("Buster") Douglas, who will always be remembered for his huge upset knockout of Mike Tyson.

IN THE RING	WON 55	LOST 9	DRAWS 4	TB 70	KO 34	W 21	WF 0	D 4	KO'd 3	L 6	LF 0	ND 2

Date	Opponent	Site	Result / Rounds		Title	Wt.
1969						
May 10	Ramon Ruiz	Buenos Aires	TKO	4	—	161
Jun 28	Ruperto Robledo	Buenos Aires	TKO	3	—	160
Aug 16	Adolfo Cejas	Azul, Argentina	D	10	—	164
1970						
Jan 17	Adolfo Cardoza	Buenos Aires	TKO	5	—	172
Mar 13	Ramon Rocha	Rosario, Argentina	TKO	9	—	169
Apr 8	Juan Aguilar	Buenos Aires	L	10	—	170
May 9	Ramon Cerrezuela	Lujan, Argentina	TKO	6	—	169
May 20	Alfredo Segura	Buenos Aires	TKO	3	—	168
Jun 24	Juan Aguilar	Buenos Aires	D	10	—	166
Jul 22	Jorge Ahumada	Buenos Aires	KO	5	—	170
Aug 14	Juan Aguilar	Mendoza, Argentina	NC	1	—	170
Sep 18	Juan Aguilar	Mendoza	L	10	—	172
Nov 28	Avenamar Peralta	Buenos Aires	L	12	For-Argentina-LH	170
1971						
Jan 9	Avenamar Peralta	Buenos Aires	W	10	—	171
Apr 7	Pedro Rimovsky	Buenos Aires	NC	1	—	173
May 24	Jorge Ahumada	Mendoza	L	10	—	169
Jun 12	Pedro Rimovsky	Buenos Aires	D	10	—	168
Jul 31	Jorge Ahumada	Buenos Aires	KO	9	—	170
Sep 11	Avenemar Peralta	Buenos Aires	TKO'd	9	—	171
Oct 30	Juan Aguilar	Buenos Aires	W	10	—	169
Dec 18	Avenemar Peralta	Buenos Aires	L	10	—	172
1972						
Jan 22	Carlos Santagada	9 de Julio, Arg.	TKO	8	—	174
May 6	Eddie Jones	Buenos Aires	W	10	—	176
Jul 22	Juan Aguilar	Buenos Aires	W	12	Won-Argentina-LH	171
Aug 19	Adolfo Cardoza	Rosario	TKO	4	—	175
Sep 2	Avenamar Peralta	Buenos Aires	W	12	Ret-Argentina-LH	172
Oct 7	Avenamar Peralta	Buenos Aires	W	12	Won-Vac-S Amer-LH	173
Nov 10	Oscar Wondryk	Venado Tuerto, Arg.	TKO	7	—	177
Dec 15	Juan Aguilar	Mendoza	D	10	—	176
1973						
Jan 29	Ruben Gonzalez	Salta, Argentina	TKO	3	—	174
Apr 14	Juan Aguilar	Buenos Aires	W	12	Ret-Argentina-LH	174
May 12 ⑩	Eddie Owens	Buenos Aires	TKO	3	—	174
Jul 14	Karl Zurheide	Buenos Aires	KO	2	—	174
Aug 10	Juan Aguilar	Tucuman, Argentina	KO	6	—	177
Sep 7	Raul Loyola	Buenos Aires	W	12	Ret-Argentine-LH	174
Nov 10	Raul Loyola	Buenos Aires	TKO	8	—	174
Dec 8	Eddie Duncan	Buenos Aires	KO	2	—	176
1974						
Feb 16	Ray Anderson	Balcarce, Argentina	KO	2	—	179
Apr 5	Ruben Gonzalez	Rio Cuarto, Argentina	KO	3	—	178
Jun 8	Jose Gonzalez	Buenos Aires	W	10	—	176
Jul 12	Domingo Silveyra	Jujuy, Argentina	TKO	4	—	181
Sep 1	Domingo Silveyra	San Juan, Argentina	TKO	5	—	182
Sep 14	Angle Oquendo	Buenos Aires	W	10	—	176

Date		Opponent	Location	Result	Rds.	Title	Wt.
Oct 5		Domingo Silveyra	Parana, Argentina	KO	4	—	178
Dec 7	Ⓦ	Len Hutchins	Buenos Aires	TKO	13	Won-Vac WBA-LH	174
1975							
Feb 15		John Griffin	Balcarce	KO	6	—	180
Apr 7	Ⓦ	Pierre Fourie	Johannesburg	W	15	Ret-WBA-LH	172
May 16		Ray J. Elson	Las Vegas	TKO	8	—	177
Jun 30	Ⓦ	Jorge Ahumada	New York	W	15	Ret-WBA-LH	174
Sep 13	Ⓦ	Pierre Fourie	Johannesburg	W	15	Ret-WBA-LH	175
1976							
Mar 28		Harald Skog	Oslo	KO	3	Ret-WBA-LH	173
Apr 8	Ⓦ	Jesse Burnett	Copenhagen	W	10	—	174
May 22	Ⓦ	Richie Kates	Johannesburg	KO	15	Ret-WBA-LH	174
Aug 21		Billy Douglas	Buenos Aires	W	10	—	178
Oct 5		Kosie Smith	Johannesburg	W	15	Ret-WBA-LH	175
1977							
Apr 6		Guillermo Aquirrezabala	Mendoza	KO	4	—	182
Jun 18	Ⓦ	Richie Kates	Rome	W	15	Ret-WBA-LH	174
Sep 17	Ⓦ	Alvaro ("Yaqui") Lopez	Rome	W	15	Ret-WBA-LH	174
Oct 19		Eddie Gregory	Turin, Italy	W	15	Ret-WBA-LH	173
1978							
Apr 8		Ramon Cerrezuela	Buenos Aires	W	10	—	179
May 6	Ⓦ	Alvaro ("Yaqui") Lopez	Via Reggio, Italy	W	15	Ret-WBA-LH	174
Jun 16		Antonio Musaldino	Mendoza	TKO	9	—	181
Jul 8		Waldemar de Oliveira	Buenos Aires	TKO	9	—	178
Aug 19		Marcos A. Tostos	General Pico, Argentina	TKO	6	—	182
Sep 15	Ⓦ	Mike Rossman	New Orleans	TKO'd	13	Lost-WBA-LH	174
1979							
Mar 10		Roberto Aguilar	San Miguel, Argentina	TKO	6	—	185
Apr 14	♛	Mike Rossman	New Orleans	TKO	10	Reg-WBA-LH	174
Nov 30	Ⓦ	Marvin Johnson	New Orleans	TKO'd	11	Lost-WBA-LH	174
1980							
Jun 14		Jesse Burnett	Anaheim, CA	L	12	—	190

Starting with the Santagada fight, Galindez racked up a streak of 22 wins and a single draw before he signed for a match with Len Hutchins on December 7, 1974, in the famed Luna Park in Buenos Aires. Light heavyweight champion Bob Foster had just retired, and the WBA announced it would consider the winner of the Galindez–Hutchins contest its new title holder. Galindez injured his knee in a car accident a month before the fight, and then, just a week before the bout, he injured his ankle horseback riding. Both times he refused to postpone, fearing that he would never get another chance at a world title. A pre-fight meal of frogs upset his stomach immediately before the match, but he had no trouble stopping Hutchins in thirteen.

At this point in his career, Galindez was a "walk-in slugger" who left himself open to the blows of a skillful boxer. All-time great middleweight Carlos Monzon, his close friend and fellow Argentine, helped Galindez focus on boxing and counterpunching rather than just whacking his opponent. Galindez successfully defended his title in a tough fifteen-round decision against Ahumada in his first fight held in the United States, but had difficulty making weight for the June 30, 1975, match in New York.

On May 22, 1976, Galindez had one of his roughest match-ups, against top contender Richie Kates in Johannesburg, South Africa. In the third round, Kates opened a deep gash over Galindez's right eye, which bled in round after punishing round for the rest of the fight. Late in the fifteenth, Galindez uncorked a left hook to the jaw, and Kates was counted out with eleven seconds left in the fight. Galindez won the rematch as well.

In 1977, Galindez triumphed over Yaqui Lopez and future champion Eddie Gregory (who later became Eddie Mustafa Muhammad). Galindez won a narrow decision over Gregory, who might have won but for points lost on fouls. For his next title defense against Mike Rossman in New Orleans on September 15, 1978, Galindez jumped rope for over an hour in a hot hotel boiler room, again struggling to make weight. He lost the thirteen-round fight and the championship.

After protracted negotiations, he agreed to fight Rossman again in the New Orleans Superdome, on April 14, 1979. Stung by the loss of his title, Galindez had worked himself into top form. Rossman opened with left jabs, winning the first round, but Galindez countered by taking a quick step forward, shooting a lunging left jab, followed by a right. Rossman fought back with jabs over Galindez's right and also won the second and third rounds. In the fourth, the challenger unleashed a furious attack that went past the bell. When referee Stanley Christodoulou ruled that Galindez had not heard the signal, Rossman's brother leapt into the ring and swung at Galindez. The ring filled with partisans of both sides until Christodoulou regained control and the fight resumed. Rossman suffered a broken hand in the fifth, and, though Galindez had dislocated his elbow, he took control and Rossman could not continue in the ninth. After the fight, Galindez said of Rossman, "He's a chicken. I'll never give him a rematch."

He did not need to. His first defense on November 30, 1979, ended with a broken jaw and an ignominious knockout at the hands of Marvin Johnson. After surgery, Galindez fought twice more. Lightly regarded Jesse Burnett knocked him down twice and beat him in twelve rounds on June 14, 1980. Galindez announced his retirement on August 28, 1980; he had suffered two detached retinas, and his doctors advised him to quit.

Always fascinated with cars, Galindez decided to try his hand at auto racing. He obtained a racing license and rode with Antonio Lizeviche in a competition on October 26, 1980. Though warned to stay inside the car if it experienced engine trouble during the race, they exited the vehicle and another race car hit them, killing them both.

In a Rome rematch, on June 18, 1977, Galindez (L) lands a left to the body of Richie Kates. The decision win was Galindez's seventh successful title defense.

KID GAVILAN
The Cuban Hawk

WELTERWEIGHT

Right-handed; 5'10½"; 118–155 lbs.

143 bouts, 6/5/1943 to 6/18/1958

Managers: Fernando Balido, Angel Lopez, and Yamil Chade

Welterweight Champion 1951–54

Hall of Fame Induction: 1990

Born: 1/6/1926, Camaguey, Cuba

Named: Gerardo Gonzalez

A regular in the early days of televised boxing, with 34 TV appearances, Kid Gavilan was well known to fans for his confounding style that included playing possum, suddenly switching strategies, and slipping punches. He imported the "bolo punch," a looping uppercut that he could swing with enough power to lift an opponent off his feet.

A worker on a sugar plantation in Cuba, Gavilan competed in amateur bouts from age twelve on. When his family moved to Havana, he was spotted by a team of managers who molded his career and eventually took him to the United States. The young fighter was named after a Havana cafe owned by manager Fernando Balido and known as El Gavilan ("the hawk").

Gavilan turned professional in 1943, at the age of sixteen. After fighting for three years in Cuba, Mexico, and Puerto Rico, he had matches in New York. By 1947, Gavilan was considered one of the top welterweight contenders, although the next year held some setbacks: a loss to veteran Ike Williams by decision, and an over-the-weight match with Sugar Ray Robinson, which Gavilan also lost by decision.

In 1949 Gavilan again met Robinson, this time for the welterweight title. Once more, Robinson proved to be too much for Gavilan and won a decision after fifteen rounds—although some observers believed the victory belonged to the Kid. Gavilan waited two years to take another shot at a world championship (vacated when Robinson moved up to middleweight), when he met Johnny Bratton, who held the NBA version of the welterweight title, in Madison Square Garden. From the first round, Bratton was in trouble, and Gavilan easily won the decision to capture the undisputed title.

Gavilan successfully defended his belt against Billy Graham, although rumors surfaced that the split decision may have resulted from underworld influence. Gavilan won a rematch with Graham and also defended the title against Carmen Basilio. In 1954, he challenged Carl ("Bobo") Olson for the

Gavilan (L) was less than one year from the welterweight title when he decisioned ranked contender Joe Miceli in New York a few days before Christmas 1950.

middleweight title. Overwhelmed by the larger man's punching power, Gavilan lost the decision. That same year, Gavilan lost the welterweight title to Johnny Saxton. Saxton won a decision, even though 19 of the 21 writers at ringside gave the fight to Gavilan. The bout may have been fixed—without Gavilan's knowledge—so that his only hope of winning would have been by knockout.

Gavilan continued to fight for four more years, compiling a 10-15-1 record. A crowd-pleaser, Gavilan showed great speed in the ring, good counter-punching ability, and stamina. His bolo punch, which traced the same motion he had used with a machete in the sugar cane fields, was dreaded by many. He held his own with top fighters of his day and was never knocked out.

IN THE RING	WON 107	LOST 30	DRAWS 6	TB 143	KO 28	W 79	WF 0	D 6	KO'd 0	L 30	LF 0

Date	Opponent	Site	Result / Rounds		Title	Wt.
1943						
Jun 5	Antonio Diaz	Havana	W	4	—	119
Jun 12	Bartolo Molina	Havana	W	4	—	118
Aug 7	Valeriano Dustet	Havana	D	6	—	119
Sep 11	Sergio Prieto	Havana	KO	5	—	—
1944						
Oct 1	Juan Villalba	Havana	KO	9	—	—
Nov 25	Esmerido Salazar	Havana	W	10	—	—
Dec 23	Miguel Acevedo	Havana	W	10	—	—
1945						
Feb 10	Esmerido Salazar	Havana	W	10	—	—
Mar 10	Jose Pedroso	Havana	W	10	—	—
Apr 21	Santiago Sosa	Havana	KO	9	—	—
May 13	Kid Bebo	Cienfuegos, Cuba	KO	4	—	—
May 26	Julio ("Yucatan Kid") Jimenez	Havana	W	10	—	135
Jun 23	Pedro Ortega	Havana	W	10	—	132
Jul 7	Jose Pedroso	Havana	KO	4	Won-Cuba-L	135
Aug 4	Julio Jiminez	Mexico City	W	10	—	—
Aug 26	Pedro Ortega	Mexico City	KO	6	—	—
Sep 22	Carlos Malacara	Mexico City	L	10	—	—
Nov 5	Carlos Malacara	Havana	W	10	—	135
Nov 17	Johnny Suarez	Havana	W	10	—	132
1946						
Jan 26	Kid Bururu	Havana	W	10	—	134
Feb 9	Kid Bururu	Havana	W	10	—	133
Mar 2	Jose R. Zorilla	Bayamon, PR	KO	4	—	—
Mar 9	Santiago Sosa	Havana	W	10	—	—
Apr 5	Tony Martinez	Mexico City	L	10	—	135
Jun 25	Chico Varona	Havana	W	10	—	—
Aug 4	Hankin Barrow	Havana	KO	7	—	—
Aug 24	Jack Larrimore	Havana	KO	3	—	—
Sep 7	Hankin Barrow	Havana	W	10	—	—
Nov 1	Johnny Ryan	New York	KO	5	—	—
Dec 2	Johnny Williams	New York	W	10	—	144
Dec 13	Johnny Williams	New York	W	10	—	144
1947						
Jan 28	Julio Pedroso	Havana	W	10	—	145
Feb 8	Jose Garcia Alvarez	Havana	W	10	—	145
Feb 22	Pablo Roca	Havana	W	10	—	145
Mar 12	Nick Moran	Havana	W	10	—	146

Date		Opponent	Location	Result	Rounds	Notes	Weight
Apr 26		Vince Gambill	Havana	KO	2	—	144
Aug 11		Charlie Williams	Newark	W	10	—	—
Aug 18		Bobby Lee	Baltimore	W	10	—	—
Sep 2		Doug Ratford	Newark	L	10	—	—
Sep 15		Charley Millan	Baltimore	KO	1	—	—
Sep 18		Billy Justine	Philadelphia	W	8	—	—
Oct 23		Billy Nixon	Philadelphia	W	8	—	—
Nov 3		Bee Bee Wright	Baltimore	TKO	10	—	—
Dec 29		Buster Tyler	New York	D	10	—	144
1948							
Jan 12	⑩	Gene Burton	New York	D	10	—	147
Jan 23		Joe Curcio	New York	TKO	2	—	146
Feb 13		Vinnie Rossano	New York	W	10	—	—
Feb 27	⑩	Ike Williams★	New York	L	10	—	141
Apr 13		Doug Ratford	Brooklyn	L	10	—	142
Apr 26	⑩	Tommy Bell	Philadelphia	W	10	—	—
May 28		Rocco Rossano	New York	KO	1	—	—
Jul 22		Roman Alvarez	New York	W	10	—	147
Aug 12		Buster Tyler	New York	W	10	—	—
Sep 23	♛	Sugar Ray Robinson★	New York	L	10	—	—
Oct 21		Vinnie Rossano	Washington	TKO	6	—	—
Nov 12		Tony Pellone	New York	W	10	—	147
Dec 11		Abdul Ben Buker	Havana	W	10	—	147
1949							
Jan 28	⑩	Ike Williams★	New York	W	10	—	—
Apr 1	⑩	Ike Williams★	New York	W	10	—	—
May 2		Al ("Red") Priest	Boston	W	10	—	—
Jun 7		Cliff Hart	Syracuse, NY	KO	2	—	145
Jul 11	♛	Sugar Ray Robinson★	Philadelphia	L	15	For-World-W	144
Sep 9		Rocky Castellani	New York	W	10	—	150
Oct 14	⑩	Beau Jack★	Chicago	W	10	—	—
Oct 21	⑩	Lester Felton	Detroit	L	10	—	145
Nov 21	⑩	Laurent Dauthuille	Montreal	W	10	—	151
Dec 17		Bobby Lee	Havana	W	10	—	146
1950							
Feb 10	⑩	Billy Graham★	New York	L	10	—	146
Mar 6		Otis Graham	Philadelphia	W	10	—	148
Mar 20	⑩	Robert Villemain	Montreal	L	10	—	149
May 8	⑩	George Costner	Philadelphia	L	10	—	—
May 26		George Small	New York	W	10	—	151
Jun 8		Mike Koballa	Brooklyn	W	10	—	151
Jun 19		Bobby Mann	Hartford, CT	W	10	—	155
Jul 2		Sonny Horne	Brooklyn	W	10	—	151
Jul 13		Phil Burton	Omaha, NE	W	10	—	149
Aug 15		Johnny Greco	Montreal	KO	6	—	—
Oct 23		Tommy Ciarlo	New Haven, CT	D	10	—	—
Oct 30	⑩	Eugene Hairston	Scranton, PA	L	10	—	—
Nov 17	⑩	Billy Graham★	New York	W	10	—	—
Dec 4		Tony Janiro	Cleveland	W	10	—	—
Dec 22	⑩	Joe Miceli	New York	W	10	—	—
1951							
Jan 26	⑩	Paddy Young	New York	W	10	—	—
Feb 19		Tommy Ciarlo	Caracas, Venezuela	W	10	—	—
Mar 10		Tommy Ciarlo	Havana	TKO	8	—	—
Mar 30	⑩	Eugene Hairston	New York	W	10	—	—
Apr 20		Aldo Minelli	New York	W	10	—	—
May 18	♛	Johnny Bratton	New York	W	15	Won-Vac World-W	145
Jul 16		Fitzie Pruden	Milwaukee	W	10	—	—
Aug 29	⑩	Billy Graham★	New York	W	15	Ret-World-W	145

Date		Opponent	Location	Result	Rds	Title	Wt
Oct 4		Bobby Rosado	Havana	TKO	7	—	—
Nov 7		Tony Janiro	Detroit	TKO	4	—	—
Nov 28	⑩	Johnny Bratton	Chicago	D	10	—	—
Dec 14	⑩	Walter Cartier	New York	TKO	10	—	—

1952

Date		Opponent	Location	Result	Rds	Title	Wt
Feb 4	⑩	Bobby Dykes	Miami	W	15	Ret-World-W	147
Feb 28		Don Williams	Boston	W	10	—	—
May 19		Ralph Zannelli	Providence, RI	W	10	—	—
May 28		Fitzie Pruden	Indianapolis	TKO	6	—	—
Jul 7	⑩	Gil Turner	Philadelphia	TKO	11	Ret-World-W	146
Aug 16		Mario Diaz	Buenos Aires, Argentina	W	10	—	—
Sep 6		Rafael Merentino	Buenos Aires	TKO	9	—	—
Sep 13		Eduardo Lausse	Buenos Aires	W	10	—	—
Oct 5	⑩	Billy Graham★	Havana	W	15	Ret-World-W	146

1953

Date		Opponent	Location	Result	Rds	Title	Wt
Jan 13		Aman Peck	Tampa	W	10	—	—
Jan 21		Vic Cardell	Washington, DC	W	10	—	—
Feb 11	⑩	Chuck Davey	Chicago	TKO	10	Ret-World-W	146
Apr 14		Livio Minelli	Cleveland	W	10	—	—
May 2	⑩	Danny Womber	Syracuse	L	10	—	—
Jun 10		Italo Scortichini	Detroit	W	10	—	—
Jul 15	⑩	Ramon Fuentes	Milwaukee	W	10	—	—
Aug 26		Ralph Jones	New York	W	10	—	—
Sep 18	⑩	Carmen Basilio★	Syracuse	W	15	Ret-World-W	146
Nov 13	⑩	Johnny Bratton	Chicago	W	15	Ret-World-W	146

1954

Date		Opponent	Location	Result	Rds	Title	Wt
Feb 23		Johnny Cunningham	Miami Beach	W	10	—	—
Mar 8		Livio Minelli	Boston	W	10	—	—
Apr 2	♛	Carl ("Bobo") Olson	Chicago	L	15	For-World-M	155
Oct 20	⑩	Johnny Saxton	Philadelphia	L	15	Lost-World-W	145

1955

Date		Opponent	Location	Result	Rds	Title	Wt
Feb 4		Ernie Durando	New York	W	10	—	—
Feb 23	⑩	Hector Constance	Miami Beach	L	10	—	—
Mar 16		Bobby Dykes	Miami	L	10	—	—
Jun 2		Luigi Cemulini	Santa Clara, Cuba	KO	3	—	—
Jul 23		Cirilo Gil	Buenos Aires	W	10	—	—
Aug 13		Juan Bautista Burgues	Montevideo, Uruguay	KO	7	—	—
Sep 3	⑩	Eduardo Lausse	Buenos Aires	L	12	—	—
Dec 3		Dogomar Martinez	Montevideo	L	10	—	—

1956

Date		Opponent	Location	Result	Rds	Title	Wt
Feb 7		Peter Waterman	London	L	10	—	147
Mar 29		Germinal Ballarin	Paris	L	10	—	—
Apr 24		Peter Waterman	London	W	10	—	—
May 13		Louis Trochon	Marseilles, France	D	10	—	—
Aug 18		Jimmy Beecham	Havana	W	10	—	149
Oct 13	⑩	Tony DeMarco	Boston	L	10	—	—
Nov 13		Chico Vejar	Los Angeles	W	10	—	—
Dec 4		Walter Byars	Boston	L	10	—	148
Dec 20	⑩	Ramon Fuentes	Los Angeles	L	10	—	152

1957

Date		Opponent	Location	Result	Rds	Title	Wt
Feb 26	⑩	Vince Martinez	Newark	L	10	—	148
Apr 24		Del Flanagan	St. Paul, MN	L	10	—	—
Jun 17	⑩	Vince Martinez	Jersey City, NJ	L	10	—	—
Jul 31	⑩	Gaspar Ortega	Miami Beach	W	10	—	—
Oct 22	⑩	Gaspar Ortega	Los Angeles	L	12	—	146
Nov 20		Walter Byars	Chicago	W	10	—	—

1958

Date		Opponent	Location	Result	Rds	Title	Wt
Feb 19	⑩	Ralph Jones	Miami Beach	L	10	—	—
Apr 4	⑩	Ralph Jones	Philadelphia	W	10	—	—
Jun 18		Yama Bahama	Miami Beach	L	10	—	—

MIDDLEWEIGHT

Right-handed; 5'10", 140–175 lbs.

133 bouts, 10/2/1948 to 11/6/1967

Middleweight Champion 1963–65

Hall of Fame Induction: 1993

Born: 7/16/1930, Brooklyn, NY

Named: Carmine Orlando Tilelli

An example of persistence and professionalism, Joey Giardello did not win a championship until he was 33 years old, an age at which many fighters have already retired. A self-taught brawler who built a record of wins that spanned the era from post-World War II through the 1960s, Giardello combined his dodging, dancing style with quick on-target jabs , often opening up his opponents for the knockout.

Giardello turned professional in 1948 at the age of eighteen, without the benefit of organized amateur experience. By 1952, he had won recognition as a top middleweight contender. He fought his first important matches in 1952 and 1953 with Billy Graham. In the three-fight series, the unheralded Giardello began by upsetting Graham, who was eight years older and far more experienced in the ring. In the rematch, the ringside judges initially gave Giardello the split decision, but two commissioners of the New York State Athletic Commission changed one of the judge's scores, giving the win to Graham. Giardello sued, and the case went to New York's Supreme Court. The court ruled that the commissioners did not have the authority to change the scorecard, and Giardello was acknowledged as the winner once again. His victory restored, Giardello faced Graham for a third time, with Graham taking the decision.

Giardello continued to fight top contenders over the next several years, but he did not receive a title shot until he challenged Gene Fullmer for the NBA middleweight crown in April 1960. The match took place in the Montana State University field house in Bozeman and went a bitter and bruising fifteen rounds—with each boxer protesting the other's tactics—before being declared a draw. Years later, Giardello still expressed anger about this bout, calling Fullmer "the dirtiest fighter in the book." Fullmer, who claimed Giardello had fractured his skull with a headbutt, unhesitatingly returned the charge. The score was never settled; Fullmer and Giardello never fought again.

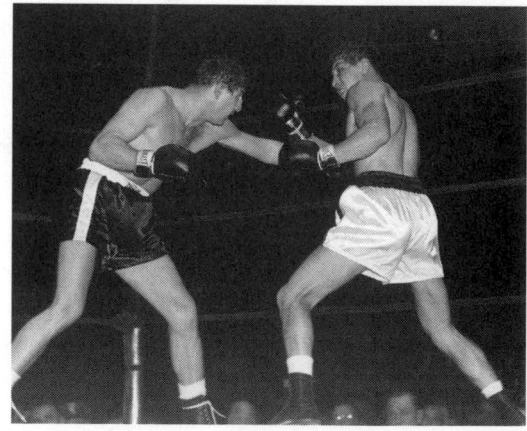

The result was in doubt long after this December 1952 Garden meeting between Billy Graham and Joey Giardello (R). After the NYSAC reversed the win by Giardello, a court reconfirmed the original decision.

In 1963, Giardello's moment finally arrived when he was signed to fight Dick Tiger for the world middleweight championship, which Tiger had wrested from Fullmer the year before. Giardello fought defensively and scored with jabs and hooks to win the fifteen-rounder in Atlantic City. Middleweight champion at last, Giardello held onto the title for two years. He defended it once, winning over Ruben Carter in 1964, then lost it in a rematch with Tiger in 1965.

Giardello fought twice in 1966 and twice in 1967 before retiring at 37. In a long, sometimes frustrating career, Giardello racked up a hundred victories.

IN THE RING	WON 100	LOST 25	DRAWS 7	TB 133	KO 32	W 68	WF 0	D 7	KO'd 4	L 21	LF 0	ND 1

Date	Opponent	Site	Result / Rounds		Title	Wt.
1948						
Oct 2	Johnny Noel	Trenton, NJ	KO	2	—	154
Oct 10	Jimmy Larkin	Atlantic City	KO	1	—	154
Nov 7	Bobby Clark	Wilkes-Barre, PA	W	4	—	—
Nov 20	Johnny Brown	Reading, PA	KO	4	—	—
Dec 16	Johnny Madison	Atlantic City	KO	1	—	154
Dec 30	Willie Wigfall	Philadelphia	KO	1	—	—
1949						
Feb 24	Clyde Diggs	Philadelphia	D	6	—	—
Mar 15	Don Ennis	Reading	KO	4	—	—
Apr 7	Bill Montgomery	Philadelphia	KO	1	—	—
Apr 25	Ray Morris	Wilkes-Barre	W	4	—	—
Apr 28	Joe Aurillo	Philadelphia	W	6	—	—
May 2	Emerson Charles	Philadelphia	W	4	—	—
Jun 6	Henry Vonsavage	Philadelphia	KO	2	—	—
Jun 20	Ray Hass	Philadelphia	KO	3	—	—
Jul 13	Leroy Fleming	Washington, DC	KO	1	—	—
Nov 14	Mitchell Allen	Philadelphia	W	6	—	—
Dec 5	Jim Dockery	Philadelphia	KO	2	—	—
1950						
Jan 5	Johnny Fry	Philadelphia	W	6	—	—
Jan 16	Joe DiMartino	New Haven, CT	L	8	—	—
Jan 26	Johnny Bernardo	Philadelphia	W	8	—	—
Feb 9	Johnny Bernardo	Philadelphia	W	8	—	—
Mar 23	Armando Amanini	Brooklyn	W	8	—	156
Mar 27	Steve Sabatino	Philadelphia	KO	1	—	158
Mar 29	Johnny Brown	Allentown, PA	W	6	—	—
Apr 20	Tommy Varsos	Brooklyn	KO	1	—	—
May 4	Hurley Sanders	Brooklyn	W	8	—	—
May 17	Carey Mace	New York	KO'd	8	—	—
Aug 25	Al Berry	Scranton, PA	KO	1	—	—
Sep 26	Ted DiGiammo	Wilkes-Barre	KO	1	—	158
Oct 16	Bruce Ubaldo	Wilkes-Barre	W	8	—	—
Oct 26	Harold Green	Brooklyn	KO'd	6	—	—
Nov 27	Gene Roberts	Philadelphia	D	8	—	—
Dec 18	Leroy Allen	Philadelphia	KO	5	—	—
1951						
Jan 6	Freddie Lott	Brooklyn	W	8	—	—
Feb 10	Jan Henri	Philadelphia	W	8	—	—
Feb 22	Hal Sampson	Brooklyn	W	8	—	—

Date		Opponent	Location	Result	Rounds		
Feb 24		Tony Wolfe	Philadelphia	KO	3	—	—
Mar 15		Roy Wouters	Philadelphia	L	8	—	—
Mar 29		Primos Cutler	Philadelphia	W	8	—	—
Apr 12		Roy Wouters	Philadelphia	W	8	—	—
Apr 30	⑩	Ernie Durando	Scranton	W	10	—	—
May 25		Gus Rubicini	New York	L	8	—	—
Aug 13		Otis Graham	Philadelphia	W	8	—	—
Aug 27		Johnny Noel	Philadelphia	W	8	—	—
Sep 14		Tommy Bazzano	New York	W	6	—	—
Oct 8		Tony Amato	New York	KO	7	—	—
Nov 13	⑩	Rocky Castellani	Scranton	L	10	—	—
Dec 12		Bobby Dykes	Miami Beach	L	10	—	—
1952							
Jan 9		Sal DiMartino	Miami Beach	D	10	—	—
Mar 28		Sammy Giuliani	New York	D	8	—	—
May 5	⑩	Joe Miceli	Scranton	D	10	—	—
Jun 5		Roy Wouters	Philadelphia	W	6	—	—
Jun 23	⑩	Pierre Langlois	Brooklyn	W	10	—	—
Aug 4	⑩	Billy Graham★	Brooklyn	W	10	—	—
Sep 15		Georgie Small	Brooklyn	W	10	—	—
Oct 13		Joey Giambra	Brooklyn	W	10	—	—
Nov 11		Joey Giambra	Buffalo	L	10	—	—
Dec 19	⑩	Billy Graham★	New York	W	10	—	—
1953							
Feb 2		Harold Green	Brooklyn	W	10	—	—
Mar 6	⑩	Billy Graham★	New York	L	12	—	—
Apr 7	⑩	Gil Turner	Philadelphia	W	10	—	—
May 30		Hurley Sanders	Newark	W	10	—	—
Jun 26	⑩	Ernie Durando	New York	W	10	—	—
Sep 29	⑩	Johnny Saxton	Philadelphia	L	10	—	—
Oct 26		Walter Dartier	Brooklyn	W	10	—	—
Nov 23		Tuzo Portuguez	Brooklyn	W	10	—	—
1954							
Jan 8		Garth Panter	New York	TKO	5	—	—
Feb 5		Walter Cartier	New York	TKO	1	—	—
Mar 19	⑩	Willie Troy	New York	TKO	7	—	—
May 21	⑩	Pierre Langlois	New York	L	10	—	—
Jun 11	⑩	Bobby Jones	New York	W	10	—	—
Jul 7		Billy Kilgore	Philadelphia	W	10	—	—
Sep 24		Tiger Jones	Philadelphia	W	10	—	—
1955							
Jan 25		Al Andrews	Norfolk, VA	W	10	—	—
Feb 15		Andy Mayfield	Miami Beach	KO	8	—	—
Mar 1		Peter Mueller	Milwaukee	KO	2	—	—
1956							
Feb 11		Tim Jones	Trenton, NJ	TKO	10	—	—
Mar 10		Hurley Sanders	Paterson, NJ	W	10	—	161
Mar 27		Joe Shaw	Philadelphia	W	10	—	—
May 7		Charlie Cotton	New York	L	10	—	160
May 28		Charlie Cotton	New York	L	10	—	—
Jul 2		Tony Baldoni	New York	KO	1	—	—
Jul 26		Franz Szuzina	Milwaukee	W	10	—	—
Aug 28		James Bussey	Miami Beach	TKO	9	—	161
Sep 28	⑩	Bobby Boyd	Cleveland	KO	5	—	—
Nov 15		Charlie Cotton	Milwaukee	W	10	—	—
Dec 14		Charlie Cotton	Cleveland	W	10	—	—

Date		Opponent	Location	Result	Rounds		
1957							
Feb 6		Randy Sandy	Chicago	W	10	—	—
Mar 27	⑩	Willie Vaugh	Kansas City, MO	ND	10	—	—
May 17	⑩	Rory Calhoun	Cleveland	W	10	—	—
Jul 2		Joe Gray	Detroit	KO	6	—	—
Jul 17		Chico Vejar	Louisville, KY	W	10	—	—
Sep 27		Bobby Lane	Cleveland	KO	7	—	—
Nov 5		Wilf Greaves	Denver	W	10	—	—
Dec 27	⑩	Tiger Jones	Miami Beach	W	10	—	—
1958							
Feb 12		Franz Szuzina	Philadelphia	W	10	—	—
May 5	⑩	Rory Calhoun	San Francisco	W	10	—	—
Jun 11		Franz Szuzina	Washington, DC	W	10	—	—
Jun 30	⑩	Joey Giambra	San Francisco	L	10	—	—
Nov 19	⑩	Spider Webb	San Francisco	TKO'd	7	—	—
1959							
Jan 28	⑩	Tiger Jones	Louisville	L	10	—	—
May 6	⑩	Holley Mims	Washington, DC	W	10	—	—
Jun 16	⑩	Del Flanagan	St. Paul, MN	KO	1	—	—
Aug 11		Chico Vejar	St. Paul	W	10	—	—
Sep 30	⑩	Dick Tiger★	Chicago	L	10	—	—
Nov 4	⑩	Dick Tiger★	Cleveland	W	10	—	—
1960							
Apr 20	♛	Gene Fullmer★	Bozeman, MT	D	15	For-NBA-M	158
Sep 27		Clarence Hinnant	Billings, MT	TKO	3	—	—
Oct 11	⑩	Terry Downes	London	L	10	—	160
Dec 1		Peter Mueller	Cologne, Germany	L	10	—	—
1961							
Mar 6	⑩	Ralph Dupas	New Orleans	L	10	—	—
May 15		Wilf Greaves	Philadelphia	TKO	9	—	162
Jul 10	⑩	Henry Hank	Detroit	L	10	—	—
Sep 12	⑩	Jesse Smith	Philadelphia	W	10	—	161
Nov 6	⑩	Jesse Smith	Chicago	W	10	—	163
Dec 12		Joe DeNucci	Boston	D	10	—	161
1962							
Jan 30	⑩	Henry Hank	Philadelphia	W	10	—	162
Jul 9		Jimmy Beecham	St. Paul	W	10	—	—
Aug 6	⑩	George Benton	Philadelphia	L	10	—	—
Nov 12		Johnny Morris	Baltimore	W	10	—	—
1963							
Feb 25		Wilf Greaves	Jacksonville, FL	W	10	—	—
Mar 25		Ernie Burford	Philadelphia	W	10	—	161
Jun 24		Sugar Ray Robinson★	Philadelphia	W	10	—	—
Dec 7	♛	Dick Tiger★	Atlantic City	W	15	Won-World-M	158
1964							
Apr 17		Rocky Rivero	Cleveland	W	10	—	—
May 22		Rocky Rivero	Cleveland	W	10	—	—
Dec 14	⑩	Ruben Carter	Philadelphia	W	15	Ret-World-M	160
1965							
Apr 23		Gil Diaz	Cherry Hill, NJ	W	10	—	—
Oct 21	⑩	Dick Tiger★	New York	L	15	Lost-World-M	160
1966							
Sep 22		Cash White	Reading	W	10	—	168
Dec 5		Nate Collins	San Francisco	TKO'd	8	—	—
1967							
May 22		Jack Rodgers	Pittsburgh	L	10	—	—
Nov 6		Jack Rodgers	Philadelphia	W	10	—	—

WILFRED GOMEZ
Bazooka

FEATHERWEIGHT

Right-handed; 5'5"; 121–142 lbs.

48 bouts, 11/16/1974 to 7/19/1989

WBC Super Bantamweight Champion 1977–83,
WBC Featherweight Champion 1984,
Jr. Lightweight Champion 1985–86

Hall of Fame Induction: 1995

Born: 10/29/1956, Las Monjas, PR

Dubbed in 1994 by *The Ring* as the greatest junior featherweight (super bantamweight, in WBC parlance) of all time, Wilfredo Gomez successfully defended this title seventeen times, each time by knockout. A champion in three divisions, Gomez was a titleholder for nearly a decade. A skillful boxer with a repertoire of powerhouse punches, Gomez was inducted into the Hall of Fame the first year he was eligible.

A native of Puerto Rico, Gomez had an excellent amateur record that included a world amateur title won in Havana in 1974. He first fought professionally in Panama with a 1974 draw with Jacinto Fuentes. After that fight, Gomez knocked out 32 consecutive opponents, including Fuentes. A loss by knockout

Gomez's (R) powerful right grotesquely distorts the jaw of Derrick Holmes. The referee called a halt to this August 22, 1980 match after Holmes was knocked down eight times.

IN THE RING	WON 44	LOST 3	DRAWS 1	TB 48	KO 42	W 2	WF 0	D 1	KO'd 3	L 0	LF 0

Date		Opponent	Site	Result / Rounds		Title	Wt.
1974							
Nov 16		Jacinto Fuentes	Panama City	D	6	—	120
Dec 21		Mario Hernandez	San Jose, CA	KO	1	—	—
1975							
Feb 16		Jorge Bernal	Panama City	TKO	1	—	119
Mar 2		Antonio DaSilva	Panama City	KO	2	—	118
May 3		Jose Jimenez	Panama City	KO	1	—	120
Jun 21		Jacinto Fuentes	Panama City	KO	2	—	—
Aug 2		Clotilde Garcia	Managua, Nicaragua	KO	3	—	—
Sep 19		Joe Guevara	San Juan, PR	TKO	6	—	120
Dec 20	⑩	Andres Hernandez	San Juan	TKO	8	—	119
1976							
Feb 20		Cornell Hall	San Juan	KO	3	—	120
Apr 5		Rick Quijano	San Juan	TKO	1	—	120
May 8		Sak Lempthong	San Juan	TKO	3	—	122
Jul 19		Albert Davila	San Juan	TKO	3	—	120
Aug 16		Tony Rocha	San Juan	TKO	2	—	120
Oct 11		Jose Medel	San Juan	KO	4	—	122
1977							
Feb 12		John Meza	San Juan	TKO	2	—	118
May 21	♛	Dong-Kyun Yum	Hato Rey, PR	KO	12	Won-WBC-JFE (SB)	121
Jul 11	⑩	Raul Tirado	Hato Rey	KO	5	Ret-WBC-JFE (SB)	122
1978							
Jan 19		Royal Kobayashi	Kitakyushu, Japan	KO	3	Ret-WBC-JFE (SB)	121
Apr 8		Juan Lopez	Bayamon, PR	TKO	7	Ret-WBC-JFE (SB)	121
Jun 2		Sakad Porntavee	Korat, Thailand	TKO	3	Ret-WBC-JFE (SB)	121
Sep 9		Leonardo Cruz	San Juan	TKO	13	Ret-WBC-JFE (SB)	122
Oct 28		Carlos Zarate★	Hato Rey	TKO	5	Ret-WBC-JFE (SB)	121
1979							
Mar 9		Nestor ("Baba") Jimenez	New York	KO	5	Ret-WBC-JFE (SB)	122
May 21		Nelson Cruz-Tamariz	New York	KO	2	—	125
Jun 16		Julio Hernandez	Hato Rey	TKO	5	Ret-WBC-JFE (SB)	122
Sep 28		Carlos Mendoza	Las Vegas	TKO	10	Ret-WBC-JFE (SB)	122
Oct 26	⑩	Nicky Perez	New York	KO	5	Ret-WBC-JFE (SB)	122
1980							
Feb 3		Ruben Valdez	Las Vegas	TKO	6	Ret-WBC-JFE (SB)	122
Apr 27		Eddie Ndukwu	San Juan	TKO	4	—	129
Aug 22		Derrik Holmes	Las Vegas	TKO	5	Ret-WBC-JFE (SB)	122
Dec 13	⑩	Jose Cervantes	Miami	KO	3	Ret-WBC-JFE (SB)	122
1981							
Jun 20		Raul Silva	San Juan	KO	3	—	128
Aug 21	♛	Salvador Sanchez★	Las Vegas	TKO'd	8	For-WBC-FE	126
1982							
Jan 9		Jose Gonzalez	San Juan	TKO	7	—	129
Feb 20		Jose Soto	San Juan	KO	2	—	125
Mar 27	⑩	Juan Meza	Atlantic City	TKO	6	Ret-WBC-JFE (SB)	121
Jun 11		Juan Lopez	Las Vegas	KO	10	Ret-WBC-JFE (SB)	121

Date		Opponent	Location	Result	Round	Title	
Aug 18	Ⓦ	Ruberto Rubaldino	San Juan	KO	8	Ret-WBC-JFE (SB)	122
Dec 3	Ⓦ	Lupe Pintor	New Orleans	TKO	14	Ret-WBC-JFE (SB)	121
1983							
Apr 23		Ivan Zamuco	Ponce, PR	TKO	3	—	133
Dec 14		Eladio Santana	Hato Rey	TKO	2	—	133
1984							
Mar 31	♛	Juan LaPorte	Hato Rey	W	12	Won-WBC-FE	125
Dec 8	Ⓦ	Azumah Nelson	San Juan	KO'd	11	Lost-WBC-FE	125
1985							
May 19	♛	Rocky Lockridge	San Juan	W	15	Won-World (WBA)-JL	129
1986							
May 24	Ⓦ	Alfredo Layne	San Juan	TKO'd	9	Lost-World (WBA)-JL	130
1988							
Jul 30		Mario Gonzalez	Miami Beach	TKO	6	—	138
1989							
Jul 19		Mario Salazar	Hallandale, FL	TKO	2	—	142

to Salvador Sanchez interrupted Gomez's nearly perfect record, and he never had to submit to the judges' ruling again until he won a decision over Juan LaPorte in 1984.

In 1977, Gomez fought the nearly invincible Dong-Kyun Yum for the WBC super bantamweight title. It was Gomez's seventeenth pro fight. In round one, Yum knocked Gomez down with a sweeping left hook. The shocked Gomez allowed Yum to control rounds two and three as well. By round four, Gomez had recovered and he unleashed a variety of punches to seize control of the bout. In the twelfth, Gomez knocked Yum out—Yum's first knockout in 62 fights—and was the new champion. Gomez would later call this victory his greatest thrill in boxing.

In 1978, Gomez defended his title against Hall of Famer Carlos Zarate. At that time, Zarate was undefeated in 52 bouts. Zarate took the initiative in the first three rounds, although Gomez scored frequently. In the fourth, Gomez exploded, knocking Zarate down three times in a round which lasted an extra fifteen seconds. Gomez floored Zarate once more in the fifth before the contest was stopped.

Gomez's knockout string continued until he challenged Sanchez in Las Vegas in 1981 for the WBC featherweight title. In a fight called "The Battle of the Little Giants," fans saw Sanchez knock Gomez down twice before stopping him in

Gomez (R) sends Nestor ("Baba") Jimenez down to the canvas in a March 9, 1979 super bantamweight title defense in New York. This bout was the seventh of seventeen successful title defenses for Gomez.

the eighth round. A proposed rematch never took place due to Sanchez's death in an automobile accident.

After this loss, Gomez returned to the super bantamweight division where he continued unbeaten. He KO'd contenders Juan Meza, Roberto Rubaldino, and Lupe Pintor in 1982. In 1983, he relinquished his title and moved up to featherweight. In 1984, Gomez challenged Juan LaPorte for the WBC featherweight title. Gomez won a twelve-round decision to capture the title. Azumah Nelson dethroned him in Gomez's first title defense, knocking him out in eleven in San Juan in December 1984.

Gomez was undaunted by this loss, however, and five months later, won his third championship when he decisioned Rocky Lockridge for the world junior lightweight belt, a title he held for just under a year before losing it to Alfredo Layne. Three times a champion, Gomez fought once in 1988 and once in 1989 before retiring with a secure reputation as an excellent puncher with fine defensive skills.

BILLY GRAHAM

WELTERWEIGHT

Right-handed; 5'8"; 127–156 lbs.
126 bouts, 4/14/1941 to 4/1/1955
Manager: Irving Cohen
Hall of Fame Induction: 1992
Born: 9/9/1922, New York, NY
Named: William Walter Graham
Died: 1/22/1992

Though never a champion, Billy Graham won over one hundred fights and made innumerable friends in a career which lasted fourteen years. Born on the East Side of New York, Graham was encouraged to box by his father and began fighting at the local Catholic Boys' Club. Legend has it that at the age of eleven, he beat a youngster named Walker Smith, who would later become known as Sugar Ray Robinson. As a teenager, Graham was denied entrance to the Golden Gloves competition because of a heart murmur.

Graham turned professional in 1941. For the first five years of his career, he fought exclusively in the New York/New Jersey area and was undefeated in his first 58 fights. Though Graham was ranked the tenth-best lightweight in 1946 in the annual rankings by *The Ring*, he did not achieve national prominence until 1950. By then a veteran of over 90 fights, Graham fought the popular Kid Gavilan twice, with each winning a decision.

Kid Gavilan (L) was ruled the winner of this August 29, 1951 title defense against Billy Graham. Ringside observers gave the bout to Graham all the way. Reportedly gangsters "got to" one of the judges.

IN THE RING	WON 102	LOST 15	DRAWS 9	TB 126	KO 26	W 76	WF 0	D 9	KO'd 0	L 15	LF 0

Date	Opponent	Site	Result / Rounds		Title	Wt.
1941						
Apr 14	Connie Savoie	New York	KO	1	—	—
May 5	Frankie Van	New York	W	4	—	—
May 19	Jimmy Kemp	New York	D	4	—	—
Jun 9	Joey Manfro	New York	D	4	—	—
Jun 24	Bobby Henry	New York	W	4	—	—
Jul 30	Joey Agro	New York	D	4	—	—
Sep 30	Bobby Henry	White Plains, NY	W	4	—	—
Oct 13	Bobby Henderson	Brooklyn	W	4	—	—
Nov 10	Bobby Henderson	New York	W	4	—	—
Nov 18	Bobby Henderson	White Plains	W	4	—	—
Nov 24	Mike Martinez	New York	KO	3	—	—
Dec 9	Louis LaSalle	White Plains	D	4	—	—
Dec 18	Al Guido	New York	W	4	—	132
1942						
Jan 19	Joe Maldonado	New York	W	4	—	—
Jan 26	Julian Malavez	New York	KO	3	—	—
Feb 2	Bobby Henry	New York	KO	2	—	—
Feb 17	Harry Diduck	Brooklyn	W	6	—	—
Feb 19	Terry Amico	Elizabeth, NJ	KO	2	—	—
Feb 24	Harry Diduck	New York	W	6	—	—
Mar 3	Al Guido	Brooklyn	W	6	—	—
Mar 23	Al Guido	New York	W	6	—	—
Apr 1	Lew Maxwell	Elizabeth	W	6	—	—
Apr 7	Davey Crawford	New York	W	6	—	—
Apr 16	Tom Sawyer	Elizabeth	KO	1	—	—
Apr 27	Al Simmons	New York	KO	1	—	—
Apr 30	Lew Maxwell	Elizabeth	W	6	—	—
May 15	Moe Weiss	New York	W	4	—	—
Jun 1	Bob Root	New York	W	6	—	—
Jun 5	Jimmy Anest	Elizabeth	W	6	—	—
Jun 9	Wallace Brown	New York	D	6	—	—
Jul 3	Bobby Henderson	Elizabeth	W	6	—	—
Jul 9	Jeff Holloway	Brooklyn	KO	5	—	—
Jul 23	Ted Christie	Newark	KO	2	—	—
Aug 1	Cedric Flournoy	New York	KO	3	—	—
Sep 14	Gus Levine	New York	W	8	—	—
Sep 19	Julian Malavez	Brooklyn	W	6	—	—
Oct 12	Johnny Rudd	New York	TKO	2	—	—
Oct 15	Thaddeus Cabey	Elizabeth	KO	3	—	—
Oct 27	Mickey LaRosa	Brooklyn	KO	5	—	—
Nov 5	Lew Maxwell	Jersey City, NJ	W	6	—	—
Nov 13	Joey Varoff	New York	D	6	—	—
1944						
Apr 13	Ralph Pacheco	Hyde Park, NY	W	6	—	—
Apr 19	Jackie Smallwood	Elizabeth	KO	1	—	—
May 4	Sammy Mammone	Hyde Park	W	6	—	—
May 10	Sammy Mammone	Elizabeth	W	6	—	—
May 31	Doug Carter	Elizabeth	W	6	—	—
Jun 26	George Johnson	New York	TKO	5	—	—

Date	Opponent	Location	Result	Rounds		
Jun 28	Johnny Williams	Elizabeth	KO	4	—	—
Jul 10	Jimmy Pierce	New York	W	6	—	—
Jul 17	Julian Malavez	Newark	W	6	—	—
Jul 21	Jackie Connor	Long Branch, NJ	TKO	6	—	—
1945						
Mar 5	Tommy Mills	New York	W	6	—	—
Mar 17	Herbie Solomon	Brooklyn	W	6	—	—
Mar 31	Jeff Holloway	Brooklyn	W	8	—	—
Apr 21	Johnny Williams	Brooklyn	W	8	—	—
May 25	Joey Manfro	New York	W	6	—	—
Aug 13	Johnny Rinaldi	New York	TKO	4	—	—
Aug 27	Donnie Maes	New York	TKO	1	—	—
Sep 11	Tony Pellone	New York	L	10	—	—
Oct 8	Cabey Lewis	New York	W	10	—	—
1946						
Mar 25	Charley Milan	Baltimore	W	10	—	—
Apr 15	Pat Scanlon	New York	TKO	6	—	—
May 8	Pedro Biesca	New York	W	8	—	—
May 13	Frankie Carto	New York	KO	9	—	—
May 20	Jimmy Joyce	Baltimore	W	10	—	—
Aug 20	Vic Costa	New York	W	8	—	—
Aug 30 ⑩	Tony Pellone	New York	L	10	—	—
Oct 15	Cleo Shans	New York	W	10	—	141
Oct 25	Doll Rafferty	New York	W	10	—	141
1947						
Jan 17	Ruby Kessler	New York	W	10	—	141
Mar 21 ⑩	Tippy Larkin	New York	L	10	—	139
May 27	Ernie Petrone	Brooklyn	W	8	—	141
Jun 2 ⑩	Aldo Minelli	New York	W	8	—	142
Sep 12	Billy Seep	Worcester, MA	KO	2	—	—
Oct 13	Pat Giordano	Rochester, NY	W	10	—	—
Oct 24	Willie Beltram	New York	W	10	—	—
Nov 21	Rocco Rossano	New York	W	10	—	—
1948						
Jan 20	Jimmy Joyce	New York	TKO	5	—	—
Feb 2	Patsy Brandino	Brooklyn	W	10	—	—
Jun 21	Patsy Brandino	New York	W	8	—	—
Jul 16	Maxie Starr	New York	W	8	—	—
Aug 26 ⑩	Terry Young	New York	W	10	—	—
Dec 2	Joe Lucignano	New York	W	8	—	—
Dec 13	Billy Lee	Newark	W	8	—	—
1949						
Jan 26	Fitzie Pruden	New York	W	10	—	—
Feb 7	Eddie Thomas	London	L	10	—	—
Mar 4 ⑩	Paddy DeMarco	New York	L	10	—	—
Apr 9	Mike Koballa	Brooklyn	W	8	—	—
Jun 7	Sonny Hampton	Wilkes-Barre, PA	W	10	—	—
Jul 8	Jimmy Sanders	Long Beach, NY	W	10	—	—
Sep 19	James Cox	Miami	KO	3	—	—
Oct 19	Jean Walczak	New York	W	10	—	—
Nov 23	Tony LaBua	New York	W	10	—	—
1950						
Jan 18	Tony Pellone	New York	W	10	—	—
Feb 10 ⑩	Kid Gavilan★	New York	W	10	—	—
Apr 14	Phil Burton	Wilkes-Barre	W	10	—	—

Date		Opponent	Location	Result	Rounds	Notes	Weight
Apr 18		Jimmy Sanders	Cleveland	W	10	—	—
Jul 14		Tommy Bazzano	Long Beach, NY	W	10	—	145
Aug 14		Sammy Mastrean	Brooklyn	W	10	—	145
Oct 24		Kid Dussart	Toledo, OH	W	10	—	—
Nov 17	⑩	Kid Gavilan ★	New York	L	10	—	—
Dec 19		Tommy Ciarlo	New York	W	8	—	—
1951							
Aug 9		Billy Jenkins	North Adams, MA	W	8	—	—
Aug 29	♛	Kid Gavilan ★	New York	L	15	For-World-W	145
Oct 8		Mario Trigo	Milwaukee	D	10	—	—
Oct 22		Jimmy Brown	Holyoke, MA	KO	4	—	—
Nov 1		Johnny Cesario	Canton, OH	W	10	—	—
Nov 27		Danny Stepanovitch	Cincinnati	W	10	—	—
1952							
Feb 15		Jimmy Herring	New York	W	10	—	—
Mar 24		Mike Gillo	Holyoke	W	10	—	—
Apr 14		Art Soto	San Francisco	W	10	—	—
May 16	⑩	Rocky Castellani	New York	D	10	—	—
Aug 4	⑩	Joey Giardello ★	Brooklyn	L	10	—	—
Aug 20		Carmen Basilio ★	Chicago	W	10	—	—
Oct 5	♛	Kid Gavilan ★	Havana	L	15	For-World-W	146
Dec 19	⑩	Joey Giardello ★	New York	L	10	—	—
1953							
Jan 29	⑩	Art Aragon	Los Angeles	W	10	—	—
Mar 6	⑩	Joey Giardello ★	New York	W	12	—	—
Jun 6	⑩	Carmen Basilio ★	Syracuse, NY	L	12	—	—
Jul 25	⑩	Carmen Basilio ★	Syracuse	D	12	—	—
Dec 18	⑩	Paddy Young	New York	W	10	—	—
1954							
Jun 10		Charlie Simmons	Danbury, CT	TKO	6	—	—
Jul 19		Chris Christensen	Brooklyn	L	10	—	—
Oct 21	⑩	Ramon Fuentes	Los Angeles	L	10	—	—
1955							
Mar 4		Chico Vejar	New York	L	10	—	—
Apr 1		Chico Vejar	Syracuse	L	10	—	—

In 1951, Graham challenged Gavilan for the world welterweight title. Although experts agreed that Graham dominated the fight, Gavilan won the decision. Regarding the verdict, matchmaker Teddy Brenner said, "If a fighter ever won a fight, Graham won that fight. It ranks among the worst decisions I've ever seen." In Brenner's autobiography, he stated that Arthur Schwartz, one of the judges in the fight, had been pressured to give the decision to Gavilan by "certain figures." Apparently, before the fight, Irving Cohen, Graham's manager, had refused to give a percentage of Graham's contract to underworld denizen Frankie Carbo. The New York State Athletic Commission reviewed the matter in 1985 but did not change the decision.

Graham lost his rematch with Gavilan in Havana. He both won and lost to Joey Giardello and Carmen Basilio in 1952 and 1953, and retired two years later. Never a hard puncher, Graham did not record many knockouts in his career, but he was never knocked down either. A popular fighter, Graham won the respect of the entire boxing community.

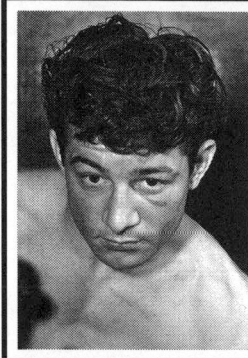

MIDDLEWEIGHT

Right-handed; 5'7"; 147–162 lbs.

83 bouts, 3/31/1942 to 9/17/1952

Managers: Irving Cohen and Jack Hurley

Middleweight Champion 1947–48

Hall of Fame Induction: 1991

Born: 1/1/1922, New York, NY

Named: Thomas Rocco Barbella

Died: 5/22/90

Though Rocky Graziano often found himself embroiled in controversy during his boxing career, he emerged as one of the most popular fighters of the 1940s and early '50s. Born in New York City, Graziano overcame an impoverished, delinquent boyhood to become the middleweight champion of the world. After a stint in reform school, Graziano entered the Metropolitan AAU boxing tournament in New York as a replacement for another fighter. Graziano won the tournament—his first organized boxing experience. Graziano served time in prison at Riker's Island and later, while in the Army, in military prison for striking an officer. He officially began his professional boxing

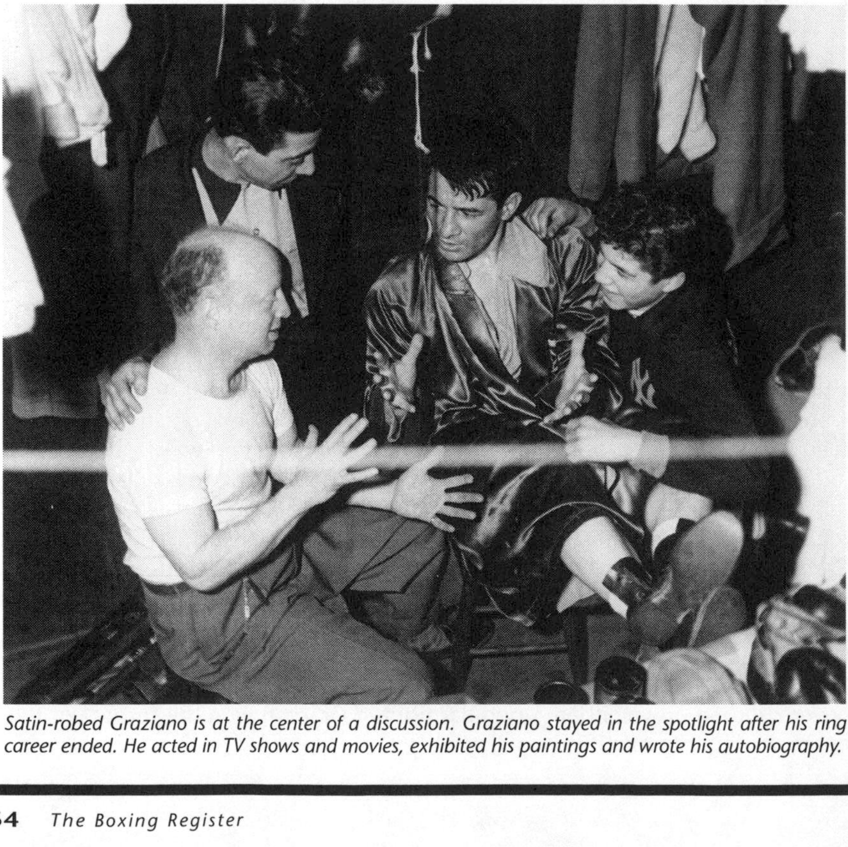

Satin-robed Graziano is at the center of a discussion. Graziano stayed in the spotlight after his ring career ended. He acted in TV shows and movies, exhibited his paintings and wrote his autobiography.

IN THE RING	WON 67	LOST 10	DRAWS 6	TB 83	KO 52	W 14	WF 1	D 6	KO'd 3	L 7	LF 0

Date	Opponent	Site	Result / Rounds		Title	Wt.
1942						
Mar 31	Curtis Hightower	Brooklyn	KO	2	—	148
Apr 6	Mike Mastandrea	New York	KO	3	—	—
Apr 14	Kenny Blackmar	Brooklyn	KO	1	—	—
Apr 20	Godfrey Howell	New York	D	4	—	—
Apr 28	Charley Ferguson	Brooklyn	L	4	—	—
May 4	Ed Lee	New York	KO	4	—	—
May 12	Godfrey Howell	Brooklyn	KO	4	—	—
May 25	Lou Miller	New York	D	6	—	—
1943						
Jun 11	Gilbert Vasquez	Brooklyn	KO	1	—	—
Jun 16	Joe Curcio	Elizabeth, NJ	KO	4	—	—
Jun 24	Frankie Falco	Brooklyn	KO	5	—	—
Jul 8	Johnny Attelly	Brooklyn	TKO	2	—	—
Jul 22	Georgie Stevens	Brooklyn	KO	1	—	—
Jul 27	Randy Drew	Long Island City, NY	KO	1	—	149
Aug 12	Charley McPherson	Brooklyn	W	6	—	—
Aug 20	Ted Apostoli	New York	W	4	—	148
Aug 24	Tony Grey	Long Island City	KO	6	—	—
Sep 10	Joe Agosta	New York	L	6	—	—
Sep 21	Sonny Wilson	Brooklyn	W	8	—	151
Oct 5	Freddie Graham	Brooklyn	KO	1	—	150
Oct 13	Jimmy Williams	Elizabeth	TKO	2	—	151
Oct 27	Charley McPherson	Elizabeth	D	6	—	151
Nov 12	Steve Riggio	New York	L	6	—	149
Nov 30	Freddie Graham	Jersey City, NJ	W	8	—	—
Dec 6	Charley McPherson	New York	W	6	—	—
Dec 27	Milo Theodorescu	Newark	TKO	1	—	—
1944						
Jan 4	Harry Gray	Jersey City	W	8	—	—
Jan 7	Jerry Pittro	New York	TKO	1	—	—
Jan 18	Phil Enzenga	Brooklyn	TKO	5	—	—
Feb 9	Steve Riggio	New York	L	6	—	—
Feb 24	Manny Morales	Highland Park, NJ	KO	4	—	—
Mar 4	Leon Anthony	Brooklyn	KO	1	—	—
Mar 8	Harry Gary	Elizabeth	W	6	—	—
Mar 14	Ray Rovelli	Brooklyn	W	8	—	152
Apr 10	Bobby Brown	Washington, DC	KO	5	—	—
May 9	Freddie Graham	Washington, DC	KO	3	—	—

career in 1942, although he had fought so-called amateur bouts for compensation before that.

By 1945, Graziano had started to make a name for himself, knocking out Billy Arnold and Bummy Davis. In 1946, the title war between Graziano and middleweight champ Tony Zale commenced. Zale ultimately got the best of Graziano but not until Graziano had worn the crown for a year. It started when Graziano challenged Zale for the championship in New York in a fight *The Ring's* International Ratings Panel called the fourth-greatest of all time. Both fighters had strong

Date		Opponent	Location	Result	Rds	Notes	No.
May 29		Tommy Mollis	Washington, DC	TKO	7	—	149
Jun 7		Larney Moore	Brooklyn	KO	2	—	—
Jun 27		Frankie Terry	Brooklyn	TKO	6	—	—
Jul 21		Tony Reno	Brooklyn	W	8	—	—
Aug 14		Jerry Fiorello	Long Island City	W	8	—	—
Sep 15		Frankie Terry	New York	D	8	—	151
Oct 6		Danny Kapilow	New York	D	10	—	152
Oct 24		Bernie Miller	Brooklyn	TKO	2	—	154
Nov 3	⑩	Harold Green	New York	L	10	—	150
Dec 22	⑩	Harold Green	New York	L	10	—	—
1945							
Mar 9	⑩	Billy Arnold	New York	TKO	3	—	—
Apr 17		Solomon Stewart	Washington, DC	KO	4	—	—
May 25		Al ("Bummy") Davis	New York	TKO	4	—	—
Jun 29	⑩	Freddie ("Red") Cochrane	New York	KO	10	—	153
Aug 24	⑩	Freddie ("Red") Cochrane	New York	KO	10	—	154
Sep 28	⑩	Harold Green	New York	KO	3	—	153
1946							
Jan 18		Sonny Horne	New York	W	10	—	155
Mar 29		Marty Servo	New York	TKO	2	—	152
Sep 27	♛	Tony Zale★	New York	KO'd	6	For-World-M	154
1947							
Jun 10		Eddie Finazzo	Memphis, TN	TKO	1	—	—
Jun 16		Jerry Fiorello	Toledo, OH	TKO	5	—	—
Jul 16	♛	Tony Zale★	Chicago	TKO	6	Won-World-M	155
1948							
Apr 5		Sonny Horne	Washington, DC	W	10	—	160
Jun 10	⑩	Tony Zale★	Newark	KO'd	3	Lost-World-M	158
1949							
Jun 21		Bobby Claus	Wilmington, DE	KO	2	—	—
Jul 18		Joey Agosta	W. Springfield	KO	2	—	—
Sep 14	⑩	Charley Fusari	New York	TKO	10	—	159
Dec 6		Sonny Horne	Cleveland	W	10	—	—
1950							
Mar 6		Joe Curcio	Miami	TKO	1	—	162
Mar 31		Tony Janiro	New York	D	10	—	—
Apr 24		Danny Williams	New Haven, CT	KO	3	—	—
May 9		Vinnie Cidone	Milwaukee	TKO	3	—	160
May 16		Henry Brimm	Buffalo	KO	4	—	160
Oct 4		Gene Burton	Chicago	KO	7	—	160
Oct 16		Pete Mead	Milwaukee	KO	3	—	—
Oct 27		Tony Janiro	New York	W	10	—	—
Nov 27		Honey Johnson	Philadelphia	KO	4	—	—
1951							
Mar 19		Reuben Jones	Miami	KO	3	—	—
May 21		Johnny Greco	Montreal	KO	3	—	—
Jun 18		Freddy Lott	Baltimore	KO	5	—	—
Jul 10		Cecil Hudson	Kansas City	TKO	3	—	—
Aug 6		Chuck Hunter	Boston	WD	2	—	—
Sep 19		Tony Janiro	Detroit	TKO	10	—	—
1952							
Feb 18		Eddie O'Neill	Louisville, KY	TKO	4	—	—
Mar 27		Roy Wouters	Minneapolis	TKO	1	—	—
Apr 16	♛	Sugar Ray Robinson★	Chicago	KO'd	3	For-World-M	159
Sep 17		Chuck Davey	Chicago	L	10	—	—

crowd appeal and the fans went crazy as Zale and Graziano traded explosive punches. Zale knocked Graziano down in the first round, then, just before the bell ended the third round, Graziano sent Zale through the ropes. Zale recovered to knock Graziano out with a left hook in the sixth.

In their rematch the next year in Chicago, Graziano got his revenge. Zale cut Graziano early and punished him severely in the third round, but Graziano recovered to knock Zale down in the sixth and then battered him at will along the ropes before the referee stopped the fight. In 1948, Zale knocked Graziano out in three to reclaim the title.

The Zale fights serve as prime examples of Graziano's style. A great slugger, Graziano was not a clever boxer. He absorbed a tremendous amount of punishment while he waited for the opening he needed to try for a knockout. His record of 52 knockouts in 83 fights is proof of his great punching ability.

Before the third Zale fight, Graziano's prison record was made public and he temporarily lost his license to box in New York for not reporting an attempted bribe. The ban was hard on Graziano, and many observers, including noted boxing writer W.C. Heinz believed the nine-month penalty to be unduly harsh. When Graziano then backed out of a scheduled fight in California with former champion Fred Apostoli, he drew the ire of West Coast boxing officials.

In 1952, Graziano went up against against the middleweight champion Sugar Ray Robinson for one last title attempt. In the third round, Graziano floored Robinson, but Robinson quickly recovered and knocked Graziano out before the round was finished. Graziano fought just once more before retiring. He then wrote an extremely successful autobiography titled *Somebody Up There Likes Me*, which was later made into a movie starring Paul Newman. The colorful Graziano then had a lengthy career as an actor and commercial spokesman.

Defending champ Tony Zale (L) is frozen by Graziano's deadly overhand right. On July 16, 1947, Graziano took the title with a 6th-round TKO.

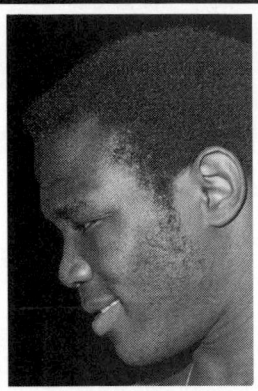

MIDDLEWEIGHT

Right-handed; 5'7½"; 144–162 lbs.

112 bouts, 6/2/1958 to 7/30/1977

Managers: Gil Clancy and Howard Albert

Welterwt. Champ 1961, 1962–63, 1963–66; Middlewt. Champ 1966–67, 1967–68

Hall of Fame Induction: 1990

Born: 2/3/1938, St. Thomas, Virgin Islands

Named: Emile Alphonse Griffith

Emile Griffith held the welterweight championship three times and the middleweight championship twice. Born in the Virgin Islands, Griffith moved to New York when he was nineteen and found work as a stock boy at a millinery. Howard Albert, the owner of the millinery and later Griffith's co-manager, encouraged his employee to try boxing and sent him to Gil Clancy, who would ultimately serve as Griffith's co-manager and trainer. Under Clancy's tutelage, Griffith won the New York Golden Gloves and the Inter-City tournament in 1957. He turned professional the next year at age twenty.

Griffith quickly found success as a welterweight. He won 21 of his first 23 fights and in 1961, earned a shot at the welterweight title held by Benny ("Kid") Paret. In the fight, held at the Miami Beach Convention Hall, Paret had a slim lead until the thirteenth round when Griffith plied him with a left hook followed by a right

Griffith (R) retained his welterweight title in a decision over Luis Rodriguez in June 1964 at Las Vegas— the fourth and final fight of their classic series.

IN THE RING	WON 85	LOST 24	DRAWS 2	TB 112	KO 23	W 62	WF 0	D 2	KO'd 2	L 21	LF 1	NC 1

Date	Opponent	Site	Result / Rounds		Title	Wt.
1958						
Jun 2	Joe Parham	New York	W	4	—	—
Jun 23	Bobby Gibson	New York	W	4	—	—
Jul 21	Martin Leaks	New York	W	4	—	147
Oct 6	Art Cunningham	New York	W	6	—	146
Nov 17	Sergio Rios	New York	KO	3	—	—
Dec 15	Larry Jones	New York	KO	5	—	146
1959						
Jan 26	Gaylord Barnes	New York	KO	5	—	148
Feb 9	Willie Johnson	New York	KO	5	—	—
Feb 23	Barry Allison	New York	KO	5	—	—
Mar 23	Bobby Shell	New York	W	10	—	148
Apr 27	Mel Barker	New York	W	10	—	—
May 25	Willie Stevenson	New York	W	10	—	147
Aug 7	Kid Fichique	New York	W	10	—	—
Oct 26	Randy Sandy	New York	L	10	—	—
Nov 23	Ray Lancaster	New York	TKO	7	—	147
1960						
Jan 8	Roberto Pena	New York	W	10	—	—
Feb 12	⑩ Gaspar Ortega	New York	W	10	—	147
Mar 11	⑩ Denny Moyer	New York	W	10	—	150
Apr 26	⑩ Denny Moyer	Portland, OR	L	10	—	—
Jun 3	⑩ Jorge Fernandez	New York	W	10	—	147
Jul 25	⑩ Jorge Fernandez	New York	W	10	—	150
Aug 25	⑩ Florentino Fernandez	New York	W	10	—	—
Oct 22	Willie Toweel	New York	TKO	8	—	147
Dec 17	⑩ Luis Rodriguez★	New York	W	10	—	—
1961						
Apr 1	♛ Benny ("Kid") Paret	Miami Beach	KO	13	Won-World-W	145
Jun 3	⑩ Gaspar Ortega	Los Angeles	TKO	12	Ret-World-W	145
Jul 29	⑩ Yama Bahama	New York	W	10	—	—
Sep 30	⑩ Benny ("Kid") Paret	New York	L	15	Lost-World-W	147
Nov 4	Stanford Bulla	Hamilton, NY	TKO	4	—	—
Dec 23	Isaac Logart	New York	W	10	—	151
1962						
Feb 3	Johnny Torres	St. Thomas, VI	W	10	—	153
Mar 24	♛ Benny ("Kid") Paret	New York	TKO	12	Reg-World-W	144
Jul 13	⑩ Ralph DuPas	Las Vegas	W	15	Ret-World-W	145
Aug 18	⑩ Denny Moyer	Tacoma, WA	W	10	—	—
Oct 6	Don Fullmer	New York	W	10	—	—
Oct 17	⑩ Teddy Wright	Vienna	W	15	Won-Vac EBU World-JM	149
Dec 8	⑩ Jorge Fernandez	Las Vegas	TKO	9	Ret-World-W	145
1963						
Feb 3	Chris Christensen	Copenhagen, Denmark	TKO	9	Ret-EBU World-JM	152
Mar 21	⑩ Luis Rodriguez★	Los Angeles	L	5	Lost-World-W	145
Jun 8	♛ Luis Rodriguez★	New York	W	15	Reg-World-W	146
Aug 10	Holly Mims	Saratoga Springs, NY	W	10	—	—
Oct 5	Jose Gonzalez	San Juan	W	10	—	—
Dec 20	Rubin ("Hurricane") Carter	Pittsburgh	TKO'd	1	—	—
1964						
Feb 10	⑩ Ralph DuPas	Sydney	KO	3	—	149
Mar 11	Juan Duran	Rome	NC	7	—	—

Date		Opponent	Location	Result	Rds	Title	Wt
Apr 14	⑩	Stan Harrington	Honolulu	KO	4	—	—
Jun 12	⑩	Luis Rodriguez★	Las Vegas	W	15	Ret-World-W	146
Sep 22	⑩	Brian Curvis	London	W	15	Ret-World-W	145
Dec 1		Dave Charnley	Wembley, England	TKO	9	—	148

1965

Date		Opponent	Location	Result	Rds	Title	Wt
Jan 21	⑩	Manuel Gonzalez	Houston	L	10	—	149
Mar 30	⑩	Jose Stable	New York	W	15	Ret-World-W	146
Jun 14	⑩	Eddie Pace	Honolulu	W	10	—	149
Aug 20	⑩	Don Fullmer	Salt Lake City	L	12	—	150
Sep 14		Gabe Terronez	Fresno, CA	KO	4	—	148
Oct 4		Harry Scott	Kensington, England	TKO	7	—	154
Dec 10	⑩	Manuel Gonzalez	New York	W	15	Ret-World-W	146

1966

Date		Opponent	Location	Result	Rds	Title	Wt
Feb 3		Johnny Brooks	Las Vegas	W	10	—	155
Apr 25	♛	Dick Tiger★	New York	W	10	Won-World-M	160
Jul 13	⑩	Joey Archer	New York	W	15	Ret-World-M	160

1967

Date		Opponent	Location	Result	Rds	Title	Wt
Jan 23	⑩	Joey Archer	New York	W	15	Ret-World-M	160
Apr 17	⑩	Nino Benvenuti★	New York	L	15	Lost-World-M	160
Sep 29	♛	Nino Benvenuti★	Flushing, NY	W	15	Reg-World-M	160
Dec 15		Remo Golfarini	Rome	KO	6	—	157

1968

Date		Opponent	Location	Result	Rds	Title	Wt
Mar 4	⑩	Nino Benvenuti★	New York	L	15	Lost-World-M	160
Jun 11		Andy Heilman	Oakland	W	12	—	—
Aug 6	⑩	Joe Harris	Philadelphia	W	12	—	157
Oct 29	⑩	Stan Hayward	Philadelphia	L	10	—	156

1969

Date		Opponent	Location	Result	Rds	Title	Wt
Feb 3	⑩	Andy Heilman	New York	W	10	—	156
May 12	⑩	Stan Hayward	New York	W	12	—	155
Jul 11		Dick DiVeronica	Syracuse, NY	TKO	7	—	152
Aug 15		Art Hernandez	Sioux Falls, SD	W	10	—	—
Oct 18	♛	Jose Napoles★	Inglewood, CA	L	15	For-World-W	144

1970

Date		Opponent	Location	Result	Rds	Title	Wt
Jan 28	⑩	Doyle Baird	Cleveland	W	10	—	—
Mar 11		Carlos Marks	New York	W	12	—	156
Jun 4	⑩	Tom Bogs	Copenhagen	W	10	—	—
Jul 15	⑩	Dick Tiger★	New York	W	10	—	—
Oct 17		Danny Perez	St. Thomas	W	10	—	—
Nov 10		Nate Collins	San Francisco	W	10	—	—

1971

Date		Opponent	Location	Result	Rds	Title	Wt
Mar 23	⑩	Rafael Gutierrez	San Francisco	W	10	—	156
Apr 10		Juan Ramos	St. Thomas	KO	2	—	—
May 3		Ernie Lopez	Las Vegas	W	10	—	—
Jul 26		Nessim Cohen	New York	W	10	—	—
Sep 25	♛	Carlos Monzon★	Buenos Aires	TKO'd	14	For-World-M	160
Dec 10		Danny McAloon	New York	W	10	—	—

1972

Date		Opponent	Location	Result	Rds	Title	Wt
Jan 31		Armando Muniz	Anaheim, CA	W	10	—	156
Feb 21		Jacques Kechichian	Paris	W	10	—	
Mar 30	⑩	Ernie Lopez	Los Angeles	W	10	—	153
Sep 16		Joe DeNucci	Boston	W	10	—	156
Oct 11		Joe DeNucci	Boston	W	12	—	156
Dec 18	⑩	Jean Bouttier	Paris	LD	7	—	—

1973

Date		Opponent	Location	Result	Rds	Title	Wt
Mar 12		Max Cohen	Paris	D	10	—	154
Jun 2	♛	Carlos Monzon★	Monte Carlo, Monaco	L	15	For-World-M	157
Nov 2		Manny Gonzalez	Tampa	W	10	—	—
Nov 19	⑩	Tony Mundine	Paris	L	10	—	—

1974							
Feb 5	⑩	Tony Licata	Boston	L	12	For-Vac NABF-M	160
May 25		Renato Garcia	Monte Carlo	W	10	—	—
Oct 9	⑩	Bennie Briscoe	Philadelphia	W	10	—	160
Nov 22	⑩	Vito Antuofermo	New York	L	10	—	—
Dec 10	⑩	Donato Paduano	Montreal	W	10	—	157
1975							
May 31	⑩	Jose Duran	Cali, Columbia	L	10	—	—
Jul 23		Leo Saenz	Landover, MD	W	10	—	157
Aug 9		Elijah Makhatini	Johannesburg	L	10	—	—
Nov 7		Jose Chirino	Albany, NY	W	10	—	—
1976							
Feb 9		Loucif Hamani	Paris	L	10	—	—
Jun 26	⑩	Bennie Briscoe	Monte Carlo	D	10	—	—
Sep 18	♛	Eckhard Dagge	Berlin	L	15	For-WBC-JM	151
Oct 24		Dino Del Cid	Cartagena, Columbia	TKO	4	—	—
Dec 4		Frank Reiche	Hamburg, Germany	TKO	10	—	—
1977							
Feb 2		Christy Elliott	New York	W	10	—	—
Apr 15		Joel Bonnetaz	Periqueux, France	L	1	—	—
Jul 19		Mayfield Pennington	Louisville, KY	L	10	—	159
Jul 30	⑩	Alan Minter	Monte Carlo	L	10	—	—

to knock him out. Griffith lost the rematch in a split decision. Griffith believed he had won the fight, and his opinion was shared by twelve boxing writers at ringside.

Six months later, Griffith met Paret for the third and final time in Madison Square Garden in front of 7,600. Though knocked down early, Griffith controlled the fight and by the twelfth round was in such command that he blasted Paret along the ropes with multiple punches before referee Ruby Goldstein stopped him. Paret died soon after the fight as a result of this beating and residual damage done by his previous opponent, Gene Fullmer. Paret's death wore heavily on Griffith. "I would have quit," he said later, "but I didn't know how to do anything but fight."

Griffith did continue to fight, though perhaps with less of a will to finish off his opponents. He defended his welterweight title once before adding the new junior middleweight crown to his accomplishments with a win over Teddy Wright in Austria in 1962. Griffith lost the welterweight title to Luis Rodriguez in 1963 but decisioned Rodriguez the same year to win it back. Although he suffered a stunning one-round knockout at the hands of Ruben ("Hurricane") Carter in Pittsburgh late in 1963, the loss did not occur in a title fight.

Griffith defended his welterweight titles against several top contenders before going up a class in 1966 to take the world middleweight title with a decision over Dick Tiger. Nino Benvenuti beat Griffith the next year to claim the title, but in the rematch, Griffith battered Benvenuti, cutting his eye, mouth and nose. Both judges gave Griffith the fight, with the referee calling it a draw. Griffith lost to Benvenuti in their third fight, the opener for the new Madison Square Garden.

Griffith continued to fight for nine more years, losing title bids to welterweight Jose Napoles and middleweight Carlos Monzon. A very likable fan favorite and a fixture of Madison Square Garden main events, Griffith combined speed, aggressiveness, and determination to post 85 victories in his career.

MARVELOUS MARVIN HAGLER

MIDDLEWEIGHT

Left-handed; 5'9½"; 155–163 lbs.

67 bouts, 5/18/1973 to 4/6/1987

Managers:
Goody and Pat Petronelli

Middleweight Champion 1980–87

Hall of Fame Induction: 1993

Born: 5/23/1954, Newark, NJ

Marvelous Marvin Hagler successfully defended his middleweight title twelve times—second only to Carlos Monzon's fourteen title defenses. One of boxing's few southpaw champions, Hagler's heroic good looks were incidental to his astounding ring skills. He was a devastating puncher as well as an elegant boxer who could adapt his defense to any opponent's style.

Born in Newark, New Jersey, Hagler moved as a child with his family to Brockton, Massachusetts, the same town which produced Rocky Marciano. Hagler idolized Mickey Mantle and Willie Mays as a boy and dreamed of a baseball career until Floyd Patterson's emergence on the sports scene convinced him that he wanted to become a boxer.

In Brockton, Hagler started boxing under the direction of Goody and Pat

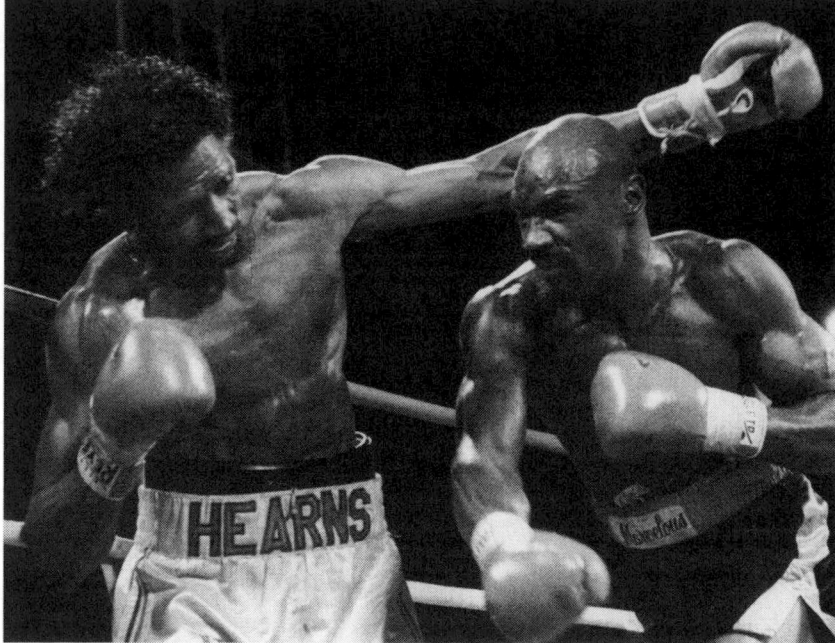

Shaved head glistening, Hagler follows through with a powerful right sending Tommy ("Hit Man") Hearns to the canvas at 2:01 of the 3rd in their April 15, 1985 bout at Caesar's Palace in Las Vegas.

IN THE RING	WON 62	LOST 3	DRAWS 2	TB 67	KO 52	W 9	WF 1	D 2	KO'd 0	L 3	LF 0

Date	Opponent	Site	Result / Rounds		Title	Wt.
1973						
May 18	Terry Ryan	Brockton, MA	TKO	2	—	160
Jul 25	Sonny Williams	Boston	W	6	—	160
Aug 8	Muhammad Smith	Boston	KO	2	—	163
Oct 6	Don Wigfall	Brockton	W	8	—	160
Oct 26	Cove Green	Brockton	TKO	4	—	161
Nov 18	Cocoa Kid	Brockton	KO	2	—	160
Dec 7	Manny Freitas	Portland, ME	TKO	1	—	161
Dec 18	James Redford	Boston	TKO	4	—	162
1974						
Feb 5	Bob Harrington	Boston	TKO	5	—	161
Apr 5	Tracy Morrison	Boston	TKO	8	—	162
May 4	Jim Redford	Brockton	TKO	2	—	157
May 30	Curtis Phillips	Portland	KO	5	—	162
Jul 16	Robert Williams	Boston	TKO	3	—	159
Aug 13	Peachy Davis	New Bedford, MA	KO	1	—	160
Aug 30	Sugar Ray Seales	Boston	W	10	—	156
Oct 29	Morris Jordan	New Bedford	TKO	4	—	162
Nov 16	George Green	Brockton	KO	1	—	155
Nov 26	Sugar Ray Seales	Seattle	D	10	—	158
Dec 20	D.C. Walker	Boston	KO	2	—	159
1975						
Feb 15	Don Wigfall	Brockton	KO	5	—	158
Mar 31	Joey Blair	Boston	KO	2	—	160
Apr 14	Jimmy Owens	Boston	W	10	—	160
May 24	Jimmy Owens	Brockton	WD	6	—	160
Aug 7	Jesse Bender	Portland, ME	KO	1	—	159
Sep 30	Lamont Lovelady	Boston	TKO	7	—	161
Dec 20	Johnny Baldwin	Boston	W	10	—	160
1976						
Jan 13	⑩ Bobby Watts	Philadelphia	L	10	—	157
Feb 7	Matt Donovan	Boston	TKO	2	—	160
Mar 9	⑩ Willie Monroe	Philadelphia	L	10	—	161
Jun 2	Bob Smith	Taunton, MA	TKO	5	—	162
Aug 3	D.C. Walker	Providence, RI	TKO	6	—	160
Sep 14	Eugene Hart	Philadelphia	TKO	8	—	160
Dec 21	George Davis	Boston	TKO	6	—	162
1977						
Feb 15	Willie Monroe	Boston	TKO	12	Won-NABF-M	160
Mar 16	Reggie Ford	Boston	KO	3	—	161
Jun 10	Roy Jones	Hartford, CT	TKO	3	—	159
Aug 23	Willie Monroe	Philadelphia	TKO	2	—	159
Sep 24	Ray Phillips	Boston	TKO	7	—	158
Oct 15	Jim Henry	Providence	W	10	—	160
Nov 26	⑩ Mike Colbert	Boston	KO	12	Ret-NABF-M	160
1978						
Mar 4	Kevin Finnegan	Boston	TKO	9	—	158
Apr 7	Doug Demmings	Los Angeles	TKO	8	—	158
May 13	Kevin Finnegan	Boston	TKO	7	—	160
Aug 24	⑩ Bennie Briscoe	Philadelphia	W	10	—	159
Nov 11	Willie Warren	Boston	TKO	7	—	158

1979							
Feb 3		Ray Seales	Boston	TKO	1	—	161
Mar 12		Bob Patterson	Providence	TKO	3	—	162
May 26		Jaime Thomas	Portland	KO	3	—	158
Jun 30		Norberto Cabrera	Monte Carlo	TKO	8	—	160
Nov 30	♛	Vito Antuofermo	Las Vegas	D	15	For-World-M	158
1980							
Feb 16	Ⓦ	Loucif Hamani	Portland	TKO	2	—	161
Apr 19		Bobby Watts	Portland	TKO	2	—	158
May 17		Marcos Geraldo	Las Vegas	W	10	—	160
Sep 27	♛	Alan Minter	Wembley, England	TKO	3	Won-World-M	160
1981							
Jan 17	Ⓦ	Fulgencio Obelmejias	Boston	TKO	8	Ret-World-M	159
Jun 13	Ⓦ	Vito Antuofermo	Boston	TKO	5	Ret-World-M	160
Oct 3	Ⓦ	Mustafa Hamsho	Rosemont, IL	TKO	11	Ret-World-M	157
1982							
Mar 7		William Lee	Atlantic City	KO	1	Ret-World-M	158
Oct 31	Ⓦ	Fulgencio Obelmejias	San Remo, Italy	KO	5	Ret-World-M	158
1983							
Feb 11	Ⓦ	Tony Sibson	Worcester, MA	KO	6	Ret-World-M	158
May 27	Ⓦ	Wilford Scypion	Providence	KO	4	Ret-World-M	160
Nov 10		Roberto Duran	Las Vegas	W	15	Ret-World-M	157
1984							
Mar 30	Ⓦ	Juan Roldan	Las Vegas	KO	10	Ret-World-M	159
Oct 19	Ⓦ	Mustafa Hamsho	New York	KO	3	Ret-World-M	159
1985							
Apr 15	Ⓦ	Thomas ("Hit Man") Hearns	Las Vegas	KO	3	Ret-World-M	159
1986							
Mar 10	Ⓦ	John Mugabi	Las Vegas	KO	11	Ret-World-M	159
1987							
Apr 6		Sugar Ray Leonard★	Las Vegas	L	12	Lost-World-M	160

Petronelli, who remained as his co-managers for many years. He compiled a fine amateur record, including winning the 1973 national Amateur Athletic Union middleweight championship. He first fought professionally in May of that same year, with a second-round technical knockout of Terry Ryan.

Hagler won fourteen fights in a row before facing his first real test in Boston against former Olympic champion, Sugar Ray Seales. The fighters were closely matched, but Hagler won the ten-round decision. In a rematch several months later, they fought to a draw. In 1976, Hagler journeyed to Philadelphia and lost two hotly contested ten-round decisions to ranked fighters, Bobby ("Boogalou") Watts and Willie ("The Worm") Monroe.

By 1977, Hagler had earned a place as one of the top middleweight contenders in the annual rankings of *The Ring*. He took the NABF middleweight title from Monroe in 1977 and successfully defended it against contender Mike Colbert later that year.

Hagler did not receive a shot at the world middleweight title until 1979, when he fought Vito Antuofermo in Las Vegas. The bout was called a draw, angering Hagler who claimed he had won the fight. Less than a year later, Hagler took the title from new world champion, Alan Minter, in England. Hagler opened cuts around Minter's left eye and dominated the fight after the first round, forcing the referee to stop the fight in the third with Minter bleeding profusely.

Hagler showed his true mettle as champion. Every one of his fights from the victory over Minter to the end of his career was a championship bout. His first defense was against Fulgencio Obelmejias of Venezuela, a ranked fighter with an unblemished record of wins. Obelmejias was battered mercilessly by Hagler for eight rounds in Boston before the referee stopped the fight. In a rematch in San Remo, Italy the next year, Hagler knocked out the big Venezuelan in five.

Hagler never ducked a contender and recorded knockouts in eleven of his twelve winning title defenses. His one victory by unanimous decision came over the great Roberto Duran, who although aging was still a formidable opponent. The WBC refused to recognize the bout as a title contest because it went fifteen and not twelve rounds, but Hagler was still generally acknowledged to be the champ. His victory over Thomas Hearns included an exciting first round which boxing historian Herbert Goldman labeled as one of the best first rounds of all time. The two slugged it out at a ferocious pace. Hagler won the hard-fought second round and dominated in the third when he knocked Hearns down with three vicious rights. The referee intervened and called a knockout.

In 1987, Hagler faced Sugar Ray Leonard, who was making a comeback after five years away from the ring. In one of the most ballyhooed fights ever, the gifted Leonard won a split decision, which years later Hagler still claims should have been his. Hagler resisted pressure to return to the ring and embarked instead on a film career in Europe. His mastery of punches, ability to fight as both a right- and left-hander, and his intimidating ring demeanor have not been matched in the middleweight division since his retirement.

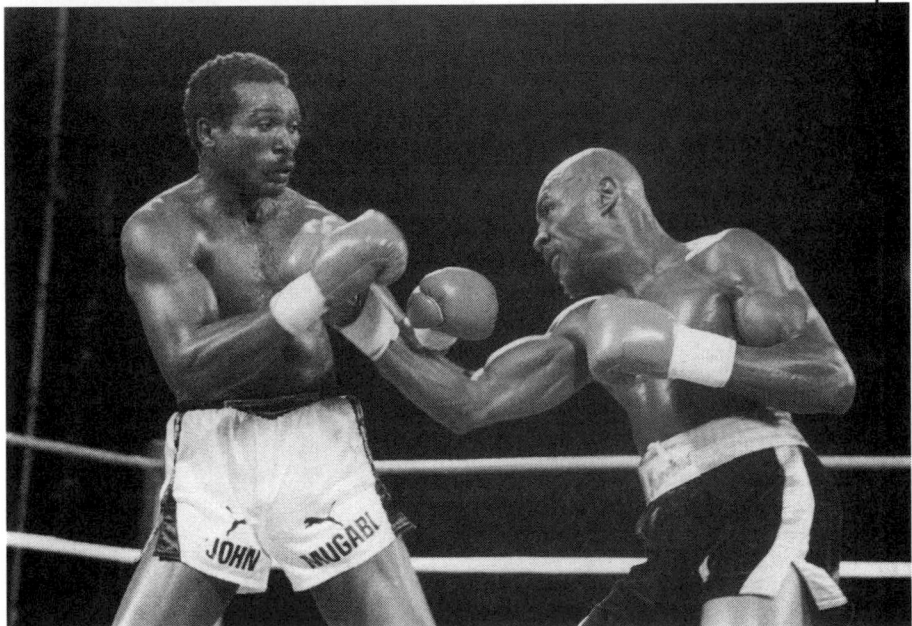

With biceps bulging, Marvelous Marvin Hagler thrusts a right through the defenses of southpaw John ("The Beast") Mugabi. Hagler retained the middleweight crown on March 10, 1986 in Las Vegas.

MASAHIKO ("FIGHTING") HARADA

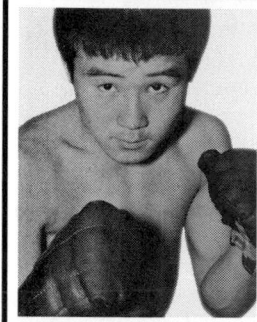

BANTAMWEIGHT

Right-handed; 5'4"; 111–127 lbs.

62 bouts, 2/21/1960 to 1/6/1970

Manager: Takeshi Sasazaki

Flyweight Champ 1962–63,
Bantamweight Champ 1965–68

Hall of Fame Induction: 1995

Born: 4/5/1943, Setagaya Ward, Tokyo, Japan

Masahiko ("Fighting") Harada won championships in two weight classes—and came within a point of winning in a third—at a time when there were only ten weight divisions. He is the first fighter to win both the flyweight and bantamweight world titles. The son of a Tokyo gardener, Harada trained at home for two years before turning professional at sixteen. Harada dispatched 26 of the first 27 opponents and, by 1962, had earned a shot at the flyweight championship held by Pone Kingpetch of Thailand. Harada was just nineteen. The fight was held in Tokyo with 12,000 Japanese fans cheering Harada on. Displaying the aggressive style which was likened to a windmill or a typhoon, Harada knocked Kingpetch out in the eleventh round to win the title.

Harada (R) sends a sharp right to the jaw of flyweight champion Pone Kingpetch on October 10, 1962 in Tokyo. His buzzsaw attack climaxed with an 11th-round knockout, and Harada took the title.

IN THE RING	WON **55**	LOST **7**	DRAWS **0**	TB 62	KO 22	W 33	WF 0	D 0	KO'd 2	L 5	LF 0

Date	Opponent	Site	Result / Rounds		Title	Wt.
1960						
Feb 21	Isami Masui	Tokyo	TKO	4	—	—
Mar 2	Mitsuo Motohashi	Tokyo	W	4	—	—
Mar 27	Goro Iwamoto	Tokyo	KO	3	—	—
Apr 4	Yuichi Noguchi	Tokyo	W	4	—	—
Apr 13	Ken Morita	Tokyo	W	4	—	—
Jun 10	Masatake Ogura	Tokyo	TKO	3	—	—
Jun 26	Ken Morita	Tokyo	KO	1	—	—
Jul 18	Masaru Kodangi	Tokyo	TKO	3	—	—
Sep 1	Yukio Suzuki	Tokyo	W	4	—	—
Oct 28	Sadayoshi Yoshida	Tokyo	KO	4	—	—
Nov 7	Hachiro Arai	Tokyo	W	4	—	—
Dec 11	Yoshinori Hikita	Tokyo	KO	3	—	—
Dec 24	Hiroyuki Ebihara	Tokyo	W	6	—	—
1961						
Jan 5	Takeshi Nakamura	Tokyo	W	6	—	—
Jan 28	Riichi Tanaka	Tokyo	W	6	—	—
Mar 5	Yasuo Fujita	Tokyo	W	6	—	—
May 1	Ray Perez	Tokyo	W	10	—	—
Jun 19	Shigeru Ito	Tokyo	W	10	—	—
Jul 31	Akio Maki	Tokyo	TKO	8	—	—
Sep 9	Sombang Banbung	Tokyo	KO	5	—	—
Oct 9	Akio Maki	Osaka, Japan	W	10	—	—
Dec 10	Ryoji Shiratori	Nagoya, Japan	KO	6	—	—
1962						
Jan 12	Kozo Nagata	Tokyo	W	10	—	—
Mar 18	Tadao Kawamura	Tokyo	W	10	—	—
May 4	Baby Espinosa	Tokyo	W	10	—	—
Jun 15	Edmundo Esparza	Tokyo	L	10	—	—
Jul 23	Little Rufe	Tokyo	W	10	—	—
Oct 10	⑩ Pone Kingpetch	Tokyo	KO	11	Won-World-FL	111
1963						
Jan 12	⑩ Pone Kingpetch	Bangkok	L	15	Lost-World-FL	112
Mar 21	Tetsuro Kawai	Tokyo	W	10	—	117
May 5	Jose Cejuda	Okinawa, Japan	KO	1	—	—
Jun 19	Thira Loedjalengabo	Nagoya	TKO	6	—	—
Aug 7	Dommy Balajada	Tokyo	W	10	—	118
Sep 26	⑩ Joe Medel	Tokyo	TKO'd	6	—	118
Nov 25	Emile de Leon	Tokyo	W	10	—	—
1964						
Jan 2	Avelino Estrada	Tokyo	KO	5	—	—
Feb 14	Somsak Laemphafa	Osaka	KO	2	—	—
Jul 6	⑩ Ray Asis	Los Angeles	W	10	—	120
Sep 17	Oscar Reyes	Tokyo	W	10	—	—

Date		Opponent	Location	Result		Notes	Weight
Oct 29		Katsutoshi Aoki	Tokyo	KO	3	—	—
1965							
Jan 4		Dommy Froilan	Tokyo	TKO	6	—	123
May 17	♛	Eder Jofre★	Nagoya	W	15	Won-World-B	117
Jul 28		Katsuo Saito	Tokyo	W	12	—	123
Nov 30	⑩	Alan Rudkin	Tokyo	W	15	Ret-World-B	117
1966							
Feb 15		Soo Kang Soo	Nagoya	W	12	—	—
Jun 1	⑩	Eder Jofre★	Tokyo	W	15	Ret-World-B	118
Aug 1		Dio Espinosa	Sapporo, Japan	W	10	—	124
Oct 25		Antonio Herrera	Osaka	W	12	—	—
1967							
Jan 3	⑩	Joe Medel	Nagoya	W	15	Ret-World-B	117
Apr 4		Tiny Palacio	Fukuoka City, Japan	W	12	—	—
Jul 4	⑩	Bernardo Caraballo	Tokyo	W	15	Ret-World-B	118
Sep 25		Hajime Taroura	Osaka	KO	2	—	—
Nov 28		Soo Bok Kwon	Okayama, Japan	KO	8	—	—
1968							
Feb 26	⑩	Lionel Rose	Tokyo	L	15	Lost-World-B	117
Jun 5		Dwight Hawkins	Tokyo	W	10	—	126
Sep 4		Nobuo Chiba	Sano, Japan	TKO	7	—	—
Dec 4		Roy Amolong	Tokyo	KO	2	—	—
1969							
Apr 2		Alton Colter	Tokyo	L	10	—	127
Jun 5		Vil Tumulak	Nagoya	W	10	—	126
Jul 28	♛	Johnny Famechon	Sydney	L	15	For-WBC-FE	125
Oct 1		Pat Gonzales	Fukui City, Japan	KO	8	—	—
1970							
Jan 6	♛	Johnny Famechon	Tokyo	TKO'd	14	For-WBC-FE	126

Within months, Harada lost the rematch to Kingpetch in a disputed decision. The fight was held on Kingpetch's home turf, and Harada had to contend with the extremely hostile and unruly crowd that blocked his entrance to the ring. Although all three judges decided in Kingpetch's favor, the Associated Press scored the fight 72–67 for Harada.

Harada had such difficulty making the weight for the flyweight division that he moved up to bantamweight after his loss to Kingpetch and, in 1965, he challenged the unbeaten Eder Jofre of Brazil for the bantamweight championship. At the time, Jofre was considered by many ring experts to be the greatest fight-

DECISIONS

RINGFACT

Two Hall of Famers have won the greatest number of fights by decision. Maxie Rosenbloom was victorious in 186 fights that went to the scorecards. Willie Pep took 165 decisions. (So-called "newspaper decisions" are not counted in this tally.)

Nineteen-year-old, 111-pound Masahiko ("Fighting") Harada, who was ranked only tenth in his division entering the fight, is exhaltant after wresting the flyweight title from Pone Kingpetch.

er, of any weight, then boxing. Employing his characteristic aggressive style, Harada earned a decision over Jofre to win his second title.

Australian fighter Lionel Rose came to Tokyo in 1968 to win a fifteen-round decision over Harada and take the bantamweight title. Undaunted, Harada then attempted to attain what he later called "his dream of taking the triple crown." In 1969, Harada met another Australian, Johnny Famechon, for the WBC featherweight championship. The two fought a close and hotly contested battle. It was initially announced that referee and sole judge Willie Pep had scored the bout a draw. However, a review of Pep's scorecard indicated that he had actually scored the bout 70 to 69 in Famechon's favor. Famechon was awarded the victory. Harada had knocked Famechon down three times and was judged by the Australian sportswriters at ringside to have beaten their countryman. Harada lost a rematch with Famechon and then retired.

In retirement, Harada had a successful career as an actor in Japan before returning to boxing as a trainer.

BEAU JACK

LIGHTWEIGHT

Right-handed; 5'6"; 126–145 lbs.

113 bouts, 5/20/1940 to 8/12/1955

Managers: Joe Caron 1940–41, Bowman Milligan 1941–42, Chick Wergeles 1942–51

NY World Lightweight Champion 1942–43, 1943–44

Hall of Fame Induction: 1991

Born: 4/1/1921, Augusta, GA

Named: Sidney Walker

Died: 2/9/2000

Along with Ike Williams and Bob Montgomery, the man they called Beau Jack delighted boxing fans of the 1940s and '50s with his courageous, attacking style. Barely literate and with little pretense to being anything but a good fighter, Jack came from a poor Southern background. Born Sidney Walker, Jack first started fighting as a child in Georgia. Often, he and five or more other black youths would be blindfolded and placed in a ring to fight each other for the entertainment of white spectators.

When he was eighteen, Jack had a job shining shoes at the Augusta National Golf Club, the home of the Masters. Impressed with his fighting ability, golf legend Bobby Jones and others gave Jack enough money to go to Massachusetts and receive formal boxing training. He trained ardently, a habit he followed throughout his career and, a year later, turned professional in Holyoke, Massachusetts. He continued to fight in the Holyoke area until mid-1941 when he was first signed for bouts in New York.

In late 1942, Jack faced Tippy Larkin in Madison Square Garden for the vacant New York world lightweight title. Larkin landed a few good punches, but the fight was all Jack's. He knocked Larkin down in the first round, then swarmed over him with punches thrown from all angles. In the third round, Jack ended the fight with a knockout.

A titleholder at 21, Jack embarked on an ambitious schedule, fighting against three top contenders—and future Hall of Famers —in a three-month period. He won two decisions over Fritzie Zivic and one from Henry Armstrong. He then

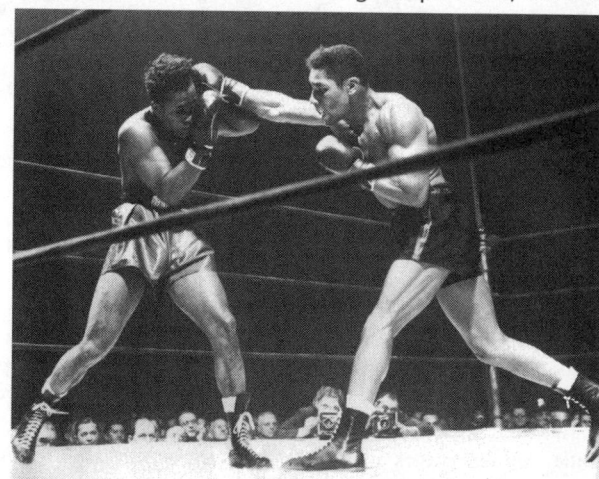

Beau Jack (R) headlines the Madison Square Garden card in this ten-round decision over contender Willie Joyce on December 14, 1945. Jack's 21 main-event bouts at the Garden drew a total of over 335,000 fans.

IN THE RING	WON 83 LOST 24 DRAWS 5	TB 113	KO 40	W 43	WF 0	D 5	KO'd 4	L 20	LF 0	ND 1

Date	Opponent	Site	Result / Rounds		Title	Wt.
1940						
May 20	Frankie Allen	Holyoke, MA	D	4	—	—
May 27	Billy Bannick	Holyoke	KO	3	—	—
Jun 17	Jackie Parker	Holyoke	L	4	—	—
Jul 14	Joe Polowitzer	New Haven, CT	L	6	—	—
Jul 21	Joe Polowitzer	New Haven	W	6	—	—
Aug 19	Jackie Parker	Holyoke	L	4	—	—
Aug 26	Carlo Daponde	Holyoke	W	4	—	—
Sep 2	Jackie Small	Holyoke	KO	4	—	—
Sep 16	Ollie Barbour	Holyoke	KO	3	—	—
Sep 30	Tony Dupre	Holyoke	TKO	2	—	—
Oct 14	Abe Cohen	Holyoke	KO	3	—	—
Oct 21	Ritchie Jones	Holyoke	KO	3	—	—
Nov 14	Joey Stack	Holyoke	W	6	—	—
Dec 2	Jimmy Fox	Holyoke	W	6	—	—
Dec 16	Young Buff	Holyoke	KO	1	—	—
Dec 30	Mel Neary	Holyoke	KO	5	—	—
1941						
Jan 27	Joey Silva	Holyoke	L	6	—	—
Feb 10	Joe Rivers	Holyoke	TKO	4	—	—
Feb 24	Lenny Isrow	Holyoke	TKO	3	—	—
Mar 10	Nickey Jerome	Holyoke	KO	3	—	—
Mar 24	Joey Silva	Holyoke	W	6	—	—
Apr 7	Tony Iacovacci	Holyoke	KO	6	—	—
Apr 21	Bob Reilly	Holyoke	TKO	7	—	—
Apr 28	Harry Gentile	Holyoke	TKO	1	—	—
May 5	⑩ Chester Rico	Holyoke	D	8	—	—
May 19	George Salamone	Holyoke	KO	8	—	126
Jun 2	⑩ Tommy Spiegel	Holyoke	W	8	—	137
Jun 16	George Zengaras	Holyoke	W	8	—	—
Aug 5	Minnie DeMore	Brooklyn	TKO	3	—	—
Aug 14	Al Roth	Brooklyn	TKO	6	—	—
Aug 26	Guillermo Puente	New York	W	6	—	—
Sep 19	Al Reid	New York	KO	7	—	—
Oct 14	⑩ Tommy Spiegel	Brooklyn	W	8	—	—
Oct 31	Guillermo Puente	New York	W	8	—	—
Dec 1	Joe Rivers	Brooklyn	KO	3	—	—
Dec 8	Freddie Archer	New York	L	8	—	—
Dec 29	Freddie Archer	New York	L	8	—	—
1942						
Jan 5	Carmelo Fenoy	Holyoke	W	10	—	—
May 22	⑩ Bobby ("Poison") Ivy	New York	W	8	—	—
Jun 23	Guillermo Puente	New York	KO	1	—	—
Jul 3	Bobby McIntire	Fort Hamilton, KY	TKO	6	—	—
Jul 7	Cosby Linson	Long Island City, NY	TKO	8	—	—
Aug 1	Ruby Garcia	Elizabeth, NJ	KO	6	—	—
Aug 18	Carmine Fatta	New York	KO	1	—	—
Aug 28	Billy Murray	New York	W	10	—	—
Sep 22	Joe Torres	Washington, DC	KO	4	—	—

Date		Opponent	Location	Result	Rounds	Notes	Weight
Oct 2	⑩	Chester Rico	New York	W	8	—	138
Oct 12		Terry Young	New York	W	10	—	—
Nov 13	⑩	Allie Stolz	New York	TKO	7	—	132
Dec 18		Tippy Larkin	New York	KO	3	Won-Vac NY World-L	132
1943							
Feb 5	⑩	Fritzie Zivic★	New York	W	10	—	137
Mar 5	⑩	Fritzie Zivic★	New York	W	12	—	136
Apr 2		Henry Armstrong★	New York	W	10	—	135
May 21	⑩	Bob Montgomery★	New York	L	15	Lost-NY World-L	135
Jun 21		Maxie Starr	Washington, DC	KO	6	—	—
Jul 19		Johnny Hutchinson	Philadelphia	TKO	6	—	135
Oct 4		Bobby Ruffin	New York	L	10	—	140
Nov 19	♛	Bob Montgomery★	New York	W	15	Reg-NY World-L	132
1944							
Jan 7	⑩	Lulu Costantino	New York	W	10	—	—
Jan 28	⑩	Sammy Angott★	New York	D	10	—	—
Feb 15		Maxie Berger	Cleveland	W	10	—	—
Mar 3	⑩	Bob Montgomery★	New York	L	15	Lost-NY World-L	134
Mar 17	⑩	Al ("Bummy") Davis	New York	W	10	—	138
Mar 31	⑩	Juan Zurita	New York	W	10	—	136
Aug 4	♛	Bob Montgomery★	New York	W	10	—	—
1945							
Dec 14	⑩	Willie Joyce	New York	W	10	—	144
1946							
Jan 4		Morris Reif	New York	KO	4	—	143
Feb 8	⑩	Johnny Greco	New York	D	10	—	142
May 31	⑩	Johnny Greco	New York	W	10	—	141
Jul 8	⑩	Sammy Angott★	Washington, DC	TKO	7	—	142
Aug 19		Danny Kapilow	Washington, DC	W	10	—	—
Oct 22		Buster Tyler	Elizabeth	L	10	—	—
1947							
Feb 21	⑩	Tony Janiro	New York	TKO'd	4	—	—
Nov 3		Humberto Zavala	St. Louis	KO	4	—	141
Dec 16		Frankie Vigeant	Hartford, CT	W	10	—	—
Dec 29		Billy Kearns	Providence, RI	W	10	—	—
1948							
Jan 5		Jimmy Collins	New Haven	KO	2	—	140
Jan 23	⑩	Johnny Bratton	Chicago	TKO	8	—	—
Feb 20	⑩	Terry Young	New York	L	10	—	141
Apr 9	⑩	Johnny Greco	Montreal	W	10	—	—
May 24	⑩	Tony Janiro	Washington, DC	W	10	—	—
Jul 12	♛	Ike Williams★	Philadelphia	TKO'd	6	For-World-L	134
Oct 28		Eric Boon	Washington, DC	TKO	3	—	—
Nov 23		Chuck Taylor	Philadelphia	TKO	3	—	—
Dec 17		Leroy Willis	Detroit	W	10	—	139
1949							
Jan 17		Jackie Weber	Boston	W	10	—	—
Mar 28	⑩	Johnny Greco	Montreal	L	10	—	—
Jul 13		Eddie Giosa	Washington, DC	W	10	—	—
Aug 31		Johnny Gonsalves	Oakland	W	10	—	—
Sep 6		Tote Martinez	Los Angeles	W	10	—	—
Sep 30		Livio Minelli	Chicago	W	10	—	—
Oct 14	⑩	Kid Gavilan★	Chicago	L	10	—	—
Dec 16	⑩	Tuzo Portuguez	New York	L	10	—	142

1950							
Apr 3		Joey Carkido	Hartford	L	10	—	142
Apr 14		Lew Jenkins	Washington, DC	TKO	5	—	—
May 8		Jackie Weber	Providence	TKO	7	—	—
May 22		Johnny Potenti	Boston	W	10	—	141
Jun 28		Ronnie Harper	Indianapolis	TKO	5	—	141
Jul 8		Sonny West	Springfield, MA	ND	3	—	137
Jul 17		Bobby Timpson	Atlanta	TKO	6	—	—
Oct 4		Philip Kim	Honolulu	W	10	—	141
Nov 14	⑩	Frankie Fernandez	Honolulu	L	10	—	—
1951							
Jan 1		Fitzie Pruden	Milwaukee	L	10	—	—
Jan 18	⑩	Del Flanagan	Minneapolis	L	10	—	—
Jan 31		Emil Barao	Hartford	W	10	—	—
Mar 5	⑩	Ike Williams★	Providence	L	10	—	—
Mar 30		Leroy Willis	New Orleans	W	10	—	—
Apr 16	⑩	Gil Turner	Philadelphia	L	10	—	—
May 21	⑩	Gil Turner	Philadelphia	TKO'd	8	—	—
1955							
Jan 20		Eddie Green	Columbia, SC	W	10	—	—
Apr 9		Ike Williams★	Augusta, GA	D	10	—	—
Jul 4		Willie Johnson	Daytona Beach, FL	W	10	—	—
Aug 12		Ike Williams★	Augusta	TKO'd	9	—	—

faced Bob Montgomery in the first of three title fights in Madison Square Garden, where Jack had become a regular main-event attraction. Montgomery was a dangerous fighter, light on his feet and in possession of a full arsenal of punches. Jack was a good match for this aggressive contender and had Montgomery in trouble in the first round but, as the fight continued, Montgomery took control. By the end of fifteen, both of Jack's eyes were almost swollen shut, and his lips were puffy. Montgomery won the unanimous decision and the New York world lightweight title.

In the rematch a few months later, Jack turned the tables on Montgomery. He used great speed, bolo punch uppercuts, and a sharp jab to take the bout. Though Jack absorbed some punishment, he did not tire as he had in the first fight, and he won the unanimous decision to regain the title. In 1944, the pair fought for a third time. A crowd of 19,006 filled Madison Square Garden to see these two enemies meet again in a furious contest that at times resembled a wrestling match. Jack jabbed furiously but Montgomery's barrage of blows was too much for him. Montgomery won the decision. In their fourth bout, Jack won a non-title rematch with the proceeds going for war bonds.

In 1948, Jack challenged Ike Williams for the world lightweight title but was knocked out in six rounds. Jack fought Williams three more times but could not beat him before retiring in 1955. Jack's energetic, swarming style made him a fan favorite, especially in Madison Square Garden. He fought there 27 times and headlined 21 cards, many of which drew crowds of close to 20,000. After leaving the ring, Jack worked at the Fontainebleau Hotel in Miami Beach, pursuing the only other occupation he had ever had—shining shoes.

LEW JENKINS

LIGHTWEIGHT

Right-handed; 5'7"; 125–144 lbs.

110 bouts, 12/2/1935 to 4/14/1950

Managers: Benny Woodhall, Frank Bachman, and Hymie Kaplan

Lightweight Champion 1940-41

Hall of Fame Induction: 1999

Born: 12/4/1916, Milburn, TX

Named: Verlin E. Jenkins

Lew Jenkins was a powerful boxer whose career was hampered by drinking and carousing. Yet after he retired, Jenkins was considered a hero in the armed services.

Jenkins was the son of a travelling blacksmith and cotton picker. After his father's death, Lew joined the T.J. Tidwell carnival, where he earned 25 cents a day to fight men—of all sizes—in the boxing and wrestling tent.

In 1936, Jenkins joined the army but continued boxing. He won the welterweight championship of Fort Bliss, Texas, and boxed professionally while on furlough. Jenkins left the army in 1938 to box full time, reeling off seven straight knockouts in Dallas. When Jenkins married, his wife, Katie, took charge of his career. After Katie determined that they would have to move to a larger city to make a living in the ring, the couple relocated first to Chicago and then New York.

Katie created quite a stir when she and her husband appeared at the famed Stillman's Gym and asked for a locker. Lou Stillman replied that women were not allowed in the gym, but under a withering barrage of salty language from Katie, he gave in.

Once in New York, Jenkins began working under the care of experienced managers and soon racked up ten straight wins, including knockouts over highly regarded fighters like future junior welterweight champion Tippy Larkin.

The Larkin victory earned Jenkins a May 10, 1940 chance at the lightweight title held by Lou Ambers. But success led Lew and Katie to

Katie Jenkins often worked the corner in her husband 's fights.

IN THE RING	WON 66	LOST 39	DRAWS 5	TB 110	KO 46	W 19	WF 1	D 5	KO'd 12	L 27	LF 0

Date	Opponent	Site	Result / Rounds		Title	Wt.
1935						
Dec 2	Lee ("Moon") Mullins	Phoenix, AZ	W	8	—	—
1936						
Mar 5	Fay Koskey	Silver City, NM	W	4	—	—
1937						
—	Jimmy Maddox	—	D	8	—	—
—	Rudolfo Ramirez	—	KO'd	8	—	—
Apr 12	Billy Firpo	Houston	L	6	—	—
Aug 1	Ray Serrano	Houston	W	4	—	—
1938						
Jan 11	Ray Serrano	Houston	D	6	—	—
Jan 14	Kid Levy	Dallas	KO	5	—	—
Jan 28	Young Ernst	Dallas	KO	5	—	—
Feb 4	Jackie Conway	Dallas	KO	2	—	—
Feb 18	Frankie Graham	Dallas	KO	4	—	—
Mar 11	Louis Arriola	Dallas	KO	5	—	—
Mar 18	Ray Serrano	Dallas	KO	2	—	—
Apr 1	Jackie Sharkey	Dallas	KO	2	—	—
Apr 8	Lew Feldman	Dallas	W	10	—	—
Apr 28	Wesley Ramey	Dallas	L	10	—	—
May 27	Bobby Britton	Dallas	KO'd	7	—	—
Jun 17	Evening Thunder	Dallas	KO	3	—	—
Jul 29	Chino Alvarez	Dallas	KO'd	8	—	—
Aug 23	Zeke Castro	Los Angeles	W	6	—	—
Sep	Cullen Williams	Corpus Christi, TX	KO	5	—	—
Sep 16	Jackie Griffin	Dallas	W	6	—	—
Sep 23	Carlos Malacara	Dallas	L	10	—	—
Sep 30	Don Eddy	Dallas	KO	8	—	—
Oct 6	Luis Orozco	Dallas	KO	1	—	—
Oct 20	Carl Faust	Dallas	KO	8	—	—
Nov 3	Carl Faust	Dallas	KO	8	—	—
Nov 9	Sammy Musco	Corpus Christi	D	10	—	—
Nov 17	Lew Feldman	Dallas	L	10	—	—
Dec 2	Sammy Musco	Dallas	W	10	—	—
Dec 16	Wesley Ramey	Dallas	L	10	—	—
Dec 23	Pedro Ortega	San Antonio	L	8	—	—
Dec 29	Ted Tellos	Dallas	W	8	—	—
1939						
Jan 6	Joe Law	Chicago	W	6	—	—
Jan 20	Willie Joyce	Chicago	D	10	—	—
Jan 31	Sam Scully	Houston	KO	10	—	—
Feb 17	Willie Joyce	Chicago	L	8	—	—
Feb 24	Willie Joyce	Chicago	L	8	—	—
Mar 24 ⑩	Pete Lello	Chicago	KO'd	7	—	—
May 6	Panchito Campos	Mexico City	KO	1	—	—
May 26	Jimmy Hatcher	Dallas	KO	2	—	—
Jun 19	Jorge Morelia	San Antonio	W	10	—	—
Jul 18	Bus Breese	Long Island City, NY	W	8	—	—
Aug 1	Joey Fontana	Long Island City	W	8	—	—

Date		Opponent	Location	Result	Rounds	Notes	
Aug 15		Bus Breese	Long Island City	W	8	—	—
Sep 5		Ginger Foran	Long Island City	KO	4	—	—
Sep 12		Primo Flores	Long Island City	KO	4	—	—
Oct 10		Primo Flores	New York	KO	5	—	—
Nov 21		Mike Belloise	New York	KO	8	—	—
Dec 15		Billy Marquart	New York	KO	3	—	—
1940							
Jan 24		Chino Alvarez	Dallas	KO	1	—	—
Mar 8		Tippy Larkin	New York	KO	1	—	—
May 10	♛	Lou Ambers★	New York	TKO	3	Won-World-L	132
Jul 17	♛	Henry Armstrong★	New York	TKO'd	6	—	139
Sep 16	ⓦ	Bob Montgomery★	Philadelphia	W	12	—	—
Nov 22	ⓦ	Pete Lello	New York	TKO	2	Ret-World-L	134
Dec 20	♛	Fritzie Zivic★	New York	D	10	—	135
1941							
Feb 28	ⓦ	Lou Ambers★	New York	TKO	7	—	134
May 16	ⓦ	Bob Montgomery★	New York	L	10	—	—
Aug 4		Joey Zodda	Newark, NJ	KO	3	—	—
Sep 12		Cleo McNeil	Minneapolis	KO	3	—	—
Oct 6		Freddie ("Red") Cochrane	New York	L	10	—	—
Dec 19	ⓦ	Sammy Angott★	New York	L	15	Lost-World-L	134
1942							
Feb 17		Marty Servo	Philadelphia	L	10	—	—
Mar 27		Mike Kaplan	Boston	L	10	—	—
May 13		Jack Byrd	Hot Springs, AK	L	10	—	—
May 25	ⓦ	Fritzie Zivic★	Pittsburgh	KO'd	10	—	—
Aug 17		Cosby Linson	New Orleans	L	10	—	—
Aug 27		Carmen Notch	Detroit	L	10	—	—
Sep 22		Al Tribuani	Wilmington, DE	L	10	—	137
Nov 18		Chato Gonzalez	Las Vegas	KO	2	—	144
Dec 4	ⓦ	Henry Armstrong★	Portland, OR	KO'd	8	—	—
Dec 22		John Thomas	Los Angeles	TKO'd	5	—	137
1943							
Jul 28		Steve Rosina	Oran, Algeria	KO	2	—	—
Aug 6		Chick Broussard	Oran	W	3	—	—
1945							
Dec 3	ⓦ	Jimmy Doyle	Cleveland	KO'd	4	—	—
1946							
Jan 15		Jerry Zullo	Salem, MA	KO	2	—	139
Jan 25		Jack Garrity	Danbury, CT	KO	1	—	139
Jan 29		Johnny Cool	Manchester, NH	WF	2	—	139
May 21		Henry Majcher	Houston	L	10	—	—
Jun 14		Lou Flyer	Dallas	KO'd	6	—	—
Sep 26		Tony Davila	Waco, TX	KO	1	—	—
Nov 20		Ted ("Mustang") Garcia	Galveston, TX	KO	9	—	—
Dec 13		Hubert Gray	Dallas	KO	10	—	—
Dec 20		Nick Castiglione	Chicago	KO	4	—	—
1948							
Dec 10		Andres Balderas	El Paso, TX	KO	3	—	—
1949							
Jan 17		Rene Camacho	Philadelphia	KO	2	—	—
Jan 31		Chuck Burton	Philadelphia	KO	9	—	—
Feb 28		Percy Bassett	Philadelphia	L	10	—	—
Mar 17		Santa Bucca	Philadelphia	KO	4	—	—
Mar 28		Joey Carkido	Philadelphia	KO	4	—	—

Apr 11	Bobby Timpson	Philadelphia	KO	10	—	—
May 2	Eddie Giosa	Philadelphia	L	10	—	—
Jun 6	Jimmy Collins	Philadelphia	W	8	—	—
Jun 21	Mario Marino	Allentown, PA	KO	2	—	—
Jul 1	Beppe Cosalanti	Long Beach, CA	L	10	—	134
Aug 1	Lou Joyce	Allentown	W	8	—	—
Aug 17	Don Williams	Worcester, MA	L	10	—	—
Sep 1	Bob Sandberg	Milwaukee	L	10	—	—
Sep 21	Don Williams	Worcester	L	10	—	—
Sep 30	Eddie Giosa	Philadelphia	W	10	—	—
Oct 20	Ike Jenkins	Philadelphia	W	8	—	—
Nov 14	Calvin Smith	Philadelphia	L	10	—	—
Dec 5	Johnny DeFazi	Newark	KO	8	—	—
Dec 19	Iggy Vaccari	Boston	KO	9	—	—
1950						
Jan 9	Al Pennino	Newark	KO	3	—	140
Jan 25	Walter Haines	New York	L	8	—	138
Jan 31	Rafael Lastre	Toledo, OH	KO'd	10	—	138
Mar 6	Carmen Basilio★	Syracuse, NY	L	10	—	—
Apr 14	Beau Jack★	Washington, DC	KO'd	6	—	—

excessive drinking and revelry. While Jenkins trained fairly diligently, he was spotted the day of the fight in Toots Shor's famous bar, having a few. Still, at fight time Jenkins performed well, knocking down Ambers several times. In the third, he floored the champ and Ambers failed to beat the count, suffering the first knockout defeat of his career.

As champion, Jenkins's drinking and rowdy escapades escalated. He eschewed training for his next fight, a non-title bout against welterweight champion Henry Armstrong. On the day of the fight, he escaped from his locked hotel room to go on a binge with friends visiting from Texas. His trainer, Willie Ketchum, tracked Jenkins down and dragged him to the ring where Armstrong knocked Jenkins down seven times before referee Arthur Donovan stopped the fight.

A car accident preceded Jenkins's non-title rematch with Ambers. Jenkins drove into a bridge, but was unhurt. After the weigh-in, however, he got so drunk that he had to be helped into the ring. Somehow, he held on through the sixth round and then finished Ambers with a knockout in the seventh. Jenkins next suffered whiplash in a drunken motorcycle accident shortly before a fight with Freddie ("Red") Cochrane. He removed his neck brace the day of the fight, self-administering doses of whiskey during the bout. Cochrane won a ten-round decision.

On December 19, 1941, Jenkins's stormy title reign came to an end. Still suffering from his various injuries, he could do little to defend himself in the fight against Sammy Angott, who took the decision and the title.

Katie left Jenkins. He was broke. After losing nine of ten fights in 1942, he enlisted in the Coast Guard. Resuming his boxing career in 1945, he won seven of his first ten bouts, but was no longer considered a contender. He reenlisted in the army, and remarried while in the service, yet he was drawn back to boxing in 1949. He lost the last four bouts of his career.

Jenkins served with distinction in the Korean War, earning a Silver Star, and continued to serve until 1963. Jenkins is buried in Arlington National Cemetery.

EDER JOFRE

FEATHERWEIGHT

Right-handed; 5'4"; 116–126 lbs.

78 bouts, 3/26/1957 to 10/8/1976

NBA Bantamwt. Champ 1960–61,
Bantamwt. Champ 1961–65,
WBC Featherwt. Champ 1973–74

Hall of Fame Induction: 1992

Born: 3/26/1936, Sao Paulo, Brazil

Although not well known to American boxing fans—he only fought three times in the United States—Eder Jofre of Brazil held three championship titles during his long career, with thirteen years separating his first from his last title victory. Jofre retired for three years late in his career before re-establishing himself not only as an international contender, but as a champion.

Jofre's father and others in his family were active in boxing and wrestling, and Jofre started boxing at a very young age. As an amateur, he represented Brazil in the 1956 Olympics, going to the quarterfinals before being eliminated.

He turned professional the next year and compiled a record of 34-0-2, earning him a chance to fight for the vacant NBA bantamweight title against Eloy Sanchez in 1960. The fight in Los Angeles was Jofre's second bout outside South America. Jofre knocked Sanchez out in the sixth with a hook-cross combination to the jaw. The next year, Jofre scored a technical knockout over Piero Rollo in Rio de Janeiro to claim the vacant world bantamweight title.

Referee Willie Pep halted this bout in the tenth round as Jofre (L) beat EBU champ Johnny Caldwell in Sao Paulo on January 18, 1962. Caldwell's manager threw in the towel to stop the slaughter.

IN THE RING	WON 72	LOST 2	DRAWS 4	TB 78	KO 50	W 22	WF 0	D 4	KO'd 0	L 2	LF 0

Date		Opponent	Site	Result / Rounds		Title	Wt.
1957							
Mar 26		Raul Lopez	Sao Paulo, Brazil	KO	3	—	—
Apr 23		Raul Lopez	Sao Paulo	TKO	5	—	—
May 5		Osvaldo Perez	Sao Paulo	TKO	1	—	—
Jun 7		Osvaldo Perez	Sao Paulo	KO	2	—	—
Jun 14		Juan Gonzalez	Sao Paulo	TKO	5	—	—
Jul 5		Raul Jamie	Sao Paulo	W	10	—	—
Jul 19		Raul Jamie	Sao Paulo	W	10	—	—
Aug 16		Ernesto Miranda	Sao Paulo	D	10	—	—
Sep 6		Ernesto Miranda	Sao Paulo	D	10	—	—
Oct 31		Luis Jimenez	Sao Paulo	TKO	8	—	—
Dec 13		Adolfo Pendas	Sao Paulo	W	10	—	—
Dec 22		Carlos Galisans	Rio de Janeiro	W	8	—	—
1958							
Jan 24		Avelino Romero	Sao Paulo	KO	2	—	—
Mar 7		Cristobal Galisans	Sao Paulo	TKO	6	—	—
Apr 13		German Escudero	Sao Paulo	KO	2	—	—
Apr 27		German Escudero	Rio de Janeiro	KO	2	—	—
May 14		Ruben Caceres	Montevideo, Uruguay	D	10	—	—
Jul 18		Juan Acebal	Sao Paulo	KO	2	—	—
Aug 9		Roberto Olmedo	Sao Paulo	KO	5	—	—
Sep 12		Jose Casas	Sao Paulo	W	10	—	—
Oct 9		Jose Casas	Sao Paulo	KO	5	—	—
Nov 14		Jose Smecca	Sao Paulo	TKO	7	—	—
Dec 12		Roberto Castro	Sao Paulo	KO	2	—	—
1959							
Mar 23		Aniceto Pereyra	Sao Paulo	W	10	—	—
Apr 20		Salustiano Suarez	Sao Paulo	KO	4	—	—
Jun 4		Leo Espinosa	Sao Paulo	W	10	—	—
Jun 28		Angel Bustos	Sao Paulo	KO	1	—	—
Jul 19		Salustiano Suarez	Sao Paulo	KO	4	—	—
Jul 31		Ruben Caceres	Sao Paulo	KO	7	—	—
Oct 9		Angel Bustos	Rio de Janeiro	KO	3	—	—
Oct 30		Gianni Zuddas	Sao Paulo	W	10	—	—
Dec 12	⑩	Danny Kid	Sao Paulo	W	10	—	—
1960							
Feb 19	⑩	Ernesto Miranda	Sao Paulo	W	15	Won-S Am-B	118
Jun 10	⑩	Ernesto Miranda	Sao Paulo	KO	3	Ret-S Am-B	118
Jul 15		Claudio Barrientos	Sao Paulo	KO	8	—	122
Aug 18	⑩	Jose Medel	Los Angeles	KO	10	—	—
Sep 30		Ricardo Moreno	Sao Paulo	TKO	6	—	—
Nov 18	⑩	Eloy Sanchez	Los Angeles	KO	6	Won-Vac NBA-B	118
Dec 16		Billy Peacock	Sao Paulo	KO	2	—	—
1961							
Mar 25	⑩	Piero Rollo	Rio de Janeiro	TKO	10	Won-Vac World-B	118
Apr 18		Sugar Ray	Sao Paulo	KO	2	—	—
Jul 26		Sadao Yaoita	Sao Paulo	KO	10	—	—
Aug 19		Ramon Arias	Caracas, Venezuela	KO	7	Ret-World-B	118
Dec 6		Fernando Soto	Sao Paulo	KO	8	—	—

1962							
Jan 18	♛	Johnny Caldwell	Sao Paulo	TKO	10	Ret-World-B	117
May 4	⑩	Herman Marquez	San Francisco	KO	10	Ret-World-B	117
Sep 11	⑩	Jose Medel	Sao Paulo	KO	6	Ret-World-B	117
1963							
Apr 4	⑩	Katsutoshi Aoki	Tokyo	KO	3	Ret-World-B	118
May 18		Johnny Jamito	Quezon, Philippines	TKO	12	Ret-World-B	117
1964							
Nov 27	⑩	Bernardo Caraballo	Bogota, Columbia	KO	7	Ret-World-B	117
1965							
May 17	⑩	Fighting Harada★	Nagoya, Japan	L	15	Lost-World-B	118
Nov 5	⑩	Manny Elias	Sao Paulo	D	10	—	—
1966							
Jun 1	♛	Fighting Harada★	Tokyo	L	15	For-World-B	116
1969							
Aug 27		Rudy Corona	Sao Paulo	KO	6	—	—
1970							
Jan 30		Nevio Carbi	Sao Paulo	W	10	—	—
May 29		Manny Elias	Sao Paulo	W	10	—	—
Sep 25		Roberto Wong	Sao Paulo	KO	3	—	—
Nov 7		Giovanni Girgenti	Sao Paulo	W	10	—	—
1971							
Mar 26		Jerry Stokes	Sao Paulo	KO	2	—	—
Jul 9		Domenico Chilorio	Sao Paulo	W	10	—	—
Sep 10		Terry Jumao	Sao Paulo	W	10	—	—
Oct 29		Roberto Porcel	Sao Paulo	KO	2	—	—
1972							
Mar 24		Guillermo Morales	Sao Paulo	KO	6	—	—
Apr 28		Felix Figueroa	Sao Paulo	W	10	—	—
Jun 30		Jose Bisbal	Sao Paulo	KO	2	—	—
Aug 18		Shig Fukuyama	Sao Paulo	TKO	9	—	—
Sep 29		Djiemei Belhadf	Sao Paulo	KO	3	—	—
1973							
May 5	♛	Jose Legra	Brasilia, Brazil	W	15	Won-WBC-FE	125
Jul 21		Godfrey Stevens	Sao Paulo	KO	4	—	—
Aug 25		Frankie Crawford	Bauru, Brazil	W	10	—	—
Oct 21		Vicente Saldivar	Salvador, Brazil	KO	4	Ret-WBC-FE	124
1975							
Jan 3		Filiberto Herrera	Jundiai, Brazil	W	10	—	—
1976							
Feb 24		Enzo Farinelli	Porto Alegre, Brazil	KO	4	—	—
May 1		Michael Lefevbre	Brasilia	KO	3	—	—
May 29		Pasquale Mortibelli	Sao Paulo	KO	4	—	—
Jul 2		Gitano Jimenez	Sao Paulo	W	10	—	—
Aug 13	⑩	Juan Lopez	Sao Paulo	W	10	—	—
Oct 8	⑩	Octavio Gomez	Sao Paulo	W	12	—	—

Jofre won his next ten fights, all by knockout, to maintain a firm hold on the bantamweight belt. In 1965, he traveled to Nagoya, Japan for a title bout with the former flyweight champion, Fighting Harada. Making the weight for his title defenses had been a continual struggle for Jofre and, in Japan, he once again had trouble. Two pounds over at the weigh-in, Jofre had to go for an hour's run in order to get down to the necessary weight. The fight didn't go Jofre's way. Harada's intense, attacking style proved to be too much for him, and Harada won a split decision to take the title. Jofre complained that referee Barney Ross lost control of the fight and allowed Harada to butt and hold throughout the match. In a rematch the next year in Tokyo, Harada again won a fifteen-round decision.

After this second loss to Harada, Jofre retired. Three years later, in 1969, he was back, this time fighting as a featherweight. It may have seemed that a comeback at age 33 was doomed, but Jofre showed that he still had the classic boxing skills and punching ability which had won him the bantamweight title. He was 37 when he won a 1973 majority decision over Jose Legra to take the world featherweight title. He was stripped of the title the next year for failure to defend, but continued to fight for another two years before retiring for good.

In retirement, Jofre has been active in politics in Brazil, where he continues to enjoy great popularity. He is one of the few vegetarians to hold a world title.

After campaigning for most of his career as a bantamweight, Eder Jofre moved up to featherweight and took the WBC's version of that championship from Spain's José Legra in Brasilia on May 5, 1973.

INGEMAR JOHANSSON

Ingo

HEAVYWEIGHT

Right-handed; 6'½", 192–207 lbs.

28 bouts, 12/5/1952 to 4/21/1963

Manager: Edwin Ahlquist

Heavyweight Champion 1959–60

Hall of Fame Induction: 2002

Born: 10/16/1932, Gothenburg, Sweden

A heavyweight champion who upset Floyd Patterson in his prime, Ingemar Johansson made a lasting impression on boxing fans with his likeable personality, unique training methods, and potent right hand.

Johansson was born in Sweden, and from the time he was a small boy he carried a potent punch. His father was a maintenance foreman, and Johansson followed the same job path after he quit school at age fifteen.

He embarked on his amateur boxing career on February 17, 1948, and won a decision over his first opponent. In all, Johansson would compile a 60-11 amateur record. As a member of the European Golden Gloves team in 1951, he knocked out American Ernest Fann in the second round of their bout. In the 1952 Olympics, Johansson represented Sweden and reached the championship match, where he faced Eddie Sanders of the United States. Unfortunately, Johansson was disqualified in the second round for "not trying." He was disgraced in the eyes of his countrymen and the entire boxing community, and it would be years before he finally received his silver medal.

Johansson began fighting for pay in exhibitions with a traveling circus, but his formal boxing career started with a fourth-round knockout of Robert Masson on December 5, 1952. Johansson won his next four fights, but was then forced to temporarily hang up his gloves while he served a stint in the Swedish Navy. After his discharge, he continued to rack up victories, culminating in a September 30, 1956, win over Franco Cavicchi in thirteen rounds to claim the European heavyweight title. That year, *The Ring* ranked Johansson as the seventh-best contender for the heavyweight championship held by Floyd Patterson.

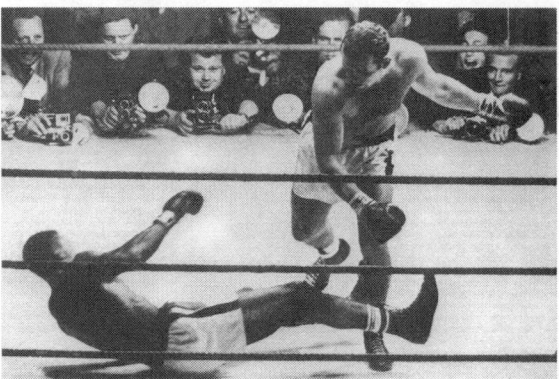

Johansson uncorked three powerful knockdown rights in his important 9/14/1958 fight with Californian Eddie Machen. Machen failed to rise from the third and Johannson won in 2:16 of the first round.

IN THE RING	WON 26	LOST 2	DRAWS 0	TB 28	KO 17	W 8	WF 1	D 0	KO'd 2	L 0	LF 0

Date	Opponent	Site	Result / Rounds		Title	Wt.
1952						
Dec 5	Robert Masson	Gothenburg, Sweden	KO	4	—	—
1953						
Feb 6	Emile Bentz	Gothenburg	KO	2	—	—
Mar 6	Lloyd Barnett	Gothenburg	W	6	—	—
Mar 12	Erik Jensen	Copenhagen	W	6	—	—
Dec 4	Raymond Degl'Innocenti	Gothenburg	KO	2	—	—
1954						
Nov 5	Werner Wiegand	Gothenburg	TKO	5	—	—
1955						
Jan 6	Ansel Adams	Gothenburg	W	6	—	—
Feb 13	Kurt Schiegl	Stockholm	KO	5	—	—
Mar 4	Aldo Pellegrini	Gothenburg	WF	5	—	—
Apr 3	Uber Bacilieri	Stockholm	W	8	—	—
Jun 12	Günther Nürnberg	Dortmund, Germany	KO	7	—	—
Aug 28	Hein ten Hoff	Gothenburg	TKO	1	—	—
1956						
Feb 24	Joe Bygraves	Gothenburg	W	8	—	—
Apr 15	Hans Friedrich	Stockholm	W	10	—	—
Sep 30	Franco Cavicchi	Bologna, Italy	TKO	13	Won-European-H	—
Dec 28	Peter Bates	Gothenburg	KO	2	—	—
1957						
May 19	Henry Cooper	Stockholm	TKO	5	Ret-European-H	—
Dec 13	Archie McBride	Gothenburg	W	10	—	—
1958						
Feb 21	Joe Erskine	Gothenburg	KO	13	Ret-European-H	197
Jul 13	Heinz Neuhaus	Gothenburg	TKO	4	—	197
Sep 14 ⑩	Eddie Machen	Gothenburg	TKO	1	—	198
1959						
Jun 26 ♛	Floyd Patterson★	New York	TKO	3	Won-World-H	196
1960						
Jun 20 ⑩	Floyd Patterson★	New York	KO'd	5	Lost-World-H	194
1961						
Mar 13 ♛	Floyd Patterson★	Miami	KO'd	6	For-World-H	206
1962						
Feb 9	Joe Bygraves	Gothenburg	TKO	7	—	200
Apr 15	Wim Snoek	Stockholm	KO	5	—	198
Jun 17	Dick Richardson	Gothenburg	KO	8	Reg-European-H	202
1963						
Apr 21 ⑩	Brian London	Stockholm	W	12	—	207

Johansson successfully defended his European crown with knockout victories over Henry Cooper and Joe Erskine, yet he and his advisor Edwin Ahlquist—a Swedish manager and promoter—realized that Johansson would have to do more than beat up Europe's best to earn recognition in the U.S. and a shot at the world championship. With that goal in mind, Ahlquist arranged for top contender Eddie Machen to come to Gothenburg to fight Johansson. Johansson knocked Machen down three times and finally put him out in the first round of the fight, September 14, 1958. The victory over Machen propelled Johansson to *The Ring*'s top contender spot, and Patterson agreed to meet him for a title match.

Johansson moved his operation to Grossinger's, a resort in the Catskills, where he started training rigorously for the upcoming fight. His unusual methods attracted much attention. He brought his parents, his sister, and even his fiancée with him, though women were normally not allowed in a fighter's training camp. His running schedule was far tougher than the norm—six miles a day—and he trained at night because the fight was to take place at night. Johansson refused to use his fearsome right hand in sparring, and he rounded out his training with swimming and dancing.

Johansson was a heavy underdog as the day of the fight—June 26, 1959—approached, and many ridiculed his training regimen. In front of 19,000 fans in Yankee Stadium, the battle began quietly, with little action in the first round. In the second, Patterson scored with lefts to Johansson's face, but in the third spectators witnessed one of the most action-packed rounds in heavyweight championship history. Patterson threw two jabs to the face. Johansson responded with a left jab and then a right that knocked Patterson down for a nine count. Another right and left sent Patterson tumbling again. The champion got up, but another Johansson right, hitting behind the ear, toppled him to the canvas for a third time. An uppercut knocked Patterson down for a count of six, and a swinging right connected for the fifth knockdown of the round, while a left and right combination floored the now bleeding Patterson yet again. The champ gamely rose to his feet only to be met by a looping right that put him down for the seventh time. At this point, referee Ruby Goldstein stopped the fight.

The first Patterson match showed Johansson at his boxing best, a skillful fighter who looked for openings to fire his right hand, a pounding weapon that earned nicknames like "Hammer of Thor," "Toonder and Lighting," and "Ingo's Bingo."

Referee Ruby Goldstein has seen enough after Floyd Patterson suffers his seventh third-round knockdown. The first of the three Patterson–Johannson fights ended with Ingemar Johannson becoming the first European Heavyweight Champion of the World in 25 years.

The Associated Press named Johansson its Athlete of the Year for 1959, an honor rarely bestowed on a boxer.

Johansson's rematch with Patterson took place at the Polo Grounds on June 20, 1960, in front of 32,000 fans, and the belt changed hands again. This time Patterson led through the first four rounds, then put Johansson down for a nine count in the fifth, followed immediately by a knockout— both falls on powerful left hooks. The brawling fighters met for a third time, on March 13, 1961, at Convention Hall in Miami Beach. This time Johansson knocked Patterson down twice in the first round, but Patterson pulled off a win when Ingo failed to beat the count in the sixth.

After these two defeats, Johansson returned to Europe. He would never fight again in the United States—a choice that he would later regret. He did regain the European heavyweight title when he knocked out Dick Richardson in June of 1962, yet after barely decisioning Brian London in a fight where he was literally saved by the bell, on April 21, 1963, Johansson knew it was time to retire.

Johansson has led an active life outside of the ring. While still in boxing, he appeared on television with Dinah Shore and joined her in a duet. He also acted in a television production of Hemingway's *The Killers,* and worked as a boxing correspondent for Swedish TV. In July 1959, at the peak of Johansson's fame, rocker Johnny Lion released a song entitled "Ingemar Johannson" on the B-side of his single, *Haunted Heart.* Johansson also starred is a 1960 suspense film, *48 Hours to Live,* in which a scientist is held hostage on a secluded island by nuclear weapon-seeking terrorists. Johansson has owned a fishing boat, a restaurant, and a motel, and was involved in the construction business both in Europe and the United States. He also was an importer of fish and prefabricated houses to the U.S.

Though not a typical boxer, for a short period Johansson held that elusive and imposing title: "Heavyweight Champion of the World."

With palm trees as a background, Johannson holds a public workout at Miami Beach before his third and final fight with Floyd Patterson.

LIGHT HEAVYWEIGHT

Right-handed; 5'10"; 170–177 lbs.

87 bouts, 1946 to 3/30/1971

NBA Lt. Heavywt. Champ 1961–62,
Lt. Heavywt. Champ 1962–63

Hall of Fame Induction: 1993

Born: 8/9/1928, Manayunk, PA

Appreciated by the connoisseurs of boxing if not by casual fans, Harold Johnson was one of the best technical boxers of all time. As a measure of Johnson's greatness, he was either champion or a ranked contender every year except one from 1951 to 1964.

Although Johnson's father, Phil, had been a professional fighter, the young Johnson did not learn to box at home. He ran away to join the Navy at age fifteen and while there, had one amateur bout and boxed an exhibition with Hall of Famer Billy Conn. With this minimal amateur experience, Johnson turned professional upon his discharge from the Navy in 1946.

Johnson reeled off 24 straight wins at the start of his career before losing a decision in ten rounds to Archie Moore. Jersey Joe Walcott put Johnson out in three rounds in 1950, one of the few times Johnson was knocked out. At times fighting heavyweight as well as light heavyweight opponents, Johnson won most of his bouts. By 1951, he was recognized by *The Ring* as one of the top contenders in the light heavyweight division.

Moore continued to be the man to beat, as far as Johnson was concerned. In a four-month period in late 1951 and early 1952, Johnson and Moore fought three times. Each fight went ten rounds; Johnson lost two and won one. Johnson suffered one more loss in 1952, to Bob Satterfield, whom he later KO'd in two. The year 1953 yielded only wins for Johnson.

In 1954, Johnson faced Moore, who by then had become light heavyweight champion for the fifth time.

Harold Johnson had a total of seven fights against other Hall of Famers. He battled Moore (five times), Charles, and Walcott.

With Moore's title at stake, Johnson battled hard. He knocked Moore down in the tenth and was winning the fight through the thirteenth. In the fourteenth, Moore charged out of his corner to hit Johnson with a hard right. Then he unleashed a barrage of punches with both hands before knocking Johnson down with a crushing left hook. Johnson made it to his feet but was so groggy, referee Ruby Goldstein stopped the fight

A mystery surrounding a 1955 fight in Philadelphia caused a slowdown in Johnson's career. In the second round, Johnson inexplicably fell to the canvas, giving the fight to opponent Julio Mederos. Although barbiturates were found in Johnson's urine, he claimed ignorance of the source and blamed his condition

IN THE RING	WON 76	LOST 11	DRAWS 0	TB 87	KO 32	W 44	WF 0	D 0	KO'd 5	L 6	LF 0

Date		Opponent	Site	Result / Rounds		Title	Wt.
1946							
—		Joe Riley	Wilmington, DE	KO	2	—	—
—		Charley Lester	Wilmington,	KO	2	—	—
—		Jack Simon	Allentown, PA	KO	4	—	—
Oct 25		Randy Ingram	Philadelphia	KO	4	—	—
1947							
Jan 10		Frank Lowry	Philadelphia	KO	2	—	—
Jan 24		Chappie Manning	Reading, PA	W	6	—	—
Feb 10		Jimmy Holden	Allentown	KO	4	—	—
Feb 17		Joe Van Loan	Philadelphia	KO	2	—	—
Mar 10		Tony Gillo	Philadelphia	W	6	—	—
Apr 28		Leon Szymurski	Philadelphia	KO	3	—	—
May 26		Fred Lester	Philadelphia	KO	8	—	—
Jul 8		Tommy Ruth	Philadelphia	KO	6	—	—
Aug 4		Al Pinel	Philadelphia	W	6	—	—
Oct 6		Eddie Beazley	Philadelphia	KO	1	—	—
Nov 6		Jimmy Moore	Atlantic City	KO	5	—	—
Nov 24		Herbie Katz	Philadelphia	KO	1	—	—
Dec 11		Kid Wolfe	Atlantic City	W	8	—	—
1948							
Mar 1		Kenny Harris	Philadelphia	W	8	—	—
Mar 29		Kenny Harris	Philadelphia	W	10	—	—
May 13		Vernon Williams	Atlantic City	W	8	—	—
Sep 28		Augustino Guedes	Philadelphia	KO	3	—	176
Nov 9		Jim Holden	Allentown	W	8	—	—
Dec 14		Willie Brown	Philadelphia	KO	7	—	—
1949							
Feb 24		Arturo Godoy	Philadelphia	W	10	—	—
Apr 26	⑩	Archie Moore★	Philadelphia	L	10	—	—
Jun 16	⑩	Henry Hall	Milwaukee	W	10	—	173
Jul 25	⑩	Henry Hall	Milwaukee	W	10	—	—
Oct 26	⑩	Jimmy Bivins★	Philadelphia	W	10	—	—
Dec 7	⑩	Bert Lytell	Dayton, OH	W	10	—	—
1950							
Feb 8	⑩	Jersey Joe Walcott★	Philadelphia	KO'd	3	—	—
Dec 18		Harry Daniels	Philadelphia	KO	2	—	—

1951							
Jan 22		Dusty Wilkerson	Philadelphia	KO	4	—	—
Feb 9		Chuck Hunter	New York	W	8	—	—
Jun 18		Elkins Brothers	Philadelphia	KO	10	—	—
Jul 23		Chubby Wright	Philadelphia	W	10	—	—
Sep 24	⑩	Archie Moore★	Philadelphia	L	10	—	—
Dec 10	⑩	Archie Moore★	Milwaukee	W	10	—	—
1952							
Jan 29	⑩	Archie Moore★	Toledo, OH	L	10	—	—
Mar 17	⑩	Clarence Henry	Philadelphia	W	10	—	—
Aug 6	⑩	Bob Satterfield	Chicago	L	10	—	—
Sep 16		Leonard Morrow	Toledo	TKO	3	—	—
Oct 6	⑩	Bob Satterfield	Philadelphia	KO	2	—	—
Nov 24		Nino Valdes	Brooklyn	W	10	—	—
1953							
Jan 16	⑩	Jimmy Slade	New York	W	10	—	—
Mar 21		Bill Gilliam	Toledo	W	10	—	—
May 11		Toxie Hall	Miami	W	10	—	—
Sep 8	⑩	Ezzard Charles★	Philadelphia	W	10	—	—
Nov 7		Henry Hall	Milwaukee	W	10	—	—
Nov 19		Chubby Wright	Hershey, PA	W	10	—	—
1954							
Jan 29	⑩	Jimmy Slade	New York	W	10	—	—
Feb 15		Charlie Williams	Miami	KO	8	—	—
Mar 17	⑩	Paul Andrews	Chicago	W	10	—	—
Aug 11	♛	Archie Moore★	New York	TKO'd	14	For-World-LH	172
Oct 8	⑩	Billy Smith	Philadelphia	KO'd	2	—	—
Dec 7		Julio Mederos	Miami Beach	W	10	—	—
Dec 22	⑩	Marty Marshall	Detroit	W	10	—	—
1955							
Feb 11	⑩	Paul Andrews	New York	KO	6	—	—
May 6		Julio Mederos	Philadelphia	TKO'd	2	—	—
1956							
Dec 8		Bert Whitehurst	Portland, ME	W	10	—	179
1957							
Mar 12		Bob Satterfield	Miami Beach	W	10	—	—
May 31	⑩	Clarence Hinnant	New York	KO	1	—	—
Sep 20	⑩	Wayne Bethea	Philadelphia	W	10	—	—
Dec 17		Sid Peaks	Toledo	KO	5	—	—
1958							
Jan 17		Bert Whitehurst	Syracuse, NY	W	10	—	—
Apr 15		Oliver Wilson	Hartford, CT	KO	2	—	—
Dec 3		Howard King	Chicago	W	10	—	—
Dec 15		Rudy Watkins	Philadelphia	KO	6	—	—
1959							
Aug 4		Johnny York	Pittsfield, IL	TKO	6	—	—
Nov 11	⑩	Sonny Ray	Chicago	TKO	10	—	—
1960							
May 4		Clarence Floyd	Philadelphia	W	10	—	—
1961							
Feb 7		Jesse Bowdry	Miami Beach	TKO	9	Won-Vac NBA-LH	172
Apr 24	⑩	Von Clay	Philadelphia	KO	2	Ret-NBA-LH	174
Jul 1	⑩	Eddie Machen	Atlantic City	W	10	—	181
Aug 29	⑩	Eddie Cotton	Seattle	W	15	Ret-NBA-LH	173

1962							
May 12	⑩	Doug Jones	Philadelphia	W	15	Won-Vac World-LH	171
Jun 23	⑩	Gustav Scholz	Berlin	W	15	Ret-World-LH	172
1963							
Mar 19		Tommy Merrill	Scranton, PA	KO	9	—	—
Jun 1	⑩	Willie Pastrano ★	Las Vegas	L	15	Lost-World-LH	173
Dec 6	⑩	Henry Hank	Philadelphia	W	10	—	—
1964							
Apr 20		Hank Casey	Santa Monica, CA	KO	8	—	176
1966							
Jan 7		Johnny Persol	New York	L	10	—	176
Dec 6		Pekka Kokkonen	Vienna	W	10	—	—
1967							
May 1		Herschel Jacobs	New Orleans	W	10	—	—
Aug 7	⑩	Eddie Jones	New Orleans	W	10	—	—
1968							
Mar 2	⑩	Lothan Stengel	Frankfurt, Germany	W	10	—	170
Jun 11		Johnny Alford	Miami Beach	W	10	—	—
1971							
Mar 30		Herschel Jacobs	New York	TKO'd	3	—	177

on an adulterated orange he had been given before the fight. Johnson passed a lie detector test clearing his name, but the uproar resulted in a three-month suspension of boxing in Pennsylvania, by order of the governor.

Following this incident, Johnson found it more difficult to gain bouts. Moore was reluctant to fight him again, and it was not until 1961, after Moore had forfeited his crown for inactivity, that Johnson finally got another chance at a light heavyweight title. He knocked out Jesse Bowdry in Miami Beach to win the vacant NBA title. Muhammad Ali, on the undercard that night, was reportedly very impressed with Johnson.

Johnson unified the title when he decisioned Doug Jones in convincing fashion in 1962. He held the undisputed world championship for one year before losing on a decision to a last-minute replacement, Willie Pastrano. Johnson continued to fight for five years and even made a brief comeback in 1971 at 42. Though never a great favorite of the fans, Johnson earned the respect of those inside boxing. Asked why he never put Johnson in a nationally televised fight, matchmaker Teddy Brenner said cryptically, "Harold Johnson represents perfection in the art of boxing, and there is no room in this world for perfection."

Johnson was recognized as champ by the NBA in 1961. The following year he gained universal recognition.

ISMAEL LAGUNA
The Santa Isabel Tiger

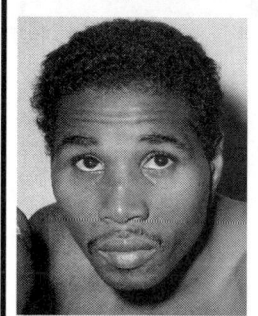

LIGHTWEIGHT

Right-handed; 5'9"; 116–137 lbs.

75 bouts, 1/8/1961 to 9/13/1971

Manager: Hector ("Tato") Valdes

Lightweight Champion 1965, 1970

Hall of Fame Induction: 2001

Born: 6/28/1943, Colon, Panama

One of the top lightweights of the 1960s, Ismael Laguna twice reigned as world lightweight champion. A twin and one of ten children in his family, Laguna idolized the boxers who trained at a local gym, and he would spend his time there after school. The boxers, for their part, took a liking to Laguna and taught him the rudiments of boxing. After competing as an amateur, he turned pro as a bantamweight on January 8, 1961, knocking out Antonio Morgan in the second round.

Fighting exclusively in Colon and Panama City, Laguna won his first 27 bouts, nineteen of them with knockout victories. Along the way, he captured the Panamanian featherweight title with a knockout over Pedro Ortiz. Laguna suffered his first defeat in Bogata, Columbia, a decision on June 8, 1963, that went to Antonio Herrera. He returned to Panama to knock Herrera out in the rematch on Laguna's home turf. The following year, Laguna lost a decision to Hall of Famer Vicente Saldivar, who would soon be the featherweight champion, but nevertheless rose to the top-contender spot in *The Ring* rankings.

Given his five-foot, nine-inch frame, it was not difficult for Laguna to advance to the lightweight division. On April 10, 1965, he received his first title shot against lightweight champ Carlos Ortiz, a Hall of Famer. Before 18,000 fans in Panama City, the fight opened with Laguna aggressively taking charge, throwing swift jabs and punishing shots to the body. Ortiz made an attempt to slow Laguna down, rushing inside, but Laguna countered with swift punches and

Laguna (R) regains his world lightweight title with a March 3, 1970, TKO victory over Armando ("Mando") Ramos in Los Angeles. Laguna's uppercut is an effective weapon.

IN THE RING	WON 65	LOST 9	DRAWS 1	TB 75	KO 37	W 28	WF 0	D 1	KO'd 0	L 9	LF 0

Date	Opponent	Site	Result / Rounds		Title	Wt.
1961						
Jan 8	Antonio Morgan	Colon, Panama	KO	2	—	—
Jan 22	Eduardo Frutos	Colon	W	4	—	—
Mar 5	Javier Valle	Panama City	W	4	—	116
Mar 26	Carlos Real	Panama City	W	4	—	117
Apr 16	Jose Pacheco	Panama City	TKO	3	—	118
Apr 30	Ernest Campbell	Panama City	W	6	—	116
May 21	Battling Escudero	Colon	KO	2	—	117
Jun 4	Killer Solomon	Colon	KO	7	—	—
Jun 25	Claudio Martinez	Colon	KO	4	—	116
Aug 27	Enrique Hitchman	Panama City	W	10	—	117
Oct 15	Euro Partides	Panama City	KO	4	—	118
Dec 1	Hector Hicks	Colon	KO	5	—	—
1962						
Jan 14	Eloy Sanchez	Colon	KO	3	—	—
Mar 2	Castor Castillo	Maracaibo, Venezuela	W	10	—	—
Apr 15	Nelson Estrada	Panama City	KO	7	—	—
Jun 3	Jorge Uzcategui	Colon	KO	2	—	—
Jun 10	Agustin Carmona	Panama City	KO	6	—	119
Jun 24	Carlos Celis	Panama City	KO	3	—	—
Jul 29	Jorge Salazar	Panama City	KO	6	—	—
Sep 16	Pedro Ortiz	Panama City	TKO	7	Won-Panama-FE	123
Oct 28	Beresford Francis	Colon	KO	5	—	123
Nov 18	Enrique Hitchman	Colon	KO	2	—	121
Dec 16	Tony Herrera	Panama City	KO	2	—	124
1963						
Jan 20	Bobby Gray	Colon	KO	9	—	—
Feb 22	Juan Ramirez	Panama City	W	10	—	125
Mar 17 ⑩	Auburn Copeland	Panama City	W	10	—	125
May 21	Filiberto Nava	Panama City	KO	3	—	127
Jun 8 ⑩	Antonio Herrera	Bogota	L	10	—	127
Jul 21 ⑩	Don Johnson	Panama City	KO	3	—	126
Aug 24	Eduardo ("Lalo") Guerrero	Panama City	W	10	—	126
Sep 15 ⑩	Antonio Herrera	Panama City	TKO	7	—	126
Nov 18 ⑩	Rafiu King	Paris	W	10	—	—
1964						
Jan 26	Pedro Miranda	Colon	KO	4	—	—
Feb 21	Orispo Dos Santos	São Paulo, Brazil	KO	7	—	—
Mar 9	Angel Robinson Garcia	Paris	W	10	—	—
Jun 1 ⑩	Vicente Saldivar★	Tijuana, Mexico	L	10	—	—
Jul 6	Kid Anahuac	Los Angeles	KO	8	—	130
Aug 2 ⑩	Vicente Derado	Panama City	W	10	—	132
Oct 25	Percy Hayles	Panama City	TKO	7	—	134
Dec 19	Sebastiao Nascimento	Panama City	W	10	—	132
1965						
Apr 10 ♛	Carlos Ortiz★	Panama City	W	15	Won-World-L	132
Jun 20	Raul Soriano	Panama City	KO	8	—	136
Jul 17 ⑩	Nicolino Loche	Buenos Aires	D	10	—	136
Nov 13 ⑩	Carlos Ortiz★	San Juan, PR	L	15	Lost-World-L	133

1966

Date		Opponent	Location	Result	Rounds	Title	Weight
Feb 19	♛	Carlos Hernandez	Panama City	TKO	8	—	133
Mar 19	♛	Gabriel ("Flash") Elorde★	Manila	L	10	—	134
Jul 28		Al Grant	Los Angeles	W	10	—	135
Oct 2		Percy Hayles	Kingston, Jamaica	KO	6	—	135
Dec 3		Daniel Guanin	Panama City	KO	8	—	135

1967

Date		Opponent	Location	Result	Rounds	Title	Weight
Mar 10	⑩	Frankie Narvaez	New York	W	10	—	134
Apr 2		Vicente Rivas	Panama City	KO	5	—	135
Jun 3		Alfredo Urbina	Panama City	W	10	—	136
Aug 16	♛	Carlos Ortiz★	New York	L	15	For-World-L	135
Oct 28	⑩	Paul Armstead	Panama City	W	10	—	133

1968

Date		Opponent	Location	Result	Rounds	Title	Weight
Feb 26		Ray Adigun	Paris	W	10	—	—
Apr 15		Bud Anderson	Philadelphia	TKO	10	—	131
Apr 29	⑩	Frankie Narvaez	San Juan	W	10	—	136
Jul 17		Victor Melendez	New York	W	10	—	136
Aug 20	⑩	Lloyd Marshall	New York	TKO	9	—	136
Oct 7		Gabe LaMarca	Portland, ME	KO	7	—	—
Oct 22		Grady Ponder	Miami Beach	W	10	—	137
Nov 15		Ramon Blanco	New York	W	10	—	136

1969

Date		Opponent	Location	Result	Rounds	Title	Weight
Mar 1		Curly Aguirre	Panama City	KO	4	—	—
Mar 31		Maurice Tavant	Paris	W	10	—	—
May 24		Eugenio Espinosa	Quito, Ecuador	L	10	—	135
Jul 5		Eugenio Espinosa	Panama City	W	10	—	135
Jul 14		Gennaro Soto	New York	W	10	—	136

1970

Date		Opponent	Location	Result	Rounds	Title	Weight
Jan 10		Jose Luis Vallejo	Colon	KO	3	—	—
Mar 3	♛	Armando ("Mando") Ramos	Los Angeles	TKO	9	Reg-World-L	135
Jun 6		Ishimatsu Suzuki	Panama City	TKO	13	Ret-World-L	135
Sep 26	⑩	Ken Buchanan★	San Juan	L	15	Lost-World-L	134

1971

Date		Opponent	Location	Result	Rounds	Title	Weight
Mar 6		Lloyd Marshall	Panama City	W	10	—	137
Apr 3	⑩	Chango Carmona	Panama City	W	10	—	135
Jun 22		Eddie Linder	Miami Beach	L	10	—	—
Sep 13	♛	Ken Buchanan★	New York	L	15	For-World-L	135

out-boxed the champion. In the seventh round, Laguna's hard-hitting combinations opened a gash in Ortiz's mouth and split open his left eye. Ortiz came back in the ninth, hammering his opponent with a left to the head, a right to his midsection, and another right that sent Laguna reeling into the ropes. Yet the attack did not faze Laguna, and he came back with both fists flying to end the Ortiz rally. For the rest of the bout, Laguna was clearly in command and he won a majority decision, with referee Jersey Joe Walcott's card showing 143-132, one judge's card showing 149-137, and the other judge inexplicably scoring the battle 145-145. The latter judge escaped the arena with police protection, and Laguna was the champion.

In the rematch seven months later in San Juan, Ortiz capitalized on his superior strength and nearly ended the fight in both the twelfth and thirteenth rounds, but Laguna toughed it out and lasted for the full fifteen rounds. The decision, however, went to Ortiz, and he recaptured his championship title. On August 16, 1967, the two came together for another match, this time meeting in Shea Stadium in New York. Laguna eluded the bull-like rushes of Ortiz, but he failed to mount a strong attack, and the belt stayed with the champion in a fifteen-round decision.

Laguna won fourteen of his next fifteen fights, earning him another shot at the lightweight title, which was now held by Mando Ramos. Fifteen thousand fans packed the Los Angeles Sports Arena, Ramos's home turf. Laguna went on the attack and opened cuts over both of Ramos's eyes, and by the ninth round, Ramos could not continue. Laguna was again the champion.

Laguna successfully defended his title against Ishimatsu Suzuki, then faced Hall of Famer Ken Buchanan. Though he was favored, Laguna found he had his hands full with Buchanan. The latter scored well in the twelfth round especially, and the split decision went to Buchanan. A year later, on September 13, 1971, in Madison Square Garden, the two fighters came together once more. Laguna changed his plan of attack, attempting to brawl with Buchanan, but lost another fifteen-round decision to the champion. Faced with defeat, Laguna retired.

Laguna was a complete fighter, possessed of a strong jab and a knockout punch, and combining great boxing skill with impressive resilience. Described as a "tall, immaculate boxer," he knocked out almost half of his opponents and was not once knocked to the canvas during his 75 fights.

In retirement, Laguna resided in Panama City, where he remained an extremely popular figure. Unlike many boxers, he had not squandered his ring earnings. He moved on to promote some fights, until weakened by sickle cell anemia.

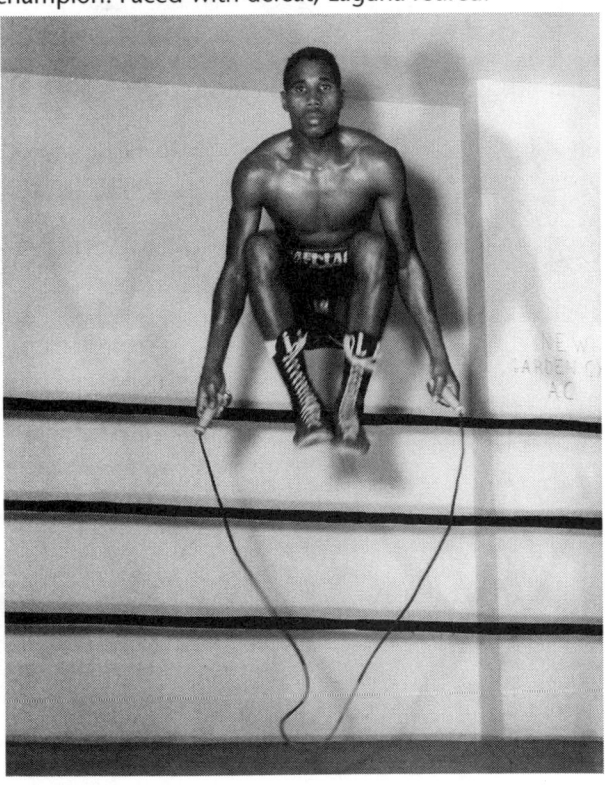

Laguna shows amazing leg spring in this high-flying jump rope demonstration.

JAKE LaMOTTA
The Bronx Bull

MIDDLEWEIGHT

Right-handed; 5'8"; 154–175 lbs.

106 bouts, 3/3/1941 to 4/14/1954

Managers: Mike Capriano and Joey LaMotta

Middleweight Champion 1949–51

Hall of Fame Induction: 1990

Born: 7/10/1921, Bronx, NY

Named: Giacobe LaMotta

Jake LaMotta, perennial opponent of Sugar Ray Robinson, was a tough, cagey fighter. He fought with a brutal will to win and was a master of playing possum in the ring. LaMotta's fame was given an extra dimension by the Academy Award-winning movie, *Raging Bull*, in which the fighter was portrayed by Robert DeNiro.

Born in New York, LaMotta was a street fighter who ran afoul of the law as a youth and spent some time in reform school. He began boxing in his teens, fought as an amateur for two years, then turned pro at the age of eighteen. He quickly made a name for himself and by 1942, was ranked by *The Ring* as the sixth-best middleweight contender. That year he fought Sugar Ray Robinson in the first of their six match-ups. LaMotta lost the ten-round decision, but in 1943, he became the first to beat the then-undefeated Robinson. LaMotta also battled Hall of Famer Fritzie Zivic four times in seven months in 1943 and 1944, losing only once.

Battered and swollen, LaMotta (R) summons his last reserves to knock out Laurent Dauthuille with a mere thirteen seconds remaining before the final bell in this September 1950 Motor City meeting.

IN THE RING	WON 83	LOST 19	DRAWS 4	TB 106	KO 30	W 53	WF 0	D 4	KO'd 4	L 15	LF 0

Date	Opponent	Site	Result / Rounds		Title	Wt.
1941						
Mar 3	Charley Mackley	New York	W	4	—	167
Mar 14	Tony Gillo	Bridgeport, CT	W	6	—	—
Apr 1	Johnny Morris	White Plains, NY	TKO	4	—	174
Apr 8	Joe Fredericks	White Plains	KO	1	—	—
Apr 15	Stanley Goicz	White Plains	W	4	—	—
Apr 22	Lorne McCarthy	White Plains	W	4	—	—
Apr 26	Monroe Crewe	Brooklyn	W	4	—	169
May 20	Johnny Cihlar	Brooklyn	W	4	—	170
May 27	Johnny Morris	New York	W	4	—	167
Jun 9	Lorenzo Strickland	Woodhaven, NY	W	4	—	—
Jun 16	Lorenzo Strickland	New York	W	6	—	166
Jun 23	Johnny Morris	New York	KO	3	—	—
Jul 15	Joe Baynes	Long Island City, NY	W	6	—	166
Aug 5	Joe Shikula	Long Island City	D	6	—	166
Aug 11	Cliff Koerkle	New York	W	6	—	166
Sep 24	Jimmy Reeves	Cleveland	L	10	—	167
Oct 7	Lorenzo Strickland	White Plains	W	8	—	167
Oct 20	Jimmy Reeves	Cleveland	L	10	—	166
Nov 14	Jimmy Casa	New York	W	6	—	162
Dec 22	Nate Bolden	Chicago	L	10	—	—
1942						
Jan 27	Frankie Jamison	New York	W	8	—	162
Mar 3	Frankie Jamison	New York	W	8	—	163
Mar 18	Lorenzo Strickland	New York	W	10	—	161
Apr 7	Lou Schwartz	New York	KO	9	—	160
Apr 21	Buddy O'Dell	New York	W	10	—	158
May 12	⑩ Jose Basora	New York	D	10	—	159
Jun 2	Vic Dellicurti	New York	W	10	—	157
Jun 16	⑩ Jose Basora	New York	L	10	—	158
Jul 28	Lorenzo Strickland	New York	W	8	—	160
Aug 28	⑩ Jimmy Edgar	New York	W	10	—	160
Sep 8	Vic Dellicurti	New York	W	10	—	158
Oct 2	⑩ Sugar Ray Robinson★	New York	L	10	—	157
Oct 20	Wild Bill McDowell	New York	TKO	5	—	162
Nov 6	Henry Chmielewski	Boston	W	10	—	—
1943						
Jan 2	⑩ Jimmy Edgar	Detroit	W	10	—	161
Jan 15	⑩ Jackie Wilson	New York	W	10	—	161
Jan 22	Charley Hayes	Detroit	TKO	6	—	—
Feb 5	⑩ Sugar Ray Robinson★	Detroit	W	10	—	160
Feb 26	⑩ Sugar Ray Robinson★	Detroit	L	10	—	160
Mar 19	Jimmy Reeves	Detroit	KO	6	—	—
Mar 30	Ossie Harris	Pittsburgh	W	10	—	161
May 12	Tony Ferrara	Cincinnati	KO	6	—	160
Jun 10	⑩ Fritzie Zivic★	Pittsburgh	W	10	—	155
Jul 12	⑩ Fritzie Zivic★	Pittsburgh	L	15	—	157
Sep 17	⑩ Jose Basora	Detroit	W	10	—	162
Oct 11	Johnny Walker	Philadelphia	TKO	2	—	164
Nov 12	⑩ Fritzie Zivic★	New York	W	10	—	161

1944

Jan 14	⑩	Fritzie Zivic★	Detroit	W	10	—	—
Jan 28		Ossie Harris	Detroit	W	10	—	—
Feb 25		Ossie Harris	Detroit	W	10	—	—
Mar 17	⑩	Coley Welch	Boston	W	10	—	—
Mar 31		Sgt. Lou Woods	Chicago	W	10	—	162
Apr 21	⑩	Lloyd Marshall	Cleveland	L	10	—	160
Sep 29	⑩	George Kochan	Detroit	W	10	—	162
Nov 3	⑩	George Kochan	Detroit	TKO	9	—	—

1945

Feb 23	⑩	Sugar Ray Robinson★	New York	L	10	—	157
Mar 19		Lou Schwartz	Norfolk, VA	KO	1	—	161
Mar 28		George Costner	Chicago	KO	6	—	—
Apr 19	⑩	Vic Dellicurti	New York	W	10	—	163
Apr 27	⑩	Bert Lytell	Boston	W	10	—	160
Jul 6		Tommy Bell	New York	W	10	—	161
Aug 10	⑩	Jose Basora	New York	TKO	9	—	159
Sep 17		George Kochan	New York	KO	9	—	162
Sep 26	⑩	Sugar Ray Robinson★	Chicago	L	12	—	159
Nov 13		Coolidge Miller	New York	KO	3	—	165
Nov 23		Walter Woods	Boston	KO	8	—	—
Dec 7		Charley Parham	Chicago	TKO	6	—	159

1946

Jan 11	⑩	Tommy Bell	New York	W	10	—	161
Mar 29		Marcus Lockman	Boston	W	10	—	163
May 24		Joe Reddick	Boston	W	10	—	162
Jun 13	⑩	Jimmy Edgar	Detroit	D	10	—	156
Aug 7	⑩	Holman Williams	Detroit	W	10	—	—
Sep 12		Bob Satterfield	Chicago	KO	7	—	—
Oct 25		O'Neill Bell	Detroit	KO	2	—	159
Dec 6		Anton Raadik	Chicago	W	10	—	162

1947

Mar 14	⑩	Tommy Bell	New York	W	10	—	161
Jun 6	⑩	Tony Janiro	New York	W	10	—	154
Sep 3		Cecil Hudson	Chicago	L	10	—	—
Nov 14	⑩	Billy Fox	New York	TKO'd	4	—	167

1948

Jun 1		Ken Stribling	Washington, DC	TKO	5	—	164
Sep 7		Burl Charity	New York	TKO	6	—	166
Oct 1		Johnny Colan	New York	TKO	10	—	165
Oct 18		Vern Lester	Brooklyn	W	10	—	165
Dec 3		Tommy Yarosz	New York	W	10	—	164

1949

Feb 21	⑩	Laurent Dauthuille	Montreal	L	10	—	161
Mar 25	⑩	Robert Villemain	New York	W	12	—	160
Apr 18		O'Neill Bell	Detroit	KO	4	—	167
May 18		Joey DeJohn	Syracuse, NY	TKO	8	—	162
Jun 16	♛	Marcel Cerdan★	Detroit	TKO	10	Won-World-M	158
Dec 9	⑩	Robert Villemain	New York	L	10	—	165

1950

Feb 3		Dick Wagner	Detroit	TKO	9	—	170
Mar 28		Chuck Hunter	Cleveland	TKO	6	—	168
May 4		Joe Taylor	Syracuse	W	10	—	169
Jul 12	⑩	Tiberio Mitri	New York	W	15	Ret-World-M	159
Sep 13	⑩	Laurent Dauthuille	Detroit	KO	15	Ret-World-M	159

1951						
Feb 14		Sugar Ray Robinson★	Chicago	TKO'd 13	Lost-World-M	160
Jun 27	⑩	Bob Murphy	New York	TKO'd 7	—	175
1952						
Jan 28	⑩	Norman Hayes	Boston	L 10	—	169
Mar 5		Eugene Hairston	Detroit	D 10	—	168
Apr 9	⑩	Norman Hayes	Detroit	W 10	—	167
May 21		Eugene Hairston	Detroit	W 10	—	168
Jun 11	⑩	Bob Murphy	Detroit	W 10	—	169
Dec 31	⑩	Danny Nardico	Coral Gables, FL	TKO'd 8	—	—
1954						
Mar 11		Johnny Pretzie	W. Palm Beach, FL	KO 4	—	169
Apr 3		Al McCoy	Charlotte, NC	KO 1	—	168
Apr 14		Billy Kilgore	Miami Beach	L 10	—	167

LaMotta lost two decisions to Robinson in 1945. He continued to box well, but was not given a chance at the middleweight title. Later, LaMotta testified before a U.S. Senate Anti-Monopoly Subcommittee that he was denied a title fight because he refused to become involved with mobsters. In the same hearings, however, LaMotta said he took a dive in a 1947 fight with Billy Fox in return for a promise that he could fight for the title.

In 1949, LaMotta finally got his chance at the middleweight title, against Marcel Cerdan. The match was held at Briggs Stadium in Detroit before 22,183 fans. After he wrestled Cerdan to the canvas in the first round, injuring Cerdan's left shoulder, LaMotta easily controlled the fight. He was given the victory when Cerdan failed to answer the bell for the tenth round. The chance of a rematch, first delayed by a claim of injury by LaMotta, was lost forever when Cerdan was killed in a plane crash.

LaMotta had two amazing fights left in his career. In 1950, he scored a fifteenth-round knockout of Laurent Dauthuille. Dauthuille, who dominated through most of the bout, fell victim in the twelfth round to LaMotta's trick of feigning serious injury. When Dauthuille came in close, LaMotta unleashed a flurry of blows. LaMotta, still behind in the fifteenth, gathered the strength for one last foray. He knocked Dauthuille out with thirteen seconds to go in the fight.

Actor Robert DeNiro (L) played Jake LaMotta (R) in the acclaimed biographical movie, Raging Bull.

LaMotta lost his final fight with Robinson, held on Valentine's Day, 1951 in Chicago Stadium. The two seemed fairly well matched in the early going, but as time went on, Robinson's pummeling of LaMotta became painful to watch. That LaMotta could still stand amazed the ringside experts. With LaMotta still on his feet but Robinson clearly the winner, the fight was stopped in the thirteenth round. LaMotta fought for another three years before turning to acting and other pursuits.

SUGAR RAY LEONARD

WELTERWEIGHT

Right-handed; 5'10"; 141–168 lbs.

40 bouts, 2/5/1977 to 3/1/1997

1976 Olympic Light Welterweight Gold Medalist

WBC Welterweight Champ 1979–80, 1980–81, World Welterweight Champ 1981–82, WBA Junior Middleweight Champ 1981, WBC Middleweight Champ 1987, WBC Light Heavyweight Champ 1988, WBC Super Middleweight Champ 1988–90

Hall of Fame Induction: 1997

Born: 5/17/1956, Wilmington, NC

Named: Ray Charles Leonard

Sugar Ray Leonard first captured the public's imagination with an electrifying gold medal performance in the 1976 Olympics, and his popular appeal has never diminished. Fast, powerful, and stylish in the ring, Leonard has proven to be one of the greatest boxers of the modern era. His stellar career brought him world championships in five weight classes, over $100 million in earnings, and fame that spread far beyond boxing.

Leonard was thirteen years old when he started training at a recreation center in Palmer Park, Maryland under the guidance of Janks Morton and Dave Jacobs. In 1972, at just sixteen, Leonard advanced to the quarterfinals of the Olympic trials. Other amateur honors followed as Leonard won the national junior light-

Two young future Hall of Famers contested the welterweight championship on November 30, 1979 in Las Vegas. Challenger Leonard (R), 23 years old, defeated titleholder Wilfred Benitez, only 21.

IN THE RING	WON 36	LOST 3	DRAWS 1	TB 40	KO 25	W 11	WF 0	D 1	KO'd 1	L 2	LF 0

Date		Opponent	Site	Result / Rounds		Title	Wt.
1977							
Feb 5		Luis Vega	Baltimore	W	6	—	141
May 14		Willie Rodriguez	Baltimore	W	6	—	141
Jun 10		Vinnie DeBarros	Hartford, CT	TKO	3	—	142
Sep 24		Frank Santore	Baltimore	KO	5	—	142
Nov 5		Agustin Estrada	Las Vegas	KO	5	—	145
Dec 17		Hector Diaz	Washington	KO	2	—	145
1978							
Feb 4		Rocky Ramon	Baltimore	W	8	—	143
Mar 1		Art McKnight	Dayton, OH	TKO	7	—	145
Mar 19		Javier Muniz	New Haven, CT	KO	1	—	144
Apr 13		Bobby Haymon	Landover, MD	TKO	3	—	147
May 13		Randy Milton	Utica, NY	TKO	8	—	—
Jun 3		Rafael Rodriguez	Baltimore	W	10	—	147
Jul 18		Dick Ecklund	Boston	W	10	—	146
Sep 9	⑩	Floyd Mayweather	Providence, RI	TKO	9	—	146
Oct 6	⑩	Randy Shields	Baltimore	W	10	—	147
Nov 3		Bernardo Prada	Portland, ME	W	10	—	146
Dec 9	⑩	Armando Muniz	Springfield, MA	TKO	6	—	149
1979							
Jan 11	⑩	Johnny Gant	Landover	TKO	8	—	146
Feb 11		Fernand Marcotte	Miami Beach	TKO	8	—	149
MarË 24		Daniel Gonzalez	Tucson	KO	1	—	147
Apr 21	⑩	Adolfo Viruet	Las Vegas	W	10	—	145
May 20		Marcos Geraldo	New Orleans	W	10	—	153
Jun 24	⑩	Tony Chiaverini	Las Vegas	TKO	4	—	151
Aug 12	⑩	Pete Ranzany	Las Vegas	TKO	4	Won-NABF-W	147
Sep 28	⑩	Andy Price	Las Vegas	KO	1	Ret-NABF-W	146
Nov 30	♛	Wilfred Benitez★	Las Vegas	TKO	15	Won-WBC-W	146
1980							
Mar 31	⑩	Davey ("Boy") Green	Landover	KO	4	Ret-WBC-W	147
Jun 20	⑩	Roberto Duran	Montreal	L	15	Lost-WBC-W	145
Nov 25	♛	Roberto Duran	New Orleans	TKO	8	Reg-WBC-W	146
1981							
Mar 28		Larry Bonds	Syracuse, NY	TKO	10	Ret-WBC-W	145
Jun 25	♛	Ayub Kalule	Houston	KO	9	Won-WBA-JM	153
Sep 16	♛	Thomas ("Hit Man") Hearns	Las Vegas	TKO	14	Won-World-W	146
1982							
Feb 15	⑩	Bruce Finch	Reno	TKO	3	Ret-World-W	146
1984							
May 11		Kevin Howard	Worcester, MA	TKO	9	—	149
1987							
Apr 6	♛	Marvelous Marvin Hagler★	Las Vegas	W	12	Won-WBC-M	160
1988							
Nov 7	♛	Don Lalonde	Las Vegas	TKO	9	Won-WBC-SM & LH	167

1989							
Jun 12	⑩	Thomas ("Hit Man") Hearns	Las Vegas	D	12	Ret-WBC-SM	160
Dec 7	♛	Roberto Duran	Las Vegas	W	12	Ret-WBC-SM	168
1991							
Feb 9	♛	Terry Norris	New York	L	12	For-WBC-JM	154
1997							
Mar 1	⑩	Hector ("Macho") Camacho	Atlantic City	TKO'd	5	For-IBC-M	159

weight title in 1972; national Golden Gloves titles in 1973, 1974, and 1975; AAU championships in 1974 and 1975; the North American junior welterweight title in 1974 and 1975; and the Pan American Games championship in 1975.

Leonard capped his amateur career by striking gold in the 1976 Olympics in the light welterweight division. As part of the U.S. team that produced four other gold medal winners (Leon Spinks, Michael Spinks, Howard Davis, and Leo Randolph), Leonard tore through five opponents before winning the top honors with a decision over Andres Aldama of Cuba. The national television audience saw Leonard as a charismatic, personable young man who, as ABC-TV's Howard Cosell

Trading canvas for hardwood for one evening, Leonard drives past Pernell ("Sweet Pea") Whitaker in a charity basketball game held at Norfolk State University in Norfolk, Virginia on August 29, 1990. Whitaker's team came out on top.

Leonard (L) floored Thomas ("Hit Man") Hearns in Las Vegas in their September 16, 1981 welterweight unification bout. The referee stopped the contest in the 14th round and declared Leonard the winner.

reported, went into the ring with a picture of his girlfriend taped to his shoe.

Initially, Leonard hoped his Olympic stardom would lead to commercial endorsements and enough money to go to college and also to help care for his ailing parents. When no endorsement offers arrived, he decided to turn professional. Morton and Jacobs stayed with him, and Maryland attorney Mike Trainer also came on the scene. Partly on the advice of Ali and Cosell, Trainer and Leonard hired Angelo Dundee as manager.

CBS televised Leonard's pro debut on February 5, 1977 against Luis ("the Bull") Vega. The fight drew a record crowd of 10,170 to the Baltimore Civic Center. Leonard's win by decision earned him $40,000 (a then-record paycheck for a pro debut), while Vega took home just $650. By the end of 1978, Leonard had won all seventeen of his fights, including three victories over ranked opponents. *The Ring* rated him the third-best welterweight contender. In 1979, Leonard beat an impressive lineup of ranked contenders and was given a shot at the WBC welterweight title held by Wilfred Benitez. For this much-anticipated bout, Benitez penned a contract for $1 million and Leonard $1.2 million.

Although Benitez evaded more blows than any of Leonard's previous opponents, Leonard downed the champ with a jab in the third. Benitez fought gamely and well until late in the last round when Leonard knocked Benitez down with a left uppercut, then followed with a devastating combination that convinced referee Carlos Padilla to stop the fight. Just six seconds short of the final bell, Leonard had won his first world title.

Despite his speed and power, some considered Leonard a bit of a hot dog who liked to play to the crowd and imitate the Ali shuffle. His first fight with Roberto Duran made it clear, however, that Leonard was as tough as they come. On June 20, 1980, he faced former lightweight champion Duran—one of the most aggressive and fearsome fighters ever.

Rankled by an exchange of pre-fight insults with Duran, Leonard entered the ring angry and tried to slug it out in the early going. Leonard fired effective combinations, but Duran was able to work inside to counteract Leonard's speed. The fight went the full fifteen rounds, many of them scored even, but Duran won the unanimous decision with scores of 6-4-5, 6-5-4, and 3-2-10.

Five months later Leonard faced Duran again at the Superdome in New Orleans. Leonard peppered Duran's head with swift jabs. When Duran tried to bull him into the ropes, Leonard eluded his charges and responded with rights to the head and uppercuts to the body. While Duran won a couple of rounds, Leonard remained firmly in control. As the fight went on, Leonard taunted the faltering Duran. With sixteen seconds to go in the eighth, Duran threw up his hands and said to the referee, "No mas" (no more), and thus gave up the fight and the championship.

On June 25, 1981, Leonard took a world title in a second weight class when he knocked out WBA world junior middleweight champ (and previously undefeated) Ayub Kalule in the ninth round. Next Leonard, the WBC welterweight champ, faced WBA champ Thomas ("Hit Man") Hearns in a unification bout. The fighters traded punches in the early rounds with Leonard developing a swelling under one eye. In the sixth Leonard unleashed a flurry of punches, breaking through Hearns' defense. From the eighth through the twelfth, Hearns outboxed Leonard and worked on his eye, which was beginning to close. In the thirteenth round Leonard caught Hearns with a right to the temple and then pummeled him with 24 unanswered blows. Hearns went through the ropes, but the referee ruled that Leonard had pushed him so it was not judged a knockdown. Behind on all three judges' scorecards, Leonard finished off Hearns in the fourteenth, when the referee stopped the fight and granted him a TKO victory.

On November 9, 1982, Leonard announced that his June 1982 surgery for a detached retina had convinced him to hang up his gloves. Nevertheless, he came back in 1984 to fight unheralded Kevin Howard. Howard knocked him down, but Leonard recovered to score a TKO in the ninth. Dissatisfied with his performance, Leonard again said he was retiring.

He returned from this second retirement to fight long-time middleweight champion Marvelous Marvin Hagler, whom Leonard believed could be vulnerable. Held on April 6, 1987 at Caesar's Palace in Las Vegas, the fight drew 15,336 and earned Leonard approximately $12 million. Though he had fought only once in the past five years, Leonard looked fresh, and his gritty performance earned him a split-decision victory in a match *The Ring* called the Fight of the Year and the Upset of the Year. Leonard then retired with the middleweight title.

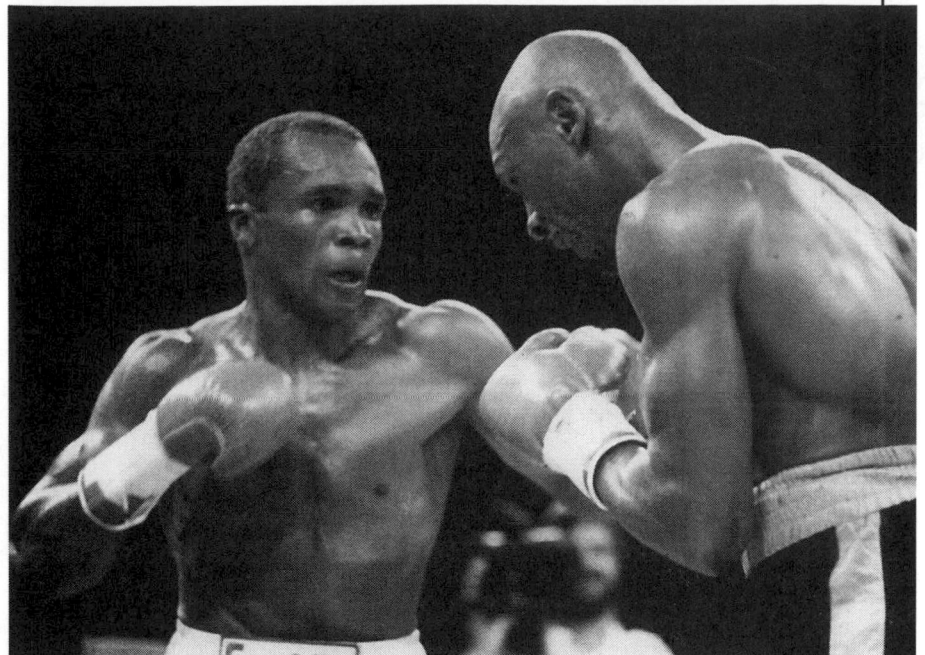

Two legends of modern boxing squared off when Leonard (L) met Marvelous Marvin Hagler for the WBC middleweight crown. In a thrilling, closely contested match in Las Vegas on April 6, 1987, Leonard took the split decision.

A year and a half later, Leonard boxed again, facing WBC light heavyweight champ Don Lalonde at the super middleweight limit of 168. Lalonde agreed to the weight so that the fight could be for both the super middleweight and light heavyweight titles. Knocked down early, Leonard recovered to stop Lalonde in the ninth. He followed that fight with a controversial draw with Hearns (in which Hearns scored two knockdowns) and a win-by-decision over Duran in a rubber match. Leonard then trimmed down to fight for the WBC super welterweight title held by Terry Norris but Norris totally dominated the fight to win easily by decision.

Although it appeared that Leonard had retired for good after the February 1991 Norris fight, he returned to the ring on February 28, 1997 at the age of forty against Hector ("Macho") Camacho. Leonard, hindered by a torn calf muscle, could not handle the younger Camacho, who knocked him down in the fifth shortly before the fight was stopped. At this writing, Leonard still has plans to continue his career.

Despite his checkered comeback attempts, Leonard compiled an outstanding lifetime record. He is revered as a great fighter and perhaps the best non-heavyweight since Sugar Ray Robinson. With boxing as a springboard, Leonard has become a well-known sports figure, earning such honors as *Sports Illustrated* Sportsman of the Year. In retirement Leonard has endorsed products and worked as a boxing commentator and actor.

CHARLES ("SONNY") LISTON

HEAVYWEIGHT

Right-handed; 6'1"; 198–226 lbs.

54 bouts, 9/2/1953 to 6/29/1970

Heavyweight Champion 1962–64

Hall of Fame Induction: 1991

Born: 5/8/1932, St. Francis County, AR

Died: 12/30/1970

One of the triumvirate of great heavyweight champions of the early 1960s, Sonny Liston blasted Floyd Patterson out of the throne only to be tossed out himself by a sassy young kid named Cassius Clay. Liston, an ex-convict with a cold stare that made him the bane of weigh-ins, was scary in the ring and unreadable in private life. The twists in Liston's career were influenced as much by his reputation as a bad man as by his formidable boxing skills.

Liston was born in rural Arkansas into an enormous family of 24 brothers and sisters. At about the age of thirteen, he fled his grindingly poor environment and moved to St. Louis to join his mother. St. Louis street life bred in Liston a propensity for crime. After a conviction for armed robbery, he was sentenced to two concurrent five-year terms in the Missouri State Penitentiary. While in prison,

In a reprise of the fight a year earlier in which he took the title from Floyd Patterson, fearsome Sonny Liston pummels Patterson with a right hook en route to a 1st-round KO July 22, 1963 in Las Vegas.

IN THE RING	WON **50**	LOST **4**	DRAWS **0**	TB 54	KO 39	W 11	WF 0	D 0	KO'd 3	L 1	LF 0

Date		Opponent	Site	Result / Rounds		Title	Wt.
1953							
Sep 2		Don Smith	St. Louis	TKO	1	—	200
Sep 17		Ponce De Leon	St. Louis	W	4	—	200
Nov 21		Benjamin Thomas	St. Louis	W	6	—	198
1954							
Jan 24		Martin Lee	St. Louis	TKO	6	—	201
Mar 31		Stanley Howlett	St. Louis	W	6	—	203
Jun 24		John Summerlin	Detroit	W	8	—	206
Aug 10		John Summerlin	Detroit	W	8	—	201
Sep 7	⑩	Marty Marshall	Detroit	L	8	—	—
1955							
Mar 1		Neil Welch	St. Louis	W	8	—	202
Apr 21	⑩	Marty Marshall	St. Louis	TKO	6	—	202
May 5		Emil Brtko	Pittsburgh	TKO	5	—	202
May 25		Calvin Butler	St. Louis	TKO	2	—	206
Sep 13		John Gray	Indianapolis	TKO	6	—	—
Dec 13		Larry Watson	St. Louis	TKO	4	—	209
1956							
Mar 6		Marty Marshall	Pittsburgh	W	10	—	203
1958							
Jan 29		Bill Hunter	Chicago	KO	2	—	210
Mar 11		Benjamin Wise	Chicago	KO	4	—	210
Apr 3		Bert Whitehurst	St. Louis	W	10	—	—
May 14		Julio Mederos	Chicago	TKO	3	—	204
Aug 6	⑩	Wayne Bethea	Chicago	TKO	1	—	206
Oct 7		Frankie Daniels	Miami Beach	KO	1	—	212
Oct 24		Bert Whitehurst	St. Louis	W	10	—	212
Nov 18		Ernie Cab	Miami Beach	TKO	8	—	211
1959							
Feb 18	⑩	Mike De John	Miami Beach	TKO	6	—	210
Apr 15		Cleveland Williams	Miami Beach	TKO	3	—	212
Aug 5		Geraldo Valdez	Chicago	KO	3	—	211
Dec 9		Willi Besmanoff	Cleveland	TKO	7	—	210
1960							
Feb 23		Howard King	Miami Beach	TKO	8	—	212
Mar 21		Cleveland Williams	Houston	TKO	2	—	212
Apr 25	⑩	Roy Harris	Houston	TKO	1	—	212
Jul 18	⑩	Zora Folley	Denver	KO	3	—	212
Sep 7	⑩	Eddie Machen	Seattle	W	12	—	211
1961							
Mar 8		Howard King	Miami Beach	KO	3	—	219
Dec 4		Albert Westphal	Philadelphia	KO	1	—	—
1962							
Sep 25	♛	Floyd Patterson★	Chicago	KO	1	Won-World-H	214
1963							
Jul 22	⑩	Floyd Patterson★	Las Vegas	KO	1	Ret-World-H	215
1964							
Feb 25	⑩	Cassius Clay★	Miami Beach	TKO'd	7	Lost-World-H	218

1965							
May 25	♛	Muhammad Ali★	Lewiston, ME	KO'd	1	For-World-H	218
1966							
Jun 29		Gerhard Zech	Stockholm	KO	7	—	221
Aug 19		Amos Johnson	Gothenburg, Sweden	KO	3	—	218
1967							
Mar 30		Dave Bailey	Gothenburg	KO	1	—	221
Apr 28		Elmer Rush	Stockholm	TKO	6	—	223
1968							
Mar 16		Bill McMurray	Reno	KO	4	—	223
May 23		Billy Joiner	Los Angeles	TKO	8	—	222
Jul 6		Henry Clark	San Francisco	TKO	7	—	219
Oct 14		Sonny Moore	Phoenix	KO	3	—	221
Nov 3		Willie Earls	Juarez, Mexico	KO	2	—	—
Nov 12		Roger Rischer	Pittsburgh	KO	3	—	219
Dec 10		Amos Lincoln	Baltimore	KO	2	—	215
1969							
Mar 28		Billy Joiner	St. Louis	W	10	—	219
May 19		George Johnson	Las Vegas	TKO	7	—	217
Sep 23		Sonny Moore	Houston	KO	3	—	226
Dec 6	⑩	Leotis Martin	Las Vegas	KO'd	9	For-Vac NABF-H	219
1970							
Jun 29		Chuck Wepner	Jersey City, NJ	TKO	10	—	219

Liston began to participate, for the first time, in a formal boxing program under the direction of the prison chaplain. Paroled in 1952, he started fighting on the amateur level. An extremely talented boxer, he won the 1953 National Golden Gloves title.

Liston turned professional later in 1953 and won fourteen of his first fifteen fights. His budding career was derailed when he got into a fight with a St. Louis policeman and was again sent to prison. It is believed that Liston may have been the victim of police harassment. Upon his release, Liston continued his climb up the rungs of the heavyweight ladder. In 1958, *The Ring* ranked him as the ninth-best contender for the heavyweight title. By 1960, the venerable boxing publication ranked him the number one challenger.

Heavyweight champ Floyd Patterson was in no hurry to sign for a title match against Liston. Liston's incredibly strong jab, great left hook, strong right, and good boxing skills had destroyed many strong opponents. In addition, Liston's criminal past and the reputed underworld connections of those involved in handling him did not make him an attractive opponent for a title shot.

Finally, in 1962, Patterson agreed to meet Liston in Comiskey Park in Chicago. The end for Patterson was abrupt. Liston, who seldom allowed anyone to go the distance, hammered Patterson with two left hooks and a right to knock him out in the first round. Less than a year later, Patterson was back for the rematch and Liston did it again: a first-round knockout reaffirmed him as the world's top heavyweight.

Then along came the brash-talking Cassius Clay, a pretty fighter who was Liston's opposite in too many ways to count. Some observers said the world-weary Liston was confused by Clay. Clay quipped where Liston stared, he danced where Liston stood firm. As the fight, held in February 1964 in Miami Beach, developed, Clay proved too fast for Liston. He slammed at the champ with lightning punches, then slipped out of the way. During the fifth round, Clay's vision was impaired when some ointment Liston's handlers had applied to Liston's cuts, and perhaps to his shoulders or gloves, got into Clay's eyes. Although Clay begged his cornermen to cut off his gloves, they urged him to keep fighting. In the sixth, Clay's eyes began to clear and he dominated the fight again. When the bell rang to start round seven, Liston did not come out, claiming an injured shoulder. Questions about the reasons for Liston's poor performance were never answered.

The circumstances of Liston's rematch with Clay in Lewiston, Maine the next year are equally murky. Clay, by then known as Muhammad Ali, knocked Liston down in the first round. Ali was slow in retreating to a neutral corner for the count and Liston stayed down for some time. Referee Jersey Joe Walcott motioned for the fighters to continue after Liston got up. Then Nat Fleischer, editor of *The Ring*, shouted to Walcott that the fight should be stopped because Liston had been down for too long. The fight ended there. Once again, rumors of a fix were never substantiated.

Liston continued to fight for another six years. He was knocked out by Leotis Martin in his second-to-last fight, a bid for the vacant NABF heavyweight title. His seventeen-year career ended in 1970 when he died in his home in Las Vegas under suspicious circumstances. Officially, the cause of death was listed as lung congestion and heart failure. Unofficially, the death appeared to be the result of a heroin overdose, and some police officials and Liston associates believed that Liston was murdered.

A nimble big man, Liston once demonstrated his jump rope skills on the Ed Sullivan show. Here he turns a headstand, wearing his "anti-foul" protector.

JOE LOUIS
The Brown Bomber

HEAVYWEIGHT

Right-handed; 6'1½"; 188–218 lbs.

70 bouts, 7/4/1934 to 10/26/1951

Managers: Julian Black
and John Roxborough 1934–49,
Marshall Miles 1950–51

Heavyweight Champion 1937–49

Hall of Fame Induction: 1990

Born: 5/13/1914, Lafayette, AL

Named: Joseph Louis Barrow

Died: 4/12/1981

Joe Louis dominated the sport of boxing from the 1930s into the 1950s. He was arguably the best heavyweight champion ever and, in an era when blacks were still riding in the back of the bus, was widely respected as an individual. Fans didn't just like Louis, they loved him. He was also a hero to a generation of younger boxers, some of whom faced him in his post-championship years.

Born in Alabama, Louis moved to Detroit as a child and first became involved in boxing there at Brewster's Gym. In his first amateur bout, Louis was knocked down seven times. He was seldom knocked down again. He won the 1934 National AAU light heavyweight title and ended his amateur career that year with a record of 53 wins and three losses.

Twenty-two-year-old Louis hands Hall of Famer Jack Sharkey his final defeat with a 3rd-round knockout on August 18, 1936 in New York. This was the first fight for Louis after his loss to Schmeling.

IN THE RING	WON 68	LOST 3	DRAWS 0	TB 71	KO 54	W 13	WF 1	D 0	KO'd 2	L 1	LF 0

Date		Opponent	Site	Result / Rounds		Title	Wt.
1934							
Jul 4		Jack Kracken	Chicago	TKO	1	—	—
Jul 12		Willie Davies	Chicago	TKO	3	—	—
Jul 30		Larry Udell	Chicago	TKO	2	—	—
Aug 13		Jack Kranz	Chicago	W	8	—	—
Aug 27		Buck Everett	Chicago	KO	2	—	—
Sep 11		Alex Borchuk	Detroit	TKO	4	—	—
Sep 26		Adolph Wiater	Chicago	W	10	—	—
Oct 24		Art Sykes	Chicago	KO	8	—	—
Oct 31		Jack O'Dowd	Detroit	KO	2	—	—
Nov 14		Stanley Poreda	Chicago	KO	1	—	—
Nov 30		Charley Massera	Chicago	KO	3	—	188
Dec 14	⑩	Lee Ramage	Chicago	TKO	8	—	—
1935							
Jan 4	⑩	Patsy Perroni	Detroit	W	10	—	—
Jan 11		Hans Birkie	Pittsburgh	TKO	10	—	—
Feb 21	⑩	Lee Ramage	Los Angeles	TKO	2	—	—
Mar 8		Donald ("Red") Barry	San Francisco	TKO	3	—	—
Mar 29	⑩	Natie Brown	Detroit	W	10	—	—
Apr 12		Roy Lazer	Chicago	TKO	3	—	—
Apr 22*		Biff Bennett	Dayton, OH	KO	1	—	—
Apr 25*		Roscoe Toles	Flint, MI	KO	6	—	—
May 3*		Willie Davies	Peoria, IL	KO	2	—	—
May 7*		Gene Stanton	Kalamazoo, MI	KO	3	—	—
Jun 25	⑩	Primo Carnera	New York	TKO	6	—	—
Aug 7		King Levinsky	Chicago	TKO	1	—	—
Sep 24	⑩	Max Baer★	New York	KO	4	—	—
Dec 14		Paolino Uzcudun	New York	TKO	4	—	—

Some boxing historians believe these bouts were exhibition matches.

Louis's first professional fight was a one-round knockout win. Louis followed that victory up with seventeen more in less than a year. After his first year as a pro, Louis was rated the ninth-top contender for the heavyweight title by *The Ring* in its annual rankings. In 1935, he knocked out former champions Primo Carnera and Max Baer to vault to the status of top contender.

Louis suffered his first defeat when he faced another former champion, Max Schmeling of Germany, in Yankee Stadium before a crowd of 60,000. Louis was knocked down in the fourth round and, though he did inflict damage on Schmeling, trailed throughout the fight. Schmeling caught Louis with two overhand rights in the twelfth and knocked him out.

In 1937, Louis met champion James J. Braddock for the heavyweight title in Comiskey Park in Chicago. Braddock knocked Louis down early on but, as the fight continued, Louis dominated. A crushing straight right to Braddock's head finished the champion off in the eighth.

Louis had become the first black heavyweight champion since Jack Johnson and as such was a tremendous source of pride for black Americans. Promoter Mike

1936							
Jan 17	⑩	Charley Retzlaff	Chicago	KO	1	—	199
Jun 19	⑩	Max Schmeling★	New York	KO'd	12	—	198
Aug 18		Jack Sharkey★	New York	KO	3	—	199
Sep 22	⑩	Al Ettore	Philadelphia	KO	5	—	203
Oct 9		Jorge Brescia	New York	KO	3	—	202
Dec 14		Eddie Simms	Cleveland	TKO	1	—	—
1937							
Jan 11*		Steve Ketchel	Buffalo	KO	2	—	—
Jan 29	⑩	Bob Pastor	New York	W	10	—	203
Feb 17		Natie Brown	Kansas City	TKO	4	—	206
Jun 22	♛	James J. Braddock	Chicago	KO	8	Won-World-H	197
Aug 30	⑩	Tommy Farr	New York	W	15	Ret-World-H	197
1938							
Feb 23	⑩	Nathan Mann	New York	KO	3	Ret-World-H	200
Apr 1		Harry Thomas	Chicago	KO	5	Ret-World-H	202
Jun 22	⑩	Max Schmeling★	New York	KO	1	Ret-World-H	198
1939							
Jan 25	♛	John Henry Lewis★	New York	KO	1	Ret-World-H	200
Apr 17		Jack Roper	Los Angeles	KO	1	Ret-World-H	201
Jun 28	⑩	Tony Galento	New York	TKO	4	Ret-World-H	200
Sep 20	⑩	Bob Pastor	Detroit	KO	11	Ret-World-H	200
1940							
Feb 9	⑩	Arturo Godoy	New York	W	15	Ret-World-H	203
Mar 29	⑩	Johnny Paychek	New York	KO	2	Ret-World-H	201
Jun 20	⑩	Arturo Godoy	New York	TKO	8	Ret-World-H	199
Dec 16		Al McCoy	Boston	TKO	6	Ret-World-H	202
1941							
Jan 31	⑩	Red Burman	New York	KO	5	Ret-World-H	202
Feb 17		Gus Dorazio	Philadelphia	KO	2	Ret-World-H	203
Mar 21	⑩	Abe Simon	Detroit	TKO	13	Ret-World-H	202
Apr 8		Tony Musto	St. Louis	TKO	9	Ret-World-H	203
May 23	⑩	Buddy Baer	Washington, DC	WD	7	Ret-World-H	201
Jun 18	⑩	Billy Conn★	New York	KO	13	Ret-World-H	199
Sep 29	⑩	Lou Nova	New York	TKO	6	Ret-World-H	202
1942							
Jan 9	⑩	Buddy Baer	New York	KO	1	Ret-World-H	206
Mar 27	⑩	Abe Simon	New York	KO	6	Ret-World-H	207
1946							
Jun 19	⑩	Billy Conn★	New York	KO	8	Ret-World-H	207
Sep 18	⑩	Tami Mauriello	New York	KO	1	Ret-World-H	211
1947							
Dec 5	⑩	Jersey Joe Walcott★	New York	W	15	Ret-World-H	211
1948							
Jun 25	⑩	Jersey Joe Walcott★	New York	KO	11	Ret-World-H	213
1950							
Sep 27	♛	Ezzard Charles★	New York	L	15	For-World-H	218
Nov 29		Cesar Brion	New York	W	10	—	—
1951							
Jan 3		Freddie Beshore	Detroit	TKO	4	—	—
Feb 7		Omelio Agramonte	Miami	W	10	—	—
Feb 23		Andy Walker	San Francisco	TKO	10	—	—
May 2		Omelio Agramonte	Detroit	W	10	—	—
Jun 15	⑩	Lee Savold	New York	KO	6	—	—
Aug 1		Cesar Brion	San Francisco	W	10	—	—
Aug 15		Jimmy Bivins★	Baltimore	W	10	—	—
Oct 26	⑩	Rocky Marciano★	New York	KO'd	8	—	212

Some boxing historians believe this bout was an exhibition match.

Jacobs and Louis's managers, Julian Black and John Roxborough, made sure that Louis did not do anything in public which would lower him in the critical eyes of white America. For instance, Louis was directed not to smile after defeating a white opponent. Whatever he felt inside, Louis allowed himself to be guided in this way, perhaps because he already possessed an uncommon sense of dignity. When some called Louis "a credit to his race," sportswriter Jimmy Cannon commented, "Yes, Louis is a credit to his race— the human race."

Sugar Ray Robinson (LC) and Joe Louis (RC) share a laugh in their Army uniforms on August 29, 1943 at Mitchell Field, New York.

In 1938, Louis got a chance to avenge his loss to Schmeling in Yankee Stadium in front of a colossal crowd of 75,000. Louis sent them home early with a one-round knockout of Schmeling, whom German leaders had put forward as an Aryan figurehead. Louis, who was seen as a standard-bearer for all Americans, had

Max Schmeling hears the count of ten in the first round of his June 22, 1938 return match with Louis. The reigning champ is placidly victorious in the fourth defense of his heavyweight title.

met President Franklin D. Roosevelt at the White House before the fight, which indicated the importance assigned to the match.

Louis continued to defend his title successfully. Though some of his opponents were disparaged as members of the "Bum of the Month Club," Louis handled them all. In June of 1941, he fought one of his most memorable fights against former light heavyweight champion Billy Conn. Fighting before another large crowd of 54,487 in the Polo Grounds, Conn gave a Louis a good battle and was leading after twelve rounds. Louis's corner told Louis that he needed a knockout to win. The champ rose to the occasion and knocked Conn out with a flurry of punches in the thirteenth round.

Louis fought twice in 1942 and donated his purses to the war effort. He then enlisted in the Army and fought 96 exhibitions before some two million GIs in the United States, North Africa, and Europe. Louis received the Legion of Merit for his work in this regard and further endeared himself to the American public with his comment that the United States would win the war because "we're on God's side."

After the war, Louis fought the long-awaited rematch with Conn and knocked him out in the eighth round. The next year Louis fought the tough Jersey Joe

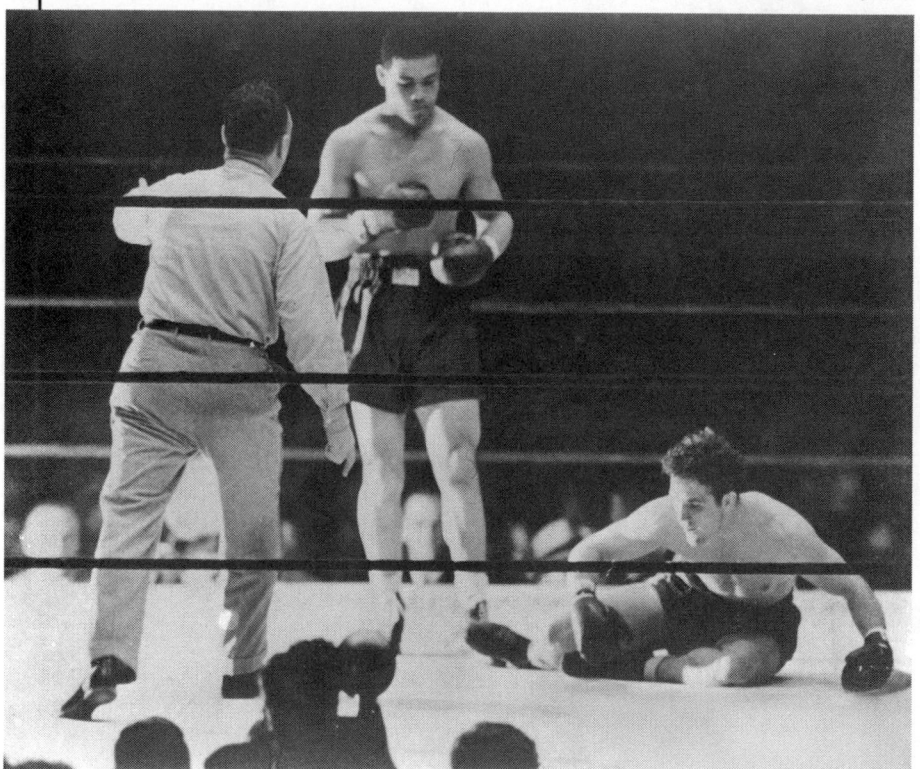

Louis stands over Hall of Famer Billy Conn who slipped to the canvas in the first round of their June 18, 1941 bout. In the thirteenth round, Louis, behind on the scorecards, knocked out Conn.

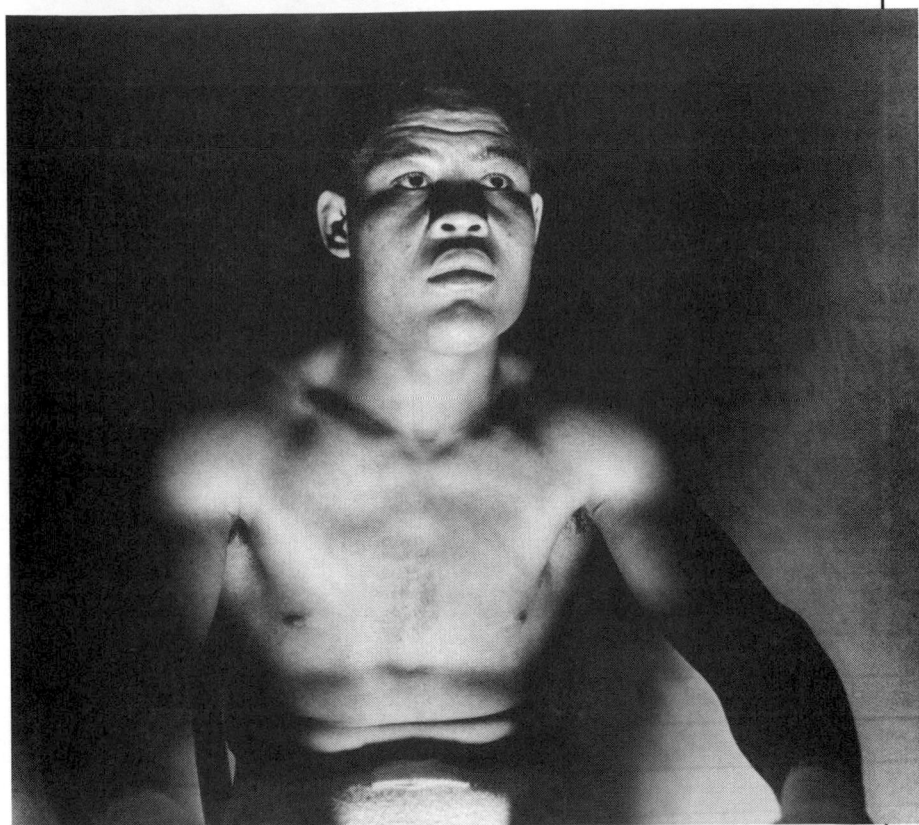

Despite his long career, Louis was only knocked to the canvas a total of ten times. Accomplishing this feat were Schmeling (2), Braddock, Galento, Buddy Baer, Jersey Joe Walcott (3), and Marciano (2).

Walcott, struggling to come in under 212 pounds as the contract specified. In Madison Square Garden before 18,194, Louis retained the title though he was knocked down in the first and fourth rounds. He won a split decision which many believed should have gone to Walcott. Louis knocked Walcott out in the rematch and, soon thereafter, announced his retirement.

In 1950, Louis made a comeback and lost by decision to Ezzard Charles in his bid to regain the championship. He then won eight fights in a row before facing the up-and-coming Rocky Marciano, who knocked him out in the eighth round. Louis then retired for good. Ring experts point to his great left jab, left hook, and powerful right, as well as his solid boxing skills, to rank Louis at or near the top of the all-time list of heavyweights. After retiring, he struggled to settle longstanding Internal Revenue Service problems by working in various business-es. He also worked as a wrestler, a wrestling referee, and as a greeter for a Las Vegas hotel. For the rest of his life, he maintained an association with the fight game, and remained much admired by both the boxing community and the general public.

HEAVYWEIGHT

Right-handed; 5'11"; 178–192 lbs.

49 bouts, 3/17/1947 to 9/21/1955

Managers: Gene Caggiano, Al Weill

Heavyweight Champion 1952–56

Hall of Fame Induction: 1990

Born: 9/1/1923, Brockton, MA

Named: Rocco Francis Marchegiano

Died: 8/31/1969

Rocky Marciano fought 49 times as a professional and never lost once. To date, he is the only heavyweight champion of the world to retire undefeated. Easy-going and gentle outside the ring, Marciano could be a hellish opponent. He offered a stolid resistance to whatever came his way, and the blockbuster punches that made him famous were some of the most dangerous ever thrown.

Marciano was born in Brockton, Massachusetts, just outside Boston. According to legend, he told his father he would one day be heavyweight champ of the world, but the young Marciano also dreamed of becoming a catcher in major league baseball. Although an uncle showed him the rudiments of boxing, Marciano didn't apply himself seriously until he did a stint in the Army. After leaving

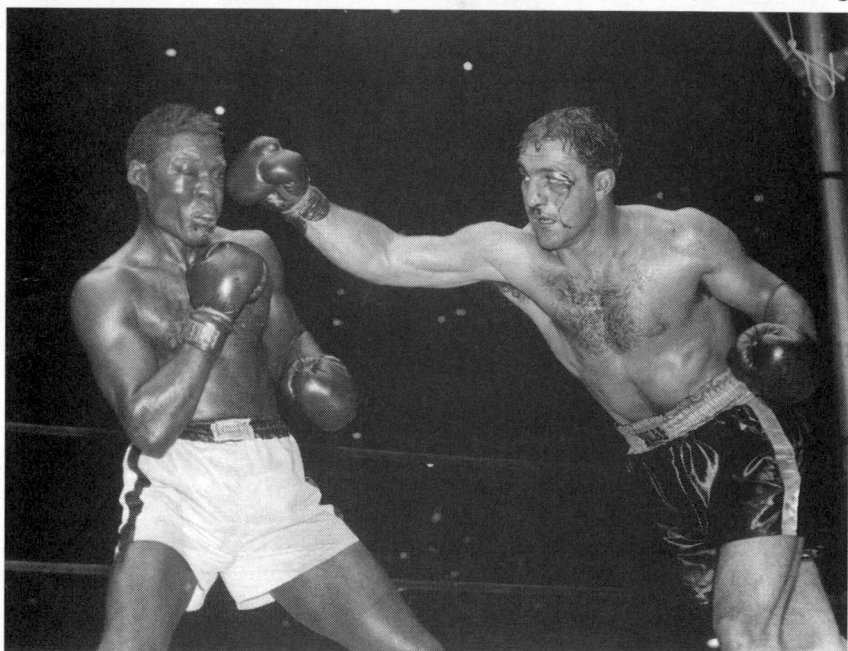

Blood trailing down his face, Marciano (R) unleashes "Susie Q" (his powerful right-hand punch) at Ezzard Charles in the first of his two successful 1954 title defenses.

the service, Marciano boxed as an amateur and won top honors in a New England Golden Gloves tournament.

As a novice, Marciano displayed great power but little control. In training, he sometimes swung his punches with so much momentum he fell down. He was a crude slugger that few expected to go very far. He was also considered too short, too light, and lacking the necessary reach to contend with heavyweights. Marciano's reach was only 68" (for comparison, Muhammad Ali's reach was 82"),

IN THE RING	WON 49	LOST 0	DRAWS 0	TB 49	KO 43	W 6	WF 0	D 0	KO'd 0	L 0	LF 0

Date	Opponent	Site	Result / Rounds		Title	Wt.
1947						
Mar 17	Lee Epperson	Holyoke, MA	KO	3	—	192
1948						
Jul 12	Harry Bilzarian	Providence, RI	TKO	1	—	185
Jul 19	John Edwards	Providence	KO	1	—	186
Aug 9	Bobby Quinn	Providence	KO	3	—	183
Aug 23	Eddie Ross	Providence	KO	1	—	184
Aug 30	Jimmy Weeks	Providence	TKO	1	—	184
Sep 13	Jerry Jackson	Providence	TKO	1	—	183
Sep 20	Bill Hardeman	Providence	KO	1	—	182
Sep 30	Gil Cardione	Washington, DC	KO	1	—	179
Oct 4	Bob Jefferson	Providence	TKO	2	—	178
Nov 29	Pat Connolly	Providence	TKO	1	—	185
Dec 14	Gilley Ferron	Philadelphia	TKO	2	—	180
1949						
Mar 21	Johnny Pretzie	Providence	TKO	5	—	183
Mar 28	Artie Donato	Providence	KO	1	—	182
Apr 11	James Walls	Providence	KO	3	—	183
May 2	Jimmy Evans	Providence	TKO	3	—	183
May 23	Don Mogard	Providence	W	10	—	181
Jul 18	Harry Haft	Providence	KO	3	—	184
Aug 16	Pete Louthis	New Bedford, MA	KO	3	—	184
Sep 26	Tommy Di Giorgio	Providence	KO	4	—	179
Oct 10	Ted Lowry	Providence	W	10	—	180
Nov 7	Joe Dominic	Providence	KO	2	—	185
Dec 2	Pat Richards	New York	TKO	2	—	181
Dec 19	Phil Muscato	Providence	TKO	5	—	183
Dec 30	Carmine Vingo	New York	KO	6	—	180
1950						
Mar 24	⑩ Roland La Starza	New York	W	10	—	183
Jun 5	Eldridge Eatman	Providence	TKO	3	—	189
Jul 10	Gino Buonvino	Boston	TKO	10	—	188
Sep 18	Johnny Shkor	Providence	KO	6	—	190
Nov 13	Ted Lowry	Providence	W	10	—	186
Dec 18	Bill Willson	Providence	KO	1	—	190
1951						
Jan 29	Keene Simmons	Providence	TKO	8	—	191
Mar 20	Harold Mitchell	Hartford, CT	TKO	2	—	186
Mar 26	Art Henri	Providence	TKO	9	—	186

Date		Opponent	Location	Result	Round	Title	Weight
Apr 30		Red Applegate	Providence	W	10	—	185
Jul 12	⑩	Rex Layne	New York	KO	6	—	185
Aug 27		Fred Beshore	Boston	TKO	4	—	187
Oct 26	⑩	Joe Louis★	New York	KO	8	—	187
1952							
Feb 13		Lee Savold	Philadelphia	KO	6	—	186
Apr 21		Gino Buonvino	Providence	KO	2	—	189
May 12		Bernie Reynolds	Providence	KO	3	—	186
Jul 28	⑩	Harry Matthews	New York	KO	2	—	187
Sep 23	♛	Jersey Joe Walcott★	Philadelphia	KO	13	Won-World-H	184
1953							
May 15	⑩	Jersey Joe Walcott★	Chicago	KO	1	Ret-World-H	184
Sep 24	⑩	Roland La Starza	New York	TKO	11	Ret-World-H	185
1954							
Jun 19	⑩	Ezzard Charles★	New York	W	15	Ret-World-H	187
Sep 17	⑩	Ezzard Charles★	New York	KO	8	Ret-World-H	187
1955							
May 16	⑩	Don Cockell	San Francisco	TKO	9	Ret-World-H	189
Sep 21	⑩	Archie Moore★	New York	KO	9	Ret-World-H	188

one of the smallest of any heavyweight champion, which forced him to fight his opponents at close range. But Trainer Charley Goldman saw the potential in Marciano and taught him to fight from a crouch that made him very difficult to hit. Marciano spent countless hours training to perfect the lessons taught him by Goldman.

Marciano turned professional in 1947 with a third-round knockout of Lee Epperson. He went on to record sixteen consecutive knockouts, nine in the first round. Indeed, a look at Marciano's career record shows that few fighters ever went the distance with him. By 1950, Marciano was ranked tenth among heavyweight contenders in the annual rankings by The Ring. In 1951, his name became a household word when he fought Joe Louis, who had come out of retirement. Louis was old but still a master of the ring. Marciano had the edge in the close fight and in the eighth, knocked Louis down with a left hook to the jaw. He followed that up with a flurry of punches and ended the fight with a powerful right to the jaw.

In 1952, Marciano took the world heavyweight title from Jersey Joe Walcott, a fierce defender of his crown. The memorable battle was held at Philadelphia's Municipal Stadium before 40,379 fans. Walcott opened up by knocking Marciano down in the first round. From then on, it was a bloody contest. Both fighters inflicted significant damage, including multiple cuts. After twelve rounds, Walcott was ahead on the cards of both judges and the referee. The only way Marciano could win was by knockout. In the thirteenth, Marciano plunged a crushing right into Walcott's jaw. "Susie Q," Marciano's pet name for his piston-like right, had done her job. Walcott was out and Marciano was the new world champion. A rematch with Walcott ended much more abruptly, with a one-round knockout confirming Marciano's right to the title.

Marciano twice defended his title against former champ Ezzard Charles, winning both bouts. In 1955, he entered the ring against light heavyweight champion Archie Moore, a master boxer and ring veteran whose age hadn't caught up with him. Moore knocked Marciano down in the second, but Marciano recovered and knocked Moore out in the ninth. After this fight, Marciano retired. He left behind an unblemished record and the memory of his powerful punching ability. Well-liked, Marciano also left behind many friends. He died in a plane crash in 1969, en route to a personal appearance in Des Moines, Iowa.

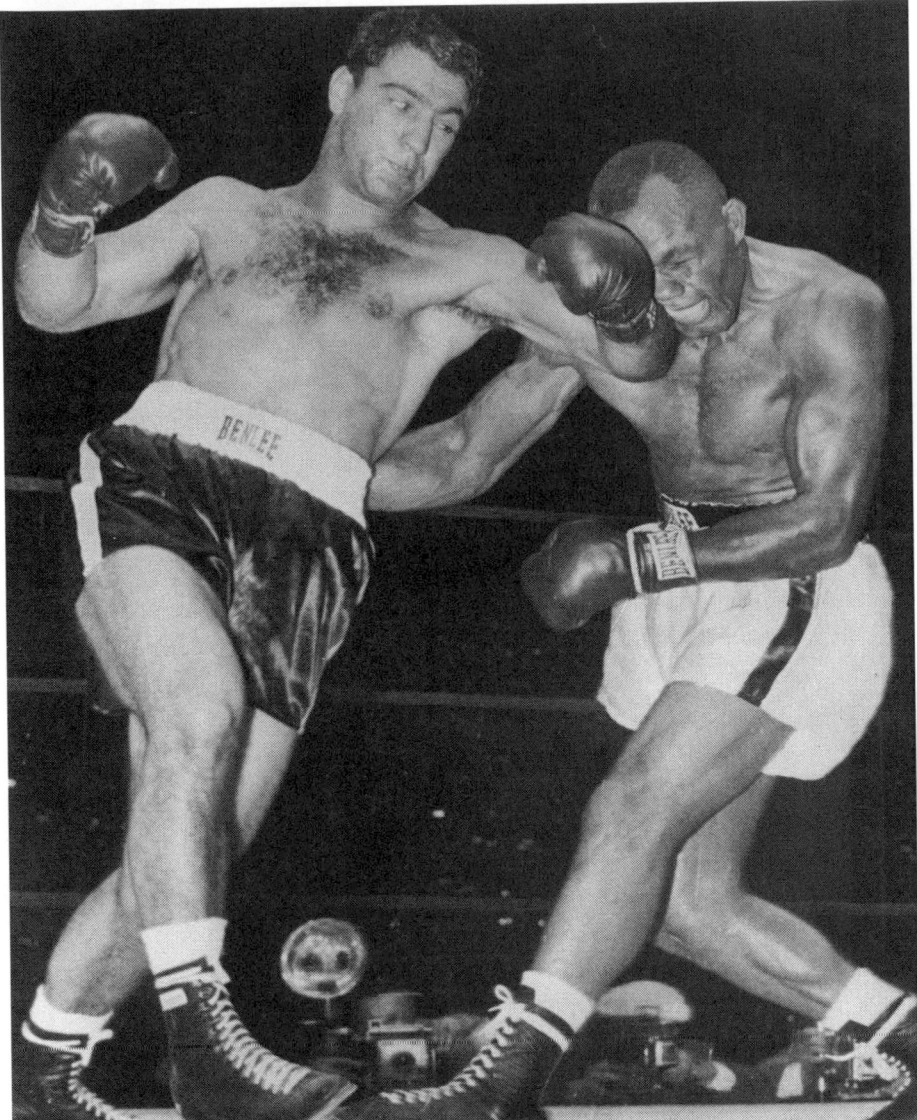

Marciano (L) crushes Jersey Joe Walcott with a left and a trailing forearm. With Walcott ahead on the cards, Marciano took him out in the 13th round on September 23, 1952.

LIGHT HEAVYWEIGHT

Right-handed; 6'1"; 173–196 lbs.
115 bouts, 1/13/1941 to 5/17/1958
Manager: Jack ("Doc") Kearns
Light Heavyweight Champ 1950–52
Hall of Fame Induction: 1994
Born: 3/28/1922, Cleveland, OH
Named: Giuseppe Antonio Berardinelli
Died: 6/2/2001

Joey Maxim used solid boxing skills to win 82 fights and the world light heavyweight championship in the span of a seventeen-year career. Maxim teamed with Jack Dempsey's former trainer, Jack ("Doc") Kearns, to face the best fighters of his era, and he was the first man to beat Floyd Patterson.

Maxim began boxing professionally in Cleveland at eighteen. Never a strong puncher, he did not record a knockout until his tenth fight. Maxim was sternly tested in 1942 when he twice lost decisions to future Hall of Famer Ezzard Charles. The next year, he suffered the only knockout of his career—a first-rounder at the hands of Curtis Sheppard.

Building up his record, Maxim won the first of three fights with the venerable Jersey Joe Walcott. Three years later, in 1949, he decisioned Gus Lesnevich to win the American light heavyweight title. At the close of that year, *The Ring* ranked Maxim as the top contender for the light heavyweight championship held by Freddie Mills. In 1950, Maxim travelled to England to face Mills in a fight held before a capacity crowd at Earl's Court in London. The favored Mills struck early but without enough power to knock out the

Joey Maxim's most troublesome career opponent was Ezzard Charles. He met Charles five times between 1942 and 1951 and lost all five decisions.

IN THE RING	WON **82**	LOST **29**	DRAWS **4**	TB 115	KO 21	W 61	WF 0	D 4	KO'd 1	L 27	LF 1

Date		Opponent	Site	Result / Rounds		Title	Wt.
1941							
Jan 13		Bob Perry	Cleveland	W	4	—	—
Jan 27		Frank McBride	Chicago	W	8	—	—
Feb 17		Orlando Trotter	Chicago	L	8	—	—
Apr 29		Bob Perry	Cleveland	W	6	—	—
Jul 11		Tony Paoli	Cleveland	W	10	—	—
Jul 28		Johnny Trotter	Chicago	W	8	—	—
Sep 13		Lee Oma	Youngstown, OH	W	8	—	—
Sep 15		Nate Bolden	Chicago	W	10	—	—
Oct 6		Bill Peterson	Chicago	W	10	—	—
Oct 27		Oliver Shanks	Chicago	TKO	5	—	—
Dec 1	⑩	Red Burman	Cleveland	W	10	—	—
1942							
Jan 16	⑩	Booker Beckwith	Chicago	L	10	—	—
Mar 11	⑩	Herbie Katz	Cleveland	KO	6	—	—
Mar 23	⑩	Lou Brooks	Baltimore	W	10	—	—
Apr 20		Frank Green	Chicago	KO	2	—	—
May 11		Charles Roth	Chicago	LF	2	—	—
Jun 1		Charles Roth	Chicago	KO	4	—	—
Jun 22	⑩	Jimmy Bivins★	Cleveland	L	10	—	—
Jul 10	⑩	Lou Brooks	Wilmington, DE	W	10	—	—
Jul 27		Curtis Sheppard	Pittsburgh	W	10	—	—
Aug 10		Altus Allen	Chicago	L	10	—	—
Aug 27		Jack Marshall	Chicago	KO	8	—	—
Sep 22		Shelton Bell	Pittsburgh	W	10	—	181
Oct 5		Hubert Hood	Chicago	W	8	—	—
Oct 13		Larry Lane	Akron, OH	W	10	—	—
Oct 27	⑩	Ezzard Charles★	Pittsburgh	L	10	—	181
Dec 1	⑩	Ezzard Charles★	Cleveland	L	10	—	—
1943							
Jan 18		Clarence Brown	Chicago	W	10	—	182
Feb 15		Clarence Brown	Chicago	W	10	—	188
Mar 10	⑩	Curtis Sheppard	Cleveland	KO'd	1	—	—
Mar 31	⑩	Curtis Sheppard	Cleveland	W	10	—	—
Apr 26		Al Jordan	Chicago	W	10	—	—
Aug 9	⑩	Nate Bolden	Chicago	W	10	—	175
Oct 29	⑩	Buddy Scott	Chicago	W	10	—	195
Dec 1		Claudio Villar	Cleveland	KO	6	—	—
1944							
Jan 31		Georgie Parks	Washington, DC	W	10	—	—
Apr 28		Buddy Walker	Detroit	W	10	—	—
May 29	⑩	Bob Garner	Chicago	W	10	—	—
Jun 26		Frank Androff	Chicago	W	10	—	189
Jul 27	⑩	Lloyd Marshall	Cleveland	L	10	—	—
Dec 19		Johnny Flynn	Cleveland	L	10	—	—
1945							
Feb 2		Johnny Flanagan	Chicago	W	8	—	—
Apr 16		Clarence Brown	Detroit	W	10	—	—
Nov 26		Cleo Everett	Detroit	W	10	—	—

1946

Date		Opponent	Location	Result	Rounds		
Mar 4		Howard Williams	Detroit	W	10	—	—
Mar 11		John Thomas	New York	L	10	—	185
Mar 27		Ralph DeJohn	Buffalo	TKO	1	—	—
Apr 1		Buddy Walker	Baltimore	W	10	—	186
Apr 9	⑩	Phil Muscato	Buffalo	L	10	—	—
May 7		Charley Eagle	Buffalo	D	10	—	—
May 14	⑩	Phil Muscato	Buffalo	W	12	—	—
Aug 2	⑩	Phil Muscato	Rochester, NY	W	10	—	—
Aug 14		Henry Cooper	Chicago	W	10	—	—
Aug 28	⑩	Jersey Joe Walcott★	Camden, NJ	W	10	—	—
Oct 10		Clarence Jones	Akron	W	10	—	—
Oct 16		Bearcat Jones	Toledo, OH	KO	5	—	—
Nov 12		Jim Ritchie	St. Louis	D	10	—	179
Dec 3		Jimmy Webb	Houston	KO	6	—	—
Dec 12		Al Velez	El Paso, TX	W	10	—	—
Dec 17		Jack Marshall	Houston	W	10	—	—

1947

Date		Opponent	Location	Result	Rounds		
Jan 6	⑩	Jersey Joe Walcott★	Philadelphia	L	10	—	—
Jan 28		Marty Clark	Miami	TKO	7	—	—
May 12		Charlie Roth	Louisville	KO	4	—	—
Jun 23	⑩	Jersey Joe Walcott★	Los Angeles	L	10	—	—
Sep 8		Clarence Jones	Wheeling, WV	KO	5	—	—
Sep 17		John Thomas	Cleveland	W	10	—	—
Nov 12	⑩	Bob Foxworth	Chicago	W	10	—	—
Dec 8	⑩	Billy Thompson	Philadelphia	W	10	—	—

1948

Date		Opponent	Location	Result	Rounds		
Jan 9		Olle Tandberg	New York	W	10	—	179
Feb 2		Bob Sikes	Little Rock, AR	W	10	—	—
Feb 13		Tony Bosnich	San Francisco	W	10	—	—
Mar 22	⑩	Pat Valentino	San Francisco	D	10	—	—
Apr 27		Louis Berlier	Houston	W	10	—	—
May 7		Francisco de la Cruz	El Paso	W	10	—	—
May 27		Roy Hawkins	Tacoma, WA	W	10	—	—
Jun 7	⑩	Pat Valentino	San Francisco	D	10	—	—
Jun 22	⑩	Joe Kahut	Portland, OR	W	10	—	—
Jun 29		Bill Peterson	Seattle	W	10	—	—
Sep 28		Bill Peterson	Portland	W	10	—	—
Oct 19	⑩	Joe Kahut	Portland	L	15	—	—
Nov 12		Bob Satterfield	Chicago	W	10	—	—
Dec 7		Jimmy Bivins★	Cleveland	W	10	—	182

1949

Date		Opponent	Location	Result	Rounds		
Feb 28	⑩	Ezzard Charles★	Cincinnati	L	15	—	—
May 23	⑩	Gus Lesnevich	Cincinnati	W	15	Won-Vac Amer-LH	175
Oct 25	⑩	Joe Kahut	Cincinnati	TKO	5	—	181
Nov 30		Pat McCafferty	Wichita, KS	TKO	4	—	—
Dec 9		Bill Peterson	Grand Rapids, MI	W	10	—	—

1950

Date		Opponent	Location	Result	Rounds		
Jan 24	♛	Freddie Mills	London	KO	10	Won-World-LH	174
Apr 19		Joe Dawson	Omaha, NE	KO	2	—	—
May 12		Bill Petersen	Memphis, TN	KO	6	—	—
Sep 25		Johnny Swanson	Huntington, WV	KO	3	—	—

Date		Opponent	Location	Result	Rounds	Title	
Oct 10		Bill Petersen	Salt Lake City	W	10	—	—
Nov 22		Big Boy Brown	Moline, IL	W	10	—	—
Dec 11	Ⓚ	Dave Whitlock	San Francisco	KO	4	—	—
1951							
Jan 27		Hubert Hood	Indianapolis	KO	3	—	—
May 30	♛	Ezzard Charles★	Chicago	L	15	For-World-H	181
Aug 22	Ⓚ	Bob Murphy	New York	W	15	Ret-World-LH	173
Dec 12	Ⓚ	Ezzard Charles★	San Francisco	L	12	—	—
1952							
Mar 6		Ted Lowry	St. Paul, MN	W	10	—	—
Jun 25		Sugar Ray Robinson★	New York	TKO	14	Ret-World-LH	173
Dec 17	Ⓚ	Archie Moore★	St. Louis	L	15	Lost-World-LH	174
1953							
Mar 4	Ⓚ	Danny Nardico	Miami	W	10	—	—
Jun 24	♛	Archie Moore★	Ogden, UT	L	15	For-World-LH	175
1954							
Jan 27	♛	Archie Moore★	Miami	L	15	For-World-LH	174
Jun 7	Ⓚ	Floyd Patterson★	Brooklyn	W	8	—	177
Nov 24	Ⓚ	Paul Andrews	Chicago	W	10	—	—
1955							
Apr 13	Ⓚ	Carl ("Bobo") Olson★	San Francisco	L	10	—	—
Jun 28	Ⓚ	Willie Pastrano★	New Orleans	L	10	—	—
1956							
Sep 29		Edgardo Jose Romero	Vancouver, B.C.	W	10	—	196
1957							
Jan 25	Ⓚ	Eddie Machen	Miami Beach	L	10	—	192
May 3	Ⓚ	Eddie Machen	Louisville, KY	L	10	—	—
Jun 18		Carl ("Bobo") Olson★	Portland, OR	L	10	—	—
1958							
Apr 11		Heinz Neuhaus	Stuttgart, Germany	L	10	—	—
Apr 27		Mino Bozzano	Milan, Italy	L	10	—	—
May 17		Ulli Ritter	Mannheim, Germany	L	10	—	—

challenger. Surprising many observers, Maxim knocked Mills out in the tenth round with a left to the jaw and a right cross to the chin.

In 1951, Maxim attempted to move up in class with a challenge to Ezzard Charles, who was by then the heavyweight champion. In this, their fourth meeting, Maxim lost the decision. The next year brought Maxim two of his most important fights. The first took place in June in Yankee Stadium before 48,000 sweltering fans on a night when the temperature exceeded 100°F. Maxim was defending his title against Sugar Ray Robinson, a two-time champion who was attempting to win a belt in a third weight class. Robinson fought all-out and was ahead on the judges' cards when he failed to answer the bell for the fourteenth round. The exhausted Robinson had apparently not paced himself for going the distance with Maxim. Maxim had fought a sound fight and received credit for a knockout.

Six months later Maxim lost his title to Archie Moore on a decision. Maxim met Moore two more times but came away defeated. One of the final victories of his career was an eight-round decision over a young Floyd Patterson. After winning just one of his last nine fights, Maxim retired in 1958.

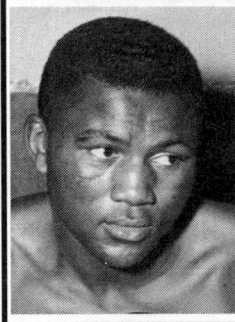

L I G H T W E I G H T

Right-handed; 5'8"; 133–143 lbs.

97 bouts, 10/23/1938 to 3/27/1950

Managers: Frankie Thomas 1938–44,
Joe Gramby 1944–47

NY World Lightweight Champ 1943,
1944–47

Hall of Fame Induction: 1995

Born: 2/10/1919, Sumter, SC

Died: 8/25/1998

One of the top lightweights in an era which included Hall of Famers Beau Jack and Ike Williams, Bob Montgomery won acclaim for his aggressive, take-no-prisoners approach. His intense boxing style led sportswriter Johnny Webster of the *Philadelphia Inquirer* to dub Montgomery, the "Bobcat" because of Montgomery's way of continually moving forward and pawing an opponent until he got him.

Born in South Carolina, Montgomery followed a brother to Philadelphia at the age of fifteen and shortly thereafter began boxing. Montgomery quickly came under the tutelage of Joe Gramby, who would eventually become Philadelphia's most influential black manager. Fighting primarily in the Philadelphia area in the late 1930s and early '40s, Montgomery quickly achieved designation as *The Ring*'s top lightweight contender for the year 1941. Never one to shy away from a tough fight, Montgomery split two non-title bouts with lightweight champ Lew Jenkins and lost two non-title bouts by decision to Sammy Angott.

In May 1943, Montgomery challenged Hall of Famer Beau Jack for the New York world lightweight title. Montgomery dominated the Madison Square Garden

The lightweight title was disputed during Montgomery's tenure. While he held the NY world belt, Angott, Zurita, and Williams were the NBA champs.

fight, effectively countering Jack's furious attacks with skillful combinations. This first meeting began a memorable series with Jack. The pair would duel three more times. In the title rematch in November, Jack upset the heavily favored Montgomery before another large crowd in the Garden to reclaim the crown. They met again in 1944 in Madison Square Garden, where Montgomery withstood a frantic effort by Jack in the tenth, eleventh, and twelfth rounds. Montgomery won on

IN THE RING	WON 75	LOST 19	DRAWS 3	TB 97	KO 37	W 38	WF 0	D 3	KO'd 3	L 16	LF 0

Date	Opponent	Site	Result / Rounds		Title	Wt.
1938						
Oct 23	Young Johnny Buff	Atlantic City	KO	2	—	—
Oct 27	Pat Patucci	Atlantic City	KO	2	—	—
Nov 4	Eddie Stewart	Philadelphia	KO	2	—	—
Nov 10	Joe Beltrante	Atlantic City	KO	3	—	—
Nov 17	Red Rossi	Atlantic City	KO	2	—	—
Dec 8	Jackie Sheppard	Atlantic City	W	8	—	—
1939						
Jan 19	Harvey Jacobs	Atlantic City	KO	1	—	—
Feb 2	Charley Burns	Atlantic City	W	8	—	—
Feb 23	Jay Macedon	Atlantic City	W	8	—	—
Mar 9	Billy Miller	Atlantic City	KO	2	—	—
Mar 16	Frankie Saia	Philadelphia	KO	4	—	—
Mar 30	Benny Berman	Atlantic City	W	8	—	—
Apr 13	Young Raspi	Atlantic City	KO	6	—	—
Apr 20	Eddie Guerra	Atlantic City	W	8	—	—
May 1	George Zengaras	Philadelphia	D	10	—	—
May 23	Norment Quarles	Philadelphia	KO	4	—	—
Jun 15	Charley Burns	Atlantic City	KO	2	—	—
Jun 21	Tommy Rawson	Philadelphia	KO	1	—	—
Jul 3	Frankie Wallace	Philadelphia	W	10	—	—
Aug 14	Jimmy Murray	Philadelphia	KO	3	—	—
Aug 24	Ray Ingram	Atlantic City	W	10	—	—
Oct 5	Charles Gilley	Atlantic City	KO	6	—	—
Oct 23	Mike Evans	Philadelphia	W	10	—	—
Nov 10	Tommy Spiegel	Philadelphia	L	10	—	—
Nov 17	Mike Evans	Philadelphia	KO	1	—	—
1940						
Jan 29	Al Nettlow	Philadelphia	D	10	—	—
Mar 11	Al Nettlow	Philadelphia	W	10	—	—
Jun 3	Al Nettlow	Philadelphia	W	12	—	—
Jul 5	Jimmy Vaughn	Atlantic City	KO	2	—	—
Sep 16	♛ Lew Jenkins★	Philadelphia	L	10	—	136
Nov 7	Norment Quarles	Atlantic City	D	10	—	—
Nov 25	♛ Sammy Angott	Philadelphia	L	10	—	—
1941						
Jan 29	Julie Kogon	Brooklyn	W	8	—	—
Feb 7	Al Nettlow	New York	W	8	—	—
Mar 3	George Zengaras	Philadelphia	TKO	3	—	—
Apr 28	Nick Peters	Philadelphia	TKO	3	—	—
May 16	♛ Lew Jenkins★	New York	W	10	—	—

Date		Opponent	Location	Result	Rds	Notes	No.
Jun 16		Manuel Villa	Baltimore	KO	1	—	—
Jun 30		Wishy Jones	Washington, DC	TKO	6	—	—
Jul 3		Frankie Wallace	Atlantic City	KO	3	—	—
Jul 14		Luther ("Slugger") White	Baltimore	W	10	—	—
Sep 8		Mike Kaplan	Philadelphia	W	10	—	—
Oct 10		Davey Day	Chicago	KO	1	—	—
Oct 24		Julie Kogon	Chicago	W	10	—	—
Oct 30		Frankie Wallace	Williamsport, PA	KO	5	—	—
Dec 8		Jimmy Garrison	Philadelphia	TKO	4	—	—
1942							
Jan 5		Mayon Padlo	Philadelphia	KO	8	—	—
Mar 6	♛	Sammy Angott★	New York	L	12	—	—
Apr 20	⑩	Joey Peralta	Philadelphia	W	10	—	—
May 8		Carmen Notch	Toledo, OH	W	10	—	—
Jul 7	♛	Sammy Angott★	Philadelphia	L	12	—	—
Aug 13	⑩	Bobby Ruffin	New York	W	10	—	—
Oct 6	⑩	Maxie Shapiro	Philadelphia	L	10	—	—
Dec 1	⑩	Maxie Shapiro	Philadelphia	W	10	—	—
1943							
Jan 8	⑩	Chester Rico	New York	TKO	8	—	—
Feb 22	⑩	Lulu Costantino	Philadelphia	W	10	—	—
Apr 5		Roman Alvarez	Philadelphia	KO	4	—	—
Apr 30		Gene Johnson	Scranton, PA	W	10	—	—
May 3		Henry Vasquez	Holyoke, MA	W	8	—	—
May 21	♛	Beau Jack★	New York	W	15	Won-NY World-L	134
Jul 4		Al Reasoner	New Orleans	KO	6	—	139
Jul 30	⑩	Frankie Wills	Washington, DC	W	10	—	—
Aug 23	⑩	Fritzie Zivic★	Philadelphia	W	10	—	136
Oct 25		Petey Scalzo	Philadelphia	TKO	6	—	—
Nov 19	⑩	Beau Jack★	New York	L	15	Lost-NY World-L	133
1944							
Jan 7	⑩	Joey Peralta	Detroit	W	10	—	—
Jan 25	⑩	Ike Williams★	Philadelphia	KO	12	—	—
Feb 18	⑩	Al ("Bummy") Davis	New York	KO'd	1	—	—
Mar 3	♛	Beau Jack★	New York	W	15	Reg-NY World-L	135
Apr 28	⑩	Joey Peralta	Chicago	W	10	—	—
Aug 4	⑩	Beau Jack★	New York	L	10	—	—
1945							
Feb 13		Cecil Hudson	Los Angeles	W	10	—	140
Mar 20		Genaro Rojo	Los Angeles	TKO	8	—	—
May 8	⑩	Nick Moran	Los Angeles	L	10	—	—
Jul 9	⑩	Nick Moran	Philadelphia	W	10	—	135
1946							
Feb 3		Bill Parsons	New Orleans	W	10	—	—
Feb 15		Leo Rodak	Chicago	W	10	—	138
Mar 8	⑩	Tony Pellone	New York	W	10	—	139
Mar 21		Ernie Petrone	New Haven, CT	KO	4	—	137
Jun 28	⑩	Allie Stolz	New York	KO	13	Ret-NY World-L	134
Jul 29		George LaRover	Springfield, MA	W	10	—	—
Aug 19		Wesley Mouzon	Philadelphia	KO'd	2	—	—
Nov 26		Wesley Mouzon	Philadelphia	TKO	8	Ret-NY World-L	135
1947							
Jan 20		Eddie Giosa	Philadelphia	TKO	5	—	—
Feb 7	⑩	Tony Pellone	Detroit	L	10	—	140

Feb 25		Joey Barnum	Los Angeles	KO	7		—	—
Mar 31	⑩	Jesse Flores	San Francisco	KO	3		—	138
May 12		George LaRover	Philadelphia	W	10		—	—
Jun 2		Julie Kogon	New Haven	W	10		—	137
Jun 9		Frankie Cordino	Springfield	W	10		—	—
Aug 4	♔	Ike Williams ★	Philadelphia	KO'd	6	For-Vac World-L		133
Nov 24		Livio Minelli	Philadelphia	L	10		—	—
Dec 22		Joey Angelo	Boston	L	10		—	—
1950								
Feb 3		Aldo Minelli	Washington, DC	L	10		—	—
Feb 27		Johnny Greco	Montreal	L	10		—	142
Mar 9		Don Williams	Worcester, MA	L	10		—	—
Mar 27		Eddie Giosa	Philadelphia	L	10		—	143

a split decision and once again relieved Jack of the title. In yet another tough battle, Jack prevailed on points in a non-title ten-rounder.

Montgomery's two fights with Ike Williams are also memorable for their ferocity. Montgomery may have had a personal grudge against Williams. In any case, in their first fight, a non-title contest in 1944, he administered a terrific beating to Williams, punishing him for twelve rounds before knocking him out.

The two met again in 1947. Williams, by then holder of the NBA lightweight crown, put his title on the line, while Montgomery followed suit with his New York title. For five rounds, the two combatants engaged in an extremely hard-fought, even battle. In the sixth, Williams knocked Montgomery down twice, and the referee stopped the fight. This bout was ranked as one of the twenty greatest fights of all time in a 1981 poll by *The Ring*.

After that, Montgomery fought six more bouts and lost them all. However, those late-career losses do not detract from his reputation as one of the best lightweights of all time.

Early in his career, Montgomery fought a gruelling schedule. He had nineteen fights in 1939, all in Philadelphia or Atlantic City.

MIDDLEWEIGHT

Right-handed; 5'11½"; 151–166 lbs.

100 bouts, 2/6/1963 to 8/29/1977

Middleweight Champion 1970–77

Hall of Fame Induction: 1990

Born: 8/7/1942, Santa Fe, Argentina

Died: 1/8/1995

The greatest middleweight champion of the 1970s and possibly one of the greatest middleweights of all time, Carlos Monzon dominated the division as few had before him. Monzon beat all comers and, with time, overcame critics' complaints that he did not face particularly tough competition.

Born in Argentina, Monzon started his professional career in 1963. He fought an average of once a month in the early stages of his career and posted a record of 29-3-6, with one no-contest, before capturing the Argentine middleweight title in 1966. The next year, he added the South American middleweight title. By 1968, Monzon had achieved sufficient international stature to be ranked eighth in the rankings compiled by *The Ring*.

In 1970, Monzon faced Hall of Famer Nino Benvenuti in a challenge for the world middleweight title. Monzon took the championship in convincing fashion, knocking out Benvenuti in the twelfth round with a right to the head. Monzon also won the rematch, stopping Benvenuti in the third round. Monzon successfully defended his belt a record fourteen times. He vanquished such notables as Emile Griffith, Jose Napoles, and Rodrigo Valdez.

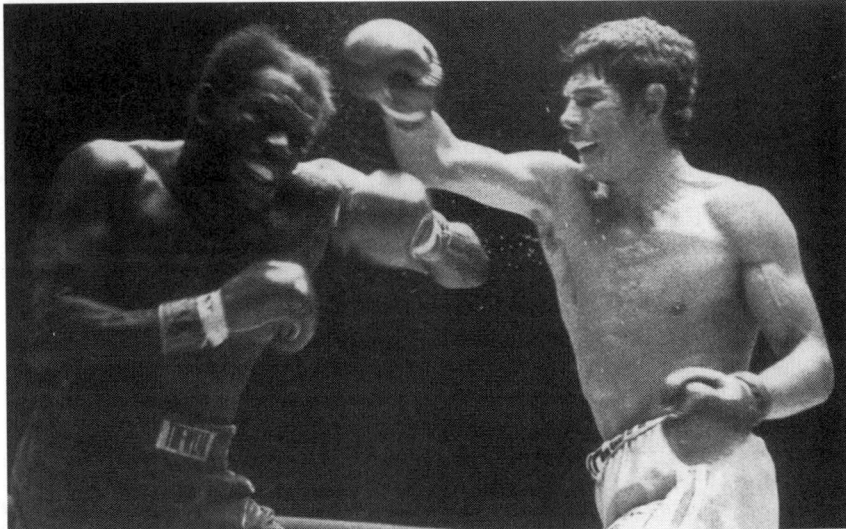

Veteran boxer Emile Griffith, who had lost the middleweight title three years earlier to Nino Benvenuti, recoils from a Monzon (R) right hook on September 25, 1971 in Buenos Aires. Griffith went in 14.

IN THE RING	WON 87	LOST 3	DRAWS 9	TB 100	KO 59	W 28	WF 0	D 9	KO'd 0	L 3	LF 0	NC 1

Date	Opponent	Site	Result / Rounds		Title	Wt.
1963						
Feb 6	Ramon Montenegro	Rafaela, Argentina	KO	2	—	—
Mar 13	Albino Veron	Vila, Argentina	NC	1	—	—
Apr 9	Albino Veron	Santa Fe, Argentina	TKO	2	—	155
Apr 26	Mario Suarez	Posadas, Argentina	TKO	7	—	153
May 3	Raul Rivas	Posadas	TKO	5	—	151
May 31	Jose N. Rodriguez	Parana, Argentina	KO	5	—	—
Jul 17	Andres Cejas	Buenos Aires	TKO	4	—	158
Aug 9	Lisandro Guzman	Cordoba, Argentina	TKO	3	—	158
Aug 28	Antonio Aguilar	Buenos Aires	L	10	—	158
Oct 18	Benito Sanchez	Reconquista, Argentina	KO	8	—	—
Dec 6	Rene Sosa	Parana	KO	6	—	157
1964						
Jan 17	Roberto Carabajal	Parana	KO	8	—	157
Jun 13	Angel Coria	Mar Del Plata, Argentina	W	8	—	—
Jun 28	Felipe Cambeiro	Rio de Janeiro	L	8	—	159
Jul 10	Roberto Carabajal	Tostado, Argentina	W	10	—	—
Jul 24	Walter Villa	Ceres, Argentina	KO	9	—	—
Aug 14	Juan Diaz	Villa Angela, Argentina	TKO	9	—	—
Sep 4	Americo Vaca	Parana	KO	3	—	159
Sep 25	Francisco Olea	Tostado	TKO	9	—	—
Oct 9	Alberto Massi	Cordoba	L	10	—	160
Oct 28	Francisco Gelabert	Buenos Aires	TKO	4	—	160
Nov 18	Celedonio Lima	Buenos Aires	D	10	—	158
1965						
Jan 8	Andres Selpa	Mar Del Plata	D	10	—	161
Mar 11	Andres Selpa	Santa Fe	W	10	—	154
Apr 9	Emilio Ale-Ali	Tucuman, Argentina	D	10	—	158
May 19	Anibal Cordoba	Buenos Aires	W	10	—	158
Jul 14	Alberto Redondo	Buenos Aires	TKO	8	—	159
Aug 1	Felipe Cambeiro	Sao Paulo, Brazil	W	8	—	157
Aug 14	Manoel Severino	Rio de Janeiro	D	8	—	158
Aug 28	Manoel Severino	Rio de Janeiro	D	8	—	157
Oct 6	Gregorio Gomez	Buenos Aires	W	10	—	157
Nov 17	Celedonio Lima	Buenos Aires	KO	5	—	159
Dec 8	Antonio Aguilar	Buenos Aires	W	10	—	157
Dec 29	Carlos Salinas	Buenos Aires	W	10	—	158
1966						
Feb 4	Ramon Rocha	Santa Fe	W	10	Won-Argentina State-M	156
Feb 17	Norberto Juncos	Santa Fe	TKO	7	—	157
Apr 29	Ismael Hamze	San Nicolas, Argentina	TKO	9	—	158
Jun 3	Marcos Bustos	Rio Gallegos, Argentina	D	10	—	159
Jul 8	Benito Sanchez	San Pereyra, Argentina	KO	4	—	—
Sep 3	Jorge Fernandez	Buenos Aires	W	12	Won-Argentina-M	157
Oct 1	Angel Coria	Mar Del Plata	W	10	—	161
Nov 18	Luis Pereyra	Santa Fe	TKO	2	—	160
Dec 2	Alberto Massi	Santa Fe	TKO	8	—	161
Dec 23	Marcelo Farias	San Cristobal, Argentina	KO	3	—	—

1967

Date	Opponent	Location	Result	Rd	Title	Wt
Jan 13	Carlos Salinas	Santa Fe, Argentina	KO	8	—	159
Jan 27	Eudoro Robledo	Charata, Argentina	TKO	4	—	163
Feb 15	Alberto Massi	San Francisco, Argentina	W	10	—	—
Mar 9	Osvaldo Marino	Santa Fe	TKO	7	—	158
Mar 25	Angel Coria	Mar Del Plata	KO	6	—	161
Apr 9	Benito Sanchez	Santa Elena, Argentina	TKO	3	—	—
May 6	Bennie Briscoe	Buenos Aires	D	10	—	157
Jun 10	Jorge Fernandez	Buenos Aires	W	12	Won-S Am-M	157
Jul 29	Antonio Aguilar	Buenos Aires	KO	9	—	160
Aug 16	Tito Marshall	Buenos Aires	W	10	—	158
Sep 8	Ramon Rocha	Rosario, Argentina	W	10	—	160
Oct 6	Carlos Estrada	Trelew, Argentina	TKO	7	—	—
Oct 20	Ramon Rocha	San Juan, Argentina	TKO	7	—	—
Nov 18	Tito Marshall	Buenos Aires	W	10	—	159

1968

Date	Opponent	Location	Result	Rd	Title	Wt
Apr 15	Juan Aguilar	Mendoza, Argentina	D	10	—	159
May 17	Alberto Massi	Cordoba	W	10	—	160
Jun 19	Juan Aguilar	Buenos Aires	W	10	—	158
Jul 5	Benito Sanchez	Chaco, Argentina	KO	4	—	159
Aug 14	Doug Huntley	Buenos Aires	KO	4	—	159
Oct 23	Charlie Austin	Buenos Aires	W	10	—	160
Dec 7	Johnny Brooks	Buenos Aires	W	10	—	160
Dec 20	Emilio Ale-Ali	Mendoza	W	10	—	159

1969

Date	Opponent	Location	Result	Rd	Title	Wt
Jan 10	Ruben Orrico	Santa Fe	KO	9	Ret-S Am-M	159
Mar 14	Mario Taborda	Chaco	KO	3	—	162
Apr 25	Carlos Salinas	Parana	D	10	—	161
Jun 6	Carlos Salinas	Parana	TKO	7	—	161
Jul 5	Harold Richardson	Buenos Aires	TKO	3	—	159
Aug 9	Tom Bethea	Buenos Aires	W	10	—	159
Sep 5	Emilio Ale-Ali	Tucuman	TKO	7	—	161
Sep 27	Manoel Severino	Buenos Aires	KO	6	Ret-S Am-M	159
Dec 12	Carlos Estrada	Santa Fe	KO	2	—	162

1970

Date		Opponent	Location	Result	Rd	Title	Wt
Feb 2		Antonio Aguilar	Rosario	KO	6	Ret-Argentina-M	159
Mar 7		Juan Aguilar	Santa Fe	TKO	9	—	164
Apr 17		Adolfo Cardozo	Buenos Aires	TKO	3	—	166
Jul 18		Eddie Pace	Buenos Aires	W	10	—	160
Sep 19		Candy Rosa	Buenos Aires	KO	4	—	162
Nov 7	♛	Nino Benvenuti★	Rome	KO	12	Won-World-M	159
Dec 20		Charley Austin	Buenos Aires	KO	2	—	161

1971

Date		Opponent	Location	Result	Rd	Title	Wt
Feb 19		Domingo Guerrero	Salta, Argentina	TKO	2	—	161
Mar 6		Roy Lee	Santa Fe	TKO	2	—	162
May 7	⑩	Nino Benvenuti★	Monte Carlo, Monaco	TKO	3	Ret-World-M	159
Sep 25	⑩	Emile Griffith★	Buenos Aires	TKO	14	Ret-World-M	159
Dec 4	⑩	Fraser Scott	Buenos Aires	TKO	3	—	161

1972

Date		Opponent	Location	Result	Rd	Title	Wt
Mar 4	⑩	Denny Moyer	Rome	TKO	5	Ret-World-M	159
Jun 17	⑩	Jean-Claude Bouttier	Paris	TKO	13	Ret-World-M	159
Aug 19		Tom Bogs	Copenhagen	TKO	5	Ret-World-M	159
Nov 11	⑩	Bennie Briscoe	Buenos Aires	W	15	Ret-World-M	158

1973

Date		Opponent	Location	Result	Rd	Title	Wt
May 5		Lee Roy Dale	Rome	KO	5	—	164
Jun 2	⑩	Emile Griffith★	Monte Carlo, Monaco	W	15	Ret-World-M	159

Sep 29	⑩	Jean-Claude Bouttier	Paris	W	15	Ret-World-M	159
1974							
Feb 9	⑩	Jose Napoles ★	Paris	TKO	7	Ret-World-M	159
Oct 5	⑩	Tony Mundine	Buenos Aires	KO	7	Ret-World (WBA)-M	160
1975							
Jun 30	⑩	Tony Licata	New York	TKO	10	Ret-World (WBA)-M	159
Dec 13	⑩	Gratien Tonna	Paris	KO	5	Ret-World (WBA)-M	159
1976							
Jun 26	♛	Rodrigo Valdez	Monte Carlo	W	15	Ret-World-M	159
1977							
Jul 30	⑩	Rodrigo Valdez	Monte Carlo	W	15	Ret-World-M	159

Monzon's two fights with Valdez at the end of his career validated his strength as a champion. Valdez held the WBC title, which Monzon had forfeited in 1974. Monzon won the first fight, although Valdez believed he deserved the decision. In the rematch, Valdez knocked down Monzon in the second round, but the tenacious 35-year-old champion rose from the canvas to win a unanimous decision. Monzon then retired from the ring, with fourteen of his last sixteen fights having been successful title defenses.

Monzon was never knocked out at any time in his career and never even lost a fight after 1964. In analyzing his greatness, boxing experts have pointed to his superior height and reach as compared to most middleweights, as well as his great boxing intelligence, superior power, and possession of a complete arsenal of punches.

Monzon's extraordinary competence did not extend to his life outside the squared circle. In 1988, Monzon was convicted of murdering his estranged lover and sentenced to eleven years in prison. Then, in 1995, while returning to prison after a furlough for good behavior, Monzon was killed when the car he was driving ran off a country road.

Carlos Monzon (R) throws a quick combination at dazed Tony Licata while retaining his WBA middleweight crown. The 10-round knockout took place in Madison Square Garden on June 30, 1975.

ARCHIE MOORE
The Old Mongoose

LIGHT HEAVYWEIGHT

Right-handed; 5'11"; 157–206 lbs.

229 bouts, 1/31/1936 to 3/15/1963

Managers: Kid Bandy, George Wilsman, Cal Thompson, Felix Thurman, Jack Richardson, Jimmy Johnston, Charley Johnston, Jack ("Doc") Kearns

Light Heavyweight Champ 1952–62 *(NBA withdrew recognition in 1960)*

Hall of Fame Induction: 1990

Born: 12/13/1913, Benoit, MS

Named: Archibald Lee Wright

Died: 12/9/1998

Archie Moore recorded more knockouts than anyone else in the long history of boxing, with 131 lights-out punches. Moore's career lasted 27 years, and it seemed as if "The Old Mongoose" would never stop fighting. Respected by both fans and his boxing colleagues, Moore stayed active through the pre-war, post-war, and television ages.

Born in Mississippi around 1913, Moore moved to St. Louis as a youth. He was convicted of stealing money from a streetcar and served two years in reform school, where he learned to box. Moore then joined the Civilian Conservation Corps and boxed in amateur tournaments while off duty. Moore had turned professional by 1936, fighting as a middleweight. He boxed in the St. Louis area for a year, then moved to San Diego. Seeking tougher competition, he went to Australia in 1940. On his return, he sported a record of 41-4-3, which caught the boxing world's attention. That year, *The Ring* ranked Moore as the fourth-best middleweight contender.

By 1945, Moore had moved up to light heavyweight and held the position of top contender. *The Ring* considered him one of the top light heavyweights in every year from 1945 to 1951. But though he fought steadily, Moore was passed over for a championship bout. Willing to go anywhere to get a fight, Moore toured South America in 1951. In many ways, his plight was similar to that of Charley Burley. Black and not managed properly, both fighters were arguably too good to get top fights.

In 1952, at an age when most fighters had long retired, Moore finally received a shot at the light heavyweight title, then held by Joey Maxim. Fighting before a crowd of 12,610 in his hometown of St. Louis, Moore attacked Maxim relentlessly. Although Maxim

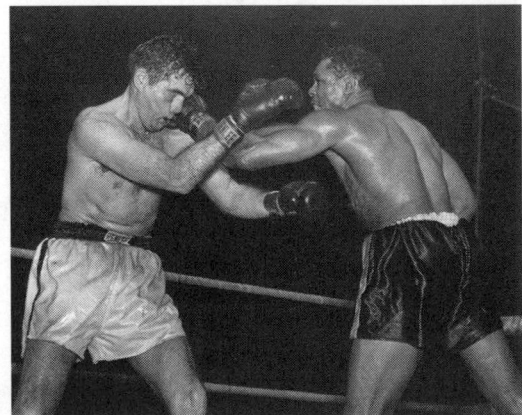

Four days after his 39th birthday, Moore finally got a shot at the light heavyweight title. Although he didn't score a knockout, Moore (R) battered champion Joey Maxim for 15 rounds and took the decision.

IN THE RING	WON **183**	LOST **24**	DRAWS **10***	TB 218	KO 131	W 52	WF 0	D 10*	KO'd 7	L 15	LF 2	NC 1

*includes 1 TD

Date	Opponent	Site	Result / Rounds		Title	Wt.
1936						
Jul 14	Murray Allen	Quincy, IL	KO	6	—	—
Aug	Sammy Christian	Quincy	D	6	—	—
Sep 30	Murray Allen	Keokuk, IA	KO	3	—	—
Oct 9	Sammy Jackson	St. Louis	W	5	—	—
Dec 8	Sammy Jackson	St. Louis	D	5	—	—
1937						
Jan 5	Dynamite Payne	St. Louis	KO	1	—	—
Jan 18	Johnny Davis	Quincy	KO	3	—	—
Feb 2	Joe Huff	St. Louis	KO	2	—	—
Mar 23	Ham Pounder	Ponce City, AR	KO	2	—	—
Apr 9	Charley Dawson	Indianapolis	KO	5	—	—
Apr 23	Karl Martin	Indianapolis	KO	1	—	—
May 1	Franky Hatfield	—	KO	1	—	—
Jun 1	Al Dublinsky	—	KO	1	—	—
Aug 19	Deacon Logan	St Louis	KO	3	—	—
Sep 1	Billy Adams	Cincinnati	L	8	—	—
Sep 9	Sam Slaughter	Indianapolis	W	10	—	—
Sep 17	Charley Dawson	St. Louis	KO	5	—	—
Nov 16	Sammy Christian	St Louis	W	5	—	—
Dec 1	Sammy Jackson	—	KO	8	—	—
1938						
Jan 7	Carl Lautenschlager	St. Louis	KO	2	—	—
May 20	Jimmy Brent	San Diego	KO	1	—	—
May 27	Ray Vargas	San Diego	KO	3	—	—
Jun 24	Johnny Romero	San Diego	L	10	—	—
Jul 22	Johnny Sykes	San Diego	KO	1	—	—
Aug 5	Lorenzo Pedro	San Diego	W	10	—	—
Sep 02	Johnny Romero	San Diego	KO	8	—	—
Sep 16	Frank Rowsey	San Diego	KO	3	—	—
Sep 27	Tom Henry	Los Angeles	KO	4	—	—
Oct 1	Bob Llanes	—	KO	2	—	—
Nov 22	Ray Lyle	St. Louis	KO	2	—	—
Dec 7	Bob Turner	St. Louis	KO	2	—	—
1939						
Jan 20	Jack Moran	St. Louis	KO	1	—	—
Mar 2	Domenic Ceccarelli	St. Louis	KO	1	—	—
Apr 1	Marty Simmons	Minneapolis	W	10	—	—
Apr 20	⑩ Teddy Yarosz	St. Louis	L	10	—	—
Jul 21	Jack Coggins	San Diego	NC	8	—	—
Sep 1	Jack Coggins	San Diego	W	10	—	—
Sep 22	Bobby Seaman	San Diego	KO	7	—	—
Nov 13	Freddy Dixon	Phoenix	TD	8	—	—
Nov 27	Billy Day	Phoenix	KO	8	—	—
Dec 7	Honeyboy Jones	San Diego	W	10	—	—
Dec 29	Shorty Hogue	San Diego	L	6	—	—
1940						
Mar 30	Jack McNamee	Melbourne	KO	4	—	—
Apr 18	⑩ Ron Richards	Sydney	KO	10	—	158
May 9	Atilio Sabatino	Sydney	KO	5	—	—

Date		Opponent	Location	Result	Rds	Title	Wt
May 12		Joe Delaney	Adelaide, Australia	KO	7	—	—
Jun 2		Frank Lindsay	Hobart, Tasmania	KO	4	—	—
Jun 27		Fred Henneberry	Sydney	KO	7	—	—
Jul 11	⑩	Ron Richards	Sydney	W	12	—	159
Oct 18		Pancho Ramirez	San Diego	KO	5	—	—
Dec 5		Shorty Hogue	San Diego	L	6	—	—
1941							
Jan 17		Clay Rowan	San Diego	KO	1	—	—
Jan 31		Shorty Hogue	San Diego	L	10	—	—
Feb 26		Eddie Booker	San Diego	D	10	—	161
1942							
Jan 28		Bobby Britton	Phoenix	KO	3	—	—
Feb 27		Guero Martinez	San Diego	KO	2	—	—
Mar 17		Jimmy Casino	San Francisco	KO	5	—	—
Oct 30		Shorty Hogue	San Diego	KO	2	—	—
Nov 6		Tabby Romero	San Diego	KO	2	—	159
Nov 27	⑩	Jack Chase	San Diego	W	10	—	158
Dec 11	⑩	Eddie Booker	San Diego	D	12	For-CA-M	158
1943							
May 8	⑩	Jack Chase	San Diego	W	15	Won-CA-M	159
Jul 1		Willard Hogue	San Diego	TKO	5	—	160
Jul 28		Eddie Cerda	San Diego	KO	3	—	158
Aug 2	⑩	Jack Chase	San Francisco	L	15	Lost-CA-M	160
Aug 16		Aaron Wade	San Francisco	L	10	—	157
Nov 5		Kid Hermosillo	San Diego	KO	5	—	—
Nov 26	⑩	Jack Chase	Hollywood	W	10	—	—
1944							
Jan 7		Amado Rodriguez	San Diego	KO	1	—	—
Jan 21		Eddie Booker	Hollywood	KO'd	8		
Mar 24		Roman Starr	Hollywood	TKO	2	—	166
Apr 21	⑩	Charley Burley★	Hollywood	L	10	—	164
May 19		Kenny La Salle	San Diego	W	10	—	166
Aug 11		Louis Mays	San Diego	KO	3	—	171
Aug 18		Jimmy Hayden	San Diego	KO	5	—	170
Sep 1		Battling Monroe	San Diego	KO	6	—	171
Dec 18	⑩	Nate Bolden	New York	W	10	—	164
1945							
Jan 11		Joey Jones	Boston	KO	1	—	—
Jan 29		Bob Jacobs	New York	KO	9	—	166
Feb 12		Nap Mitchell	Boston	KO	6	—	—
Apr 2	⑩	Nate Bolden	Baltimore	W	10	—	—
Apr 23		Teddy Randolph	Baltimore	KO	9	—	—
May 21	⑩	Lloyd Marshall	Cleveland	W	10	—	—
Jun 18		George Kochan	Baltimore	KO	6	—	—
Jun 26	⑩	Lloyd Marshall	Cleveland	TKO	10	—	162
Aug 22	⑩	Jimmy Bivins★	Cleveland	TKO'd	6	—	168
Sep 17	⑩	Cocoa Kid	Baltimore	KO	8	—	—
Oct 22	⑩	Holman Williams	Baltimore	L	10	—	—
Nov 12		Odell Riley	Detroit	KO	6	—	—
Nov 26	⑩	Holman Williams	Baltimore	TKO	11	—	169
Dec 13		Colion Chaney	St. Louis	KO	5	—	170
1946							
Jan 28	⑩	Curtis Sheppard	Baltimore	W	12	—	172
Feb 5		Georgie Parks	Washington, DC	TKO	1	—	170
May 2		Verne Escoe	Orange, NJ	TKO	7	—	175
May 20	⑩	Ezzard Charles★	Pittsburgh	L	10	—	174

Date		Opponent	Location	Result	Rds	Title	Wt
Aug 19		Buddy Walker	Baltimore	KO	4	—	173
Sep 9		Shamus O'Brien	Baltimore	KO	2	—	—
Oct 23	⑩	Billy Smith	Oakland	D	12	For-CA-M	171
Nov 6	⑩	Jack Chase	Oakland	D	10	—	171

1947

Date		Opponent	Location	Result	Rds	Title	Wt
Mar 18	⑩	Jack Chase	Los Angeles	KO	9	Won-CA-M	173
Apr 11		Rusty Payne	San Diego	W	10	—	176
May 5	⑩	Ezzard Charles★	Cincinnati	L	10	—	—
Jun 16	⑩	Curtis Sheppard	Washington, DC	W	10	—	—
Jul 14		Bert Lytell	Baltimore	W	10	—	—
Jul 30		Bobby Zander	Oakland	W	12	Ret-CA-M	175
Sep 8		Jimmy Bivins	Baltimore	KO	9	—	—
Nov 10		George Fitch	Baltimore	KO	6	—	—

1948

Date		Opponent	Location	Result	Rds	Title	Wt
Jan 13	⑩	Ezzard Charles★	Cleveland	KO'd	8	—	—
Apr 12		Dusty Wilkerson	Baltimore	KO	7	—	—
Apr 19	⑩	Doc Williams	Newark	KO	7	—	—
May 5	⑩	Billy Smith	Cincinnati	W	10	—	—
Jun 2	⑩	Leonard Morrow	Oakland	KO'd	1	Lost-CA-M	175
Jun 28	⑩	Jimmy Bivins★	Baltimore	W	10	—	172
Aug 2		Ted Lowry	Baltimore	W	10	—	172
Sep 20	⑩	Billy Smith	Baltimore	KO	4	—	—
Oct 15	⑩	Henry Hall	New Orleans	L	10	—	—
Nov 1		Lloyd Gibson	Washington, DC	LD	4	—	—
Nov 15	⑩	Henry Hall	Baltimore	W	10	—	—
Dec 6		Bob Amos	Washington, DC	W	10	—	—
Dec 27	⑩	Doc Williams	Baltimore	KO	7	—	—

1949

Date		Opponent	Location	Result	Rds	Title	Wt
Jan 10		Alabama Kid	Toledo, OH	KO	4	—	—
Jan 31		Bob Satterfield	Toledo	KO	3	—	—
Mar 4		Alabama Kid	Columbus, OH	KO	3	—	—
Mar 23		Dusty Wilkerson	Philadelphia	KO	6	—	—
Apr 11	⑩	Jimmy Bivins★	Toledo	KO	8	—	—
Apr 26	⑩	Harold Johnson★	Philadelphia	W	10	—	—
Jun 13		Clinton Bacon	Indianapolis	LD	6	—	—
Jun 27		Bob Sikes	Indianapolis	KO	3	—	—
Jul 29		Esco Greenwood	North Adams, MA	KO	2	—	—
Oct 4		Bob Amos	Toledo	W	10	—	171
Oct 24		Phil Muscato	Toledo	TKO	6	—	181
Dec 6	⑩	Doc Williams	Hartford, CT	KO	8	—	175
Dec 13	⑩	Leonard Morrow	Toledo	KO	10	—	—

1950

Date		Opponent	Location	Result	Rds	Title	Wt
Jan 31	⑩	Bert Lytell	Toledo	W	10	—	175
Jul 31		Vernon Williams	Chicago	KO	2	—	—

1951

Date		Opponent	Location	Result	Rds	Title	Wt
Jan 2		Billy Smith	Portland, OR	TKO	8	—	—
Jan 28		John Thomas	Panama City	KO	1	—	—
Feb 21		Jimmy Bivins★	New York	TKO	9	—	—
Mar 13		Abel Cestac	Toledo	W	10	—	—
Apr 26		Herman Harris	Flint, MI	TKO	4	—	—
May 14		Art Henri	Baltimore	TKO	4	—	—
Jun 9		Abel Cestac	Buenos Aires	TKO	10	—	—
Jun 23		Karel Sys	Buenos Aires	D	10	—	—
Jul 8		Alberto Lovell	Buenos Aires	KO	1	—	—
Jul 15		Vicente Quiroz	Montevideo, Uruguay	KO	6	—	—
Jul 26		Vicente Carabajal	Cordoba, Argentina	TKO	3	—	—

Jul 28		Americo Capitanelli	Tucuman, Argentina	TKO	3		—	—
Aug 5		Rafael Miranda	Tucuman	TKO	4		—	—
Aug 17		Alfredo Lagay	Bahia Blanca, Argentina	KO	3		—	—
Sep 5		Embrell Davison	Detroit	KO	1		—	—
Sep 24	⑩	Harold Johnson★	Philadelphia	W	10		—	—
Oct 29		Chubby Wright	St. Louis	TKO	7		—	—
Dec 10	⑩	Harold Johnson★	Milwaukee	L	10		—	—
1952								
Jan 29	⑩	Harold Johnson★	Toledo	W	10		—	—
Feb 27	⑩	Jimmy Slade	St. Louis	W	10		—	—
May 19	⑩	Bob Dunlap	San Francisco	KO	6		—	—
Jun 26	⑩	Clarence Henry	Baltimore	W	10		—	—
Jul 25		Clint Bacon	Denver	TKO	4		—	—
Dec 17	♛	Joey Maxim★	St. Louis	W	15	Won-World-LH	172	
1953								
Jan 27		Toxie Hall	Toledo	KO	4			
Feb 16		Leonard Dugan	San Francisco	TKO	8		—	
Mar 3		Sonny Andrews	Sacramento, CA	KO	5		—	
Mar 11	⑩	Nino Valdes	St. Louis	W	10		—	
Mar 17		Al Spaulding	Spokane, WA	KO	3		—	
Mar 30		Frank Buford	San Diego	TKO	9		—	—
Jun 24	⑩	Joey Maxim★	Ogden, UT	W	15	Ret-World-LH	173	
Aug 22		Reinaldo Ansaloni	Buenos Aires	TKO	4		—	
Sep 12		Dogomar Martinez	Buenos Aires	W	10		—	
1954								
Jan 27	⑩	Joey Maxim★	Miami	W	15	Ret-World-LH	175	
Mar 9	⑩	Bob Baker	Miami	TKO	9		—	
Jun 7		Bert Withehurst	New York	KO	6		—	—
Aug 11	⑩	Harold Johnson★	New York	TKO	14	Ret-World-LH	173	
1955								
May 2	⑩	Nino Valdes	Las Vegas	W	15		—	—
Jun 22	⑩	Carl ("Bobo") Olson★	New York	KO	3	Ret-World-LH	175	
Sep 21	♛	Rocky Marciano★	New York	KO'd	9	For-World-H	188	
1956								
Feb 20		Howard King	San Francisco	W	10		—	197
Feb 27		Bob Dunlap	San Diego	KO	1		—	196
Mar 17		Frankie Daniels	Hollywood	W	10		—	194
Mar 27		Howard King	Hollywood	W	10		—	191
Apr 10		Willie Bean	Richmond, VA	TKO	5		—	—
Apr 16		George Parmentier	Seattle	TKO	3		—	—
Apr 26		Sonny Andrews	Edmonton, Alb.	KO	4		—	—
Apr 30		Gene Thompson	Tucson	TKO	3		—	—
Jun 5	⑩	Yolande Pompey	London	TKO	10	Ret-World-LH	174	
Jul 25		James Parker	Toronto	TKO	9			190
Sep 8		Roy Shire	Ogden	TKO	3		—	—
Nov 30	⑩	Floyd Patterson★	Chicago	KO'd	5	For-Vac World-H	187	
1957								
May 1		Hans Kalbfell	Essen, Germany	W	10		—	206
Jun 2		Alain Cherville	Stuttgart, Germany	TKO	6		—	—
Sep 20	⑩	Tony Anthony	Los Angeles	TKO	7	Ret-World-LH	175	
Oct 31		Bob Mitchell	Vancouver, B.C.	TKO	5		—	192
Nov 5		Eddie Cotton	Seattle	W	10		—	193
Nov 29		Roger Rischer	Portland, OR	KO	4		—	—
1958								
Jan 18		Luis Ignacio	Sao Paulo, Brazil	W	10		—	—
Feb 1		Julio Neves	Rio de Janeiro	KO	3		—	—

Date		Opponent	Location	Result	Rnd		
Mar 4		Bert Withehurst	San Bernardino, CA	TKO	10	—	—
Mar 10		Bob Albright	Vancouver	TKO	7	—	—
May 2		Willi Besmanoff	Louisville, KY	W	10	—	—
May 17		Howard King	San Diego	W	10	—	—
May 26		Charlie Norkus	San Francisco	W	10	—	—
Jun 9		Howard King	Sacramento	W	10	—	—
Aug 4		Howard King	Reno	D	10	—	199
Dec 10	⑩	Yvon Durelle	Montreal	KO	11	Ret-World-LH	173
1959							
Mar 9		Sterling Davis	Odessa, TX	TKO	3	—	—
Aug 12	⑩	Yvon Durelle	Montreal	KO	3	Ret-World-LH	174
1960							
May 25		Willi Besmanoff	Indianapolis	TKO	10	—	206
Sep 13		George Abinet	Dallas	TKO	3	—	195
Oct 29	⑩	Giulio Rinaldi	Rome	L	10	—	190
Nov 28		Buddy Turman	Dallas	W	10	—	—
1961							
Mar 25		Buddy Turman	Manila	W	10	—	201
May 12		Clifford Gray	Nogales, Mexico	KO	4	—	185
Jun 10	⑩	Giulio Rinaldi	New York	W	15	Ret-World-LH	174
Oct 23		Pete Rademacher	Baltimore	TKO	6	—	198
1962							
Mar 30	⑩	Alejandro Lavorante	Los Angeles	TKO	10	—	197
May 7		Howard King	Tijuana, Mexico	KO	1	—	190
May 28	⑩	Willie Pastrano★	Los Angeles	D	10	—	201
Nov 15	⑩	Cassius Clay★	Los Angeles	TKO'd	4	—	197
1963							
Mar 15		Mike DiBiase	Phoenix	TKO	3	—	206

stayed in the fight for the full fifteen rounds, Moore dominated him with his powerful punching and easily won the unanimous decision. He held the light heavyweight title for the next six years.

In 1955, Moore attempted to move up to the heavyweight title by fighting the undefeated Rocky Marciano in Yankee Stadium. Moore knocked Marciano down in the second round with a right but he was up at the count of two. Marciano knocked Moore down in the sixth, eighth, and ninth rounds, the last time for the knockout. After Marciano's retirement, Moore fought Floyd Patterson for the title but fell in five.

In 1958, Moore engaged in a memorable defense of his light heavyweight title against Yvon Durelle in Montreal's Forum. Managed by Hall of Famer Jack Kearns since the victory over Maxim, Moore was a strong favorite. However, Durelle knocked Moore down three times in the first round and again in the fifth. But from then on, Moore used his left to weaken Durelle, knocking him down in the seventh and finishing him off with a short right in the eleventh.

Moore continued to fight, even after New York and the NBA stripped him of his belts for failure to defend the light heavyweight title. In 1962, Muhammad Ali, who had briefly trained with Moore but had disagreed with the old man's instructions, knocked him out in the fourth round. Moore's date of birth is disputed, but his age in the Ali fight hovered somewhere around 50. After fighting just once more, The Old Mongoose retired. He remained active in boxing as a trainer, embarked on a film career, and worked with youth.

JOSE NAPOLES
Mantequilla

WELTERWEIGHT

Right-handed; 5'7½"; 127–153 lbs.

84 bouts, 8/2/1958 to 12/6/1975

Welterwt. Champ 1969–70, 1971–75

Hall of Fame Induction: 1990

Born: 4/13/1940, Santiago de Cuba, Oriente, Cuba

Jose Napoles earned the nickname "Mantequilla" (Spanish for "butter") because of his smooth style. A native of Cuba, Napoles began fighting as a small boy in the Santiago slums under the tutelage of his three uncles. He worked odd jobs in Havana gyms so that he could watch fighters train. As an amateur, Napoles compiled an astonishing 114–1 record. He turned pro in 1958 and won his first time out, with a one-punch knockout. Early in his career, fighting exclusively in Havana, Napoles battled as a featherweight and as a lightweight.

Napoles fled Cuba soon after Fidel Castro banned professional boxing there. Napoles explained, "I have no interest in politics. I wanted to make a decent liv-

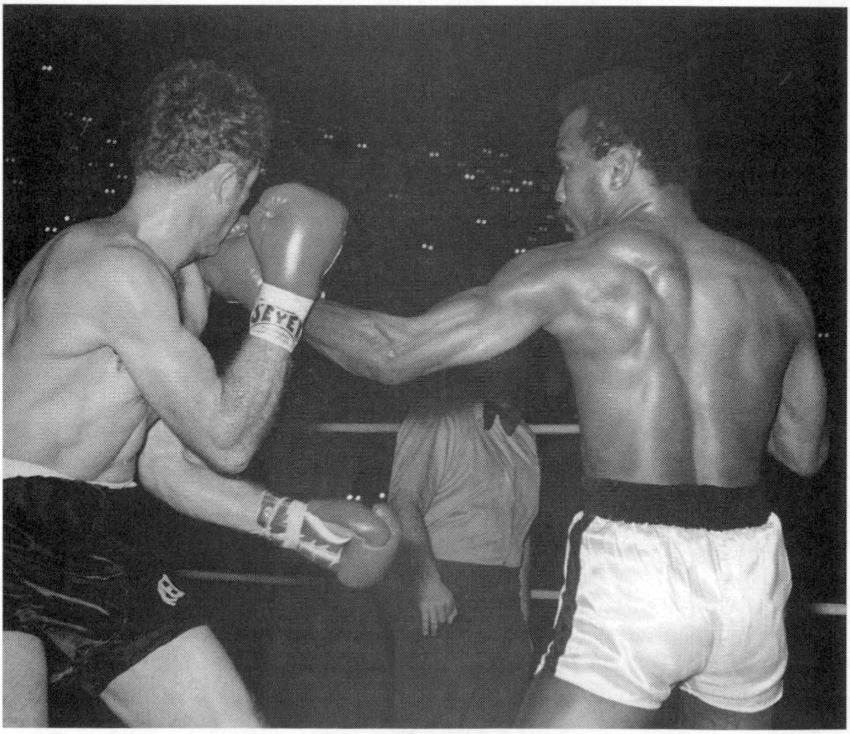

A left to the jaw by Napoles (R) twists Ernie ("Indian Red") Lopez during their first title fight, February 1970 at the Fabulous Forum in Inglewood, CA. Napoles won by TKO in the last scheduled round.

IN THE RING	WON **77***	LOST **7**	DRAWS **0**	TB 84	KO 54	W 22	WF 1*	D 0	KO'd 4	L 3	LF 0

*includes 1 TW

Date	Opponent	Site	Result / Rounds		Title	Wt.
1958						
Aug 2	Julio Rojas	Havana	KO	1	—	—
Oct 11	Eurispides Guerra	Havana	KO	4	—	—
Nov 29	Felix Pomares	Havana	TKO	2	—	—
1959						
Feb 21	Armando Castillo	Havana	W	4	—	—
May 16	Juan Bacallao	Havana	TKO	4	—	—
Jul 11	Cloroaldo Hernandez	Havana	TKO	3	—	—
Jul 25	Cristobal Gonzalez	Havana	W	10	—	—
Aug 22	Hilton Smith	Havana	L	10	—	127
Oct 3	Chris Gonzalez	Havana	W	8	—	—
1960						
Jan 2	Isaac Espinosa	Havana	W	10	—	131
Feb 20	Diwaldo Ventosa	Havana	W	10	—	133
May 21	Angel Garcia	Havana	W	10	—	132
Jul 2	Leslie Grant	Havana	W	10	—	—
Oct 15	Tony Padron	Havana	W	10	—	—
Nov 26	Rolando Morales	Havana	W	10	—	—
1961						
Jan 28	Guillermo Valdez	Havana	W	10	—	—
Mar 19	Rolando Morales	Havana	W	10	—	133
Mar 29	Enrique Carabeo	Havana	TKO	9	—	—
1962						
Jul 21	Enrique Camarena	Mexico City	KO	2	—	134
Aug 25	Kid Anahuac	Mexico City	KO	9	—	135
Sep 29	Bobby Cervantes	Mexico City	TKO	2	—	135
Nov 10	Tony Perez	Los Mochis, Mexico	W	10	—	—
1963						
Jan 5	Tony Perez	Hermosillo, Mexico	L	10	—	—
Feb 9	Jorge Gutierrez	Mexico City	TKO	7	—	134
Mar 30	Baby Vasquez	Mexico City	W	10	—	135
Apr 27 ⑩	Alfredo Urbina	Mexico City	L	10	—	135
May 27	Raul Soriano	Tijuana	KO	4	—	135
Aug 19	Pulga Serrano	Tijuana	TKO	10	—	—
Oct 23	Francisco Cancio	Mexico City	KO	1	—	136
Nov 16	Tony Perez	Mexico City	TKO	3	—	—
Nov 30	L.C. Morgan	Caracas, Venezuela	KO	7	—	—
1964						
Mar 1	Taketeru Yoshimoto	Tokyo	KO	1	—	—
Apr 25 ⑩	Alfredo Urbina	Mexico City	TKO	1	—	135
Jun 22 ⑩	Carlos Hernandez	Caracas	TKO	7	—	—
Aug 15	Eduardo Moreno	Culiacan, Mexico	TKO	5	—	—
Nov 14 ⑩	Alfredo Urbina	Mexico City	KO	3	—	—
1965						
Jan 1	Carlos Rios	Laguna, Mexico	TKO	7	—	140
Feb 28	L.C. Morgan	Monterrey, Mexico	KO	3	—	143
Mar 25 ⑩	Giordano Campari	Caracas	TKO	2	—	—
Aug 3 ⑩	Eddie Perkins	Juarez, Mexico	W	10	—	—

Date		Opponent	Location	Result	Rnd	Title	Wt
Dec 11	⑩	Adolph Pruitt	Mexico City	TKO	3	—	—

1966

Date		Opponent	Location	Result	Rnd	Title	Wt
Feb 12	⑩	Johnny Santos	Mexico City	KO	3	—	138
Apr 17		Al Grant	Reynosa, Mexico	TKO	4	—	—
Jul 27		Humberto Trottman	Juarez	TKO	2	—	140
Aug 22		L.C. Morgan	Reynosa	TKO'd	4	—	138
Oct 30		Jimmy Fields	San Luis Potosi, Mexico	TKO	10	—	
Dec 17	⑩	Eugenio Espinoza	Mexico City	TKO	6	—	140

1967

Date		Opponent	Location	Result	Rnd	Title	Wt
Jun 4		Johnny Brooks	Merida, Mexico	KO	7	—	—
Jul 10		L.C. Morgan	Tijuana	TKO	2	—	—
Sep 11		Johnny De Peiza	Juarez	TKO	10	—	140
Dec 3		Charlie Watson	Merida	KO	5	—	—

1968

Date		Opponent	Location	Result	Rnd	Title	Wt
Feb 18		Mike Cruz	Tampico, Mexico	TKO	4	—	137
Apr 29		Herbie Lee	Tijuana	TKO	4	—	139
Jun 2		Peter Cobblah	Mexico City	W	10	—	141
Jun 14		Leroy Roberts	Los Angeles	TKO	1	—	145
Jul 15		Eddie Pace	Tijuana	W	10	—	144
Nov 4		Des Rea	Inglewood, CA	TKO	5	—	144
Dec 22		Lennox Beckles	Mexico City	KO	1	—	148

1969

Date		Opponent	Location	Result	Rnd	Title	Wt
Feb 15		Fate Davis	Mexico City	TKO	7	—	144
Apr 18	♛	Curtis Cokes	Inglewood	TKO	13	Won-World-W	143
Jun 29	⑩	Curtis Cokes	Mexico City	TKO	10	Ret-World-W	145
Oct 12	⑩	Emile Griffith★	Inglewood	W	15	Ret-World-W	144

1970

Date		Opponent	Location	Result	Rnd	Title	Wt
Feb 15	⑩	Ernie ("Indian Red") Lopez	Inglewood	TKO	15	Ret-World-W	145
Aug 14		Fighting Mack	Inglewood	KO	3	—	—
Oct 5		Pete Toro	New York	TKO	9	—	150
Dec 3	⑩	Billy Backus	Syracuse, NY	TKO'd	4	Lost-World-W	144

1971

Date		Opponent	Location	Result	Rnd	Title	Wt
Mar 27		Manuel Gonzalez	Mexico City	KO	6	—	148
Jun 4	♛	Billy Backus	Inglewood	TKO	8	Reg-World-W	146
Jul 2		David Melendez	Mexico City	TKO	5	—	—
Aug 23	⑩	Jean Josselin	Inglewood	KO	5	—	—
Oct 17		Esteban Osuna	Mexico City	W	10	—	150
Dec 14	⑩	Hedgemon Lewis	Los Angeles	W	15	Ret-World-W	145

1972

Date		Opponent	Location	Result	Rnd	Title	Wt
Mar 28		Ralph Charles	Wembley, England	KO	7	Ret-World-W	146
Jun 10	⑩	Adolph Pruitt	Monterrey	KO	2	Ret-World-W	146
Aug 5		Edmundo Leite	Mexico City	TKO	2	—	147

1973

Date		Opponent	Location	Result	Rnd	Title	Wt
Feb 28	⑩	Ernie Lopez	Los Angeles	KO	7	Ret-World-W	146
Jun 23	⑩	Roger Menetrey	Grenoble, France	W	15	Ret-World-W	146
Sep 22	⑩	Clyde Gray	Toronto	W	15	Ret-World-W	147

1974

Date		Opponent	Location	Result	Rnd	Title	Wt
Feb 9	♛	Carlos Monzon★	Monte Carlo	KO'd	7	For-World-M	153
Aug 3	⑩	Hedgemon Lewis	Mexico City	TKO	9	Ret-World-W	145
Dec 14	⑩	Horacio Saldano	Mexico City	KO	3	Ret-World-W	146

1975

Date		Opponent	Location	Result	Rnd	Title	Wt
Mar 30	⑩	Armando Muniz	Acapulco	TW	12	Ret-World-W	147
Jul 12	⑩	Armando Muniz	Mexico City	W	15	Ret-World (WBC)-W	146
Dec 6	⑩	John Stracey	Mexico City	TKO'd	6	Lost-World (WBC)-W	147

ing for my wife and son, so I went to Mexico City and resumed my boxing career."

By 1962, Napoles was considered the tenth-best junior welterweight in *The Ring*'s annual rankings. In 1967, Napoles moved up to welterweight. He earned a title shot in 1969 against Curtis Cokes in the Fabulous Forum in Los Angeles. Napoles knocked Cokes out in thirteen rounds to win the championship. The battered Cokes had a cut mouth and bloody nose, and both eyes were almost swollen shut. In their rematch two months later in Mexico City, Napoles knocked out Cokes in the tenth.

Napoles defended this belt three times, winning a decision over Emile Griffith, and a TKO over Ernie Lopez before losing to Billy Backus, of Canastota, New York. That fight, which took place in Syracuse, New York late in 1970, was stopped because of serious cuts around Napoles's eyes. Napoles won the rematch in June 1971 with an eighth-round TKO. Having regained the title, Napoles defended it six times before attempting to move up to middleweight.

In 1974, Napoles challenged Hall of Famer Carlos Monzon for the middleweight crown. However, Monzon proved to be too much for Napoles, who was stopped in seven rounds. Still welterweight champ, Napoles defended this title four more times, in each case against a top-ten contender, until he lost to John Stracey on a sixth-round TKO in December 1975. Napoles retired after the Stracey fight. Although susceptible to cuts, Napoles was a stylish boxer who possessed a wide array of left-hand punches, a fine right uppercut, and great speed.

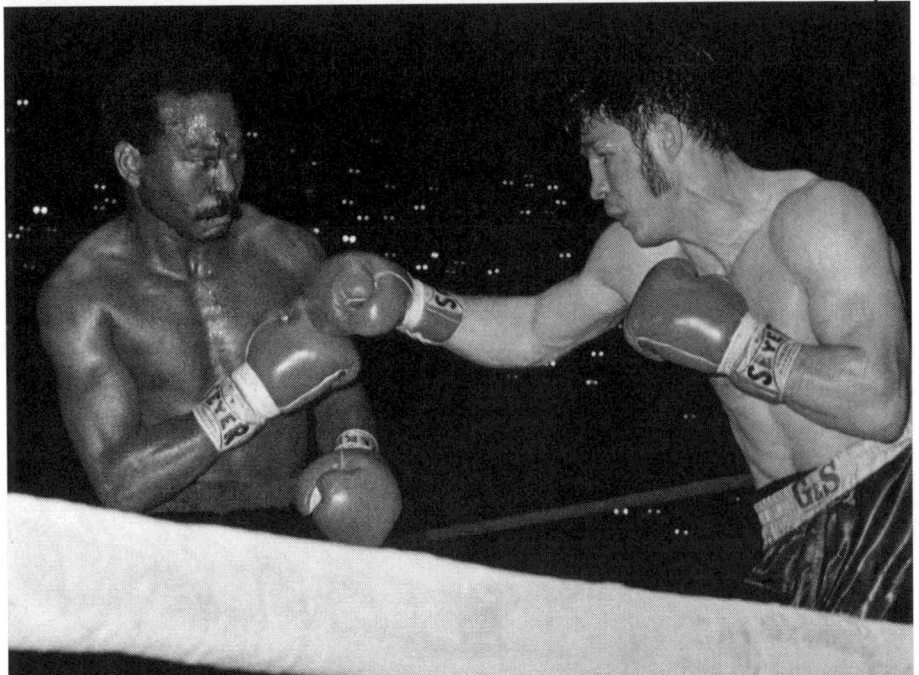

Courageous Billy Backus (R) traded punches with Napoles in their June 4, 1971 rematch. The ringside physician stopped the bout in the eighth after an examination of Backus's bruised face.

KEN NORTON

HEAVYWEIGHT

Right-handed; 6'3"; 200–224 lbs.
50 bouts, 11/14/1967 to 5/11/1981
Manager: Bob Biron
WBC Heavyweight Champion 1978
Hall of Fame Induction: 1992
Born: 8/9/1943, Jacksonville, IL
Named: Kenneth Howard Norton

Ken Norton's name is inextricably linked to that of Muhammad Ali. Norton fought Ali three times and handed "The Greatest" the second defeat of his career, the result of a jaw-fracturing punch in the first round. Asked in a 1992 interview what he thought he would be most remembered for, Norton replied, "Fighting Ali." Nevertheless, Norton was a key player in the heavyweight wars of the 1960s and '70s. He was an aggressive fighter who could move with a confusing fluidity and who commanded a dangerous repertoire of punches.

Unlike many fighters, Norton did not grow up boxing or dreaming of becoming a fighter. He played football, basketball, and track in high school and received

Still trim and powerful at 37, Ken Norton (L) pounds journeyman fighter Tex Cobb in San Antonio on November 7, 1980. Norton took the 10-round decision. This proved to be his next-to-last fight.

IN THE RING	WON 42	LOST 7	DRAWS 1	TB 50	KO 33	W 9	WF 0	D 1	KO'd 4	L 3	LF 0

Date	Opponent	Site	Result / Rounds		Title	Wt
1967						
Nov 14	Grady Brazell	San Diego	KO	9	—	201
1968						
Jan 16	Sam Wyatt	San Diego	W	6	—	—
Feb 6	Harold Dutra	Sacramento, CA	KO	3	—	210
Mar 26	Jimmy Gilmore	San Diego	KO	7	—	—
Jul 23	Wayne Kindred	San Diego	TKO	6	—	203
Dec 5	Cornell Nolan	Los Angeles	KO	6	—	207
1969						
Feb 11	Joe Hemphill	Woodland Hills, CA	TKO	3	—	206
Feb 20	Wayne Kindred	Los Angeles	KO	9	—	205
Mar 31	Pedro Sanchez	San Diego	TKO	2	—	203
May 29	Bill McMurray	Los Angeles	TKO	7	—	202
Jul 25	Gary Bates	San Diego	KO	8	—	—
Oct 21	Julius Garcia	San Diego	KO	3	—	210
1970						
Feb 4	Aaron Eastling	Las Vegas	KO	2	—	—
Mar 13	Stanford Harris	San Diego	KO	3	—	—
Apr 7	Bob Mashburn	Cleveland	KO	4	—	—
May 8	Ray Ellis	San Diego	KO	2	—	—
Jul 2	⑩ Jose Luis Garcia	Los Angeles	KO'd	8	—	207
Aug 29	Cookie Wallace	San Diego	KO	4	—	—
Sep 26	Chuck Leslie	Woodland Hills	W	10	—	205
Oct 16	Roby Harris	San Diego	KO	2	—	205
1971						
Apr 24	Steve Carter	Woodland Hills	TKO	3	—	208
Jun 12	Vic Brown	Santa Monica, CA	KO	5	—	211
Aug 19	Chuck Haynes	Santa Monica	KO	10	—	207
Sep 30	James Woody	San Diego	W	10	—	209
1972						
Feb 17	Charlie Harris	San Diego	KO	3	—	—
Mar 17	Jack O'Halloran	San Diego	W	10	—	212
Jun 5	Herschel Jacobs	San Diego	W	10	—	206
Jun 30	James Woody	San Diego	TKO	7	—	209
Nov 21	Henry Clark	Stateline, NV	KO	9	—	—
Dec 13	Charlie Reno	San Diego	W	10	—	208
1973						
Mar 31	⑩ Muhammad Ali★	San Diego	W	12	Won-NABF-H	210
Sep 10	⑩ Muhammad Ali★	Los Angeles	L	12	Lost-NABF-H	205
1974						
Mar 26	♛ George Foreman	Caracas, Venezuela	KO'd	2	For-World-H	212
Jun 25	Boone Kirkman	Seattle	TKO	8	—	—
1975						
Mar 4	Reco Brooks	Oklahoma City, OK	KO	1	—	224
Mar 24	⑩ Jerry Quarry	New York	TKO	5	Won-NABF-H	218
Aug 14	Jose Luis Garcia	St Paul, MN	TKO	5	—	218

1976							
Jan 3		Pedro Lovell	Las Vegas	KO	5	—	220
Apr 30		Ron Stander	Landover, MD	KO	5	—	224
Jul 10		Larry Middleton	San Diego	TKO	10	—	220
Sep 28	♛	Muhammad Ali★	New York	L	15	For-World-H	217
1977							
May 11	⑩	Duane Bobick	New York	TKO	1	—	222
Sep 14		Lorenzo Zanon	Las Vegas	TKO	5	—	223
Nov 5	⑩	Jimmy Young	Las Vegas	W	15	—	—
1978							
Jun 8	⑩	Larry Holmes	Las Vegas	L	15	Lost-WBC-H	220
Nov 10		Randy Stephens	Las Vegas	KO	4	—	—
1979							
Mar 23	⑩	Earnie Shavers	Las Vegas	TKO'd	1	—	—
Sep 19	⑩	Scott Le Doux	Bloomington, MN	D	10	—	223
1980							
Nov 7		Randall ("Tex") Cobb	San Antonio, TX	W	10	—	218
1981							
May 11	⑩	Gerry Cooney	New York	TKO'd	1	—	218

a scholarship to Northeast Missouri State, which he attended for two years. It wasn't until Norton joined the Marine Corps that he began boxing. In the Marines, Norton compiled a 24-2 amateur record and won the All-Marine heavyweight title three times. He also won a title in the Pan American Games trials.

Norton turned pro in 1967 at the relatively advanced age of 24 with a knockout of Grady Brazell. He fought primarily in the Southern California area and won his first sixteen fights before suffering a knockout loss to Jose Luis Garcia, the first ranked contender he ever faced. This was a loss he avenged five years later. By 1972, Norton appeared in the number nine slot in *The Ring*'s annual ranking of top contenders.

In March 1973, Norton faced Ali for the NABF heavyweight title in a fight broadcast on national television from the San Diego Sports Arena. Ali had failed to train adequately for the match and had trouble avoiding Norton's advances. Norton, who was in top form, broke Ali's jaw in the first round. Although Ali went the distance, the injury took its toll and Norton won on a split decision. Ali won the rematch in Los Angeles in September with a blistering final round. Again the result was a split decision. Norton then faced George Foreman in March 1974 in Caracas for the heavyweight championship. Foreman won easily, knocking Norton out in the second round.

Norton beat Jerry Quarry in New York in 1975 with a fifth-round TKO to take the NABF heavyweight title. Seeking a world title, Norton again faced Ali, acknowledged as champion once more after a win over Foreman. The fight was held in Yankee Stadium in 1976 in front of 30,296 fans. Norton led early on but Ali recovered and won a unanimous decision, though Norton clearly believed that he had won the fight.

Norton was awarded the WBC heavyweight title when Leon Spinks refused to honor an agreement to defend his title against Norton. Norton defended his awarded championship against Larry Holmes and lost a close decision in a very exciting bout.

Norton's pressing style combined with a hook to the body and a right upper-cut to the head made him a formidable foe. But after losing to Earnie Shavers and Gerry Cooney in one-round knockouts, he retired.

Norton, whose undeniable good looks were affected very little by boxing, had a brief acting career. His son, Ken Norton, Jr., grew up to become a linebacker with the San Francisco 49ers and the Dallas Cowboys and has played in three Super Bowls.

Norton (R) jolts Jerry Quarry, a heavyweight who also faced Ali and Frazier, with a straight left to the jaw. Norton won the NABF heavyweight title with a 5th-round TKO on March 24, 1975 in New York.

RUBEN OLIVARES

El Puas

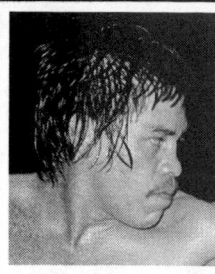

FEATHERWEIGHT

Right-handed; 5'5½"; 112–135 lbs.

104 bouts, 1/4/1965 to 3/12/1988

Bantamwt. Champ 1969–70, 1971–72,
WBA Featherweight Champ 1974,
WBC Featherweight Champ 1975

Hall of Fame Induction: 1991

Born: 1/14/1947, Mexico City, Mexico

Considered by many to be the best bantamweight of all time, Ruben Olivares twice won the world bantamweight title and twice won versions of the world featherweight title. Olivares started his career in his native Mexico with an impressive record. He knocked out his first 23 opponents and 54 of his first 57 opponents. In the other three bouts, Olivares took one decision, one win on a foul, and one draw. Overall, Olivares recorded 78 knockouts in his fourteen-year career.

Olivares captured the world bantamweight title at the Fabulous Forum in Inglewood, California knocking out Lionel Rose in the fifth round in August 1969. In 1970, also at the Forum, Olivares suffered his first loss when Chucho Castillo scored a technical knockout in the fourteenth round to take the title. The next year Olivares again fought Castillo at the Forum before a crowd of 18,456. The

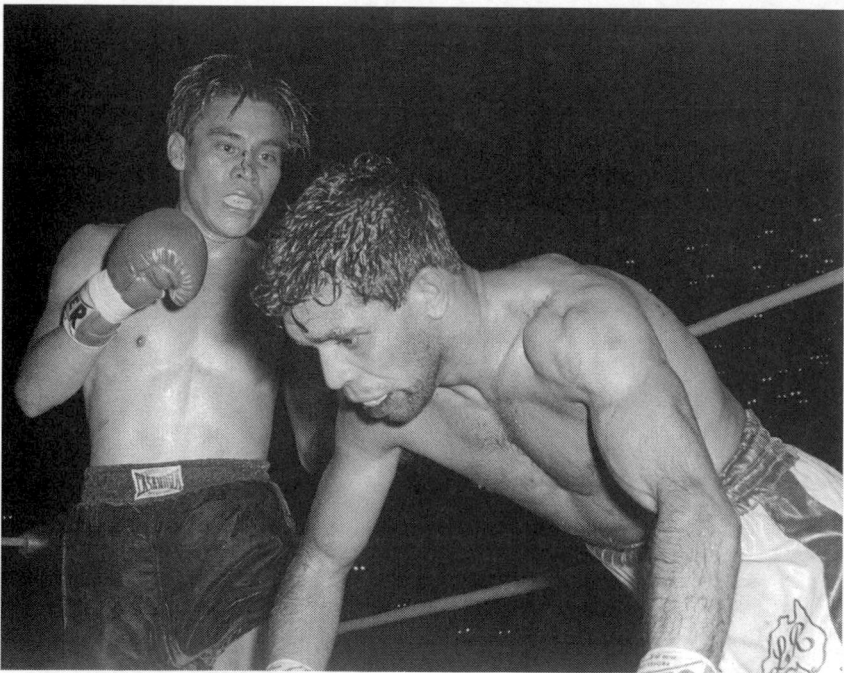

Olivares (L) knocks champion Lionel Rose of Australia into a glassy-eyed daze in the 5th round to seize the world bantamweight championship on August 22, 1969 in the Fabulous Forum in Inglewood, CA.

IN THE RING	WON 88	LOST 13	DRAWS 3	TB 104	KO 78	W 9	WF 1	D 3	KO'd 9	L 4	LF 0

Date	Opponent	Site	Result / Rounds		Title	Wt.
1965						
Jan 4	Isidro Sotelo	Cuernavaca, Mexico	KO	1	—	—
Jan 18	Freddy Garcia	Cuernavaca	KO	1	—	—
Feb 1	Geronimo Cisneros	Mexico City	TKO	3	—	—
Feb 16	Francisco Silva	Gomez Palacio, Mexico	TKO	6	—	113
Apr 1	Tony Gallegos	Gomez Palacio	KO	4	—	112
Aug 14	Nemesio Zenil	Mexico City	TKO	2	—	112
Sep 8	Jorge Ruiz	Torreon, Mexico	TKO	8	—	—
Oct 20	Mateo Jaimes	Mexico City	TKO	5	—	112
Nov 24	Pablo Martinez	Mexico City	TKO	2	—	—
1966						
Jan 17	Reynaldo De La Cerda	Mexico City	TKO	3	—	112
Feb 16	Eduardo Alvarado	Mexico City	TKO	2	—	112
Mar 12	Gallito Camacho	Mexico City	TKO	1	—	114
Apr 4	Juan Molina	Mexico City	TKO	2	—	112
May 19	Emetrio Campas	Tampico, Mexico	TKO	4	—	113
Jun 12	Alfonso Cazares	Mexico City	TKO	2	—	112
Jun 23	German Guzman	Tampico	TKO	4	—	113
Jul 10	Gerardo Lujano	Mexico City	TKO	5	—	113
Aug 7	Oscar Rivas	Tampico	TKO	3	—	—
Sep 1	Ramiro Garcia	Mexico City	KO	9	—	112
Sep 30	Monito Aguilar	Tampico	TKO	3	—	—
Oct 18	Rafael Macias	Mexico City	TKO	5	—	112
Dec 17	Daniel Gutierrez	Mexico City	TKO	10	—	112
1967						
Feb 5	Antonio Leal	Mexico City	KO	1	—	114
Mar 8	Felipe Gonzalez	Mexicali, Mexico	W	10	—	115
Jun 7	Julio Guerrero	Mexico City	KO	4	—	114
Jul 14	Angel Hernandez	Leon, Mexico	KO	5	—	116
Jul 29	German Bastidas	Mexico City	D	10	—	—
Sep 6	Grillo Aguilar	Poza Rica, Mexico	KO	5	—	113
Sep 20	Gustavo Sosa	Puebla, Mexico	TKO	3	—	115
Oct 14	Ushiwakamaru Harada	Mexico City	TKO	2	—	—
Nov 3	Chamaco Castillo	Veracruz, Mexico	TKO	5	—	117
Nov 19	Felipe Gonzalez	La Paz, Mexico	TKO	6	—	—
1968						
Jan 28	German Bastidas	Mexico City	TKO	5	—	—
Mar 3	Pornchai Popraigam	La Paz	TKO	9	—	117
Mar 30	⑩ Salvatore Burruni	Mexico City	TKO	3	—	—
Apr 27	Manuel Arnal	Mexico City	WD	6	—	—
May 20	Kid Gavilan	Puebla	KO	4	—	120
Jun 8	⑩ Octavio Gomez	Mexico City	KO	5	—	116
Jun 25	Enrique Yepes	Jalapa, Mexico	KO	5	—	119
Jul 11	Gary Garber	Torreon	TKO	3	—	118
Aug 10	Tiny Palacio	Mexico City	KO	6	—	118
Aug 28	Bernabe Fernandez	Inglewood	TKO	3	—	119
Sep 15	Antoine Porcel	Mexico City	KO	1	—	115
Oct 11	Wally Brooks	Mexico City	KO	1	—	—
Nov 23	Jose Medel	Monterrey, Mexico	KO	8	—	—

1969							
Jan 26	⑩	Kazuyoshi Kanazawa	Mexico City	TKO	2	—	118
Feb 23		Jose Bisbal	Mexico City	KO	3	—	117
Mar 9		Carlos Zayas	Tuxtla Gutierrez, Mexico	TKO	7	—	118
Mar 17		Ernie De La Cruz	Inglewood	TKO	9	—	121
May 6		Frank Adame	Nogales, Mexico	KO	2	—	120
May 23	⑩	Takao Sakurai	Inglewood	KO	6	—	117
Jun 29		Nene Jun	Mexico City	TKO	1	—	120
Aug 22	♛	Lionel Rose	Inglewood	KO	5	Won-World-B	118
Oct 27		Shigeyoshi Oki	Juarez, Mexico	KO	3	—	122
Dec 12	⑩	Alan Rudkin	Inglewood	KO	2	Ret-World-B	117
1970							
Feb 22		Angel Hernandez	Acambaro, Mexico	KO	3	—	122
Mar 18		Romy Ruelas	San Antonio, TX	TKO	6	—	122
Apr 18	⑩	Chucho Castillo	Inglewood	W	15	Ret-World-B	117
Jul 22		Shuji Chiyoda	Chicago	W	10	—	124
Aug 14		Jose Arranz	Inglewood	TKO	3	—	123
Sep 11		Guillermo Rodriguez	Acapulco	KO	5	—	125
Oct 16	⑩	Chucho Castillo	Inglewood	TKO'd	14	Lost-World-B	118
1971							
Mar 4		Chung-Sul Park	Guadalajara, Mexico	KO	6	—	118
Apr 3	♛	Chucho Castillo	Inglewood	W	15	Reg-World-B	118
May 19		Tsujio Mineyama	Tijuana	TKO	3	—	125
Jun 7		Yambito Blanco	Managua, Nicaragua	KO	5	—	125
Jul 11	⑩	Efren Torres	Guadalajara	TKO	4	—	120
Aug 23		Valentin Galeano	Inglewood	TKO	9	—	120
Oct 25		Kazuyoshi Kanazawa	Nagoya, Japan	TKO	14	Ret-World-B	117
Dec 14	⑩	Jesus Pimentel	Inglewood	TKO	11	Ret-World-B	118
1972							
Mar 19	⑩	Rafael Herrera	Mexico City	KO'd	8	Lost-World-B	117
Aug 19		Godfrey Stevens	Monterrey	W	10	—	124
Nov 14	⑩	Rafael Herrera	Inglewood	L	10	—	121
1973							
Apr 28		Walter Seeley	Inglewood	TKO	2	—	126
Jun 23	⑩	Bobby Chacon	Inglewood	TKO	9	Won-Vac NABF-FE	126
Sep 4	⑩	Art Hafey	Monterrey	TKO'd	5	—	126
Dec 2		Francisco Durango	Matamoros, Mexico	W	10	—	—
1974							
Mar 4	⑩	Art Hafey	Inglewood	W	12	Ret-NABF-FE	126
May 14		Adrian Zapanta	Juarez	KO	2	—	123
Jul 9		Zensuke Utagawa	Inglewood	KO	7	Won-Vac WBA-FE	125
Aug 31		Enrique Garcia	Monterrey	TKO	5	—	126
Oct 6		Carlos Mendoza	Juarez	TKO	6	—	129
Nov 23		Alexis Arguello★	Inglewood	KO'd	13	Lost-WBA-FE	125
1975							
Apr 7		Benjamin Ortiz	Tijuana	KO	6	—	—
Jun 20	♛	Bobby Chacon	Inglewood	TKO	2	Won-WBC-FE	125
Sep 20	⑩	David Kotey	Inglewood	L	15	Lost-WBC-FE	126
Dec 4	⑩	Danny Lopez	Inglewood	KO'd	7	—	—
1976							
Jun 2		Pajet Lupikanete	Los Angeles	KO	1	—	128
Jul 30		Fernando Cabanela	Los Angeles	W	10	—	125
Nov 19	⑩	Jose Cervantes	Los Angeles	KO'd	6	—	122
1977							
Aug 20	⑩	Bobby Chacon	Inglewood	L	10	—	—
Dec 6		Ricky Gutierrez	San Antonio	W	10	—	—

1978						
Apr 28	Jose Luis Ramirez	Obregon, Mexico	TKO	2	—	128
Oct 18	Shig Fukuyama	Houston	KO	2	—	—
Nov 20	Isaac Vega	Houston	TKO	3	—	—
1979						
Apr 22	Guillermo Morales	Tuxtla Gutierrez	D	10	—	—
Jun 30	Adrian Zapanta	Albuquerque, NM	KO	2	—	—
Jul 21 ♛	Eusebio Pedroza★	Houston	TKO'd	12	For-WBA-FE	125
1980						
Mar 7	Carlos Serrano	Chicago	KO	5	—	—
Apr 25	Sergio Reyes	Nuevo Laredo, Mexico	TKO	7	—	—
Aug 24	Rafael Gandarilla	McAllen, TX	TKO'd	9	—	128
1981						
Nov 24	Margarito Marquez	Houston	L	10	—	—
1986						
Feb 25*	Roman Almaguer	Inglewood	D	4	—	133
1988						
Mar 12*	Ignacio Madrid	Mexico City	KO'd	4	—	135

Some official records do not include these four-round bouts.

fight started slowly with little action until Castillo rocked Olivares in the sixth. Olivares then started to take charge. He mixed left hooks and right crosses to win easily by unanimous decision and regain his bantamweight title.

Olivares retained the belt for about a year before losing it to challenger Rafael Herrera, who knocked him out in the eighth round. Shortly thereafter, Olivares moved up to the featherweight division, where he quickly found success. Again fighting at the Forum, he faced Zensuke Utagawa of Japan for the vacant WBA featherweight title. Olivares dominated the entire fight, pounding Utagawa with close shots to the body. In the seventh, Olivares knocked Utagawa down three times. Utagawa got up twice but could not recover from the third knockdown, and Olivares was the champion.

In his first defense of the title, Olivares lost the belt to Hall of Famer Alexis Arguello on a thirteenth-round knockout. Seven months later, Olivares won the WBC version of the featherweight belt with an impressive victory over Bobby Chacon, stopping him in two rounds. Olivares failed to defend the title successfully, losing a decision to David Kotey in his next fight.

Olivares fought for another five years and suffered six of his thirteen career defeats during this period. After a five-year layoff, he made two brief comeback attempts, but failed to secure a win. The hard-partying Olivares will be remembered as a superb knockout artist and the greatest draw ever to Inglewood's Fabulous Forum.

Promoter George Parnassus and Olivares after he regained the title from Castillo in April 1971.

MIDDLEWEIGHT

Right handed; 5'10½"; 135–178 lbs.
111 bouts, 8/19/1944 to 11/22/1966
Manager: Sid Flaherty, Herbert Campos
Hall of Fame Induction: 2000
Born: 7/11/1928, Honolulu, HI
Named: Carl Elmer Olson
Died: 1/16/2002

Carl ("Bobo") Olson's colorful career ensured his lasting fame. His father was a Swedish immigrant who went to Hawaii during World War I, and Olson was nicknamed the "Hawaiian Swede."

Olson learned fighting on the streets of Honolulu, sometimes brawling with grown men. His parents broke up when he was only twelve, and he found work on a dairy farm and at odd jobs. As news of his fighting prowess spread, the young Olson participated in amateur bouts and bootleg fights against servicemen, some of whom had been professionals before enlisting.

Olson's first professional bout took place on August 19, 1944, when the sixteen-year-old knocked out Bob Correa in just two rounds. Sid Flaherty, a boxing manager who was serving in Hawaii as a sergeant in the army, was impressed enough with Olson's performance to sign him to a contract, and he took Olson with him to San Francisco after the war.

Olson won eight fights in 1946 and 1947 before he lost his California State Boxing Commission license for being underage. He returned to Hawaii and came under the management of Herbert Campos. The next four years, Olson fought in Hawaii, Manila, and Australia, where he won 30 of 33 fights. His toughest opponent was Australian Dave Sands, a highly regarded middleweight title contender, who held the British Empire middleweight title. Sands knocked Olson down in the first round, but Olson battled back and lasted the full twelve rounds before losing a close decision on May 20, 1950.

Just seven months later, on October 26,

During WWII, the teenaged Bobo Olson took part in many bootleg bouts, most against professionals competing with a special military exemption stationed in Hawaii. He picked up a lot of experience from these bouts, along with his two trademark tattoos.

IN THE RING	WON 99	LOST 16	DRAWS 2	TB 117	KO 49	W 50	WF 0	D 2	KO'd 7	L 9	LF 0

Date	Opponent	Site	Result / Rounds		Title	Wt.
1944						
Aug 19	Bob Correa	Honolulu	TKO	2	—	135
Aug 28	Ben Ramos	Honolulu	TKO	4	—	—
Sep 10	Young Pancho	Honolulu	W	4	—	—
1945						
Nov 23	Art Robinson	San Francisco	KO	4	—	—
Dec 10	Bobby Jones	San Francisco	KO	2	—	159
1946						
Jan 7	Obie Wooten	San Francisco	KO	1	—	—
Jan 14	Vepe Watson	San Francisco	KO	1	—	160
Jan 28	Pedro Jimenez	San Francisco	KO	4	—	160
Feb 4	Chuck Ross	San Francisco	W	6	—	158
Feb 25	Delaware Bradby	San Francisco	KO	3	—	—
— —	Lavelle Perrin	San Francisco	KO	3	—	—
— —	Lloyd Wagner	San Francisco	KO	3	—	—
— —	Jackie Downlee	San Francisco	KO	2	—	—
Jul 19	Trader Horne	Honolulu	TKO	2	—	163
Jul 26	Johnny Boski	Honolulu	KO	4	—	166
Aug 19	Johnny Boski	Honolulu	KO	3	—	162
Sep 9	Jackie Ryan	Honolulu	TKO	6	—	156
Oct 7	Wayne Powell	Honolulu	TKO	4	—	160
Dec 2	Wayne Powell	Honolulu	TKO	4	—	161
1947						
Jan 28	Gil Mojica	Honolulu	W	10	—	162
Mar 21	Candy McDaniels	Honolulu	W	10	—	158
May 2	Leroy Wade	Honolulu	TKO	5	—	160
Jun 20	Paul Lewis	Honolulu	W	10	—	157
Jul 4	George Duke	Honolulu	L	10	—	158
Aug 19	George Duke	Honolulu	W	10	—	158
Nov 22	Boy Brooks	Manila	L	10	—	157
Dec 17	Nai Som Pong	Manila	TKO	3	—	—
1948						
Jan 17	Boy Brooks	Manila	W	12	—	153
Apr 7	Flashy Sebastian	Manila	KO	7	—	—
May 11	Bobby Castro	Honolulu	W	8	—	—
Jul 20	Charley Cato	Honolulu	W	8	—	159
Oct 12	Boy Brooks	Honolulu	TKO	3	—	153
Oct 26	Kenny Watkins	Honolulu	W	10	—	—
Dec 14	Johnny Boski	Honolulu	KO	1	—	163
1949						
Jan 11	Paulie Perkins	Honolulu	KO	2	—	—
Mar 15	Anton Raadik	Honolulu	KO	7	—	—
Jun 3	Tommy Yarosz	Honolulu	W	10	—	163
Jul 26	Milo Savage	Honolulu	W	10	—	—
Aug 23	Art Hardy	Honolulu	KO	3	—	164
Nov 22	Johnny Duke	Honolulu	W	10	—	—
Dec 13	Earl Turner	Honolulu	W	10	—	—
1950						
Feb 22	Don Lee	Honolulu	W	10	—	165

Date		Opponent	Location	Result	Rounds	Title	Weight
Mar 20	⑩	Dave Sands	Sydney, Australia	L	12	—	—
Apr 25		Roy Miller	Honolulu	KO	5	—	—
May 22		Otis Graham	Honolulu	W	10	—	157
Sep 5		Henry Brimm	Honolulu	W	10	—	164
Oct 26	♛	Sugar Ray Robinson★	Philadelphia	KO'd	12	For-Penn World-M	159

1951

Date		Opponent	Location	Result	Rounds	Title	Weight
Mar 20		Art Soto	Honolulu	W	10	—	—
May 7		Lloyd Marshall	Honolulu	KO	5	—	—
Jul 9		Chuck Hunter	San Francisco	W	10	—	—
Jul 27		Charlie Cato	Richmond, CA	KO	3	—	—
Aug 27		Bobby Jones	San Francisco	W	10	—	—
Oct 3	⑩	Dave Sands	Chicago	L	10	—	—

1952

Date		Opponent	Location	Result	Rounds	Title	Weight
Feb 12		Woody Harper	Sacramento, CA	W	10	—	—
Feb 15		Tommy Harrison	Hollywood, CA	W	10	—	—
Mar 13	♛	Sugar Ray Robinson★	San Francisco	L	15	For-World-M	159
May 6		Woody Harper	Richmond	KO	7	—	—
May 19	⑩	Walter Cartier	Brooklyn	KO	5	—	—
Jun 6		Jimmy Beau	New York	W	10	—	—
Jul 12	⑩	Robert Villemain	San Francisco	W	10	—	—
Aug 27	⑩	Eugene Hairston	New York	KO	7	—	—
Nov 20	⑩	Lee Sala	San Francisco	KO	2	—	—
Dec 18	⑩	Norman Hayes	San Francisco	W	10	—	—

1953

Date		Opponent	Location	Result	Rounds	Title	Weight
Feb 7	⑩	Norman Hayes	Boston	W	10	—	—
Mar 16		Garth Panter	Butte, MT	W	10	—	—
Jun 19	⑩	Paddy Young	New York	W	15	Won-Amer-M	160
Oct 21	⑩	Randy Turpin★	New York	W	15	Won-Vac-World-M	159

1954

Date		Opponent	Location	Result	Rounds	Title	Weight
Jan 23		Joe Rindone	San Francisco	KO	5	—	—
Apr 2	♛	Kid Gavilan	Chicago	W	15	Ret-World-M	159
Jun 15		Jesse Turner	Honolulu	TKO	8	—	166
Jul 7		Pedro Gonzales	Oakland	KO	4	—	—
Aug 20	⑩	Rocky Castellani	San Francisco	W	15	Ret-World-M	160
Nov 3		Garth Panter	Richmond, VA	KO	8	—	—
Dec 15	⑩	Pierre Langlois	San Francisco	TKO	11	Ret-World-M	159

1955

Date		Opponent	Location	Result	Rounds	Title	Weight
Feb 16	⑩	Ralph ("Tiger") Jones	Chicago	W	10	—	—
Mar 12		Willie Vaughn	Hollywood	W	10	—	—
Apr 13	⑩	Joey Maxim★	San Francisco	W	10	—	169
Jun 22	♛	Archie Moore★	New York	KO'd	3	For-World-LH	170
Aug 13		Jimmy Martinez	Portland, OR	W	10	—	—
Aug 26		Joey Giambra	San Francisco	W	10	—	—
Dec 9	⑩	Sugar Ray Robinson★	Chicago	KO'd	2	Lost-World-M	159

1956

Date		Opponent	Location	Result	Rounds	Title	Weight
May 18	♛	Sugar Ray Robinson★	Los Angeles	KO'd	4	For-World-M	160

1957

Date		Opponent	Location	Result	Rounds	Title	Weight
Jun 18		Joey Maxim★	Portland, OR	W	10	—	—
Aug 17	⑩	Pat McMurtry	Portland	KO'd	2	—	—

1958

Date		Opponent	Location	Result	Rounds	Title	Weight
Oct 28		Don Grant	Oakland	TKO	7	—	173
Nov 25		Paddy Young	Oakland	KO	6	—	—
Dec 16		Tommy Villa	Fresno, CA	TKO	5	—	175

1959

Date		Opponent	Location	Result	Rounds	Title	Weight
Mar 30		Rory Calhoun	San Francisco	W	10	—	174

Aug 25		George Kartalian	Fresno	KO	5	—	176
1960							
Apr 7		Roque Maravilla	Portland	KO	7	—	—
May 5		Al Sparks	Vancouver, BC	KO	5	—	—
Jun 6	⑩	Mike Holt	Johannesburg	W	10	—	—
Aug 31	⑩	Doug Jones	Chicago	KO'd	6	—	—
1961							
Jan 19		Bobby Daniels	Spokane, WA	W	10	—	—
Feb 16		Floyd Buchanan	Victoria, BC	KO	3	—	—
Aug 14		Roque Maravilla	Oakland	W	10	—	177
Sep 11		Sixto Rodriguez	San Francisco	L	10	—	178
Oct 23		Sixto Rodriguez	San Francisco	W	10	—	—
Nov 14		Roy Smith/Yancy D	Honolulu	KO	8	—	—
1962							
Jan 12		Al Williams	Honolulu	W	10	—	175
Jan 19		Artie Dixon	Honolulu	W	10	—	177
Apr 3		Pete Rademacher	Honolulu	L	10	—	—
Jun 3		Lennart Risberg	Stockholm	KO	6	—	—
Dec 14	⑩	Giulio Rinaldi	Rome	D	10	—	—
1963							
Jan 25		Al Williams	Eugene, OR	TKO	5	—	175
Apr 30		Sonny Ray	Honolulu	KO	8	—	—
May 14		Jesse Bowdry	Honolulu	W	10	—	178
Oct 21		Jose Menno	San Francisco	W	10	—	176
Dec 9		Hank Casey	San Francisco	D	10	—	176
1964							
Mar 27	⑩	Wayne Thornton	San Francisco	W	10	—	176
Jun 19	⑩	Johnny Persol	New York	L	10	—	—
Aug 28	⑩	Wayne Thornton	New York	W	10	—	—
Nov 27	⑩	Jose Torres★	New York	KO'd	1	—	175
1965							
Jun 24		Andy Kendall	Reno	W	10	—	174
Sep 23		Fred Roots	Reno	KO	3	—	—
1966							
Jul 11		Piero Del Papa	San Francisco	W	10	—	—
Nov 22	⑩	Don Fullmer	Oakland	L	10	—	—

1950, Olson traveled to Philadelphia to challenge Sugar Ray Robinson for his Pennsylvania world middleweight title. Robinson, far more experienced than his opponent, knocked Olson out with a combination that ended in a left to the stomach in the twelfth round. About eighteen months later, Olson again faced Robinson, this time for the world middleweight championship in San Francisco. He gave Robinson a good battle in the first ten rounds, but Robinson fought back in the last five and won a narrow decision, though he had to be helped from the ring.

When Robinson retired and his title was declared vacant, two Europeans and two Americans were chosen for a four-man tournament to crown the new champ. Olson decisioned Paddy Young to face Randy Turpin for the title on October 21, 1953, in front of 19,000 fans in Madison Square Garden. Turpin got off to a good start, stunning Olson in the first and winning the first three rounds convincingly. Olson took charge after that and sent Turpin down in the tenth for a nine count. Olson won the title and wept with joy when the decision was announced. He was declared *The Ring*'s Fighter of the Year for 1953.

The next year saw more of the same with successful title defenses against Hall of Famer and welterweight champion Kid Gavilan, Rocky Castellani, and Pierre Langlois. Olson won non-title bouts against Joe Rindone, Jesse Turner, Pedro Gonzales, and Garth Panter. His great year earned him another major pugilistic award: the Boxing Writers Association of America's Edward J Neil Trophy for Fighter of the Year.

In 1955, Olson easily decisioned former light heavyweight champion Joey Maxim at the Cow Palace in San Francisco, and decided to aim for the heavyweight championship held by Rocky Marciano. He needed the light heavyweight title first, and so Olson signed to face champion Archie Moore on June 22 in the Polo Grounds. He won the first two rounds and opened cuts on Moore's face, but in the third, Moore put him down for the count with a right to the jaw. Olson earned $125,000 for the fight but did not see a penny of the winnings because of tax problems.

Olson was about to lose his middleweight title. On December 9, 1955, in Chicago Stadium, Robinson, having emerged from his brief retirement, knocked Olson out in the second round with a left hook. In the rematch, Olson unleashed a solid attack to Robinson's body for three rounds, but fell victim to a Robinson combination in the fourth and was knocked out.

Olson (L) sends a driving right just over the shoulder of Bobby Jones. Jones, holder of both the California welterweight and middleweight titles, dropped a ten-round decision to Olson in San Francisco on August 27, 1951.

At the same time, Olson's personal life came under heavy scrutiny when *Confidential* magazine revealed that he had two wives, Helen and Jane, and ten children between them. Both women knew about the arrangement, but they weren't happy with it. Helen filed for divorce, delivering another financial blow to Olson, though it allowed him to legally marry Jane.

Olson briefly retired after his last loss at Robinson's hands, but returned to the ring on June 18, 1957, with a decision over Maxim. He attempted to move up to heavyweight, but was knocked out in two rounds by Pat McMurtry. On June 6, 1960, Olson decisioned highly regarded light heavyweight contender Mike Holt. Unfortunately, Doug Jones knocked Olson out in his next fight. Olson returned to *The Ring*'s rankings in 1962 as the fifth place light heavyweight contender with a knockout over Lennart Risberg and a draw against Giulio Rinaldi.

In 1964, Olson sandwiched two wins over formidable light heavyweight Wayne Thornton around a loss to contender Johnny Persol. He was then pitted against Hall of Famer Jose Torres for an opportunity to fight for the title held by Willie Pastrano. Olson was knocked out in the first round, ending his title hopes for good. He fought four more times before retiring after a loss to Don Fullmer.

After leaving the ring, Olson worked in California as recreation director for the pre-apprentice program of the Operating Engineers Union. He also worked in public relations for the Teamsters Union and made numerous personal appearances.

A shot to the body staggers Kid Gavilan (L) to the ropes. Gavilan stepped up in weight to challenge Olson for the middleweight crown, but he couldn't withstand the champ's powerful right. Olson took the fifteen-round decision in Chicago on April 2, 1954.

CARLOS ORTIZ

LIGHTWEIGHT

Right-handed; 5'7"; 134–145 lbs.

70 bouts, 2/14/1955 to 9/20/1972

Jr. Welterwt. Champ 1959–60,
Lightwt. Champ 1962–65, 1965–68

Hall of Fame Induction: 1991

Born: 9/9/1936, Ponce, PR

Born in Puerto Rico, Carlos Ortiz first learned to fight on the streets of New York, where his family moved when he was eight. Battling neighborhood toughs who taunted him because of his ethnic heritage, Ortiz developed physical skills, as well as a will to win, which would later help him in the ring. He started boxing as an amateur at the Madison Square Boys Club. Turning professional at the age of eighteen, he won his first 20 fights.

In 1959, Ortiz fought crafty Kenny Lane for the vacant world junior welterweight title. Ortiz had lost to Lane the year before in a ten-round decision in Miami Beach, but this time he avenged the defeat, stopping Lane in the second round. The junior welterweight crown had not been contested in thirteen years and had limited value, but Ortiz defended it three times in 1960. He KO'd Bat-

Ortiz (L) keeps Kenny Lane at bay with a jab. He beat Lane on points to keep his lightweight title on April 11, 1964. The two fighters twice met earlier as junior welterweights, splitting the results.

IN THE RING	WON 61	LOST 7	DRAWS 1	TB 70	KO 30	W 31	WF 0	D 1	KO'd 1	L 6	LF 0	NC 1

Date	Opponent	Site	Result / Rounds		Title	Wt.
1955						
Feb 14	Harry Bell	New York	KO	1	—	—
Feb 28	Morris Hodnett	New York	KO	1	—	—
May 13	Danny Roberts	New York	KO	3	—	—
May 30	Juan Pacheco	New York	KO	2	—	—
Jun 24	Jimmy DeMura	Syracuse, NY	W	6	—	—
Aug 10	Tony DeCola	New York	W	6	—	—
Aug 22	Armand Bush	New York	W	6	—	—
Sep 19	Hector Rodriguez	New York	KO	2	—	—
Oct 3	Leroy Graham	New York	KO	2	—	—
Oct 29	Al Duarte	Boston	KO	4	—	—
Nov 12	Lem Miller	Boston	W	8	—	—
Dec 10	Charley Titone	Paterson, NJ	KO	2	—	133
1956						
Jan 9	Ray Portilla	New York	W	8	—	135
Feb 17	Ray Portilla	New York	W	8	—	139
May 25	Johnny Gorman	New York	W	6	—	138
Jul 30	Tommy Salem	New York	W	10	—	—
Oct 27	Mickey Northrup	Hollywood	W	10	—	—
Dec 15	Phil Kim	Hollywood	TKO	9	—	139
Dec 31	Gale Kerwin	New York	W	10	—	135
1957						
Jan 23	Bobby Rogers	Chicago	W	10	—	136
Mar 2	Lou Filippo	Hollywood	NC	9	—	138
Apr 9	Lou Filippo	Hollywood	KO	7	—	—
May 7	Ike Vaughn	Miami Beach	W	10	—	—
May 29	Felix Chiocca	Chicago	W	10	—	—
Sep 23	Harry Bell	New York	W	10	—	137
1958						
Feb 28	Tommy Tibbs	New York	W	10	—	—
May 9	⑩ Joe Lopes	Hollywood	W	10	—	—
Jun 27	⑩ Johnny Busso	New York	L	10	—	—
Sep 19	⑩ Johnny Busso	New York	W	10	—	137
Oct 28	⑩ Dave Charnley	London	W	10	—	—
Dec 31	⑩ Kenny Lane	Miami Beach	L	10	—	135
1959						
Apr 13	⑩ Len Matthews	Philadelphia	TKO	6	—	—
Jun 12	⑩ Kenny Lane	New York	TKO	2	Won-Vac World-JW	139
1960						
Feb 4	⑩ Battling Torres	Los Angeles	KO	10	Ret-World-JW	137
Jun 15	⑩ Duilio Loi	San Francisco	W	15	Ret-World-JW	137
Sep 1	⑩ Duilio Loi	Milan	L	15	Lost-World-JW	138
1961						
Feb 2	⑩ Cisco Andrade	Los Angeles	W	10	—	—
May 10	♛ Duilio Loi	Milan	L	15	For-World-JW	136
Sep 2	⑩ Doug Vaillant	Miami Beach	W	10	—	139
Nov 18	⑩ Paolo Rosi	New York	W	10	—	—

1962							
Apr 21	♛	Joe Brown★	Las Vegas	W	15	Won-World-L	134
Aug 1	⑩	Arthur Persley	Manila	W	10	—	—
Nov 7	⑩	Kazuo Takayama	Tokyo	W	10	—	—
Dec 3	⑩	Teruo Kosaka	Tokyo	KO	5	Ret-World-L	134
1963							
Apr 7	⑩	Doug Vaillant	San Juan, PR	TKO	13	Ret-World-L	134
Sep 18		Pete Acera	Honolulu	KO	7	—	—
Oct 22		Maurice Cullen	London	W	10	—	—
1964							
Feb 15		Flash Elorde★	Manila	TKO	14	Ret-World-L	135
Apr 11	⑩	Kenny Lane	San Juan	W	15	Ret-World-L	135
Dec 14		Dick Divola	Boston	KO	1	—	—
1965							
Apr 10	⑩	Ismael Laguna★	Panama City	L	15	Lost-World-L	134
Nov 13	♛	Ismael Laguna★	San Juan	W	15	Reg-World-L	135
1966							
Apr 7	⑩	Nicolino Locche	Buenos Aires	D	10	—	138
Jun 20	⑩	Johnny Bizzarro	Pittsburgh	TKO	12	Ret-World-L	135
Oct 22	⑩	Sugar Ramos★	Mexico City	TKO	5	Ret-World-L	134
Nov 28		Flash Elorde★	New York	KO	14	Ret-World-L	135
1967							
Jul 1	⑩	Sugar Ramos★	San Juan	TKO	4	Ret-World-L	135
Aug 16	⑩	Ismael Laguna★	New York	W	15	Ret-World-L	135
1968							
Jun 29	⑩	Carlos Teo Cruz	Santo Domingo, D.R.	L	15	Lost-World-L	135
1969							
Nov 21		Edmundo Leite	New York	W	10	—	—
1971							
Dec 1		Jimmy Ligon	Las Vegas	KO	3	—	—
1972							
Jan 8		Bill Whittenburg	Miami	KO	7	—	145
Jan 20		Terry Rondeau	Portland, ME	TKO	4	—	139
Jan 31		Ivelaw Eastman	Waltham, MA	TKO	2	—	144
Feb 19		Leo DiFiore	San Juan	KO	2	—	—
Mar 20		Junior Varney	Ponce, PR	KO	2	—	—
May 1		Greg Potter	Los Angeles	W	10	—	142
Jun 3		Gerardo Ferrat	Chicago	KO	3	—	—
Aug 1		Johnny Copeland	Oklahoma City, OK	KO	3	—	—
Sep 20	⑩	Ken Buchanan★	New York	TKO'd	6	—	—

tling Torres in Los Angeles and won a fifteen-round decision over Italian Duilio Loi. Months later, Ortiz lost the belt to Loi on a controversial decision in Loi's hometown of Milan. Ortiz faced Loi in Milan again in 1961 and again lost a fifteen-round decision.

But for Ortiz, a much more worthy goal was the lightweight title. In 1962, he got his chance, facing Joe ("Old Bones") Brown in a nationally televised match in Las Vegas. Ortiz devised a strategy for the fight which involved peppering Brown with left jabs and avoiding a slugfest with the seasoned veteran. The strategy worked to perfection, and Ortiz won a lopsided decision.

He maintained the lightweight championship until 1965 when he lost a decision to Ismael Laguna. Ortiz regained the title the following year, with a deci-

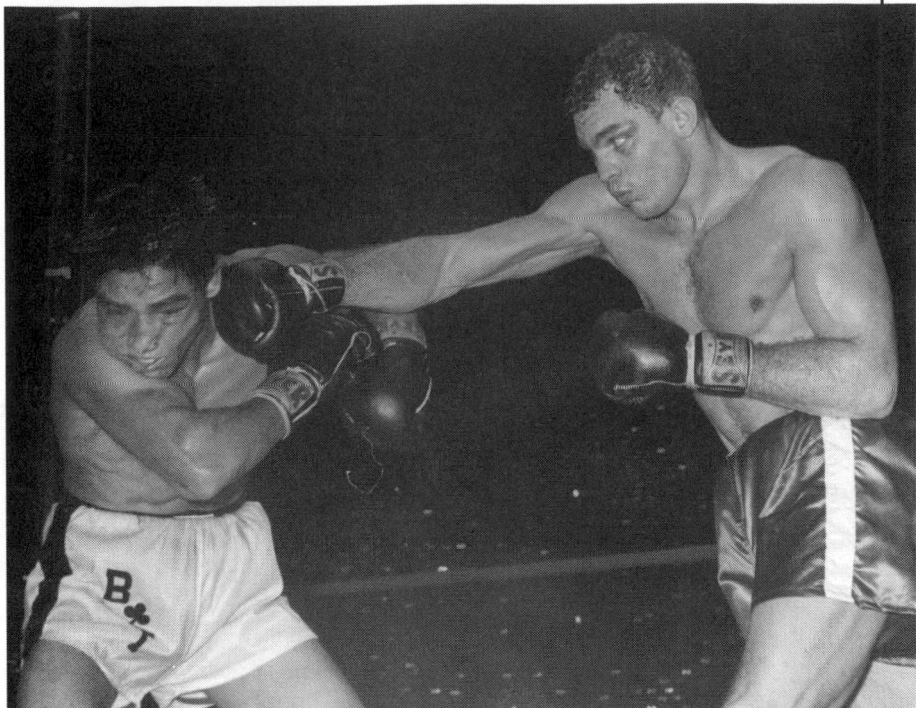

Ortiz (R) scorches Battling Torres with an overhand right in his first title defense on February 4, 1960. Ortiz was the first junior welterweight champion (140-pound limit) to campaign in thirteen years.

sion over Laguna and held it until 1968 when he lost a controversial split decision to Carlos Teo Cruz in Cruz's native Dominican Republic. Ortiz retired briefly, then made a comeback in 1971 and 1972 which ended in defeat at the hands
of former champion lightweight Ken Buchanan.

FIXES

The Sweet Science has often been tainted by talk of fixed fights. While the vast
majority of bouts are on the level, some matches have certainly been rigged for the
benefit of gamblers.

• In Tom Sharkey's nine-round win over Jim Corbett, the Corbett corner-man who
jumped in the ring causing a loss by foul was apparently a plant on the Sharkey
camp's payroll.

• Was he bribed? Wild West legend Wyatt Earp was refereeing a Tom Sharkey–Bob
Fitzsimmons bout in 1896 and disqualified a legitimate knock-out punch by Fitzsimmons, giving the victory to Tom Sharkey as a win by foul.

• Jake LaMotta admitted to having taken a dive, in exchange for a
future title shot opportunity, in his four-round TKO loss to Billy Fox.

RINGFACT

MANUEL ORTIZ

BANTAMWEIGHT

Right-handed; 5'4"; 112–137 lbs.

127 bouts, 2/25/1938 to 12/10/1955

Managers: Noel Johnson 1938–1941, Tommy Farmer and Johnny Rogers 1941–1951

Bantamweight Champion 1942–1947, 1947–1950

Hall of Fame Induction: 1996

Born: 7/2/1916, Corona, CA

Died: 5/31/1970

Twice bantamweight champ, Manuel Ortiz defended his title more times than any other champion except Joe Louis. Born in California, Ortiz left school for work after one year of high school. At nineteen, he attended an amateur boxing match. When one of the scheduled fighters failed to appear, Ortiz's friends persuaded him to enter the ring. He knocked down his opponent on the way to a victory. Thus encouraged, Ortiz began training for an amateur career. He won the Southern California amateur flyweight title, the California Golden Gloves, and a national amateur title.

Although his professional debut was a loss, Ortiz improved under the direction of Noel Johnson. Within two years, he compiled a 17-9 record, with a knockout win over Jackie Jurich, and a fourth-place flyweight ranking from *The Ring*.

In 1941, Ortiz hired manager Tommy Farmer. Farmer coached Ortiz, seconded him, lived with him during training, and cooked his meals. Moving up to bantamweight, Ortiz was rated second-best contender for the title held by Lou Salica. In August 1942, a fight with Salica—and the title—went to Ortiz but, because the bout lasted only twelve rounds, it was not recognized by New York. Ortiz settled this matter in a rematch the next year, with an eleventh-round knockout.

In a non-title bout in Paris on November 14, 1949, Ortiz (L) has Theo Medina in trouble. Ortiz took the ten-round decision.

IN THE RING	WON 96	LOST 28	DRAWS 3	TB 127	KO 49	W 47	WF 0	D 3	KO'd 1	L 27	LF 0

Date	Opponent	Site	Result / Rounds		Title	Wt.
1938						
Feb 25	⑩ Benny Goldberg	Hollywood	L	4	—	—
Mar 25	Frenchy Savidan	Hollywood	W	4	—	—
Apr 14	Serio Mendoza	Hollywood	W	4	—	—
May 3	General Padilla	Los Angeles	KO	4	—	—
May 17	Santos Lugo	Los Angeles	KO	4	—	—
Jun 3	Sammy LaPorte	Hollywood	W	4	—	—
Jun 24	Frenchy Savidan	Hollywood	W	4	—	—
Jul 5	Pablo Dano	Los Angeles	L	6	—	—
Aug 5	⑩ Benny Goldberg	Hollywood	W	6	—	—
Aug	Tony Navarro	El Centro, CA	KO	3	—	—
Sep 30	Richie Lemos	Hollywood	W	6	—	—
Oct 21	Richie Lemos	Hollywood	W	10	—	—
Nov 8	⑩ David Young	Los Angeles	L	10	—	—
Nov	⑩ Benny Goldberg	Hollywood	L	10	—	—
Dec 6	Bernie Reyes	Los Angeles	W	10	—	—
1939						
Jan 2	⑩ Small Montana	Stockton, CA	L	10	—	—
Feb	Donnie Maes	El Centro	L	10	—	—
Feb	Ken Martinez	El Centro	KO	3	—	—
Mar 14	⑩ Jackie Jurich	San Jose, CA	TKO	7	—	—
Apr 11	Tommy Cobb	San Jose	W	10	—	—
May	Sammy LaPorte	El Centro	KO	7	—	—
Jun 9	⑩ Jackie Jurich	Hollywood	L	10	—	—
Aug	Bobby Leyvas	Yuma, AZ	L	10	—	—
Sep 15	⑩ Lou Salica	Hollywood	L	10	—	—
Oct 26	Horace Mann	San Jose	W	10	—	—
Dec	Cyril Josephs	San Jose	KO	5	—	—
Dec 14	Elwood Romero	Sacramento, CA	W	10	—	—
1940						
Jan 30	♛ Little Dado	Stockton	D	10	—	—
Mar 22	Andy Vasquez	Hollywood	TKO	5	—	—
Apr 5	⑩ Jackie Jurich	Hollywood	KO	9	—	—
Apr 20	Panchito Villa	Mexico City	W	10	—	—
May 18	Panchito Villa	Mexico City	L	10	—	—
Oct 9	Panchito Villa	Mexico City	KO	7	—	—
1941						
Jan 10	⑩ Rush Dalma	Hollywood	KO	3	—	—
Feb	Jose Robleto	Calexito, CA	TKO	6	—	—
Mar 14	⑩ Lupe Cardoza	Sacramento	KO	9	—	—
Apr 4	⑩ Carlos Chavez	Hollywood	D	10	—	—
May 20	Jesus Llanes	El Centro	W	10	—	—
May 9	⑩ Carlos Chavez	Hollywood	W	10	—	118
Jun 6	Lou Transparenti	Hollywood	KO	7	—	—
Aug 8	⑩ Tony Olivera	Hollywood	L	10	—	—
Nov 7	Donnie Maes	Hollywood	W	10	—	—
Nov 21	Johnny Grady	San Diego	W	10	—	—
1942						
Jan 2	⑩ Tony Olivera	Hollywood	W	10	Won-CA State-B	117
Mar 6	Little Pancho	Hollywood	TKO	7	—	—

Date		Opponent	Location	Result	Rds	Title	Rating
May 8	⑩	Kenny Lindsay	Hollywood	KO	6	—	—
May 30	⑩	Leonardo Lopez	Tijuana	TKO	—	—	—
Jul 3		Elwood Romero	Hollywood	TKO	6	—	—
Aug 7	♛	Lou Salica	Hollywood	W	12	Won-World-B	116
Sep 25		Bobby Carroll	San Diego	KO	5	—	121
Oct 9		Nat Corum	Portland, OR	W	10	—	121
Oct 30		Nat Corum	Hollywood	KO	6	—	—
1943							
Jan 1		Kenny Lindsay	Portland	W	10	Ret-World-B	117
Jan 27		Georgie Freitas	Oakland	TKO	10	Ret-World-B	117
Mar 10	⑩	Lou Salica	Oakland	TKO	11	Ret-World-B	117
Apr 2		Pedro Ramirez	Hollywood	KO	6	—	—
Apr 16		Jose Robleto	San Diego	W	10	—	123
Apr 28		Lupe Cardoza	Fort Worth, TX	KO	6	Ret-World-B	118
May 26		Jose Robleto	Long Beach, CA	W	15	Ret-World-B	118
Jun 25	⑩	Tony Olivera	Hollywood	TKO	7	—	—
Jul 12		Jose Robleto	Seattle	TKO	7	Ret-World-B	117
Aug 13	⑩	Leonardo Lopez	Hollywood	W	10	—	—
Sep 4		Filio Gonzalez	Mexico City	W	10	—	—
Oct 1	⑩	Leonardo Lopez	Hollywood	KO	4	Ret-World-B	117
Nov 23	⑩	Benny Goldberg	Los Angeles	W	15	Ret-World-B	117
1944							
Mar 14	⑩	Ernesto Aguilar	Los Angeles	W	15	Ret-World-B	118
Apr 4	⑩	Tony Olivera	Los Angeles	W	15	Ret-World-B	117
May 19		Pee Wee Lewis	Hollywood	TKO	9	—	124
Jun 29	⑩	Larry Bolvin	Boston	W	10	—	125
Jul 17		Willie Pep★	Boston, MA	L	10	—	—
Aug 29	⑩	Enrique Bolanos	Los Angeles	TKO	6	—	123
Sep 12	⑩	Luis Castillo	Los Angeles	TKO	4	Ret-World-B	118
Sep 30	⑩	Carlos Chavez	Hollywood	W	10	—	123
Nov 14	⑩	Luis Castillo	Los Angeles	KO	9	Ret-World-B	117
Nov 22	⑩	Lorenzo Safora	Oakland	W	10	—	122
1945							
Jan 12		Jose ("Baby") Gonzalez	Hollywood	W	10	—	123
Jan 26		Bert White	San Diego	KO	7	—	123
Nov 2		Horace Leftwich	San Diego	W	10	—	—
Nov 12		Jose Andreas	Dallas	W	10	—	—
Nov 20		Proctor Heinold	San Antonio, TX	W	10	—	—
1946							
Feb 15		Eli Golindo	Hollywood	KO	4	—	123
Feb 25	⑩	Luis Castillo	San Francisco	KO	13	Ret-World-B	117
Mar 19	⑩	Carlos Chavez	Los Angeles	D	15	—	122
Apr 22		Horace Leftwich	San Francisco	W	10	—	—
May 18		Kenny Lindsay	Hollywood	TKO	5	Ret-World-B	118
Jun 10		Jackie Jurich	San Francisco	KO	11	Ret-World-B	118
Jul 12	⑩	David Young	Honolulu	KO	7	—	122
Oct 22	⑩	Carlos Chavez	Los Angeles	L	12	—	125
1947							
Jan 6	⑩	Harold Dade	San Francisco	L	15	Lost-World-B	118
Mar 11	♛	Harold Dade	Los Angeles	W	15	Reg-World-B	117
May 30	⑩	David Young	Honolulu	W	15	Ret-World-B	118
Oct 15		Manny Ortega	El Paso, TX	TKO'd	8	—	—
Dec 20	⑩	Tirso Del Rosario	Manila, Philippines	W	15	Ret-World-B	118
1948							
Apr 27		Joey Dolan	Portland	TKO	6	—	—
May 25	⑩	Henry Davis	Honolulu	W	10	—	—

Date		Opponent	Location	Result	Rounds	Title	Wt
Jul 4	⑩	Memo Valero	Mexicali, Mexico	TKO	8	Ret-World-B	117
Sep 28		Lauro Salas	Los Angeles	L	10	—	133
Oct 29		Buddy Jacklich	Hollywood	KO	8	—	—
Dec 14		Maxie Docusen	Los Angeles	L	10	—	—
1949							
Jan 1		Jose Cardenas	Mexicali	W	10	—	—
Mar 1		Dado Marino	Honolulu	W	15	Ret-World-B	118
Mar 29	⑩	Henry Davis	Honolulu	L	10	—	—
Apr 26	⑩	Lauro Salas	Los Angeles	W	10	—	122
May 15		Baby Mickey	Sonora, Mexico	KO	5	—	—
May 20		Pinky Peralta	Mexico City	KO	5	—	—
Jun 25		Roberto Coaury	Veracruz, Mexico	L	10	—	—
Jun 29		Roberto Carvajal	Merida, Mexico	W	10	—	—
Jul 16	⑩	Memo Valero	Mexico City	KO	7	—	—
Jul 23		Tony Vasquez	Tampico, Mexico	KO	4	—	—
Aug 29		Jimmy Cooper	Washington, DC	L	10	—	—
Oct 3	⑩	Ronnie Clayton	Manchester, England	L	10	—	—
Oct 26	⑩	Jackie Paterson	Glasgow, Scotland	W	10	—	—
Nov 14	⑩	Theo Medina	Paris	W	10	—	—
1950							
Mar 7		Harold Dade	Los Angeles	W	10	—	132
May 31	⑩	Vic Toweel	Johannesburg	L	15	Lost-World-B	117
Nov 10		Jackie McCoy	Hollywood	W	10	—	—
Dec 5	⑩	Eddie Chavez	San Jose	L	10	—	—
1951							
Jan 26	⑩	Lauro Salas	Hollywood	L	10	—	—
Mar 3		Bonnie Espinosa	Manila	KO	8	—	—
Jun 2		Tirso del Rosario	Manila	L	10	—	—
Jul 17		Jackie Graves	Los Angeles	L	10	—	—
Sep 3	⑩	Eddie Chavez	Santa Clara, CA	L	10	—	—
1953							
Mar 6		Manuel Hernandez	Mexicali	TKO	6	—	—
1955							
Jun 10		Manuel Hernandez	Ensenada, Mexico	KO	4	—	—
Jul 22		Memo Valero	Mexicali	KO	3	—	—
Aug 16		Papelero Sanchez	Mexicali	KO	3	—	—
Dec 10		Enrique Esqueda	Mexico City	L	10	—	—

He defended his title eight times in 1943 and four times in 1944. That year, he also won a decision over Larry Bolvin and lost another to Hall of Famer Willie Pep. After a reduced schedule in 1945 because of military service, Ortiz successfully defended his title four more times in 1946. At the beginning of 1947, Harold Dade beat Ortiz to take the bantamweight title. Two months later Ortiz recovered it by decision. That year he also suffered the only knockout of his career, dished out by Manny Ortega.

Ortiz defended his crown far less frequently during his second reign, fighting only four title challengers in three years, before facing Vic Toweel in 1950. Twelve years younger than Ortiz and fighting in his hometown of Johannesburg, South Africa, Toweel took the title in a fifteen-round decision.

Ortiz continued to fight for five more years before hanging up his gloves at 42. In retirement, he owned a farm, a ranch and a nightclub, but when these ventures failed, he worked at a series of odd jobs until his death from a liver ailment on May 31, 1970.

LASZLO PAPP

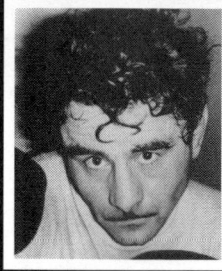

MIDDLEWEIGHT

Left-handed; 5'5½"; 160 lbs.
29 bouts, 5/19/1957 to 10/11/1964
1948 Olympic Middleweight
Gold Medalist
1952, 1956 Olympic Light
Middleweight Gold Medalist
Hall of Fame Induction: 2001
Born: 3/25/1926, Budapest, Hungary

Laszlo Papp had one of the most unusual careers of any fighter in the International Boxing Hall of Fame. As a youth in Hungary, Papp initially preferred soccer, track, and wrestling to boxing. After much cajoling, his friends persuaded him to join them at the Budapest Railwayman's Club to learn the sport. Papp quickly displayed a natural flair for fighting. Club officials decided to keep him under wraps by restricting him to fights in the outlying provinces. On October 6, 1945, a tournament was held at Budapest's Sports Hall to select a team to represent Hungary in an upcoming series of matches against Austria. Papp was asked to step in at the last minute to fill a cancellation, and he knocked out his opponent in the second round to earn a place on the Hungarian national team. Papp easily won his bout in Austria, starting a long career of international triumphs.

Papp had 50 amateur boxing wins (47 by knockout) before he represented Hungary as a middleweight at the 1948 London Olympics. He won all five of his matches and the gold medal.

American medalists usually turn pro shortly after their Olympic victories, to cash in on their fame. Because Papp's native Hungary was, at that time, a part of the Soviet-ruled Eastern Bloc, he wasn't permitted to compete professionally. Relegated to the ranks of amateur pugilism, Papp con-

Boxing Illustrated correspondent Jose Alvarez congratulates Papp after his 1963 eighth-round knockout of Luis Folledo in Madrid.

IN THE RING	WON 27	LOST 0	DRAWS 2	TB 29	KO 15	W 12	WF 0	D 2	KO'd 0	L 0	LF 0

Date	Opponent	Site	Result / Rounds		Title	Wt.
1957						
May 19	Alois Brand	Cologne, Germany	W	4	—	—
Jun 15	Herbert Sowa	Dortmund, Germany	W	4	—	—
Jun 28	Gerhard Moll	Hamburg, Germany	W	6	—	—
1958						
Oct 17	Hugo Koehler	Vienna	KO	6	—	—
Dec 15	Francois Anewy	Paris	KO	3	—	—
1959						
Feb 9	Andre Drille	Paris	W	10	—	—
Mar 16	Jean Ruellet	Vienna	W	10	—	—
Apr 13	Germinal Ballarin	Paris	D	10	—	—
Sep 10	Bill Tate	Vienna	KO	3	—	—
1960						
Feb 10	Lou Perry	Vienna	W	10	—	—
Sep 23	Erich Walter	Vienna	KO	9	—	—
Oct 1	Mohammed Boudib	Agram, Yugoslavia	KO	7	—	—
Dec 26	Giancarlo Garbelli	Milan, Italy	D	10	—	—
1961						
Feb 20	Sauveur Chiocca	Paris	W	10	—	—
Apr 8	Moussa Sangare	Vienna	W	10	—	—
Sep 10	Peter Mueller	Cologne	TKO	8	—	—
Oct 13	Peter Mueller	Vienna	TKO	4	—	—
Dec 2	Michel Francois	Frankfurt	KO	2	—	—
1962						
Mar 21	Ralph ("Tiger") Jones	Vienna	W	10	—	—
May 16	Christian Christensen	Vienna	TKO	7	Won-Eur-M	160
Nov 19	Hippolyte Annex	Paris	TKO	9	Ret-Eur-M	160
1963						
Feb 6	George Aldridge	Vienna	KO	15	Ret-Eur-M	160
Mar 30	Peter Mueller	Dortmund	TKO	4	Ret-Eur-M	160
May 17	Randy Sandy	Vienna	W	10	—	—
Jun 14	Eddie Cotton	Cologne	KO	7	—	—
Dec 6	Luis Folledo	Madrid	TKO	8	Ret-Eur-M	—
1964						
Mar 13	Harry Scott	Vienna	W	10	—	—
Jul 2	Christian Christensen	Copenhagen	KO	4	Ret-Eur-M	160
Oct 9	Mick Leahy	Vienna	W	15	Ret-Eur-M	160

tinued to accumulate honors, including two victories at the European amateur championships and three wins at the World Student Games.

But Papp made his greatest impact on the boxing scene in the Olympic Games. He slimmed down one weight class and earned two more gold medals as a light middleweight in 1952 and 1956. Times were difficult in Hungary in the early 1950s. Opportunities to train were difficult to secure, and jobs—required even for Olympic-grade athletes—were scarce. Fortunately, Papp found employment that helped build up his strength and endurance. At work, his duties included carrying heavy packages up and down stairs.

In the semifinals of the latter competition, Papp decisioned Zbiginiew Pietrykowski, who had stopped him short of the three-round amateur limit for the first time in his career earlier that year in Warsaw. He also decisioned future light heavyweight champion and Hall of Famer Jose Torres in the finals. The short-lived Hungarian revolt against Soviet occupation took place just before the Hungarian team left for the 1956 Olympics in Melbourne, Australia. Papp was a devoted Roman Catholic and was deeply saddened by the death and suffering resulting from the repression of the Hungarian revolt. His belief was that his participation in the 1956 Olympics, at a time when his nation was experiencing such trauma, would help turn the world's attention to Hungary's plight. Though a third of the Hungarian team defected to the West after the Games, Papp was among the athletes who returned to their homeland.

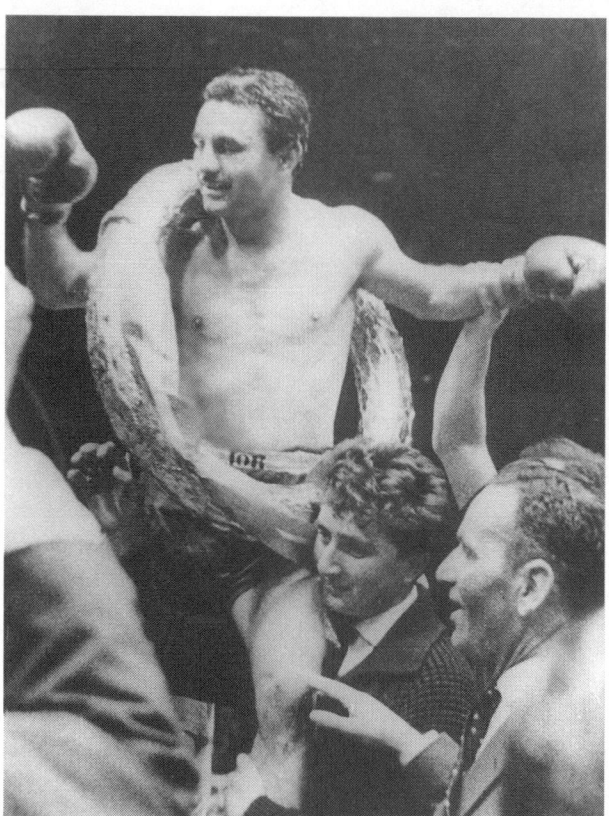

Papp stood alone as the first Olympic boxer to win three gold medals. Since then, Cubans Teofilo Stevenson (in 1972, 1976, and 1980) and Felix Savon (in 1992, 1996, and 2000) have matched this Herculean feat, but it has never been surpassed. After winning three gold medals, Papp wished to test his skill against professional boxers, who were naturally barred from Olympic competition. In an unprecedented move, Hungary allowed Papp to compete professionally. Through his ring earnings, or perhaps from a more direct government grant, Papp acquired the use of a villa on the Danube and an ex-

Hoisted onto his supporters' shoulders like the heroes of old, Papp joyously celebrates his victory over Christian Christensen in Vienna on May 16, 1962, to take the European middleweight title.

pensive car. His wife and son were allowed to travel much more frequently than most Hungarians, shuttling between Budapest and Vienna, where Papp trained.

In the ring, Papp met his first professional opponent on May 19, 1957, winning a four-round decision over Alois Brand in Cologne, Germany. At 31, Papp was considered old for the sport, especially since he was just making his debut. He won his next six fights, including a wild brawl with Andre Drille who knocked Papp down twice before succumbing to the Hungarian. Papp floored Drille down five times to win the ten-round decision. On April 13, 1959, Papp faced Germinal Ballarin in Paris. Although most observers believed that he won seven of ten rounds, the fight was called a draw. Of greater consequence was a broken hand that Papp suffered during the fight. He did not fight again for six months. The next year, Papp defeated American Lou Perry, but he broke his left hand again, this time so severely that he required surgery. Though he was out of action for another seven months, he won his first two fights before recording a draw against Giancarlo Garbelli in Milan, though this may have been the result of hometown scoring.

On March 21, 1962, Papp faced his first well-known American opponent, Ralph ("Tiger") Jones, a former middleweight contender who had once beaten Sugar Ray Robinson. Papp knocked Jones down three times to win an easy decision. In his next fight, at the Vienna City Hall on May 16, Papp fought European champion Christian Christensen for the latter's title. Each man was cut in the second round, yet Papp held the advantage in the first three, scoring with right hooks. Indeed, his right hook was an effective weapon for the left-handed Papp, who was able to lead with both hands and was an effective boxer/puncher. Christensen won the fourth round, but in the fifth Papp floored him with a hard right hook, and in the seventh another blow opened a cut near Christensen's eye. At the end of the round, the referee stopped the fight at the orders of the ringside doctor. Papp was champion.

The next year, he won all five of his fights, including a knockout victory over ranked contender Luis Folledo. He advanced to the fourth contender spot for 1963, and held the position in 1964, defeating ranked contender Mick Leahy.

In 1964, there was some concern that Papp would be forced to abandon his career to coach the Hungarian Olympic team, but he was allowed to continue fighting. In early 1965, it appeared that he might at last receive a title shot against middleweight champion Joey Giardello. Earlier rumored fights against champions Paul Pender and Dick Tiger had fallen through. Before a date was set for the Giardello match, Papp was ordered back to Hungary. Officially, it was announced that his "professional career would not be compatible with our [Hungary's] socialist principles." Speculation as to the reasons for the decision ranged from envy of his financial success and his refusal to coach the '64 Olympic team to worry that, at 38, he might not remain undefeated for much longer. Papp regretted the decision, stating, "I'm very sorry about all this. I was hoping they would change their minds, but the ruling was definite—I am not supposed to box as a professional anymore."

In retirement, Papp served for many years as coach of the Hungarian boxing team.

W I L L I E   P A S T R A N O
Willie The Wisp

LIGHT HEAVYWEIGHT

Right handed; 5'11¾"; 143–191 lbs.

84 bouts, 9/10/1951 to 3/30/1965

Managers: Whitey Esneault and Angelo Dundee

Light Heavyweight Champ 1963–65

Hall of Fame Induction: 2001

Born: 11/27/1935, New Orleans

Named: Wilfred Raleigh Pastrano

Died: 12/6/1997

Willie Pastrano was perhaps the foremost practitioner of the busy jabbing, constant-motion "New Orleans–style" of fighting. Pastrano was obese as a youngster and was mercilessly taunted and beaten by neighborhood kids. He was known as "Fatmeat" for weighing 200 pounds at age ten. When he came home in tears, his father forced him to fight his tormentors. Ralph Dupas, Pastrano's friend and future world junior middleweight champ, took him to Whitey Esneault's boxing gym to get him in shape and teach him how to fight. By the time he was thirteen, Pastrano had slimmed down to featherweight size. At fourteen, he was knocked down in a street fight and vowed to give up fighting if he were ever knocked down again.

Pastrano turned pro at the age of fifteen with a four-round decision over Domingo Rivera in New Orleans on September 10, 1951. After five wins and a draw with Alvin Pellegrini, Esneault sent Pastrano to Angelo Dundee to train in Miami Beach. Fighting almost exclusively in New Orleans and Miami Beach, he compiled a 21-4-3 record through 1953, but in 1954 he won all seven of his fights, including decisions over Bobby Dykes and the tough Jackie LaBua.

Though Pastrano was light for the division, Dundee usually matched him with heavyweights, where the purses were larger. In 1955, Pastrano had another banner year, winning decisions over Hall of Famer Joey Maxim, ranked light heavyweight Chuck Spieser, and former ranked heavyweight Rex Layne. 1956 saw more of the same, with decisions over Spieser, future heavyweight contender Pat McMurtry, and

Hall of Famer Angelo Dundee (R) started training Pastrano at Miami Beach in the summer of 1952.

IN THE RING	WON 63	LOST 13	DRAWS 8	TB 84	KO 14	W 49	WF 0	D 8	KO'd 2	L 11	LF 0

Date	Opponent	Site	Result / Rounds		Title	Wt.
1951						
Sep 10	Domingo Rivera	New Orleans	W	4	—	—
Sep 17	Frank Speed	New Orleans	W	4	—	—
Oct 1	Jimmy Connino	New Orleans	W	4	—	—
Oct 22	Domingo Rivera	New Orleans	W	4	—	—
1952						
Apr 1	Alvin Boudreaux	New Orleans	W	4	—	144
Apr 21	Alvin Pellegrini	New Orleans	D	4	—	143
Jul 1	Buzz Brown	Miami Beach	KO	2	—	—
Jul 8	John Chaney	Miami Beach	W	6	—	—
Jul 22	Al McCoy	Miami Beach	KO	2	—	—
Jul 28	Jim Carter	Pensacola, FL	KO	4	—	—
Aug 5	Sonny Luciano	Miami Beach	W	8	—	—
Aug 19	Sonny Luciano	Miami Beach	W	8	—	—
Sep 8	Johnny Capitano	New Orleans	W	6	—	—
Oct 6	Alvin Pellegrini	New Orleans	L	6	—	—
Oct 14	Lonnie Rylant	New Orleans	KO	3	—	—
Nov 17	Alvin Pellegrini	New Orleans	W	6	—	—
Nov 24	Alvin Boudreaux	New Orleans	KO	2	—	—
Dec 15	Alvin Pellegrini	New Orleans	D	8	—	—
1953						
Jan 26	Alfredo LaGrutta	New Orleans	W	8	—	—
Feb 24	Emerson Butcher	New Orleans	W	8	—	—
Mar 3	Chic Boucher	Miami Beach	KO	3	—	—
Mar 16	Roger Trevino	New Orleans	W	8	—	—
Apr 6	Chato Hernandez	New Orleans	W	8	—	—
May 25	Johnny Cesario	New Orleans	L	8	—	—
Jul 14	Del Flanagan	Miami Beach	L	8	—	—
Sep 22	Elmer Beltz	Miami Beach	D	10	—	—
Oct 5	Elmer Beltz	New Orleans	W	8	—	—
Nov 30	Italo Scortichini	New Orleans	L	10	—	—
1954						
Mar 29	Jimmy Martinez	New Orleans	W	10	—	—
Apr 12	Jacques Royer-Crecy	New Orleans	W	10	—	—
Jun 18	Tommy Hatcher	Mobile, AL	KO	1	—	—
Aug 9	Tommy Bazzano	New Orleans	KO	8	—	—
Aug 24	Jimmy Martinez	Miami Beach	W	10	—	—
Sep 14	Jackie LaBua	Miami Beach	W	10	—	—
Nov 23	Bobby Dykes	Miami Beach	W	10	—	—
1955						
Mar 1	Tony Johnson	Miami Beach	W	10	—	—
Mar 23	Al Andrews	Chicago	W	10	—	—
Apr 22	Willie Troy	Chicago	D	10	—	—
Jun 28	⑩ Joey Maxim★	New Orleans	W	10	—	—
Jul 27	⑩ Chuck Spieser	Chicago	W	10	—	—
Oct 3	Paddy Young	New Orleans	W	10	—	—
Nov 18	Joey Rowan	New York	W	10	—	—
Dec 19	⑩ Rex Layne	New Orleans	W	10	—	185

1956

Jan 27	⑩	Chuck Spieser	Miami Beach	D	10	—	182
Apr 4		Johnny Arthur	New Orleans	W	10	—	—
May 30	⑩	Chuck Spieser	New Orleans	W	10	—	182
Aug 24		Pat McMurtry	Tacoma, WA	W	10	—	186
Dec 26		Charlie Norkus	Miami Beach	W	10	—	189

1957

Feb 20		John Holman	Louisville, KY	W	10	—	187
May 14		Neal Welch	Miami Beach	W	10	—	—
Jun 11		Roy Harris	Houston	L	10	—	—
Sep 10		George Peyton	Miami Beach	KO	8	—	191
Oct 22		Dick Richardson	London	W	10	—	188
Nov 27	⑩	Willie Besmanoff	Miami Beach	W	10	—	—

1958

Feb 25	⑩	Brian London	London	W	10	—	—
Apr 21		Joe Bygraves	Leicester, England	W	10	—	188
Jun 15		Franco Cavicchi	Bologna, Italy	W	10	—	—
Aug 25		Tommy Thompson	Colombus, OH	KO	4	—	186
Sep 30	⑩	Brian London	London	KO'd	5	—	189

1959

Feb 24		Joe Erskine	London	L	10	—	—
Jul 24		Alonzo Johnson	Louisville	L	10	—	—
Aug 30		Tom Davis	Knoxville, TN	KO	4	—	—
Dec 7		Charley Pavlis	Tampa, FL	W	10	—	180

1960

Jan 20		Jerry Luedee	Miami Beach	W	10	—	177
Apr 9		George Kartalian	Augusta, GA	KO	6	—	—
May 6		Alonzo Johnson	Louisville	W	10	—	—
Jun 1	⑩	Sonny Ray	Chicago	W	10	—	—
Sep 16	⑩	Chic Calderwood	Glasgow, Scotland	L	10	—	—
Dec 27	⑩	Jesse Bowdry	Miami Beach	L	10	—	—

1961

Aug 6		Lennart Risberg	Stockholm	D	12	—	—

1962

May 1		Tom McNeeley	Boston	W	10	—	—
May 28	⑩	Archie Moore★	Los Angeles	D	10	—	—
Jun 25		Billy Ryan	New Orleans	W	10	—	—
Sep 8		Rodolfo Diaz	Miami Beach	W	10	—	184

1963

Feb 9	⑩	Wayne Thornton	New York	L	10	—	—
Mar 23	⑩	Wayne Thornton	New York	D	10	—	175
May 4	⑩	Wayne Thornton	Las Vegas	W	10	—	—
Jun 1	♛	Harold Johnson★	Las Vegas	W	15	Won-World-LH	174
Aug 31		Ollie Wilson	Jacksonville, FL	W	10	—	—
Sep 20	⑩	Gregorio Peralta	Miami Beach	L	10	—	179
Nov 30		Mike Holt	Johannesburg	W	10	—	—

1964

Apr 10	⑩	Gregorio Peralta	New Orleans	KO	6	Ret-World-LH	174
Nov 30	⑩	Terry Downes	Manchester, England	KO	11	Ret-World-LH	174

1965

Mar 30	⑩	Jose Torres★	New York	KO'd	9	Lost-World-LH	174

former contender Charlie Norkus. The next year he met Roy ("Cut and Shoot") Harris, with a strong possibility that the winner of the fight would get a title shot against heavyweight champ Floyd Patterson. Pastrano clearly lost the decision.

In 1958, for the first time in his career, Pastrano was stopped within the distance by Brian London, whom he had previously defeated. The referee stopped the fight after five rounds because of a cut on Pastrano's eyelid. He won only six of his next nine fights.

While in Louisville for a fight, Pastrano sparred with a young amateur named Cassius Clay. Afterwards, he told Dundee he would only fight Clay again if he was paid for it. "Angie, this kid's got it. I know it," said Pastrano. Some credit Pastrano with helping Ali develop his distinctive style.

Dundee and Pastrano now decided that he should fight at his more natural weight class of light heavyweight. After stripping Archie Moore of its title, the NBA set up a tournament in which Hall of Famer Harold Johnson would face the winner of a Pastrano–Jesse Bowdry fight for the championship. Pastrano lost a unanimous decision to Bowdry on December 27, 1960, in Miami Beach. Pastrano fought only once in the next sixteen months. In 1962, he fought Archie Moore to a draw.

Light heavyweight champion Johnson now turned to Pastrano after fights with Mauro Mina and Henry Hank fell through because of injuries. Pastrano was reluctant, but when offered $21,500, he agreed to the match, held at the Las Vagas Convention Center on June 1, 1963. Pastrano, a five-to-one underdog, used jabs and occasional rights while moving from side to side to pile up points, sometimes switching to right jabs from a southpaw stance to confuse Johnson. Pastrano won a narrow decision to become the champion.

Pastrano successfully defended his title twice before facing Jose Torres on March 30, 1965, in Madison Square Garden. Torres attacked him from the start and bloodied his nose in the first round, then knocked him down in the sixth.

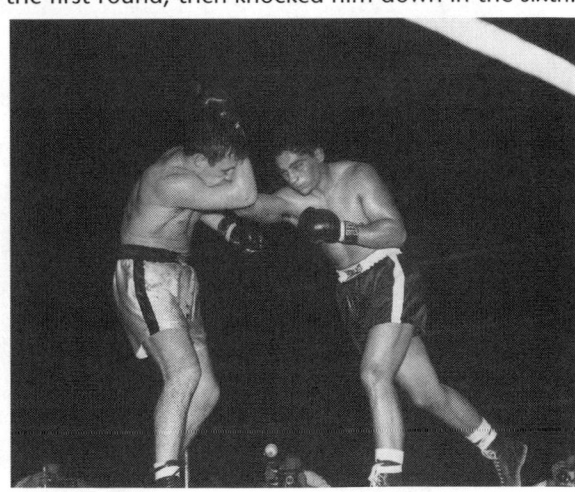

Referee Johnny Lobiano wouldn't allow a dazed Pastrano to answer the bell in the tenth, and true to his word so long ago, he never fought again.

Retirement was not kind to Pastrano, and he developed a serious heroin habit that he finally managed to kick in 1969. Finally, he returned to New Orleans and worked in a youth boxing program, managing a few fighters. Pastrano died of cancer in New Orleans on December 6, 1997.

Pastrano's (R) first New York fight was against Joey Rowan on November 18, 1955. His eyes swollen to slits, Pastrano connects with a solid right.

FLOYD PATTERSON

HEAVYWEIGHT

Right-handed; 6'; 163–200 lbs.

64 bouts, 9/12/1952 to 9/20/1972

Manager: Cus D'Amato

1952 Olympic Middleweight Gold Medalist

Heavyweight Champion 1956-59, 1960-62

Hall of Fame Induction: 1991

Born: 1/4/1935, Waco, NC

Floyd Patterson's pleasant face and demeanor belied the ferocity he showed in the ring. A quiet tiger, Patterson was seldom the favorite in his bouts with other past and future champions, but he was the youngest heavyweight yet to win the title, and he wore the crown twice. He was also among the lightest of the modern heavyweight champions, never topping 200 pounds.

Patterson was born into a large family in North Carolina, but he grew up in one of New York's toughest black ghettos. He got into trouble early in life and spent some time in reform school, where he first learned to box. He was discovered by manager Cus D'Amato, who helped build him into championship material. (D'Amato would later present Mike Tyson to the boxing world.) Patterson

Keeping his left held high, Patterson (L) goes at aging Archie Moore with a straight right. Patterson took the title with a fifth-round KO in this matchup to replace retired champ Rocky Marciano.

IN THE RING	WON 55	LOST 8	DRAWS 1	TB 64	KO 40	W 15	WF 0	D 1	KO'd 5	L 3	LF 0

Date	Opponent	Site	Result / Rounds		Title	Wt.
1952						
Sep 12	Eddie Godbold	New York	TKO	4	—	164
Oct 6	Sammy Walker	Brooklyn	TKO	2	—	166
Oct 21	Lester Johnson	New York	TKO	3	—	165
Dec 19	Lalu Sabotin	Brooklyn	TKO	5	—	167
1953						
Jan 28	Chester Mieszala	Chicago	TKO	5	—	163
Apr 3	Dick Wagner	Brooklyn	W	8	—	166
Jun 1	Gordon Wallace	Brooklyn	TKO	3	—	165
Oct 19	Wes Bascom	Brooklyn	W	8	—	166
Dec 14	Dick Wagner	Brooklyn	TKO	5	—	167
1954						
Feb 15	Yvon Durelle	Brooklyn	W	8	—	167
Mar 30	Sam Brown	Washington, DC	TKO	2	—	167
May 10	Jesse Turner	Brooklyn	W	8	—	167
Jun 7	⑩ Joey Maxim★	Brooklyn	L	8	—	165
Jul 12	Jacques Royer-Crecy	New York	TKO	7	—	168
Aug 2	Tommy Harrison	Brooklyn	TKO	1	—	164
Sep 14	Alvin Williams	Brooklyn	W	8	—	169
Oct 11	Ferdinand Esau	New York	W	8	—	169
Oct 22	Joe Gannon	New York	W	8	—	170
Nov 19	⑩ Jimmy Slade	New York	W	8	—	169
1955						
Jan 7	⑩ Willie Troy	New York	TKO	5	—	166
Jan 17	Don Grant	Brooklyn	TKO	5	—	168
Mar 17	Ferdinand Esau	Oakland	TKO	10	—	174
Jun 23	Yvon Durelle	Newcastle, DE	TKO	5	—	170
Jul 6	Archie McBride	New York	KO	7	—	170
Sep 8	Alvin Williams	Moncton, N.B.	TKO	8	—	177
Sep 29	⑩ Dave Whitlock	San Francisco	TKO	3	—	175
Oct 13	Calvin Brad	Los Angeles	KO	1	—	175
Dec 8	⑩ Jimmy Slade	Los Angeles	TKO	7	—	178
1956						
Mar 12	Jimmy Walls	New Britain, CT	TKO	2	—	183
Apr 10	Alvin Williams	Kansas City	KO	3	—	183
Jun 8	⑩ Tommy Jackson	New York	W	12	—	178
Nov 30	⑩ Archie Moore★	Chicago	KO	5	Won-Vac World-H	182
1957						
Jul 29	⑩ Tommy Jackson	New York	TKO	10	Ret-World-H	184
Aug 22	Pete Rademacher	Seattle	KO	6	Ret-World-H	187
1958						
Aug 18	⑩ Roy Harris	Los Angeles	TKO	13	Ret-World-H	184
1959						
May 1	⑩ Brian London	London	KO	11	Ret-World-H	182
Jun 26	⑩ Ingemar Johansson★	New York	TKO'd	3	Lost-World-H	182
1960						
Jun 20	♛ Ingemar Johansson★	New York	KO	5	Reg-World-H	190
1961						
Mar 13	⑩ Ingemar Johansson★	Miami Beach	KO	6	Ret-World-H	194

Dec 4		Tom McNeeley	Toronto	KO	4	Ret-World-H	188
1962							
Sep 25	⑩	Sonny Liston★	Chicago	KO'd	1	Lost-World-H	189
1963							
Jul 22	♛	Sonny Liston★	Las Vegas	KO'd	1	For-World-H	194
1964							
Jan 6		Dante Amonti	Stockholm	TKO	8	—	192
Jul 5	⑩	Eddie Machen	Stockholm	W	12	—	192
Dec 12		Charles Powell	San Juan, PR	KO	6	—	197
1965							
Feb 1	⑩	George Chuvalo	New York	W	12	—	197
May 14		Tod Herring	Stockholm	TKO	3	—	196
Nov 22	♛	Muhammad Ali★	Las Vegas	TKO'd	12	For-World-H	196
1966							
Sep 29		Henry Cooper	London	KO	4	—	193
1967							
Feb 13		Willie Johnson	Miami Beach	KO	3	—	200
Mar 30		Bill McMurray	Pittsburgh	KO	1	—	197
Jun 9	⑩	Jerry Quarry	Los Angeles	D	10	—	194
Oct 28	⑩	Jerry Quarry	Los Angeles	L	12	—	195
1968							
Sep 14	♛	Jimmy Ellis	Stockholm	L	15	For-WBA-H	188
1970							
Sep 15		Charlie Green	New York	KO	10	—	186
1971							
Jan 16		Levi Forte	Miami Beach	TKO	2	—	192
Mar 29		Roger Russell	Philadelphia	TKO	9	—	190
May 26		Terry Daniels	Cleveland	W	10	—	190
Jul 17		Charley Polite	Erie, PA	W	10	—	190
Aug 21		Vic Brown	Buffalo	W	10	—	189
Nov 23		Charlie Harris	Portland, OR	KO	6	—	195
1972							
Feb 11	⑩	Oscar Bonavena	New York	W	10	—	191
Jul 14		Pedro Agosto	New York	TKO	6	—	193
Sep 20	⑩	Muhammad Ali★	New York	TKO'd	7	For-NABF-H	188

trained and fought in D'Amato's Gramercy Park Gym and compiled a fine amateur record. In 1952, he won a gold medal in the 165-pound class at the Olympic Games in Helsinki.

Patterson then turned professional, fighting as a light heavyweight. He won his first twelve bouts before losing a decision to Hall of Famer Joey Maxim, then went on to win another 23 straight fights. By 1956, he was picked for a shot at the world heavyweight title (which Rocky Marciano had vacated upon his retirement) in a bout with veteran fighter Archie Moore. Moore was older and slower, but he was also a master of the ring who had beaten the best men of his time, and the odds were heavily in his favor. But Patterson had trained hard and he made short work of Moore, knocking him out in the fifth round. At 21, Patterson had become heavyweight champion of the world.

Patterson is often criticized for the string of second-rate challengers he accepted, but D'Amato refused to match him with any fighter controlled by promoter James Norris and his corrupt International Boxing Club. Patterson therefore found few worthy opponents, and D'Amato was forced to import fighters for private bouts with Patterson to keep him sharp. When Swedish champion Ingemar Johansson appeared on the scene in 1959, a genuine championship fight was in the offing. This time, Patterson was the favorite, but after two hard-fought rounds, Johansson caught Patterson with a powerful right cross that put the champ down in the third. Patterson got up and was knocked down again a half-dozen times before referee Ruby Goldstein called an end to the fight.

A year later, Patterson was back, looking to regain the title. Patterson shook off the effects of a Johansson right in round two and, in the fifth, he knocked Johansson down with a sweeping left hook. Johansson got up only to meet a second left hook that put him down for good. Patterson thus became the first man to regain the heavyweight championship. The two fought a third time, in March 1961, in a wild melee in which Patterson was knocked down twice and Johansson once in the first round. Patterson triumphed with a sixth-round knockout. Patterson KO'd Tom McNeeley in December 1961 in a title bout, then faced

a boxer many said he had been avoiding: Sonny Liston. Here D'Amato, who was criticized for being overly protective of his fighter, and Patterson parted ways.

The match with Liston was one of the shortest title fights on record. Within two minutes, Patterson was sprawled on the canvas and Liston was champ. In the rematch, Liston again took Patterson out in one. Patterson had two more shots at the title but lost both, to Muhammad Ali and Jimmy Ellis. After a second loss to Ali in 1972, Patterson retired. His distinctive peek-a-boo style—keeping his gloves high in front of his face—had led him to win 55 fights and two world championships. Since retirement, Patterson has remained active in boxing. His son Tracy has had a very successful career in the ring, largely under his father's management. In 1995, Governor George Pataki appointed Patterson chairman of the New York State Athletic Commission to replace Randy Gordon as the overseer of boxing and wrestling in the Empire State.

Floyd Patterson won his 1952 Olympic gold medal in the 165-pound class by knocking out Romania's Vasile Tita in just 74 seconds.

EUSEBIO PEDROZA

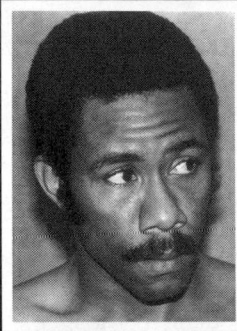

FEATHERWEIGHT

Left handed; 5'9"; 117–137 lbs.

50 bouts, 12/1/1973 to 11/21/1992

Manager: Santiago Del Rio

WBA Featherweight Champion 1978–85

Hall of Fame Induction: 1999

Born: 3/2/1953, Panama City

One of the top featherweight fighters of the 1970s and 80s, Eusebio Pedroza held his WBA featherweight championship title from 1978 to 1985, successfully defending it an impressive nineteen times.

Pedroza grew up in the poor Maranon neighborhood of Panama City. He boxed professionally by age twenty, winning his first bout with a knockout victory over Julio Garcia. Competing as a bantamweight, he won fourteen of his first fifteen fights.

Pedroza received a title shot against WBA bantamweight champion Alfonso Zamora in Mexicali, Mexico, April 3, 1976. Zamora, champion and 1972 Olympic silver medalist at only 22, stood undefeated and had won all his 24 fights by knockout. Although at 5'9" Pedroza was seven inches taller than his opponent and faster, in spite of this size difference, he could not defeat Zamora. The champ knocked Pedroza out in the second round with his much-vaunted left hook.

By 1978, Pedroza had moved up to featherweight, and on April 15, 1978, he again went up against a champion, this time WBA featherweight title-holder Cecilio Lastra. The Lastra–Pedroza matchup was held in Panama City, before more than 12,000 Pedroza fans; he did not disappoint them. Pedroza beat Lastra onto the canvas in the third round, closed his eye later in the same round, and floored him twice in the thirteenth, ending the fight and winning the title.

Pedroza (R) unleases a combination to the head of then-undefeated Bernard Taylor in their October 16, 1982, meeting in Charlotte, NC. Just starting his third year as a pro, Taylor took champion Pedroza to a fifteen-round draw.

Though Pedroza faced a wide

IN THE RING	WON 42* LOST 6 DRAWS 1	TB 50	KO 26	W 15	WF 0	D 1	KO'd 3	L 3	LF 0	NC 1

*includes 1 TW

Date	Opponent	Site	Result / Rounds		Title	Wt.
1973						
Dec 1	Julio Garcia	Panama City	TKO	4	—	120
Dec 22	Jose Santana	Panama City	W	4	—	122
1974						
Feb 8	Jorge Bernal	Panama City	W	6	—	121
Mar 1	Loitolier Chacon Plata	Panama City	TKO	1	—	121
Mar 30	Jacinto Fuentes	Panama City	KO	1	—	117
May 4	Ricardo Vega	Panama City	TKO	2	—	117
Jun 14	Ernesto Davis	Panama City	KO	1	—	120
Jul 20	Vicente Worrell	Panama City	KO	1	—	119
Sep 14	Senen Rios	Panama City	TKO	6	—	120
1975						
Jan 15	Alfonso Perez	Panama City	TKO'd	3	—	124
Feb 22	Ernesto Mathias	Panama City	TW	8	—	120
Mar 21	Benicio Sosa	David, Panama	W	10	—	118
Apr 26	Marcos Britton	Panama City	KO	4	—	120
Jul 19	Guillermo Almengot	Panama City	TKO	7	—	122
Nov 5	Orlando Amores	Panama City	TKO	9	—	119
1976						
Apr 3 ♛	Alfonso Zamora	Mexicali, Mexico	KO'd	2	For-World-B	118
Jun 12	Pablo Jimenez	Panama City	W	10	—	125
Jul 11	Oscar Reyes Arnal	Caracas	TKO'd	6	—	127
1977						
Apr 2	Jose Santana	Panama City	W	10	—	126
May 14	Reynaldo Hidalgo	Panama City	TKO	9	—	126
Nov 26	Rodolfo Francis	Panama City	TKO	7	—	126
1978						
Apr 15 ⑩	Cecilio Lastra	Panama City	TKO	13	Won WBA-FE	125
Jul 2	Ernesto Herrera	Panama City	TKO	12	Ret-WBA-FE	126
Nov 27	Enrique Solis	San Juan, PR	W	15	Ret-WBA-FE	126
1979						
Jan 9	Royal Kobayashi	Tokyo	TKO	14	Ret-WBA-FE	126
Apr 7 ⑩	Hector Carrasquilla	Panama City	TKO	11	Ret-WBA-FE	126
Jul 21	Ruben Olivares★	Houston	TKO	12	Ret-WBA-FE	126
Nov 17	Johnny Aba	Port Moresby, New Guinea	TKO	11	Ret-WBA-FE	126
1980						
Jan 22	Spider Nemoto	Tokyo	W	15	Ret-WBA-FE	126
Mar 29	Juan Malvarez	Panama City	KO	9	Ret-WBA-FE	125
Jul 20	Sa-Wang Kim	Seoul	KO	8	Ret-WBA-FE	126
Oct 4 ⑩	Rocky Lockridge	McAfee, NJ	W	15	Ret-WBA-FE	126
1981						
Jan 17	Raul Silva	Panama City	TKO	4	—	129
Feb 14	Pat Ford	Panama City	KO	13	Ret-WBA-FE	125
Aug 1 ⑩	Carlos Pinango	Caracas	KO	7	Ret-WBA-FE	126

Dec 5	Bashew Sibaca	Panama City	KO	5	Ret-WBA-FE	126
1982						
Jan 24	⑩ Juan LaPorte	Atlantic City	W	15	Ret-WBA-FE	125
Jul 17	Rudy Alpizar	Panama City	NC	2		130
Oct 16	⑩ Bernard Taylor	Charlotte, NC	D	15	Ret-World-FE	126
1983						
Apr 24	⑩ Rocky Lockridge	San Remo, Italy	W	15	Ret-World-FE	126
Oct 22	⑩ Jose Caba	St. Vincent, Italy	W	15	Ret-World-FE	126
1984						
May 27	Angel Levy	Maracaibo, Venezuela	W	15	Ret-World-FE	126
Jun 23	Gerald Hayes	Panama City	TKO	10		132
1985						
Feb 2	Jorge Lujan	Panama City	W	15	Ret-World-FE	126
Jun 8	⑩ Barry McGuigan	London	L	15	Lost-World-FE	126
1986						
Aug 9	Edgar Castro	Panama City	L	10	—	132
1991						
Oct 25	Tomas Rodriguez	Miami	W	8	—	136
Dec 15	Jorge Romero	Miami	W	10	—	134
1992						
Mar 14	Tomas Quinones	Antibes, France	TKO	3	—	135
Nov 21	Mauro Gutierrez	Detroit	L	10	—	137

variety of fighters in his lengthy title reign, he never received the opportunity to unify the title against WBC champions like Danny "Little Red" Lopez and Hall of Famer Salvador Sanchez, both of whom garnered more widespread acclaim than did Pedroza.

Pedroza sported a reach of 68 inches, far more than most of his featherweight competitors. He had a fine jab and good boxing skills, and unlike many tall fighters, Pedroza also performed well on the inside. He became known for his bolo punches and his ability to wear down an opponent with a blistering body attack. Often, he was also criticized as a dirty fighter.

Though his first title defense was a twelve-round knockout victory over Ernesto Herrera in his hometown of Panama City, Pedroza's title fights took him around the world. In 1979, Pedroza retained his championship in four title matches, including a knockout victory over Hall of Famer Ruben Olivares, an all-time great slightly past his prime.

The next year saw four more title defenses, the final one against undefeated future junior lightweight champ Rocky Lockridge, October 4, 1980, at the Playboy Club in McAfee, New Jersey. Lockridge dominated the first six rounds getting the champ on the ropes in the fifth and twice stunning the champion with rights and hooks. By the seventh Pedroza began to take command with his left jab. The ninth and tenth saw Pedroza fire effective shots to the body and follow with hard, short counters to the chest and head. The champ came away with a split decision; the rematch two years later went to Pedroza by decision. Televised on CBS, the fight brought Pedroza to the attention of U.S. boxing fans.

On January 24, 1982, Pedroza fought one of the most controversial battles of his career against Juan LaPorte in Atlantic City. LaPorte jumped out to a fast start, winning the first three rounds with right-hand leads and hooks, and staggered Pedroza twice. Yet by the ninth, LaPorte appeared to be tiring. Pedroza used every weapon in his arsenal, fighting after the bell, using his elbows inside, frequently hitting LaPorte below the belt and using illegal kidney punches, as well as his famed bolo punch and an effective uppercut. Despite two points deducted by the referee, he won the decision by a narrow margin on all three cards. LaPorte later called Pedroza, "the dirtiest fighter I ever fought." LaPorte's manager Howie Albert filed protests with both the WBA and the New Jersey State Athletic Commission, alleging that Pedroza was using drugs or stimulants, in addition to committing at least 34 fouls. The WBA upheld the original decision in the fight, and Pedroza kept his title.

Pedroza remained champion until June 8, 1985, when he faced Barry McGuigan in London. McGuigan won a solid, unanimous decision and knocked Pedroza down in the seventh round. The next year, Pedroza retired after losing a decision to Edgar Castro. Pedroza became a well-known political figure in Panama, serving in Congress and as boxing coordinator at the National Sports Institute. After the U.S. invasion of Panama, he ended his retirement and fought four times in 1991 and 1992 before retiring again. In retirement, Pedroza worked for the government as chief of General Services. He now owns a pig farm.

Juan LaPorte lost a split decision to Pedroza (R) in a tough 1982 Atlantic City title brawl that was punctuated with complaints from LaPorte's corner about low blows and other rough stuff.

WILLIE PEP
Will o' the Wisp

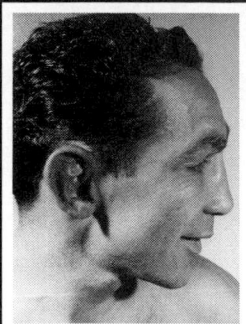

FEATHERWEIGHT

Right-handed; 5'5½"; 105–139 lbs.

242 bouts, 7/3/1940 to 3/16/1966

Manager: Lou Viscusi

Featherweight Champion 1942–48, 1949–50

Hall of Fame Induction: 1990

Born: 9/19/1922, Middletown, CT

Named: Guiglermo Papaleo

Willie Pep is one of the biggest winners in the history of boxing. In 242 contests, Pep emerged victorious 230 times. Fighting as a featherweight, Pep developed a ring artistry that veteran boxing observers still admire. His style of boxing has been likened to tap dancing with gloves on. He once won a round without even throwing a punch because his tactical movements kept his opponent completely off-balance.

Pep rose through the amateur ranks in his home state of Connecticut, winning that state's amateur flyweight championship in 1938 and the Connecticut State Amateur Bantamweight Championship in 1939. He turned professional the following year. After winning over 50 fights in a little over two years, Pep challenged Chalky Wright for the New York version of the world featherweight championship. Pep did not hurt Wright but scored often enough to win the decision. At twenty, Pep was the youngest champion to win a title in 40 years.

Pep continued to win and became the sole claimant to the world feather-

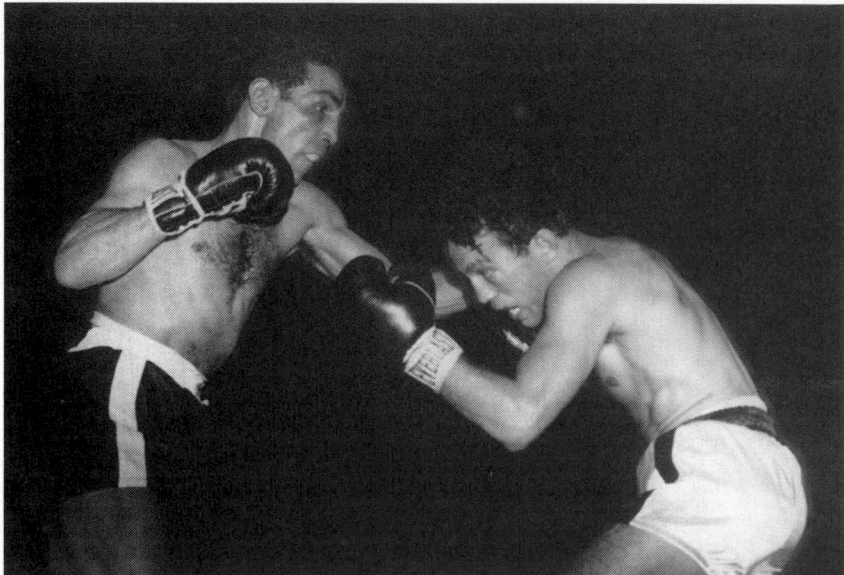

Pat Marcune (R) is in trouble as Pep intently probes for weaknesses. On June 5, 1953, in New York, Marcune fell in ten on a TKO. Today, Pep is a frequent visitor to the International Boxing Hall of Fame.

IN THE RING	WON 230	LOST 11	DRAWS 1	TB 242	KO 65	W 165	WF 0	D 1	KO'd 6	L 5	LF 0

Date	Opponent	Site	Result / Rounds		Title	Wt.
1940						
Jul 3	James McGovern	Hartford, CT	W	4	—	105
Jul 25	Joey Marcus	Hartford	W	4	—	—
Aug 8	Joey Wasnick	New Haven, CT	KO	3	—	—
Aug 29	Tommy Burns	Hartford	KO	1	—	—
Sep 5	Joey Marcus	New Britain, CT	W	6	—	—
Sep 19	Jack Moore	Hartford	W	6	—	—
Oct 3	Jimmy Riche	Waterbury, CT	TKO	3	—	—
Oct 24	Jimmy McAllister	New Haven	W	6	—	—
Nov 22	Carlo Daponde	New Britain	TKO	6	—	—
Nov 29	Frank Topazio	New Britain	TKO	5	—	—
Dec 6	Jim Mutane	New Britain	KO	2	—	—
1941						
Jan 28	Augie Almeida	New Haven	TKO	6	—	—
Feb 3	Joe Echevarria	Holyoke, MA	W	6	—	—
Feb 10	Don Lyons	Holyoke	KO	2	—	—
Feb 17	Ruby Garcia	Holyoke	W	6	—	—
Mar 3	Ruby Garcia	Holyoke	W	6	—	—
Mar 25	Marty Shapiro	Hartford	W	6	—	—
Mar 31	Joey Gatto	Holyoke	KO	2	—	—
Apr 14	Henry Vasquez	Holyoke	W	6	—	—
Apr 22	Joey Silva	Hartford	W	6	—	—
May 6	Lou Puglese	Hartford	KO	2	—	—
May 12	Johnny Cockfield	Holyoke	W	6	—	—
Jun 24	Eddie De Angelis	Hartford	TKO	3	—	—
Jul 16	Jimmy Gilligan	Hartford	W	8	—	—
Aug 1	Harry Hintlian	Manchester, CT	W	6	—	—
Aug 5	Paul Frechette	Hartford	TKO	3	—	—
Aug 12	Eddie Flores	Thompsonville, MI	KO	1	—	—
Sep 26	Jackie Harris	New Haven	TKO	1	—	—
Oct 10	Carlos Manzano	New Haven	W	8	—	—
Oct 22	Connie Savoie	Hartford	KO	2	—	—
Nov 7	Billie Spencer	Los Angeles	W	4	—	—
Nov 24	Dave Crawford	Holyoke	W	8	—	—
Dec 12	Ruby Garcia	New York	W	4	—	—
1942						
Jan 8	Joey Rivers	Fall River, MA	KO	4	—	—
Jan 16	Sammy Parrotta	New York	W	4	—	—
Jan 27	Abie Kaufman	Hartford	W	8	—	—
Feb 10	Angelo Callura	Hartford	W	8	—	—
Feb 24	Willie Roache	Hartford	W	8	—	—
Mar 18	Johnny Compo	New Haven	W	8	—	—
Apr 14	Spider Armstrong	Hartford	KO	4	—	—
May 4	Curley Nichols	New Haven	W	8	—	—
May 12	Aaron Seltzer	Hartford	W	8	—	—
May 26	Joey Iannotti	Hartford	W	8	—	—
Jun 23	Joey Archibald	Hartford	W	10	—	—
Jul 21	Abe Denner	Hartford	W	12	—	—
Aug 1	Joey Silva	Waterbury	TKO	7	—	—
Aug 10	⑩ Pedro Hernandez	Hartford	W	10	—	—
Aug 20	Nat Litfin	West Haven, CT	W	10	—	—
Sep 1	⑩ Bobby ("Poison") Ivy	Hartford	TKO	10	—	—
Sep 10	Frank Franconeri	New York	TKO	1	—	—
Sep 22	Vince Dell'Orto	Hartford	W	10	—	—
Oct 5	Bobby McIntire	Holyoke	W	10	—	—

Date		Opponent	Location	Result	Rounds		Title
Oct 16		Joey Archibald	Providence, RI	W	10	—	128
Oct 27		George Zengaras	Hartford	W	10	—	130
Nov 20	♛	Albert ("Chalky") Wright★	New York	W	15	Won-World-FE	125
Dec 14		Jose Aponte Torres	Washington, DC	KO	7	—	—
Dec 21		Joey Silva	Jacksonville, FL	TKO	9	—	128

1943

Date		Opponent	Location	Result	Rounds		Title
Jan 4		Vince Dell'Orto	New Orleans	W	10	—	129
Jan 19		Bill Speary	Hartford	W	10	—	—
Jan 29	⑩	Allie Stolz	New York	W	10	—	—
Feb 11		Davey Crawford	Boston	W	10	—	—
Feb 15		Bill Speary	Baltimore	W	10	—	—
Mar 2		Lou Transparenti	Hartford	KO	6	—	—
Mar 19	⑩	Sammy Angott★	New York	L	10	—	130
Mar 29		Bobby McIntire	Detroit	W	10	—	—
Apr 9	⑩	Sal Bartolo	Boston	W	10	—	—
Apr 19		Angel Aviles	Tampa, FL	W	10	—	—
Apr 26	⑩	Jackie Wilson	Pittsburgh	W	12	—	—
Jun 8	⑩	Sal Bartolo	Boston	W	15	Ret-World-FE	126

1944

Date		Opponent	Location	Result	Rounds		Title
Apr 4		Leo Francis	Hartford	W	10	—	133
Apr 20		Harold Lacey	New Haven	W	10	—	—
May 1		Jackie Leamus	Philadelphia	W	10	—	—
May 19		Frankie Rubino	Chicago	W	10	—	—
May 23		Joey Bagnato	Buffalo	KO	2	—	—
Jun 6		Julie Kogon	Hartford	W	10	—	—
Jul 7	⑩	Willie Joyce	Chicago	W	10	—	127
Jul 17	⑩	Manuel Ortiz★	Boston	W	10	—	—
Aug 4	⑩	Lulu Costantino	Waterbury	W	10	—	—
Aug 29	⑩	Joey Peralta	Springfield, MA	W	10	—	—
Sep 19	⑩	Cabey Lewis	Hartford	KO	8	—	—
Sep 29	⑩	Albert ("Chalky") Wright★	New York	W	15	Ret-World-FE	125
Oct 25		Jackie Leamus	Montreal	W	10	—	—
Nov 14	⑩	Cabey Lewis	Hartford	W	10	—	126
Nov 27		Pedro Hernandez	Washington, DC	W	10	—	128
Dec 5	⑩	Albert ("Chalky") Wright★	Cleveland	W	10	—	128

1945

Date		Opponent	Location	Result	Rounds		Title
Jan 23		Ralph Walton	Hartford	W	10	—	—
Feb 5	⑩	Willie Roache	New Haven	W	10	—	127
Feb 19	⑩	Phil Terranova	New York	W	15	Ret-World-FE	124
Oct 30		Paulie Jackson	Hartford	W	8	—	130
Nov 5		Mike Martyk	Buffalo	TKO	5	—	—
Nov 26		Eddie Giosa	Boston	W	10	—	—
Dec 5		Harold Gibson	Lewiston, ME	W	10	—	130
Dec 13		Jimmy McAllister	Baltimore	D	10	—	—

1946

Date		Opponent	Location	Result	Rounds		Title
Jan 15		Johnny Virgo	Buffalo	KO	2	—	—
Feb 13		Jimmy Joyce	Buffalo	W	10	—	—
Mar 1		Jimmy McAllister	New York	KO	2	—	129
Mar 26	⑩	Jackie Wilson	Kansas City, MO	W	10	—	—
Apr 8		Georgie Knox	Providence	KO	3	—	130
May 6		Ernie Petrone	New Haven	W	10	—	128
May 13		Joey Angelo	Providence	W	10	—	—
May 22		Jose Aponte Torres	St. Louis	W	10	—	—
May 27		Jimmy Joyce	Minneapolis	W	8	—	127
Jun 7	⑩	Sal Bartolo	New York	KO	12	Ret-World-FE	126
Jul 10		Harold Gibson	Buffalo	TKO	7	—	—
Jul 25	⑩	Jackie Graves	Minneapolis	TKO	8	—	—
Aug 26		Doll Rafferty	Milwaukee	KO	6	—	131
Sep 4		Walter Kolby	Buffalo	TKO	5	—	—
Sep 17		Maurice LaChance	Hartford	KO	3	—	—
Nov 1		Paulie Jackson	Minneapolis	W	10	—	—

Date		Opponent	Location	Result	Rds	Title	
Nov 15		Tomas Beato	Waterbury	KO	2	—	128
Nov 27	Ⓚ	Albert ("Chalky") Wright★	Milwaukee	KO	3	—	—

1947

Jun 17		Victor Flores	Hartford	W	10	—	—
Jul 1		Joey Fortuna	Albany, NY	KO	5	—	—
Jul 8		Leo LeBrun	Norwalk, CT	W	8	—	—
Jul 11		Jean Barriere	North Adams, MA	KO	4	—	—
Jul 15		Paulie Jackson	New Bedford, MA	W	10	—	—
Jul 23		Humberto Sierra	Hartford	W	10	—	—
Aug 22	Ⓚ	Jock Leslie	Flint, MI	TKO	12	Ret-World-FE	125
Oct 21		Jean Barriere	Portland, ME	KO	1	—	—
Oct 27		Archie Wilmer	Philadelphia	W	10	—	—
Dec 22		Alvaro Estrada	Lewiston, NY	W	10	—	—
Dec 30		Maurice LaChance	Manchester	TKO	8	—	—

1948

Jan 6		Pedro Biesca	Hartford	W	10	—	129
Jan 12		Jimmy McAllister	St. Louis	W	10	—	—
Jan 19		Joey Angelo	Boston	W	10	—	—
Feb 24		Humberto Sierra	Miami	TKO	10	Ret-World-FE	125
May 7		Leroy Willis	Detroit	W	10	—	—
May 19		Cabey Lewis	Milwaukee	W	10	—	—
Jun 17	Ⓚ	Miguel Acevedo	Minneapolis	W	10	—	—
Jun 25		Luther Burgess	Flint	W	10	—	—
Jul 28		Young Junior	Utica, NY	KO	1	—	—
Aug 3		Teddy Davis	Hartford	W	10	—	128
Aug 17		Teddy Davis	Hartford	W	10	—	—
Sep 2		Johnny Dell	Waterbury	TKO	8	—	—
Sep 10	Ⓚ	Paddy DeMarco	New York	W	10	—	128
Oct 12		Chuck Burton	Jersey City, NJ	W	8	—	—
Oct 19		John LaRusso	Hartford	W	10	—	—
Oct 29	Ⓚ	Sandy Saddler★	New York	KO'd	4	Lost-World-FE	125
Dec 20		Hermie Freeman	Boston	W	10	—	—

1949

Jan 17		Teddy Davis	St. Louis	W	10	—	127
Feb 11	♛	Sandy Saddler★	New York	W	15	Reg-World-FE	126
Jun 6		Luis Ramos	New Haven	W	10	—	131
Jun 14		Al Pennino	Pittsfield, MA	W	10	—	131
Jun 20		John LaRusso	Springfield	W	10	—	—
Jul 12		Jean Mougin	Syracuse, NY	W	10	—	—
Sep 20		Eddie Compo	Waterbury	TKO	7	Ret-World-FE	126
Dec 12		Harold Dade	St. Louis	W	10	—	—

1950

Jan 16	Ⓚ	Charley Riley	St. Louis	KO	5	Ret-World-FE	123
Feb 6		Roy Andrews	Boston	W	10	—	—
Feb 22		Jimmy Warren	Miami	W	10	—	129
Mar 17	Ⓚ	Ray Famechon	New York	W	15	Ret-World-FE	124
May 15		Art Llanos	Hartford	KO	2	—	130
Jun 1		Terry Young	Milwaukee	W	10	—	129
Jun 26		Bobby Timpson	Hartford	W	10	—	127
Jul 25		Bobby Bell	Washington, DC	W	10	—	130
Aug 2		Proctor Heinold	Scranton, PA	W	10	—	131
Sep 8	Ⓚ	Sandy Saddler★	New York	TKO'd	8	Lost-World-FE	124

1951

Jan 30		Tommy Baker	Hartford	TKO	4	—	—
Feb 26		Billy Hogan	Sarasota	TKO	2	—	—
Mar 5		Carlos Chavez	New Orleans	W	10	—	—
Mar 26		Pat Iacobucci	Miami	W	10	—	—
Apr 17		Neftali Ortiz	St. Louis	TKO	5	—	—
Apr 27		Eddie Chavez	San Francisco	W	10	—	—
Jun 4		Jesus Compos	Baltimore	W	10	—	—
Sep 4		Corky Gonzales	New Orleans	W	10	—	—

Date		Opponent	Location	Result		Notes	
Sep 26	♛	Sandy Saddler★	New York	TKO'd	9	For-World-FE	125

1952

Apr 29		Santiago Gonzales	Tampa	W	10	—	—
May 5		Kenny Leach	Columbus, GA	W	10	—	—
May 10		Buddy Baggett	Aiken, SC	KO	5	—	—
May 21		Claude Hammond	Miami Beach	W	10	—	—
Jun 30	⑩	Tommy Collins	Boston	TKO'd	6	—	—
Sep 3		Billy Lima	Pensacola, FL	W	10	—	—
Sep 11		Bobby Woods	Vancouver, B.C.	W	10	—	—
Oct 1		Armand Savoie	Chicago	W	10	—	—
Oct 20		Billy Lima	Jacksonville	W	10	—	—
Nov 5		Manny Castro	Miami Beach	TKO	5	—	—
Nov 19		Fabela Chavez	St. Louis	W	10	—	—
Dec 5		Jorge Sanchez	West Palm Beach, FL	W	10	—	—

1953

Jan 19		Billy Lauderdale	Nassau, Bahamas	W	10	—	—
Jan 27		Davey Mitchell	Miami Beach	W	10	—	—
Feb 10		Jose Alvarez	San Antonio, TX	W	10	—	—
Mar 31		Joey Gambino	Tampa	W	10	—	—
Apr 7		Noel Paquette	Miami Beach	W	10	—	—
May 13		Jackie Blair	Dallas	W	10	—	—
Jun 5		Pat Marcune	New York	TKO	10	—	—
Nov 21		Sonny Luciano	Charlotte, NC	W	10	—	—
Dec 4		Davey Allen	West Palm Beach	W	10	—	—
Dec 8		Billy Lima	Houston	KO	2	—	—
Dec 15		Tony Longo	Miami Beach	W	10	—	—

1954

Jan 19		David Seabrooke	Jacksonville	W	10	—	—
Feb 26	⑩	Lulu Perez	New York	TKO'd	2	—	—
Jul 24		Mike Turcotte	Mobile, AL	W	10	—	—
Aug 18		Til LeBlanc	Moncton, N.B.	W	10	—	—
Nov 1		Mario Colon	Daytona Beach, FL	W	10	—	—

1955

Mar 11		Myrel Olmstead	Bennington, VT	W	10	—	—
Mar 22		Charley Titone	Holyoke	W	10	—	—
Mar 30		Gil Cadilli	San Francisco	L	10	—	—
May 18		Gil Cadilli	Detroit	W	10	—	—
Jun 1		Joey Cam	Boston	TKO	4	—	—
Jun 14		Mickey Mars	Miami Beach	TKO	7	—	—
Jul 12		Hector Rodriguez	Bridgeport, CT	W	10	—	—
Sep 13		Jimmy Ithia	Hartford	TKO	6	—	—
Sep 27		Pappy Gault	Holyoke	W	10	—	—
Oct 10		Charley Titone	Brockton, MA	W	10	—	—
Nov 29		Pappy Gault	Tampa	W	10	—	—
Dec 12		Lee Carter	Houston	TKO	4	—	127
Dec 28		Andy Arel	Miami Beach	W	10	—	128

1956

Mar 13		Kid Campeche	Tampa	W	10	—	128
Mar 27		Buddy Baggett	Beaumont, TX	W	10	—	127
Apr 17		Jackie Blair	Hartford	W	10	—	—
May 22		Manuel Armenteros	San Antonio	TKO	7	—	—
Jun 19		Russ Tague	Miami Beach	W	10	—	—
Jul 4		Hector Bacquette	Lawton, OK	KO	4	—	—

1957

Apr 23		Cesar Morales	Ft. Lauderdale, FL	W	10	—	—
May 10		Manny Castro	Florence, SC	W	10	—	—
Jul 16		Manny Castro	El Paso, TX	W	10	—	—
Jul 23		Russ Tague	Houston	W	10	—	—
Dec 17		Jimmy Connors	Boston	W	10	—	—

1958

Jan 14		Tommy Tibbs	Boston	L	10	—	—

Mar 31	Prince Johnson	Holyoke	W	10	—	—
Apr 8	George Stephany	Bristol, CT	W	10	—	129
Apr 14	Cleo Ortiz	Providence	W	10	—	129
Apr 29	Jimmy Kelly	Boston	W	10	—	129
May 20	Bobby Singleton	Boston	W	10	—	—
Jun 23	Pat McCoy	New Bedford, MA	W	10	—	—
Jul 1	Bobby Soares	Athol, MA	W	10	—	128
Jul 17	Bobby Bell	Norwood, MA	W	10	—	128
Aug 4	Luis Carmona	Presque Isle, ME	W	10	—	131
Aug 9	Jesse Rodrigues	Painesville, OH	W	10	—	129
Aug 26	Al Duarte	North Adams, MA	W	10	—	129
Sep 20	♛ Hogan ("Kid") Bassey	Boston	TKO'd	9	—	129
1959						
Jan 26	⑩ Sonny Leon	Caracas, Venezuela	L	10	—	130
1965						
Mar 12	Hal McKeever	Miami	W	8	—	139
Apr 26	Jackie Lennon	Philadelphia	W	6	—	—
May 21	Johnny Gilmore	Norwalk	W	6	—	—
Jul 26	Benny Randell	Quebec City, Mon.	W	10	—	—
Sep 28	Johnny Gilmore	Philadelphia	W	6	—	134
Oct 1	Willie Little	Johnstown, PA	KO	3	—	—
Oct 4	Tommy Haden	Providence	TKO	3	—	—
Oct 14	Sergio Musquiz	Phoenix	KO	5	—	—
Oct 25	Ray Coleman	Tucson, AZ	TKO	5	—	—
1966						
Mar 16	Calvin Woodland	Richmond, VA	L	6	—	—

weight title when he won a decision over NBA titleholder Phil Terranova in 1945. Pep's career was temporarily derailed when he suffered serious injuries in a plane crash in 1947. Pep defied those who said he would never fight again by winning a ten-round decision over Victor Flores barely five months after the accident.

Though he had lost a non-title bout to the heavier Sammy Angott, Pep continued to be unbeaten at the featherweight level until he faced Sandy Saddler in 1948 at Madison Square Garden. Saddler gave Pep more trouble than any other opponent in his 26-year career. In this first of their four title bouts over the years, Saddler knocked Pep out in the fourth round, and questions arose because Pep had performed so badly. In the rematch at Madison Square Garden in 1949, Pep took many punches but boxed a clever fight and won a decision over Saddler to regain his championship. With cuts over each eye and on both cheeks, Pep felt he was vindicated of the allegations concerning the first fight. In 1981, *The Ring* rated the rematch one of the ten greatest bouts of all time.

Pep and Saddler met for a third time in Yankee Stadium in 1950 before 38,781 fans. Saddler cut Pep early and knocked him down in the third round. Pep won the next three rounds but Saddler battered Pep in the seventh, and Pep failed to answer the bell for the eighth, claiming a dislocated shoulder. These two warriors met for a last time in 1951 at New York's Polo Grounds. The crowd of 13,786 witnessed a wild melee complete with heeling, gouging, tripping, butting, pushing, shoving, and wrestling. Nat Fleischer labeled the bout "a disgraceful brawl." Pep suffered a technical knockout when he retired after the ninth round. Pep continued to box until 1959 and made a comeback in 1965 at the age of 42. The clever "Will o' the Wisp" is remembered as a consummate boxer.

PASCUAL PEREZ
El Terrier

FLYWEIGHT

Right-handed; 5′; 104–112 lbs.

92 bouts, 12/5/1952 to 3/15/1964

Manager: Lazaro Koci

1948 Olympic Flywt. Gold Medalist

Flyweight Champion 1954–60

Hall of Fame Induction: 1995

Born: 3/4/1926, Tupungate, Mendoza, Argentina

Died: 1/22/1977

Considered by many to be the finest flyweight in the modern era of boxing, Pascual Perez did not follow the usual path to stardom as a boxer. After a strong amateur career, Perez took time off and did not fight professionally until he was 26.

Born in Argentina, Perez grew up working in his family's vineyard. Despite his family's opposition to his boxing, Perez, inspired by his idol, Argentine heavyweight Luis Angel Firpo, became a top amateur. He won the flyweight gold medal in the 1948 Olympic Games but then dropped out of boxing and worked as a janitor in government civil service. Finally, in 1952, in an effort to earn more money, he fought and won his first professional fight.

Perez then reeled off 22 straight wins—21 by knockout—and within a year proved he was the best flyweight in Argentina. In July, 1954 world flyweight champion Yoshio Shirai of Japan came to Buenos Aires to test Perez's mettle in

Chin tucked low, globetrotting champion Perez (R) won on points over Dommy Ursua in his December 15, 1958 title defense in Manila. President Juan Peron of Argentina keenly followed Perez's career.

IN THE RING	WON 84	LOST 7	DRAWS 1	TB 92	KO 57	W 27	WF 0	D 1	KO'd 3	L 4	LF 0

Date	Opponent	Site	Result / Rounds		Title	Wt.
1952						
Dec 5	Jose Ciorino	Gerli, Argentina	TKO	4	—	—
Dec 19	Jorge Flores	San Fernando, Argentina	KO	3	—	—
1953						
Jan 3	Ramon Stronatti	Mendoza, Argentina	TKO	2	—	—
Feb 20	Mario Ahumada	Mendoza	TKO	3	—	—
Mar 16	Miguel Carrasco	Mendoza	KO	5	—	—
Mar 30	Juan Godoy	Buenos Aires	KO	4	—	—
Nov 11	Marcelo Quiroga	Buenos Aires	TKO	4	Won-Argentina-FL	104
Nov 25	Eduardo Lliuzzi	Buenos Aires	TKO	1	—	—
Dec 23	Hernan Rojas	Mendoza	KO	2	—	—
Dec 30	Roberto Romero	Uspallata, Argentina	KO	2	—	—
1954						
Jan 8	Nestor Rojas	Catamarca, Argentina	TKO	2	—	—
Jan 19	Jose Luna	Tucuman, Argentina	TKO	2	—	—
Jan 29	Antonio Zapata	Catamarca	TKO	5	—	—
Feb 6	Marcelo Quiroga	Buenos Aires	TKO	4	—	—
Feb 12	Nestor Rojas	Tandil, Argentina	KO	3	—	—
Feb 24	Nicolas Paez	Buenos Aires	KO	1	—	—
Mar 12	Pablo Sosa	Catamarca	KO	6	—	—
Mar 24	Pablo Sosa	Buenos Aires	KO	2	—	—
Apr 22	Juan Bishop	Buenos Aires	W	10	—	—
May 19	Vicente Bruno	Buenos Aires	TKO	3	—	—
Jun 5	Domingo Sandoval	Comodoro Rivadavia, Arg.	KO	4	—	—
Jun 12	Pablo Sosa	Comodoro Rivadavia	TKO	8	—	—
Jun 25	Marcelo Quiroga	La Plata, Argentina	KO	4	—	—
Jul 24 ♛	Yoshio Shirai	Buenos Aires	D	10	—	108
Nov 26 ♛	Yoshio Shirai	Tokyo	W	15	Won-World-FL	109
1955						
Apr 13	Alberto Barenghi	Buenos Aires	KO	3	—	—
May 30 ⑩	Yoshio Shirai	Tokyo	KO	5	Ret-World-FL	108
Aug 26	Alberto Palomeque	Catamarca	KO	4	—	—
Oct 22 ⑩	Danny Kidd	Buenos Aires	W	10	—	—
1956						
Jan 11 ⑩	Leo Espinosa	Buenos Aires	W	15	Ret-World-FL	107
Feb 10	Antonio Gomez	Mar Del Plata, Argentina	W	10	—	—
Mar 21	Antonio Gomez	Buenos Aires	TKO	8	—	—
Mar 31	Marcelo Quiroga	Mendoza	W	10	—	—
Jun 8	Ricardo Valdez	Bahia Blanca, Argentina	TKO	6	—	—
Jun 15	Pablo Sosa	Martinez, Argentina	KO	4	—	—
Jun 30 ⑩	Oscar Suarez	Montevideo, Uruguay	TKO	11	Ret-World-FL	108
Aug 3	Ricardo Valdez	Tandil	KO	5	—	109
Aug 25	Hector Almaraz	Rosario, Argentina	KO	3	—	—
Sep 6	Conrado Moreira	Sao Paulo, Brazil	W	10	—	—
Sep 28	Hernan Rojas	Asuncion, Paraguay	TKO	8	—	—
Dec 12	Conrado Moreira	Buenos Aires	W	10	—	—
1957						
Mar 30 ⑩	Dai Dower	Buenos Aires	KO	1	Ret-World-FL	107
Jul 12	Luis Jimenez	Babilonia, Argentina	W	10	—	—
Aug 2	Urbieta Sosa	Santa Fe, Argentina	TKO	4	—	—

Date		Opponent	Location	Result	Rd	Title	
Aug 17		Pablo Sosa	Tandil	KO	3	—	—
Sep 13		Conrado Moreira	La Plata	W	10	—	—
Dec 7	⑩	Young Martin	Buenos Aires	KO	3	Ret-World-FL	108
1958							
Mar 22		Ricardo Valdez	Moron, Argentina	KO	8	—	—
Apr 19	⑩	Ramon Arias	Caracas, Venezuela	W	15	Ret-World-FL	107
Aug 9		Tito Ragone	Ciudad Trujillo, D.R.	W	10	—	—
Nov 22		Tito Ragone	Willemstad, Curacao	W	10	—	—
Dec 15	⑩	Dommy Ursua	Manila	W	15	Ret-World-FL	109
1959							
Jan 16	⑩	Sadao Yaoita	Tokyo	L	10	—	110
Feb 18	⑩	Kenji Yonekura	Tokyo	W	10	—	—
Aug 10	⑩	Kenji Yokenura	Tokyo	W	15	Ret-World-FL	107
Nov 5	⑩	Sadao Yaoita	Osaka, Japan	KO	13	Ret-World-FL	107
1960							
Apr 16	⑩	Pone Kingpetch	Bangkok	L	15	Lost-World-FL	112
Sep 22	♛	Pone Kingpetch	Los Angeles	TKO'd	8	For-World-FL	110
1961							
Mar 18		Hugo Villarreal	Avellaneda, Argentina	TKO	4	—	—
Apr 1		Juan Moreira	Quilmes, Argentina	W	10	—	—
Apr 9		Pablo Sosa	San Pedro, Argentina	KO	3	—	—
May 13		Juan Montevero	General Roca, Argentina	TKO	6	—	—
May 19		Francisco Bahamondez	Cipolletti, Argentina	TKO	3	—	—
Jul 8		Hugo Villarreal	Punta Alta, Argentina	KO	3	—	—
Jul 15		Juan Montevero	Rio Gallegos, Argentina	KO	5	—	—
Jul 29		Wladimiro Torres	Rio Gallegos	KO	8	—	—
Aug 19		Simon Rios	Trelew, Argentina	KO	6	—	—
Sep 5		Wladimiro Torres	Bolivar, Argentina	KO	3	—	—
Oct 12		Jose Diaz	Esquel, Argentina	KO	7	—	—
Oct 21		Alberto Garcia	Rosario	TKO	6	—	—
Dec 22		Rodolfo Trivis	Cordoba, Argentina	W	10	—	—
1962							
Jan 27		Demetrio Acosta	9 de Julio, Argentina	KO	2	—	—
Feb 23		Ursino Bernal	Balcarce, Argentina	W	10	—	—
Mar 2		Rodolfo Trivis	Miramar, Argentina	W	10	—	—
Apr 21		Ursino Bernal	Tucuman	TKO	6	—	—
Apr 27		Juan Moreira	Salta, Argentina	KO	3	—	—
May 2		Martin Luque	Santiago del Estero, Arg.	TKO	5	—	—
May 19		Cirilo Avellaneda	Formosa, Argentina	KO	5	—	—
Jun 9		Rodolfo Trivis	Tucuman	W	10	—	—
Jun 15		Martin Luque	Jujuy, Argentina	KO	5	—	—
Dec 8		Juan Moreira	Cordoba	TKO	9	—	—
1963							
Jan 25		Cirilo Avellaneda	Villa Dolores, Argentina	W	10	—	—
Feb 1		Miguel Herrera	San Luis, Argentina	W	10	—	—
Feb 16		Rodolfo Trivis	Montevideo	W	10	—	—
Apr 5		Juan Moreira	Villa Dolores	W	10	—	—
Apr 12		Cirilo Avellaneda	Bahia Blanca	KO	7	—	—
Apr 30	⑩	Leo Zulueta	Manila	L	10	—	112
Jun 16		Manuel Moreno	Panama City	W	10	—	—
Jul 26	⑩	Bernardo Caraballo	Bogota, Colombia	L	10	—	112
Aug 9		Adolfo Osses	Guayaquil, Ecuador	W	10	—	—
Oct 19	⑩	Efren Torres	Guadalajara, Mexico	TKO'd	3	—	109
1964							
Mar 15		Eugenio Hurtado	Panama City	TKO'd	6	—	107

a non-title fight. The two fought to a draw, setting the stage for a title fight four months later in Tokyo. Shirai was seven inches taller than the challenger, whom fight experts gave little chance of dethroning the champion. However, Perez fought inside and battered Shirai to earn a fifteen-round decision. Called "El Terrier" in his home country, the diminutive Perez was known for the tremendous drive contained within his 5′ frame. He returned to Argentina a conquering hero.

Perez knocked Shirai out in their rematch and commenced to defend his title against all comers. He defeated top-ten contenders Leo Espinoza and Oscar Suarez in 1956, and Dai Dower and Young Martin in 1957. He triumphed in title bouts in Caracas and Manila in 1958 and fought exclusively in Japan in 1959, defending his title twice against top Japanese contenders. The end for the diminutive Argentine came in 1960 when he faced Pone Kingpetch in Bangkok. Although Kingpetch was ten years younger and eight inches taller, El Terrier put up a valiant effort but lost a split decision. The fight ended with both men cut around the eyes.

Perez made his only appearance in the United States when he faced Kingpetch in a rematch in Los Angeles. Perez could not mount an effective attack against Kingpetch, and the referee stopped the fight in the eighth round. Though past his prime, Perez continued to fight until he was 38, campaigning successfully against secondary competition.

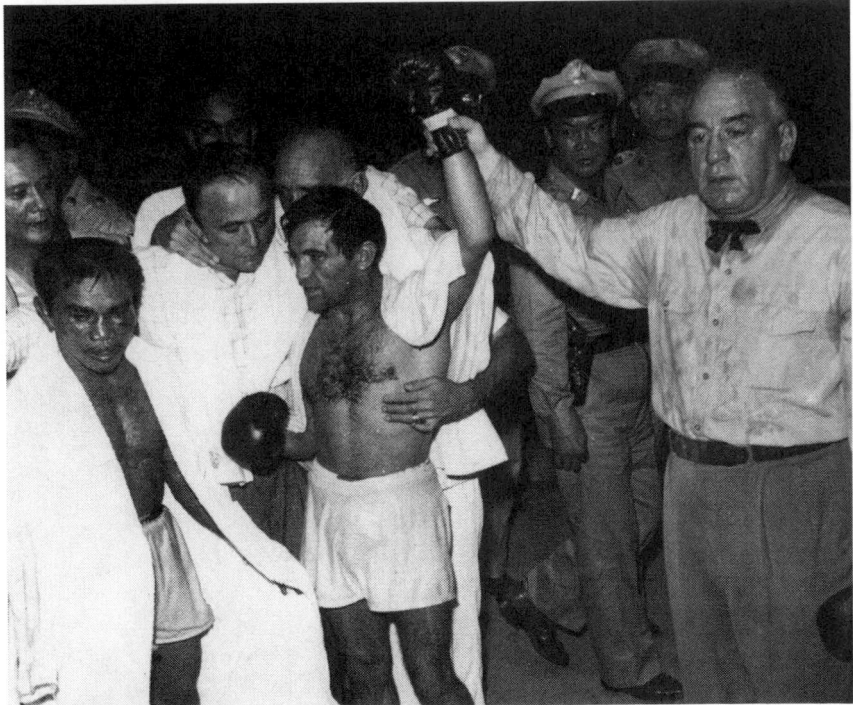

An exhausted Pascual Perez (R) wins the unanimous decison over Dommy Ursua in their 1958 bout. His left eye badly swollen, Ursua suffered the defeat in Rizal Memorial Football Stadium, Manila's soccer venue.

AARON PRYOR
The Hawk

JUNIOR WELTERWEIGHT

Right-handed; 5'6½"; 135–140 lbs.

40 bouts, 11/12/1976 to 12/4/1990

WBA Junior Welterweight Champion 1980–83, IBF Junior Welterweight Champion 1984–85

Hall of Fame Induction: 1996

Born: 10/20/1955, Cincinnati, OH

One of the most thrilling fighters of the late 1970s and early '80s, Aaron Pryor compiled an outstanding 39-1 record in a career known as much for personal turmoil as for brilliant performance. Born in Cincinnati, Pryor was one of seven children in a poor family. He spent much of his time on the streets but, by age 13, he had found his way to a gym and learned to box. As an amateur, he won 204 of 220 fights and two national Golden Gloves titles. Representing the U.S. 21 times in international competition, he only lost once—in the finals of the 1975 Pan-American Games.

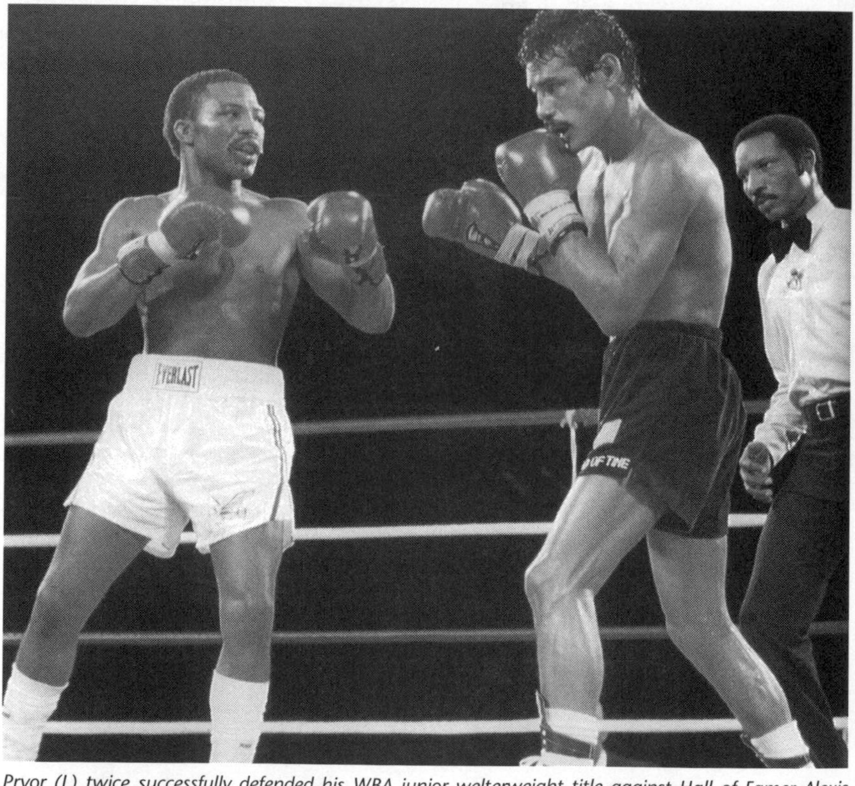

Pryor (L) twice successfully defended his WBA junior welterweight title against Hall of Famer Alexis Arguello. Both bouts ended in knockout wins, but Pryor suffered lasting eye damage in one of the fights.

Despite his excellent amateur record, Pryor never fought in the Olympics. When the 1976 trials were held in Cincinnati, he was favored in his weight class, but lost by decision to Howard Davis, who eventually took the gold medal. Davis beat Pryor again in the box-off at the Olympic training camp in Vermont, but some observers believe Pryor was denied an Olympic shot because of official concern about his behavior outside the ring.

As a result, Pryor was unable to use the 1976 Olympics as a springboard to a professional career as did Davis, Sugar Ray Leonard, and Leon and Michael Spinks. Pryor turned professional on November 12, 1976 knocking out former kick boxer Larry Smith in the second round to earn $400. By contrast, Davis earned $250,000 for his first pro fight.

IN THE RING	WON 39	LOST 1	DRAWS 0	TB 40	KO 35	W 4	WF 0	D 0	KO'd 1	L 0	LF 0

Date	Opponent	Site	Result / Rounds		Title	Wt.
1976						
Nov 12	Larry Smith	Cincinnati	TKO	2	—	137
1977						
Feb 1	Larry Moore	Cincinnati	TKO	4	—	139
Feb 24	Harvey Wilson	Cincinnati	TKO	1	—	139
Mar 12	Nicky Wills	Lincoln Heights, OH	KO	1	—	139
Mar 26	Isaac Vega	Cincinnati	KO	2	—	141
May 7	Jose Resto	Cincinnati	W	8	—	140
Sep 3	Melvin Young	Covington, KY	TKO	4	—	140
Oct 7	Johnny Summerhays	Cincinnati	W	8	—	139
Nov 4	Angel Cintron	Cincinnati	KO	3	—	141
1978						
Jan 16	Roberto Tijerina	Cincinnati	KO	2	—	136
Mar 1	Ron Pettigrew	Dayton, OH	TKO	5	—	140
Mar 10	Alfred Franklin	Cincinnati	TKO	3	—	136
May 3	Scotty Foreman	Miami Beach	TKO	6	—	138
Jul 18	Marion Thomas	Dayton	KO	8	—	139
1979						
Mar 16	Johnny Copeland	Cincinnati	KO	7	—	139
Apr 13	Norman Goins	Cincinnati	KO	9	—	140
Apr 27	Freddie Harris	Dayton	KO	3	—	137
May 11	Al Ford	Cincinnati	TKO	4	—	140
Jun 23	Jose Fernandez	Cincinnati	KO	1	—	141
Oct 20	Alfonso Frazer	Cincinnati	TKO	5	—	136
1980						
Feb 24	Juan Garcia	Las Vegas	KO	1	—	138
Mar 16	⑩ Julio Valdez	Miami	TKO	4	—	136
Apr 13	Leonidas Asprilla	Kansas City, MO	TKO	10	—	134
Jun 20	Carl Crowley	Cincinnati	KO	1	—	143
Aug 2	♛ Antonio Cervantes ★	Cincinnati	KO	4	Won-WBA-JW	138
Nov 1	Danny Myers	Dayton	TKO	3	—	138
Nov 22	Gaetan Hart	Cincinnati	TKO	6	Ret-WBA-JW	138

1981							
Jun 27	⑩	Lennox Blackmoore	Las Vegas	TKO	2	Ret-WBA-JW	140
Nov 14	⑩	Dujuan Johnson	Cleveland	TKO	7	Ret-WBA-JW	139
1982							
Mar 21	⑩	Miguel Montilla	Atlantic City	TKO	12	Ret-WBA-JW	139
Jul 4		Akio Kameda	Cincinnati	TKO	6	Ret-WBA-JW	139
Nov 12		Alexis Arguello★	Miami	TKO	14	Ret-WBA-JW	140
1983							
Apr 2	⑩	Sang-Hyun Kim	Atlantic City	TKO	3	Ret-WBA-JW	140
Sep 9		Alexis Arguello★	Las Vegas	KO	10	Ret-WBA-JW	140
1984							
Jun 22		Nick Furlano	Toronto	W	15	Ret-IBF-JW	139
1985							
Mar 2	⑩	Gary Hinton	Atlantic City	W	15	Ret-IBF-JW	140
1987							
Aug 8		Bobby Joe Young	Sunrise, FL	KO'd	7	—	148
1988							
Dec 15		Herminio Morales	Rochester, NY	KO	3	—	146
1990							
May 16		Darryl Jones	Madison, WI	KO	3	—	154
Dec 4		Roger Choate	Norman, OK	TKO	7	—	148

Still, defeating one opponent after another, Pryor was bound to be noticed. Fighting mostly in Cincinnati under manager Buddy LaRosa, he gained a reputation as a hard hitter who went after opponents with reckless abandon. By mid-1980, he had scored knockouts in 22 of his first 24 fights, and applied the same treatment to Antonio ("Kid Pambele") Cervantes to take the WBA junior welterweight championship. In an attempt to unify the title, promoter Harold Smith lined up a fight for Pryor with the WBC junior welterweight titleholder, Saoul Mamby. Before this match came off, however, Pryor's wife shot him during a domestic dispute.

The resulting delay, coupled with some legal difficulties involving promoter Smith, ended hopes of a unification bout. A falling-out with La Rosa then cost Pryor a fight with Roberto Duran, which would have paid him $750,000.

Pryor defended his title five times by knockout before he entered "The Ring of Fire" with Alexis Arguello in 1982 for the most memorable fight of his career. Having held the featherweight, junior lightweight and lightweight titles, Arguello was aiming to be the first fighter in history to win four world titles in four weight classes.

From the opening bell in Miami's Orange Bowl, Pryor was on the attack. He threw 130 punches in the first round. In the second, Arguello twice caught Pryor with strong rights. In the view of Arguello's agent, Bill Miller, the second punch "would have decapitated anybody else," but Pryor was barely fazed. After thirteen rounds, Pryor was ahead on two cards and Arguello on one. In the fourteenth, Pryor snapped Arguello's head back with a hook, then sent him to the ropes with a series of furious blows. Defenseless, Arguello took 23 more punches before the fight was stopped. On the canvas for four minutes, Arguello collapsed again on the way to his dressing room.

Pryor defended his crown eight times, readily dominating his weight class. But after beating Arguello in their rematch, he announced his retirement and relinquished his title.

Missing the ring and also needing to fund a serious drug habit, Pryor came back less than a year later. He won a few fights and was awarded the IBF's junior welterweight championship, but by 1985 had lost the crown because of inactivity.

Plagued by a worsening drug addiction and a detached retina which eventually led to severe vision loss in one eye, Pryor came back again two years later for the only loss of his career, to Bobby Joe Young. Although because of his vision problem, Pryor should not have been licenced, he fought three more times before retiring for good in 1990.

In 1991, Pryor was imprisoned after pleading guilty to a reduced charge of drug abuse. Drained of all his earnings by crack addiction, Pryor left prison to live

Alexis Arguello (L) is counted out in the tenth round on September 9, 1983 in his second defeat at the hands of triumphant Aaron Pryor.

on the streets, often going days without food or sleep. After nearly dying from bleeding ulcers, he began to turn his life around. He now works training fighters in Cincinnati and is active in a local church. In spite of all his problems outside the ring, fight fans remember Pryor for his ceaseless attack and a capacity to take the best punches an opponent could throw.

FEATHERWEIGHT

Right handed; 5'4½"; 124–138 lbs.
66 bouts, 10/5/1957 to 4/25/1972
Manager: Cuco Conde
Featherweight Champion 1963–64
Hall of Fame Induction: 2001
Born: 12/2/1941, Matanzas, Cuba
Named: Ultiminio Ramos Zaqueira

Ultiminio ("Sugar") Ramos was a fine, strong, intense fighter with a big right hand. Unfortunately he is also remembered as Davey Moore's opponent in the fight that led to Moore's untimely death.

Ramos was born into a very large, very poor family. One of twenty-two children, he began boxing at an early age and turned professional at fifteen, with a knockout victory over Rene Arce on October 5, 1957. Ramos won nineteen of his first twenty fights, with only a single draw against featherweight title contender Ike Chestnut, marring his otherwise perfect record. One opponent, José ("Tigre") Blanco, died after a Ramos knockout.

On February 27, 1960, he went twelve rounds for the first time when he decisioned Orlando Castillo to take the Cuban featherweight title. He knocked out his opponents in his five remaining fights in 1960 and advanced to the second contender spot in *The Ring*. When Fidel Castro banned all professional sports, including boxing, in 1961, Ramos left Cuba for Mexico. That year, he suffered his first defeat on a disqualification after four rounds to Rafael Camacho.

In 1962, Ramos made his first trip to the United States, knocking out Eddie Garcia in an L.A. bout. He decisioned one of the top featherweights, Rafiu King, and also knocked out the highly regarded Jose Luis Cruz in just two rounds.

Now ranked as top contender, Ramos had earned a shot at Davey Moore's featherweight title. A crowd of 26,000 attended the triple-header of championship bouts at Dodger Stadium on March 21, 1963: welterweight champ Emile Griffith faced number-one contender Luis Rodriguez, Battling Torres and Roberto Cruz vied for the vacant junior welterweight crown, and Ramos faced Moore. Moore dominated the first two rounds, but as the fight wore on, Ramos took command, sending Moore to the ropes in the tenth. A quick series

Ramos sits in his corner, dazed, after suffering a serious cut over his left eye. Referee Billy Conn stopped his October 22, 1966, challenge for the lightweight championship and declared Carlos Ortiz the winner by TKO.

IN THE RING	WON 55	LOST 7	DRAWS 4	TB 66	KO 40	W 14	WF 1	D 4	KO'd 4	L 2	LF 1

Date	Opponent	Site	Result / Rounds		Title	Wt.
1957						
Oct 5	Rene Arce	Havana	KO	2	—	—
Nov 30	Inocencio Cartas	Havana	KO	3	—	—
1958						
Jan 11	Juan Machado	Havana	KO	2	—	—
Feb 7	Carlos Suarez	Ranchuelo, Cuba	KO	3	—	—
Apr 12	Felix Pomares	Havana	KO	2	—	—
May 24	Humberto De La Rosa	Havana	KO	4	—	—
Jul 5	Hector Medina	Havana	KO	3	—	—
Jul 19	Manuel Perdomo	Havana	W	6	—	125
Aug 9	Wilfredo Gonzalez	Ciunfuegos, Cuba	KO	2	—	—
Sep 20	Al Castillo	Havana	KO	5	—	—
Oct 11	Augusto Narvalle	Havana	WF	6	—	—
Nov 8	Jose ("Tiger") Blanco	Havana	KO	8	—	—
Dec 4	Antonio Coria	Havana	KO	4	—	—
1959						
Feb 14	Orlando Castillo	Havana	KO	10	—	—
Mar 28	Wally Livingston	Havana	KO	10	—	128
May 9	Angel Guerrero	Havana	KO	4	—	127
Jun 29	Victor Leon	Caracas	W	10	—	—
Aug 1	Johnny Bean	Havana	KO	3	—	—
Oct 31 ⑩	Ike Chestnut	Caracas	D	10	—	—
Nov 20	Francisco Barraez	Matanzas, Cuba	W	10	—	—
1960						
Feb 27	Orlando Castillo	Havana	W	12	Won Cuban-FE	124
Apr 1	Tony Padron	Caracas	KO	4	—	—
May 28	Vernon Lynch	Havana	TKO	7	—	127
Aug 17	Tony Pardon	Havana	KO	8	—	—
Aug 28	Jesus Santamaria	Colon, Panama	KO	9	—	—
Dec 30	Sergio Gomez	Havana	KO	9	—	—
1961						
Jan 23	Jesus Santamaria	Panama	KO	6	—	—
Feb 8	Edwin Sykes	Panama	KO	4	—	—
Apr 22	Juan Ramirez	Mexico City	TD	7	—	128
May 8 ⑩	Felix Cervantes	Tijuana	KO	3	—	130
May 27	Ramon ("Bobby") Cervantes	Guadalajara, Mexico	KO	4	—	132
Jun 17	Alfredo Urbina	Mexico City	W	10	—	131
Sep 2	Alfredo Urbina	Mexico City	D	10	—	132
Sep 30	Kid Anahuac	Guadalajara	W	10	—	131
Dec 13	Rafael Camacho	Puebla, Mexico	LF	4	—	131
1962						
Jan 12	Eddie Garcia	Los Angeles	KO	9	—	131
Mar 26 ⑩	Rafiu King	Paris	W	10	—	126
May 11 ⑩	Danny Valdez	Los Angeles	TKO	7	—	126
Jul 15	Baby Vasquez	Mexico City	W	10	—	133
Sep 3	Baby Vasquez	Tijuana	KO	10	—	135
Oct 20	Eloy Sanchez	Mexico City	KO	3	—	127
Dec 30 ⑩	Jose Luis Cruz	Mexico City	KO	2	—	—

1963							
Mar 21	♛	Davey Moore	Los Angeles	TKO	10	Won-World-FE	125
Jul 13	⑩	Rafiu King	Mexico City	W	15	Ret-World-FE	125
Oct 12		Sammy McSpadden	London	TKO	2	—	135
Nov 9		Kid Anahuac	Los Mochis, Mexico	KO	8	—	—
1964							
Jan 10	⑩	Vicente Derado	Los Angeles	W	10	—	132
Feb 28	⑩	Mitsunori Seki	Tokyo	TKO	6	Ret-World-FE	126
May 9	⑩	Floyd Robertson	Accra, Ghana	W	15	Ret-World-FE	125
Sep 26	⑩	Vicente Saldivar★	Mexico City	TKO'd	12	Lost-World-FE	124
1965							
Apr 18		Antonio Rosales	Acapulco, Mexico	W	10	—	131
Jun 4		Delfino Rosales	Ciudad Juarez, Mexico	KO	1	—	—
Aug 24		Raul Soriano	Tijuana	KO	6	—	—
Dec 11		Raul Soriano	Mexico City	KO	2	—	—
1966							
Feb 12		Antonio Herrera	Mexico City	W	10	—	133
Oct 22	♛	Carlos Ortiz★	Mexico City	KO'd	5	For-World-L	134
1967							
Jul 1	♛	Carlos Ortiz★	San Juan	TKO'd	4	For-World-L	132
1969							
Jun 29		Rudy Gonzalez	Mexico City	KO	2	—	137
Sep 30	⑩	Chango Carmona	Tijuana	TKO	7	—	135
Dec 14	⑩	German Gastelbondo	Vera Cruz, Mexico	KO	1	—	—
1970							
Mar 26		Raul Rojas	Los Angeles	W	10	—	—
Aug 7	⑩	Mando Ramos	Los Angeles	L	10	—	—
1971							
Jan 5		Antonio Amaya	Monterrey, Mexico	L	10	—	135
Oct 15	⑩	Jimmy Robertson	Los Angeles	D	10	—	—
1972							
Mar 24		Lyle Randolph	Chicago	KO	7	—	—
Apr 25		Cesar Sinda	Inglewood, CA	TKO'd	10	—	138

of lefts and rights drove Moore to the centerfield side of the ring, and then a left hook knocked him down, his head landing against the lowest of the three ring ropes. Moore got up at the count of three, but by the end of the round a Ramos right had Moore draped over the ropes. Before the start of the eleventh, Moore's manager, Willie Ketchum, told the referee that Moore could not continue.

Ramos was champion. Moore talked with reporters for about 40 minutes after the fight, then slipped into unconsciousness. He never woke again and died on March 23. When Ramos heard of Moore's death, he wept. An investigation revealed that Moore's death was caused by his head hitting the bottom rope. Calls came for the banning of the entire sport, including Bob Dylan's song, *Who Killed Davey Moore?*.

Ramos continued his boxing career. He decisioned Rafiu King in his first title defense and then traveled to Tokyo to face Mitsunori Seki, the top contender, on February 28, 1964, at Kuramae Sumo Stadium. Ramos was in command from the start, opening a cut over Seki's eye in the fifth. In the sixth, Ramos felled Seki with a right to the jaw and the contender took an eight count. When the action resumed, Ramos unleashed a flurry of lefts and rights, which put Seki down again.

His manager, Iwao Wakamatsu, afraid of a repeat of the Moore incident, screamed for the ref to stop the fight.

In his next match, Ramos flew to Africa to face another contender, Floyd Robertson of Ghana, at the Accra Sports Stadium. Ramos initially won a split decision, with Ramon Velazquez, chairman of the Mexican Boxing Commission, and Ed Lassman, president of the WBA, giving the fight to Ramos, and referee Jack Hart giving the nod to Robertson. After the decision was announced, the crowd reacted angrily, and the Ghana Boxing Authority declared the bout "no contest," and then awarded the victory to Robertson. The WBA and the rest of the boxing world stuck by the original decision, and Ramos retained his title.

The Ghana fight was Ramos's last successful defense. In his next bout, he faced Hall of Famer Vicente Saldivar in Mexico City on September 26, 1964. Both fighters went at each other with reckless fury and, by the seventh round, Ramos's face was covered in blood. He could not answer the bell for the twelfth.

Nearly two years later, Ramos challenged Hall of Famer Carlos Ortiz for the world lightweight title in Mexico City, a locale where Ramos was a fan favorite. A deep cut in Ramos's left eyelid, which would require 22 stitches to close, caused referee Billy Conn to stop the fight in the fifth. Unhappy with Conn's decision, a portion of the crowd rioted and twenty minutes later Mexican Boxing Commission Chairman Velazquez ordered Ortiz to return to the ring and resume fighting. Ortiz refused. Velazquez then declared Ramos the lightweight champion, but as with the Ghana decision, the boxing community at large did not recognize the hometown decision. In the rematch the next year, Ortiz proved his dominance by knocking Ramos out in four rounds. Following his defeat, Ramos announced his retirement.

After several failed business ventures, Ramos returned to the ring. He won the first four fights of his comeback before dropping a ten-round split decision to Mando Ramos in a spirited battle before a sellout crowd of 10,400. That bout was considered one of the greatest fights ever hosted at the Olympic Auditorium.

After a heartbreaker, in which referee John Thomas stopped Ramos's fight with Cesar Sinda in the final moments—with Ramos ahead on all three cards—Ramos left boxing for good.

Referee George Latka brings a halt to the tragic Ramos vs. Davey Moore bout in the tenth round. After a left hook sent Moore down to the bottom rope, he rose and continued to fight. A subsequent flurry by Ramos forced Moore through the ropes and ended the fight.

MIDDLEWEIGHT

Right-handed; 5'11"; 134–165 lbs.

202 bouts, 10/4/1940 to 11/10/1965

Manager: George Gainford

Welterweight Champion 1946–51,
Middleweight Champion 1951,
1951–52, 1955, 1957, 1958–60

Hall of Fame Induction: 1990

Born: 5/3/1921, Detroit, MI

Named: Walker Smith, Jr.

Died: 4/12/1989

The real Ray Robinson has faded into boxing obscurity, while the boy who subbed for him in an amateur bout became one of the sweetest fighters in history. Walker Smith, who adopted the name Sugar Ray Robinson, won the world middleweight title on five separate occasions—a record that is likely to stand for a long time.

Born in Detroit, Robinson was first exposed to boxing in his teens at the same Brewster Gym where Joe Louis had learned to fight. Robinson later moved to New York and started fighting in amateur bouts there. He won the New York Golden Gloves featherweight title in 1940 and turned pro that year at age twenty.

He made his debut at Madison Square Garden with a quick two-round victory.

Robinson (R) suffered a defeat in a ten-round contest in Chicago on January 19, 1955 at the hands of Ralph ("Tiger") Jones. This was just the third bout after Robinson's return from his 1952 retirement.

IN THE RING	WON 175	LOST 19	DRAWS 6	TB 202	KO 109	W 66	WF 0	D 6	KO'd 1	L 18	LF 0	NC 2

Date		Opponent	Site	Result / Rounds		Title	Wt.
1940							
Oct 4		Joe Echevarria	New York	TKO	2	—	—
Oct 8		Silent Stafford	Savannah, GA	KO	2	—	—
Oct 22		Mistos Grispos	Bronx	W	6	—	—
Nov 11		Bobby Woods	Philadelphia	KO	1	—	—
Dec 9		Norment Quarles	Philadelphia	TKO	4	—	—
Dec 13		Oliver White	New York	TKO	3	—	—
1941							
Jan 4		Henry LaBarba	Brooklyn	TKO	1	—	—
Jan 13		Frankie Wallace	Philadelphia	KO	1	—	—
Jan 31		George Zengaras	New York	W	6	—	—
Feb 8		Benny Cartagena	Brooklyn	TKO	1	—	—
Feb 21		Bobby McIntire	New York	W	6	—	134
Feb 27		Gene Spencer	Detroit	TKO	5	—	—
Mar 3		Jimmy Tygh	Philadelphia	KO	8	—	—
Apr 14		Jimmy Tygh	Philadelphia	TKO	1	—	—
Apr 24		Charley Burns	Atlantic City	KO	1	—	—
Apr 30		Joe Ghnouly	Washington, DC	TKO	3	—	134
May 10		Vic Troise	Brooklyn	TKO	1	—	—
May 19		Nick Castiglione	Philadelphia	KO	1	—	—
Jun 16		Mike Evans	Philadelphia	KO	2	—	—
Jul 2	⑩	Pete Lello	New York	TKO	4	—	—
Jul 21	⑩	Sammy Angott★	Philadelphia	W	10	—	—
Aug 27		Carl Guggino	Long Island City, NY	TKO	3	—	—
Aug 29		Maurice Arnault	Atlantic City	KO	1	—	—
Sep 19		Maxie Shapiro	New York	TKO	3	—	—
Sep 25		Marty Servo	Philadelphia	W	10	—	—
Oct 31	⑩	Fritzie Zivic★	New York	W	10	—	—
1942							
Jan 16	⑩	Fritzie Zivic★	New York	TKO	10	—	—
Feb 20		Maxie Berger	New York	TKO	2	—	—
Mar 20	⑩	Norman Rubio	New York	TKO	8	—	—
Apr 17		Harvey Dubs	Detroit	TKO	6	—	—
Apr 30		Dick Banner	Minneapolis	KO	2	—	—
May 28		Marty Servo	New York	W	10	—	—
Jul 31	♛	Sammy Angott★	New York	W	10	—	—
Aug 21		Ruben Shank	New York	KO	2	—	—
Aug 27	⑩	Tony Motisi	Chicago	KO	1	—	—
Oct 2	⑩	Jake LaMotta★	New York	W	10	—	145
Oct 19	⑩	Izzy Jannazzo	Philadelphia	W	10	—	—
Nov 6		Vic Dellicurti	New York	W	10	—	—
Dec 1	⑩	Izzy Jannazzo	Cleveland	TKO	8	—	—
Dec 14		Al Nettlow	Philadelphia	TKO	3	—	—
1943							
Feb 5	⑩	Jake LaMotta★	Detroit	L	10	—	144
Feb 19	⑩	Jackie Wilson	New York	W	10	—	142
Feb 26	⑩	Jake LaMotta★	Detroit	W	10	—	145
Apr 30		Freddie Cabral	Boston	KO	1	—	—
Jul 1	⑩	Ralph Zannelli	Boston	W	10	—	—

Aug 27	⑩	Henry Armstrong★	New York	W	10	—	—

1944

Oct 13	⑩	Izzy Jannazzo	Boston	TKO	2	—	—
Oct 27		Sgt. Lou Woods	Chicago	TKO	9	—	147
Nov 17	⑩	Vic Dellicurti	Detroit	W	10	—	—
Dec 12		Richard ("Sheik") Rangel	Philadelphia	TKO	2	—	—
Dec 22		Georgie Martin	Boston	TKO	7	—	—

1945

Jan 10		Billy Furrone	Washington, DC	TKO	2	—	148
Jan 16		Tommy Bell	Cleveland	W	10	—	—
Feb 14		George Costner	Chicago	KO	1	—	147
Feb 24	⑩	Jake LaMotta★	New York	W	10	—	148
May 14	⑩	Jose Basora	Philadelphia	D	10	—	—
Jun 15	⑩	Jimmy McDaniels	New York	KO	2	—	145
Sep 18		Jimmy Mandell	Buffalo	TKO	5	—	—
Sep 26	⑩	Jake LaMotta★	Chicago	W	12	—	150
Dec 4	⑩	Vic Dellicurti	Boston	W	10	—	—

1946

Jan 14		Dave Clark	Pittsburgh	TKO	2	—	148
Feb 5		Tony Riccio	Elizabeth, NJ	TKO	4	—	147
Feb 15		O'Neill Bell	Detroit	KO	2	—	—
Feb 26		Cliff Beckett	St. Louis	KO	4	—	147
Mar 4	⑩	Sammy Angott★	Pittsburgh	W	10	—	147
Mar 14		Izzy Jannazzo	Baltimore	W	10	—	—
Mar 21		Freddy Flores	New York	KO	5	—	150
Jun 12		Freddy Wilson	Worcester, MA	KO	2	—	156
Jun 25		Norman Rubio	Union City, NJ	W	10	—	—
Jul 12		Joe Curcio	New York	KO	1	—	149
Aug 15		Vinnie Vines	Albany, NY	KO	6	—	—
Sep 25		Sidney Miller	Elizabeth	KO	3	—	—
Oct 7		Ossie Harris	Pittsburgh	W	10	—	152
Nov 1		Cecil Hudson	Detroit	KO	6	—	—
Nov 6		Artie Levine	Cleveland	KO	10	—	150
Dec 20	⑩	Tommy Bell	New York	W	15	Won-Vac World-W	146

1947

Mar 27		Bernie Miller	Miami	TKO	3	—	157
Apr 3		Fred Wilson	Akron, OH	KO	3	—	—
Apr 8		Eddie Finazzo	Kansas City, MO	TKO	4	—	—
May 16	⑩	Georgie Abrams	New York	W	10	—	150
Jun 24	⑩	Jimmy Doyle	Cleveland	TKO	8	Ret-World-W	146
Aug 21		Sammy Secreet	Akron	KO	1	—	—
Aug 29		Flashy Sebastian	New York	KO	1	—	152
Oct 28	⑩	Jackie Wilson	Los Angeles	TKO	7	—	161
Dec 10		Billy Nixon	Elizabeth	TKO	6	—	—
Dec 19		Chuck Taylor	Detroit	TKO	6	Ret-World-W	146

1948

Mar 4		Ossie Harris	Toledo, OH	W	10	—	—
Mar 16		Henry Brimm	Buffalo	W	10	—	—
Jun 28	⑩	Bernard Docusen	Chicago	W	15	Ret-World-W	146
Sep 23	⑩	Kid Gavilan★	New York	W	10	—	—
Nov 15		Bobby Lee	Philadelphia	W	10	—	152

1949

Feb 10		Gene Buffalo	Wilkes-Barre, PA	KO	1	—	—
Feb 15		Henry Brimm	Buffalo	D	10	—	—

Date		Opponent	Location	Result	Rounds	Title	Weight
Mar 25		Bobby Lee	Chicago	W	10	—	—
Apr 11		Don Lee	Omaha, NE	W	10	—	—
Apr 20		Earl Turner	Oakland, NE	TKO	8	—	—
Jun 7		Freddie Flores	New Bedford, MA	TKO	3	—	—
Jun 20		Cecil Hudson	Providence, RI	TKO	5	—	—
Jul 11	⑩	Kid Gavilan★	Philadelphia	W	15	Ret-World-W	147
Aug 24	⑩	Steve Belloise	New York	KO	7	—	153
Sep 9		Benny Evans	Omaha	TKO	5	—	—
Sep 12		Charley Dotson	Houston	KO	3	—	—
Nov 9		Don Lee	Denver	W	10	—	—
Nov 13		Vern Lester	New Orleans	KO	5	—	—
1950							
Jan 30		George LaRover	New Haven, CT	TKO	4	—	153
Feb 13		Al Mobley	Miami	TKO	6	—	151
Feb 22		Aaron Wade	Savannah	KO	3	—	—
Feb 27		Jean Walzack	St. Louis	W	10	—	—
Mar 22	⑩	George Costner	Philadelphia	KO	1	—	154
Apr 21		Cliff Beckett	Columbus, OH	TKO	3	—	—
Apr 28	⑩	Ray Barnes	Detroit	W	10	—	—
Jun 5	⑩	Robert Villemain	Philadelphia	W	15	Won-Vac PA World-M	155
Aug 9	⑩	Charley Fusari	Jersey City, NJ	W	15	Ret-World-W	147
Aug 25		Jose Basora	Scranton, PA	KO	1	Ret-PA World-M	155
Sep 4		Billy Brown	New York	W	10	—	—
Oct 16		Joe Rindone	Boston	KO	6	—	—
Oct 26		Carl ("Bobo") Olson★	Philadelphia	KO	12	Ret-PA World-M	158
Nov 8		Bobby Dykes	Chicago	W	10	—	—
Nov 27		Jean Stock	Paris	TKO	2	—	—
Dec 9		Luc Van Dam	Brussels	KO	4	—	—
Dec 16		Jean Walzack	Geneva	W	10	—	—
Dec 22	⑩	Robert Villemain	Paris	TKO	9	—	—
Dec 25		Hans Stretz	Frankfurt, Germany	KO	6	—	—
1951							
Feb 14	♛	Jake LaMotta★	Chicago	TKO	13	Won-World-M	155
Apr 5		Holly Mims	Miami	W	10	—	—
Apr 9		Don Ellis	Oklahoma City, OK	KO	1	—	—
May 21		Kid Marcel	Paris	TKO	5	—	—
May 26		Jean Wanes	Zurich, Switzerland	W	10	—	—
Jun 10		Jan de Bruin	Antwerp, Belgium	TKO	8	—	—
Jun 16		Jean Walzack	Liege, Belgium	TKO	6	—	—
Jun 24		Gerhard Hecht	Berlin	NC	2	—	—
Jul 1		Cyrille Delannoit	Turin, Italy	TKO	3	—	—
Jul 10	⑩	Randy Turpin★	London	L	15	Lost-World-M	155
Sep 12	♛	Randy Turpin★	New York	TKO	10	Reg-World-M	157
1952							
Mar 13	⑩	Carl ("Bobo") Olson★	San Francisco	W	15	Ret-World-M	157
Apr 16	⑩	Rocky Graziano★	Chicago	KO	3	Ret-World-M	157
Jun 25	♛	Joey Maxim★	New York	TKO'd	14	For-World-LH	157
1955							
Jan 5		Joe Rindone	Detroit	KO	6	—	—
Jan 19	⑩	Ralph ("Tiger") Jones	Chicago	L	10	—	—
Mar 29		Johnny Lombardo	Cincinnati	W	10	—	—
Apr 14		Ted Olla	Milwaukee	TKO	3	—	—
May 4		Garth Panter	Detroit	W	10	—	—
Jul 22	⑩	Rocky Castellani	San Francisco	W	10	—	—

Date		Opponent	Location	Result	Rounds	Title	Weight
Dec 9	♛	Carl ("Bobo") Olson★	Chicago	KO	2	Reg-World-M	159
1956							
May 18	⑩	Carl ("Bobo") Olson★	Los Angeles	KO	4	Ret-World-M	159
Nov 10		Bob Provizzi	New Haven	W	10	—	—
1957							
Jan 2	⑩	Gene Fullmer★	New York	L	15	Lost-World-M	160
May 1	♛	Gene Fullmer★	Chicago	KO	5	Reg-World-M	159
Sep 23	⑩	Carmen Basilio★	New York	L	15	Lost-World-M	160
1958							
Mar 25	♛	Carmen Basilio★	Chicago	W	15	Reg-World-M	159
1959							
Dec 14		Bob Young	Boston	TKO	2	—	—
1960							
Jan 22	⑩	Paul Pender	Boston	L	15	Lost-World-M	159
Apr 2		Tony Baldoni	Baltimore	KO	1	—	165
Jun 10	♛	Paul Pender	Boston	L	15	For-World-M	158
Dec 3	♛	Gene Fullmer★	Los Angeles	D	15	For-NBA-M	158
1961							
Mar 4	♛	Gene Fullmer★	Las Vegas	L	15	For-NBA-M	159
Sep 25		Wilf Greaves	Detroit	W	10	—	—
Oct 21	⑩	Denny Moyer	New York	W	10	—	159
Nov 20		Al Hauser	Providence	TKO	6	—	—
Dec 8		Wilf Greaves	Pittsburgh	KO	8	—	161
1962							
Feb 17	⑩	Denny Moyer	New York	L	10	—	159
Apr 27		Bobby Lee	Port of Spain, Trinidad	KO	2	—	—
Jul 9		Phil Moyer	Los Angeles	L	10	—	—
Sep 25	⑩	Terry Downes	London	L	10	—	—
Oct 17		Diego Infantes	Vienna	KO	2	—	—
Nov 10		Georges Estatoff	Lyons, France	TKO	6	—	—
1963							
Jan 30	⑩	Ralph Dupas	Miami Beach	W	10	—	162
Feb 25		Bernie Reynolds	Santo Domingo, D.R.	KO	4	—	—
Mar 11		Billy Thornton	Lewiston, ME	KO	3	—	—
May 5		Maurice Robinet	Sherbrooke, Que.	KO	3	—	—
Jun 24	⑩	Joey Giardello★	Philadelphia	L	10	—	—
Oct 14		Armand Vanucci	Paris	W	10	—	160
Nov 9		Fabio Bettini	Lyons	D	10	—	—
Nov 16		Emile Saerens	Brussels	KO	8	—	—
Nov 29		Andre Davier	Grenoble, France	W	10	—	—
Dec 9		Armand Vanucci	Paris	W	10	—	160
1964							
May 19		Gaylord Barnes	Portland, OR	W	10	—	—
Jul 8		Clarence Riley	Pittsfield, MA	TKO	6	—	—
Jul 27		Art Hernandez	Omaha	D	10	—	—
Sep 3		Mick Leahy	Paisley, Scotland	L	10	—	—
Sep 28		Yolande Leveque	Paris	W	10	—	—
Oct 12		Johnny Angel	London	TKO	6	—	162
Oct 24		Jackie Cailleau	Nice, France	W	10	—	—
Nov 7		Jean Baptiste Rolland	Calen, France	W	10	—	—
Nov 14		Jean Beltritti	Marseilles, France	W	10	—	—
Nov 27		Fabio Bettini	Rome	D	10	—	—

1965							
Mar 6		Jimmy Beecham	Kingston, NY	KO	2	—	—
Apr 4		East Basting	Savannah	KO	1	—	—
Apr 28		Gary ("Rocky") Randall	Norfolk, VA	KO	3	—	—
May 5		Gary ("Rocky") Randall	Jacksonville, FL	W	8	—	—
May 24		Memo Ayon	Tijuana, Mexico	L	10	—	—
Jun 1	⑩	Stan Harrington	Honolulu	L	10	—	—
Jun 24		Harvey McCullough	Richmond, VA	W	10	—	—
Jul 12		Ferd Hernandez	Las Vegas	L	10	—	160
Jul 27		Harvey McCullough	Richmond	W	10	—	—
Aug 10	⑩	Stan Harrington	Honolulu	L	10	—	—
Sep 15		Bill Henderson	Norfolk	NC	2	—	160
Sep 23		Harvey McCullough	Philadelphia	W	10	—	—
Oct 1		Peter Schmidt	Johnstown, PA	W	10	—	—
Oct 5		Neil Morrison	Richmond	TKO	2	—	—
Oct 20		Rudolph Bent	Steubenville, OH	KO	3	—	—
Nov 10	⑩	Joey Archer	Pittsburgh	L	10	—	—

Robinson rapidly moved through the welterweight ranks, and the next year, he defeated Sammy Angott and Fritzie Zivic. *The Ring* already ranked him as the top welterweight contender by 1941. The next few years brought victories over Angott, Zivic, Jackie Wilson, Henry Armstrong, and—beginning a long and bitter rivalry—Jake LaMotta.

By 1946, Robinson had gained the admiration of ring devotees for his lightning speed, impeccable timing, solid punching power, and graceful style. That year, Robinson faced Tommy Bell for the vacant welterweight title. Robinson outpointed Bell to take the belt. He defended the welterweight title five times through 1950, one with a win over the tough Kid Gavilan, and meanwhile annexed Pennsylvania's world middleweight title with a victory over Robert Villemain.

Now solidly in middleweight territory, Robinson met his old foe LaMotta in a challenge for the middleweight crown. He and LaMotta had fought five times up to then, with Robinson winning four of their fierce battles. On Valentine's Day in 1951, Robinson faced LaMotta for the sixth time in Chicago Stadium in front of 14,802 fans. It was an ugly, brutal fight from which neither man came away unscathed. After eight rounds of mutual battering, LaMotta led on two cards and Robinson on one. Robinson took control in the ninth. By the twelfth, he had complete command of the fight. LaMotta was bloody and staggering when the referee stopped the fight with one minute left in the thirteenth round.

Robinson took his newly won title to Europe, where he was upset by Randy Turpin, who won the championship in London on a decision. In a rematch back in the United States, Robinson stopped Turpin in the tenth round to reclaim the title. Robinson defended the middleweight crown twice in 1952, with a fifteen-round decision over Bobo Olson in March and a three-round KO of Rocky Graziano in April.

Robinson now wanted to join the light heavies and in 1952, on a blistering hot day in Yankee Stadium, he challenged Joey Maxim for the light heavyweight

The popular Robinson lived extravagantly in the 1950s and early '60s. At times his entourage included a voice coach, drama instructor, barber, golf pro, masseur, secretary, trainers, and a dwarf mascot.

title. Robinson seized the fight early, scoring at will and dancing away from Maxim's offensive thrusts. The first nine rounds were almost all Robinson. Maxim took the tenth. Robinson won the eleventh and the twelfth, but he was visibly wilting in the intense heat. He flagged in the thirteenth and could not answer the bell for the fourteenth round. Officially, the loss was recorded as a knockout, the first and only KO of Robinson's career.

Robinson then retired but was back in January 1955. By December, he had reclaimed the middleweight title by knocking out Olson in two rounds. Robinson lost the title in 1957 to Gene Fullmer, but he won it back for the fourth time with a knockout in their rematch. That same year Robinson faced Hall of Famer Carmen Basilio in Yankee Stadium before 35,000 fans. The aging Robinson came into the match as the underdog. Robinson got off to a good start and won the first four rounds, cutting Basilio's eye and nose. Basilio pressed forward and won four of the next five rounds. The two great champions battled toe-to-toe for the rest of the fight. When the result was announced, Basilio was the winner by a split decision. In the rematch, Robinson, though fighting a virus, dominated the fight and closed Basilio's left eye. An exhausted Robinson won the decision and the championship for the fifth time.

He lost the title in 1960 to Paul Pender by decision and was defeated in their rematch as well. After two failed attempts to win the NBA middleweight title from Fullmer, the 40-year-old Robinson received no more opportunities for title fights.

He finally retired from the ring at the age of 44. In retirement, Robinson had some acting roles, ran a popular Harlem nightclub, and established the Sugar Ray Robinson Youth Foundation. He suffered from Alzheimer's Disease in his last years and ultimately died from it.

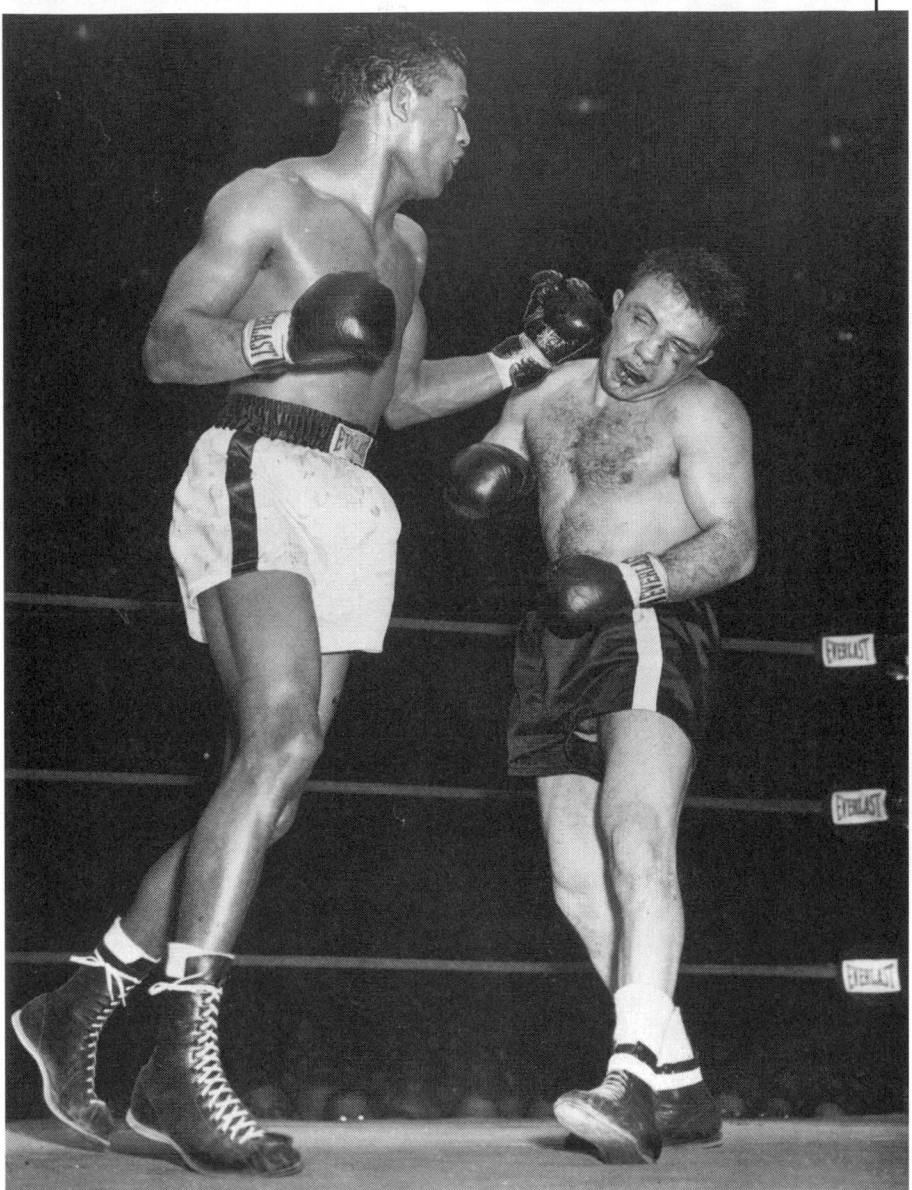

It was called the "St. Valentine's Day massacre" after Robinson (L) battered the determined and courageous Jake LaMotta for nearly 13 rounds to take the middleweight title in Chicago on February 14, 1951.

WELTERWEIGHT

Right-handed; 5'8"; 144–162 lbs.
121 bouts, 6/2/1956 to
4/12/1972
Manager: Ernesto Corrales
Welterweight Champion 1963
Hall of Fame Induction: 1997
Born: 6/17/1937, Camaguey, Cuba
Named: Luis Manuel Rodriguez
Died: 7/1/1996

Luis Rodriguez was a top welterweight of the 1960s, along with his frequent rival and fellow Hall of Famer, Emile Griffith. Rodriguez and Griffith fought four times, each bout going to the scorecards. Rodriguez won the only unanimous decision in the series; Griffith took the rest on splits.

Born in Camaguey, Cuba, the city that had produced Kid Gavilan, Rodriguez grew up in poverty and, while still a boy, had to work selling newspapers and shining shoes. Rodriguez learned to box and won a Cuban national Golden Gloves title, knocking out ten consecutive opponents. His first pro fight was a three-round knockout on June 2, 1956. Except for one bout that was stopped by rain, Rodriguez won all of his first 35 fights. Manager Ernesto Corrales took Rodriguez to Florida and signed him with Angelo Dundee as co-manager. Rodriguez decisioned a series of strong opponents and earned *The Ring*'s ranking as the top contender for the welterweight crown in 1959.

Despite his top-contender status in 1959, 1960, and 1962 (he was fourth in 1961), Rodriguez did not get a chance to fight for the title. Still, "El Feo," or "The Ugly One," as Rodriguez was called, continued to achieve great success. On December 17, 1960, he met Griffith in Madison Square Garden in a non-title contest. Griffith was awarded a split decision, possibly because of his status as champion.

Over the next two years, Rodriguez won fourteen of fifteen fights, and on March 21, 1963, he finally fought Griffith for the title in Dodger Stadium in Los Angeles before 26,142 fans. In a close fight, Rodriguez took the unanimous decision. The rematch in the Garden two months later was another close battle. The official decision was split in favor of Griffith, but most writers at ringside believed that Rodriguez had won.

In his final bout with Grif-

Rodriguez faced Hall of Famer Emile Griffith (L) four times. The two fighters were so closely matched, Griffith once commented that both deserved to be champion.

IN THE RING	WON 107	LOST 13	DRAWS 0	TB 121	KO 49	W 57	WF 1	D 0	KO'd 3	L 10	LF 0	NC 1

Date	Opponent	Site	Result / Rounds		Title	Wt.
1956						
Jun 2	Lazaro Hernandez	Havana	KO	3	—	—
Jul 21	Vicente Reyes	Havana	W	4	—	—
Oct 20	Julian Yanes	Havana	W	4	—	—
Nov 28	Pablo Cardenas	Havana	KO	2	—	—
Dec 15	Jose Hernandez	Havana	NC	2	—	—
1957						
Jan 12	Jose Hernandez	Havana	KO	5	—	—
Feb 16	Guillermo Diaz	Havana	W	6	—	144
Mar 23	Vicente Reyes	Havana	W	6	—	—
May 18	Vicente Reyes	Havana	W	6	—	—
Jun 22	Antonio Salas	Havana	W	8	—	—
Jul 20	Guillermo Diaz	Havana	WF	6	—	—
Sep 28	Gomeo Brennan	Havana	W	8	—	—
Nov 15	Rolando Rodriguez	Havana	W	8	—	—
1958						
Feb 8	Benny Paret	Havana	W	10	—	—
Mar 29	Rolando Rodriguez	Havana	KO	4	—	—
Apr 19	Tony Armenteros	Havana	W	10	—	—
Jul 26	Charley Scott	Havana	KO	9	—	144
Aug 9	Benny Paret	Havana	W	10	—	—
Sep 20	Kid Fichique	Havana	W	12	Won-Cuba-W	144
Nov 22	Juan Padilla	Havana	W	10	—	—
1959						
Feb 21	Joe Miceli	Havana	KO	5	—	—
May 9	Cecil Shorts	Havana	KO	9	—	144
Jun 17	⑩ Virgil Akins	Miami Beach	W	10	—	—
Aug 26	⑩ Rudell Stitch	Louisville, KY	W	10	—	—
Oct 3	Larry Baker	Havana	W	10	—	—
Oct 21	⑩ Isaac Logart	Miami Beach	W	10	—	—
Dec 23	⑩ Garnet ("Sugar") Hart	Miami Beach	W	10	—	—
1960						
Feb 10	Carl Hubbard	Miami Beach	KO	4	—	—
Mar 2	Chico Vejar	Miami Beach	W	10	—	149
Apr 7	Alvaro Gutierrez	Los Angeles	TKO	4	—	146
May 26	Alfredo Cota	Los Angeles	KO	2	—	145
Jul 6	Virgil Akins	Louisville	W	10	—	147
Aug 17	Basil Campbell	Havana	KO	5	—	—
Oct 24	Mel Collins	Tampa, FL	W	10	—	147
Nov 16	Yama Bahama	Miami Beach	W	10	—	—
Nov 28	⑩ Johnny Gonsalves	Oakland, CA	W	10	—	—
Dec 17	⑩ Emile Griffith★	New York	L	10	—	—
1961						
Feb 21	Lyle Mackin	Oakland	TKO	5	—	—
Mar 22	Johnny Gonsalves	Oakland	W	10	—	—
Apr 15	Alvaro Gutierrez	Mexico City	KO	5	—	146
May 13	Alfredo Cota	Guadalajara, Mexico	KO	4	—	147
Aug 3	⑩ Curtis Cokes	Dallas	L	10	—	—
Sep 13	Guy Sumlin	Miami Beach	KO	5	—	—

Date		Opponent	Location	Result	Rounds	Title	Weight
Oct 24		Jose Gonzalez	Miami Beach	TKO	7	—	152
Dec 2	⑩	Curtis Cokes	Miami Beach	W	10	—	—
1962							
Jan 27	⑩	Federico Thompson	New York	W	10	—	150
Mar 17		Ricardo Falech	Miami Beach	TKO	3	—	147
May 4	⑩	Yama Bahama	New York	TKO	3	—	151
Jun 30		Gene Armstrong	New York	TKO	8	—	—
Aug 29		Ernie Burford	Miami Beach	KO	7	—	151
Nov 6		Santiago Gutierrez	San Antonio, TX	KO	3	—	—
Dec 12		Mel Collins	Miami Beach	W	10	—	—
1963							
Jan 19	⑩	Joey Giambra	Miami Beach	W	10	—	150
Mar 21	♛	Emile Griffith★	Los Angeles	W	15	Won-World-W	146
Jun 8	⑩	Emile Griffith★	New York	L	15	Lost-World-W	146
Aug 17	⑩	Denny Moyer	Miami Beach	KO	9	—	—
Oct 18		Wilbert McClure	New York	W	10	—	150
Dec 27		Wilbert McClure	Miami Beach	W	10	—	151
1964							
Mar 20		Holly Mims	New York	W	10	—	151
Apr 3		Jesse Smith	Miami Beach	W	10	—	151
Jun 12	♛	Emile Griffith★	Las Vegas	L	15	For-World-W	146
Nov 14		L.C. Morgan	Mexico City	KO	2	—	—
1965							
Feb 13	⑩	Rubin ("Hurricane") Carter	New York	W	10	—	—
Mar 26		Johnny Smith	Los Angeles	KO	10	—	149
Apr 21		Garland Randall	Tampa	W	10	—	147
Jul 16		Memo Ayon	Los Angeles	TKO	3	—	150
Jul 26		Jose Asumpcion	Las Vegas	W	10	—	150
Aug 3		Charley Austin	Phoenix, AZ	W	10	—	152
Aug 26	⑩	Rubin ("Hurricane") Carter	Los Angeles	W	10	—	150
Oct 4		Johnny Morris	Philadelphia	TKO	2	—	150
Nov 16		Cecil Mott	Miami Beach	KO	4	—	—
Dec 2	⑩	Eddie Pace	Los Angeles	W	10	—	—
Dec 21		Joe Louis Murphy	Albuquerque, NM	KO	4	—	—
1966							
Jan 18		Fred McWilliams	Phoenix	TKO	9	—	152
Jan 25		Joey Limas	Albuquerque	TKO	4	—	149
Mar 7		George Benton	Albuquerque	TKO	9	—	152
Apr 11		Percy Manning	Philadelphia	L	10	—	151
May 7		Tommy Caldwell	San Juan, PR	TKO	2	—	150
Jul 6	⑩	Curtis Cokes	New Orleans	TKO'd	15	—	146
Sep 9		Juarez de Lima	Rosario, Argentina	KO	3	—	—
Sep 24		Ruben Orrico	Rosario	TKO	4	—	—
1967							
Jan 21		Manuel Alvarez	Mar del Plata, Argentina	KO	8	—	—
Feb 7		Esteban Osuna	Rosario	W	10	—	—
Mar 20		Bennie Briscoe	San Juan	W	10	—	—
Jun 4		Rocky Rivero	San Juan	W	10	—	153
Jun 17		Jimmy Lester	Oakland	W	10	—	—
Sep 7	⑩	Ferd Hernandez	Oakland	W	10	—	—
Sep 29		Phil Robinson	Caracas, Venezuela	KO	3	—	—
Oct 21		Marvin McFarland	Caracas	W	10	—	—
Nov 6		Percy Manning	Caracas	TKO	1	—	—
Dec 15		Bennie Briscoe	New York	W	10	—	—

1968						
Feb 6	Charley Austin	Miami Beach	TKO	6	—	154
Mar 26	Carl Moore	Miami Beach	W	10	—	—
May 7	Teddy Wright	Miami Beach	W	10	—	156
Jun 3	Vicente Rondon	San Juan	L	10	—	154
Jul 18	Vicente Rondon	San Juan	W	10	—	—
Sep 4	Rudy Rodriguez	Key West, FL	TKO	4	—	—
Nov 15	⑩ Joe Shaw	New York	W	10	—	153
1969						
Jan 21	Dub Huntley	Miami Beach	W	10	—	157
Feb 20	Robert Williams	Tampa	KO	7	—	—
Mar 31	Rafael Gutierrez	San Diego	TKO	6	—	—
Jul 8	Eddie Owens	Miami Beach	KO	7	—	158
Aug 12	David Beckles	Miami Beach	TKO	2	—	158
Sep 23	Tom Bethea	Miami Beach	W	10	—	—
Nov 22	♛ Nino Benvenuti ★	Rome	KO'd	11	For-World-M	156
1970						
Feb 10	Porter Rolle	Miami Beach	KO	4	—	—
Mar 17	Joe Cokes	Miami Beach	TKO	4	—	—
Apr 14	Willie Warren	Miami Beach	W	10	—	—
Jun 16	Kirkland ("Baby Boy") Rolle	Miami	KO	5	—	162
Jul 31	Jose Gonzalez	San Juan	L	10	—	—
Aug 20	⑩ Fraser Scott	Seattle	W	10	—	—
Dec 1	J.C. Ponder	Miami Beach	KO	5	—	—
1971						
Jan 26	⑩ Bobby Cassidy	Miami Beach	W	10	—	—
Apr 7	Tony Mundine	Melbourne	KO	1	—	—
May 25	⑩ Bunny Sterling	London	L	10	—	—
Aug 3	⑩ Rafael Gutierrez	San Francisco	KO'd	6	—	—
Nov 1	Mike Padgett	Greenwood, CA	KO	2	—	—
Nov 30	Dave Hilton	Miami Beach	W	10	—	—
1972						
Mar 16	Mike Lancaster	Seattle	L	10	—	161
Apr 12	Donato Paduano	Montreal	L	10	—	—

fith, Rodriguez lost another hotly contested split decision. Rodriguez was the second-ranked welterweight contender in 1966. When he moved up to middleweight, *The Ring* considered him that division's top contender in 1967, second in 1968, and third in 1969.

On November 22, 1969, in Rome, Rodriguez went after Nino Benvenuti's middleweight crown. Rodriguez outboxed Benvenuti for ten rounds, but fell to a knock-out left hook in the eleventh. Rodriguez remained a highly rated contender for the next year, but he began losing as often as he won, and he retired at the age of 34. He had won over a hundred fights.

In retirement the affable Rodriguez trained amateur boxers for the City of Miami. He died in 1996 at the age of 59.

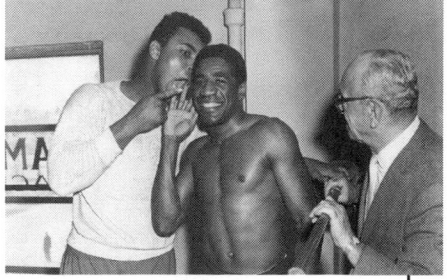

In the presence of Philadelphia boxing promoter Herman Taylor (R), Cassius Clay offers the good-natured Rodriguez some counsel at Miami Beach's Fifth Street Gym.

MATTHEW SAAD MUHAMMAD

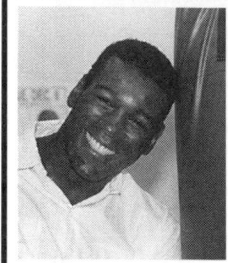

LIGHT HEAVYWEIGHT

Right-handed; 5'11"; 171–187 lbs.

58 bouts, 1/14/1974 to 3/21/1992

WBC Light Heavyweight Champion 1979–81

Hall of Fame Induction: 1998

Born: 6/16/54, Jenkintown, PA

Named: Maxwell Antonio Loach

In a sport that is filled with stories of athletes who rose from humble beginnings to become world champions, few can rival the history of Matthew Saad Muhammad.

Born Maxwell Antonio Loach near Philadelphia, Saad Muhammad was orphaned as a very young child. He and his older brother lived with his aunt who, when she could not afford to care for both children, told Saad Muhammad's brother to lose him. His brother took him to the Benjamin Franklin Parkway and ran away. The lost child was taken to a Catholic shelter where the nuns named him Matthew after the saint and Franklin after the place where he was found.

In and out of reform school as a youth, Saad Muhammad's life took a turn when he saw Muhammad Ali sparring in a local Philadelphia gym. He decided to become a fighter. Saad Muhammad turned professional in 1974, fighting as Matthew Franklin. The next year Muhammad lost a decision to Eddie Gregory who later, as Eddie Mustafa Muhammad, became WBA light heavyweight champion. Saad Muhammad knocked Gregory down in the first round but then fought

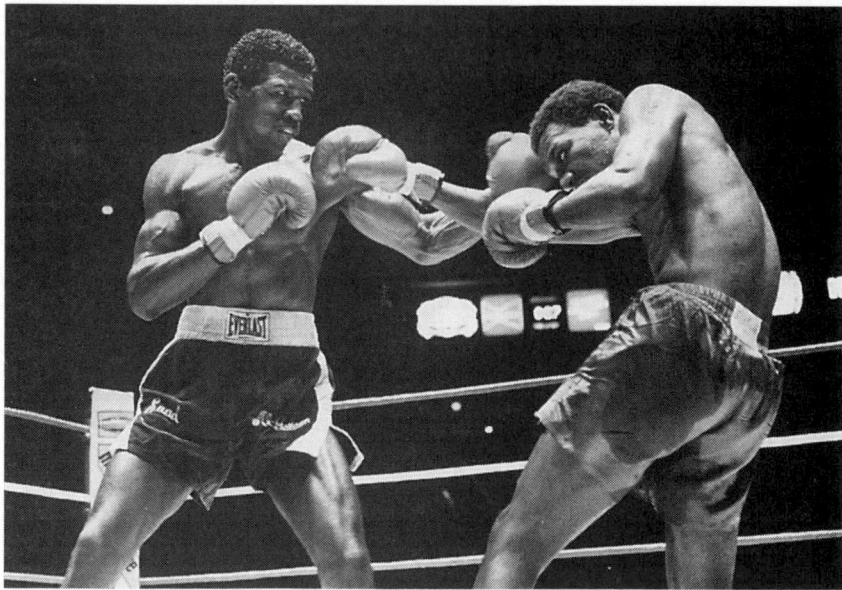

Saad Muhammad (L) connects with a left jab as he racks up points on the way to a ten-round decision over Larry Davis on September 9, 1983 in New York.

IN THE RING	WON 39	LOST 16	DRAWS 3	TB 58	KO 29	W 10	WF 0	D 3	KO'd 8	L 8	LF 0

Date	Opponent	Site	Result / Rounds		Title	Wt.
1974						
Jan 14	Billy Early	Philadelphia	KO	2	—	—
Feb 25	Bele Apolosa	Paris	W	4	—	—
Mar 11	Roy Ingram	Philadelphia	W	4	—	—
May 22	Joe Middleton	Philadelphia	KO	5	—	—
Jul 15	Joe Jones	Philadelphia	KO	3	—	—
Sep 10	Lloyd Richardson	Philadelphia	TKO	4	—	—
Oct 22	Joe Middleton	Alexandria, VA	KO	2	—	—
Dec 10	Wayne Magee	Philadelphia	L	6	—	—
1975						
Feb 25	Vandell Woods	Philadelphia	KO	6	—	174
Jul 24	Roosevelt Brown	Philadelphia	TKO	4	—	173
Oct 21	Wayne Magee	Philadelphia	D	6	—	—
1976						
Feb 13	Harold Carter	Baltimore	W	10	—	—
May 21	Mate Parlov	Milan	W	8	—	—
Jul 17	Marvin Camel	Stockton, CA	W	10	—	174
Sep 15	Bobby Walker	Scranton	TKO	4	—	177
Oct 23	Marvin Camel	Missoula, MT	L	10	—	175
Dec 3	Mate Parlov	Trieste, Italy	D	10	—	—
1977						
Mar 11	Eddie Gregory	Philadelphia	L	10	—	176
Apr 21	Joe Maye	Wilmington, DE	W	10	—	175
Jun 23	Ed Turner	Philadelphia	TKO	6	—	—
Jul 26 ⑩	Marvin Johnson	Philadelphia	KO	12	Won-Vac-NABF-LH	175
Sep 17	Billy Douglas	Philadelphia	KO	6	Ret-NABF-LH	175
Nov 1	Lee Royster	Philadelphia	W	10	—	—
1978						
Feb 10 ⑩	Richie Kates	Philadelphia	TKO	6	Ret-NABF-LH	175
Jun 19	Dale Grant	Philadelphia	TKO	5	—	178
Aug 16	Fred Bright	Newark	KO	8	—	—
Oct 24 ⑩	Yaqui Lopez	Philadelphia	TKO	11	Ret-NABF-LH	175
1979						
Apr 22 ⑩	Marvin Johnson	Indianapolis	TKO	8	Won-WBC-LH	175
Aug 18 ⑩	John Conteh	Atlantic City	W	15	Ret-WBC-LH	172
1980						
Mar 29 ⑩	John Conteh	Atlantic City	TKO	4	Ret-WBC-LH	175
May 13	Louis Pergaud	Halifax	KO	5	Ret-WBC-LH	174
Jul 13 ⑩	Yaqui Lopez	McAfee, NJ	TKO	14	Ret-WBC-LH	174
Nov 28 ⑩	Lottie Mwale	San Diego	KO	4	Ret-WBC-LH	175
1981						
Feb 28	Vonzell Johnson	Atlantic City	TKO	11	Ret-WBC-LH	174
Apr 25 ⑩	Murray Sutherland	Atlantic City	KO	9	Ret-WBC-LH	175
Sep 26 ⑩	Jerry Martin	Atlantic City	TKO	11	Ret-WBC-LH	172
Dec 19	Dwight Braxton	Atlantic City	TKO'd	6	Lost-WBC-LH	174
1982						
Apr 17	Pete McIntyre	Atlantic City	TKO	2	—	174
Aug 7 ♛	Dwight Braxton	Philadelphia	KO'd	6	For-WBC-LH	175

1983						
Mar 23	Eric Winbush	Atlantic City	TKO'd	3	—	176
Sep 9	Larry Davis	New York	TKO	10	—	172
1984						
Feb 11 ⑩	Willie Edwards	Detroit	TKO'd	11	For-NABF-LH	175
1986						
Jan 10	Chris Wells	Hallendale, FL	TKO	6	—	187
Feb 21	Uriah Grant	Fort Lauderdale	L	10	—	176
Nov 15	Tomas Polo-Ruiz	Port of Spain, Trinidad	W	10	—	—
1987						
Jan 30	Pat Strachan	Nassau, Bahamas	L	10	—	—
Jun 26	James Coakley	Nassau	KO	3	—	—
Dec 4	Bobby Thomas	Weirton, WV	W	10	—	175
1988						
Mar 8	Lee Harris	Richmond	TKO	1	—	176
Oct 21	Frank Swindell	Newark	TKO'd	1	—	179
1989						
Oct 24	Kevin Wagstaff	Brisbane, Australia	D	8	—	—
1990						
Feb 16	Markus Bott	Hamburg	TKO'd	3	—	—
1991						
Feb 26	Ed Mack	Philadelphia	L	8	—	174
May 9	Anton Josipovic	Novisad, Yugoslavia	L	8	—	—
Aug 15	Govonor Chavers	Marbella, Spain	KO	1	—	—
Oct 5	Michael Green	Woodbridge, VA	L	8	—	176
Oct 29	Andrew Maynard	Washington, DC	TKO'd	3	—	176
1992						
Mar 21	Jason Waller	Fredericksburg, VA	KO'd	2	—	186

cautiously the whole remainder of the bout. After this defeat, Muhammad vowed that he would no longer be a defensive fighter.

In 1977, he faced Marvin Johnson for the vacant North American Boxing Federation light heavyweight championship in Philadelphia at the Spectrum. Saad Muhammad knocked Johnson out in the twelfth round.

Saad Muhammad successfully defended this regional title three times before facing Johnson for the WBC light heavyweight title in Johnson's hometown of Indianapolis on April 22, 1979. A sparse crowd of 7,000 witnessed what ESPN boxing commentator Al Bernstein called "one of the most incredible brawls any light heavyweights ever staged." Both fighters were hurt from the first round on. In the early going, southpaw Johnson pressed the action, with Saad Muhammad counterpunching. By the fifth round Johnson had a bloody nose and a cut under his right eye, while Saad Muhammad had cuts under both eyes. In the seventh, Saad Muhammad scored with fifteen unanswered punches to leave Johnson wobbly at the bell. In the eighth round, Johnson opened a gash over Saad Muhammad's left eye. Knowing the action could be stopped at any time, Saad Muhammad unleashed a barrage of punches that finally knocked Johnson down. Although Johnson got up at the count of nine, the referee stopped the fight. *The Ring* later named the eighth round its Round of the Year.

In his very next fight, Saad Muhammad, who adopted his Muslim name after winning the light heavyweight title, won a decision over former champion

John Conteh. Another bloody and damaging brawl, the fight aroused controversy over the use of a substance by Saad Muhammad's cut man, Adolph Ritaccio. Some of the substance applied to Saad Muhammad's cuts apparently got on his gloves and then affected Conteh's vision. The WBC suspended Ritaccio for one year and ordered a rematch. Saad Muhammad won the 1980 encounter with a fourth-round TKO.

On July 13, 1980 Saad Muhammad fought Yaqui Lopez, whom he had previously beaten in an NABF title defense, in a bout televised from the Playboy Club in McAfee, New Jersey. Through seven rounds neither fighter gave an inch. In the eighth Lopez caught Saad Muhammad with a hook to the chin, then issued two dozen shots to the head. Saad Muhammad rallied and staggered Lopez before the end of the round. In the fourteenth he dropped Lopez four times before the referee stopped the fight, which *The Ring* later named Fight of the Year.

Saad Muhammad defended his title four more times, all by knockout, before meeting Dwight Braxton (later, Dwight Muhammad Qawi) in Atlantic City on December 19, 1981. Saad Muhammad was pummeled by Braxton before the referee stopped the fight in the tenth. In the rematch (dubbed "the Liberty Brawl") in Philadelphia, Saad Muhammad was battered and bloody by the second round and was knocked down in the third. Braxton scored a technical knockout in the sixth.

Saad Muhammad continued to fight for another ten years, finally hanging up his gloves in 1992. During his later career, he owned a limousine service and a seafood restaurant. He also worked as a model and was offered the movie role in "Rocky III" that eventually went to Mr. T. Saad Muhammad currently trains fighters in Atlantic City and New Orleans.

As he did in many fights, Saad Muhammad (L) had to rally to defeat excellent light heavyweight Yaqui Lopez on July 13, 1980 in a tough, nationally-televised bout.

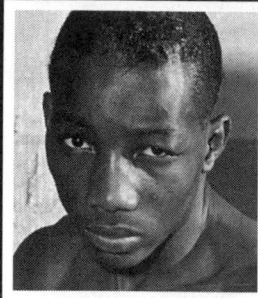

FEATHERWEIGHT

Right-handed; 5'8½"; 124–130 lbs.

162 bouts, 3/7/1944 to 4/14/1956

Manager: Charley Johnston

Featherweight Champion 1948–49,
Jr. Lightweight Champion 1949–50,
Featherweight Champion 1950–57

Hall of Fame Induction: 1990

Born: 6/23/1926, Boston, MA

One of the top featherweights of all time, Sandy Saddler is best remembered for his four brawls with Willie Pep. Few opponents ever fought as viciously or with as much determination as did Saddler and Pep. And few fighters ever worked as hard as Saddler in his quest to be champion. Tall for his weight and possessing a 70" reach, Saddler was a strong puncher. Over the course of his career, he knocked out 103 opponents.

Saddler was born in Boston of West Indian parents and grew up in Harlem, where he learned to box. After about 50 amateur bouts, he turned professional in 1944 at age seventeen when a last-minute substitute was needed for a scheduled bout. Though he won that fight, Saddler lost his second bout by knockout

On December 14, 1948, several weeks after Saddler (L) seized the featherweight championship from Willie Pep, editor Nat Fleischer presented Saddler with The Ring *belt to commemorate his achievement.*

IN THE RING	WON 144	LOST 16	DRAWS 2	TB 162	KO 103	W 41	WF 0	D 2	KO'd 1	L 14	LF 1

Date	Opponent	Site	Result / Rounds		Title	Wt.
1944						
Mar 7	Earl Roys	Hartford, CT	W	8	—	118
Mar 21	Jock Leslie	Hartford	KO'd	3	—	118
Mar 27	Al King	Holyoke, MA	KO	2	—	—
Apr 17	Joe Landry	Holyoke	KO	1	—	—
May 8	Jose Aponte Torres	Trenton, NJ	W	6	—	—
May 15	Jose Aponte Torres	Holyoke	W	6	—	—
May 23	Domingo Diaz	Jersey City, NJ	W	6	—	—
Jun 13	Jose Aponte Torres	Union City, PA	W	8	—	—
Jun 15	Lou Alter	Fort Hamilton, NY	L	6	—	119
Jun 23	Lou Alter	New York	D	4	—	116
Jul 11	Clyde English	Dexter, NY	W	6	—	—
Jul 18	Benny Saladino	Brooklyn	KO	3	—	—
Jul 25	Al Pennino	Brooklyn	W	6	—	—
Aug 8	Georgie Knox	Brooklyn	KO	3	—	—
Aug 18	Clifford Smith	New York	W	6	—	117
Nov 11	Manuel Torres	Brooklyn	W	6	—	—
Nov 13	Ken Tompkins	Newark	KO	1	—	—
Nov 24	Manuel Torres	New York	KO	5	—	—
Nov 28	Percy Lewis	Jersey City	KO	1	—	—
Dec 12	Tony Oshiro	Jersey City	KO	2	—	—
Dec 16	Earl Mintz	Brooklyn	KO	2	—	—
Dec 26	Midget Mayo	Newark	KO	3	—	—
1945						
Jan 13	Tony Oshiro	Brooklyn	W	6	—	—
Jan 15	Mickey Johnson	Newark	KO	1	—	—
Jan 22	Joey Puig	New York	KO	1	—	126
Jan 26	Benny May	New Brunswick, NJ	W	6	—	—
Feb 19	Joey Gatto	New York	KO	1	—	—
Mar 10	Harold Gibson	Brooklyn	W	6	—	—
Mar 19	Joe Montiero	New York	KO	4	—	—
Mar 22	Georgie Knox	Camden, NJ	KO	4	—	—
Apr 2	Jimmy Allen	Newark	KO	1	—	—
Apr 19	Willie Anderson	Detroit	KO	5	—	—
Apr 30	Chilindrina Valencia	Detroit	KO	9	—	—
Jun 18	Caswell Harris	Baltimore	KO	3	—	—
Jun 25	Bobby Washington	Allentown, PA	KO	2	—	—
Jun 29	Leo Methot	New York	KO	1	—	126
Jul 23	Herbert Jones	Baltimore	KO	3	—	—
Jul 24	Joe Montiero	Brooklyn	KO	5	—	125
Jul 30	Luis Rivera	New York	KO	4	—	—
Aug 16	Louis Langley	Brooklyn	KO	1	—	—
Aug 20	Bobby English	Providence, RI	KO	3	—	122
Aug 27	Earl Mintz	Providence	KO	1	—	—
Sep 21	Richie Myashiro	New York	W	6	—	120
Dec 3	Benny Daniels	Holyoke	W	6	—	—
Dec 14	Joe Montiero	Boston	W	8	—	131
Dec 21	Filiberto Osario	New York	W	6	—	127

1946

Date		Opponent	Location	Result	Rounds		Weight
Jan 17		Arvey Bowie	Orange, NJ	KO	1	—	129
Feb 18		Bobby McQuillar	Detroit	L	10	—	—
Apr 8		Ralph LaSalle	New York	KO	1	—	128
Apr 11		Johnny Wolgast	Atlantic City	W	8	—	—
Apr 25		Pedro Firpo	Atlantic City	W	8	—	—
Jun 13		Cedric Flournoy	Detroit	KO	4	—	—
Jul 10		George Cooper	Brooklyn	KO	7	—	—
Jul 23	⑩	Phil Terranova	Detroit	L	10	—	—
Aug 5		Dominic Amoroso	Providence	KO	2	—	130
Aug 22		Pedro Firpo	Brooklyn	W	10	—	122
Oct 10		Jose Rodriguez	Atlantic City	KO	3	—	—
Nov 12		Art Price	Detroit	W	10	—	—
Dec 9		Clyde English	Holyoke	KO	3	—	—
Dec 26		Luis Marquez	Jamaica, NY	KO	2	—	—
Dec 30		Leonard Caesar	Newark	KO	2	—	—

1947

Date		Opponent	Location	Result	Rounds		Weight
Jan 20		George Brown	Holyoke	KO	4	—	—
Jan 27		Humberto Zavala	New York	KO	7	—	128
Feb 7		Larry Thomas	Asbury Park, NJ	KO	2	—	—
Mar 8		Leonardo Lopez	Mexico City	KO	2	—	124
Mar 29		Carlos Malacara	Mexico City	W	10	—	130
Apr 14	⑩	Cabey Lewis	New York	W	10	—	—
May 2		Joe Brown★	New Orleans	KO	3	—	—
May 9		Melvin Bartholomew	New Orleans	W	10	—	130
Jun 3		Jimmy Carter★	Washington, DC	D	10	—	—
Jul 26	⑩	Oscar Calles	Caracas, Venezuela	KO	5	—	—
Aug 14		Leslie Harris	Atlantic City	KO	5	—	—
Aug 29	⑩	Miguel Acevedo	New York	KO	7	—	127
Sep 17		Angelo Ambrosano	Jamaica	KO	2	—	—
Oct 3	⑩	Humberto Sierra	Minneapolis	L	10	—	—
Oct 13		Al Pennino	New York	KO	4	—	130
Oct 26		Lino Garcia	Caracas	KO	5	—	—
Nov 9		Emilio Sanchez	Caracas	KO	5	—	—
Dec 5		Lino Garcia	Havana	KO	3	—	128
Dec 13		Orlando Zulueta	Havana	W	10	—	127

1948

Date		Opponent	Location	Result	Rounds		Weight
Feb 2		Charley Noel	Holyoke	W	10	—	—
Feb 9		Joey Angelo	New York	W	10	—	—
Mar 5		Archie Wilmer	New York	W	8	—	129
Mar 8		Thompson Harmon	Holyoke	TKO	8	—	—
Mar 23		Bobby Timpson	Hartford	W	10	—	128
Apr 10		Luis Monagas	Caracas	KO	3	—	—
Apr 17		Jose Diaz	Caracas	KO	8	—	—
Apr 26		Young Tanner	Oranjestad, Aruba	KO	5	—	—
May 24		Harry LaSane	Holyoke	W	10	—	—
Jun 29	⑩	Chico Rosa	Honolulu	L	10	—	124
Aug 16		Kid Zefine	Panama City	TKO	2	—	126
Aug 23		Aguilino Allen	Panama City	TKO	2	—	126
Oct 11		Willie Roache	New Haven, CT	TKO	3	—	—
Oct 29	♛	Willie Pep★	New York	KO	4	Won-World-FE	124
Nov 19		Tomas Beato	Bridgeport, CT	TKO	2	—	126
Nov 29		Dennis Pat Brady	Boston	W	10	—	—
Dec 7		Eddie Giosa	Cleveland	KO	2	—	129

Date		Opponent	Location	Result	Rd	Notes	
Dec 17	⑩	Terry Young	New York	TKO	10	—	128

1949

Date		Opponent	Location	Result	Rd	Notes	
Jan 17		Young Finnegan	Panama City	KO	5	—	—
Feb 11	⑩	Willie Pep★	New York	L	15	Lost-World-FE	124
Mar 21		Felix Ramirez	Newark	W	10	—	—
Apr 18		Ermano Bonetti	Philadelphia	KO	2	—	—
Jun 2		Jim Keery	London	KO	4	—	138
Jun 23		Luis Ramos	New York	KO	5	—	—
Jul 15		Gordon House	New York	TKO	5	—	—
Aug 2		Chuck Burton	Pittsfield, MA	KO	5	—	—
Aug 8		Johnny Rowe	Brooklyn	KO	8	—	—
Aug 24		Alfredo Escobar	Los Angeles	TKO	9	—	128
Sep 2		Harold Dade	Chicago	W	10	—	—
Sep 20		Proctor Heinold	Schenectady, NY	KO	2	—	—
Oct 28	⑩	Paddy DeMarco	New York	TKO	9	—	—
Nov 7		Leroy Willis	Toledo, OH	W	10	—	130
Dec 6		Orlando Zulueta	Cleveland	W	10	Won-Vac World-JL	127

1950

Date		Opponent	Location	Result	Rd	Notes	
Jan 16		Paulie Jackson	Caracas	KO	1	—	—
Jan 22		Pedro Firpo	Caracas	KO	1	—	—
Feb 6		Chuck Burton	Holyoke	KO	1	—	—
Feb 20		Luis Ramos	Toronto	TKO	3	—	129
Apr 10		Reuben Davis	Newark	TKO	7	—	—
Apr 18	⑩	Lauro Salas	Cleveland	TKO	9	Ret-World-JL	130
Apr 29		Jesse Underwood	Waterbury, CT	W	10	—	—
May 25	⑩	Miguel Acevedo	Minneapolis	TKO	6	—	—
Jun 19		Johnny Forte	Toronto	KO	3	—	—
Jun 30		Leroy Willis	Long Beach, NY	TKO	2	—	131
Sep 8	♛	Willie Pep★	Bronx	TKO	8	Reg-World-FE	124
Oct 12		Harry LaSane	St. Louis	W	10	—	—
Nov 1	⑩	Charley Riley	St. Louis	W	10	—	—
Dec 6	⑩	Del Flanagan	Detroit	L	10	—	—

1951

Date		Opponent	Location	Result	Rd	Notes	
Jan 23		Jesse Underwood	Buffalo	W	10	—	—
Feb 28		Diego Sosa	Havana	KO	2	Ret-World-JL	129
Mar 27	⑩	Lauro Salas	Los Angeles	TKO	6	—	—
Apr 3		Freddie Herman	Los Angeles	TKO	5		
May 5		Harry LaSane	Hershey, PA	W	10	—	—
Jun 2		Alfredo Prada	Buenos Aires	KO	4	—	—
Jun 16		Oscar Flores	Buenos Aires	KO	1	—	—
Jun 22		Mario Salinas	Santiago, Chile	KO	5	—	—
Jun 30		Angel Olivieri	Buenos Aires	KO	5	—	—
Aug 20		Hermie Freeman	Philadelphia	TKO	5	—	—
Aug 27	⑩	Paddy DeMarco	Milwaukee	L	10	—	—
Sep 26	⑩	Willie Pep★	New York	TKO	9	Ret-World-FE	125
Dec 7	⑩	Paddy DeMarco	New York	L	10	—	—

1952

Date		Opponent	Location	Result	Rd	Notes	
Jan 14	⑩	George Araujo	Boston	L	10	—	—
Mar 3		Armand Savoie	Montreal	LD	4	—	—
Mar 17	⑩	Tommy Collins	Boston	TKO	5	—	—

1954

Date		Opponent	Location	Result	Rd	Notes	
Jan 15	⑩	Bill Bossio	New York	TKO	9	—	—
Mar 4		Charlie Slaughter	Akron, OH	TKO	4	—	—
Apr 1		Augie Salazar	Boston	TKO	7	—	—

May 17		Hoacine Khalfi	New York	L	10	— —
Jul 5		Libby Manzo	New York	KO	10	— —
Aug 30		Jackie Blair	Caracas	TKO	1	— —
Sep 27	⑩	Baby Ortiz	Caracas	TKO	3	— —
Oct 25	⑩	Ray Famechon	Paris	TKO	6	— —
Dec 10		Bobby Woods	Spokane, WA	W	10	— —
1955						
Jan 17		Lulu Perez	Boston	KO	4	— —
Feb 25	⑩	Teddy Davis	New York	W	15	Ret-World-FE 124
Apr 5		Kenny Davis	Butte, MT	TKO	5	— —
May 24	⑩	Joe Lopes	Sacramento, CA	L	10	— —
Jul 8		Shigeji Kaneko	Tokyo	TKO	6	— —
Jul 20	⑩	Flash Elorde ★	Manila	L	10	— 129
Dec 12		Dave Gallardo	San Francisco	TKO	7	— 131
1956						
Jan 18	⑩	Flash Elorde ★	San Francisco	TKO	13	Ret-World-FE 126
Feb 13		Curley Monroe	Providence	TKO	3	— —
Apr 14	⑩	Larry Boardman	Boston	L	10	— —

to the more experienced Jock Leslie. This was the only time Saddler was knocked out in his 162-fight career.

Saddler started as a bantamweight, then quickly moved up to featherweight and earned recognition in 1946 as the seventh-best featherweight contender in the annual rankings by *The Ring*. With his phenomenal string of knockouts, Saddler probably deserved a title shot long before Pep finally agreed to fight him, but in October 1948, the stage was set for the first of their four encounters for the featherweight championship. Saddler dominated the fight. He cut Pep in the first round, knocked him down twice in the third, and finally knocked him out in the fourth. In the rematch the next year, Pep was at the top of his form and regained the championship with an outstanding display of boxing skill. Pep was badly battered—he received eleven stitches after the bout—but Saddler lost the unanimous decision.

In December 1949, Saddler won a decision over Orlando Zulueta in Cleveland to take the vacant world junior lightweight title. He held this title for two years,

WHEN TO QUIT

A perennial problem for successful fighters is knowing when to hang up the gloves and find a day job. Several great boxers would have enjoyed perfect records if they had known when to quit. James J. Jeffries was coaxed out of his undefeated retirement to stand as a "white hope" against the first African-American heavyweight champion, Jack Johnson. Jeffries, out of shape after a six-year layoff, was KO'd in fifteen rounds. Michael Spinks's only career defeat was against Mike Tyson, with Spinks re-entering the ring after a 21-month hiatus. Spinks weighed in at a career-high 212 for his last bout.

 RINGFACT

Terry Young (R) could duck, but he couldn't hide. In his eighteenth bout of the year, Saddler beat Young by a TKO in ten on December 17, 1948. Saddler was a rough-and-tumble fighter who gave no quarter.

successfully defending it twice. In September 1950, Saddler was back in Pep's face for another go at the featherweight title. The match was a rouser, with each fighter flying at the other with a relentless will to inflict damage. Saddler knocked Pep down in the third with a left hook, then peppered him with body punches. As the match went on, it developed into an no-holds-barred brawl. Saddler won when an exhausted Pep could not answer the bell for the eighth round. Saddler had reclaimed his title, but Pep wanted a rematch and the two met again a year later. Their fourth meeting was the most grim of all and involved even more wrestling, gouging, tripping and other illegal maneuvers than any of their earlier fights. Saddler won with the TKO in the ninth round. As a result of their actions in this bout, both fighters were suspended briefly by the New York State Athletic commission.

Saddler spent the next two years in the Army and was allowed to retain his featherweight championship. When he returned to the ring, he re-established his hold on the title by beating contenders Teddy Davis in 1955 and Flash Elorde in 1956. He retained the title until announcing his retirement in 1957 after suffering serious eye injuries in an auto accident.

VICENTE SALDIVAR
Zurdo de Oro (Lefty of Gold)

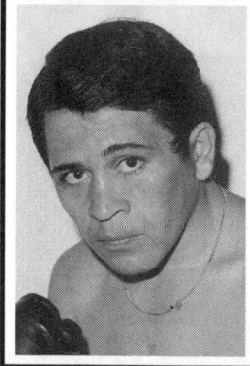

FEATHERWEIGHT

Left-handed; 5'3"; 124–128 lbs.

41 bouts, 2/18/1961 to 10/20/1973

Manager: Adolpho Perez

Featherweight Champion 1964–67

WBC Featherweight Champion 1970

Hall of Fame Induction: 1999

Born: 5/3/1943, Mexico City

Named: Vicente Samuel Saldivar Garcia

Died: 7/18/1985

Vicente Saldivar retired as featherweight champion at 24, only to return to the ring and regain the title by the time he was twenty-seven.

Born in one of the poorest sections of Mexico City, Saldivar learned to fight on the streets. He was introduced to organized boxing by his father, who was an avid fight fan. Although Saldivar wanted to box, his first priority was helping to support his family, and he became an apprentice printer. But he soon met boxing referee Ernesto Arcos, who gave the eager Saldivar boxing instruction. After learning the rudiments from Arcos, Saldivar came under the tutelage of trainer Jose Merino. Though only seventeen, Saldivar was chosen to represent Mexico in the 1960 Olympic Games. He did not fare well at the games, but he gained valuable ring experience and learned from the top boxers he observed.

Saldivar (L) is all smiles after taking the featherweight crown from Sugar Ramos in Mexico City on September 26, 1964.

IN THE RING	WON 38	LOST 3	DRAWS 0	TB 41	KO 27	W 10	WF 1	D 0	KO'd 2	L 0	LF 1

Date		Opponent	Site	Result / Rounds		Title	Wt.
1961							
Feb 18		Baby Palacios	Oaxaca, Mexico	KO	1	—	125
Mar 22		Frijol Gonzalez	Oaxaca	KO	4	—	—
Apr 16		Eduardo Meza	Oaxaca	KO	3	—	—
May 20		Babe Lopez	Leon, Mexico	KO	3	—	—
Oct 14		Jose Luis Mora	Huachinango, Mexico	W	10	—	126
Dec 3		Juan Rodriguez	Leon	TKO	6	—	128
1962							
Jan 6		Ernesto Beltran	Acapulco	KO	6	—	127
Feb 8		Rosendo Martinez	Huachinango	TKO	5	—	128
Mar 18		Juan Zavala	Tuxtla, Mexico	KO	10	—	—
Apr 4	⑩	Jorge Salazar	Matamoros, Mexico	KO	4	—	—
May 2		Gennaro Gonzalez	Mexico City	WF	8	—	—
Jun 27		Indio Fernandez	Mexico City	TKO	6	—	—
Aug 22		Alberto Soto	Mexico City	TKO	2	—	—
Oct 11		Luis Hernandez	Los Mochis, Mexico	KO	1	—	—
Nov 17		Jose Lopez	Monterrey	W	10	—	—
Dec 16	⑩	Jorge Salazar	Matamoros	KO	5	—	—
Dec 29		Baby Luis (Emiro Durgel)	Mexico City	LF	7	—	—
1963							
Mar 16		Luis Hernandez	Los Mochis	KO	2	—	—
Apr 19		Dwight Hawkins	Monterrey	KO	5	—	—
Jun 12		Baby Luis (Emiro Durgel)	Mexico City	TKO	8	—	—
Jul 13		Eloy Sanchez	Mexico City	KO	1	—	—
Sep 21		Beresford Francis	Mexico City	TKO	2	—	126
Dec 16		Felix Gutierrez	Cuernavaca, Mexico	TKO	3	—	—
1964							
Feb 8		Juan Ramirez	Mexico City	TKO	2	Won-Mex-FE	126
Apr 4		Eduardo Guerrero	Mexico City	W	12	Ret-Mex-FE	126
Jun 1	⑩	Ismael Laguna★	Tijuana	W	10	—	127
Sep 26	♛	Ultiminio ("Sugar") Ramos★	Mexico City	TKO	12	Won-World-FE	125
Dec 6		Delfino Rosales	Leon, Mexico	TKO	11	Ret-Mex-FE	126
1965							
Feb 13		Eduardo Torres	Guadalajara	KO	4	—	—
May 7	⑩	Raul Rojas	Los Angeles	TKO	15	Ret-World-FE	124
Sep 7	⑩	Howard Winstone	London	W	15	Ret-World-FE	125
1966							
Feb 12	⑩	Floyd Robertson	Mexico City	KO	2	Ret-World-FE	125
Aug 7	⑩	Mitsunori Seki	Mexico City	W	15	Ret-World-FE	124
1967							
Jan 29	⑩	Mitsunori Seki	Mexico City	TKO	7	Ret-World-FE	124
Jun 15	⑩	Howard Winstone	Cardiff, Wales	W	15	Ret-World-FE	125
Oct 14	⑩	Howard Winstone	Mexico City	TKO	12	Ret-World-FE	125
1969							
Jul 18	⑩	Jose Legra	Inglewood, CA	W	10	—	—
1970							
May 9	♛	Johnny Famechon	Rome	W	15	Reg-WBC-FE	126
Dec 11	⑩	Kuniaki Shibata	Tijuana	TKO'd	14	Lost-WBC-FE	125

1971							
Jul 15	⑩	Frankie Crawford	Los Angeles	W	10	—	—
1973							
Oct 20	♛	Eder Jofre★	Salvador, Brazil	KO'd	4	For-WBC-FE	125

On February 19, 1961, Saldivar began his professional career with a first-round knockout of Baby Palacios in Oaxaca, Mexico. Saldivar defeated his first sixteen opponents, thirteen of them by knockout, before losing to Baby Luis on December 29, 1962, on a disqualification. He defeated his next six opponents, all by knockouts, including a Baby Luis rematch. Saldivar's impressive record earned him a shot at the Mexican featherweight title against Juan Ramirez, whom he knocked out in the second round to win the crown. After defending his championship once, Saldivar faced his first world title contender in Hall of Famer Ismael Laguna on June 1, 1964, in Tijuana. Laguna was *The Ring*'s top-ranked contender in 1964, yet Saldivar earned a decision in ten rounds and the right to challenge world featherweight champion Sugar Ramos.

The title fight was held in Mexico City on September 26, 1964. Ramos and Saldivar gave the fans a good show, going at each other with reckless abandon. As the fight wore on, Ramos's face was covered in blood, but the champion fought on through the pain. By the twelfth round, however, Ramos could not answer the bell, and the 21-year-old Saldivar was the new world champion. The title fight served as a showcase for Saldivar's style. He fought as a southpaw and had tremendous power in both his right and left hands. He was able to box at a furious pace, an ability he believed he owed to an abnormally slow heart rate.

Saldivar was a busy champion. After knocking out Delfino Rosales, he traveled to the United States for the first time and faced Raul Rojas at Memorial Coliseum in Los Angeles on May 7, 1965. After a quick start, he rocked Rojas in the sixth round with a left to the head. Throwing off the blow, Rojas was able to win the next round; Saldivar cut Rojas above the eye in the eighth; Rojas retaliated by cutting Saldivar's cheek in the ninth. Finally, Saldivar took control of the fight. In the fifteenth round, he pummeled Rojas with rights and lefts to the head and body before the referee stopped the fight with only ten seconds to go.

For his next defense, Saldivar met European featherweight champ Howard Winstone in London. Winstone outboxed Saldivar in the early going, but the champion came back strong to retain his title. This was only the first of three meetings between Saldivar and Winstone. On June 15, 1967, at Ninian Stadium in Cardiff, Wales, under the eyes of 30,000 fans, the two met again. Winstone opened quickly with jabs and rights, while Saldivar often missed his clever opponent. Saldivar worked the body in the middle of the fight, but Winstone continued to score with jabs. Finally, Saldivar's heavy body punches began to weaken Winstone. Saldivar was then able to move his attack to the head, and in the fourteenth he knocked Winstone down. He retained control in the fifteenth and won a close decision. After his third victory over Winstone in a twelve-round knockout in Mexico City on October 14, 1967, the 24-year-old Saldivar announced his retirement. Standing in the center of the ring, Zurdo de Oro (Lefty of Gold), as he was known in his native country, shocked his fans by pronouncing, "I have made more money as a boxer than I can ever spend. I am tired of always training and never having any fun while I am still young. . . . This was my last fight." Many in the crowd wept.

However, like many boxers who retire early, Saldivar could not stay away for long. On July 18, 1969, he won a ten-round decision over Jose Legra. Legra had defeated Winstone to win the vacant WBC featherweight title, then lost the title to Johnny Famechon. On May 9, 1970, Saldivar met Famechon at the Palazza dello Sport in Rome, before a crowd of about 16,000, for a chance to regain the WBC title and general recognition as world champion. Saldivar took to the attack. Although he suffered a badly puffed eye, he continued to be the aggressor. Saldivar won a clear-cut decision by scores of 71-68, 72-68, and 73-70.

Saldivar's second reign as champion was short lived. In his very next fight, he was knocked him out by Kuniaki Shibata in the thirteenth round—the first time Saldivar had been stopped short of the distance. In this bout, Saldivar was plagued by serious cuts around his eyes. After decisioning Frankie Crawford seven months after his loss, Saldivar did not fight for over two years. He then faced Hall of Famer Eder Jofre in another bid for the featherweight title. Saldivar was knocked out by Jofre in four rounds. He retired for good at the age of 30, and trained boxers in Mexico until he suffered a fatal heart attack at the age of 42.

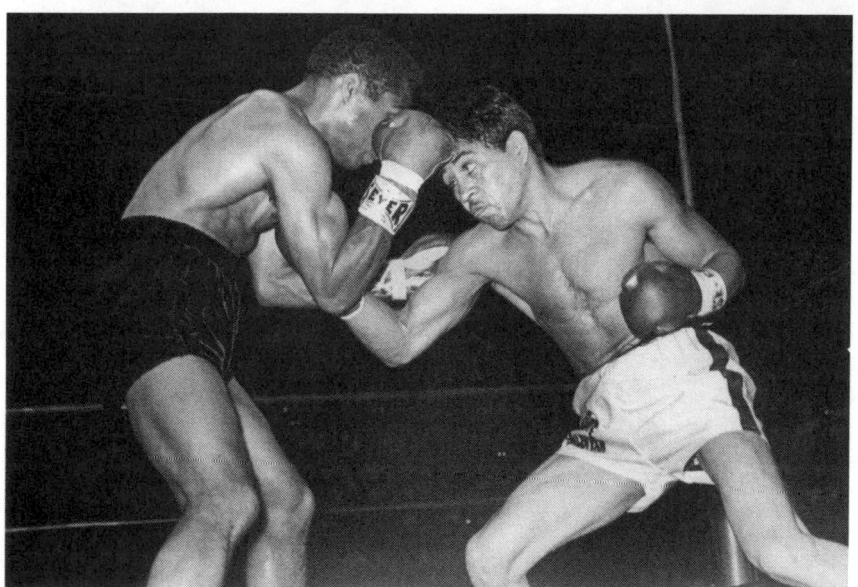

Raul Rojas (L) fails to block a Saldivar shot in Saldivar's first title defense, and his first fight outside Mexico, in Los Angeles on May 7, 1965.

Right-handed; 5'7"; 117–129 lbs.

46 bouts, 5/4/1975 to 7/21/1982

Manager: Cristobal Rosas

WBC Featherwt. Champ 1980–82

Hall of Fame Induction: 1991

Born: 1/26/1959, Santiago Tianguistenco, Mexico

Died: 8/12/1982

Thoughts about the career of Salvador Sanchez must invariably turn to the tragic and early end of his life. Sanchez was only 23 years old when he died after his Porsche collided with a pickup truck in Mexico. Nevertheless, Sanchez had a brilliant seven-year career that culminated in a championship.

Sanchez began his career in 1975 at the age of sixteen and won his first eighteen fights before losing to Antonio Becerra in a bid to obtain the vacant Mexican bantamweight title. He first rose to international prominence in 1979, when he appeared in the eighth position in *The Ring*'s world rankings for featherweights.

In 1980, Sanchez challenged the colorful WBC featherweight champion, Danny ("Little Red") Lopez for his belt. Sanchez thrashed the champion from the

In his fifth defense of the WBC featherweight belt at Caesar's in Las Vegas, Sanchez (L) feints with his left and prepares to unload on Roberto Castanon with his right. Sanchez won by 10th-round TKO.

IN THE RING	WON 44	LOST 1	DRAWS 1	TB 46	KO 32	W 12	WF 0	D 1	KO'd 0	L 1	LF 0

Date	Opponent	Site	Result / Rounds		Title	Wt.
1975						
May 4	Al Gardeno	Veracruz, Mexico	KO	3	—	—
May 25	Miguel Ortiz	Misantla, Mexico	KO	3	—	—
Aug 10	Victor Martinez	Misantla	KO	2	—	—
Oct 19	Cesar Lopez	Misantla	KO	4	—	—
Nov 25	Candido Sandoval	Mexico City	TKO	7	—	—
Dec 11	Fidel Trejo	Mexico City	W	8	—	—
1976						
Jan 24	Juan Granados	Mexico City	TKO	3	—	117
Feb 25	Javier Solis	Mexico City	TKO	7	—	—
Mar 31	Serafin Pacheco	Mexico City	TKO	4	—	—
Apr 24	Jose Chavez	Mexico City	TKO	7	—	118
May 26	Fidel Trejo	Mexico City	KO	6	—	—
Jul 5	Pedro Sandoval	Mexico City	TKO	9	—	121
Aug 11	Joel Valdez	Mexico City	TKO	9	—	—
Oct 31	Saul Montana	Nuevo Laredo, Mexico	TKO	9	—	118
Dec 25	Antonio Leon	Mexico City	TKO	10	—	119
1977						
Feb 5	Raul Lopez	Mexicali, Mexico	TKO	10	—	—
Mar 12	Daniel Felizardo	Mexico City	KO	5	—	118
May 21	Rosalio Badillo	Mexico City	TKO	5	—	—
Sep 9	Antonio Becerra	Mazatlan, Mexico	L	12	For-Vac Mexico-B	118
Nov 11	Jose Soto	Los Mochis, Mexico	W	10	—	—
Dec 5	Eliseo Cosme	Mexico City	W	10	—	—
1978						
Apr 15	Juan Escobar	Los Angeles	D	10	—	—
Jul 1	Jose Sanchez	Mexico City	W	10	—	—
Aug 13	Hector Cortez	Mazatlan	TKO	7	—	—
Sep 26	Francisco Ponce	Houston	KO	2	—	129
Nov 21	Edwin Alarcon	San Antonio, TX	TKO	9	—	—
Dec 16	Jose Santana	Mexico City	TKO	2	—	126
1979						
Feb 3	Carlos Mimila	Mexico City	KO	3	—	129
Mar 13	James Martinez	San Antonio	W	10	—	—
May 19	Salvador Torres	Mexico City	TKO	7	—	126
Jun 17	Fel Clemente	San Antonio	W	12	—	126
Jul 22	Rosalio Muro	San Luis Potosi, Mexico	KO	3	—	125
Aug 7	Felix Trinidad	Houston	KO	5	—	127
Sep 25 ⑩	Richard Rozelle	Los Angeles	TKO	3	—	128
Dec 15	Rafael Gandarilla	Guadalajara, Mexico	TKO	5	—	—
1980						
Feb 2 ♛	Danny Lopez	Phoenix	TKO	13	Won-WBC-FE	125
Apr 12 ⑩	Ruben Castillo	Tucson	W	15	Ret-WBC-FE	126
Jun 21 ⑩	Danny Lopez	Las Vegas	TKO	14	Ret-WBC-FE	126

Sep 13	⑩	Patrick Ford	San Antonio	W	15	Ret-WBC-FE	126
Dec 13	⑩	Juan LaPorte	El Paso, TX	W	15	Ret-WBC-FE	126
1981							
Mar 22	⑩	Roberto Castanon	Las Vegas	TKO	10	Ret-WBC-FE	126
Jul 11	⑩	Nicky Perez	Los Angeles	W	10	—	129
Aug 21		Wilfredo Gomez★	Las Vegas	TKO	8	Ret-WBC-FE	126
Dec 12	⑩	Pat Cowdell	Houston	W	15	Ret-WBC-FE	126
1982							
May 8		Rocky Garcia	Dallas	W	15	Ret-WBC-FE	126
Jul 21	⑩	Azumah Nelson	New York	TKO	15	Ret-WBC-FE	126

sixth to the thirteenth round, when the referee called for an end to the slaughter. Nine of Sanchez's last ten fights were title defenses, including a victory over Hall of Famer Wilfredo Gomez. Sanchez dominated the previously unbeaten Gomez and then knocked him out in the eighth.

In an interview shortly before his death, Sanchez spoke of his desire to move up to lightweight and fight Alexis Arguello. He expressed no particular desire to

Sanchez (L) holds off Hall of Famer and junior featherweight champ Wilfredo Gomez, who put on four extra pounds and challenged for Sanchez's belt. It was Sanchez by an eighth-round TKO.

In his ninth defense in just a little over two years since winning the WBC featherweight title, Sanchez (R) faced Azumah Nelson, a tough customer from Ghana, on July 21, 1982 in Madison Square Garden. Sanchez floored Nelson (R) in the 15th round and won by TKO. Twenty-two days later, Sanchez died in an early morning accident north of Mexico City. His sports car crashed into a heavily-laden truck.

unify the featherweight title as he considered his WBC belt to have the widest recognition.

Although Sanchez recorded thirty-two knockouts in his forty-six fights, he was not considered a big puncher. His primary skill was as a boxer and an observant tactician. As Sanchez said, "The KO's come through undermining my opponents." Sanchez greatly admired the ring artistry of Jose Napoles, Ruben Olivares, and Sugar Ray Leonard.

PAPERWEIGHTS

Many fight fans assume that the bantamweight division was the lightest contested division until the flyweight class was introduced in England in 1909. In fact, the 105-pound division was contested in America as the "paperweight" class from the 1890s through at least 1910. The term "flyweight" wasn't generally accepted for 105-pounders in the U.S. until the New York State Athletic Commission adopted new standards in 1920. Johnny Coulon was the last well-known paperweight champ, winning the title by besting Kid Murphy in Peoria, Illinois in 1908. Coulon successfully defended the title three times before moving up to bantamweight.

RINGFACT

MAX SCHMELING
The Black Uhlan

HEAVYWEIGHT

Right-handed; 6'1"; 175–195 lbs.

70 bouts, 8/2/1924 to 10/31/1948

Managers: Arthur Bulow 1924–28, Joe Jacobs 1928–38

Heavyweight Champion 1930–32

Hall of Fame Induction: 1992

Born: 9/28/1905, Klein Luckaw, Brandenburg, Germany

Named: Maximillian Adolph Otto Siegfried Schmeling

At one time a very hated man in the United States, Max Schmeling was an excellent boxer and sportsman who proved himself worthy of the world heavyweight championship. Schmeling was a victim of his times, held up by Nazi Germany as an example of Aryan supremacy. His fights became symbolic of a much greater struggle, but Schmeling the man was simply a good fighter who wanted to reach the top.

Schmeling turned professional in his native Germany in 1924. Initially fighting as a light heavyweight, he won the German light heavyweight title in 1926 with a one-round knockout of Max Diekmann (who had handed Schmeling his first defeat two years earlier). In the next couple of years, Schmeling took the European light heavyweight and German heavyweight titles. In late 1928, Schmeling began fighting in the United States and became known to American audiences. A strong puncher with both hands and the owner of an especially

Franklin Roosevelt meets Max Schmeling on June 1, 1930 after watching a training session in Kingston, NY. FDR was then governor of New York. Schmeling was preparing for his title fight with Sharkey.

IN THE RING	WON 56	LOST 10	DRAWS 4	TB 70	KO 39	W 14	WF 3	D 4	KO'd 5	L 5	LF 0

Date	Opponent	Site	Result / Rounds		Title	Wt.
1924						
Aug 2	Hans Czapp	Dusseldorf, Germany	KO	6	—	—
Sep 20	Willy Louis	Duisburg, Germany	KO	1	—	—
Sep 22	Pietrus Van Der Veer	Dusseldorf	KO	3	—	—
Oct 4	Rocky Knight	Cologne, Germany	W	8	—	—
Oct 10	Max Diekmann	Berlin	TKO'd	4	—	—
Oct 31	Fred Hammer	Cologne	KO	3	—	—
Dec 4	Hans Breuer	Cologne	KO	2	—	—
Dec 7	Battling Marthar	Dusseldorf	KO	3	—	—
Dec 17	Helmuth Hartig	Berlin	KO	1	—	—
Dec 26	Jimmy Lygget	Cologne	WD	4	—	—
1925						
Jan 18	Johnny Kloudts	Cologne	KO	2	—	—
Jan 20	Joe Mehling	Berlin	W	6	—	—
Mar 1	Leon Randol	Cologne	KO	4	—	—
Mar 15	Alf Baker	Cologne	KO	3	—	—
Apr 3	Jimmy Lygget	Berlin	D	8	—	—
Apr 28	Fred Hammer	Bonn, Germany	W	8	—	—
May 9	Jack Taylor	Cologne	L	10	—	—
Jun 14	Leon Randol	Brussels, Belgium	D	10	—	—
Sep 1	Larry Gains	Cologne	KO'd	2	—	—
Nov 8	Rene Compere	Cologne	W	8	—	—
1926						
Feb 12	Max Diekmann	Berlin	D	8	—	—
Mar 19	Willy Louis	Cologne	KO	1	—	—
Jul 13	August Vongehr	Berlin	KO	1	—	—
Aug 24	Max Diekmann	Berlin	KO	1	Won-Germany-LH	175
Oct 1	Hermann Van't Hoff	Berlin	WD	8	—	—
1927						
Jan 13	Jack Stanley	Berlin	KO	8	—	—
Jan 23	Louis Wilms	Breslau, Poland	KO	8	—	—
Feb 4	Joe Mehling	Dresden, Germany	KO	3	—	—
Mar 12	Leon Sebilo	Dortmund, Germany	KO	2	—	—
Apr 8	Francis Charles	Berlin	KO	8	—	—
Apr 26	Stanley Glen	Hamburg, Germany	KO	1	—	—
May 7	Robert Larsen	Frankfurt, Germany	W	10	—	—
May 17	Raoul Paillaux	Frankfurt	KO	3	—	—
Jun 19	Fernand Delarge	Dortmund	KO	14	Won-Europe-LH	175
Jul 13	Jack Taylor	Hamburg	W	10	—	—
Aug 7	Willem Westbroeck	Essen, Germany	KO	1	—	—
Sep 2	Robert Larsen	Berlin	KO	3	—	—
Oct 2	Louis Clement	Dortmund	KO	6	—	—
Nov 6	Hein Domogergen	Leipzig, Germany	KO	7	Ret-Europe-LH	175
Dec 2	Gypsie Daniels	Berlin	W	10	—	—
1928						
Jan 6	Michele Bonaglia	Berlin	KO	1	Ret-Europe-LH	175
Feb 25	Gypsie Daniels	Frankfurt	KO'd	1	—	—
Mar 11	Ted Moore	Dortmund	W	10	—	—

Apr 4		Franz Diener	Berlin	W	15	Won-Germany-H	188
Nov 23		Joe Monte	New York	KO	8	—	—
1929							
Jan 4		Joe Sekyra	New York	W	10	—	—
Jan 22		Pietro Corri	Newark	KO	1	—	—
Feb 1	⑩	Johnny Risko	New York	TKO	9	—	—
Jun 27	⑩	Paolino Uzcudun	New York	W	15	—	189
1930							
Jun 12	⑩	Jack Sharkey★	New York	WD	4	Won-Vac World-H	188
1931							
Jul 3	⑩	Young Stribling★	Cleveland	TKO	15	Ret-World-H	189
1932							
Jun 21	⑩	Jack Sharkey★	Long Island, NY	L	15	Lost-World-H	188
Sep 26		Mickey Walker★	Long Island	TKO	8	—	—
1933							
Jun 8	⑩	Max Baer★	New York	TKO'd	10	—	—
1934							
Feb 13	⑩	Steve Hamas	Philadelphia	L	12	—	—
May 12		Paulino Uzcudun	Barcelona	D	12	—	—
Aug 26		Walter Neusel	Hamburg	TKO	9	—	—
1935							
Mar 10	⑩	Steve Hamas	Hamburg	KO	9	—	—
Jul 7		Paolino Uzcudun	Berlin	W	12	—	—
1936							
Jun 19	⑩	Joe Louis★	New York	KO	12	—	—
1937							
Dec 14		Harry Thomas	New York	KO	8	—	—
1938							
Jan 30		Ben Foord	Hamburg	W	12	—	—
Apr 16		Steve Dudad	Hamburg	KO	5	—	—
Jun 22	♛	Joe Louis★	New York	KO'd	1	For-World-H	193
1939							
Jul 2		Adolf Heuser	Stuttgart, Germany	KO	1	Won-Europe-H	195
1947							
Sep 28		Werner Vollmer	Frankfurt	KO	7	—	—
Dec 7		Hans Draegenstein	Hamburg	W	10	—	—
1948							
May 23		Walter Neusel	Hamburg	L	10	—	—
Oct 2		Hans Draegenstein	Kiel, Germany	KO	9	—	—
Oct 31		Reifdel Vogt	Berlin	L	10	—	—

destructive short right hook, Schmeling was the second-ranked heavyweight contender in *The Ring*'s annual rankings in 1929.

In 1930, Schmeling met Jack Sharkey in Yankee Stadium for the vacant heavyweight title. More than 80,000 fans were curious to see who would succeed Gene Tunney, who had given up the crown two years earlier. The first three rounds were fast and furious. In the fourth Schmeling momentarily stunned Sharkey, but Sharkey retaliated with a left to the body, knocking Schmeling down. Schmeling claimed that he had been fouled by a low blow. The officials supported his contention and awarded him the title. This was the only time the heavyweight crown had changed hands on a foul, and the manner in which he won the championship did not make Schmeling particularly popular in the U.S.

Schmeling defended his title against Young Stribling in 1931. American fans were anxious to get the title back from Europe, and knockout artist Stribling was their hope. Schmeling hammered at Stribling for fourteen rounds and finally finished him in the fifteenth. By now, Sharkey was fidgeting for a rematch. The two intervening years had been enough to turn the tables, and Sharkey won a fifteen-round decision to take the title.

Schmeling continued to box. He demolished Mickey Walker in a fight that had fans calling for it to be stopped, then was himself the victim of a vicious battering by Max Baer. In 1936, Schmeling fought young Joe Louis, then unbeaten. Schmeling knocked Louis down in the fourth round, the first time anyone had ever floored the Brown Bomber, and dropped Louis to his knees for the ten-count in the twelfth. Schmeling was again in line for the championship and signed for a match with the current champion James J. Braddock. The fight never took place because American boxing officials did not want to risk losing the heavyweight title to Europe.

But when Joe Louis became champion, a match was allowed in 1938. The contest was fraught with social and political implications. Louis became America's flagbearer against all that was evil in Adolf Hitler's reign. Schmeling was publicized by the German government as an example of the superiority of the German "race" and way of life. (Stories later surfaced that Schmeling had hid Jewish youths in his hotel during Kristallnacht and had helped Jews escape Germany during the war.) Louis made short work of Schmeling, knocking him out with such fury in the first round that Schmeling screamed. The Nazis quickly cut the radio broadcast in Germany. Schmeling, who served as a paratrooper in the German military, continued to box after World War II until 1948, before beginning a long period of employment with Coca-Cola in Germany.

This sequence shows Jack Sharkey (R) landing the low blow to Schmeling that caused a disqualification by foul. Schmeling became champion—the only time the heavyweight title changed hands on a foul.

MICHAEL SPINKS
The Spinks Jinx

HEAVYWEIGHT

Right-handed; 6'2½"; 165–212 lbs.

32 bouts, 4/17/1977 to 6/27/1988

1976 Olympic Middlewt. Gold Medalist

WBA Light Heavywt. Champ 1981–83,
Light Heavywt. Champ 1983–85,
Heavywt. Champ 1985–88

Hall of Fame Induction: 1994

Born: 7/13/1956, St. Louis, MO

Michael Spinks accomplished what no other light heavyweight champion had ever been able to achieve. Spinks became the first light heavyweight champ to move up in class and grab the heavyweight crown when he defeated Larry Holmes in 1985. Light heavyweights on the Hall of Famer roster such as Tommy Loughran, Bob Foster, Archie Moore, and Billy Conn had all failed in bids to win the heavyweight title. Though sometimes overshadowed by his older brother Leon, heavyweight champion in 1978, Michael was a top-shelf fighter who lost only one fight in his nine-year career.

Born in St. Louis, Spinks gained national prominence when he represented the United States in the 1976 Olympics as a middleweight. Spinks was one of five Americans to win gold medals at the Montreal games, along with brother Leon, Sugar Ray Leonard, Howard Davis, and Leo Randolph. Spinks did not immediately turn pro but worked for a time in a chemical plant. Convinced in 1977 by flamboyant promoter Butch Lewis to join the pro ranks, Spinks quickly found success in the light heavyweight division.

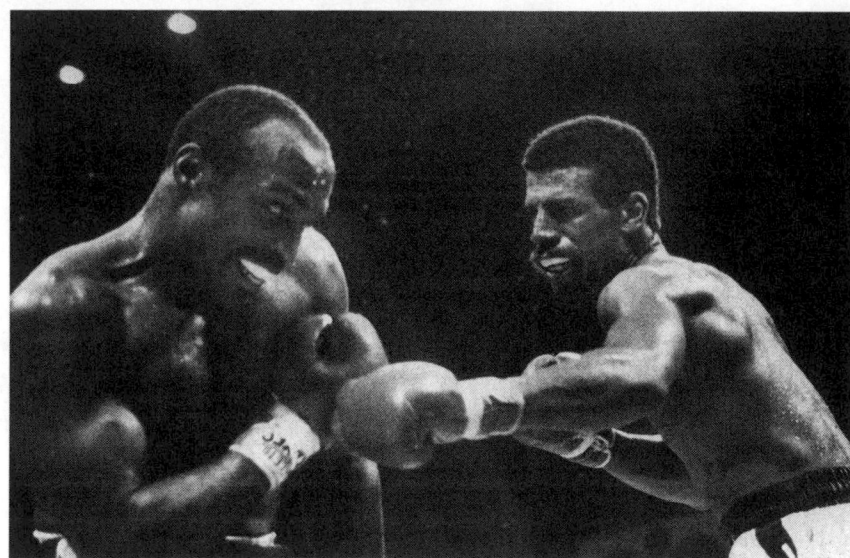

En route to a fifteen-round victory to unify the light heavyweight title, Spinks (R) goes after formidable Dwight Muhammad Qawi (originally Dwight Braxton), the WBC champ. They fought in Atlantic City.

Spinks won his first sixteen fights, which included victories over former champion John Conteh as well as ranked contenders Yaqui Lopez and Marvin Johnson. The record put Spinks in line for a championship bout with WBA title holder Eddie

IN THE RING	WON 31	LOST 1	DRAWS 0	TB 32	KO 21	W 10	WF 0	D 0	KO'd 1	L 0	LF 0

Date	Opponent	Site	Result / Rounds		Title	Wt.
1977						
Apr 17	Eddie Benson	Las Vegas	KO	1	—	165
May 9	Luis Rodriguez	St. Louis	W	6	—	165
Jun 1	Joe Borden	Montreal	KO	2	—	167
Aug 23	Jasper Brisbane	Philadelphia	TKO	1	—	166
Sep 13	Ray Elson	Los Angeles	KO	1	—	168
Oct 21	Gary Summerhays	Las Vegas	W	8	—	169
1978						
Feb 15	Tom Bethea	Las Vegas	W	8	—	170
Dec 15	Eddie Phillips	White Plains, NY	TKO	4	—	170
1979						
Nov 24	Marc Hans	Bloomington, MN	TKO	1	—	180
1980						
Feb 1	Johnny Wilburn	Louisville	W	8	—	175
Feb 4	Ramon Ronquillo	Atlantic City	TKO	6	—	174
May 4	Murray Sutherland	Kiamesha Lake, MI	W	10	—	179
Aug 2	David Conteh	Baton Rouge	TKO	9	—	177
Oct 18 ⑩	Yaqui Lopez	Atlantic City	TKO	7	—	176
1981						
Jan 24	Willie Taylor	Philadelphia	TKO	8	—	176
Mar 28 ⑩	Marvin Johnson	Atlantic City	KO	4	—	176
Jul 18 ♛	Mustafa Muhammad	Las Vegas	W	15	Won-WBA-LH	175
Nov 7	Vonzell Johnson	Atlantic City	TKO	7	Ret-WBA-LH	173
1982						
Feb 13	Mustapha Wasajja	Atlantic City	KO	6	Ret-WBA-LH	173
Apr 11 ⑩	Murray Sutherland	Atlantic City	KO	8	Ret-WBA-LH	172
Jun 12 ⑩	Jerry Celestine	Atlantic City	TKO	8	Ret-WBA-LH	173
Sep 18 ⑩	John Davis	Atlantic City	TKO	9	Ret-WBA-LH	173
1983						
Mar 18 ♛	Dwight Braxton	Atlantic City	W	15	Won-Vac World-LH	173
Nov 25 ⑩	Oscar Rivadeneyra	Vancouver, B.C.	TKO	10	Ret-World-LH	173
1984						
Feb 25 ⑩	Eddie Davis	Atlantic City	W	12	Ret-World-LH	175
1985						
Feb 23 ⑩	David Sears	Atlantic City	TKO	3	Ret-World-LH	170
Jun 6 ⑩	Jim MacDonald	Las Vegas	TKO	8	Ret-World-LH	175
Sep 21 ♛	Larry Holmes	Las Vegas	W	15	Won-World (IBF)-H	200
1986						
Apr 19 ⑩	Larry Holmes	Las Vegas	W	15	Ret-World (IBF)-H	205
Sep 6	Steffan Tangstad	Las Vegas	TKO	4	Ret-World (IBF)-H	201
1987						
Jun 15	Gerry Cooney	Atlantic City	TKO	5	—	208
1988						
Jun 27 ♛	Mike Tyson	Atlantic City	KO'd	1	Lost-World-H	212

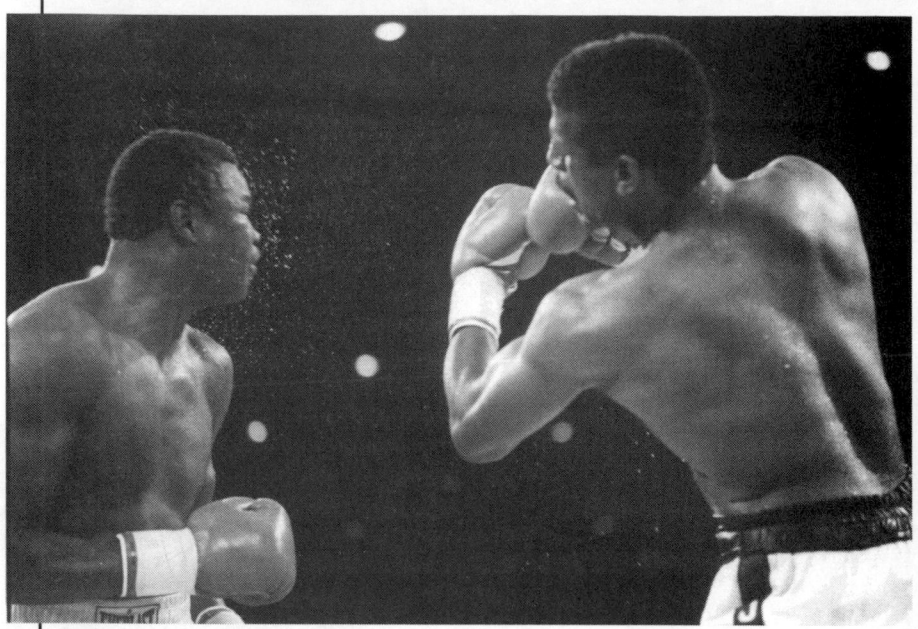

Spinks twice beat heavyweight great Larry Holmes. The first victory gave Spinks the title. In their April 19, 1986 rematch, he connects with a left hook to Holmes's jaw, on the way to another decision.

Mustafa Muhammad in July 1981 in Las Vegas. Muhammad was a powerful but ungraceful fighter, dangerous in his unpredictability. He was unquestionably the most formidable opponent Spinks had faced to date. Spinks fell behind early, shaken by Muhammad's flailing attacks, but from the fifth round on Spinks dominated the bout. He used his superior control to cut the champion over both eyes and he knocked Muhammad down in the twelfth. Spinks's arsenal of uppercuts, overhand lefts, and body shots earned him the unanimous decision.

Spinks was in championship territory now, and fourteen of the remaining fifteen fights in his career were title defenses or challenges. In the period from November 1981 to September 1982, he defended the light heavyweight title five times, vanquishing all comers with knockouts in nine or fewer rounds. Tough Jerry Celestine went down in eight in Atlantic City, reduced to helplessness by Spinks's insistent attack.

In 1983, Spinks unified the light heavyweight title with a fifteen-round decision over Dwight Braxton. He defended the title four times through June 1985. Building on this success, Spinks seized the opportunity to challenge the undefeated heavyweight champion Larry Holmes. Holmes was aging but he had destroyed every contender that had come his way in seven years and was expected to retain his crown. But Spinks outmaneuvered the champ and won a fifteen-round decision at the Riviera Hotel in Las Vegas. He kept Holmes from initiating the action with his vaunted jab and he avoided battling the larger man inside. He used a variety of tactics to score enough to win the fight without allowing Holmes to hurt him.

Holmes demanded a rematch and the two met again in April 1986 in Las Vegas. Intent on taking Spinks out early, Holmes was all over the smaller man in the first rounds, but Spinks again used his excellent ring skills to stay out of serious trouble. It wasn't until the fourteenth round that Holmes caught him with a strong right, slamming him into the ropes. Spinks sagged but did not fall. He came back in the fifteenth to box expertly, and the judges awarded him the decision. Boxing's warring governing bodies then intervened, and both the WBA and WBC stripped Spinks of his titles for granting Holmes a rematch in violation of their rules. Holmes later went on to meet defeat at the hands of Mike Tyson.

Spinks took out ferocious Gerry Cooney in a non-title bout, and then went up against Tyson to see who really was the world champion. As it turned out, it was Tyson all the way. Tyson destroyed him in under two minutes. Spinks then retired, having gone further than any light heavyweight in boxing history.

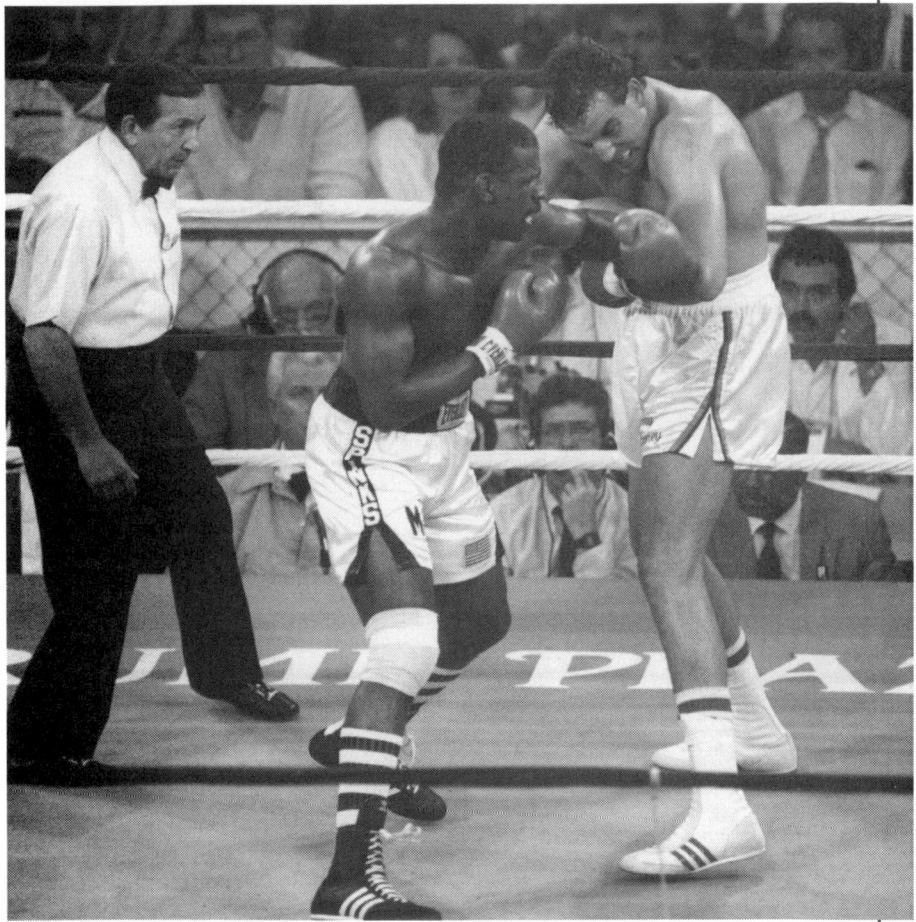

Giant Gerry Cooney (R) hunches his shoulders as he struggles to defend himself from a Spinks on-slaught. Spinks won in five on June 15, 1987 at Atlantic City. This bout was Spinks's last win.

Dick Tiger

LIGHT HEAVYWEIGHT

Right-handed; 5'8"; 156–175 lbs.

81 bouts, Oct. 1952 to 7/15/1970

Manager: Jersey Jones

WBA Middlewt. Champ 1962–63, Middlewt. Champ 1963, 1965–66, Light Heavywt. Champ 1966–68

Hall of Fame Induction: 1991

Born: 8/14/1929, Amaigbo, Orlu, Nigeria

Named: Richard Ihetu

Died: 12/14/1971

Dick Tiger earned wide admiration not only for his considerable boxing skills—as evidenced by world championship victories in two weight classes—but also for his gentlemanly demeanor and his efforts on behalf of the impoverished Biafran people in his home country of Nigeria.

Tiger started fighting professionally in Nigeria at the age of 23 and built up a good record there for three years before Jack Farnsworth, an English insurance salesman and creator of the Nigerian Boxing Board of Control, sent him to Liverpool to train under Peter Benencko. Tiger had difficulty adjusting to life in England and to the style of British fighters and lost his first four fights after the move. Before long, however, he found his footing and won the British Empire middleweight title in 1958, defeating Pat McAteer.

In 1959, Tiger began to campaign extensively in the United States where he experienced both success and popularity, with a 11-2-1 record. In October 1962, he was given a chance at the NBA crown held by Hall of Famer Gene Fullmer. In Candlestick Park in San Francisco, Tiger scored a convincing fifteen-round decision over Fullmer, whose eyes were seriously cut and bleeding from well-placed shots from Tiger.

Later that year the New York State Athletic Commission, European Boxing Union and the British Boxing Board

Tiger enlisted in the Biafran army after war broke out in Nigeria. In the ring, he held the middle- and light heavyweight titles.

IN THE RING	WON 61	LOST 17	DRAWS 3	TB 81	KO 26	W 35	WF 0	D 3	KO'd 2	L 15	LF 0

Date	Opponent	Site	Result / Rounds		Title	Wt.
1952						
Oct	Simon Eme	Lagos, Nigeria	KO	2	—	—
Nov	Easy Dynamite	Lagos	KO	1	—	—
Dec	Mighty Joe	Lagos	W	8	—	—
1953						
Jan	Lion Ring	Lagos	TKO	6	—	—
Feb	Simon Eme	Lagos	W	8	—	—
Mar	Koko Kid	Lagos	W	8	—	—
Apr	Black Power	Lagos	W	8	—	—
May 6	Tommy West	Lagos	TKO'd	7	For-Nigeria-M	160
Oct	Bolaji Johnson	Lagos	W	8	—	—
1954						
Feb	Robert Nuanne	Lagos	KO	2	—	—
May	Tommy West	Lagos	W	12	Won-Nigeria-M	160
Jul	Roy Fargbemy	Lagos	W	8	—	—
Nov	Peter Okptra	Lagos	KO	8	—	—
1955						
Jan	Koko Kid	Amaigbo, Nigeria	TKO	6	—	—
Mar	Super Human Power	Lagos	W	8	—	—
May	John Ama	Lagos	KO	2	—	—
Dec 8	Alan Dean	Liverpool, England	L	6	—	—
1956						
Jan 27	Gerry McNally	Blackpool, England	L	8	—	161
Mar 2	Jimmy Lynas	Blackpool	L	8	—	162
Mar 22	George Roe	Liverpool	L	8	—	162
May 3	Dennis Rowley	Liverpool	KO	1	—	164
May 10	Alan Dean	Liverpool	W	8	—	163
May 28	Wally Scott	West Hartlepool, England	TKO	4	—	—
Jul 2	Jimmy Lynas	West Hartlepool	W	8	—	—
Oct 18	Alan Dean	Liverpool	L	6	—	—
Nov 9	Alan Dean	Blackpool	W	8	—	—
1957						
Apr 29	Johnny Read	London	TKO	2	—	165
May 14	Terry Downes	London	TKO	5	—	162
Jun 4	Marius Dori	London	TKO	7	—	—
Jul 15	Willie Armstrong	West Hartlepool	L	8	—	—
Jul 25	Alan Dean	Liverpool	W	8	—	—
Sep 9	Phil Edwards	Cardiff, Wales	W	10	—	163
Oct 21	Jean Poison	Cardiff	W	10	—	—
Nov 11	Pat McAteer	Cardiff	D	10	—	—
Nov 29	Paddy Delargy	Birmingham, England	TKO	6	—	—
1958						
Jan 13	Jean Ruellet	Hull, England	W	8	—	—
Feb 3	Jimmy Lynas	Manchester, England	TKO	7	—	—
Feb 25	Johnny Read	London	TKO	6	—	—
Mar 27	Pat McAteer	Liverpool	KO	9	Won-Brit Emp-M	160
May 1	Billy Ellaway	Liverpool	TKO	2	—	—

Date		Opponent	Location	Result	Rounds	Title	Weight
Jun 24	⑩	Spider Webb	London	L	10	—	—
Oct 14	⑩	Yolande Pompey	London	W	10	—	—

1959

Date		Opponent	Location	Result	Rounds	Title	Weight
Mar 19		Randy Sandy	Liverpool	L	10	—	—
May 12		Randy Sandy	London	W	10	—	—
Jun 5	⑩	Rory Calhoun	New York	D	10	—	—
Jul 17	⑩	Rory Calhoun	Syracuse, NY	L	10	—	—
Sep 2	⑩	Gene Armstrong	Camden, NJ	W	10	—	—
Sep 30	⑩	Joey Giardello★	Chicago	W	10	—	—
Nov 4	⑩	Joey Giardello★	Cleveland	L	10	—	—
Dec 30	⑩	Holly Mims	Chicago	W	10	—	—

1960

Date		Opponent	Location	Result	Rounds	Title	Weight
Feb 24		Gene Armstrong	Chicago	W	10	—	—
Apr 1		Victor Zalazar	Boston	W	10	—	161
Jun 22		Wilf Greaves	Edmonton, Alb.	L	15	Lost-Brit Emp-M	160
Nov 30		Wilf Greaves	Edmonton	TKO	9	Reg-Brit Emp-M	160

1961

Date		Opponent	Location	Result	Rounds	Title	Weight
Feb 18		Gene Armstrong	New York	TKO	9	—	—
Apr 15		Spider Webb	New York	TKO	6	—	160
May 15	⑩	Hank Casey	New Orleans	W	10	—	160
Dec 16		Bill Pickett	New York	W	10	—	160

1962

Date		Opponent	Location	Result	Rounds	Title	Weight
Jan 20	⑩	Floro Fernandez	Miami Beach	KO	6	—	160
Mar 31	⑩	Henry Hank	New York	W	10	—	—
Oct 23	♛	Gene Fullmer★	San Francisco	W	15	Won-WBA-M	159

1963

Date		Opponent	Location	Result	Rounds	Title	Weight
Feb 23	⑩	Gene Fullmer★	Las Vegas	D	15	Ret-WBA-M	160
Aug 10	⑩	Gene Fullmer★	Ibadan, Nigeria	TKO	7	Won-Vac World-M	159
Dec 7	⑩	Joey Giardello★	Atlantic City	L	15	Lost-World-M	159

1964

Date		Opponent	Location	Result	Rounds	Title	Weight
Jul 31		Jose Gonzalez	New York	TKO	6	—	—
Sep 11		Don Fullmer	Cleveland	W	10	—	—
Oct 16	⑩	Joey Archer	New York	L	10	—	—

1965

Date		Opponent	Location	Result	Rounds	Title	Weight
Mar 12		Rocky Rivero	New York	TKO	6	—	169
May 20	⑩	Rubin Carter	New York	W	10	—	163
Oct 21	♛	Joey Giardello★	New York	W	15	Reg-World-M	158

1966

Date		Opponent	Location	Result	Rounds	Title	Weight
Feb 18		Peter Mueller	Dortmund, Germany	KO	3	—	162
Apr 25		Emile Griffith★	New York	L	15	Lost-World-M	160
Dec 16	♛	Jose Torres★	New York	W	15	Won-World-LH	175

1967

Date		Opponent	Location	Result	Rounds	Title	Weight
Feb 5		Abraham Tomica	Port Harcourt, Nigeria	W	10	—	—
May 16	⑩	Jose Torres★	New York	W	15	Ret-World-LH	175
Nov 17	⑩	Roger Rouse	Las Vegas	TKO	12	Ret-World-LH	175

1968

Date		Opponent	Location	Result	Rounds	Title	Weight
May 24	⑩	Bob Foster★	New York	KO'd	4	Lost-World-LH	175
Oct 25		Frank DePaula	New York	W	10	—	167

1969

Date		Opponent	Location	Result	Rounds	Title	Weight
May 26	⑩	Nino Benvenuti★	New York	W	10	—	166
Nov 14	⑩	Andy Kendall	New York	W	10	—	—

1970

Date		Opponent	Location	Result	Rounds	Title	Weight
Jul 15	⑩	Emile Griffith★	New York	L	10	—	—

Tiger cut up Gene Fullmer (R) and stripped him of his WBA middleweight title on October 23, 1962. These two rivals battled three times in less than a year. Tiger won two; one fight was called a draw.

of Control all recognized Tiger as middleweight champion. *The Ring* further honored Tiger by naming him its Fighter of the Year for 1962.

In 1963, Tiger lost the title to Hall of Famer Joey Giardello but regained it in a return match decision in 1965. He was again named *The Ring*'s Fighter of the Year. At age 36, Tiger faced a stern challenge from welterweight champion, Emile Griffith. The younger Griffith fought brilliantly, outboxing Tiger to win a decision.

Tiger continued fighting, in part to gain aid for the people of Biafra. He moved up in class and outpointed Jose Torres to win the light heavyweight title in 1966. He retained the title until 1968 when he faced the great Bob Foster, who was nine years younger, seven inches taller, and had a reach advantage of eight inches. Foster did what no other fighter had accomplished up until then: he knocked Tiger out in the fourth round, a session *The Ring* later called the most exciting round of 1968.

Tiger continued to fight for two more years to recoup from the confiscation of his property by the Nigerian government. He retired in 1971 and went to live in his beloved Biafra, where he died of cancer less than six months later. His old rival Fullmer called Tiger "a great competitor and champion and, most important, a gentleman."

JOSE TORRES
Chegui

LIGHT HEAVYWEIGHT

Right-handed; 5'10"; 150–182 lbs.

45 bouts, 5/24/1958 to 7/14/1969

1956 Olympic Light Middleweight Silver Medalist

Light Heavyweight Champ 1965–66

Hall of Fame Induction: 1997

Born: 5/3/1936, Playa Ponce, Puerto Rico

Named: Jose Luis Torres

Today Jose Torres is almost as well known as a boxing writer and administrator as for his considerable achievements in the ring. However, his other successes will never obscure his greatness as a fighter.

Growing up in Puerto Rico, Torres was a street fighter. When he was sixteen, he stole a car. Although he was cleared in court, Torres volunteered to join the U.S. Army to turn his life around. He joined the boxing team where his natural talent was developed by army trainers.

Torres won the Caribbean army title in 1954. After transferring to Fort Meade in Maryland in 1955, Torres continued to claim amateur crowns including the Maryland State AAU title, the Second Army championship, and the All-Army and All-Service titles. Torres represented the U.S. in the 1956 Olympics in the light middleweight division. He took a silver medal in the finals in Melbourne, losing a 3-2 decision to Hungary's Laszlo Papp.

Torres (L) was 17-0-1 on April 1, 1961 when he faced Bobby Barnes in Paterson, NJ's Plaza Ballroom. He triumphed with a 3rd-round KO.

IN THE RING	WON 41	LOST 3	DRAWS 1	TB 45	KO 29	W 12	WF 0	D 1	KO'd 1	L 2	LF 0

Date	Opponent	Site	Result / Rounds		Title	Wt.
1958						
May 24	Gene Hamilton	Brooklyn	KO	1	—	—
Jun 7	Walter Irby	Brooklyn	W	6	—	—
Jun 21	Joe Salvato	Brooklyn	KO	4	—	—
Jul 5	Wes Lowery	Brooklyn	W	6	—	—
Aug 18	Benny Doyle	Los Angeles	KO	1	—	—
Sep 29	Otis Woodard	New York	KO	5	—	160
Oct 13	Frankie Anselm	New York	KO	9	—	158
Nov 3	Burke Emery	New York	TKO	5	—	164
Dec 4	Ike Jenkins	New York	KO	5	—	—
1959						
Feb 26	Eddie Wright	New York	KO	5	—	—
Mar 19	Leroy Oliphant	New York	TKO	3	—	162
Apr 23	Joe Shaw	New York	KO	5	—	—
Jun 27	Al Andrews	New York	KO	6	—	—
Sep 26	⑩ Benny Paret	San Juan, PR	D	10	—	—
1960						
Jan 30	Randy Sandy	Elizabeth, NJ	W	10	—	162
Mar 15	Tony Dupas	Buffalo	W	10	—	—
Jun 11	Randy Sandy	New York	W	10	—	—
1961						
Feb 17	Gene Hamilton	San Juan	KO	4	—	—
Apr 1	Bobby Barnes	Paterson, NJ	TKO	3	—	—
May 23	Bob Young	Boston	TKO	5	—	164
Jun 5	Mel Collins	Boston	KO	7	—	164
Jun 27	Ike White	Boston	TKO	3	—	160
Oct 31	Georgie Price	Houston	KO	2	—	—
Nov 28	Tony Montano	Houston	KO	4	—	—
1962						
Apr 10	Jimmy Watkins	Utica, NY	KO	7	—	—
Jul 27	Dulio Nunez	San Juan	KO	7	Won-PR-M	160
Dec 14	Al Hauser	Boston	KO	3	—	—
1963						
May 26	Florentino Fernandez	San Juan	KO'd	5	—	—
Oct 9	Don Fullmer	Teaneck, NJ	W	10	—	—
1964						
Jan 3	Jose Gonzalez	New York	W	10	Ret-PR-M	160
Apr 21	Walker Simmons	New York	TKO	8	—	173
May 15	Wilbert McClure	New York	W	10	—	161
Jun 22	Frankie Olevera	New Bedford, MA	KO	5	—	—
Jul 20	Walker Simmons	New Bedford	TKO	6	—	—
Sep 4	Gomeo Brennan	Miami Beach	W	10	—	—
Nov 27	⑩ Carl ("Bobo") Olson★	New York	KO	1	—	170
1965						
Mar 30	♛ Willie Pastrano★	New York	TKO	9	Won-World-LH	171
Jul 31	Tom McNeeley	San Juan	W	10	—	182
1966						
May 21	⑩ Wayne Thornton	Flushing, NY	W	15	Ret-World-LH	175
Aug 15	⑩ Eddie Cotton	Las Vegas	W	15	Ret-World-LH	173

Oct 15		Chic Calderwood	San Juan	KO	2	Ret-World-LH	175
Dec 16	Ⓦ	Dick Tiger★	New York	L	15	Lost-World-LH	175
1967							
May 16	♛	Dick Tiger★	New York	L	15	For-World-LH	175
1968							
Apr 1	Ⓦ	Bob Dunlop	Sydney	TKO	6	—	175
1969							
Jul 14		Charlie Green	New York	KO	2	—	178

Torres left the Army and turned professional in 1958 with a first-round knock-out of Gene Hamilton. Fighting under the tutelage of Hall of Famer Cus D'Amato, Torres mastered the distinctive peekaboo style of fighting—hands held high to shield the face—similar to another of D'Amato's protégés, Floyd Patterson. Fighting as a middleweight, Torres won his first thirteen bouts before fighting to a draw with future welterweight champ Benny ("Kid") Paret. He won another string of thirteen before Florentino Fernandez knocked him out in five rounds in San Juan in 1963.

Although Torres had a record of 26-1-1 to this point, he had very little to show for it financially until he gained the sponsorship of Brooklyn real estate dealer Cain Young. Young got Torres a fight with the third-ranked light heavyweight Carl ("Bobo") Olson by guaranteeing Olson $10,000. Though still a comparatively light 170 pounds, Torres moved up a weight class and faced Olson at Madison Square Garden on November 27, 1964. (Torres had never fought in the Garden because of D'Amato's opposition to the corrupt International Boxing Club, controllers of the arena for over a decade.) In a one-round knockout, Torres devas-

Torres (L) confers with his derby-hatted trainer, Hall of Famer Cus D'Amato (C).

tated Olson with a four-punch combination—a left hook to the kidney followed by a right cross, left hook, and a right uppercut, all to the jaw. *The Ring* rated this as the Round of the Year for 1964.

The victory over Olson gave Torres a shot at the light heavyweight title held by Willie Pastrano. Held in Madison Square Garden on March 30, 1965, the fight drew 18,112 fans and a gate of $239,956. A large contingent of Puerto Rican fans rooted for Torres, who attacked Pastrano with fiery aggression. He bloodied Pastrano's nose in the first round and, in the sixth, slammed the champion with a left hook to the body that took him to the canvas—the first time Pastrano had ever been floored. *The Ring* would later label this round the best of 1965. Pastrano held on through nine but could not answer the bell for the tenth. Torres was the new champion, and his friend, novelist Norman Mailer, hosted a victory party whose guests included James Baldwin, George Plimpton, and Senator Jacob Javits.

Torres successfully defended the title three times in 1966. On December 16, 1966, Torres' title reign came to an end when Hall of Famer Dick Tiger defeated him in a close decision. Five months later, Tiger won a decision in a rematch. Torres only fought twice more. When Charlie Green knocked him down in the first round of their July 14, 1969 fight, Torres decided it was time to retire. He knocked Green out in two, but he never fought again, thus ending his career with a victory.

Mailer and fellow writers Pete Hamill and Budd Schulberg encouraged Torres to pursue writing. He authored boxing books *Sting Like a Bee,* about Muhammad Ali, and *Fire and Fear,* a study of Mike Tyson, and has written numerous articles for newspapers and magazines. Torres campaigned for Senators Robert Kennedy and George McGovern and has worked on issues affecting Puerto Rico.

Torres served five years as chairman of the New York State Athletic Commission, from 1983 to 1988. He was also president of the World Boxing Organization (WBO) from 1993 to 1995. The eloquent Torres appeared as an announcer on Spanish language telecasts of the USA Network's "Tuesday Night Fights."

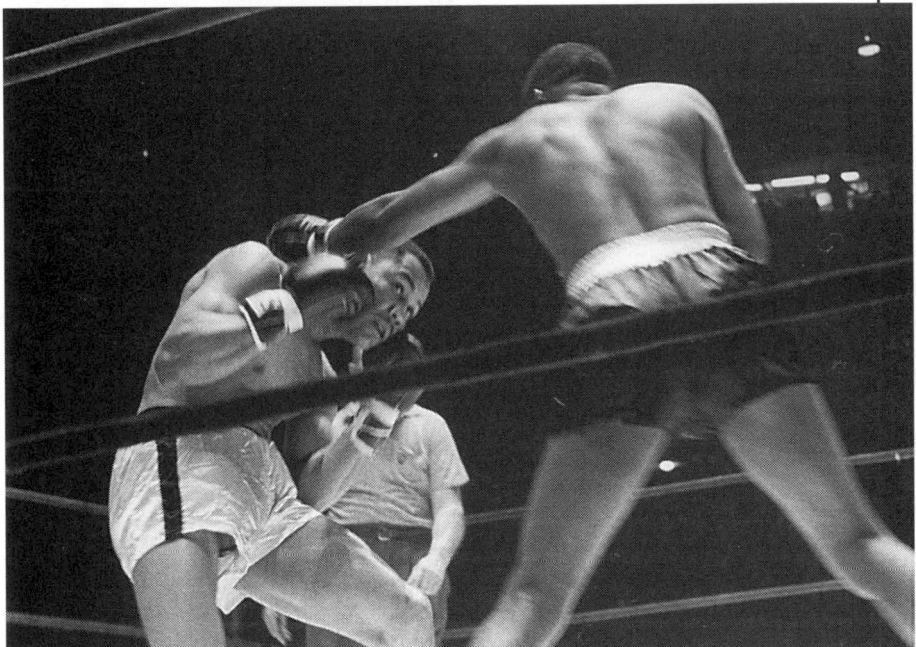

Torres dispatched Al Hauser in three rounds in their December 14, 1962 Boston match-up. That gave Torres ten consecutive knockout victories.

RANDY TURPIN
The Leamington Licker

MIDDLEWEIGHT

Right-handed; 5'9½"; 156–175 lbs.

75 bouts, 9/17/1946 to 9/1/1964

Manager: George Middleton

Middleweight Champion 1951

Hall of Fame Induction: 2001

Born: 6/7/1928, Leamington, Warwickshire, England

Named: Randolph Adolphus Turpin

Died: 5/17/1966

Randy Turpin's triumphant 64 day reign as the middleweight champion of the world is somewhat tarnished by his tragic life outside the ring.

Turpin's father, Lionel, was a native of British Guiana. Wounded and exposed to mustard gas while serving in World War I, he was sent to convalesce in England where he met and married the daughter of a bare-knuckle fighter. Randy Turpin was born just a few months before his father's death.

Turpin and his brothers became well known as fighters, his brother Dick winning the Lonsdale Belt as the British middleweight champion and Jackie Turpin boxing professionally as a featherweight. Randy was dubbed "Leamington Licker," or simply Licker, because he could lick anyone in a fight.

Turpin won three British junior titles. In 1945, he won the ABA welterweight title, and he secured the ABA middleweight title the next year. In what was perhaps his most memorable amateur fight, he knocked out Harold Anspach of the United States boxing team to help England defeat the Americans five to three in a special tournament. Around this time, Turpin served as a cook in the Royal Navy. While on leave, he ingested a poisonous substance and had to have his stomach pumped. He was charged with attempted suicide, though the case was soon dropped. Already, his tortured personal life was impacting his boxing career.

Turpin turned professional on September 17, 1946, with a first-round knockout of Gordon Griffiths, and he rolled on to an 18-0-1 record before losing a decision to Albert Finch on April 26, 1948. Some blamed this loss, and a knockout at the hands of Jean Stock five months later, on tumult between Turpin and his wife. Arrested later for assaulting her, Turpin was not convicted.

After the British Boxing Board of Control rescinded its rule prohibiting blacks from fighting for its titles, Dick Turpin won the middleweight championship. Although Randy was qualified to fight for the title, the brothers had vowed never to face each other in the ring. When Finch dethroned Dick, Turpin got his chance not only to try for the title, but also to avenge his own

The three fighting Turpin brothers (L to R): Randy, Jackie, and Dick.

Date	Opponent	Site	Result / Rounds		Title	Wt.
1946						
Sep 17	Gordon Griffiths	London	TKO	1	—	—
Nov 19	Des Jones	London	W	6	—	—
Dec 26	Bill Blything	Birmingham, England	KO	1	—	—
1947						
Jan 14	Jimmy Davis	London	KO	4	—	157
Jan 24	Dai James	Birmingham	KO	3	—	—
Feb 18	Johnny Best	London	TKO	1	—	159
Mar 18	Bert Hyland	London	KO	1	—	161
Apr 1	Frank Dolan	London	TKO	2	—	161
Apr 15	Tommy Davies	London	KO	2	—	162
Apr 28	Bert Sanders	London	W	6	—	—
May 12	Ron Coopers	Oxford, England	TKO	4	—	—
May 27	Jury VII	London	W	6	—	158
Jun 3	Mark Hart	London	W	6	—	—
Jun 23	Leon Fouquet	Coventry, England	KO	1	—	156
Sep 9	Jimmy Ingle	Coventry	TKO	3	—	—
Oct 20	Mark Hart	London	D	6	—	—
1948						
Jan 26	Freddie Price	Coventry	KO	1	—	—
Feb 17	Gerry McCready	London	TKO	1	—	—
Mar 16	Vince Hawkins	London	W	8	—	—
Apr 26	Albert Finch	London	L	8	—	—
Jun 28	Alby Hollister	Birmingham	W	8	—	—
Sep 21	Jean Stock	London	TKO'd	5	—	—
1949						
Feb 7	Jackie Jones	Coventry	TKO	5	—	—
Feb 21	Doug Miller	London	W	8	—	—
Mar 25	Mickey Laurent	Manchester, England	TKO	3	—	—
May 3	William Poli	London	WF	4	—	160
Jun 20 ⑩	Cyrille Delannoit	Birmingham	TKO	8	—	—
Aug 22	Jean Wanes	Manchester	TKO	3	—	—
Sep 19	Roy Wouters	Coventry	TKO	5	—	—
Nov 15	Pete Mead	London	TKO	5	—	160
1950						
Jan 31	Gilbert Stock	London	W	8	—	162
Mar 6	Richard Armah	Croydon, England	TKO	6	—	161
Apr 24	Gus Degouve	Nottingham, England	W	8	—	161
Sep 5	Eli Elandon	Watford, England	KO	2	—	—
Oct 17	Albert Finch	London	KO	5	Won-British-M	160
Nov 13	Jose Alamo	Abergavenny, England	KO	2	—	—
Dec 12 ⑩	Tommy Yarosz	London	WF	8	—	—
1951						
Jan 22	Eduardo Lopez	Birmingham	KO	1	—	—
Feb 27	Luc Van Dam	London	KO	1	Won-Vac Eur-M	160
Mar 19	Jean Stock	Leicester, England	TKO	5	—	—
Apr 16	Billy Brown	Birmingham	KO	2	—	—
May 7	Jan DeBruin	Coventry	KO	6	—	—
Jun 5	Jackie Keough	London	TKO	7	—	—

Date		Opponent	Location	Result	Rounds	Title
Jul 10	♛	Sugar Ray Robinson★	London	W	15	Won-World-M 158
Sep 12	⑩	Sugar Ray Robinson★	New York	TKO'd	10	Lost-World-M 159
1952						
Feb 12		Alex Buxton	London	TKO	7	— —
Apr 22		Jacques Hairabedjian	London	KO	3	— —
Jun 10	⑩	Don Cockell	London	TKO	11	Won-Vac Commonwealth-LH 175
Oct 21	⑩	George Angelo	London	W	15	Won-Vac Commonwealth-M 160
1953						
Jan 19		Victor d'Haes	Birmingham	KO	7	— —
Feb 16		Duggie Miller	Leicester	W	10	— —
Mar 17		Walter Cartier	London	WF	2	— —
Jun 9		Charles Humez	London	W	15	Ret-Eur-M 160
Oct 21	⑩	Carl ("Bobo") Olson★	New York	L	15	For-Vac-World-M 157
1954						
Mar 30		Olle Bengtsson	London	W	10	— —
May 2	⑩	Tiberio Mitri	Rome	TKO'd	1	Lost-Eur-M 160
1955						
Feb 15		Ray Schmitt	Birmingham	WF	8	— —
Mar 8		Jose Gonzalez	London	KO	7	— —
Apr 26		Alex Buxton	London	KO	2	Ret-Commonwealth-LH 175
Sep 19		Polly Smith	Birmingham	W	10	— —
Oct 18		Gordon Wallace	London	KO'd	4	— —
1956						
Apr 17		Sandro D'Ottavio	Birmingham	TKO	6	— —
Jun 18		Jacques Bro	Birmingham	KO	5	— —
Sep 21	⑩	Hans Stretz	Hamburg	L	10	— —
Nov 26		Alex Burton	Leicester	TKO	5	Ret-British-LH 175
1957						
Jun 11		Arthur Howard	Leicester	W	15	Ret-British-LH 175
Sep 17		Ahmed Boulgroune	London	TKO	9	— 171
Oct 28		Sergio Burchi	Birmingham	TKO	2	— 172
Nov 25		Uwe Janssen	Leicester	TKO	8	— —
1958						
Feb 1		Wim Snoek	Birmingham	W	10	— —
Apr 21		Eddie Wright	Leicester	TKO	7	— 176
Jul 22		Redvers Sangoe	Oswestry, Eng.	TKO	4	— —
Sep 9	⑩	Yolande Pompey	Birmingham	KO'd	2	— 175
1963						
Mar 19		Eddie Marcano	Wisbech, Eng.	KO	6	— —
1964						
Sep 1		Charles Seguna	Malta	TKO	2	— —

previous loss, as well as his brother's. On October 17, 1950, he knocked out Finch in five rounds, and four months later, he added the European middleweight title to his collection with a first-round knockout of Luc Van Dam. Four more knockout victories followed, setting the stage for Turpin's greatest triumph.

Sugar Ray Robinson, the middleweight champion of the world (with only one loss in one hundred and 35 fights), was touring Europe. On July 10, 1951, Robinson put his title on the line against Turpin before 18,000 fans at Earl's Court in London. Robinson was the heavy favorite, yet Turpin's unorthodox, spread-legged stance confused the champ, and Turpin scored with a strong left and outmuscled Ray in the clinches. He won the decision in a fight that ranks with the biggest upsets of all time.

Unfortunately, Turpin did not fare well in the rematch, held 64 days later at the Polo Grounds. Robinson felled Turpin in the tenth with a right to the jaw. By the end of the round, Robinson had his battered opponent pinned against the ropes. Referee Ruby Goldstein stopped the fight with eight seconds remaining. The ring death of George Flores in a bout eleven days earlier may have colored the referee's decision, but most observers supported Goldstein's call.

Turpin returned to England and knocked out Don Cockell in the eleventh round to win the vacant British Empire light heavyweight title. He followed up with a decision over George Angelo for the Empire middleweight title. Turpin next outpointed Charlie Humez in London in a bout to select the European to meet an American contender for the now-vacant middleweight title.

Turpin came to the United States to face Carl ("Bobo") Olson in Madison Square Garden on October 21, 1953. He had not trained properly for the fight, reportedly distracted by arguments with his brother Dick, and separation from his girlfriend. Turpin won the first three rounds, but it was Olson who came away with the title in a fifteen-round decision. Before he could return to Britain, Turpin was arrested on an assault charge brought by a 24-year-old woman. Authorities dropped the criminal case, but his accuser forced Turpin into a settlement in civil court.

Back in the ring, Turpin lost the European middleweight title to Tiberio Mitri in a first-round knockout. He then moved up to light heavyweight and won the British title. Despite his success, he retired after a second-round knockout loss to Yolande Pompey on September 9, 1958, fighting only twice more, five and six years later.

In retirement, the embittered Turpin realized that he had frittered away most of his ring earnings and owed significant back taxes to the British government. Turpin found work in his manager's scrap yard. Later, he and his second wife operated a small transport café. Eventually, he filed for bankruptcy.

On May 14, 1966, Turpin received a final demand from the tax authorities for a settlement. His café also faced condemnation to make room for a garage. On May 17, Turpin took his seventeen-month-old daughter, Carmen, to an attic bedroom, shot her, and then shot and killed himself. Carmen survived.

Randy Turpin (L) floors Don Cockell in the third round of their June 10, 1952, London battle for the British Light Heavyweight title. Turpin won in the eleventh, when the referee stopped the fight.

JERSEY JOE WALCOTT

HEAVYWEIGHT

Right-handed; 6'; 165–197 lbs.

72 bouts, 9/9/1930 to 5/15/1953

Managers: Sonny Banks,
Felix Bocchicchio 1945–53

Heavyweight Champion 1951–52

Hall of Fame Induction: 1990

Born: 1/31/1914, Merchantville, NJ

Named: Arnold Raymond Cream

Died: 2/25/1994

Jersey Joe Walcott was 33 years old before he was given a chance to fight for the heavyweight championship. It took four more years before he attained his goal. On a slow rise through the professional ranks, Walcott literally outlived the color bar that kept many black boxers of the 1930s and '40s from meeting their full potential. He was a master of defense as well as a fearless attacker, and he never ducked a challenge.

Born Arnold Cream, Walcott took his name in honor of his idol, the great Joe Walcott of Barbados. He was sixteen when he fought in his first professional bout in his native New Jersey. Early in his career, Walcott trained briefly with Jack Blackburn and was scheduled to accompany him to Chicago when Blackburn was assigned to train Joe Louis. Walcott's career might have been different

Tommy Gomez crumbles as Walcott (R) stands ready to hand out more punishment. The third round of their August 1946 fight proved to be the last. Walcott was about a year away from his first title shot.

IN THE RING	WON 53	LOST 18	DRAWS 1	TB 72	KO 33	W 19	WF 1	D 1	KO'd 6	L 12	LF 0

Date		Opponent	Site	Result / Rounds		Title	Wt.
1930							
Sep 9		Cowboy Wallace	Vineland, NJ	KO	1	—	165
Oct 10		Jimmy O'Toole	Camden, NJ	TKO	4	—	165
Oct 24		Frankie Matthews	Camden	TKO	4	—	165
1931							
Apr 20		Carl Mays	Atlantic City	KO	2	—	—
1933							
May 5		Bob Norris	Camden	KO	1	—	—
Jul 28		Henry Taylor	Camden	TKO	1	—	176
Nov 16		Henry Taylor	Philadelphia	L	6	—	179
1935							
Jan 1		Al Lang	Camden	KO	1	—	—
Feb 2		Lew Alva	Camden	KO	3	—	—
Oct 1		Pat Roland	Camden	TKO	4	—	—
Oct 29		Joe King	Camden	KO	1	—	175
Nov 26		Roxie Allen	Camden	KO	7	—	—
1936							
Jan 21	⑩	Al Ettore	Camden	TKO'd	8	—	—
Mar 16		Willie Reddish	Philadelphia	W	10	—	—
Apr 28		Joe Colucci	Camden	KO	4	—	—
Jun 16		Lou LaPage	Coney Island, NY	KO	6	—	188
Jun 22		Phill Johnson	Philadelphia	KO	3	—	188
Jul 14		Billy Ketchell	Camden	D	10	—	—
Aug 1		Young Passarella	Camden	W	8	—	—
Aug 15		Billy Ketchell	Camden	W	10	—	—
Sep 1		Billy Ketchell	Camden	L	10	—	187
1937							
May 22	⑩	Tiger Jack Fox	New York	KO'd	8	—	—
Sep 3		Joe Lipps	Atlantic City	KO	2	—	183
Sep 25		Elmer Ray	New York	KO	3	—	—
Oct 9		George Brothers	New York	L	8	—	—
1938							
Jan 10		Fred Fiducia	Philadelphia	W	8	—	—
Jan 20		Jim Whitest	Philadelphia	W	8	—	—
Mar 25		Art Sykes	Philadelphia	KO	4	—	—
Apr 12		Lorenzo Pack	Camden	KO	4	—	—
May 10	⑩	Tiger Jack Fox	Camden	L	10	—	—
Jun 14		Roy Lazer	Fairview,NJ	L	8	—	—
Dec 23		Bob Tow	Camden	W	8	—	—
1939							
Aug 14		Al Boros	Newark	W	8	—	—
Nov 18		Curtis Sheppard	New York	W	8	—	—
1940							
Jan 19		Tiger Red Lewis	Philadelphia	KO	6	—	—
Feb 12	⑩	Abe Simon	Newark	KO'd	6	—	—

Date		Opponent	Location	Result	Rounds	Notes	Weight
1941							
Jun 27		Columbus Gant	Memphis, TN	KO	3	—	—
1944							
Jun 7		Felix Del Paoli	Batesville, NJ	W	8	—	—
Jun 28		Ellis Singleton	Batesville	KO	3	—	—
1945							
Jan 11		Jackie Saunders	Camden	TKO	2	—	183
Jan 25		Skippy Allen	Camden	L	8	—	182
Feb 22		Austin Johnson	Camden	W	6	—	—
Mar 15		Skippy Allen	Camden	W	8	—	—
Aug 2	⑩	Joe Baksi	Camden	W	10	—	188
Sep 20		Johnny Denson	Camden	KO	2	—	—
Oct 23		Steve Dudas	Paterson, NJ	KO	5	—	—
Nov 12	⑩	Lee Q. Murray	Baltimore	WD	9	—	—
Dec 10	⑩	Curtis Sheppard	Baltimore	KO	10	—	192
1946							
Jan 30		Skippy Allen	Camden	KO	3	—	192
Feb 25	⑩	Jimmy Bivins★	Cleveland	W	10	—	196
Mar 20		Al Blake	Camden	KO	4	—	192
May 24	⑩	Lee Oma	New York	W	10	—	191
Aug 16		Tommy Gomez	New York	TKO	3	—	191
Aug 28	⑩	Joey Maxim★	Camden	L	10	—	—
Nov 15	⑩	Elmer Ray	New York	L	10	—	191
1947							
Jan 6	⑩	Joey Maxim★	Philadelphia	W	10	—	—
Apr 3	⑩	Elmer Ray	Miami	W	10	—	192
Jun 23	⑩	Joey Maxim★	Los Angeles	W	10	—	—
Dec 5	♛	Joe Louis★	New York	L	15	For-World-H	194
1948							
Jun 25	♛	Joe Louis★	New York	KO'd	11	For-World-H	194
1949							
Jun 22	⑩	Ezzard Charles★	Chicago	L	15	For-Vac NBA-H	195
Aug 14		Olle Tandberg	Stockholm	KO	5	—	—
1950							
Feb 8	⑩	Harold Johnson★	Philadelphia	KO	3	—	—
Mar 3	⑩	Omelio Agramonte	New York	KO	7	—	—
Mar 13		Johnny Shkor	Philadelphia	KO	1	—	197
May 28		Hein Hoff	Mannheim, Germany	W	10	—	195
Nov 24	⑩	Rex Layne	New York	L	10	—	—
1951							
Mar 7	♛	Ezzard Charles★	Detroit	L	15	For-World-H	193
Jul 18	♛	Ezzard Charles★	Pittsburgh	KO	7	Won-World-H	194
1952							
Jun 5	⑩	Ezzard Charles★	Philadelphia	W	15	Ret-World-H	196
Sep 23	⑩	Rocky Marciano★	Philadelphia	KO'd	13	Lost-World-H	196
1953							
May 15	♛	Rocky Marciano★	Chicago	KO'd	1	For-World-H	197

had he gone, but he was stricken with typhoid and never made the trip.
Walcott fought as a second-tier attraction for several years. He had the respon-
sibility of supporting his mother and siblings, but pay for a fair-to-middling black
boxer was often skimpy. Sometimes Walcott simply could not afford to box, and
he held down a variety of jobs or subsisted on welfare. He married and over the

Ezzard Charles (L) and Walcott met three times for the unified heavyweight title. March 7, 1951—Charles successfully defended his crown. July 18, 1951—Walcott won the title. June 5, 1952—Walcott kept the belt.

years fathered six children. By 1941, Walcott was fighting only once or twice a year and his career seemed to be winding down.

Then in 1945, perhaps because of the loss of fighters during World War II or perhaps because color had become less important, doors started to open for Walcott. He began to be signed for bouts with better opposition and, for the first time, he earned a place in *The Ring*'s annual top ten ratings.

In 1947, Walcott was put up against Joe Louis for the heavyweight championship of the world. The fight was held in Madison Square Garden. Walcott knocked Louis down twice and nearly closed his left eye. At the end of fifteen, referee Ruby Goldstein indicated that Walcott had won, but two judges scored the fight in favor of Louis, and Jersey Joe lost the split decision. He got another chance a year later, but Louis was better prepared and knocked Walcott out in the eleventh round. Walcott's first two tries to take the title from Ezzard Charles also failed. However, in July 1951, in Pittsburgh's Forbes Field, Walcott knocked Charles out with a thunderous left hook. At the age of 37—some said he was older—Walcott was the champion. After winning the rematch with Charles, Walcott lost the title in September 1952 to Rocky Marciano, who bounded up from a first-round knockdown to drop Walcott in the thirteenth. After Marciano knocked him out in the first round of the rematch in 1953, Walcott retired.

After leaving the ring, Walcott worked as a boxing and wrestling referee, as a sheriff in New Jersey, as chairman of the New Jersey State Athletic Commission, and as a director of special projects for New Jersey Governor Brendan Byrne. Assessing Walcott's career, esteemed trainer Eddie Futch called him "one of the finest technicians in heavyweight boxing history."

ISIAH ("IKE") WILLIAMS

LIGHTWEIGHT

Right-handed; 5'9½"; 125–150 lbs.

153 bouts, 3/15/1940 to 8/12/1955

Managers: Connie McCarthy 1940–46, Frank ("Blinky") Palermo 1946–55

NBA Lightweight Champion 1945–47, Lightweight Champion 1947–51

Hall of Fame Induction: 1990

Born: 8/2/1923, Brunswick, GA

Died: 9/5/1994

Lightweight champion for six years, Ike Williams was known as a relentless fighter who also demonstrated grace and finesse in the ring. He started boxing as an amateur in 1938 and made his professional debut in 1940. He won the NBA lightweight championship in Mexico City in 1945 when he knocked out Juan Zurita in the second round.

Williams's career was sidetracked after his victory over Zurita when he had a dispute with his manager, Connie McCarthy, and decided to go out on his own. The then-powerful Managers Guild blackballed Williams for his action.

The boycott was effective and Williams had great difficulty securing fights, until he agreed to be managed by Frank ("Blinky") Palermo. Palermo straightened out Williams's problems with the guild and got him a rematch with Bob Montgomery, who then held the New York version of the lightweight title. Williams fought masterfully and knocked Montgomery out in the sixth.

For much of the time he owned the title, Williams engaged in over-the-weight non-title matches where his strong jab, formidable straight right, and a fine defense served him well. Williams held the lightweight title until 1951 when Jimmy Carter soundly defeated him in Madison Square Garden.

According to testimony Williams gave to the Kefauver committee during the Senate's investigation of organized crime's ties to boxing, Palermo often suggested that Williams throw fights. Although he testified that he had never taken a dive, he did admit to the committee that he carried Enrique Bolanos and had put forth less than his best effort at other times. Williams said he sometimes never saw a penny of his purses.

Williams (R) puts contender Enrique Bolanos on the canvas, but this successful lightweight title defense went the full 15 rounds. The bout took place on May 25, 1948.

IN THE RING	WON 125	LOST 24	DRAWS 5	TB 154	KO 60	W 65	WF 0	D 5	KO'd 6	L 18	LF 0

Date	Opponent	Site	Result / Rounds		Title	Wt.
1940						
Mar 15	Carmine Fatta	New Brunswick, NJ	W	4	—	—
Mar 29	Billy George	New Brunswick	W	4	—	—
Apr 1	Patsy Gall	Hazleton, PA	D	6	—	—
May 10	Billy Hildebrand	Morristown, NJ	L	6	—	—
Jun 17	Billy Hildebrand	Mt. Freedom, NJ	TKO	6	—	—
Jul 19	Joe Romero	Mt. Freedom	KO	2	—	—
Sep 9	Pete Kelly	Trenton, NJ	KO	2	—	—
Nov 11	Tony Maglione	Trenton	L	8	—	—
1941						
Jan 6	Tommy Fontana	Trenton	W	8	—	—
Feb 19	Carl Zullo	Perth Amboy, NJ	TKO	2	—	—
Mar 5	Joey Zodda	Perth Amboy	L	6	—	—
Mar 19	Joe Genovese	Perth Amboy	W	5	—	—
Apr 9	Johnny Rudolph	Perth Amboy	W	6	—	—
Apr 14	Hugh Civatte	Trenton	KO	3	—	—
Oct 1	Freddie Archer	Perth Amboy	L	8	—	—
Oct 27	Benny Williams	Newark	D	6	—	—
Nov 3	Vince DeLia	Newark	W	6	—	—
Dec 16	Eddie Dowe	Perth Amboy	W	6	—	—
1942						
Jan 26	Eddie Dowe	Newark	W	6	—	—
Mar 26	Pedro Firpo	Atlantic City	W	8	—	—
Apr 10	Angelo Panatellas	Atlantic City	KO	5	—	—
Apr 24	Willie Roache	Perth Amboy	W	8	—	—
May 7	Abie Kaufman	Atlantic City	W	8	—	—
Jun 29	Ivan Christie	Newark	KO	5	—	—
Jul 29	Angelo Maglione	Trenton	KO	3	—	—
Aug 13	Jan Ruby Garcia	Atlantic City	W	8	—	—
Sep 10	Charley Davis	Elizabeth, NJ	W	8	—	—
Oct 20	Gene Burton	White Plains, NY	KO	4	—	—
Dec 7	Bob Gunther	Trenton	W	8	—	131
Dec 21	Sammy Daniels	Baltimore	W	6	—	—
1943						
Jan 29	Jerry Moore	New York	W	6	—	—
Feb 22	Sammy Daniels	Philadelphia	KO	2	—	—
Feb 23	Bobby McQuillar	Cleveland	KO	3	—	135
Mar 8	Bill Speary	Philadelphia	KO	2	—	—
Apr 2	Rudy Giscombe	New York	TKO	3	—	132
Apr 5	Ruby Garcia	Philadelphia	W	8	—	—
Apr 21	Joe Genovese	Cleveland	TKO	4	—	—
May 7 ⑩	Maurice LaChance	Boston	W	8	—	—
May 17	Ray Brown	Philadelphia	W	10	—	—
Jul 19	Jimmy Hatcher	Philadelphia	TKO	6	—	—
Aug 24	Tommy Jessup	Hartford, CT	TKO	5	—	131
Aug 31	Johnny Bellus	Hartford	W	10	—	131
Sep 13	Jerry Moore	W. Springfield, MA	W	10	—	—
Oct 1 ⑩	Maurice LaChance	Boston	TKO	4	—	—
Oct 22	Ed Perry	New Orleans	KO	2	—	—
Oct 29	Gene Johnson	New Orleans	W	10	—	—
Nov 8	Johnny Hutchinson	Philadelphia	KO	3	—	—
Dec 13	Mayon Padlo	Philadelphia	W	10	—	—

1944

Date		Opponent	Location	Result	Rnd	Title	Weight
Jan 25	⑩	Bob Montgomery★	Philadelphia	KO'd	12	—	—
Feb 28		Ellis Phillips	Philadelphia	TKO	1	—	—
Mar 13		Leo Francis	Trenton	W	8	—	138
Mar 27	⑩	Joey Peralta	Philadelphia	TKO	9	—	—
Apr 10		Leroy Saunders	Holyoke, MA	KO	5	—	—
Apr 17		Mike Delia	Philadelphia	KO	1	—	—
May 16	⑩	Luther ("Slugger") White	Philadelphia	W	10	—	—
Jun 7	⑩	Sammy Angott★	Philadelphia	W	10	—	135
Jun 23		Cleo Shans	New York	TKO	10	—	136
Jul 10		Joey Pirrone	Philadelphia	KO	1	—	—
Jul 20		Julie Kogon	New York	W	10	—	—
Aug 29		Jimmy Hatcher	Washington	W	10	—	—
Sep 6	⑩	Sammy Angott★	Philadelphia	W	10	—	—
Sep 19		Freddie Dawson	Philadelphia	KO	4	—	135
Oct 18		Johnny Green	Buffalo	KO	2	—	—
Nov 2		Ruby Garcia	Baltimore	TKO	7	—	—
Nov 13		Willie Joyce	Philadelphia	L	10	—	134
Dec 5	⑩	Lulu Costantino	Cleveland	W	10	—	136
Dec 12		Dave Castilloux	Buffalo	TKO	5	—	—

1945

Date		Opponent	Location	Result	Rnd	Title	Weight
Jan 8	⑩	Willie Joyce	Philadelphia	W	12	—	—
Jan 22		Mike Berger	Philadelphia	KO	4	—	—
Mar 2	⑩	Willie Joyce	New York	L	12	—	133
Mar 26		Dorsey Lay	Philadelphia	KO	3	—	—
Apr 18	♔	Juan Zurita	Mexico City	KO	2	Won-NBA-L	131
Jun 8	⑩	Willie Joyce	New York	L	10	—	—
Aug 14		Charley Smith	Union City, NJ	W	10	—	137
Aug 28		Gene Burton	Philadelphia	W	10	—	—
Sep 7	⑩	Nick Moran	New York	W	10	—	134
Sep 19	⑩	Sammy Angott★	Pittsburgh	TKO'd	6	—	136
Nov 26		Wesley Mouzon	Philadelphia	D	10	—	135

1946

Date		Opponent	Location	Result	Rnd	Title	Weight
Jan 8		Charley Smith	Trenton	W	10	—	136
Jan 20	⑩	Johnny Bratton	New Orleans	W	10	—	—
Jan 28	⑩	Freddie Dawson	Philadelphia	D	10	—	135
Feb 14		Cleo Shans	Orange, NJ	W	10	—	137
Feb 22		Ace Miller	Detroit	W	10	—	—
Mar 11		Eddie Giosa	Philadelphia	TKO	4	—	—
Apr 8		Eddie Giosa	Philadelphia	TKO	1	—	—
Apr 30	⑩	Enrique Bolanos	Los Angeles	TKO	8	Ret-NBA-L	134
Jun 12	⑩	Bobby Ruffin	Brooklyn	TKO	5	—	138
Aug 6		Ivan Christie	Norwalk, CT	KO	2	—	138
Sep 4	⑩	Ronnie James	Cardiff, Wales	KO	9	Ret-NBA-L	134

1947

Date		Opponent	Location	Result	Rnd	Title	Weight
Jan 27	⑩	Gene Burton	Chicago	L	10	—	139
Apr 14		Frankie Conti	Allentown, PA	TKO	7	—	137
Apr 25		Willie Russell	Columbus, OH	W	10	—	—
May 9	⑩	Ralph Zannelli	Boston	W	10	—	139
May 26		Juste Fontaine	Philadelphia	TKO	4	—	—
Jun 20	⑩	Tippy Larkin	New York	KO	4	—	—
Aug 4	♔	Bob Montgomery★	Philadelphia	KO	6	Won-Vac World-L	133
Sep 29		Doll Rafferty	Philadelphia	KO	4	—	—
Oct 10		Talmadge Bussey	Detroit	TKO	9	—	—
Dec 12	⑩	Tony Pellone	New York	W	10	—	—

1948

Date		Opponent	Location	Result	Rnd	Title	Weight
Jan 13		Doug Carter	Camden, NJ	W	10	—	138
Jan 26	⑩	Freddie Dawson	Philadelphia	W	10	—	137
Feb 9		Livio Minelli	Philadelphia	W	10	—	—

Date		Opponent	Location	Result	Rnd	Note	Wt
Feb 27	⑩	Kid Gavilan★	New York	W	10	—	136
May 5		Rudy Cruz	Hartford	W	10	—	—
May 25	⑩	Enrique Bolanos	Los Angeles	W	15	Ret-World-L	135
Jul 12	⑩	Beau Jack★	Philadelphia	TKO	6	Ret-World-L	135
Sep 23	⑩	Jesse Flores	New York	KO	10	Ret-World-L	134
Nov 8		Buddy Garcia	Philadelphia	KO	1	—	—
Nov 18		Billy Nixon	Philadelphia	TKO	4	—	—

1949

Date		Opponent	Location	Result	Rnd	Note	Wt
Jan 17	⑩	Johnny Bratton	Philadelphia	W	10		— —
Jan 28	⑩	Kid Gavilan★	New York	L	10	—	—
Apr 1	⑩	Kid Gavilan★	New York	L	10	—	—
Apr 23		Vince Turpin	Cleveland	TKO	6	—	—
Jun 21		Irvin Steen	Los Angeles	W	10	—	141
Jul 21	⑩	Enrique Bolanos	Los Angeles	TKO	4	Ret-World-L	135
Aug 3		Benny Walker	Oakland	W	10	—	—
Sep 30		Doug Ratford	Philadelphia	W	10	—	—
Oct 24		Al Mobley	Trenton	W	10	—	141
Nov 14		Jean Walzack	Philadelphia	W	10	—	—
Dec 5	⑩	Freddie Dawson	Philadelphia	W	15	Ret-World-L	135

1950

Date		Opponent	Location	Result	Rnd	Note	Wt
Jan 20	⑩	Johnny Bratton	Chicago	TKO	8	—	143
Feb 17	⑩	Sonny Boy West	New York	KO	8	—	141
Feb 27	⑩	John L. Davis	Seattle	W	10	—	141
Jun 2	⑩	Lester Felton	Detroit	W	10	—	144
Jul 12	⑩	George Costner	Philadelphia	L	10	—	143
Aug 7	⑩	Charley Salas	Washington, DC	L	10	—	—
Sep 26	⑩	Charley Salas	Washington, DC	W	10	—	—
Oct 2	⑩	Joe Miceli	Milwaukee	L	10	—	—
Nov 23	⑩	Joe Miceli	Milwaukee	W	10	—	—
Dec 12		Dave Marsh	Akron, OH	TKO	9	—	—
Dec 18	⑩	Rudy Cruz	Philadelphia	W	10	—	—

1951

Date		Opponent	Location	Result	Rnd	Note	Wt
Jan 5		Jose Maria Gatica	New York	TKO	1	—	—
Jan 22		Ralph Zannelli	Providence, RI	KO	5	—	—
Jan 31		Vic Cardell	Detroit	TKO	9	—	—
Feb 19	⑩	Joe Miceli	Philadelphia	L	10	—	—
Mar 5		Beau Jack★	Providence	W	10	—	—
Apr 11		Fitzie Pruden	Chicago	W	10	—	—
May 25	⑩	Jimmy Carter★	New York	TKO'd	14	Lost-World-L	135
Aug 2		Don Williams	Worcester, MA	L	10	—	—
Sep 10	⑩	Gil Turner	Philadelphia	TKO'd	10	—	—

1952

Date		Opponent	Location	Result	Rnd	Note	Wt
Mar 17		Johnny Cunningham	Baltimore	KO	5	—	—
Mar 26	⑩	Chuck Davey	Chicago	TKO'd	5	—	—
Nov 24		Pat Manzi	Syracuse, NY	TKO	7	—	—

1953

Date		Opponent	Location	Result	Rnd	Note	Wt
Jan 12	⑩	Carmen Basilio★	Syracuse	L	10	—	—
Mar 9		Claude Hammond	Trenton	W	10	—	—
Mar 28		Vic Cardell	Philadelphia	W	10	—	—
Apr 20		Billy Andy	Trenton	W	10	—	—
May 18		Billy Andy	Erie, PA	W	10	—	—
Jun 8		George Johnson	Trenton	TKO'd	8	—	—
Sep 17		Dom Zimbardo	Newark	TKO	2	—	—
Nov 9		Jed Black	Fort Wayne, IN	L	10	—	—

1954

Date		Opponent	Location	Result	Rnd	Note	Wt
Jul 2		Rafael Lastre	Havana	L	10	—	—

1956

Date		Opponent	Location	Result	Rnd	Note	Wt
Apr 9		Beau Jack★	Augusta, GA	D	10	—	—
Aug 12		Beau Jack★	Augusta	TKO	9	—	—

ALBERT ("CHALKY") WRIGHT

FEATHERWEIGHT

Right-handed; 5'7½"; 124–135 lbs.
206 bouts, 2/23/1928 to 3/9/1948
Manager: Eddie Walker
Featherweight Champ 1941–42
Hall of Fame Induction: 1997
Born: 2/10/1912, Durango, Mexico
Named: Albert Garfield Wright
Died: 8/12/1957

A small, plucky fighter whose career started in the 1920s, Chalky Wright persevered for thirteen years and over 140 fights before he won a championship belt.

Most sources list Wright's birthplace as Durango, Mexico. Officially, his date of birth is February 10, 1912, but many believed that he was much older. When Wright's father abandoned his mother shortly after the boy was born, she moved her young family to the Los Angeles area. As a young man, Wright turned to prizefighting more for survival than glory, and in his first bout in 1926, he decisioned Nilo Balles.

Wright (L) relinquished his world featherweight title to the legendary Willie Pep in a 15-round decision in Madison Square Garden on November 20, 1942.

IN THE RING	WON 150	LOST 40	DRAWS 15	TB 206	KO 75	W 75	WF 0	D 15	KO'd 7	L 33	LF 0	NC 1

Date	Opponent	Site	Result / Rounds		Title	Wt.
1928						
Feb 23	Nilo Balles	San Bernardino, CA	W	4	—	—
Apr 12	Nilo Balles	San Bernardino	KO	3	—	—
May 3	Val Martin	San Bernardino	W	4	—	—
May 31	Victor Acosta	San Bernardino	KO	2	—	—
Jul 12	Young Valentino	San Bernardino	D	4	—	—
Jul 26	Ray Davis	San Bernardino	L	4	—	—
Aug 23	Joe Hernandez	San Bernardino	L	4	—	—
Sep 13	Joe Hernandez	San Bernardino	D	4	—	—
Nov 22	Ray Davis	San Bernardino	W	4	—	—
Dec 13	Louie Contreras	San Bernardino	D	6	—	—
Dec 20	Ray Davis	San Bernardino	W	6	—	—
1929						
Jan 17	Patsy Callope	San Bernardino	KO	2	—	—
Feb 7	Joey Valarde	San Bernardino	L	6	—	—
Mar 28	Paul Hardy	San Bernardino	KO	3	—	—
Apr 9	Harry Wallinger	Los Angeles	D	4	—	—
Apr 18	Johnny Mason	San Bernardino	W	6	—	—
May 2	Ray Billobas	San Bernardino	D	6	—	—
Jul 5	Frisco Landa	El Centro, CA	L	4	—	—
Sep 12	Pal Shoaf	San Bernardino	W	4	—	—
Oct 7	Kid Avelino	Los Angeles	W	4	—	—
Oct 10	Harry Purdue	San Bernardino	W	4	—	—
Oct 24	Harry Barrere	San Bernardino	W	6	—	—
Nov 11	Ray Cervantes	Los Angeles	W	4	—	—
1930						
May 8	Clayton Gouyd	Pasadena, CA	W	6	—	—
Jun 12	Jimmy Mack	Pasadena	W	6	—	—
Jun 17	Frisco Landa	San Bernardino	W	6	—	—
Jun 26	Ray Navarro	Pasadena	KO	5	—	—
Jul 5	Frisco Landa	El Centro	L	4	—	—
Jul 21	Sammy Seaman	Los Angeles	D	6	—	—
Aug 12	Sid Torres	Los Angeles	W	6	—	—
Sep 16	Manuel Trevino	Los Angeles	KO	3	—	—
Oct 7	Kid Avelino	Los Angeles	W	6	—	—
Oct 21	Martin Cane	Los Angeles	KO	4	—	—
Oct 24	Mose Bailey	San Diego	D	6	—	—
Nov 7	Johnny Lee	San Diego	KO	3	—	—
Nov 10	Ray Cervantes	Los Angeles	W	4	—	—
Nov 14	Jerry Duffy	San Diego	W	6	—	—
Nov 18	Ray Cervantes	Los Angeles	W	6	—	—
Dec 12	Ramon Montoya	San Diego	L	10	—	—
1931						
Jan 13	Huerta Evans	Los Angeles	L	6	—	—
Feb 13	Ray Butler	San Diego	W	10	—	—
Mar 10	Ernie Chacon	Los Angeles	W	4	—	—
Mar 31	Mike Cordova	Los Angeles	W	4	—	—
May 1	Claude Roberts	San Diego	W	6	—	—
Aug 6	Marty Zuniga	Sacramento	D	6	—	—
Aug 11	Baby Jack Dempsey	Los Angeles	KO	2	—	—
Sep 15	Mike Cordova	Los Angeles	W	6	—	—

Date		Opponent	Location	Result	Rounds		
Oct 8		Huerta Evans	San Bernardino	W	8	—	—
Oct 29		Huerta Evans	San Bernardino	D	10	—	—
Nov 24		Clemente Avila	Los Angeles	W	6	—	—
1932							
Jan 12		Tony Tassi	Los Angeles	KO	4	—	—
Feb 8		Ramon Montoya	San Diego	W	6	—	—
Feb 16		Marty Zuniga	Los Angeles	D	6	—	—
Apr 29		Al Greenfield	San Diego	W	6	—	—
May 3		Willie Davies	Los Angeles	W	4	—	—
May 18		Jose Pimental	San Francisco	KO	2	—	—
Jun 7		Huerta Evans	Los Angeles	KO	5	—	—
Jul 12		Al Greenfield	Los Angeles	W	4	—	—
Aug 26		Johnny Minella	San Diego	W	6	—	—
Sep 2		Mose Bailey	San Diego	D	6	—	—
Oct 11		Jess Macy	Los Angeles	KO	1	—	—
Oct 19		Kid Ponce	Long Beach, CA	KO	2	—	—
Nov 15		Baby Jack Dempsey	Los Angeles	KO	1	—	—
Nov 22		Al Greenfield	Los Angeles	W	4	—	—
Dec 15		Benny Garcia	Ventura, CA	W	6	—	—
1933							
Jan 6		Pedro Villanueva	Ventura	W	6	—	—
Apr 11		Mickey Cohen	Los Angeles	KO	3	—	—
May 3		Whitey Neil	Portland, OR	W	6	—	—
Aug 22		Whitey Neil	Portland	W	6	—	—
Sep 1		Huerta Evans	San Francisco	KO	4	—	—
Sep 5		Willie Jabura	Los Angeles	KO	3	—	—
Oct 17	⑩	Eddie Shea	Los Angeles	KO'd	1	For-CA-130 lbs	—
1934							
Apr 17		Jimmy Alvarado	Los Angeles	KO	2	—	—
May 1		Albert Ladou	Los Angeles	W	4	—	—
May 25		Frankie Venegas	El Centro	KO	5	—	—
Jun 8	♛	Freddie Miller★	El Centro	L	10	—	—
Jun 29		Perfecto Lopez	Ventura	W	6	—	—
Oct 8		Mose Butch	Pittsburgh	L	10	—	—
Nov 17		Lew Monte	Brooklyn	L	6	—	—
1935							
Feb 2	⑩	Baby Arizmendi	Mexico City	KO'd	4	—	—
Feb 16		Chico Cisneros	Mexico City	L	10	—	—
Apr 6		Mark Diaz	Sacramento	KO	4	—	—
May 10	⑩	Pablo Dano	Watsonville, CA	KO'd	2	—	—
1936							
Mar 28		Claude Varner	Vancouver	W	10	—	—
Apr 17		Buzz Brown	Butte, MT	W	10	—	—
May 21		Eddie Spina	Tacoma, WA	W	10	—	—
Aug 20		Cecil Payne	Tacoma	D	10	—	—
Sep 29		Doug Wirth	Portland	KO	1	—	—
1937							
May 18		Sonny Valdez	Los Angeles	W	6	—	—
Jun 14		Bobby Gray	Los Angeles	KO	5	—	—
Jul 21		Norbert Meehan	Oakland, CA	KO	5	—	—
Aug 17		Georgie Hansford	Los Angeles	D	10	—	—
Sep 7		Georgie Hansford	Los Angeles	W	10	—	—
Oct 5		Baby Arizmendi	Los Angeles	L	10	—	—
Oct 19		Babe Santella	Los Angeles	KO	1	—	—
Nov 30		Buss Breese	Los Angeles	W	10	—	—
1938							
Feb 1	♛	Henry Armstrong★	Los Angeles	TKO'd	3	—	—
Aug 17		Al Reid	New York	KO	4	—	—
Nov 7		Cristobal Jaramillo	New York	W	8	—	—

Date		Opponent	Location	Result	Rounds	Title	Rating
Nov 25		Vince Dell'Orto	New York	W	6	—	—
Dec 5		Pete De Grasse	New York	KO	5	—	—
Dec 26		Joey Ferrando	New York	L	8	—	—
1939							
Jan 3		Tommy Speigel	Brooklyn	W	10	—	—
Jan 14		Johnny Rohrig	Brooklyn	W	8	—	—
Jan 31		Lew Feldman	Brooklyn	L	8	—	—
Feb 14		Johnny Bellus	New York	L	8	—	—
Mar 10		Joe DeJesus	New York	KO	2	—	—
Mar 21		Red Guggino	Brooklyn	W	8	—	—
Apr 27		Dan McAllister	Liverpool, England	KO	5	—	—
May 25		George Daly	London	W	8	—	—
Jun 8	⑩	Kid Tanner	Liverpool	KO	7	—	—
Aug 8		Teddy Baldwin	Garfield, NJ	W	8	—	—
Aug 21		Billy Bullock	Baltimore	KO	5	—	—
Sep 18		Lew Feldman	Baltimore	L	10	—	—
Dec 1		Young Rightmire	New York	W	6	—	—
1940							
Jan 16		Sammy Julian	Brooklyn	W	8	—	128
Jan 29		Paul Junior	Portland, ME	L	10	—	—
Feb 19		Frankie Gilmore	Baltimore	W	10	—	—
Feb 22		Mike Martinez	Baltimore	KO	3	—	—
Mar 11		Charley Gomer	Baltimore	KO	4	—	—
Apr 1	⑩	Tommy Speigel	Baltimore	W	10	—	—
Apr 29	⑩	Cocoa Kid	Baltimore	L	10	—	—
Jun 24		Saverio Turiello	Baltimore	W	10	—	—
Jul 15		Joey Silva	Baltimore	KO	7	—	—
Aug 12		Paul Junior	Philadelphia	KO	5	—	—
Sep 9		Joey Ferrando	Baltimore	KO	4	—	—
Oct 7		Teddy Baldwin	Philadelphia	KO	4	—	—
Dec 9	⑩	Pete Leto	Baltimore	L	10	—	127
1941							
Jan 6		Johnny Williams	New York	KO	5	—	127
Jan 14		Norment Quarles	Jersey City, NJ	W	8	—	—
Feb 4		Norman Rahn	Jersey City	KO	2	—	—
Feb 19		Frank Terranova	Allentown, PA	KO	6	—	—
Feb 24		Maurice Arnault	Baltimore	KO	2	—	—
Mar 6		Texas Lee Harper	Washington, DC	KO	3	—	—
Mar 17		Charles Schnaupoff	Wilkes-Barre, PA	KO	5	—	—
May 1		Charley Varre	New York	W	8	—	—
May 22	⑩	Sal Bartolo	New York	W	8	—	128
May 29		Norment Quarles	Atlantic City	W	8	—	—
Jun 3		Guillermo Puentes	Long Island City, NY	KO	5	—	128
Jun 17		Lloyd Pine	Wilkes-Barre	KO	2	—	—
Jun 24		Bobby McIntire	Long Island City	KO	5	—	—
Jul 17	⑩	Jackie Wilson	Baltimore	W	10	—	—
Aug 5		Paco Villa	Long Island City	KO	6	—	—
Sep 11	♛	Joey Archibald	Washington, DC	KO	11	Won-World-FE	124
Oct 2		Joey Peralta	Wilkes-Barre	L	10	—	—
Oct 14		Leo Rodak	Washington, DC	W	10	—	—
Oct 31		Ray Lunny	San Francisco	W	10	—	—
Nov 28		Jesse Morales	San Diego	KO	6	—	—
1942							
Jan 13	⑩	Bobby Ruffin	New York	L	10	—	129
Feb 3	⑩	Richie Lemos	Los Angeles	KO	6	—	—
Feb 19		Ritchie Fontaine	Oakland	W	10	—	—
Mar 24		Jorge Morelia	Los Angeles	KO	6	—	—
Apr 6		Vern Bybee	San Francisco	L	10	—	—
May 7	⑩	Lulu Constantino	New York	W	8	—	—

Date		Opponent	Location	Result	Rnd	Title	Wt
Jun 19	⑩	Harry Jeffra	Baltimore	TKO	10	Ret-World-FE	124
Jul 13		Lou Transparenti	Baltimore	KO	4	—	—
Aug 6	⑩	Allie Stoltz	New York	L	10	—	—
Aug 15		Tommy ("Curley") St. Angelo	Springfield, MA	KO	2	—	—
Aug 27		Joey Marinelli	Detroit	KO	2	—	—
Sep 25	⑩	Lulu Constantino	New York	W	15	Ret-World-FE	125
Oct 13		Carlos ("No No") Cuebas	Hartford, CT	KO	4	—	—
Oct 20		Henry Vasquez	New Haven, CT	KO	8	—	130
Nov 20		Willie Pep★	New York	L	15	Lost-World-FE	125
1943							
Jan 15	⑩	Joey Peralta	New York	W	10	—	130
Feb 15		Morris Parker	Newark	KO	4	—	—
Feb 23	⑩	Joey Peralta	St. Louis	W	10	—	—
Mar 10		Joey Pirrone	Cleveland	KO	3	—	—
May 17		Frankie Carto	Baltimore	KO	8	—	—
May 25		Billy Pinti	Brooklyn	KO	4	—	130
Jun 4	⑩	Phil Terranova	New York	KO	5	—	125
Jul 3		Kid National	Havana	KO	8	—	127
Jul 21	⑩	Lulu Constantino	Cleveland	L	10	—	—
Aug 9		Angel Avila	Washington, DC	KO	7	—	—
Oct 26		Patsy Spataro	Brooklyn	TKO	2	—	132
Nov 8		Billy Banks	Philadephia	KO	5	—	—
Nov 19		Al Reasoner	New Orleans	KO	2	—	—
1944							
Jan 25		Baby Al Brown	Panama City	KO	5	—	—
Feb 10		Alberto Carlos	Panama City	KO	6	—	—
Mar 5		Young Finnegan	Panama City	D	10	—	—
May 1		Clyde English	Scranton, PA	KO	7	—	—
May 22		Sammy Daniels	Baltimore	KO	8	—	—
Jun 5		Vince Dell'Orto	Washington, DC	KO	3	—	—
Jul 10		Ruby Garcia	Houston	KO	8	—	—
Jul 17		Johnny Cockfield	Norfolk, VA	KO	5	—	—
Sep 29	♛	Willie Pep★	New York	L	15	For-World-FE	125
Dec 5	♛	Willie Pep★	Cleveland	L	10	—	132
1945							
Feb 5	⑩	Willie Joyce	Philadelphia	L	10	—	—
Apr 9		Jackie Wilson	Baltimore	NC	7	—	—
Apr 17	⑩	Willie Joyce	Los Angeles	W	10	—	—
Jul 31		Henry Jordan	Brooklyn	KO	6	—	133
Aug 28	⑩	Enrique Bolanos	Los Angeles	W	10	—	—
Sep 21		Humberto Zavala	New York	W	10	—	132
Oct 5	⑩	Bobby Ruffin	Detroit	W	10	—	129
Nov 2		Leroy Willis	Detroit	W	10	—	—
Dec 14		Johnny Bratton	New Orleans	W	10	—	—
1946							
Jan 25		Pedro Firpo	New York	W	10	—	134
Feb 19	⑩	Enrique Bolanos	Los Angeles	L	10	—	133
Mar 5		Georgie Hansford	Milwaukee	KO	4	—	—
Mar 27		Frankie Moore	Oakland	KO'd	1	—	—
Apr 17		Frankie Moore	Oakland	L	10	—	135
Aug 27		Johnny Dell	New York	L	10	—	134
Oct 15	⑩	Enrique Bolanos	Los Angeles	L	10	—	131
Nov 27	♛	Willie Pep★	Milwaukee	KO'd	3	—	—
1947							
May 19		Frankie Saucedo	Juarez, Mexico	D	10	—	—
Jun 24		Larry Cisneros	Albuquerque, NM	L	10	—	—
1948							
Mar 9		Ernie Hunick	Salt Lake City	TKO'd	3	—	—

Fighting exclusively in California against unranked opponents, Wright racked up a record of 48-7-11 in his first five years of fighting. In the next five years he fought less frequently and, for a time, worked as a chauffeur for the glamorous comedic actress Mae West. Wright posted a dismal 0–6 record against ranked fighters, including Freddie Miller and Henry Armstrong. However, Armstrong was impressed with Wright's boxing style and hired him as a sparring partner to help him sharpen up for a fight with Barney Ross. Wright performed so well in these sparring sessions that manager Eddie Walker added Wright to his stable. Wright started winning again and in 1938 was ranked as the sixth-best featherweight by *The Ring*.

Wright finally got a chance to fight for the featherweight title against champion Joey Archibald on September 11, 1941 in Washington DC's Griffith Stadium. Wright started quickly and dominated the fight. He knocked Archibald down twice before finishing him off with a left hook to the body and a right to the jaw in the eleventh.

After successfully defending his title twice, Wright lost the championship to the undefeated Willie Pep at Madison Square Garden on November 20, 1942. Yet even after Wright lost the title, he impressed schooled observers as a consummate boxer. Reporter Stanley Woodward, after he watched Wright's five-round knockout of Phil Terranova, wrote in the June 6, 1943 *New York Tribune*:

"It was the first time we ever had seen Chalky and we came away convinced that he is the greatest boxer and smartest operator and the most efficient puncher of his time.... Every move he makes is the perfect illustration for a treatise on how to box. He walks out flatfooted, conserving his ancient legs. He blocks nonchalantly and slips punches by moving his head just enough. When he hits he doesn't miss. The one-two with which he knocked down the outclassed Terranova in the second round was the most perfect punch seen in the Garden since Joe Louis was a civilian."

In a 1944 rematch following Pep's discharge from the Navy, Wright got in some shots, but Pep's incredible defensive skills prevailed. (This bout is also noteworthy in that it was the first televised fight sponsored by The Gillette Safety Razor Company.) Two months later Wright again lost to Pep. Although he continued to fight for four more years, Wright was definitely past his prime. He won only one of his last ten fights and suffered a knockout loss to Pep. After Ernie Hunick knocked him out in three rounds, Wright announced his retirement.

The fact that he was unable to defeat Hall of Famer Willie Pep should not detract from Wright's accomplishments. He took on all comers, including lightweights and welterweights. He possessed a fine left hook and a strong right. He could box on the outside or mix it up in close. Distinguished boxing historian Hank Kaplan described Wright as "a good all-around boxer-puncher."

In retirement Wright lost most of his ring earnings gambling. He was working in a bakery when he moved back to his mother's house after a dispute with his wife. On August 12, 1957, his mother came home to find Wright slumped in the bathtub, dead after a fall.

TONY ZALE
The Man of Steel

MIDDLEWEIGHT

Right-handed; 5'8"; 154–164 lbs.

87 bouts, 6/11/1934 to 9/21/1948

Managers: Harry Shall 1934–36, John Zale 1936–37, Sam Pian and Art Winch 1937–48

NBA Middlewt. Champ 1940–41, Middlewt. Champ 1941–47, 1948

Hall of Fame Induction: 1991

Born: 5/29/1913, Gary, IN

Named: Anthony Florian Zaleski

Died: 3/21/1997

Tony Zale has been called the greatest comeback fighter in the history of boxing. Few, if any, have equaled Zale's ability to withstand a tremendous beating and then rebound to take charge of a fight which appeared to be totally lost.

Zale grew up under the haze of steel town Gary, Indiana. He and his brothers had been active in amateur boxing, but Zale did not turn to fighting in earnest until he was about to graduate from high school and saw the steel mills looming as his most likely place of employment. "I didn't want those mills," recalled Zale later in his career.

Zale did work in the mills but only as a day job while he compiled a solid amateur record of 87-8 before making his professional debut in 1934. He boxed

Rocky Graziano crashes to the canvas after a pile driver body punch and a left hook by Zale. This fight, the first of three battles between these two well-matched warriors, took place in September 1946.

in the Chicago area for five years and was recognized as the tenth-best middle-weight contender in *The Ring*'s annual rankings of 1939. Under the guidance of the managerial team of Art Winch and Sam Pian, Zale had his first major fight, a non-title bout with NBA middleweight champion, Al Hostak. The unheralded Zale surprised Hostak and took the decision. Six months later the two squared off for the title with Zale winning by knockout in thirteen. In 1941, Zale unified the middleweight championship with a decision over the New York champion, Georgie Abrams. After a rather lackluster loss to the light heavyweight Billy Conn, Zale joined the Navy for the duration of World War II.

IN THE RING	WON 67	LOST 18	DRAWS 2	TB 87	KO 45	W 22	WF 0	D 2	KO'd 5	L 13	LF 0

Date	Opponent	Site	Result / Rounds		Title	Wt.
1934						
Jun 11	Eddie Allen	Chicago	W	4	—	—
Jun 15	Johnny Simpson	Chicago	W	4	—	—
Jun 21	Bobby Millsap	Chicago	KO	1	—	—
Jun 25	Johnny Liston	Chicago	KO	3	—	—
Jul 2	Ossie Jefferson	Chicago	KO	3	—	—
Jul 9	Lou Bartell	Chicago	W	4	—	—
Jul 16	Einar Hedquist	Chicago	KO	4	—	—
Jul 30	Bobby Millsap	Chicago	W	4	—	—
Aug 6	Bruce Wade	Peoria, IL	KO	3	—	—
Aug 13	Billy Hood	Chicago	L	6	—	—
Aug 15	George ("Billy") Black	Chicago	L	6	—	—
Aug 27	Wilbur Stokes	Chicago	W	8	—	—
Sep 3	Mickey Misko	Chicago	L	8	—	—
Sep 17	Mickey Misko	Chicago	KO	4	—	—
Oct 8	Young Jack Blackburn	Chicago	W	8	—	—
Oct 22	Frankie Misko	Chicago	KO	6	—	—
Oct 28	Jackie Schwartz	Milwaukee	KO	4	—	—
Nov 5	Jack Chavez	Chicago	W	8	—	—
Nov 26	Kid Leonard	Peoria	L	10	—	—
Dec 17	Jack Gibbons	Chicago	L	10	—	—
Dec 28	Joey Bazzone	Chicago	L	6	—	—
1935						
Feb 25	Jack Blackburn	Chicago	W	6	—	—
Mar 11	Max Elling	Chicago	W	8	—	—
Mar 27	Frank Glover	Cincinnati	KO'd	9	—	—
May 6	Johnny Phagan	Chicago	TKO'd	6	—	—
Jul 2	Dave Clark	Chicago	L	5	—	—
1936						
Apr 13	Jack Moran	Chicago	D	5	—	—
1937						
Jul 26	Elby Johnson	Chicago	W	4	—	—
Aug 17	Emanuel Davila	Chicago	L	4	—	—
Sep 17	Elby Johnson	Chicago	TKO	3	—	—
Oct 11	Billy Brown	Chicago	KO	1	—	—
Oct 18	Bobby Gerry	Chicago	KO	2	—	—
Nov 1	Nate Bolden	Chicago	L	5	—	—
Nov 10	Leon Jackson	Gary, IN	W	6	—	—
Nov 22	Nate Bolden	Chicago	W	6	—	—

1938

Date		Opponent	Location	Result	Rounds	Title	Weight
Jan 3		Nate Bolden	Chicago	W	8	—	—
Jan 24		Henry Schaft	Chicago	W	8	—	—
Feb 21		Jimmy Clark	Chicago	KO'd	1	—	—
Mar 28		King Wyatt	Chicago	W	8	—	—
May 16		Bobby LaMonte	Chicago	TKO	5	—	—
Jun 13		Jimmy Clark	Chicago	TKO	8	—	—
Jul 18		Billy Celebron	Chicago	D	10	—	—
Aug 22		Billy Celebron	Chicago	L	10	—	—
Oct 10		Tony Cisco	Chicago	W	10	—	—
Oct 31		Jimmy Clark	Chicago	TKO	2	—	—
Nov 18		Enzo Iannozzi	Chicago	W	6	—	—

1939

Date		Opponent	Location	Result	Rounds	Title	Weight
Jan 2	⑩	Nate Bolden	Chicago	L	10	—	—
May 1		Johnny Shaw	Chicago	KO	5	—	—
May 23		Babe Orgovan	New York	W	6	—	—
Aug 14		Milton Shivers	Chicago	KO	3	—	—
Oct 6		Sherman Edwards	Chicago	TKO	3	—	—
Nov 3		Al Wardlow	Youngstown, OH	KO	3	—	—
Nov 11		Eddie Meleski	Chicago	KO	1	—	—
Dec 12		Babe Orgovan	Chicago	KO	3	—	—

1940

Date		Opponent	Location	Result	Rounds	Title	Weight
Jan 29	♛	Al Hostak	Chicago	W	10	—	—
Feb 29		Enzo Iannozzi	Youngstown	KO	4	—	—
Mar 29	⑩	Ben Brown	Chicago	KO	3	—	—
Jun 12		Baby Kid Chocolate	Youngstown	KO	4	—	—
Jul 19	♛	Al Hostak	Seattle	TKO	13	Won-NBA-M	158
Aug 21	⑩	Billy Soose	Chicago	L	10	—	—
Nov 19		Fred Apostoli	Seattle	W	10	—	—

1941

Date		Opponent	Location	Result	Rounds	Title	Weight
Jan 1		Tony Cianciola	Milwaukee	TKO	7	—	—
Jan 10		Steve Mamakos	Chicago	W	10	—	—
Feb 21		Steve Mamakos	Chicago	KO	14	Ret-NBA-M	159
May 28	⑩	Al Hostak	Chicago	KO	2	Ret-NBA-M	158
Jul 23		Ossie Harris	Chicago	KO	1	—	—
Aug 16		Billy Pryor	Milwaukee	KO	9	—	—
Nov 28	⑩	Georgie Abrams	New York	W	15	Won-Vac World-M	—

1942

Date		Opponent	Location	Result	Rounds	Title	Weight
Feb 13	⑩	Billy Conn★	New York	L	12	—	—

1946

Date		Opponent	Location	Result	Rounds	Title	Weight
Jan 7		Bobby Giles	Kansas City	KO	4	—	162
Jan 17		Tony Gillo	Norfolk, VA	KO	5	—	—
Feb 7		Oscar Boyd	Des Moines, IA	KO	3	—	159
Feb 26		Bobby Claus	Houston	KO	4	—	—
Apr 12		Ira Hughes	Houston	KO	2	—	—
May 2		Eddie Rossi	Memphis, TN	KO	4	—	—
Sep 27	⑩	Rocky Graziano★	New York	KO	6	Ret-World-M	160

1947

Date		Opponent	Location	Result	Rounds	Title	Weight
Feb 3		Deacon Logan	Omaha, NE	TKO	6	—	162
Feb 12		Len Wadsworth	Wichita, KS	KO	3	—	—
Mar 20		Tommy Charles	Memphis	KO	4	—	—
Apr 1		Al Timmons	Kansas City, KS	KO	5	—	—
May 8		Cliff Beckett	Youngstown	KO	6	—	—
Jul 16	⑩	Rocky Graziano★	Chicago	TKO'd	6	Lost-World-M	159

1948

Date		Opponent	Location	Result	Rounds	Title	Weight
Jan 23		Al Turner	Grand Rapids, MI	KO	5	—	—
Mar 8		Bobby Claus	Little Rock, AR	KO	4	—	—
Mar 19		Lou Woods	Toledo, OH	KO	3	—	—
Jun 10	♛	Rocky Graziano★	Newark	KO	3	Reg-World-M	158
Sep 21	⑩	Marcel Cerdan★	Jersey City, NJ	TKO'd	12	Lost-World-M	159

On his return from the war, Zale, still viewed as the world champion, engaged in a series of career-defining battles: three all-out struggles with Hall of Famer Rocky Graziano. The two first met in Yankee Stadium before a crowd of 39,827. Most observers expected Zale to fall to Graziano, who was nine years younger. In one of the most brutal battles on record, the fighters went at each other as if their killer instincts had been released. Zale dropped Graziano in the first round, but was knocked down in the second. Graziano then battered and cut Zale until he was so groggy from punches at the end of the fifth, he mistook his opponent's corner for his own. Fans yelled for referee Ruby Goldstein to stop the fight, but the veteran official allowed it to continue. Then, astoundingly, Zale came out for the sixth round as if it were the first. In under two minutes, Graziano was on the canvas, victim of a Zale knockout.

There was a rematch in 1947 and a rubber match in 1948, both as vicious and unrelenting as the initial battle. Graziano, although bleeding from several cuts, won the first by battering Zale to insensibility by the sixth round. Zale took the second with a third-round knockout to reclaim his title.

Within three months, 35-year-old Zale faced Marcel Cerdan in a title defense. He was knocked out in twelve rounds. After this fight, the great battler retired. Zale briefly returned to the ring to play himself in the movie version of Graziano's autobiography, *Somebody Up There Likes Me*.

Gaunt Tony Zale (L) knocks out Rocky Graziano in the third round of their third meeting on June 10, 1948 in Newark, NJ. Over 21,000 fans witnessed the fight, held in Ruppert Stadium.

CARLOS ZARATE

BANTAMWEIGHT

Right-handed; 5'8"; 111–127 lbs.

65 bouts, 2/2/1970 to 2/29/1988

WBC Bantamweight Champion
1976–79

Hall of Fame Induction: 1994

Born: 5/23/1951, Tepito, Mexico

One of the top fighters of the 1970s, bantamweight Carlos Zarate is most notable for his record of knockout wins. Of his first 47 fights, an amazing 46 ended in knock-out victories. And all but eight of the knockouts occurred in five rounds or less.

Born in Tepito, Mexico, Zarate became a professional boxer at the age of eighteen. He fought exclusively in his homeland for the first four years of his career, building up a strong record of knockouts, many in the second round. In 1972, only one fighter went more than two rounds with Zarate.

In 1976, Zarate fought for only the second time outside Mexico when he challenged Rodolfo Martinez at the Fabulous Forum in Inglewood, California for the WBC bantamweight title. Zarate had a pattern of approaching his opponent carefully at first, then relentlessly stalking him until the perfect moment occurred to

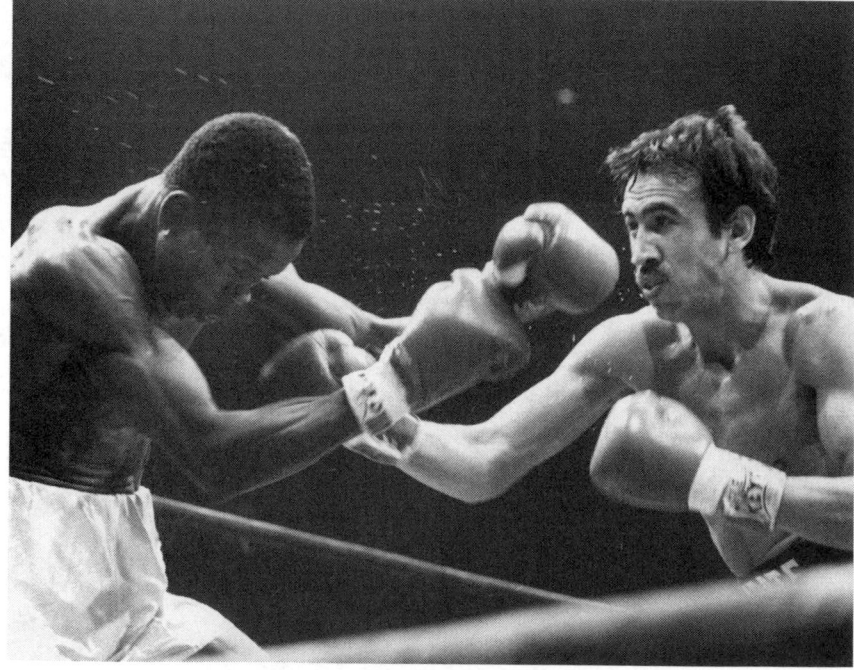

Back in the ring after his first loss, Carlos Zarate (R) keeps his WBC bantamweight title with a three-round shellacking of Mensah Kpalongo (from Togo, West Africa) on March 10, 1979 in Inglewood, CA.

IN THE RING	WON 61	LOST 4*	DRAWS 0	TB 65	KO 58	W 3	WF 0	D 0	KO'd 2	L 1	LF 1*

*includes 1 TL

Date	Opponent	Site	Result / Rounds		Title	Wt.
1970						
Feb 2	Luis Castaneda	Cuernavaca, Mexico	KO	3	—	111
Mar 2	Jose Pavon	Cuernavaca	KO	1	—	—
Apr 1	Costenito Sotelo	Villahermosa, Mexico	KO	2	—	—
Nov 17	Nuno Temix	Villahermosa	TKO	3	—	—
Dec 18	Alfredo Perez	Acapulco	KO	2	—	116
1972						
Jan 28	Emiliano Mayoral	Acapulco	TKO	3	—	—
Feb 7	Jose Gonzalez	Tampico, Mexico	KO	2	—	—
Mar 19	Jose Morales	Mexico City	TKO	2	—	115
Aug 19	Jesus Escobedo	Monterrey, Mexico	KO	2	—	116
Oct 8	Arturo Patino	Ciudad Madero, Mexico	KO	2	—	113
Oct 31	Armando Carrasco	Villahermosa	KO	2	—	116
Dec 3	Juan Perez	La Paz, Mexico	TKO	2	—	—
1973						
Jun 2	Juan Perez	La Paz	KO	2	—	—
Jul 12	Francisco Pino	Cuernavaca	KO	2	—	—
Aug 21	Al Torres	Tijuana, Mexico	TKO	5	—	—
Oct 2	Antonio Castaneda	Tijuana	TKO	9	—	117
Nov 1	Eduardo Miranda	Tijuana	KO	5	—	—
Dec 11	Sixto Perez	Tijuana	KO	2	—	—
1974						
Jan 30	Victor Ramirez	Mexico City	W	10	—	118
Feb 22	Carlos Armenta	Matamoros, Mexico	KO	1	—	—
Apr 9	Alfonso Ibarra	Tijuana	KO	2	—	117
May 3	Chamaco Limon	Monterrey	KO	3	—	117
May 25	Juan Ordonez	Mexico City	KO	3	—	119
Aug 3	Magallo Lozada	Mexico City	TKO	5	—	119
Oct 27	Francisco Cruz	Mexicali, Mexico	TKO	2	—	118
Nov 23	James Martinez	Los Angeles	TKO	7	—	118
1975						
Feb 4	Alberto Cabanig	Ciudad Victoria, Mexico	TKO	4	—	—
Mar 14	Joe Guevara	Inglewood, CA	TKO	4	—	117
Jun 20	Orlando Amoros	Inglewood	KO	3	—	118
Aug 16	Jose Sanchez	Mexico City	TKO	3	—	118
Sep 20	Benicio Sosa	Inglewood	TKO	4	—	—
Oct 11	Jorge Torres	Guadalajara, Mexico	TKO	9	—	118
Dec 7	Nestor Jimenez	Mexicali	KO	2	—	—
1976						
Mar 27	Cesar Deciga	Monterrey	TKO	4	—	—
May 8 ♛	Rodolfo Martinez	Inglewood	KO	9	Won-WBC-B	116
Jun 26	Felix Illanos	Mexicali	KO	2	—	—
Aug 2	Antonio Paredes	Chihuahua, Mexico	TKO	2	—	—

Date		Opponent	Location	Result	Rds	Title	
Aug 28	⑩	Paul Ferreri	Inglewood	TKO	12	Ret-WBC-B	117
Nov 13		Waruinge Nakayama	Culiacan, Mexico	KO	4	Ret-WBC-B	118
1977							
Feb 5		Fernando Cabanela	Mexico City	TKO	3	Ret-WBC-B	118
Apr 23	♔	Alfonso Zamora	Inglewood	TKO	4	—	119
Oct 29		Danilo Batista	Los Angeles	TKO	6	Ret-WBC-B	116
Dec 2		Juan Rodriguez	Madrid	TKO	5	Ret-WBC-B	117
1978							
Feb 25	⑩	Albert Davila	Inglewood	TKO	8	Ret-WBC-B	118
Apr 22		Andres Hernandez	San Juan, PR	TKO	13	Ret-WBC-B	118
Jun 9		Emilio Hernandez	Las Vegas	KO	4	Ret-WBC-B	118
Sep 30		Rudy Gonzalez	Matamoros	KO	4	—	121
Oct 28	♔	Wilfredo Gomez★	Hato Rey, PR	TKO'd	5	For-WBC-JFE (SB)	122
1979							
Mar 10		Mensah Kpalongo	Inglewood	KO	3	Ret-WBC-B	118
May 1		Celso Chairez	Houston	TKO	5	—	—
Jun 3	⑩	Lupe Pintor	Las Vegas	L	15	Lost-WBC-B	117
1986							
Feb 25		Adam Garcia	Inglewood	W	4	—	127
Apr 12		Jose De La Dora	Zacapu, Mexico	KO	3	—	—
May 5		Hector Napoles	Torreon, Mexico	KO	2	—	—
May 23		Jesus Muniz	Chicago	W	10	—	123
Jul 19		Alejandro Garcia	Juarez, Mexico	KO	2	—	—
Sep 13		Gerardo Esparza	Zapopan, Mexico	KO	5	—	—
Nov 21		Eddie Rodriguez	San Jose, CA	TKO	3	—	126
Dec 13		Alex Galvan	Fresno, CA	TKO	7	—	125
1987							
Feb 20		Francis Childs	San Jose	KO	4	—	124
May 5		John Boyd	Los Angeles	TKO	5	—	126
Jun 19		Tony Montoya	San Jose	KO	3	—	126
Aug 15		Richard Savage	Mexico City	TKO	5	—	—
Oct 16	♔	Jeff Fenech★	Sydney	TL	4	For-WBC-JFE (SB)	122
1988							
Feb 29		Daniel Zaragoza	Inglewood	TKO'd	10	For-WBC-JFE (SB)	122

launch a knockout punch. Zarate used this technique on Martinez, whom he knocked down in the fifth round and KO'd in the ninth to win the title.

Though not sanctioned as a title fight, the greatest ring victory Zarate scored came when he stopped undefeated WBA bantamweight champion Alfonso Zamora in four rounds in 1977. Zarate dominated Zamora, knocking him down three times.

Zarate tried to move up in class and win the WBC junior featherweight title but was defeated in five rounds by Hall of Famer Wilfredo Gomez. Later, it was revealed that Zarate had climbed into the ring against Gomez while suffering from the flu.

After losing a controversial decision to his former stable mate Lupe Pintor in 1979, Zarate asked the WBC to reverse the decision. Jose Sulaiman, President of the WBC, agreed that the decision appeared to be incorrect but would not change it.

Zarate then left the fight game, only to make a comeback after almost seven years of inactivity. He continued to build on his stupendous record, winning twelve fights in a row, but his last two fights were losses. He failed in a WBC junior featherweight title bid against Jeff Fenech in Sydney in 1987. His last fight was in February, 1988 against Daniel Zaragoza, again for the WBC junior featherweight crown. Zaragoza scored a technical knockout in the tenth round. Zarate then hung up the gloves again.

An intense Carlos Zarate (R) pounds Paul Ferreri. Zarate ended his first title defense with a 12th-round TKO on August 28, 1976 in the Fabulous Forum. This bout was Zarate's 38th consecutive win.

FRITZIE ZIVIC
The Croat Comet

WELTERWEIGHT

Right-handed; 5'9"; 130–153 lbs.

232 bouts, 10/5/1931 to 1/17/1949

Managers: Luke Carney 1931–42,
Louis Stokan 1942–49

Welterweight Champion 1940–41

Hall of Fame Induction: 1993

Born: 5/8/1913, Pittsburgh, PA

Died: 5/16/1984

Carrying the dubious distinction of being one of the most openly dirty fighters in the history of boxing, Fritzie Zivic was also one of the most popular. His bouts set attendance records at Madison Square Garden, and a Zivic fight was almost always guaranteed to set the crowd roaring. One of five boxing brothers from Pittsburgh, Zivic turned professional as a featherweight in 1931. He generally met with success but, in 1935 and 1936, lost eight fights in a row, a sour streak that might have discouraged a less-dedicated fighter. Nevertheless, in 1936 *The Ring* ranked Zivic as one of the top contenders for the welterweight title.

In his rise to the top, Zivic faced such notables as fellow Pittsburghers Billy Conn and Charley Burley, losing his only meeting with Conn and two out of three

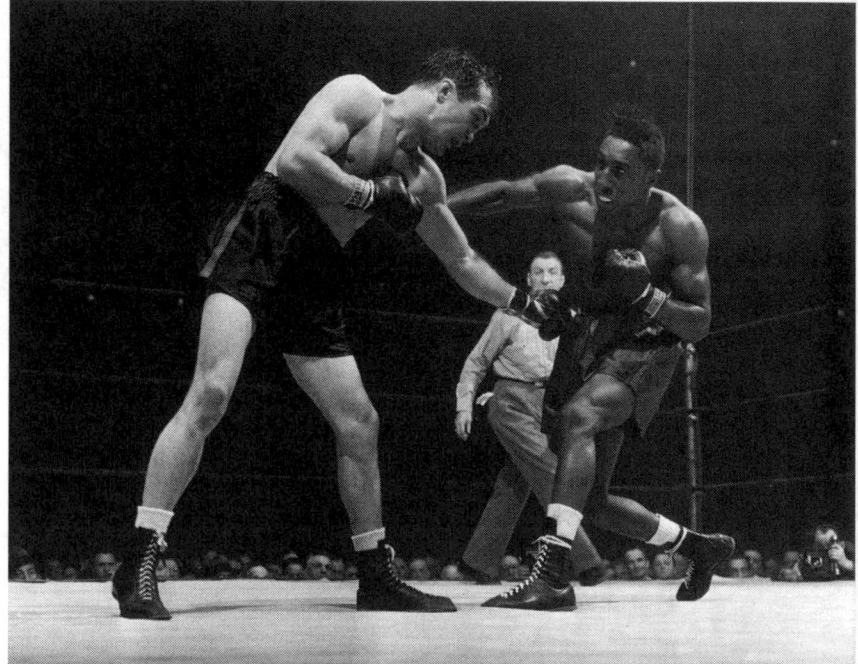

Zivic's (L) punch looks south of the border as Billy Arnold swings a roundhouse right. Zivic took the eight-round decision in 1945. After losing his crown in 1941, Zivic never had another title shot.

IN THE RING	WON 159	LOST 64	DRAWS 9	TB 233	KO 80	W 78	WF 1	D 9	KO'd 4	L 60	LF 0	ND 1

Date	Opponent	Site	Result / Rounds		Title	Wt.
1931						
Oct 5	Al Rettinger	Pittsburgh	TKO	1	—	—
Nov 16	Steve Senich	Pittsburgh	L	6	—	—
1932						
Jan 1	Paddy Gilmore	Pittsburgh	KO	4	—	—
Mar 4	Elmer Kozak	Pittsburgh	TKO	4	—	—
Jun 9	Young Lowstetter	Millvale, PA	W	6	—	—
Jun 22	Steve Senich	North Braddock, PA	L	6	—	—
Sep 26	Jim Dorsey	Pittsburgh	KO	4	—	—
Oct 14	Terry Waner	Pittsburgh	TKO	3	—	—
Nov 18	Jerry Clements	Pittsburgh	L	6	—	—
Dec 13	Billy Criggin	Pittsburgh	W	4	—	—
1933						
Jan 30	George Schlee	Pittsburgh	TKO	2	—	—
Feb 8	Steve Senich	Pittsburgh	KO	2	—	—
Mar 24	U.S. Carpenter	Pittsburgh	KO	4	—	—
Apr 10	Eddie Brannon	Pittsburgh	KO	6	—	—
Apr 28	Patsy Hennigan	Pittsburgh	W	6	—	—
Jun 26	Don Asto	Pittsburgh	W	6	—	—
Jul 10	Don Asto	Pittsburgh	KO	3	—	—
Aug 7	Joey Greb	Millvale	W	10	—	—
Oct 12	Joe Pimental	Pasadena, CA	KO	4	—	—
Nov 3	Gus Vagas	San Francisco	KO	2	—	—
Nov 23	Don Miller	Pasadena	KO	3	—	—
Dec 4	Homer Foster	Pico, CA	D	4	—	—
Dec 15	Vincent Martinez	Hollywood	W	4	—	—
Dec 27	Rudy Ayon	Pico	W	4	—	—
1934						
Jan 5	Luis Carranza	Los Angeles	W	6	—	—
Jan 23	Baby Sal Sorio	Los Angeles	KO	2	—	—
Jan 30	Lloyd Smith	Los Angeles	D	6	—	—
Feb 22	Perfecto Lopez	Los Angeles	W	6	—	—
Apr	Phil Rios	Los Angeles	W	6	—	—
May 8	Lloyd Smith	Los Angeles	D	6	—	—
Jul 2	Eddie Ran	Pittsburgh	W	10	—	—
Jul 25	Joe Firpo	Lake Conneaut, PA	W	8	—	—
Sep 2	Harry Carlton	Pittsburgh	W	10	—	—
Oct 25	Laddie Tonelli	Chicago	KO'd	3	—	—
1935						
Feb 4	⑩ Jimmy Leto	Holyoke, MA	L	10	—	—
Feb 18	Johnny Jadick	Washington, DC	L	10	—	—
Mar 10	K.O. Pete Castillo	Holyoke	W	10	—	—
Mar 25	Dominic Mancini	Pittsburgh	D	10	—	—
Apr 2	Dominic Mancini	Pittsburgh	KO	11	—	—
Apr 16	Marty Gornick	Steubenville, OH	KO	5	—	—
Apr 29	Freddie Chenowyth	Chicago	W	8	—	—
May 6	Sammy Chivas	Chicago	KO	3	—	—
May 30	Eddie Adams	Kent, OH	KO	8	—	—
Jul 1	⑩ Lou Ambers★	Pittsburgh	L	10	—	—

Jul 15		Jackie McFarland	Millvale	W	10	—	—
Aug 1		Mike Barto	Millvale	W	12	—	—
Aug 8	⑩	Joey Ferrando	Jersey City, NJ	L	10	—	—
Sep 30		Tony Herrera	Pittsburgh	L	10	—	—
Oct 4		George Salvadore	New York	L	6	—	—
Dec 16		Billy Celebron	Chicago	L	10	—	—

1936

Jan 13	⑩	Eddie Cool	Pittsburgh	L	10	—	—
Jan 27	⑩	Joey Ferrando	New York	L	8	—	—
Feb 24		Chuck Woods	Pittsburgh	L	10	—	—
Apr 27		Gene Buffalo	Atlantic City	L	10	—	—
May 22		Billy Celebron	St. Louis	KO	1	—	—
Jun 9		Tony Falco	Pittsburgh	KO	8	—	—
Jun 27		Al Manfredo	St. Louis	W	10	—	—
Jul 2		Lou Jallos	Steubenville, OH	W	10	—	—
Jul 6		Laddie Tonelli	Pittsburgh	KO	4	—	—
Jul 22		Mickey Duris	Johnstown, PA	W	12	—	—
Jul 30		Laddie Tonelli	Pittsburgh	TKO	6	—	—
Aug 12	⑩	Cleo Locatelli	Brooklyn	L	10	—	—
Sep 28		Jackie McFarland	Canton, OH	W	10	—	—
Oct 5		Johnny Durso	Pittsburgh	KO	2	—	—
Oct 16		Chuck Woods	St. Louis	KO	6	—	—
Nov 9		Gaston LeCadre	Pittsburgh	W	10	—	—
Dec 2	⑩	Harry Dublinsky	Pittsburgh	KO	6	—	—
Dec 28		Billy Conn ★	Pittsburgh	L	10	—	—

1937

Feb 11		Johnny Jadick	Pittsburgh	KO	6	—	—
Mar 1		Bobby Pacho	Pittsburgh	W	10	—	—
Apr 6		Chuck Woods	Detroit	W	10	—	—
May 27		Tony Petroskey	Muskegon, MI	W	10	—	—
Oct 29		Frankie Portland	Clarksburg, WV	KO	2	—	—
Nov 18		Jimmy Reilly	McKeesport, PA	KO	1	—	—
Dec 25		Tommy Bland	Pittsburgh	L	10	—	—

1938

Jan 1		Harold Brown	Chicago	W	10	—	—
Feb 14		Frankie Blair	Pittsburgh	W	10	—	—
Mar 7		Tommy Bland	Pittsburgh	TKO	8	—	—
Mar 21	⑩	Charley Burley ★	Pittsburgh	W	10	—	—
Apr 12		Remo Fernandez	Detroit	W	10	—	—
May 29		Petey Mike	Brooklyn	KO	1	—	—
Jun 13	⑩	Charley Burley ★	Pittsburgh	L	10	—	—
Jun 20		Ercole Buratti	Pittsburgh	KO	4	—	—
Jul 9		Eddie Conley	Walnut Beach, PA	KO	6	—	—
Jul 12		Phil Furr	Pittsburgh	TKO	3	—	—
Aug 2		Joe Lemieux	Newark	TKO	4	—	—
Aug 12		Joe Pennino	Coney Island, NY	W	8	—	—
Aug 22		Steve Kahley	Newark	KO	3	—	—
Aug 26		Mickey Paul	Long Beach, NY	KO	3	—	—
Sep 13		Bobby Pacho	Newark	W	10	—	—
Oct 3		Paul Cortlyn	Newark	KO	4	—	—
Oct 10		Jay Macedon	Newark	TKO	5	—	—
Oct 27		Salvy Saban	Pittsburgh	W	10	—	—
Nov 15		Frankie Blair	Brooklyn	W	8	—	—
Nov 21		Al Hamilton	Columbus, OH	KO	5	—	—

Date		Opponent	Location	Result	Rounds	Title	Weight
Dec 7		Vincent Pimpinella	Pittsburgh	W	10	—	—
Dec 26		Howell King	Toledo, OH	ND-D	10	—	—
1939							
Jan 5		Al Costello	Columbus	KO	2	—	—
Jan 20		Jackie Burke	St. Louis	W	10	—	—
Feb 10		Eddie Booker	New York	W	8	—	—
Feb 15		Charlie Bell	Columbus	KO	3	—	—
Mar 20		Nick Pastore	Miami	KO	9	—	—
Mar 29		Bobby Britton	Miami	W	10	—	—
Apr 20		Tiger Kid Walker	St. Louis	KO	1	—	—
May 9		Kenny LaSalle	Houston	L	10	—	—
May 16		Al Traino	Rochester, NY	W	10	—	—
Jun 5		Kenny LaSalle	Pittsburgh	W	10	—	—
Jul 11		Jackie Burke	St. Louis	W	10	—	—
Jul 17	⑩	Charley Burley★	Pittsburgh	L	10	—	—
Sep 5		Pete DeRuzza	Pittsburgh	KO	6	—	—
Sep 12		Ralph Gizzy	Pittsburgh	KO	2	—	—
Oct 24		Kid Azteca	Houston	W	10	—	—
Oct 30		Milo Theodorescu	Pittsburgh	W	10	—	—
Nov 18		Billy Lancaster	Brooklyn	TKO	7	—	—
Dec 9		Wicky Harkins	Philadelphia	KO	9	—	—
Dec 27	⑩	Milt Aron	Chicago	KO'd	8	—	—
1940							
Jan 22	⑩	Mike Kaplan	Philadelphia	W	10	—	—
Mar 4		Saverio Turiello	Philadelphia	KO	1	—	—
Mar 7		Remo Fernandez	Cleveland	TKO	7	—	—
Mar 14		Johnny Barbara	Chicago	W	10	—	—
Apr 8		Johnny Barbara	Philadelphia	· L	10	—	—
May 3		Mansfield Driskell	Detroit	W	10	—	—
May 7		Johnny Barbara	Philadelphia	L	10	—	—
May 21		Ossie Harris	Pittsburgh	W	10	—	—
Jun 24		Johnny Rinaldi	Pittsburgh	KO	1	—	—
Jul 8		Ossie Harris	Pittsburgh	W	10	—	—
Jul 22		Leonard Bennett	Chicago	KO	4	—	—
Aug 5		Kenny LaSalle	Pittsburgh	W	10	—	—
Aug 28	⑩	Sammy Angott★	Pittsburgh	W	10	—	—
Oct 4	♛	Henry Armstrong★	New York	W	15	Won-World-W	145
Nov 15		Al Davis	New York	WD	2	—	—
Nov 26		Ronnie Beaudin	Buffalo	KO	2	—	—
Dec 20		Lew Jenkins★	New York	D	10	—	142
1941							
Jan 17	⑩	Henry Armstrong★	New York	TKO	12	Ret-World-W	145
Mar 17		Saverio Turiello	Pittsburgh	W	10	—	149
Mar 20		Felix Garcia	Baltimore	KO	2	—	—
Apr 4		Dick Demeray	Minneapolis	KO	4	—	150
Apr 18	⑩	Mike Kaplan	Boston	L	10	—	—
May 2	⑩	Tony Marteliano	New York	W	10	—	149
Jul 2		Al Davis	New York	TKO	10	—	—
Jul 14		Johnny Barbara	Philadelphia	W	12	—	—
Jul 29	⑩	Freddie ("Red") Cochrane	Newark	L	15	Lost-World-W	145
Sep 15		Milt Aron	Pittsburgh	KO	5	—	—
Oct 31	⑩	Sugar Ray Robinson★	New York	L	10	—	—
Nov 26		Phil Furr	Washington, DC	W	10	—	—
Dec 1		Harry Weekly	Cleveland	TKO	9	—	—
Dec 12		Young Kid McCoy	New York	D	10	—	—

1942

Date		Opponent	Location	Result	Rounds		
Jan 16	⑩	Sugar Ray Robinson★	New York	TKO'd	10	—	—
Feb 8		Raul Carrabantes	Pittsburgh	W	10	—	—
Feb 27	⑩	Tony Motisi	Chicago	L	10	—	—
Mar 9	⑩	Izzy Jannazzo	Pittsburgh	TKO	5	—	—
Mar 30		Bill McDowell	Newark	TKO	6	—	—
Apr 13		Maxie Berger	Pittsburgh	W	10	—	—
Apr 23		Reuben Shank	Minneapolis	L	10	—	—
May 25	⑩	Lew Jenkins★	Pittsburgh	TKO	10	—	—
Jun 4		Reuben Shank	Minneapolis	W	10	—	—
Jun 22		Bobby Britton	Wilkes-Barre, PA	TKO	4	—	—
Jun 29	⑩	Norman Rubio	Newark	L	10	—	—
Jul 27	⑩	Norman Rubio	Pittsburgh	TKO	9	—	—
Aug 13		Garvey Young	New York	TKO	6	—	—
Sep 10		Freddie ("Red") Cochrane	New York	W	10	—	—
Sep 21		Johnny Walker	Philadelphia	W	10	—	—
Oct 13		Tito Taylor	Milwaukee	W	10	—	—
Oct 26	⑩	Henry Armstrong★	San Francisco	L	10	—	—
Nov 16	⑩	Richard ("Sheik") Rangel	San Francisco	L	10	—	—
Dec 15		Carmen Notch	Pittsburgh	W	10	—	150

1943

Date		Opponent	Location	Result	Rounds		
Feb 5	♛	Beau Jack★	New York	L	10	—	145
Feb 16		Mayon Padlo	Pittsburgh	W	10	—	149
Mar 5	♛	Beau Jack★	New York	L	12	—	147
Apr 30		Johnny Roszina	Milwaukee	TKO	8	—	—
Jun 10	⑩	Jake LaMotta★	Pittsburgh	L	10	—	151
Jul 12	⑩	Jake LaMotta★	Pittsburgh	W	15	—	151
Aug 9		Young Kid McCoy	Pittsburgh	TKO	4	—	—
Aug 23	♛	Bob Montgomery★	Philadelphia	L	10	—	144
Sep 10		Vinnie Vines	New York	KO	1	—	—
Oct 15	⑩	Jose Basora	Detroit	L	10	—	—
Oct 29		Bobby Richardson	Chicago	W	10	—	149
Nov 12	⑩	Jake LaMotta★	New York	L	10	—	149
Dec 20	⑩	Ralph Zannelli	Boston	L	10	—	—

1944

Date		Opponent	Location	Result	Rounds		
Jan 3		Ossie Harris	Pittsburgh	KO	10	—	—
Jan 14	⑩	Jake LaMotta★	Detroit	L	10	—	—
Mar 27		Harry Teaney	Milwaukee	W	10	—	—
Mar 29	⑩	Freddie Archer	Elizabeth, NJ	L	10	—	—
Jun 26	⑩	Tommy Bell	Pittsburgh	L	10	—	—
Aug 1		Pete DeRuzza	Houston	TKO	8	—	—
Sep 12		Felix Morales	San Antonio, TX	KO	2	—	—
Sep 26		Artie Dorrell	Galveston, TX	KO	7	—	—
Oct 16		Tommy Roman	Shreveport, LA	L	10	—	150
Oct 18		Pat Saia	Dallas	TKO	8	—	—
Nov 14		Chick Hirst	Houston	KO	5	—	—
Nov 29		Manuel Villa	Dallas	KO	6	—	—
Dec 12		Kid Azteca	San Antonio	W	10	—	—

1945

Date		Opponent	Location	Result	Rounds		
Jan 5	⑩	Billy Arnold	New York	W	8	—	—
Feb 22		Kid Estrada	Camp Maxey, TX	KO	2	—	—
Mar 6		Bill McDowell	Galveston	W	10	—	—
Mar 22		Ben Evans	Galveston	KO	8	—	—
Apr 3		Manuel Villa	San Antonio	KO	8	—	—
May 7		Kid Azteca	San Antonio	W	10	—	—

Date		Opponent	Location	Result	Rounds		
May 8		Pat Saia	Beaumont, TX	W	10	—	—
Jun 12		Baby Zavala	San Antonio	KO	4	—	—
Jul 3		Reuben Shank	Pittsburgh	L	10	—	—
Jul 10		Ossie Harris	Pittsburgh	L	10	—	—
Jul 16		Bill McDowell	New Orleans	L	10	—	—
Sep 12		Paul Altman	Houston	L	10	—	—
Sep 18		Billy Deeg	Oklahoma City, OK	W	10	—	152
Oct 20		Joe Reddick	Brooklyn	L	10	—	152
Nov 2	⑩	Freddie Archer	New York	L	10	—	153
Nov 13		Joe Curcio	Elizabeth, NJ	L	10	—	—
Dec 10		Cecil Hudson	New York	L	10	—	150
1946							
Jan 15	⑩	Al ("Red") Priest	Boston	L	10	—	—
Feb 1		O'Neill Bell	Detroit	L	10	—	—
Feb 25		Aaron Perry	Washington, DC	L	10	—	150
Mar 19		Levi Southall	Kansas City	W	10	—	—
Mar 26		Tony Elizondo	San Antonio	L	10	—	—
Apr 5		Manuel Villa	El Paso, TX	D	10	—	—
Apr 12		Lincoln Stanley	Portland, OR	W	10	—	—
Apr 18		Don Lee	Hollywood	W	10	—	148
Apr 29		Howard Bleyhl	Omaha, NE	L	10	—	—
May 1		Joey Martinez	Wichita, KS	TKO	8	—	147
May 14	⑩	Jackie Wilson	Hollywood	L	10	—	147
May 27		Tommy Lemmon	Milwaukee	L	10	—	146
Oct 29		Russell Wilhite	Memphis, TN	TKO	5	—	146
Nov 12		Al Mobley	Trenton, NJ	L	8	—	—
Nov 18		Jimmy McGriff	Washington, DC	D	10	—	—
Dec 2		Ralph Zannelli	Providence, RI	L	10	—	—
Dec 6		Pete Mead	Grand Rapids, MI	L	10	—	—
Dec 10		Bobby Britton	Memphis	W	10	—	—
1947							
Jan 8		Clyde Gordon	Miami	L	10	—	—
Feb 15		Kid Azteca	Mexico City	KO'd	5	—	—
1948							
Oct 28		Eddie Steele	Macon, GA	D	10	—	—
1949							
Jan 12		Al Reid	Macon	W	10	—	—
Jan 17		Eddie Steele	Augusta, GA	W	10	—	—

to Burley. He beat tough Sammy Angott in 1940, which won him a shot at the welterweight championship held by Henry Armstrong. In a well-attended fight in Madison Square Garden, Zivic upset the heavily favored Armstrong. It was a close bout. Zivic withstood Armstrong's body blows and targeted his opponent's eyes, vulnerable from previous batterings, nearly closing them in the final rounds. In the last round, Zivic knocked down the exhausted Armstrong just before the ending bell.

Zivic won the rematch with Armstrong with a TKO in twelve but lost his title to Red Cochrane in 1941. Though he continued to fight for eight years, he never received another chance to fight for the title. Zivic's reputation for hitting low while hitting high to distract the referee, grinding his laces into cuts or just worrying ring wounds until they became serious seemed to enhance rather than diminish his appeal as a ring hero. He was well liked by the sporting world and later enjoyed a reputation as an entertaining after-dinner speaker.

BOXING AT THE
MOVIES

Since the beginning of motion pictures, the sport of boxing has been one of the cinema's favorite subjects. In 1894, when Thomas Edison set up a kinetograph in his West Orange, New Jersey laboratory, he filmed heavyweight champion James J. Corbett in an exhibition match. Since then, boxing has been featured in documentaries, dramas, and comedies, both full-length movies and shorts, and many real-life boxers have starred in films about non-boxing subjects.

In many ways, this marriage of pugilism and cinema is a match made in heaven. The inherent drama of flying fists in "mano a mano" combat coupled with the small and easy-to-film ring make boxing a natural for the big screen. Of course, boxing's often-sordid reputation is another draw for filmmakers, who have made many pictures about fixed fights and broken fighters. The colorful lives of many real-life boxers are readily transferable to film. John L. Sullivan, Jake LaMotta, Joe Louis, and Muhammad Ali all led fascinating lives, and possessed a ready-made fan base that would flock to movies about their heroes.

While most boxing movies are fictional, the earliest significant ring films were recordings of actual fights. Even though boxing was illegal in many jurisdictions, showing filmed matches, legally held elsewhere, was not. Thus, in the first decade of the 1900s boxing films took the place of live legal matches in some parts of the country. These screen displays of boxing helped maintain popular interest in the sport and provided a source of additional revenue for the boxing community. Before long, however, moralist opponents to boxing, and parties motivated by racism, formed a coalition—with groups such as the United Society of Christian Endeavor, the Anti-Saloon League of America, and the California Federation of Women's Clubs—to lobby state legislatures to ban movie house showings of the 1910 Jack Johnson-James Jeffries fight. Among their objections was the belief that blacks would riot against whites if they witnessed Johnson's victory.

Soon, at least fifteen states and the District of Columbia passed laws prohibiting the showing of all films of prize fights. In 1912, Congress passed a law banning the transportation of fight films in interstate commerce for the purpose of public exhibition. The next ten years saw many violations of the new law, and enforcement was spotty at best. In 1927, a federal judge instructed a jury that transportation of the film was different from screening of the film, which was not illegal. Finally, in 1940, Congress repealed its earlier law.

It is, however, the fictionalized biographies of boxers, rather than films of actual fights, that have etched the deepest mark in cinematic history. One of the most successful boxing biographies was *Gentleman Jim*, a 1942 movie about James J. Corbett, starring Errol Flynn in the title role. Unlike some sports movies, Warner Brothers released *Gentleman Jim* as a major feature film. Great pains were taken to film realistic fight scenes, with Hall of Famer Freddie Steele doubling for Flynn. Wrestling great Strangler Lewis was also a double.

Three years later, Sullivan himself was the focus of *The Great John L.*, which starred Greg McClure and featured Rory Calhoun as Corbett. Another accomplished boxing film, was the now-seldom-seen *Joe Louis Story* (1953), which starred Coley Wallace. A movie with an almost all-black

Wallace Beery and Jackie Cooper in "The Champ" (1931).

cast, it avoided the patronizing depiction of African Americans typical of that era. Footage of some of Louis's actual fights was interwoven with staged segments. Hall of Famer Barney Ross's life was dramatized in the 1957 film *Monkey on My Back*. The movie covered his boxing career, WWII heroics, and battle against drug addiction.

Hall of Famer Rocky Graziano's autobiography of his rise from the New York slums to the world middleweight championship was captured on film in *Somebody Up There Likes Me* (1956). James Dean was originally slated to play the part of Graziano, but the role went to Paul Newman instead, who gave a fine performance in an early starring role. Sal Mineo and Steve McQueen also appeared in the film.

Perhaps the greatest boxing movie of all time and one of the all-time best sports films is *Raging Bull* (1980), directed by Martin Scorsese. Based on Hall of Famer Jake LaMotta's autobiography, the graphically violent film led to Robert DeNiro's best actor Academy Award for his portrayal of LaMotta.

More recently, Denzel Washington starred as boxer Rubin ("Hurricane") Carter in *The Hurricane* (1999), the middleweight who spent years in prison for a crime he did not commit. In 2001, the movie *Ali* was released to favorable reviews and garnered an Oscar nomination for Will Smith's portrayal of Muhammad Ali and for Jon Voight's supporting role as Howard Cosell. (Voight also starred in two earlier boxing films, *The All American Boy* in 1973 and the 1979 version of *The Champ*.) Other fine boxing movies include *Body and Soul, The Harder They Fall, The Set-Up, Fat City,* the original *Kid Galahad* and *The Milky Way*.

Though few of them emerged as great actors, actual boxers have appeared in many movies throughout the years. Muhammad Ali starred as himself in the often-fanciful story of his life up until 1977, *The Greatest,* and appeared in the 1981 version of *Body and Soul*. He also had a brief role in *Requiem for a Heavyweight* (1962) an excellent film starring Anthony Quinn as the over-the-hill boxer Mountain Rivera. After he fails to lose a fight to a boxer played by Ali, Rivera is forced to humiliate himself to save the life of his manager, played by Jackie Gleason. Mickey Rooney turned in a fine performance as Rivera's trainer, while Jack Dempsey, Barney Ross, and Willie Pep all appeared in the movie as well.

Hall of Famer Max Baer had a successful acting career that included a starring role in *The Prizefighter and the Lady* (1933) with Myrna Loy. In the film's climactic scene, Baer rose from the canvas to fight a draw with Primo Carnera, who was playing himself. Carnera refused to be defeated on film, though in real life Baer knocked him out in their 1934 championship fight. Dempsey, James Jeffries, and former heavyweight champion Jess Willard all played themselves in the movie.

Billy Conn, Joe Louis, Maxie Rosenbloom, Tony Zale, Archie Moore, Joe Frazier, Jersey Joe Walcott, Jose Torres, and Sugar Ray Robinson are among the numerous fighters who dabbled in film at some point in their careers.

Like Paul Newman in *Somebody Up There Likes Me*, actors' careers have been jumpstarted by roles in boxing movies. In *Golden Boy* (1939), based on a play by Clifford Odets, William Holden had his first major role as an excellent but impoverished violinist who enters the ring to make some money. (Holden beat out John Garfield, Robert Taylor, Robert Cummings, Tyrone Powers, and Henry Fonda for the role.) A talented boxer, Holden's character worries about injuring his hands and ending the violin career his father always wanted for him. The 1949 film *Champion* launched Kirk Douglas. Douglas earned an Academy Award nomination for his portrayal of a boxer who ruthlessly climbs to the top of the middleweight ranks only to become a tool of a crime syndicate.

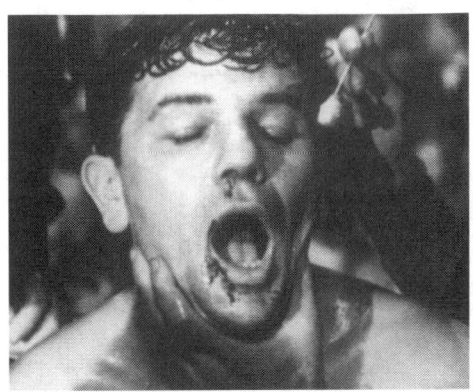

John Garfield in "Body and Soul" (1947).

Any list of career-making boxing movies would be incomplete without *Rocky*, the story of a Philadelphia club fighter who gets a shot at the world championship held by Apollo Creed (Carl Weathers). *Rocky* won Oscars for best picture, best director, and best editing, spawned four sequels, and made its leading actor and screenwriter, Sylvester Stallone, into a world-famous superstar.

Other famous names that starred in boxing movies include some of Hollywood's best and brightest stars, like John Garfield, James Cagney, Robert Taylor, Tony Curtis, James Earl Jones, Humphrey Bogart, Danny Kaye, Elvis Presley, Douglas Fairbanks Jr., Barbra Streisand, and Robert Ryan.

Rocky and *Raging Bull* were not the only boxing films to capture Academy Awards. In 1996, *When We Were Kings* won best documentary feature for its account of the famous "Rumble in the Jungle" in 1974, the fight where Ali reclaimed his heavyweight championship by knocking out George Foreman. *Here Comes Mr. Jordan*, a 1941 flight of fancy about a boxer who dies before his time and is temporarily returned to earth to win the heavyweight championship, won for best original story and best screenplay. An earlier movie, *The Champ* (1932), won for best original story as well, and garnered its star, Wallace Beery, a statue for best actor, despite its sometimes overly sentimental plot.

From the early raw footage of real bouts to the masterful Academy Award winning boxing dramas, no other sport has been so regularly, faithfully, and powerfully depicted in American cinema.

THE
NON-COMBATANTS
Boxing's Supporting Cast

THE ATTENTION OF MOST boxing fans is, of course, focussed on the combatants in the ring, but the sport could never have achieved its success and visibility without a host of behind-the-scenes personalities. The International Boxing Hall of Fame honors the contributions of such individuals in a section titled "Non-Participants." These inductees include promoters, matchmakers, managers, trainers, patrons, referees, writers, and broadcasters. In contrast to the Hall's other inductees, non-combatant members do not have to be retired before they are honored.

The stories of these important figures in boxing, some of whom started their careers as fighters, are integral to the rich history of the sport.

THOMAS S. ANDREWS
Writer and Publisher

A successful boxing promoter in Milwaukee, Thomas S. Andrews made his greatest contributions to the sport through his writing and publishing efforts. Andrews's books were invaluable resources for boxing devotees and participants in the early decades of the twentieth century. He edited and published *T.S. Andrews' World Sporting Annual* from 1903 through 1938. This publication, which covered all sports but featured boxing, included complete lists of champions, cumulative records, and other boxing information. Andrews also wrote a record book of boxing from its earliest beginnings. Titled *Ring Battles of the Centuries,* it was first published in 1914. Hall of Fame Induction: 1992.

RAY ARCEL
Trainer

One of the most respected men in the history of boxing, Ray Arcel trained a record twenty world champions. Born in Terre Haute, Indiana in 1899, Arcel grew up in a tough New York City neighborhood.

He learned his trade from Frank ("Doc") Bagley, who once managed Gene Tunney and Dai Dolling, who handled Harry Wills, Jack Britton, and Johnny Dundee. In 1923, Arcel developed his first champion, flyweight Frankie Genaro. In 1925, he helped bantamweight Charley Phil Rosenberg lose 37 pounds in three months in preparation for a winning title fight. From 1925 to 1934, Arcel worked in partnership with trainer Whitey Bimstein. Among the champions Arcel and Bimstein handled were Jackie ("Kid") Berg, Lou Brouillard, and Sixto Escobar. Arcel also worked with Barney Ross, and managed and trained his early idol, Benny Leonard, in a comeback try.

Arcel first handled a heavyweight champion when he trained James J. Braddock for his bout with Joe Louis, which Braddock lost. Over the next several years, Arcel trained fourteen Louis opponents before producing one who could beat the Brown Bomber. In 1950, Arcel and Ezzard Charles—who won a decision over Louis—ended the parade which had come to be called "The Meat Wagon." During this period Arcel also guided many fighters in lower weight classes to championships. The list includes Tony Marino, Ceferino Garcia, Billy Soose, and Tony Zale.

In the early fifties, Arcel apparently ran afoul of organized crime after arranging fights for the ABC television network. The matches competed with other network television fights run by the International Boxing Club (IBC), reputed to have underworld ties. In September 1953, in front of a Boston hotel, Arcel was struck on the head with a lead pipe. Many believed that the assault was related to his work in television. Arcel recovered but dropped out of boxing soon after the incident.

Not until the early seventies did Arcel return. He trained Peppermint Frazier for a title bid, then began an eight-year association with Roberto Duran, seeing Duran to a win in his first meeting with Sugar Ray Leonard. Arcel broke with Duran following the second match with Leonard in 1980, when Duran uttered his famous "no mas" and quit the fight.

Arcel capped his career with three years of work with Larry Holmes, training him for his title defense versus Gerry Cooney in 1982. For that fight, Arcel teamed with Eddie Futch. He then retired but continued to follow boxing and to comment on the sport until his death on March 6, 1994. Arcel trained over two thousand boxers and won the admiration and respect of his fighters, his peers, and the media. Hall of Fame Induction: 1991.

BOB ARUM
Promoter

There was nothing in the first 35 years of Bob Arum's life that hinted at his future as one of boxing's greatest promoters and a Hall of Fame inductee. Born in Brooklyn on December 8, 1931, Arum was the son of orthodox Jewish parents. He graduated from New York University in 1953, and then studied law at Harvard, where he graduated cum laude in 1956. Arum served in the tax division of the United States Department of Justice under Attorney Generals Robert F. Kennedy and Robert Morgenthau from 1961 to 1965. In 1962, he was assigned to investigate allegations that part of the proceeds of the Sonny Liston–Floyd Patterson fight in Chicago were sneaked out of the country to avoid taxes. Thus, through a criminal investigation, Arum first became acquainted with many of boxing's leading figures.

Arum's next brush with the boxing world came when he recommended to a client that he hire a black commentator to support flagging ticket sales for the Ernie Terrell–George Chuvalo heavyweight bout. The client hired football great Jim Brown, and it was Brown who introduced Arum to Muhammad Ali. This additional contact with boxing inspired Arum to found a fight promotion company, Main Bouts, Inc. Surprisingly, he had never even seen a boxing match until he promoted Ali–Chuvalo in March 1966. He promoted many more Ali fights, including bouts against Henry Cooper, Brian London, Karl Mildenberger, Cleveland Williams, and Terrell. When Ali lost his boxing license for refusing to enter the army, Arum assisted with his legal defense.

In 1970, Arum formed Top Rank, Inc, and to this day he continues to promote under the Top Rank banner. Though initially known for his association with Ali, he branched out to promote many other contests in all weight classes. Arum has promoted over one thousand cards, including 27 fights featuring Ali, twenty with Marvelous Marvin Hagler, and fourteen with George Foreman. Indeed, some of the best-known and highest-grossing fights of the last 35 years have been promoted by Arum, including Hagler–Sugar Ray Leonard, Hagler–Thomas Hearns, Leonard–Roberto Duran I, Foreman–Evander Holyfield, Foreman–Moorer, Ali–Joe Frazier II, and both Ali–Leon Spinks bouts. Arum promotes fan favorite and multiple-title-holder Oscar De La Hoya.

Arum has long appreciated the role of pay-per-view, closed circuit, and cable television in the sport and is savvy at using these media to his advantage. In 1980, he initiated a long-running and profitable association between ESPN and Top Rank.

"My essential strength as a promoter," Arum told *KO Magazine*, "is that I'm a good administrator. I'm also able to run a promotion in a dispassionate manner. And there's no great trick in selling a fight to a network or cable system. What really calls on one's ability is the big closed-circuit and pay-per-view fights. That's what I specialize in."

In recent years, Arum has taken a stance in favor of open scoring. Although some boxing enthusiasts like the suspense inherent in the present system, he believes that fairer scoring will be achieved if judges' cards were displayed as a bout progressed.

In his long career, Arum has had his share of legal battles, many of them with his rival Don King. At the racketeering trial of former International Boxing Federation president Bob Lee, Arum admitted that he made improper payments to encourage the IBF to sanction one of his fights.

Still one of the top promoters, he currently promotes Floyd Mayweather, Jr., Paulie Ayala, and Oscar de la Hoya. Hall of Fame Induction: 1999.

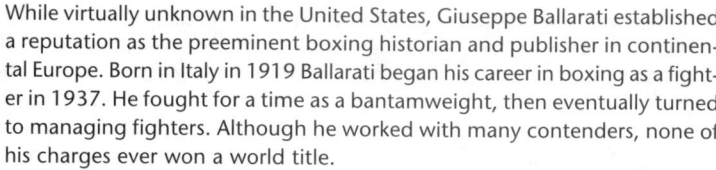

GIUSEPPE BALLARATI
Publisher and Historian

While virtually unknown in the United States, Giuseppe Ballarati established a reputation as the preeminent boxing historian and publisher in continental Europe. Born in Italy in 1919 Ballarati began his career in boxing as a fighter in 1937. He fought for a time as a bantamweight, then eventually turned to managing fighters. Although he worked with many contenders, none of his charges ever won a world title.

However, it is not for fighting or managing that Ballarati is a Hall of Famer. First published in 1962 and subsequently published annually for the next three decades, Ballarati compiled *La Bibbia del Pugilato*, a compendium of boxing records and statistics akin to *The Ring Record Book*. He also published a series of books about the sport's all-time greats, which translates to Champions of the Past.

A boxing purist, Ballarati was extremely concerned about the proliferation of sanctioning bodies. Hall of Fame Induction: 1999.

GEORGE BENTON
Trainer

Using the knowledge he gained during his twenty years as a professional boxer, George Benton became one of the sport's top trainers. Born on May 15, 1933, in Philadelphia, Benton became interested in boxing at an early age. He frequented a gym run by Joe Rose, and at the age of twelve or thirteen was left in charge of the gym when Rose was away. He was an active amateur boxer at age fourteen and turned professional at sixteen, establishing a record of 30-2-1 before joining the army at 23. The highlight of Benton's early career was a victory over future middleweight contender Holly Mims in 1952. He resumed his career after leaving the army and in 1962 was rated by *The Ring* as the third-best contender for the middleweight title. That year he decisioned Hall of Famer Joey Giardello.

Known as a stylish, clever boxer with a strong punch, Benton never fought for a middleweight title. In part, this was because the champions avoided him, but he also lost key fights to Willie Dockery in 1958 and to Rubin ("Hurricane") Carter in 1963—bouts which could have been a springboard to capturing the title. Benton continued fighting until 1970. In addition to his victory over Giardello, he defeated Freddie Little and Jimmy Ellis, who both held world titles at one time, and compiled a record of 61-13-1, with 36 knockouts. Benton was still an active fighter when he was shot on a Philadelphia street by a man who had a beef with one of Benton's brothers.

Unable to fight again, Benton spent a short time as a numbers writer. He then worked with a few fighters before being hired by Joe Frazier to train fighters in his gym when Eddie Futch was unavailable. Benton added to his ring knowledge—especially the psychological aspects of training—by working with Futch.

Benton came to prominence as a trainer when his fighter, Leon Spinks, upset Muhammad Ali to win the heavyweight title. Benton counseled Spinks to stay on top of Ali and jab at his left shoulder to prevent Ali from throwing his own jab in the later rounds. However, after Spinks won the championship, his camp froze Benton out until shortly before the Spinks–Ali rematch. Because he wasn't permitted to speak with Spinks after each round,

Benton left the arena in disgust before the end of the fight in which Ali was victorious.

In the 80s, Benton began working for managers Shelly Finkel and Lou Duva. After the 1984 Olympics, he and Duva took control of the professional careers of U.S. Olympic team members Evander Holyfield, Meldrick Taylor, and Pernell ("Sweetpea") Whitaker. The three went on to become champions and household names in boxing. When Holyfield took the heavyweight title from Buster Douglas, Benton was working the corner.

Hall of Famer Duva and Benton managed and trained seventeen champions before Benton, dubbed "The Professor" for his knowledge and teaching ability, broke with the Duva family Main Events, Inc. enterprise. After his departure from Main Events, Benton worked with fighters including: Mike McCallum, Rocky Lockridge, and Michael Moorer.

Though they may have parted on a sour note, Benton graciously acknowledged Lou Duva's role in his success in his Hall of Fame induction speech. A two-time recipient of the Boxing Writers Association of America's John F.X. Condon Award for the Trainer of the Year, Benton is now in semiretirement. Hall of Fame Induction: 2001.

JACK BLACKBURN
Trainer

Jack Blackburn had a fine career as a fighter but is honored in the Hall of Fame for his even greater achievement as the trainer of Joe Louis. Born in Versailles, Kentucky in 1883, Blackburn was the son of a minister. He moved with his family to Terre Haute, Indiana, where he first began boxing, then headed to Pittsburgh and Philadelphia to continue his ring career. He was quick, had a fine jab, and a powerful left hook, and though he weighed only 135 pounds, often fought much larger men. He made good showings against such greats as Joe Gans and Sam Langford (who outweighed him by 45 pounds), and he gave Philadelphia Jack O'Brien all he could handle in a no-decision bout in 1908.

In January 1909, Blackburn's career was derailed when he went on a shooting spree in Philadelphia. In the midst of an argument, he killed three people, including his wife. He was convicted of manslaughter and sentenced to ten to fifteen years in prison. Blackburn, who gave boxing lessons to the warden and his children, was released on good behavior after four years and eight months.

Blackburn returned to professional boxing, taking on opponents such as Ed ("Gunboat") Smith and Harry Greb. He retired from fighting in 1923 after losing by knockout to Panama Joe Gans and Ray Pelkey. Blackburn posted an official career record of 38-3-12 with 50 no-decisions. He claimed to have fought 385 times.

Blackburn then became a trainer and guided weak puncher Sammy Mandell to the lightweight title in 1926. Blackburn also trained Bud Taylor, who won the bantamweight title in 1927. Blackburn also worked briefly with Jersey Joe Walcott in Philadelphia.

Blackburn at first expressed skepticism about Louis, predicting that a black heavyweight would not have many opportunities. Nevertheless, Blackburn worked tirelessly with Louis, schooling him on every aspect of fighting, such as balance, stepping forward when throwing a punch, and hitting with accuracy. According to Hall of Fame trainer Eddie Futch, Blackburn changed Louis from a "box and move" type to a more aggressive fighter. Though Blackburn was tough on Louis, the two grew close and called each other "Chappie." Louis later said, "Chappie made a fighter out of me. He was my closest friend."

Blackburn had problems with drinking and with arthritis during the time he trained Louis. Blackburn's health deteriorated and, in 1942, he died of a heart attack. Hall of Fame Induction: 1992.

WILLIAM A. BRADY
Manager and Promoter

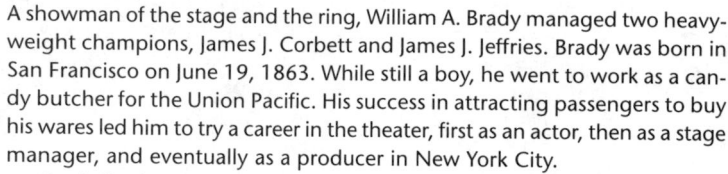

A showman of the stage and the ring, William A. Brady managed two heavy-weight champions, James J. Corbett and James J. Jeffries. Brady was born in San Francisco on June 19, 1863. While still a boy, he went to work as a can-dy butcher for the Union Pacific. His success in attracting passengers to buy his wares led him to try a career in the theater, first as an actor, then as a stage manager, and eventually as a producer in New York City.

Brady first hired up-and-coming heavyweight James J. Corbett as an actor, but quickly took on the job of managing Corbett's fighting career. After seeing him box an exhibition with John L. Sullivan, Brady was convinced that his charge had a very promising future. He commissioned Charles T. Vincent to write a play about a genteel prizefighter called "Gentleman Jack," in which Corbett was to have the starring role. To generate more publicity for Corbett, Brady pitted him against three opponents on the same night. Corbett knocked out the first two and outboxed the third.

Brady arranged a Corbett-Sullivan bout, littering New York with posters that heralded the appearance of the "new champion Corbett" at the New York Garden the week after the fight. Corbett did in fact defeat Sullivan, and "Gentleman Jack" was a big hit at the box office. After Bob Fitzsimmons defeated Corbett, Brady amicably ended his association with the deposed champion.

Two years later Brady returned to boxing as the manager of Corbett's former sparring partner, James J. Jeffries. Brady leased the Bauer Pavilion at Coney Island to stage a cham-pionship bout between Jeffries and Fitzsimmons. Jeffries won, and Brady had his second world champion. But Brady's efforts to parlay Jeffries' victory into a theatrical tour did not prove as successful as his earlier venture with Corbett.

Brady was very successful in the theater, producing more than 260 plays. He also participated in the nascent motion picture industry and, with Thomas Edison, staged an 1884 Corbett-Peter Cortney bout that was filmed for the Kineograph Company and widely distributed. From 1915 to 1922, Brady was head of the National Association of the Mo-tion Picture Industry. In 1937 his daughter, Alice Brady, won an Academy Award for best supporting actress for her role in "Old Chicago."

Brady died of heart failure on January 6, 1950. Hall of Fame Induction: 1998.

TEDDY BRENNER
Matchmaker

Teddy Brenner made matches based on two guidelines: Would he buy a tick-et, and was the public interested? This standard did not always endear him to managers who wanted their fighters to go up against easy competition, but it made for hundreds of exciting fights that fans willingly paid to see. Surviving boxing's power struggles and unsavory influences, Brenner ar-ranged matches not only for greats such as Muhammad Ali and Sugar Ray Robinson, but also for tyros in whom he saw championship potential.

Born in New York, Brenner got his start in boxing after World War II, arranging fights in New Brunswick, New Jersey for his close friend Irving Cohen. In 1947, Brenner began his off-and-on association with Madison Square Garden, working as an assistant matchmaker. When the Garden lost its booking rights in a dispute with the Boxing Managers' Guild, Brenner moved to Laurel Gardens in Newark, New Jersey as a promoter. When the International Boxing Club (IBC) took over promotion at Madison Square Garden, Brenner returned there to work as assistant matchmaker to Al Weill. Brenner booked preliminary matches at the Garden and cards at St. Nicholas Arena, also in New York. In 1950, Brenner left the IBC, alleging Weill had ordered him to make a match for a fixed fight.

Brenner ran operations at the Coney Island Velodrome and also worked for the Long Beach Stadium in New York. In 1952, Brenner became the matchmaker for the Eastern Parkway Arena in Brooklyn, site of the Dumont television network's broadcasts of Monday night fights. This arena became famous as the "House of Upsets" because of Brenner's good, even matches. It was here that Brenner gave Floyd Patterson and Gene Fullmer their first national exposure. Fifty-seven of the 156 television bouts made by Brenner at Eastern Parkway were later booked by the IBC as return matches in Madison Square Garden.

By 1955, Eastern Parkway was struggling with declining television ratings, and Brenner moved to St. Nicholas Arena for four years. In 1959, with the breakup of the IBC, Brenner moved back to Madison Square Garden, where he stayed as matchmaker for fourteen years. His bookings included Muhammad Ali's first fights in New York, the first fights in the new Madison Square Garden, the first Ali–Frazier meeting, Roberto Duran's first bout in the United States, and George Foreman's first fights.

In 1973, when Harry Markson retired, Brenner assumed the presidency of Madison Square Garden Boxing, Inc. His boss, Sonny Werblin, fired him in 1978 because Werblin wanted to do business with Don King. In 1980, Brenner joined Bob Arum's Top Rank, Inc., where he stayed as an advisor after retiring from full-time matchmaking. He died January 7, 2000. Hall of Fame Induction: 1993.

LESTER BROMBERG
Writer

Lester Bromberg was one of the nation's finest boxing writers, but boxing played only a part in his long and successful career in journalism. Born in Brooklyn on March 12, 1909, Bromberg reported for the *Brooklyn Eagle* after graduating from high school, assigned to the city news beat. He next joined the *New York Post*, where he was scholastic sports editor for three years before moving to the *New York World Telegram*. There, he covered high school athletics for another seven years before he became the paper's boxing writer. By the early 1950s, Bromberg was one of only three full-time boxing writers in New York, and his lengthy career spanned countless world title bouts, beginning with the second Louis–Schmeling fight in 1938. After 35 years at the *World Telegram*, he moved his colums to the *New York Post*.

In addition to writing his regular columns, Bromberg wrote two books on boxing, *World's Champs* in 1958 and *Boxing's Unforgettable Fights* in 1962. He also wrote articles on the sport for numerous publications like *Sport* and *The Saturday Evening Post*. Boxing historian Herbert G. Goldman said, "The late Mr. Bromberg who covered the fight game extensively for many, many years, was so knee-deep in the business and happenings of boxing that he was probably one of the last of the real day-to-day information diggers among the boxing journalists." Well regarded in the fighting world, Bromberg also achieved legendary status as a gourmand, once consuming a 113-ounce steak in a single sitting! In retirement, Bromberg continued to write freelance articles on boxing. He died February 21, 1989. Hall of Fame Induction: 2001.

JIMMY CANNON
Journalist

Jimmy Cannon was one of the most respected sports columnists in the United States in the post-World War II period, writing with a distinctive flair and an abiding respect for the athletes he covered.

Cannon was born in 1910 in Greenwich Village. He left school in ninth grade for a job as a copy boy with the *New York Daily News*, and he remained a newspaperman for the rest of his life. Writing dispatches on the Lindbergh kidnapping trial, Cannon attracted the attention of Damon Runyon, who advised him to write sports and helped him get a job with a Hearst newspaper. Like Runyon, Cannon was attracted to the bookies, gamblers, and talent agents who frequented New York's nightspots. In his reports from the front as a correspondent for *Stars and Stripes* during the war, Cannon developed his signature style—what David Remnick described in *King of the World* as "florid, sentimental prose with an underpinning of hard-bitten wisdom, and urban style that he had picked up in candy stores and nightclubs and from Runyon, Ben Hecht, and Westbrook Pegler."

After the war, Cannon became a sports columnist for the *New York Post*, under the title "Jimmy Cannon Says." He frequently wrote about boxing, and penned the memorable line that Joe Louis was "a credit to his race: the human race." He often wrote columns entitled "Nobody Asked Me, But..." in which he would string together a series of seemingly random observations, a style of writing still popular among news columnists today.

In 1959, Cannon moved to the New York *Journal American*, but he also wrote for *PM* and his column was syndicated by King Features and Hearst—the first $1,000-a-week columnist. Cannon wrote often about corruption in the boxing world, though he treated the individual athletes with great regard. He did not appreciate the new type of sportswriter who emerged in the 50s and 60s, an irreverent breed who looked at stories beyond the game, dubbing them "chipmunks," because they were always chattering away in the press box.

Cannon was a distinctive presence wherever he went, his bushy black eyebrows, thick-rimmed glasses, wide-brimmed hats, plaid jackets, and striped ties marking him out in a crowd. He was extremely dedicated to his column, and though he suffered a stroke in 1971, he continued to write until his death in 1973. In addition to the International Boxing Hall of Fame, Cannon is a member of the National Sportscasters and Sportswriters Association Hall of Fame. Hall of Fame Induction: 2002.

JOHN GRAHAM CHAMBERS
Author of Queensberry Rules

Although not often heralded, John Graham Chambers made an important contribution to the development of boxing when he devised the Marquess of Queensberry Rules on which the modern sport is based. Born in Carmarthenshire, Wales in 1843, Chambers attended Magdalene College at Cambridge where he met John Sholto Douglas, the eighth Marquess of Queensberry. The two shared an interest in boxing. An accomplished oarsman, Chambers rowed for Cambridge and went on to coach the Cambridge crew. In 1866, he founded the Amateur Athletic Club and later played a key role in organizing Britain's Amateur Athletic Association. In 1867, Chambers created a set of twelve rules to govern boxing, which established the mandatory use of gloves, the ten-count for a knockout, and three-minute rounds. Douglas agreed to sponsor the regulations which led to them being known as the Queensberry Rules. Hall of Fame Induction: 1990.

DON CHARGIN
Promoter

From "Wonder Boy" to elder statesman, Don Chargin's long boxing career has covered every aspect of the sport. He first became interested in boxing when his father took him to a Manuel Ortiz fight in 1940. In high school, Chargin became captain of the boxing team before an injury forced him from the squad his senior year. His coach kept him involved in boxing as an unofficial assistant. After graduation, Chargin worked at a variety of odd jobs and spent his free time at gyms, working as a second, trainer, or in whatever role was available.

On Labor Day, 1950, the 21-year-old Chargin—who had been turned down repeatedly for a promoter's license because of his age—staged his first boxing promotion at the Washington Baseball Park in Santa Clara. A good crowd turned out for the event, a match between local attraction Eddie Chavez and Hall of Famer Manuel Ortiz, which ended in a ten-round victory for Chavez. Chargin was inspired by the $16,000 he netted for the card and went on to promote fights in Oakland, Stockton, Fresno, Richmond, Merced, and San Jose. Scant financial success in these ventures led him to briefly abandon promoting and turn to managing. He directed the ring career of flyweight contender Keeny Teran, who lost a shot at Flash Elorde's title when he was arrested on a narcotics charge.

With his father's encouragement, Chargin returned to promoting in the late fifties, primarily in Oakland and at his Bonanza Club in Sacramento. His promotions in Oakland's Auditorium included bouts between Bobo Olson and Don Grant, Olson and Paddy Young, and Joey Gambia and Chico Vejar.

When the Coliseum Arena opened next to the Oakland-Alameda County Coliseum, Chargin staged the first pro-boxing event there. The main event was a Andy Heilman–Jimmy Lester middleweight bout. At different stages of Chargin's long career, he promoted bouts featuring all three generations of the fighting Lester family, including his father, Top Row Allen, and Lester's son, Jimmy Lester Jr. The late 60s saw Chargin host two WBA heavyweight title elimination fights at the Coliseum Arena: Thad Spencer vs. Jerry Quarry and Quarry vs. Jimmy Ellis.

Though his promotional base was in northern California, Chargin was a long-time matchmaker for Hall of Famer Aileen Eaton at the Olympic Auditorium in Los Angeles. In 1970, Chargin pitted Hall of Famer Ismael Laguna against Mando Ramos for the latter's lightweight title. He also staged Sugar Ramos against Mando Ramos on August 7, 1970, at the Olympic, the toughest fight Chargin ever witnessed. During the 70s, he booked bouts at the LA Sports Arena, including Danny ("Little Red") Lopez–Bobby Chacon.

Chargin remained active in boxing, promoting in Northern California with such notables as Tony Lopez and Loreto Garza, and staging a 1995 bout at the ARCO Arena between heavyweight great Lennox Lewis and Lionel Butler. In 2001, Chargin promoted the Willie Jorrin and Oscar Larrios match for the WBC super bantamweight championship in Sacramento. Don Chargin Productions is a joint effort of Don and his wife Lorraine. Together they won the 2001 James J. Walker Award for Long and Meritorious service to Boxing. A promoter for more than half a century, Chargin shows no signs of slowing down. Hall of Fame Induction: 2001.

RALPH CITRO
Statistician and Cutman

Since the day in 1938 when he first walked into a YMCA gym in Youngstown, Ohio, Ralph Citro has been an amateur fighter, trainer, gym owner, manager, matchmaker, cutman, statistician, and record keeper.

Boxing as an amateur after a WWII stint in the marines, Citro compiled an 18-3 record before he hung up his gloves, explaining, "If I can't beat Willie Pep and Sandy Saddler, I might as well give it up." Citro stayed involved in boxing as a trainer in a Camden, New Jersey, gym while he worked for the Post Office in Blackwood. In 1958, he opened Blackwood Gym, where he trained and managed fighters while also selling insurance. Around this time, Hall of Famer Jersey Joe Walcott—then fight promoter at the Camden Convention Hall—asked for Citro's help as a trainer. Though Citro trained several fighters, including Walcott's son, and worked for a while as a matchmaker, his venture with Walcott proved unsuccessful.

Citro began work as a cutman, so impressing boxer Gaten Hart with his corner work at a bout in Canada that he was hired by the fighter. According to Citro, Hart averaged 43 stitches per fight, so a cutman was extremely important. When Hart defeated contender Ralph Racine, keeping him from a title shot against Hilmer Kenty, Citro kept Hart in the fight despite two bleeding eyes and a bloody nose. Emanuel Steward, who handled Kenty for the Kronk stable in Detroit, was so impressed with Citro's work that he hired him to work as cutman with fighters like Kenty and Thomas Hearns. By his own estimate, Citro has worked 125 title bouts; he was in the corner for both of Hearns's bouts with Sugar Ray Leonard and worked for sixteen of Riddick Bowe's fights, including his heavyweight championship triumph over Evander Holyfield.

In 1981, Citro began Computer Boxing Update, a database of boxing records for use by commissions, matchmakers, promoters, managers, and the media. He maintained the Update for thirteen years, publishing ten annual volumes before his retirement in 1993. Computer Boxing Update continues today as *The Boxing Record Book* by Fight Fax, Inc.

Citro, however, did not retire from the field of boxing. From 1993 to 2000 he served as director of the International Boxing Research Organization, a group devoted to maintaining the accuracy of historical boxing records. He also wrote a book, *So You Want to be a Cornerman*, as a guide for aspiring seconds. In recognition of his varied contributions to the sport, the Boxing Writers Association of America named Citro as the 1992 recipient of the James J. Walker Award for Long and Meritorious Service to Boxing. Hall of Fame Induction: 2001.

GIL CLANCY
Trainer and Manager

Gil Clancy, although well-known in the 1980s and '90s as a boxing announcer, earned his place in the Hall of Fame for his work managing and training fighters. Born in 1922, Clancy was a schoolteacher who first began to work with young boxers at a Police Athletic League (PAL) gym in Queens. He then moved to another PAL facility in the Bronx, where he worked as a trainer until eleven o'clock every night, after putting in a full day teaching school.

Clancy's first protege to make it as a professional was Ralph ("Tiger") Jones, who although he never became a champion, won over 50 fights in a twelve-year career and defeated Hall of Famers Sugar Ray Robinson, Kid Gavilan, and Joey Giardello. Clancy also trained and managed Emile Griffith, the great welter- and middle-weight, for his whole career. Middleweight champion Rodrigo Valdez and heavyweight contender Jerry Quarry thrived under Clancy's guidance. He also trained George Foreman.

In 1978, Clancy worked for three years as the matchmaker for Madison Square Garden. He then turned his attention to announcing and became highly successful as a boxing analyst for CBS and other networks, including HBO. In the 1990s, Clancy came out of retirement to work with Oscar de la Hoya. The Boxing Writers Association honored Clancy in 1967 and again in 1973 with the Al Buck Memorial Award given to the manager of the year. Hall of Fame Induction: 1993.

JAMES W. COFFROTH
Promoter

James W. Coffroth was the first large-scale boxing promoter. Born in California in 1872, Coffroth worked as a clerk in the Surrogate Court in San Francisco, but he had a great interest in boxing and would often travel east to see important matches. He became friendly with New York promoter Jim Kennedy, and the two began to promote fights on the West Coast. Coffroth was able to secure a permit to stage boxing events in San Francisco from Abe Ruef, the local political power broker.

Their first fight of national interest was a heavyweight championship match between James Jeffries and Gus Ruhlin in 1901. The bout ended when Ruhlin's manager threw in the sponge between the fifth and sixth rounds, the first time in American boxing history a fight had ended that way. It went into the books as a fifth-round knockout and established a precedent for scoring rules. When Kennedy died in 1903, Coffroth went on to promote events in California for another twelve years.

Other notable fights promoted by Coffroth include Corbett–Jeffries, Bob Fitzsimmons–George Gardner, Battling Nelson–Joe Gans, and Stanley Ketchel–Jack Johnson. Coffroth instituted the practice of paying fighters a percentage of the gate receipts. He was also aware of the value of publicity and held frequent press conferences.

As competition grew and the political climate changed, Coffroth lost his permits for bouts in San Francisco and moved his operations to the nearby towns of Colma and Daly City. Coffroth lost out to rival Tex Rickard on the mammoth Jeffries–Johnson fight. In sealed bids, Coffroth bid $100,000. Rival Tex Rickard bid $120,000 in gold.

Coffroth made most of his money in horse racing and continued operating tracks long after he retired from boxing promotion. He died in 1943. Hall of Fame Induction: 1991.

IRVING COHEN
Manager

Irving Cohen managed over 500 fighters in a career spanning more than 30 years. Though his stable included one world champion, Rocky Graziano, he is best remembered for his integrity in an often sordid profession.

Born on January 2, 1904, in Vilna, Russia, Cohen left home for the land of opportunity. Though Cohen boxed as an amateur, he didn't immediately find a career in the sport, and even worked as a lingerie salesman before becoming a fight manager. Calm, quiet, and distinguished, the 5'6" Cohen did not fit the stereotype of the loud, insensitive, cigar-chomping manager.

Cohen's first promising fighter was Sammy Garcia, who came to him in 1935. When Garcia began to attract attention, Cohen was instructed to meet with Jimmy Doyle, a New York racketeer involved in boxing. When Cohen met Doyle and his associates at the office of Hall of Famer Jimmy Johnson, Doyle threatened to throw Cohen out the window if he refused to relinquish control of Garcia. Cohen replied steadily, "Jimmy, if I go out that window, you're coming with me." The racketeer backed off for good.

Cohen skillfully and carefully guided his best fighter, Graziano, to the top—not an easy task given Rocky's disinterest in training. Cohen brought Graziano along slowly and, for a while, even had him live with his own family. When Graziano moved on to acting after his retirement from the ring, he asked Cohen to continue as his manager, but Cohen refused, saying he knew nothing about the entertainment industry.

Besides Graziano, Cohen also managed Hall of Famer Billy Graham. When Sugar Ray Robinson vacated the welterweight title in 1951 to move up to middleweight, Graham and Kid Gavilan were the two top contenders. The corrupt International Boxing Club controlled much of the sport at this time, and IBC president James D. Norris and mobster Frankie Carbo—the power behind Norris—allegedly met with Cohen to discuss a championship matchup. They offered Cohen's fighter a title shot if they could have a piece of Graham. Cohen told Graham and Graham's father about the offer. But the Grahams nixed it, largely because of their loyalty to and admiration for Cohen.

Rumors of skullduggery abounded when Gavilan and Graham finally met in Madison Square Garden on August 29, 1951. An anonymous phone call to Cohen on the day of the fight led him to believe that Graham could only win by knockout, since the referees and judges were "committed" to picking Gavilan. The caller told Cohen which officials would be assigned to the contest. An upset Cohen went to the offices of the New York State Athletic Commission to lodge a complaint, but his fears were dismissed by the commission. Gavilan won a split decision in a fight that many thought should have belonged to Graham. Teddy Brenner, a protege of Cohen, recounted a deathbed confession from one of the judges, avowing that the fight was fixed. In 1985, the New York State Athletic Commission rejected an appeal that would have reversed the decision, in part because the confessing judge was said to have died under circumstances that made a deathbed revelation impossible.

Cohen managed other notable fighters, like Walter Cartier, Irish Bob Murphy, Terry Young, Freddie Russon, and Joey Fontana. Cohen also promoted fights at New York area clubs such as the St. Nicholas Arena and Sunnyside Garden, and managed the famous Stillman's Gym in its final years. When diagnosed with glaucoma in the mid-60s, Cohen heeded his doctor's advice to slow down and retired to Florida. Cohen died on June 25, 1991, in Scottsdale, Arizona. Hall of Fame Induction: 2002.

CUS D'AMATO
Manager

Cus D'Amato earned a reputation as one of the most forthright and honest men in boxing. He guided Floyd Patterson and Jose Torres to world titles and was instrumental in launching Mike Tyson's career. Top trainers Teddy Atlas, Kevin Rooney, and Joe Fariello all learned their trade from D'Amato.

Born in 1908 in New York, D'Amato grew up as one of five brothers and learned to fight in the streets. At the age of 22, he opened the Empire Sporting Club with Jack Barrow at the Gramercy Gym. The purpose of the club was to develop young boxers. D'Amato was devoted to the gym and actually lived there for years. He was very attentive to his boxers, and his belief in his young stars was important to their success. He built the neophyte Patterson into an Olympic gold medal winner and then world heavyweight champion, and he later guided Jose Torres to the light heavyweight championship. Both Torres and Patterson continued responsible careers after boxing, Torres as a writer and member of the New York State Athletic Commission, Patterson most recently as head of the New York State Athletic Commission.

Once Patterson won the championship, D'Amato carefully selected his opponents both with an eye towards maximizing revenues for his fighter and thwarting the International Boxing Club (IBC). Although it meant bypassing many top challengers, D'Amato refused to match his fighter in any bout promoted by the powerful but corrupt IBC. The IBC was eventually found to be in violation of anti-trust laws and was dissolved. However, D'Amato's stance had the unintended effect of decreasing interest in boxing because Patterson fought infrequently and did not face many top contenders.

After Patterson's and Torres's careers had ended, D'Amato worked in relative obscurity for some years, surfacing briefly as a possible trainer for Wilt Chamberlain when the basketball great considered going into the ring. D'Amato then moved to Catskill, New York, where he opened a gym. He began to work with Mike Tyson who was in a nearby reform school. D'Amato did much to develop Tyson into a top heavyweight contender, but he died in 1985 before Tyson became the youngest world heavyweight titleholder in history. Hall of Fame Induction: 1995.

JEFF DICKSON
Promoter

Although he was an American, Jeff Dickson made his mark as a boxing promoter in Paris and throughout Europe. Born in Natchez, Mississippi, Dickson found a job as a newsboy at age seven. He continued in journalism as a war photographer, travelling to Europe in 1917. When World War I ended the next year, Dickson was stationed in Paris as part of the Signal Corps. For a fee, Dickson staged "war" pictures of American soldiers still in Paris who had seen no action before the armistice, complete with trenches dug by himself, actors in rented German uniforms, and action shots of "combat"—a very profitable scheme.

After his demobilization, Dickson remained in France, becoming a newsreel cameraman and travelling throughout Europe. He became friendly with the owner of the Salle Wagram—the major fight venue of Paris—and began lending him money. When the business failed, Dickson took it over and, after promoting fight cards there, moved to the larger Palais des Sports in 1924.

At the Palais des Sports and throughout Europe at venues in London, Berlin, Brussels, Rome, Barcelona, and Oslo, Dickson used his unique public relations sense to stage boxing matches. He also staged skating events, six-day bicycle races, bull fights, hockey, basketball, tennis, and wrestling matches, animal shows, and other extravaganzas. To promote a fight between Primo Carnera and Paulino Uzcudun, this master of publicity won the hearts of the Spanish public by staging a bullfight—with himself as matador! His victory over the bull led the Spanish press to support a fight they and the public had originally opposed because it was promoted by a foreigner. An amazing 85,000 people attended the fight, confirming not only Dickson's skills, but the public appeal of Carnera, whom Dickson afterwards took to London to meet Reggie Meen.

Dickson's unusual approach to running a promotion also extended to the way he managed his arenas. He had no objection to riots after unpopular decisions. In fact, he had a special retractable net installed around the ring, in case angry fans at the Palais des Sports threw bottles or other debris from the balconies. Although Dickson, like all good promoters, was a hard-nosed businessman, each year during the Christmas season he invited about twenty thousand poor and orphaned children to a free festival, where athletes, actors, and comedians entertained, and candy, food, and toys were given away to all comers.

Dickson realized that a successful promotion needed good fighters. To that end, Dickson had scouts comb European gyms for promising young boxers to bring into his fold. After the appropriate training, he would match these novices with proven fighters to see if they showed promise.

Dickson regularly visited New York, but Paris remained his home, and he lived there until the day before the Germans captured the city during World War II. He then returned to the United States and re-enlisted in the U.S. Army. Dickson was killed in action when his plane was shot down during a bombing raid over Germany. Hall of Fame Induction: 2000.

ARTHUR DONOVAN
Referee

Arthur Donovan refereed fourteen heavyweight championship fights from 1933 to 1946. The son of Professor Mike Donovan, the noted American middleweight champion and boxing instructor, Donovan was born on August 13, 1891 and grew up around boxers, and Gentleman Jim Corbett befriended the youngster when he came for a visit. Against his father's wishes, Donovan boxed professionally for a time, under an assumed name.

When his father retired as boxing instructor at the New York Athletic Club, Donovan took the job and held it for exactly fifty years to the minute. He also served two tours in the military, and after World War I, tried unsuccessfully to revive his boxing career. In 1923, James Farley, New York State Athletic Commissioner, urged Donovan to become a referee. Donovan agreed and was immediately called for important fights. He became a favorite of fans, who often asked him for autographs. Donovan officiated at twenty Joe Louis fights, including both Schmeling bouts. After retiring as a referee, Donovan continued in his instructor's job, which he had never left. He died on September 1, 1980.

Donovan's son, Art, is a well-known television personality and was enshrined in the Pro Football Hall of Fame after a career with the Baltimore Colts. Hall of Fame Induction: 1993.

MICKEY DUFF
Promoter and Manager

Mickey Duff was the dominant force in British boxing for nearly 30 years, and his influence on the sport spread across the globe. Born Monek Prager on June 7, 1929, near Krakow, Poland, Duff was the son, grandson, and great-grandson of rabbis. He was exposed to the ugliness of anti-Semitism at a young age, when he saw he grandfather beaten by thugs. In 1938, Duff and his parents moved to London's East End.

To avoid the air raids during the war, Duff was sent to a Jewish hostel in Gateshead, where he received his first formal exposure to boxing. He reached the finals of the London schoolboys' boxing tournament, but his family did not approve of his participation. At the young age of twelve, Duff argued with his father and vowed never to speak to him again, but he adopted the name "Mickey Duff" to avoid embarrassing his family. "Mickey" was an anglicized version of his given name, while "Duff" was a character played by James Cagney in *Cash and Carry*.

Duff entered professional boxing at the age of fifteen and amassed a 55-8-6 record in four years, before deciding that he would have more success outside the ring. He served briefly as a trainer and cutman but made his real mark as a matchmaker, quickly displaying a skill for choosing the right fighter for a match based on talent and character. Though he started out at small venues, by 1960 Duff was working for London promoter Harry Levene and booking fights in Wembley, Manchester, Glasgow, and Cardiff. He later worked for another promoter in Royal Albert Hall and served as matchmaker/director for the Anglo-American Sporting Clubs of the London Hilton and Manchester Piccadilly hotels. Duff matched Sugar Ray Robinson at his first event for the Hilton.

As his influence and reputation continued to grow, Duff became an independent manager and promoter, involved in fistic events all over the world, though he focused his attention in England. There, he replaced Hall of Famer Jack Solomons as the country's premier promoter. The first world champion with whom he worked was Terry Downes. Over the course of his career, he was involved with eighteen more champions or former champs. These included Howard Winstone, John Conteh, Barry McGuigan, Lloyd Honeyghan, and Cornelius Boza-Edwards. Additionally, Duff set up Mike Tyson's first eighteen bouts at the request of Tyson handler Jim Jacobs.

Duff's influence began to wane and Frank Warren replaced him as England's top boxing figure. Duff decried the influence of Warren, Don King, and Bob Arum on the sport he loved, and he retired from boxing in 1999, after his fighter Billy Schwer was defeated in a bid for the world lightweight title. At about the same time, he wrote his autobiography, entitled *Twenty and Out*. The title referred to the number of world champions he would have handled, had Schwer been victorious. A promoter and manager with first-hand experience in the ring, Duff was a major figure in the boxing world for nearly 50 years. Hall of Fame Induction: 1999.

ANGELO DUNDEE
Trainer

Angelo Dundee is best known for his work as the trainer of Muhammad Ali. Born in Philadelphia in 1923, Dundee was originally named Angelo Mirena, Jr. He changed his name to Dundee after his older brother Joe adopted it in honor of Hall of Famer Johnny Dundee. In the Army in World War II, Dundee boxed a couple of times and worked as a corner man in service bouts.

After the war, Dundee moved to New York to do corner work for his brother Chris, who was then a fight manager. He also spent a great deal of time in Stillman's Gym, watching the action and learning from great trainers such as Charley Goldman, Ray Arcel, Bill Gore, Whitey Bimstein, and Chickie Ferrara. In 1950, Dundee took over the management of his first fighter, Bill Bossio, and in 1952, he was hired as chief second and cut man for Carmen Basilio, who won both the welterweight and middleweight titles. He later became Basilio's trainer.

During the 1950s, Dundee built up a stable of fighters, although Basilio was his only champion. Then in 1960, Dundee was hired to train a fighter who would change his life:

Cassius Clay, later known as Muhammad Ali. Dundee enjoyed working with the superbly talented boxer, even if Ali at times resisted his advice, and he remained in the Ali camp for over twenty years. Ali credited Dundee not only for getting him through some crisis points in key fights, but with having faith in him after Ali lost to Joe Frazier and Ken Norton.

At the same time he was training Ali, Dundee handled other champions. On March 21, 1963, two of his charges won world titles on the same card in Los Angeles. Ultiminio ("Sugar") Ramos knocked out Davey Moore to win the featherweight title, and Luis Rodriguez decisioned Emile Griffith to win the welterweight title. Two other fighters in the Dundee stable, Ralph Dupas and Willie Pastrano, won titles in 1963 in the junior middleweight and light heavyweight divisions.

Dundee also trained Jose Napoles, who won the welterweight title in 1969. Napoles lost the title when Billy Backus stopped him on cuts in 1970. On the night of the Backus fight, Dundee was with Ali and his services as the best cut man in boxing were not available. Napoles won the rematch with Dundee back in his corner.

As Ali's career wound down, Dundee took on a new high-profile fighter, Sugar Ray Leonard. Under Dundee's direction, Leonard became an outstanding fighter and perhaps the most popular boxer of the post-Ali era. Other champions trained or managed by Dundee include Pinklon Thomas, Slobodan Kacar, and Michael Nunn. Most recently, Dundee worked with the 46-year-old George Foreman in his 1994 comeback win over Michael Moorer for the heavyweight championship.

Howard Cosell said of Dundee, "If I had a son who wanted to be a fighter, the only man I would entrust him to would be Angelo Dundee." Hall of Fame Induction: 1992.

CHRIS DUNDEE
Manager and Promoter

Although he was never a professional fighter, Chris Dundee's life was boxing. He managed approximately three hundred fighters, promoted hundreds of bouts, and ran a famous gym. Born in Philadelphia in 1908, Dundee began life with the name Cristofo Mirena. Like his brothers Angelo, who became a top trainer, and Joe, a club fighter, he adopted the name used by Hall of Famer Johnny Dundee.

In 1928, Dundee started managing fighters. He shepherded Midget Wolgast to the world flyweight title in 1930, Ken Overlin to the New York version of the world middleweight title in 1941, and Ezzard Charles to the world heavyweight title in 1949.

Starting in 1932, Dundee also acted as a boxing promoter, putting on shows in the Norfolk, Washington, and Baltimore areas. In 1950, with the completion of the Miami Beach Convention Hall, Dundee moved his base of operations there and promoted boxing and wrestling at that venue for 27 years. He succeeded in putting on a large number of cards annually, even as promoters in similar-sized cities were going out of business. Some of the important bouts he promoted included the Harold Johnson–Jesse Bowdry light heavyweight championship fight, the world welterweight title fight in which Emile Griffith first defeated Benny ("Kid") Paret, and the famous world heavyweight title fight in which Muhammad Ali defeated Sonny Liston.

After relinquishing his exclusive hold on the Miami Beach hall, Dundee worked for British promoter Chris Wilson. For approximately 30 years, Dundee also owned and operated the famous Fifth Street Gym in Miami Beach, where Ali and many other prominent fighters trained. He died on November 16, 1998. Hall of Fame Induction: 1994.

DON DUNPHY
Broadcaster

Don Dunphy enjoyed a long career behind the mike calling fights at ringside for radio and then television audiences. In his forty-year career, Dunphy called the blow-by-blow of over two thousand fights, with over two hundred of them for titles, including 50 heavyweight championships.

Born in New York in 1908, Dunphy went to Manhattan College, where he was a college correspondent for a number of New York newspapers. After graduating, Dunphy worked for a time at the New York Coliseum, broadcasting hockey and wrestling from the site. He also hosted a daily sports show, for no pay, on radio station WHOM, and worked at WINS as a spotter for football broadcasts before getting air time himself, mostly doing ticker tape re-creations. He worked Newark Bears minor league baseball games and, in 1936, assisted at broadcasts of Cornell University football games. In 1937, Dunphy became the sports director at WINS, a job he held for the next ten years. He also hosted a popular boxing talk show on WINS on Saturday afternoons.

In 1939, Dunphy ventured into local fight broadcasts, and in 1941, he auditioned for radio sponsor Gillette Safety Razor Company by calling the Gus Lesnevich–Anton Christoforidis fight at Madison Square Garden. He got the job and his next broadcast was the first Joe Louis–Billy Conn fight. Dunphy called fights on radio for Gillette for nineteen years.

In 1960, Dunphy moved over to television and called fights on the ABC network for four years. He also worked fights for WOR-TV and continued to call many championship fights on radio. By the 1970s and early '80s, Dunphy had retired from network television, but he was still very much in demand on closed-circuit telecasts, calling such fights as Ali–Frazier I, and Ali–Foreman. His final complete blow-by-blow of a major fight was the first Sugar Ray Leonard–Thomas Hearns fight in 1981.

Dunphy worked with color man Bill Corum for many years. He was also paired with such celebrity broadcasting partners as Muhammad Ali, Pearl Bailey, Flip Wilson, and Ryan O'Neal. Throughout his career, Dunphy broadcast New York Yankee games, the Cotton Bowl, track events, bowling, basketball, and horse racing. Dunphy died July 22, 1998. Hall of Fame Induction: 1993.

LOU DUVA
Trainer and Manager

Lou Duva has been a boxer, manager, trainer, matchmaker, and promoter, but his career did not really take off until he was almost 60. Born in New York on May 28, 1922, Duva moved to Paterson, New Jersey as a child. At fifteen Duva boxed for five dollars a fight before dropping out of school to join the Civilian Conservation Corps. After working with the Corps in Oregon, Duva returned home and won the New Jersey Diamond Gloves welterweight championship.

During World War II, Duva taught boxing at Camp Hood, Texas. After the war, he went to Florida where he worked in his parents' restaurant and boxed on the side. Back in New Jersey, he started a trucking business but, whenever he had the opportunity, Duva went to Stillman's Gym in New York to be around boxing. Duva later worked as a bail bondsman before becoming president of the local Teamsters union. During this time he promoted many small boxing shows in the Paterson area. His most significant promotion was the Joey Giardello-Dick Tiger middleweight championship in 1963.

In 1977, Lou's son Dan, a law school graduate, organized the family's boxing operations as a promotional company called Main Events. Duva served as manager, with his son as promoter and matchmaker. When Main Events linked up with rock promoter Shelly Finkel, who excelled at recruiting talent, it became a major player in the sport. In 1981, Main Events won promotional rights to the Sugar Ray Leonard-Thomas Hearns bout that grossed $34 million.

Duva sought more talented boxers to join the Main Events stable, sometimes serving as manager, sometimes as trainer. He also signed top amateur fighters such as 1984 Olympians Pernell Whitaker, Mark Breland, and Evander Holyfield. Duva worked the corner for these fighters and other stars of the 1980s and 1990s, including Bobby Czyz, Livingstone Bramble, Darrin Van Horn, Meldrick Taylor, and Michael Moorer. On February 4, 1989, Duva was in Las Vegas when Breland won the WBA welterweight title by knocking out Seung-Soon Lee. The very next day Duva was ringside in Atlantic City when Van Horn won the IBF junior middleweight title over Robert Hines. In 1996, Lou suffered the loss of his son Dan to a brain tumor. Dino, Dan's younger brother, took over as Main Events president.

Duva is known for fierce devotion to his fighters which, combined with his pugnacious demeanor, has resulted in some unorthodox activities in the ring. He once charged at a referee with whom he disagreed. He almost attacked Don King after the latter shouted "something rude" at Duva following Mike Tyson's knockout of Duva's charge, Tyrell Biggs.

Duva was part of the melee that took place after Andrew Golota, Duva's fighter, was disqualified in his first fight with Riddick Bowe. Duva, who had suffered a heart attack more than fifteen years before, had to be carried out of the ring on a stretcher. In 1999, Lou Duva, along with son Dino and daughter Donna Brooks, departed Main Events after a dispute with Dan's widow, Kathy Duva. The new company Duva Boxing promotes a new young corps of fighters. Hall of Fame Induction: 1998.

AILEEN EATON
Promoter

Aileen Eaton, the only female member of the International Boxing Hall of Fame, staged top boxing promotions at the Olympic Auditorium in Los Angeles for almost forty years.

Eaton, born Aileen Goldstein in Vancouver, British Columbia, on February 5, 1909, did not originally intend to pursue a career ringside. A widowed mother of two in need of a job to support her children, Eaton left law school and entered the world of boxing as a private secretary to Frank A. Garbutt, president of the Los Angeles Athletic Club, which owned the Olympic Auditorium. In 1942, Garbutt asked Eaton to find out why boxing promotions at the Olympic lost money. When she reported back that the current promoter was incompetent, Garbutt told her to find a new one. She selected Cal Eaton, an inspector for the California State Athletic Commission. Eaton soon joined Cal's staff and learned the fine arts of publicity, advertising, and matchmaking. She ultimately married Cal, and served as his co-promoter.

The first fight card Eaton helped promote drew 2,212 fans on July 21, 1942, to watch Jack Chase decision Big Boy Hogue in the main event. While Cal Eaton was officially the promoter, Aileen quickly became closely involved in all aspects of boxing promotions at the Olympic.

Eaton staged weekly shows at the Olympic from 1942 to 1980. While it was not unusual for a fight club to hold regular weekly events in the 40s, by the 70s such regularity was rare. By some accounts, the Olympic was the only one of around four hundred 1940s venues still holding weekly fight cards into the late 70s. After Cal died in 1966, Eaton functioned as the Olympic's sole promoter, assisted by two Hall of Fame matchmakers, George Parnassus beginning in 1957, and then Don Chargin.

Eaton's promotional achievements are almost too numerous to list. She staged over 2,500 cards, 10,000 fights, and 100 title fights. In addition to regular bouts at the Olympic, she staged promotions at other L.A. sites, like Dodger Stadium, the Los Angeles Sports Arena, and the Coliseum. She promoted the championship triple-header in Dodger Stadium on March 21, 1963 in which Sugar Ramos faced champion Davey Moore for the featherweight title, welterweight title-holder Emile Griffith fought number-one contender Luis Rodriquez, and Battling Torres and Roberto Cruz vied for the vacant junior welterweight crown, in front of 26,000 fans. Another notable Eaton promotion was the Lauro Salas upset of heavily favored Jimmy Carter for the lightweight title, a bout held at the Olympic on May 14, 1952. Eaton also promoted contests with Sugar Ray Robinson, George Foreman, Joe Frazier, Carmen Basilio, Floyd Patterson, Archie Moore, Manuel Ortiz, Ike Williams, Mando Ramos, Art Aragon, Danny Lopez, Carlos Palomino, and Muhammad Ali. Additionally, Eaton had a hand in the Las Vegas promotion of the Sugar Ray Leonard–Wilfred Benitez fight. Eaton credited herself with giving Muhammad Ali the idea for his "I am the greatest" shtick.

Aileen Eaton's sons, Mike and Gene LeBell gained fame as professional wrestlers. Gene won two consecutive national Judo championships and worked as a stunt man in over 1,000 movies and TV shows. Eaton stopped promoting fights at the Olympic in 1980, and two years later she was appointed as a commissioner of the California State Athletic Commission, the first person with boxing industry experience ever appointed to that organization. Eaton died on November 7, 1987. Hall of Fame Induction: 2002.

PIERCE EGAN
Historian

All students of boxing history owe a debt of gratitude to Pierce Egan, the first boxing historian. He was the most popular and successful of English sports journalists, and the public eagerly sought out his vivid descriptions of bare knuckle bouts in the London *Weekly Dispatch.*

Egan was born in England, probably in 1772. He began publishing his magnum opus, *Boxiana,* in 1812. A history of boxing containing biographical sketches of fighters, round-by-round descriptions of fights, and other information about the sport and its participants, the work was issued in monthly paperbound sections and sold by subscription. By 1813, enough material had been issued to create the first book-length volume, and, by 1829, Egan published *Boxiana* as a five-volume set with an additional volume contributed by Jon Bee (John Babcock). Egan's work is often cited by writers discussing the early days of fisticuffs.

Egan also wrote plays, songs, novels, epigrams, and a dictionary of slang; he also appeared on stage as an actor. His knowledge of London's seamier elements lent richness to his reports of criminal trials. His 1821 bestseller, *Life in London,* is said to have inspired and influenced Charles Dickens. Egan died in 1849. Hall of Fame Induction: 1991.

NATHANIEL S. FLEISCHER
Writer and Publisher

Nat Fleischer is best known for founding *The Ring* magazine in 1922. He published this "bible of boxing" until his death in 1972. Born in New York on November 3, 1887, Fleischer grew up participating in a variety of sports including boxing. He graduated from City College of New York in 1908, then worked for the *New York Press* while pursuing studies at New York University. He left NYU after causing an explosion in the chemistry lab.

Fleischer eventually became sports editor of the *Press* and, when the newspaper merged with the *Morning Sun,* Fleischer became sports editor of the reconstituted *Sun Press.* As the paper's owner, Frank A. Munsey, bought a succession of newspapers, Fleischer became sports editor of each until 1929, when he left to devote full attention to his magazine. *The Ring* quickly became the authoritative voice on boxing.

The magazine's annual rankings of fighters were highly influential. When Fleischer first came up with the idea, he asked Tex Rickard to make the selections. After Rickard's death, Jack Dempsey made the choices for a year. Ultimately, Fleischer decided that *The Ring* staff and correspondents were best qualified to rank fighters. Fleischer also used the magazine to speak out on matters such as corruption or the influence of television. Fleischer became a kind of moral voice for boxing, advocating more extensive physical examinations for fighters, padded rings, and a halt to fights where one of the combatants had been seriously cut.

Fleischer strongly believed that titles should be won and lost in the squared circle. Although he denigrated Muhammad Ali's abilities at times and referred to him as Cassius Clay long after he had changed his name, Fleischer continued to list Ali as champion after he had been stripped of his title for refusing induction into the armed services.

In addition to the magazine, Fleischer published *Nat Fleischer's Ring Record Book and Boxing Encyclopedia* annually, beginning in 1941. The record book continued to be published until 1987. Fleischer also wrote many books about boxing, including *Black Dynamite,* a series on great African-American boxers; a history of the heavyweight championship; an autobiography; a history of wrestling; and several technical boxing manuals.

Fleischer was one of the founders of the Boxing Writers Association and twice received its James J. Walker Award for long and meritorious service to boxing. The organization named the Nathaniel S. Fleischer Award after him to honor fine boxing writing. Fleischer also established a (no longer extant) museum and hall of fame in the offices of *The Ring.* Throughout his life, Fleischer fought for what he believed was best for the sport of boxing. He died on June 25, 1972. Hall of Fame Induction: 1990.

RICHARD K. FOX
Writer and Publisher

Second only to his frequent nemesis, John L. Sullivan, Richard K. Fox did more than anyone to popularize boxing in the late nineteenth century. Fox gave the sport extensive coverage in his tabloid, *The National Police Gazette,* and by helping to organize key ring contests. Born in Belfast, Ireland in 1846, Fox came to the United States in 1874 with less than five dollars in his pocket.

Within two years, he had taken over the financially troubled *Police Gazette* and expanded its quota of sensational, lurid tales of crime, sex, and scandal.

He built up the distribution network until the *Gazette* was available nationally and in 26 countries around the world.

By the 1880s, the *Gazette* had a circulation of 150,000. In addition to accounts of murders and pictures of showgirls, the paper contained news of sporting events. When sales of issues covering the 1880 Joe Goss–Paddy Ryan fight leaped to 400,000, Fox decided to make the *Gazette* the "leading prize ring authority in America."

Fox's role in boxing grew after his first meeting with John L. Sullivan. According to legend, the two encountered each other at Harry Hill's saloon in New York. Sullivan supposedly insulted Fox by refusing to come to his table, and Fox seemed to bear a long grudge. His paper gave considerable column inches to Sullivan and his exploits, but often portraying the champion in a negative light.

Fox backed a succession of challengers to the "Boston Strongboy," among them Paddy Ryan, Tug Wilson, Herbert Slade, and Jake Kilrain. Fox named champions in several weight classes and bestowed upon them the *Police Gazette* Diamond Belt. Fox backed his champion Kilrain against Sullivan in the last bare knuckle heavyweight championship bout, which Sullivan won.

Although the *Police Gazette* declined in the twentieth century, when Fox died in 1922 he was a wealthy man leaving an estate of over $1.5 million. The colorful Fox, known for his Prince Albert coat and top hat, contributed greatly to the growth of boxing by publicizing fighters and bouts, backing fighters financially, and helping to establish standardized weight classes. Fox's successes also helped spur the development of regular sports sections in daily newspapers. Hall of Fame Induction: 1997.

EDDIE FUTCH
Trainer and Manager

One of the finest trainers in boxing history, Eddie Futch was in the winning corner each of the first two times Muhammad Ali was defeated. Born in Hillsboro, Mississippi in 1911, Futch moved to Detroit as a child and grew up in the rough Black Bottom neighborhood. Although only 5'7", Futch starred on a crack semi-pro basketball team which travelled to such cities as Chicago and Pittsburgh to play.

When lack of funds kept Futch from going to college, he turned to boxing. He won the Detroit Athletic Association championship as a lightweight in 1932 and the Detroit Golden Gloves in 1933. Futch worked at the same gym as the young Joe Louis, who liked to spar with Futch because of the smaller man's speed and cleverness.

Futch's plans for a pro career ended when doctors discovered that he had a heart murmur. He began training amateur fighters in his spare time and, in the 1940s, started to develop pro fighters. He then left boxing for several years, but returned in the early 1950s. Futch's first champion was Don Jordan, who won the welterweight title in 1958. Even with this success, Futch needed to work other jobs, including a long stint with the post office. Futch trained Hall of Famer Bob Foster and helped him to the world light heavyweight championship.

In 1966, Futch began training Joe Frazier, helping him to develop his bob-and-weave, which made the compact fighter even more difficult to hit. Under his guidance, Frazier won the heavyweight title during Muhammad Ali's enforced exile. When Frazier met Ali in the so-called "Fight of the Century," Futch instructed Frazier to back Ali into the ropes and work the body before moving to the head. He also instructed Frazier to make Ali throw right up-percuts which would leave him open to a left hook. Following Futch's instructions, Frazier won the fight over the previously unbeaten Ali. After the death of Yank Durham, Frazier's manager, Futch took over his managerial duties as well. Futch made the decision not to send the battered Frazier out for the fifteenth round in the "Thrilla in Manila."

Futch also handled Ken Norton for many years and was in his corner when Norton beat Ali. Futch's strategy of having Norton jab every time Ali jabbed, left Ali open to attack and led to Norton's victory. Futch also worked with Larry Holmes, Alexis Arguello, and Michael Spinks. When Spinks fought Holmes, Futch declined to work in either corner. Futch was the recipient of the James J. Walker Award for long and meritorious service to boxing in 1982. He also won the Al Buck Award as manager of the year in 1975 and the John Condon Award as trainer of the year in 1991. Active well into his eighties, Futch recently trained Riddick Bowe and Wayne McCullough. By the time he finally announced his retirement in January 1998, Futch had helped 22 fighters earn world titles. Futch died on October 10, 2001. Hall of Fame Induction: 1994.

BILL GALLO
Cartoonist

While an accomplished sportswriter, Bill Gallo is best known for his work as a sports cartoonist with the *New York Daily News*. Born December 28, 1922, Gallo learned about the newspaper business and boxing from his father, Fran-cisco ("Frank") Gallo, a reporter and editor for the Spanish language news-paper *La Prensa*. Gallo had to grow up quickly when his father died, leaving the eleven-year-old to finish school while working a variety of jobs to support his family.

Following high school graduation in 1941, Gallo became a copyboy at the *Daily News*, but his career was cut short by the war. In 1942, he enlisted in the marines, where he saw plenty of action in the Pacific Theater, including the invasion of Iwo Jima. Back in New York after the war, Gallo became an apprentice in the art department of the *Daily News*, and attended the Cartoonists and Illustrators School at Columbia University at the same time. In 1954, he penned his first full cartoon, "Hitting Spree," recounting a boxing match.

During the 1950s, Gallo worked under the *Daily News* sports cartoonist, Leo O'Mealia, replacing him when O'Mealia died in 1960. In describing his own style, Gallo stated, "I've always tried to make it easy on the reader, whether I'm writing or drawing. Make it sim-ple and natural on his eyes so he doesn't have to strain and wonder, 'Who is this? What is that?'"

Despite his 60 years in the newspaper business—with time out for military service—Gallo shows no signs of quitting, and to date he has penned over 14,000 cartoons. His drawings have also appeared in *The Sporting News* and several have a place in the National Baseball Hall of Fame and Museum in Cooperstown, New York. Gallo has also written a regular column for the *Daily News*, and while he is not afraid to criticize sports and ath-letes—in both his cartoons and his column—he has earned the respect of those he cov-ers. Joe DiMaggio was a special admirer of Gallo's work, and wanted original copies of every cartoon that featured the "Yankee Clipper."

In addition to his induction into the International Boxing Hall of Fame, Gallo has received numerous other honors. He has won ten Reuben Awards from the National Cartoonists Society as best sports cartoonist of the year, and in 1999, he earned the Milt Caniff Lifetime Achievement Award. In 1981, he received the James J. Walker Award for Long and Meritorious Service to Boxing from the Boxing Writers Association of America, and in 2001 he was inducted into the National Black Sports and Entertainment Hall of Fame for his role in helping black athletes, one of only three Caucasians selected for this honor. In 2000, he published a book showcasing his cartoons, entitled *Drawing a Crowd: Bill Gallo's Greatest Sports Moments.*

Boxing writer Bert Randolph Sugar said, "No one on the sports scene today can capture that scene in words and pictures like Bill Gallo. No one, but no one!"

While Gallo has covered many different athletes in his long career, the distinguished writer and cartoonist has singled out boxers for their "nobility." Hall of Fame Induction: 2001.

CHARLEY GOLDMAN
Trainer

The man who shaped Rocky Marciano into a champion, Charley Goldman also trained four other world champions and, in his younger days, had a successful career as a fighter himself. Born Israel Goldman in Warsaw, Poland in 1888, Goldman grew up in the tough Red Hook section of Brooklyn and learned to fight in the streets. He left school in the fourth grade and began fighting in the back of bars to earn spending money. He turned professional at the age of fifteen.

Goldman fought mostly as a bantamweight. He idolized Terry McGovern and started wearing his trademark derby hat in imitation of McGovern. He fought bantamweight champion Johnny Coulon in a no-decision bout in 1912. Goldman retired in 1914 with a recorded tally of 36-6-11 and 84 no-decision bouts. Goldman claimed that he actually fought about 400 times.

Goldman quickly found success as a trainer. In 1914, he trained Al McCoy, who won the middleweight title. With the passage of the Walker Law legalizing boxing in 1920, Goldman teamed with manager Al Weill. After five years, Goldman left boxing and moved to Newburgh, New York to open a roadhouse, although Weill still occasionally sent him fighters to train.

In the mid-1930s, Goldman returned to New York and training fulltime. Although he often worked with Weill's boxers, he also handled other fighters. He worked with such champions as lightweight Lou Ambers, welterweight Marty Servo, and featherweight Joey Archibald. But in the late 1940s and '50s, Goldman gained his greatest fame training Rocky Marciano. When Goldman first saw him, Marciano had a strong punch but a crude style. Employing his philosophy of improving upon but not changing a fighter's basic style, Goldman strengthened Marciano's defense, left jab, and left hook. Marciano worked tirelessly to implement Goldman's instructions, and, of course, won the world championship.

Goldman was well liked and respected by the trainers, sportswriters, and others who frequented Stillman's Gym. For many years, he spent about six hours a day at Stillman's and then went to a C.Y.O. gym to work with very young fighters. He died of a heart attack in 1968. Hall of Fame Induction: 1992.

RUBY GOLDSTEIN
Referee

Famed referee Ruby Goldstein also had a distinguished career as a fighter. Born on the East Side of New York in 1907, Goldstein learned to box at the Henry Street Settlement House and started boxing in amateur tournaments at the age of sixteen. He turned pro in 1925 with a second-round knockout of Al Vano. He was nicknamed "the Jewel of the Ghetto."

Goldstein won his first 23 fights before Ace Hudkins knocked him out and he compiled an early record of 50 wins in 55 bouts. However, after losing five fights by knockout, including one to Hall of Famer Jimmy McLarnin, Goldstein realized that he didn't have what it took to become a champion. Nevertheless, he continued to fight until 1937, retiring after winning a decision over Kid Bon Bon.

After leaving the ring, Goldstein remained on the fringes of boxing, and he also managed a pool hall. He started to referee while in the Army during World War II. He served as referee when Joe Louis fought exhibitions at military installations.

After his discharge, Goldstein continued to officiate. His first heavyweight title fight was the first Joe Louis–Jersey Joe Walcott match. Goldstein scored the fight for Walcott, while the two judges scored the fight in Louis's favor. Many observers thought that Walcott had won. When Louis was asked about Goldstein's scoring, he replied, "I know Ruby. He calls 'em like he sees 'em."

Louis's comment helped build Goldstein's reputation and, from then on, he officiated at many important fights, including the first Zale–Graziano match and the Robinson–Maxim light heavyweight championship fight (where the 104° heat conquered Goldstein in the tenth round and Robinson in the fourteenth). Goldstein officiated for the Emile Griffith–Benny ("Kid") Paret fight in which Paret was killed in the ring. That event bothered Goldstein greatly, and he retired after working one more fight.

Goldstein worked for longtime employer Schenley Distillers and wrote a column for *The Ring,* before retiring to Miami Beach. He died on April 22, 1984. Hall of Fame Induction: 1994.

MURRAY GOODMAN
Publicist

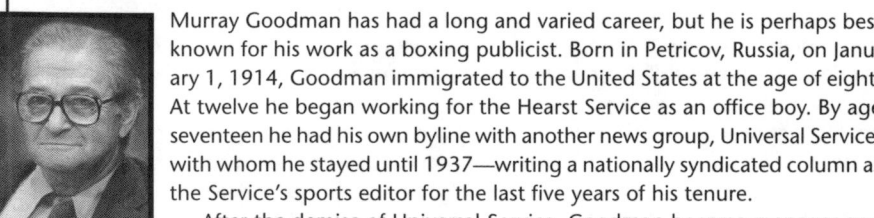

Murray Goodman has had a long and varied career, but he is perhaps best known for his work as a boxing publicist. Born in Petricov, Russia, on January 1, 1914, Goodman immigrated to the United States at the age of eight. At twelve he began working for the Hearst Service as an office boy. By age seventeen he had his own byline with another news group, Universal Service, with whom he stayed until 1937—writing a nationally syndicated column as the Service's sports editor for the last five years of his tenure.

After the demise of Universal Service, Goodman became manager and publicist to the well-known "Clown Prince of Baseball," Al Schacht, with whom he worked for eight years, including collaboration on two books. During his time with Schacht, Goodman also served as the sports and publicity director for the Infantile Paralysis Fund of New York.

Goodman next served briefly as publicity director for the Jumping Brook Resort in Neptune, New Jersey, where he arranged for heavyweight contender Tami Mauriello to train, and then as the promotion and tournament director of the short-lived and long-forgotten World Professional (Tennis) League.

Goodman then began a direct association with boxing, when he was hired by the Tournament of Champions promotional organization to handle publicity for Marcel Cerdan before the Cerdan–Tony Zale middleweight championship fight. The Tournament of Champions later became the International Boxing Club and dominated the world of fight promotion in the late 1940s and 50s from its base of operations at the old Madison Square Garden. Goodman handled publicity for both Garden fights and IBC's national promotions held outside of New York.

Around 1960, Goodman left the IBC, working for the Yonkers Raceway before briefly becoming the public relations director for the New York Titans (later the Jets) of the American Football League. He also promoted the Dick Tiger–Joey Giardello middleweight title fight.

Goodman next headed to the sports division of the advertising and public relations division of Richard Kerr, Inc., where he helped publicize many major fights through the late 60s and early 70s. He and his son Bobby then opened Murray Goodman Associates, creating publicity for the two greatest promoters of recent times, Hall of Famers Don King and Bob Arum.

In his long career, Goodman publicized fights involving such notables as Joe Louis, Sugar Ray Robinson, Marcel Cerdan, Muhammad Ali, Rocky Graziano, Kid Gavilan, Sugar Ray Leonard, Bob Foster, Ken Norton, and Larry Holmes. In 1969, he received the James J. Walker Award for Long and Meritorious Service to Boxing from the Boxing Writers Association of America. He is credited with originating the S. Rae Hickok Professional Athlete of the Year Award, sponsored by the Hickok Manufacturing Company, and awarded annually from 1950 to 1976. Goodman wrote seventeen books—none of them about boxing—before his death on March 8, 1996. Hall of Fame Induction: 1999.

REG GUTTERIDGE
Broadcaster and Journalist

Over the last half century, Reg Gutteridge has been one of the best known figures in British and international boxing circles and is also heir to the legacy of one of Britain's greatest boxing families. His grandfather, Arthur Gutteridge, was a professional fighter, who was on the card at the opening of the National Sporting Club at Covent Garden in 1898 and reportedly gave boxing lessons to Rudyard Kipling. Reg's father, Dick Gutteridge, and his uncle, Jack Gutteridge, were identical twins, both well known in boxing circles as amateur fighters, club and school coaches, professional trainers, and seconds. They were known as the "Trainers of Champions."

It was, perhaps, inevitable that Gutteridge would follow in his family's boxing tradition. He has spent his life covering boxing, both as a writer and a broadcaster. Born in Islington, England, in 1924, his father let him hold the boxers' robes at Bethnal Green when he was only ten. Gutteridge even fought a few times as an amateur, but it was soon apparent to him that a life inside the ring was not his best career opportunity. In 1938, Gutteridge left school and got a job as a messenger with the London *Evening News*. He served in the British Army during WWII, and lost half his left leg in 1944 to a land mine in Normandy.

After the war, Gutteridge returned to the *Evening News*, where he became the paper's boxing correspondent, a position he held until the paper merged with another publication in 1980. Gutteridge has also written numerous columns and articles for boxing publications in Great Britain and the United States, and has authored or coauthored several books about boxing, including *Boxing: The Great Ones, Mike Tyson: The Release of Power, The Big Punchers,* and his autobiography, *Uppercuts and Dazes.*

For decades, Gutteridge also has been a boxing broadcaster for British radio and television. In 1991, the Boxing Writers' Association of America awarded him the Sam Taub Award for Excellence in Broadcasting Journalism.

Gutteridge found that he actually preferred his longstanding BBC television duties to print journalism. "I enjoyed the TV work; writing for a newspaper is much harder. Before you start you look at a blank page and it's like a desert."

Throughout his long career, Gutteridge has traveled the globe and has developed close relationships with some of the fighters he has covered. He once lured Muhammad Ali to the set of the British edition of *This is Your Life,* and Ali let Gutteridge interview him between rounds of his 1973 fight with Rudi Lubbers. When Gutteridge was hospitalized with blood poisoning, he awoke to find Ali praying at his bedside.

Besides his induction into the International Boxing Hall of Fame, Gutteridge has received another great honor: In 1995, Queen Elizabeth II awarded Gutteridge an Order of the British Empire for his service to boxing. Hall of Fame Induction: 2002.

JOE HUMPHREYS
Announcer

The first ring announcer to be inducted into the International Boxing Hall of Fame, Joe Humphreys earned this honor by announcing tens of thousands of fights in a career that lasted from 1890 until his death in 1936.

Born on New York City's Lower East Side on October 19, 1872, Humphreys was orphaned at the age of ten and received only limited schooling. He became involved in boxing as a mascot of the Nonpareil Athletic Club. Known as "Joe the Beaut" for his good looks and fine singing voice, Humphreys first announced a fight at a benefit for an injured boxer. Humphreys sang on the program and impressed the crowd with his booming voice and commanding presence.

As a reward for his work in the political campaign of Big Tim Sullivan of Tammany Hall in the late 1890s, Humphreys received the announcing assignment at the Broadway Athletic Club. Early in his career, Humphreys worked without a microphone. He also served as public address announcer for the New York Yankees but quit when owner Frank Farrell wanted him to use a megaphone. "I myself am the loudspeaker," Humphreys said indignantly.

Humphreys had the unique ability to know how to handle a fight crowd that was about to turn into an unruly mob. His announcement of "Quiet, please, quiet" instantly commanded a crowd's attention. In Yankee Stadium on May 20, 1927, prior to the Jack Sharkey–Jim Maloney bout, Humphreys quelled a disturbance over the previous bout by asking the crowd to pray for Charles Lindbergh, who had just embarked on his historic transatlantic flight earlier that day.

Some of the most noteworthy fights Humphreys introduced were the Jack Dempsey–Georges Carpentier "Battle of the Century" at Boyle's Thirty Acres in New Jersey, Dempsey–Luis Firpo, and the second Dempsey–Gene Tunney fight. Humphreys was also co-manager of Hall of Famer Terry McGovern. Humphreys died of a heart attack on July 11, 1936, in Fairhaven, New Jersey. Hall of Fame Induction: 1997.

SAM ICHINOSE
Promoter

Sam Ichinose, the greatest boxing promoter in Hawaiian history, was born on November 12, 1907. He dropped out of Lahainaluna High School after his fumble in the football game against traditional rival Maui High School led to a Maui touchdown and defeat for his team. He then considered a career in boxing, but lost his first and only amateur bout. When professional boxing was legalized in Hawaii in 1929, Ichinose decided to work in the fight game, and began his new career by managing a fighter named Freddie Gomez. Ichinose dubbed Gomez, "Mexicali Rose" because of his Irish and Mexican heritage. Ichinose's experience with Gomez led him to other fighters, and by 1952, he was promoting fights in Japan, Indonesia, and Europe in addition to his home base of Hawaii where—with partner Ralph Yempuku—he promoted under the Boxing Enterprises banner. He often went to the continental United States to publicize his fighters, where his penchant for displaying a hang-dog expression when talking to sportswriters led to his nickname "Sad Sam."

In his lengthy career, Ichinose was instrumental in Ben Villaflor's rise to the world junior lightweight championship. He also managed Dado Marino to the world flyweight championship and worked with Hall of Famer Bobo Olson.

In 1981, the year of his retirement, Ichinose tried to obtain a license for Muhammad Ali to fight in Hawaii, but the Hawaii Boxing Commission refused his application. In addition to his career in boxing, he owned Sad Sam's Bar, which remained in business for over three decades. Ichinose served a two-year term in the Territorial House of Representatives, and was both a city and county supervisor. Ichinose is also a member of the Hawaii Sports Hall of Fame. He died on January 24, 1993. Hall of Fame Induction: 2000.

JIMMY JACOBS
Manager and Film Historian

Jimmy Jacobs is primarily known to boxing for his vast collection of fight films, but he was also a fight manager and, as a young man, a handball champion. Born in St. Louis in 1930, Jacobs grew up in Los Angeles and, while he excelled in baseball, football, and basketball, his primary sport was handball. He was a six-time national singles handball champion and a six-time national doubles champion. Handball experts credit him with first using the ceiling shot.

Jacobs was also a boxing enthusiast and, in his travels to other countries to give handball exhibitions, he began to acquire films of old fights which were no longer available in this country. In 1961, Jacobs joined forces with another collector, Bill Cayton, to restore and preserve the films. Their corporation, The Big Fights, Inc., produced over one thousand boxing features with the old films as a base. Three of their productions were nominated for Academy Awards.

In addition to his film collecting, Jacobs also managed fighters with Cayton. The pair handled three world champions: Wilfred Benitez, Edwin Rosario, and Mike Tyson. As a manager, Jacobs was content to let the trainer determine the fight strategy and training regimen.

Jacobs died on March 23, 1988 after a long struggle with leukemia. He was hailed in both the boxing and handball worlds for his successes and fine character. Along with his spot in the Boxing Hall of Fame, Jacobs is an inductee of the Handball Hall of Fame. Hall of Fame Induction: 1993.

MIKE JACOBS
Promoter

Following in the footsteps of Tex Rickard, Mike Jacobs ruled as the dominant boxing promoter of the 1930s and '40s. Born in New York City in 1880, Jacobs came from a poor family and went to work as a boy, selling newspapers and candy on Coney Island excursion boats. Noticing that ticket purchases for the boats were often confusing to prospective passengers, Jacobs began scalping boat tickets. He then bought concession rights on all the boats docked at the Battery, sold train tickets to recent immigrants, and eventually ran his own ferryboats.

Jacobs then became the premier ticket scalper in New York, buying and selling theater, opera, or sports events tickets. He began backing events himself—any sort of venture he believed would profit in the end—including charity balls, bike races, and circuses.

Jacobs met Rickard at the Gans–Nelson fight in 1904, Rickard's first promotion, and helped Rickard become active in the New York area. Jacobs profited from Rickard's ventures, both from ticket sales and from investing in Rickard's promotions.

After Rickard's death in 1929, Jacobs focussed his money-making talents elsewhere until sportswriters Damon Runyon, Ed Frayne, and Bill Farnsworth of the Hearst newspaper chain arranged for him to stage Hearst's annual Milk Fund boxing benefit at the Bronx Coliseum. In 1933, the three reporters and Jacobs formed the Twentieth Century Sporting Club to promote boxing. Jacobs used the Hippodrome in New York as his primary venue. The Club's initial bout was staged in January 1934 between Barney Ross and Billy Petrolle.

In 1935, Jacobs signed the young heavyweight Joe Louis to an exclusive contract. Louis's first bout in Yankee Stadium grossed $328,655, while his fight with Max Baer grossed over $1 million. Jacobs's link to Louis, the biggest attraction in boxing, solidified his position as a top promoter. This was borne out when he staged the Tournament of Champions on September 23, 1937 in Yankee Stadium in which four world championship bouts were fought. Following on this success, Madison Square Garden leased the arena and the outdoor Madison Square Garden Bowl to the Twentieth Century Sporting Club.

Jacobs now had complete control of boxing in New York. In 1938, his relationship with the Garden changed from tenant-landlord to a partnership. At about that time, Jacobs became the sole shareholder of the Twentieth Century Sporting Club, paying off Runyon and forcing the other two partners out. Through the rest of the 1930s and into the postwar period, Jacobs was unmatched as a promoter, reaching his peak with the second Louis–Billy Conn fight, which brought in almost two million dollars. Every fight that Louis fought as a champion was promoted by Jacobs. In his heyday, the stretch on Manhattan's 49th Street between Broadway and Eighth Avenue was known as "Jacob's Beach."

Jacobs suffered a cerebral hemorrhage in 1946 but remained in charge of the organization with his relative Sol Strauss operating the club on a day-to-day basis. When Louis decided to retire and then go into business with the group that became the International Boxing Club, the Twentieth Century Sporting Club ceased to function. Jacobs remained in ill health and died in January 1953. Hall of Fame Induction: 1990.

JAMES J. JOHNSTON
Promoter and Manager

Known as the "Boy Bandit," James J. Johnston was a top manager and promoter for many years, as well as one of the more colorful figures in boxing history. Born in Liverpool, England, on November 28, 1875, Johnston was twelve when his parents moved to Hell's Kitchen in New York City. Although his parents were Irish, his English accent led him into many fights in that Irish neighborhood. Johnston quit school at thirteen and went to work with his father at an iron foundry.

Johnston toyed with professional boxing, but had limited success and moved on to helping Billy Newman operate fight clubs in New York. When Charles Harvey, a fight manager specializing in importing fighters from England, asked Johnston to become his assistant, he gladly accepted. Together, Harvey and Johnston brought over noteworthy fighters like Hall of Famers Owen Moran, Jim Driscoll, and Ted ("Kid") Lewis. Harvey's stable grew so large, he had trouble getting matches for all his fighters, so Johnston devised a plan whereby each fighter was paired with a promoter in need of a card. This arrangement worked well until the fighters began to make side deals among themselves that resulted in less than scintillating bouts.

While still working for Harvey, Johnston promoted fights at St. Nicholas Rink, later St. Nicholas Arena, in the years before WWI. He frequently used Harvey's fighters, which led other managers to complain of favoritism, but Johnston was more concerned with ticket sales than fairness. He staged midget boxing matches and brought in a suffragette speaker, which was sure to draw hecklers. Johnston's other stunts included having a white man with yellow face paint masquerade as a Chinese champion, and another man pose as a gypsy fighter. These tactics seem tawdry today, but Johnston won great acclaim in boxing circles of the time.

After his success at St. Nicholas Rink, Johnston was invited to promote at Madison Square Garden in 1914, and for brief periods before and after World War I, he promoted at both the Rink and the Garden. Although he no longer was associated with Harvey, he continued to manage some fighters, including George Rodel—whom he falsely claimed was a veteran of the Boer War—and Lewis. He also continued to use shady tactics in and out of the ring. He planted the idea that Rodel had a weak heart in the mind of Jess Willard, whose last bout had resulted in his opponent's accidental death. Willard's fear of killing Rodel made him lose the newspaper decision.

Johnston became promoter/manager at Tex Rickard's "New" Madison Square Garden from 1933–1937, where he promoted three heavyweight title fights in which the belt changed hands: Primo Carnera–Jack Sharkey, Carnera–Max Baer, and Baer–Jim Braddock. Johnston lost control of the heavyweight division to Mike Jacobs when the latter matched Braddock against Joe Louis in Chicago, and later lost out to Jacobs at the Garden as well.

Still, Johnston continued to manage fighters—he goaded Joe Lewis into a rematch against his charge, Bob Pastor, even after Pastor did little but run from Lewis in their first fight—and spent countless hours during World War II speaking at veteran's hospitals. The Boxing Writers Association of America awarded him the James J. Walker Award for Long and Meritorious Service to Boxing in 1945. He died of heart failure on May 7, 1946, just after attending a fight at St. Nicholas Arena. Marcus Griffin authored a fine early biography of Johnston in 1933—Damon Runyon contributed a foreword to—*Wise Guy. James J. Johnston—A Rhapsody in Fistics*. Hall of Fame Induction: 1999.

JACK KEARNS
Manager

Best known as heavyweight champion Jack Dempsey's manager, Jack ("Doc") Kearns spent over 60 years in boxing. Kearns and Dempsey, both rough-and-tumble characters with a great zest for life, were partners for six years.

Born in 1882, Kearns grew up in the state of Washington. When he was fourteen, he joined the Alaska Yukon gold rush by stowing away on a freighter. The young Kearns did not strike it rich and, on returning home, worked as a ranch hand. He also accepted pay in return for helping to smuggle Chinese immigrants into the United States. He gravitated toward boxing and, in 1900, first fought professionally in Billings, Montana. Kearns later claimed to have had over 60 professional bouts.

Kearns spent a year in prison for fighting in a street brawl. He operated a bar and a boxing club in Spokane. But San Francisco, then the boxing center of the nation, was the place to be, and Kearns eventually found his way there. He thrived in the active boxing world and quickly started managing and promoting fights. Harry Wills was prominent among the boxers he managed.

In 1917, Kearns and Dempsey met. Though Kearns claimed Dempsey came to his aid in a bar fight, others said that Kearns had seen him fight in New York and was impressed with his crude power. Kearns guided Dempsey to the championship in 1919 with a victory over Jess Willard. He was a master of publicity and was largely responsible for making possible the first million-dollar gate in boxing history when Dempsey fought Georges Carpentier. Kearns' managerial acumen also allowed Dempsey to receive $300,000 for a fight in Shelby, Montana which virtually bankrupted the town.

Dempsey split with Kearns after the Dempsey–Firpo fight in 1923. Dempsey and his new wife, actress Estelle Taylor, believed that Kearns had been mishandling the fighter's funds. The parting was acrimonious and involved multiple lawsuits.

Although Kearns's greatest success was with Dempsey, he remained active as a fight manager until his death on July 17, 1963. Among the other fighters he managed were Hall of Famers Joey Maxim, Archie Moore, and Mickey Walker. He spent five years in the employ of the International Boxing Club, setting matches. When asked to testify before the Kefauver committee, Kearns positively impressed the panel of senators and did not prove to be directly linked to the organized crime figures who heavily influenced the International Boxing Club. Kearns has also been credited with staging the first fight in Las Vegas—a 1955 bout between Moore and Nino Valdes. Hall of Fame Induction: 1990.

DON KING
Promoter

Don King has been involved in every aspect of promotion, from setting up world championship bouts in far-flung locales to selling broadcast rights to major television networks and pay-per-view channels. With persistence and energy, King has taken an innovative approach to boxing promotion for 25 years. His name is inextricably linked to a long list of multi-million dollar purses and gates.

King grew up in Cleveland, where as a young man he became involved in running gambling operations. At age 23 and again twelve years later, King was involved in homicides connected to the gambling business. He was convicted in the second incident and served more than four years in prison, where he read voraciously, devouring the classics and works of philosophy. For a time, King also owned a nightclub in Cleveland called the New Corner Tavern, where such musicians as Erroll Garner, B.B. King, and Lloyd Price performed.

King first became involved in boxing promotion in 1972 when, with Don Elbaum, he organized a boxing benefit for the black-owned Forest City Hospital in Cleveland. King got Muhammad Ali to box ten exhibition rounds with an assortment of fighters and Cleveland radio personalities. The evening's festivities, which also included a concert featuring Marvin Gaye, Lou Rawls, and Wilson Pickett, brought in $81,000.

King went on to promote several fighters, including heavyweight Earnie Shavers. His first widespread public acclaim came with the "Rumble in the Jungle" heavyweight championship fight matching George Foreman and Muhammad Ali in Kinshasa, Zaire on October 30, 1974. The fight was the first to offer a $10 million purse—guaranteed by the Zairian government!

Working independently, King then promoted Ali's championship defense against Chuck Wepner, in Cleveland. With Bob Arum, King promoted Ali's third fight with Joe Frazier, "The Thrilla in Manila," on October 1, 1975. He then went on to assemble a series of big-name fights, including many featuring Larry Holmes. "The Last Hurrah," Ali's failed 1980 comeback attempt against Holmes in Las Vegas, was a King production that brought in the first $6 million live gate. Other notable King promotions include Leonard–Duran I (co-promoted with Bob Arum), in which Leonard was the first fighter ever guaranteed a $10 million purse, and the "Grand Slam of Boxing," featuring four world championship fights headlined by Julio Cesar Chavez. The latter show drew a paid attendance of 132,274 to Mexico City's Estadio Azteca.

King has promoted a total of over 500 championship fights, with as many as six on one card. He has owned and operated his own cable and pay-per-view television networks and was involved in promoting singer Michael Jackson's smash-hit "Victory Tour." He promoted Mike Tyson's first comeback fight, on August 19, 1995, which generated over $90 million worldwide and set a U.S. pay-per-view record. King's November 1996 show pitting Tyson against Evander Holyfield brought in $14 million—the highest-ever revenues from a live gate. Tyson-Holyfield II topped the previous pay-per-view record with approximately 1.9 million buys.

A man of apparent contrasts, King has donated millions to charitable organizations while continuing to have brushes with the law. His unparalleled influence over boxing has led to money disputes with some fighters and further appearances in court. Named by *Sports Illustrated* as one of the "most influential sports figures of the past 40 years," King's activities led him to be named "Promoter of the Century" by the WBA and the "Greatest Promoter of All Time" by the IBF and WBC. In 1997, the NAACP awarded King its prestigious President's Award. Only two years before, acclaimed writer Jack Newfield documented King's history in the revealing book: *Only in America: The Life and Crimes of Don King*.

Age 65 at the time of his induction into the Hall of Fame, Don King's strong personality, distinctive "electric" stand-up hair, and flowery speech peppered with the catchphrase "Only in America" have made him a well-known figure throughout the world.

Among King's recent promotional coups was the "2001 Middleweight World Championship Series" which led to the crowning of Bernard Hopkins as the first undisputed middleweight champ since Marvelous Marvin Hagler. Hall of Fame Induction: 1997.

TITO LECTOURE
Promoter

The only South American promoter in the International Boxing Hall of Fame, Juan Carlos ("Tito") Lectoure gained worldwide recognition—in a career spanning 31 years—for both himself and his primary venue, the storied Luna Park in Buenos Aires, Argentina.

Luna Park was opened in 1932 by Lectoure's uncle, the first Argentine lightweight champion Jose Lectoure, and Ismael Pace. The original arena lacked even a roof, but it was remodelled into a fully enclosed stadium seating about 25,000. Inspired by his uncle, Lectoure decided to become a boxer himself, and he sparred with Archie Moore when "The Old Mongoose" was training for a fight at Luna Park.

Though he served in the army and attended college, Lectoure's true calling was boxing, and early on he became involved in the operations of Luna Park. After Pace and Jose Lectoure died within five years of each other in the 1950s, Tito's aunt put the nineteen-year-old Lectoure in charge of the arena. At first he worked under the tutelage of Luna Park's official promoter, Juan Manual Morales, but soon staged his first personally promoted card on September 14, 1956. It was an auspicious date—September 14 is "Boxer Day" to Argentine fight fans, celebrating Luis Firpo's 1923 match against Jack Dempsey.

Lectoure staged an incredible two fights per week at Luna Park, on Wednesdays and Saturdays, for 31 years, a total of 2,976 cards. The Wednesday night fights were a special challenge, since they were televised. In addition to managing all the boxing events at Luna Park, Lectoure was responsible for securing the services of every other show at the arena, including circuses, ice shows, and even the Harlem Globetrotters. He also operated the spacious Luna Park Gymnasium, where one hundred fighters could train at one time.

Lectoure's impact on the world of boxing extended beyond Argentina. In 1966, he staged his first world title bout at Luna Park, pitting WBA flyweight champion Horacio Accavallo against former champ Hiryoki Ebihara in a sold-out fight. He promoted five world title fights at his arena for Niccolino Loche, who was perhaps Lectoure's favorite boxer. By the end of his career, he had sponsored 24 world title fights at Luna Park. Perhaps the highlight of those two dozen bouts was the Carlos Monzon–Emile Griffith middleweight championship match in 1971, which set a South American box office record and was televised in the United States on ABC's *Wide World of Sports*. Twelve Argentine fighters became world champions while working under Lectoure's promotion. In addition, Hall of Famers Archie Moore, Sandy Saddler, Kid Gavilian, Joe Brown, Carlos Ortiz, Ismael Laguna, Eder Jofre, and Antonio Cervantes fought at Luna Park.

Lectoure, a shrewd promoter with a knack for finding matches that were attractive to the paying public, was involved as a promoter or co-promoter in another one hundred world title fights at other venues. Highly respected for his business acumen, boxing knowledge, and character, Lectoure left boxing in 1987. The last bout that he promoted was a welterweight fight between Arce Rossi and Ramón Abeldaño on October 17, 1987. Next Lectoure turned his promotional skills to the arts. Luna Park hosted events with the like of Luciano Pavarotti, the Bolshoi Ballet and a great array of plays and concerts. He died March 1, 2002 in Buenos Aires. Hall of Fame Induction: 2000.

A.J. LIEBLING
Writer

One of boxing's greatest chroniclers, A.J. Liebling wrote about the sport with a brilliance and wit that may never be surpassed. In a series of essays for *The New Yorker*, Liebling interpreted boxing's mayhem and beauty for a wide audience. Liebling spent many an hour at ringside, but his best writing sprang from his connections behind the scenes. He knew the players and could reflect their voices with spellbinding realism. He wrote about boxing with a wry honesty that neither glamorized nor vilified its violence.

Born in New York, Liebling went to Dartmouth College before being expelled for not attending chapel. He then attended and graduated from the Columbia School of Journalism and went to work at *The New York Times*, which fired him for an alleged lack of attention to detail. He then worked for newspapers in Providence, Rhode Island, lived in Paris where he studied medieval history, and worked for five years for *The New York World Telegram.*

In 1935, Liebling began a 28-year association with *The New Yorker*, which lasted until his death in 1963. He wrote on a number of subjects including politics, war, food, horse racing, and the media. His essays on boxing appeared in *The New Yorker* from 1951 until his death and have been collected in two books, *The Sweet Science* and *A Neutral Corner.* Hall of Fame Induction: 1992.

LORD LONSDALE
Patron

As the first president of the National Sporting Club, which governed boxing in England from 1891 to 1929, Hugh Cecil Lowtner, the fifth Earl of Lonsdale, helped establish the club as the major force in English boxing. He donated the original Lonsdale belts presented to English champions.

Lonsdale's great wealth allowed him to live a life of leisure and luxury. He had a genuine love for and knowledge of boxing. He was taught to box by Hall of Famer Jem Mace. In an era when boxing was not considered respectable, Lonsdale was one of the few aristocrats to take an interest in seeing that bouts took place fairly under proper rules. He appeared in court to assist boxers prosecuted for ring fatalities. He also had a role in the development of the original Queensberry Rules and the padded boxing glove. As president of the National Sporting Club, Lonsdale expanded his efforts to legitimize boxing. Starting in 1909 the National Sporting Club began awarding the Lonsdale Belt, named after their patron. It was originally presented to the champion in each British weight division and the holder could keep the belt if it was won and then defended two times. The belt was first won by Freddie Welsh in 1909 for winning the British lightweight title. Heavyweight Henry Cooper was the first person to win three Lonsdale Belts outright. The belt is still won today and awarded by the British Boxing Board of Control although to keep it you must win and defend it three times. Hall of Fame Induction: 1990.

HARRY MARKSON
Publicist and Promoter

Harry Markson was involved in the promotion of boxing matches for 40 years, from the time of Joe Louis to the time of Muhammad Ali. Born in Kingston, New York, Markson graduated from Union College and worked as a sportswriter for the *Bronx Home News*. In 1933, he became a part-time publicity man for Madison Square Garden. Four years later, he became publicity director for promoter Mike Jacobs and his 20th Century Sporting Club. At that time, Jacobs was the premier promoter in boxing, handling Joe Louis's fights and other major New York bouts.

In 1948, Jacobs made Markson managing director of the 20th Century Sporting Club. When the International Boxing Club (IBC), controlled by James Norris, replaced Jacobs and 20th Century as the promotional entity at Madison Square Garden, Markson took a top position with the IBC. An anti-trust ruling eventually forced Norris to untangle himself from a web of interlocking entities, and Markson became the top executive in charge of boxing for the Madison Square Garden Corporation. In 1968, he became president of Madison Square Garden Boxing, Inc. He held that position until 1973, when he retired to a consulting position.

Although Norris and his organization were associated with organized crime figures, Markson managed to avoid their influence. He helped schedule the two championship fights which opened the new Madison Square Garden: Joe Frazier–Buster Mathis and Emile Griffith–Nino Benvenuti. He also played a key role in the staging of Ali–Frazier I at Madison Square Garden in 1971. In 1963, Markson received the James J. Walker Award of the Boxing Writers Association for long and meritorious service to the sport. A lover of classical music, Markson brought an air of refinement to an often crude game. Markson died November 10, 1998 at the age of 92. Hall of Fame Induction: 1992.

ARTHUR MERCANTE
Referee

Arthur Mercante refereed 145 world championship fights in a career that started in 1954. Born in Brockton, Massachusetts in 1920, Mercante has lived in New York state since he was eight. He boxed as an amateur and made the Golden Gloves finals in 1938. He attended New York University and was a member of the varsity football and swimming teams. After graduating in 1942, Mercante served four years in the navy under Gene Tunney as a recruit training and physical rehabilitation specialist. One of Mercante's duties was to referee in service bouts.

After World War II, Mercante coached and officiated boxing at the amateur level. In 1954, he became licensed as a professional referee. His first world title fight was the second Johansson–Patterson heavyweight title bout on June 20, 1960. Other notable matches he has handled include Paret–Thompson, Ali–Frazier I, Frazier–Foreman I, and Ali–Norton III.

Mercante showed his toughness in the ring when he officiated the Ernie Terrell–Bob Foster fight in 1964. During the fight, Foster slugged him with a punch intended for Terrell. Mercante shook off the blow and continued in the ring until he stopped the fight to protect the battered Foster. Foster was upset that the fight was stopped, but his manager told him he shouldn't complain since his best shot hadn't even hurt the referee.

Mercante has occasionally served as a color commentator on fights broadcasts and has been paired with such well-known announcers as Chris Schenkel, Al Michaels, and Howard Cosell. Mercante finally retired on September 29, 2001 after refereeing Richardo Lopez's eighth round knockout of Zolani Petelo in their Madison square Garden IBF junior flyweight title bout. For many years Mercante also worked for the Hempstead, New York Department of Parks and Recreation. Mercante's son, Arthur Jr., is also a prominent referee. Hall of Fame Induction: 1995.

DAN MORGAN
Manager

One of the most colorful characters in boxing history, Dan Morgan always had an opinion or an amusing anecdote to offer about any fight or any fighter. Born in New York on July 3, 1873, Morgan began boxing as an amateur at the Chelsea A.C. Gym and turned professional in 1894. After Phil Kelley knocked him out in the fifteenth round of a fight at Brooklyn's Pelican Club, Morgan hung up his gloves and became a manager.

In 1904, Morgan opened what he claimed was the first fight manager's office in New York City, and also served as his own press agent. During a newspaper campaign to drum up interest in one of his fighters, Morgan prepared a 15,000-word publicity brochure. He presented this treatise to Tad Dorgan, well-known writer, humorist, and cartoonist—then sports editor of *The New York Journal*—who, stunned at the length of the article, asked, "Shall I call you 'One-Word Morgan' or simply 'Dumb Dan'?" Morgan replied, "Keep my bum's name in the paper and you can call me anything you want." Dorgan ran the entire brochure in his paper, and even added eight cartoons, and the name "Dumb Dan" stuck with Morgan—the price of his publicity success.

Among the hundreds of fighters managed by Morgan were world middleweight champion Al McCoy and Hall of Famers Battling Levinsky and Jack Britton. Morgan gave up managing McCoy in disgust after the light-hitting title holder—derisively known as the "Cheese Champion"—ran off a series of loses in non-title, no-decision bouts. Morgan's favorite fighter was Britton; he marveled at the durable welterweight's willingness to test his skills in the ring over three hundred times. Morgan managed fighters until 1925, when the strain led his doctor to recommend retirement.

In retirement, Morgan continued to advise and coach both amateur and professional boxers, including Max Schmeling. Under Morgan's tutelage Schmeling defeated Joe Louis with a knockout in their first meeting. Morgan also claimed to have helped James Braddock defeat Max Baer for the heavyweight championship by placing an attractive blond at ringside and drawing Baer's attention to her, distracting him and allowing Braddock to triumph. He also kept up his work in publicity, helping to win public attention for fights promoted by Mike Jacobs and Jim Norris. Yet Morgan regarded most of the fighters he encountered at this stage of his career as vastly inferior to the previous generation of greats.

Morgan made countless appearances at banquets and dinners and visited veteran's hospitals where he told stories about boxing and even staged boxing shows for the patients. As a result of this charitable work, Morgan received the Boxing Writers Association of America's James J. Walker Award for Long and Meritorious Service to Boxing in 1948. He died on July 7, 1955, at the age of 82. Hall of Fame Induction: 2000.

WILLIAM MULDOON
Trainer and Official

A trainer of championship boxers, William Muldoon was a powerful athlete in his own right, and later became the head of the first modern boxing commission. Born in Belfast, New York in 1845, Muldoon fought for the North in the Civil War. As a youth, he was a wrestler of some renown, and he continued to wrestle in the army. He competed in the "Greco-Roman" wrestling style of the day—which barred holds below the waist. After the war, Muldoon became a bouncer and then a policeman in New York City. Known as "The Solid Man" and "The Iron Duke," he wrestled in both professional and amateur matches, defeating the police department champion as well as English wrestler Edwin Bibby.

Muldoon served six years on the police force, then quit to open a bar which was popular with boxers and wrestlers as well as bankers and financiers. He toured the country with boxing champion John L. Sullivan, and the two posed, wrestled, boxed, and performed feats of strength in exhibitions. He also acted in stage plays including the role of Charles the Wrestler in *As You Like It*.

A great believer in physical fitness, Muldoon opened the Muldoon Hygienic Institute in Purchase, New York. Here, he trained Sullivan for his famous fight with Jake Kilrain, whipping the overweight, out-of-shape Sullivan into fighting trim. Supposedly, Muldoon had to threaten the champ with a baseball bat to get him to follow the training regimen and wrestled Sullivan into submission when he wanted to go out for a drink. Sullivan entered the ring in excellent condition and won the Kilrain fight. Muldoon also trained Kid McCoy and Jack Dempsey, The Nonpareil.

After the Walker Law legalized boxing in New York State in 1920, Muldoon was appointed to chair the New York State Athletic Commission. In this role, Muldoon attempted to bar known gamblers from attending fights, established a no-smoking rule for bouts, and pushed for improved sanitary conditions for boxers. Muldoon was opposed to mixed-race bouts and was voted out of the chairmanship after he refused to approve a fight between heavyweight champion Jack Dempsey and the great black fighter Harry Wills. Nevertheless, Muldoon remained on the commission until 1929.

Muldoon later joined with Gene Tunney to award the Tunney-Muldoon Trophy to world heavyweight champions. He died of cancer in 1933, at the age of 88, having been associated with boxing since its bare knuckle days. Hall of Fame Induction: 1996.

GILBERT ODD
Writer

The premier modern British boxing writer, Gilbert Odd has contributed much to the sport as a reporter, historian, and record keeper. Born in England in 1902, Odd developed a great fascination for boxing as a boy. After a short amateur boxing career, he became a ringside correspondent at the age of eighteen for the British weekly boxing publication, *Boxing*. In 1941, he started a ten-year stint as the editor of *Boxing*, by then called *Boxing News*.

In 1944, Odd joined with G.W. Whiting to publish *The Boxers Annual* , a compendium of both amateur and professional records. Odd also launched another record book, known as *Boxing News Authors' and Record Book*. After leaving his position as editor, Odd continued to write hundreds of articles on boxing and became known as the top boxing historian in England. In addition to the many articles, Odd has written over a dozen books, including *Ali—The Fighting Prophet* (1975), *The Fighting Blacksmith* (1976), *The Encyclopedia of Boxing* (1983), and *Kings of the Ring* (1985).

Odd served as a member of the British Boxing Board of Control from 1961 to 1969, and is a founding member of the Boxing Writers Club. Odd has also broadcast boxing on radio and television, and he is the only journalist to be made an honorary member of the National Sporting Club. Odd died on May 12, 1996. Hall of Fame Induction: 1995.

TOM O'ROURKE
Manager

One of boxing's greatest managers, Tom O'Rourke was at the pinnacle of his success at the end of the nineteenth and the beginning of the twentieth centuries. Born in Boston on May 13, 1856, O'Rourke enjoyed fighting as a youth, but his great talent as an athlete was rowing. Professionally, he turned his attention to boxing, managing his first fighter, Jack Havlin, in a bloody battle against Ike Weir, "The Belfast Spider," on July 20, 1887, a bout that ended in a draw after 61 grueling rounds.

It was not until 1889 that a truly great fighter came under O'Rourke's stewardship—Hall of Famer George Dixon. After seeing Dixon match the much heavier Paddy Kelly in a fifteen-round draw at Boston's Cribb Club, O'Rourke was so impressed that he immediately became Dixon's manager. He took Dixon to England, at a time when Americans fighters did not often campaign overseas. Under his guidance, Dixon became the bantamweight champion in 1891, and then the featherweight titleholder in 1892, when he took part in the three-day Carnival of Champions at New Orleans' Olympia Club. It was a significant match for another reason: Dixon was allowed to take part in a mixed-race bout, a rarity for the South at that time, and a tribute to O'Rourke's managerial skills. Dixon remained the featherweight champ until 1900.

O'Rourke managed another Hall of Famer, the original Joe Walcott, who became welterweight champion under O'Rourke's direction. O'Rourke took Walcott and Dixon on a "meet all comers" tour, bringing along his own ring, slightly smaller than the standard size, thus giving his own fighters an advantage in controlling the bout. The highly regarded Sailor Tom Sharkey fought under O'Rourke's banner when he lost to heavyweight champion Jim Jeffries in 1899.

In addition to managing fighters, O'Rourke operated boxing clubs in New York, including the Lenox Club, the National Sporting Club, and the Broadway. He also ran the Delavan Hotel in the same city. During the nineteen teens O'Rourke managed the career of German-American heavyweight Al Palzer. The big, powerful puncher's career was abruptly ended when he was shot and killed by his father. O'Rourke continued to maintain an active role in boxing through the 20s. In 1923 he helped stage title bouts at the Polo Grounds: Hall of Famers Johnny Kilbane and Johnny Dundee, each against Eugene Criqui for the featherweight belt; and Pancho Villa versus Jimmy Wilde for the flyweight title. O'Rourke was then appointed by the New York State Athletic Commission to the position of boxing judge. He also served as a NYSAC Inspector.

One June 19, 1936, O'Rourke collapsed with a fatal heart attack in Max Schmeling's dressing room at Yankee Stadium, just before Schmeling's first fight against Joe Louis. Active in boxing for almost 50 years, the canny O'Rourke left an indelible mark on the sport's history. Hall of Fame Induction: 1999.

DAN PARKER
Sports Editor and Columnist

Damon Runyon called Dan Parker "the most constantly brilliant of all sports-writers." In his 38 years as a columnist for *The New York Daily Mirror,* and, at the very end of his career, *The New York Journal-American,* Parker was a fre-quent crusader against corruption in boxing, wrestling, and other sports. He is credited with doing the most in print to expose the crooked International Boxing Club (IBC), which in the 1950s had a stranglehold on boxing promo-tion nationwide.

Parker, whose bulk was memorable (he stood 6'4" tall and weighed over 200 pounds), wrote about every sport from baseball to horse racing. He was noted for his humor as well as his compassion for losers or the unlucky, but he was relentless in his exposure of payoffs and fixes. At one time, he discovered that wrestling promoters were printing up cards based on the "winners" of matches that hadn't taken place yet. Parker reported the winners' names in advance of the matches, infuriating the promoters.

Parker showed not only a strong moral sense but great courage in writing about the underworld connections to boxing. His columns helped spark the investigations that re-sulted in the breakup of the IBC and the conviction of mobster Frankie Carbo and others. Apparently impervious to threats, Parker wrote as his conscience directed. "There's always been larceny in boxing," Parker told a *Newsweek* interviewer in 1964, "and when I've seen it, I've written it."

Parker was born in Waterbury, Connecticut in 1893. After graduating from high school, he worked first as a reporter, then city editor and sportswriter at *The Waterbury American.* He joined the staff of the Hearst chain's *Daily Mirror* in 1924 and, within two years, launched his column. He wrote for the *Mirror* until it folded in 1963 and, although the rest of the staff moved on, remained in the paper's defunct newsroom for another year filing columns for the *Journal-American.* He also wrote for *The Ring, The Saturday Evening Post,* and *Sport,* among other publications.

Parker was honored by his peers several times during his career. He won the Headlin-ers' Award for sportswriting in 1949; received the New York Newspaper Guild's Page One award in 1951, 1956, and 1961; and the National Sportscasters and Sportswriters award in 1960. He was inducted into the National Sportscasters and Sportswriters Hall of Fame. In memory of his friend and fellow sportswriter, Parker established the Damon Runyon fund for cancer research. Parker died in 1967. Hall of Fame Induction: 1996.

GEORGE PARNASSUS
Promoter

George Parnassus was one of the top promoters in boxing history. He ex-panded the range of boxing venues and saw the value in promoting fight-ers in the smaller weight classes. Born in Methone, Greece in 1897, Parnas-sus followed his brother to the United States in 1916 and first found work as a waiter and dishwasher. Eventually, he and his brother saved enough money to purchase a restaurant in Phoenix, Arizona. The restaurant happened to be located across the street from a fight gym. Legend has it that the fighters began running up unpaid bills at the restaurant, and Parnassus began man-aging them to settle the debts.

As a manager, Parnassus had great success with Mexican boxers, such as lightweight champ Juan Zurita, Enrique Bolanos, bantamweight champ Raton Macias, and Jose Beccera. In the late 1950s, Parnassus moved from managing to matchmaking and promoting. In 1957 he became the matchmaker for the Olympic Auditorium in Los Angeles. Parnassus's shrewd matchmaking ability helped save the Olympic from financial ruin.

Parnassus excelled in matching fighters in smaller weight classes when his rivals were concentrating on the heavyweights. He promoted a bantamweight title bout between Jose Beccera and Alphonse Halimi and a junior welterweight championship match between Carlos Ortiz and Battling Torres on the same card at the massive Los Angeles Coliseum, which had not previously been used for boxing. The event was a huge success and gave Parnassus a well-deserved reputation as one of the greatest promoters in the world.

In the 1960s, Parnassus staged fights in such diverse locales as Wales, Mexico, Japan, Thailand, Argentina, Italy, and England. During this period, Parnassus helped establish and finance the World Boxing Council (WBC). Starting in 1966, Parnassus staged successful bouts in Jack Kent Cooke's new venue, The Fabulous Forum in Los Angeles. Ruben Olivares and Jose Napoles were his top draws during this period.

Throughout his career, Parnassus always aimed for top quality shows. He declared, "The thing is not to be the richest promoter in the world, but to be the best." His honesty and fairness were highly valued in professional boxing. Parnassus died of a heart attack in 1975. Hall of Fame Induction: 1991.

MARQUESS OF QUEENSBERRY
Patron

Although his association with boxing was rather tangential, John Sholto Douglas, the eighth Marquess of Queensberry, gained lasting fame when he sponsored the rules compiled by his friend John Graham Chambers. Douglas became acquainted with Chambers at Magdalene College at Cambridge and in 1867, he agreed to lend the new rules his name and patronage. The Queensberry Rules, as they came to be known, did much to establish universally recognized standards of fairness by which boxing matches could be conducted. The rules, the basis for the boxing regulations of today, included the establishment of three-minute rounds with one-minute rest periods between rounds. They also ushered out the bare-knuckle era by mandating the use of boxing gloves.

An avid boxing enthusiast, Douglas succeeded to his hereditary title in 1858 and died in 1900. Hall of Fame Induction: 1990.

GEORGE ("TEX") RICKARD
Promoter

George ("Tex") Rickard led boxing into the era of million-dollar gates, huge crowds, and fights at Madison Square Garden. Born in Missouri in 1871, Rickard left school at age nine and, while still a youngster, worked cattle drives from Texas to Montana. At 21, he became a town marshal in Henrietta, Texas. He also tried cattle ranching in Brazil. In 1894, he went to Alaska and discovered gold, although he later remarked that he sold his claim for too low a price. When the Klondike gold rush started, Rickard ran a hotel in Dawson known as the Northern. He made a sizable fortune before going broke in the boom-and-bust economy. He opened another version of the Northern in Nome and stayed in Alaska for the next twelve years.

Rickard followed gold prospectors to Nevada, where he opened another hotel called the Northern, before boxing caught his fancy. Local business leaders wanted to stage a boxing match to publicize the growing community. Rickard had recently attended a boxing match in New York, so he was given the task of making the arrangements. He tried unsuccessfully to sign Terry McGovern and Jimmy Britt—the two fighters he had seen in New York, but then landed Joe Gans and Battling Nelson for $30,000. The gate receipts from the fight, held on Labor Day, 1906, were $69,715, the largest ever for a boxing match.

Although Rickard was no boxing expert, he saw the earning potential of the sport. Backed by Montana mining interests, Rickard outbid James Coffroth among others for the right to promote the James J. Jeffries–Jack Johnson fight. The fight was held in Reno on July 4, 1910. Rickard helped recoup the money paid to the fighters by selling the film rights for $101,000. The fight drew 15,760 fans who paid $270,775 to see the spectacle.

Rickard believed in getting top attractions, publicizing them, and charging high prices for the tickets. When he shifted his base of operations to New York following the passage of the Walker Law which legalized boxing in the state, Rickard made successful overtures to the upper strata of society. He was also skillful in dealing with politicians to facilitate the promotion of his fights.

At the urging of Jack Dempsey's manager, Jack ("Doc") Kearns, Rickard agreed to promote the Jess Willard–Dempsey championship fight in Toledo, Ohio in 1919. Although that match was not one of Rickard's most successful promotions, it set the stage for another Dempsey fight held at Boyle's Thirty Acres near Jersey City on July 2, 1921. Rickard matched heavyweight champion Dempsey with light heavyweight champion Georges Carpentier. Although Dempsey outweighed Carpentier by about twenty pounds, Rickard raised interest in the fight to never-before-seen levels. He played on the fact that Carpentier had been a French war hero in World War I, while Dempsey had avoided military service. Dempsey won the fight easily, but the real story was the gate. More than 80,000 fans paid a record $1,789,238. Five years later in a Rickard promotion, 120,757 paid $1,895,733 to watch Gene Tunney upset Dempsey. The rematch held in Soldier Field in Chicago drew 104,943 with a gate of $2,658,660.

Rickard developed Madison Square Garden into a top boxing venue. With help from Nat Fleischer and others in site selection and financing, Rickard built a new Madison Square Garden at 49th Street and Eighth Avenue, which became known as "The House That Tex Built." The New York Rangers hockey team was named after Rickard as a wordplay on "Texas Rangers." Rickard built another famed sports arena in Boston. Originally dubbed the "Boston Madison Square Garden," the name was shortened to Boston Garden shortly after its November 1928 opening. The facility served as home to the Boston Bruins and Celtics for nearly 70 years.

Rickard also helped Nat Fleischer start *The Ring* magazine and compiled the first annual top-ten-contender ratings for the magazine. At the time of his death on January 6, 1929, Rickard was planning on expanding his base of operations to Florida and England.

Rickard was no saint. He once told Dempsey to carry an opponent for a few rounds and he refused to promote a match between black heavyweight Harry Wills and Dempsey. However, he brought boxing into the modern era with his large-scale promotions. Hall of Fame Induction: 1990.

IRVING RUDD
Publicist

One of the last, great, old-time press agents, Irving Rudd had nothing but disdain for the new-school, public relations flacks, who conducted business from a cushy seat in a fancy restaurant and never saw the inside of a gym. Rudd's boxing career stretched across much of twentieth century boxing. He worked for three of the century's premier promoters: Mike Jacobs, Don King, and Bob Arum, and he worked with champs from Louis to Leonard. Born in Brooklyn on October 13, 1917, Rudd became an enthusiastic sports fan—especially of the Dodgers. In 1933, working as a reporter for his high school newspaper, he interviewed Hall of Famer Max Baer, who was in town to promote his movie, *The Prizefighter and the Lady*. Baer took a liking to Rudd, and invited him to spend a week with him in Baltimore, his next tour stop. The following year, Rudd spent several weekends at Baer's training camp in Asbury Park, New Jersey, and it is Baer whom Rudd credits for getting him into boxing.

After high school, Rudd worked as a bookkeeper at the Fulton Fish Market, but a day's trip to Stillman's Gym proved propitious: Big Al Douglas, owner of the Harlem fight club called the Rockland Palace, offered Rudd work as a press agent for $18 a week. Rudd quickly accepted and thrived in his new position. He worked at several such small boxing venues in the years that followed, including the Eastern Parkway Arena, the Ridgewood Grove Arena, and the Queensboro Arena. He also assisted Hall of Fame promoter Mike ("Uncle Mike") Jacobs.

With smaller fighting clubs quickly losing audiences to the allure of television, Rudd left boxing to work for the Dodgers as promotions director, staying until their 1958 move to Los Angeles. Rudd next went to work for the Yonkers Raceway. His most famous publicity stunt there involved repainting its sign incorrectly to spell "Racewya," drawing much attention. He remained at the track until 1969, when he became the public relations director of New York's Off Track Betting agency.

In 1976, Rudd returned to boxing, drumming up publicity for the Muhammad Ali–Ken Norton championship fight at Yankee Stadium. He then worked for Don King during the time of the scandal-ridden U.S. Boxing Championships. Not long after, he moved to Bob Arum's Top Rank, Inc., where he developed a close friendship with Thomas Hearns. Rudd pulled off an outrageous publicity coup during his promotion of the Hagler–Hearns fight. He succeeded in convincing the IRS that Hagler and Hearns would be ideal spokesmen for a huge public service TV campaign to "file early." For weeks before their scheduled showdown the two combatants appeared on living rooms throughout the country. In his lengthy career, Rudd was involved in over 100 title fights and over 2,000 fights in all. He was awarded the Boxing Writers Association of America's James J. Walker Award for Long and Meritorious Service to Boxing in 1985.

Rudd, also known as "Unswerving Irving" and the "Happy Rabbit" continued with Top Rank, Inc., until his retirement in 1991. Credited with a unique ability to serve both his employer and the press, he was always available for the media, and often gave them great quotes. When someone said to him that broadcaster Howard Cosell was his own worst enemy, Rudd responded, "Not while I'm alive." He recounted his many contacts with the colorful figures of sports in his book—co-written with Stan Fischler—*The Sporting Life: The Duke and Jackie, Pee Wee, Razor, Phil, Ali, Mushky Jackson and Me*. Rudd died on June 2, 2000. Hall of Fame Induction: 1999.

DAMON RUNYON
Writer

Perhaps best known for his depictions of gamblers, bookies, and gangsters—characters who came to be known as "Runyonesque" (the musical *Guys and Dolls* is based on one of his short stories)—Damon Runyon was also a first-rate sportswriter. In his long career, he covered boxing, baseball, and horse racing, along with many other sports, and was involved in boxing as a manager and promoter.

Born Alfred Damon Runyan on October 4, 1884, in Manhattan, Kansas, where his father was the publisher of the *Manhattan Enterprise*, Runyan's name was changed accidently to Runyon when it appeared that way in a byline. After his mother fell sick with consumption, the family moved to Colorado, where she died when Runyon was only seven. His sisters were sent to live with their grandmother, but Runyon remained under the nominal care of his father. While he received very little in the way of parental guidance and was a troublemaker at school, he did develop a strong interest in writing and had a poem published in the Pueblo *Chieftain*. The next year, at twelve years old, he got a job as a reporter at the Pueblo *Evening Express*.

During the Spanish-American War, Runyon served as a bugler, primarily in the Philippines. After leaving the military, he worked for various Colorado newspapers before moving to the *Denver Post* in 1905. Fired the very next year, he moved to another Denver paper, *The Rocky Mountain News*. In addition to his newspaper work, Runyon wrote verses and short stories that appeared in national magazines.

In 1910, Runyon traveled to New York, where he soon found a job as a sportswriter for the *American*, and dropped the "Alfred" from his byline. Runyon covered baseball's New York Giants from 1911 to 1920 and began to know the city and its colorful characters. In covering games, he often wrote about personalities and subjects only tangentially related to the game itself. He did not keep a scorecard, and the paper ran a play-by-play account next to his report. Over time, especially after becoming a columnist, Runyon changed his schedule so that he came home at dawn, slept until noon, worked in the afternoon and early evening, and then went to restaurants and clubs for the rest of the night. In addition to sportswriting, Runyon also reported on courtroom trials and covered the U.S. Army's pursuit of the infamous bandit Pancho Villa in Mexico. He also traveled to Europe during World War I to gather news from the front.

When Jack Dempsey arrived on the New York scene, he looked up Runyon on the advice of a mutual friend. Runyon reported some of his fights, including his triumph over Jess Willard for the heavyweight title. During the course of his career, Runyon covered many fights and he also managed some fighters, though not very successfully. His involvement in setting up matches for Mrs. Hearst's Milk Fund charity boxing benefits in the 20s led him to a partnership with sportswriters Ed Frayne and Bill Farnsworth, and Hall of Fame promoter Mike Jacobs in the Twentieth Century Sporting Club. Jacobs bought out Runyon and took sole control of the promotional enterprise about ten years later.

Besides his newspaper work, Runyon published many short stories, the majority of which dealt with the colorful characters he saw in New York. At least a half dozen of these stories were eventually made into movies, including *Little Miss Marker*, which made a star of Shirley Temple, and *Guys and Dolls*.

In 1938, Runyon developed throat cancer. An operation in 1944 left him unable to speak, and for the remainder of his life, Runyon communicated by writing notes. He died on December 10, 1946. The Damon Runyon Memorial Fund for Cancer Research was established by his close friend, columnist Walter Winchell. Now known as the Damon Runyon Memorial Cancer Foundation, the organization has raised over $135 million to combat the disease.

In addition to the International Boxing Hall of Fame, Runyon is a member of the National Sportscasters and Sportswriters Association Hall of Fame. In 1967, the Baseball Writer's Association of America posthumously awarded him the J.G. Taylor Spink Award, given by the National Baseball Hall of Fame for meritorious contributions to baseball writing. Hall of Fame Induction: 2002.

GEORGE SILER
Referee

A well-known and respected referee in the early days of American boxing, George Siler officiated at a time when the Marquess of Queensberry Rules were first introduced and boxing was evolving from bare knuckle to gloved fisticuffs. Born in 1846, Siler officiated at the James J. Corbett–Bob Fitzsimmons heavyweight championship fight in 1897. Corbett admonished Siler for counting too slowly when he knocked Fitzsimmons down in the sixth round. Later, Siler counted Corbett out after Fitzsimmons floored him.

Siler also refereed such important fights as Fitzsimmons–James J. Jeffries, Fitzsimmons–Peter Maher, and Tom Sharkey–Jeffries. As the third man in the Joe Gans–Battling Nelson bout, Siler gave the fight to Gans after Nelson landed several low blows in the 42nd round. Siler had a reputation for honesty in an era when not all officials shared that virtue. He was also very knowledgeable about the sport and wrote about it as a newspaper correspondent. Siler died in 1908. Hall of Fame Induction: 1995.

SAM SILVERMAN
Promoter

Sam Silverman promoted over 10,000 fights in New England in his 40 years in boxing. He was a colorful figure in the fight game, a rotund man with finely tailored suits, white-on-white shirts, an ever-present cigar, and a new Cadillac every year. He always maintained a good relationship with the press, realizing the role the news media played in helping his promotions.

Silverman was born on December 25, 1909, and attended Boston University as a journalism major. Short of funds, he dropped out of school and turned to boxing. His lack of success in the ring led him to try his hand at managing, then matchmaking, and finally, promoting. Though Silverman's operation was centered in Boston, he staged matches throughout New England. Many of his promotions involved "name" fighters, but Silverman put on financially viable shows in many areas with only local boxers. In the mid-1930s, he promoted shows in an average of eleven different cities per week. In the 60s, Silverman staged weekly shows in Worcester, Lowell, and Framingham, Massachusetts; Bangor, Portland, and Lewiston, Maine; Providence, Rhode Island, and Boston, where he was known as "Subway Sam." Fight fans could take the subway to bouts all over the city, in venues like Boston Garden, the Boston Arena, the Mechanics Building, Fenway Park, the Rollaway Arena in Revere, and even at the elite Harvard Club, where Silverman was quoted as complaining about the vichyssoise served in the Club dining room: "I thought you said this was a class joint. The damn chef gives us cold soup."

Silverman was involved in the promotion of about 25 championship matches, including Sugar Ray Robinson–Paul Pender and Tony DeMarco–Carmen Basilio. Further, Silverman promoted 32 of Rocky Marciano's 49 fights. Though liked by many, he also had his share of enemies. He fought off knife-wielding assailants in London, escaped injury from a bullet through his window, and a dynamite explosion in the basement of his building when he and his family were out. The fearless Silverman took on the powerful and corrupt International Boxing Club, and sued the promotional behemoth for $9,000,000, alleging that it was a monopoly. He ultimately settled for $150,000.

Silverman was so singularly devoted to boxing, that he had only disdain for other sports. He called the Celtics a "bunch of giraffes," the Bruins "foreigners playing a foreign game," and said of the Red Sox, they "put you to sleep." While boxing's fortunes waxed and waned, he remained active as a promoter. Into the 1970s, he staged regular cards in Boston, Portland, and Peabody, Massachusetts. On July 8, 1977, Silverman drove fighter Al Romano home from Geneva, New York, after a small boxing card. After dropping Romano off at his house, Silverman was continuing to his own home when his car went off the road in Cambridge and crashed. Silverman died the next day. Over two decades later, he is still remembered as one of the top regional promoters of the twentieth century, a man who held an unshakable commitment to boxing. Hall of Fame Induction: 2002.

JACK SOLOMONS
Promoter

The foremost promoter in the history of British boxing, Jack Solomons brought top American fighters to England in the post-World War II period, when boxing enthusiasm in that country was at its peak. Solomons spent close to 50 years in the sport, during which he staged 26 title fights.

Born into a family of fish marketers, Solomons's first import to Britain was live carp. He became involved in boxing in the 1930s as the manager of Eric Boone and as operator of the Devonshire Club, a boxing venue for up-and-coming London talent. He also worked as a matchmaker for the leading promoters before venturing into his own shows. His first big promotion was the Bruce Woodcock–Jack London British heavyweight title fight.

In 1946, when he brought American world light heavyweight champion Gus Lesnevich to England to face Freddie Mills, he opened the door to many more transatlantic matches. A connection with Hall of Famer Mike Jacobs, then the preeminent American promoter, helped to provide Solomons with the best American talent. Solomons quickly became the most important man in British boxing. He had the best fighters, and he created an air of theatrical excitement around his fights that greatly advanced the sport's popularity. The Sugar Ray Robinson–Randy Turpin middleweight title fight in 1951 was perhaps Solomons's most memorable production. The program cover for this bout showed not the fighters, but Solomon's bow-tie clad, cigar-chomping countenance.

Competition and the growth of television gradually reduced Solomons's influence, but he continued to stage many important bouts until his death in 1979. He brought Muhammad Ali (then known as Cassius Clay) to England in 1963 to fight Henry Cooper, and he opened the private World Sporting Club and staged many promotions through its auspices. Hall of Fame Induction: 1995.

EMANUEL STEWARD
Trainer and Manager

One of the most successful trainers and managers active in boxing today, Emanuel Steward has turned an obscure Detroit community center into a top training ground for boxers. Under Steward's leadership, the famous Kronk Center Gym continues to produce champion-level fighters.

Steward was born in West Virginia in 1944. His interest in boxing began at age eight, when he was given a pair of Jack Dempsey boxing gloves. He grew up fighting other boys, sometimes in illegal smokers that his father ran to entertain adults. When his parents separated, Steward moved with his mother to Detroit. He continued fighting, both in the streets and in organized competition. At age twelve, he began training at Brewster's Gym, the same gym where Joe Louis got his start. Steward wasn't a hard hitter, but he compiled an amateur record of 94-3 and won a 1963 National Golden Gloves title. Steward then coached amateur boxers for three years while working at a variety of jobs, until he gave up boxing altogether while studying to become an electrician.

In 1969, Steward's father asked him to look after his half-brother, James, who was fifteen. Steward took his brother to a local gym named after a Detroit city councilman, John Kronk, and soon guided James to a Detroit Golden Gloves title. He became a part-time coach at Kronk and, in 1971, seven of his charges won Golden Gloves championships. The next year, although Steward had become a master electrician at Detroit Edison where he supervised 200 employees, he left that career to work full-time in the amateur program at the gym, while holding other part-time jobs.

Steward took his first fighter into the professional ranks when Thomas Hearns debuted in 1977. Steward has since developed such great boxers as Mike McCallum, Dennis Andries, Hilmer Kenty, Jimmy Paul, Duane Thomas, and Michael Moorer.

As a trainer and manager, Steward preaches balance and even weight distribution for his fighters. He believes in varied but strenuous training sessions—often held in hot, humid conditions—and he insists on total control of his fighters leading up to a fight. He oversees his fighters' diets to keep their energy levels high. He gets to know his boxers well and motivates each of them accordingly.

Recently, Steward has trained heavyweight champ Lennox Lewis, Evander Holyfield, Oscar de la Hoya, and Prince Naseem Hamed. On February 1, 2002 he began work as the National Director of Coaching for USA Boxing. USA Boxing is the governing body of Olympic-style boxing in the U.S. Stewart is dedicated to building a winning U.S. team to compete in the 2004 Olympic Games. Hall of Fame Induction: 1996.

LONGEST FIGHT

The longest fight on record was a 110-round marathon between Andy Bowen and Jack Burke held April 6, 1893 in New Orleans. This epic gloved battle lasted seven hours and nineteen minutes. The referee called it no contest when both men were unable to continue.

RINGFACT

SAM TAUB
Broadcaster

Considered the first great boxing broadcaster, Sam Taub was associated with the sport for over 60 years. A longtime sports writer and editor for the *New York Morning Telegraph*, Taub pioneered live blow-by-blow announcing of boxing matches on radio. At the end of his career, Taub estimated that he had seen almost 12,000 fights and had broadcast 7,500.

He started working the "Friday Night Fights" on the NBC Radio Network in 1924, first with Angelo Palange and later with broadcasting legend Bill Stein. Taub's voice became well known in broadcasts from many New York City boxing venues, including Madison Square Garden. At the height of his activity, Taub broadcast six boxing or wrestling shows a week. He was replaced at NBC by Don Dunphy in 1941. The last fight Taub called was the second Rocky Graziano–Tony Zale fight in 1947.

Taub also hosted "The Hour of Champions" on New York radio station WHN. The show aired for 24 years, and featured interviews with sports personalities. Taub also wrote for *The Ring* from the magazine's earliest days, and for decades, until his death in 1979 he contributed a column called "Up and Down Old Broadway."

In 1958, the Boxing Writers Association awarded Taub the James J. Walker Award for long and meritorious service to boxing. In 1978, the same group created "The Sam Taub Award" for excellence in broadcast boxing journalism. Taub was the first recipient. Hall of Fame Induction: 1994.

HERMAN TAYLOR
Promoter

Herman ("Muggsy") Taylor, born in Philadelphia on May 1, 1887, was one of the top promoters in boxing history. As a young man Taylor got a job with promoter Jack McGuigan, distributing placards about upcoming fights, setting up the ring and seating, selling concessions, even sweeping floors. The experience affected him for the rest of his life.

Taylor actually fought twice as a flyweight and retired 2-0, but his boxing future was on the business side of the sport. In 1912, he purchased the Broadway Athletic Club and, in 1916, he formed a partnership with Bobby Gunnis. The pair, dubbed the "Boy Promoters," were the first to bring fights to Philadelphia's major stadiums. (Years later Taylor promoted the first fight at the Spectrum when, in 1967, Joe Frazier knocked out Tony Doyle in two rounds.)

In 1926, Taylor and Gunnis did much of the behind-the-scenes work for Tex Rickard's first Jack Dempsey-Gene Tunney heavyweight championship match, a fight which 120,757 fans paid $1,895,733 to see. The final Taylor-Gunnis promotion took place in 1936 when Joe Louis knocked out Philadelphian Al Ettore in five rounds before 55,000 people at Municipal Stadium. Gunnis suffered a heart attack and died a week before the fight.

On his own, Taylor continued to stage entertaining and profitable fights. He co-promoted the Joe Louis-Tony Galento heavyweight championship match, Sugar Ray Robinson bouts, Louis-Gus Dorazio, and the Ike Williams-Bob Montgomery battles.

In 1952, Taylor staged three championship fights in Philadelphia. In the first on June 5, Jersey Joe Walcott defeated Ezzard Charles in a heavyweight championship match. On July 7, Kid Gavilan knocked out Gil Turner to retain the welterweight crown, and on September 23, 1952, Rocky Marciano won the heavyweight championship by knocking out Walcott in the thirteenth.

Taylor lost his license for a time in the early sixties amid hints that a match on one of his cards was fixed. He rebounded, however, to stage the Harold Johnson-Doug Jones light heavyweight title fight in 1962 and continued to promote fights through 1975. Even at the time of his death on June 27, 1980, it was said the ninety-three-year-old promoter was still looking to promote another fight. Hall of Fame Induction: 1998.

JAMES J. WALKER
Politician

James J. ("Jimmy") Walker, the famous New York City mayor of the Roaring Twenties, was a career politician who made an invaluable contribution to the development of boxing. In his days as minority leader of the New York State Senate, he sponsored the Walker Law, which legalized boxing in the state and provided a model for its regulation by state athletic commissions.

Walker was a native New Yorker, born in 1881. He trained as a lawyer and was elected to the state Assembly in 1909. In 1915, he was elected to the state Senate, eventually becoming minority leader in 1921. He introduced the bill that would legalize boxing in 1920. In 1925, Walker was elected mayor of New York. He was a popular leader even though he had come to symbolize the free-wheeling life of speakeasies and Tammany Hall improprieties. Shortly after his reelection in 1929, rumors of corruption surfaced, and Walker was investigated by a committee of the state legislature. Evidence of graft was uncovered and, in 1932, Governor Franklin D. Roosevelt summoned Walker to Albany to explain his actions. Shortly thereafter, Walker resigned as mayor.

Walker had a great fondness for boxing and was often seen at ringside at major New York fights. He was a regularly featured speaker at the Boxing Writers Association annual dinners and, in 1940, received that organization's award for long and meritorious service to boxing. The award was renamed the James J. Walker Memorial Award after Walker's death in 1946. The writers group had earlier honored Walker with its Edward J. Neil Memorial Award for outstanding contributions to boxing.

Walker's life story was made into a movie starring former professional boxer and legendary comedian, Bob Hope. Hall of Fame Induction: 1992.

DEBUT WAS TITLE FIGHT

Jack Skelly, a Brooklyn friend of Hall of Famers "The Nonpareil" Jack Dempsey and Jack McAuliffe was also a fine boxer. He is unique in fistic history because his first professional fight, on September 6, 1892, was a featherweight title match against reigning world champion George Dixon.

RINGFACT

Heavyweight Ch
Sonny Liston

HEROES AND HISTORY

The International Boxing Hall of Fame

ALI WAS THERE. He took an early morning jog through the streets of the village. Archie Moore, Jersey Joe Walcott, Carmen Basilio, Jake LaMotta, Sandy Saddler, Jose Napoles, Emile Griffith, Bob Foster, Billy Conn, Kid Gavilan, Ike Williams, and Willie Pep—they were all there, too.

The occasion that brought these boxing greats—and the memories of so many others—together was the first induction weekend, June 8, 9 and 10, 1990 at the International Boxing Hall of Fame in Canastota, New York. Forty-six boxers, from the earliest bare knuckle brawlers to modern heroes like Muhammad Ali and Joe Frazier, were chosen by a panel of over 100 boxing writers and historians to become the first members of the Hall of Fame. In addition, seven men who contributed outside the ring to boxing's growth through the years were also honored. The inimitable promoter Tex Rickard, Nat Fleischer of The Ring magazine, and manager of champions, Jack Kearns, topped this list.

On the second weekend of each successive June, more inductees have been installed, increasing the membership in the Hall to over 150.

Boxing Arrives by Canal Boat

Canastota has a rich boxing heritage which makes it an ideal home for the International Boxing Hall of Fame. This small central New York town (population: 5,000) is located about twenty miles east of Syracuse on the New York State Thruway. It was once a thriving stop on the Erie Canal, which linked it to New York City and Buffalo. When the canal builders and barge crews brought bare knuckle fighting and boxing news to the town, the locals took up the sport enthusiastically. In 1895, the first projection of a motion picture film, with a device known as the Biograph, took place in Canastota. Appropriately, the film showed boxers sparring.

In the twentieth century, boxing gyms and clubs flourished in Canastota, and an active amateur program continues there today. For many years, the American Legion sponsored amateur boxing teams, and high schools in the Canastota area competed in boxing until the late 1940s. In addition to its own boxing tradition, Canastota is close to Syracuse, a major boxing venue for many years. More recently, the nearly Turning Stone Casino, owned by the Oneida Indian Nation, has begun hosting high profile, nationally televised professional boxing matches. Their handsome facility hosted the much hyped bout between the daughters of Muhammad Ali and Joe Frazier. A boxing program at Turning Stone has become a regular Friday night feature of the annual Induction Weekend.

A Town's Determination

Canastota is most proud, however, of the two champions its boxing environment eventually produced: native sons Carmen Basilio, welter- and middleweight champion in the late 1950s, and Basilio's nephew Billy Backus, welterweight champ in 1970 and '71.

In August 1982, two American Legionnaires and

longtime Canastota residents, Joe Bonaventura and Farrell Miller, were particularly struck by an article written by Mike Milmoe, editor of the *Canastota Bee-Journal*, on the 25th anniversary of Basilio's victory over Sugar Ray Robinson for the middleweight title. Something ought to be done, thought Bonaventura and Miller, to commemorate the accomplishments of the boy who once worked in the onion fields just outside of town and grew up to become a world champion. That the Canastota area had also produced another champion in Backus, as well as strong welterweight contender Dickie DiVeronica, ranked eighth-best in his weight division in the early 1960s, redoubled the sense that the town had something to crow about.

A movement was started to raise $30,000 in donations from local businesses to construct a showcase featuring memorabilia from the careers of Basilio and Backus. The showcase, a brick structure with tall picture windows and overhanging roof, was built directly across the street from the future site of the Hall of Fame. It was dedicated in August, 1984.

This success gave impetus to the group that had already established itself as the Boxing Hall of Fame, Inc. to plan and build a shrine for the sport and its stars from around the world. *The Ring* had at one time inducted members into a Hall of Fame

The bronze statue of Carmen Basilio (left) is one of three life-size boxer sculptures on display at the Hall of Fame. Basilio was the proud recipient of this commemorative championship belt (above), presented by The Ring magazine.

located in its offices. However, that hall never established an existence independent of the magazine and did not survive changes in the publication's ownership and offices.

Many Canastota residents put their energies behind the effort to establish a new Hall of Fame, and local boxing enthusiast Edward Brophy became the Hall's executive director. The Hall's founders secured two state grants for $50,000 for a feasibility study and other preliminary work. Twenty-five area residents pledged $1,000 each, and the village and township councils approved small annual appropriations. A location near the Thruway, and agreements from collectors to donate boxing

The huge fist of Ken Norton dominates this display of plaster fist casts from the Hall of Fame's unique collection. Emile Griffith's, Joey Giardello's, and Ruben Olivares's fists are displayed in the foreground.

memorabilia to the museum were lined up, and four years later, the 2,000 square-foot facility opened its doors to the public. The Hall has seen two major expansions since its opening, and further plans, including a new library facility, are in the works. The village continues to actively support the Hall, and many residents have contributed a decade or more of service. Don Ackerman, has served as the Board of Director's second president for the past sixteen years. Charter board members Mike Milmoe, Don Cerio, and Paul Basilio (Carmen's brother) each has served eighteen years. The efforts of many townsfolk have been instrumental in the Hall's success.

INSIDE THE HALL

Once you walk through the doors of the International Boxing Hall of Fame, as the authors of *The Volvo Guide to Halls of Fame* found, "you are immediately thrown into the colorful and unforgiving world of flesh and flash." Exhibits include the "Wall of Fame," where each inductee is represented with a plaque including a photo and brief biography, and boxing fans will glory in the Hall's collection of ring accoutrements. Championship belts, plaster casts of famous fists, and the robes, trunks, and gloves of storied fighters are prominently displayed. The mystique of Joe Louis's trademark purple trunks or the gloves Rocky Marciano wore when he fought Jersey Joe Walcott is inescapable.

The Hall owes its unique collection of fist casts to Dr. Walter H. Jacobs, a dentist who applied his knowledge of plaster casting to making lifelike models of the hands of the great ring heroes of his day. Jacobs created exact likenesses of fists belonging to champions Jack Dempsey, Jack Johnson, Benny Leonard, and many others. The mammoth fist of former heavyweight champion Primo Carnera dwarfs all the other fists on display. The collection grows each year as living honorees join in fist-casting on the induction weekends.

Other displays in the Hall include tickets and programs from famous fights, and historic copies of *The Ring*. In addition, a collection of equipment Harold Johnson used in training shows the different gloves and protective devices used in preparing for a fight. An exhibit of the tools used by cut men gives the boxing fan a rare opportunity to see firsthand what a cornerman uses to control cuts. In addition to these and other exhibits videotapes of great fights and fighters are shown on monitors located throughout the museum.

The Hall of Fame also boasts an extensive boxing library, available for use by the general public by appointment. The library's holdings include annual editions of the Ring Record Book, biographies and autobiographies of boxing figures, and many other books dealing with the sport. Of special interest to the boxing enthusiast is the collection of boxing magazines and programs, most notably the complete bound volumes of *The Ring*. The museum also has a gift shop, replete with boxing collectibles.

THE VOTE

Members of the Hall of Fame fall into five categories: Modern, Old-Timer, Pioneer, Non-Participant and Observer, and are chosen by a vote of 150 boxing experts, historians, and writers. (The *Boxing Register* groups the last two categories as Non-combatants.) The voters hail from all parts of the globe, including Australia, South Africa, Italy and other parts of Europe, Canada, Argentina, Japan, and the United States. In order to be placed on the ballot, individuals must first clear a pre-screening committee of boxing historians. Modern fighters are additionally required to have been retired for five years. Non-participants can

Tickets, posters, and programs of historic fights are on display.

Each June, the Hall of Fame Induction Weekend brings together an amazing cast of boxing immortals. This photo shows part of the inaugural class of inductees from 1990. Front row: Sandy Saddler, Ike Williams, Kid Gavilan, Willie Pep, Jake LaMotta, Carmen Basilio. Back row: Billy Conn, Jose Napoles, Jersey Joe Walcott, Muhammad Ali, Emile Griffith, Bob Foster, Archie Moore.

be elected to the Hall of Fame even if they are still active, assuming they have achieved enough in their careers to merit selection.

The current ballots contain 45 modern-day fighters and from fifteen to forty names in the other categories. The board of directors of the Hall of Fame determines how many people are to be inducted each year. At present, approximately four Moderns, four Old-Timers, three Non-Participants, and one Pioneer are to be elected each year. The candidates who accrue the most votes are those who become inductees. Ballots are mailed out on November 1 each year with the announcement of the new class of inductees coming in mid-January.

THE FESTIVITIES

The high point of the year at the International Boxing Hall of Fame is the Hall of Fame Weekend in June, when new members are inducted. Famous boxers, past and present, pour into town. The atmosphere is casual, and members of the public are

quite likely to be able to talk with and get autographs from some of the sport's heroes.

Besides the induction ceremony itself, the weekend features many other boxing-related activities, such as live boxing, a golf tournament where fans can play golf with the boxing greats, a cocktail party, a banquet, and a parade of champions through the town. In addition, the public can attend ringside lectures given by fighters and other prominent figures in the sport. For those interested in boxing memorabilia, a large boxing collectibles show is held in the Canastota High School gym.

As an added attraction, a celebrity serves as Grand Marshal of the parade. Female boxing champion Christy Martin and celebrities from the entertainment world such as Mr. T, John Amos, Sherman Hemsley, Danny Aiello, Bo Derek, Al Lewis, and Tony Sirico have each taken a turn.

That the Hall of Fame Weekend is so well run and that the events come off without a hitch is a tribute to Executive Director Brophy, his staff, and his army of volunteers. Forty committee chairpersons begin planning the June event the previous November. In the last month before the event, they are helped by about 150 local volunteers and 100 organizations which help with the various events. The Hall of Fame Weekend is well publicized and draws thousands of boxing fans to Canastota each year.

Though it is still relatively new, the International Boxing Hall of Fame is rapidly living up to its nickname: "The Showplace of Boxing."

SELECT BIBLIOGRAPHY

BOOKS

Anderson, Dave. *In the Corner: Boxing's Greatest Trainers Talk about Their Art.* New York: William Morrow & Company, 1991.

Andre, Sam, and Nat Fleischer. *A Pictorial History of Boxing: From the Bare-Knuckle Days to the Present.* New York: Carol Publishing Group, 1989.

Armstrong, Henry. *Gloves, Glory and God: An Autobiography.* 1957.

Arnold, Peter. *All Time Greats of Boxing.* Edison, NJ: Book Sales, 1993.

Ashe, Arthur R., Jr. *A Hard Road to Glory: A History of the African-American Athlete.* 4 vols. New York: Amistad Press, 1988.

Astor, Gerald. " . . . and a credit to his race": The Hard Life and Times of Joseph Louis Barrow, a. k. a. Joe Louis.* New York: Saturday Review Press, 1974.

Baker, Mark Allen. *Complete Guide to Boxing Collectibles.* Iola, WI: Krause Publications, 1995.

Bordman, Gerald Martin. *The Oxford Companion to American Theatre.* Oxford: Oxford U. Press, 1992.

Brenner, Teddy, and Barney Nagler. *Only the Ring was Square.* Englewood Cliffs, N.J.: Prentice-Hall, 1981.

Breslin, Jimmy. *Damon Runyon: A Life.* New York: Ticknor & Fields, 1991.

Bromberg, Lester. *Boxing's Unforgettable Fights.* Ronald Press, 1962.

Cannon, Jack and Tom Cannon. *Nobody Asked Me, But... (The World of Jimmy Cannon).* New York: Holt, Rinehart, and Winston, 1978.

Cantwell, Robert. *The Real McCoy: The Life and Times of Norman Selby.* Princeton, N.J.: Auerbach Publishers, 1971.

Castleman, H., and W. J. Podrazik. *Watching TV: Four Decades of American Television.* New York: McGraw-Hill, 1982

Clark, Tom. *The World of Damon Runyon.* New York: Harper & Row, 1978.

Collins, Nigel. *Boxing Babylon: Behind the Shadowy World of the Prize Ring.* New York: Carol Publishing Group, 1990.

Corbett, Jim. *My Life and Fights.* John Ousely, 1910.

Cornell, Phil. *Drawing a Crowd: Bill Gallo's Greatest Sports Moments.* New York: Jonathan David, 2000.

Cosell, Howard. *Cosell.* Chicago: Playboy Press, 1973.

Cosell, Howard. *I Never Played the Game.* New York: William Morrow & Company, 1985.

Cramer, Richard Ben. *Joe DiMaggio: The Hero's Life.* New York: Simon & Schuster, 2000

De Cristofaro, S. *Boxing's Greatest Middleweights.* Rochester, N.Y. (26 Everett Dr., Rochester 14624): S. De Cristofaro, 1982.

Deghy, Guy. *Noble and Manly: The History of the National Sporting Club.* London: Hutchinson, 1956

Dempsey, Jack, and Barbara P. Dempsey. *Dempsey.* New York: HarperCollins, 1977.

Dibble, Roy F. *John L. Sullivan; an Intimate Narrative.* Boston: Little, Brown, and Company, 1925.

Dickson, Paul, and Robert Skole. *The Volvo Guide to Halls of Fame: The Traveler's Handbook of North America's Most Inspiring and Entertaining Attractions.* Washington, DC: Living Planet Press, 1995.

Donovan, Arthur J. Jr. *Fatso: Football When Men Were Really Men.* New York: William Morrow & Company, 1988.

Dundee, Angelo, and Mike Winters. *I Only Talk Winning.* Chicago: Contemporary Books, 1985.

Durant, John. *The Heavyweight Champions.* London: Arco Publications, 1961.

Fleischer, Nat. *Black Dynamite.* 5 vols. New York: Ring Athletic Library, 1938–47.

Fleischer, Nat. *50 Years at Ringside.* New York: Greenwood Press, 1969.

Fleischer, Nat. *Jack Dempsey.* New Rochelle, N.Y.: Arlington House,1972.

Fleischer, Nat. *The Heavyweight Championship: An Informal History of Heavyweight Boxing from 1719 to the Present Day.* London: Putnam, 1949.

Fleischer, Nat. *The Michigan Assassin: The Saga of Stanley Ketchel.* New York: Ring Book Shop, 1946.

Fleischer, Nat, Bert Sugar, and Herbert G. Goldman et. al., eds. *The Ring Record Book & Boxing Encyclopedia.* 46 vols. 1941–1967. New York: Ring Book Shop and others.

Fried, Ronald K. *Corner Men: Great Boxing Trainers.* New York: Four Walls Eight Windows, 1991.

Fullerton, Hugh. *Two Fisted Jeff.* Consolidated Book Publishers, 1929.

Gallico, Paul. *Farewell to Sport.* New York: A.A. Knopf, 1938.

Gipe, George. *The Great American Sports Book.* New York: Doubleday & Company, 1978.

Goldstein, Ruby and Frank Graham. *Third Man in the Ring.* Westport, CT: Greenwood Publishing Group, 1986.

Golesworthy, Maurice. *Encyclopaedia of Boxing.* London: Robert Hale, 1988.

Gorn, Elliot J. *Manly Art: Bare-Knuckle Prize Fighting in America.* Ithaca, NY: Cornell University Press, 1986.

Graziano, Rocky, and Rowland Barber. *Somebody Up There Likes Me: The Story of My Life Until Today.* New York, Simon and Schuster, 1955.

Hassan, John. *1998 ESPN Information Please Sports Almanac.* New York: Warner Books, 1997.

Harding, John. *Lonsdale's Belt: The Story of Boxing's Greatest Prize.* London: Robson Books, 1994.

Hauser, Thomas. *Muhammad Ali: His Life & Times.* New York: Simon & Schuster, 1991.

Heller, Peter. *In This Corner!* New York: Simon & Schuster, 1973.

Isenberg, Michael. *John L. Sullivan and His America.* Urbana, Illinois: U. of Illinois Press, 1994.

Johnston, Alexander. *Ten—and Out! The Complete Story of the Prize Ring in America.* New York: I. Washburn, 1927.

Kearns, Jack, and Oscar Fraley. *The Million Dollar Gate.* New York: Macmillan, 1966.

Lardner, Rex. *The Legendary Champions.* New York: American Heritage Press, 1972.

Liebling, A. J. *A Neutral Corner: Boxing Essays.* New York: Simon & Schuster, 1992.

Liebling, A. J. *The Sweet Science.* Westport, CT: Greenwood Publishing Group, 1973.

Louis, Joe, Edna Rust, and Art Rust, Jr. *Joe Louis: My Life.* New York: Harcourt Brace Jovanovich, 1978.

McCallum, John. *Encyclopedia of World Boxing Champions.* Radnor, PA: Chilton Book Company, 1975.

McCallum, John. *The World Heavyweight Boxing Championship.* Radnor, PA: Chilton, 1974

McIlvanney, Hugh. *McIlvanney On Boxing: An Anthology.* London: Mainstream Publishing, 1996.

McNeil, Alex. *Total Television.* New York: Viking Penguin, 1980.

Mead, Chris. *Champion: Joe Louis, Black Hero in White America.* New York: Scribner, 1985.

Menke, Frank G. *The Encyclopedia of Sports.* 6th ed. New York: A. S. Barnes, 1978.

Miles, Henry Downes. *Pugilistica: The History of British Boxing.* 3 vols. Edinburgh: John Grant, 1906.

Moore, Archie. *Any Boy Can: The Archie Moore Story.* Englewood Cliffs, N.J.: Prentice-Hall, 1971.

Mullan, Harry. *The Great Book of Boxing.* New York: Crescent Books, 1987.

Mullan, Harry. *The Illustrated History of Boxing.* New York: Crescent Books, 1987.

Mullan, Harry. *The Ultimate Encyclopedia of Boxing.* Edison, New Jersey: Chartwell Books, 1996.

Nagler, Barney. *James Norris and the Decline of Boxing.* Indianapolis: Bobbs Merrill Co., 1964.

Nelson, Battling. *Life, Battles, and Career of Battling Nelson, Lightweight Champion of the World.* self published, 1908.

Newfield, Jack. *Only in America: The Life and Crimes of Don King.* New York: William Morrow & Company, 1995.

Odd, Gilbert E. *Boxing: The Great Champions.* London: Hamlyn, 1974.

Odd, Gilbert E. *The Fighting Blacksmith: A Biography of Bob Fitzsimmons.* London: Pelham, 1976.

Odd, Gilbert E. *Encyclopedia of Boxing.* Edison, NJ: Book Sales, 1989.

Patterson, Floyd, and Milton Gross. *Victory Over Myself.* Pelham Books, 1962.

Pepe, Phil. *Come Out Smokin': Joe Frazier, The Champ Nobody Knew.* New York: Coward McCann & Geoghegan, 1972.

Porter, David L., ed. *Biographical Dictionary of American Sports: Basketball and Other Indoor Sports.* Westport, CT: Greenwood Publishing Group, 1989.

Reid, J.C. *Bucks and Bruisers: Pierce Egan and Regency England*. London: Routledge & Kegan Paul, 1971.

Remnick, David. *King of the World*. New York: Random House, 1998.

Robinson, Sugar Ray, and Dave Anderson. *Sugar Ray*. New York: Viking Press, 1970.

Ross, Barney. *No Man Stands Alone: The True Story of Barney Ross*. Philadelphia: Lippincott, 1957.

Sammons, Jeffrey T. *Beyond the Ring: The Role of Boxing in American Society*. Champaign, IL: U. of Illinois Press, 1988.

Skehan, Everett M. *Rocky Marciano: Biography of a First Son*. Boston: Houghton Mifflin, 1977.

Sugar, Bert Randolph. *The 100 Greatest Boxers of All Time*. New York: Bonanza Books, 1984.

Sugar, Bert Randolph. *One Hundred Years of Boxing: A Pictorial History of Modern Boxing, 1882-1982*. New York: Smithmark Publishers, 1982.

Sugar, Bert Randolph and The Editors Of Ring Magazine. *The Great Fights: A Pictorial History Of Boxing's Greatest Bouts*. New York: Gallery Books, 1981

Suster, Gerald. *Champions of the Ring: The Lives and Times of Boxing's Heavyweight Heroes*. Jersey City, NJ: Parkwest Publications, 1994.

Torres, Jose. *Fire & Fear: The Inside Story of Mike Tyson*. New York: Warner, 1989.

Variety Obituaries, Vol. 1-10. New York: Garland, 1988.

Vecchione, Joseph J., ed. *The New York Times Book of Sports Legends*. New York: Times Books, 1991.

Walsh, Peter. *Men of Steel: The Lives and Times of Boxing's Middleweight Champions*. London: Robson Books, 1993.

Weston, Stanley, and Steven Farhood. *The Ring: Chronicle of Boxing*. London: Hamlyn, 1993.

Wignall, Trevor C. *The Story of Boxing*. New York: Brentano's, 1924

Wiley, Ralph. *Serenity: A Book about Fighters, Why They Fight & How It Feels to Be One*. New York: Henry Holt & Company, 1989.

Young, A.S. ("Doc"). *Sonny Liston: The Champion Nobody Wanted*. Johnson Publishing Co., 1963.

INTERNET SOURCES

3615, Boxing Avenue
www.boxing-records.com

ABCNews.com
www.abcnews.go.com

Amazon.com www.amazon.com

Cyber Boxing Zone
www.cyberboxingzone.com

Denver Press Club Online
www.pressclub.org

ESPN
msn.espn.go.com

Fightnews.com
www.fightnews.com

Guardian Unlimited
www.guardian.co.uk

International Boxing Hall of Fame
www.ibhof.com

Latino Legends in Sports
www.latinosportslegends.com

Nando Sportserver
www.sportserver.com

Nando Times, The
www.nando.net

National Baseball Hall of Fame and Museum
www.baseballhalloffame.org

NSSA Hall of Fame
www.nssahalloffame.com

Official Pete Sanstol Web Site
home.talkcity.com/
BleacherSt/boxofdaylight

Pegasos
Kirjasto.sci.fi

Pocono Record
www.poconorecord.com

Schneider Publishing Company
www.schneiderpublishing.com

Travel & Sports, Puerto Rico MasterGuide
www.travelandsports.com

Upcomingmovies.com
www.upcomingmovies.com

PHOTO CREDITS

Photographs, etchings, drawings and other illustrations used in this book are from the collections of *The Ring* magazine (including the Stanley Weston Collection), The International Boxing Hall of Fame, Sports Legends Photos, Inc. and from the private collections of the authors.

The photograph of Dan Parker is from UPI/CORBIS–BETTMAN.

Andrew Gillis of Cascadilla Photography took photographs of the International Boxing Hall of Fame expressly for this book.

Other individual photographers and studios, where known, are listed below:

20th Century Sporting Club—Jenkins

Ace Photographers—Joe Brown

Sam Andre—Jenkins in corner

Bill Apter—Chandler vs. Murata, Don Dunphy, Lou Duva, Eddie Futch, Gallo, Wilfredo Gomez, Goodman, Harry Markson, Pedroza vs. LaPorte, Aaron Pryor, Rudd, Salvador Sanchez, Sanchez vs. Nelson (2), Spinks vs. Braxton

D. Arnow—Benny Leonard

Al Bello—Arthur Mercante

Scott K. Brown—Leonard Basketball

Les Clark—Lennox Lewis

David Corona—Ortiz vs. Torres

Louis Dummett—Saddler & Fleischer

Theo Ehret—Ali vs. Norton, Alexis Arguello, Foster vs. Quarry, Emile Griffith, Laguna vs. Ramos, Napoles, Napoles vs. Backus, Napoles vs. Lopez, Olivares, Olivares & Parnassus, Olivares vs. Rose, George Parnassus, Saldivar, Carlos Zarate, Zarate vs. Ferreri

Gunther—Griffith vs. Rodriguez, Liston handstand, Liston vs. Patterson, Ortiz vs. Lane

Guttenstein—Bob Fitzsimmons

David Jones—Chris Dundee

Jim Laurie—Hagler vs. Hearns

Lavin—Mickey Duff

LeConte—Norton vs. Quarry

Ray Monaco—LaMotta & DeNiro

Frank Monell—Basilio vs. Saxton

A.C. McManus—Spinks vs. Cooney

National N.Y.—Charley Burley

Charlotte Peters—Benton, Pedroza, Pedroza vs. Taylor

P.A. Reuter—Dick Tiger

Bert Roberts—Harry Wills

D. Rowe—Buchanan vs. Cullen

Salas—Giardello vs. Graham

Sax—Saad Muhammad vs. Lopez

Russ Scott—Pep vs. Leslie

M. Smith—Robinson portrait

Paul Thompson—Jack Dillon

Von Romerheim Studio—Kid Chocolate

D.L. Waite—Benitez vs. Hope, Hagler vs. Mugabi, Sanchez vs. Castanon, Sanchez vs. Gomez, Spinks vs. Holmes

John Wood—Jack Dempsey (The Nonpareil)

INDEX

Names and page references in **boldface** indicate Hall of Fame inductees and their biographies.

Page references in *italics* indicate photo captions.

Harvey, Len, *150*

Hauser, Al, *551*

Havlin, Jack, 625

Hearns, Thomas ("Hitman"), 259, 319, *372*, 375, *411*, 412, 413, 629

Heenan, John C., 13, **26**, 29, 34, 37

Heeney, Tom, 203

Heinz, W.C., 367

Herera, Aurelio, 178

Herford, Al, 108

Herman, "Pekin" Kid, 122

Herman, Pete, *122*, **122–123**, 198, 213, 215

Hernandez, Art, *260*

Herrera, Antonio, 400

Herrera, Ernesto, 486

Herrera, Rafael, 457

Herrick, Joe, 114

Hickey, Dan, 62, 63

Hogarth, William, 25

Hollands, John, 38

Holmes, Derrick, *356*

Holmes, Jack, 36

Holmes, Larry, 226, 237, 453, *540*, *542*, 542–543, 590, 610, 619

Holyfield, Evander, 231, 619

Hope, Maurice, *259*, 259

Hopkins, Bernard, 231, 619

Hostak, Al, 195, 571

Howard, Kevin, 412

Hudkins, Ace, 209

Hughes, Al, 256

Humez, Charlie, 555

Humphreys, Joe, *116*, 148, **614**

Humphries, Richard, *12*, 32

Hunsaker, Tunney, 234

Hurley, Battling, 180

Hurley, Jack, 182

Hurst, Sam, 31

Hutchins, Len, 346

Hyer, Jacob, 12

Hyer, Tom, 12

■

Ichinose, Sam, 615

Ingelston, George, 27

International Boxing Club (IBC), 224–225, 230, 482, 550, 590, 600, 601, 613, 626, 632

International Boxing Council (IBC), 47

International Boxing Federation (IBF), 44, 47, 591

International Boxing Hall of Fame, 636–643

International Boxing Managers Guild, 224

International Boxing Union (IBU), 44

Iriarte, Miguel, 307

J

Jack, Beau, *380*, **380–383**, 432–433, 435

Jackson, John, 24, **27**, 32

Jackson, Peter, 79, *124*, **124–125**, 128

Jackson, Young Peter, 185

Jacobs, Dave, 408, 411

Jacobs, Dr. Walter H., 641

Jacobs, Jimmy, 258, 259, **615–616**

Jacobs, Mike, 65, 224, 419, 421, **616**, 630

Jeannette, Joe, *126*, **126–127**, 143, 170–171, 216

Jeffra, Harry, 103

Jeffries, James J., 79, 105, 125, **128–129**, 190, 526, 586, 594, 599

 as referee, 70, *180*, 180–181

 v. Johnson, 51, *128*, 128–129, 132, 584, 628

Jeffries, Young Jim, *76*, 77

Jenkins, Katie, *384*, 384, 387

Jenkins, Lew, 53, 238, *384*, **384–387**, 432

Jimenez, Nestor ("Baba"), *359*

Jofre, Eder, 378–379, *388*, **388–391**, *391*, 531

Johansson, Ingemar, *392*, **392–395**, *394*, 395, 483

Johnson, Battling Jim, 126, 171

Johnson, Fred, 96

Johnson, Harold, 223, 273, *396*, **396–399**, 399

Johnson, Jack, 70–71, 77, 78, 105, *130*, **130–133**, *133*, 142, 526

 v. Jeannette, 126, 127

 v. Jeffries, 51, *128*, 128–129, 132, 584, 628

 v. Ketchel, *132*, 132, 135, 222

 v. McVey, 170–171

Johnson, Marvin, 347, 520, 541

Johnson, Tom, 16, **28**

Johnston, James J., 199, **617**

Joiner, Herschel, 173

Jones, Aaron, 37

Jones, Bobby (fighter), *462*

Jones, Bobby (golfer), 380

Jones, Doug, 230, 235, 328, 330, 334, 399, 463

Jones, Gorilla, 194

Jones, Ralph ("Tiger"), 475, *506*, 598–599

Jones, Roy, Jr., 231

Jordan, Don, 225, 609

Joyce, Willie, *380*

Jurich, Jackie, 157

K

Kalbhenn, Johnny, 326

Kalule, Ayub, 412

Kane, Peter, 156–157

Kansas, Rocky, *158*, 158–159, 198

Kates, Richie, *347*, 347

Kearns, Alfred "Soldier," 148

Kearns, Jack, 89, 114, 208, 428, **618**

Kelly, Hugo, 92, 134, 180

Kendrick, Jim, 80

Kennedy, Billy, 174

Kennedy, Jim, 599

Kenny, Burt, 114

Ketchel, Al, 220

Ketchel, Stanley, *132*, 132, **134–135**, 142, 185, 222

 v. Papke, 134, *180*, 180–181

Ketchum, Willie, 292, 387, 504

Keyes, Bert, 164

Kid Chocolate, 61, 73, *136*, **136–137**, 140–141, 269

Kid Chocolate, Baby, 306

Kilbane, Johnny, 55, 100, *134*, *138*, **138–149**, 146, 198, 215

Kilrain, Jake, 40, 44, 78, 174

King, Don, 226, 230, 231, **618–619**, 629

King, Rufiu, 502, 504

King, Tom, 26, **29**, 31

Kingpetch, Pone, *376*, 376, *379*, 497

King Tut, 182

Ki-Soo Kim, 263

Klaus, Frank, 181

Knight, Charles, 24

Kouidri, Omar, 296